PHILIP'S

WORLD REFERENCE
ATLAS

PICTURE ACKNOWLEDGEMENTS:

Page 9 (centre left) – NASA: Olympus Mons, *The Universe Revealed*, page 47 (top).
Page 10 – Science Photo Library/National Optical Astronomy Observationaries:
Sun's corona (blue) *The Universe Revealed*, page 21.
Page 12 – Royal Greenwich Observatory, Herstmonceaux: Sun maximum,
Joy of Knowledge Science and Technology (c 1976 pic), page 221.
Page 13 – NASA: UV shot of prominences *Joy of Knowledge Science and Technology*,
page 223 (c 1976).
Page 14 – NASA: Mercury from Mariner. *The Universe Revealed*, page 25.
Page 15 – NASA: Venus (Octopus Publishing Group Ltd).
Page 16 (centre) – NASA: *Joy of Knowledge Science and Technology*, page 192.
Page 16 (bottom) – NASA: *The Universe Revealed*, page 35.
Page 17 – NASA: *The Universe Revealed*, page 47 (bottom).
Page 18 – NASA: Jupiter and Io (Octopus Publishing Group Ltd).
Page 19 – NASA: Saturn (Octopus Publishing Group Ltd).
Page 20 – NASA/Science Photo Library: Uranus.
Page 21 (centre) – NASA: Triton, moon of Neptune. *The Universe Revealed*, page 74.
Page 21 (bottom) – Space Telescope Science Institute/NASA/Science Photo Library:
Hubble computer images of Pluto hemispheres.
Page 23 – NASA: comet Hale-Bopp. *The Universe Revealed*, page 78.
Page 24 – NASA: asteroid Ida. *The Universe Revealed*, page 80.

The Solar System and the Physical Earth compiled by Richard Widdows.

PHILIP'S
WORLD REFERENCE
ATLAS

CHANCELLOR
PRESS

This 2000 edition published
by Chancellor Press, an imprint of Bounty Books,
a division of Octopus Publishing Group Ltd.,
2-4 Heron Quays, London, E14 4JP.

Copyright (c) 2000 Octopus Publishing Group Ltd.
Maps and index (c) 2000 George Philip Ltd.
Cartography by Philip's

ISBN: 0 75370 310 6

A CIP catalogue record for this book is available from the British Library.

Produced by Toppan (HK) Ltd.

Printed in China

CONTENTS

THE SOLAR SYSTEM

THE PHYSICAL EARTH

THE MAP SECTION

INDEX

SOLAR SYSTEM: EVOLUTION

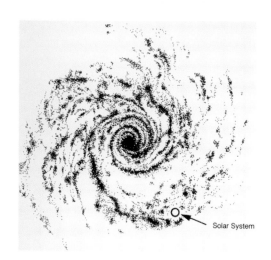

ABOUT 15 BILLION years ago, time and space began with the most colossal explosion in cosmic history: the "Big Bang" that initiated the Universe. According to current theory, in the first millionth of a second of its existence it expanded from a dimensionless point of infinite mass and density into a fireball about 30 billion km (18.6 billion miles) across – and has been expanding at a phenomenal rate ever since.

It took almost a million years for the primal fireball to cool enough for atoms to form. They were mostly hydrogen, still the most abundant material in the Universe. But the new matter was not evenly distributed around the young Universe, and a few billion years later atoms in relatively dense regions began to cling together under the influence of gravity, forming distinct masses of gas separated by vast expanses of empty space.

At the beginning these first proto-galaxies were dark places – the Universe had cooled – but gravitational attraction continued its work, condensing matter into coherent lumps inside the galactic gas clouds. About three billion years later, some of these masses had contracted so much that internal pressure produced the high temperatures necessary to cause nuclear fusion: the first stars were born.

There were several generations of stars, each feeding on the wreckage of its extinct predecessors as well as the original galactic gas swirls. With each new generation, progressively larger atoms were forged in stellar furnaces and the galaxy's range of elements, once restricted to hydrogen, grew larger. About ten billion years after the Big Bang, a star formed on the outskirts of our galaxy with enough matter left over to create a retinue of planets. Some 4.6 billion years after that, a few planetary atoms had evolved into structures of complex molecules that lived, breathed and, eventually, pointed telescopes at the sky.

These early astronomers found that their Sun was just one of more than 100 billion stars in our home galaxy alone – the number of grains of rice it would take to fill a cathedral. Our galaxy, in turn, forms part of a local group of 25 or so similar structures, some much larger than ours. The most distant galaxy so far observed lies about 13.1 billion light-years away – and one light-year is some 9,461 million km (5,879 million miles).

ABOVE Our Solar System is located in one of the home galaxy's spiral arms, a little under 28,000 light-years away from the galactic centre and orbiting around it in a period of about some 200 million years. There are at least 100 million other galaxies in the Universe.

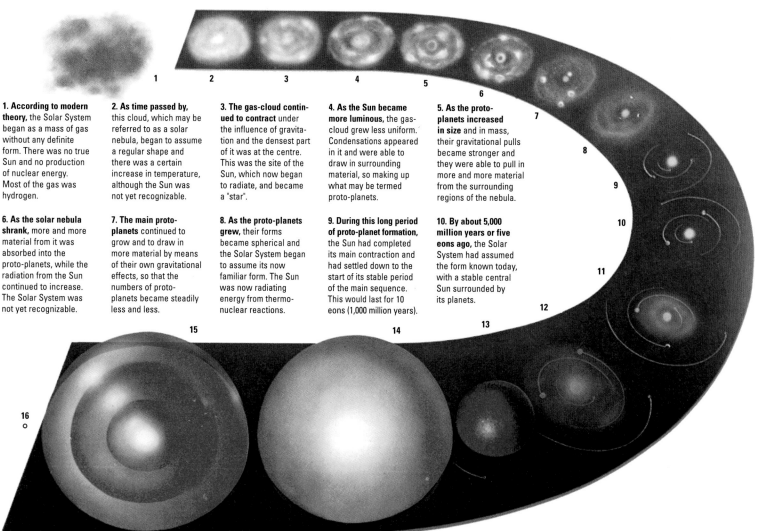

1. According to modern theory, the Solar System began as a mass of gas without any definite form. There was no true Sun and no production of nuclear energy. Most of the gas was hydrogen.

2. As time passed by, this cloud, which may be referred to as a solar nebula, began to assume a regular shape and there was a certain increase in temperature, although the Sun was not yet recognizable.

3. The gas-cloud continued to contract under the influence of gravitation and the densest part of it was at the centre. This was the site of the Sun, which now began to radiate, and became a "star".

4. As the Sun became more luminous, the gas-cloud grew less uniform. Condensations appeared in it and were able to draw in surrounding material, so making up what may be termed proto-planets.

5. As the proto-planets increased in size and in mass, their gravitational pulls became stronger and they were able to pull in more and more material from the surrounding regions of the nebula.

6. As the solar nebula shrank, more and more material from it was absorbed into the proto-planets, while the radiation from the Sun continued to increase. The Solar System was not yet recognizable.

7. The main proto-planets continued to grow and to draw in more material by means of their own gravitational effects, so that the numbers of proto-planets became steadily less and less.

8. As the proto-planets grew, their forms became spherical and the Solar System began to assume its now familiar form. The Sun was now radiating energy from thermo-nuclear reactions.

9. During this long period of proto-planet formation, the Sun had completed its main contraction and had settled down to the start of its stable period of the main sequence. This would last for 10 eons (1,000 million years).

10. By about 5,000 million years or five eons ago, the Solar System had assumed the form known today, with a stable central Sun surrounded by its planets.

11. In perhaps 5,000 million years from now the Sun will have exhausted its supply of available hydrogen and its structure will change. The core will shrink and the surface expand considerably, with a lower surface temperature.

12. The next stage of solar evolution will be expansion to the red giant stage, with luminosity increased by 100 times. The size of the globe will increase with the overall increase in energy output, and the inner planets will be destroyed.

13. With a further rise in core temperature, the Sun will begin to burn its helium, causing a rapid rise in temperature and increase in size. The Earth can hardly hope to survive this phase of evolution as the Sun expands to 50 times its size.

14. By now the Sun will be at its most unstable, with an intensely hot core and a rarefied atmosphere. The helium burning helium will give the so-called "helium flash". After a temporary contraction the Sun will be 400 times its present size.

15. Different kinds of reactions inside the Sun will lead to an even greater increase of core temperature. The system of planets will no longer exist in the form we know today, but the supply of nuclear energy will be almost exhausted.

16. When all the nuclear energy is used up, the Sun (as all stars eventually do) will collapse, very rapidly on the cosmic scale, into a small dense and very feeble white dwarf. It will continue to shine because it will still be contracting gravitationally.

Formation of the planets

The planets and larger satellites can be divided into two distinct classes. Mercury, Venus, Earth and Mars are all rocky "terrestrials", while Jupiter, Saturn, Uranus and Neptune are the large gaseous Jovian planets. Pluto can be classified, along with the large icy moons of the gas giants, as a third type. The terrestrial planets are closer to the Sun, have smaller masses and radii, and are more dense than the Jovian planets. These are big, low in density and have extensive satellite systems and rings.

The basic difference between the two families arose as a consequence of the temperature difference within the proto-solar cloud. This allowed icy material to condense well beyond the asteroid belt, producing cold proto-planets which effectively collected vast amounts of gas. The inner planets were too small and too hot to retain large amounts of original atmosphere in the face of the strong winds from the Sun.

Beyond the Solar System

Far beyond the gas giants, and outside the erratic orbit of Neptune, lie two regions of space that have intrigued astronomers since their discovery in the last half of the 20th century.

The Kuiper belt, named after one of the scientists who predicted its existence, is a disc of debris lying between about 35 and 100 astronomical units from the Sun; an astronomical unit (AU) is the average distance from the Earth to the Sun – 149,597,870km (92,958,350 miles). The first object was located there in 1992, so dim it was 10 million times fainter than the faintest stars seen by eye. It is now estimated that this belt may contain up to a billion comets, with a total mass just 1% of Earth.

Astronomers have now found over 60 Kuiper belt objects orbiting farther from the Sun than Neptune and Pluto, taking between 160 and 720 years to orbit the Sun. The smallest object seen is roughly 100km (60 miles) across, while the largest is 500 km (300 miles) in diameter, slightly smaller than Neptune's moon Triton. Indeed, Triton could be a body captured from the Kuiper belt, and Pluto and its moon Charon could be among its members.

Much further out in space is the Oort cloud, named in 1950 after the Dutch astronomer who identified it as a source of long-period comets. This is a rough sphere of rocky and icy debris left over from the solar nebula from which the Solar System formed. A vast size, it lies between 30,000 and 100,000AU from the Sun, a distance where gravity from passing stars could perurb it, sending comets in towards the Sun.

Future of the Solar System

We now know that dramatic consequences are in store for these terrestrial planets as a result of the dramatic changes that will happen to the Sun. Astronomers calculate that our star will be hot enough in 3 billion years to boil Earth's oceans away, leaving the planet a burned-out cinder, a dead and sterile place. Four billion years on, the Sun will balloon into a giant star, engulfing Mercury and becoming 2,000 times brighter than it is now. Its light will be intense enough to melt Earth's surface and turn the icy moons of the giant planets into globes of liquid.

Such events are in the almost inconceivably distant future, of course. For the present the Sun continues to provide us with an up-close laboratory of stellar astrophysics and evolution.

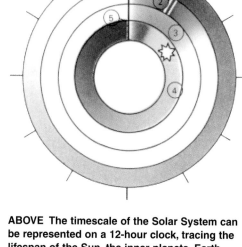

ABOVE The timescale of the Solar System can be represented on a 12-hour clock, tracing the lifespan of the Sun, the inner planets, Earth and the outer planets from the inner circle outwards. At the 12 o'clock position [1] the Solar System is created; after 4,000 million years, conditions on Earth are favourable for life [2]; as a red giant the Sun engulfs the inner planets [3] before collapsing as a white dwarf [4] and, possibly, end its long life as a brown dwarf [5].

BELOW The distance of the outermost planets – Jupiter, Saturn, Uranus, Neptune and Pluto – will save them from the Sun's helium burn, and each will continue its orbit. More precise predictions for their future are not possible.

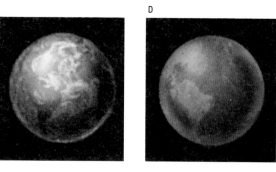

LEFT Olympus Mons is the largest volcano in the Solar System. Its peak rises to a staggering 27km (16.8 miles) above the mean surface level of Mars. More than three times as high as Earth's Mount Everest, it has a diameter of some 520km (323 miles). Olympus Mons is surrounded by a huge cliff up to 6km (3.7 miles) high, where the lower flanks appear to have fallen away in a gigantic landslide.

This collapse may have generated the peculiar blocky terrain of ridges separated by flat areas, the Olympus Mons aureole, that extends from the base of the cliff up to 1,000km (600 miles) from the volcano's summit. This contains a nested set of volcanic craters, the largest of them 80km (50 miles) across.

BELOW The lifespan of the Earth started from the material of the solar nebula [A] which at first had no regular form. When it reached its present size [B] the original hydrogen atmosphere had already been lost and replaced by a new one, caused by gases sent out from the interior. Life could begin and today the Earth is moving in a settled orbit round a stable star, so that it is habitable [C]. But this state of affairs will not persist indefinitely: long before the Sun enters the red giant stage, most scientists believe, the Earth will be overheated, the oceans will boil, and the atmosphere will be driven off [D]. Finally, the only planet known to have had life will be completely destroyed [E].

A   B   C   D   E

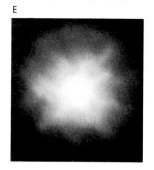

SOLAR SYSTEM: PROFILE

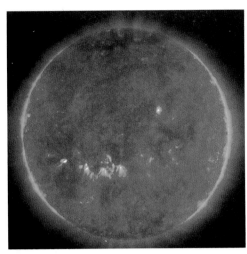

ABOVE The Sun's outer corona in ultraviolet light. The bright regions are areas of intense magnetism. This part of the corona is at a temperature of around 1,000,000°C. All the components of the Solar System are tethered by the immense gravitational pull of the Sun, the star whose thermonuclear furnaces provide them with virtually all their heat and light.

BELOW The planets of the Solar System shown to the same scale. On the right is a segment of the Sun [1]; from its surface rises a huge prominence [2]. Then come the inner planets: Mercury [3], Venus [4], Earth [5] with its Moon [6], and Mars [7]. Mars has two dwarf satellites Phobos [8] and Deimos [9], exaggerated here – if shown to the correct scale, they would be too small to be seen without a microscope.

A TINY PART of one of the millions of galaxies (collections of stars) that make up the known Universe, the Solar System orbits at a mean distance of 29,700 light-years from the centre of our own galaxy, the "Milky Way". The present distance is 27,700 light-years, and it will reach the minimum distance of 27,600 in around 15 million years' time. It comprises one star, which we call the Sun, nine principal planets, and various bodies of lesser importance, including the satellites that attend some of the planets and a range of cosmic debris, notably asteroids, meteors and comets.

The system is entirely dependent on the Sun, which is by far the most massive body and the only one to be self-luminous: the remaining members of the Solar System shine by reflected sunlight and appear so brilliant in our skies that it is not always easy to remember that in universal terms they are nowhere near as large or important as they appear.

The inner planets

The planets are divided into two well-defined groups. First come the four relatively small planets of Mercury, Venus, Earth and Mars, with diameters ranging from 12,756km (7,926 miles) for Earth down to only 4,878km (3,031 miles) for Mercury.

Then come the asteroids [10], of which even the largest is only about 913 (567 miles) in diameter. Beyond lie the giant planets: Jupiter [11], with its four largest satellites Io [12], Europa [13], Ganymede [14] and Callisto [15]; Saturn [16] with its retinue of satellites, of which the largest is Titan [17]; Uranus [18] with its many satellites; Neptune [19] with its large satellite Triton [20]; and finally misfit Pluto [21].

These planets have various factors in common. All, for example, have solid surfaces and are presumably made up of similar materials, although Earth and Mercury are more dense than Mars and Venus.

Although their orbits do not in general depart much from the circular, the paths of Mercury and Mars are considerably more eccentric than those of Earth and Venus. Mercury and Venus are known as the "inferior planets" because their orbits lie inside that of Earth; they show lunar-type phases from new to full and remain in the same region of the sky as the Sun. While Mercury and Venus are unattended by any satellites, Earth has one satellite (our familiar Moon) and Mars has two, Phobos and Deimos, both of which are very small and different in nature from the Moon.

Beyond Mars comes a wide gap, in which move thousands of small worlds known as the asteroids, or minor planets. Even Ceres, the largest, is only about 913km (567 miles) in diameter. This is much larger than was once thought, but still small by planetary standards. It is not therefore surprising that the asteroids remained hidden until relatively recent times, with Ceres discovered only in 1801. Just one of this new multitude, Vesta, is ever visible from Earth without the aid of a telescope.

The outer planets

Far beyond the main asteroid belt come the four giant planets of Jupiter, Saturn, Uranus and Neptune. These worlds are quite different from the terrestrial planets: they are fluid (that is, gas or liquid) rather than solid bodies with very dense atmospheres. Their masses are so great that they have been able to retain much of their original hydrogen; the escape velocity of Jupiter, for instance, is 60km (37 miles) per second as against

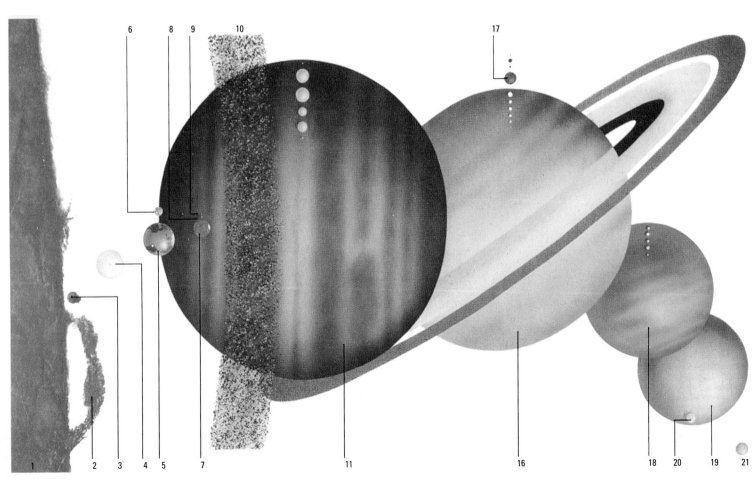

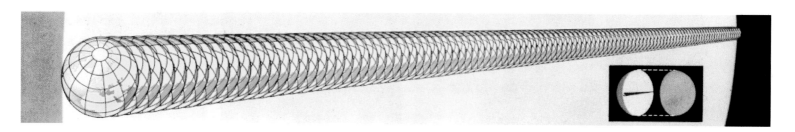

only 11.2km (7 miles) per second for Earth. Their mean distances from the Sun range from 778 million km (483 million miles) for Jupiter out to 4,497 million km (2,794 million miles) for Neptune. Conventional diagrams of the Solar System tend to be misleading as far as scale is concerned; it is tempting, for example, to assume that Saturn and Uranus are lying next to each other when in fact the distance of Uranus from the Earth's orbit is about twice that of Saturn.

The giant planets have various points in common, but differ markedly in detail. Their densities are comparatively low and the density of Saturn is actually less than that of water. Although Jupiter is seen solely by reflected sunlight, the planet does generate some heat of its own. However, even though the core temperature must be high, it is not nearly high enough for nuclear reactions to begin, so that Jupiter, though massive, cannot be compared to a star like the Sun.

Planetary discoveries

Five of the planets – Mercury, Venus, Mars, Jupiter and Saturn – have been known from ancient times, since all are prominent naked-eye objects. Uranus, just visible with the naked eye, was discovered fortuitously in 1781 by William Herschel and Neptune was added to the list of known planets in 1846 as a result of mathematical investigations carried out concerning movements of Uranus. All the giants are attended by satellites; Jupiter has 16 moons, Saturn 20, Uranus 15 and Neptune eight. Several of these are of planetary size, with diameters almost equal to Mercury's.

The outermost known planet is Pluto, discovered in 1930 by astronomers at the Lowell Observatory, Flagstaff, Arizona. It is far from another giant, being smaller than the Earth, and is usually ranked as a terrestrial-type planet, even though little is known about it.

Pluto's origin was long a mystery because of its size, rocky composition and highly unusual orbit. In recent years, however, it has become apparent that Pluto orbits within a "swarm" of tens of thousands of still smaller worlds orbiting well beyond the region of Neptune.

RIGHT The ecosphere is the region around the Sun in which a planet can be at a suitable temperature for life as we conceive it to exist – assuming that the planet is of Earth "type". The inner yellow zone [1] is way too hot, and beyond the ecosphere [orange, 2], temperatures will become too low [3]. Earth [4] lies in the middle of the ecosphere, enjoying a near-perfect set of balanced conditions for life. Inhospitable Venus [5] orbits at the very inner limit and barren Mars [6] at the outer, but recent probes have proved that neither has the prerequisites for evolution. The best hope of finding life as we know it seems now to rest with a similar ecosphere – in one of the billions of other solar systems in the Universe.

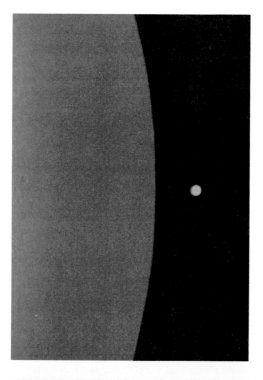

ABOVE Shown here in cross-section, the Sun has an equatorial diameter of 1,392,000km (865,000 miles), 109 times that of Earth. Despite the fact that its volume is more than a million times that of Earth, its mass is only 333,000 times greater because the density is lower: the mean specific gravity, on a scale where water = 1, is only 1.4.

LEFT While the Sun is the body on which the entire Solar System depends, and is more massive than all the planets combined, it is an ordinary main sequence star with a magnitude of +5 – small when compared with a giant star. The diagram shows the Sun alongside a segment of the red supergiant Betelgeuse, which marks Orion's right shoulder. Betelgeuse is of spectral class M2 – a very cool star – but has an absolute magnitude of –5.5. Its diameter is 300 to 400 times that of the Sun, and its globe is large enough to contain Earth's orbit. In 5 million years' time the Sun's life cycle will make it a modest red giant in its own right, and the solid inner planets of the Solar System will be destroyed by the heat and light that results from its phenomenal expansion.

THE SUN

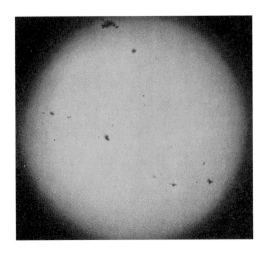

ABOVE The "solar maximum" of 1958, pictured here, was the most energetic phase of the solar cycle ever recorded, and sunspots are clearly visible. Occurring where there is a local strengthening of the Sun's magnetic field, sunspots are regions in the photosphere that are cooler than their surroundings and therefore appear darker. Varying in size from 1,000 to 50,000km (600 to 30,000 miles) and occasionally up to 200,000km (125,000 miles), they comprise a dark central region called the umbra, and a grey outer region, the penumbra. Their duration varies from a few hours to several weeks, or months for the biggest ones.

The number of spots visible depends on the stage of the solar cycle. This is fairly regular and lasts around 11 years and is part of a longer 22-year solar cycle, but at the intervening "spot minima" the disc may remain featureless for several days or even weeks. The exact cause of sunspots is not fully understood – and no theory has been able to explain their disappearance between 1645 and 1715.

Sunspots are seen to move across the face of the Sun as it rotates. Most appear in pairs, but often complex groups emerge. They can be seen if you project an image of the Sun onto a piece of white paper or card.

THE SUN is a star, one of 100,000 million stars in our galaxy. In the Universe as a whole it is insignificant – classed as a yellow dwarf star with a spectrum of type G – but in our planetary system it is the all-important controlling body.

Immensely larger than Earth, the Sun has a diameter of 1,392,000km (865,000 miles). Though big enough to contain more than a million bodies the volume of Earth, its mass is only 1.99×10^{30} kg – approximately 333,000 times that of Earth. The reason why it is not as massive as might be expected is that its density is lower than that of an Earth-type planet. The mean value for the specific gravity is 1.409 (that is, 1.409 times an equal volume of water), but the Sun is not homogenous and density, pressure and temperature all increase rapidly beneath the brilliant outer surface towards the centre. It consists of about 70% hydrogen (by weight) and some 28% helium, with the remainder mostly oxygen and carbon.

The Sun lies some 32,000 light-years from the centre of our galaxy and takes approximately 200 million years to complete one journey round the galactic nucleus. It has an axial rotation period of 25.4 days at its equator, but because the Sun does not rotate in the manner of a solid body, this period is considerably longer near the solar poles.

In ordinary light the Sun appears to have a clear edge. This is because only a 500-km (300-mile) layer of its atmosphere, the photosphere, is at the correct temperature to emit light at visible wavelengths – a very small layer in comparison to the star's vast diameter.

The Sun's magnetic field

Overall, the Sun's magnetic field is roughly the same strength as Earth's, but the mechanism is entirely different. The Sun is not a solid body but a plasma created by heat removing the electrons of hydrogen atoms to leave negatively charged electrons and, possibly, positively charged ions. Magnetic fields can be created by the motion of electrically charged particles, and the Sun's turbulence and rotation create localized fields.

As the Sun rotates, the magnetic field lines get "trapped" and move around with the rotation. As the top layers bubble with convection the field lines become twisted up, and this squashing together increases the strength of the magnetic field in those areas. These intense pockets cause many of the phenomena seen on the Sun, notably sunspots.

Prominences and flares

The part of the solar atmosphere lying immediately above the photosphere is called the chromosphere ("colour sphere") because it has a characteristically reddish appearance. This is also the region of the large and brilliant prominences. To observe the prominences, instruments based on the principle of the spectroscope are used. There are two main types of prominences: eruptive and quiescent. Eruptive prominences are in violent motion and have been observed extending to more than 50,000km (312,500 miles) above the Sun's surface; quiescent prominences are much more stable and may hang in the chromosphere for days before breaking up. Both are most common near the peak of the solar cycle of activity.

Prominences are often associated with major spot-groups. Active groups also produce "flares", which are not usually visible, although a few have been seen. The flares are short-lived and emit streams of particles as well as short-wave radiation. These emissions have marked effects on Earth, producing magnetic storms or disturbances of Earth's magnetic field that affect radio communications and compasses. They also produce the beautiful solar lights or aurorae.

The solar wind

Less dense areas of the corona, the outer layer of the Sun, called coronal holes by astronomers, appear where the Sun's magnetic field opens to interplanetary space rather than looping back down. These areas are believed to be the major source of the solar wind, where charged particles, mainly protons and electrons, stream out into the interplanetary medium.

It is this emission that has a strong effect on the tails of comets, forcing them to point away from the Sun. Even when it reaches Earth, the wind's velocity exceeds 950km (590 miles) per second.

BELOW The structure of the Sun cannot be drawn to an accurate scale, and attempts at full cross-sections are misleading. In the core, about 400,000km (250,000 miles) across, continual nuclear transformations create energy and the temperature is perhaps 15 million °C (27 million °F). Further out in the solar interior, the radiative zone [1], about 300,000km (200,000 miles) wide, diffuses radiation randomly, and temperatures range from 15 million to 1 million °C. In the convective layer [2] heat travels outward for 200,000km (125,000 miles) on convection currents, cooling from a million to 6,000°C (11,000°F). The relatively rarefied photosphere [3], the fairly well-defined "sphere of light" from which energy is radiated into space and where temperatures average 5,500°C (10,000°F), is surprisingly narrow – only 500km (300 miles) wide; because it is the layer of the Sun that radiates in visible wavelengths, this is the part of the Sun that we see, including the sunspots [4].

RIGHT Like all stars the Sun's energy is generated by nuclear reactions taking place under extreme conditions in the core. Here the Sun is continually converting four hydrogen atoms into one helium atom. The amount of energy produced in each individual reaction is tiny, but the Sun is converting 600,000 million kg (1,325,000 million lb) of hydrogen into helium every single second. The Sun's total power output, its luminosity, is 3.9×10^{26} watts (the equivalent of a million, million, million, million 100-watt light bulbs).

Powerhouse of a star

It is a mistake to think of the Sun burning in the same way that a fire burns. A star made up entirely of coal, and radiating as fiercely as the Sun does, would not last long on the cosmic scale, and astronomers believe that the Sun is at least 5,000 million years old.

The source of solar energy is to be found in nuclear transformations. Hydrogen is the main constituent and near the core, where the temperatures and pressures are so extreme that the second lightest element, helium, is formed from hydrogen nuclei by nuclear fusion. It takes four hydrogen nuclei to make one nucleus of helium; in the process a little mass is lost, being converted into a large amount of energy. The energy produced keeps the Sun radiating: the loss of mass amounts to four million tonnes per second. This may seem significant, but it is negligible compared with the total mass of the Sun – and there is enough hydrogen available to keep the Sun shining in its present form for at least another 5,000 million years.

Eventually the hydrogen will start to become exhausted and the Sun will change its structure drastically. According to current theory, it will pass through a red giant stage, when it will have a luminosity at least 100 times as great as it does today. Once all its nuclear fuel has been used up, it will start to collapse into a small dense star of the type known as a white dwarf. Earth will have long gone: it will not survive the heat of the Sun's red giant stage, and along with the other inner planets will be totally destroyed.

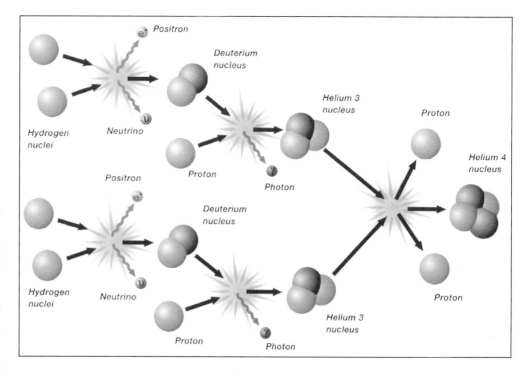

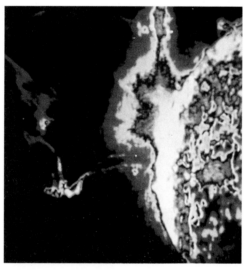

LEFT A solar prominence photographed by astronauts on board Skylab. In this extreme ultraviolet shot the colours are false: they represent the degree of radiation intensity from red, through yellow and blue, to purple and white, where the activity is most intense. This picture could only be taken with equipment carried above the layers of the Earth's atmosphere.

When viewed face-on against the bright photosphere, prominences are known as filaments. Narrow jets of gas called spicules can also be observed at the limb of the Sun. They move at around 20–30km (12–18 miles) a second from the lower chromosphere into the inner corona, and fall back or fade away after a few minutes. Flares, intense outpourings of energy, occur in complex sunspot groups, and can cause auroral activity and storms on Earth.

Above the photosphere lies the chromosphere [5], meaning "sphere of colour", and so-called because of its rosy tint when seen during a total solar eclipse. This is the region of flares and prominences [6], where the temperature rises from 6,000 to 50,000°C; temperature here is purely a measure of the speeds at which the atomic particles are moving and does not necessarily indicate extra "heat". In the chromosphere there are spicules [7], masses of high-temperature gases shooting up into the immensely rarefied corona [8], where temperatures can reach 1 million °C (1,800,000°F) – possibly due to the action of the Sun's magnetic field. Streamers [9] issue from the corona, which has no definite boundary and extends millions of kilometres out into space, eventually thinning to become the radiation we call the "solar wind". Together with the Sun's magnetic field, the solar wind dominates a vast indeterminate region of space called the heliosphere.

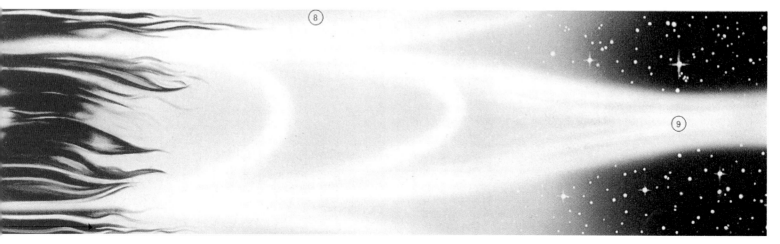

MERCURY

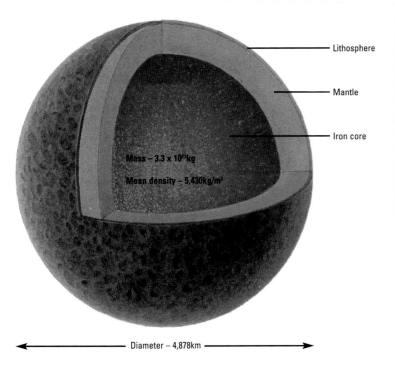

- Lithosphere
- Mantle
- Iron core

Mass – 3.3 x 10²³kg

Mean density – 5,430kg/m³

Diameter – 4,878km

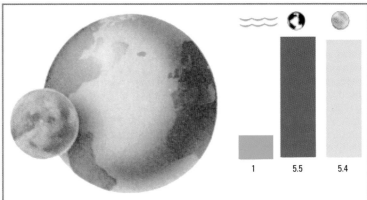

1   5.5   5.4

ABOVE With a diameter of 4,878km (3,031miles), Mercury is dwarfed by Earth and is the Solar System's smallest planet after Pluto. However, its mean density (5.4 times that of water) is similar to Earth's. A small planet must contain a lot of iron to have so high a density, and astronomers believe that Mercury has twice as much, by proportion, as any other planet. Its iron core, thought to extend out to three-quarters of its entire radius, is surrounded by a mantle of rock and a thick hard crust. Mercury has a very tenuous and thin atmosphere, mostly hydrogen and helium, with a ground pressure only two-trillionths that of Earth.

THE "FASTEST" planet, Mercury takes just 88 Earth days to orbit its massive close neighbour, the Sun – probably the reason the Romans named it after the fleet-footed messenger of the gods. It is the closest planet to the Sun and suffers the widest extremes of temperature: at noon, when the Sun is directly overhead, the temperature can soar to as high as 470°C (880°F), while during the long Mercurian night it can plunge to below –175°C (–283°F).

Mercury's orbit is elliptical: its aphelion (farthest point from the Sun) is 69,800,000km (43,400,000 miles), and its perihelion (closest point to the Sun) is 46,000,000km (28,600,000 miles).

The elusive planet

Although its existence has been known since the dawn of history, and it can appear to be brighter than the brightest star, Mercury is notoriously difficult to observe. This is because it is always too close to the Sun in the sky. The angle between Mercury and the Sun can never exceed 28°; this means that Mercury is lost in the Sun's glare because it sets no more than two hours after the Sun and rises no more than two hours before it. Once or twice a year, you may be able to see Mercury shining like a bright star close to the western horizon after sunset, or close to the eastern horizon before sunrise.

Mercury orbits the Sun in only 88 Earth days and undertakes the Earth at intervals of, on average, 115.88 days. On these occasions, Mercury lies between the Sun and Earth, but because of the tilt of its orbit (7°), usually passes above or below the Sun when viewed from Earth. Occasionally, when the alignment is right, Mercury passes directly in front of the Sun and can be seen as a small dot moving slowly across its face: such an event is called a transit. The alignments that allow transits of Mercury to take place occur only in the months of May or November, and the dates of early 21st-century transits are 7 May 2003, 8 November 2006, 9 May 2016, and 11 November 2019.

Until the 1960s, most astronomers believed that Mercury took exactly the same time to rotate on its axis as it took to orbit the Sun: one hemisphere would always face toward the Sun and constantly

suffer its boiling heat, while the other was in constant darkness. However, radar measurements carried out since then have shown that this is not the case: Mercury rotates every 58.65 Earth days, precisely two-thirds of its orbital period or year.

Mercury's magnetic puzzle

The strength of the magnetic field at Mercury's surface is very low: only about 1% that of the Earth's. This is only just strong enough to deflect most of the incoming solar wind and to form a magnetosphere around the planet. Nevertheless, Mariner

10's discovery of the magnetic field came as a surprise to most astronomers. According to conventional theory, a planet can only sustain a magnetic field if it has an electrically conductive liquid interior and rotates rapidly on its axis.

Although Mercury has a large iron core, this should in theory have cooled and solidified by now because of the planet's small size. The presence of a magnetic field suggests that at least part of the deep interior must still be liquid – but even if this is the case, Mercury's slow rotation still makes the presence of a magnetic field puzzling.

RIGHT A mosaic of Mercury created from images taken by Mariner 10, the first two-planet probe, on its outward journey in March 1974. The craft flew within 703km (437 miles) of the planet, and in three encounters during 1974–75 took more than 12,000 images covering over half its surface. Images returned by Mariner 10 revealed that most of Mercury's surface is heavily cratered from impacts by meteorites, asteroids and comets, with many over 200km (125 miles) wide. As on the Moon, some are surrounded by lighter-coloured ejecta – material splashed out by the impacts. The largest feature pictured by the probe was the Caloris Basin, measuring 1,300km (800 miles) across.

VENUS

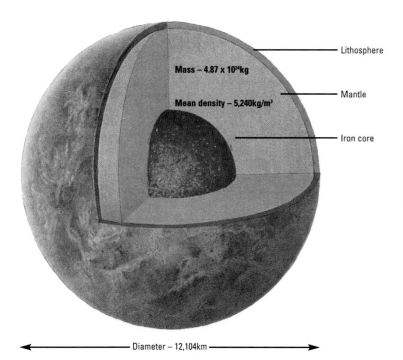

Lithosphere

Mass – 4.87 x 10²⁴kg

Mantle

Mean density – 5,240kg/m³

Iron core

— Diameter – 12,104km —

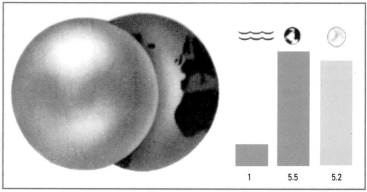

ABOVE The similarity in size, mass and density led to astronomers regarding Venus and Earth as "sister planets", formed at much the same time and part of space, but incredible heat and pressure make Venus an inhospitable body. Its internal structure, however, is probably much the same, with a nickel-iron core surrounded by a silicate mantle. The Mariner 2 probe of 1962 discovered it has a much weaker magnetic field than Earth, suggesting it may not have a liquid outer core. The lack of a strong magnetic field may also be a result of the planet's slow rotation of 243 days. Venus also rotates "backwards" (retrograde) as compared to other planets, but the reason remains a mystery.

TO THE NAKED EYE Venus is a splendid object and, as the evening and morning "star", is far brighter than any celestial object except the Sun and Moon – the reason it was named after the goddess of beauty. Telescopically, however, it has always been a disappointment, shrouded in cloud and, until very recently, mystery.

The orbit of Venus is nearer to circular than any planet, and the mean distance from the Sun – an average of 108,200,000km (67,200,000 miles) varies little. This revolution period is 224.7 Earth days, while the rotation takes 243 days.

Analysis of the sunlight reflected from the Venusian clouds revealed that the atmosphere was chiefly composed of carbon dioxide, and radio measurements suggested the surface was extremely hot. Space probe soundings of the atmosphere and surface later revealed a world completely devoid of all forms of water and confirmed searing surface temperatures that reached 480°C (895°F).

As if this were not enough, the dense atmosphere crushes down on the planet with a pressure 90 times that at the Earth's surface; a human being standing unprotected on the rock-strewn landscape of Venus would be simultaneously roasted, crushed and asphyxiated.

A dead planet

Liquid water is an essential ingredient for life as we know it, and without any water source it is extremely unlikely that any form of life ever existed on the planet. Venus's proximity to the Sun means that it probably started out with less water than the Earth – any water there would probably have existed as vapour rather than as liquid.

Even after the planets formed, the more intense solar radiation on Venus would have driven what little water remained from its atmosphere by breaking up the water molecules into their constituent parts of hydrogen and oxygen. Hydrogen is a very light gas and would have escaped off into space, while the oxygen would have been absorbed by the planet's surface. Even the rain of watery, icy comets that must have impacted Venus during its history was apparently insufficient to prevent the planet drying out.

The Venusian atmosphere

When the interiors of both Venus and Earth heated up from radioactivity, a great deal of volcanic activity occurred, causing vast amounts of carbon dioxide to be released. On Earth, the oceans dissolved some of this gas and carbonate rocks were formed, but on Venus there were no oceans and the carbon dioxide stayed in the atmosphere.

Findings in 1978 from the US Pioneer Venus 2 spacecraft, which parachuted through the atmosphere, established that Venus has sulphuric acid clouds concentrated in a layer at heights of 48–58km (30–36 miles) above the surface. Drops of the acid develop just like drops of water in our own clouds and when they are large enough, they fall as acid rain. However, this corrosive rain never reaches Venus' surface because the temperature difference, 13.3°C (56°F) at the top of the clouds and an oven-like 220°C (430°F) underneath them, causes them to evaporate at about 31km above the ground. Below this level, the Venera and Pioneer probes revealed that the atmosphere is remarkably clear, though the surface, subject to a fierce greenhouse effect, lies under a permanent overcast.

RIGHT This view of Venus was taken from 760,000km (450,000 miles) by Mariner 10's television cameras in 1974, en route to Mercury. Individual TV frames were computer-enhanced using invisible ultraviolet light: the blue appearance of the planet does not represent true colour, but is the result of darkroom processing of the images to enhance the UV markings on the clouds. It is this cloud cover that accounts for the brilliance of Venus. The picture is viewed with the predominant swirl at the South Pole. The clouds rotate 60 times faster than the planet's slow 243 days, taking only four days to go around Venus once, a rapid motion driven by the heating of the atmosphere by the nearby Sun.

EARTH

THE "THIRD rock from the Sun" is the heaviest of the stony planets and the most dense of all planets. The difference in size and mass between Earth and Venus is slight but Mars is much smaller

What makes Earth unique, however, is the fact that it has the perfect physical and chemical credentials for the evolution of life; slightly closer to the Sun, or slightly farther away, and life could not have developed. The "ecosphere", or the region in which solar radiation will produce tolerable conditions for terrestrial-type life, extends from just inside the orbit of Venus out to that of Mars. Until about 1960, it was thought that such life might exist throughout the region, but spaceprobes have shown both Venus and Mars to be incapable of creating and sustaining any form of life.

Approximately equal in density as well as size and mass, Venus absorbs about the same amount of solar energy as Earth because of the high reflecting power of its cloud. It was not until 1967, when the surface temperature of Venus was shown to register up to 480°C (895°F), that it was commonly accepted that advanced terrestrial life could develop only within a very limited zone.

Temperature depends not only on the distance of the planet from the Sun or the composition of its atmosphere; there is also the axial rotation period to be taken into account. Earth spins round once in approximately 24 hours, and the rotation period of Mars is only 37 minutes longer, but Mercury and Venus are very different – the periods are 58.7 days and 243 days respectively, leading to very peculiar "calendars". Were Earth a slow spinner, the climatic conditions would be both unfamiliar and hostile.

An atmosphere must not only enable living creatures to breathe, but also protect the planet from lethal short-wave radiations from space. There is no danger on the surface of Earth because the radiations are blocked out by layers in the upper atmosphere; had Earth been more massive, it might have been able to retain at least some of its original hydrogen (as the giants Jupiter and Saturn have done) and the resulting atmosphere might have been unsuitable for life.

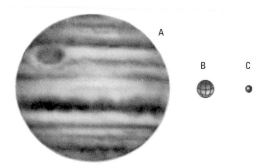

ABOVE The relative sizes of Jupiter [A], Earth [B] and Mercury [C]. Jupiter is the largest planet, Mercury the smallest (excluding the extraordinary misfit Pluto), and while Earth is intermediate in size, it is more nearly comparable with Mercury in the context of the Solar System. Earth is the largest of the so-called terrestrial planets – Mercury, Venus, Earth, Mars, Pluto – but far inferior in size even to the smallest of the four "gas giants", Neptune.

ABOVE Seen from space, Earth will show phases – just as the Moon does to us. These five photographs shown were taken from a satellite over a period of 12 hours.

RIGHT Earth as captured above the Moon's surface from an Apollo spacecraft. The contrast between the barren landscape of the Moon and the near-perfect balance of land, cloud and ocean on Earth is startling. Our planet is the only home of known life in the Solar System, though spheres in the same section of their ecospheres may well exist in the Universe.

Earth is unique in having a surface that is largely covered with water; thus although it is the largest of the four inner planets its land surface is much less than that of Venus and equal to that of Mars. There can be no oceans or even lakes on Mars, because of the low atmospheric pressure, and none on the Moon or Mercury, which are to all intents and purposes without atmosphere. On Venus the surface temperature is certainly too high for liquid water to exist, so that the old, intriguing picture of a "carboniferous" Venus, with luxuriant vegetation flourishing in a swampy and moist environment, has had to be given up.

Because Earth is so exceptional, it has been suggested that it was formed in a manner different from that of the other planets, but this is almost certainly not the case. The age of Earth, as measured by radioactive methods, is approximately 4,600 million years (4.6 eons) and studies of the lunar rocks show that the age of the Moon is the same; there is no reason to doubt that the Earth and all other members of the Solar System originated by the same process, and at about the same time, from the primeval solar nebula.

[For detailed profile of Earth, see pages 28–29; for Earth statistics, see page 54]

MARS

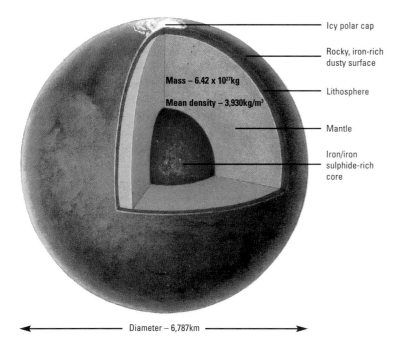

Mass – 6.42 x 10²³kg

Mean density – 3,930kg/m³

- Icy polar cap
- Rocky, iron-rich dusty surface
- Lithosphere
- Mantle
- Iron/iron sulphide-rich core

Diameter – 6,787km

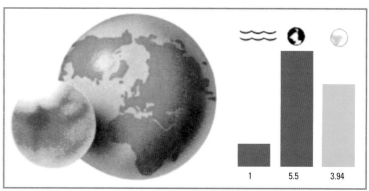

ABOVE The surface area of Mars is 28% that of Earth. Its diameter of 6,787km (4,217 miles) is a just over half that of Earth, and about twice that of the Moon. It has only a tenth of Earth's mass. Observations suggest that Mars contains an iron-rich core, about 1,700km (1,050 miles) in diameter. The low density of Mars compared to the other terrestrial planets hints that this core may also contain a significant amount of sulphur. Apparently, this core is not convecting enough to create as strong a magnetic field as Earth: indeed, it was not until 1997 that Mars Global Surveyor detected its weak and patchy magnetic field.

LIKE EARTH, Mars experiences seasons. Varying between 207 million km and 249 million km (129 and 158 million) miles from the Sun, its orbit is not circular and it is much closer to the Sun during the southern summer than in the northern summer, so that southern Martian summers are warmer than northern ones. But because the planet moves faster when it is closer to the Sun they are shorter and southern winters longer and colder than those in the north; one result is that the southern residual cap retains some frozen carbon dioxide (which melts at a lower temperature) as well as water.

In the late 1960s the Mariner 4, 6 and 7 spacecraft confirmed that the surface resides under only a thin atmosphere of carbon dioxide, with a pressure of only one hundredth of that at the Earth's surface at most, and in places even lower. They also revealed that Mars is cold, with mean annual temperatures ranging from –58°C (–72°F) at the equator to –123°C (–189°F) at the poles. At these temperatures and low pressures liquid water cannot currently exist on the Martian surface, although the Mariner and subsequent Viking pictures revealed evidence for the ancient action of flowing water.

RIGHT A mosaic image of the Schiaparelli hemisphere created from images taken by the Viking orbiter in 1980. Mars was once considered the likeliest of planets to share Earth's cargo of life, the seasonal expansion of dark patches strongly suggesting vegetation and the icecaps indicating the presence of water.

However, close inspection by spacecraft brought disappointment: some combination of chemical reactions, erosion and dark dust deposited by strong winds account for the "vegetation", and the "icecaps", though comprising a permanent layer of water ice, are covered from autumn to spring by a cover of carbon dioxide frost. Whatever oxygen the planet once possessed is now locked up in the iron-bearing rock that covers its cratered surface and gives it its characteristic red colour. The large crater near the centre is Schiaparelli, about 500km (370 miles) in diameter.

Mars is smaller and less "massive" than Earth or Venus, and so has a lower surface gravity and cannot hold on to a dense atmosphere. Mars' lower volume means that it could not generate and retain the same amount of internal heat as Venus or Earth, and does not maintain the same level of volcanic activity.

The core is surrounded by a molten rocky mantle denser and perhaps three times as rich in iron oxide as that of the Earth, overlain by a thin crust. The lack of plate tectonics and absence of current volcanic activity implies this mantle is also non-convecting – though one massive feature, the 4,500-km (2,800-mile) long Valles Marineris, may be a fracture in the crust caused by internal stresses.

Mars has two small moons, Phobos and Deimos, two potato-shape asteroids that were once captured by the planet's gravity.

JUPITER

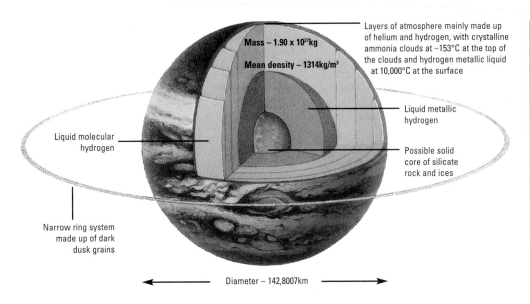

Mass – 1.90 x 10²⁷kg

Mean density – 1314kg/m³

Layers of atmosphere mainly made up of helium and hydrogen, with crystalline ammonia clouds at –153°C at the top of the clouds and hydrogen metallic liquid at 10,000°C at the surface

Liquid metallic hydrogen

Liquid molecular hydrogen

Possible solid core of silicate rock and ices

Narrow ring system made up of dark dusk grains

Diameter – 142,8007km

Jupiter's mean density is only 1.3 times that of water *(right)*, but the outer layers are tenuous and the core is far denser. The Earth's axis is tilted at an angle of 23¹/₂° from the perpendicular to the plane of orbit, but Jupiter's is only just over 3° *(below)*.

1   5.5   1.3

23.5°   3.1°

FAR BEYOND the main asteroid belt, at a mean distance of 778,300,000km (483,600,000 miles) from the Sun, lies Jupiter, the largest of the planets. This huge globe could swallow up 1,300 bodies the volume of Earth but its mass – despite being nearly three times as much as the other planets combined – is only 318 times that Earth because Jupiter is much less dense.

The planet is mostly gas, under intense pressure in its lower atmosphere above a core of fiercely compressed hydrogen and helium. The upper layers form strikingly coloured rotating belts, outward signs of the intense storms created by its rapid rotation of less than ten hours. This also means that the equator tends to bulge, and like Saturn the planet is clearly flattened at the poles: Jupiter's equatorial diameter is 143,000km (89,000 miles), whereas the polar diameter is less than 135,000km (84,000 miles).

When viewing the planet, you can only see the outermost part of its very deep atmosphere, which has several layers of cloud of different composition and colour. Jupiter rotates so fast that it spins the clouds into bands in which various spots, waves and other dynamic weather systems occur. The banded patterns in Jupiter's clouds arise because of the existence of convection cells in the atmosphere. The giant spots between, and sometimes within,

the bands are giant eddies, or rotating masses of cloudy air, similar to enormous versions of our earthly hurricanes. Other weather systems, often of contrasting colour, appear embedded in the layers.

The Great Red Spot

While most of Jupiter's spots are short-lived, the Great Red Spot, by far the largest, is the notable exception. Under observation for over 300 years, it sometimes disappears but always returns, and has been prominent this time around since the mid-1960s. Occurring at a latitude of around 23° south, it is a huge, complex, cloudy vortex – variable in size but always far larger than the diameter of Earth – rotating in an anti-clockwise direction.

The "GRS" is believed to be a two-dimensional vortex which spirals outwards away from areas of high pressure, so although it appears like a hurricane it is a high- rather than low-pressure phenomenon. The reasons for its constant position and its characteristic colour, however, remain unclear.

Jupiter's rings

Recent investigations by spaceprobes have shown an orbiting ring system and discovered several previously unknown moons, and Jupiter has at least 16. The ring system is composed of three major

components. The main ring is some 7,000km (4,350 miles) wide and has an average radius of about 126,000km (80,000 miles). At its inner edge this merges into the halo, a faint doughnut-shaped ring about 20,000km (12,400 miles) across, which extends over half the distance to the planet itself. Just outside the main ring is a faint gossamer ring made of fine material, extending out past the orbit of the innermost satellite Amalthea. These rings are not only more tenuous than Saturn's but are also darker, probably comprising dust rather than ice.

The magnetic field

Jupiter has a strong magnetic field, caused by the planet still cooling from its time of formation and constantly collapsing in on itself under its own gravitational pull. This gives off heat, producing dynamic convection movements in the fluid metallic interior. Coupled with the spin of Jupiter's rapid rotation, it produces an extensive magnetic field about 20,000 times stronger than that of the Earth – one which constantly alters size and shape in response to changes in the solar wind.

LEFT Voyager 1 took this photo of Jupiter and the innermost of its four Galilean satellites, Io, in 1979, with Io about 420,600km (260,000 miles) above Jupiter's Great Red Spot. The picture was taken about 20 million km (12,400,000 miles) from the planet. Slightly larger than our Moon, Io is the densest large object in the outer Solar System and most volcanically active, spewing material up to 300km (200 miles) into the air; in 1996, when Galileo detected an iron core and magnetic field, it found the moon's surface features had changed radically since the satellite was imaged by Voyager just 17 years before.

Jupiter's main moons are group-named after Galileo because it was his identification of their orbiting the planet that eventually led him to support Copernicus's revolutionary views that Earth revolved round the Sun. They are Europa, Callisto and Ganymede, the largest satellite in the Solar System and bigger than Mercury and Pluto, orbiting Jupiter at a distance of just over 1 million km (620,000 miles).

SATURN

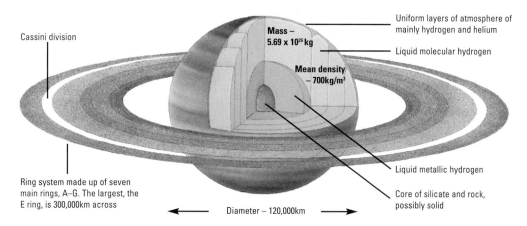

Cassini division

Ring system made up of seven main rings, A–G. The largest, the E ring, is 300,000km across

Mass – 5.69 x 10²⁶ kg

Mean density – 700kg/m³

Diameter – 120,000km

Uniform layers of atmosphere of mainly hydrogen and helium

Liquid molecular hydrogen

Liquid metallic hydrogen

Core of silicate and rock, possibly solid

Saturn

Earth to same scale

1   5.5   1.3

OUTERMOST OF the planets known to ancient man and named after the Roman god of agriculture, Saturn lies at a mean distance of 1,427 million km (88 million miles) from the Sun and has a revolution period of 29.46 years. The second largest planet in the Solar System, its polar diameter of 120,000km (75,000 miles) is considerably less than its equatorial diameter.

Astronomers believe the temperatures in the core of Saturn exceed 11,700°C (21,000°F), and the atmosphere must be deeply convective since this is the only plausible way to transport the interior heat to levels where it can be radiated to space. Like its neighbours Jupiter and Uranus, Saturn radiates more energy into space than it receives from the Sun.

The atmosphere of Saturn broadly resembles that of Jupiter: it has 80–90% hydrogen, 10–20% helium and less than 1% traces of other gases, including methane and ammonia detected by Earth-based and Voyager spectroscopy. Because the cloud layers are cooler than those of Jupiter, they tend to be thicker and more uniform in shape, forming deeper in the atmosphere. Saturn's distinctive hazy yellow hue, plus the deeper orange-yellow of Titan, largest of its 18 moons, are thought to be caused by deep haze layers of condensed hydrocarbons.

Saturn's magnetosphere is smaller than that of Jupiter, though it still extends well beyond the orbits of the outer moons, while the field is about 30 times weaker than that of its huge neighbour.

ABOVE Though not as large as Jupiter, Saturn's globe is of impressive size – its volume is 1,000 times that of Earth. The mean density of Saturn is only 0.7 that of water, far less than any other planet, and it would float if it were dropped into an ocean. The low density is due to the preponderance of hydrogen.

RIGHT Voyager 2 returned this view of Saturn in 1981, when the spacecraft was approaching the large, gaseous planet at about 1 million km (620,000 miles) a day.

The so-called "ribbon-like" feature in the white cloud band marks a high-speed jet at about 47° north; there, the westerly wind speeds are about 530km/h (330mph). Although less pronounced than on Jupiter, the bands, storms, ovals and eddies are all evident here, too, caused by the same combination of rapid rotation (just under 10 hours and 14 minutes) and convective atmosphere.

Saturn's stunning ring system – hundreds or even thousands of narrow ringlets – are grouped, giving the impression of broad bands, each of which has been designated a letter. Brighter than those of other outer planets and no more than 1.5km thick, they comprise millions of small objects ranging in size from tiny stones to rocks several metres long, and are composed at least in part of water ice, possibly plus rocky particles with icy coatings.

The bright A and B rings and the fainter C ring are visible from Earth through a telescope. The space between the A and B rings is called the Cassini division, while the much narrower Encke division splits the A ring. The complex structure is due to the gravitational effects of the satellites, which orbit close to and within the rings.

Saturn has 18 named satellites, six of them icy (resembling the three outer moons of Jupiter) and the others small and rocky. The unique atmosphere of Titan, second largest moon in the Solar System after Ganymede, make it the odd one out. About every 15 years we see Saturn's rings edge-on because of the orbital geometry between Saturn and Earth.

URANUS

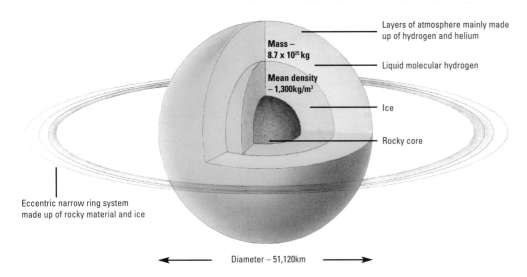

Layers of atmosphere mainly made up of hydrogen and helium

Mass – 8.7 x 10²⁵ kg

Mean density – 1,300kg/m³

Liquid molecular hydrogen

Ice

Rocky core

Eccentric narrow ring system made up of rocky material and ice

Diameter – 51,120km

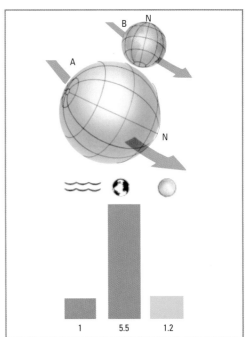

DISCOVERED BY William Herschel in 1781, Uranus appears as a smooth, aqua-coloured sphere with very subtle hints of bands, but this calm facade gives no hint of a history fraught with spectacular catastrophe: at some stage a mighty collision wrenched the young planet off its axis. As a result the planet is tipped over on its side so that its rotation axis lies almost in the plane of the planet's orbit, giving rise to the most striking seasonal changes. Another collision may have been responsible for the fantastic geology of its moon Miranda.

Uranus has a mean distance from the Sun of 2,869,600,000km (1,783 million miles) and a revolution period of just over 84 years. Its basic composition is the same as the other giant planets and similar to that of the Sun – predominantly hydrogen (about 80%) with some helium (15%), the remainder of the atmosphere being methane, hydrocarbons (molecular mixtures of carbon, nitrogen, hydrogen and oxygen) and other trace elements.

RIGHT The tilt of Uranus's axis [A] compared to Earth [B] is 98°, unique in the Solar System. Its density is 1.2 times that of water, more than Jupiter and Saturn but far less than Earth.

Uranus' colour is caused by the small amount of methane – probably less than 3% – that preferentially absorbs red light, meaning the reflected sunlight we see is greenish-blue.

Temperatures at the outer layers of the atmosphere are very cold, about –200°C (330°F), but pressures and temperatures rise with depth and the hydrogen and helium transform from gas to a liquid state. At still greater depth, a transition occurs to a thick, viscous, partly solidified layer of highly compressed liquid water, which may have traces of ammonia and methane. Deep within the centre of Uranus, at extremely high pressure, a core of rocky material is thought to exist, with a mass almost five times that of Earth.

BELOW A composite image of Uranus, the striking but featureless blue planet, and five of its 15 moons, made from photographs taken by Voyager 2 in 1986. The moons (clockwise from top left) are Umbriel, Oberon, Titania, Miranda and Ariel. While an unexplained jumble of huge geological features dominates Miranda, tectonic activity has given Ariel the youngest surface of the moons. Voyager 2's discovery of 10 moons tripled Uranus's known total, while in 1997 two unnamed satellites, probably captured asteroids, were found by the Palomar Observatory. In 1977, astronomers discovered that Uranus has a ring system: there are nine well-defined rings, plus a fainter one and a wider fuzzy ring.

NEPTUNE

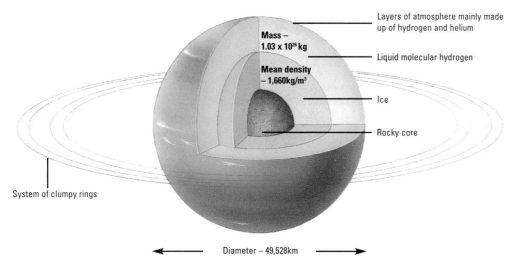

Mass –
1.03 x 10²⁶ kg

Mean density
– 1,660kg/m³

Layers of atmosphere mainly made up of hydrogen and helium

Liquid molecular hydrogen

Ice

Rocky core

System of clumpy rings

← Diameter – 49,528km →

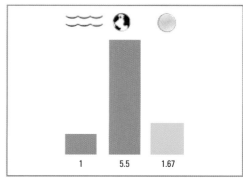

1   5.5   1.67

ABOVE Densest of the four main outer planets, Neptune's mass is 17.1 times that of Earth. Its almost circular orbit is always more than 4 billion km (2.5 billion miles) from Earth. Its rotation period is just over 16 hours.

A NEAR TWIN to Uranus in size, Neptune has a similar atmospheric make-up and internal structure, though its magnetic field is 60% weaker. A gas giant surrounded by clumpy rings and eight moons, it takes 164.8 years to orbit the Sun.

Unlike Uranus, which has no detectable internal heat source, Neptune has the strongest internal heat source of all the giant planets. It radiates almost three times more heat than equilibrium conditions would predict, as opposed to Jupiter and Saturn, which radiate about twice as much energy as expected.

Clouds and storms are the main features of Neptune's dynamic atmosphere. Dominating all is the Great Dark Spot, a hurricane-like storm in the southern hemisphere about half the size of Earth. Like all Neptune's weather conditions, it is constantly and rapidly changing. Neptune's winds are among the fastest in the Solar System, dwarfed only by Saturn's high-speed equatorial jet.

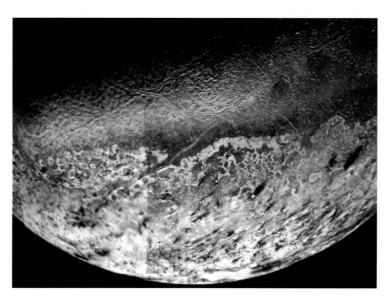

LEFT The southern hemisphere of Triton, largest of Neptune's eight moons, pictured from Voyager 2 in 1989. The large, lighter-coloured area is the polar icecap, probably nitrogen. Because of its retrograde and highly inclined orbit, it is thought Triton was captured by the gravitational pull of Neptune. Tiny Nereid was also known before 1989, when Voyager discovered six more satellites.

PLUTO

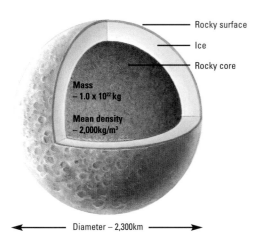

Rocky surface

Ice

Rocky core

Mass
– 1.0 x 10²² kg

Mean density
– 2,000kg/m³

← Diameter – 2,300km →

ABOVE Pluto has an average density about twice that of water ice, implying its interior is composed of rock; about 30% of its volume is thought to be water ice. Like Earth, Pluto's atmosphere is primarily nitrogen gas, but the changing surface pressure never exceeds about 10 millibars – around one hundred thousandth of the pressure on Earth at sea level.

FARTHEST PLANET from the Sun, Pluto's tiny size (smaller than Mercury) and rocky composition (like the terrestrial planets of the inner system) make it a real misfit among the gas giants of the outer system. In both size and surface constituents it is similar to Triton, a moon of Neptune, and many astronomers believe it is a former satellite of Neptune somehow separated from its parent.

Pluto has a long, elliptical and tilted orbit that takes over 248 Earth years to complete, of which about 20 years are inside the orbit of Neptune, the last occasion being from 1979 to 1999. Discovered only in 1930, its size and distance from Earth make it difficult to study, despite its high reflectivity: in our sky it is less than one 36,000th of a degree across – the equivalent of a walnut at a range of 50km (30 miles). It is thought that the surface of Pluto is largely nitrogen ice, with methane and carbon monoxide ices as impurities. At nearly half its size, the mysterious Charon (discovered in 1978) is the Solar System's largest moon in relation to its parent planet. Pluto did not form in isolation: it is simply the largest relic in space past Neptune left over from the formation of the Solar System.

RIGHT Hubble Space Telescope (HST) images from 1994 showing two hemispheres of Pluto. The two main images have been computer processed to show rotation and bring out the differences in brightness on the surface; the original "raw" images are at the top left of each panel. Twelve bright regions have been identified, including a large north polar cap.

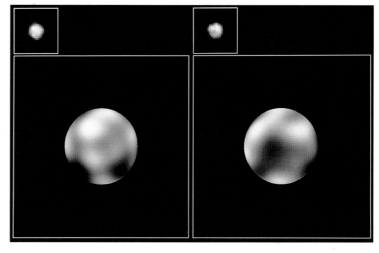

THE MOON

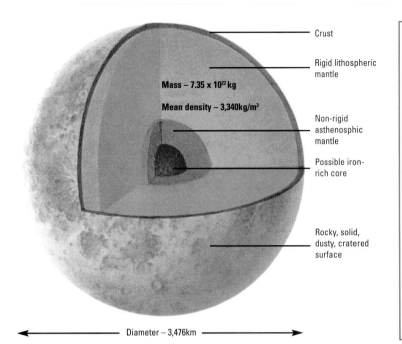

Crust

Rigid lithospheric mantle

Mass – 7.35 x 10²² kg

Mean density – 3,340kg/m³

Non-rigid asthenosphic mantle

Possible iron-rich core

Rocky, solid, dusty, cratered surface

Diameter – 3,476km

The average diameter of the Moon is 3,475km (2,159 miles), 0.27 times Earth. It has a mass of about 1/81 that of Earth, its surface gravity is one-sixth of Earth, and its density is 3.344 times that of water. It orbits the Earth at a mean distance of 384,199 km (238,731 miles) at an average speed of 3,683km/h (2,289mph) in relation to the Earth. It orbits its parent in 27.3 days.

BECAUSE THE Moon is about 400 times smaller than the Sun, but about 400 times closer to Earth, humans have always seen them as roughly the same size. While the Moon is tiny in cosmic terms, however, its diameter is more than a quarter that of Earth, considerably more than Pluto and well over 70% that of Mercury. Despite its bright appearance it is a dark body, illuminated only by light reflected from the Sun.

Analysis of lunar samples suggests that the Moon was formed from the remnant of a Mars-sized body that collided with the juvenile planet Earth in a giant impact some 4,500 billion years

LEFT The lunar "seas" were formed, either by internal accretion or by impact, at an early stage development of Moon and Earth surfaces around 4,000 million years ago [1]. The general aspect of the Moon then must have been similar to that of today, although the basins were not filled. The surface of both the Earth and the Moon then remained the same for a considerable period. Some 2,000 million years ago the basins on the Moon were filled in; 1,000 million years later [4] lunar activity was almost over, while Earth has since seen fabulous change.

ago. Any iron-rich core this body may have had appears to have been absorbed into the Earth's core, while the Moon grew out of the mostly rocky debris thrown into space by the crash. The lack of a large, fluid core explains the almost total lack of a magnetic field, which registers only one ten millionth of the strength of Earth's.

The Moon's characteristic dark patches – the face of the "Man in the Moon" – are low-lying regions once flooded by outpourings of basaltic lava, which scientists have dated as between 3 and 4 billion years ago. Known as the lunar seas (Latin *maria*, singular *mare*), they have appeared never to have contained any water, nor indeed any liquid.

Only about 59% of the Moon's surface is directly visible from Earth. Reflected light takes 1.25 seconds to reach us – compared to 8 minutes 27.3 seconds for light from the Sun. With the Sun overhead the temperature on the lunar equator can reach 117.2°C (243°F), and at night it can sink to –162.7°C (–261°C). An astronaut has only a sixth of his normal weight on the Moon, though his mass is unaltered. There is no local surface colour and the lunar sky is black, even when the Sun is above the horizon. There is no air or water – and there has never been any form of life.

BELOW After the dark patches of the lunar seas, huge craters are the most noticeable features on the Moon. Once presumed volcanic in origin, it is now accepted they were caused by the impact of asteroids and comets travelling at tens of kilometres a second. Around 30 times the size of the foreign bodies that created them, the craters are always roughly circular unless, rarely, the angle of impact was extremely oblique. The Moon's lack of any atmosphere means that its surface remains unprotected from any form of impactors – an atmospheric layer, as on Earth, helps to burn up any encroaching objects – and this, combined with the fact that it has no geological processes, means that no crater is ever worn away or changed . . . except by the arrival of another foreign body.

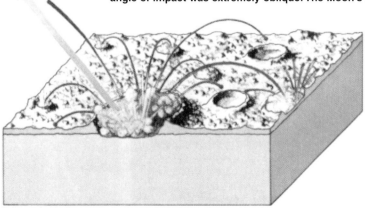

COMETS

A GREAT COMET, with a brilliant head and a tail stretching way across the sky, is a spectacular object – and it is easy to understand they caused such terror in ancient times. Comets have always been regarded as unlucky and fear of them is still not dead in some primitive societies.

Yet a comet is not nearly as important as it may look: it is made up of small rock and ice particles and tenuous gas. On several occasions Earth passed through a comet's tail without suffering the slightest damage. Since Edmund Halley first calculated the paths of several comets in 1695 – including Halley's, whose period is 76 years and which last appeared in 1986 – astronomers have found over 600 such bodies orbiting the Sun.

Analysis of a comet

At the heart of every comet is the nucleus, a solid mass of ice that also contains small solid particles of rock called "dust". Most nuclei are between 1 and 10km (0.6 and 6 miles) across, though they can reach 100km (60 miles). The dark thin crust of icy dust that covers them reflects only 4% of sunlight, making them difficult to detect when distant from the Sun. Over 80% of the ice is simple water ice – the nucleus of Halley's comet contains more than 300,000 tonnes of it – and another 10% or more is frozen carbon dioxide and carbon monoxide. The coma and tails appear only when the comet approaches the Sun, which can be from any angle; as the comet recedes the tail disappears.

Because a comet nucleus shrinks every time it passes the Sun – Halley's by perhaps about a metre (3ft) on each orbit – no comet can have been in its present orbit since the birth of the Solar System. It is now believed that while some comets come from the Kuiper belt beyond Pluto, far more spend most of their time in the Oort cloud much farther out in space. Collisions occur, too: in 1994 at least 21 fragments of Shoemaker-Levy 9 exploded in Jupiter's upper atrmosphere, and Jupuiter may well have swept up many comets from farther out in the Solar System in the past.

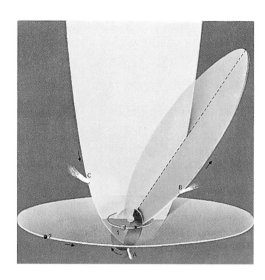

RIGHT There are three main classes of comet. The faint short-period comets [A] often have their aphelia (furthest points from the Sun) at approximately the distance of Jupiter's orbit [1], and their periods amount to a few years. Long-period comets [B] have aphelia near or beyond Neptune's orbit [2], though Halley's is the only conspicuous member of the class. Comets with very long periods [C] have such great orbital eccentricities that the paths are almost parabolic. Apart from Halley's, all the really brilliant comets are of this type. Half the known comets orbit almost entirely within the paths of Jupiter and Saturn, taking 20 or so years; the quickest, Encke, takes just 3.3 years. At the other extreme there are comets with huge orbits: Hyakutake, last seen in 1996, will not be near the Sun again for another 14,000 years.

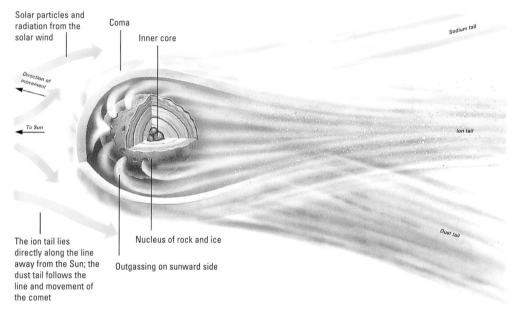

Solar particles and radiation from the solar wind

Coma

Inner core

Sodium tail

Direction of movement

To Sun

Ion tail

Dust tail

The ion tail lies directly along the line away from the Sun; the dust tail follows the line and movement of the comet

Nucleus of rock and ice

Outgassing on sunward side

LEFT Hale-Bopp had its perihelion (closest approach to the Sun) in 1997, and it was easily seen with the naked eye from much of Earth for several days. Spectroscopy revealed 38 types of gas present in the comet's coma.

BELOW Following its visit in 1910, Halley's comet last returned to perihelion in 1986. Although not as bright as the great "non-periodical" comets, the increase and decline of the tail is clearly shown. As it approached perihelion the tail developed enormously; after the closest approach to the Sun the tail contracted, so that when the comet was last seen the tail had disappeared altogether. The seventh picture shows the tail shortly before perihelion.

ABOVE A comet has an irregular nucleus of rock and ice. As it nears the Sun, the ice vaporizes and combines with dust to produce the coma or head, hiding the nucleus from our view. The gas or ion tail, often blue and comprising charged electrons (ions) caught up in the solar wind, streams away from the direction of the Sun for up to 100 million km (60 million miles); the dust tail, often white in reflected sunlight, comprises tiny grains of rock and can stretch for up to 10 million km (6 million miles) behind the comet. When observing comet Hale-Bopp in 1997 astronomers also discovered a new type, the sodium tail, which accelerates a straight neutral gas tail up to 10 million km (6 million miles) behind the comet.

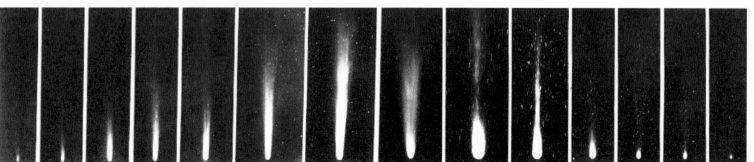

ASTEROIDS AND METEOROIDS

SINCE THE BEGINNING of the 19th century, astronomers have catalogued more than 8,000 asteroids orbiting our Sun, and at least 10,000 more have been observed. It is estimated that there are at least a million of these rocky bodies with diameters of over 1km (0.6 miles), their numbers making nonsense of their previous description the "minor planets". Along with comets and meteoroids, they are better described as "space debris", though 95% are found in the main asteroid belt between Mars and Jupiter. Some tiny examples find their way to Earth as meteorites, but our knowledge of their formation and composition remains limited.

Asteroid orbits

The main belt asteroids are not smoothly distributed in cloud between Mars and Jupiter. There are gaps in the main belt where very few asteroids exist. These were discovered by an American astronomer, Daniel Kirkwood, and are known as the Kirkwood gaps and mark places where the orbital period would be a simple fraction of Jupiter's. For example, an asteroid orbiting the Sun at a distance of 375 million km (233 million miles) would complete exactly three orbits while Jupiter orbited the Sun once. It would feel a gravitational tug from Jupiter, away from the Sun, every orbit, and quickly be moved out of that position.

However, in some places more asteroids are seen than expected: one such place is Jupiter's orbit. A swarm of a few hundred asteroids is found 60° ahead of and behind Jupiter in the same orbit. Known as the Trojans, they orbit the Sun at the same rate as Jupiter, but hardly ever come close enough to the planet for their orbits to be disturbed.

Swarms can also be found within the main belt of asteroids. These are known as asteroid families, and are formed when two larger asteroids collide. Astronomers then see the resulting fragments as many smaller asteroids sharing similar orbits around the Sun.

ABOVE The asteroid Ida as photographed by the Galileo spacecraft on its way to Jupiter in 1993. Galileo discovered a small moon, seen here on the right, orbiting at about 100km (60 miles); named Dactyl by surprised scientists, this irregularly shaped satellite measures only 1.7 cu. km (0.4 cu. miles). Galileo also passed the asteroids Gaspra and Mathilde, like Ida heavily cratered by small asteroids and meteorites: one crater on Mathilde was estimated at about 10km (6 miles) deep, huge in relation to the body's size.

Formation and composition of asteroids

For some time it was thought that the asteroids were the debris of a collision that destroyed a "missing" planet, but it now seems unlikely that a large planet ever formed between Mars and Jupiter – mainly because of the latter's gravitational field. Most of the mass present in that region during the early days of the Solar System was probably rotating in elliptical orbits and ended up colliding with the planets, their satellites or even the Sun.

No asteroid has ever been shown to have an atmosphere, so the light we see must be sunlight reflected from the surface. An asteroid's composition depends on its distance from the Sun. In the inner main belt nearest Mars, they are made of silicate rocks (minerals containing silicon and oxygen) similar to those found on Earth. These are called "S-type" asteroids. In the middle of the belt are mostly "C-type": these appear to have rocks containing carbon, similar to some types of meteorites landing on Earth.

The outer belt has asteroids that are so dark they only reflect 5% of the sunlight that reaches them, and are very red. Our best assumption about these "D-type" asteroids is that there is a large amount of ices such as water ice and frozen carbon monoxide

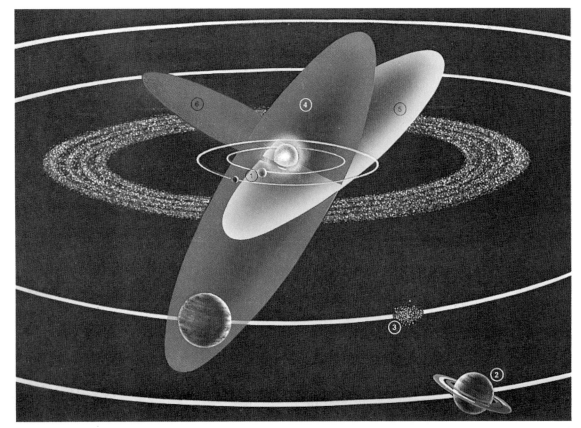

LEFT The orbits of the planets from Earth [1] out to Saturn [2], together with some notable asteroids (the illustration is not to scale). While most asteroids move in the region between the orbits of Mars and Jupiter, the so-called Trojan asteroids [3] move in the same orbit as Jupiter. They keep their distance, however, and collisions are unlikely to occur: one group moves 60° ahead of the planet and the other group 60° behind, though they move round for some distance to either side of their mean positions.

Hidalgo [4] has a path which is highly inclined and so eccentric – much like a comet – that its aphelion (farthest point from the Sun) is not far from the orbit of Saturn. Amor [5] and Apollo [6] belong to the so-called "Earth-grazing" asteroid group. All the Earth-grazers are very small: Amor has a diameter of 8km (5 miles) and Apollo only about 2km (1.25 miles). Both satellites of Mars, Phobos and Deimos, are asteroids captured by the gravitational pull of the planet.

mixed in with the rock, and that charged particles from the solar wind hitting them have created chemical reactions to form the dark red colour.

This change in asteroid make-up is logical if they were formed at the beginning of the Solar System, as this change in composition fits in with theories about how the planets formed. In addition, since their formation, asteroids nearer the Sun have been heated more than those farther out; this means that, over time, more ice melted and escaped. Farther away, lower temperatures mean that less of the ice has melted.

Asteroids undergo some of the most violent temperature changes in the Solar System. One asteroid, Icarus, actually approaches closer to the the Sun than the baked planet Mercury. At its perihelion (closest point), only 28 million km (17 million miles), its surface can reach more than 900°C (500°F); just 200 Earth days later it has reached its aphelion (farthest point), 295 million km (183 million miles) from the warmth of the Sun in the cool space beyond Mars.

Asteroids and Earth

In 1937 Hermes, a mere 1km (0.6 miles) in diameter, passed just 780,000km (485,000 miles) from Earth, less than twice the distance of the Moon. What would happen if such an object hit Earth? Besides the tremendous heat, enough rock and dust would be deposited in the atmosphere to change the climate all over the Earth, while if it landed near water, huge tsunamis would devastate cities on the edge of the ocean all over the globe. Indeed, it is now widely thought that the impact of an asteroid or comet 65 million years ago, producing a crater 180km (112 miles) wide in the Yucatan Peninsula of Mexico assisted in the extinction of the dinosaurs. Luckily for us, it's estimated that such devastating impacts are likely to happen only once every 100 million years or so.

Meteors

Commonly known as shooting stars, meteors are flashes of light caused by particles of rock entering the Earth's atmosphere at altitudes of around 100km (60 miles), most of them only the size of a grain of sand. As they travel at between 10 and 30km (6 to 18 miles) per second, friction with the air molecules rapidly heats them to thousands of degrees, and they vaporize in a flash of heat. Larger and therefore brighter meteors are known as fireballs, and can be anything from the size of a small pebble up to a large boulder. Before the rocks enter our atmosphere, they are following their own orbit about the Sun.

A "meteor shower" occurs when Earth passes through one of the meteor streams, belts of dust

RIGHT The sizes of the first four asteroids to be discovered, Ceres [C], Vesta [D], Pallas [E] and Juno [F], together with the irregularly-shaped Eros [B], are compared here with the Moon [A]. Being so small, the diameters are difficult to measure: earlier assessments of Ceres gave 685km (426 miles), but new methods show that it is much larger at 913km (567 miles). Still the largest known asteroid, Ceres is two-fifths the size of Pluto. It was the first asteroid to be identified, by the Italian astronomer Guiseppe Piazzi in 1801.

While Ceres and some other large asteroids are spherical, most are elongated and lumpy. All are pitted with craters – one on Mathilde is 10km (6 miles) deep. The average rotation period of an asteroid is eight hours, but while Florentina takes only three hours to spin once, Mathilde takes 17 days. They almost certainly originate from the time of the formation of the Solar System and are not remnants of a large planet that disintegrated, as was once thought. The largest asteroid is less than 1% of the mass of the Moon, and the known asteroids combined are less than 10% of Earth's mass. The first encounter by a space probe was made by the Galileo mission in 1989.

particles sharing their orbits with comets but too heavy to be swept out of the Solar System. For example, the Leonid shower shares the orbit of comet Temple-Tuttle. The best showers occur on 12 August and 13 December each year. They are called the Perseid meteor shower and the Geminid meteor shower because their radiant points appear to be in the constellations of Perseus and Gemini.

Meteorites

While meteoroids usually burn up in the atmosphere, some are big enough to make it through the atmosphere without being completely vaporized and reach the ground; they are then called meteorites. Scientists estimate that about 300,000 meteorites reach the surface of the Earth every year, though many fall in the oceans or remote forests,

deserts and mountains. Even those that fall near towns and cities can remain undiscovered, since many look like ordinary rocks to the untrained eye. Some meteorites are tiny particles, while others weigh up to 200 tonnes. Meteoroids weighing more than about 100 tonnes that don't break up are not decelerated as much as lighter bodies, and produce impressive impact craters.

When chemically analysed, there are many different types of meteorite. The most common finds are called chondrites, and appear to be the same type of iron- and silicon-bearing rock that S-type asteroids are made from. Much rarer are the carbonaceous chondrites, which have large amounts of carbon and appear to have come from the middle of the asteroid belt. Finally, about 10% of meteorites are the heavier stony-iron and iron-nickel type.

RIGHT Research suggests that craters such as the Barringer in Arizona, 1.6km (1 mile) wide and 180m (600ft) deep, was formed by nickel-iron meteorites up to about 50,000 years ago. Burning up as they plunged through the atmosphere, they shattered the Earth's outer layer of rock on impact (*top right*). Because of their high speed they burrowed into the ground, causing friction, heat, compression and shock-waves, culminating in a violent explosion that left the huge crater. More than 130 craters have so far been identified, though many more were created before being subsequently destroyed by geological activity and erosion.

TIME AND MOTION

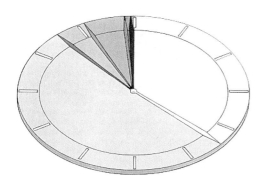

ABOVE A "clock" of the Earth's history, with 12 hours representing the 4,600 million years the world has been in existence. The first 2 hours and 52 minutes are still obscure, but the earliest rocks are then formed – though the planet remains a lifeless desert until 04.20, when bacterial organisms first appear.

Eons of time drag by until just after 10.30, when there is an explosion of invertebrate life in the oceans. Dinosaurs wander the land by 11.36, only to die out and replaced by birds and mammals 25 minutes later. Hominids arrive about 30 seconds before noon – and the last tenth of a second covers human civilization.

The oldest rocks of the great Precambrian shields of North America, Africa and Australia convey dates of up to about 3,500 million years ago. Only the past 570 million years show an abundance of plant and animal life. The most widely found fossil remains from any period are called index fossils and are used to correlate various rock formations of the same age.

THE BASIC unit of time measurement is the day, one rotation of the Earth on its axis. The subdivision of the day into hours, minutes and seconds is simply for our convenience. The present Western calendar is based on the "solar year", the 365.24 days the Earth takes to orbit the Sun.

Calendars based on the movements of the Sun and Moon, however, have been used since ancient times. The average length of the year, fixed by the Julian Calendar introduced by Julius Caesar, was about 11 minutes too long, and the cumulative error was eventually rectified in 1582 by the Gregorian Calendar. Pope Gregory XIII decreed that the day following 4 October that year was in fact 15 October, and that century years do not count as leap years unless they are divisible by 400. Britain did not adopt the reformed calendar until 1752 – by which stage it was lagging 11 days behind the continent; the Gregorian Calendar was imposed on all its possessions, including the American colonies, with all dates preceding 2 September marked O.S., for Old Style.

The seasons are generated by a combination of the Earth's revolution around the Sun and the tilt of its axis of 23½°. The solstices (from the Greek *sol*, sun, and *stitium*, standing) are the two times in the year when the Sun is overhead at one of the Tropics of Cancer and Capricorn, 23½° North and South, furthest from the Equator. The equinoxes (from the Greek *aequus*, equal, and *nox*, night) are the two times in the year when day and night are of equal length due to the Sun being overhead at the Equator. The longest and shortest days in each hemisphere fall on or around the solstices, and are opposites in each hemisphere.

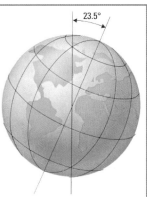

The Earth's axis is inclined at 23.5° to the perpendicular to the orbital plane. This angle accounts for the complex seasonal variations in climate, notably in mid-latitudes. The varying distance of the Earth from the Sun has only a minor effect.

DEFINITIONS OF TIME

Year: The time taken by the Earth to revolve around the Sun, or 365.24 days.
Month: The approximate time taken by the Moon to revolve around the Earth. The 12 months of the year in fact vary from 28 days (29 in a Leap Year – once every 4 years to offset the difference between the calendar and the solar year) to 31 days.
Week: An artificial period of 7 days. Unlike days, months and years – but like minutes and seconds – it is not based on astronomical time.
Day: The time taken by the Earth to complete one rotation (spin) on its axis.
Hour: A day comprises 24 hours, divided into hours a.m. (*ante meridiem*, before noon) and p.m. (*post meridiem*, after noon) – though time-tables use the 24-hour system from midnight.

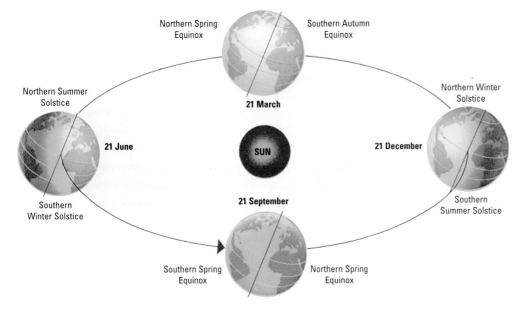

Northern Spring Equinox

Southern Autumn Equinox

Northern Summer Solstice

Northern Winter Solstice

21 March

21 June

SUN

21 December

Southern Winter Solstice

Southern Summer Solstice

21 September

Southern Spring Equinox

Northern Spring Equinox

LEFT Seasons occur because the Earth's axis is tilted at a constant angle of 23½° as it spins. When the Northern Hemisphere is tilted to a maximum extent towards the Sun, on 21 June, the Sun is overhead at noon at the Tropic of Cancer (23½° North): this is midsummer, or the summer solstice, in this hemisphere.

On 22 or 23 September the Sun is overhead at the Equator, and day and night are of equal length throughout the world: this is the autumn or fall equinox in the Northern Hemisphere. On 21 or 22 December, the Sun is overhead at the Tropic of Capricorn (23½° South), the winter solstice in the Northern Hemisphere. The overhead Sun then tracks north, until on 21 March it is overhead at the Equator: this is the spring equinox in the Northern Hemisphere.

In the Southern Hemisphere the seasons are the reverse of those in the Northern Hemisphere: autumn corresponds to spring and winter to summer.

21 June

21 December

N

N

N. Pole: 24 hours daylight

N. Pole: 24 hours darkness

10½ hours daylight

12 hours daylight

0°

SUN'S RAYS

13½ hours daylight

13½ hours daylight

0°

12 hours daylight

10½ hours daylight

S

S. Pole: 24 hours darkness

S. Pole: 24 hours daylight

S

LEFT The Sun appears to "rise" in the east, reach its highest point at noon, and then "set" in the west, to be followed by night. In reality it is not the Sun that is moving but the Earth, rotating ("spinning" on its axis) from west to east. At the summer solstice in the Northern Hemisphere (21 June), the area inside the Arctic Circle has total daylight and the area inside the Antarctic Circle has total darkness. The opposite occurs at the winter solstice on 21 or 22 December. At the Equator, the length of day and night are almost equal all year round, with seasonal variations in between.

RIGHT The Moon rotates more slowly than the Earth, making one complete turn on its axis in just over 27 days. Since this corresponds to its period of revolution around the Earth, the Moon always presents the same hemisphere or face to us, and we never see its "dark side".

The interval between one full Moon and the next (and thus also between two new Moons) is about 29½ days – a lunar month. The apparent changes in the shape of the Moon are caused by its changing position in relation to the Earth; like the planets, the Moon produces no light of its own and shines only by reflecting the rays of the Sun.

BELOW The Earth rotates through 360° in 24 hours, and therefore moves 15° every hour. The world is divided into 24 standard time zones, each centred on lines of longitude at 15° intervals, 7½° on either side of its central meridian.

The prime or Greenwich meridian, based on the Royal Observatory in London, lies at the centre of the first zone. All places to the west of Greenwich are one hour behind for every 15° of longitude; places to the east are ahead by one hour for every 15°.

When it is 12 noon at the Greenwich meridian, at 180° east it is midnight of the same day – while at 180° west the day is only just beginning. To overcome this problem the International Dateline was established, approximately following the 180° meridian. If you travelled from Japan (140° east) to Samoa (170° west) you would pass from the night into the morning of the same day.

While some countries cope with several time zones (Russia experiences no fewer than 11), others "bend" the meridians to incorporate their territory in certain zones, and China, despite crossing five, follows just one. Others, including Iran and India, employ differences of half an hour.

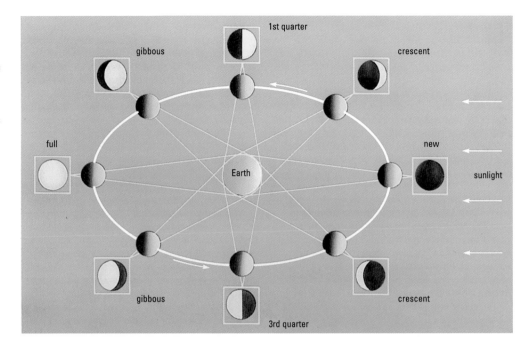

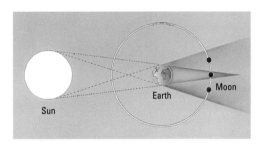

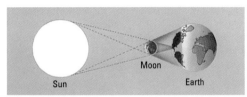

LEFT A solar eclipse occurs when the Moon passes between the Sun and the Earth. It will cause a partial eclipse of the Sun if the Earth passes through the Moon's outer shadow, or a total eclipse if the inner cone shadow crosses the Earth's surface. A total eclipse was visible in much of the Northern Hemisphere in 1999.

LEFT In a lunar eclipse the Earth's shadow crosses the Moon and, as with the solar version, provides either a partial or total eclipse. Eclipses do not occur every month because of the 5° difference between the plane of the Moon's orbit and the plane in which the Earth moves. In the 1990s, for example, only 14 eclipses were possible – seven partial and seven total – and each was visible only from certain and variable parts of the world.

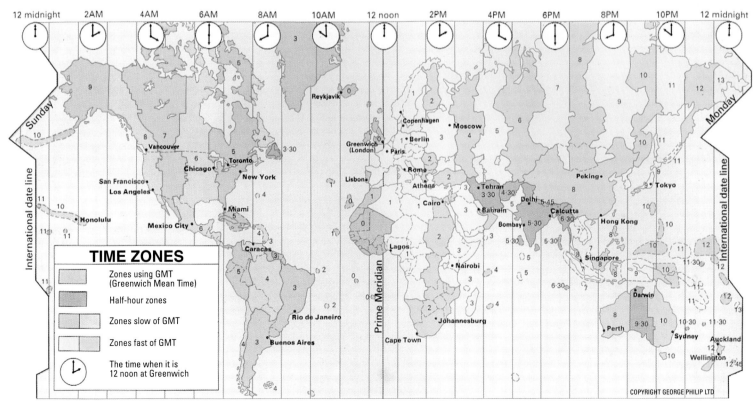

27

ANATOMY OF THE EARTH

THE EARTH is made up of several concentric shells, like the bulb of an onion. Each shell has its own particular chemical composition and physical properties. These layers are grouped into three main regions: the outermost is called the crust, which surrounds the mantle, and the innermost is the core. The solid, low-density crust on which we live is no thicker in relation to the Earth than an eggshell, taking up only 1.5% of the planet's volume. While the chemical distinction between crust and mantle is important, as far as physical processes go they behave as a single unit termed the lithosphere. It is a common fallacy that if you could drill through the Earth's crust you would find a molten mass: even well below the brittle outer shell that forms part of the lithosphere, the convecting part of the the mantle is still essentially solid, and pockets of liquid rock (magma) are relatively rare.

While the chemical composition of the crust and upper mantle is well known, little is absolutely certain about the layers beneath.

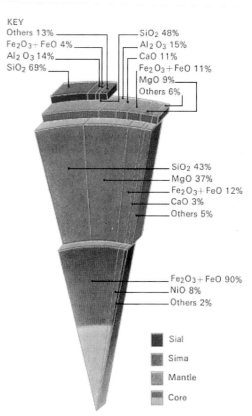

BELOW The Earth's crust varies in thickness from 40km (25 miles) under the continents to 5km (3 miles) under the seafloor. With the top of the mantle it forms the rigid lithosphere [1], which overlies a "plastic" layer, the asthenosphere [2], on which it may move. The upper mantle [3] goes down to about 700km (430 miles), where it overlies the lower mantle [4].

From the surface the temperature inside the Earth increases by 30°C for every kilometre (85°F for every mile), so that the asthenosphere is close to melting point. At 50km (30 miles), in the upper mantle, it reaches 800°C (1,480°F). After around 100km (60 miles) the rate of increase slows dramatically, and scientists now estimate the temperature to be 2,500°C (4,600°F) at the boundary of the lower mantle and core [5] – a depth of 2,900km (1,800 miles).

The mantle is separated from the outer core [6], which seismic observations suggest is in a liquid state. The density jumps from 5.5g/cm for the lower mantle to 10g/cm for the outer core, where it increases downwards to 12 or 13g/cm. The liquid outer core gives way to a solid inner core [7] at around 5,150km (3,200 miles] from the surface. Although the core is only around 16% of the Earth by volume, it represents 32% of its mass; it is thought to consist mostly of iron and some nickel, a hypothesis that fits the data and is inspired by iron-nickel meteorites which are probably the remnants of another planet. The temperature at the centre of the Earth (8) is estimated at least 3,000°C (5,400°F), and could be as high as 5,000°C (9,000°F).

ABOVE The Earth is composed of three main but unequal layers – the crust, mantle and core. The crust is subdivided into continental and oceanic material. The upper continental crust is mostly granite, abundant in <u>si</u>licon and <u>al</u>uminium – hence the term sial; over oceanic areas, and underlytng the continental sial, is a lighter material, essentially basalt and rich in <u>si</u>licon and <u>ma</u>gnesium – hence the term sima. The mantle comprises rock, rich in magnesium and iron silicates, and the dense core probably consists mainly of iron and nickel oxides, almost certainly in a molten condition. Heat is transferred to the surface by convection and conduction: in the solid layers it is probably transferred by conduction, and in the liquid layers it moves by convection₂

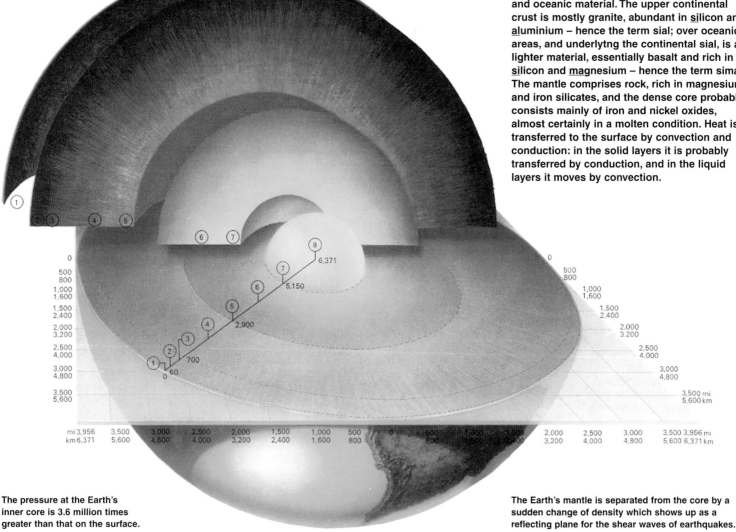

The pressure at the Earth's inner core is 3.6 million times greater than that on the surface.

The Earth's mantle is separated from the core by a sudden change of density which shows up as a reflecting plane for the shear waves of earthquakes.

THE MAGNETIC EARTH

As the Earth spins on its axis, the fluid layer of the outer core allows the mantle and solid crust to rotate relatively faster than the inner core. As a result, electrons in the core move relative to those in the mantle and crust. It is this electron movement that constitutes a natural dynamo and produces a magnetic field similar to that produced by an electric coil.

The Earth's magnetic axis is inclined to its geographical axis by about 11°, and the magnetic poles don't coincide with the geographic north and south poles. The Earth's magnetic axis is continually changing its angle in relation to the geographic axis, but over a long time – some tens of thousands of years – an average relative position is established.

A compass needle points to a position some distance away from the geographical north and south poles. The difference (the declination), varies from one geographical location to the next, with small-scale variations in the Earth's magnetism. The magnetosphere is the volume of space in which the Earth's magnetic field predominates.

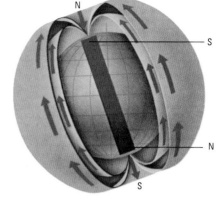

ABOVE The magnetic field originating inside the Earth makes up about 90% of the field observed at ground level: the remainder is due to currents of charged particles coming from the Sun and to the magnetism of rocks in the crust. The difference in rotation speed between the liquid outer core and the mantle creates a dynamo effect.

ABOVE The Earth's magnetic field is like that of a giant natural bar magnet placed inside the Earth, with its magnetic axis inclined at a small angle to the geographical axis. The poles of a compass needle are attracted by the magnetic poles of the Earth so that one end points to the north magnetic pole and the other to the south magnetic pole.

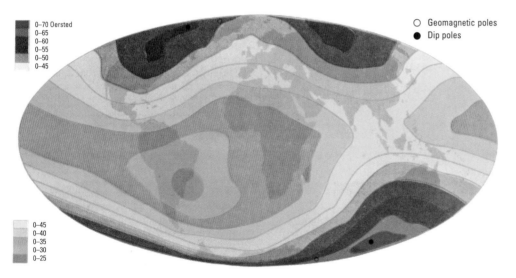

○ Geomagnetic poles
● Dip poles

LEFT The intensity of the Earth's magnetic field is strongest at the poles and weakest in the equatorial regions. If the field were purely that of a bar magnet in the centre of the Earth and parallel to the spin axis, the lines of equal intensity would follow the lines of latitude and the magnetic poles would coincide with the geographic poles. In reality, however, the "bar magnet" field is inclined at about 11° to the spin axis and so are its geomagnetic poles.

Neither is the real field purely that of a bar magnet. The "dip poles", where the field direction is vertical (downwards at the north pole and upwards at the south dip pole), are themselves offset in respect to the geomagnetic poles – each by a different amount so that the south dip pole is not exactly opposite the north dip pole. Oersted is a traditional unit of magnetic field strength.

BELOW Until recent times taking account of the difference between the magnetic and geographic poles was crucial in navigation. The needle of a ship's magnetic compass, for example, swings to a position where its ends point to north and south along a line of force of the Earth's magnetic field. In navigation today, the magnetic compass is often replaced by the motor-driven gyrocompass, which indicates true north.

RIGHT The magnetosphere is the region in which the Earth's magnetic field can be detected. It would be symmetrical were it not for the "solar wind", electrically-charged particles from the Sun [A], which distort it to a teardrop shape. The particles meet the Earth's magnetic field at the shock front [1]. Behind this is a region of turbulence and inside the turbulent region is the magnetopause [2], the boundary of the magnetic field. The Van Allen belts [3] are two zones of high radiation in the magnetopause. The inner belt consists of high-energy particles produced by cosmic rays, the outer comprises solar electrons.

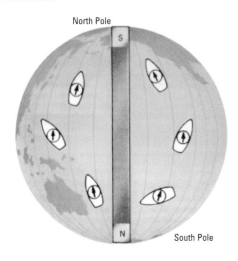

North Pole

South Pole

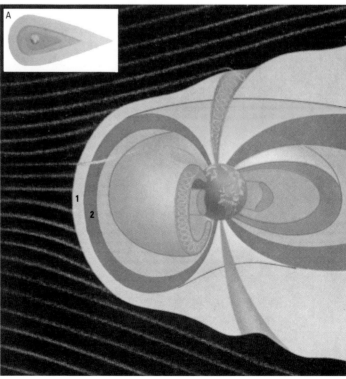

THE RESTLESS EARTH

THE THEORY of plate tectonics was advanced in the late 1960s and has had a revolutionary effect on the earth sciences. It is a unifying, all-embracing theory, offering a plausible and logical explanation for many of the Earth's varied structural phenomena, ranging from continental drift to earthquakes and mountain building.

The crust of the Earth, which together with the upper mantle forms the lithosphere, consists of rigid slabs called plates that are slowly but constantly moving their position in relation to each other. The plates are bounded by oceanic ridges, trenches and transform faults. Oceanic ridges are formed where two plates are moving apart, leaving a gap which is continuously filled by magma (molten rock) rising from the asthenosphere, on which the plates "float". As the magma cools, new crust is created on the ridges and becomes part of the oceanic plates.

This is the phenomenon known as seafloor spreading. Spreading rates, though slow, are not negligible: the North Atlantic is opening up by 4cm (1.6 in) a year, and the fastest rate is found at the East Pacific Rise, which creates 10cm (4 in) of new crust every year – 1,000km (620 miles) in the relatively short geological time of 10 million years.

Trenches as well as mountain ranges are formed where two plates converge. One of the plates slides steeply under the other and enters the mantle: the world's deepest trench, the Mariana, was formed when the Pacific plate was forced under the far smaller Philippine plate. Since the volume of the Earth does not change, the amount of crust created at the ridges is balanced by that destroyed at the trenches in an endless cycle of movement.

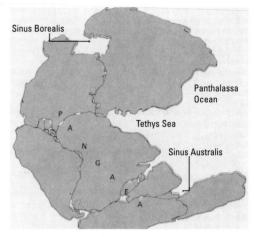

ABOVE First put forward by the German meteorologist Alfred Wegener in 1912, the theory of continental drift suggests the continents once formed a single land mass, Pangaea. The initial break-up created a northern mass, Laurasia, and a southern one, Gondwanaland, named after a province in India.

135 million years ago

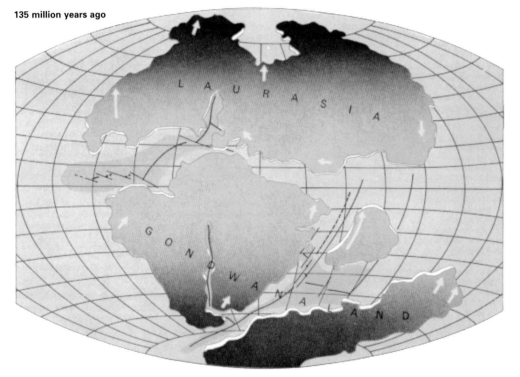

65 million years ago

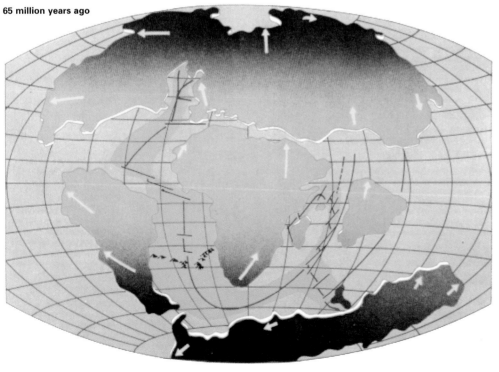

LEFT A map of Pangaea cannot be accurately constructed. The most suitable fit of the land masses is obtained by matching points midway down the continental slope, at about 200m (650ft). The easiest areas to fit together are the continents of Africa and South America, and while the linking of the northern lands is possible with a certain degree of accuracy, much remains to be learned of the complex fit of India, Antarctica and Australia with Africa and South America. The break-up of Pangaea began about 200 million years ago, and by the end of the Jurassic period, about 135 million years ago, the North Atlantic and Indian Oceans had become firmly established. The Tethys Sea was being diminished by the Asian land mass rotating in an anti-clockwise direction, and South America had begun to move away from Africa to form the South Atlantic.

LEFT By the end of the Cretaceous period, about 65 million years ago, the South Atlantic had grown, Madagascar had parted from Africa and India had continued northwards. Antarctica was moving away from the central land mass, though still linked with Australia. The North Atlantic rift forked at the north, starting to form the island of Greenland.

Geological evidence that the continents were once linked is provided by distinctive rock formations that can be assembled into continuous belts when South America and Africa are juxtaposed; by the processes of mountain building, notably India grinding into Asia and crumpling up sediments to form the Himalayas; and by the dovetailed distribution of many plants and animals.

Perhaps the most important impetus to the theory of continental drift came from the twin theories of plate tectonics and seafloor spreading, which developed rapidly from the 1960s. One of the weakest points in Wegener's argument centred on the tremendous forces needed to drive the continents apart. The new plate theories, which have been substantially proven, provide an explanation of the source of the necessary power. Even so, much has still to be learned about the original continent.

RIGHT The debate about continental drift was followed by a more radical idea: plate tectonics. The basic theory proposes that the Earth's crust comprises a series of rigid plates that "float" on a softer layer of the mantle, and are moved about by continental convection currents within the Earth's interior. These plates slowly converge and diverge along margins marked by seismic (earthquake) activity.

Converging plates form either trenches (where the oceanic plate sinks below the lighter continental rock), or mountain ranges. The theory not only supports the notion of continental drift: it also explains the paradox that while there have always been oceans, none of the present seabeds contain sediments more than 150 million years old.

The six major mobile plates (the American, Eurasian, African, Indo-Australian, Pacific and Antarctic) contain smaller plates such as the Arabian and West Indian plates which "absorb" the geometrical discrepancies between major plates by creating or destroying compensating amounts of crustal material.

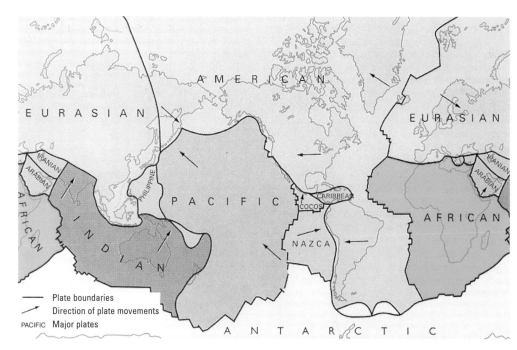

— Plate boundaries
↗ Direction of plate movements
PACIFIC Major plates

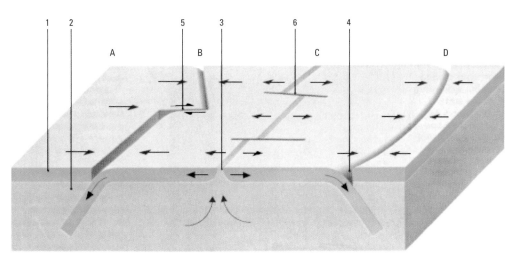

ABOVE The plate tectonics theory sees the Earth's lithosphere [1] as a series of rigid but mobile slabs called plates [A,B,C,D]. The lithosphere floats on a "plastic" layer called the asthenosphere [2]. There are three types of boundaries. At the mid-oceanic ridges [3], upwelling of mantle material occurs and new seafloor is formed. A trench [4] is formed where one plate of oceanic crust slides beneath the other, which may be oceanic or continental. The third type of boundary is where two plates slide past one another, creating a transform fault [5,6]. These link two segments of the same ridge [6], two ocean trenches [5] or a ridge to a trench. Plates move from ridges and travel like conveyor belts towards the trenches.

BELOW Collision zones are where two plates, each carrying a continental mass, meet. When one of the plates is forced beneath the other, the buoyant continental material is pushed upwards in a series of high overthrusts and folds, producing great mountain ranges. The Himalayas, formed when the northward-moving Indian plate crunched up against the Eurasian plate, were the result of such forces – as were other leading fold mountains such as the Alps in Europe (African/Eurasian plates), the Andes in South America (Nazca/American) and the western Rockies (Pacific/American).

50 million years ahead

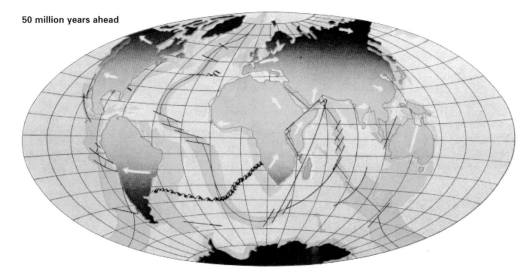

LEFT The continents are still drifting, and there is no reason to expect them to stop. This is how the world may look 50 million years from now if drift is maintained as predicted. The most striking changes in this "new world" are the joining of the Atlantic and Pacific Oceans; the splitting away from the USA of Baja California and the area west of the San Andreas fault line; the northward drift of Africa; the breaking away of that part of the African continent east of the present-day Great Rift Valley; and Australia's continued journey north towards Asia. The majority of the great continent of Antarctica, however, remains in its present southerly position. Plant fossils found in Antarctica's coal seams – remnants of its tropical past hundreds of millions of years ago – are among many examples of evidence supporting the tectonic theory of continent drift.

EARTHQUAKES

A N EARTHQUAKE is the sudden release of energy in the form of vibrations and tremors caused by compressed or stretched rock snapping along a fault in the Earth's surface. Rising lava under a volcano can also produce small tremors. It has been estimated that about a million earthquakes occur each year, but most of these are so minor that they pass unnoticed. While really violent earthquakes occur about once every two weeks, fortunately most of these take place under the oceans, and only rarely do they produce tsunamis.

Slippage along a fault is initially prevented by friction along the fault plane. This causes energy, which generates movement, to be stored up as elastic strain, similar to the effect created when a bow is drawn. Eventually the strain reaches a critical point, the friction is overcome and the rocks snap past each other, releasing the stored-up energy in the form of earthquakes by vibrating back and forth. Earthquakes can also occur when rock folds that can no longer support the elastic strain break to form a fault.

Shockwaves

Seismic or shockwaves spread outwards in all directions from the focus of an earthquake, much as sound waves do when a gun is fired. There are two main types of seismic wave: compressional and shear. Compressional waves cause the rock particles through which they pass to shake back and forth in the direction of the wave, and can be transmitted through both solids and liquids; they are therefore able to travel through the Earth's core. Shear waves make the particles vibrate at right-angles to the direction of their passage, and can

travel only through solids; at the boundary of lower mantle and liquid outer core, they are reflected back to the Earth's surface. Neither type of seismic wave physically moves the particles – it merely travels through them.

Compressional waves, which travel 1.7 times faster than shear waves, are the first ones to be distinguished at an earthquake recording station. Consequently seismologists refer to them as primary (P) waves and to the shear waves as secondary (S) waves. A third wave type is recognized by seismologists – the long (L) wave which travels slowly along the Earth's surface, vertically or horizontally. It is L waves that produce the most violent shocks.

Measuring earthquakes

The magnitude of earthquakes is usually rated according to either the Richter or the Modified Mercalli scales, both formulated in the 1930s. Developed by the US geologist Charles Richter, the Richter scale measures the total energy released by a quake with mathematical precision, each upward step representing a tenfold increase in shockwave power. A magnitude of 2 is hardly felt, while a magnitude of 7 is the lower limit of an earthquake that has a devastating effect over a large area. Theoretically there is no upper limit, but the largest measured have been rated at between 8.8 and 8.9. The 12-point Mercalli scale, named after the Italian seismologist Guiseppe Mercalli, is based on damage done and thus varies in different places. It ranges from I (noticed only by seismographs) to XII (total destruction); intermediate points include VII (collapse of substandard buildings) and IX (conspicuous cracks in the ground).

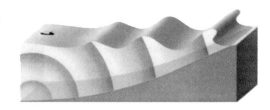

Tsunamis

Tsunami is the Japanese word for a seismic sea wave; they are often called tidal waves, though they have no connection with tides. Tsunamis are caused mainly by seismic disturbances below the seafloor (oceanic earthquakes), but also by submarine landslides and volcanic eruptions. Other tidal waves can be due to the surge of water when the barometric pressure is exceptionally low, such as in a hurricane. At sea, the height of the wave is seldom more than 60–90cm (2–3ft), but the wave length may be as long as 200km (120 miles), generating speeds of up to 750km/h (450mph).

Although the height of the crest is low out to sea, tsunamis have immense energy, which, as they lose speed in more shallow water, is converted into an increase in height. The waves, on reaching the shore, may be 40m (125ft) or more high. The most destructive tsunamis occur in the northern Pacific.

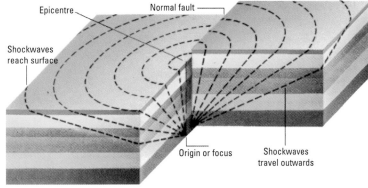

Epicentre — Normal fault —
Shockwaves reach surface
Origin or focus — Shockwaves travel outwards

LEFT An earthquake takes place when two parts of the Earth's surface move suddenly in relation to each other along a crack called a fault. The point from which this movement originates is called the focus, usually located at depths between 8 and 30km (5 to 18 miles), and the point on the surface directly above this is called the epicentre. Shockwaves move outwards from the focus in a curved pattern; while speed varies with the density of rock, intensity decreases the farther the waves travel.

BELOW Earthquakes occur in geologically sensitive areas of the world such as mid-oceanic ridges and mountain-building regions, and can be classified according to the depth of their focus. Deep focus quakes occur at depths of between 300 and 650km (185-400 miles), intermediate focus quakes from 55 to 240km (35-150 miles), and shallow focus quakes from the surface down to a depth of 55km (35 miles).

EARTHQUAKE ZONES

Major earthquake zones
Areas experiencing frequent earthquakes

The highest magnitude recorded on the Richter scale is 8.9, for a quake that killed 2,990 people in Japan on 2 March 1933. The most devastating earthquake ever affected three provinces of central China on 2 February 1556, when it is believed that about 830,000 people perished. The highest toll in modern times was at Tangshan, eastern China, on 28 July 1976: the original figure of over 655,000 deaths has since been twice revised by the Chinese government to stand at 242,000.

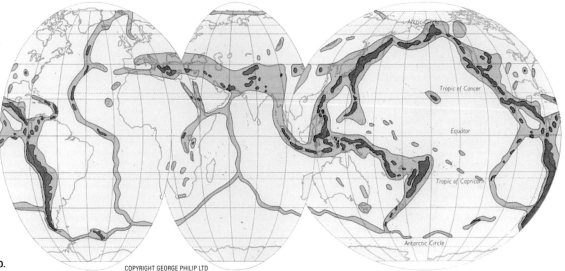

COPYRIGHT GEORGE PHILIP LTD

VOLCANOES

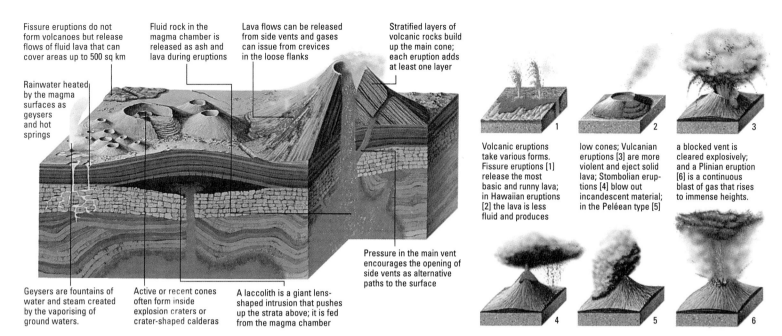

Fissure eruptions do not form volcanoes but release flows of fluid lava that can cover areas up to 500 sq km

Fluid rock in the magma chamber is released as ash and lava during eruptions

Lava flows can be released from side vents and gases can issue from crevices in the loose flanks

Stratified layers of volcanic rocks build up the main cone; each eruption adds at least one layer

Rainwater heated by the magma surfaces as geysers and hot springs

Geysers are fountains of water and steam created by the vaporising of ground waters.

Active or recent cones often form inside explosion craters or crater-shaped calderas

A laccolith is a giant lens-shaped intrusion that pushes up the strata above; it is fed from the magma chamber

Pressure in the main vent encourages the opening of side vents as alternative paths to the surface

Volcanic eruptions take various forms. Fissure eruptions [1] release the most basic and runny lava; in Hawaiian eruptions [2] the lava is less fluid and produces

low cones; Vulcanian eruptions [3] are more violent and eject solid lava; Stombolian eruptions [4] blow out incandescent material; in the Peléean type [5]

a blocked vent is cleared explosively; and a Plinian eruption [6] is a continuous blast of gas that rises to immense heights.

THE WORLD'S most spectacular natural displays of energy, volcanoes are responsible for forming large parts of the Earth's crust. Volcanoes occur when hot liquefied rock beneath the crust is pushed up by pressure to the surface as molten lava. They are found in places where the crust is weak – the mid-ocean ridges and their continental continuations, and along the collision edges of crustal plates. Some volcanoes erupt in an explosive way, throwing out rocks and ash, while others are effusive and lava flows out of the vent. Some, such as Mount Fuji in Japan, are both.

An accumulation of lava and cinders creates cones of various sizes and shapes. As a result of many eruptions over centuries Mount Etna in Sicily has a circumference of more than 120km (75 miles). Craters at rest are often filled by a lake – and the mudflow caused by an eruption can be as destructive as a lava flow and, because of its speed, even more lethal.

Despite the increasingly sophisticated technology available to geologists to monitor volcanoes, like earthquakes they remain both dramatic and unpredictable. For example, in 1991 Mount Pinatubo, located 100km (60 miles) north of the Philippines capital Manila, suddenly burst into life without any warning after lying dormant for over six centuries.

Most of the world's active volcanoes are located in a belt round the Pacific Ocean, on the edge of the Pacific crustal plate, called the "Ring of Fire" – a circle of fear that threatens over 400 million people. However, the soils formed by the weathering of volcanic rocks are usually exceptionally fertile, and despite the dangers large numbers of people have always lived in the shadows of volcanoes.

Climatologists believe that volcanic ash, if ejected high into the atmosphere, can influence temperature and weather conditions generally over a massive area and for several years afterwards. It has been estimated that the 1991 eruption of Mount Pinatubo in the Philippines threw up more than 20 million tonnes of dust and ash over 30km (18 miles) into the atmosphere, and it is widely believed that this accelerated the depletion of the ozone layer over large parts of the globe.

There are far more volcanoes on the seafloor than on the land, however. These "seamounts" exist because the oceanic crust is newer and thinner than continental crust and easily pierced by the underlying magma. The Pacific Ocean alone is thought to have more than 10,000 underwater volcanoes over 3,000m (9,850ft) high.

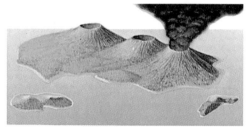

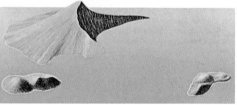

ABOVE Situated in the Sunda Strait of Indonesia, Krakatau was a small volcanic island inactive for over 200 years when, in August 1883, two-thirds of it was destroyed by a violent erruption. It was so powerful that the resulting tidal wave killed 36,000 people. Indonesia has the greatest concentration of volcanoes with 90, 12 of which are active.

VOLCANIC ZONES

- · Volcanoes
- — Seafloor spreading centre
- Ocean trench
- Continental shelf

Structure

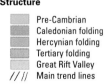

- Pre-Cambrian
- Caledonian folding
- Hercynian folding
- Tertiary folding
- Great Rift Valley
- // || Main trend lines

Of the 850 volcanoes to produce recorded eruptions, nearly three-quarters lie in the "Ring of Fire" that surrounds the Pacific Ocean on the edge of the Pacific plate.

SHAPING THE LANDSCAPE

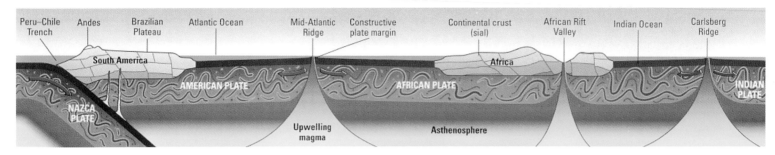

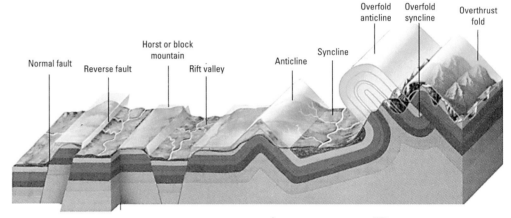

ABOVE A view of seafloor spreading along the Equator from the west coast of South America to the centre of the Indian Ocean. On the left, the Nazca plate has been subducted beneath the American plate to push up the Andes.

RIGHT A normal fault results when vertical movement causes the surface to break apart, while compression leads to a reverse fault. Horizontal movement causes shearing, known as a tear or strike-slip fault. When the rock breaks in two places, the central block may be pushed up in a "horst", or sink in a rift valley. Folds occur when rock strata are squeezed and compressed. Layers bending up form an anticline, those bending down form a syncline.

THE VAST ridges that divide the Earth beneath the world's oceans mark the boundaries between tectonic plates that are gradually moving in opposite directions. As the plates shift apart, molten magma rises from the mantle to seal the rift and the seafloor spreads towards the land masses. The rate of spreading has been calculated at about 40mm (1.6in) a year in the North Atlantic Ocean.

Near the ocean shore, underwater volcanoes mark the lines where the continental rise begins. As the plates meet, much of the denser oceanic crust dips beneath the continental plate at the "subduction zone" and falls back to the magma.

Mountains are formed when pressures on the Earth's crust caused by continental drift become so intense that the surface buckles or cracks. This happens where oceanic crust is subducted by continental crust, or where two tectonic plates collide: the Rockies, Andes, Alps, Urals and Himalayas all resulted from such impacts. These are known as fold mountains because they were formed by the compression of the sedimentary rocks, forcing the surface to bend and fold like a crumpled rug.

The other main mountain-building process occurs when the crust is being stretched or compressed so violently that the rock strata breaks to create faults, allowing rock to be forced upwards in large blocks; or when the pressure of magma inside the crust forces the surface to bulge into a dome, or erupts to form a volcano. Large and more complex mountain ranges may well reveal a combination of these features.

AGENTS OF EROSION

Destruction of the landscape, however, begins as soon as it is formed. Wind, ice, water and sea, the main agents of erosion, maintain a constant assault that even the hardest rocks cannot withstand. Mountain peaks may dwindle by only a few millimetres a year, but if they are not uplifted by further movements of the Earth's crust they will eventually disappear. Over millions of years, even great mountain ranges can be reduced to a low, rugged landscape.

Water is the most powerful destroyer: it has been estimated that 100 billion tonnes of rock are washed into the oceans each year. Three Asian rivers alone account for a fifth of this total – the Hwang Ho in China, and the Ganges and the Brahmaputra in Bangladesh.

When water freezes, its volume increases by about 9%, and no rock is strong enough to resist this pressure. Where water has penetrated fissures or seeped into softer rock, a freeze followed by a thaw may result in rockfalls or earthslides, creating major destruction in minutes.

Over much longer periods, acidity in rain water breaks down the chemical composition of porous rocks such as limestone, eating away the rock to form deep caves and tunnels. Chemical decomposition also occurs in river beds and glacier valleys, hastening the process of mechanical erosion.

Like the sea, rivers and glaciers generate much of their effect through abrasion, pounding or tearing the land with the debris they carry. Yet as well as destroying existing landforms they also create new ones, many of them spectacular. Prominent examples include the Grand Canyon, the vast deltas of the Mississippi and the Nile, the rock arches and stacks off the south coast of Australia, and the deep fjords cut by glaciers in British Columbia, Norway and New Zealand.

While landscapes evolve from a "young" mountainous stage, through a "mature" hilly stage to an "old age" of lowland plain, this long-term cycle of erosion is subject to interruption by a number of crucial factors, including the pronounced effects of plate tectonics and climate change.

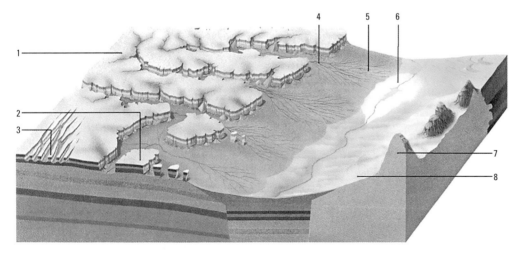

ABOVE The topography of a desert is characterized by the relative absence of the chemical weathering associated with water, and most erosion takes place mechanically through wind abrasion and the effect of heat – and cold.

Mesas [1] are large flat-topped areas with steep sides, while the butte [2] is a flat isolated hill, also with steep sides. Elongated in the direction of the prevailing wind, yardangs [3] comprise tabular masses of resistant rock resting on undercut pillars of softer material. Alluvial fans [5] are pebble-mounds deposited in desert deltas by flash floods, usually at the end of a wadi [4]. A saltpan [6] is a temporary lake of brackish water, also formed by flash floods. An inselberg [7] is an isolated hill rising from the plain, and a pediment [8] is a gently inclining rock surface.

Shaping forces: ice

Many of the world's most dramatic landscapes have been carved by icesheets and glaciers. During the Ice Ages of the Pleistocene epoch (over 10,000 years ago) up to a third of the land surface was glaciated; even today a tenth is still covered in ice – the vast majority locked up in the huge icesheets of Antarctica and Greenland.

Valley glaciers are found in mountainous regions throughout the world, except Australia. In the relatively short geological time scale of the recent Ice Ages, glaciers accomplished far more carving of the topography than rivers and wind.

They are formed from compressed snow, called névé, accumulating in a valley head or cirque. Slowly the glacier moves downhill, moving at rates of between a few millimetres and several metres a day, scraping away debris from the mountains and valleys through which it passes. The debris, or moraine, adds to the abrasive power of the ice. The sediments are transported by the ice to the edge of the glacier, where they are deposited or carried away by meltwater streams.

Shaping forces: rivers

From their origins as small upland rills and streams channelling rainfall, or as springs releasing water that has seeped into the ground, all rivers are incessantly at work cutting and shaping the landscape on their way to the sea.

In highland regions flow may be rapid and turbulent, pounding rocks to cut deep gorges and V-shaped valleys through softer rocks, or tumbling as waterfalls over harder ones.

As they reach more gentle slopes, rivers release some of the pebbles and heavier sediments they have carried downstream, flow more slowly and broaden out. Levées or ridges are raised along their banks by the deposition of mud and sand during floods. In lowland plains the river drifts into meanders, depositing layers of sediment, especially on the inside of bends where the flow is weakest. As the river reaches the sea it deposits its remaining load, and estuaries are formed where the tidal currents are strong enough to remove them; if not, the debris creates a delta.

Shaping forces: the sea

Under the constant assault from tides and currents, wind and waves, coastlines change faster than most landscape features, both by erosion and by the building up of sand and pebbles carried by the sea. In severe storms, giant waves pound the shoreline with rocks and boulders; but even in much quieter conditions, the sea steadily erodes cliffs and headlands, creating new features in the form of sand dunes, spits and salt marshes. Beaches, where sand and shingle have been deposited, form a buffer zone between the erosive power of the waves and the coast. Because it is composed of loose materials, a beach can rapidly adapt its shape to changes in wave energy.

Where the coastline is formed from soft rocks such as sandstones, debris may fall evenly and be carried away by currents from shelving beaches. In areas with harder rock, the waves may cut steep cliffs and wave-cut platforms; eroded debris is deposited as a terrace. Bays and smaller coves are formed when sections of soft rock are carved away between headlands of harder rock. These are then battered by waves from both sides, until the headlands are eventually reduced to rock arches, which as stacks are later separated from the mainland.

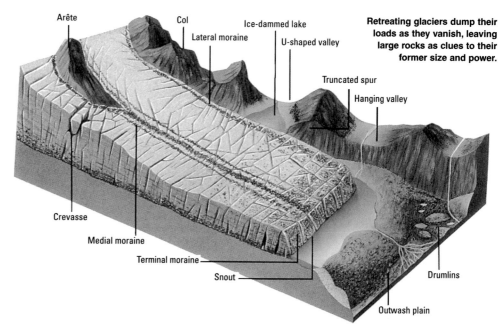

Arête · Col · Ice-dammed lake · Lateral moraine · U-shaped valley · Truncated spur · Hanging valley · Crevasse · Medial moraine · Terminal moraine · Snout · Drumlins · Outwash plain

Retreating glaciers dump their loads as they vanish, leaving large rocks as clues to their former size and power.

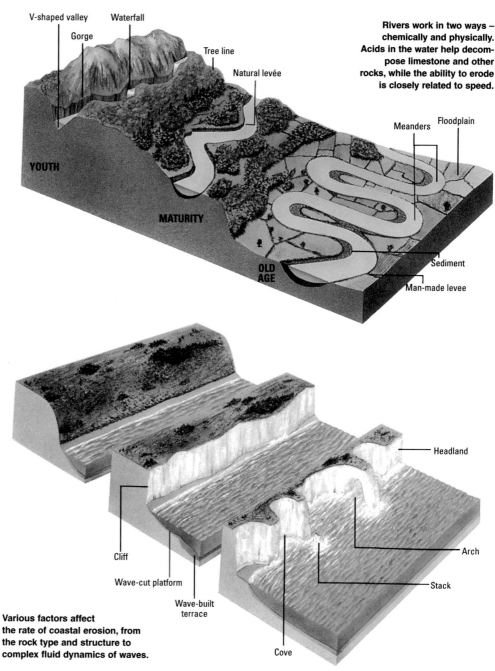

V-shaped valley · Waterfall · Gorge · Tree line · Natural levée · YOUTH · MATURITY · OLD AGE · Meanders · Floodplain · Sediment · Man-made levee

Rivers work in two ways – chemically and physically. Acids in the water help decompose limestone and other rocks, while the ability to erode is closely related to speed.

Cliff · Wave-cut platform · Wave-built terrace · Cove · Headland · Arch · Stack

Various factors affect the rate of coastal erosion, from the rock type and structure to complex fluid dynamics of waves.

OCEANS: SEAWATER

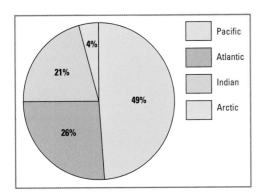

50 m

100 m

150 m

200 m

ABOVE In the strictest geographical sense the Earth has only three oceans – Atlantic, Indian and Pacific. The legendary "Seven Seas" would require these to be divided at the Equator and the addition of the smaller Arctic Ocean. Geographers do not recognize the Antarctic Ocean (much less the "Southern Ocean") as a separate entity.

The Earth is a watery planet: almost 71% of its surface is covered by its oceans and seas. This great liquid cloak gives our planet its characteristic and beautiful blue appearance from space, and is one of the two obvious differences between the Earth and its two near-neighbours, Venus and Mars. The other difference is the presence of life – and the two are closely linked.

ABOVE When sunlight strikes the surface of the ocean between 3% and 30% of it is immediately reflected. The amount reflected depends on the angle at which the light strikes – the smaller the angle the greater the reflection – which varies with latitude and the seasons.

Penetration of sunlight is selectively reduced according to wavelength. Radiation at the red or long-wave end of the visible spectrum is absorbed near the surface of the water, while the shorter blue wavelengths are scattered, giving the sea its characteristic blue colour.

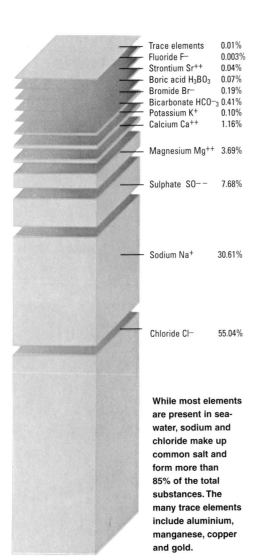

Trace elements	0.01%
Fluoride F–	0.003%
Strontium Sr++	0.04%
Boric acid H_3BO_3	0.07%
Bromide Br–	0.19%
Bicarbonate HCO_3^-	0.41%
Potassium K+	0.10%
Calcium Ca++	1.16%
Magnesium Mg++	3.69%
Sulphate SO– –	7.68%
Sodium Na+	30.61%
Chloride Cl–	55.04%

While most elements are present in seawater, sodium and chloride make up common salt and form more than 85% of the total substances. The many trace elements include aluminium, manganese, copper and gold.

$\mathbf{E}$ARTH IS something of a misnomer for our planet; "Ocean" would be a more suitable name, since the oceans and seas cover 70.8% of its total surface area. The oceans are not separate areas of water but form one continuous oceanic mass, and (as with some continental divisions) the boundaries between them are arbitrary lines drawn for convenience. The vast areas of interconnected oceans contain 97.2% of the world's total water supply.

The study of oceans, including their biology, chemistry, geology and physics, has now become a matter of urgency, because the future of humans on Earth may well depend on our knowledge of the ocean's potential resources not only of minerals and power but also of food.

Composition of seawater

The most obvious resource of the oceans is the water itself. But seawater is salty, containing sodium chloride (common salt), which makes it unsuitable for drinking or farming. One kilogramme (2.2lb) of seawater contains about 35g (1.2oz) of dissolved materials, of which chloride and sodium together make up nearly 30g (1oz) or about 85%.

Seawater is a highly complex substance in which 73 of the 93 natural chemical elements are present in measurable or detectable amounts. Apart from chloride and sodium it contains appreciable amounts of sulphate, magnesium, potassium and calcium, which together add up to over 13% of the total. The remainder, less than 1%, is made up of bicarbonate, bromide, boric acid, strontium, fluoride, silicon and various trace elements. Because the volume of the oceans is so great, there are substantial amounts of some trace elements: seawater contains more gold, for example, than there is on land, even though it's in a very low concentration of four-millionths of one part per million.

Also present in seawater are dissolved gases from the atmosphere, including nitrogen, oxygen and carbon dioxide. Of these, oxygen is vital to marine organisms. The amount of oxygen in seawater varies according to temperature. Cold water can contain more oxygen than warm water, but cold water in the ocean depths, which has been out of contact with the atmosphere for a long period, usually contains a much smaller amount of oxygen than surface water.

Other chemicals in seawater that are important to marine life include calcium, silicon and phosphates, all of which are used by marine creatures to form shells and skeletons. For building cells and tissue, marine organisms extract phosphates, certain nitrogen compounds, iron and silicon. The chief constituents of seawater – chloride, sodium, magnesium and sulphur – are hardly used by marine organisms.

Density, light and sound

The density of seawater is an important factor in causing ocean currents and is related to the interaction of salinity and temperature. The temperature of surface water varies between –2°C and 29°C (28°F and 85°F); ice will begin to form if the temperature drops below –2°C (28°F).

The properties of light passing through seawater determine the colour of the oceans. Radiation at the red or long-wave end of the spectrum is absorbed near the surface of the water, while the shorter blue wavelengths are scattered, giving the sea its characteristic colour.

The depth to which light can penetrate is important to marine life. In clear water light may reach to 110m (360ft), whereas in muddy coastal waters it may penetrate to only 15m (50ft). Below about 1,000m (3,300ft) there is virtually no light at all.

The most active zone in the oceans is the sunlit upper layer, falling to about 200m (650ft) at the edge of the continental shelf, where the water is moved around by windblown currents. This is the

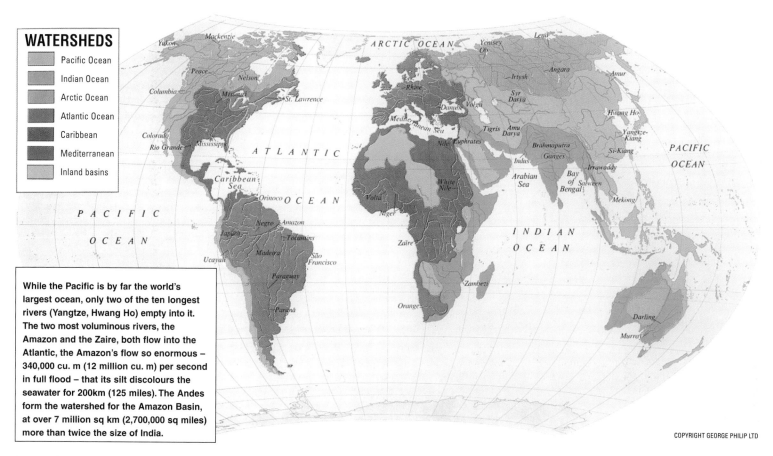

WATERSHEDS

- Pacific Ocean
- Indian Ocean
- Arctic Ocean
- Atlantic Ocean
- Caribbean
- Mediterranean
- Inland basins

While the Pacific is by far the world's largest ocean, only two of the ten longest rivers (Yangtze, Hwang Ho) empty into it. The two most voluminous rivers, the Amazon and the Zaire, both flow into the Atlantic, the Amazon's flow so enormous – 340,000 cu. m (12 million cu. m) per second in full flood – that its silt discolours the seawater for 200km (125 miles). The Andes form the watershed for the Amazon Basin, at over 7 million sq km (2,700,000 sq miles) more than twice the size of India.

home of most sealife and acts as a membrane through which the ocean breathes, absorbing great quantities of carbon dioxide and partly exchanging it for oxygen.

As the depth increases light fades and temperatures fall until just before around 950m (3,000ft), when there is a marked temperature change at the thermocline, the boundary between the warm surface zones and the cold deep zones.

Water is a good conductor of sound, which travels at about 1,507m (4,954ft) per second through seawater, compared with 331m (1,087ft) per second through air. Echo-sounding is based on the meas-urement of the time taken for sound to travel from a ship to the seafloor and back again. However, temperature and pressure both affect the speed of sound, causing the speed to vary by about 100m (330ft) per second.

The salinity of the oceans

The volume of dissolved salts in seawater is called the salinity. The average salinity of seawater ranges between 33 and 37 parts of dissolved material per 1,000 parts of water. Oceanographers express these figures as 33 parts per thousand (33⁰/oo) to 37⁰/oo.

The salinity of ocean water varies with local conditions. Large rivers or melting ice reduce salin-ity, for example, whereas it is increased in areas with little rainfall and high evaporation.

To produce fresh water from seawater the dis-solved salts must be separated out. This desalination can be carried out by electrical, chemical and change of phase processes. Change of phase processes involve changing the water into steam and distilling it, or changing it into ice, a process that also expels the salt. Eskimos have used sea ice as a source of fresh water for centuries, while primitive coastal tribes still take salt from the sea by damming water in pools and letting it evaporate in the Sun.

RIGHT The average salinity of seawater ranges between 33 and 37 parts of dissolved material per 1,000 parts of water. While the most saline water is generally found in semi-enclosed seas in temperate and tropical areas such as the Gulf of Mexico, Mediterranean and the Red Sea (where high rates of evaporation can produce a figure of 41 parts per thousand), the Baltic Sea, which receives large quantities of freshwater from rivers and melting snow, has a remarkably low salinity of 7.2⁰/oo.

In the oceans themselves, the least saline waters occur in areas of high freshwater discharge such as the edge of the Antarctic icecap and the mouths of large rivers. The most pronounced regional example of this is Southeast Asia, where a string of massive rivers – including the Ganges, Brahmaputra, Irrawaddy, Salween, Mekong, Si Kiang, Yangtze and Hwang Ho – flow into the coastal area from the Bay of Bengal to the Yellow Sea.

If the salt in the oceans were precipitated, it would cover the Earth's land areas with a layer more than 150m (500ft) thick.

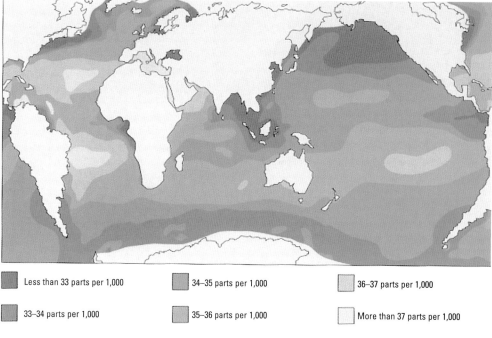

- Less than 33 parts per 1,000
- 33–34 parts per 1,000
- 34–35 parts per 1,000
- 35–36 parts per 1,000
- 36–37 parts per 1,000
- More than 37 parts per 1,000

THE OCEANS: CURRENTS

NO PART of the ocean is completely still – although, in the ocean depths, the movement of water is often extremely slow. Exploration of the deeper parts of the oceans has revealed the existence of marine life. If the water were not in motion, the oxygen on which all lifeforms depend would soon be used up and not replaced. No life would therefore be possible.

Prevailing winds sweep surface water along to form drift currents. These surface currents do not conform precisely with the direction of the prevailing wind because of the Coriolis effect caused by the rotation of the Earth. This effect, which increases away from the Equator, makes currents in the Northern Hemisphere veer to the right of the wind direction and currents in the Southern Hemisphere veer to the left. The result is a general clockwise circulation of water in the Northern Hemisphere and an anticlockwise circulation in the Southern.

Other factors affecting currents are the configuration of the ocean bed and the shapes of land masses. For example, in the Atlantic Ocean the North Equatorial Current flows towards the West Indies. Most of this current is channelled into the Gulf of Mexico where it veers northeastwards, bursting into the Atlantic between Florida and Cuba as the Gulf Stream.

OCEAN CURRENTS

Winter in Northern Hemisphere

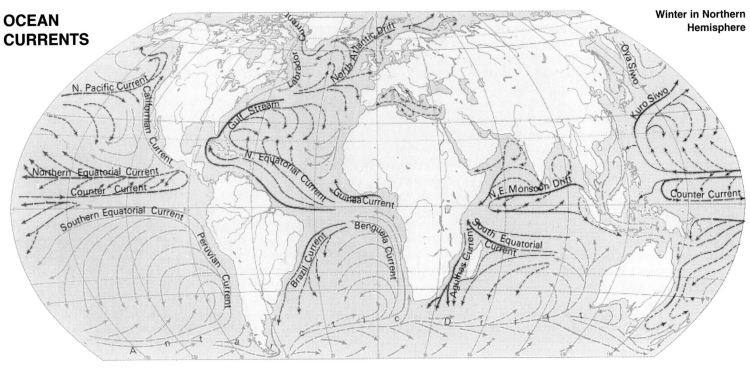

(cold currents are shown in blue, warm currents in red)

Summer in Northern Hemisphere

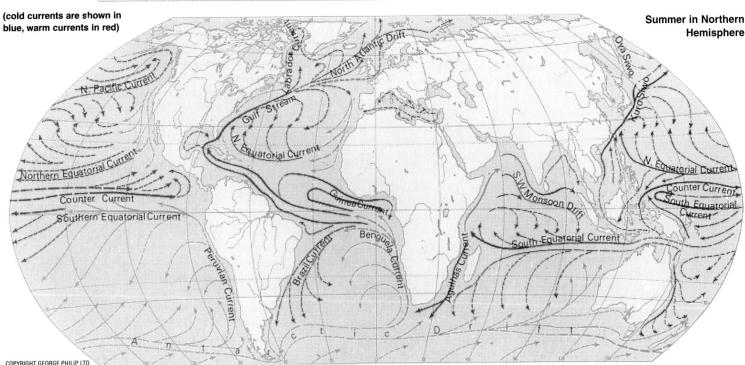

ABOVE The world's surface currents circulate in a clockwise direction in the Northern Hemisphere and in an anticlockwise direction in the Southern Hemisphere. These circulatory systems are called gyres. There are two large clockwise gyres in the Northern Hemisphere (North Atlantic and North Pacific) and three anticlockwise gyres in the Southern (South Atlantic, South Pacific and Indian Ocean).

Beneath the surface are undercurrents whose direction may be opposite to those at the surface. Under the Gulf Stream off the eastern USA lies a large, cold current flowing south from the Arctic. The Gulf Stream finally splits: while the North Atlantic Drift branches past eastern Greenland and western Europe, part of the current returns southwards to complete the gyre. Surface cold currents in the Northern Hemisphere generally flow southwards. In the Southern Hemisphere, cold water circulates around Antarctica, while offshoots flow northwards. The warm currents are very strong in tropical and subtropical regions, and include the various Equatorial currents.

The causes of currents that are not powered by winds are related to the density of ocean water, which varies according to temperature and salinity. Heating at the Equator causes the water to become less dense, while cooling round the poles has the opposite effect. Salinity is affected by the inflow of fresh water from rivers, melting ice and rainfall, and by evaporation. A high rate of evaporation increases the salinity and therefore the density.

Effects of ocean currents

One of the most important effects of ocean currents is that they mix ocean water and so affect directly the fertility of the sea. Mixing is especially important when subsurface water is mixed with surface water. The upwelling of subsurface water may be caused by strong coastal winds that push the surface water outwards, allowing subsurface water to rise up. Such upwelling occurs off the coasts of Peru, California and Mauritania, where subsurface water rich in nutrients (notably phosphorus and silicon) rises to the surface, stimulating the growth of plankton which provides food for great shoals of fish, such as Peruvian anchovies.

Water has a high heat capacity and can retain heat two and a half times as readily as land. The heat of the Sun absorbed by water around the Equator is transported north and south by currents. Part of the North Atlantic Drift flows past Norway, warming offshore winds and giving northwest Europe a winter temperature that is 11°C (20°F) above the average for those latitudes. The northward-flowing Peru and Benguela currents have a reverse effect, bringing cooler weather to the western coasts of South America and southern Africa.

In such ways, currents have a profound effect on climate. Currents from polar regions can also create hazards for shipping: the Labrador and East Greenland currents carry icebergs and pack ice into shipping lanes, and fog often occurs where cold and warm currents meet, most persistently off the coast of Newfoundland.

RIGHT Surface currents are caused largely by prevailing winds. The Coriolis effect caused by the rotation of the Earth results in the deflection of currents to the right of the wind direction in the Northern Hemisphere. In the same manner, the surface motion drags the subsurface layer at an angle to it, and so on.

Each layer moves at a slower speed than the one above it and at a greater angle from the wind. The spiral created has the overall effect of moving the water mass above the depth of frictional resistance at an angle of about 90° from the wind direction, while surface currents move at around 45°. The same effect reverses the direction of draining water from a bath in the Northern and Southern hemispheres.

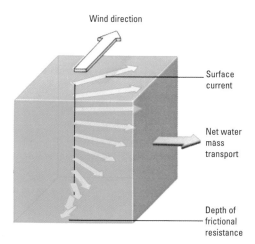

Wind direction
Surface current
Net water mass transport
Depth of frictional resistance

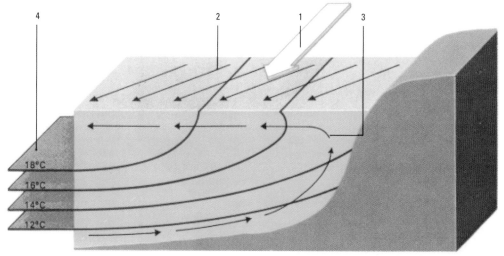

18°C
16°C
14°C
12°C

ABOVE Upwelling occurs when a longshore wind [1] pushes surface water away from a coast at an angle [2], allowing deeper water to rise [3]. The deeper water is not only colder [4] but usually rich in nutrients, and areas where upwelling occurs are often exceptional fishing grounds. A good example are the waters off the west coast of South America, the most productive in the world before the upwelling was suppressed by successive years of El Niño.

EL NIÑO

El Niño is the most dramatic and influential of current reversals, producing devastating effects. Its 1997–98 visit was the most damaging yet, triggering (among other things) floods and landslides in northwest South America, storms in California, drought in southern Africa, monsoon failure in India and widespread rainforest fires in Southeast Asia. Estimates put the cost of the property damage alone as high as US$33 billion.

As the previous worst case in 1982–83 showed, the commercial cost is colossal and far-reaching. This includes declining fish stocks in the eastern Pacific (the anchovy catch dropped by over 90%), frost-wrecked orange groves in Florida, crop losses in Africa and brush fires in Australia.

While El Niño is unpredictable in both power and frequency – it used to appear every 2 to 7 years – the phenomenon now occurs more often, including five consecutive seasons from 1990 to 1994. It usually lasts about three months but can be far longer. The name was originally given by

The El Niño sequence begins in the western Pacific. The mass of warm water (white in centre), 8°C higher than in the east and generally kept in check by the prevailing westerly trade winds, breaks free of its moorings as these winds subside and moves in an equatorial swell towards South America. There it raises both sea temperatures and sea levels, suppressing the normal upwelling of the cold and nutrient-rich Peruvian current. Meanwhile, the western Pacific waters cool (purple) as the warm water is displaced.

The movement of such vast amounts of

warm water results in chaotic changes to wind patterns, in turn creating freak weather conditions well outside the Pacific tropics. The passage of El Niño's warm water is also tracked by rainfall, leading to droughts in Southeast Asia and Australia and excessive levels of precipitation in South America.

This sequence traces El Niño's passage from March 1997 *(above left)* to October 1998 *(below right)*, when normal oceanic conditions were finally resumed – until the next time. In 1983, 1987 and 1995 El Niño was followed by the cool current La Niña ("the little girl").

Oceans: Waves and Tides

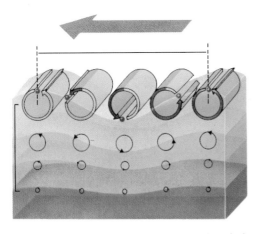

ABOVE Most waves are generated by the wind. As a wave travels in deep water, however, the water particles don't move up and down but rotate in circular orbits. As depth increases, the rotations of the water particles diminish rapidly – the reason why submarines escape the effects of severe storms at sea.

BECAUSE THEY affect coastal areas, waves and tides are the most familiar features of oceans and seas for most of us, but sometimes the energies of waves, tides and high winds combine with devastating effect. In January 1953 a high spring tide, storm waves and winds of 185km/h (115mph) combined to raise the level of the North Sea by 3m (10ft) higher than usual. This "surge" caused extensive flooding in eastern England, but in the Netherlands over 4% of the country was inundated: 1,800 people died and about 30,000 houses were destroyed or damaged by the seawater.

The motion of waves

While some wave motion occurs at great depth along the boundary of two opposing currents, most waves are caused by the wind blowing over an open stretch of water. This area where the wind blows is known as the "fetch". Waves there are confused and irregular and are referred to as a "sea". As they propagate beyond the fetch they combine into more orderly waves to form a "swell", which travels for long distances beyond the fetch. Waves are movements of oscillation – that is, the shape of the wave moves across the water, but the water particles rotate in a circular orbit with hardly any lateral movement. As a result, if there is no wind or current, a corked bottle bobs up and down in the waves, but is more or less stationary.

At sea, waves seldom exceed 12m (40ft) in height, although one 34m (115ft) high was accurately measured in the Pacific Ocean in 1933. Such a wave requires a long fetch measuring thousands of kilometres and high-speed winds.

Waves that break along a seashore may have been generated by storms in mid-ocean or by local winds. As a wave approaches shallow water, which is defined as a depth of half a wave length, it "feels" the bottom, gradually slowing down, and the crests tend to crowd together. When the water in front of a wave is insufficient to fill the wave form, the rotating orbit – and hence the wave – breaks. There are two main kinds of breakers: spilling breakers occur on gently sloping beaches, when the crests spill over to form a mass of surf, while plunging breakers occur on steeper slopes.

BELOW Waves have dimensions of both length and height. The wave length [14] is the distance between one crest [5] and another – in this case a peaking wave [4] – and between two crests is a trough [11]. The wave height [6] is the distance between the crest and the trough. If wave action ceased, the water would settle at the "still water level" [8]. Wave action extends to the wave base [7], where rotation becomes negligible. Wave distortion is caused by frictional drag on the seabed: if waves pass over a sand-bar [10], a spilling breaker [9] may form. Sometimes, waves in shallow water move the whole body of the water forward in translation waves [2] towards the shore [1].

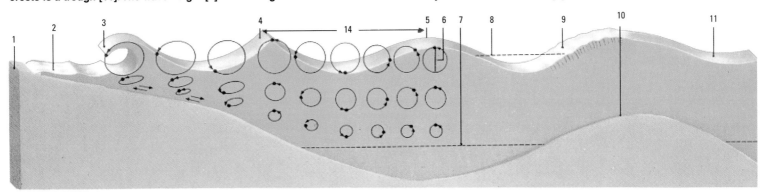

RIGHT Tides are the alternate rises and falls of the sea's surface level, caused by the gravitational pull of the Moon and the Sun. Although the Moon is much smaller than the Sun, it is much closer to Earth and its effect on the oceans is more than twice that of the Sun. The configurations of coasts and seafloors can accentuate these forces, while barometric pressure and wind effects can also superimpose an added "surge" element.

In the open sea the tidal range is small and in enclosed basins, such as the Mediterranean, it is little more than 30cm (12in). However, in shallow seas it may be more than 6m (20ft) and in tidal estuaries 12–15m (40–50ft). The highest tidal range recorded is about 16m (53ft) in the Bay of Fundy, which divides the peninsula of Nova Scotia from the Canadian mainland of New Brunswick.

In some 60 estuaries, such as Hangchow Bay in China and the Severn in England, tidal bores occur. These are bodies of water with a wall-like front that surge up rivers, formed because the estuaries act as funnels, leading to a rise in the height of the water. At spring tides the Hangchow bore attains heights of 7.5m (25ft) and speeds of 27km/h (17mph).

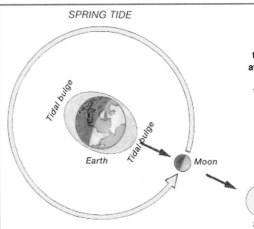

The effect is the same if the Moon and Sun are aligned on opposite sides of the Earth (at the time of full Moon). Thus the tides are greatest at the time of new Moon and full Moon (spring tides). Tides are less pronounced when the Sun, Moon and Earth are not aligned, and are least strong when the three are at right-angles to each other (near the Moon's first and third quarters). In this situation solar and lunar forces compete: the lunar tide wins, but the difference between high and low tides is much less (neap tides).

When the Moon and Sun are roughly in the same direction (around the time of the new Moon), they each pull the oceans on the near side of the Earth towards them. They also pull the Earth towards them, away from the oceans on the far side of the Earth. The effect is to produce two bulges on opposite sides of the Earth. These will not rotate with the Earth but will stay with the forces that produced them, causing two high tides and two low tides a day.

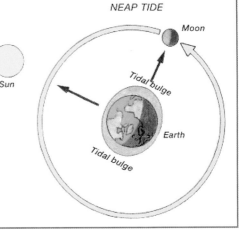

OCEANS: THE SEAFLOOR

THE DEEP ocean floor was once thought to be flat, but maps compiled from readings made by sonar equipment show that it's no more uniform than the surface of the continents. Here are not just the deepest trench – the Challenger Deep of the Pacific's Mariana Trench plunges 11,022m (36,161ft) – but also the Earth's longest mountain chains and its tallest peaks.

The vast underwater world starts in the shallows of the seaside. Surrounding the land masses is the shallow continental shelf, composed of rocks that less dense than the underlying oceanic crust. The shelf drops gently to around 200m (650ft), where the seafloor suddenly falls away at an angle of 3° to 6° via the continental slope. Submarine canyons such as the 1.5km (5,000ft) gorge off Monterey, California are found on the continental slopes. They can be caused either by river erosion before the land was submerged by the sea, or by turbidity currents – underwater avalanches that carry mud, pebbles and sand far out to sea, scouring gorges out of both slope rock and sediment.

The third stage, the continental rise, made up of sediments washed down from the shelves, is more gradual, with gradients varying from 1 in 100 to 1 in 700. At an average depth of 5,000m (9,000ft) there begins the aptly named abyssal plain, massive submarine depths where sunlight fails to penetrate and only creatures specially adapted to deal with the darkness and the pressure can survive.

Underwater highlands

While the abyss contains large plains it is broken by hills, volcanic seamounts and mid-ocean ridges. Here new rock is being continually formed as magma rises through the Earth's crust, pushing the tectonic plates on each side apart towards the continents in the process called seafloor spreading.

Taken from base to top, many of the seamounts which rise from these plains rival and even surpass the biggest of continental mountains in height. Mauna Kea, Hawaii's highest peak, reaches 10,203m (33,475ft), some 1,355m (4,380ft) more than Mount Everest, though only 4,205m (13,795ft) is above sea level. Nearby is Mauna Loa, the world's biggest active volcano, over 84% of which is hidden from view.

Life in the ocean depths

Manned submersibles have now established that life exists even in the deepest trenches, where the pressure reaches 1,000 "atmospheres" – the equivalent of the force of a tonne bearing down on every sq cm (6.5 tons per sq in).

Further exploration in the pitch-black environment of the oceanic ridges has revealed extraordinary forms of marine life around the scalding hot vents: creatures include giant tubeworms, blind shrimps, and bacteria, some of which are genetically different from any other known lifeforms.

In 1996 an analysis of one micro-organism revealed that at least half its 1,700 or so genes were hitherto unknown. Based on chemicals, not sunlight, this alien environment may well resemble the places where life on Earth first began.

ABOVE Continental shelves are the regions immediately off the land masses, and there are several different types. Off Europe and North America the shelf has a gentle relief, often with sandy ridges and barriers [A]. In high latitudes, floating ice wears the shelf smooth [B], and in clear tropical seas a smooth shelf may be rimmed with a coral barrier such as the Great Barrier Reef off eastern Australia, leaving an inner lagoon area "dammed" by the reef [C].

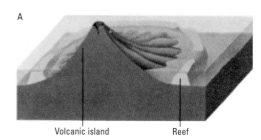

A

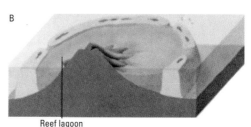

Volcanic island   Reef

B

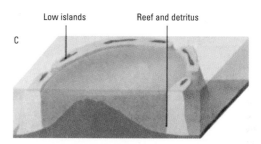

Reef lagoon

Low islands   Reef and detritus

C

ABOVE The most intriguing of coral features, an atoll is a ring or horseshoe-shaped group of coral islands. Organisms with skeletons of calcium carbonate, corals grow in warm, fairly shallow water to depths of about 90m (300ft), but the depth of coral in many atolls is much greater than this.

The prevailing theory is that the coral began to form as a reef in the shallows of a volcanic island [A]. While the sea level began to rise and the island slowly sank [B], the coral growth kept pace with these gradual changes, leaving an atoll of hard limestone around its remnant [C]. In this way, coral can reach depths of up to 1,600m (5,250ft).

The world's largest atoll is Kwajalein in the Marshall Islands, in the central Pacific. Its slender 283-km (176-mile) coral reef encloses a lagoon of 2,850 sq km (1,100 sq miles).

RIGHT The seafloor consists of different zones, the most shallow being the continental shelf that lies between the coast and the 200m (650ft) depth contour. The shelf area occupies 7.5% of the seafloor and corresponds to the submerged portion of the continental crust. Beyond, the downward slope increases abruptly to form the continental slope (8.5%), an area that may be dissected by submarine canyons. The continental slope meets the abyssal basins at a more gentle incline (the continental rise). The basins lie at depths of 4,000m (13,200 ft) and feature mountain ranges and hills.

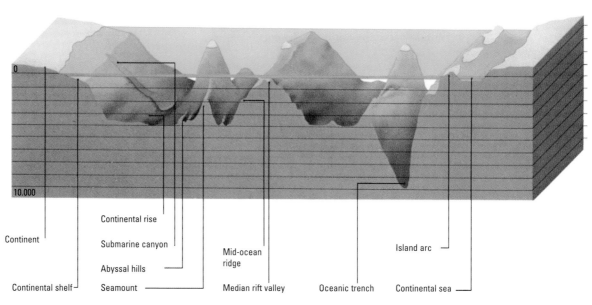

Continent

Continental shelf

Continental rise

Submarine canyon

Abyssal hills

Seamount

Mid-ocean ridge

Median rift valley

Oceanic trench

Island arc

Continental sea

THE ATMOSPHERE AND CLOUDS

THE ORIGIN of the atmosphere was closely associated with the origin of the Earth. When the Earth was still a molten ball, it was probably surrounded by a large atmosphere of cosmic gases, including hydrogen, that were gradually lost into space. As the Earth began to develop a solid crust over a molten core, gases such as carbon dioxide, nitrogen and water vapour were slowly released to form an atmosphere with a composition not unlike the present emissions from volcanoes. Further cooling probably led to massive precipitation of water vapour – so that today it occupies less than 4% by volume of the atmosphere. At a much later stage, the oxygen content of the atmosphere was created by green plants releasing oxygen.

Extending from the Earth's surface far into space, the atmosphere is a meteor shield, a radiation deflector, a thermal blanket and a source of chemical energy for the Earth's diverse lifeforms. Five-sixths of its total mass is located in the first 15 km (9 miles), the troposphere, which is no thicker in relative terms than the skin of an onion. Almost all the phenomena we call the weather occur in this narrow layer.

RIGHT Because air is easily compressed, the atmosphere becomes "squashed" by gravity. Thus the bulk of the atmosphere lies in the troposphere, occupying a volume of about 6 billion cu. km (1,560 million cu. miles). As air density decreases with altitude, the very much smaller amounts of air present in the strato-sphere (19%) and the ionosphere and above (1%) occupy an increasingly greater volume.

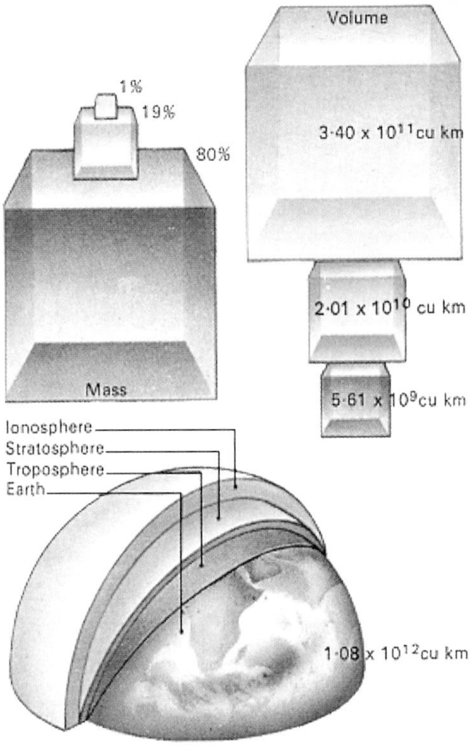

Volume

3·40 x 10^11 cu km

2·01 x 10^10 cu km

5·61 x 10^9 cu km

1%
19%
80%

Mass

Ionosphere
Stratosphere
Troposphere
Earth

1·08 x 10^12 cu km

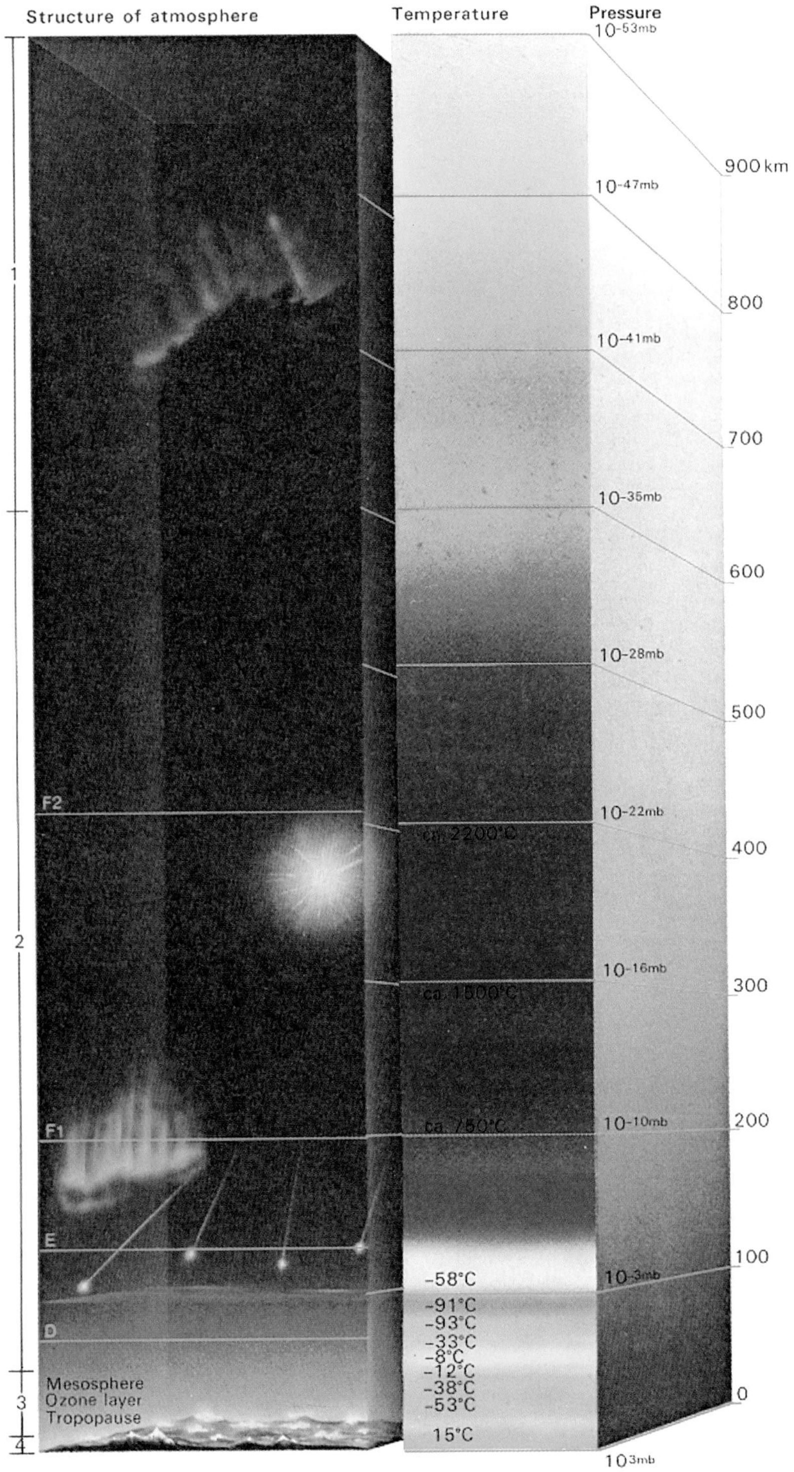

LEFT The discovery by British scientists of the hole in the ozone layer over Antarctica in 1985 triggered a growing interest in the structure of the atmosphere.

LAYERS OF THE ATMOSPHERE

1. EXOSHERE
The atmosphere's upper layer has no clear outer boundary, merging imperceptibly with interplanetary space. Its lower boundary, at an altitude of around 400km (250 miles), is almost equally vague. The exosphere is mainly composed of hydrogen and helium in changing proportions: helium vanishes with increasing altitude, and above 2,400km (1,500 miles) it is almost entirely hydrogen.

2. IONOSPHERE
Gas molecules in the ionosphere, mainly helium, oxygen and nitrogen, are ionized – electrically charged – by the Sun's radiation. Within the ionosphere's range of 50 to 400km (30 to 250 miles) they group themselves into four layers, known conventionally as D, E, F1 and F2, all of which can reflect radio waves of differing frequencies. The high energy of ionospheric gas gives it a notional temperature of more than 2000°C (3,600°F), although its density is negligible. The auroras – *aurora borealis* and its southern counterpart, *aurora australis* – occur in the ionosphere when charged particles from the Sun interact with the Earth's magnetic fields, at their strongest near the poles.

3. STRATOSPHERE
Separated at its upper and lower limits by the distinct thresholds of the stratopause and the tropopause, the stratosphere is a remarkably stable layer between about 15km and 50km (9 and 30 miles). Its temperature rises from –55°C (–67°F) at its lower extent to approximately 0°C (32°F) near the stratopause, where a thin layer of ozone – increasingly depleted with the acceleration in pollution by CFCs since the 1970s – absorbs ultraviolet radiation believed to cause skin cancer, cataracts and damage to the immune system in humans. Stratospheric air contains enough ozone to make it poisonous, although it is far too rarified to breathe. Overall, the stratosphere comprises 80% nitrogen, 18% oxygen, 1% argon and 1% ozone. "Mother-of-pearl" or nacreous cloud occurs at about 25km (15 miles).

4. TROPOSPHERE
The narrowest of all the atmospheric layers, the troposphere extends up to 15km (9 miles) at the Equator but only 8km (5 miles) at the poles. Since this thin region contains about 85% of the atmosphere's total mass and almost all of its water vapour, it is also the realm of the Earth's weather. Temperatures fall steadily with increasing height by about 1°C for every 100 metres (1.5°F for every 300 feet) above sea level. The main constituents are nitrogen (78%), oxygen (21%) and argon (1%).

Structure of atmosphere | Temperature | Pressure

10^-53mb

900 km

10^-47mb

800

10^-41mb

700

10^-35mb

600

10^-28mb

500

10^-22mb

400

F2

10^-16mb

300

ca. 2200°C

ca. 1500°C

ca. 750°C

10^-10mb

200

F1

10^-3mb

100

E

–58°C
–91°C
–93°C
–33°C
–8°C
–12°C
–38°C
–53°C

D

Mesosphere
Ozone layer
Tropopause

15°C

0

10^3mb

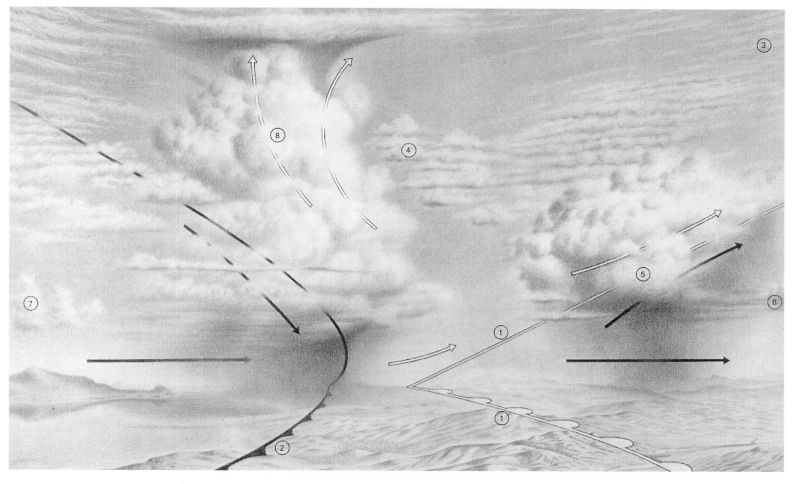

ABOVE The different cloud types are best illustrated within the context of the familiar mid-latitude frontal depression. Here a schematic, generalized Northern Hemisphere depression is viewed from the south as it moves eastwards, with both warm [1] and cold [2] fronts clearly visible. Over the warm front the air rises massively and slowly over the great depth of the atmosphere. This results in a fairly complete suite of layer-type clouds ranging from ice-crystal cirrus [3] and fluffy altocumulus [4] to grey-based nimbostratus [5].

The precipitation area often associated with such cloud types, and especially with nimbostratus, usually lies ahead of the surface warm front and roughly parallel to it [6]. Turbulence may cause some clouds to rise and produce heavy convective rainfall, as well as the generally lighter and more widespread classical warm front rainfall. Stratus often occupies the warm sector, but a marked change occurs at the cold front. Here the wind veers (blowing in a more clockwise direction) and cumulus clouds [7], brilliant white in sunlight, are often found in the cold air behind the front.

At the front itself the atmosphere is often unstable and cumulus clouds grow into dramatic cumulonimbus formations [8]. The canopy of cirrus clouds – of all types – may extend over the whole depression and is often juxtaposed with the anvil shape of the nimbus. These cloud changes are accompanied by changes in pressure, wind temperature and humidity as the fronts pass.

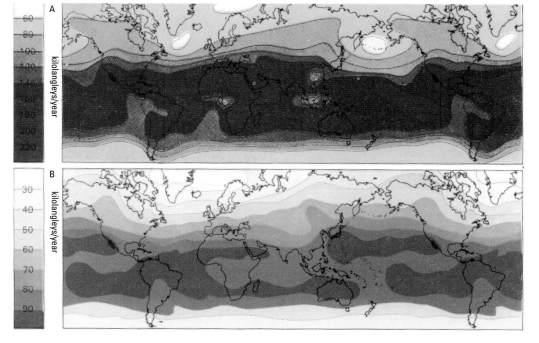

LEFT Temperatures in the atmosphere and on Earth result mainly from a balance of radiation inputs and outputs. Average annual solar radiation reaching the Earth, measured in kilolangleys – one calorie absorbed per sq cm (0.15 sq in) is highest in hot desert areas [A].

Comparison with the average annual long-wave radiation back from the Earth's surface [B] shows an overall surplus radiation for nearly all latitudes, but this is absorbed in the atmosphere and then lost in space, ensuring an overall balance. The extreme imbalance of incoming radiation between equatorial and polar latitudes is somewhat equalized through heat transfers by atmosphere and oceans. This balancing transfer between surplus and deficit radiation is greatest in mid-latitudes, where most cyclones and anticyclones occur.

WINDS AND THE WEATHER

WIND IS the movement of air, and large-scale air movements, both horizontal and vertical, are crucial in shaping weather and climate. The chief forces affecting horizontal air movements are pressure gradients and the Coriolis effect.

Pressure gradients are caused by the unequal heating of the atmosphere by the Sun. Warm equatorial air is lighter and therefore has a lower pressure than cold, dense, polar air. The strength of air movement from areas of high to low pressure – known as the pressure gradient – is proportional to the difference in pressure.

Along the Equator is a region called the doldrums, where the Sun's heat warms the rising air. This air eventually spreads out and flows north and south away from the Equator. It finally sinks at about 30°N and 30°S, creating subtropical high-pressure belts (the horse latitudes), from which trade winds flow back towards the Equator and westerlies flow towards the mid-latitudes.

The Coriolis effect is the deflection of winds caused by the Earth's rotation, to the right in the Northern Hemisphere and to the left in the Southern. As a result, winds don't flow directly from the point of highest pressure to the lowest; those approaching a low-pressure system are deflected round it rather than flowing directly into it. This creates air systems, with high or low pressure, in which winds circulate round the centre. Horizontal air movements are important around cyclonic (low-pressure) and anticyclonic (high-pressure) systems. Horizontal and vertical movements combine to create a pattern of prevailing global winds.

Weather and depressions

To most of us "weather" means rain and sunshine, heat and cold, clouds and wind. Humidity and visibility might be added to the list. If not precise in terminology, this layman's catalogue comprises the six main elements which also comprise weather for meteorologists: in their language they are precipitation, air temperature, cloud cover, wind velocity, humidity and barometric pressure.

Depressions occur when warm air flows into waves in a polar front while cold air flows in behind it, creating rotating air systems that bring changeable weather. Along the warm front (the boundary on the ground between the warm and cold air), the warm air flows upwards over the cold air, producing a sequence of clouds that help forecasters predict a depression's advance.

Along the cold front the advancing cold air forces warm air to rise steeply, and towering cumulonimbus clouds form in the rising air. When the cold front overtakes the warm front, the warm air is pushed up to form an occluded front. Cloud and rain persist along occlusions until temperatures equalize, the air mixes, and the depression dies out.

BELOW The world's zones of high and low pressure are both areas of comparative calm, but between them lie the belts of prevailing winds. West of Africa, wind patterns are remarkably constant between summer and winter, but in much of the east variations are caused by monsoons (reversals of wind flows) stemming in part from the unequal heating of land masses and the sea.

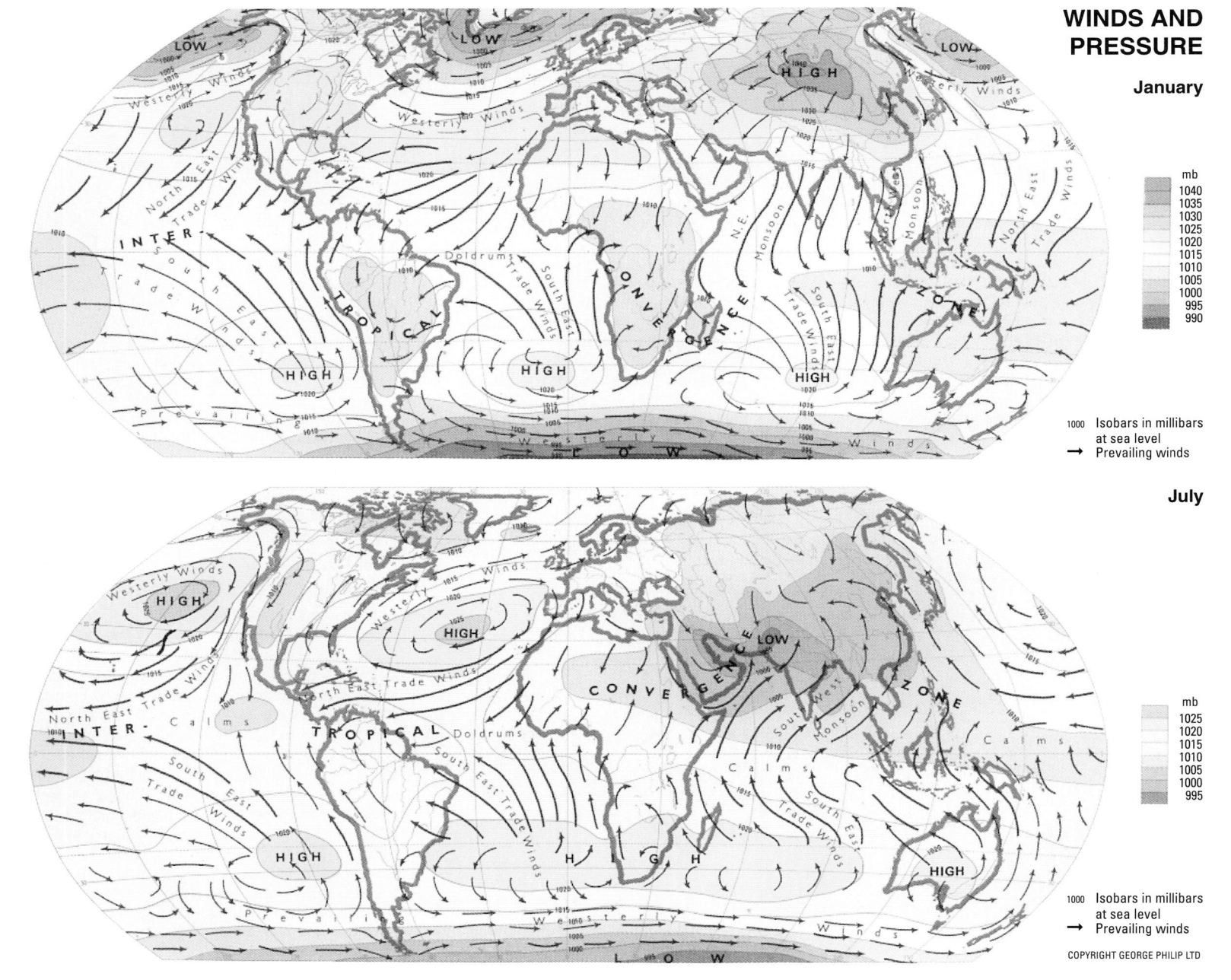

WINDS AND PRESSURE

January

mb
1040
1035
1030
1025
1020
1015
1010
1005
1000
995
990

1000 Isobars in millibars at sea level
→ Prevailing winds

July

mb
1025
1020
1015
1010
1005
1000
995

1000 Isobars in millibars at sea level
→ Prevailing winds

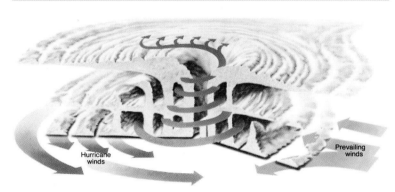

➡ Warm air	
➡ Cool air	
➡ Cold air	

▲▲▲▲ Warm front	H = High pressure
▲▲▲▲ Cold front	L = Low pressure

ABOVE The Earth's atmosphere acts as a giant heat engine. The temperature differences between the poles and the Equator provide the thermal energy to drive atmospheric circulation, both horizontal and vertical. In general, warm air at the Equator rises and moves towards the poles at high levels and cold polar air moves towards the Equator at low levels to replace it. Air also flows north and south from the high-pressure belts called the horse latitudes, and these airflows meet up with cold, dense air flowing from the poles along the polar front.

The basic global pattern of prevailing winds is complicated by the rotation of the Earth (which causes the Coriolis effect), by cells of high-pressure and low-pressure systems (depressions) and by the distribution and configuration of land and sea.

ABOVE Hurricanes consist of a huge swirl of clouds rotating round a calm centre – the "eye" – where warm air is sucked down. Hurricanes may be 400km (250 miles) in diameter and they extend through the troposphere, which is about 15-20km (9-12 miles) thick. Clouds, mainly cumulonimbus, are arranged in bands round the eye, the tallest forming the wall of the eye. Cirrus clouds usually cap the hurricane.

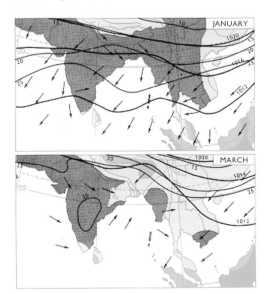

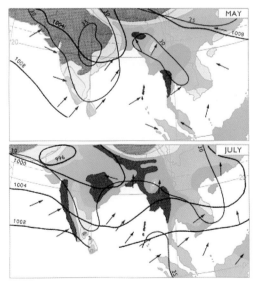

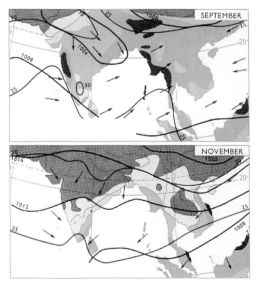

ABOVE "Monsoon" is the term given to the seasonal reversal of wind direction, most noticeably in South and Southeast Asia, where it results in very heavy rains. In January a weak anticyclone in northern India gives the clear skies brought by northeasterly winds; in March temperatures increase and the anticyclone subsides, sea breezes bringing rain to coastal areas; by May the north is hot and a low pressure area begins to form, while the south is cooler with some rain; in July the low-pressure system over India caused by high temperatures brings the Southwest Monsoon from the high-pressure area in the south Indian Ocean; in September the Southwest Monsoon – with its strong winds, cloud cover, rain and cool temperatures – begins to retreat from the northwest; by the end of the cycle in November the subcontinent is cool and dry, though still wet in the southeast.

Monthly rainfall

mm		
400	100	
200	50	25

——— Isotherms in °Celsius (reduced to sea level)

——— Isobars in mb

◄— Prevailing winds

WORLD CLIMATE

CLIMATE IS weather in the longer term, the seasonal pattern of hot and cold, wet and dry, averaged over time. Its passage is marked by a ceaseless churning of the atmosphere and the oceans, further agitated by the Earth's rotation and the motion it imparts to moving air and water.

There are many classifications of world climate, but most are based on a system developed in the early 19th century by the Russian meteorologist Vladimir Köppen. Basing his divisions on two main features, temperature and precipitation, and using a code of letters, he identified five main climatic types: tropical (A), dry (B), warm temperate (C),

cool temperate (D) and cold (E). Each of these main regions was then further subdivided. (A highland mountain category was added later to account for the variety of climatic zones found in mountainous areas due to changes caused by altitude.)

Although latitude is a major factor in determining climate, other factors add to the complexity. These include the influence of ocean currents, different rates of heating and cooling of land and ocean, distance from the sea, and the effect of mountains on winds. New York, Naples and the Gobi Desert all share the same latitude, for example, but their climates are very different.

Climates are not stable indefinitely. Our planet regularly passes through cool periods – Ice Ages probably caused by the recurring long-term oscillations in the Earth's orbital path from almost circular to elliptical every 95,000 years, variations in the Earth's tilt from 21½° to 24½° every 42,000 years, and perhaps even fluctuations in the Sun's energy output. In the present era, the Earth is closest to the Sun in the middle of winter in the Northern Hemisphere and furthest away in summer; 12,000 years ago, at the height of the last Ice Age, northern winter fell with the Sun at its most distant.

Studies of these cycles suggest that we are now

CLIMATIC ZONES

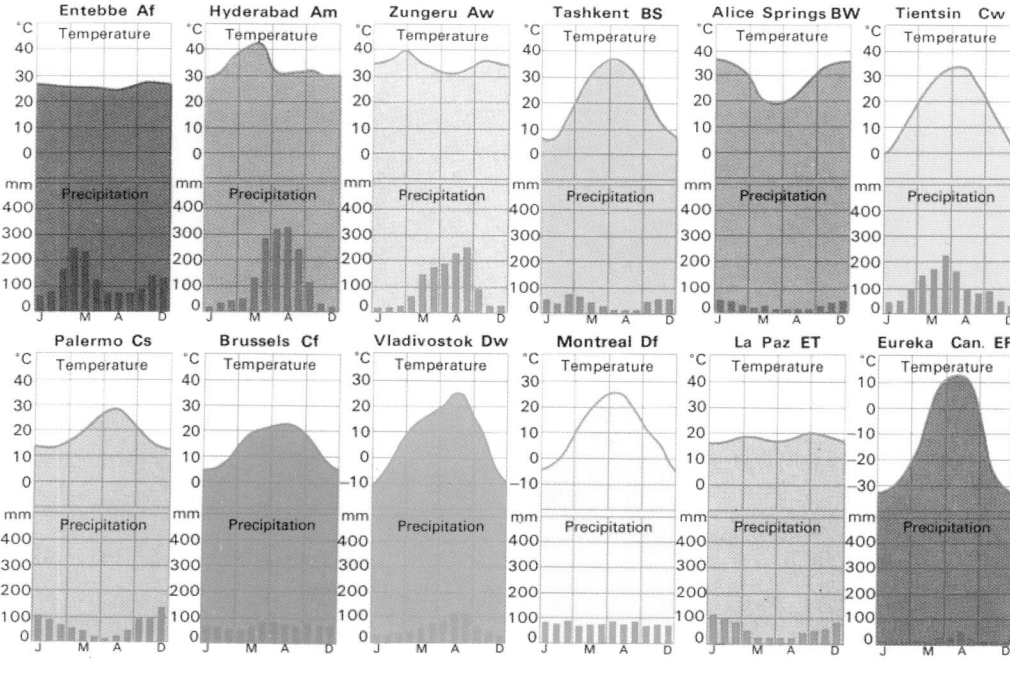
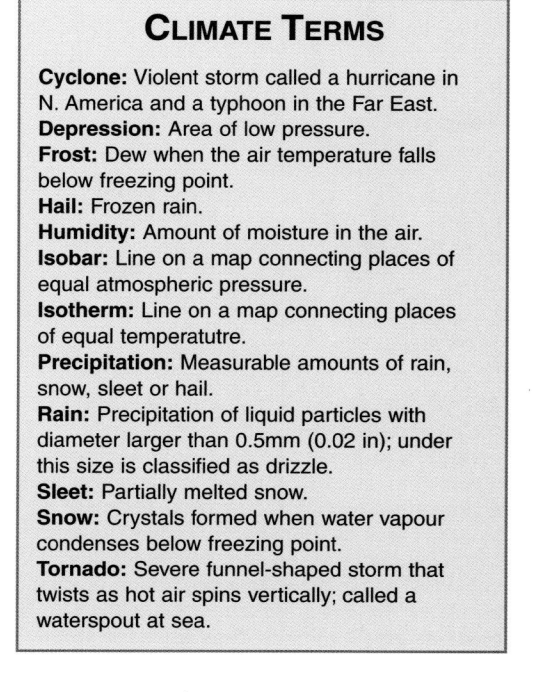

Af Equatorial forest
Am Monsoon forest
Aw Savanna

BS Steppe
BW Desert
Cw Dry winters
Cs Dry summers
Cf Rain at all seasons

Dw Dry winters
Df Rain at all seasons
ET Tundra
EF Polar

Tropical climates			Dry climates		Warm temperate climates			Cool temperate climates		Cold climates	
Af	Am	Aw	BS	BW	Cw	Ca	Cf	Dw	Df	ET	EF

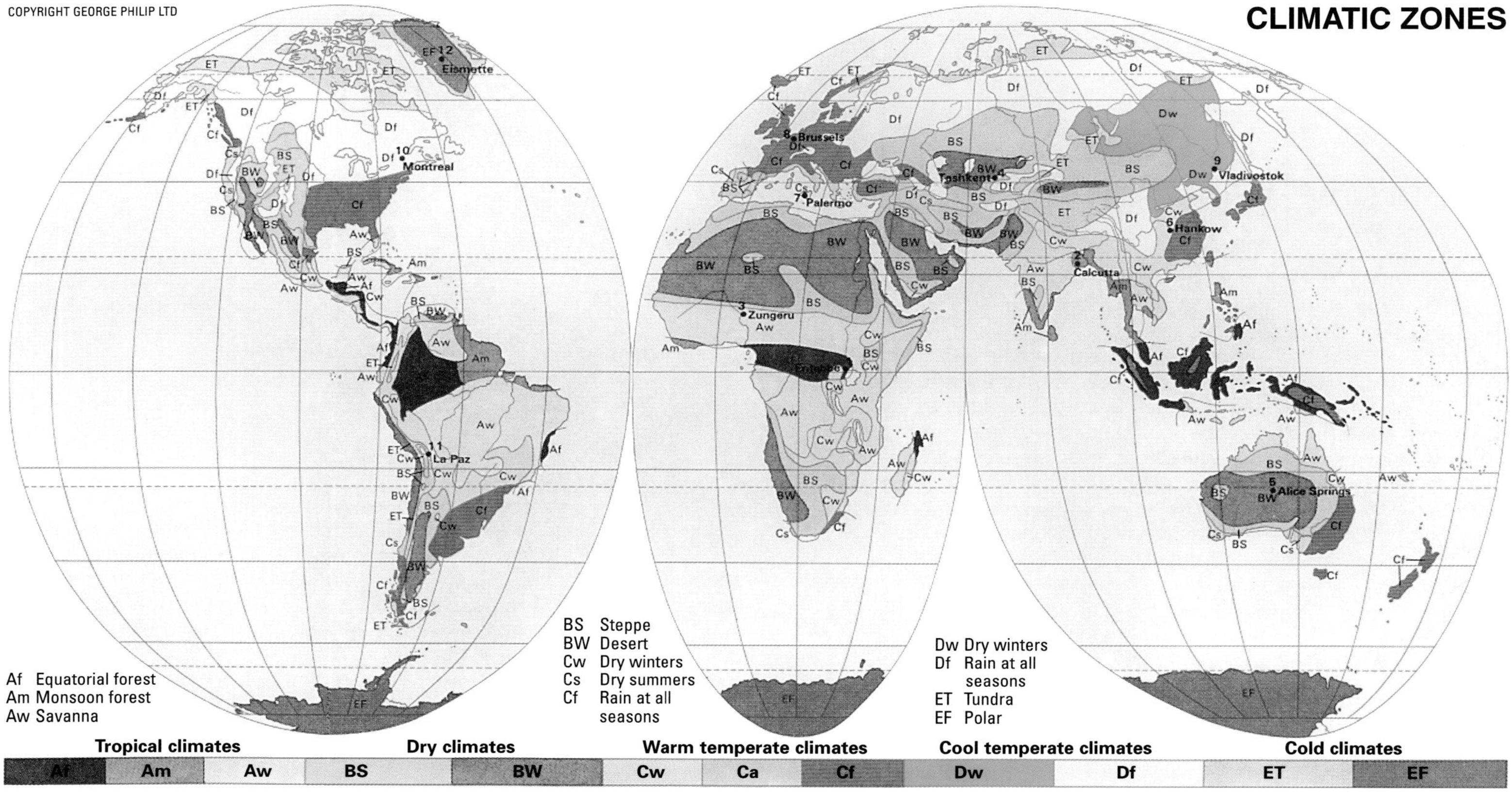

CLIMATE TERMS

Cyclone: Violent storm called a hurricane in N. America and a typhoon in the Far East.
Depression: Area of low pressure.
Frost: Dew when the air temperature falls below freezing point.
Hail: Frozen rain.
Humidity: Amount of moisture in the air.
Isobar: Line on a map connecting places of equal atmospheric pressure.
Isotherm: Line on a map connecting places of equal temperatutre.
Precipitation: Measurable amounts of rain, snow, sleet or hail.
Rain: Precipitation of liquid particles with diameter larger than 0.5mm (0.02 in); under this size is classified as drizzle.
Sleet: Partially melted snow.
Snow: Crystals formed when water vapour condenses below freezing point.
Tornado: Severe funnel-shaped storm that twists as hot air spins vertically; called a waterspout at sea.

in an interglacial period, but with a new glacial period on the way. For the forseeable future, however, the planet is likely to continue heating up because of global warming, caused largely by the burning of fossil fuels and deforestation. Figures show that average temperatures rose 1.7°C (0.9°F) in the 20th century, with most of that increase coming after about 1970, and despite attempts to stabilize the situation it's likely that the trend will continue. Such changes would not redraw Köppen's divisions, but they would make a significant difference to many local climates, with a dramatic effect on everything from agriculture to architecture.

CLIMATE RECORDS

TEMPERATURE

Highest recorded shade temperature: Al Aziziyah, Libya, 58°C (136.4°F), 13 Sep. 1922.

Highest mean annual temperature: Dallol, Ethiopia, 34.4°C (94°F), 1960-66.

Longest heatwave: Marble Bar, Western Australia, 162 days over 37.8°C (100°F), 23 October 1923 to 7 April 1924.

Lowest recorded temperature: Vostock Station, Eastern Antarctica, 21 July 1985, −89.2°C (−128.6°F)

(Lowest recorded temperature (outside poles): Verkhoyansk, Siberia, −68°C (−90°F), 6 February 1933.

Lowest mean annual temperature: Plateau Station, Antarctica, −56.6°C (−72.0°F).

PRECIPITATION

Longest drought: Calama, N. Chile – no recorded rainfall in 400 years to 1971.

Wettest place (12 months): Cherrapunji, Meghalaya, NE. India, 26,470mm (1,040 in), August 1860 to August 1861; Cherrapunji also holds the record for the most rainfall in a month: 2,930mm (115 in), July 1861.

Wettest place (average): Tututendo, Colombia, mean annual rainfall of 11,770mm (463.4 in).

Wettest place (24 hours): Cilaos, Réunion, Indian Ocean, 1,870mm (73.6 in), 15-16 March 1952.

Heaviest hailstones: Gopalganj, Bangladesh, up to 1.02kg (2.25lb), 14 April 1986 (92 people were killed).

Heaviest snowfall (continuous): Bessans, Savoie, France, 1,730mm (68 in) in 19 hours, 5-6 April 1969.

Heaviest snowfalls (season/year): Paradise Ranger Station, Mt Rainier, Washington, USA, 31,102mm (1,224.5 in), 19 February 1971 to 18 February 1972.

Conversions
°C = (°F -32) x ⁵/₉; °F = (°C x ⁹/₅) + 32; 0°C = 32°F
1 mm = 0.0394 in (100 mm = 3.94 in); 1 in = 25.4 mm

TEMPERATURE

Average temperature in January

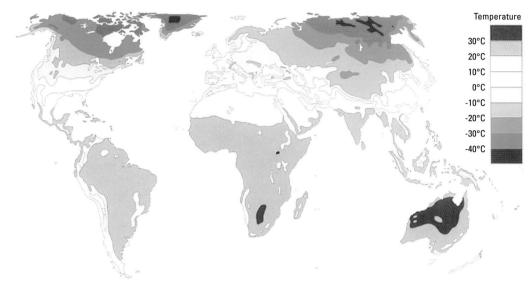

Temperature

30°C
20°C
10°C
0°C
-10°C
-20°C
-30°C
-40°C

Average temperature in July

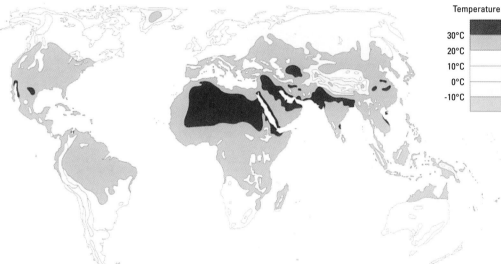

Temperature

30°C
20°C
10°C
0°C
-10°C

RAINFALL

Average annual precipitation

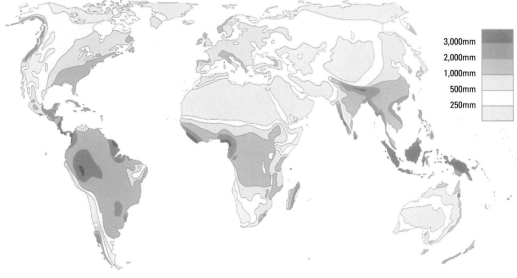

3,000mm
2,000mm
1,000mm
500mm
250mm

THE WORLD'S WATER

FRESH WATER is essential to all life on Earth, from the humblest bacterium to the most advanced technological society. Yet freshwater resources form a minute fraction of our 1.36 billion cu. km (326 million cu. miles) of water: most human needs must be met from the 2,000 cu. km (480 cu. miles) circulating in rivers.

Agriculture accounts for huge quantities: without large-scale irrigation, most of the world's people would starve. Since fresh water is just as essential for most industrial processes, the combination of growing population and advancing industry has put supplies under increasing strain.

Fortunately water is seldom used up: the planet's water cycle circulates it efficiently, at least on a global scale. More locally, however, human activity can cause severe shortages: water for industry and agriculture is being withdrawn from many river basins and underground aquifers faster than natural recirculation can replace it – a process exacerbated by global warming.

The demand for water has led to tensions between an increasing number of nations as supplies are diverted or hoarded. Both Iraq and Syria, for example, have protested at Turkey's dam-building programme, which they claim drastically reduces the flow of Tigris and Euphrates water to their land.

The water cycle

Oceanic water is salty and unsuitable for drinking or farming. In some desert regions, where fresh sources are in short supply, seawater is desalinated to make fresh water, but most of the world is constantly supplied with fresh water by the natural process of the water or hydrological cycle, which relies on the action of two factors: gravity and the Sun's heat.

Over the oceans, which cover almost 71% of the Earth's surface, the Sun's heat causes evaporation, and water vapour rises on air currents and winds. Some of this vapour condenses and returns directly to the oceans as rain, but because of the circulation of the atmosphere, air bearing large amounts is carried over land, where it falls as rain or snow.

Much of this precipitation is quickly re-evaporated by the Sun. Some soaks into the soil, where it is absorbed by plants and partly returned to the air through transpiration; some flows over the land surface as run-off, which flows into streams and rivers; and some rain and melted snow

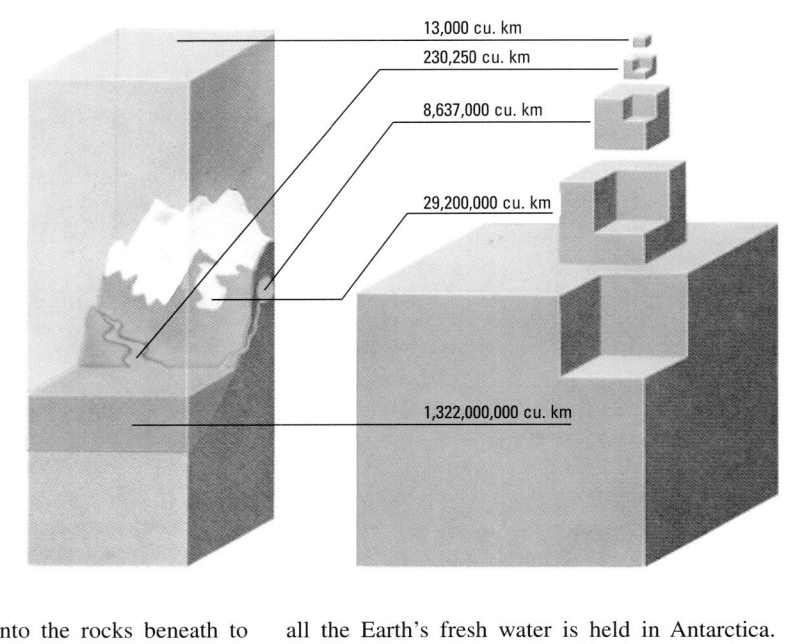

13,000 cu. km
230,250 cu. km
8,637,000 cu. km
29,200,000 cu. km
1,322,000,000 cu. km

seeps through the soil into the rocks beneath to form ground water.

In polar and high mountainous regions most precipitation is in the form of snow. There it is compacted into ice, forming icesheets and glaciers. The force of gravity causes these bodies of ice to move downwards and outwards, and they may eventually return to the oceans where chunks of ice break off at the coastline to form icebergs. Thus all the water that does not return directly to the atmosphere gradually returns to the sea to complete the water cycle. This continual movement of water and ice plays a major part in the erosion of land areas.

Of the total water on land, more than 75% is frozen in icesheets and glaciers, and two-thirds of

all the Earth's fresh water is held in Antarctica. Twice the size of Australia, this frozen continent contains ice to depths of 3,500m (11,500ft) and land is covered in ice to an average depth of more than 2,000m (6,500ft). However, Antarctica receives very little precipitation, not even in the form of snow. It is, effectively, a polar desert.

Most of the rest of the water on land (about 22%) is collected below the Earth's surface and is called ground water; comparatively small but crucially important quantities are in lakes, rivers and in the soil. Water that is held in the soil and that nourishes plant growth is called capillary water: it is retained in the upper few metres by molecular attraction between the water and soil particles.

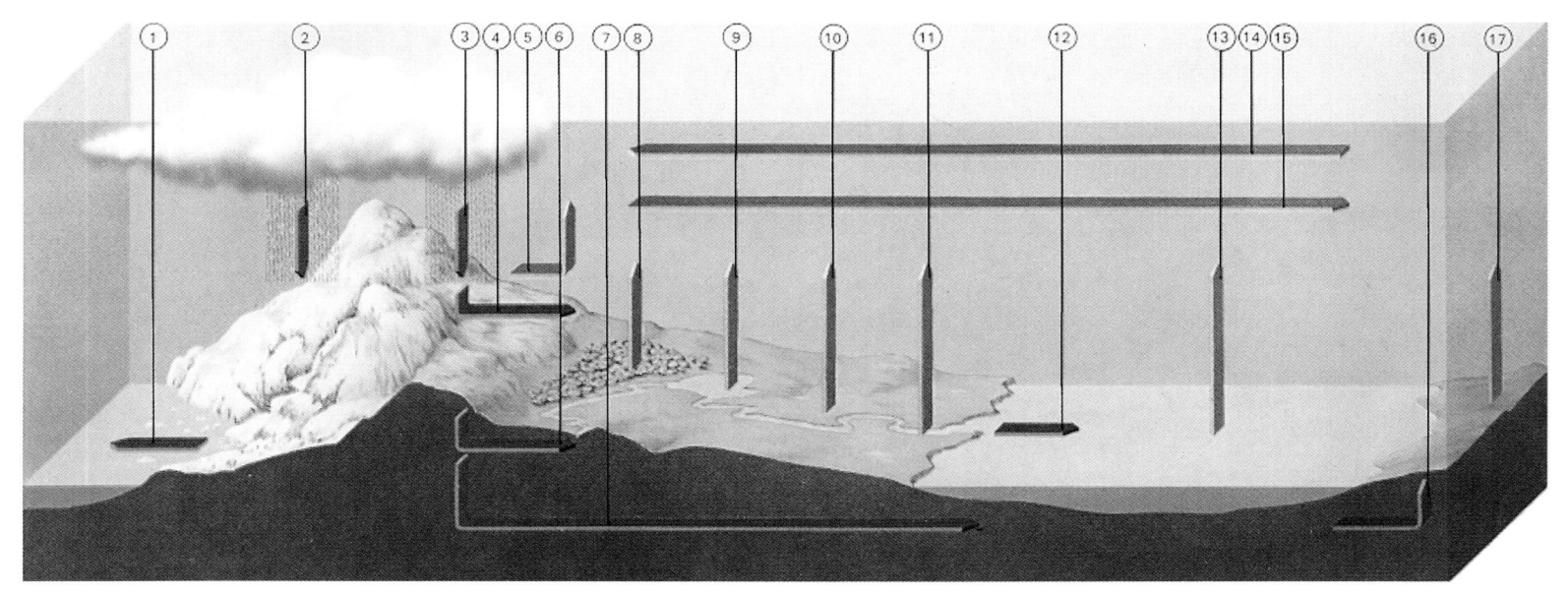

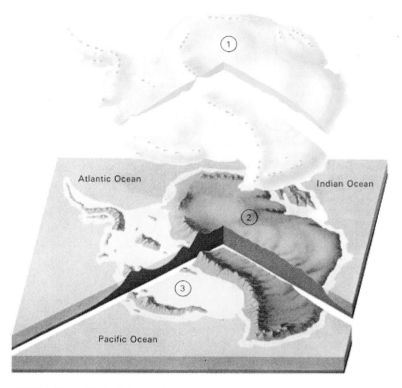

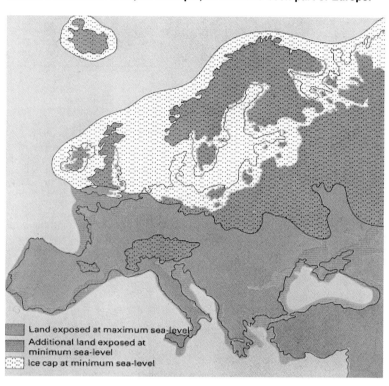

BELOW Ice in the form of icesheets and glaciers now covers 10% of the world's land area, but during the last glacial period, between about 110,000 and 10,000 years ago, icesheets covered up to 30% of the land. At periods of maximum glaciation, sea levels were 180m (600ft) lower than at the present time because of the large amount of water frozen in the ice. Many of today's islands were joined to adjacent continental masses: the British Isles, for example, would have been part of Europe.

Land exposed at maximum sea-level
Additional land exposed at minimum sea-level
Ice cap at minimum sea-level

ABOVE While 75% of the world's fresh water is frozen, continental icesheets are now found only in Antarctica and Greenland. In Antarctica the ice [1] covers the land [2] but also permanently frozen sea [3]. Beneath the ice the terrain is rugged and variable in height, but because of the weight of the ice, about 40% of the land is depressed below sea level.

BELOW Almost all our water supply is 3 billion years old, and all of it cycles endlessly through the hydrosphere, though at very different rates. Water vapour circulates over days, even hours, and deep ocean water over millennia, while icecap water remains solid for millions of years.

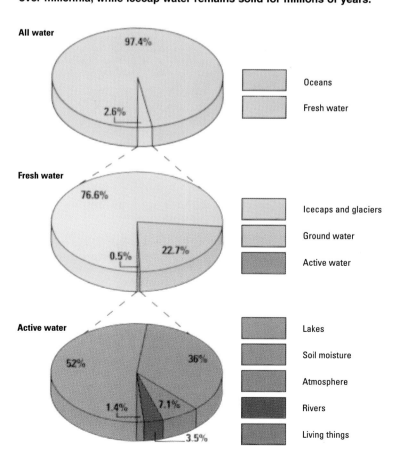

All water
97.4%
2.6%
Oceans
Fresh water

Fresh water
76.6%
0.5%
22.7%
Icecaps and glaciers
Ground water
Active water

Active water
52%
36%
1.4%
7.1%
3.5%
Lakes
Soil moisture
Atmosphere
Rivers
Living things

BELOW Rivers are the most visible part of the water cycle. The drainage pattern of a river and its tributaries is related primarily to the type of rocks on which it formed or flows. On rocks of equal or similar resistance (A), a dendritic pattern develops; in areas of alternating hard and soft rock (B), the water follows the softer rock to form a trellis pattern; and a radial pattern (C), forms on and around and rock domes and volcanoes.

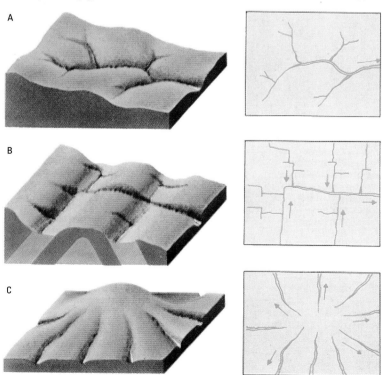

UNDERGROUND WATER

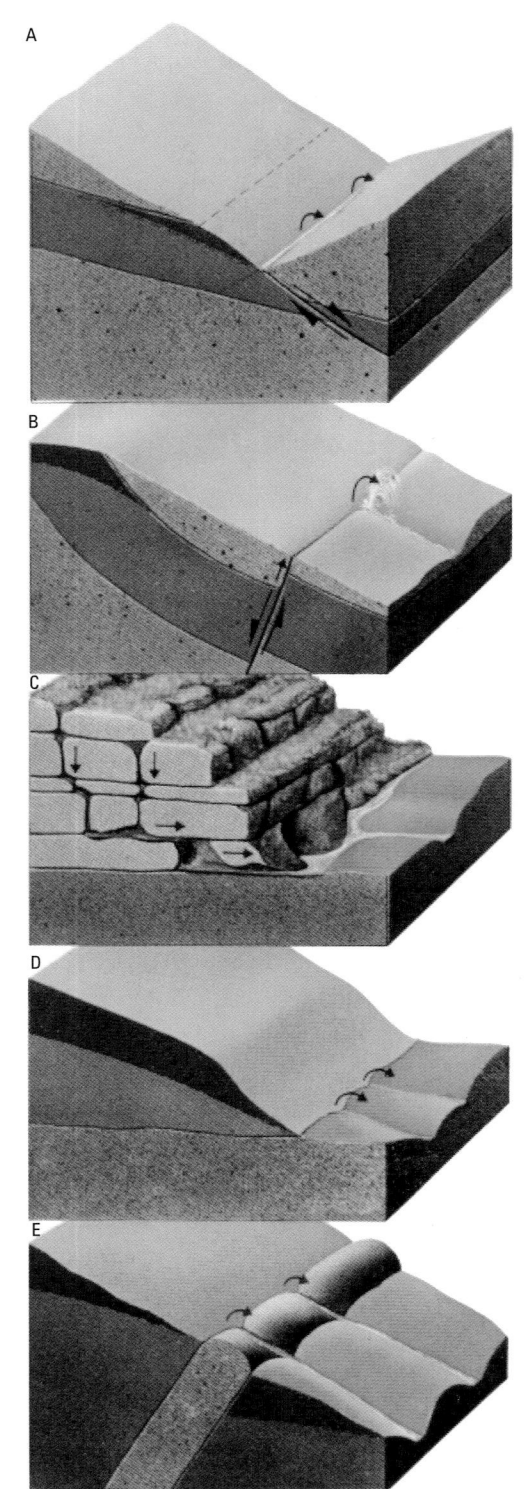

GROUND WATER enters permeable rocks through what is called the zone of intermittent saturation, a layer that may retain water after continued rain but which soon dries up. Beneath this lies a rock zone where the pores or crevices are filled with water. Called the zone of saturation, this usually begins within 30m (100ft) of the surface, extending downwards until it reaches impermeable rock, through which it cannot percolate, lying below the water-holding layer (aquifer). The top of the saturated zone is the water table which, despite its name, is not level. It is often arched under hills, while beneath the softer rocks of plains it generally lies closer to the surface. The water table also varies in level during the year, depending on the amount of rainfall. In some places the water table intersects the surface, forming features such as oases in desert hollows, lakes, swamps and springs. Some springs

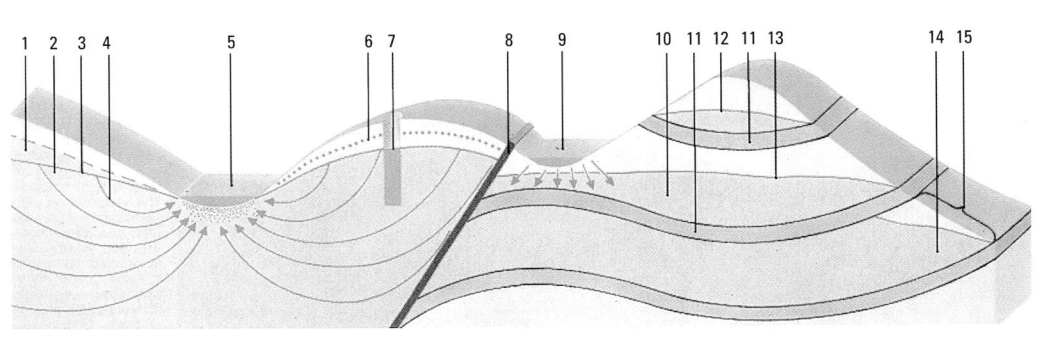

ABOVE Ground water seeps through the zone of intermittent saturation [1] until it reaches an impermeable layer, above which it forms the zone of saturation or aquifer [2,10]. The upper surface of the aquifer forms the water table [3,13], above which is the capillary fringe [6]. Because the capillary fringe is not saturated, wells [7] must be sunk to the water table.

Impermeable dikes [8] block the flow of ground water. In uniform material the water follows paths [4] that curve down and up again towards the nearest stream. If an aquifer is part of a series of strata including several impermeable layers [11], a "perched" water table [12] may result; if it lies between two impermeable strata it is said to be "confined" [14].

The recharge area [15] of the water table is where water enters the confined aquifer. A stream below the water table is called a gaining stream [5], while a stream flowing above it is known as a losing stream [9] because it loses water by seepage.

ABOVE The lowest level of the water table, reached at the driest time of the year, is called the permanent water table, and wells must be drilled to this depth if they are to guarantee a supply of water throughout the seasons.

Artesian springs and wells are found where ground water is under pressure, and in artesian wells water is forced to the surface by hydrostatic pressure. The water table [1] in the confined aquifer [2] lies near the top of the dipping layers. A well [4] drilled through the top impervious layer [3] is not an artesian well because the head of hydrostatic pressure [6] is not sufficient to force water to the surface; in such wells the water must be pumped or drawn to the surface.

The top of an artesian well [5] lies below the level of the head of hydrostatic pressure and so water gushes to the surface. Artesian springs [8] may occur along joints or faults [7] where the head of hydrostatic pressure is sufficient to force the water up along the fault.

Areas with artesian wells are called artesian basins. Artesian water is obtained from porous sandstone aquifers that underlie the Great Basin of Australia, which are supplied with water from rain that falls on the Eastern Highlands of Queensland and New South Wales. In the London and Paris artesian basins the water has been so heavily tapped in recent centuries that the water level has dropped below the level of the well-heads.

contain so much mineral substance in solution that their water is used for medicinal purposes and spa towns have grown up around them.

While sandstone is a highly porous rock through which water percolates easily, limestone is a permeable but non-porous rock. Ground water can seep through its maze of joints, fissures and caves, with apertures enlarged by the chemical action of rainwater containing dissolved carbon dioxide.

BELOW Limestone surfaces are often eroded into blocks called clints [1]. Surface streams flow into dissolved sink-holes [2] that lead to a deep chimney [3]; pot-holes [7] are dry chimneys. Gours [4] are ridges formed as carbonate is precipitated from turbulent water. Streams flow at the lowest level of the galleries [17], and abandoned galleries [13] are common. A siphon [12] occurs where the roof is below water level. Streams reappear at resurgences [20], and abandoned resurgences [19] may provide entrances to caves.

Stalactites [5] include macaroni stalactites [6], curtain stalactites or drapes [11] and "eccentric" stalactites [16], formed by water being blown sideways; stalagmites [14] sometimes have a fir-cone shape [15] caused by splashing, or resemble stacked plates [8]. Stalactites and stalagmites may also merge to form columns [10]. Signs of ancient humans [18] have been found in many caves, and they still harbour a variety of animal life adapted to the environment, including colourless shrimps and sightless newts – often called blind fish – which live in the dark pools [9].

Rain coming off the Atlantic Ocean and Mediterreanean Sea and falling on the Atlas Mountains of Morocco and Algeria then drains into porous rocks underlying the northern parts of the Sahara Desert. The water seeps through these rocks which, wherever they come to the surface, give rise to fertile oases.

BELOW As rain falls, it dissolves carbon dioxide from the atmosphere and becomes a weak carbonic acid that attacks carbonate rock (limestone and dolomite) by transforming it into the soluble bicarbonate. Carbonate rocks are crisscrossed by vertical cracks and horizontal breaks along bedding planes [A]. Some geologists believe the caves were formed when the rock was saturated by water; others reckon they formed gradually by solution [B] into a major cave network [C]. Limestone caves contain many features formed from calcium carbonate.

VEGETATION AND SOIL

THE DISTRIBUTION of natural resources over the Earth's surface is far from even. The whereabouts of mineral deposits depends on random events in a remote geological past, while patches of fertile soil depend on more recent events such as the flow of rivers or the movement of ice.

For agriculture, the activity that has been basic to the survival of humanity and our huge increase in population, about a fifth of the Earth's surface is barred by ice or perennially frozen soil; a fifth is arid or desert; and another fifth is composed of highlands too cold, rugged or barren for the cultivation of crops. Between 5% and 10% of the remainder has no soil, either because it has been scraped by ice or because it is permanently wet or flooded. This leaves only 30% to 35% of the land surface where food production is even possible.

The importance of soil

The whole structure of life on Earth, with its enormous diversity of plant and animal types, is dependent on a mantle of soil which is rich in moisture and nutrients.

Soil is a result of all the processes of physical and chemical weathering on the barren, underlying rock mass of the Earth that it covers, and varies in

BELOW The map illustrates the natural "climax" vegetation of a region, as dictated by its climate and topography. In the vast majority of cases, however, human agricultural activity has drastically altered the pattern of vegetation. Western Europe, for example, lost most of its broadleaf forest many centuries ago, and in many areas irrigation has gradually turned natural semi-desert into productive land.

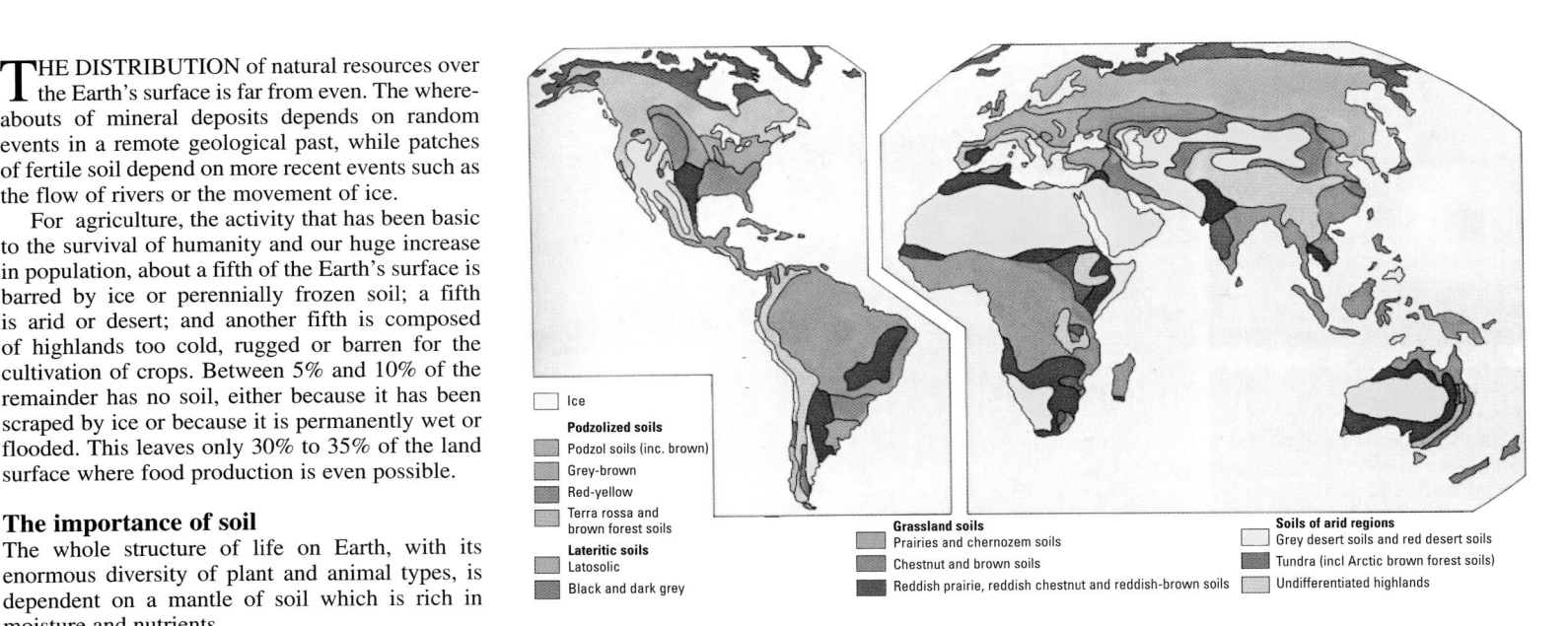

Ice

Podzolized soils
Podzol soils (inc. brown)
Grey-brown
Red-yellow
Terra rossa and brown forest soils

Lateritic soils
Latosolic
Black and dark grey

Grassland soils
Prairies and chernozem soils
Chestnut and brown soils
Reddish prairie, reddish chestnut and reddish-brown soils

Soils of arid regions
Grey desert soils and red desert soils
Tundra (incl Arctic brown forest soils)
Undifferentiated highlands

depth from a few centimetres to several metres. The depth of soil is measured either by the distance to which plants send down their roots, or by the depth of soil directly influencing their systems. In some places only a very thin layer is necessary to support life.

Soil remains an unconsolidated mass of inorganic particles until it acquires a minimum organic content and plants take root and deposit their "litter". As the organic matter accumulates, fine humus builds up in the upper soil horizons, enriching them chemically and providing an environment for a wide variety of lifeforms. In the course of time

plants, fungi, bacteria, worms, insects and burrowing animals such as rodents and moles reproduce in the soil and thrive in the complex ecosystem of a mature soil.

Formation of soil is the result of the complex interaction of five major elements – the parent rock (the source of the vast bulk of soil material), land topography, time, climate and decay. However, by far the most single important factor in the development of soil is climate, with water essential to all chemical and biological change. As it percolates through, water both leaches the surface layers and deposits material in the subsoil.

NATURAL VEGETATION

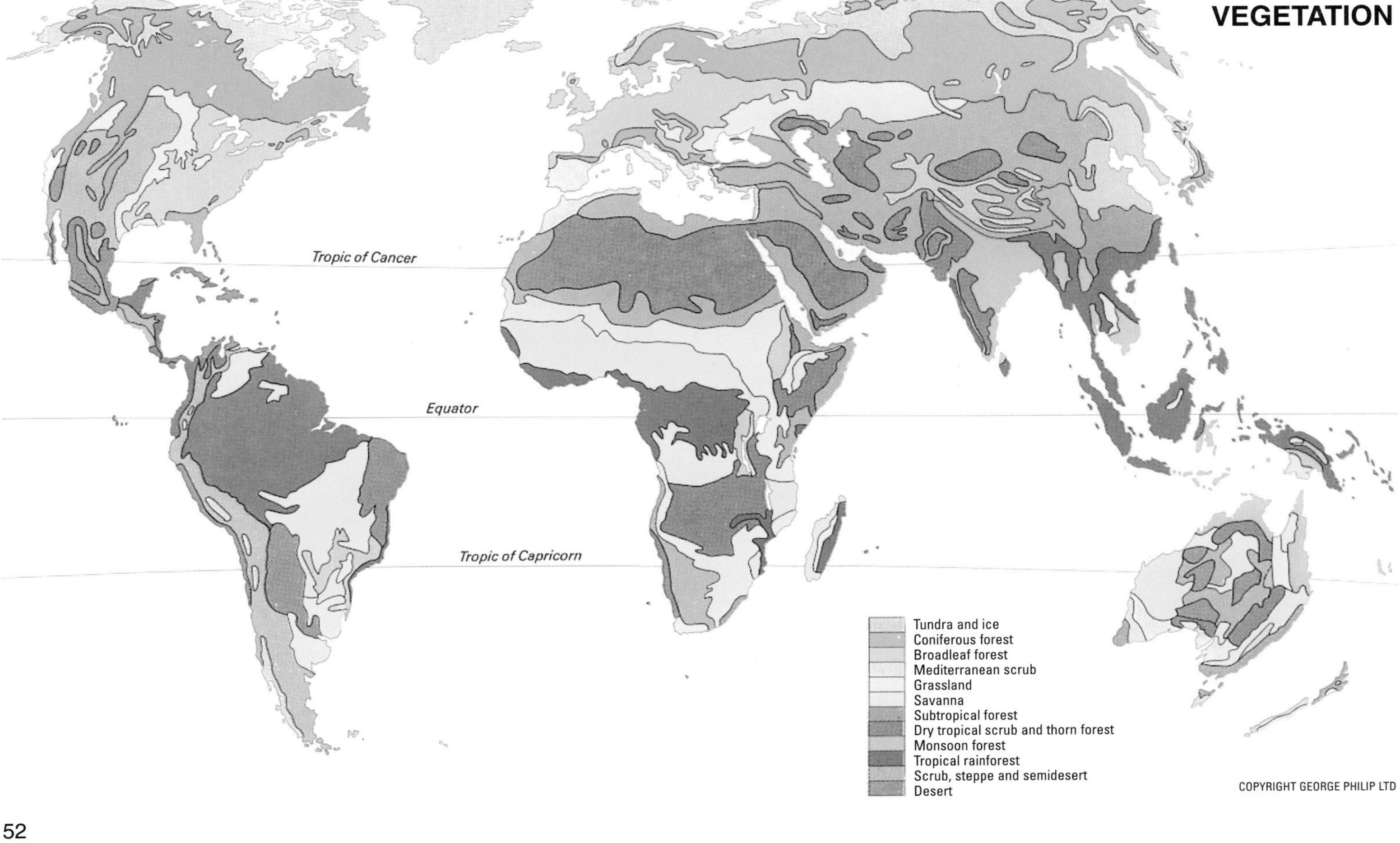

Tropic of Cancer

Equator

Tropic of Capricorn

Tundra and ice
Coniferous forest
Broadleaf forest
Mediterranean scrub
Grassland
Savanna
Subtropical forest
Dry tropical scrub and thorn forest
Monsoon forest
Tropical rainforest
Scrub, steppe and semidesert
Desert

RIGHT Some legume crops, such as clover, can obtain nitrogen from the air by the process known as fixation, but most plants need additional inorganic nitrogen and this element is the one most widely used in fertilizers.

Nitrogen undergoes a natural cycle. Together with its compounds it is involved in five basic processes: fixation of nitrogen from the air by micro-organisms and by lightning; use by plants of nitrates in the soil to make proteins; ammonium compound production in decaying plant and animal matter; nitrification of these to nitrites and then to nitrates; and denitrification of ammonium compounds back to nitrogen gas.

Nitrogen is removed from the soil whenever we consume food, but is replaced by the artificial addition of nitrogenous fertilizers to the soil by farmers. In its many forms nitrogen accounts for almost half of the world consumption of fertilizers: phosphoros makes up another 30% and potassium, the remaining primary nutrient, accounts for most of the balance.

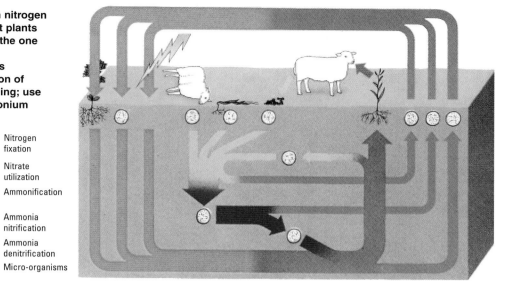

- Nitrogen fixation
- Nitrate utilization
- Ammonification
- Ammonia nitrification
- Ammonia denitrification
- Micro-organisms

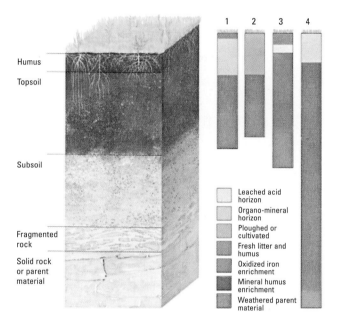

Humus
Topsoil

Subsoil

Fragmented rock

Solid rock or parent material

- Leached acid horizon
- Organo-mineral horizon
- Ploughed or cultivated
- Fresh litter and humus
- Oxidized iron enrichment
- Mineral humus enrichment
- Weathered parent material

RIGHT Soil is identified by composition and colour. The tundra soil [1] has a dark, peaty surface. Light-coloured desert soil [2] is coarse and poor in organic matter. Chestnut-brown soil [3] and chernozem [4] – Russian for "black earth" – are humus-rich grassland soils typical of the central Asian steppes and prairies of North America. The reddish, leached latosol [5] of tropical savannas has a very thin but rich humus layer. Podzolic soils are typical of northern climates where rainfall is heavy but evaporation is slow: they include the organically rich brown forest podzol [6], the grey-brown podzol [8], and the grey-stony podzol [9] that supports mixed growths of conifers and hardwoods. All are relatively acid. The red-yellow podzol [9] is quite highly leached.

ABOVE Profile 1 is of acid brown earth found in temperate climates – this one on sandy rock – and 2 is a cultivated brown earth of the same region. Grey leached podzol [3] is typical of wet, cool climates such as the taiga in Russia – while oxisol [4], a thick red soil containing iron compounds, is found in humid, tropical lands with high chemical and biological activity.

BELOW The soil is a complex ecosystem. A cubic metre of fertile soil teems with more than 1,000 million individual forms of life, from microscopic organisms through insects and earthworms to large animals such as burrowing rodents. In the steppes, for example, these include marmots, susliks, hamsters and mole rats. All play an important part in helping to

aerate the soil and to accelerate the processes of decay and humus formation.

The role of soil bacteria is perhaps the most crucial: they not only "fix" nitrogen from the air in a form that plants can use, but also promote the essential processes of decay. As they decay, plants provide the fine organic humus litter vital to healthy soil life.

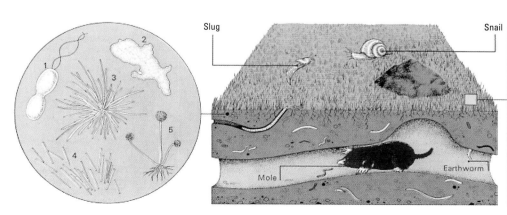

Slug
Snail
Mole
Earthworm

1. Bacterium
2. Protozoan
3. Alga
4. Virus
5. Fungus
6. Eelworm
7. Earwig
8. Woodlouse
9. Mite
10. Centipede
11. Millipede
12. Spider
13. Ant
14. Springtail
15. Cricket
16. Cockchafer lava

THE EARTH IN FIGURES

Mean distance from the Sun	149,500,000km (92,860,000 miles)
Average speed around the Sun	108,000km/h (66,600mph)
Age	approx. 4,500,000,000 years
Mass	5,975 million million million tonnes
Density	5,515 times that of water
Volume	1,083,207,000,000cu. km (260,000,000,000 cu. miles)
Area	509,450,000sq km (196,672,000sq miles)
Land surface	149,450,000sq km (57,688,000sq mi) – 29.3% of total
Water surface area	360,000,000sq km (138,984,000sq mi) – 70.7% of total
Equatorial circumference	40,075km (24,902 miles)
Polar circumference	40,008km (24,860 miles)
Equatorial diameter	12,756km (7,926 miles)
Polar diameter	12,714km (7,900 miles)

INSIDE THE EARTH

	Density (g/cm)	Temperature		State	Thickness	
Sial	2.8	⋞ 500°C	(930°F)	Solid	0-30km	(0-18miles)
Sima	2.9	⋞ 650°C	(1,200°F)	Solid	20-80km	(12-50miles)
Upper mantle	4.3	⋞ 800°C	(1,480°F)	Molten	c. 700km	(435miles)
Lower mantle	5.5	⋞ 2,500°C	(4,600°F)	Solid	c. 1,700km	(1,050miles)
Outer core	10.0	⋞ 3,000°C	(5,400°F)	Molten	c. 2,100km	(1,305miles)
Inner core	13.5	⋞ 5,000°C	(9,000°F)	Solid	c. 1,370km	(850miles)

SELECTED EARTH RECORDS

Greatest tides	Bay of Fundy, Nova Scotia, Canada, 16.3m (53.5ft)
Deepest gorge	Colca River, Peru, 3,205m (10,515ft)
Longest gorge	Grand Canyon, Arizona, USA, 350km (217 miles)
Deepest lake	Lake Baikal, Siberia, Russia, 1,620m (5,315ft)
Highest navigable lake	Lake Titicaca, Peru/Bolivia, 3,812m (12,506ft)
Deepest cave	Réseau Jean Bernard, Haute-Savoie, France, 1,602m (5,256ft)
Longest cave system	Mammoth Cave, Kentucky, USA, 560km (348 miles)
Deepest valley	Kali Gandaki, Nepal, 5,883m (19,300ft)
Longest glacier	Lambert-Fisher Ice Passage, Antarctica, 515km (320 miles)
Deepest depression	Dead Sea, Israel/Jordan, 395m (1,296ft)

The area of the Earth covered by sea is estimated at over 70% of the total. Occupying almost a hemisphere, the Pacific Ocean accounts for nearly half the oceans if adjacent seas are included, and 35.5% of the surface area of the world. The average depth of the hydro-sphere is calculated at 3,554m (11,660ft), almost five times the figure for average height of land.

Over 41% of the Earth's surface is covered by continental land masses, with 29% above water, with a mean height of 756m (2,840ft) above sea level. The Eurasian land mass is the largest with an area (including islands) of 53,698,000 sq km (20,733,000 sq miles). The Afro-Asian land mass, artificially severed by the Suez Canal, covers 84,702,000 sq km (32,704,000 sq miles) – or 57.2% of the Earth's land mass.

LARGEST ISLANDS

	sq km	sq miles
Europe		
Great Britain [8]	229,880	88,700
Iceland	103,000	39,800
Ireland	84,400	32,600
Novaya Zemlya (N)	48,200	18,600
Sicily	25,500	9,800
Corsica	8,700	3,400
Asia		
Borneo [3]	744,360	287,400
Sumatra [6]	473,600	182,860
Honshu [7]	230,500	88,980
Celebes	189,000	73,000
Java	126,700	48,900
Luzon	104,700	40,400
Mindanao	95,000	36,700
Hokkaido	78,400	30,300
Sakhalin	76,400	29,500
Sri Lanka	65,600	25,300
Africa		
Madagascar [4]	587,040	226,660
Socotra	3,600	1,400
Réunion	2,500	965
North America		
Greenland [1]*	2,175,600	839,800
Baffin Island [5]	508,000	196,100
Victoria Island [9]	212,200	81,900
Ellesmere Island [10]	212,000	81,800
Cuba	110,860	42,800
Newfoundland	96,000	37,100
Hispaniola	76,200	29,400
Jamaica	11,400	4,400
Puerto Rico	8,900	3,400
South America		
Tierra del Fuego	47,000	18,100
Falkland Island (E)	6,800	2,600
Oceania		
New Guinea [2]	821,030	317,000
New Zealand (S)	150,500	58,100
New Zealand (N)	114,700	44,300
Tasmania	67,800	26,200
Hawaii	10,450	4,000

* Geographers consider Australia to be a continental land mass

LARGEST INLAND LAKES AND SEAS

	Location	sq km	sq mi
Europe			
Lake Ladoga	Russia	17,700	6,800
Lake Onega	Russia	9,700	3,700
Saimaa system	Finland	8,000	3,100
Vänern	Sweden	6,500	2,100
Asia			
Caspian Sea [1]	W. Central Asia	371,800	143,550
Aral Sea* [6]	Kazakhstan/Uzbekistan	33,640	13,000
Lake Baikal [9]	Russia	30,500	11,780
Tonlé Sap	Cambodia	20,000	7,700
Lake Balkhash	Kazakhstan	18,500	7,100
Africa			
Lake Victoria [3]	East Africa	68,000	26,000
Lake Tanganyika [7]	Central Africa	33,000	13,000
Lake Malawi [10]	East Africa	29,600	11,430
Lake Chad*	Central Africa	25,000	9,700
Lake Turkana	Ethiopia/Kenya	8,500	3,300
Lake Volta†	Ghana	8,480	3,250
North America			
Lake Superior [2]	Canada/USA	82,350	31,800
Lake Huron [4]	Canada/USA	59,600	23,010
Lake Michigan [5]	USA	58,000	22,400
Great Bear Lake [8]	Canada	31,800	12,280
Great Slave Lake	Canada	28,500	11,000
Lake Erie	Canada/USA	25,700	9,900
Lake Winnipeg	Canada	24,400	9,400
Lake Ontario	Canada/USA	19,500	7,500
Lake Nicaragua	Nicaragua	8,200	3,200
South America			
Lake Titicaca‡	Bolivia/Peru	8,300	3,200
Lake Poopó	Peru	2,800	1,100
Australia			
Lake Eyre§	Australia	8,900	3,400
Lake Torrens§	Australia	5,800	2,200
Lake Gairdner§	Australia	4,800	1,900

* Shrinking in area due to environmental factors; until the 1980s it was the world's 4th largest
† Artificial lake created by Akosombo Dam (1966)
‡ Lake Maracaibo, in Venezuela, is far larger at 13,260 sq km (5,120 sq miles), but is linked to the Caribbean by a narrow channel and therefore not an "inland" lake
§ Salt lakes that vary in size with rainfall

BEAUFORT WIND SCALE

Named after the 19th-century British naval officer who devised it, the Beaufort Scale assesses wind speed according to its effects. Originally designed in 1806 as an aid for sailors, it has since been adapted for use on land and was internationally recognised in 1874.

Scale	Wind speed		Name
	km/h	mph	
0	0-1	0-1	Calm
1	1-5	1-3	Light air
2	6-11	4-7	Light breeze
3	12-19	8-12	Gentle breeze
4	20-28	13-18	Moderate
5	29-38	19-24	Fresh
6	39-49	25-31	Strong
7	50-61	32-38	Near gale
8	62.74	39-46	Gale
9	75-88	47-54	Strong gale
10	89-102	55-63	Storm
11	103-117	64-72	Violent storm
12	118+	73+	Hurricane

WINDCHILL FACTORS

A combination of cold and wind makes the human body feel cooler than the actual air temperature. The charts below give approximate equivalents for combinations of wind speed and temperature. In sub-zero temperatures even moderate winds will significantly reduce effective temperatures: if human skin was exposed to winds of 48km/h (30mph) in a temperature of −34°C (−30°F) it would freeze solid in 30 seconds.

Temp. °C	Wind speed (km/h)				Temp. °F	Wind speed (mph)			
	16	32	48	64*		10	20	30	40*
15	11	9	8	6	30	16	4	−2	−5
10	6	3	2	−1	20	3	−10	−18	−21
5	1	4	−5	−8	10	−9	−24	−33	−37
0	−8	−14	−17	−19	0	−2	−39	−49	−53
−5	−14	−21	−25	−27	−10	−34	−53	−6	−69
−10	−20	−28	−33	−35	−20	−46	−67	−79	−84
−15	−26	−36	−40	−43	−30	−58	−81	−93	−100
−20	−32	−42	−48	−51	−40	−71	−95	−109	−115

*Wind speeds of more than about 64km/h (40mph) have only a marginal cooling effect

THE CONTINENTS

Continent	Area			Highest point above sea level			Lowest point below sea level		
	sq km	sq miles	%		metres	feet		metres	feet
Asia	44,500,000	17,179,000	29.8	Mt Everest (China/Nepal)	8,848	29,029	Dead Sea, Israel/Jordan	−396	−1,302
Africa	30,302,000	11,697,000	20.3	Mt Kilimanjaro, Tanzania	5,895	19,340	Lake Assal, Djibouti	−153	−502
North America	24,454,000	9,442,000	16.2	Mt McKinley, Alaska	6,194	20,321	Death Valley, California, USA	−86	−282
South America	17,793,000	6,868,000	11.9	Mt Aconcagua, Argentina	6,960	22,834	Peninsular Valdés, Argentina	−40	−131
Antarctica	14,100,000	5,443,000	9.4	Vinson Massif	4,897	16,066	*		
Europe	9,957,000	3,843.000	6.7	Mt Elbrus, Russia	5,633	18,481	Caspian Sea, W. Central Asia	−28	−92
Oceania	8,945,000	3,454,000	5.7	Puncak Jaya (Ngga Pulu), Indonesia	5,029	16,499	Lake Eyre (N), South Australia	−15	−50

*The Bentley trench (−2,540m/−8,333ft) is englacial and therefore not a surface point

THE OCEANS

Ocean	Area			Average depth		Greatest known depth			
	sq km	sq miles	%	metres	feet		metres	feet	
Pacific	179,679,000	69,356,000	49.9	4,300	14,100	Mariana Trench	11,022	36,161	
Atlantic	92,373,000	35,657,000	25.7	3,700	12,100	Puerto Rico Deep*	9,200	30,138	
Indian	73,917,000	28,532,000	20.5	3,900	12,800	Java Trench	7,450	24,442	
Arctic	14,090,000	5,439,000	3.9	1,330	4,300	Molloy Deep	5,608	18,399	

*7th deepest trench in the world; 8 of the deepest 10, including 1-6, are in the Pacific Ocean

LONGEST RIVERS

	Outflow	km	miles
Europe			
Volga	Caspian Sea	3,700	2,300
Danube	Black Sea	2,850	1,770
Ural*	Caspian Sea	2,535	1,575
Asia			
Yangtze [3]	Pacific Ocean	6,380	3,960
Yenisey-Angara [5]	Arctic Ocean	5,550	3,445
Hwang Ho [6]	Pacific Ocean	5,464	3,395
Ob-Irtysh [7]	Arctic Ocean	5,410	3,360
Mekong [9]	Pacific Ocean	4,500	2,795
Amur [10]	Pacific Ocean	4,400	2,730
Africa			
Nile [1]	Mediterranean	6,620	4,140
Zaire (Congo) [8]	Atlantic Ocean	4,670	2,900
Niger	Atlantic Ocean	4,180	2,595
Zambezi	Indian Ocean	3,540	2,200
North America			
Mississippi-Missouri[4]	Gulf of Mexico	6,020	3,740
Mackenzie	Arctic Ocean	4,240	2,630
Mississippi	Gulf of Mexico	3,780	2,350
Missouri	Mississippi	3,780	2,350
Yukon	Pacific Ocean	3,185	1,980
Rio Grande	Gulf of Mexico	3,030	1,880
Arkansas	Mississippi	2,840	1,450
Colorado	Pacific Ocean	2,330	1,445
South America			
Amazon [2]	Atlantic Ocean	6,450	4,010
Paraná-Plate	Atlantic Ocean	4,500	2,800
Purus	Amazon	3,350	2,080
Madeira	Amazon	3,200	1,990
Sao Francisco	Atlantic Ocean	2,900	1,800
Australia			
Murray-Darling	Southern Ocean	3,750	2,830
Darling	Murray	3,070	1,905
Murray	Southern Ocean	2,575	1,600
Murrumbidgee	Murray	1,690	1,050

* Flows through Europe and Asia

HIGHEST MOUNTAINS

	Location	metres	feet		Location	metres	feet
Europe				Ruwenzori	Uganda/Zaire	5,109	16,762
Elbrus*	Russia	5,642	18,510				
Mont Blanc† ‡	France/Italy	4,807	15,771	**North America**			
Monte Rosa‡	Italy/Switzerland	4,634	15,203	Mt McKinley (Denali) ‡	USA (Alaska)	6,194	20,321
Also				Mt Logan	Canada	5,959	19,551
Matterhorn (Cervino)‡	Italy/Switzerland	4,478	14,691	Citlaltépetl (Orizaba)	Mexico	5,700	18,701
Jungfrau	Switzerland	4,158	13,642	Mt St Elias	USA/Canada	5,489	18,008
Grossglockner	Austria	3,797	12,457	Popocatépetl	Mexico	5,452	17,887
Mulhacen	Spain	3,478	11,411	*Also*			
Etna	Italy (Sicily)	3,340	10,958	Mt Whitney	USA	4,418	14,495
Zugspitze	Germany	2,962	9,718	Tajumulco	Guatemala	4,220	13,845
Olympus	Greece	2,917	9,570	Chirripo Grande	Costa Rica	3,837	12,589
Galdhopiggen	Norway	2,468	8,100	Pico Duarte	Dominican Rep.	3,175	10,417
Ben Nevis	UK (Scotland)	1,343	4,406				
				South America			
Asia§				Aconcagua#	Argentina	6,960	22,834
Everest	China/Nepal	8,848	29,029	Ojos del Salado	Argentina/Chile	6,863	22,516
K2 (Godwin Austen)	China/Kashmir	8,611	28,251	Pissis	Argentina	6,779	22,241
Kanchenjunga‡	India/Nepal	8,598	28,208	Mercedario	Argentina/Chile	6,770	22,211
Lhotse‡	China/Nepal	8,516	27,939	Huascarán‡	Peru	6,768	22,204
Makalu‡	China/Nepal	8,481	27,824				
Cho Oyu	China/Nepal	8,201	26,906	**Oceania**			
Dhaulagiri‡	Nepal	8,172	26,811	Puncak Jaya	Indonesia (W Irian)	5,029	16,499
Manaslu (Kutang)‡	Nepal	8,156	26,758	Puncak Trikora	Indonesia (W Irian)	4,750	15,584
Nanga Parbat	Kashmir	8,126	26,660	Puncak Mandala	Indonesia (W Irian)	4,702	15,427
Annapurna‡	Nepal	8,078	26,502	Mt Wilhelm	Papua New Guinea	4,508	14,790
Also				*Also*			
Pik Kommunizma	Tajikistan	7,495	24,590	Mauna Kea	USA (Hawaii)	4 205	13 796
Ararat	Turkey	5,165	16,945	Mauna Loa	USA (Hawaii)	4,170	13,681
Gunong Kinabalu	Malaysia (Borneo)	4.101	13,455	Mt Cook (Aorangi)	New Zealand	3,753	12,313
Fuji-san (Fujiyama)	Japan	3,776	12,388	Mt Kosciusko	Australia	2,237	7,339
Africa				**Antarctica**			
Kilimanjaro	Tanzania	5,895	19,340	Vinson Massif	—	4,897	16,066
Mt Kenya	Kenya	5,199	17,057	Mt Tyree	—	4,965	16,289

* The Caucasus Mountains include 14 other peaks higher than Mont Blanc, the highest point in non-Russian Europe
† The highest point is in France; the highest point wholly in Italian territory is 4,760m (15,616ft)
‡ Many mountains, especially in Asia, have two or more significant peaks; only the highest ones are listed here
§ The ranges of Central Asia have more than 100 peaks over 7,315m (24,000ft); thus the first 10 listed here constitute the world's 10 highest mountains   # Highest mountain outside Asia

HIGHEST WATERFALLS

Name	Total height		Location	River	Highest fall	
	m	ft			m	ft
Angel	979	3,212	Venezuela	Carrao	807	2,648
Tugela	947	3,110	Natal, South Africa	Tugela	410	1,350
Utigård	800	2,625	Nesdale, Norway	Jostedal Glacier	600	1,970
Mongefoseen	774	2,540	Mongebekk, Norway	Monge	—	—
Yosemite	739	2,425	California, USA	Yosemite Creek	739	2,425
Østre Mardøla Foss	656	2,154	Eikisdal, Norway	Mardals	296	974
Tyssestrengane	646	2,120	Hardanger, Norway	Tysso	289	948
Cuquenán	610	2,000	Venezuela	Arabopó	—	—
Sutherland	580	1,904	Otago, New Zealand	Arthur	248	815
Takkakaw	502	1,650	British Columbia, Canada	Daly Glacier	365	1,200
Ribbon	491	1,612	California, USA	Ribbon Fall Stream	491	1,612

The greatest falls by volume are the Boyoma (formerly Stanley) Falls on the Zaïre (formerly Congo), with a mean annual flow of 17,000 cu m/sec (600,000 cu ft/sec). The Niagara Falls come 4th and the Victoria Falls 9th in terms of volume, though both are relatively modest in height.

NOTABLE EARTHQUAKES*

Year	Location	Magnitude†	Deaths
1906	San Francisco, USA	8.3	503
1908	Messina, Italy	7.5	83,000
1920	Gansu (Kansu), China	8.6	180,000
1923	Yokohama, Japan	8.3	143,000
1927	Nan Xian, China	8.3	200,000
1932	Gansu (Kansu), China	7.6	70,000
1933	Sanriku, Japan	8.9 ‡	2,990
1935	Quetta, India §	7.5	60,000
1939	Chillan, Chile	8.3	28,000
1963	Skopje, Yugoslavia #	6.0	1,000
1964	Anchorage, Alaska	8.4	131
1970	N. Peru	7.7	86,794
1976	Guatemala	7.5	22,778
1976	Tangshan, China	8.2	242,000
1985	Mexico City, Mexico	8.1	4,200
1988	NW. Armenia	6.8	55,000
1990	N. Iran	7.7	36,000
1993	Maharastra, India	6.4	30,000
1995	Kobe, Japan	7.2	5,000
1995	Sakhalin Island, Russia	7.5	2,000
1997	NE Iran	7.1	2,400
1998	Takhar, Afghanistan	6.1	4,200
1999	NW Turkey	8.2	22,000
1999	Taiwan	7.6	4,600

* Since 1900   † On the Richter scale   ‡ Highest ever recorded   § Now Pakistan   # Now Macedonia

Understanding Maps

Mapmaking
While small areas can be mapped by plane (flat) surveying, larger areas must be done by geodesy, which takes into account the Earth's curvature. A variety of instruments and techniques is used to determine the position, height and extent of features – data essential to the cartographic process. Instruments such as graduated metal rods, chains, tapes and portable radar or radio transmitters are used for measuring distances, and the theodolite is used for angles. With measured distances and angles, further distances and angles as well as heights are calculated by triangulation.

Latitude and longitude
Accurate positioning of points on the Earth's surface is made possible by reference to latitude and longitude. Parallels of latitude are drawn west-east around the globe and numbered by degrees north and south of the Equator (0° of latitude). Meridians of longitude are drawn north-south and numbered by degrees east and west and the prime meridian (0° of longitude) which passes through the Royal Observatory at Greenwich in southeast London. Latitude and longitude are indicated by blue lines on the maps, and are straight or slightly curved according to the projection used.

Representing relief
Height and gradient can be represented on a map in many ways. Hachuring, in which fine lines follow the direction of the greatest slope, can give an excellent impression of the landscape but the lines may obscure other information. Hill shading, the representation of a landscape illuminated from one direction, is used alone or with colours. Contours can also be separated by colour and intermediate heights given as spot heights. These techniques are now often used in conjunction with sophisticated computerized technology, including digitalization.

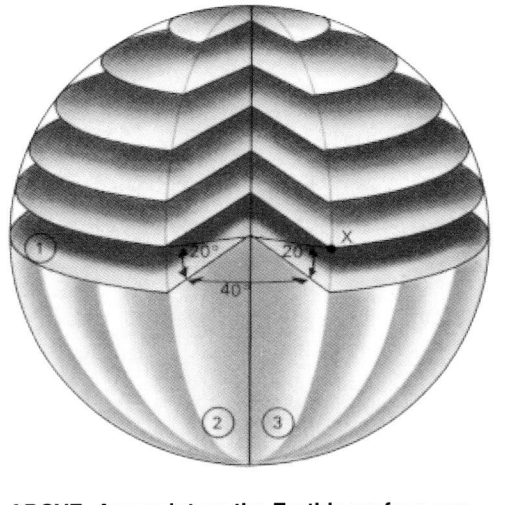

RIGHT Reference to lines of longitude and latitude is the easiest and most common way of determining the relative positions of places on different maps, and for plotting compass directions.

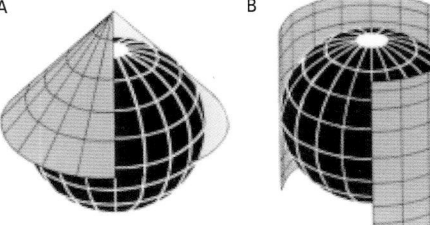

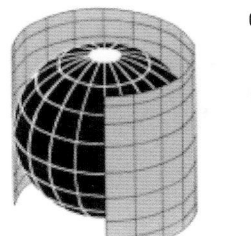

ABOVE Any point on the Earth's surface can be located in terms of longitude and latitude – in degrees, minutes and seconds east or west of the prime meridian for longitude, and north or south of the Equator for latitude. The latitude of X (the angle between X, the centre of the Earth and the plane of the Equator [1]) equals 20°, while its longitude (the angle between between the plane of the prime meridian [2] and that passing through X and the North and South Poles [3]) equals 40°.

Projections
A map projection is the systematic depiction on a plane surface of the imaginary lines of latitude or longitude from a globe of the Earth. This network of lines is called the graticule and forms the framework on which an accurate depiction of the world is made. The basis of any map, the graticule, is constructed sometimes by graphical means but often by using mathematical formulas to give the intersections plotted as x and y co-ordinates.

The choice of projection is governed by the properties the cartographer wishes the map to possess, the map scale and also the extent of the area to be mapped. Since the globe is three-dimensional, it is not possible to depict its surface on a two-dimensional plane without distortion. Preservation of one of the basic properties involved – area, distance or shape – can only be secured at the expense of the others, and the choice of projection is often a compromise solution.

Map projections are constructions designed to maintain certain selected relationships of the Earth's surface. Most of the projections used for large-scale atlases, selected primarily to minimize distortion of size and distance, fall into one of three categories – conic [A], cylindrical [B] or azimuthal [C]. Each involves plotting the forms of the Earth's surface on a grid of lines of latitude and longitude, which may be shown as parallels, curved lines or radiating spokes (see below).

Conical projections use the projection of the graticule from the globe onto a cone which is tangential to a line of latitude (termed the standard parallel). This line is always an arc and scale is always true along it. Because of its method of construction it is used mainly for maps depicting the temperate latitudes around the standard parallel – that is, where there is least distortion.

Cylindrical projections are constructed by the projection of the graticule from the globe onto a cylinder tangential to the globe, and permit the whole of the Earth's surface to be depicted on one map. Though they can depict all the land masses, there is colossal exaggeration of area and shape towards the poles at the expense of equatorial regions: Greenland, for example, grows to almost the size of Africa. However, the best known example, named after the pioneering 16th-century cartographer Gerardus Mercator, has been invaluable to navigators because any straight line drawn on it is a line of constant bearing.

Azimuthal projections, sometimes called zenithal, are constructed by the projection of part of the graticule from the globe onto a plane tangential to any single point on it. This plane may be tangential to the equator (equatorial case), the poles (polar case) or any other point (oblique case). Any straight line drawn from the point where the plane touches the globe is the shortest distance from that point and is known as a great circle.

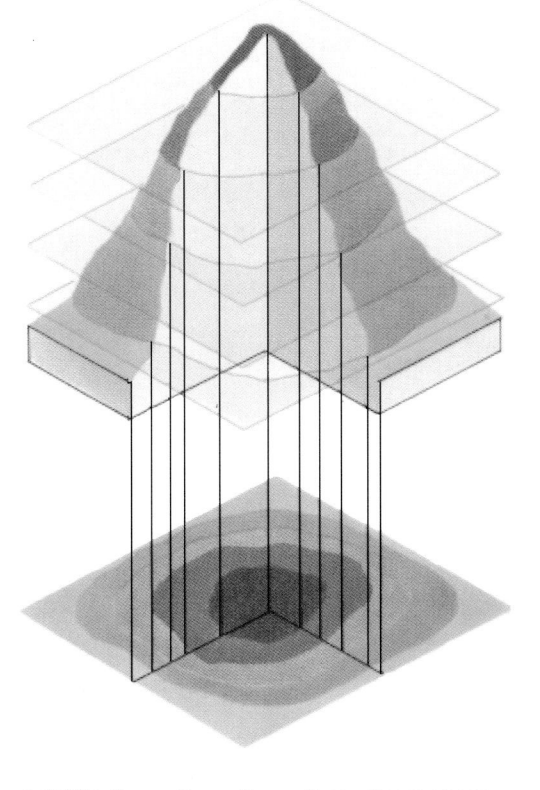

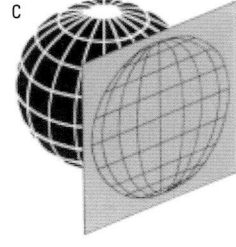

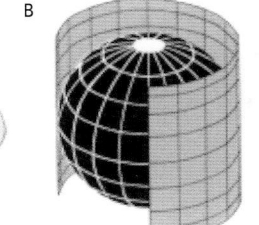

LEFT Most of the projections used for large-scale atlases, selected primarily to minimize distortion of size and distance, fall into one of three principal categories – conic [A], cylindrical [B] or azimuthal [C].

ABOVE Recording a three-dimensional shape on a flat surface can be achieved by contour scaling. Here the cross-sections of a hill at heights of 50, 100, and 150 metres (or feet) are projected onto a map of the hill. The topography of the hill can be visualized fairly well from such a map when graduated colour is employed – the closer the gradations the steeper the slope – though the crudeness of the contour intervals loses some finer detail.

WORLD MAPS

SETTLEMENTS

■ PARIS   ■ Berne   ◉ Livorno   ◎ Brugge   ◎ Algeciras   ○ Frejus   ○ Oberammergau   ○ Thira

Settlement symbols and type styles vary according to the scale of each map and indicate the importance
of towns on the map rather than specific population figures

∴   Ruins or Archæological Sites   Wells in Desert

ADMINISTRATION

International Boundaries

International Boundaries
(Undefined or Disputed)

Internal Boundaries

National Parks

Country Names
NICARAGUA

Administrative
Area Names
KENT
CALABRIA

International boundaries show the *de facto* situation where there are rival claims to territory

COMMUNICATIONS

Principal Roads

Other Roads

Road Tunnels

Passes

⊕   Airfields

Principal Railways

Railways
Under Construction

Other Railways

Railway Tunnels

Principal Canals

PHYSICAL FEATURES

Perennial Streams

Intermittent Streams

Perennial Lakes

Intermittent Lakes

Swamps and Marshes

Permanent Ice
and Glaciers

▲ 8848   Elevations in metres

▼ 8500   Sea Depths in metres

1134   Height of Lake Surface
Above Sea Level in metres

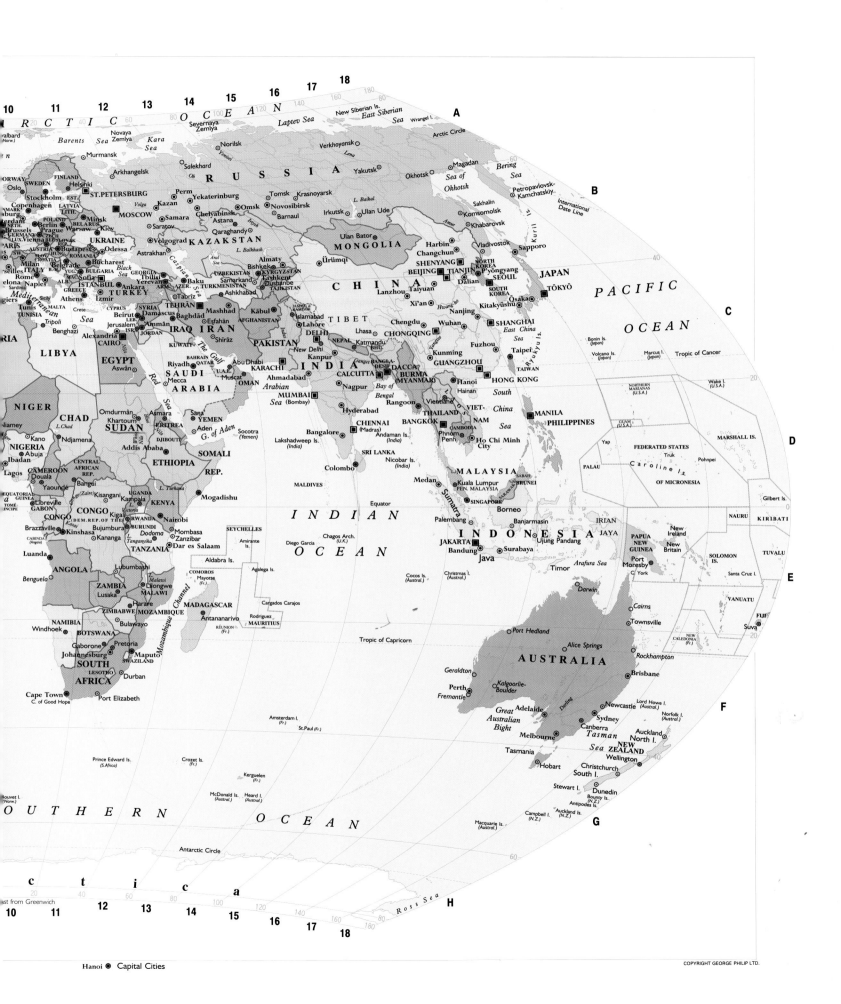

Hanoi ● Capital Cities

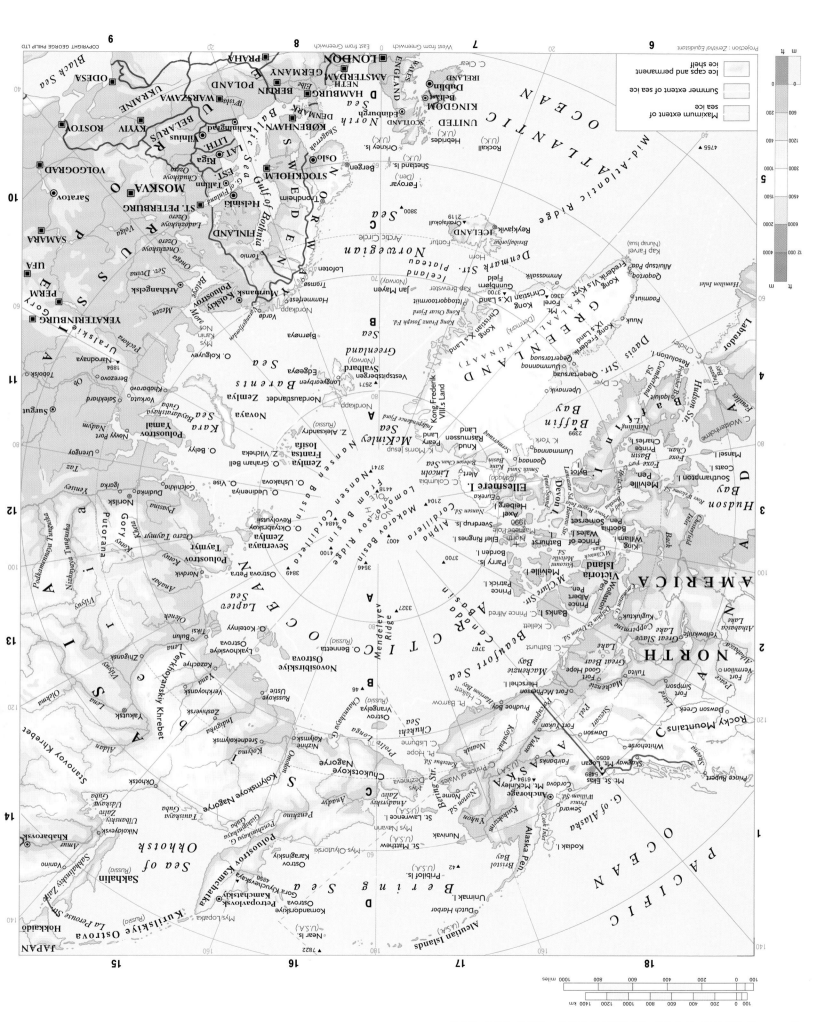

Projection: Zenithal Equidistant

Maximum extent of sea ice

Summer extent of sea ice

Ice caps and permanent ice shelf

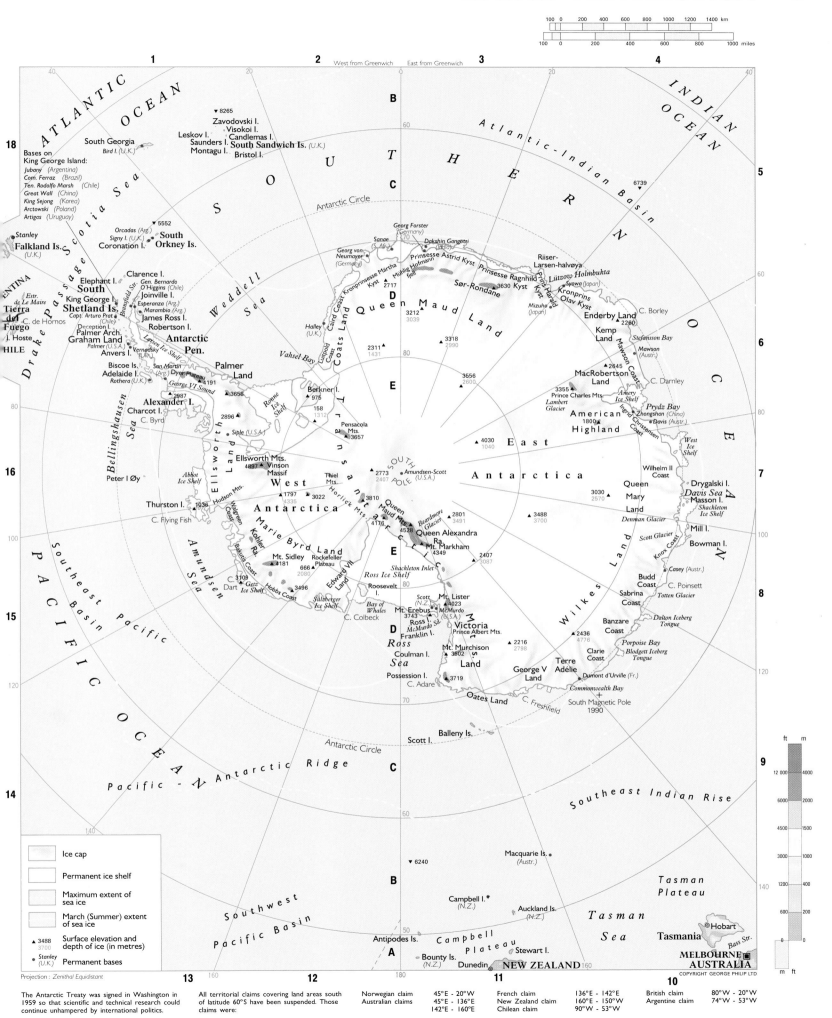

Projection : Zenithal Equidistant

The Antarctic Treaty was signed in Washington in 1959 so that scientific and technical research could continue unhampered by international politics.

All territorial claims covering land areas south of latitude 60°S have been suspended. Those claims were:

Norwegian claim	45°E - 20°W	French claim	136°E - 142°E	British claim	80°W - 20°W
Australian claims	45°E - 136°E	New Zealand claim	160°E - 150°W	Argentine claim	74°W - 53°W
	142°E - 160°E	Chilean claim	90°W - 53°W		

Legend:
- Ice cap
- Permanent ice shelf
- Maximum extent of sea ice
- March (Summer) extent of sea ice
- ▲ 3488 / 3700 Surface elevation and depth of ice (in metres)
- Stanley (U.K.) Permanent bases

Bases on King George Island:
Jubany (Argentina)
Com. Ferraz (Brazil)
Ten. Rodolfo Marsh (Chile)
Great Wall (China)
King Sejong (Korea)
Arctowski (Poland)
Artigas (Uruguay)

ATLANTIC

OCEAN

Norwegian Sea

North Sea

Baltic Sea

Mediterranean Sea

Adriatic Sea

Black Sea

Caspian Sea

Caspian Depression

Iberian Peninsula

Alps

Carpathians

Scandinavia

Lapland

North European Plain

Central Russian Uplands

Ukraine

Caucasus

Anatolia (Asia Minor)

Mesopotamia

Kurdistan

Armenia

Iceland

British Isles

Great Britain

Ireland

Faroe Is.

Shetland Is.

Orkney Is.

Hebrides

Ben Nevis 1347

Snowdon 1085

Thames

Severn

Land's End

C. Clear

Celtic Sea

Irish Sea

English Channel

Ushant

Brittany

Bay of Biscay

Gironde

Garonne

Loire

Seine

Meuse

Ardennes

Rhine

Weser

Elbe

Jutland

Helgoland

Bornholm

Öland

Gotland

Åland

G. of Finland

G. of Riga

G. of Bothnia

Finland

L. Ladoga

L. Onega

White Sea

Kola Pen.

Kanin Pen.

Pechora

Ob

Ural

Volga

Kama

Don

Donets

Dnieper

Dniester

Prut

Crimea

Sea of Azov

Str. of Kerch

Danube

Wallachia

Transylvanian Alps

Plain of Hungary

Tisza

Mureş

Drava

Sava

Bakony Forest

Dinaric Alps

Apennines

Tatra 2655

Moravian Hts.

Bohemian Forest

Sudeten

Erzgebirge

Harz

Black Forest

Vosges

Jura

Massif Central

Cévennes

Rhône

Mont Blanc 4807

Puy de Sancy 1886

Pyrenees

Pico de Aneto 3404

Ebro

Douro

Old Castile

New Castile

Cantabrian Mts.

Sierra de Estrela

C. da Roca

C. de São Vicente

C. Trafalgar

C. da Tagus

Str. of Gibraltar

Sierra Morena

Sierra Nevada · Mulhacén 3743

Guadalquivir

Guadiana

Andalusia

Ibiza

Majorca

Minorca

Balearic Is.

G. of Lions

Ligurian Sea

Corsica

Sardinia

Str. of Bonifacio

Tyrrhenian Sea

Sicily · Etna 3340

Calabria

Str. of Messina

Malta

Pantelleria

C. Bon

C. Blanc

Ionian Sea

Ionian Is.

C. Matapan

Morea

Pindus

Olympus 2917

Balkans

Rhodope

Aegean Sea

Crete

Rhodes

Cyprus

Taurus Mts.

Pontine Mts.

Erciyas Dağı 3770

L. Tuz

Kızıl Irmak

Mt. Ida 1766

Dardanelles

Sea of Marmara

Bosporus

Str. of Otranto

Gran Sasso d'Italia 2914

Vesuvius 1277

Tiber

Po

Inn

Danube

Oder

Vistula

Niemen

Dvina

Dvina

Neva

L. Chudskoye

Rybinsk Res.

Oka

Volga

Terek

Kura

Araks

L. Urmia

L. Van

Tigris

Euphrates

Ararat 5165

Elbrus 5642

Manych

Kuban

N. Dvina

Mezen

Onega

Pechora

Narodnaya 1894

Telpos Iz 1617

Volga Hts.

Obshchi Syrt

Ural

Arctic Circle

Roraima

Rockall

North Cape

Nordkinn

Inari

Torne

Kemi

Lindesnes

Skagerrak

Kattegat

Göta

Vänern

Vättern

Mälaren

Saaremaa

Lofoten

Vesterålen

Trøndelag

Kebnekaise 2117

Galdhøpiggen 2469

Hekla 1491

Öraefajökull 2119

Plateau of the Shotts

Atlas

Rif

Wallachia

Pripet

Bug

Projection: Bonne

West from Greenwich

East from Greenwich

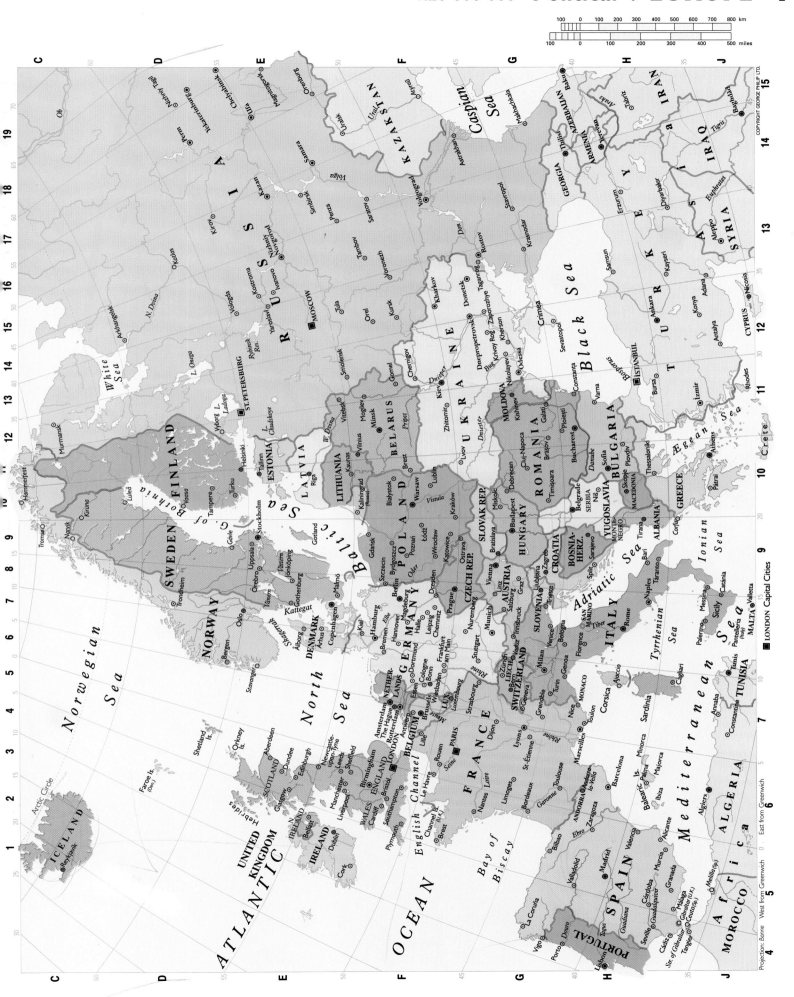

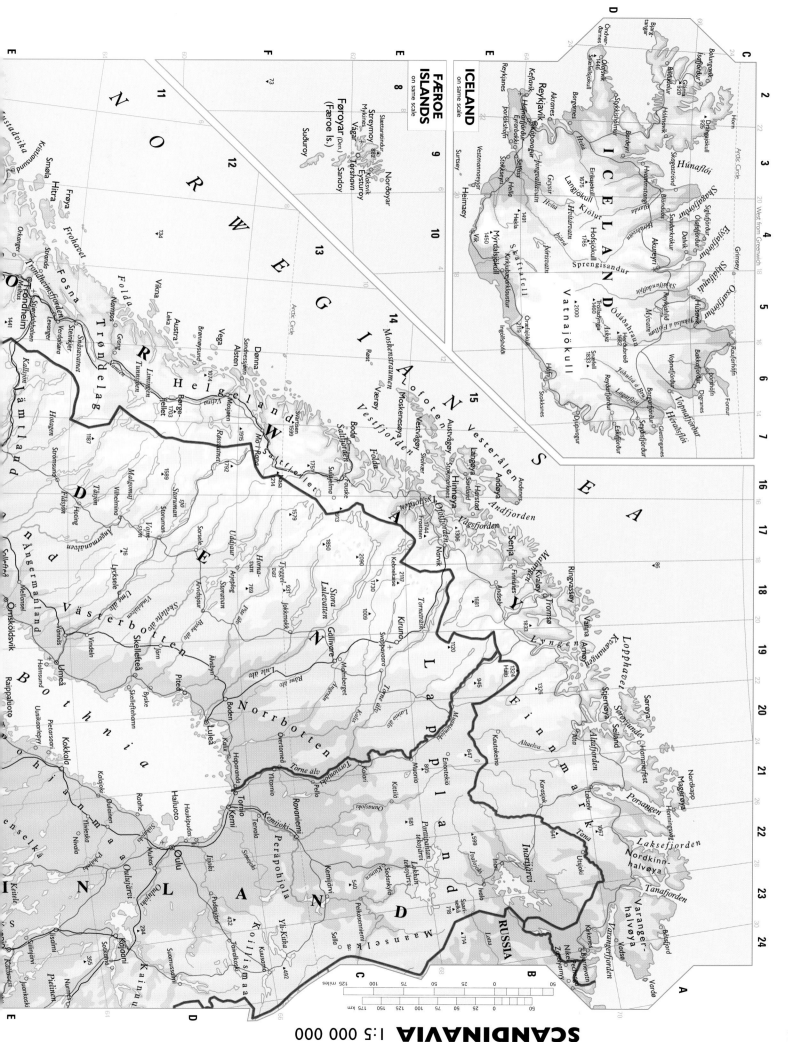

SCANDINAVIA 1:5 000 000

ICELAND
on same scale

FÆROE
ISLANDS
on same scale

9

Projection: Conical with two standard parallels

East from Greenwich

Countries / Regions
ESTONIA · LATVIA · LITHUANIA · POLAND · GERMANY · DENMARK · RUSSIA · BELORUSSIA · FINLAND

Seas and Gulfs
Gulf of Bothnia · Gulf of Finland · Gulf of Riga · BALTIC SEA · Kattegat · Skagerrak · Ålands hav · Oslofjorden · Mälaren · Vättern · Vänern · Daugava

Major cities and places

Finland: Helsinki (Helsingfors), Espoo, Tampere, Turku (Åbo), Pori, Rauma, Kotka, Lahti, Lappeenranta, Mikkeli, Jyväskylä, Kouvola, Porvoo, Vantaa, Hyvinkää, Hämeenlinna, Hanko, Naantali, Salo, Forssa, Nokia, Valkeakoski, Mänttä, Keuruu, Heinola, Kuusankoski, Loviisa, Kurikka, Kauhajoki, Jalasjärvi, Parkano, Kankaanpää, Kristinankaupunki, Kaskinen, Uusikaupunki, Vammala

Estonia: Tallinn, Tartu, Pärnu, Narva, Viljandi, Paide, Rakvere, Kohtla-Järve, Haapsalu, Kuressaare, Kärdla, Valga, Võru, Hiiumaa (Dagö), Saaremaa (Ösel), Muhu, Vormsi, Naissaar

Latvia: Riga, Jelgava, Liepāja, Ventspils, Daugavpils, Jūrmala, Valmiera, Cēsis, Sigulda, Ogre, Tukums, Talsi, Dobele, Saldus, Bauska, Aizkraukle, Jēkabpils, Rēzekne, Madona, Gulbene, Preili, Limbaži, Roja

Lithuania: Vilnius, Kaunas, Šiauliai, Panevėžys, Klaipėda, Alytus, Marijampolė, Utena, Ukmergė, Telšiai, Tauragė, Plungė, Kretinga, Mažeikiai, Radviliškis, Kėdainiai, Jonava, Raseiniai, Šilutė, Palanga, Neringa, Druskininkai, Varėna

Kaliningrad (Russia): Kaliningrad (Russia), Sovetsk, Chernyakhovsk, Gvardeysk, Zelenogradsk, Baltiysk, Bagrationovsk

Sweden: STOCKHOLM, Göteborg (Gothenburg), Malmö, Uppsala, Västerås, Örebro, Norrköping, Linköping, Jönköping, Borås, Helsingborg, Lund, Gävle, Sundsvall, Hudiksvall, Söderhamn, Falun, Borlänge, Karlstad, Eskilstuna, Södertälje, Nyköping, Kalmar, Karlskrona, Växjö, Halmstad, Landskrona, Trelleborg, Ystad, Kristianstad, Nässjö, Motala, Mjölby, Värnamo, Ljungby, Visby, Slite, Roma, Mariestad, Lidköping, Skövde, Trollhättan, Uddevalla, Vänersborg, Kungsbacka, Varberg, Falkenberg

Norway: Oslo, Bergen, Stavanger, Drammen, Kristiansand, Hamar, Lillehammer, Gjøvik, Sandefjord, Tønsberg, Moss, Fredrikstad, Sarpsborg, Skien, Porsgrunn, Larvik, Notodden, Kongsberg, Arendal, Haugesund, Egersund, Flekkefjord, Lillesand, Mandal, Voss, Førde, Florø, Volda, Ålesund, Kongsvinger, Elverum, Røros

Denmark: KØBENHAVN (Copenhagen), Århus, Ålborg, Odense, Esbjerg, Randers, Kolding, Horsens, Vejle, Roskilde, Helsingør, Næstved, Slagelse, Svendborg, Frederikshavn, Hjørring, Viborg, Herning, Silkeborg, Holstebro, Nykøbing, Køge, Korsør, Sønderborg, Åbenrå, Haderslev, Flensburg, Skive, Struer, Thisted, Skagen, Ringkøbing, Skanderborg

Poland: Gdańsk, Gdynia, Sopot, Słupsk, Koszalin, Kołobrzeg, Elbląg, Malbork, Tczew, Starogard Gdański, Wejherowo, Lębork, Bytów, Darłowo

Germany: Rostock, Kiel, Lübeck, Wismar, Stralsund, Greifswald, Neumünster, Rendsburg, Schleswig, Flensburg, Fehmarn, Rügen, Usedom

Islands and physical features
Gotland, Öland, Bornholm, Åland (Ahvenanmaa), Gotska Sandön, Fårö, Hiddensee, Sjælland, Fyn, Lolland, Falster, Møn, Langeland, Læsø, Anholt, Samsø, Als, Sylt, Fanø, Rømø, Nordfriesische Inseln, Ostfriesische Inseln, Helgoland

Dalarna, Härjedalen, Hälsingland, Medelpad, Gästrikland, Uppland, Västmanland, Södermanland, Närke, Småland, Blekinge, Skåne, Halland, Bohuslän, Dalsland, Värmland, Götaland, Dovrefjell, Jotunheimen, Rondane, Gudbrandsdalen, Østerdalen, Telemark, Hardangervidda, Hallingdal, Valdres, Nordfjord, Romsdalen, Jostedalsbreen, Sognefjorden, Hardangerfjorden, Folgefonni

Göta älv, Göta kanal, Glåma, Lågen, Klarälven, Dalälven, Österdalälven, Västerdalälven, Ljusnan, Ljungan

Deutsche Bucht, Mecklenburger Bucht, Fehmarn Belt, Store Bælt, Lille Bælt, Kieler Bucht, Store Bælt, Limfjorden

Grid reference letters
F · G · H · J · K

Grid reference numbers
12 · 13 · 14 · 15 · 16 · 17 · 18 · 19 · 20 · 21

Scale
m / ft — 2000 · 1500 · 1000 · 500 · 200 · 0
ft — 6000 · 4500 · 3000 · 1500 · 600 · 0

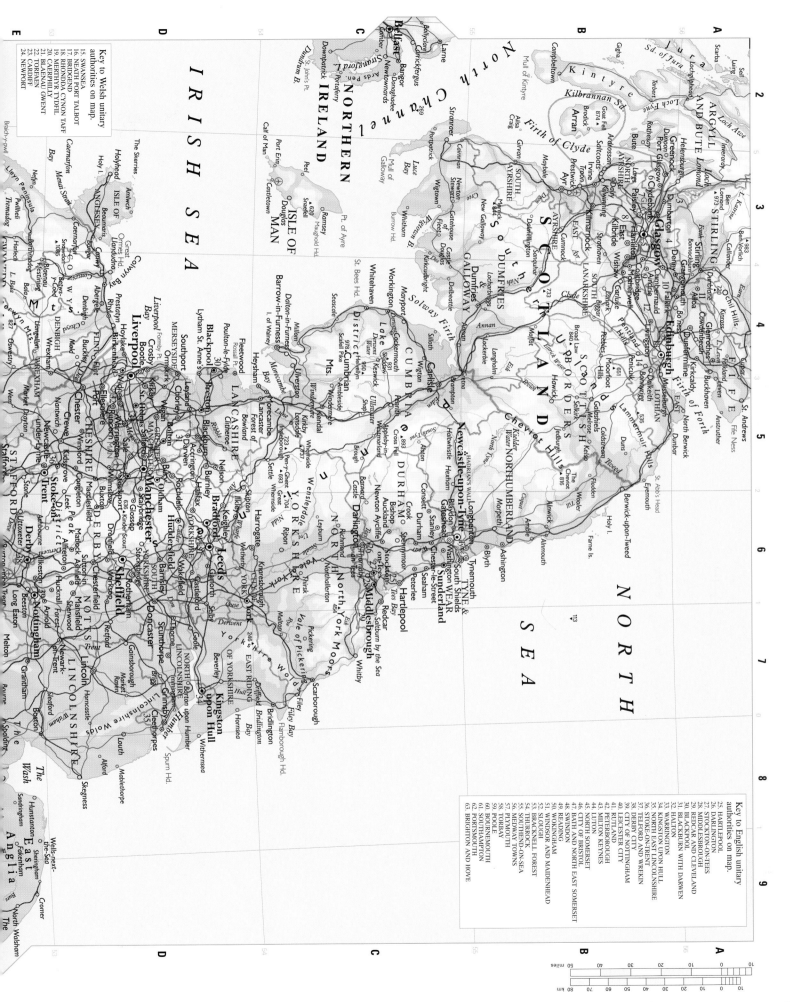

Key to Welsh unitary authorities on map.
15. SWANSEA
16. NEATH PORT TALBOT
17. BRIDGEND
18. RHONDDA CYNON TAFF
19. MERTHYR TYDFIL
20. CAERPHILLY
21. BLAENAU GWENT
22. TORFAEN
23. CARDIFF
24. NEWPORT

Key to English unitary authorities on map.
25. HARTLEPOOL
26. DARLINGTON
27. STOCKTON-ON-TEES
28. MIDDLESBROUGH
29. REDCAR AND CLEVELAND
30. BLACKPOOL
31. BLACKBURN WITH DARWEN
32. HALTON
33. WARRINGTON
34. KINGSTON UPON HULL
35. NORTH EAST LINCOLNSHIRE
36. NORTH LINCOLNSHIRE
37. STOKE-ON-TRENT
38. DERBY CITY
39. NOTTINGHAM
40. TELFORD AND WREKIN
41. RUTLAND
42. PETERBOROUGH
43. MILTON KEYNES
44. LUTON
45. NORTH SOMERSET
46. CITY OF BRISTOL
47. BATH AND NORTH EAST SOMERSET
48. SWINDON
49. READING
50. WOKINGHAM
51. WINDSOR AND MAIDENHEAD
52. SLOUGH
53. BRACKNELL FOREST
54. THURROCK
55. SOUTHEND-ON-SEA
56. MEDWAY TOWNS
57. PLYMOUTH
58. TORBAY
59. POOLE
60. BOURNEMOUTH
61. SOUTHAMPTON
62. PORTSMOUTH
63. BRIGHTON AND HOVE

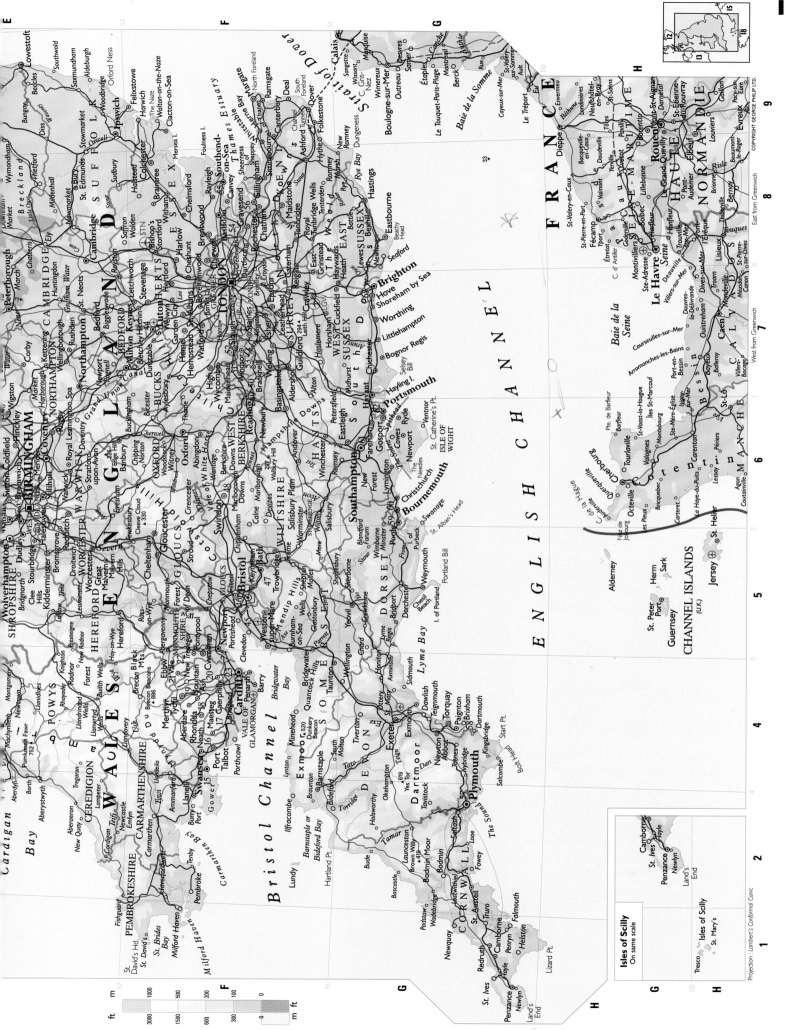

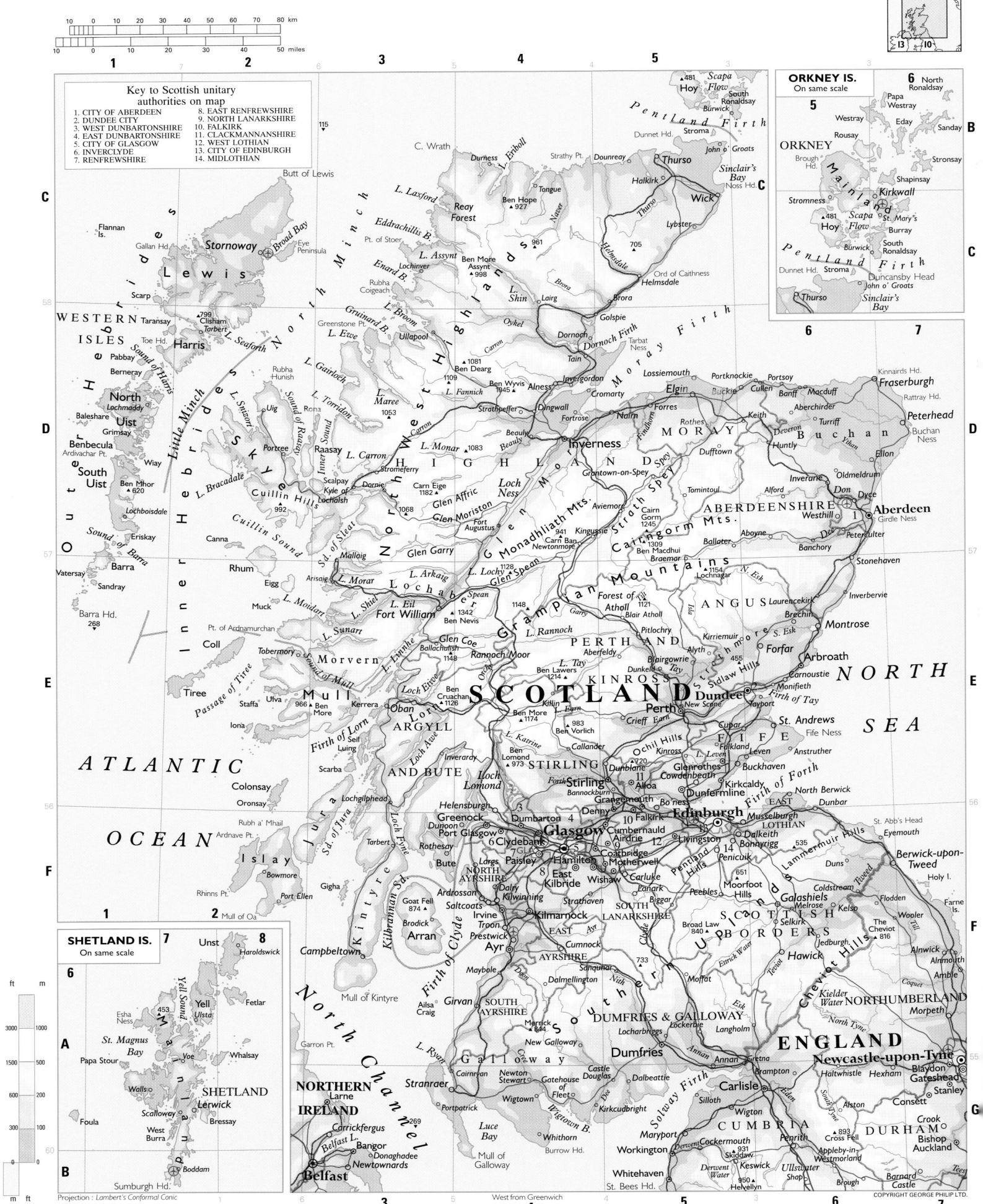

10 0 10 20 30 40 50 60 70 80 km
10   0   10   20   30   40   50 miles

Key to Scottish unitary authorities on map

1. CITY OF ABERDEEN
2. DUNDEE CITY
3. WEST DUNBARTONSHIRE
4. EAST DUNBARTONSHIRE
5. CITY OF GLASGOW
6. INVERCLYDE
7. RENFREWSHIRE
8. EAST RENFREWSHIRE
9. NORTH LANARKSHIRE
10. FALKIRK
11. CLACKMANNANSHIRE
12. WEST LOTHIAN
13. CITY OF EDINBURGH
14. MIDLOTHIAN

ORKNEY IS.
On same scale

ORKNEY

North Ronaldsay
Papa Westray
Westray
Sanday
Rousay
Eday
Stronsay
Brough Hd.
Stromness
Shapinsay
Kirkwall
Mainland
St. Mary's
481
Hoy
Scapa Flow
Burray
South Ronaldsay
Dunnet Hd. Stroma
Duncansby Head
Thurso
John o' Groats
Sinclair's Bay

SHETLAND IS.
On same scale

Unst
Haroldswick
Esha Ness
453
Yell Sound
Yell
Fetlar
St. Magnus Bay
Ulsta
Papa Stour
Yoe
Whalsay
Walls
Mainland
Foula
SHETLAND
Lerwick
Bressay
Scalloway
West Burra
Boddam
Sumburgh Hd.

Projection : Lambert's Conformal Conic

ATLANTIC OCEAN

WESTERN ISLES
Flannan Is.
Gallan Hd.
Broad Bay
Stornoway
Eye Peninsula
Lewis
Butt of Lewis
Scarp
799 Clisham
Tarbet
Toe Hd.
Harris
Taransay
L. Seaforth
Pabbay
Berneray
North Uist
Baleshare
Grimsay
Benbecula
Ardivachar Pt.
South Uist
Lochmaddy
Lochboisdale
Barra
Vatersay
Sandray
Eriskay
Barra Hd. 268

Sound of Harris
Wiay
Ben Mhor 620

C. Wrath
Durness
L. Eriboll
Strathy Pt.
Dounreay
Reay Forest
Ben Hope 927
Tongue
Naver
Halkirk
Dunnet Hd.
Stroma
Thurso
Pentland Firth
John o' Groats
Wick
Lybster
Helmsdale
961
705
Ord of Caithness
Brora
Golspie
Dornoch
Dornoch Firth
Tarbat Ness
Moray Firth

Eddrachillis B.
Pt. of Stoer
L. Laxford
Ben More Assynt 998
Lochinver
Enard B.
Rubha Coigeach
Ullapool
Gruinard B.
Greenstone Pt.
L. Broom
L. Ewe
L. Maree
1053
Rubha Hunish
Uig
Portree
Raasay
Scalpay
Kyle of Lochalsh
Dornie
Stromeferry
Carn Eige 1182
1068
992
Cuillin Hills
Glen Affric
Glen Moriston
Fort Augustus
Loch Ness
L. Monar 1083
Carron
Beauly
Beauly
Strathpeffer
Dingwall
Fortrose
Cromarty
Invergordon
Alness
Tain
Lairg
L. Shin
Oykel
Brora
Strath Spey
Grantown-on-Spey
Aviemore
Cairn Gorm 1245
Kingussie
Newtonmore
Ben Macdhui 1309
Braemar
941
1154 Lochnagar
MORAY
Elgin
Lossiemouth
Portknockie Portsoy
Buckie
Cullen
Banff
Macduff
Forres
Nairn
Rothes
Keith
Aberchirder
Turriff
Dufftown
Huntly
Deveron
Tomintoul
Alford
Inverurie
Oldmeldrum
Don
Dyce
Westhill
1
Aberdeen
Girdle Ness
Peterculter
Banchory
Aboyne
Ballater
Stonehaven
N. Esk
Laurencekirk
Inverbervie
Brechin
S. Esk
Forfar
Montrose
Arbroath
Carnoustie
Monifieth
Tayport
Firth of Tay
Dundee
St. Andrews
Fife Ness
Anstruther
Crail
Buckhaven
Leven
Kirkcaldy
North Berwick
Dunbar
St. Abb's Head
Eyemouth
Berwick-upon-Tweed
Coldstream
Flodden
Wooler
The Cheviot 816
Alnwick
Almouth
Amble
Coquet
Morpeth
NORTHUMBERLAND
Newcastle-upon-Tyne
Gateshead
Blaydon
Stanley
Consett
Crook
Bishop Auckland
DURHAM
Barnard Castle
Tees

HIGHLAND
Fraserburgh
Kinnairds Hd.
Rattray Hd.
Peterhead
Buchan Ness
Ellon
BUCHAN
ABERDEENSHIRE
Caingorm Mts.
Grampian Mountains
Forest of Atholl 1121
Blair Atholl
Pitlochry
Aberfeldy
Kirriemuir
Alyth
Blairgowrie
Dunkeld
Coupar
ANGUS
Sidlaw Hills
455
Strathmore
Perth
New Scone
PERTH AND KINROSS
L. Tay
Ben Lawers 1214
Killin
Crieff
Comrie
Ben More 1174
Callander
Lochearnhead
L. Earn
Ben Vorlich 983
720
L. Katrine
Ben Lomond 973
Stirling
Dunblane
STIRLING
Bannockburn
Bo'ness
Alloa
Dunfermline
Cowdenbeath
Glenrothes
Cupar
Kinross
L. Leven
Falkland
Ochil Hills
FIFE
Firth of Forth
Bo'ness
Grangemouth
Falkirk
Denny
Cumbernauld
Airdrie
Coatbridge
Motherwell
Wishaw
Carluke
Lanark
Livingston
Dalkeith
Musselburgh
EAST LOTHIAN
Bonnyrigg
Penicuik
Moorfoot Hills
535
Peebles
651
Lammermuir Hills
Duns
Galashiels
Melrose
Selkirk
SCOTTISH BORDERS
Kelso
Jedburgh
Hawick
Cheviot Hills
Kielder Water
North Tyne
Langholm
Ettrick Water
Teviot
Esk
Broad Law 840
Biggar
Moffat
SOUTH LANARKSHIRE
Strathaven
East Kilbride
Hamilton
Larkhall
Clyde
733
Sanquhar
Cumnock
Dalmellington
EAST AYRSHIRE
Kilmarnock
Ayr
Prestwick
Troon
Irvine
Saltcoats
Ardrossan
Kilwinning
Dalry
NORTH AYRSHIRE
Largs
Paisley
Greenock
Port Glasgow
Dumbarton
Clydebank
Glasgow
Rutherglen
Maybole
Girvan
Ailsa Craig
SOUTH AYRSHIRE
Dalmellington
Nith
New Galloway
Merrick 844
L. Ryan
Stranraer
Cairnryan
Portpatrick
Newton Stewart
Gatehouse of Fleet
Wigtown
Whithorn
Kirkcudbright
Castle Douglas
Dalbeattie
Dumfries
DUMFRIES & GALLOWAY
Galloway
Lockerbie
Locharbriggs
Annan
Gretna
Brampton
Carlisle
Solway Firth
Silloth
Wigton
Maryport
Workington
Cockermouth
931 Skiddaw
893
Cross Fell
Penrith
Appleby-in-Westmorland
CUMBRIA
Alston
Haltwhistle
Hexham
Whitehaven
St. Bees Hd.
Derwent Water
Keswick
Helvellyn 950
Ullswater
Shap
Brough
Eden

Inverness
Loch Ness
Glen Affric
Monadhliath Mts.
Fort Augustus
L. Lochy 1128
Glen Spean
Ben Nevis 1342
Fort William
Glen Coe 1148
Ballachulish
Rannoch Moor
L. Rannoch
Glen Garry
Garry
L. Arkaig
Spean
1148
Mallaig
Arisaig
L. Morar
Loch Eil
L. Shiel
L. Linnhe
Glen Coe
Ben Cruachan 1126
L. Etive
Loch Awe
Ben More 966
Kerrera
Oban
Loch Lomond
SCOTLAND
Ben Lomond
Inveraray
ARGYLL AND BUTE
Lochgilphead
Tarbert
Loch Fyne
Helensburgh
Dunoon
Rothesay
Bute
Gigha
Tarbert
Kintyre
Campbeltown
Mull of Kintyre
Mull of Oa
Islay
Bowmore
Port Ellen
Rhinns Pt.
Jura
Sd. of Jura
Scarba
Lochgilphead
Colonsay
Oronsay
NORTH CHANNEL
Garron Pt.
Larne
Carrickfergus
Belfast L.
Bangor
NORTHERN IRELAND
Belfast
Donaghadee
Newtownards
Mull of Galloway
Burrow Hd.
Luce Bay
Wigtown B.

ATLANTIC OCEAN
Skye
Cuillin Sound
Sd. of Sleat
Rhum
Eigg
Muck
Canna
Coll
Tobermory
Pt. of Ardnamurchan
Morvern
Sound of Mull
Mull
Ben More 966
Ulva
Staffa
Iona
Tiree
Passage of Tiree
Lorn
Firth of Lorn
Seil
Luing
Jura

NORTH SEA

ENGLAND

North Minch
Little Minch
The Minch
Inner Sound
Inner Hebrides
Outer Hebrides
North West Highlands
HIGHLAND

115

58

57

56

55

COPYRIGHT GEORGE PHILIP LTD.

West from Greenwich

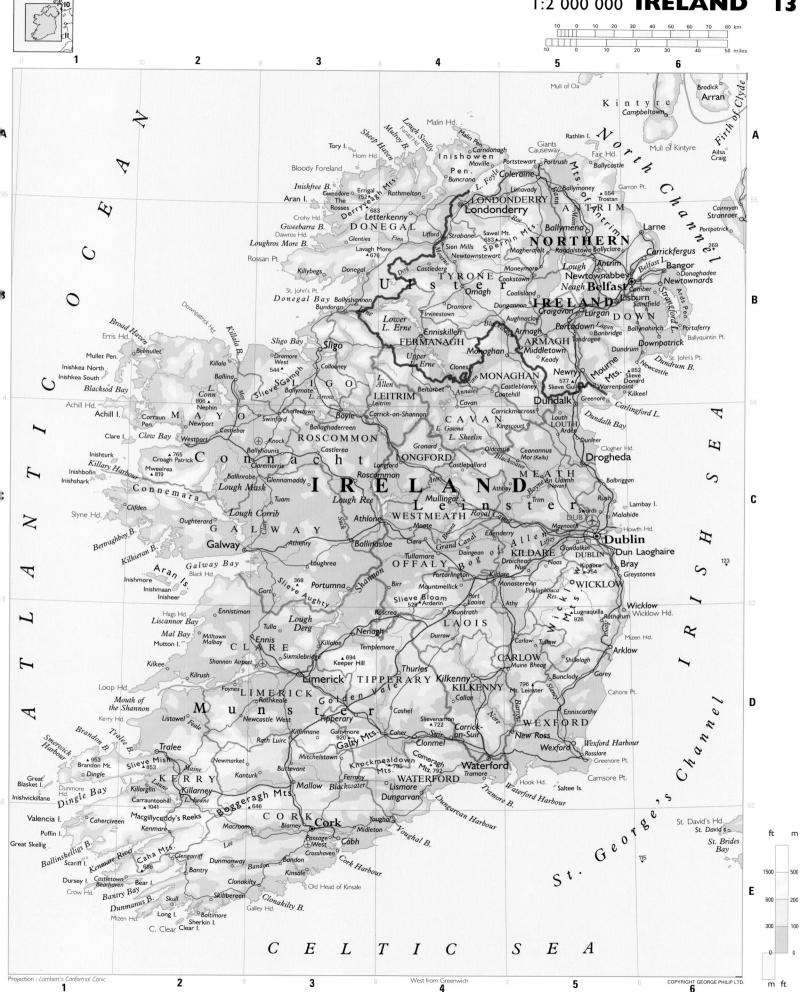

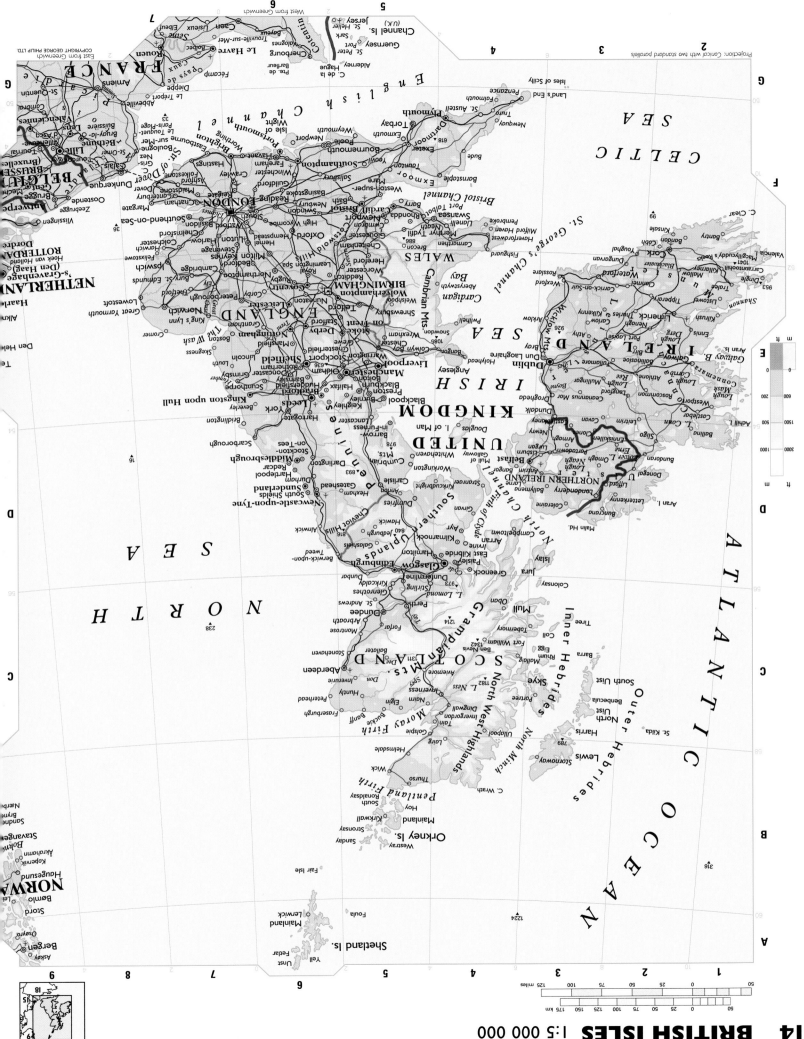

Projection: Conical with two standard parallels

COPYRIGHT GEORGE PHILIP LTD.
East from Greenwich

West from Greenwich

Underlined towns give their name to the
administrative area in which they stand.

Projection: Conical with two standard parallels

East from Greenwich

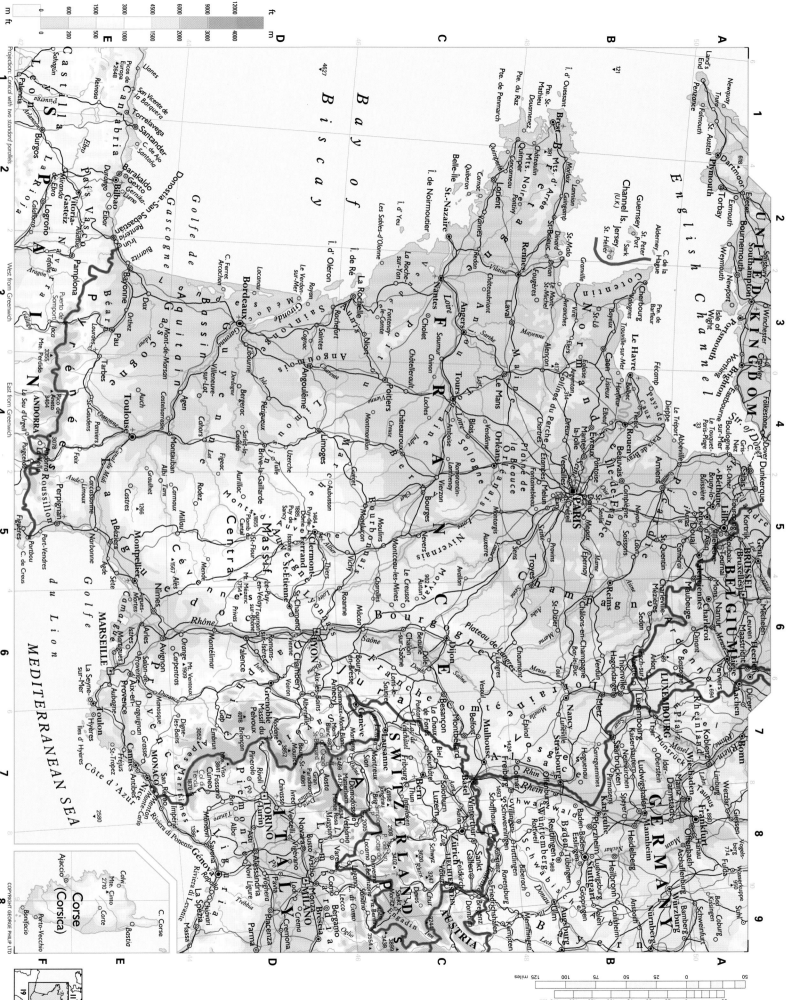

50   0   25   50   75   100   125   150   175 km
50   0   25   50   75   100   125 miles

Projection: Conical with two standard parallels
COPYRIGHT GEORGE PHILIP LTD
West from Greenwich   0   East from Greenwich

A map of Spain and Portugal, with parts of France, Algeria and Morocco. Principal labels include:

FRANCE — Montpellier, Béziers, Narbonne, Toulouse, Carcassonne, Foix, Pau, Bayonne, Biarritz, Golfe du Lion, Gascogne, Pyrénées, Andorra

SPAIN — MADRID, Barcelona, Zaragoza, Valencia, Sevilla, Málaga, Bilbao, San Sebastián, Pamplona, Lleida, Tarragona, Burgos, Valladolid, Salamanca, Córdoba, Granada, Murcia, Alicante, Cartagena, Almería, Cádiz, Huelva, Toledo, Cuenca, Albacete, Vitoria-Gasteiz, Logroño, Santander, Gijón, Oviedo, A Coruña (La Coruña), Santiago de Compostela, Vigo, Ourense (Orense), León, Castilla y León, Castilla–La Mancha, Andalucía, Sierra Nevada, Sierra Morena, Guadalquivir, Ebro

PORTUGAL — LISBOA, Porto, Coimbra, Braga, Bragança, Évora, Beja, Faro, Setúbal, Algarve, Tejo, Douro, Guadiana

MOROCCO — Tanger, Tetouan, Ceuta (Sp.), Melilla (Sp.), Gibraltar (U.K.)

ALGERIA — ALGER, Oran, Mostaganem, Blida, Tiaret

Islands: Mallorca (Palma de Mallorca), Menorca, Eivissa (Ibiza), Formentera — Islas Baleares

Seas: ATLANTIC OCEAN, MEDITERRANEAN SEA, Bay of Biscay, Golfo de Valencia, G. de Cádiz, Costa Brava, Costa Blanca, Costa del Sol

ft   m
6000 2000
4500 1500
3000 1000
1500   500
 600   200
   0   0

East from Greenwich

COPYRIGHT GEORGE PHILIP LTD.

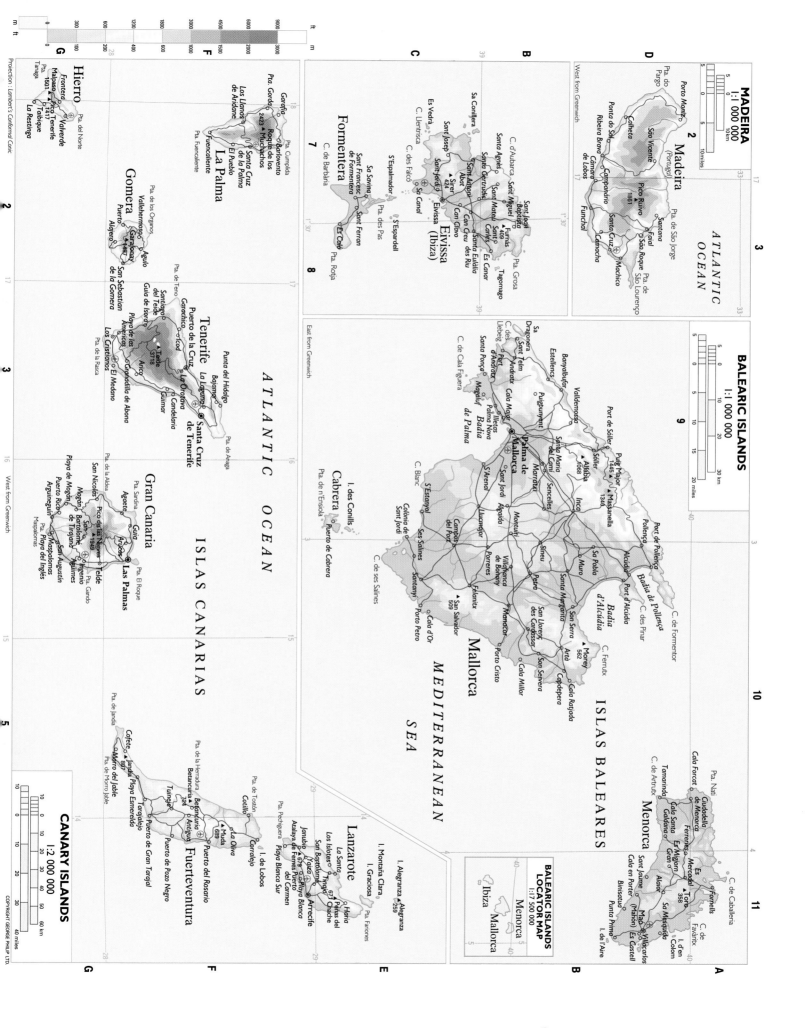

MADEIRA
1:1 000 000

Madeira (Portugal)

West from Greenwich

ATLANTIC OCEAN

Porto do Pargo
Porto Moniz
Calheta
Ponta do Sol
Ribeira Brava
Câmara de Lobos
São Vicente
Santana
Faial
São Roque
Santa Cruz
Funchal
Pico Ruivo 1861
Machico
Pta. de São Jorge
Pta. de São Lourenço
Campanário
Camacha

BALEARIC ISLANDS
1:1 000 000

East from Greenwich

Sa Dragonera
Sant Telm
Andratx
Port d'Andratx
C. de Cala Figuera
C. des Llebeig
Estellencs
Banyalbufar
Valldemossa
Puigpunyent
Palma Nova
Magaluf
Illetes
Badia de Palma
Palma de Mallorca
Santa Maria del Camí
Marratxí
S'Arenal
Port de Sóller
Puig Major 1445
Sóller
Massanella 1346
Alfàbia 1068
Inca
Santa Ponça
Sant Jordi
Algaida
Montuïri
Llucmajor
Sencelles
Binissalem
Petra
Sineu
Muro
Sa Pobla
Santa Margarita
Port d'Alcúdia
Alcúdia
Badia d'Alcúdia
Pollença
Port de Pollença
C. des Pinar
C. de Formentor
Porreres
Vilafranca de Bonany
Felanitx
Sant Salvador 509
Campos del Port
Colònia de Sant Jordi
Ses Salines
C. de ses Salines
Santanyí
Cala d'Or
Porto Petro
Porto Cristo
Cala Millor
Artà
Morey 562
Capdepera
Cala Rajada
Son Servera
Son Sierra
Sant Llorenç des Cardassar
Manacor
C. Ferrutx
C. Blanc
S'Estanyol

I. des Conills
Cabrera
Puerto de Cabrera
Pta. de n'Ensiola

MEDITERRANEAN SEA

Mallorca

ISLAS BALEARES

BALEARIC ISLANDS
LOCATOR MAP
1:17 500 000

Ibiza
Menorca
Mallorca

Menorca
Pta. Nati
Ciutadella de Menorca
Cala Forcat
Cala Santa Galdana
Tamarinda
C. de Artrutx
Ferreries
Es Migjorn Gran
Alaior
Es Mercadal
Toro 358
Maó (Mahón)
Sant Jaume
Villacarlos
Binisafua
Punta Prima
I. de l'Aire
C. de Favàritx
Sa Mesquida
Es Grau
Colom
Es Castell
I. den Colom
Fornells
C. de Caballería

MADEIRA

Eivissa (Ibiza)
Sa Conillera
C. d'Aubarca
Santa Agnès
Sant Antoni Abat
Santa Gertrudis
Sant Mateu
Santa Eulàlia
Sant Joan Baptista
Sant Miguel
Siesta 424
Can Creu des Riu
Can Clavo
Es Canar
Sant Josep
Sant Jordi
Sant Carles
Tagomago
Eivissa (Ibiza)
Pta. Grosa
C. Llentrisca
Es Vedrà
C. des Falcó
Sa Talaia 409
S'Espalmador
Pta. des Pas
Sa Savina
Sant Francesc
Formentera
Sant Ferran
C. de Barbària
Es Caló
Pta. Roja
S'Espardell

ISLAS CANARIAS

ATLANTIC OCEAN

CANARY ISLANDS
1:2 000 000

COPYRIGHT GEORGE PHILIP LTD.

Projection : Lambert's Conformal Conic

West from Greenwich

Hierro
Pta. del Norte
Frontera
Valverde
Pico Tenerife 1501
Malpaso 1417
Tamaduste
La Restinga
Pta. de Orchilla
Pta. Salmor

Gomera
Pta. de los Órganos
Vallehermoso
Agulo
Hermigua
Garajonay 1487
San Sebastián de la Gomera
Alajeró
Puerto
Playa de Santiago

La Palma
Pta. Gorda
Barlovento
Garafía
Santa Cruz de la Palma
Roque de los Muchachos 2423
Los Llanos de Aridane
El Paso
Pta. Cumplida
Fuencaliente
Pta. Fuencaliente

Tenerife
Pta. de Teno
Santiago del Teide
Buenavista
Garachico
Icod
Guía de Isora
La Orotava
Puerto de la Cruz
La Laguna
Teide 3718
Santa Cruz de Tenerife
Arico
Adeje
Granadilla de Abona
Los Cristianos
Playa de las Américas
Güímar
Candelaria
El Médano
Punta del Hidalgo
Bajamar
Pta. de Anaga
Pta. de la Rasca

Gran Canaria
Pta. Sardina
Agaete
Guía
Gáldar
Pico de las Nieves 1949
San Nicolás
Pta. de la Aldea
Mogán
Puerto Rico
Puerto de Mogán
San Bartolomé de Tirajana
Arucas
Telde
Ingenio
Agüimes
Santa Lucía
San Agustín
Maspalomas
Playa del Inglés
Arguineguín
Las Palmas
Gando
Pta. Gando
Pta. El Roque

ATLANTIC OCEAN

Fuerteventura
Pta. de Jandía
Cofete
Morro del Jable
Pta. de Morro Jable
Pta. de la Herradura
Playa Esmeralda
Jandía Playa
Betancuria
Bégonvura 724
Antigua
Muda 689
Tuineje
Gran Tarajal
Puerto del Rosario
Tarajalejo
Puerto de Gran Tarajal
Puerto de Pozo Negro
La Oliva
Corralejo
Cotillo
Pta. de Tostón
I. de Lobos

Lanzarote
La Santa
Tinajo
Peñas del Chache 671
Haría
Órzola
I. Graciosa
I. Montaña Clara
I. Alegranza
Alegranza 289
Pta. Fariones
San Bartolomé
Los Islotes
Atalaya de Femés 607
Arrecife
Playa Blanca
Playa Blanca del Carmen
Femés
Yaiza
Puerto del Carmen
Pta. Pechiguera
Playa Blanca Sur
Janubio

ISLAS CANARIAS

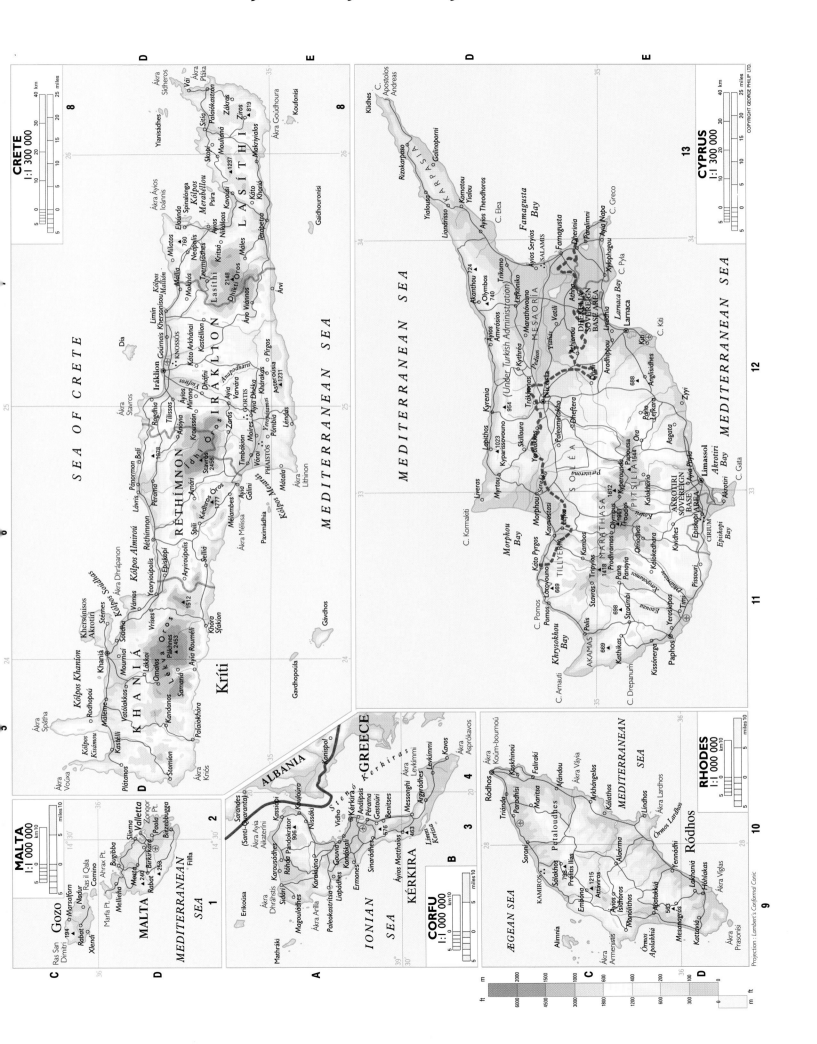

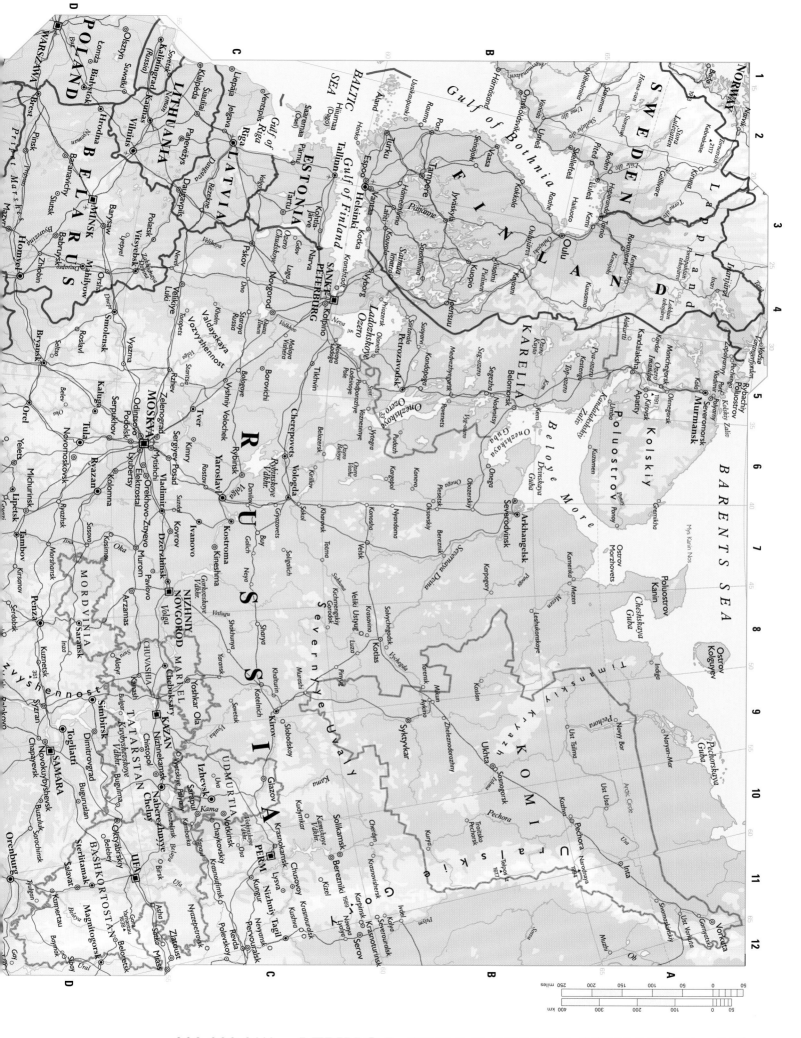

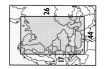

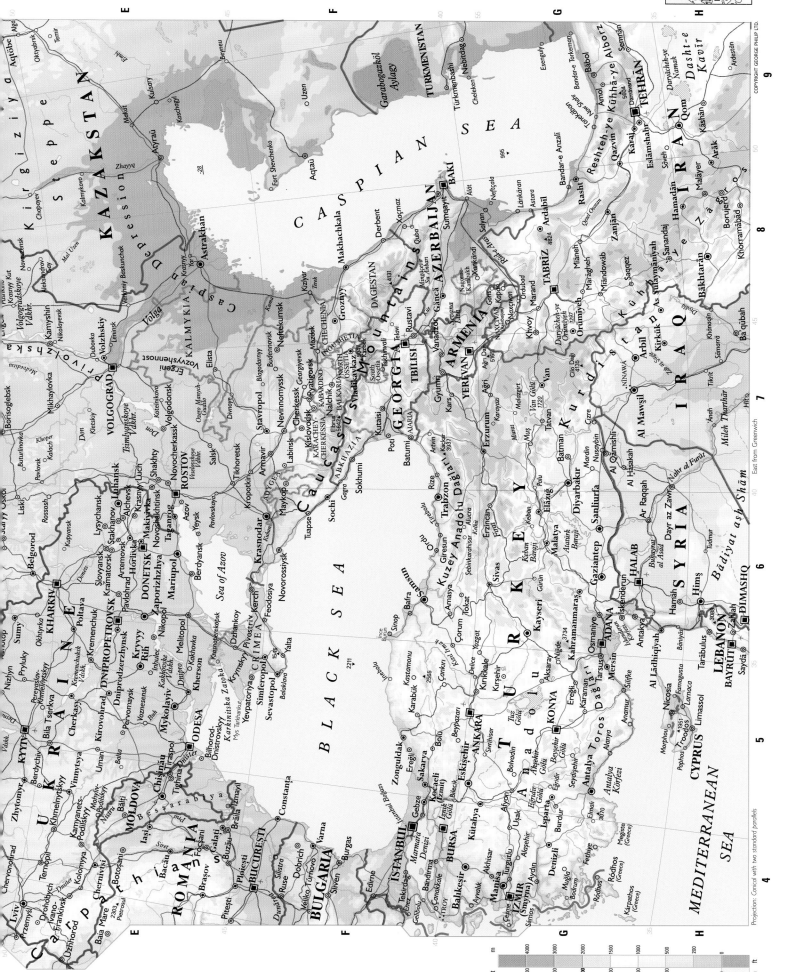

Projection: Conical with two standard parallels

East from Greenwich

CASPIAN SEA

BLACK SEA

MEDITERRANEAN SEA

KAZAKSTAN

TURKMENISTAN

AZERBAIJAN

ARMENIA

GEORGIA

IRAN

IRAQ

SYRIA

LEBANON

CYPRUS

TURKEY

UKRAINE

ROMANIA

BULGARIA

MOLDOVA

DAGESTAN

CHECHENIA

Sea of Azov

Caucasus Mountains

m   ft
4000   12 000
3000   9000
2000   6000
1500   4500
1000   3000
500   1500
200   600
0   0
ft   m

RUSSIA
1 Adygea
2 Karachey-Cherkessia
3 Kabardino-Balkaria
4 North Ossetia
5 Ingushetia
6 Chechenia
7 Dagestan
8 Mordvinia
9 Chuvashia
10 Mari El
11 Tatarstan
12 Udmurtia
13 Khakassia
AZERBAIJAN
14 Naxçivan
GEORGIA   UKRAINE
15 Ajaria   17 Crimea
16 Abkhazia

Projection: Conical Orthomorphic with two standard parallels

East from Greenwich

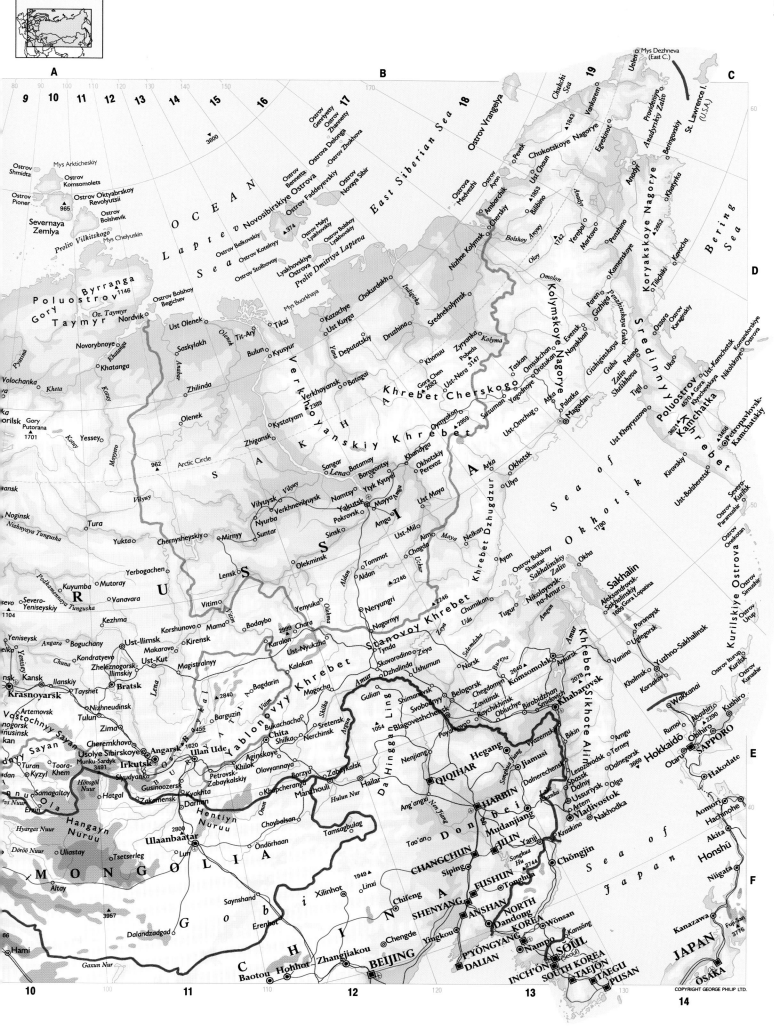

A   B   C

9 10 11 12 13 14 15 16 17 18 19

Mys Dezhneva
(East C.)
Uelen

St. Lawrence I.
(U.S.A.)

ARCTIC OCEAN

Chukchi Sea

East Siberian Sea

Bering Sea

Ostrov Shmidta
Mys Arkticheskiy
Ostrov Komsomolets
Ostrov Oktyabrskoy Revolyutsii
Ostrov Pioner
Ostrov Bolshevik
Severnaya Zemlya

Prolio Vilkitskogo
Mys Chelyuskin

Laptev Sea

Novosibirskiye Ostrova

Ostrov Genriyetty
Ostrov Zhannety
Ostrova Delonga
Ostrov Zhokhova

Ostrov Vrangelya

Koryakskoye Nagorye

Poluostrov Kamchatka

Sredinnyy Khrebet

Petropavlovsk-Kamchatskiy

Sea of Okhotsk

Sakhalin

Kurilskiye Ostrova

Hokkaidō
SAPPORO
Hakodate

Honshū

JAPAN
ŌSAKA

Krasnoyarsk

R U S S I A

MONGOLIA

Ulaanbaatar

G o b i

C H I N A

BEIJING

Baotou Hohhot Zhangjiakou

Chengde

QIQIHAR

HARBIN

CHANGCHUN

JILIN

SHENYANG
ANSHAN
FUSHUN

DALIAN

NORTH KOREA
PYŎNGYANG
Nampo

SOUTH KOREA
SŎUL
INCH'ŎN
TAEJŎN
TAEGU
PUSAN

Sea of Japan

Vladivostok

Khabarovsk

Yuzhno-Sakhalinsk

10 100 11 110 12 120 13 130 14

COPYRIGHT GEORGE PHILIP LTD.

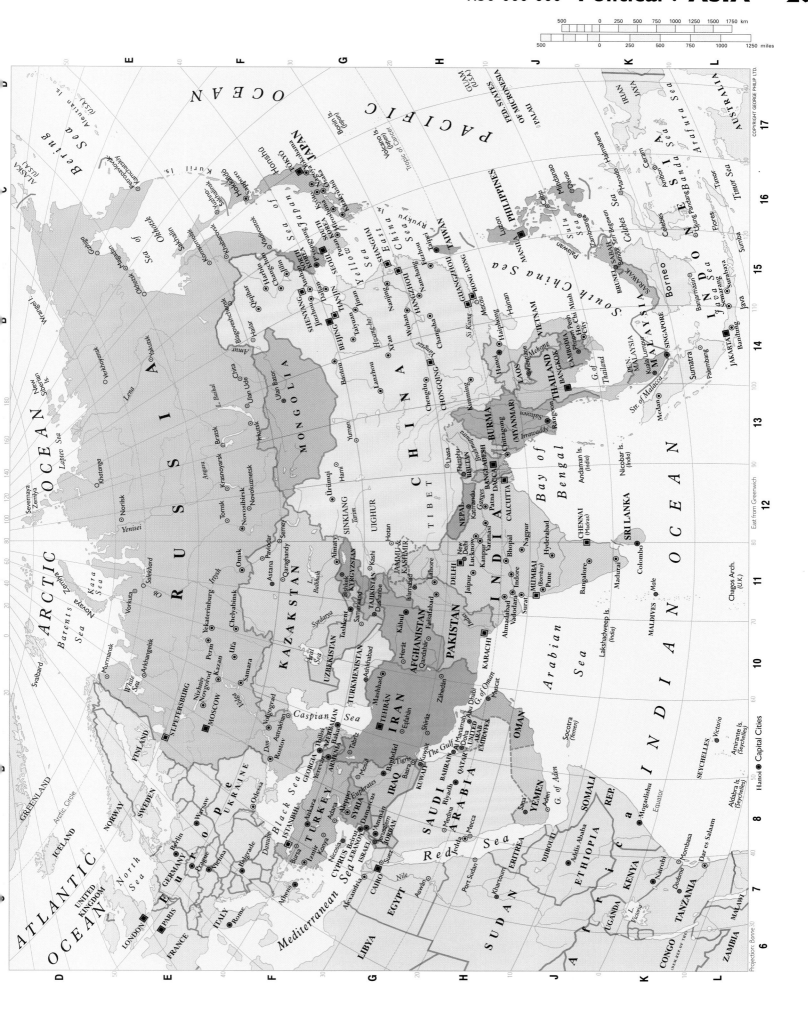

Projection: Bonne

Hanoi ● Capital Cities

JAPAN 1:5 000 000

RUSSIA

CHINA

HEILONG JIANG

JILIN

NORTH KOREA

SEA OF JAPAN

SEA OF OKHOTSK

HOKKAIDO

TŌHOKU

Khrebet Sikhote Alin

Lake Khanka

La Perouse Strait
(Sōya-Kaikyo)

Sakhalin (Russia)

Nemuro-Kaikyo

Tsugaru-Kaikyo

Ishikari-Wan (Otaru-Wan)

Hidaka-Sammyaku

Ishikari-Sammyaku

Kitami-Sammyaku

Selected place names

Jiamusi, Hegang, Fujin, Naoli He, Songhua Jiang, Shuangyashan, Boli, Qitaihe, Huanan, Jixi, Jinkou, Hulin, Mishan, Muling He, Dongning, Dongfanghong, Wusuli Jiang, Bikin, Lespilinoye, Rakitnoye, Dalnerechensk, Novokachlinsk, Kamen Rybolov, Lipovtsy, Marizovka, Suyfun, Suifenhe, Pogranichny, Razdolnoye, Ussuriysk, Spassk, Dalniy, Kirovskiy, Ariadnoye, Arsenev, Gornyy, Yakovlevka, Krasnorechenskiy, Lifudzin, Kovalerovo, Dalnegorsk, Rudnaja Pristan, Plastun, Terney, Velikaya Kema, Amgu, Svetlaya, Olga, Margaritovo, Valentin, Preobrazheniye, Nakhodka, Vladivostok, Artem, Sichan, Lazo, Dunay, Slavyanka, Zaliv Petra Velikogo, Trudovoye, Kraskino, Khasan, Hunchun, Najin, Unggi, Chŏngjin, Suiyang

Wakkanai, Rebun-Tō, Rishiri-Tō, Teshio, Haboro, Rumoi, Otaru, Ishikari, Ebetsu, SAPPORO, Chitose, Tomakomai, Muroran, Hakodate, Esashi, Matsumae, Ōma, Ōhata, Mutsu, Aomori, Hirosaki, Odate, Noshiro, Akita, Honjō, Sakata, Tsuruoka, Yamagata, Sendai, Ishinomaki, Shiogama, Fukushima, Sōma, Shinjo, Yamagata

Abashiri-Wan, Shari, Shiretoko-Misaki, Ostrov Kunashir, Nemuro, Akkeshi, Kushiro, Kushiro-Gawa, Hiroo, Erimo-Misaki, Urakawa, Samani, Obihiro, Tokachi-Gawa, Monbetsu, Engaru, Kitami, Yūbetsu, Mombetsu, Asahigawa, Furano, Biei, Bibai, Iwamizawa, Yūbari, Horoi

Niigata, Niitsu, Ryōtsu, Aikawa, Sado, Murakami, Murakami, Nagaoka, Shibata, Kashiwazaki

1:5 000 000
km 50 25 0 25 50 75 100 125 150 175
miles 50 25 0 25 50 75 100 125

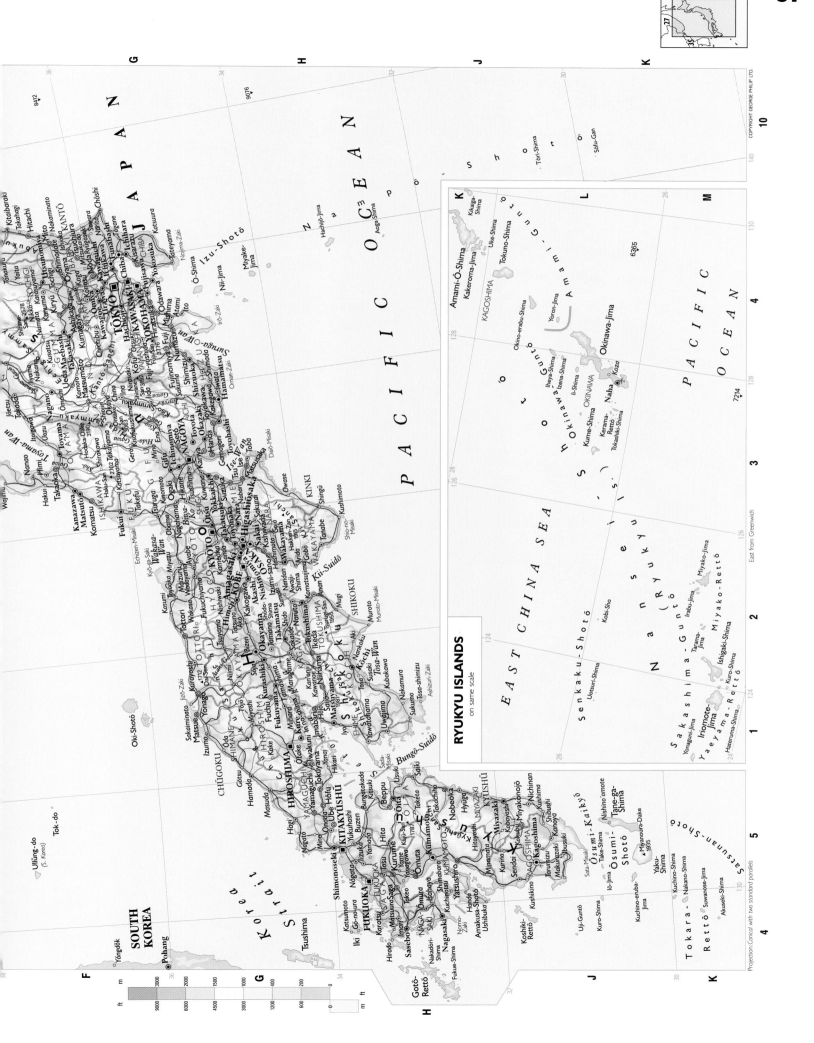

31

P A C I F I C   O C E A N

J A P A N

TŌKYŌ
KAWASAKI
YOKOHAMA
NAGOYA
KYŌTO
ŌSAKA
KŌBE
HIROSHIMA
KITAKYŪSHŪ
FUKUOKA
NAGASAKI
KAGOSHIMA

SOUTH
KOREA

SHIKOKU

KYŪSHŪ

E A S T   C H I N A   S E A

RYUKYU ISLANDS
on same scale

N a n s e i   I s.   (R y u k y u
R e t t ō)

KAGOSHIMA

Amami-Ō-Shima

Okinawa-jima
OKINAWA
Naha

P A C I F I C   O C E A N

Sakashima-Guntō

Miyako-Rettō
Ishigaki-Shima

COPYRIGHT GEORGE PHILIP LTD.

East from Greenwich

Projection: Conical with two standard parallels

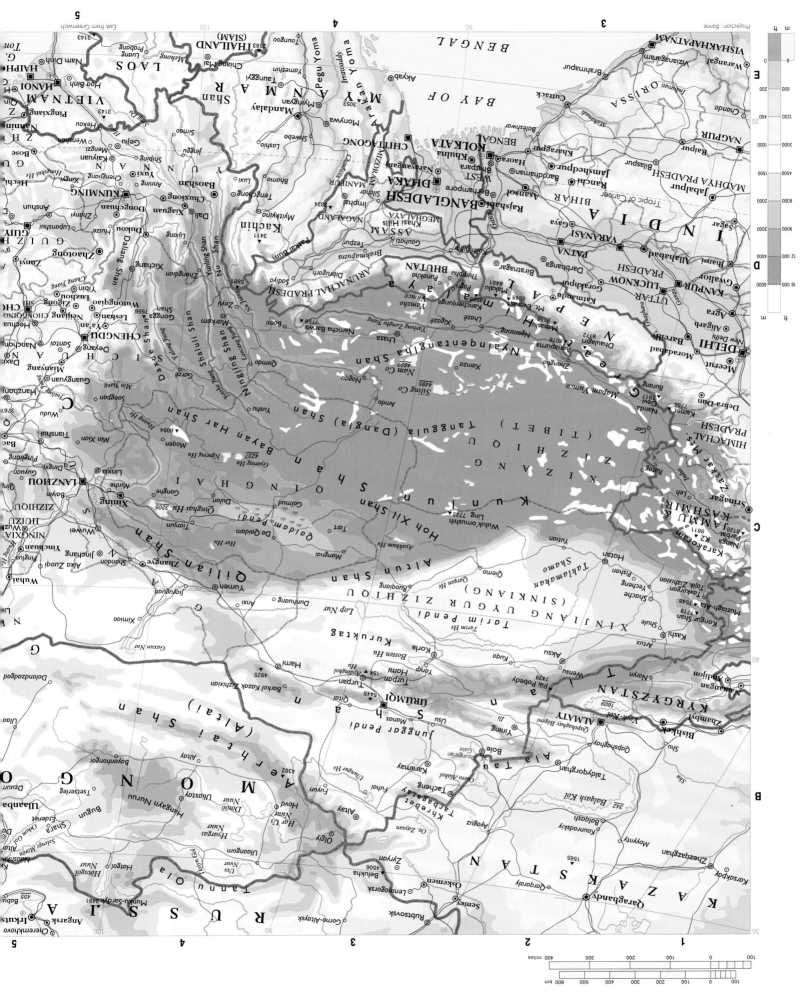

27
40
38 37

6 7 8 9

110

L. Baykal
Ulan Ude
-kalskiy
Chita
Bukachacha
Sretensk
Nerchinsk
Olovyannaya
Borzya
Priargunsk
Manzhouli
Hulun
Nur
Hailar

tiyn
uu
Saynshand
Borhoyn Tal
Erenhot
Sonid
Youqi
aotou
Hohhot
Datong
Yuanping

Gulian
Shimanovsk
Svobodnyy
Chegdomyn
Komsomolsk
Yilehuli
Shan
Blagoveshchensk
Aihui
Bureya
Orogen Zizhiqi
Nenjiang
Butha Qi
QIQIHAR
Daqing Anda
Suihua
HARBIN
Shuangcheng Fuyu
Dongbei
(Manchuria)
CHANGCHUN JILIN
Shuangliao
Tongliao Siping Liaoyuan
Tieling FUSHUN
Chaoyang SHENYANG
Liaoyang Benxi
ANSHAN
Yingkou Dandong

Hegang
Jiamusi
Shuangyashan
Yichun
Bei'an
Qianjin
Hulin
Bikin Mishan
Jixi
Mudanjiang
Dunhua Vladivostok
Changbai Yanji
Shan Baihe
Tonghua
Chöngjin

Sakhalin

Poronaysk
Mys Terpeniya
Vanino
Tartarskiy
Proliv
La Perouse Str.
Wakkanai
Kitami
Asahigawa 2290
Hokkaidō
SAPPORO
Otaru Muroran
Hakodate
Erimo-misaki
Tsugaru-Kaikyō
Aomori
Hachinohe
Morioka
Akita
Ishinomaki
Sakata
Sado Yamagata Sendai
Niigata Fukushima
Jōetsu Kōriyama
Wajima Utsunomiya
Takaoka Mito
Kanazawa TŌKYŌ KAWASAKI
Komatsu NAGOYA YOKOHAMA
Fuji-San Shizuoka
3776 Hamamatsu

SEA OF
JAPAN

Khabarovsk
Khrebet Sikhote Alin
L. Khanka
Ussuriysk
Artem
Nakhodka
Hunchun
Kimchaek
Hamhung
Hŭngnam
Wŏnsan

NORTH
KOREA
P'YŎNGYANG
Namp'o
Haeju Kaesŏng Ch'unch'ŏn
SŎUL (SEOUL)
INCH'ŎN SOUTH
KOREA
TAEJŎN
Kunsan TAEGU
Chŏnju Masan PUSAN
KWANGJU
Mokp'o
Cheju-do

YELLOW
SEA

Korea Strait

KYŌTO
OSAKA
KŌBE Sakai
Wakayama
Okayama
Kure Shimonoseki
HIROSHIMA Shikoku
Matsue
Matsuyama Kōchi
KITAKYUSHU
FUKUOKA
Sasebo
Nagasaki Kumamoto
Kyūshū
Miyazaki
Kagoshima
Yaku-Shima Tane-ga-Shima

EAST CHINA
SEA

Amami-Ō-Shima
Tokuno-Shima

Ryūkyū-rettō

Okinawa-Jima
Naha

PACIFIC

Tropic of Cancer

OCEAN

SOUTH CHINA
SEA

PHILIPPINES
Babuyan Is.
Batan Is.

Nampō-Shotō

B
N
40
C
A
P
A
N
J
D
30
E
20

50

MONGOLIA
MONGGOL
ZIZHIQU
(INNER MONGOLIA)
Xilinhot
Duolun
Chifeng
Zhangjiakou
Xuanhua
BEIJING
(PEKING)
BEIJING SHI
Baoding
Anci
TANGSHAN
TIANJIN
TIANJIN SHI
HEBEI
Cangzhou
Bo Hai
TAIYUAN
SHIJIAZHUANG
Handan
JINAN
ZIBO
Weifang
QINGDAO
SHANDONG
Rizhao
Lianyungang
Qingjiang
Yancheng
Nantong
SHANGHAI
Suzhou SHANGHAI
NANJING Wuxi
HANGZHOU
NINGBO
Shaoxing
LINHAI
Wenzhou
ZHEJIANG
Jinhua
Quzhou
Shangrao
NANCHANG
JIANGXI
Fuzhou
Nanping
FUJIAN
FUZHOU
Putian
Quanzhou
Xiamen
Zhangzhou
Mei Xian
Chaozhou
Shantou
GUANGDONG
GUANGZHOU
(CANTON)
Foshan
HONG KONG
Macau
Zhuhai
Jiangmen
Zhaoqing
Yangjiang
Maoming
Zhanjiang
Hainan Dao
HAINAN
1879
acheng
Haikou
Haixia

HUANG HO
Huang He (Hoang Ho)
Grand Canal
HENAN
ZHENGZHOU
XI'AN
Luoyang
Kaifeng
Shangqiu
Huaibei
Xuzhou
JIANGSU
Hongze
Hu
HUBEI
WUHAN
HEFEI
ANHUI
Huainan
Bengbu
Chang Jiang
(Yangtze)
Wuhu
TAIWAN
(FORMOSA)
T'AIPEI
Chilung
Hsinchu
T'aichung
Changhua
Yu Shan
3997
T'ainan
T'aitung
KAOHSIUNG
P'ingtung
Taiwan Strait

COPYRIGHT GEORGE PHILIP LTD.

Projection: Conical with two standard parallels

BEIJING (PEKING)

ZHENGZHOU XIAN TAIYUAN SHIJIAZHUANG LANZHOU BAOTOU HOHHOT

Huang He (Yellow River)

Qin Ling Tsinling Shan Lü Liang Shan Tai Hang Shan Helan Shan Yin Shan Daqing Shan Lang Shan

Mu Us Shamo (Ordos) Tengger Shamo Baiyu Shan Yabrai Shan

NINGXIA HUIZU ZIZHIQU

M O N G O L I A

DORNOGOVI DUNDGOVI ÖVÖRHANGAY SÜHBAATAR

Galbin Gobi Guryan Sayhanguul

GREAT WALL

150 miles
200 km

m ft

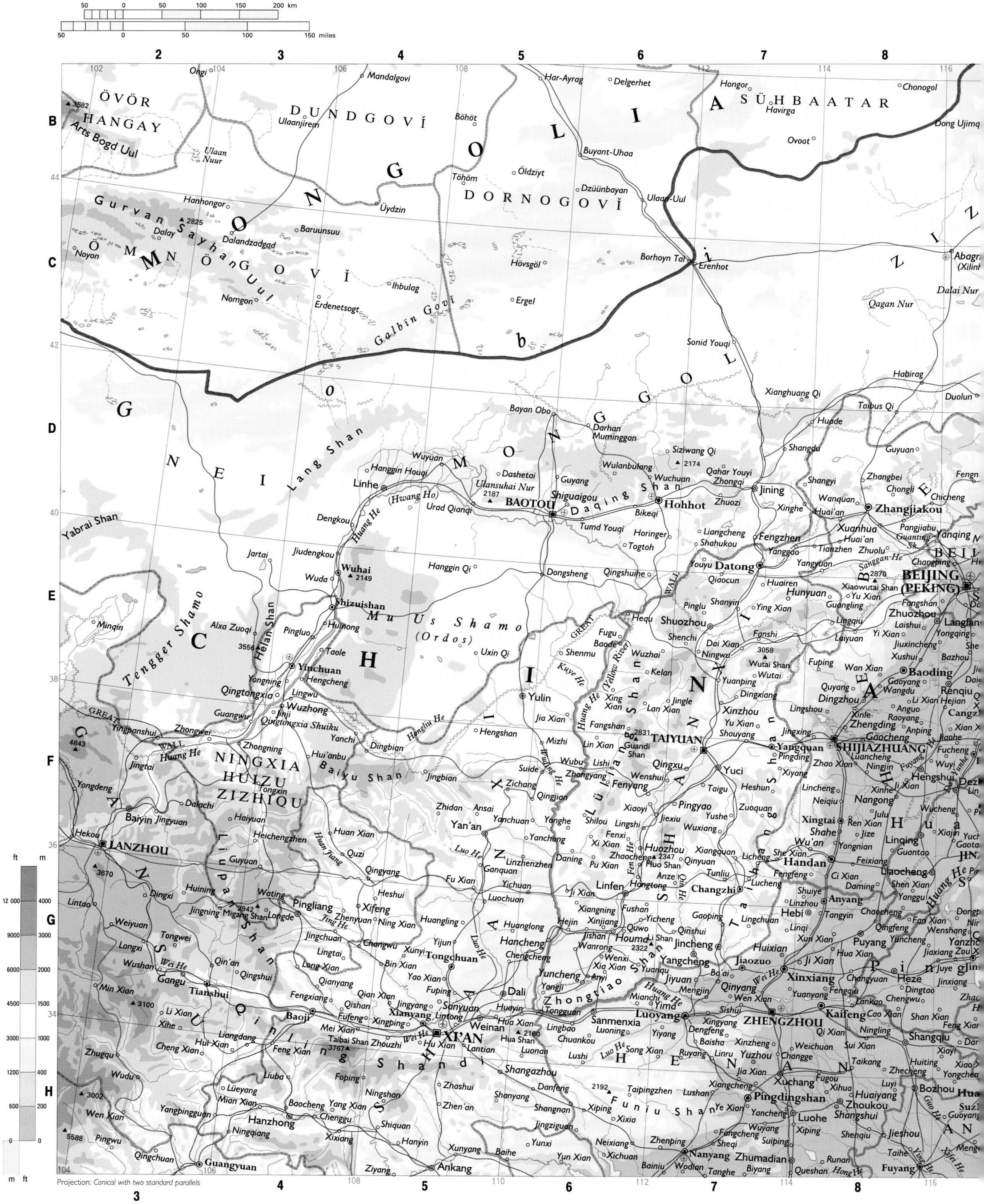

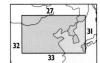

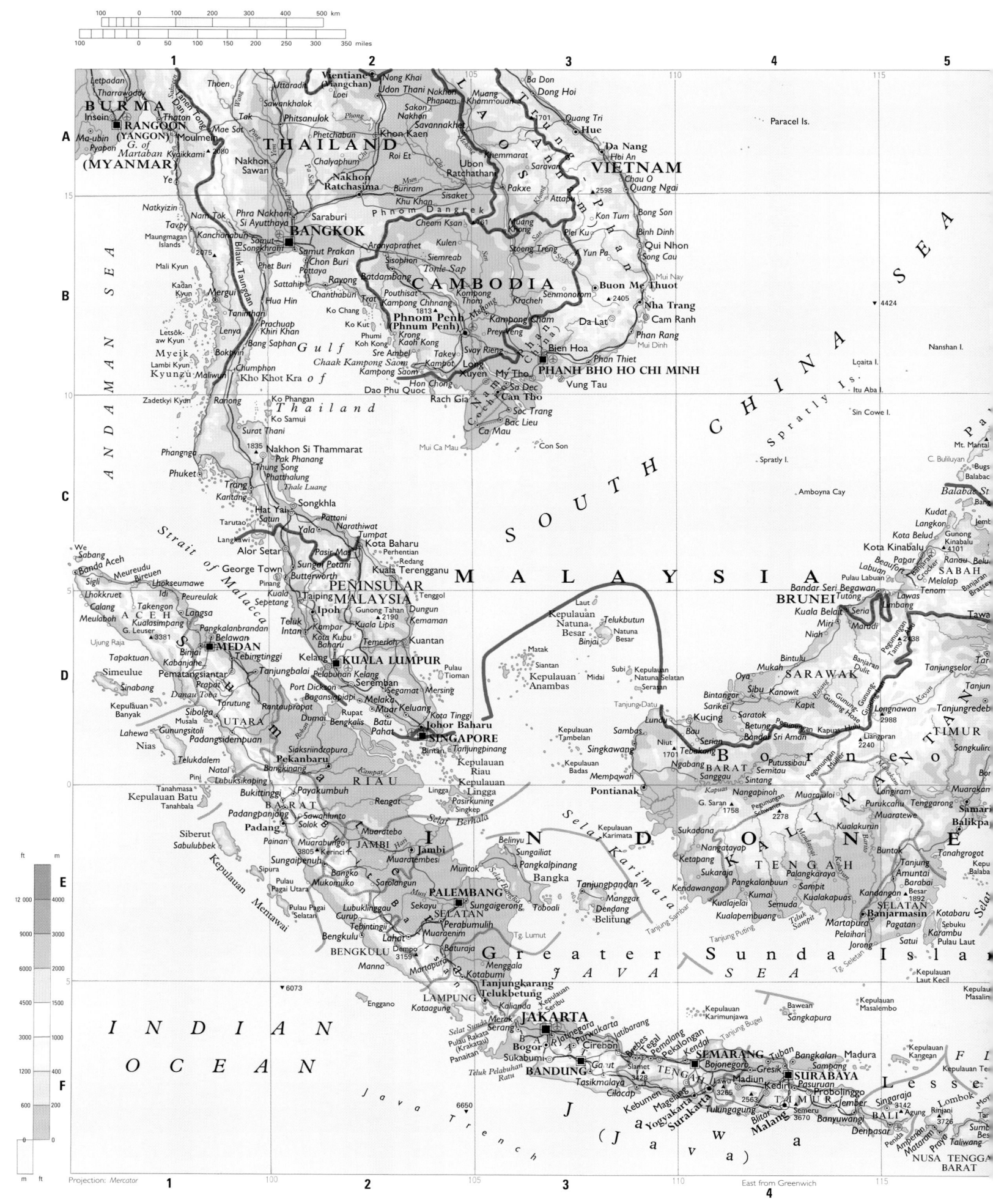

Projection: *Mercator*

East from Greenwich

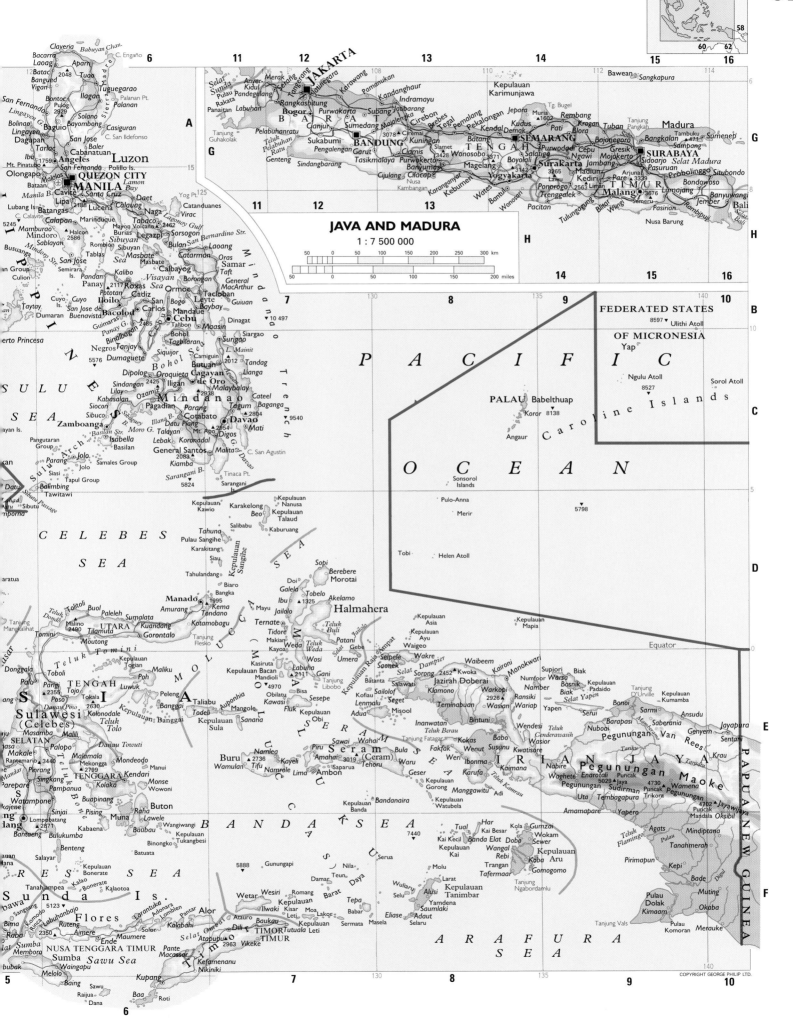

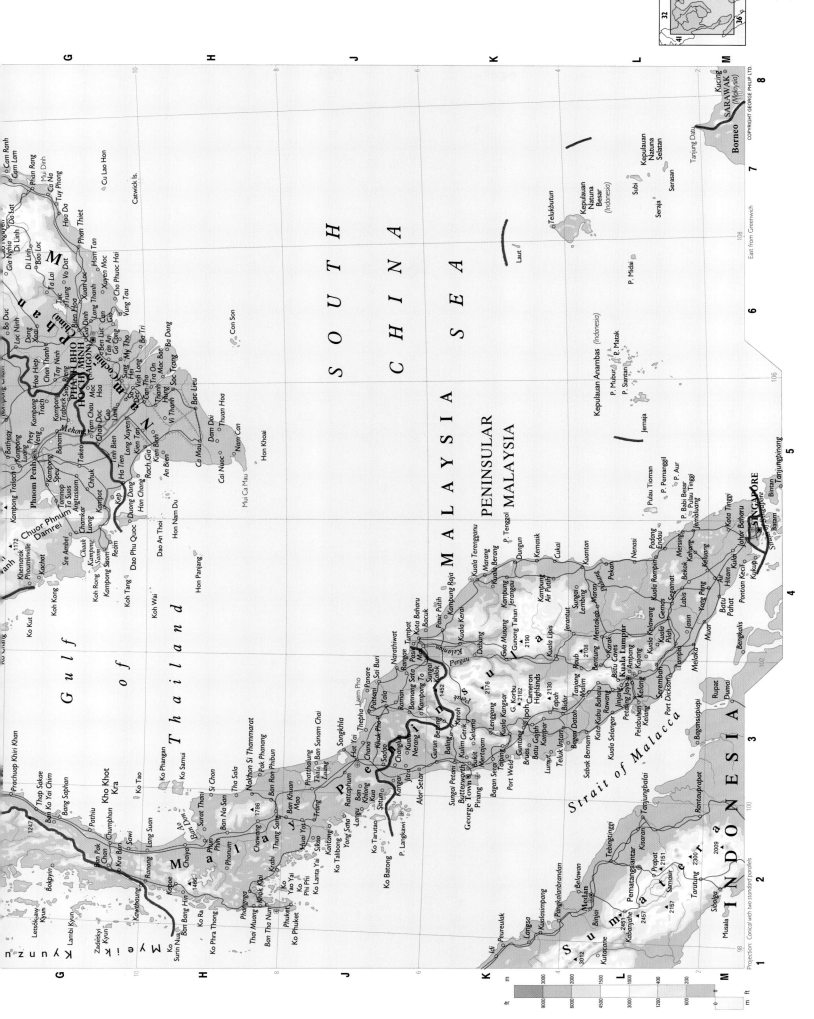

SOUTH

CHINA

SEA

Gulf

of

Thailand

M A L A Y S I A

PENINSULAR
MALAYSIA

I N D O N E S I A

Strait of Malacca

Borneo

SARAWAK
(Malaysia)
Kucing

Kepulauan
Natuna
Selatan

Kepulauan
Natuna
Besar
(Indonesia)

Kepulauan Anambas (Indonesia)

Tanjung Datu

SINGAPORE

Kuala Lumpur

George Town

Medan

S u m a t r a

COPYRIGHT GEORGE PHILIP LTD.

East from Greenwich

Projection: Conical with two standard parallels

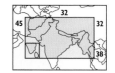

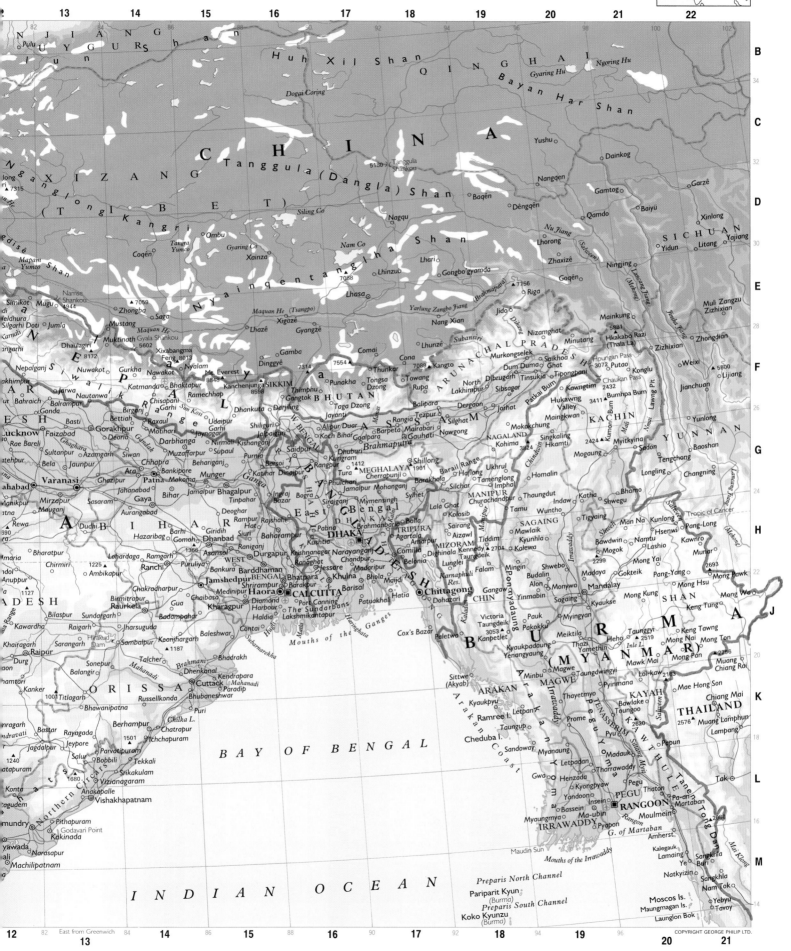

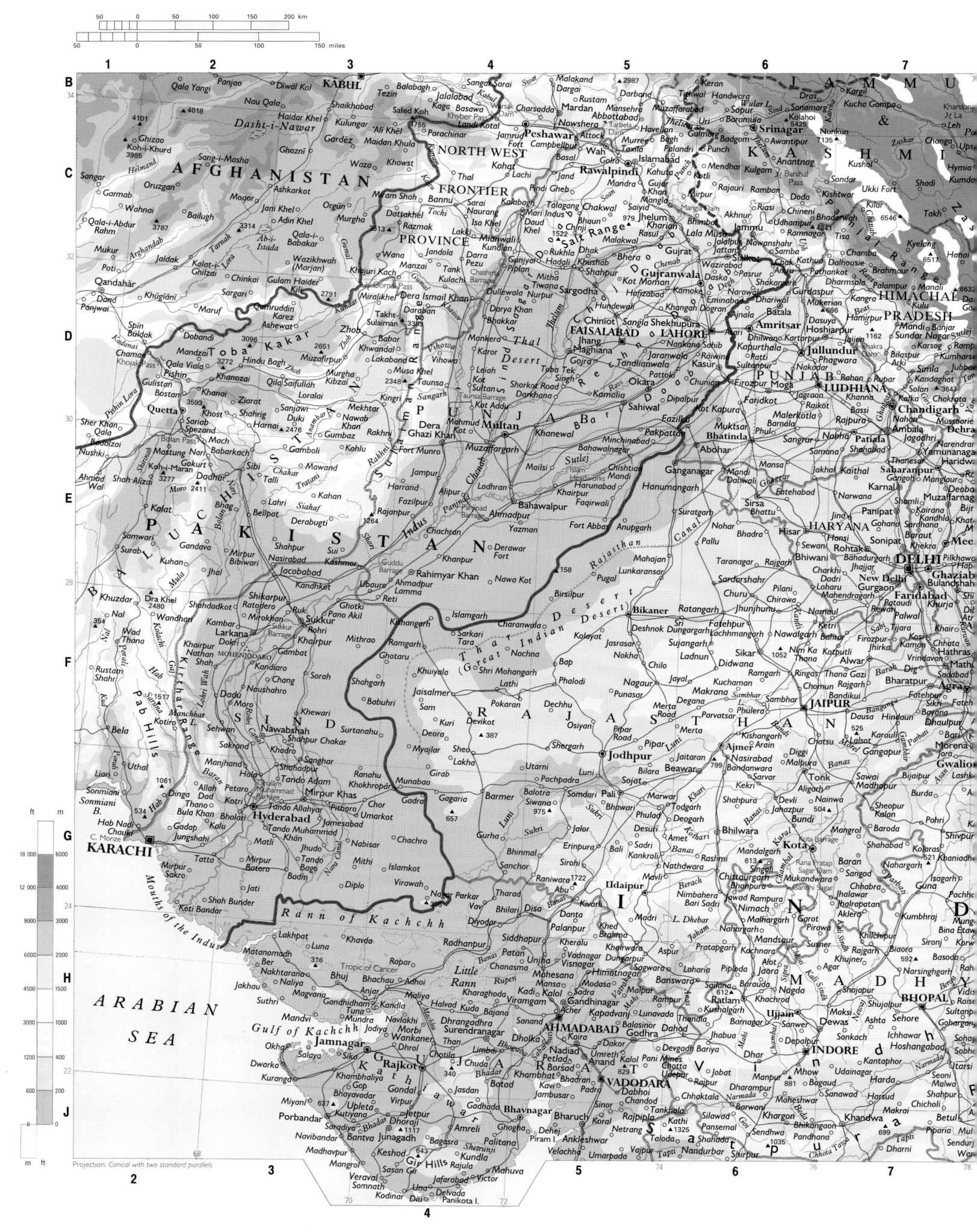

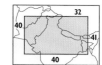

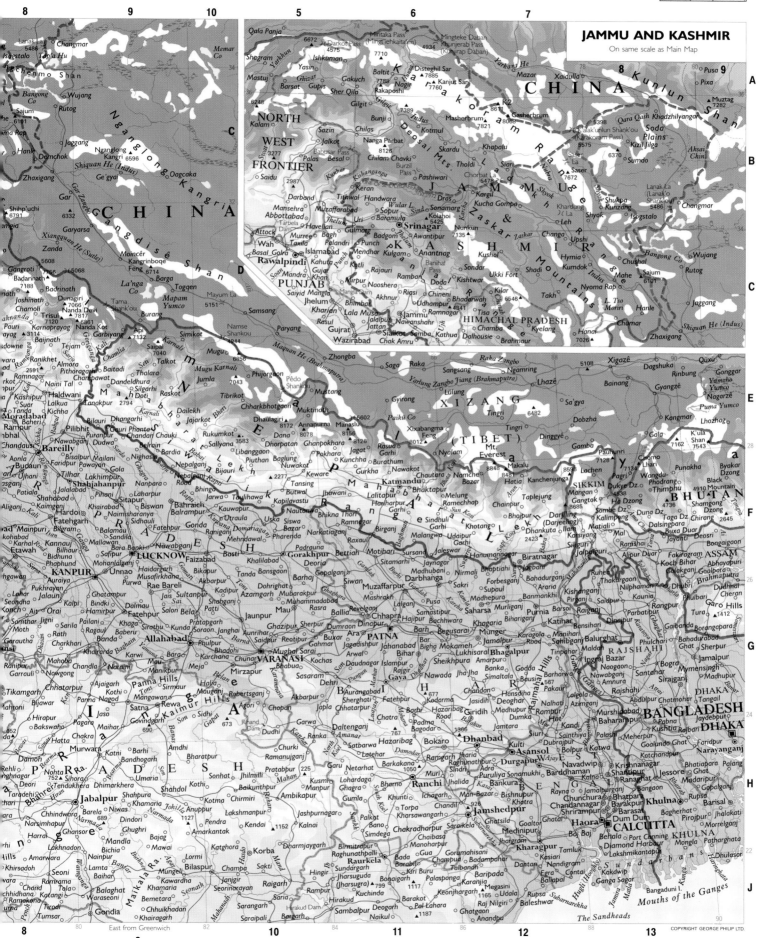

JAMMU AND KASHMIR
On same scale as Main Map

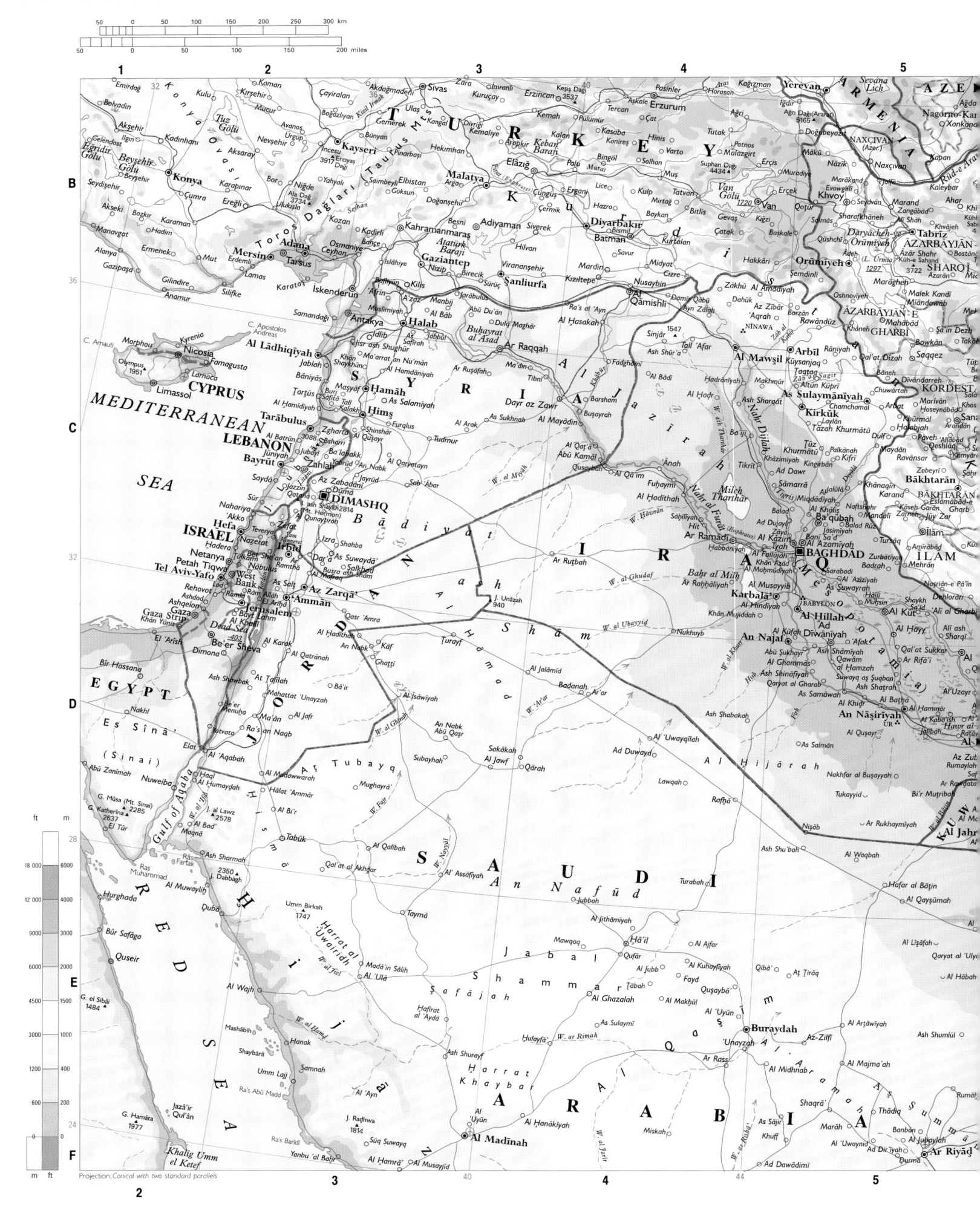

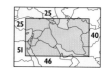

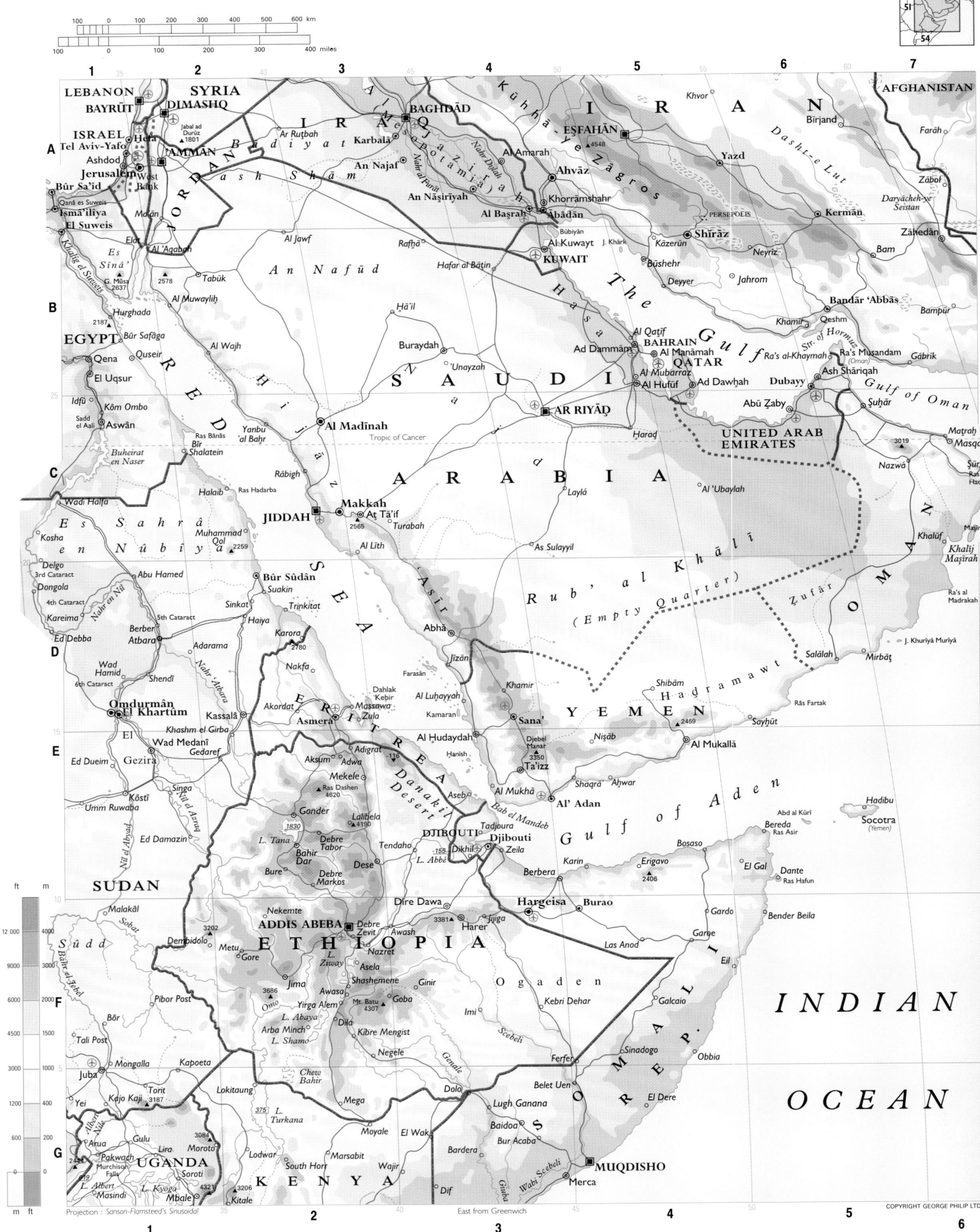

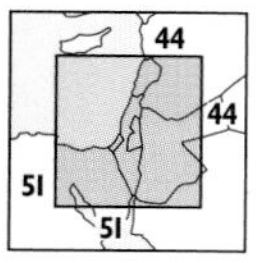

44
44
51
51

10 0 10 20 30 40 50 60 70 80 100 km
10 0 10 20 30 40 50 60 miles

Map labels

CYPRUS
Paphos
Episkopi
Episkopi Bay
Limassol
Akrotiri Bay
C. Gata

M E D I T E R R A N E A N

S E A

Ḥims (Homs)
Al Ḥamīdīyah
Tall Kalakh
Shinshār
Furqlus
Al Mīnā'
ASH SHAMĀL
Al Ḥirmil
Al Qusayr
ḤIMS
Tarābulus (Tripoli)
Zgharta
Ḥalbā
3088
Bsharri
Al Burayj
2464
Al Qaryatayn
Al Batrūn
Al Labwah
Jubayl
Qarṭabā
2616
An Nabk
Bi'r Ghadir
Ibrāhīm
Ba'labakk
Yabrūd
Jūniyah
Bikfayyā
2628
J. Sannīn
BAYRŪT (Beirut)
Alayh
Zaḥlah
Sirghāyā
SYRIA
Ash Shuwayfāt
Ḥawsh Mūssá
Al Quṭayfah
Ad Dāmūr
1942
Az Zabadānī
Dumayr
Khān Abū Shāmat
al Bārūk
LEBANON
DIMASHQ
Saydā (Sidon)
J. ash Shaykh (Mt. Hermon)
A'waj
Dūmā
Jazzīn
2814
DIMASHQ (Damascus)
An Nabaṭīyah at Taḥta
Marj 'Uyūn
Qaṭanā
AL JANŪB
Al Khiyām
Dārayyā
Al Kiswah
Al Hājānah
Sūr (Tyre)
Qiryat Shemona
Golan Heights
Burāq
AS SAFA
Nahariyya
1197
Al Qunayṭirah
As Sanamayn
Me'ona
Ar Rafid
JABAL AD DURŪZ
'Akko (Acre)
Hagalil
Zefat
Fiq
Shaykh Miskīn
DARĀ
Shahbā'
Mifraẓ Hefa
Qiryat Yam
Teverya
Yam -210
Saḥam al Jawlān
W. Al Harīr
Izra
AS SUWAYDĀ
Ḥefa (Haifa)
Qiryat Ata
(Tiberias)
Kinneret
Dar'ā
As Suwaydā
1800 Sālah
Dāliyat el Karmel
Nazerat
Yarmūk
Bușrā ash Shām
Salkhad
TEL MEGIDDO
HAZAFON
Ṭabība
Al Ramthā
CAESAREA
Afula
J. Umm ad Dara
Umm el Fahm
Bet She'an
Irbid
Salkhad
Hadera
Jenin
Ailūn
Al Mafraq
Umm al Qiṭṭayn
ISRAEL
Hanna-Karkur
Shōmrōn
1247
IRBID
Netanya
Ṭulkarm
Ṭūbās
Jarash
HAMERKAZ
SAMARIA
Herzliyya
Nāblus
Nahr az Zarqā
Bene Beraq
Ketar Sava
SHILO
AL BALQA
Tel Aviv-Yafo
Petaḥ Tiqwa
As Salt
Az Zarqā
Ramat Gan
West Bank
Wādī aṣ Sir
AMMĀN
Bat Yam
Rishon le Ziyyon
Rāmallāh
Rama
Karama
'AMMĀN
Ashdod
Rehovot
El Arīḥā (Jericho)
Na'ūr
Yavne
289
At Tunayb
Qiryat Mal'akhi
Jerusalem (Yerushalayim) (Al Quds)
Ma'dabā
Ashqelon
Qiryat Gat
Bet Shemesh
Bayt Laḥm (Bethlehem)
TEL LAKHISH
Al Khalīl (Hebron)
N. Shiqma
Gaza
Sederot
Az Zāhirīyah
-403
W. al Ḥaydān
Dhībān
Gaza Strip
Khān Yūnis
Arad
W. al Mawjib
Al Ḥadīthah
Rafaḥ
N. Besor
Be'er Sheva (Beersheba)
Sedom
W. al Ghadaf
Bûr Sa'îd (Port Said)
Bûr Fu'ad
Râs Burûn
Bor Mashash
Al Qaṭrānah
Khalîg el Tîna
Sabkhet el Bardawîl
El Daheir
Dimona
-333
Al Karak
W. al Mabrūk
Români
Bîr el 'Abd
Bîr Qaṭia
Bîr Garârât
Ha 'Arava
AL KARAK
El Qantara
Bîr el Jafir
W. 'Arîsh
HADAROM
Al Mazār
1305
W. Bá
Wâhid
Bîr Madkûr
SÎNÎ
Qezi'ot
At Ṭafilah
JORDAN
Ismâ'îlîya
Talâta
Birein
Sedé Boqér
-121
J. ash Shawmari
Khamsa
El Buheirat el Murrat el Kubra (Great Bitter L.)
892
El Quseima
Mizpe Ramon
Ba'ir
1072
Gineifo
Bîr Hasana
Hanegev
Rujm Tal'at al Jamā'ah 1736
Nijil
Mahattat 'Unayzah
W. Abu Ṣafāt
EGYPT
Bîr el Thamâda
W. el Brûk
W. Qiraiya
El 'Agrûd
Bîr ad Dabbâghât
Qa'el Jafr
G. Yi 'Allaq 1094
N. Paran
El Jafr
El Suweis (Suez)
Adabiya
Uyûn Mûsa
Nakhl
W. El Aqaba
W. Mahasham
El Kuntilla
Ma'ān
E s S î n â' (Sinai)
948 G. el Kabrît
Ain Sudr
W. el Saheira
Bîr Abu Muhammad
El Thamad
'En 'Avrona
Yotvata
Ra's an Naqb
Mahattat ash Shidîya
Bîr Bad'
Ghubbet el Bûs
Râs Matarma
Gebel el Tîh
El Wabeira
Bîr el Biarât
1592
Bi'r al Butayyiḥāt
Bi'r al Qaṭṭār
Ra's an Nāqb 1435
SAUDI
Bîr Abu Sandûq
1272
EL SUWEIS
W. Abu Ga'da
Bîr Wuseit
1165
Bîr el Heisi
Elat
Al 'Aqabah
Ḥaql
Baṭn al Ghûl
Al Mudawwarah
At Tubayq
ARABIA
Gulf of Aqaba
W. an Nuweiba
Shibh Jazîrat Sînâ'

Projection: Polyconic
East from Greenwich
COPYRIGHT GEORGE PHILIP LTD.

ft m
9000 3000
6000 2000
4500 1500
3000 1000
1200 400
600 200
0 0
m ft

━ ━ ━ 1974 Cease Fire Lines

200 0 200 400 600 800 1000 1200 1400 1600 1800 km
200 0 200 400 600 800 1000 1200 miles

NORTH
ATLANTIC
OCEAN

British Isles

E u r o p e

Carpathians

Azores

Mont Blanc 4807
Alps
Pyrénées
Corsica
Apennines
Dinaric Alps
Adriatic Sea
Black Sea
Caucasus
Elbrus 5633
Aral Sea

Caspian Sea

B. of Biscay

Iberian Peninsula

Sardinia
Sicily
Anatolia
Asia

Madeira

6578

Str. of Gibraltar
Malta
Crete
Cyprus
Levant
Mesopotamia
Tigris

Middle Atlas
High Atlas
4165
Toubkal
High Plateaux
Saharan Atlas
M e d i t e r r a n e a n   S e a
C. Bon
5121
G. of Gabès
G. of Sidra
Tripolitania
Cyrenaica
Siwa Oasis
Syrian Desert
Euphrates
The Gulf

Canary Is.
Tenerife
Anti Atlas

Arabian Desert
Red Sea
Hejaz
Mt. Sinai 2285
A r a b i a

Ras Nouâdhibou

Libyan Desert
Egypt
El Khârga
Nile

Tasili Plateau

S a h a r a

Tropic of Cancer

El Djouf
Adrar
Aïr
Bilma
Tibesti
Nubian Desert
Nubia

Hoggar
Al Kufrah

Cape Verde Is.
C. Vert
Senegambia
Gambia
Senegal

Niger
Volta
Niger
L. Chad
Bahr el Ghazal
Wadai
Dârfûr
Kordofân
White Nile
Blue Nile
Athara
Ras Dashen 4620
116
L. Tana
Barim
Bab el Mandeb
G. of Aden
Ras Asir

Fouta Djalon
S a h e l
Darfur
Ethiopian Highlands
Somali Peninsula

G u i n e a
Grain Coast
Ivory Coast
Gold Coast
Slave Coast
C. Palmas
Bight of Benin
Mt. Cameroon 4070
Bioko
Adamawa Highlands
Dar Banda
Bahr el Ghazâl
Bahr el Jebel
Shabelle
Juba

Benue
Uele
L. Turkana

Bight of Bonny
I. de Principe
Ubangi
Congo (Zaïre)
C o n g o
L. Albert
Ruwenzori
Mt. Elgon 4321
Mt. Kenya 5199

Gulf of Guinea
São Tomé
C. Lopez
Ogooué
Chutes Boyoma
5109
L. Edward
L. Kivu
Tana

Equator
Annobón
B a s i n
Congo (Zaïre)
Kasai
Sankuru
L. Victoria
5895
Kilimanjaro
Pemba I.

INDIAN
OCEAN
Seych

Cuango
Kasai
L. Tanganyika
Luapula

Ascension I.

Luvua
L. Mweru
Rungwe 2961
L. Nyasa (L. Malawi)
Aldabra Is.

Cuanza
Shaba
Bangweulu Swamp
C. Delgado
Comoros

SOUTH
ATLANTIC
OCEAN

St. Helena

Bié Plateau
Zambezi
Zambezi
Shire

Cunene
Cubango
Cuando
Victoria Falls

C. Fria
Okavango Swamps

Madagascar
2643
Ma
Réunion

Walvis Bay
Limpopo
Mozambique Channel

Namib Desert
K a l a h a r i
Delagoa B.

Tropic of Capricorn
Orange
Vaal
High Veld
Drakensberg
3482
Compass Mt. 2505
Nuweveldberge
Great Karoo
Swartberge
Algoa B.
C. of Good Hope
C. Agulhas

Tristan da Cunha

ft m
12000 4000
9000 3000
6000 2000
3000 1000
1500 500
600 200
0 0
m ft

Projection: Azimuthal Equidistant
West from Greenwich
East from Greenwich

COPYRIGHT GEORGE PHILIP LTD.

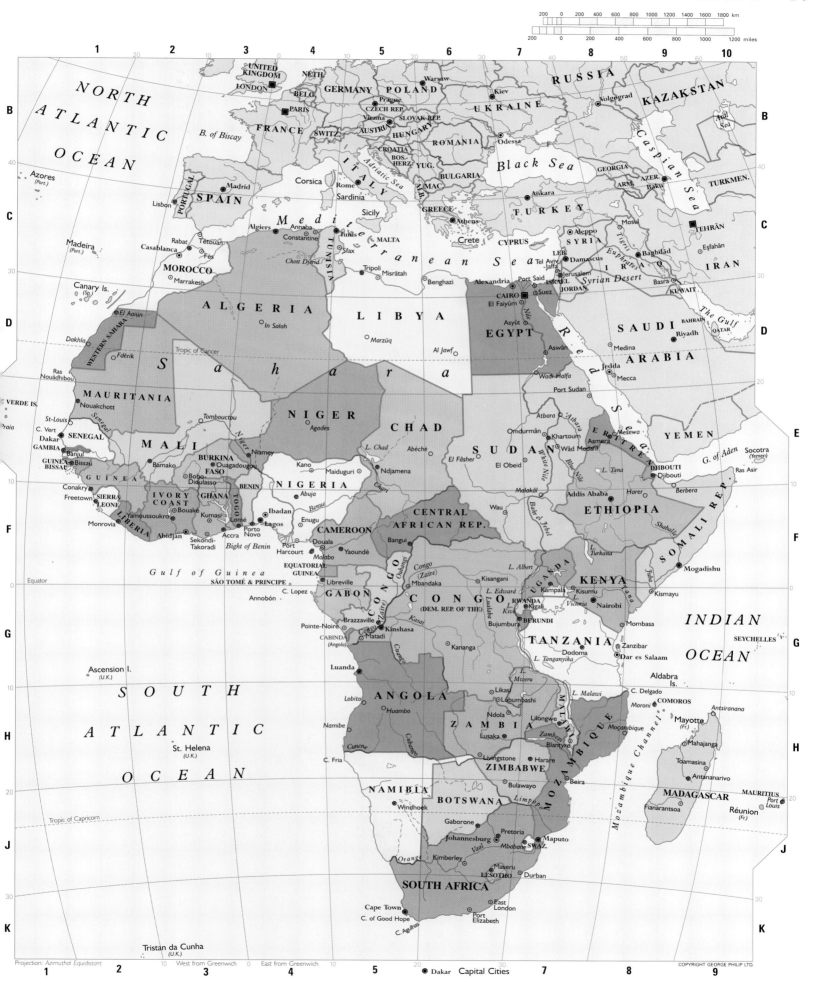

200 0 200 400 600 800 1000 1200 1400 1600 1800 km

200 0 200 400 600 800 1000 1200 miles

| | 1 | | 2 | | 3 | | 4 | | 5 | | 6 | | 7 | | 8 | | 9 | | 10 | |

B

NORTH

ATLANTIC

OCEAN

UNITED KINGDOM
LONDON
NETH.
BELG.
PARIS
GERMANY
POLAND   Warsaw
Prague
CZECH REP.
Vienna   SLOVAK REP.
SWITZ.   AUSTRIA   HUNGARY
FRANCE
B. of Biscay
CROATIA
BOS.-HERZ.   YUG.
ITALY   Adriatic Sea   ALB.   MAC.
BULGARIA
Kiev
UKRAINE
ROMANIA
Odessa
Black Sea
RUSSIA
Volgograd
KAZAKSTAN
Aral Sea
GEORGIA
ARM.   AZER.   Baku
Caspian Sea
TURKMEN.

B

Azores (Port.)

Madrid
PORTUGAL   SPAIN
Lisbon
Corsica
Rome   Sardinia
Sicily
GREECE   Athens
Crete
CYPRUS
Ankara
TURKEY
Aleppo
SYRIA
Mosul
Tigris
TEHRĀN
Eşfahān
IRAN

C

Madeira (Port.)
Casablanca
Rabat   Tétouan
Fès   Algiers   Annaba
Constantine   TUNISIA   Tunis
Sfax   MALTA
Mediterranean Sea
Benghazi
Tripoli   Misrātah
LEB.
Damascus
Tel Aviv-Jaffa   Jerusalem
ISRAEL   JORDAN
Alexandria   Port Said
Suez
Baghdād
IRAQ   Basra
KUWAIT
Syrian Desert
BAHRAIN   The Gulf
QATAR
Riyadh

C

D

MOROCCO   Marrakesh
Canary Is. (Sp.)
WESTERN SAHARA
El Aaiún
Dakhla
Fdérik
ALGERIA
In Salah
Marzūq
Al Jawf
Sahara
LIBYA
EGYPT   El Faiyûm
CAIRO
Asyût
Aswân   Nile
Wadi Halfa
Medina
Mecca
SAUDI
ARABIA
Jedda

D

Tropic of Cancer

E

Ras Nouâdhibou
VERDE IS.
Praia
Nouakchott
MAURITANIA
St-Louis
C. Vert   Dakar
SENEGAL
GAMBIA   Banjul
GUINEA-BISSAU   Bissau
Senegal
MALI
Tombouctou
NIGER
Agades
L. Chad
CHAD
Abéché
Ndjamena
SUDAN
El Fâsher
El Obeid
Omdurmân   Khartoum
Atbara   Atbara
Wâd Medani
Port Sudan
Red Sea
ERITREA
Mesewa
Asmera
YEMEN
G. of Aden
Socotra (Yemen)
Ras Asir

E

Niamey

F

Conakry
Freetown
SIERRA LEONE
Monrovia
LIBERIA
Yamoussoukro
IVORY COAST
Bouaké
Abidjan
Sekondi-Takoradi
GUINEA
Bamako
BURKINA FASO
Bobo Dioulasso   Ouagadougou
GHANA
Kumasi   TOGO
Accra   Lomé
Porto Novo
BENIN
NIGERIA
Kano   Maiduguri
Abuja
Ibadan   Enugu
Lagos
Bight of Benin
Port Harcourt
Douala
CAMEROON
Yaoundé
Malabo
EQUATORIAL GUINEA
CENTRAL AFRICAN REP.
Bangui
Benue
Wau
Bahr el Jebel
Malakâl
White Nile   Blue Nile
L. Tana
Addis Ababa
Harer
ETHIOPIA
DJIBOUTI   Djibouti
Berbera
SOMALI REP.
Mogadishu

F

G

Gulf of Guinea
SÃO TOMÉ & PRINCIPE
Libreville
C. Lopez
GABON
Annobón
Pointe-Noire
Brazzaville
CABINDA (Angola)
CONGO (Zaïre)
Mbandaka
CONGO (DEM. REP. OF THE)
Kisangani
Kinshasa
Matadi
Kananga
Kasai
Lualaba
L. Albert
L. Edward
RWANDA   Kigali
BURUNDI   Bujumbura
UGANDA   Kampala
Kisumu   Victoria
Nairobi
KENYA
L. Turkana
Juba
Tana
Mombasa
INDIAN
OCEAN
SEYCHELLES
Kismayu

G

Equator

Ascension I. (U.K.)

H

SOUTH
ATLANTIC
OCEAN
St. Helena (U.K.)
Luanda
Lobito
ANGOLA
Huambo
Namibe
C. Fria
Cunene
Cubango
Cuango
TANZANIA
Dodoma
Zanzibar
Dar es Salaam
L. Tanganyika
L. Mweru
Likasi
Lubumbashi
Ndola
ZAMBIA
Lusaka
Livingstone
L. Malawi
MALAWI
Lilongwe
Blantyre
Zambezi
Moçambique
MOZAMBIQUE
C. Delgado
Moroni   COMOROS
Mayotte (Fr.)
Antsiranana
Mahajanga
Toamasina
Antananarivo
Mozambique Channel

H

Aldabra Is.

J

Tropic of Capricorn
NAMIBIA
Windhoek
BOTSWANA
Gaborone
ZIMBABWE
Bulawayo
Harare
Beira
Limpopo
Johannesburg
Pretoria   Maputo
Mbabane   SWAZ.
Vaal
Kimberley
Orange
Maseru   LESOTHO
Durban
Fianarantsoa
MADAGASCAR
MAURITIUS   Port Louis
Réunion (Fr.)

J

K

SOUTH AFRICA
Cape Town
C. of Good Hope
C. Agulhas
Port Elizabeth
East London

K

Tristan da Cunha (U.K.)

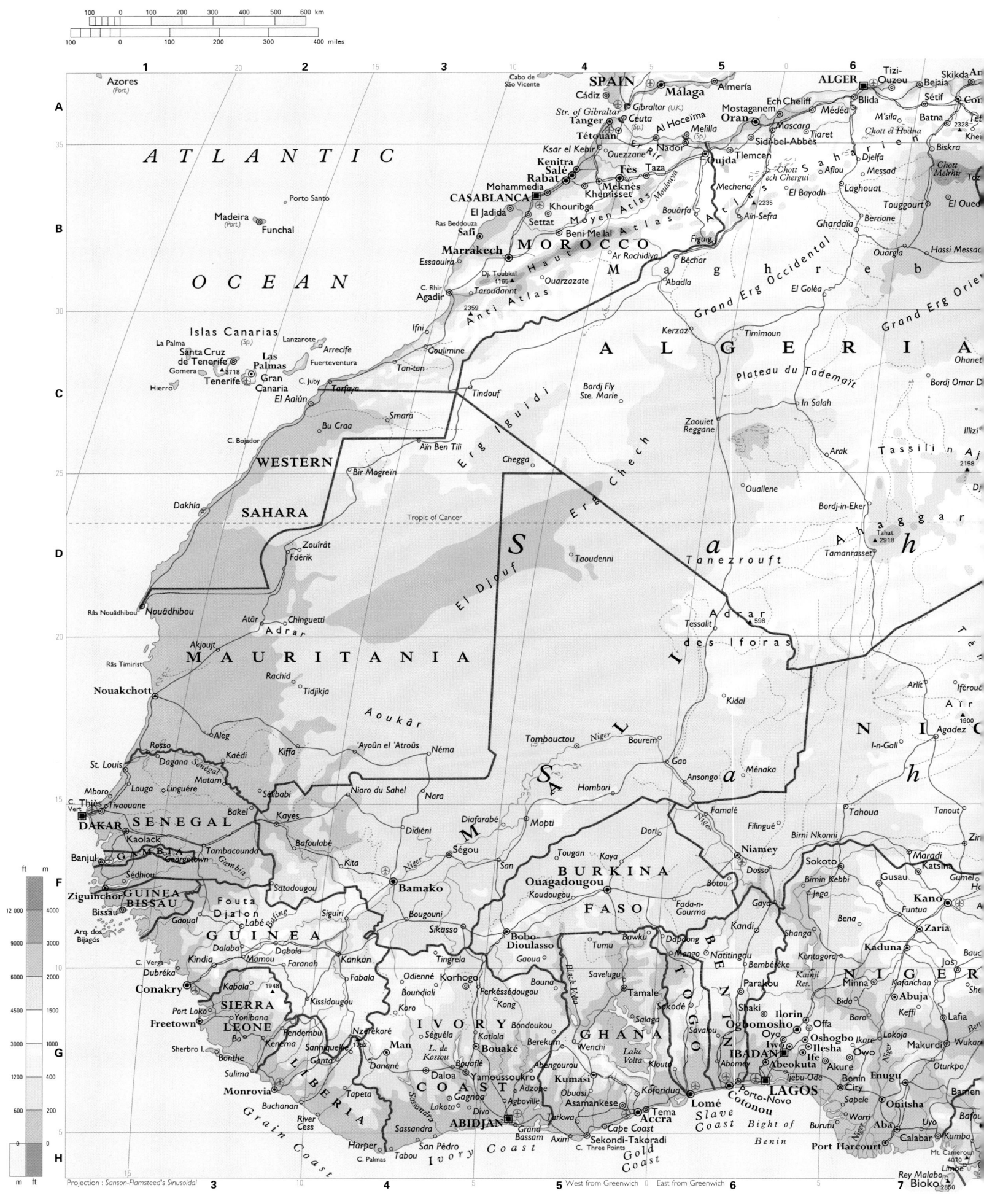

100 0 100 200 300 400 500 600 km
100 0 100 200 300 400 miles

ATLANTIC

Azores
(Port.)

Cabo de
São Vicente
SPAIN
Cádiz   Málaga   Almería
Str. of Gibraltar   Gibraltar (U.K.)   TIZI-
Tanger   Ceuta (Sp.)   Al Hoceïma   Melilla   Oran   Mostaganem   Ech Cheliff   ALGER   Ouzou   Skikda
Tétouan   (Sp.)   Oran   Sidi-bel-Abbès   Blida   Bejaïa   Sétif
Ksar el Kebir   Nador   Tlemcen   Mascara   Tiaret   M'sila   Batna
Kenitra   Salé   Fès   Taza   Oujda   Chott   Djelfa   Messad   Biskra
Rabat   Meknès   ech Chergui   Aflou   Laghouat   Chott
Mohammedia   Khemisset   Mecheria   El Bayadh   Melrhir
CASABLANCA   Khouribga   Aïn-Sefra   Ghardaïa   El Oued
El Jadida   Settat   Bouârfa   Berriane   Touggourt
Ras Beddouza   Beni Mellal   Figuig   Ouargla   Hassi Messa
Safi   MOROCCO   Ar Rachidiya   Béchar

OCEAN

Madeira
(Port.)   Funchal

Porto Santo

Marrakech   Moyen Atlas
Essaouira   Haut   Béchar   Grand Erg Occidental   Grand Erg Orie
Dj. Toubkal   Ouarzazate   Abadla
4165   Atlas   El Goléa   b
C. Rhir   Taroudannt   M   a   g   h   r   e
Agadir   Anti Atlas   El Golea
2359   ALGERIA
Ifni   Kerzaz   Timimoun
Goulimine   Bordj Fly   Plateau du Tademaït   Ohane
Tan-tan   Ste. Marie   In Salah   Bordj Omar Orie
WESTERN   Bu Craa   Tindouf   Zaouiet   Arak   Tassili n Aj
C. Juby   Tarfaya   Reggane   2158
El Aaiún   Smara   Ouallene   Bordj-in-Eker
Aïn Ben Tili   Chegga   Ahaggar
SAHARA   Tropic of Cancer   Ouallene   Tamanrasset   Tahat
Dakhla   Zouîrât   S   Taoudenni   Tessalit   2918
Fdérik   Adrar   598
Râs Nouâdhibou   Nouâdhibou   El Djouf   Tanezrouft   des Iforas
Atâr   Chinguetti   Adrar   Te
Adrar   Kidal   Arlit   Iférouâ
Akjoujt   Aïr
Râs Timirist   **MAURITANIA**   1900
Rachid   Tidjikja   NIGE
Nouakchott   Aoukâr   I-n-Gall   Agadez   h
Rosso   Aleg   'Ayoûn el 'Atroûs   Néma   Tombouctou   Niger   Bourem   Tahoua   Tanout
St. Louis   Kaédi   Kiffa   Gao
Dagana   Senegal   Matam   Nioro du Sahel   Ansongo   a   Ménaka   Birni Nkonni
Mboro   Louga   Linguère   Sélibabi   Nara   S   Hombori   Filingué
C. Vert   Thiès   Tivaouane   Bakel   Kayes   A   Famalé   Dosso
DAKAR   **SENEGAL**   Diafarabé   Mopti   Niamey   Sokoto   Maradi   Katsina
Kaolack   Bafoulabé   M   Dori   Zin
Banjul   GAMBIA   Tambacounda   Georgetown   Gambia   Kita   Didjéni   Ségou   Niger   Tougan   Kaya   Bôtou   Birnin Kebbi   Gusau
Sédhiou   San   **BURKINA**   Gaya   Jega   Zaria
Ziguinchor   **GUINEA**   Satadougou   Bamako   Bougouni   **Ouagadougou**   Fada-n-   Kandi   Shanga   **KANO**
BISSAU   Fouta   Koudougou   **FASO**   Gourma   Bembéréke   Kontagora   Kaduna
Bissau   Djalon   Siguiri   Sikasso   Bobo-   Tumu   Bawku   Dapaong   Natitingou   Bena   Funtua
Arq. dos   Gaoual   Labé   Dioulasso   Gaoua   Mango   Kainji   Minna   Abuja   Jos   Bauc
Bijagós   **GUINEA**   Dalaba   Dabola   Kankan   Odienné   Korhogo   Savelugu   Res.   Baro   Lafia
C. Verga   Kindia   Mamou   Faranah   Ferkéssédougou   Tamale   Parakou   Bida   Lokoja
Dubréka   Fabala   Boundiali   Kong   Salaga   Sokodé   Shaki   Ilorin   Offa   Kafanchan
Conakry   Kabala   1948   Kissidougou   Koro   Bouna   Savalou   Oyo   Ogbomosho   Ife   Owo   Makurdi   Wukar
Port Loko   **SIERRA**   Nzérékoré   Séguéla   Katiola   Berekum   Wenchi   Lake   Iwo   Oshogbo   Ikare   Oturkpo
Freetown   **LEONE**   1752   Man   L. de   **Bouaké**   Bondoukou   Volta   **IBADAN**   Iwo   Ilesha   Benin   Enugu
Yonibana   Kossou   **GHANA**   **Abomey**   Ejjebu-Ode   City
Bo   Kenema   Ganta   Daloa   Yamoussoukro   Kumasi   Koforidua   **LAGOS**   Benin   Onitsha
Sherbro I.   Bonthe   Danané   **IVORY**   Adzope   Obuasi   Asamankese   **Porto-Novo**   City   Sapele
Sulima   Tapeta   Agboville   Lomé   Cotonou   Warri   Aba
Monrovia   **LIBERIA**   Gagnoa   **COAST**   Divo   Slave   Oko   Calabar
Buchanan   Daloa   Axim   Tema   Coast   Bight of
River   Lakota   **ABIDJAN**   Grand   Accra   Benin   Port Harcourt
Cess   Sassandra   Bassam   Cape Coast   Mt. Cameroun
Harper   Tabou   Sekondi-Takoradi   Gold   4070
C. Palmas   San Pédro   Ivory   Coast   C. Three Points   Coast   Limbe
Grain Coast   Rey Malabo
Projection: Sanson-Flamsteed's Sinusoidal   Bioko   2850

ft m
12 000   4000
9000   3000
6000   2000
4500   1500
3000   1000
1200   400
600   200
0
m ft

West from Greenwich   East from Greenwich

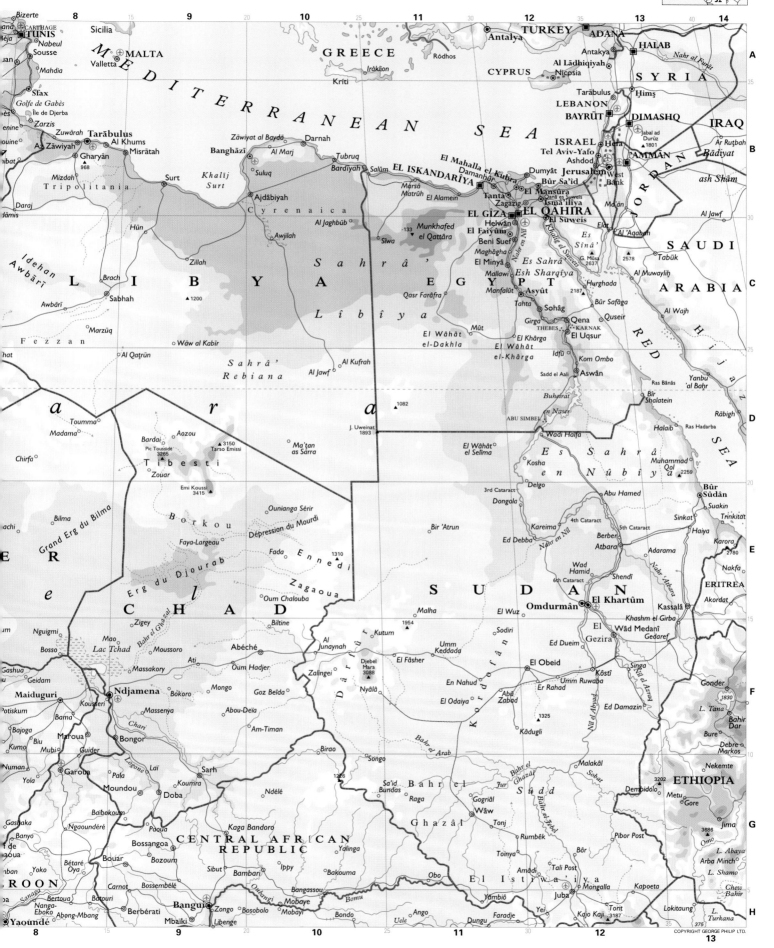

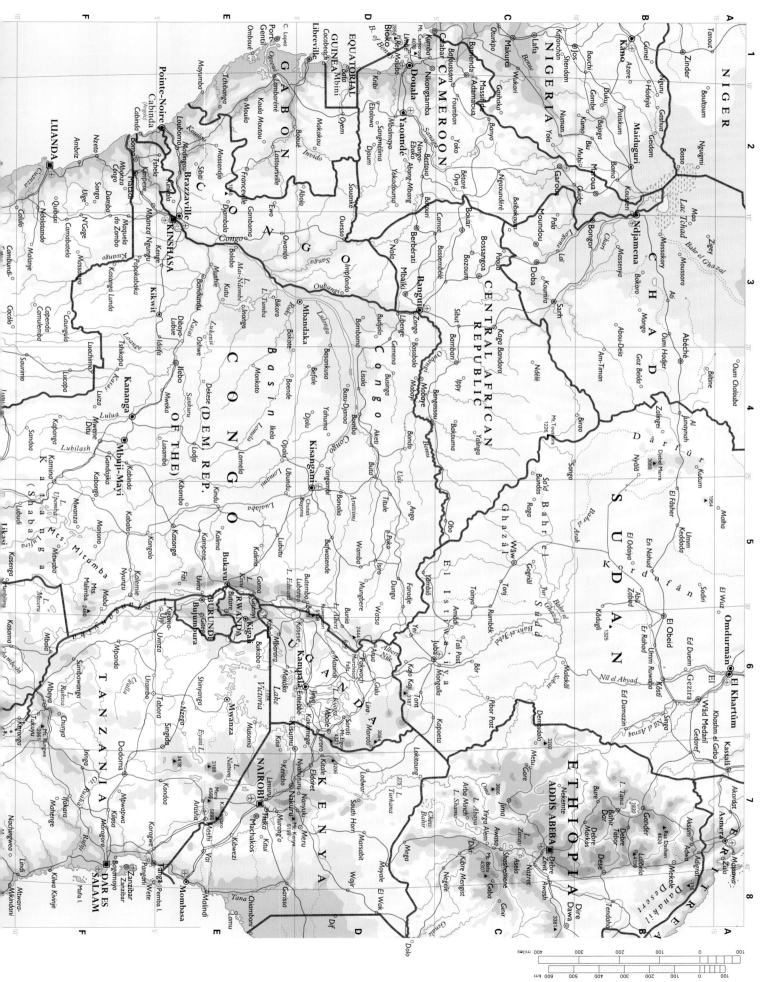

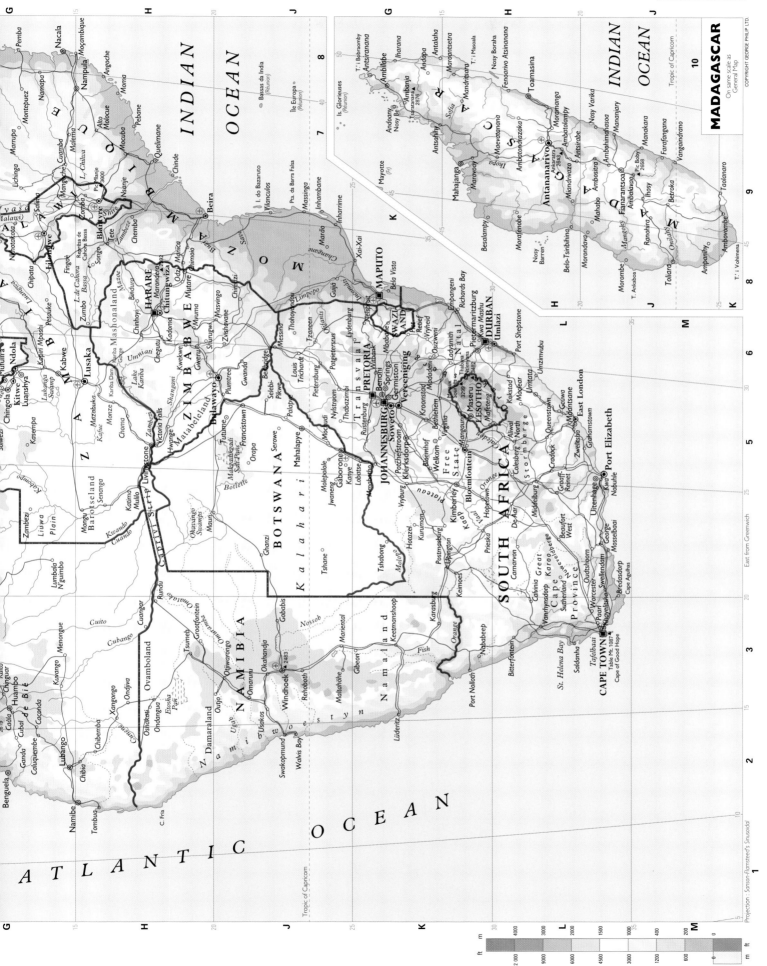

INDIAN OCEAN

ATLANTIC OCEAN

MADAGASCAR
On same scale as General Map

COPYRIGHT GEORGE PHILIP LTD.

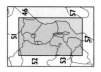

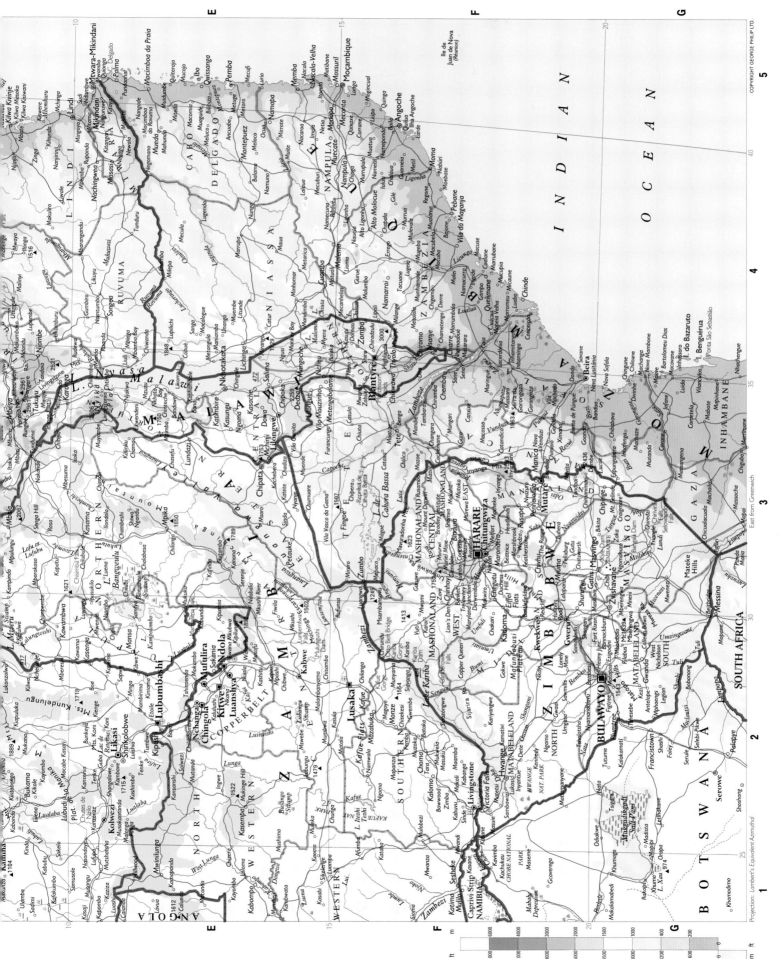

53 55

5 6 7

8

MOZAMBIQUE CHANNEL

B

ZAMBEZIA

MALAWI

ZIMBABWE

MOZAMBIQUE

MASHONALAND
CENTRAL
HARARE
Chitungwiza

MASHONALAND
EAST

MASVINGO

A

C

CHANNEL

MADAGASCAR

Antsiranana

ANTSIR-
ANANA

Mahajanga

MAHAJANGA

Toamasina

ANTANANARIVO
ANTANANARIVO

B

Antsirabe

D

NORTHERN

KRUGER
NATIONAL
PARK

PRETORIA
JOHANNESBURG
Benoni
MPUMALANGA
SWAZILAND
Maputo
MAPUTO

KWAZULU
NATAL

Pietermaritzburg
KwaMashu DURBAN
Umlazi

EASTERN
CAPE

Umtata

Morondava

MADAGASCAR

FIANARANTSOA

Toliara

C

D

INDIAN
OCEAN

MOZAMBIQUE
CHANNEL

Tropic of Capricorn

INDIAN
OCEAN

9

East from Greenwich

30

5

7

45

8

MADAGASCAR

On same scale as General Map

COPYRIGHT GEORGE PHILIP LTD.

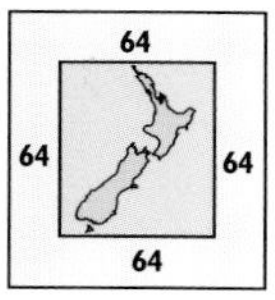

64
64 64
64

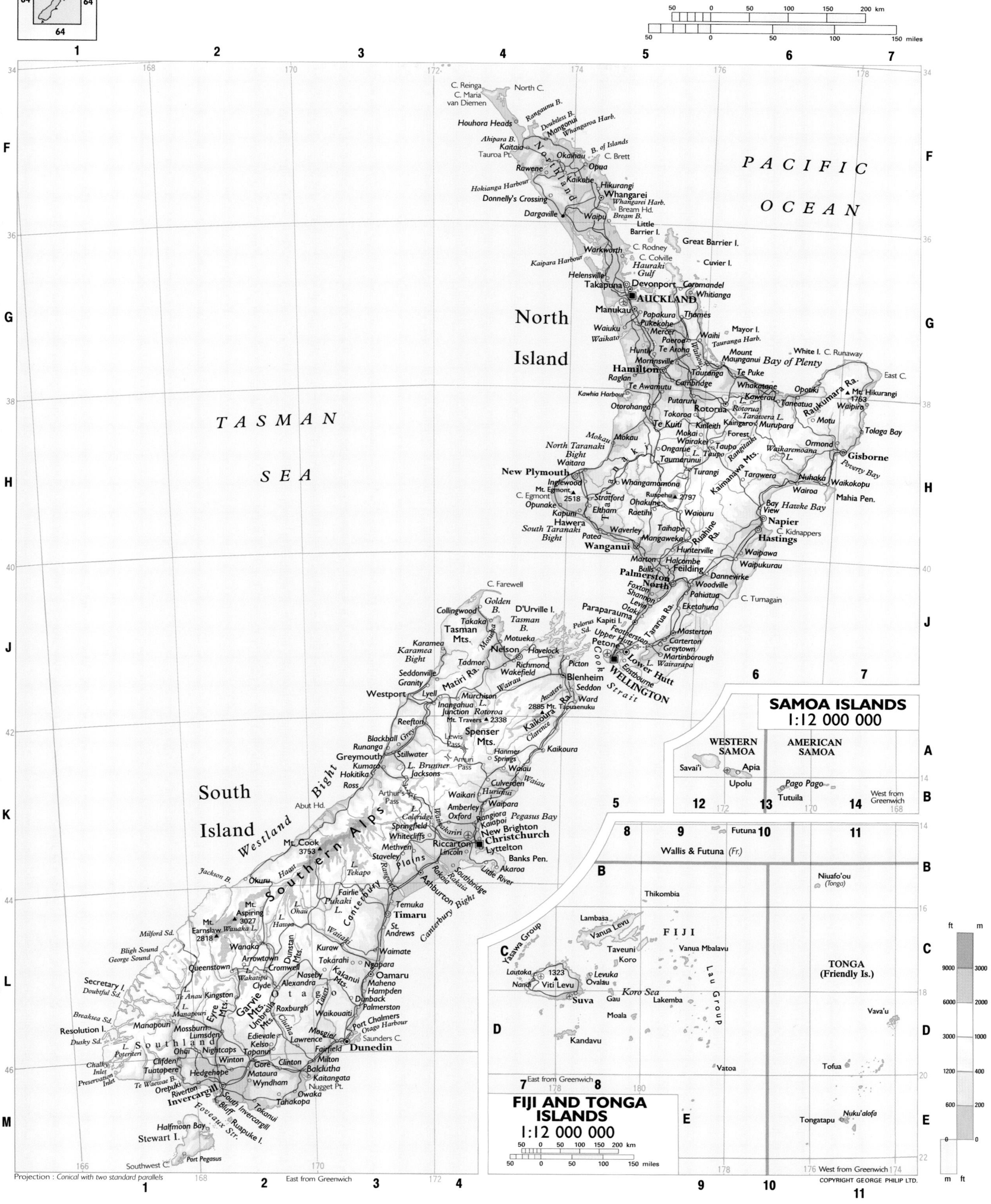

1 2 3 4 5 6 7

50 0 50 100 150 200 km
50 0 50 100 150 miles

F C. Reinga North C.
C. Maria van Diemen
Rangaunu B.
Houhora Heads Doubtless B.
Mangonui Whangaroa Harb.
Ahipara B. Kaitaia Okaihau B. of Islands
Tauroa Pt. Kaikohe C. Brett
Rawene Opua

PACIFIC
OCEAN

Hokianga Harbour Hikurangi
Whangarei
Donnelly's Crossing Whangarei Harb.
Bream Hd.
Dargaville Waipu Bream B.

Little Barrier I.

Warkworth C. Rodney Great Barrier I.
Kaipara Harbour C. Colville
Helensville Hauraki Cuvier I.
Gulf
Takapuna Devonport Coromandel
G Manukau **AUCKLAND** Whitianga
Papakura Thames
North Waiuku Pukekohe
Mercer Waihi Mayor I.
Island Waikato Paeroa Tauranga Harb.
Huntly Te Aroha Mount
Morrinsville Maunganui Bay of Plenty
Hamilton Tauranga
Raglan Cambridge Te Puke Whakatane Opotiki East C.
Kawhia Harbour Te Awamutu Raukumara Ra. Mt. Hikurangi
Putaruru Rotorua 1753
Otorohanga Tokoroa Kinleith Kaingaroa Taneatua Waipiro
Mokau Te Kuiti Mokai Wairakei Murupara Motu
TASMAN Forest Ongarue L. Taupo Tolaga Bay
Wairakei Ormond
Mokau Taumarunui L. Taupo Waikaremoana Gisborne
SEA North Taranaki Turangi Poverty Bay
Bight Whangamomona Nuhaka
Waitara Kaimanawa Mts. Tarawera Waikokopu
New Plymouth Ruapehu Mahia Pen.
H Inglewood 2797 Waiou Bay
Mt. Egmont 2518 Stratford Ohakune View Hawke Bay
C. Egmont Eltham Raetihi Waiouru Napier
Opunake Kapuni Taihape Ruahine Ra. Hastings
Hawera Waverley Mangaweka C. Kidnappers
South Taranaki Patea Marton Hunterville Waipawa
Bight Wanganui Halcombe Feilding Waipukurau
Bulls Dannevirke
Palmerston Woodville
J North Foxton Pahiatua
C. Farewell Shannon C. Turnagain
Collingwood Golden Levin Eketahuna
Takaka B. D'Urville I. Paraparaumu Masterton
Tasman Tasman Otaki Carterton
Karamea Mts. B. Kapiti I. Upper Hutt Greytown
Karamea Motueka Pelorus Sd. Petone Martinborough
Bight Nelson Havelock Picton Lower Hutt Wairarapa
Seddonville Richmond **WELLINGTON**
Granity Matiri Ra. Wakefield Blenheim Eastbourne
Westport Lyell Murchison Seddon Cook
Inangahua Ward Strait 6 7
Junction Rotoroa 2885 Mt. Tapuaenuku
K Reefton Mt. Travers 2338 Kaikoura **SAMOA ISLANDS**
Blackball Grey Spenser Clarence 1:12 000 000
Runanga Mts. Hanmer Kaikoura
Greymouth Stillwater Springs WESTERN AMERICAN
Kumara Lewis Waiau SAMOA SAMOA
South Hokitika Pass Culverden A
Ross L. Brunner Jacksons Hurunui Savai'i Apia
Island Arthur's Waikari Waipara Upolu Pago Pago
Abut Hd. Pass Oxford Pegasus Bay Tutuila West from
Rangiora Kaiapoi 12 13 14 Greenwich
Calderdale New Brighton B
Mt. Cook Springfield **Christchurch** 5 8 9 Futuna 10 11
3753 Whitecliffs Riccarton Wallis & Futuna (Fr.)
Methven Lincoln Lyttelton
L Staveley Banks Pen. B
Jackson B. Akaroa Niuafo'ou
Okuru Little River Thikombia (Tonga)
Mt. Lambasa
Aspiring Fairlie Temuka Vanua Levu
3027 Ohau Timaru FIJI C
Mt. L. St. Andrews Taveuni
Milford Sd. Earnslaw Wanaka L. Ysawa Group Koro
Bligh Sound 2818 Wanaka Waimate Lautoka 1323 Levuka TONGA
George Sound Kurow Nandi Ovalau (Friendly Is.)
Queenstown Arrowtown Ngapara Viti Levu Gau
Cromwell Oamaru Suva Koro Sea Lakemba Vava'u
Secretary I. Wakatipu Alexandra Maheno Moala D
Doubtful Sd. Clyde Hampden Kandavu Vatoa Tofua
Te Anau Kingston Roxburgh Dunback
L. Garvie Palmerston 7 East from Greenwich 8
Breaksea Sd. Manapouri Mts. Umbrella Waikouaiti **FIJI AND TONGA**
Resolution I. Mts. Port Chalmers **ISLANDS**
Dusky Sd. Southland Otago Mosgiel Otago Harbour 1:12 000 000 Tongatapu E
Poteriteri Edievale Lawrence Saunders C. 50 0 50 100 150 200 km Nuku'alofa
Clifden Nightcaps Tapanui Fairfield **Dunedin** 50 0 50 100 150 miles
Tuatapere Ohai Milton 9 10 11
Te Waewae B. Hedgehope Winton Balclutha
M Orepuki Gore Clinton Kaitangata
Riverton Mataura Kelso Nugget Pt.
Invercargill Wyndham Owaka
Bluff Ruapuke I. Tokanui Tahakopa
Foveaux Str.
Halfmoon Bay
Stewart I.
Port Pegasus
Southwest C.

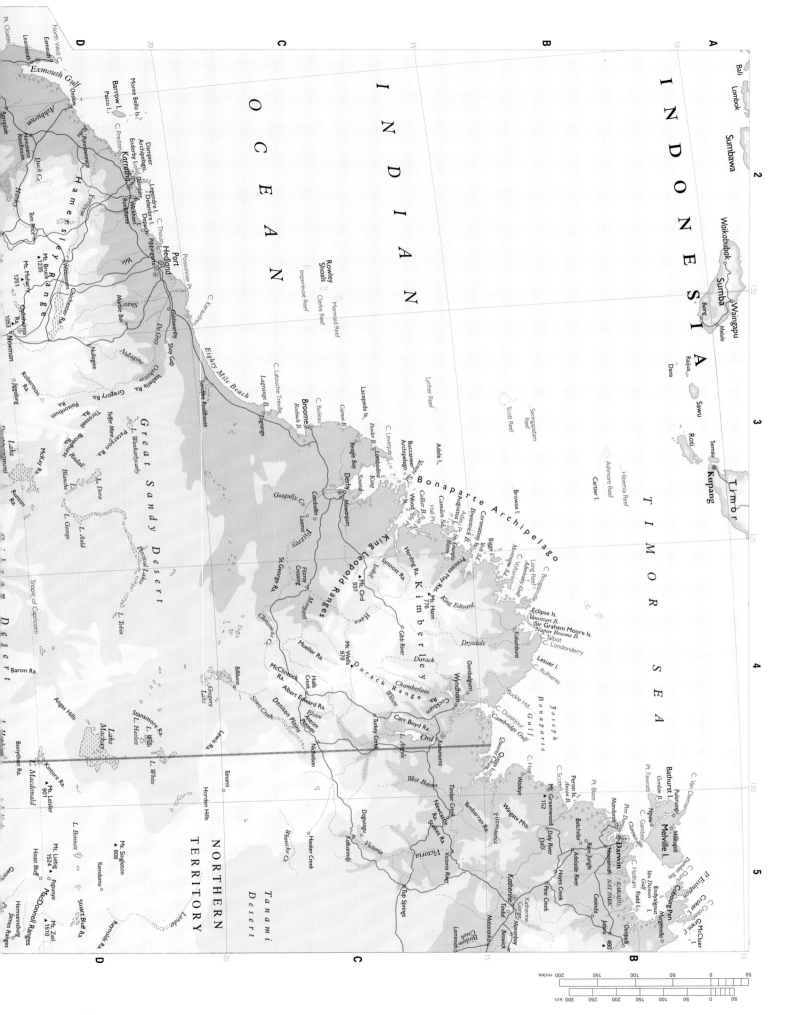

INDONESIA

Bali

Lombok

Sumbawa

Waikabubak

Sumba

Waingapu

Melolo

Baing

Dana

Rajua

Sawu

Roti

Semau

Kupang

Timor

T I M O R   S E A

Joseph Bonaparte Gulf

I N D I A N

O C E A N

Rowley Shoals

Mermaid Reef

Clerke Reef

Imperieuse Reef

Scott Reef

Serinngapatam Reef

Ashmore Reef

Hibernia Reef

Cartier I.

Browse I.

Lynher Reef

Bonaparte Archipelago

King Leopold Ranges

Kimberley

Exmouth Gulf

Onslow

Barrow I.

Pasco I.

Monte Bello Is.

Karratha

Dampier Archipelago

Port Hedland

Broome

Eighty Mile Beach

Derby

Great Sandy Desert

Tropic of Capricorn

Newman

Hamersley Range

Chichester Ra.

Great Victoria Desert

NORTHERN TERRITORY

Tanami Desert

Darwin

Melville I.

Bathurst I.

Katherine

MacDonnell Ranges

Mt. Zeil 1510

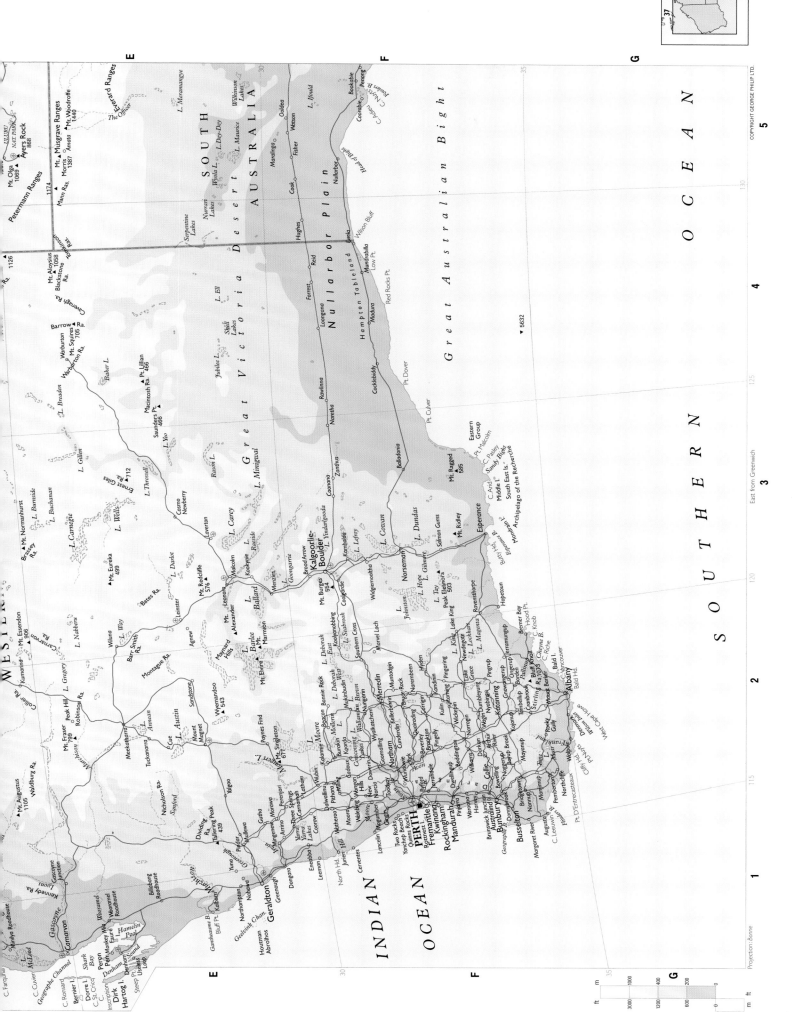

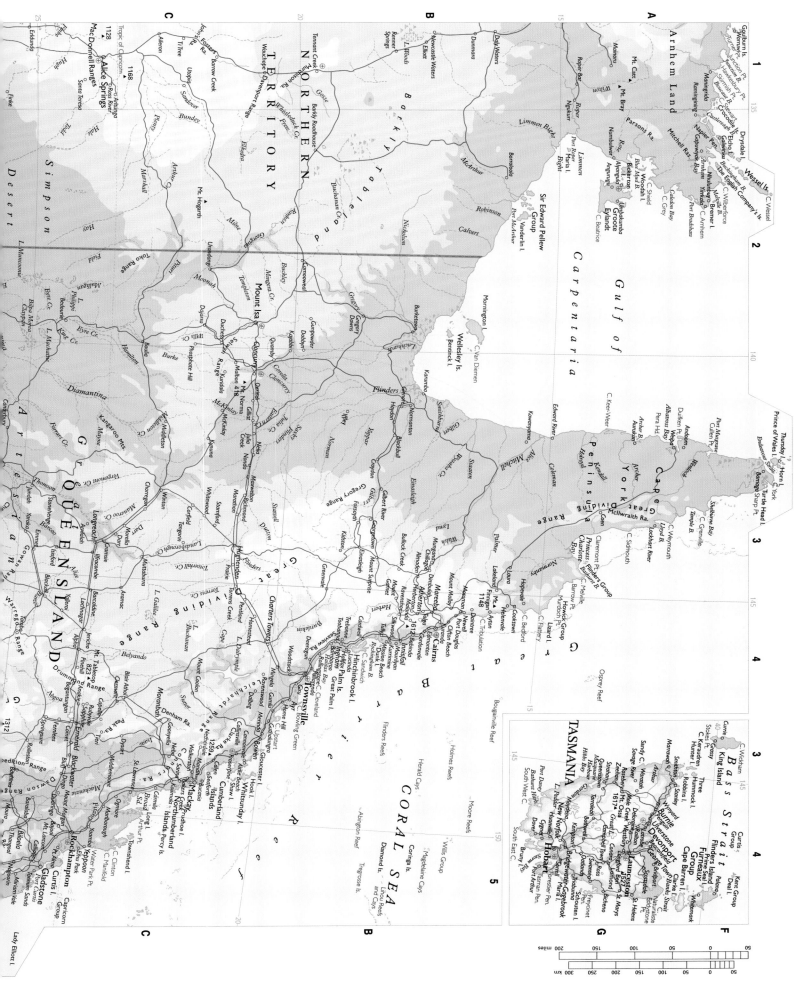

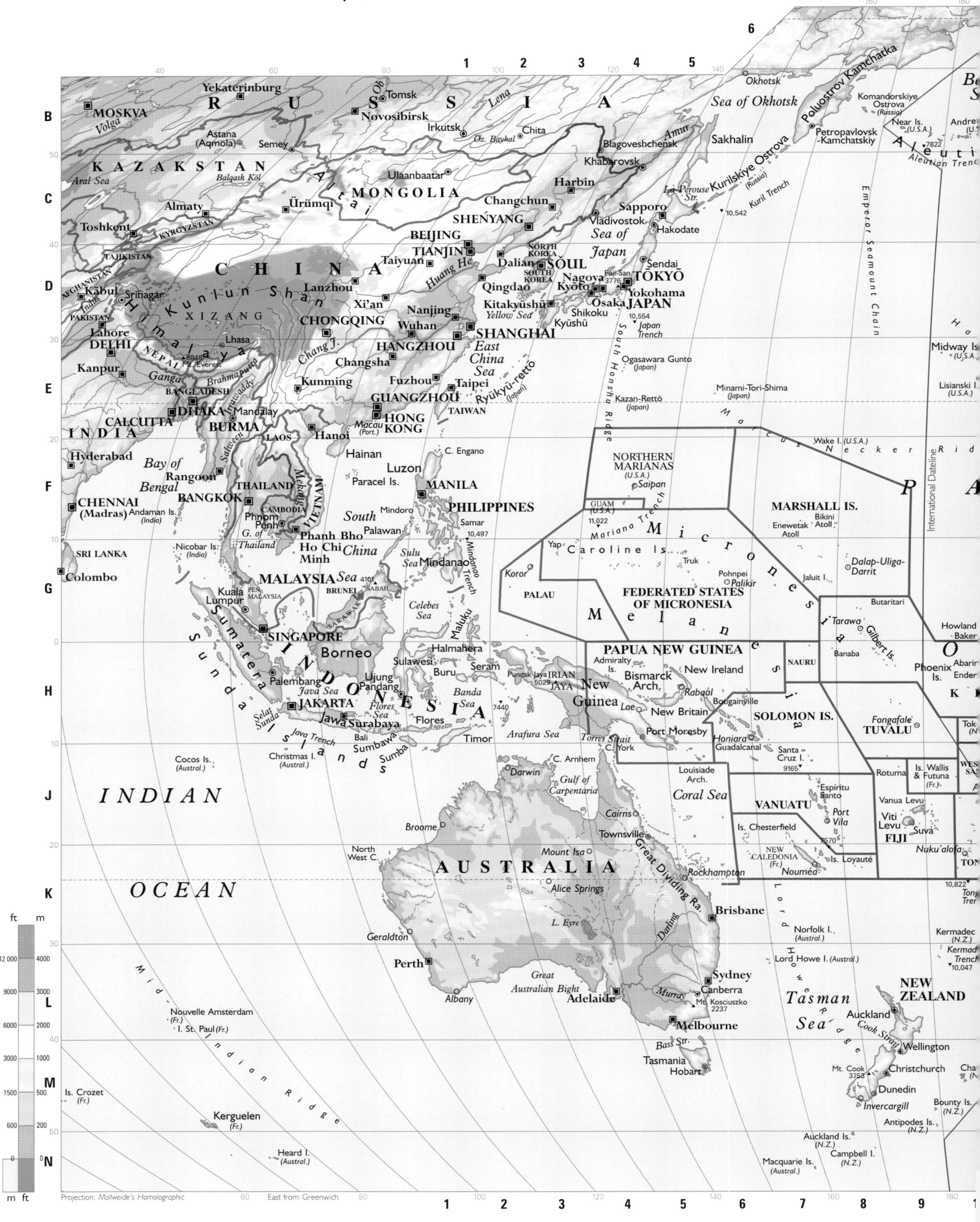

B

MOSKVA
Volga
Yekaterinburg
Tomsk
R U S S I A
Okhotsk
Sea of Okhotsk
Poluostrov Kamchatka
Be
Komandorskiye
Ostrova
(Russia)
Near Is.
(U.S.A.)
Andre
U.S.

Astana
(Aqmola)
Semey
Novosibirsk
Irkutsk
Oz. Baykal
Chita
Amur
Sakhalin
Petropavlovsk
-Kamchatskiy
7822
Aleutian Trench
Aleutia

K A Z A K S T A N
Aral Sea
Balqash Köl
Ulaanbaatar
M O N G O L I A
Blagoveshchensk
Khabarovsk
Kurilskiye Ostrova
(Russia)
La Perouse
Str.
10,542
Kuril Trench

C

Almaty
Ürümqi
Changchun
Harbin
SHENYANG
Vladivostok
Sapporo
Hakodate
Emperor Seamount Chain

Toshkent
KYRGYZSTAN
BEIJING
TIANJIN
Taiyuan
Dalian
NORTH
KOREA
SOUTH
KOREA
SÖUL
Sendai
Sea of
Japan

TAJIKISTAN
C H I N A
Lanzhou
Huang He
Qingdao
Kyoto
Osaka
Nagoya
Fuji-San
3776
TOKYO
Yokohama
JAPAN

D

AFGHANISTAN
Kabul
Srinagar
Indus
Kunlun Shan
XIZANG
Xi'an
Nanjing
Wuhan
Yellow Sea
Kitakyūshū
Shikoku
Kyūshū
10,554
Japan
Trench
South Honshu Ridge

PAKISTAN
Lahore
DELHI
Himalaya
Lhasa
+8848
Mt. Everest
CHONGQING
HANGZHOU
SHANGHAI
East
China
Sea
Ogasawara Gunto
(Japan)

Kanpur
NEPAL
Ganga
Brahmaputra
Chang J.
Changsha
Fuzhou
Taipei
Ryukyu-retto
(Japan)
Minami-Tori-Shima
(Japan)
Midway Is
(U.S.A.)

E

Hyderabad
BANGLADESH
DHAKA
Mandalay
Kunming
GUANGZHOU
HONG
KONG
Macau
(Port.)
TAIWAN
Kazan-Rettō
(Japan)
Lisianski I.
(U.S.A.)

CALCUTTA
I N D I A
Irrawaddy
BURMA
Salween
LAOS
Hanoi
Hainan
C. Engano
P

Bay of
Bengal
Rangoon
THAILAND
Mekong
Luzon
Paracel Is.
NORTHERN
MARIANAS
(U.S.A.)
Wake I. (U.S.A.)
Necker
A

F

CHENNAI
(Madras)
Andaman Is.
(India)
BANGKOK
CAMBODIA
Phnom
Penh
MANILA
PHILIPPINES
Saipan
MARSHALL IS.

SRI LANKA
Nicobar Is.
(India)
G. of
Thailand
Phanh Bho
Ho Chi
Minh
South
China
Sea
Mindoro
Samar
Palawan
10,497
GUAM
(U.S.A.)
11,022
Mariana Trench
Yap
Caroline Is.
Micronesia
Truk
Enewetak
Atoll
Bikini
Atoll
M

Colombo
MALAYSIA
Sulu
Sea
Mindanao
Mindanao Trench
Koror
Jaluit I.
Dalap-Uliga-
Darrit

G

Kuala
Lumpur
PEN.
MALAYSIA
Sea 4101
Celebes
Sea
PALAU
FEDERATED STATES
OF MICRONESIA
Pohnpei
Palikir
Butaritari

SINGAPORE
Borneo
SARAWAK
BRUNEI
SABAH
Sulawesi
Halmahera
Seram
Buru
Maluku
Melanesia
Tarawa
Banaba
Gilbert Is.
Howland
Baker
O

H

Palembang
Java Sea
I N D O N E S I A
Ujung
Pandang
Banda
Sea
Puncak Jaya
5029
IRIAN
JAYA
New
Guinea
Admiralty
Is.
Bismarck
Arch.
New Ireland
PAPUA NEW GUINEA
NAURU
Phoenix
Is.
Abarin
Ender
K

JAKARTA
Surabaya
Jawa
Bali
Flores
Sea
Flores
Banda
Sea
7440
Rabaul
New Britain
Lae
Bougainville
SOLOMON IS.
Fongafale
TUVALU
Tok
(N

J

Cocos Is.
(Austral.)
Christmas I.
(Austral.)
Java Trench
Sumbawa
Sumba
Timor
Arafura Sea
Torres Strait
C. York
Port Moresby
Honiara
Guadalcanal
Santa
Cruz I.
9165
Rotuma
Is. Wallis
& Futuna
(Fr.)
WES
SA

Selat
Sunda
Sunda Strait
Sumatera
INDIAN
Darwin
C. Arnhem
Gulf of
Carpentaria
Coral Sea
Louisiade
Arch.
Espiritu
Santo
VANUATU
Vanua Levu
Viti
Levu
Suva
Nuku'alofa
TON

Broome
North
West C.
Cairns
Townsville
Is. Chesterfield
Port
Vila
7570
FIJI

K

OCEAN
Mount Isa
NEW
CALEDONIA
(Fr.)
Rockhampton
Nouméa
Is. Loyauté
10,822
Tong
Trer

Alice Springs
A U S T R A L I A
L. Eyre
Brisbane
Norfolk I.
(Austral.)
Kermadec
(N.Z.)
Kermad
Trenc
10,047

L

Geraldton
Great
Australian Bight
Lord Howe I. (Austral.)
NEW
ZEALAND

Perth
Sydney
Canberra
Murray
Mt. Kosciuszko
2237
Tasman
Sea
Auckland
Cook Strait

Albany
Adelaide
Melbourne
Wellington

Nouvelle Amsterdam
(Fr.)
I. St. Paul (Fr.)
Bass Str.
Mt. Cook
3753
Christchurch
Cha

M

Is. Crozet
(Fr.)
Tasmania
Hobart
Dunedin
Bounty Is.
(N.Z.)

Kerguelen
(Fr.)
Invercargill
Antipodes Is.
(N.Z.)

Heard I.
(Austral.)
Auckland Is.
(N.Z.)
Campbell I.
(N.Z.)
Macquarie Is.
(Austral.)

N

Mid-Indian Ridge

ft	m
12 000	4000
9000	3000
6000	2000
3000	1000
1500	500
600	200
0	0
m	ft

Projection: Mollweide's Homolographic
East from Greenwich

Arctic Circle

ALASKA
(U.S.A.)
Anchorage

Bristol Bay

Gulf of Alaska

Prince of Wales I.
(U.S.A.) Prince Rupert
Queen Charlotte Is.
(Canada)

15

B A T I

C A N A D A

Edmonton
Calgary
Vancouver
Vancouver I. Victoria
Seattle
Portland
Boise

ROCKY Mts

Regina
Winnipeg
L. Winnipeg

Newfoundland

N O R T H

St. Lawrence
Québec
Montréal
Ottawa
Toronto
Detroit
Buffalo
Boston
St. John's

B

C

NEW YORK CITY
PHILADELPHIA
Baltimore
Washington D.C.

A T L A N T I C

D

Salt Lake City
Denver
Kansas City

CHICAGO
Pittsburgh
Cincinnati

San Francisco
Sacramento

4418

UNITED STATES

LOS ANGELES
San Diego

Phoenix

Oklahoma City
Memphis

Dallas

Atlanta

C. Hatteras

Jacksonville

Bermuda
(U.K.)

Sargasso Sea

E

Ciudad
Juárez

Houston
San Antonio

New
Orleans

Monterrey

Gulf of Mexico

Miami

BAHAMAS

O C E A N

Guadalupe
(Mex.)

Tropic of Cancer

C. San Lucas

Golfo de California

La Habana

Florida Str.

C U B A

West Indies

Honolulu
Oahu
HAWAIIAN IS.
(U.S.A.)
Hawaii

4205

Is. Revilla Gigedo
(Mex.)

Guadalajara
Puebla
MEXICO

Acapulco

Mérida

7680

9200
HAITI
DOMINICAN REP.
PUERTO
RICO
(U.S.A.)

Leeward
Is.

F

BELIZE
GUATEMALA
Guatemala
San Salvador
EL SALVADOR

JAMAICA
Kingston

HONDURAS
NICARAGUA
Managua

Caribbean Sea

BARBADOS
Windward Is.

I. Clipperton
(Fr.)

San José
COSTA
RICA
PANAMA

Barranquilla

Colón Panamá

Maracaibo

Caracas
Orinoco

VENEZUELA

G

Palmyra Is.
(U.S.A.)

West Christmas Ridge

Teraina
Tabuaeran
Kiritimati

Jarvis I.
(U.S.A.)

Equator

I. del Coco
(Costa Rica)

Medellín

I. de Malpelo
(Colombia)

Cali
COLOMBIA

Bogotá

Galápagos
(Ecuador)

Quito
ECUADOR

Guayaquil

Iquitos

C. Paliñas

Amazonas

BRAZIL

H

Malden I.
Starbuck I.

Tongareva
Pukapuka Manihiki

Vostok I.

Caroline I.

Flint I.

Is. Marquises

Trujillo

6369

PERU

LIMA

Cuzco
Arequipa

L. Titicaca

Nevada Ancohuma
6550

J

Suwarrow Is
Cook Is.
(N.Z.)

Is. de la
Société
Papeete Tahiti

FRENCH POLYNESIA

Is. Tuamotu

6866
Peru-

Arica

La Paz
BOLIVIA

Rarotonga

Is. Tubuai

Mururoa

Rapa

Tropic of Capricorn

Ducie I.

Pitcairn I.
(U.K.)

Sala-y-Gómez
(Chile)

San Félix
(Chile)

San Ambrosio
(Chile)

Iquique
Chile
Antofagasta

8050
Trench

PARAGUAY

San Miguel
de Tucumán

Asunción

K

I. de Pascua
(Chile)

Córdoba
Aconcagua
6960
Valparaíso
SANTIAGO

Arch. de
Juan Fernández
(Chile)

Rosario
BUENOS
AIRES

Porto
Alegre

URUGUAY
Montevideo
Río de la Plata

L

Concepción

ARGENTINA

SOUTH

Chile Rise

Patagonia

A T L A N T I C

M

Pacific-Antarctic Ridge

6212

O C E A N

Falkland Is.
(U.K.)

Punta Arenas
Est. de Magallanes
Tierra del Fuego

South Georgia
(U.K.)

N

C. de Hornos

West from Greenwich

COPYRIGHT GEORGE PHILIP LTD.

100 0 200 400 600 800 1000 1200 1400 km
100 0 200 400 600 800 1000 miles

A B B

ARCTIC OCEAN

Asia

Greenland

C. Dezhneva
St. Lawrence I.
Bering Strait
C. Prince of Wales
Barrow Pt.
Nunivak I.
Bering Sea
Brooks Ra.
Porcupine
Yukon
Mt. McKinley
Alaska Range
Alaska
Alaska Peninsula
Mt. S. Elias 5489
Mt. Logan 5959
Kodiak I.
Gulf of Alaska
Alexander Archipelago
Queen Charlotte Islands
Skeena
Stikine
Mt. Waddington 3994
Queen Charlotte Str.
Vancouver I.
Juan de Fuca Str.
C. Flattery
Mt. Rainier 4392
Columbia
Cascade Range
Coast Ranges
C. Blanco
C. Mendocino
Mt. Shasta 4317
Sierra Nevada
Sacramento
San Joaquin
Mt. Whitney 4418
Death Valley 86
Great Basin
Great Salt Lake
Snake
Fraser
Selkirk Mts.
Mt. Robson 3954
Rocky Mountains
Liard
Peace
Athabasca
L. Athabasca
Saskatchewan
Mackenzie Mts.
Mackenzie
Great Bear L.
Great Slave L.
Arctic Circle
Dubawnt
Back
Reindeer L.
Churchill
Nelson
L. Winnipeg
Missouri
Platte
Wasatch Ra.
Mt. Elbert 4399
Blanca Peak 4378
Grand Canyon
Colorado Plateau
Colorado
Gila
Arkansas
Red
Ozark Plateau
Mississippi
Ohio
Missouri

Beaufort Sea
Axel Heiberg I.
Sverdrup Is.
Parry Is.
M'Clure Strait
Melville I.
Banks I.
Victoria I.
Queen Elizabeth Is.
Bathurst
Devon I.
Viscount Melville Sd.
Prince of Wales
Somerset
Lancaster Sd.
Bylot I.
Ellesmere I.
Kane Basin
Gulf of Boothia
Boothia Pen.
Melville Pen.
Foxe Basin
Foxe Channel
Southampton I.
Baffin Bay
Baffin Island
Disko I.
Davis Strait
Cumberland Sd.
Frobisher B.
C. Chidley
Hudson Strait
C. Wolstenholme
Ungava Peninsula
Henrietta Maria
Belcher Is.
James Bay
Eastmain
Hudson Bay
Coast of Labrador
Laurentian Plateau
Hamilton Inlet
St. Lawrence
Gulf of St. Lawrence
Newfoundland
Str. of Belle Isle
C. Race
Cape Breton I.
Nova Scotia
Pt. Edward
Sable I.
B. of Fundy
C. Sable
Great Lakes
L. Superior
L. Michigan
L. Huron
L. Ontario
L. Erie
Niagara Falls
Mt. Washington 1917
C. Cod
Nantucket I.
Long I.
Hudson
Allegheny Mts.
Cumberland Plateau
Tennessee
Appalachian Mts.
Blue Ridge Mts.
Alabama
C. Charles
Chesapeake B.
C. Hatteras

Petermann's Peak 2940
Mt. Forel 3360
Denmark Strait
Iceland
Cape Farewell
Labrador Sea

NORTH ATLANTIC OCEAN
Sargasso Sea
Bermuda
Bahamas

PACIFIC OCEAN

Guadalupe
Lower California
Gulf of California
Western Sierra Madre
Mexican Plateau
Eastern Sierra Madre
Tropic of Cancer
Clarion Fracture Zone
C. San Lucas
C. Corrientes
Revilla Gigedo Is.
Santiago
Balsas
Popocatepetl 5452
Citlaltepetl 5700
Isthmus of Tehuantepec
Rio Grande
Mississippi River Delta
Gulf of Mexico
Gulf of Campeche
Yucatan Channel
Yucatán Peninsula
Cuba
Greater Antilles
Jamaica
Cayman Trough
Yucatan Basin
G. of Honduras
G. Gracias a Dios
Coco
Caribbean Sea
Colombian Basin
Florida
Florida Strait
Hispaniola
G. de Tehuantepec
Guatemala Trench
Central America
G. de Venezuela
Sierra Nevada de Santa Marta 5800
L. Maracaibo
Cord. de Mérida
Andes
Magdalena
G. of Darién
G. of Panamá

West from Greenwich

ft m
9000 3000
6000 2000
3000 1000
1500 500
600 200
0 0
m ft

Projection: Bonne

7 8 9 10 11 12

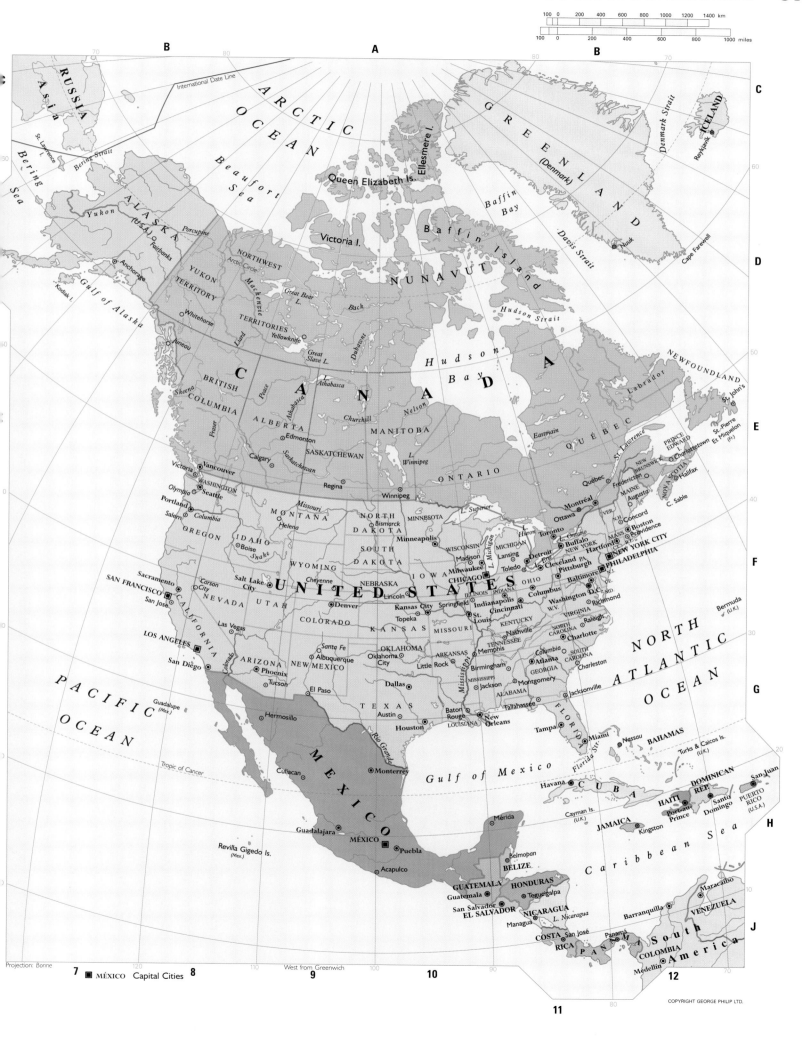

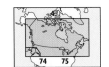

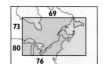

COPYRIGHT GEORGE PHILIP LTD.

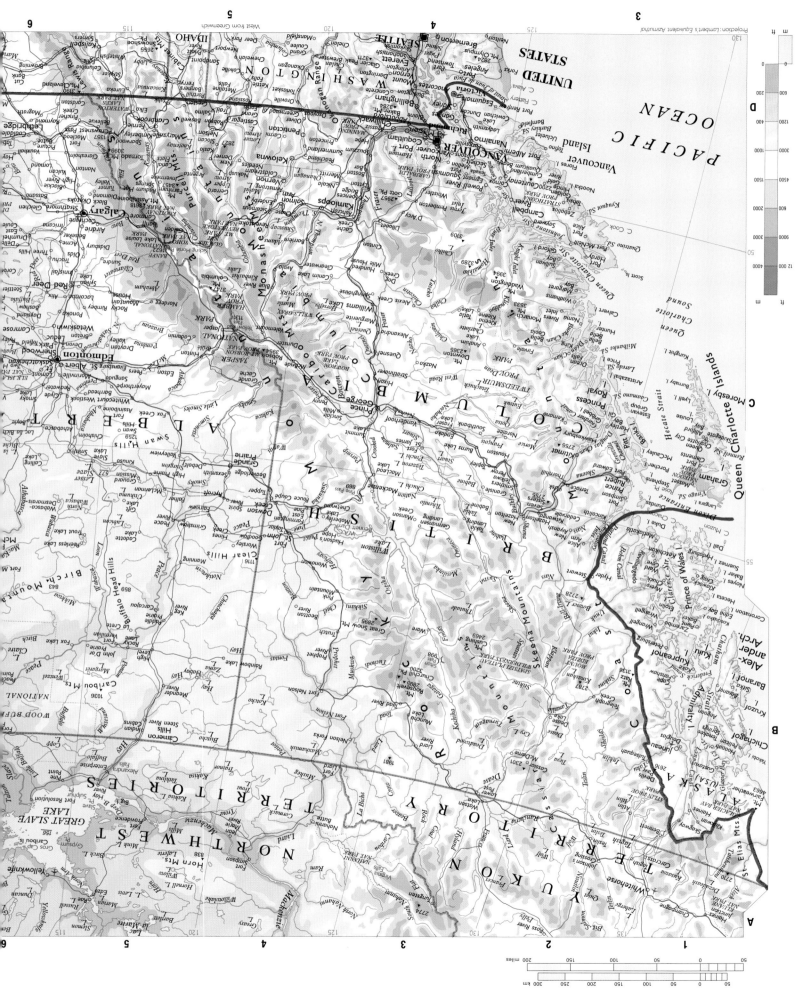

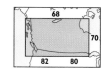

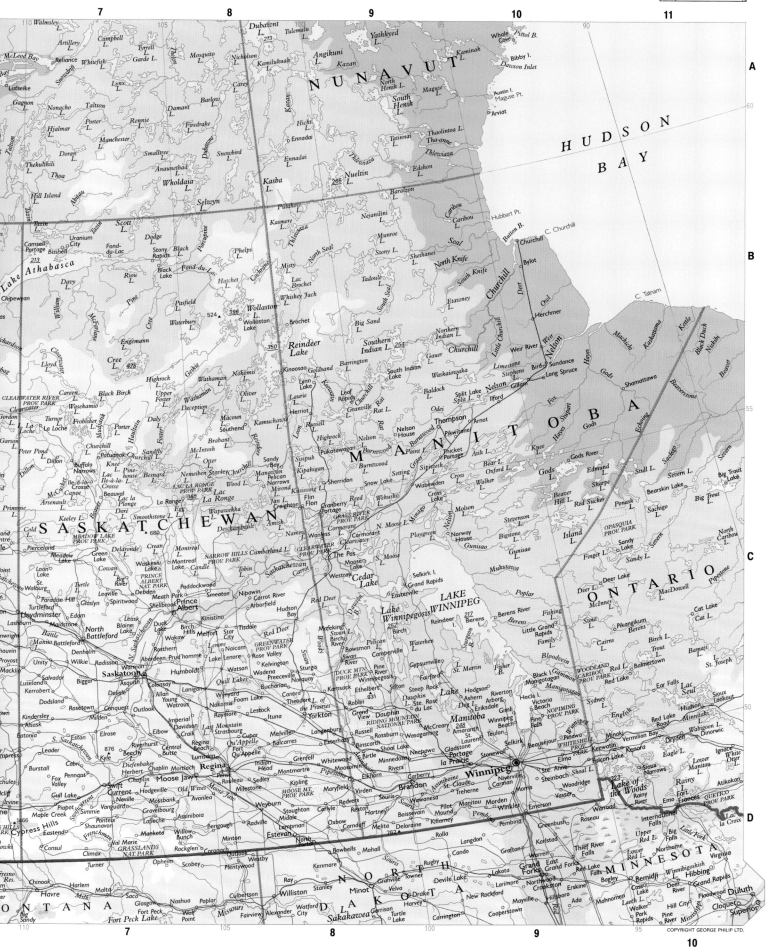

100   0   100   200   300   400   500 km
100   0   50   100   150   200   250   300   350 miles

1   2   3   4   5   6

BRITISH COLUMBIA   Mt. Assiniboine 3618   **C A**   Calgary   Kindersley   Saskatoon

Vancouver I.   VANCOUVER   Kelowna   Selkirk Mts.   Mt. 3457   High River   Red Deer   Winnipegosis   **M A N**

Str. of Georgia   Chilliwack   Lower Arrow Lake   Penticton   Nelson   Swift Current   Moose Jaw   Yorkton   Assiniboine   L. Manitoba

C. Flattery   Victoria   Bellingham   Grand Forks   Trail   Cranbrook 1396   Crowsnest Pass   Lethbridge   Medicine Hat   Regina   Moosomin   Neepaw   Dauphin

Mt. Olympus 2428   Puget Sd.   Everett   Spokane   Sandpoint   GLACIER NAT. PARK   Shelby   Milk   Glasgow   Weyburn   Estevan   Brandon   La M

Bremerton   SEATTLE   Wenatchee   Coeur d'Alene   Oreille L.   Flathead Lake   Havre   Milk   Minot   She

Tacoma   Olympia   Ellensburg   Moses Lake   Kellogg   Missoula   Great Falls   Missouri   Fort Peck L.   L. Sakakawea   Mandan   Bismarck

C. Disappointment   Aberdeen   **W A S H I N G T O N**   Yakima   Moscow   Clark Fork   Helena   Big Belt Mts. 2897   Lewistown   **N O R T H   D A K O**   Jamestown

Astoria   Centralia 4392   Mt. St. Helens   Mt. Rainier 2550   Pullman   **M O N T A N A**   Musselshell   Dickinson

C. Foulweather   PORTLAND   McMinnville   Vancouver   Walla Walla   Anaconda   Butte   Bozeman   Livingston   Billings   Mobridge   Lake Oahe

Salem   Mt. Hood 3424   The Dalles   Pendleton   La Grande   Salmon 3112   YELLOWSTONE NATIONAL PARK   Sheridan   Buffalo   Grand   Moreau

Corvallis   Albany   John Day   Blue Mountains 2712   Baker City   Salmon   Absaroka Range   Cody   Bighorn Mts. 4013   Gillette   Black Hills 2207   Rapid City   **S O U T H   D A K O**

Eugene   Springfield   Bend   Burns   Salmon River 3152   Hyndman Peak   Rexburg 4009   Grand Teton 4197   Thermopolis   Pierre   Lake Francis Case

Coos Bay   **O R E G O N**   Harney L.   Ontario   Payette   Boise   Sun Valley   Hailey   Idaho Falls   Gannett Peak 4207   Wind River Range   Riverton   Casper   Chadron   Badlands   White   Mitch

C. Blanco   Roseburg   Malheur L.   Caldwell   Nampa   **I D A H O**   Mountain Home   Pocatello   Montpelier   Bear L.   Wind River   Rawlins   Pathfinder Reservoir   Niobrara   Valentine   O'Neill

Grants Pass   Medford   Upper Klamath L.   Summer L.   Twin Falls   Burley   Rupert   Preston   Logan   **W Y O M I N G**   3131   Laramie Mts.   Scottsbluff   North Platte   **N E B R A S K**

Yreka   Klamath Falls   Goose L.   L. Albert   Winnemucca   Humboldt   Elko   Brigham City 1282   Great Salt Lake   Ogden   Evanston   Green River   Rock Springs   Laramie   Cheyenne   Sidney   North Platte

Mt. Shasta 2498 Pit.   4317   Franklin L.   Ruby Mts.   Great Salt Lake   SALT LAKE CITY 3117   Craig   Fort Collins   Greeley   Sterling   Kearney   Island

Redding   Lassen Pk. 3187   Red Bluff   Honey L.   Pyramid L.   Reese   Reno   Sparks   Carson Sink   Ely 3982   Sevier   Sandy 4123   Orem   Provo   Uinta Mts.   White   4345   Boulder   Aurora   **C O L O R A D O**   North Platte   Republican

Pt. Arena   Ukiah   Chico   Yuba City   L. Tahoe   Carson City   Walker Lake   Hawthorne   Wheeler Pk. L.   Nephi   Price   Vail   DENVER   McCook

SACRAMENTO   Santa Rosa   Napa   Roseville   **N E V A D A**   Tonopah   Richfield   3710   **U T A H**   Grand Junction   Montrose   Aspen 4399   Pikes Pk. 4301   Colorado Springs   Burlington   **K A N**   Smoky Hill   Hays   Great Bend

SAN FRANCISCO   Oakland   Stockton   Modesto   YOSEMITE NATIONAL PARK   Merced   4342   White Mts.   Cedar City   Colorado   Maab   Mt. Elbert 4399   Pueblo   Salida   Canon City   Lamar   Garden City   Dodge City   Pratt

Santa Cruz   San Jose   Salinas   Fresno   Mt. Whitney 4418   St. George   Page   Cortez   Durango   San Juan Mts. 4054   Alamosa   Blanca Pk. 4372   Walsenburg   Trinidad   La Junta   Liberal   North Canadian

Monterey   1597   Visalia   Owens L.   -86   Las Vegas   Lake Mead   Lake Powell   GRAND CANYON NATIONAL PARK   Farmington   Chuska Mts. 2989   Raton   Dalhart   Perryton

Santa Maria   Paso Robles   Tulare   Bakersfield   Ridgecrest   Henderson   Hoover Dam   Grand Canyon   Humphreys Peak 3851   Los Alamos   Santa Fe   Taos   Canadian

San Luis Obispo   Hanford   **C A L I F O R N I A**   Death Valley   Bullhead City   Kingman   Flagstaff   Gallup   Mt. Taylor 1445   Las Vegas   Tucumcari   Amarillo   Pampa   Clinton   El R

Santa Barbara   Pt. Conception   Barstow   Mojave Desert   Lake Havasu City   Prescott   Verde   Payson   Winslow   San Jose   ALBUQUERQUE   Vaughn   Borger   **O K**   Na

Glendale   Pasadena 3506   San Bernardino   Lake Havasu   **A R I Z O N A**   Baldy Pk. 3476   **N E W   M E X I C O**   Clovis   Clinton   Chickash   Lawton   Wich

LOS ANGELES   Long Beach   Anaheim   Santa Ana   Riverside   Oceanside   Salton Sea -71   Glendale   PHOENIX   Mesa   Globe   Gila   Socorro   Rio Grande   Vaughn   Roswell   Llano   Plainview   Vernon   Childress   Brazos

SAN DIEGO   El Centro   Yuma   **Sonoran Desert**   Casa Grande   Safford   Silver City   Elephant Butte Res.   Sierra Blanca Peak 3659   Alamogordo   Estacado   Lubbock   Sweetwater   Mineral Wel   Fort W

Tijuana   Mexicali   Sonoyta   Tucson   Nogales   Las Cruces   Sacramento Mts. 2730   Hobbs   Carlsbad   Lamesa   Abilene

Ensenada   **B A J A**   San Felipe 3078   **S O N O R A**   Nogales   Douglas   Ciudad Juárez   El Paso   Pecos   Midland   Big Spring   Colorado   San Angelo   Brown

San Quintín   **C A L I F O R N I A**   Caborca   Agua Prieta   Sierra   Pecos   Odessa

Pta. Baja   Sebastián Vizcaíno   I. Ángel de la Guarda   Magdalena   Ojinaga   Presidio   Alpine   Fort Stockton   **E d w a r d s   P l a t e a u**   Aus

Guadalupe (Mex.)   Bahía Sebastián Vizcaíno   I. Tiburón   Hermosillo   **C H I H U A H U A**   Rio Grande   Del Rio   San Marc

I. Cedros   Pta. Eugenia   **B A J A   CALIFORNIA   SUR**   Santa Rosalía   Guaymas   Ciudad Acuña   Uvalde   Ant

Kauai   Kapaa   Oahu   Santa Rosalía   Bolsón de   Chihuahua   Cuauhtémoc   Piedras Negras   Eagle Pass

Niihau   Kaula   Kauai Channel   Wahiawa   Kaneohe   Loreto   Ciudad Obregón   Delicias   **C O A H U I L A**   Nuevo   Laredo Ch

H   PACIFIC OCEAN   Pearl City   HONOLULU   Kaunakakai   Molokai   Lanai   Maui   Navojoa   Los Mochis   Hidalgo del Parral   Jiménez   Sabinas   Monclova   Kingsvi   Falcon Lake

HAWAII 1:10 000 000   Kaholaywe   Kihei   Wailuku   Hawaiian   Mauna Kea 4205   Mauna Loa 4169   Hilo   El Fuerte   Fuerte   **M É X I C O**   Mapimí de   Sabinas Hidalgo   Ho

Kona   Kilauea 4169   **J**   Islands   Kamuela   Mountain View   Pahala   Topolobampo   **D U R A N G O**   Torreón   Monterrey   Matam

Projection: Albers' Equal Area with two standard parallels   West from Greenwich

15   16   17   4   5   6

12 000   4000   9000   3000   6000   2000   4500   1500   3000   1000   1200   400   600   200   0   0
ft   m

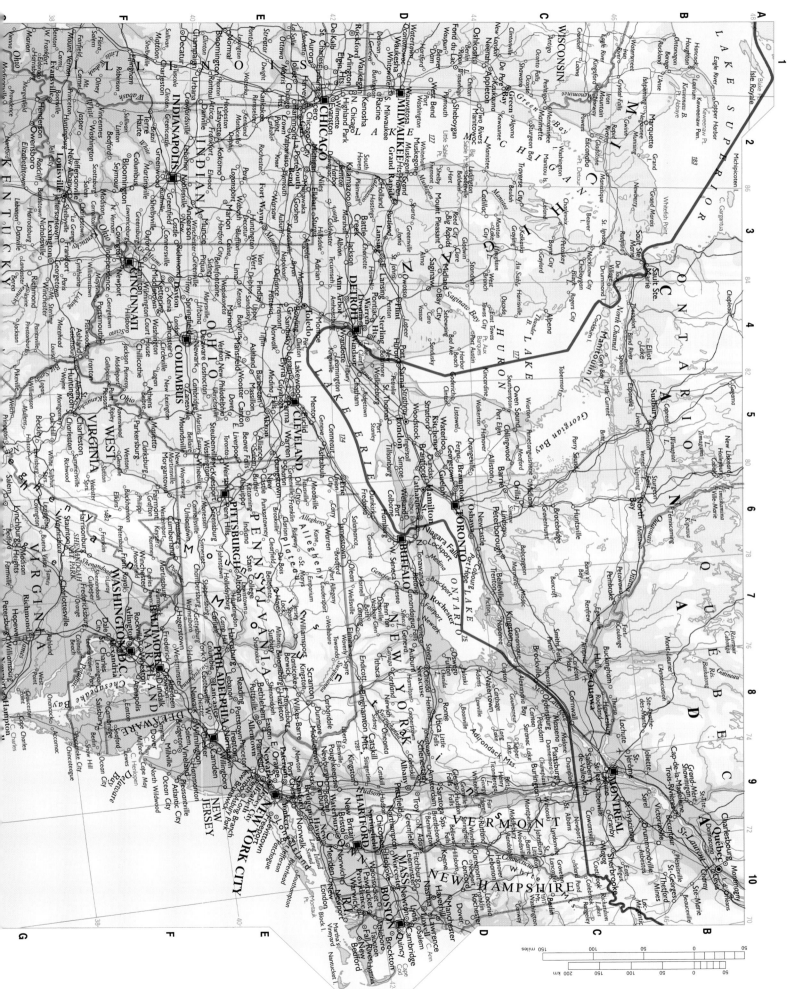

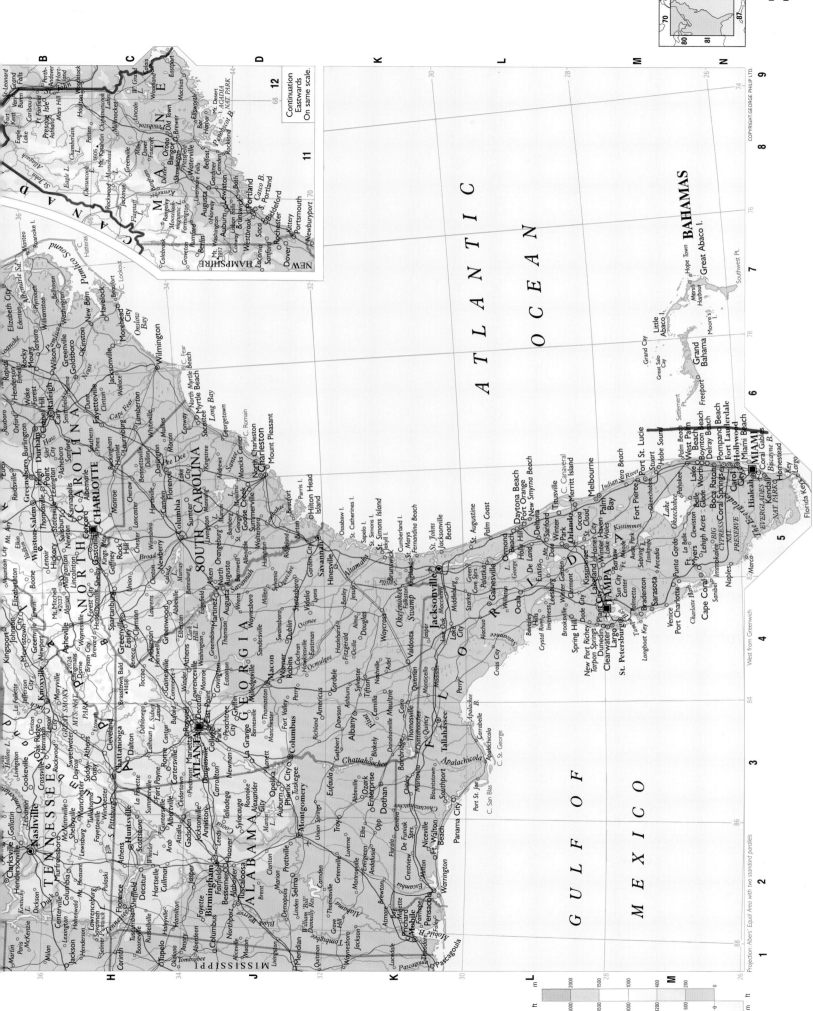

ATLANTIC

OCEAN

GULF OF

MEXICO

BAHAMAS

MAINE

NEW HAMPSHIRE

NORTH CAROLINA

SOUTH CAROLINA

GEORGIA

FLORIDA

ALABAMA

TENNESSEE

MISSISSIPPI

CANADA

Continuation Eastwards
On same scale.

Projection: Albers' Equal Area with two standard parallels

West from Greenwich

COPYRIGHT GEORGE PHILIP LTD.

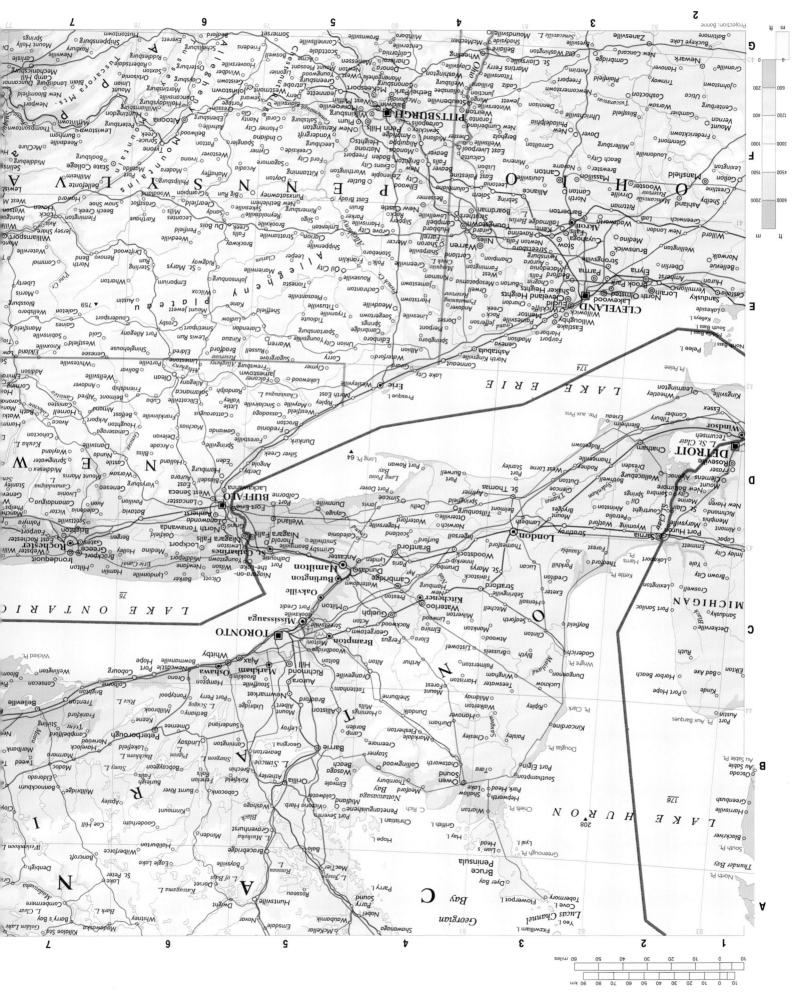

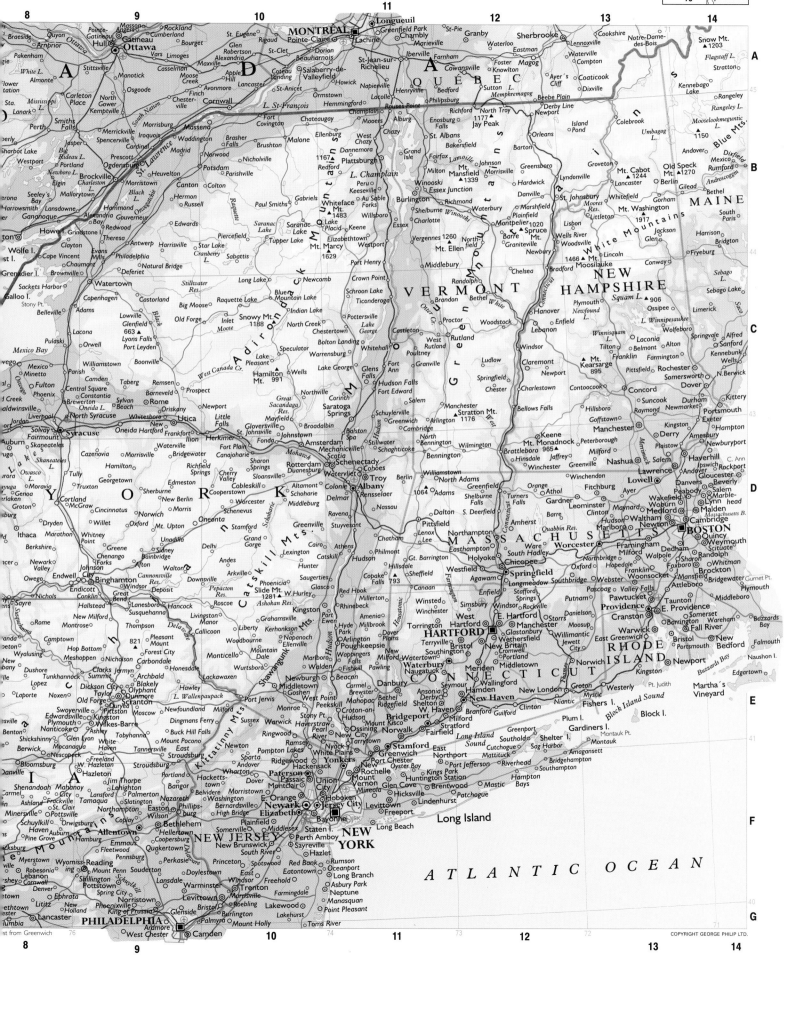

TENNESSEE

MISSISSIPPI

ARKANSAS

LOUISIANA

OKLAHOMA

TEXAS

NEW MEXICO

MEXICO

COAHUILA

CHIHUAHUA

GULF OF MEXICO

Memphis

NEW ORLEANS

Baton Rouge

DALLAS

Fort Worth

HOUSTON

SAN ANTONIO

Austin

Corpus Christi

Oklahoma City

Tulsa

Wichita

Amarillo

Lubbock

Midland

Odessa

El Paso

Laredo

Nuevo Laredo

Shreveport

Little Rock

Waco

Rio Grande

Rio Bravo del Norte

Pecos

Edwards Plateau

Stockton Plateau

Llano Estacado

Boston Mts.

Ouachita Mts.

Balcones Escarpment

BIG BEND NATIONAL PARK

CARLSBAD CAVERNS NAT. PARK

GUADALUPE MTS. NAT. PARK

Laguna Madre

Padre I.

Projection: Albers' Equal Area with two standard parallels

COPYRIGHT GEORGE PHILIP LTD.

Continuation Southwards on same scale

West from Greenwich

m ft
12 000
9000
6000
4500
3000
1500
600
400
200
0

ft
4000
3000
2000
1500
1000
400
200
0
m

Projection: Albers' Equal Area with two standard parallels

WESTERN WASHINGTON
REGION
On same scale

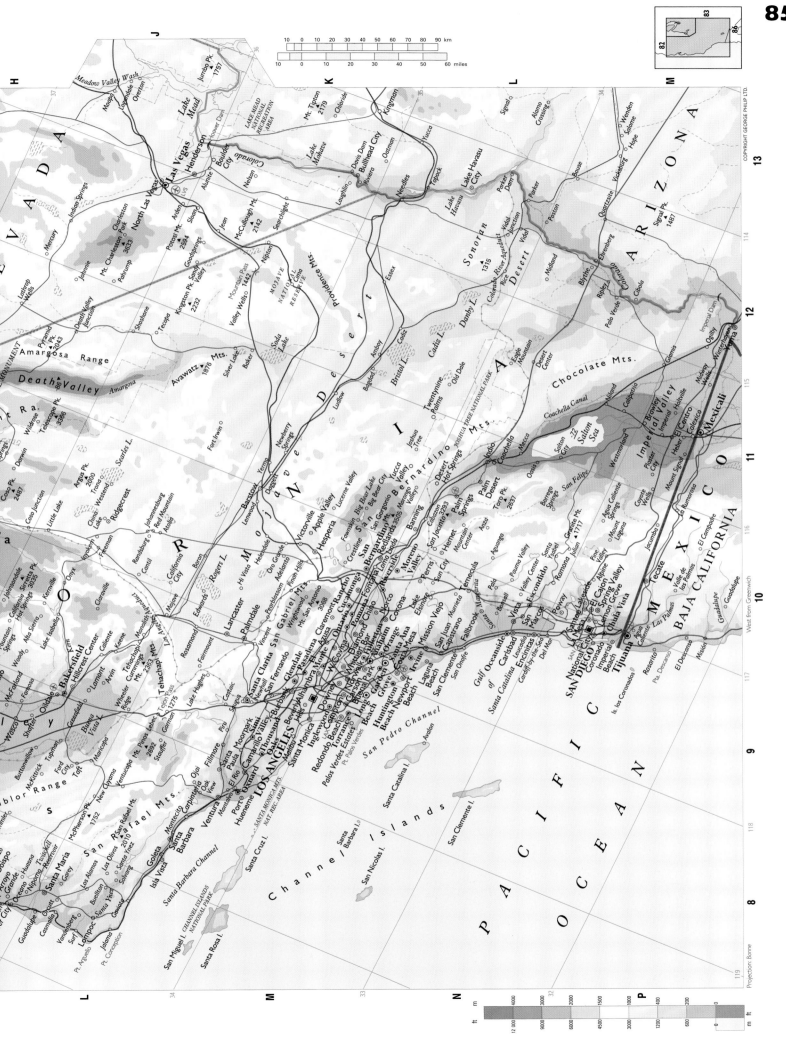

10 0 10 20 30 40 50 60 70 80 90 km

10 0 10 20 30 40 50 60 miles

J

H

K

L

M

13

12

11

10

9

8

N E V A D A

Meadow Valley Wash

Jumbo Pk. 1757

Lake Mead

LAKE MEAD
NATIONAL
RECREATION
AREA

Hoover Dam

Las Vegas

North Las Vegas

Henderson

Boulder City

Colorado

Mt. Tipton 2179

Chloride

Kingman

A R I Z O N A

Signal

Alamo Crossing

Wenden

Hope

Salome

Mt. Charleston Park 3633

McCullough Mt. 2142

Searchlight

Needles

Lake Havasu City

Parker Dam

Parker

Poston

Bouse

Quartzsite

Vicksburg

Ehrenberg

Signal Pk. 1487

M O J A V E

D E S E R T

S o n o r a n

D e s e r t

B A J A   C A L I F O R N I A

M E X I C O

Death Valley

Amargosa Range

Telescope Pk. 3366

Chocolate Mts.

Salton Sea

Imperial Valley

Mexicali

San Bernardino Mts.

JOSHUA TREE NATIONAL PARK

LOS ANGELES

San Diego

Tijuana

P A C I F I C

O C E A N

Channel Islands

CHANNEL ISLANDS
NATIONAL PARK

San Pedro Channel

Santa Catalina I.

San Clemente I.

San Nicolas I.

Santa Barbara I.

Santa Cruz I.

Santa Rosa I.

San Miguel I.

Gulf of
Santa Catalina

N

P

m   ft
12 000
9000
6000
4500
3000
1200
600
0

ft   m
4000
3000
2000
1500
1000
400
200
0

West from Greenwich

Projection Bonne

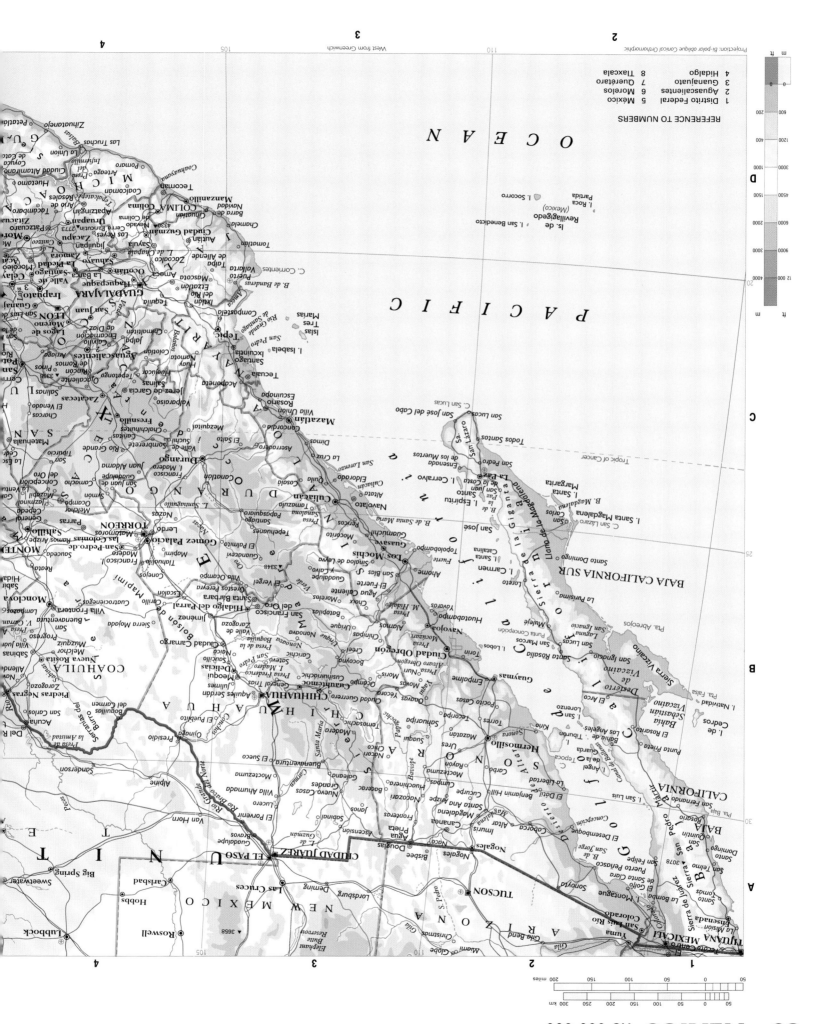

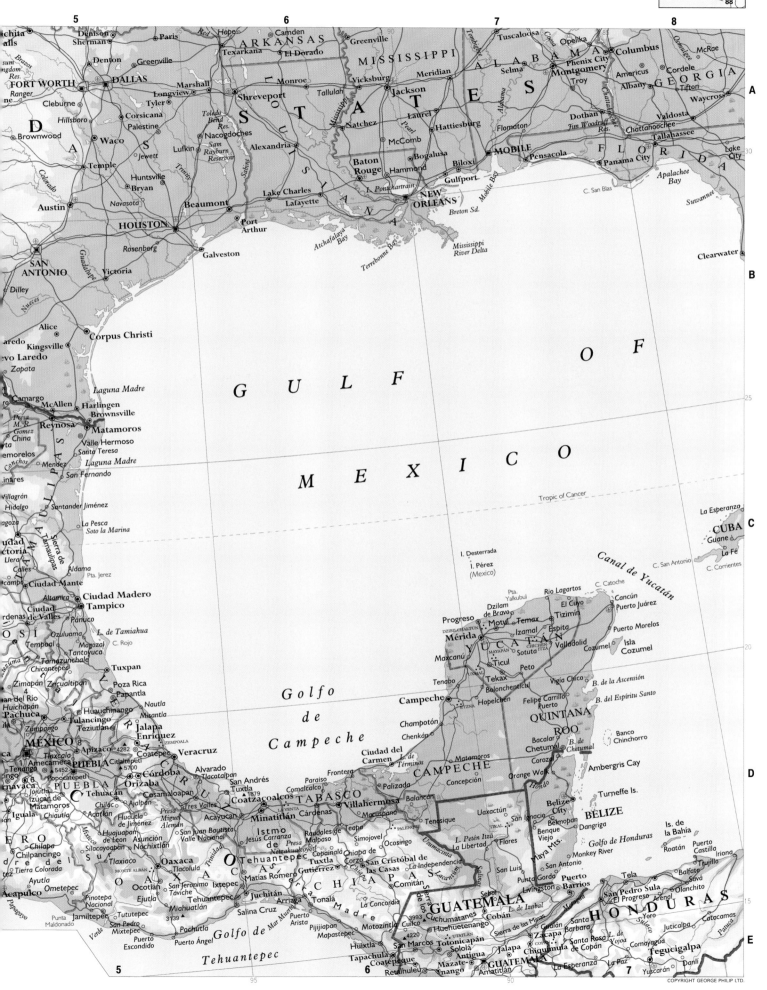

87
92 93

50 0 50 100 150 200 250 300 km
50 0 50 100 150 200 miles

5 **6** **7** **8**

A
75 70 65 60 25

A T L A N T I C

's Town
e Bight
Cat I.   San Salvador I.

Conception I.
Rum Cay

Long I.

B
Clarence
Town   Samana Cay

Crooked I.   Plana Cays

Verde   Albert   Snug   Mayaguana I.
Town   Corner
Acklins I.
Mira por vos Cay   Turks & Caicos
Hogsty Reef   (U.K.)
Little Inagua I.   Caicos Is.   Turks Is.

O C E A N

Tropic of Cancer

Lake Rosa   Great   Turks Island
Matthew   Inagua I.   Passage
Town

Moa
Baracoa   Pta. de   Î. de la
Maisi   Tortue   Monte
ntanamo   Cristi   LA ISABELA   Puerto Rico Trench
Paso de los Vientos   Cap-   Puerto   Santiago de los Cabelleros
(Windward Passage)   Haïtien   Plata   San Francisco de Macorís   Milwaukee
Jean Rabel   Port-de-   Nagua   Deep
Cap-à-   Paix   Samana   9200
Foux   G. de la   Fort Liberté   La Vega   Sanchez   Virgin Gorda
St-Marc   Gonâve   Gonaives   Cord.   Sabana de la Mar   Anegada   Sombrero (U.K.)
20
Jérémie   Î. de la Gonâve   Hinche   Central   Hato Mayor   Bayamón SAN JUAN   Virgin Is.   Anegada
Î. de la Gonâve   **HAITI**   3175   C. Engaño   Arecibo   Carolina   St. Thomas   (U.K.)   Passage
DOMINICAN   1338   Tortola   Anguilla (U.K.)
e   PORT-   San Juan   **REP.**   San Pedro   Higuey   Aguadilla   Fajardo   Road Town   St.-Martin (Fr.)
Marie   **AU-PRINCE**   L. Enriquillo   de Macorís   B. de   Carolina   Charlotte   St. Maarten   St.-Barthélemy (Fr.)
C. Carcasse   Petit   2280   Azua   San Cristóbal   Yuma   Mayagüez   Ponce   Aguas   Amalie   (Neth.)   Saba (Neth.)
Massif de la Hotte   Goâve   **SANTO**   Cumabo   Isla   Guayama   Virgin Is.   St. Eustatius   Barbuda
A)   Les Cayes   Aquin   Jacmel   **DOMINGO**   San Cristóbal   Mona   (U.S.A.)   Christiansted   (Neth.)   **ANTIGUA**
Pointe-à- Gravois   Barahona   Compostela   (U.S.A.)   Frederiksted St. Croix   St. Kitts   **& BARBUDA**
Pedernales   **PUERTO**   **ST. KITTS**   St. John's
H i s p a n i o l a   I. Beata   **RICO**   Basseterre   **& NEVIS**   Antigua
C
I. Beata   C. Beata   (U.S.A.)   Nevis   Redonda
A n t i l l e s   Montserrat   Guadeloupe Passage
(U.K.)   Ste.-Rose   Le Moule
GUADELOUPE   La Désirade
GUADELOUPE
Basse-Terre   Pointe-à-Pitre
I. des Saintes   Marie-Galante   (Fr.)
(Fr.)   Grand-Bourg
I. de Aves   Portsmouth   Dominica Passage
(Venezuela)   Roseau   **DOMINICA**

B E A N   S E A
15
Martinique Passage
Mt. Pelée   Ste.-Marie
1397   Le François
Fort-de-   Rivière-Pilote
France   **MARTINIQUE**
St. Lucia Channel   (Fr.)
Castries   **ST. LUCIA**
Soufrière

St. Vincent Passage
La Soufrière 1234 **ST. VINCENT**   Speightstown
Bridgetown
Kingstown   **& THE**   **BARBADOS**
Grenadines

D
L e s s e r   Hillsborough   **GRENADINES**
Aruba   C. San Román   Bonaire   **GRENADA**
(Neth.)   Curaçao   St. George's   **GRENADA**   60
Willemstad   **NETH.**   A n t i l l e s
Pta. Gallinas   Pen. de   **ANTILLES**   I. Blanquilla (Ven.)
Paraguaná   I. Las Aves   I. Orchila   Is. Los Hermanos   John's Mouth   Tobago
C. San Román   (Ven.)   (Ven.)   (Ven.)   Is. Los Testigos   Scarborough
Riohacha   Pen. de la   Pta.   Is. Los Roques   (Ven.)   Port of   Galera
SANTA   Uribia   Guajira   Espada   Punto   (Ven.)   I. de Margarita   La Asunción   Spain   Point
MARTA   **GUAJIRA**   Fijo   Puerto   **NUEVA**   Porlamar   Trinidad
Golfo de   Cardón   **ESPARTA**   Río   Arima
RAN-   Ciénaga   Venezuela   Coro   La Vela de Coro   Caribe   Caribe   Río Claro
ILLA   Sierra Nevada de   Altagracia   **FALCÓN**   Maracay   Cumaná   Cariaco   Pen. de Paria   **TRINIDAD**
SANTA   Santa Marta   Mene de Mauroa   Tocuyo   Puerto   Maiquetía   **SUCRE**   Carúpano   Güira   **& TOBAGO**
noa   Soledad   5800   Cabello   **CARACAS**   C. Codera   San Fernando
TICO   Sabanalarga   La Concepción   Santa Rita   Baragua   San Felipe   **DISTRITO FEDERAL**   La Guaira   Higuerote   Puerto   G. de Paria   Serpent's Mouth
Fundación   Valledupar   Cabimas   Carora   **YARACUY**   Valencia   **ARAGUA**   Río Chico   La Cruz   Barcelona   Caripito
Calamar   Agustín   Villa del   Ciudad   **LARA**   **CARABOBO**   Los Teques   Barcelona   Maturín
MAGDALENA   Codazzi   Rosario   Ojeda   **BARQUISIMETO**   Yaritagua de   Cura   **MIRANDA**   Altagracia   **MONAGAS**
10
Plato   Machiques   Mene   los Morros   San Juan   **DELTA**
Zambrano   **CÉSAR**   Lago de   Grande   El Tocuyo   San Carlos   de los Morros de Orituco   Anaco   Tucupita
Mompós   Maracaibo   Betijoque   Acarigua   **COJEDES**   Aragua de   Cantaura
ZULIA   Trujillo   **PORTUGUESA**   El Baúl   Barcelona   El Tigre   **AMACURO**
El Banco   San Carlos   **TRUJILLO**   Valle de   Santa María   Los Barrancos
Magangué   Encontrados   del Zulia   Valera   Guanare   Portuguesa   Calabozo   la Pascua   de Ipire   Soledad   Ciudad Guayana
E
NORTE   **MÉRIDA**   Mérida   Barinas   **GUÁRICO**   El Pao   Sierra Imataca
DE   Cord.   **BARINAS**   Pariaguán   El Tigre   Upata
BOLÍVAR   SANTANDER   Santa   San Fernando   Ciudad
Simití   Cúcuta   **TÁCHIRA**   Bárbara   Ciudad   San Fernando de Apure   Ciudad Bolívar   Guasipati
Bolivia   **V E N E Z U E L A**   Mapire   El Callao
aucasia   Barrancos   Bruzual   Achaguas   Apure   Orinoco   Caicara   Embalse de Guri   Tumeremo

West from Greenwich
5 70 **6** 65 **7**
COPYRIGHT GEORGE PHILIP LTD

ft   m
12 000   4000
9000   3000
6000
4500   1500
3000   1000
1200   400
600   200
0   0
m   ft

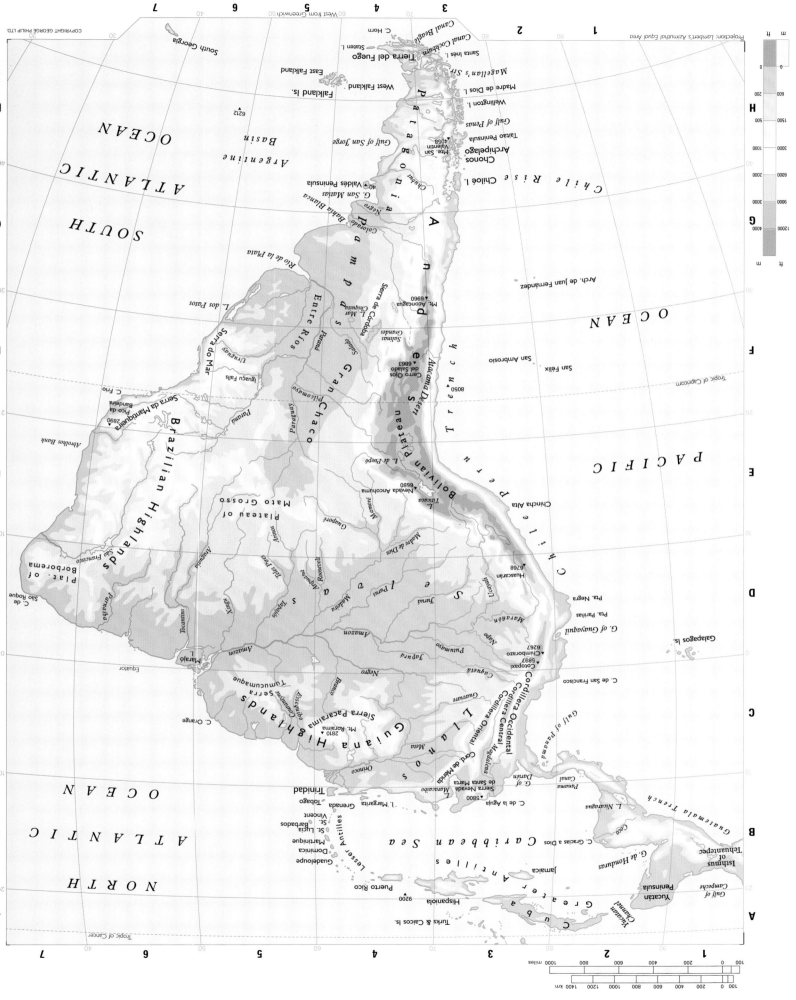

Projection: Lambert's Azimuthal Equal Area

100 0 200 400 600 800 1000 1200 1400 km
100 0 200 400 600 800 1000 miles

Tropic of Cancer

A

Havana BAHAMAS
C U B A Turks & Caicos Is. *(U.K.)*

Virgin Is. *(U.K.)*
HAITI DOMINICAN San Juan
Port-au- REP. PUERTO ST. KITTS ANTIGUA &
JAMAICA Kingston Prince RICO & NEVIS BARBUDA
(U.S.A.) Basse-Terre GUADELOUPE
DOMINICA *(Fr.)*
Fort-de-France MARTINIQUE
Castries *(Fr.)*
ST. VINCENT ST. LUCIA
Kingstown BARBADOS
GRENADA St. George's Bridgetown

N O R T H

MEXICO BELIZE
GUATEMALA HONDURAS
Guatemala Tegucigalpa *C a r i b b e a n S e a*
San Salvador NICARAGUA
EL SALVADOR
Managua COSTA San José
RICA Panamá G. of Barranquilla C. de Aruba Curaçao Port of TRINIDAD &
Darién Cartagena la Aguja Maracaibo Caracas Spain TOBAGO
P A N A M A Cúcuta Barquisimeto Valencia
Medellín San Cristóbal Orinoco Ciudad Guayana
Gulf of Panamá Bucaramanga VENEZUELA Georgetown Paramaribo
Cali Bogotá GUYANA Cayenne
SURINAM C. Orange
COLOMBIA RORAIMA FRENCH
GUIANA

A T L A N T I C

B

C

AMAPÁ
Galapagos Is. Quito Equator
(Ecuador) ECUADOR Marajó Belém
Guayaquil Napo I.
Putumayo Amazon São Luís
G. of Guayaquil Iquitos Manaus Santarém PARÁ
Marañón AMAZONAS MARANHÃO Fortaleza
Chiclayo Madeira Teresina C. de
Trujillo Juruá Purus Tapajós CEARÁ São Roque
Chimbote Pôrto Velho Xingu Tocantins RIO G. Natal
ACRE PARAÍBA DO NORTE
PERU RONDÔNIA B R A Z I L PIAUÍ Campina Grande
Callao LIMA Madre de Dios PERNAMBUCO Recife
Cuzco MATO GROSSO ALAGOAS Maceió
L. Mamoré SERGIPE
Titicaca Cuiabá Aracaju
Arequipa La Paz BOLIVIA GOIÁS Brasília B A H Í A Salvador
Cochabamba DIS. FED
Santa Cruz Goiânia
Sucre MINAS GERAIS
Iquique MATO GROSSO Belo ESPÍRITO
DO SUL Horizonte SANTO
Ribeirão Vitória
Antofagasta Salta PARAGUAY Prêto Juiz Campos
Pilcomayo Asunción Paraná SÃO PAULO de Fora R. DE J.
San Miguel PARANÁ SÃO Niterói
de Tucumán Resistencia Curitiba PAULO RIO DE
Salado Corrientes Uruguay JANEIRO
SANTA CATARINA
Córdoba RIO GRANDE
San Juan Santa Fe DO SUL Pôrto Alegre
Viña del Mar Mendoza Rosario Pelotas
Valparaíso Paraná URUGUAY
SANTIAGO BUENOS AIRES Montevideo
Talca La Plata Rio de la Plata
Concepción Bahía Mar del Plata
Colorado Blanca
Valdivia Negro Viedma
Puerto Montt
Chubut
Comodoro Rivadavia
Gulf of San Jorge

P A C I F I C

O C E A N

Tropic of Capricorn

San Félix *(Chile)*
San Ambrosio *(Chile)*

Arch. de Juan Fernández *(Chile)*

C H I L E A R G E N T I N A

Gulf of Penas

Magellan's Str.
Punta Arenas Tierra del Fuego
C. Horn

S O U T H

A T L A N T I C

O C E A N

West Falkland FALKLAND IS.
(U.K.)
Stanley
East Falkland

South Georgia
(U.K.)

D

E

F

G

H

Projection: Lambert's Azimuthal Equal Area

□ LIMA Capital Cities

West from Greenwich

COPYRIGHT GEORGE PHILIP LTD.

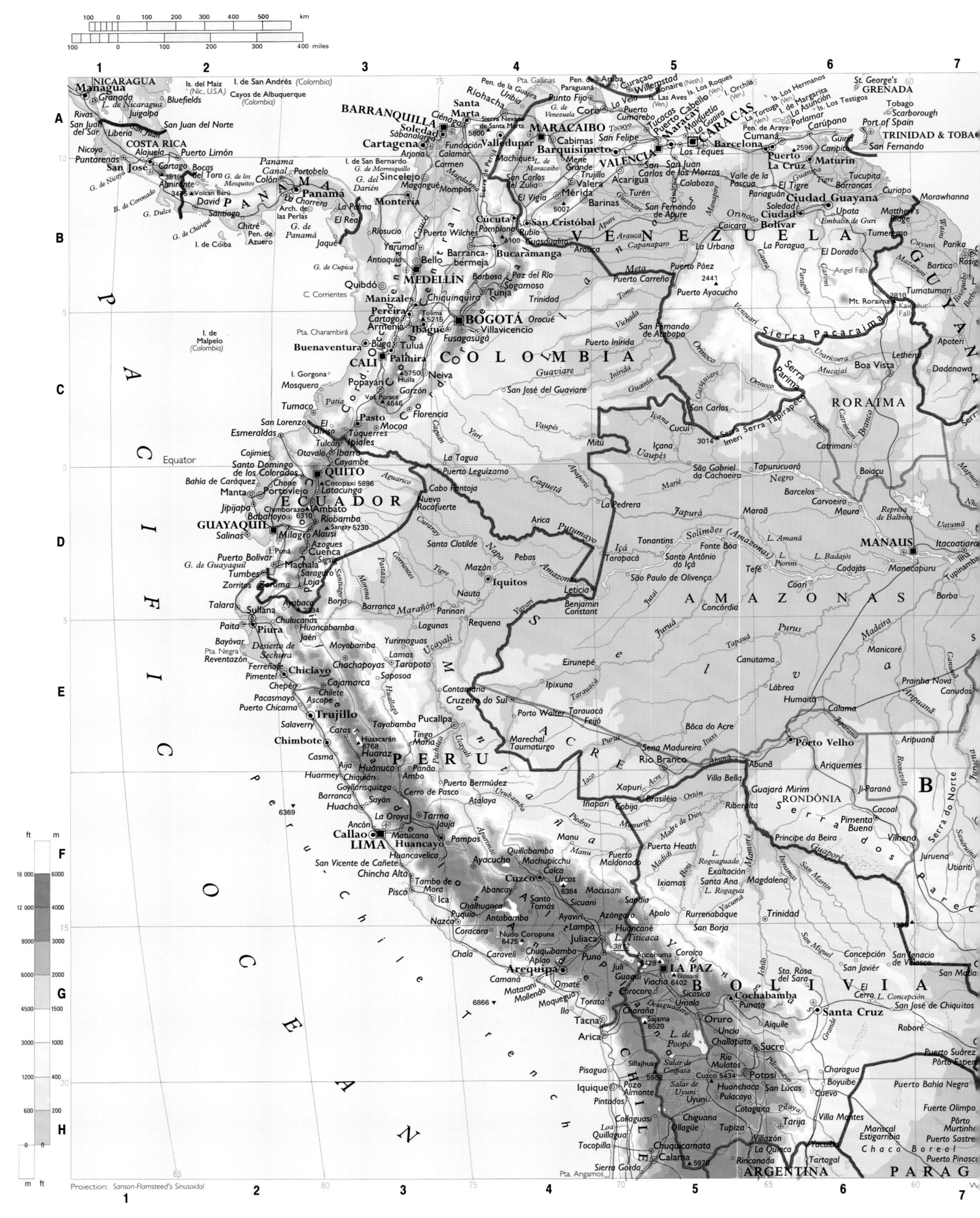

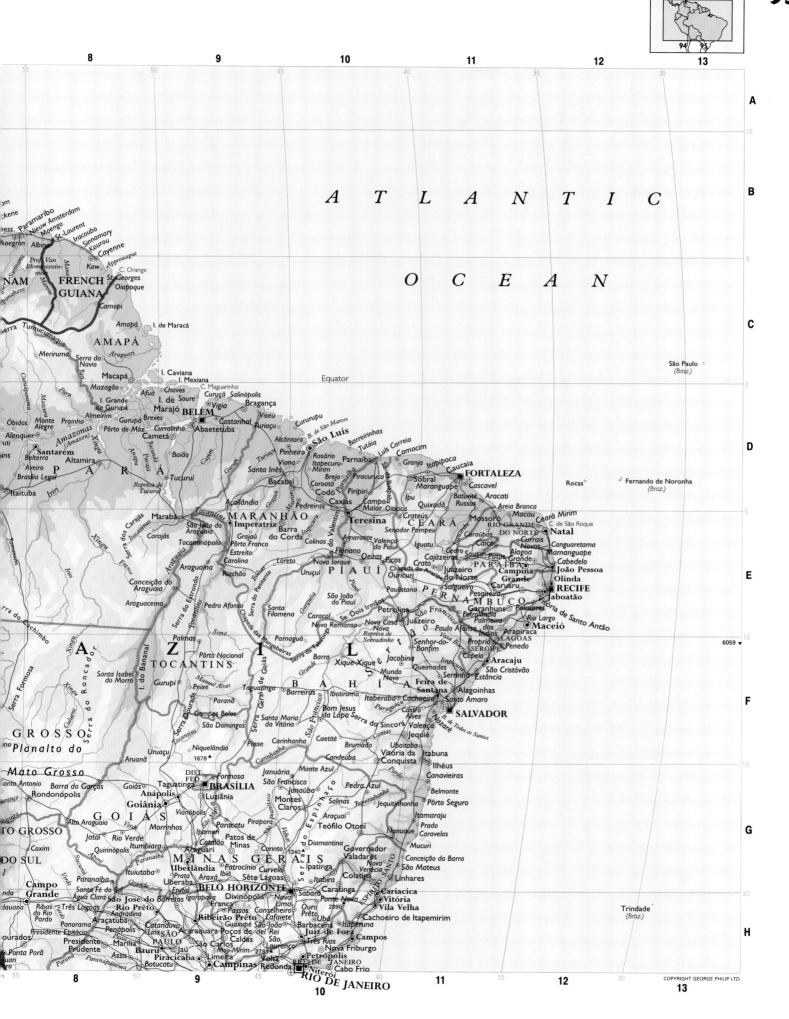

BELO HORIZONTE
Nova Lima
Itabirito

Vitória
Itaquari
Vila
Velha
Guarapari

MATO GROSSO
DO SUL

Maracaju
Nova Alvorada
do Sul

Três Lagoas
Xavantina
Mirandópolis
Panorama
Aguapeí

Andradina
Araçatuba
Birigui

Mirassol
São José
do Rio Prêto
Catanduva
Taquaritinga
Novo
Horizonte

Olímpia
Bebedouro
Jaboticabal
Pitangueiras

Batatais
Passos
São Sebastião
do Paraíso
Mococa

Represa de
Furnas

Conselheiro
Lafaiete
Congonhas

Oliveira
Campo Belo

Ouro
Prêto

Ponte Nova

Pico da
Bandeira
2880

Castelo
Cachoeiro
de Itapemirim

Sidrolândia
Nioaque
Dourados
Rio
Brilhante

Nova Andradina
do Sul

Adamantina
Santo
Anastácio
Tupã
Lins

Ribeirão
Prêto

Guaxupé

Três
Pontas
Alfenas
Casa
Branca

Varginha
Lavras
Barbacena

Santos
Dumont

Ubá
Muriaé
Carangola
Alegre

Itaperuna
Cambuci

CAMPOS

Dourados
Ponta Pora
Pedro Juan Caballero
Ivinhema
Euclides da
Cunha Paulista
Nova
Andradina
Presidente
Prudente
Martinópolis
Marília
Paraguaçu
Paulista
SÃO PAULO
Araraquara
Garça Bariri
São Carlos
Pocos de
Caldas
Pouso
Alegre
Juiz de Fora
Três
Rios
Leopoldina
Paraíba do Sul
RIO DE JANEIRO
Cabo de
São Tomé

Pôrto São José
Centenário do Sul
Paranavaí
Rancharia
Assis
Bauru
Jaú
Rio Claro
Limeira
Itajubá
2787
Serra
Cruzeiro
Volta
Redonda
Barra do Piraí
Nova Friburgo
Macaé

Amambaí
Navirai
Ivai
Nova
Esperança
Rolândia
Londrina
Santa Cruz
do Rio Pardo
Piracicaba
Americana
Ouro Fino
Mogi-Mirim
Guaratinguetá
Mansa
Barra
Angra dos
Reis
Cabo Frio
La. de Araruama

Capitán
Bado
Mundo Novo
Salto del Guaíra
Umuarama
Cianorte
Maringá
Apucarana
Araponga
Mandaguari
Campo
Mourão
Jaguariaíva
Itararé
Avaré
Botucatu
CAMPINAS
Itu
Jundiaí
Bragança
Paulista
Taubaté
Jacareí
NOVA IGUAÇU
DUQUE DE CAXIAS
SÃO GONÇALO
NITERÓI
RIO DE JANEIRO

Guaíra
Goio-Erê
Cândido de Abreu
Tibagi
Ibaiti
Joaquim
Távora
Itapetininga
SÃO PAULO
SANTO ANDRÉ
São Bernardo
do Campo
Moji das Cruzes
Ilha Grande
Bahia da Ilha Grande
Pta. de Juatinga

Tropic of Capricorn

ANIVEYU
Curuguaty
Porto Mendes
Toledo
Ubiratã
Cascavel
Sa. das Araras
Pitanga
Castro
Jaguariaíva
Itapeva
Itaporanga
Sorocaba
São José dos C.
Santos
São Vicente
Guarujá
Ilha de São Sebastião
Pta. de Boi

BRAZIL

PARANÁ

Represa de
Itaipu
Cat. del
Iguaçú

Medianeira
Cândido de Abreu
Guarapuava
Prudentópolis
Laranjeiras
do Sul
Irati
Palmeira
Ponta
Grossa
1889
CURITIBA
Antonina

Itararé
Paranapiacaba
Juquiá
Apiai
Registro
Iguape
Ilha Comprida
Ilha do Cardoso

Itanhaém

ALTO
Hernandarias
Oviedo
Ciudad
del Este
Irala
Foz do Iguaçu
Francisco
Beltrão
Bernardo
de Irigoyen
União da
Vitória
São Mateus
do Sul
Lapa
Rio Negro
Guaratuba
Matinhos
Paranaguá

PARANÁ
Eldorado
Chopim
Pato Branco
Sa. da Fartura
Porto União
São Francisco do Sul

PUÁ
Paraná
San
Pedro
Clevelândia
São Miguel
do Oeste
Palmas
Mafra
Joinville

MISIONES
Aguapeí
Corpus
Carnación
Monteagudo
Frederico
Westphalen
Xanxerê
1340
Caçador
Itajaí

Melaria
Obera
Uruguai
Chapecó
Joaçaba
Blumenau
Brusque

Leandro N. Alem
San
Javier
Erechim
Palmeira
das Missões
Campos
Novos
Santa Cecília
SANTA CATARINA
Curitibanos
Rio do Sul
São José
Ilha de Santa Catarina
Florianópolis

Santo Ângelo
Santa Rosa
Carazinho
Passo
Fundo
Lajes
São
Joaquim
1808

São
José de
Catarina

Santiago
RIO GRANDE
Cruz
Alta
Guaporé
Bento Gonçalves
Vacaria
Tubarão
Laguna
Cabo Santa Marta Grande

borja
Sa. do
Espinilho
Ijuí
Santa
Maria
Caxias do Sul
Criciúma
Araranguá

Santa Cruz
do Sul
Nôvo Hamburgo
Torres

DO SUL
Montenegro
São
Leopoldo
Taquara
Osorio

Santiago
Cachoeira do Sul
Canoas
Rio Pardo
PÔRTO ALEGRE
Viamão

egrete
do Sul
São
Gabriel
Caçapava
do Sul
Sa. Encantadas
Camaquã
Tapes

Santana do
Livramento
Dom Pedrito
Camaquã
São Lourenço
do Sul
Mostardas

overa
Santana
Bagé
Sa. do Camaquã
Canguçu

ATLANTIC

Pinheiro
Machado
Pelotas
Lagoa dos Patos

arembó
Fraile
Muerto
Gregorio
Melo
Jaguarão
São José do Norte
Rio Grande

Blanquillo
Cerro
Chato
Rio Branco
Mirim
Lagoa Mirim

arandí del Yi
Vergara
Treinta y Tres
Lagoa Mangueira

José Batlle
y Ordóñez
Lascano
Santa Vitória do Palmar
Chuy

OCEAN

Aigua
Castillos

Minas
Rocha
San Carlos
Maldonado

EVIDEO

5304

West from Greenwich

COPYRIGHT GEORGE PHILIP LTD

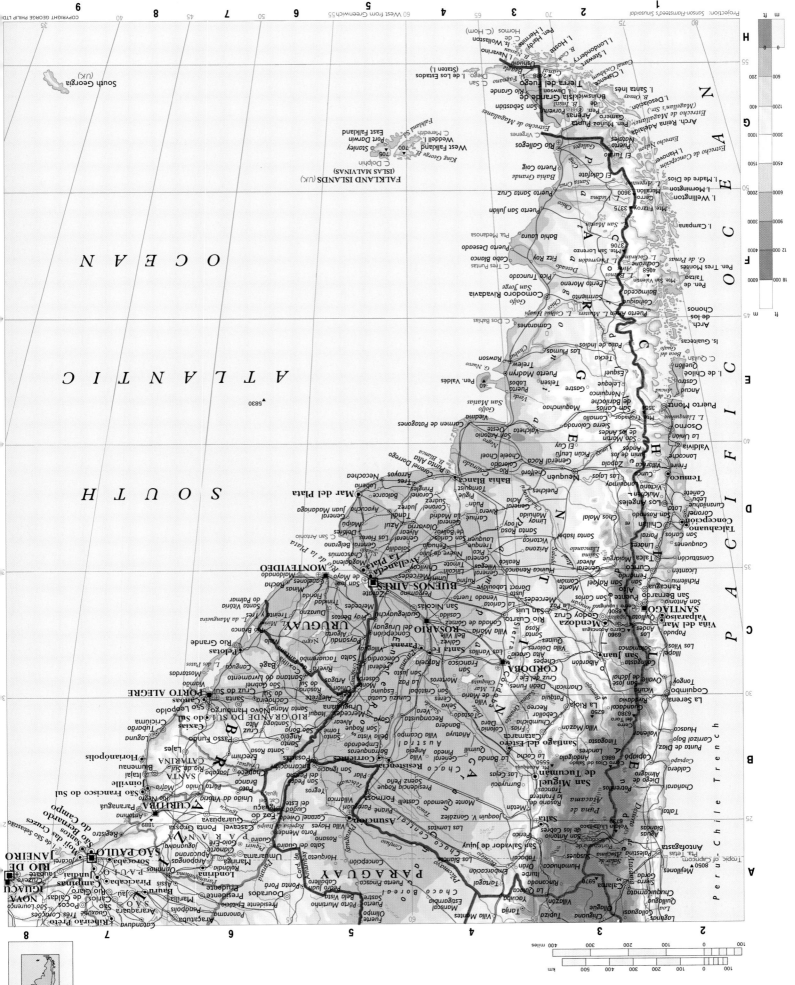

INDEX

The index contains the names of all the principal places and features shown on the World Maps. Each name is followed by an additional entry in italics giving the country or region within which it is located. The alphabetical order of names composed of two or more words is governed primarily by the first word and then by the second. This is an example of the rule:

Mīr Kūh, *Iran* . . . . **45 E8** 26 22N 58 55 E
Mīr Shahdād, *Iran* . . . . **45 E8** 26 15N 58 29 E
Mira, *Italy* . . . . **20 B5** 45 26N 12 8 E
Mira por vos Cay, *Bahamas* . **89 B5** 22 9N 74 30W
Miraj, *India* . . . . **40 L9** 16 50N 74 45 E

Physical features composed of a proper name (Erie) and a description (Lake) are positioned alphabetically by the proper name. The description is positioned after the proper name and is usually abbreviated:

Erie, L., *N. Amer.* **78 D4** 42 15N 81 0W

Where a description forms part of a settlement or administrative name however, it is always written in full and put in its true alphabetic position:

Mount Morris, *U.S.A.* **78 D7** 42 44N 77 52W

Names beginning with M' and Mc are indexed as if they were spelled Mac. Names beginning St. are alphabetised under Saint, but Sankt, Sint, Sant', Santa and San are all spelt in full and are alphabetised accordingly. If the same place name occurs two or more times in the index and all are in the same country, each is followed by the name of the administrative subdivision in which it is located. The names are placed in the alphabetical order of the subdivisions. For example:

Jackson, *Ky., U.S.A.* **76 G4** 37 33N 83 23W
Jackson, *Mich., U.S.A.* **76 D3** 42 15N 84 24W
Jackson, *Minn., U.S.A.* **80 D7** 43 37N 95 1W

The number in bold type which follows each name in the index refers to the number of the map page where that feature or place will be found. This is usually the largest scale at which the place or feature appears.

The letter and figure which are in bold type immediately after the page number give the grid square on the map page, within which the feature is situated. The letter represents the latitude and the figure the longitude.

In some cases the feature itself may fall within the specified square, while the name is outside. This is usually the case only with features which are larger than a grid square.

For a more precise location the geographical coordinates which follow the letter/figure references give the latitude and the longitude of each place. The first set of figures represent the latitude which is the distance north or south of the Equator measured as an angle at the centre of the earth. The Equator is latitude 0°, the North Pole is 90°N, and the South Pole 90°S.

The second set of figures represent the longitude, which is the distance East or West of the prime meridian, which runs through Greenwich, England. Longitude is also measured as an angle at the centre of the earth and is given East or West of the prime meridian, from 0° to 180° in either direction.

The unit of measurement for latitude and longitude is the degree, which is subdivided into 60 minutes. Each index entry states the position of a place in degrees and minutes, a space being left between the degrees and the minutes.

The latitude is followed by N(orth) or S(outh) and the longitude by E(ast) or W(est).

Rivers are indexed to their mouths or confluences, and carry the symbol → after their names. A solid square ■ follows the name of a country, while an open square □ refers to a first order administrative area.

Abbreviations used in the index

A.C.T. – Australian Capital Territory
Afghan. – Afghanistan
Ala. – Alabama
Alta. – Alberta
Amer. – America(n)
Arch. – Archipelago
Ariz. – Arizona
Ark. – Arkansas
Atl. Oc. – Atlantic Ocean
B. – Baie, Bahía, Bay, Bucht, Bugt
B.C. – British Columbia
Bangla. – Bangladesh
Barr. – Barrage
Bos.-H. – Bosnia-Herzegovina
C. – Cabo, Cap, Cape, Coast
C.A.R. – Central African Republic
C. Prov. – Cape Province
Calif. – California
Cent. – Central
Chan. – Channel
Colo. – Colorado
Conn. – Connecticut
Cord. – Cordillera
Cr. – Creek
Czech. – Czech Republic
D.C. – District of Columbia
Del. – Delaware
Dep. – Dependency
Des. – Desert
Dist. – District
Dj. – Djebel
Domin. – Dominica
Dom. Rep. – Dominican Republic
E. – East

E. Salv. – El Salvador
Eq. Guin. – Equatorial Guinea
Fla. – Florida
Falk. Is. – Falkland Is.
G. – Golfe, Golfo, Gulf, Guba, Gebel
Ga. – Georgia
Gt. – Great, Greater
Guinea-Biss. – Guinea-Bissau
H.K. – Hong Kong
H.P. – Himachal Pradesh
Hants. – Hampshire
Harb. – Harbor, Harbour
Hd. – Head
Hts. – Heights
I.(s). – Île, Ilha, Insel, Isla, Island, Isle
Ill. – Illinois
Ind. – Indiana
Ind. Oc. – Indian Ocean
Ivory C. – Ivory Coast
J. – Jabal, Jebel, Jazira
Junc. – Junction
K. – Kap, Kapp
Kans. – Kansas
Kep. – Kepulauan
Ky. – Kentucky
L. – Lac, Lacul, Lago, Lagoa, Lake, Limni, Loch, Lough
La. – Louisiana
Liech. – Liechtenstein
Lux. – Luxembourg
Mad. P. – Madhya Pradesh
Madag. – Madagascar
Man. – Manitoba
Mass. – Massachusetts

Md. – Maryland
Me. – Maine
Medit. S. – Mediterranean Sea
Mich. – Michigan
Minn. – Minnesota
Miss. – Mississippi
Mo. – Missouri
Mont. – Montana
Mozam. – Mozambique
Mt.(e) – Mont, Monte, Monti, Montaña, Mountain
N. – Nord, Norte, North, Northern, Nouveau
N.B. – New Brunswick
N.C. – North Carolina
N. Cal. – New Caledonia
N. Dak. – North Dakota
N.H. – New Hampshire
N.I. – North Island
N.J. – New Jersey
N. Mex. – New Mexico
N.S. – Nova Scotia
N.S.W. – New South Wales
N.W.T. – North West Territory
N.Y. – New York
N.Z. – New Zealand
Nebr. – Nebraska
Neths. – Netherlands
Nev. – Nevada
Nfld. – Newfoundland
Nic. – Nicaragua
O. – Oued, Ouadi
Occ. – Occidentale
Okla. – Oklahoma
Ont. – Ontario
Or. – Orientale

Oreg. – Oregon
Os. – Ostrov
Oz. – Ozero
P. – Pass, Passo, Pasul, Pulau
P.E.I. – Prince Edward Island
Pa. – Pennsylvania
Pac. Oc. – Pacific Ocean
Papua N.G. – Papua New Guinea
Pass. – Passage
Pen. – Peninsula, Péninsule
Phil. – Philippines
Pk. – Park, Peak
Plat. – Plateau
Prov. – Province, Provincial
Pt. – Point
Pta. – Ponta, Punta
Pte. – Pointe
Qué. – Québec
Queens. – Queensland
R. – Rio, River
R.I. – Rhode Island
Ra.(s). – Range(s)
Raj. – Rajasthan
Reg. – Region
Rep. – Republic
Res. – Reserve, Reservoir
S. – San, South, Sea
Si. Arabia – Saudi Arabia
S.C. – South Carolina
S. Dak. – South Dakota
S.I. – South Island
S. Leone – Sierra Leone
Sa. – Serra, Sierra
Sask. – Saskatchewan
Scot. – Scotland
Sd. – Sound

Sev. – Severnaya
Sib. – Siberia
Sprs. – Springs
St. – Saint
Sta. – Santa, Station
Ste. – Sainte
Sto. – Santo
Str. – Strait, Stretto
Switz. – Switzerland
Tas. – Tasmania
Tenn. – Tennessee
Tex. – Texas
Tg. – Tanjung
Trin. & Tob. – Trinidad & Tobago
U.A.E. – United Arab Emirates
U.K. – United Kingdom
U.S.A. – United States of America
Ut. P. – Uttar Pradesh
Va. – Virginia
Vdkhr. – Vodokhranilishche
Vf. – Vîrful
Vic. – Victoria
Vol. – Volcano
Vt. – Vermont
W. – Wadi, West
W. Va. – West Virginia
Wash. – Washington
Wis. – Wisconsin
Wlkp. – Wielkopolski
Wyo. – Wyoming
Yorks. – Yorkshire
Yug. – Yugoslavia

A Coruña

A

A Coruña, *Spain* **19 A1** 43 20N 8 25W
A Estrada, *Spain* **19 A1** 42 43N 8 27W
A Fonsagrada, *Spain* **19 A2** 43 8N 7 4W
Aachen, *Germany* **16 C4** 50 45N 6 6 E
Aalborg = Ålborg, *Denmark* **9 H13** 57 2N 9 54 E
Aalen, *Germany* **16 D6** 48 51N 10 6 E
Aalst, *Belgium* **15 D4** 50 56N 4 2 E
Aalten, *Neths.* **15 C6** 51 56N 6 35 E
Aalter, *Belgium* **15 C3** 51 5N 3 28 E
Äänekoski, *Finland* **9 E21** 62 36N 25 44 E
Aarau, *Switz.* **18 C8** 47 23N 8 4 E
Aare →, *Switz.* **18 C8** 47 33N 8 14 E
Aarhus = Århus, *Denmark* **9 H14** 56 8N 10 11 E
Aarschot, *Belgium* **15 D4** 50 59N 4 49 E
Aba,
Dem. Rep. of the Congo **54 B3** 3 58N 30 17 E
Aba, *Nigeria* **50 G7** 5 10N 7 19 E
Ābādān, *Iran* **45 D6** 30 22N 48 20 E
Ābādeh, *Iran* **45 D7** 31 8N 52 40 E
Abadla, *Algeria* **50 B5** 31 2N 2 45W
Abaetetuba, *Brazil* **93 D9** 1 40S 48 50W
Abagnar Qi, *China* **34 C9** 43 52N 116 2 E
Abai, *Paraguay* **95 B4** 25 58S 55 54W
Abakan, *Russia* **27 D10** 53 40N 91 10 E
Abancay, *Peru* **92 F4** 13 35S 72 55W
Abariringa, *Kiribati* **64 H10** 2 50S 171 40W
Abarqū, *Iran* **45 D7** 31 10N 53 20 E
Abashiri, *Japan* **30 C12** 44 0N 144 15 E
Abashiri-Wan, *Japan* **30 C12** 44 0N 144 30 E
Abay, *Kazakstan* **26 E8** 49 38N 72 53 E
Abaya, L., *Ethiopia* **46 F2** 6 30N 37 50 E
Abaza, *Russia* **26 D10** 52 39N 90 6 E
'Abbāsābād, *Iran* **45 C8** 33 34N 58 23 E
Abbay = Nîl el Azraq →,
Sudan **51 E12** 15 38N 32 31 E
Abbaye, Pt., *U.S.A.* **76 B1** 46 58N 88 8W
Abbé, L., *Ethiopia* **46 E3** 11 8N 41 47 E
Abbeville, *France* **18 A4** 50 6N 1 49 E
Abbeville, *Ala., U.S.A.* **77 K3** 31 34N 85 15W
Abbeville, *La., U.S.A.* **81 L8** 29 58N 92 8W
Abbeville, *S.C., U.S.A.* **77 H4** 34 11N 82 23W
Abbot Ice Shelf, *Antarctica* **5 D16** 73 0S 92 0W
Abbottabad, *Pakistan* **42 B5** 34 10N 73 15 E
Abd al Kūrī, *Ind. Oc.* **46 E5** 12 5N 52 20 E
Ābdar, *Iran* **45 D7** 30 16N 55 19 E
'Abdolābād, *Iran* **45 C8** 34 12N 56 30 E
Abdulpur, *Bangla.* **43 G13** 24 15N 88 59 E
Abéché, *Chad* **51 F10** 13 50N 20 35 E
Abengourou, *Ivory C.* **50 G5** 6 42N 3 27W
Åbenrå, *Denmark* **9 J13** 55 3N 9 25 E
Abeokuta, *Nigeria* **50 G6** 7 3N 3 19 E
Aber, *Uganda* **54 B3** 2 12N 32 25 E
Aberaeron, *U.K.* **11 E3** 52 15N 4 15W
Aberayron = Aberaeron,
U.K. **11 E3** 52 15N 4 15W
Aberchirder, *U.K.* **12 D6** 57 34N 2 37W
Abercorn = Mbala, *Zambia* **55 D3** 8 46S 31 24 E
Abercorn, *Australia* **63 D5** 25 12S 151 5 E
Aberdare, *U.K.* **11 F4** 51 43N 3 27W
Aberdare Ra., *Kenya* **54 C4** 0 15S 36 50 E
Aberdeen, *Australia* **63 E5** 32 9S 150 56 E
Aberdeen, *Canada* **73 C7** 52 20N 106 8W
Aberdeen, *S. Africa* **56 E3** 32 28S 24 2 E
Aberdeen, *U.K.* **12 D6** 57 9N 2 5W
Aberdeen, *Ala., U.S.A.* **77 J1** 33 49N 88 33W
Aberdeen, *Idaho, U.S.A.* **82 E7** 42 57N 112 50W
Aberdeen, *Md., U.S.A.* **76 F7** 39 31N 76 10W
Aberdeen, *S. Dak., U.S.A.* **80 C5** 45 28N 98 29W
Aberdeen, *Wash., U.S.A.* **84 D3** 46 59N 123 50W
Aberdeen, City of □, *U.K.* **12 D6** 57 10N 2 10W
Aberdeenshire □, *U.K.* **12 D6** 57 17N 2 36W
Aberdovey = Aberdyfi, *U.K.* **11 E3** 52 33N 4 3W
Aberdyfi, *U.K.* **11 E3** 52 33N 4 3W
Aberfeldy, *U.K.* **12 E5** 56 37N 3 51W
Abergavenny, *U.K.* **11 F4** 51 49N 3 1W
Abergele, *U.K.* **10 D4** 53 17N 3 35W
Abernathy, *U.S.A.* **81 J4** 33 50N 101 51W
Abert, L., *U.S.A.* **82 E3** 42 38N 120 14W
Aberystwyth, *U.K.* **11 E3** 52 25N 4 5W
Abhā, *Si. Arabia* **46 D3** 18 0N 42 34 E
Abhar, *Iran* **45 B6** 36 9N 49 13 E
Abhayapuri, *India* **43 F14** 26 24N 90 38 E
Abidjan, *Ivory C.* **50 G5** 5 26N 3 58W
Abilene, *Kans., U.S.A.* **80 F6** 38 55N 97 13W
Abilene, *Tex., U.S.A.* **81 J5** 32 28N 99 43W
Abingdon, *U.K.* **11 F6** 51 40N 1 17W
Abingdon, *U.S.A.* **77 G5** 36 43N 81 59W
Abington Reef, *Australia* **62 B4** 18 0S 149 35 E
Abitau →, *Canada* **73 B7** 59 53N 109 3W
Abitibi →, *Canada* **70 B3** 51 3N 80 55W
Abitibi, L., *Canada* **70 C4** 48 40N 79 40W
Abkhaz Republic =
Abkhazia □, *Georgia* **25 F7** 43 12N 41 5 E
Abkhazia □, *Georgia* **25 F7** 43 12N 41 5 E
Abminga, *Australia* **63 D1** 26 8S 134 51 E
Åbo = Turku, *Finland* **9 F20** 60 30N 22 19 E
Abohar, *India* **42 D6** 30 10N 74 10 E
Abolo, *Congo* **52 D2** 0 8N 14 16 E
Abomey, *Benin* **50 G6** 7 10N 2 5 E
Abong-Mbang, *Cameroon* **52 D2** 4 0N 13 8 E
Abou-Deïa, *Chad* **51 F9** 11 20N 19 20 E
Aboyne, *U.K.* **12 D6** 57 4N 2 47W
Abra Pampa, *Argentina* **94 A2** 22 43S 65 42W
Abraham L., *Canada* **72 C5** 52 15N 116 35W
Abreojos, Pta., *Mexico* **86 B2** 26 50N 113 40W
Abrud, *Romania* **17 E12** 46 19N 23 5 E
Absaroka Range, *U.S.A.* **82 D9** 44 45N 109 50W
Abu, *India* **42 G5** 24 41N 72 50 E
Abū al Abyad, *U.A.E.* **45 E7** 24 11N 53 50 E
Abū al Khaşīb, *Iraq* **45 D6** 30 25N 48 0 E
Abū 'Alī, *Si. Arabia* **45 E6** 27 20N 49 27 E
Abū 'Alī →, *Lebanon* **47 A4** 34 25N 35 50 E
Abu Dhabi = Abū Ẓāby,
U.A.E. **45 E7** 24 28N 54 22 E
Abū Du'ān, *Syria* **44 B3** 36 25N 38 15 E
Abu el Gairi, W. →, *Egypt* **47 F2** 29 35N 33 30 E
Abu Ga'da, W. →, *Egypt* **47 F1** 29 15N 32 53 E
Abū Ḥadrīyah, *Si. Arabia* **45 E6** 27 20N 48 58 E
Abu Hamed, *Sudan* **51 E12** 19 32N 33 13 E
Abū Kamāl, *Syria* **44 C4** 34 30N 41 0 E
Abū Madd, Ra's, *Si. Arabia* **44 E3** 24 50N 37 7 E
Abū Mūsā, *U.A.E.* **45 E7** 25 52N 55 3 E
Abū Şafāt, W. →, *Jordan* **47 E5** 30 24N 36 7 E
Abu Simbel, *Egypt* **51 D12** 22 18N 31 40 E
Abū Şukhayr, *Iraq* **44 D5** 31 54N 44 30 E
Abū Zabad, *Sudan* **51 F11** 12 25N 29 10 E
Abū Ẓāby, *U.A.E.* **45 E7** 24 28N 54 22 E
Abū Zeydābād, *Iran* **45 C6** 33 54N 51 45 E
Abuja, *Nigeria* **50 G7** 9 16N 7 2 E
Abukuma-Gawa →, *Japan* **30 E10** 38 6N 140 52 E
Abukuma-Sammyaku, *Japan* **30 F10** 37 30N 140 45 E
Abunã, *Brazil* **92 E5** 9 40S 65 20W
Abunã →, *Brazil* **92 E5** 9 41S 65 20W
Aburo,
Dem. Rep. of the Congo **54 B3** 2 4N 30 53 E
Abut Hd., *N.Z.* **59 K3** 43 7S 170 15 E
Acadia National Park, *U.S.A.* **77 C11** 44 20N 68 13W
Açailândia, *Brazil* **93 D9** 4 57S 47 0W
Acajutla, *El Salv.* **88 D2** 13 36N 89 50W
Acámbaro, *Mexico* **86 D4** 20 0N 100 40W
Acaponeta, *Mexico* **86 C3** 22 30N 105 20W
Acapulco, *Mexico* **87 D5** 16 51N 99 56W
Acarai, Serra, *Brazil* **92 C7** 1 50N 57 50W
Acarigua, *Venezuela* **92 B5** 9 33N 69 12W
Acatlán, *Mexico* **87 D5** 18 10N 98 3W
Acayucan, *Mexico* **87 D6** 17 59N 94 58W
Accomac, *U.S.A.* **76 G8** 37 43N 75 40W
Accra, *Ghana* **50 G5** 5 35N 0 6W
Accrington, *U.K.* **10 D5** 53 45N 2 22W
Acebal, *Argentina* **94 C3** 33 20S 60 50W
Aceh □, *Indonesia* **36 D1** 4 15N 97 30 E
Achalpur, *India* **40 J10** 21 22N 77 32 E
Acheng, *China* **35 B14** 45 30N 126 58 E
Acher, *India* **42 H5** 23 10N 72 32 E
Achill Hd., *Ireland* **13 C1** 53 58N 10 15W
Achill I., *Ireland* **13 C1** 53 58N 10 1W
Achinsk, *Russia* **27 D10** 56 20N 90 20 E
Acireale, *Italy* **20 F6** 37 37N 15 10 E
Ackerman, *U.S.A.* **81 J10** 33 19N 89 11W
Acklins I., *Bahamas* **89 B5** 22 30N 74 0W
Acme, *Canada* **72 C6** 51 33N 113 30W
Acme, *U.S.A.* **78 F5** 40 8N 79 26W
Aconcagua, Cerro,
Argentina **94 C2** 32 39S 70 0W
Aconquija, Mt., *Argentina* **94 B2** 27 0S 66 0W
Açores, Is. dos = Azores,
Atl. Oc. **50 A1** 38 44N 29 0W
Acraman, L., *Australia* **63 E2** 32 2S 135 23 E
Acre = 'Akko, *Israel* **47 C4** 32 55N 35 4 E
Acre □, *Brazil* **92 E4** 9 1S 71 0W
Acre →, *Brazil* **92 E5** 8 45S 67 22W
Acton, *Canada* **78 C4** 43 38N 80 3W
Acuña, *Mexico* **86 B4** 29 18N 100 55W
Ad Dammām, *Si. Arabia* **45 E6** 26 20N 50 5 E
Ad Dāmūr, *Lebanon* **47 B4** 33 44N 35 27 E
Ad Dawādimī, *Si. Arabia* **44 E5** 24 35N 44 15 E
Ad Dawḥah, *Qatar* **46 B5** 25 15N 51 35 E
Ad Dawr, *Iraq* **44 C4** 34 27N 43 47 E
Ad Dir'īyah, *Si. Arabia* **44 E5** 24 44N 46 35 E
Ad Dīwānīyah, *Iraq* **44 D5** 32 0N 45 0 E
Ad Dujayl, *Iraq* **44 C5** 33 51N 44 14 E
Ad Duwayd, *Si. Arabia* **44 D4** 30 15N 42 17 E
Ada, *Minn., U.S.A.* **80 B6** 47 18N 96 31W
Ada, *Okla., U.S.A.* **81 H6** 34 46N 96 41W
Adabiya, *Egypt* **47 F1** 29 53N 32 28 E
Adair, C., *Canada* **69 A12** 71 31N 71 24W
Adaja →, *Spain* **19 B3** 41 32N 4 52W
Adak I., *U.S.A.* **68 C2** 51 45N 176 45W
Adamaoua, Massif de l',
Cameroon **52 C2** 7 20N 12 20 E
Adamawa Highlands =
Adamaoua, Massif de l',
Cameroon **52 C2** 7 20N 12 20 E
Adamello, Mte., *Italy* **18 C9** 46 9N 10 30 E
Adaminaby, *Australia* **63 F4** 36 0S 148 45 E
Adams, *Mass., U.S.A.* **79 D11** 42 38N 73 7W
Adams, *N.Y., U.S.A.* **79 C8** 43 49N 76 1W
Adams, *Wis., U.S.A.* **80 D10** 43 57N 89 49W
Adam's Bridge, *Sri Lanka* **40 Q11** 9 15N 79 40 E
Adams L., *Canada* **72 C5** 51 10N 119 40W
Adams Mt., *U.S.A.* **84 D5** 46 12N 121 30W
Adam's Peak, *Sri Lanka* **40 R12** 6 48N 80 30 E
Adana, *Turkey* **25 G6** 37 0N 35 16 E
Adapazarı = Sakarya,
Turkey **25 F5** 40 48N 30 25 E
Adarama, *Sudan* **51 E12** 17 10N 34 52 E
Adare, C., *Antarctica* **5 D11** 71 0S 171 0 E
Adaut, *Indonesia* **37 F8** 8 8S 131 7 E
Adavale, *Australia* **63 D3** 25 52S 144 32 E
Adda →, *Italy* **18 D8** 45 8N 9 53 E
Addis Ababa = Addis
Abeba, *Ethiopia* **46 F2** 9 2N 38 42 E
Addis Abeba, *Ethiopia* **46 F2** 9 2N 38 42 E
Addison, *U.S.A.* **78 D7** 42 1N 77 14W
Addo, *S. Africa* **56 E4** 33 32S 25 45 E
Ādeh, *Iran* **44 B5** 37 42N 45 11 E
Adel, *U.S.A.* **77 K4** 31 8N 83 25W
Adelaide, *Australia* **63 E2** 34 52S 138 30 E
Adelaide, *Bahamas* **88 A4** 25 4N 77 31W
Adelaide, *S. Africa* **56 E4** 32 42S 26 20 E
Adelaide I., *Antarctica* **5 C17** 67 15S 68 30W
Adelaide Pen., *Canada* **68 B10** 68 15N 97 30W
Adelaide River, *Australia* **60 B5** 13 15S 131 7 E
Adelanto, *U.S.A.* **85 L9** 34 35N 117 22W
Adele I., *Australia* **60 C3** 15 32S 123 9 E
Adélie, Terre, *Antarctica* **5 C10** 68 0S 140 0 E
Adélie Land = Adélie, Terre,
Antarctica **5 C10** 68 0S 140 0 E
Aden = Al 'Adan, *Yemen* **46 E4** 12 45N 45 0 E
Aden, G. of, *Asia* **46 E4** 12 30N 47 30 E
Adendorp, *S. Africa* **56 E3** 32 15S 24 30 E
Adh Dhayd, *U.A.E.* **45 E7** 25 17N 55 53 E
Adhoi, *India* **42 H4** 23 26N 70 32 E
Adi, *Indonesia* **37 E8** 4 15S 133 30 E
Adieu, C., *Australia* **61 F5** 32 0S 132 10 E
Adieu Pt., *Australia* **60 C3** 15 14S 124 35 E
Adige →, *Italy* **20 B5** 45 9N 12 20 E
Adigrat, *Ethiopia* **46 E2** 14 20N 39 26 E
Adilabad, *India* **40 K11** 19 33N 78 20 E
Adin Khel, *Afghan.* **40 C6** 32 45N 68 5 E
Adirondack Mts., *U.S.A.* **79 C10** 44 0N 74 0W
Adjumani, *Uganda* **54 B3** 3 20N 31 50 E
Adlavik Is., *Canada* **71 A8** 55 2N 57 45W
Admiralty G., *Australia* **60 B4** 14 20S 125 55 E
Admiralty I., *U.S.A.* **72 B2** 57 30N 134 30W
Admiralty Is., *Papua N. G.* **64 H6** 2 0S 147 0 E
Adonara, *Indonesia* **37 F6** 8 15S 123 5 E
Adoni, *India* **40 M10** 15 33N 77 18 E
Adour →, *France* **18 E3** 43 32N 1 32W
Adra, *India* **43 H12** 23 30N 86 42 E
Adra, *Spain* **19 D4** 36 43N 3 3W
Adrano, *Italy* **20 F6** 37 40N 14 50 E
Adrar, *Algeria* **48 D4** 27 51N 0 11 E
Adrar, *Mauritania* **50 D3** 20 30N 7 30 E
Adrian, *Mich., U.S.A.* **76 E3** 41 54N 84 2W
Adrian, *Tex., U.S.A.* **81 H3** 35 16N 102 40W
Adriatic Sea, *Medit. S.* **20 C6** 43 0N 16 0 E
Adua, *Indonesia* **37 E7** 1 45S 129 50 E
Adwa, *Ethiopia* **46 E2** 14 15N 38 52 E
Adygea □, *Russia* **25 F7** 45 0N 40 0 E
Adzhar Republic = Ajaria □,
Georgia **25 F7** 41 30N 42 0 E
Adzopé, *Ivory C.* **50 G5** 6 7N 3 49W
Ægean Sea, *Medit. S.* **21 E11** 38 30N 25 0 E
Aerhtai Shan, *Mongolia* **32 B4** 46 40N 92 45 E
'Afak, *Iraq* **44 C5** 32 4N 45 15 E
Afándou, *Greece* **23 C10** 36 18N 28 12 E
Afghanistan ■, *Asia* **40 C4** 33 0N 65 0 E
Aflou, *Algeria* **50 B6** 34 7N 2 3 E
Africa **48 E6** 10 0N 20 0 E
'Afrīn, *Syria* **44 B3** 36 32N 36 50 E
Afton, *N.Y., U.S.A.* **79 D9** 42 14N 75 32W
Afton, *Wyo., U.S.A.* **82 E8** 42 44N 110 56W
Afuá, *Brazil* **93 D8** 0 15S 50 20W
'Afula, *Israel* **47 C4** 32 37N 35 17 E
Afyon, *Turkey* **25 G5** 38 45N 30 33 E
Afyonkarahisar = Afyon,
Turkey **25 G5** 38 45N 30 33 E
Agadès = Agadez, *Niger* **50 E7** 16 58N 7 59 E
Agadez, *Niger* **50 E7** 16 58N 7 59 E
Agadir, *Morocco* **50 B4** 30 28N 9 55W
Agaete, *Canary Is.* **22 F4** 28 6N 15 43W
Agar, *India* **42 H7** 23 40N 76 2 E
Agartala, *India* **41 H17** 23 50N 91 23 E
Agassiz, *Canada* **72 D4** 49 14N 121 46W
Agats, *Indonesia* **37 F9** 5 33S 138 0 E
Agawam, *U.S.A.* **79 D12** 42 5N 72 37W
Agboville, *Ivory C.* **50 G5** 5 55N 4 15W
Ağdam, *Azerbaijan* **44 B5** 40 0N 46 58 E
Agde, *France* **18 E5** 43 19N 3 28 E
Agen, *France* **18 D4** 44 12N 0 38 E
Āgh Kand, *Iran* **45 B6** 37 15N 48 4 E
Aginskoye, *Russia* **27 D12** 51 6N 114 32 E
Agnew, *Australia* **61 E3** 28 1S 120 31 E
Agori, *India* **43 G10** 24 33N 82 57 E
Agra, *India* **42 F7** 27 17N 77 58 E
Ağrı, *Turkey* **25 G7** 39 44N 43 3 E
Agri →, *Italy* **20 D7** 40 13N 16 44 E
Ağrı Dağı, *Turkey* **25 G7** 39 50N 44 15 E
Ağrı Karakose = Ağrı,
Turkey **25 G7** 39 44N 43 3 E
Agrigento, *Italy* **20 F5** 37 19N 13 34 E
Agrinion, *Greece* **21 E9** 38 37N 21 27 E
Agua Caliente, *Baja Calif.,
Mexico* **85 N10** 32 29N 116 59W
Agua Caliente, *Sinaloa,
Mexico* **86 B3** 26 30N 108 20W
Agua Caliente Springs,
U.S.A. **85 N10** 32 56N 116 19W
Água Clara, *Brazil* **93 H8** 20 25S 52 45W
Agua Hechicero, *Mexico* **85 N10** 32 26N 116 14W
Agua Prieta, *Mexico* **86 A3** 31 20N 109 32W
Aguadilla, *Puerto Rico* **89 C6** 18 26N 67 10W
Aguadulce, *Panama* **88 E3** 8 15N 80 32W
Aguanga, *U.S.A.* **85 M10** 33 27N 116 51W
Aguanish, *Canada* **71 B7** 50 14N 62 2W
Aguanus →, *Canada* **71 B7** 50 13N 62 5W
Aguapey →, *Argentina* **94 B4** 29 7S 56 36W
Aguaray Guazú →,
Paraguay **94 A4** 24 47S 57 19W
Aguarico →, *Ecuador* **92 D3** 0 59S 75 11W
Aguas Blancas, *Chile* **94 A2** 24 15S 69 55W
Aguas Calientes, Sierra de,
Argentina **94 B2** 25 26S 66 40W
Aguascalientes, *Mexico* **86 C4** 21 53N 102 12W
Aguascalientes □, *Mexico* **86 C4** 22 0N 102 20W
Aguilares, *Argentina* **94 B2** 27 26S 65 35W
Águilas, *Spain* **19 D5** 37 23N 1 35W
Agüimes, *Canary Is.* **22 G4** 27 58N 15 27W
Aguja, C. de la, *Colombia* **90 B3** 11 18N 74 12W
Agulhas, C., *S. Africa* **56 E3** 34 52S 20 0 E
Agulo, *Canary Is.* **22 F2** 28 11N 17 12W
Agung, *Indonesia* **36 F5** 8 20S 115 28 E
Agur, *Uganda* **54 B3** 2 28N 32 55 E
Agusan →, *Phil.* **37 C7** 9 0N 125 30 E
Aha Mts., *Botswana* **56 B3** 19 45S 21 0 E
Ahaggar, *Algeria* **50 D7** 23 0N 6 30 E
Ahar, *Iran* **44 B5** 38 35N 47 0 E
Ahipara B., *N.Z.* **59 F4** 35 5S 173 5 E
Ahiri, *India* **40 K12** 19 30N 80 0 E
Ahmad Wal, *Pakistan* **42 E1** 29 18N 65 58 E
Ahmadabad, *India* **42 H5** 23 0N 72 40 E
Aḥmadābād, *Khorāsān, Iran* **45 C9** 35 3N 60 50 E
Aḥmadābād, *Khorāsān, Iran* **45 C8** 35 49N 59 42 E
Aḥmadī, *Iran* **45 E8** 27 56N 56 42 E
Ahmadnagar, *India* **40 K9** 19 7N 74 46 E
Ahmadpur, *Pakistan* **42 E4** 29 12N 71 10 E
Ahmadpur Lamma, *Pakistan* **42 E4** 28 19N 70 3 E
Ahmedabad = Ahmadabad,
India **42 H5** 23 0N 72 40 E
Ahmednagar =
Ahmadnagar, *India* **40 K9** 19 7N 74 46 E
Ahome, *Mexico* **86 B3** 25 55N 109 11W
Ahoskie, *U.S.A.* **77 G7** 36 17N 76 59W
Ahram, *Iran* **45 D6** 28 52N 51 16 E
Ahrax Pt., *Malta* **23 D1** 35 59N 14 22 E
Āhū, *Iran* **45 C6** 34 33N 50 2 E
Ahuachapán, *El Salv.* **88 D2** 13 54N 89 52W
Ahvāz, *Iran* **45 D6** 31 20N 48 40 E
Ahvenanmaa = Åland,
Finland **9 F19** 60 15N 20 0 E
Aḥwar, *Yemen* **46 E4** 13 30N 46 40 E
Ai →, *India* **43 F14** 26 26N 90 44 E
Aichi □, *Japan* **31 G8** 35 0N 137 15 E
Aigua, *Uruguay* **95 C5** 34 13S 54 46W
Aigues-Mortes, *France* **18 E6** 43 35N 4 12 E
Aihui, *China* **33 A7** 50 10N 127 30 E
Aija, *Peru* **92 E3** 9 50S 77 45W
Aikawa, *Japan* **30 E9** 38 2N 138 15 E
Aiken, *U.S.A.* **77 J5** 33 34N 81 43W
Aileron, *Australia* **62 C1** 22 39S 133 20 E
Aillik, *Canada* **71 A8** 55 11N 59 18W
Ailsa Craig, *U.K.* **12 F3** 55 15N 5 6W
'Ailūn, *Jordan* **47 C4** 32 18N 35 47 E
Aim, *Russia* **27 D14** 59 0N 133 55 E
Aimere, *Indonesia* **37 F6** 8 45S 121 3 E
Aimogasta, *Argentina* **94 B2** 28 33S 66 50W
Aïn Ben Tili, *Mauritania* **50 C4** 25 59N 9 27W
Aïn-Sefra, *Algeria* **50 B5** 32 47N 0 37W
'Ain Sudr, *Egypt* **47 F2** 29 50N 33 6 E
Ainaži, *Latvia* **9 H21** 57 50N 24 24 E
Ainsworth, *U.S.A.* **80 D5** 42 33N 99 52W
Aiquile, *Bolivia* **92 G5** 18 10S 65 10W
Aïr, *Niger* **50 E7** 18 30N 8 0 E
Air Force I., *Canada* **69 B12** 67 58N 74 5W
Air Hitam, *Malaysia* **39 M4** 1 55N 103 11 E
Airdrie, *Canada* **72 C6** 51 18N 114 2W
Airdrie, *U.K.* **12 F5** 55 52N 3 57W
Aire →, *U.K.* **10 D7** 53 43N 0 55W
Aire, I. de l', *Spain* **22 B11** 39 48N 4 16 E
Airlie Beach, *Australia* **62 C4** 20 16S 148 43 E
Aisne →, *France* **18 B5** 49 26N 2 50 E
Ait, *India* **43 G8** 25 54N 79 14 E
Aitkin, *U.S.A.* **80 B8** 46 32N 93 42W
Aiud, *Romania* **17 E12** 46 19N 23 44 E
Aix-en-Provence, *France* **18 E6** 43 32N 5 27 E
Aix-la-Chapelle = Aachen,
Germany **16 C4** 50 45N 6 6 E
Aix-les-Bains, *France* **18 D6** 45 41N 5 53 E
Aiyion, *Greece* **21 E10** 38 15N 22 5 E
Aizawl, *India* **41 H18** 23 40N 92 44 E
Aizkraukle, *Latvia* **9 H21** 56 36N 25 11 E
Aizpute, *Latvia* **9 H19** 56 43N 21 40 E
Aizuwakamatsu, *Japan* **30 F9** 37 30N 139 56 E
Ajaccio, *France* **18 F8** 41 55N 8 40 E
Ajaigarh, *India* **43 G9** 24 52N 80 16 E
Ajalpan, *Mexico* **87 D5** 18 22N 97 15W
Ajanta Ra., *India* **40 J9** 20 28N 75 50 E
Ajari Rep. = Ajaria □,
Georgia **25 F7** 41 30N 42 0 E
Ajaria □, *Georgia* **25 F7** 41 30N 42 0 E
Ajax, *Canada* **78 C5** 43 50N 79 1W
Ajdābiyah, *Libya* **51 B10** 30 54N 20 4 E
Ajka, *Hungary* **17 E9** 47 4N 17 31 E
'Ajmān, *U.A.E.* **45 E7** 25 25N 55 30 E
Ajmer, *India* **42 F6** 26 28N 74 37 E
Ajnala, *India* **42 D6** 31 50N 74 48 E
Ajo, *U.S.A.* **83 K7** 32 22N 112 52W
Ajo, C. de, *Spain* **19 A4** 43 31N 3 35W
Akabira, *Japan* **30 C11** 43 33N 142 5 E
Akamas □, *Cyprus* **23 D11** 35 3N 32 18 E
Akanthou, *Cyprus* **23 D12** 35 22N 33 45 E
Akaroa, *N.Z.* **59 K4** 43 49S 172 59 E
Akashi, *Japan* **31 G7** 34 45N 134 58 E
Akbarpur, *Bihar, India* **43 G10** 24 39N 83 58 E
Akbarpur, *Ut. P., India* **43 F10** 26 25N 82 32 E
Akelamo, *Indonesia* **37 D7** 1 35N 129 40 E
Aketi,
Dem. Rep. of the Congo **52 D4** 2 38N 23 47 E
Akharnai, *Greece* **21 E10** 38 5N 23 44 E
Akhelóös →, *Greece* **21 E9** 38 19N 21 7 E
Akhisar, *Turkey* **21 E12** 38 56N 27 48 E
Akhnur, *India* **43 C6** 32 52N 74 45 E
Akhtyrka = Okhtyrka,
Ukraine **25 D5** 50 25N 35 0 E
Aki, *Japan* **31 H6** 33 30N 133 54 E
Akimiski I., *Canada* **70 B3** 52 50N 81 30W
Akita, *Japan* **30 E10** 39 45N 140 7 E
Akita □, *Japan* **30 E10** 39 40N 140 30 E
Akjoujt, *Mauritania* **50 E3** 19 45N 14 15W
Akkeshi, *Japan* **30 C12** 43 2N 144 51 E
'Akko, *Israel* **47 C4** 32 55N 35 4 E
Aklavik, *Canada* **68 B6** 68 12N 135 0W
Aklera, *India* **42 G7** 24 26N 76 32 E
Akmolinsk = Astana,
Kazakstan **26 D8** 51 10N 71 30 E
Akō, *Japan* **31 G7** 34 45N 134 24 E
Akola, *India* **40 J10** 20 42N 77 2 E
Akordat, *Eritrea* **46 D2** 15 30N 37 40 E
Akpatok I., *Canada* **69 B13** 60 25N 68 8W
Åkrahamn, *Norway* **9 G11** 59 15N 5 10 E
Akranes, *Iceland* **8 D2** 64 19N 22 5W
Akron, *Colo., U.S.A.* **80 E3** 40 10N 103 13W
Akron, *Ohio, U.S.A.* **78 E3** 41 5N 81 31W
Akrotiri, *Cyprus* **23 E11** 34 36N 32 57 E
Akrotiri Bay, *Cyprus* **23 E12** 34 35N 33 10 E
Aksai Chin, *India* **43 B8** 35 15N 79 55 E
Aksaray, *Turkey* **25 G5** 38 25N 34 2 E
Aksay, *Kazakstan* **25 D9** 51 11N 53 0 E
Akşehir, *Turkey* **44 B1** 38 18N 31 30 E
Akşehir Gölü, *Turkey* **25 G5** 38 30N 31 25 E
Aksu, *China* **32 B3** 41 5N 80 10 E
Aksum, *Ethiopia* **46 E2** 14 5N 38 40 E
Aktogay, *Kazakstan* **26 E8** 46 57N 79 40 E
Aktsyabrski, *Belarus* **17 B15** 52 38N 28 53 E
Aktyubinsk = Aqtöbe,
Kazakstan **25 D10** 50 17N 57 10 E
Akure, *Nigeria* **50 G7** 7 15N 5 5 E
Akureyri, *Iceland* **8 D4** 65 40N 18 6W
Akuseki-Shima, *Japan* **31 K4** 29 27N 129 37 E
Akyab = Sittwe, *Burma* **41 J18** 20 18N 92 45 E
Al 'Adan, *Yemen* **46 E4** 12 45N 45 0 E
Al Aḥsā = Hasa □,
Si. Arabia **45 E6** 25 50N 49 0 E
Al Ajfar, *Si. Arabia* **44 E4** 27 26N 43 0 E
Al Amādīyah, *Iraq* **44 B4** 37 5N 43 30 E
Al 'Amārah, *Iraq* **44 D5** 31 55N 47 15 E
Al 'Aqabah, *Jordan* **47 F4** 29 31N 35 0 E
Al Arak, *Syria* **44 C3** 34 38N 38 35 E
Al 'Aramah, *Si. Arabia* **44 E5** 25 30N 46 0 E
Al Arṭāwīyah, *Si. Arabia* **44 E5** 26 31N 45 20 E
Al 'Āṣimah = 'Ammān □,
Jordan **47 D5** 31 40N 36 30 E
Al 'Assāfīyah, *Si. Arabia* **44 D3** 28 17N 38 59 E
Al 'Ayn, *Oman* **45 E7** 24 15N 55 45 E
Al 'Ayn, *Si. Arabia* **44 E3** 25 4N 38 6 E
Al 'Azamīyah, *Iraq* **44 C5** 33 22N 44 22 E
Al 'Azīzīyah, *Iraq* **44 C5** 32 54N 45 4 E
Al Bāb, *Syria* **44 B3** 36 23N 37 29 E
Al Bad', *Si. Arabia* **44 D2** 28 28N 35 1 E
Al Bādī, *Iraq* **44 C4** 35 56N 41 32 E
Al Baḥrah, *Kuwait* **44 D5** 29 40N 47 52 E
Al Baḥral Mayyit = Dead
Sea, *Asia* **47 D4** 31 30N 35 30 E
Al Balqā' □, *Jordan* **47 C4** 32 5N 35 45 E
Al Bārūk, J., *Lebanon* **47 B4** 33 39N 35 40 E
Al Başrah, *Iraq* **44 D5** 30 30N 47 50 E
Al Baṭḥā, *Iraq* **44 D5** 31 6N 45 53 E
Al Batrūn, *Lebanon* **47 A4** 34 15N 35 40 E
Al Bayḍā, *Libya* **51 B10** 32 50N 21 44 E
Al Biqā, *Lebanon* **47 A5** 34 10N 36 10 E
Al Bi'r, *Si. Arabia* **44 D3** 28 51N 36 16 E
Al Burayj, *Syria* **47 A5** 34 15N 36 46 E
Al Faḍilī, *Si. Arabia* **45 E6** 26 58N 49 10 E

Amadeus, L.

Al Fallūjah, Iraq 44 C4 33 20N 43 55 E
Al Fâw, Iraq 45 D6 30 0N 48 30 E
Al Fujayrah, U.A.E. 45 E8 25 7N 56 18 E
Al Ghadaf, W. →, Jordan 47 D5 31 26N 36 43 E
Al Ghammās, Iraq 44 D5 31 45N 44 37 E
Al Ghazālah, Si. Arabia 44 E4 26 48N 41 19 E
Al Hâbah, Si. Arabia 44 E5 27 10N 47 0 E
Al Ḥadīthah, Iraq 44 C4 34 0N 41 13 E
Al Ḥadīthah, Si. Arabia 47 D6 31 28N 37 8 E
Al Ḥaḍr, Iraq 44 C4 35 35N 42 44 E
Al Hājānah, Syria 47 B5 33 20N 36 33 E
Al Hajar al Gharbī, Oman 45 E8 24 10N 56 15 E
Al Hāmad, Si. Arabia 44 D3 31 30N 39 30 E
Al Hamdānīyah, Syria 44 C3 35 25N 36 50 E
Al Ḥamīdīyah, Syria 47 A4 34 42N 35 57 E
Al Ḥammār, Iraq 44 D5 30 57N 46 51 E
Al Ḥamrā', Si. Arabia 44 E3 24 2N 38 55 E
Al Ḥanākīyah, Si. Arabia 44 E4 24 51N 40 31 E
Al Harīr, W. →, Syria 47 C4 32 44N 35 59 E
Al Ḥasā, W. →, Jordan 47 D4 31 4N 35 29 E
Al Ḥasakah, Syria 44 B4 36 35N 40 45 E
Al Haydān, W. →, Jordan 47 D4 31 29N 35 34 E
Al Ḥayy, Iraq 44 C5 32 5N 46 5 E
Al Ḥijarah, Asia 44 D4 30 0N 44 0 E
Al Ḥillah, Iraq 44 C5 32 30N 44 25 E
Al Hindīyah, Iraq 44 C5 32 30N 44 10 E
Al Hirmil, Lebanon 47 A5 34 26N 36 24 E
Al Hoceïma, Morocco 50 A5 35 8N 3 58W
Al Ḥudaydah, Yemen 46 E3 14 50N 43 0 E
Al Hufūf, Si. Arabia 45 E6 25 25N 49 45 E
Al Ḥumayḍah, Si. Arabia 44 D2 29 14N 34 56 E
Al Ḥunayy, Si. Arabia 45 E6 25 58N 48 45 E
Al Īsāwīyah, Si. Arabia 44 D3 30 43N 37 59 E
Al Jafr, Jordan 47 E5 30 18N 36 14 E
Al Jāfūrah, Si. Arabia 45 E7 25 0N 50 15 E
Al Jaghbūb, Libya 51 C10 29 42N 24 38 E
Al Jahrah, Kuwait 44 D5 29 25N 47 40 E
Al Jalāmīd, Si. Arabia 44 D3 31 20N 40 6 E
Al Jamalīyah, Qatar 45 E6 25 37N 51 5 E
Al Janūb □, Lebanon 47 B4 33 20N 35 20 E
Al Jawf, Libya 51 D10 24 10N 23 24 E
Al Jawf, Si. Arabia 44 D3 29 55N 39 40 E
Al Jazirah, Iraq 44 C5 33 30N 44 0 E
Al Jithāmīyah, Si. Arabia 44 E4 27 41N 41 43 E
Al Jubayl, Si. Arabia 45 E6 27 0N 49 50 E
Al Jubaylah, Si. Arabia 44 E5 24 55N 46 25 E
Al Jubb, Si. Arabia 44 E4 27 11N 42 17 E
Al Junaynah, Sudan 51 F10 13 27N 22 45 E
Al Kabā'ish, Iraq 44 D5 30 58N 47 0 E
Al Karak, Jordan 47 D4 31 11N 35 42 E
Al Karak □, Jordan 47 E5 31 0N 36 0 E
Al Kāẓim Tyah, Iraq 44 C5 33 22N 44 12 E
Al Khābūra, Oman 45 F8 23 57N 57 5 E
Al Khafji, Si. Arabia 45 E6 28 24N 48 29 E
Al Khalīl, West Bank 47 D4 31 32N 35 6 E
Al Khāliṣ, Iraq 44 C5 33 49N 44 32 E
Al Kharsānīyah, Si. Arabia 45 E6 27 13N 49 18 E
Al Khaṣab, Oman 45 E8 26 14N 56 15 E
Al Khawr, Qatar 45 E6 25 41N 51 30 E
Al Khiḍr, Iraq 44 D5 31 12N 45 33 E
Al Khiyām, Lebanon 47 B4 33 20N 35 36 E
Al Khums, Libya 51 B8 32 40N 14 17 E
Al Kiswah, Syria 47 B5 33 23N 36 14 E
Al Kūfah, Iraq 44 C5 32 2N 44 24 E
Al Kufrah, Libya 51 D10 24 17N 23 15 E
Al Kuhayfiyah, Si. Arabia 44 E4 27 12N 43 3 E
Al Kūt, Iraq 44 C5 32 30N 46 0 E
Al Kuwayt, Kuwait 44 D5 29 30N 48 0 E
Al Labwah, Lebanon 47 A5 34 11N 36 20 E
Al Lādhiqīyah, Syria 44 C2 35 30N 35 45 E
Al Līth, Si. Arabia 46 C3 20 9N 40 15 E
Al Liwā', Oman 45 E8 24 31N 56 36 E
Al Luḥayyah, Yemen 46 D3 15 45N 42 40 E
Al Madīnah, Iraq 44 D5 30 57N 47 16 E
Al Madīnah, Si. Arabia 46 C2 24 35N 39 52 E
Al Mafraq, Jordan 47 C5 32 17N 36 14 E
Al Maḥmūdīyah, Iraq 44 C5 33 3N 44 21 E
Al Majma'ah, Si. Arabia 44 E5 25 57N 45 22 E
Al Makhruq, W. →, Jordan 47 D6 31 28N 37 0 E
Al Makḥūl, Si. Arabia 44 E4 26 37N 42 39 E
Al Manāmah, Bahrain 45 E6 26 10N 50 30 E
Al Maqwa', Kuwait 44 D5 29 10N 47 59 E
Al Marj, Libya 51 B10 32 25N 20 30 E
Al Maṭlā, Kuwait 44 D5 29 24N 47 40 E
Al Mawjib, W. →, Jordan 47 D4 31 28N 35 36 E
Al Mawṣil, Iraq 44 B4 36 15N 43 5 E
Al Mayādin, Syria 44 C4 35 1N 40 27 E
Al Mazār, Jordan 47 D4 31 4N 35 41 E
Al Midhnab, Si. Arabia 44 E5 25 50N 44 18 E
Al Minā', Lebanon 47 A4 34 24N 35 49 E
Al Miqdādīyah, Iraq 44 C5 34 0N 45 0 E
Al Mubarraz, Si. Arabia 45 E6 25 30N 49 40 E
Al Mudawwarah, Jordan 47 F5 29 19N 36 0 E
Al Mughayrā', U.A.E. 45 E7 24 5N 53 32 E
Al Muḥarraq, Bahrain 45 E6 26 15N 50 40 E
Al Mukallā, Yemen 46 E4 14 33N 49 2 E
Al Mukhā, Yemen 46 E3 13 18N 43 15 E
Al Musayjīd, Si. Arabia 44 E3 24 5N 39 5 E
Al Musayyib, Iraq 44 C5 32 49N 44 20 E
Al Muwayliḥ, Si. Arabia 44 E2 27 40N 35 30 E
Al Qā'im, Iraq 44 C4 34 21N 41 7 E
Al Qalībah, Si. Arabia 44 D3 28 24N 37 42 E
Al Qāmishlī, Syria 44 B4 37 10N 41 10 E
Al Qaryatayn, Syria 47 A6 34 12N 37 13 E
Al Qaṣīm, Si. Arabia 44 E4 26 0N 43 0 E
Al Qaṭ'ā, Syria 44 C4 34 40N 40 48 E
Al Qaṭīf, Si. Arabia 45 E6 26 35N 50 0 E
Al Qatrānah, Jordan 47 D5 31 12N 36 6 E
Al Qaṭrūn, Libya 51 D9 24 56N 15 3 E
Al Qayṣūmah, Si. Arabia 44 D5 28 20N 46 7 E
Al Quds = Jerusalem, Israel 47 D4 31 47N 35 10 E
Al Qunayṭirah, Syria 47 C4 32 55N 35 45 E
Al Qurnah, Iraq 44 D5 31 1N 47 25 E
Al Quṣayr, Iraq 44 D5 30 39N 45 50 E
Al Quṣayr, Syria 47 A5 34 31N 36 34 E
Al Quṭayfah, Syria 47 B5 33 44N 36 36 E
Al 'Ubaylah, Si. Arabia 46 C5 21 59N 50 57 E
Al 'Uḍayliyah, Si. Arabia 45 E6 25 8N 49 18 E
Al 'Ulā, Si. Arabia 44 E3 26 35N 38 0 E
Al 'Uqayr, Si. Arabia 45 E6 25 40N 50 15 E
Al 'Uthmānīyah, Si. Arabia 45 E6 25 5N 49 22 E
Al 'Uwaynid, Si. Arabia 44 E5 24 50N 46 0 E
Al 'Uwayqīlah, Si. Arabia 44 D4 30 30N 42 10 E
Al 'Uyūn, Ḥijāz, Si. Arabia 44 E3 24 33N 39 35 E
Al 'Uyūn, Najd, Si. Arabia 44 E4 26 30N 43 50 E
Al 'Uzayr, Iraq 44 D5 31 19N 47 25 E
Al Wajh, Si. Arabia 44 E3 26 10N 36 30 E
Al Wakrah, Qatar 45 E6 25 10N 51 40 E
Al Wannān, Si. Arabia 45 E6 26 55N 48 24 E
Al Waqbah, Si. Arabia 44 D5 28 48N 45 33 E
Al Warī'āh, Si. Arabia 44 E5 27 51N 47 25 E
Al Wusayl, Qatar 45 E6 25 29N 51 29 E
Ala Dağ, Turkey 44 B2 37 44N 35 9 E
Ala Tau Shankou = Dzungarian Gates, Kazakstan 32 B3 45 0N 82 0 E
Alabama □, U.S.A. 77 J2 33 0N 87 0W
Alabama →, U.S.A. 77 K2 31 8N 87 57W
Alabaster, U.S.A. 77 J2 33 15N 86 49W
Alaçam Dağları, Turkey 21 E13 39 18N 28 49 E
Alachua, U.S.A. 77 L4 29 47N 82 30W
Alaérma, Greece 23 C9 36 9N 27 57 E
Alagoa Grande, Brazil 93 E11 7 3S 35 35W
Alagoas □, Brazil 93 E11 9 0S 36 0W
Alagoinhas, Brazil 93 F11 12 7S 38 20W
Alaior, Spain 22 B11 39 57N 4 8 E
Alajero, Canary Is. 22 F2 28 3N 17 13W
Alajuela, Costa Rica 88 D3 10 2N 84 8W
Alakamisy, Madag. 57 C8 21 19S 47 14 E
Alaknanda →, India 43 D8 30 8N 78 36 E
Alakurtti, Russia 24 A5 67 0N 30 30 E
Alamarvdasht, Iran 45 E7 27 37N 52 59 E
Alameda, Calif., U.S.A. 84 H4 37 46N 122 15W
Alameda, N. Mex., U.S.A. 83 J10 35 11N 106 37W
Alamo, U.S.A. 85 J11 37 22N 115 10W
Alamo Crossing, U.S.A. 85 L13 34 16N 113 33W
Alamogordo, U.S.A. 83 K11 32 54N 105 57W
Alamos, Mexico 86 B3 27 0N 109 0W
Alamosa, U.S.A. 83 H11 37 28N 105 52W
Åland, Finland 9 F19 60 15N 20 0 E
Ålands hav, Sweden 9 F18 60 0N 19 30 E
Alandur, India 40 N12 13 0N 80 15 E
Alania = North Ossetia □, Russia 25 F7 43 30N 44 30 E
Alanya, Turkey 25 G5 36 38N 32 0 E
Alaotra, Farihin', Madag. 57 B8 17 30S 48 30 E
Alapayevsk, Russia 26 D7 57 52N 61 42 E
Alaşehir, Turkey 21 E13 38 23N 28 30 E
Alaska □, U.S.A. 68 B5 64 0N 154 0W
Alaska, G. of, Pac. Oc. 68 C5 58 0N 145 0W
Alaska Peninsula, U.S.A. 68 C4 56 0N 159 0W
Alaska Range, U.S.A. 68 B4 62 50N 151 0W
Älät, Azerbaijan 25 G8 39 58N 49 25 E
Alatyr, Russia 24 D8 54 55N 46 35 E
Alausi, Ecuador 92 D3 2 0S 78 50W
Alava, C., U.S.A. 82 B1 48 10N 124 44W
Alavus, Finland 9 E20 62 35N 23 36 E
Alawoona, Australia 63 E3 34 45S 140 30 E
'Alayh, Lebanon 47 B4 33 46N 35 33 E
Alba, Italy 18 D8 44 42N 8 2 E
Alba-Iulia, Romania 17 E12 46 8N 23 39 E
Albacete, Spain 19 C5 39 0N 1 50W
Albacutya, L., Australia 63 F3 35 45S 141 58 E
Albanel, L., Canada 70 B5 50 55N 73 12W
Albania ■, Europe 21 D9 41 0N 20 0 E
Albany, Australia 61 G2 35 1S 117 58 E
Albany, Ga., U.S.A. 77 K3 31 35N 84 10W
Albany, N.Y., U.S.A. 79 D11 42 39N 73 45W
Albany, Oreg., U.S.A. 82 D2 44 38N 123 6W
Albany, Tex., U.S.A. 81 J5 32 44N 99 18W
Albany →, Canada 70 B3 52 17N 81 31W
Albardón, Argentina 94 C2 31 20S 68 30W
Albatross B., Australia 62 A3 12 45S 141 30 E
Albemarle, U.S.A. 77 H5 35 21N 80 11W
Albemarle Sd., U.S.A. 77 H7 36 5N 76 0W
Alberche →, Spain 19 C3 39 58N 4 46W
Alberdi, Paraguay 94 B4 26 14S 58 20W
Albert, L., Australia 63 F2 35 30S 139 10 E
Albert Edward Ra., Australia 60 C4 18 17S 127 57 E
Albert L., Africa 54 B3 1 30N 31 0 E
Albert Lea, U.S.A. 80 D8 43 39N 93 22W
Albert Nile →, Uganda 54 B3 3 36N 32 2 E
Albert Town, Bahamas 89 B5 22 37N 74 33W
Alberta □, Canada 72 C6 54 40N 115 0W
Alberti, Argentina 94 D3 35 1S 60 16W
Albertinia, S. Africa 56 E3 34 11S 21 34 E
Alberton, Canada 71 C7 46 50N 64 0W
Albertville = Kalemie, Dem. Rep. of the Congo 54 D2 5 55S 29 9 E
Albertville, France 18 D7 45 40N 6 22 E
Albertville, U.S.A. 77 H2 34 16N 86 13W
Albi, France 18 E5 43 56N 2 9 E
Albia, U.S.A. 80 E8 41 2N 92 48W
Albina, Surinam 93 B8 5 37N 54 15W
Albina, Ponta, Angola 56 B1 15 52S 11 44 E
Albion, Mich., U.S.A. 76 D3 42 15N 84 45W
Albion, Nebr., U.S.A. 80 E6 41 42N 98 0W
Albion, Pa., U.S.A. 78 E4 41 53N 80 22W
Alborán, Medit. S. 19 E4 35 57N 3 0W
Ålborg, Denmark 9 H13 57 2N 9 54 E
Alborz, Reshteh-ye Kūhhā-ye, Iran 45 C7 36 0N 52 0 E
Albuquerque, U.S.A. 83 J10 35 5N 106 39W
Albuquerque, Cayos de, Caribbean 88 D3 12 10N 81 50W
Alburg, U.S.A. 79 B11 44 59N 73 18W
Albury-Wodonga, Australia 63 F4 36 3S 146 56 E
Alcalá de Henares, Spain 19 B4 40 28N 3 22W
Alcalá la Real, Spain 19 D4 37 27N 3 57W
Álcamo, Italy 20 F5 37 59N 12 55 E
Alcañiz, Spain 19 B5 41 2N 0 8W
Alcântara, Brazil 93 D10 2 20S 44 30W
Alcántara, Embalse de, Spain 19 C2 39 44N 6 50W
Alcantarilla, Spain 19 D5 37 59N 1 12W
Alcaraz, Sierra de, Spain 19 C4 38 40N 2 20W
Alcaudete, Spain 19 D3 37 35N 4 5W
Alcázar de San Juan, Spain 19 C4 39 24N 3 12W
Alchevsk, Ukraine 25 E6 48 30N 38 45 E
Alcira = Alzira, Spain 19 C5 39 9N 0 30W
Alcova, U.S.A. 82 E10 42 34N 106 43W
Alcoy, Spain 19 C5 38 43N 0 30W
Alcúdia, Spain 22 B10 39 51N 3 7 E
Alcúdia, B. d', Spain 22 B10 39 47N 3 15 E
Aldabra Is., Seychelles 49 G8 9 22S 46 28 E
Aldama, Mexico 87 C5 23 0N 98 4W
Aldan, Russia 27 D13 58 40N 125 30 E
Aldan →, Russia 27 C13 63 28N 129 35 E
Aldea, Pta. de la, Canary Is. 22 G4 28 0N 15 50W
Aldeburgh, U.K. 11 E9 52 10N 1 37 E
Alder Pk., U.S.A. 84 K5 35 53N 121 22W
Alderney, U.K. 11 H5 49 42N 2 11W
Aldershot, U.K. 11 F7 51 15N 0 44W
Aledo, U.S.A. 80 E9 41 12N 90 45W
Aleg, Mauritania 50 E3 17 3N 13 55W
Alegranza, Canary Is. 22 E6 29 23N 13 32W
Alegranza, I., Canary Is. 22 E6 29 23N 13 32W
Alegre, Brazil 95 A7 20 50S 41 30W
Alegrete, Brazil 95 B4 29 40S 56 0W
Aleisk, Russia 26 D9 52 40N 83 0 E
Aleksandriya = Oleksandriya, Ukraine 17 C14 50 37N 26 19 E
Aleksandrov Gay, Russia 25 D8 50 9N 48 34 E
Aleksandrovsk-Sakhalinskiy, Russia 27 D15 50 50N 142 20 E
Além Paraíba, Brazil 95 A7 21 52S 42 41W
Alemania, Argentina 94 B2 25 40S 65 30W
Alemania, Chile 94 B2 25 10S 69 55W
Alençon, France 18 B4 48 27N 0 4 E
Alenquer, Brazil 93 D8 1 56S 54 46W
Alenuihaha Channel, U.S.A. 74 H17 20 30N 156 0W
Aleppo = Ḥalab, Syria 44 B3 36 10N 37 15 E
Alès, France 18 D6 44 9N 4 5 E
Alessándria, Italy 18 D8 44 54N 8 37 E
Ålesund, Norway 9 E12 62 28N 6 12 E
Aleutian Is., Pac. Oc. 68 C2 52 0N 175 0W
Aleutian Trench, Pac. Oc. 64 C10 48 0N 180 0 E
Alexander, U.S.A. 80 B3 47 51N 103 39W
Alexander, Mt., Australia 61 E3 28 58S 120 16 E
Alexander Arch., U.S.A. 68 C6 56 0N 136 0W
Alexander Bay, S. Africa 56 D2 28 40S 16 30 E
Alexander City, U.S.A. 77 J3 32 56N 85 58W
Alexander I., Antarctica 5 C17 69 0S 70 0W
Alexandra, Australia 63 F4 37 8S 145 40 E
Alexandra, N.Z. 59 L2 45 14S 169 25 E
Alexandra Falls, Canada 72 A5 60 29N 116 18W
Alexandria = El Iskandarîya, Egypt 51 B11 31 13N 29 58 E
Alexandria, B.C., Canada 72 C4 52 35N 122 27W
Alexandria, Ont., Canada 79 A10 45 19N 74 38W
Alexandria, Romania 17 G13 43 57N 25 24 E
Alexandria, S. Africa 56 E4 33 38S 26 28 E
Alexandria, U.K. 12 F4 55 59N 4 35W
Alexandria, La., U.S.A. 81 K8 31 18N 92 27W
Alexandria, Minn., U.S.A. 80 C7 45 53N 95 22W
Alexandria, S. Dak., U.S.A. 80 D6 43 39N 97 47W
Alexandria, Va., U.S.A. 76 F7 38 48N 77 3W
Alexandria Bay, U.S.A. 79 B9 44 20N 75 55W
Alexandrina, L., Australia 63 F2 35 25S 139 10 E
Alexandroúpolis, Greece 21 D11 40 50N 25 54 E
Alexis →, Canada 71 B8 52 33N 56 8W
Alexis Creek, Canada 72 C4 52 10N 123 20W
Alfabia, Spain 22 B9 39 44N 2 44 E
Alfenas, Brazil 95 A6 21 20S 46 10W
Alford, Aberds., U.K. 12 D6 57 14N 2 41W
Alford, Lincs., U.K. 10 D8 53 15N 0 10 E
Alfred, Maine, U.S.A. 79 C14 43 29N 70 43W
Alfred, N.Y., U.S.A. 78 D7 42 16N 77 48W
Alfreton, U.K. 10 D6 53 6N 1 24W
Alga, Kazakstan 25 E10 49 53N 57 20 E
Algaida, Spain 22 B9 39 33N 2 53 E
Ålgård, Norway 9 G11 58 46N 5 53 E
Algarve, Portugal 19 D1 36 58N 8 20W
Algeciras, Spain 19 D3 36 9N 5 28W
Algemesí, Spain 19 C5 39 11N 0 27W
Alger, Algeria 50 A6 36 42N 3 8 E
Algeria ■, Africa 50 C6 28 30N 2 0 E
Alghero, Italy 20 D3 40 33N 8 19 E
Algiers = Alger, Algeria 50 A6 36 42N 3 8 E
Algoa B., S. Africa 56 E4 33 50S 25 45 E
Algoma, U.S.A. 76 C2 44 36N 87 26W
Algona, U.S.A. 80 D7 43 4N 94 14W
Algonac, U.S.A. 78 D2 42 37N 82 32W
Algonquin Prov. Park, Canada 70 C4 45 50N 78 30W
Algorta, Uruguay 96 C5 32 25S 57 23W
Alhambra, U.S.A. 85 L8 34 8N 118 6W
Alhucemas = Al Hoceïma, Morocco 50 A5 35 8N 3 58W
'Alī al Gharbī, Iraq 44 C5 32 30N 46 45 E
'Alī ash Sharqī, Iraq 44 C5 32 7N 46 44 E
'Alī Khēl, Afghan. 42 C3 33 57N 69 43 E
Alī Shāh, Iran 44 B5 38 9N 45 50 E
'Alīābād, Khorāsān, Iran 45 C8 32 30N 57 30 E
'Alīābād, Kordestān, Iran 44 C5 35 4N 46 58 E
'Alīābād, Yazd, Iran 45 D7 31 41N 53 49 E
Aliağa, Turkey 21 E12 38 47N 26 59 E
Aliákmon →, Greece 21 D10 40 30N 22 36 E
Alicante, Spain 19 C5 38 23N 0 30W
Alice, S. Africa 56 E4 32 48S 26 55 E
Alice, U.S.A. 81 M5 27 45N 98 5W
Alice →, Queens., Australia 62 C3 24 2S 144 50 E
Alice →, Queens., Australia 62 B3 15 35S 142 20 E
Alice Arm, Canada 72 B3 55 29N 129 31W
Alice Springs, Australia 62 C1 23 40S 133 50 E
Alicedale, S. Africa 56 E4 33 15S 26 4 E
Aliceville, U.S.A. 77 J1 33 8N 88 9W
Aliganj, India 43 F8 27 30N 79 10 E
Aligarh, Raj., India 42 G7 25 55N 76 15 E
Aligarh, Ut. P., India 42 F8 27 55N 78 10 E
Alīgūdarz, Iran 45 C6 33 25N 49 45 E
Alimnia, Greece 23 C9 36 16N 27 43 E
Alingsås, Sweden 9 H15 57 56N 12 31 E
Alipur, Pakistan 42 E4 29 25N 70 55 E
Alipur Duar, India 41 F16 26 30N 89 35 E
Aliquippa, U.S.A. 78 F4 40 37N 80 15W
Alitus = Alytus, Lithuania 9 J21 54 24N 24 3 E
Aliwal North, S. Africa 56 E4 30 45S 26 45 E
Alix, Canada 72 C6 52 24N 113 11W
Aljustrel, Portugal 19 D1 37 55N 8 10W
Alkmaar, Neths. 15 B4 52 37N 4 45 E
All American Canal, U.S.A. 83 K6 32 45N 115 15W
Allagash →, U.S.A. 77 B11 47 5N 69 3W
Allah Dad, Pakistan 42 G2 25 38N 67 34 E
Allahabad, India 43 G9 25 25N 81 58 E
Allan, Canada 73 C7 51 53N 106 4W
Allanmyo, Burma 41 K19 19 30N 95 17 E
Allanridge, S. Africa 56 D4 27 45S 26 40 E
Allegany, U.S.A. 78 D6 42 6N 78 30W
Allegheny →, U.S.A. 78 F5 40 27N 80 1W
Allegheny Mts., U.S.A. 76 G6 38 15N 80 10W
Allegheny Reservoir, U.S.A. 78 E6 41 50N 79 0W
Allen, Bog of, Ireland 13 C5 53 15N 7 0W
Allen, L., Ireland 13 B3 54 8N 8 4W
Allendale, U.S.A. 77 J5 33 1N 81 18W
Allende, Mexico 86 B4 28 20N 100 50W
Allentown, U.S.A. 79 F9 40 37N 75 29W
Alleppey, India 40 Q10 9 30N 76 28 E
Aller →, Germany 16 B5 52 56N 9 12 E
Alliance, Nebr., U.S.A. 80 D3 42 6N 102 52W
Alliance, Ohio, U.S.A. 78 F3 40 55N 81 6W
Allier →, France 18 C5 46 57N 3 4 E
Alliford Bay, Canada 72 C2 53 12N 131 58W
Alliston, Canada 78 B5 44 9N 79 52W
Alloa, U.K. 12 E5 56 7N 3 47W
Allora, Australia 63 D5 28 2S 152 0 E
Alluitsup Paa = Sydprøven, Greenland 4 C5 60 30N 45 35W
Alma, Canada 71 C5 48 35N 71 40W
Alma, Ga., U.S.A. 77 K4 31 33N 82 28W
Alma, Kans., U.S.A. 80 F6 39 1N 96 17W
Alma, Mich., U.S.A. 76 D3 43 23N 84 39W
Alma, Nebr., U.S.A. 80 E5 40 6N 99 22W
Alma Ata = Almaty, Kazakstan 26 E8 43 15N 76 57 E
Almada, Portugal 19 C1 38 40N 9 9W
Almaden, Australia 62 B3 17 22S 144 40 E
Almadén, Spain 19 C3 38 49N 4 52W
Almanor, L., U.S.A. 82 F3 40 14N 121 9W
Almansa, Spain 19 C5 38 51N 1 5W
Almanzor, Pico, Spain 19 B3 40 15N 5 18W
Almanzora →, Spain 19 D5 37 14N 1 46W
Almaty, Kazakstan 26 E8 43 15N 76 57 E
Almazán, Spain 19 B4 41 30N 2 30W
Almeirim, Brazil 93 D8 1 30S 52 34W
Almelo, Neths. 15 B6 52 22N 6 42 E
Almendralejo, Spain 19 C2 38 41N 6 26W
Almere-Stad, Neths. 15 B5 52 20N 5 15 E
Almería, Spain 19 D4 36 52N 2 27W
Almirante, Panama 88 E3 9 10N 82 30W
Almiroú, Kólpos, Greece 23 D6 35 23N 24 20 E
Almond, U.S.A. 78 D7 42 19N 77 44W
Almont, U.S.A. 78 D1 42 55N 83 3W
Almonte, Canada 79 A8 45 14N 76 12W
Almora, India 43 E8 29 38N 79 40 E
Alness, U.K. 12 D4 57 41N 4 16W
Alnmouth, U.K. 10 B6 55 24N 1 37W
Alnwick, U.K. 10 B6 55 24N 1 42W
Aloi, Uganda 54 B3 2 16N 33 10 E
Alon, Burma 41 H19 22 12N 95 5 E
Alor, Indonesia 37 F6 8 15S 124 30 E
Alor Setar, Malaysia 39 J3 6 7N 100 22 E
Alot, India 42 H6 23 56N 75 40 E
Aloysius, Mt., Australia 61 E4 26 0S 128 38 E
Alpaugh, U.S.A. 84 K7 35 53N 119 29W
Alpena, U.S.A. 76 C4 45 4N 83 27W
Alpha, Australia 62 C4 23 39S 146 37 E
Alphen aan den Rijn, Neths. 15 B4 52 7N 4 40 E
Alpine, Ariz., U.S.A. 83 K9 33 51N 109 9W
Alpine, Calif., U.S.A. 85 N10 32 50N 116 46W
Alpine, Tex., U.S.A. 81 K3 30 22N 103 40W
Alps, Europe 18 C8 46 30N 9 30 E
Alsace, France 18 B7 48 15N 7 25 E
Alsask, Canada 73 C7 51 21N 109 59W
Alsasua, Spain 19 A4 42 54N 2 10W
Alsek →, U.S.A. 72 B1 59 10N 138 12W
Alsten, Norway 8 D15 65 58N 12 40 E
Alston, U.K. 10 C5 54 49N 2 25W
Alta, Norway 8 B20 69 57N 23 10 E
Alta Gracia, Argentina 94 C3 31 40S 64 30W
Alta Sierra, U.S.A. 85 K8 35 42N 118 33W
Altaelva →, Norway 8 B20 69 54N 23 17 E
Altafjorden, Norway 8 A20 70 5N 23 5 E
Altai = Aerhtai Shan, Mongolia 32 B4 46 40N 92 45 E
Altamaha →, U.S.A. 77 K5 31 20N 81 20W
Altamira, Brazil 93 D8 3 12S 52 10W
Altamira, Chile 94 B2 25 47S 69 51W
Altamira, Mexico 87 C5 22 24N 97 55W
Altamont, U.S.A. 79 D10 42 43N 74 3W
Altamura, Italy 20 D7 40 49N 16 33 E
Altanbulag, Mongolia 32 A5 50 16N 106 30 E
Altar, Mexico 86 A2 30 40N 111 50W
Altar, Desierto de, Mexico 86 B2 30 10N 112 0W
Altata, Mexico 86 C3 24 30N 108 0W
Altavista, U.S.A. 76 G6 37 6N 79 17W
Altay, China 32 B3 47 48N 88 10 E
Altea, Spain 19 C5 38 38N 0 2W
Altiplano = Bolivian Plateau, S. Amer. 90 E4 20 0S 67 30W
Alto Araguaia, Brazil 93 G8 17 15S 53 20W
Alto Cuchumatanes = Cuchumatanes, Sierra de los, Guatemala 88 C1 15 35N 91 25W
Alto del Carmen, Chile 94 B1 28 46S 70 30W
Alto del Inca, Chile 94 A2 24 10S 68 10W
Alto Ligonha, Mozam. 55 F4 15 30S 38 11 E
Alto Molocue, Mozam. 55 F4 15 50S 37 35 E
Alto Paraguay □, Paraguay 94 A4 21 0S 58 30W
Alto Paraná □, Paraguay 95 B5 25 30S 54 50W
Alton, Canada 78 C4 43 54N 80 5W
Alton, U.K. 11 F7 51 9N 0 59W
Alton, Ill., U.S.A. 80 F9 38 53N 90 11W
Alton, N.H., U.S.A. 79 C13 43 27N 71 13W
Altoona, U.S.A. 78 F6 40 31N 78 24W
Altūn Kūprī, Iraq 44 C5 35 45N 44 9 E
Altun Shan, China 32 C3 38 30N 88 0 E
Alturas, U.S.A. 82 F3 41 29N 120 32W
Altus, U.S.A. 81 H5 34 38N 99 20W
Alucra, Turkey 25 F6 40 22N 38 47 E
Alūksne, Latvia 9 H22 57 24N 27 3 E
Alunite, U.S.A. 85 K12 35 59N 114 55W
Alusi, Indonesia 37 F8 7 35S 131 40 E
Alva, U.S.A. 81 G5 36 48N 98 40W
Alvarado, Mexico 87 D5 18 40N 95 50W
Alvarado, U.S.A. 81 J6 32 24N 97 13W
Alvaro Obregón, Presa, Mexico 86 B3 27 55N 109 52W
Alvear, Argentina 94 B4 29 5S 56 30W
Alvesta, Sweden 9 H16 56 54N 14 35 E
Alvin, U.S.A. 81 L7 29 26N 95 15W
Alvinston, Canada 78 D3 42 49N 81 52W
Älvkarleby, Sweden 9 F17 60 34N 17 26 E
Alvord Desert, U.S.A. 82 E4 42 30N 118 25W
Älvsbyn, Sweden 8 D19 65 40N 21 0 E
Alwar, India 42 F7 27 38N 76 34 E
Alxa Zuoqi, China 34 E3 38 50N 105 40 E
Alyangula, Australia 62 A2 13 55S 136 30 E
Alyata = Älät, Azerbaijan 25 G8 39 58N 49 25 E
Alyth, U.K. 12 E5 56 38N 3 13W
Alytus, Lithuania 9 J21 54 24N 24 3 E
Alzada, U.S.A. 80 C2 45 2N 104 25W
Alzira, Spain 19 C5 39 9N 0 30W
Am-Timan, Chad 51 F10 11 0N 20 10 E
Amadeus, L., Australia 61 D5 24 54S 131 0 E

Amadi

Amadi, Dem. Rep. of the Congo . 54 B2 3 40N 26 40 E
Amâdi, Sudan 51 G12 5 29N 30 25 E
Amadjuak L., Canada 69 B12 65 0N 71 8W
Amagansett, U.S.A. 79 F12 40 59N 72 9W
Amagasaki, Japan 31 G7 34 42N 135 20 E
Amahai, Indonesia 37 E7 3 20S 128 55 E
Amakusa-Shotō, Japan 31 H5 32 15N 130 10 E
Åmål, Sweden 9 G15 59 3N 12 42 E
Amaliás, Greece 21 F9 37 47N 21 22 E
Amalner, India 40 J9 21 5N 75 5 E
Amamapare, Indonesia 37 E9 4 53S 136 38 E
Amambaí, Brazil 95 A4 23 5S 55 13W
Amambaí →, Brazil 95 A5 23 22S 53 56W
Amambay □, Paraguay 95 A4 23 0S 56 0W
Amambay, Cordillera de, S. Amer. 95 A4 23 0S 55 45W
Amami-Guntō, Japan 31 L4 27 16N 129 21 E
Amami-Ō-Shima, Japan 31 L4 28 0N 129 0 E
Amaná, L., Brazil 92 D6 2 35S 64 40W
Amanat →, India 43 G11 24 7N 84 4 E
Amanda Park, U.S.A. 84 C3 47 28N 123 55W
Amangeldy, Kazakstan 26 D7 50 10N 65 10 E
Amapá, Brazil 93 C8 2 5N 50 50W
Amapá □, Brazil 93 C8 1 40N 52 0W
Amarante, Brazil 93 E10 6 14S 42 50W
Amaranth, Canada 73 C9 50 36N 98 43W
Amargosa →, U.S.A. 85 J10 36 14N 116 51W
Amargosa Range, U.S.A. 85 J10 36 20N 116 45W
Amári, Greece 23 D6 35 13N 24 40 E
Amarillo, U.S.A. 81 H4 35 13N 101 50W
Amarkantak, India 43 H9 22 40N 81 45 E
Amaro, Mte., Italy 20 C6 42 5N 14 5 E
Amarpur, India 43 G12 25 5N 87 0 E
Amarwara, India 43 H8 22 18N 79 10 E
Amasya □, Turkey 25 F6 40 40N 35 50 E
Amata, Australia 61 E5 26 9S 131 9 E
Amatikulu, S. Africa 57 D5 29 3S 31 33 E
Amatitlán, Guatemala 88 D1 14 29N 90 38W
Amay, Belgium 15 D5 50 33N 5 19 E
Amazon = Amazonas →, S. Amer. 93 D9 0 5S 50 0W
Amazonas □, Brazil 92 E6 5 0S 65 0W
Amazonas →, S. Amer. 93 D9 0 5S 50 0W
Ambah, India 42 F8 26 43N 78 13 E
Ambahakily, Madag. 57 C7 21 36S 43 41 E
Ambala, India 42 D7 30 23N 76 56 E
Ambalavao, Madag. 57 C8 21 50S 46 56 E
Ambanja, Madag. 57 A8 13 40S 48 27 E
Ambarchik, Russia 27 C17 69 40N 162 20 E
Ambarijeby, Madag. 57 A8 14 56S 47 41 E
Ambaro, Helodranon', Madag. 57 A8 13 23S 48 38 E
Ambato, Ecuador 92 D3 1 5S 78 42W
Ambato, Sierra de, Argentina 94 B2 28 25S 66 10W
Ambato Boeny, Madag. 57 B8 16 28S 46 43 E
Ambatofinandrahana, Madag. 57 C8 20 33S 46 48 E
Ambatolampy, Madag. 57 B8 19 20S 47 35 E
Ambatondrazaka, Madag. 57 B8 17 55S 48 28 E
Ambatosoratra, Madag. 57 B8 17 37S 48 31 E
Ambenja, Madag. 57 B8 15 17S 46 58 E
Amberg, Germany 16 D6 49 26N 11 52 E
Ambergris Cay, Belize 87 D7 18 0N 88 0W
Amberley, N.Z. 59 K4 43 9S 172 44 E
Ambikapur, India 43 H10 23 15N 83 15 E
Ambilobé, Madag. 57 A8 13 10S 49 3 E
Ambinanindrano, Madag. 57 C8 20 5S 48 23 E
Amble, U.K. 10 B6 55 20N 1 36W
Ambleside, U.K. 10 C5 54 26N 2 58W
Ambo, Peru 92 F3 10 5S 76 10W
Ambodifototra, Madag. 57 B8 16 59S 49 52 E
Ambodilazana, Madag. 57 B8 18 6S 49 10 E
Ambohimahasoa, Madag. 57 C8 21 7S 47 13 E
Ambohimanga, Madag. 57 C8 20 52S 47 36 E
Ambohitra, Madag. 57 A8 12 30S 49 10 E
Amboise, France 18 C4 47 24N 1 2 E
Ambon, Indonesia 37 E7 3 35S 128 20 E
Amboseli, L., Kenya 54 C4 2 40S 37 10 E
Ambositra, Madag. 57 C8 20 31S 47 25 E
Ambovombe, Madag. 57 D8 25 11S 46 5 E
Amboy, U.S.A. 85 L11 34 33N 115 45W
Amboyna Cay, S. China Sea 36 C4 7 50N 112 50 E
Ambridge, U.S.A. 78 F4 40 36N 80 14W
Ambriz, Angola 52 F2 7 48S 13 8 E
Amchitka I., U.S.A. 68 C1 51 32N 179 0 E
Amderma, Russia 26 C7 69 45N 61 30 E
Amdhi, India 43 H9 23 51N 81 27 E
Ameca, Mexico 86 C4 20 30N 104 0W
Ameca →, Mexico 86 C3 20 40N 105 15W
Amecameca, Mexico 87 D5 19 7N 98 46W
Ameland, Neths. 15 A5 53 27N 5 45 E
Amenia, U.S.A. 79 E11 41 51N 73 33W
American Falls, U.S.A. 82 E7 42 47N 112 51W
American Falls Reservoir, U.S.A. 82 E7 42 47N 112 52W
American Fork, U.S.A. 82 F8 40 23N 111 48W
American Highland, Antarctica 5 D6 73 0S 75 0 E
American Samoa ■, Pac. Oc. 59 B13 14 20S 170 40W
Americana, Brazil 95 A6 22 45S 47 20W
Americus, U.S.A. 77 K3 32 4N 84 14W
Amersfoort, Neths. 15 B5 52 9N 5 23 E
Amersfoort, S. Africa 57 D4 26 59S 29 53 E
Amery Ice Shelf, Antarctica 5 C6 69 30S 72 0 E
Ames, U.S.A. 80 E8 42 2N 93 37W
Amesbury, U.S.A. 79 D14 42 51N 70 56W
Amet, India 42 G5 25 18N 73 56 E
Amga, Russia 27 C14 60 50N 132 0 E
Amga →, Russia 27 C14 62 38N 134 32 E
Amgu, Russia 27 E14 45 45N 137 15 E
Amgun →, Russia 27 D14 52 56N 139 38 E
Amherst, Burma 41 L20 16 2N 97 20 E
Amherst, Canada 71 C7 45 48N 64 8W
Amherst, Mass., U.S.A. 79 D12 42 23N 72 31W
Amherst, N.Y., U.S.A. 78 D6 42 59N 78 48W
Amherst, Ohio, U.S.A. 78 E2 41 24N 82 14W
Amherst I., Canada 79 B8 44 8N 76 43W
Amherstburg, Canada 70 D3 42 6N 83 6W
Amiata, Mte., Italy 20 C4 42 53N 11 37 E
Amidon, U.S.A. 80 B3 46 29N 103 19W
Amiens, France 18 B5 49 54N 2 16 E
Amirābād, Iran 44 C5 33 20N 46 16 E
Amirante Is., Seychelles 28 K9 6 0S 53 0 E
Amisk L., Canada 73 C8 54 35N 102 15W
Amistad, Presa de la, Mexico 86 B4 29 24N 101 0W
Amite, U.S.A. 81 K9 30 44N 90 30W
Amla, India 42 J8 21 56N 78 7 E
Amlia I., U.S.A. 68 C2 52 4N 173 30W
Amlwch, U.K. 10 D3 53 24N 4 20W
'Ammān, Jordan 47 D4 31 57N 35 52 E
'Ammān □, Jordan 47 D5 31 40N 36 30 E
Ammanford, U.K. 11 F4 51 48N 3 59W
Ammassalik = Angmagssalik, Greenland 4 C6 65 40N 37 20W
Ammon, U.S.A. 82 E8 43 28N 111 58W
Amnat Charoen, Thailand 38 E5 15 51N 104 38 E
Amnura, Bangla. 43 G13 24 37N 88 25 E
Āmol, Iran 45 B7 36 23N 52 20 E
Amorgós, Greece 21 F11 36 50N 25 57 E
Amory, U.S.A. 77 J1 33 59N 88 29W
Amos, Canada 70 C4 48 35N 78 5W
Åmot, Norway 9 G13 59 57N 9 54 E
Amoy = Xiamen, China 33 D6 24 25N 118 4 E
Ampang, Malaysia 39 L3 3 8N 101 45 E
Ampanihy, Madag. 57 C7 24 40S 44 45 E
Ampasindava, Helodranon', Madag. 57 A8 13 40S 48 15 E
Ampasindava, Saikanosy, Madag. 57 A8 13 42S 47 55 E
Ampenan, Indonesia 36 F5 8 35S 116 13 E
Amper →, Germany 16 D6 48 29N 11 55 E
Ampotaka, Madag. 57 D7 25 3S 44 41 E
Ampoza, Madag. 57 C7 22 20S 44 44 E
Amqui, Canada 71 C6 48 28N 67 27W
Amravati, India 40 J10 20 55N 77 45 E
Amreli, India 42 J4 21 35N 71 17 E
Amritsar, India 42 D6 31 35N 74 57 E
Amroha, India 43 E8 28 53N 78 30 E
Amsterdam, Neths. 15 B4 52 23N 4 54 E
Amsterdam, U.S.A. 79 D10 42 56N 74 11W
Amsterdam, I., Ind. Oc. 3 F13 38 30S 77 30 E
Amstetten, Austria 16 D8 48 7N 14 51 E
Amudarya →, Uzbekistan 26 E6 43 58N 59 34 E
Amundsen Gulf, Canada 68 A7 71 0N 124 0W
Amundsen Sea, Antarctica 5 D15 72 0S 115 0W
Amuntai, Indonesia 36 E5 2 28S 115 25 E
Amur →, Russia 27 D15 52 56N 141 10 E
Amurang, Indonesia 37 D6 1 5N 124 40 E
Amuri Pass, N.Z. 59 K4 42 31S 172 11 E
Amursk, Russia 27 D14 50 14N 136 54 E
Amyderya = Amudarya →, Uzbekistan 26 E6 43 58N 59 34 E
An Bien, Vietnam 39 H5 9 45N 105 0 E
An Hoa, Vietnam 38 E7 15 40N 108 5 E
An Nabatīyah at Tahta, Lebanon 47 B4 33 23N 35 27 E
An Nabk, Si. Arabia 44 D3 31 20N 37 20 E
An Nabk, Syria 47 A5 34 2N 36 44 E
An Nabk Abū Qaşr, Si. Arabia 44 D3 30 21N 38 34 E
An Nafūd, Si. Arabia 44 D4 28 15N 41 0 E
An Najaf, Iraq 44 C5 32 3N 44 15 E
An Nāşirīyah, Iraq 44 D5 31 0N 46 15 E
An Nhon, Vietnam 38 F7 13 55N 109 7 E
An Nu'ayrīyah, Si. Arabia 45 E6 27 30N 48 30 E
An Nuwayb'ī, W. →, Si. Arabia 47 F3 29 18N 34 57 E
An Thoi, Dao, Vietnam 39 H5 9 58N 104 0 E
An Uaimh, Ireland 13 C5 53 39N 6 41W
Anabar →, Russia 27 B12 73 8N 113 36 E
'Anabtā, West Bank 47 C4 32 19N 35 7 E
Anaconda, U.S.A. 82 C7 46 8N 112 57W
Anacortes, U.S.A. 84 B4 48 30N 122 37W
Anadarko, U.S.A. 81 H5 35 4N 98 15W
Anadolu, Turkey 25 G5 39 0N 30 0 E
Anadyr, Russia 27 C18 64 35N 177 20 E
Anadyr →, Russia 27 C18 64 55N 176 5 E
Anadyrskiy Zaliv, Russia 27 C19 64 0N 180 0 E
Anaga, Pta. de, Canary Is. 22 F3 28 34N 16 9W
'Ānah, Iraq 44 C4 34 25N 42 0 E
Anaheim, U.S.A. 85 M9 33 50N 117 55W
Anahim Lake, Canada 72 C3 52 28N 125 18W
Anáhuac, Mexico 86 B4 27 14N 100 9W
Anakapalle, India 41 L13 17 42N 83 6 E
Anakie, Australia 62 C4 23 32S 147 45 E
Analalava, Madag. 57 A8 14 35S 48 0 E
Análipsis, Greece 23 A3 39 36N 19 55 E
Anambar →, Pakistan 42 D3 30 15N 68 50 E
Anambas, Kepulauan, Indonesia 39 L6 3 20N 106 30 E
Anambas Is. = Anambas, Kepulauan, Indonesia 39 L6 3 20N 106 30 E
Anamosa, U.S.A. 80 D9 42 7N 91 17W
Anamur, Turkey 25 G5 36 8N 32 58 E
Anan, Japan 31 H7 33 54N 134 40 E
Anand, India 42 H5 22 32N 72 59 E
Anantnag, India 43 C6 33 45N 75 10 E
Ananyiv, Ukraine 17 E15 47 44N 29 58 E
Anapodháris →, Greece 23 E7 34 59N 25 20 E
Anápolis, Brazil 93 G9 16 15S 48 50W
Anapu →, Brazil 93 D8 1 53S 50 53W
Anār, Iran 45 D7 30 55N 55 13 E
Anārak, Iran 45 C7 33 25N 53 40 E
Anas →, India 42 H5 23 26N 74 0 E
Anatolia = Anadolu, Turkey 25 G5 39 0N 30 0 E
Anatsogno, Madag. 57 C7 23 33S 43 46 E
Añatuya, Argentina 94 B3 28 20S 62 50W
Anaunethad L., Canada 73 A8 60 55N 104 25W
Anbyŏn, N. Korea 35 E14 39 1N 127 35 E
Ancaster, Canada 78 C5 43 13N 79 59W
Anchor Bay, U.S.A. 84 G3 38 48N 123 34W
Anchorage, U.S.A. 68 B5 61 13N 149 54W
Anci, China 34 E9 39 20N 116 40 E
Ancohuma, Nevada, Bolivia 92 G5 16 0S 68 50W
Ancón, Peru 92 F3 11 50S 77 10W
Ancona, Italy 20 C5 43 38N 13 30 E
Ancud, Chile 96 E2 42 0S 73 50W
Ancud, G. de, Chile 96 E2 42 0S 73 0W
Anda, China 33 B7 46 24N 125 19 E
Andacollo, Argentina 94 D1 37 10S 70 42W
Andacollo, Chile 94 C1 30 14S 71 6W
Andalgalá, Argentina 94 B2 27 40S 66 30W
Åndalsnes, Norway 9 E12 62 35N 7 43 E
Andalucía □, Spain 19 D3 37 35N 5 0W
Andalusia = Andalucía □, Spain 19 D3 37 35N 5 0W
Andalusia, U.S.A. 77 K2 31 18N 86 29W
Andaman Is., Ind. Oc. 28 H13 12 30N 92 30 E
Andaman Sea, Ind. Oc. 36 B1 13 0N 96 0 E
Andamooka Opal Fields, Australia 63 E2 30 27S 137 9 E
Andapa, Madag. 53 G9 14 30S 49 30 E
Andara, Namibia 56 B3 18 2S 21 9 E
Andenes, Norway 8 B17 69 19N 16 18 E
Andenne, Belgium 15 D5 50 28N 5 5 E
Anderson, Alaska, U.S.A. 68 B5 64 25N 149 15W
Anderson, Calif., U.S.A. 82 F2 40 27N 122 18W
Anderson, Ind., U.S.A. 76 E3 40 10N 85 41W
Anderson, Mo., U.S.A. 81 G7 36 39N 94 27W
Anderson, S.C., U.S.A. 77 H4 34 31N 82 39W
Anderson →, Canada 68 B7 69 42N 129 0W
Andes, U.S.A. 79 D10 42 12N 74 47W
Andes, Cord. de los, S. Amer. 92 H5 20 0S 68 0W
Andfjorden, Norway 8 B17 69 10N 16 20 E
Andhra Pradesh □, India 40 L11 18 0N 79 0 E
Andijon, Uzbekistan 26 E8 41 10N 72 15 E
Andikíthira, Greece 21 G10 35 52N 23 15 E
Andīmeshk, Iran 45 C6 32 27N 48 21 E
Andizhan = Andijon, Uzbekistan 26 E8 41 10N 72 15 E
Andoany, Madag. 57 A8 13 25S 48 16 E
Andong, S. Korea 35 F15 36 40N 128 43 E
Andongwei, China 35 G10 35 6N 119 20 E
Andoom, Australia 62 A3 12 25S 141 53 E
Andorra ■, Europe 18 E4 42 30N 1 30 E
Andorra La Vella, Andorra 18 E4 42 31N 1 32 E
Andover, U.K. 11 F6 51 12N 1 29W
Andover, Maine, U.S.A. 79 B14 44 38N 70 45W
Andover, Mass., U.S.A. 79 D13 42 40N 71 8W
Andover, N.J., U.S.A. 79 F10 40 59N 74 45W
Andover, N.Y., U.S.A. 78 D7 42 10N 77 48W
Andover, Ohio, U.S.A. 78 E4 41 36N 80 34W
Andøya, Norway 8 B16 69 10N 15 50 E
Andradina, Brazil 93 H8 20 54S 51 23W
Andrahary, Mt., Madag. 57 A8 13 37S 49 17 E
Andramasina, Madag. 57 B8 19 11S 47 35 E
Andranopasy, Madag. 57 C7 21 17S 43 44 E
Andratx, Spain 22 B9 39 39N 2 25 E
Andreanof Is., U.S.A. 68 C2 51 30N 176 0W
Andrews, S.C., U.S.A. 77 J6 33 27N 79 34W
Andrews, Tex., U.S.A. 81 J3 32 19N 102 33W
Ándria, Italy 20 D7 41 13N 16 17 E
Andriba, Madag. 57 B8 17 30S 46 58 E
Androka, Madag. 57 C7 24 58S 44 2 E
Andropov = Rybinsk, Russia 24 C6 58 5N 38 50 E
Ándros, Greece 21 F11 37 50N 24 57 E
Andros I., Bahamas 88 B4 24 30N 78 0W
Andros Town, Bahamas 88 B4 24 43N 77 47W
Androscoggin →, U.S.A. 79 C14 43 58N 70 0W
Andselv, Norway 8 B18 69 4N 18 34 E
Andújar, Spain 19 C3 38 3N 4 5W
Andulo, Angola 52 G3 11 25S 16 45 E
Anegada I., Virgin Is. 89 C7 18 45N 64 20W
Anegada Passage, W. Indies 89 C7 18 15N 63 45W
Aneto, Pico de, Spain 19 A6 42 37N 0 40 E
Ang Thong, Thailand 38 E3 14 35N 100 31 E
Angamos, Punta, Chile 94 A1 23 1S 70 32W
Angara →, Russia 27 D10 58 5N 94 20 E
Angarsk, Russia 27 D11 52 30N 104 0 E
Angas Hills, Australia 60 D4 23 0S 127 50 E
Angaston, Australia 63 E2 34 30S 139 8 E
Angaur I., Pac. Oc. 37 C8 6 54N 134 9 E
Ånge, Sweden 9 E16 62 31N 15 35 E
Ángel, Salto = Angel Falls, Venezuela 92 B6 5 57N 62 30W
Ángel de la Guarda, I., Mexico 86 B2 29 30N 113 30W
Angel Falls, Venezuela 92 B6 5 57N 62 30W
Angeles, Phil. 37 A6 15 9N 120 33 E
Ängelholm, Sweden 9 H15 56 15N 12 58 E
Angels Camp, U.S.A. 84 G6 38 4N 120 32W
Ångermanälven →, Sweden 8 E17 62 40N 18 0 E
Ångermanland, Sweden 8 E18 63 36N 17 45 E
Angers, Canada 79 A9 45 31N 75 29W
Angers, France 18 C3 47 30N 0 35W
Ångesån →, Sweden 8 C20 66 16N 22 47 E
Angikuni L., Canada 73 A9 62 0N 100 0W
Angkor, Cambodia 38 F4 13 22N 103 50 E
Anglesey, U.K. 10 D3 53 17N 4 20W
Anglesey, Isle of □, U.K. 10 D3 53 16N 4 18W
Angleton, U.S.A. 81 L7 29 10N 95 26W
Anglisidhes, Cyprus 23 E12 34 51N 33 27 E
Angmagssalik, Greenland 4 C6 65 40N 37 20W
Ango, Dem. Rep. of the Congo 54 B2 4 10N 26 5 E
Angoche, Mozam. 55 F4 16 8S 39 55 E
Angoche, I., Mozam. 55 F4 16 20S 39 50 E
Angol, Chile 94 D1 37 56S 72 45W
Angola, Ind., U.S.A. 76 E3 41 38N 85 0W
Angola, N.Y., U.S.A. 78 D5 42 38N 79 2W
Angola ■, Africa 53 G3 12 0S 18 0 E
Angoulême, France 18 D4 45 39N 0 10 E
Angoumois, France 18 D3 45 50N 0 25 E
Angra dos Reis, Brazil 95 A7 23 0S 44 10W
Angren, Uzbekistan 26 E8 41 1N 70 12 E
Angtassom, Cambodia 39 G5 11 1N 104 41 E
Angu, Dem. Rep. of the Congo 54 B1 3 25N 24 28 E
Anguang, China 35 B12 45 15N 123 45 E
Anguilla ■, W. Indies 89 C7 18 14N 63 5W
Anguo, China 34 E8 38 28N 115 15 E
Angurugu, Australia 62 A2 14 0S 136 25 E
Angus □, U.K. 12 E6 56 46N 2 56W
Anhanduí →, Brazil 95 A5 21 46S 52 9W
Anholt, Denmark 9 H14 56 42N 11 33 E
Anhui □, China 33 C6 32 0N 117 0 E
Anhwei = Anhui □, China 33 C6 32 0N 117 0 E
Anichab, Namibia 56 C1 21 0S 14 46 E
Animas →, U.S.A. 83 H9 36 43N 108 13W
Anivorano, Madag. 57 B8 18 44S 48 58 E
Anjalankoski, Finland 9 F22 60 45N 26 51 E
Anjar, India 42 H4 23 6N 70 10 E
Anjidiv I., India 40 M9 14 40N 74 10 E
Anjou, France 18 C3 47 20N 0 15W
Anjozorobe, Madag. 57 B8 18 22S 47 52 E
Anju, N. Korea 35 E13 39 36N 125 40 E
Ankaboa, Tanjon, Madag. 57 C7 21 58S 43 20 E
Ankang, China 34 H5 32 40N 109 1 E
Ankara, Turkey 25 G5 39 57N 32 54 E
Ankaramena, Madag. 57 C8 21 57S 46 39 E
Ankaratra, Madag. 53 H9 19 25S 47 12 E
Ankazoabo, Madag. 57 C7 22 18S 44 31 E
Ankazobe, Madag. 57 B8 18 20S 47 10 E
Ankeny, U.S.A. 80 E8 41 44N 93 36W
Ankisabe, Madag. 57 B8 19 17S 46 29 E
Ankoro, Dem. Rep. of the Congo 54 D2 6 45S 26 55 E
Anmyŏn-do, S. Korea 35 F14 36 25N 126 25 E
Ann, C., U.S.A. 79 D14 42 38N 70 35W
Ann Arbor, U.S.A. 76 D4 42 17N 83 45W
Anna, U.S.A. 81 G10 37 28N 89 15W
Annaba, Algeria 50 A7 36 50N 7 46 E
Annalee →, Ireland 13 B4 54 2N 7 24W
Annam, Vietnam 38 E7 16 0N 108 0 E
Annamitique, Chaîne, Asia 38 D6 17 0N 106 0 E
Annan, U.K. 12 G5 54 59N 3 16W
Annan →, U.K. 12 G5 54 58N 3 16W
Annapolis, U.S.A. 76 F7 38 59N 76 30W
Annapolis Royal, Canada 71 D6 44 44N 65 32W
Annapurna, Nepal 43 E10 28 34N 83 50 E
Annean, L., Australia 61 E2 26 54S 118 14 E
Annecy, France 18 D7 45 55N 6 8 E
Anning, China 32 D5 24 55N 102 26 E
Anniston, U.S.A. 77 J3 33 39N 85 50W
Annobón, Atl. Oc. 49 G4 1 25S 5 36 E
Annotto Bay, Jamaica 88 C4 18 17N 76 45W
Annville, U.S.A. 79 F8 40 20N 76 31W
Áno Viánnos, Greece 23 D7 35 2N 25 21 E
Anorotsangana, Madag. 57 A8 13 56S 47 55 E
Anóyia, Greece 23 D6 35 16N 24 52 E
Anping, Hebei, China 34 E8 38 15N 115 30 E
Anping, Liaoning, China 35 D12 41 5N 123 30 E
Anqing, China 33 C6 30 30N 117 3 E
Anqiu, China 35 F10 36 25N 119 10 E
Ansai, China 34 F5 36 50N 109 20 E
Ansbach, Germany 16 D6 49 28N 10 34 E
Anshan, China 35 D12 41 5N 122 58 E
Anshun, China 32 D5 26 18N 105 57 E
Ansley, U.S.A. 80 E5 41 18N 99 23W
Anson, U.S.A. 81 J5 32 45N 99 54W
Anson B., Australia 60 B5 13 20S 130 6 E
Ansongo, Mali 50 E6 15 25N 0 35 E
Ansonia, U.S.A. 79 E11 41 21N 73 5W
Anstruther, U.K. 12 E6 56 14N 2 41W
Ansudu, Indonesia 37 E9 2 11S 139 22 E
Antabamba, Peru 92 F4 14 40S 73 0W
Antakya, Turkey 25 G6 36 14N 36 10 E
Antalaha, Madag. 57 A9 14 57S 50 20 E
Antalya, Turkey 25 G5 36 52N 30 45 E
Antalya Körfezi, Turkey 25 G5 36 15N 31 30 E
Antananarivo, Madag. 57 B8 18 55S 47 31 E
Antananarivo □, Madag. 57 B8 19 0S 47 0 E
Antanimbaribe, Madag. 57 C7 21 30S 44 48 E
Antarctic Pen., Antarctica 5 C18 67 0S 60 0W
Antarctica 5 E3 90 0S 0 0 E
Antelope, Zimbabwe 55 G2 21 2S 28 31 E
Antequera, Paraguay 94 A4 24 8S 57 7W
Antequera, Spain 19 D3 37 5N 4 33W
Antero, Mt., U.S.A. 83 G10 38 41N 106 15W
Anthony, Kans., U.S.A. 81 G5 37 9N 98 2W
Anthony, N. Mex., U.S.A. 83 K10 32 0N 106 36W
Anti Atlas, Morocco 50 C4 30 0N 8 30W
Anti-Lebanon = Ash Sharqi, Al Jabal, Lebanon 47 B5 33 40N 36 10 E
Antibes, France 18 E7 43 34N 7 6 E
Anticosti, Î. d', Canada 71 C7 49 30N 63 0W
Antigo, U.S.A. 80 C10 45 9N 89 9W
Antigonish, Canada 71 C7 45 38N 61 58W
Antigua, Canary Is. 22 F5 28 24N 14 1W
Antigua, W. Indies 89 C7 17 0N 61 50W
Antigua & Barbuda ■, W. Indies 89 C7 17 20N 61 48W
Antigua Guatemala, Guatemala 88 D1 14 34N 90 41W
Antilla, Cuba 88 B4 20 40N 75 50W
Antilles = West Indies, Cent. Amer. 89 D7 15 0N 65 0W
Antioch, U.S.A. 84 G5 38 1N 121 48W
Antioquia, Colombia 92 B3 6 40N 75 55W
Antipodes Is., Pac. Oc. 64 M9 49 45S 178 40 E
Antlers, U.S.A. 81 H7 34 14N 95 37W
Antofagasta, Chile 94 A1 23 50S 70 30W
Antofagasta □, Chile 94 A2 24 0S 69 0W
Antofagasta de la Sierra, Argentina 94 B2 26 5S 67 20W
Antofalla, Argentina 94 B2 25 30S 68 5W
Antofalla, Salar de, Argentina 94 B2 25 40S 67 45W
Anton, U.S.A. 81 J3 33 49N 102 10W
Antongila, Helodrano, Madag. 57 B8 15 30S 49 50 E
Antonibé, Madag. 57 B8 15 7S 47 24 E
Antonibé, Presqu'île d', Madag. 57 A8 14 55S 47 20 E
Antonina, Brazil 95 B6 25 26S 48 42W
Antrim, U.K. 13 B5 54 43N 6 14W
Antrim, U.S.A. 78 F3 40 7N 81 21W
Antrim □, U.K. 13 B5 54 56N 6 25W
Antrim, Mts. of, U.K. 13 A5 55 3N 6 14W
Antrim Plateau, Australia 60 C4 18 8S 128 20 E
Antsalova, Madag. 57 B7 18 40S 44 37 E
Antsirabe, Madag. 57 B8 19 55S 47 2 E
Antsiranana, Madag. 57 A8 12 25S 49 20 E
Antsohihy, Madag. 57 A8 14 50S 47 59 E
Antsohimbondrona Seranana, Madag. 57 A8 13 7S 48 48 E
Antu, China 35 C15 42 30N 128 20 E
Antwerp = Antwerpen, Belgium 15 C4 51 13N 4 25 E
Antwerp, U.S.A. 79 B9 44 12N 75 37W
Antwerpen, Belgium 15 C4 51 13N 4 25 E
Antwerpen □, Belgium 15 C4 51 15N 4 40 E
Anupgarh, India 42 E5 29 10N 73 10 E
Anuppur, India 43 H9 23 6N 81 41 E
Anuradhapura, Sri Lanka 40 Q12 8 22N 80 28 E
Anveh, Iran 45 E7 27 23N 54 11 E
Anvers = Antwerpen, Belgium 15 C4 51 13N 4 25 E
Anvers I., Antarctica 5 C17 64 30S 63 40W
Anxi, China 32 B4 40 30N 95 43 E
Anxious B., Australia 63 E1 33 24S 134 45 E
Anyang, China 34 F8 36 5N 114 21 E
Anyer-Kidul, Indonesia 37 G11 6 4S 105 53 E
Anyi, China 34 G6 35 2N 111 2 E
Anza, U.S.A. 85 M10 33 35N 116 39W
Anze, China 34 F7 36 10N 112 12 E
Anzhero-Sudzhensk, Russia 26 D9 56 10N 86 0 E
Ánzio, Italy 20 D5 41 27N 12 37 E
Aoga-Shima, Japan 31 H9 32 28N 139 46 E
Aomen = Macau, China 33 D6 22 16N 113 35 E
Aomori, Japan 30 D10 40 45N 140 45 E

Asmara

Aomori □, Japan 30 D10 40 45N 140 40 E
Aonla, India 43 E8 28 16N 79 11 E
Aosta, Italy 18 D7 45 45N 7 20 E
Aouker, Mauritania 50 E4 17 40N 10 0W
Aozou, Chad 51 D9 21 45N 17 28 E
Apa →, S. Amer. 94 A4 22 6S 58 2W
Apache, U.S.A. 81 H5 34 54N 98 22W
Apache Junction, U.S.A. 83 K8 33 25N 111 33W
Apalachee B., U.S.A. 77 L4 30 0N 84 0W
Apalachicola, U.S.A. 77 L3 29 43N 84 59W
Apalachicola →, U.S.A. 77 L3 29 43N 84 58W
Apaporis →, Colombia 92 D5 1 23S 69 25W
Aparri, Phil. 37 A6 18 22N 121 38 E
Apatity, Russia 24 A5 67 34N 33 22 E
Apatzingán, Mexico 86 D4 19 0N 102 20W
Apeldoorn, Neths. 15 B5 52 13N 5 57 E
Apennines = Appennini, Italy 20 B4 44 0N 10 0 E
Apia, W. Samoa 59 A13 13 50S 171 50W
Apiacás, Serra dos, Brazil 92 E7 9 50S 57 0W
Apizaco, Mexico 87 D5 19 26N 98 9W
Aplao, Peru 92 G4 16 0S 72 40W
Apo, Mt., Phil. 37 C7 6 53N 125 14 E
Apolakkiá, Greece 23 C9 36 5N 27 48 E
Apolakkiá, Órmos, Greece 23 C9 36 5N 27 45 E
Apollo Bay, Australia 63 F3 38 45S 143 40 E
Apolo, Bolivia 92 F5 14 30S 68 30W
Aporé →, Brazil 93 G8 19 27S 50 57W
Apostle Is., U.S.A. 80 B9 47 0N 90 40W
Apóstoles, Argentina 95 B4 28 0S 56 0W
Apostolos Andreas, C., Cyprus 23 D13 35 42N 34 35 E
Apoteri, Guyana 92 C7 4 2N 58 32W
Appalachian Mts., U.S.A. 76 G6 38 0N 80 0W
Appennini, Italy 20 B4 44 0N 10 0 E
Apple Hill, Canada 79 A10 45 13N 74 46W
Apple Valley, U.S.A. 85 L9 34 32N 117 14W
Appleby-in-Westmorland, U.K. 10 C5 54 35N 2 29W
Appleton, U.S.A. 76 C1 44 16N 88 25W
Approuague →, Fr. Guiana 93 C8 4 30N 51 57W
Aprília, Italy 20 D5 41 36N 12 39 E
Apsley, Canada 78 B6 44 45N 78 6W
Apucarana, Brazil 95 A5 23 55S 51 33W
Apure →, Venezuela 92 B5 7 37N 66 25W
Apurimac →, Peru 92 F4 12 17S 73 56W
Āqā Jarī, Iran 45 D6 30 42N 49 50 E
Aqaba = Al 'Aqabah, Jordan 47 F4 29 31N 35 0 E
Aqaba, G. of, Red Sea 44 D2 28 15N 33 20 E
'Aqabah, Khalīj al = Aqaba, G. of, Red Sea 44 D2 28 15N 33 20 E
'Aqdā, Iran 45 C7 32 26N 53 37 E
Aqmola = Astana, Kazakstan 26 D8 51 10N 71 30 E
Aqrah, Iraq 44 B4 36 46N 43 45 E
Aqtaū, Kazakstan 26 E6 43 39N 51 12 E
Aqtöbe, Kazakstan 25 D10 50 17N 57 10 E
Aquidauana, Brazil 93 H7 20 30S 55 50W
Aquiles Serdán, Mexico 86 B3 28 37N 105 54W
Aquin, Haiti 89 C5 18 16N 73 24W
Aquitain, Bassin, France 18 D3 44 0N 0 30W
Ar Rachidiya, Morocco 50 B5 31 58N 4 20W
Ar Rafid, Syria 47 C4 32 57N 35 52 E
Ar Raḥḥālīyah, Iraq 44 C4 32 44N 43 23 E
Ar Ramādī, Iraq 44 C4 33 25N 43 20 E
Ar Ramthā, Jordan 47 C5 32 34N 36 0 E
Ar Raqqah, Syria 44 C3 35 59N 39 8 E
Ar Rass, Si. Arabia 44 E4 25 50N 43 40 E
Ar Rifā'ī, Iraq 44 D5 31 50N 46 10 E
Ar Riyāḍ, Si. Arabia 46 C4 24 41N 46 42 E
Ar Ru'ays, Qatar 45 E6 26 8N 51 12 E
Ar Rukhaymīyah, Iraq 44 D5 29 22N 45 38 E
Ar Ruqayyidah, Si. Arabia 45 E6 25 21N 49 34 E
Ar Ruṣāfah, Syria 44 C3 35 45N 38 49 E
Ar Ruṭbah, Iraq 44 C4 33 0N 40 15 E
Ara, India 43 G11 25 35N 84 32 E
Arab, U.S.A. 77 H2 34 19N 86 30W
'Arab, Bahr el →, Sudan 51 G11 9 0N 29 30 E
'Arabābād, Iran 45 C8 33 2N 57 41 E
Arabia, Asia 28 G8 25 0N 45 0 E
Arabian Desert = Es Sahrâ' Esh Sharqîya, Egypt 51 C12 27 30N 32 30 E
Arabian Gulf = Gulf, The, Asia 45 E6 27 0N 50 0 E
Arabian Sea, Ind. Oc. 29 H10 16 0N 65 0 E
Aracaju, Brazil 93 F11 10 55S 37 4W
Aracati, Brazil 93 D11 4 30S 37 44W
Araçatuba, Brazil 95 A5 21 10S 50 30W
Aracena, Spain 19 D2 37 53N 6 38W
Araçuaí, Brazil 93 G10 16 52S 42 4W
'Arad, Israel 47 D4 31 15N 35 12 E
Arad, Romania 17 E11 46 10N 21 20 E
Arādān, Iran 45 C7 35 21N 52 30 E
Aradhippou, Cyprus 23 E12 34 57N 33 36 E
Arafura Sea, E. Indies 37 F9 9 0S 135 0 E
Aragón □, Spain 19 B5 41 25N 0 40W
Aragón →, Spain 19 A5 42 13N 1 44W
Araguacema, Brazil 93 E9 8 50S 49 20W
Araguaia →, Brazil 93 E9 5 21S 48 41W
Araguaína, Brazil 93 E9 7 12S 48 12W
Araguari, Brazil 93 G9 18 38S 48 11W
Araguari →, Brazil 93 C9 1 15N 49 55W
Arain, India 42 F6 26 27N 75 2 E
Arak, Algeria 50 C6 25 20N 3 45 E
Arāk, Iran 45 C6 34 0N 49 40 E
Arakan Coast, Burma 41 K19 19 0N 94 0 E
Arakan Yoma, Burma 41 K19 20 0N 94 40 E
Araks = Aras, Rūd-e →, Azerbaijan 44 B5 40 5N 48 29 E
Aral, Kazakstan 26 E7 46 41N 61 45 E
Aral Sea, Asia 26 E7 44 30N 60 0 E
Aral Tengizi = Aral Sea, Asia 26 E7 44 30N 60 0 E
Aralsk = Aral, Kazakstan 26 E7 46 41N 61 45 E
Aralskoye More = Aral Sea, Asia 26 E7 44 30N 60 0 E
Aramac, Australia 62 C4 22 58S 145 14 E
Aran I., Ireland 13 A3 55 0N 8 30W
Aran Is., Ireland 13 C2 53 6N 9 38W
Aranda de Duero, Spain 19 B4 41 39N 3 42W
Arandān, Iran 44 C5 35 23N 46 55 E
Aranjuez, Spain 19 B4 40 1N 3 40W
Aranos, Namibia 56 C2 24 9S 19 7 E
Aransas Pass, U.S.A. 81 M6 27 55N 97 9W
Aranyaprathet, Thailand 38 F4 13 41N 102 30 E
Arapahoe, U.S.A. 80 E5 40 18N 99 54W
Arapey Grande →, Uruguay 94 C4 30 55S 57 49W
Arapgir, Turkey 44 B3 39 5N 38 30 E
Arapiraca, Brazil 93 E11 9 45S 36 39W
Arapongas, Brazil 95 A5 23 29S 51 28W
Ar'ar, Si. Arabia 44 D4 30 59N 41 2 E
Araranguá, Brazil 95 B6 29 0S 49 30W
Araraquara, Brazil 93 H9 21 50S 48 0W
Ararás, Serra das, Brazil 95 B5 25 0S 53 10W
Ararat, Australia 63 F3 37 16S 143 0 E
Ararat, Mt. = Ağrı Dağı, Turkey 25 G7 39 50N 44 15 E
Araria, India 43 F12 26 9N 87 33 E
Araripe, Chapada do, Brazil 93 E11 7 20S 40 0W
Araruama, L. de, Brazil 95 A7 22 53S 42 12W
Aras, Rūd-e →, Azerbaijan 44 B5 40 5N 48 29 E
Arauca, Colombia 92 B4 7 0N 70 40W
Arauca →, Venezuela 92 B5 7 24N 66 35W
Arauco, Chile 94 D1 37 16S 73 25W
Araxá, Brazil 93 G9 19 35S 46 55W
Araya, Pen. de, Venezuela 92 A6 10 40N 64 0W
Arba Minch, Ethiopia 46 F2 6 0N 37 30 E
Arbat, Iraq 44 C5 35 25N 45 35 E
Árbatax, Italy 20 E3 39 56N 9 42 E
Arbīl, Iraq 44 B5 36 15N 44 5 E
Arborfield, Canada 73 C8 53 6N 103 39W
Arborg, Canada 73 C9 50 54N 97 13W
Arbroath, U.K. 12 E6 56 34N 2 35W
Arbuckle, U.S.A. 84 F4 39 1N 122 3W
Arcachon, France 18 D3 44 40N 1 10W
Arcade, Calif., U.S.A. 85 L8 34 2N 118 15W
Arcade, N.Y., U.S.A. 78 D6 42 32N 78 25W
Arcadia, Fla., U.S.A. 77 M5 27 13N 81 52W
Arcadia, La., U.S.A. 81 J8 32 33N 92 55W
Arcadia, Pa., U.S.A. 78 F6 40 47N 78 51W
Arcata, U.S.A. 82 F1 40 52N 124 5W
Archangel = Arkhangelsk, Russia 24 B7 64 38N 40 36 E
Archbald, U.S.A. 79 E9 41 30N 75 32W
Archer →, Australia 62 A3 13 28S 141 41 E
Archer B., Australia 62 A3 13 20S 141 30 E
Archers Post, Kenya 54 B4 0 35N 37 35 E
Arches National Park, U.S.A. 83 G9 38 45N 109 25W
Arckaringa Cr. →, Australia 63 D2 28 10S 135 22 E
Arco, U.S.A. 82 E7 43 38N 113 18W
Arcos de la Frontera, Spain 19 D3 36 45N 5 49W
Arcot, India 40 N11 12 53N 79 20 E
Arctic Bay, Canada 69 A11 73 1N 85 7W
Arctic Ocean, Arctic 4 B18 78 0N 160 0W
Arctic Red River = Tsiigehtchic, Canada 68 B6 67 15N 134 0W
Arda →, Bulgaria 21 D12 41 40N 26 30 E
Ardabīl, Iran 45 B6 38 15N 48 18 E
Ardakān = Sepīdān, Iran 45 D7 30 20N 52 5 E
Ardakān, Iran 45 C7 32 19N 53 59 E
Ardee, Ireland 13 C5 53 52N 6 33W
Arden, Canada 78 B8 44 43N 76 56W
Arden, Calif., U.S.A. 84 G5 38 36N 121 33W
Arden, Nev., U.S.A. 85 J11 36 1N 115 14W
Ardenne, Belgium 16 D3 49 50N 5 5 E
Ardennes = Ardenne, Belgium 16 D3 49 50N 5 5 E
Arderin, Ireland 13 C4 53 2N 7 39W
Ardestān, Iran 45 C7 33 20N 52 25 E
Ardivachar Pt., U.K. 12 D1 57 23N 7 26W
Ardlethan, Australia 63 E4 34 22S 146 53 E
Ardmore, Okla., U.S.A. 81 H6 34 10N 97 8W
Ardmore, Pa., U.S.A. 79 G9 39 58N 75 18W
Ardnamurchan, Pt. of, U.K. 12 E2 56 43N 6 14W
Ardnave Pt., U.K. 12 F2 55 53N 6 20W
Ardrossan, Australia 63 E2 34 26S 137 53 E
Ardrossan, U.K. 12 F4 55 39N 4 49W
Ards Pen., U.K. 13 B6 54 33N 5 34W
Arecibo, Puerto Rico 89 C6 18 29N 66 43W
Areia Branca, Brazil 93 E11 5 0S 37 0W
Arena, Pt., U.S.A. 84 G3 38 57N 123 44W
Arenal, Honduras 88 C2 15 21N 86 50W
Arendal, Norway 9 G13 58 28N 8 46 E
Arequipa, Peru 92 G4 16 20S 71 30W
Arévalo, Spain 19 B3 41 3N 4 43W
Arezzo, Italy 20 C4 43 25N 11 53 E
Arga, Turkey 44 B3 38 21N 37 59 E
Arganda, Spain 19 B4 40 19N 3 26W
Argenta, Canada 72 C5 50 11N 116 56W
Argentan, France 18 B3 48 45N 0 1W
Argentário, Mte., Italy 20 C4 42 24N 11 9 E
Argentia, Canada 71 C9 47 18N 53 58W
Argentina ■, S. Amer. 96 D3 35 0S 66 0W
Argentina Is., Antarctica 5 C17 66 0S 64 0W
Argentino, L., Argentina 96 G2 50 10S 73 0W
Argeş →, Romania 17 F14 44 5N 26 38 E
Arghandab →, Afghan. 42 D1 31 30N 64 15 E
Argolikós Kólpos, Greece 21 F10 37 20N 22 52 E
Árgos, Greece 21 F10 37 40N 22 43 E
Argostólion, Greece 21 E9 38 12N 20 33 E
Arguello, Pt., U.S.A. 85 L6 34 35N 120 39W
Arguineguín, Canary Is. 22 G4 27 46N 15 41W
Argun →, Russia 27 D13 53 20N 121 28 E
Argus Pk., U.S.A. 85 K9 35 52N 117 26W
Argyle, L., Australia 60 C4 16 20S 128 40 E
Argyll & Bute □, U.K. 12 E3 56 13N 5 28W
Århus, Denmark 9 H14 56 8N 10 11 E
Ariadnoye, Russia 30 B7 45 8N 134 25 E
Ariamsvlei, Namibia 56 D2 28 9S 19 51 E
Ariana, Tunisia 51 A7 36 52N 10 12 E
Arica, Chile 92 G4 18 32S 70 20W
Arica, Colombia 92 D4 2 0S 71 50W
Arico, Canary Is. 22 F3 28 9N 16 29W
Arid, C., Australia 61 F3 34 1S 123 10 E
Arida, Japan 31 G7 34 5N 135 8 E
Arílla, Ákra, Greece 23 A3 39 43N 19 39 E
Arima, Trin. & Tob. 89 D7 10 38N 61 17W
Arinos →, Brazil 92 F7 10 25S 58 20W
Ario de Rosales, Mexico 86 D4 19 12N 102 0W
Aripuanã, Brazil 92 E6 9 25S 60 30W
Aripuanã →, Brazil 92 E6 5 7S 60 25W
Ariquemes, Brazil 92 E6 9 55S 63 6W
Arisaig, U.K. 12 E3 56 55N 5 51W
Aristazabal I., Canada 72 C3 52 40N 129 10W
Arivonimamo, Madag. 57 B8 19 1S 47 11 E
Arizaro, Salar de, Argentina 94 A2 24 40S 67 50W
Arizona, Argentina 94 D2 35 45S 65 25W
Arizona □, U.S.A. 83 J8 34 0N 112 0W
Arizpe, Mexico 86 A2 30 20N 110 11W
Arjeplog, Sweden 8 D18 66 3N 18 2 E
Arjona, Colombia 92 A3 10 14N 75 22W
Arjuna, Indonesia 37 G15 7 49S 112 34 E
Arka, Russia 27 C15 60 15N 142 0 E
Arkadelphia, U.S.A. 81 H8 34 7N 93 4W
Arkaig, L., U.K. 12 E3 56 59N 5 10W
Arkalyk = Arqalyk, Kazakstan 26 D7 50 13N 66 50 E
Arkansas □, U.S.A. 81 H8 35 0N 92 30W
Arkansas →, U.S.A. 81 J9 33 47N 91 4W
Arkansas City, U.S.A. 81 G6 37 4N 97 2W
Arkaroola, Australia 63 E2 30 20S 139 22 E
Arkhángelos, Greece 23 C10 36 13N 28 7 E
Arkhangelsk, Russia 24 B7 64 38N 40 36 E
Arki, India 42 D7 31 9N 76 58 E
Arklow, Ireland 13 D5 52 48N 6 10W
Arkport, U.S.A. 78 D7 42 24N 77 42W
Arkticheskiy, Mys, Russia 27 A10 81 10N 95 0 E
Arkville, U.S.A. 79 D10 42 9N 74 37W
Arlanzón →, Spain 19 A3 42 3N 4 17W
Arlbergpass, Austria 16 E6 47 9N 10 12 E
Arles, France 18 E6 43 41N 4 40 E
Arlington, S. Africa 57 D4 28 1S 27 53 E
Arlington, N.Y., U.S.A. 79 E11 41 42N 73 54W
Arlington, Oreg., U.S.A. 82 D3 45 43N 120 12W
Arlington, S. Dak., U.S.A. 80 C6 44 22N 97 8W
Arlington, Tex., U.S.A. 81 J6 32 44N 97 7W
Arlington, Va., U.S.A. 76 F7 38 53N 77 7W
Arlington, Vt., U.S.A. 79 C11 43 5N 73 9W
Arlington, Wash., U.S.A. 84 B4 48 12N 122 8W
Arlington Heights, U.S.A. 76 D2 42 5N 87 59W
Arlit, Niger 50 E7 19 0N 7 38 E
Arlon, Belgium 15 E5 49 42N 5 49 E
Arltunga, Australia 62 C1 23 26S 134 41 E
Armagh, U.K. 13 B5 54 21N 6 39W
Armagh □, U.K. 13 B5 54 18N 6 37W
Armavir, Russia 25 E7 45 2N 41 7 E
Armenia, Colombia 92 C3 4 35N 75 45W
Armenia ■, Asia 25 F7 40 20N 45 0 E
Armenistís, Ákra, Greece 23 C9 36 8N 27 42 E
Armidale, Australia 63 E5 30 30S 151 40 E
Armour, U.S.A. 80 D5 43 19N 98 21W
Armstrong, B.C., Canada 72 C5 50 25N 119 10W
Armstrong, Ont., Canada 70 B2 50 18N 89 4W
Arnarfjörður, Iceland 8 D2 65 48N 23 40W
Arnaud →, Canada 69 C13 60 0N 70 0W
Arnauti, C., Cyprus 23 D11 35 6N 32 17 E
Arnett, U.S.A. 81 G5 36 8N 99 46W
Arnhem, Neths. 15 C5 51 58N 5 55 E
Arnhem, C., Australia 62 A2 12 20S 137 30 E
Arnhem B., Australia 62 A2 12 20S 136 10 E
Arnhem Land, Australia 62 A1 13 10S 134 30 E
Arno →, Italy 20 C4 43 41N 10 17 E
Arno Bay, Australia 63 E2 33 54S 136 34 E
Arnold, U.K. 10 D6 53 1N 1 7W
Arnold, U.S.A. 84 G6 38 15N 120 20W
Arnot, Canada 73 B9 55 56N 96 41W
Arnøy, Norway 8 A19 70 9N 20 40 E
Arnprior, Canada 79 A8 45 26N 76 21W
Arnsberg, Germany 16 C5 51 24N 8 5 E
Aroab, Namibia 56 D2 26 41S 19 39 E
Aron, India 42 G6 25 57N 77 56 E
Arqalyk, Kazakstan 26 D7 50 13N 66 50 E
Arrah = Ara, India 43 G11 25 35N 84 32 E
Arran, U.K. 12 F3 55 34N 5 12W
Arras, France 18 A5 50 17N 2 46 E
Arrecife, Canary Is. 22 F6 28 57N 13 37W
Arrecifes, Argentina 94 C3 34 6S 60 9W
Arrée, Mts. d', France 18 B2 48 26N 3 55W
Arriaga, Chiapas, Mexico 87 D6 16 15N 93 52W
Arriaga, San Luis Potosí, Mexico 86 C4 21 55N 101 23W
Arrilalah, Australia 62 C3 23 43S 143 54 E
Arrino, Australia 61 E2 29 30S 115 40 E
Arrow, L., Ireland 13 B3 54 3N 8 19W
Arrowhead, L., U.S.A. 85 L9 34 16N 117 10W
Arrowtown, N.Z. 59 L2 44 57S 168 50 E
Arroyo Grande, U.S.A. 85 K6 35 7N 120 35W
Ars, Iran 44 B5 37 9N 47 46 E
Arsenault L., Canada 73 B7 55 6N 108 32W
Arsenev, Russia 30 B6 44 10N 133 15 E
Árta, Greece 21 E9 39 8N 21 2 E
Artà, Spain 22 B10 39 41N 3 21 E
Arteaga, Mexico 86 D4 18 50N 102 20W
Artem, Russia 30 C6 43 22N 132 13 E
Artemovsk, Russia 27 D10 54 45N 93 35 E
Artemovsk, Ukraine 25 E6 48 35N 38 0 E
Artesia = Mosomane, Botswana 56 C4 24 2S 26 19 E
Artesia, U.S.A. 81 J2 32 51N 104 24W
Arthur, Canada 78 C4 43 50N 80 32W
Arthur →, Australia 62 G3 41 2S 144 40 E
Arthur Cr. →, Australia 62 C2 22 30S 136 25 E
Arthur Pt., Australia 62 C5 22 7S 150 3 E
Arthur River, Australia 61 F2 33 20S 117 2 E
Arthur's Pass, N.Z. 59 K3 42 54S 171 35 E
Arthur's Town, Bahamas 89 B4 24 38N 75 42W
Artigas, Uruguay 94 C4 30 20S 56 30W
Artillery L., Canada 73 A7 63 9N 107 52W
Artois, France 18 A5 50 20N 2 30 E
Artrutx, C. de, Spain 22 B10 39 55N 3 49 E
Artsyz, Ukraine 17 E15 46 4N 29 26 E
Artvin, Turkey 25 F7 41 14N 41 44 E
Aru, Kepulauan, Indonesia 37 F8 6 0S 134 30 E
Aru Is. = Aru, Kepulauan, Indonesia 37 F8 6 0S 134 30 E
Arua, Uganda 54 B3 3 1N 30 58 E
Aruanã, Brazil 93 F8 14 54S 51 10W
Aruba ■, W. Indies 89 D6 12 30N 70 0W
Arucas, Canary Is. 22 F4 28 7N 15 32W
Arun →, Nepal 43 F12 26 55N 87 10 E
Arun →, U.K. 11 G7 50 49N 0 33W
Arunachal Pradesh □, India 41 F19 28 0N 95 0 E
Arusha, Tanzania 54 C4 3 20S 36 40 E
Arusha □, Tanzania 54 C4 4 0S 36 30 E
Arusha Chini, Tanzania 54 C4 3 32S 37 20 E
Aruwimi →, Dem. Rep. of the Congo 54 B1 1 13N 23 36 E
Arvada, Colo., U.S.A. 80 F2 39 48N 105 5W
Arvada, Wyo., U.S.A. 82 D10 44 39N 106 8W
Árvi, Greece 23 E7 34 59N 25 28 E
Arviat, Canada 73 A10 61 6N 93 59W
Arvidsjaur, Sweden 8 D18 65 35N 19 10 E
Arvika, Sweden 9 G15 59 40N 12 36 E
Arvin, U.S.A. 85 K8 35 12N 118 50W
Arwal, India 43 G11 25 15N 84 41 E
Arxan, China 33 B6 47 11N 119 57 E
Aryirádhes, Greece 23 B3 39 27N 19 58 E
Aryiroúpolis, Greece 23 D6 35 17N 24 20 E
Arys, Kazakstan 26 E7 42 26N 68 48 E
Arzamas, Russia 24 C7 55 27N 43 55 E
Aş Şadr, U.A.E. 45 E7 24 40N 54 41 E
Aş Şafā, Syria 47 B6 33 10N 37 0 E
As Saffānīyah, Si. Arabia 45 E6 27 55N 48 50 E
As Safīrah, Syria 44 B3 36 5N 37 21 E
Aş Şahm, Oman 45 E8 24 10N 56 53 E
As Sājir, Si. Arabia 44 E5 25 11N 44 36 E
As Salamīyah, Syria 44 C3 35 1N 37 2 E
As Salmān, Iraq 44 D5 30 30N 44 32 E
As Salṭ, Jordan 47 C4 32 2N 35 43 E
As Sal'w'a, Qatar 45 E6 24 23N 50 50 E
As Samāwah, Iraq 44 D5 31 15N 45 15 E
As Sanamayn, Syria 47 B5 33 3N 36 10 E
As Sohar = Şuḥār, Oman 45 E8 24 20N 56 40 E
As Sukhnah, Syria 44 C3 34 52N 38 52 E
As Sulaymānīyah, Iraq 44 C5 35 35N 45 29 E
As Sulaymī, Si. Arabia 44 E4 26 17N 41 21 E
As Sulayyil, Si. Arabia 46 C4 20 27N 45 34 E
As Summān, Si. Arabia 44 E5 25 0N 47 0 E
As Suwaydā', Syria 47 C5 32 40N 36 30 E
As Suwaydā' □, Syria 47 C5 32 45N 36 45 E
As Suwayq, Oman 45 F8 23 51N 57 26 E
As Şuwayrah, Iraq 44 C5 32 55N 45 0 E
Asab, Namibia 56 D2 25 30S 18 0 E
Asad, Buḥayrat al, Syria 44 C3 36 0N 38 15 E
Asahi-Gawa →, Japan 31 G6 34 36N 133 58 E
Asahigawa, Japan 30 C11 43 46N 142 22 E
Asamankese, Ghana 50 G5 5 50N 0 40W
Asan →, India 43 F8 26 37N 78 24 E
Asansol, India 43 H12 23 40N 87 1 E
Asbesberge, S. Africa 56 D3 29 0S 23 0 E
Asbestos, Canada 71 C5 45 47N 71 58W
Asbury Park, U.S.A. 79 F10 40 13N 74 1W
Ascensión, Mexico 86 A3 31 6N 107 59W
Ascensión, B. de la, Mexico 87 D7 19 50N 87 20W
Ascension I., Atl. Oc. 49 G2 8 0S 14 15W
Aschaffenburg, Germany 16 D5 49 58N 9 6 E
Aschersleben, Germany 16 C6 51 45N 11 29 E
Ascoli Piceno, Italy 20 C5 42 51N 13 34 E
Ascope, Peru 92 E3 7 46S 79 8W
Ascotán, Chile 94 A2 21 45S 68 17W
Aseb, Eritrea 46 E3 13 0N 42 40 E
Asela, Ethiopia 46 F2 8 0N 39 0 E
Asenovgrad, Bulgaria 21 C11 42 1N 24 51 E
Aserradero, Mexico 86 C3 23 40N 105 43W
Asgata, Cyprus 23 E12 34 46N 33 15 E
Ash Fork, U.S.A. 83 J7 35 13N 112 29W
Ash Grove, U.S.A. 81 G8 37 19N 93 35W
Ash Shabakah, Iraq 44 D4 30 49N 43 39 E
Ash Shamāl □, Lebanon 47 A5 34 25N 36 0 E
Ash Shāmīyah, Iraq 44 D5 31 55N 44 35 E
Ash Shāriqah, U.A.E. 45 E7 25 23N 55 26 E
Ash Sharmah, Si. Arabia 44 D2 28 1N 35 16 E
Ash Sharqāt, Iraq 44 C4 35 27N 43 16 E
Ash Sharqi, Al Jabal, Lebanon 47 B5 33 40N 36 10 E
Ash Shaṭrah, Iraq 44 D5 31 30N 46 10 E
Ash Shawbak, Jordan 44 D2 30 32N 35 34 E
Ash Shawmari, J., Jordan 47 E5 30 35N 36 35 E
Ash Shināfīyah, Iraq 44 D5 31 35N 44 39 E
Ash Shu'bah, Si. Arabia 44 D5 28 54N 44 44 E
Ash Shumlūl, Si. Arabia 44 E5 26 31N 47 20 E
Ash Shūr'a, Iraq 44 C4 35 58N 43 13 E
Ash Shurayf, Si. Arabia 44 E3 25 43N 39 14 E
Ash Shuwayfāt, Lebanon 47 B4 33 45N 35 30 E
Asha, Russia 24 D10 55 0N 57 16 E
Ashau, Vietnam 38 D6 16 6N 107 22 E
Ashbourne, U.K. 10 D6 53 2N 1 43W
Ashburn, U.S.A. 77 K4 31 43N 83 39W
Ashburton, N.Z. 59 K3 43 53S 171 48 E
Ashburton →, Australia 60 D1 21 40S 114 56 E
Ashcroft, Canada 72 C4 50 40N 121 20W
Ashdod, Israel 47 D3 31 49N 34 35 E
Ashdown, U.S.A. 81 J7 33 40N 94 8W
Asheboro, U.S.A. 77 H6 35 43N 79 49W
Ashern, Canada 73 C9 51 11N 98 21W
Asherton, U.S.A. 81 L5 28 27N 99 46W
Asheville, U.S.A. 77 H4 35 36N 82 33W
Ashewat, Pakistan 42 D3 31 22N 68 32 E
Asheweig →, Canada 70 B2 54 17N 87 12W
Ashford, Australia 63 D5 29 15S 151 3 E
Ashford, U.K. 11 F8 51 8N 0 53 E
Ashgabat, Turkmenistan 26 F6 38 0N 57 50 E
Ashibetsu, Japan 30 C11 43 31N 142 11 E
Ashikaga, Japan 31 F9 36 28N 139 29 E
Ashington, U.K. 10 B6 55 11N 1 33W
Ashizuri-Zaki, Japan 31 H6 32 44N 133 0 E
Ashkarkot, Afghan. 42 C2 33 3N 67 58 E
Ashkhabad = Ashgabat, Turkmenistan 26 F6 38 0N 57 50 E
Āshkhāneh, Iran 45 B8 37 26N 56 55 E
Ashland, Kans., U.S.A. 81 G5 37 11N 99 46W
Ashland, Ky., U.S.A. 76 F4 38 28N 82 38W
Ashland, Mont., U.S.A. 82 D10 45 36N 106 16W
Ashland, Ohio, U.S.A. 78 F2 40 52N 82 19W
Ashland, Oreg., U.S.A. 82 E2 42 12N 122 43W
Ashland, Pa., U.S.A. 79 F8 40 45N 76 22W
Ashland, Va., U.S.A. 76 G7 37 46N 77 29W
Ashland, Wis., U.S.A. 80 B9 46 35N 90 53W
Ashley, N. Dak., U.S.A. 80 B5 46 2N 99 22W
Ashley, Pa., U.S.A. 79 E9 41 12N 75 55W
Ashmore Reef, Australia 60 B3 12 14S 123 5 E
Ashmyany, Belarus 9 J21 54 26N 25 52 E
Ashokan Reservoir, U.S.A. 79 E10 41 56N 74 13W
Ashqelon, Israel 47 D3 31 42N 34 35 E
Ashta, India 42 H7 23 1N 76 43 E
Ashtabula, U.S.A. 78 E4 41 52N 80 47W
Ashton, S. Africa 56 E3 33 50S 20 5 E
Ashton, U.S.A. 82 D8 44 4N 111 27W
Ashuanipi, L., Canada 71 B6 52 45N 66 15W
Ashville, U.S.A. 78 F6 40 34N 78 33W
Asia 28 E11 45 0N 75 0 E
Asia, Kepulauan, Indonesia 37 D8 1 0N 131 13 E
Āsīā Bak, Iran 45 C6 35 19N 50 30 E
Asifabad, India 40 K11 19 20N 79 24 E
Asinara, Italy 20 D3 41 4N 8 16 E
Asinara, G. dell', Italy 20 D3 41 0N 8 30 E
Asino, Russia 26 D9 57 0N 86 0 E
Asipovichy, Belarus 17 B15 53 19N 28 33 E
'Asīr □, Si. Arabia 46 D3 18 40N 42 30 E
Asir, Ras, Somali Rep. 46 E5 11 55N 51 10 E
Askersund, Sweden 9 G16 58 53N 14 55 E
Askham, S. Africa 56 D3 26 59S 20 47 E
Askim, Norway 9 G14 59 35N 11 10 E
Askja, Iceland 8 D5 65 3N 16 48W
Askøy, Norway 9 F11 60 29N 5 10 E
Asmara = Asmera, Eritrea 46 D2 15 19N 38 55 E

Asmera

Asmera, Eritrea **46 D2** 15 19N 38 55 E
Åsnen, Sweden **9 H16** 56 37N 14 45 E
Aspen, U.S.A. **83 G10** 39 11N 106 49W
Aspermont, U.S.A. **81 J4** 33 8N 100 14W
Aspiring, Mt., N.Z. **59 L2** 44 23S 168 46 E
Asprókavos, Ákra, Greece **23 B4** 39 21N 20 6 E
Aspur, India **42 H6** 23 58N 74 7 E
Asquith, Canada **73 C7** 52 8N 107 13W
Assam □, India **41 G18** 26 0N 93 0 E
Asse, Belgium **15 D4** 50 24N 4 10 E
Assen, Neths. **15 A6** 53 0N 6 35 E
Assiniboia, Canada **73 D7** 49 40N 105 59W
Assiniboine →, Canada **73 D9** 49 53N 97 8W
Assiniboine, Mt., Canada **72 C5** 50 52N 115 39W
Assis, Brazil **95 A5** 22 40S 50 20W
Assisi, Italy **20 C5** 43 4N 12 37 E
Assynt, L., U.K. **12 C3** 58 10N 5 3W
Astana, Kazakstan **26 D8** 51 10N 71 30 E
Āstāneh, Iran **45 B6** 37 17N 49 59 E
Astara, Azerbaijan **25 G8** 38 30N 48 50 E
Asteroúsia, Greece **23 E7** 34 59N 25 3 E
Asti, Italy **18 D8** 44 54N 8 12 E
Astipálaia, Greece **21 F12** 36 32N 26 22 E
Astorga, Spain **19 A2** 42 29N 6 8W
Astoria, U.S.A. **84 D3** 46 11N 123 50W
Astrakhan, Russia **25 E8** 46 25N 48 5 E
Asturias □, Spain **19 A3** 43 15N 6 0W
Asunción, Paraguay **94 B4** 25 10S 57 30W
Asunción Nochixtlán, Mexico **87 D5** 17 28N 97 14W
Aswa →, Uganda **54 B3** 3 43N 31 55 E
Aswân, Egypt **51 D12** 24 4N 32 57 E
Aswân High Dam = Sadd el Aali, Egypt **51 D12** 23 54N 32 54 E
Asyût, Egypt **51 C12** 27 11N 31 4 E
At Ţafilah, Jordan **47 E4** 30 45N 35 30 E
Aţ Tā'if, Si. Arabia **46 C3** 21 5N 40 27 E
Aţ Ţirāq, Si. Arabia **44 E5** 27 19N 44 33 E
Aţ Tubayq, Si. Arabia **44 D3** 29 30N 37 0 E
Atacama □, Chile **94 B2** 27 30S 70 0W
Atacama, Desierto de, Chile **94 A2** 24 0S 69 20W
Atacama, Salar de, Chile **94 A2** 23 30S 68 20W
Atalaya, Peru **92 F4** 10 45S 73 50W
Atalaya de Femes, Canary Is. **22 F6** 28 56N 13 47W
Atami, Japan **31 G9** 35 5N 139 4 E
Atapupu, Indonesia **37 F6** 9 0S 124 51 E
Atâr, Mauritania **50 D3** 20 30N 13 5W
Atari, Pakistan **42 D6** 30 56N 74 2 E
Atascadero, U.S.A. **84 K6** 35 29N 120 40W
Atasu, Kazakstan **26 E8** 48 30N 71 0 E
Atatürk Barajı, Turkey **25 G6** 37 28N 38 30 E
Atauro, Indonesia **37 F7** 8 10S 125 30 E
Atbara, Sudan **51 E12** 17 42N 33 59 E
'Atbara →, Sudan **51 E12** 17 40N 33 56 E
Atbasar, Kazakstan **26 D7** 51 48N 68 20 E
Atchafalaya B., U.S.A. **81 L9** 29 25N 91 25W
Atchison, U.S.A. **80 F7** 39 34N 95 7W
Āteshān, Iran **45 C7** 35 35N 52 37 E
Ath, Belgium **15 D3** 50 38N 3 47 E
Athabasca, Canada **72 C6** 54 45N 113 20W
Athabasca →, Canada **73 B6** 58 40N 110 50W
Athabasca, L., Canada **73 B7** 59 15N 109 15W
Athboy, Ireland **13 C5** 53 37N 6 56W
Athenry, Ireland **13 C3** 53 18N 8 44W
Athens = Athínai, Greece **21 F10** 37 58N 23 46 E
Athens, Ala., U.S.A. **77 H2** 34 48N 86 58W
Athens, Ga., U.S.A. **77 J4** 33 57N 83 23W
Athens, N.Y., U.S.A. **79 D11** 42 16N 73 49W
Athens, Ohio, U.S.A. **76 F4** 39 20N 82 6W
Athens, Pa., U.S.A. **79 E8** 41 57N 76 31W
Athens, Tenn., U.S.A. **77 H3** 35 27N 84 36W
Athens, Tex., U.S.A. **81 J7** 32 12N 95 51W
Atherley, Canada **78 B5** 44 37N 79 20W
Atherton, Australia **62 B4** 17 17S 145 30 E
Athienou, Cyprus **23 D12** 35 3N 33 32 E
Athínai, Greece **21 F10** 37 58N 23 46 E
Athlone, Ireland **13 C4** 53 25N 7 56W
Athna, Cyprus **23 D12** 35 3N 33 47 E
Athol, U.S.A. **79 D12** 42 36N 72 14W
Atholl, Forest of, U.K. **12 E5** 56 51N 3 50W
Atholville, Canada **71 C6** 47 59N 66 43W
Áthos, Greece **21 D11** 40 9N 24 22 E
Athy, Ireland **13 C5** 53 0N 7 0W
Ati, Chad **51 F9** 13 13N 18 20 E
Atiak, Uganda **54 B3** 3 12N 32 2 E
Atik L., Canada **73 B9** 55 15N 96 0W
Atikameg →, Canada **70 B3** 52 30N 82 46W
Atikokan, Canada **70 C1** 48 45N 91 37W
Atikonak L., Canada **71 B7** 52 40N 64 32W
Atka, Russia **27 C16** 60 50N 151 48 E
Atka I., U.S.A. **68 C2** 52 7N 174 30W
Atkinson, U.S.A. **80 D5** 42 32N 98 59W
Atlanta, Ga., U.S.A. **77 J3** 33 45N 84 23W
Atlanta, Tex., U.S.A. **81 J7** 33 7N 94 10W
Atlantic, U.S.A. **80 E7** 41 24N 95 1W
Atlantic City, U.S.A. **76 F8** 39 21N 74 27W
Atlantic Ocean **2 E9** 0 0 20 0W
Atlas Mts. = Haut Atlas, Morocco **50 B4** 32 30N 5 0W
Atlin, Canada **72 B2** 59 31N 133 41W
Atlin, L., Canada **72 B2** 59 26N 133 45W
Atlin Prov. Park, Canada **72 B2** 59 10N 134 30W
Atmore, U.S.A. **77 K2** 31 2N 87 29W
Atoka, U.S.A. **81 H6** 34 23N 96 8W
Atolia, U.S.A. **85 K9** 35 19N 117 37W
Atrai →, Bangla. **43 G13** 24 7N 89 22 E
Atrak = Atrek →, Turkmenistan **45 B8** 37 35N 53 58 E
Atrauli, India **42 E8** 28 2N 78 20 E
Atrek →, Turkmenistan **45 B8** 37 35N 53 58 E
Atsuta, Japan **30 C10** 43 24N 141 26 E
Attalla, U.S.A. **77 H2** 34 1N 86 6W
Attapu, Laos **38 E6** 14 48N 106 50 E
Attáviros, Greece **23 C9** 36 12N 27 50 E
Attawapiskat, Canada **70 B3** 52 56N 82 24W
Attawapiskat →, Canada **70 B3** 52 57N 82 18W
Attawapiskat L., Canada **70 B2** 52 18N 87 54W
Attica, Ind., U.S.A. **76 E2** 40 18N 87 15W
Attica, Ohio, U.S.A. **78 E2** 41 4N 82 53W
Attikamagen L., Canada **71 B6** 55 0N 66 30W
Attleboro, U.S.A. **79 E13** 41 57N 71 17W
Attock, Pakistan **42 C5** 33 52N 72 20 E
Attopeu = Attapu, Laos **38 E6** 14 48N 106 50 E
Attu I., U.S.A. **68 C1** 52 55N 172 55 E
Attur, India **40 P11** 11 35N 78 30 E
Atuel →, Argentina **94 D2** 36 17S 66 50W
Åtvidaberg, Sweden **9 G17** 58 12N 16 0 E
Atwater, U.S.A. **84 H6** 37 21N 120 37W
Atwood, Canada **78 C3** 43 40N 81 1W
Atwood, U.S.A. **80 F4** 39 48N 101 3W
Atyraū, Kazakstan **25 E9** 47 5N 52 0 E
Au Sable, U.S.A. **78 B1** 44 25N 83 20W
Au Sable →, U.S.A. **76 C4** 44 25N 83 20W
Au Sable Forks, U.S.A. **79 B11** 44 27N 73 41W
Au Sable Pt., U.S.A. **78 B1** 44 20N 83 20W
Aubagne, France **18 E6** 43 17N 5 37 E
Aubarca, C. d', Spain **22 B7** 39 4N 1 22 E
Aube →, France **18 B5** 48 34N 3 43 E
Auberry, U.S.A. **84 H7** 37 7N 119 29W
Auburn, Ala., U.S.A. **77 J3** 32 36N 85 29W
Auburn, Calif., U.S.A. **84 G5** 38 54N 121 4W
Auburn, Ind., U.S.A. **76 E3** 41 22N 85 4W
Auburn, Maine, U.S.A. **77 C10** 44 6N 70 14W
Auburn, N.Y., U.S.A. **79 D8** 42 56N 76 34W
Auburn, Nebr., U.S.A. **80 E7** 40 23N 95 51W
Auburn, Pa., U.S.A. **79 F8** 40 36N 76 6W
Auburn, Wash., U.S.A. **84 C4** 47 18N 122 14W
Auburn Ra., Australia **63 D5** 25 15S 150 30 E
Aubusson, France **18 D5** 45 57N 2 11 E
Auch, France **18 E4** 43 39N 0 36 E
Auckland, N.Z. **59 G5** 36 52S 174 46 E
Auckland Is., Pac. Oc. **64 N8** 50 40S 166 5 E
Aude →, France **18 E5** 43 13N 3 14 E
Auden, Canada **70 B2** 50 14N 87 53W
Audubon, U.S.A. **80 E7** 41 43N 94 56W
Augathella, Australia **63 D4** 25 48S 146 35 E
Aughnacloy, U.K. **13 B5** 54 25N 6 59W
Augrabies Falls, S. Africa **56 D3** 28 35S 20 20 E
Augsburg, Germany **16 D6** 48 25N 10 52 E
Augusta, Australia **61 F2** 34 19S 115 9 E
Augusta, Italy **20 F6** 37 13N 15 13 E
Augusta, Ark., U.S.A. **81 H9** 35 17N 91 22W
Augusta, Ga., U.S.A. **77 J5** 33 28N 81 58W
Augusta, Kans., U.S.A. **81 G6** 37 41N 96 59W
Augusta, Maine, U.S.A. **69 D13** 44 19N 69 47W
Augusta, Mont., U.S.A. **82 C7** 47 30N 112 24W
Augustów, Poland **17 B12** 53 51N 23 0 E
Augustus, Mt., Australia **61 D2** 24 20S 116 50 E
Augustus I., Australia **60 C3** 15 20S 124 30 E
Aukum, U.S.A. **84 G6** 38 34N 120 43W
Auld, L., Australia **60 D3** 22 25S 123 50 E
Ault, U.S.A. **80 E2** 40 35N 104 44W
Aunis, France **18 C3** 46 5N 0 50W
Auponhia, Indonesia **37 E7** 1 58S 125 27 E
Aur, Pulau, Malaysia **39 L5** 2 35N 104 10 E
Auraiya, India **43 F8** 26 28N 79 33 E
Aurangabad, Bihar, India **43 G11** 24 45N 84 18 E
Aurangabad, Maharashtra, India **40 K9** 19 50N 75 23 E
Aurich, Germany **16 B4** 53 28N 7 28 E
Aurillac, France **18 D5** 44 55N 2 26 E
Aurora, Canada **78 C5** 44 0N 79 28W
Aurora, S. Africa **56 E2** 32 40S 18 29 E
Aurora, Colo., U.S.A. **80 F2** 39 44N 104 52W
Aurora, Ill., U.S.A. **76 E1** 41 45N 88 19W
Aurora, Mo., U.S.A. **81 G8** 36 58N 93 43W
Aurora, N.Y., U.S.A. **79 D8** 42 45N 76 42W
Aurora, Nebr., U.S.A. **80 E6** 40 52N 98 0W
Aurora, Ohio, U.S.A. **78 E3** 41 21N 81 20W
Aurukun, Australia **62 A3** 13 20S 141 45 E
Aus, Namibia **56 D2** 26 35S 16 12 E
Ausable →, Canada **78 C3** 43 19N 81 46W
Auschwitz = Oświęcim, Poland **17 C10** 50 2N 19 11 E
Austin, Minn., U.S.A. **80 D8** 43 40N 92 58W
Austin, Nev., U.S.A. **82 G5** 39 30N 117 4W
Austin, Pa., U.S.A. **78 E6** 41 38N 78 6W
Austin, Tex., U.S.A. **81 K6** 30 17N 97 45W
Austin, L., Australia **61 E2** 27 40S 118 0 E
Austin I., Canada **73 A10** 61 10N 94 0W
Austra, Norway **8 D14** 65 8N 11 55 E
Austral Is. = Tubuai Is., Pac. Oc. **65 K13** 25 0S 150 0W
Austral Seamount Chain, Pac. Oc. **65 K13** 24 0S 150 0W
Australia ■, Oceania **64 K5** 23 0S 135 0 E
Australian Capital Territory □, Australia **63 F4** 35 30S 149 0 E
Australind, Australia **61 F2** 33 17S 115 42 E
Austria ■, Europe **16 E8** 47 0N 14 0 E
Austvågøy, Norway **8 B16** 68 20N 14 40 E
Autlán, Mexico **86 D4** 19 40N 104 30W
Autun, France **18 C6** 46 58N 4 17 E
Auvergne, France **18 D5** 45 20N 3 15 E
Auvergne, Mts. d', France **18 D5** 45 20N 2 55 E
Auxerre, France **18 C5** 47 48N 3 32 E
Ava, U.S.A. **81 G8** 36 57N 92 40W
Avallon, France **18 C5** 47 30N 3 53 E
Avalon, U.S.A. **85 M8** 33 21N 118 20W
Avalon Pen., Canada **71 C9** 47 30N 53 20W
Avanos, Turkey **44 B2** 38 43N 34 51 E
Avaré, Brazil **95 A6** 23 4S 48 58W
Avawatz Mts., U.S.A. **85 K10** 35 40N 116 30W
Aveiro, Brazil **93 D7** 3 10S 55 5W
Aveiro, Portugal **19 B1** 40 37N 8 38W
Āvej, Iran **45 C6** 35 40N 49 15 E
Avellaneda, Argentina **94 C4** 34 50S 58 10W
Avellino, Italy **20 D6** 40 54N 14 47 E
Avenal, U.S.A. **84 K6** 36 0N 120 8W
Aversa, Italy **20 D6** 40 58N 14 12 E
Avery, U.S.A. **82 C6** 47 15N 115 49W
Aves, Is. las, Venezuela **89 D6** 12 0N 67 30W
Avesta, Sweden **9 F17** 60 9N 16 10 E
Avezzano, Italy **20 C5** 42 2N 13 25 E
Aviá Terai, Argentina **94 B3** 26 45S 60 50W
Aviemore, U.K. **12 D5** 57 12N 3 50W
Avignon, France **18 E6** 43 57N 4 50 E
Ávila, Spain **19 B3** 40 39N 4 43W
Avila Beach, U.S.A. **85 K6** 35 11N 120 44W
Avilés, Spain **19 A3** 43 35N 5 57W
Avis, U.S.A. **78 E7** 41 11N 77 19W
Avoca, U.S.A. **78 D7** 42 25N 77 25W
Avoca →, Australia **63 F3** 35 40S 143 43 E
Avoca →, Ireland **13 D5** 52 48N 6 10W
Avola, Canada **72 C5** 51 45N 119 19W
Avola, Italy **20 F6** 36 56N 15 7 E
Avon, U.S.A. **78 D7** 42 55N 77 45W
Avon →, Australia **61 F2** 31 40S 116 7 E
Avon →, Bristol, U.K. **11 F5** 51 29N 2 41W
Avon →, Dorset, U.K. **11 G6** 50 44N 1 46W
Avon →, Warks., U.K. **11 E5** 52 0N 2 8W
Avon Park, U.S.A. **77 M5** 27 36N 81 31W
Avondale, Zimbabwe **55 F3** 17 43S 30 58 E
Avonlea, Canada **73 D8** 50 0N 105 0W
Avonmore, Canada **79 A10** 45 10N 74 58W
Avranches, France **18 B3** 48 40N 1 20W
A'waj →, Syria **47 B5** 33 23N 36 20 E
Awaji-Shima, Japan **31 G7** 34 30N 134 50 E
'Awālī, Bahrain **45 E6** 26 0N 50 30 E
Awantipur, India **43 C6** 33 55N 75 3 E
Awasa, Ethiopia **46 F2** 7 3N 38 28 E
Awash, Ethiopia **46 F3** 9 1N 40 10 E
Awatere →, N.Z. **59 J5** 41 37S 174 10 E
Awbārī, Libya **51 C8** 26 46N 12 57 E
Awe, L., U.K. **12 E3** 56 17N 5 16W
Awjilah, Libya **51 C10** 29 8N 21 7 E
Axe →, U.K. **11 F5** 50 42N 3 4W
Axel Heiberg I., Canada **4 B3** 80 0N 90 0W
Axim, Ghana **50 H5** 4 51N 2 15W
Axiós →, Greece **21 D10** 40 57N 22 35 E
Axminster, U.K. **11 G4** 50 46N 3 0W
Ayabaca, Peru **92 D3** 4 40S 79 53W
Ayabe, Japan **31 G7** 35 20N 135 20 E
Ayacucho, Argentina **94 D4** 37 5S 58 20W
Ayacucho, Peru **92 F4** 13 0S 74 0W
Ayaguz, Kazakstan **26 E9** 48 10N 80 10 E
Ayamonte, Spain **19 D2** 37 12N 7 24W
Ayan, Russia **27 D14** 56 30N 138 16 E
Ayaviri, Peru **92 F4** 14 50S 70 35W
Aydın, Turkey **21 F12** 37 51N 27 51 E
Aydin □, Turkey **25 G4** 37 50N 28 0 E
Ayer, U.S.A. **79 D13** 42 34N 71 35W
Ayer's Cliff, Canada **79 A12** 45 10N 72 3W
Ayers Rock, Australia **61 E5** 25 23S 131 5 E
Ayia Aikateríni, Ákra, Greece **23 A3** 39 50N 19 50 E
Ayia Dhéka, Greece **23 D6** 35 3N 24 58 E
Ayia Gálini, Greece **23 D6** 35 6N 24 41 E
Ayia Napa, Cyprus **23 E13** 34 59N 34 0 E
Ayia Phyla, Cyprus **23 E12** 34 43N 33 1 E
Ayia Varvára, Greece **23 D7** 35 8N 25 1 E
Áyios Amvrósios, Cyprus **23 D12** 35 20N 33 35 E
Áyios Evstrátios, Greece **21 E11** 39 34N 24 58 E
Áyios Ioánnis, Ákra, Greece **23 D7** 35 20N 25 40 E
Áyios Isidhoros, Greece **23 C9** 36 9N 27 51 E
Áyios Matthaíos, Greece **23 B3** 39 30N 19 47 E
Áyios Nikólaos, Greece **23 D7** 35 11N 25 41 E
Áyios Seryios, Cyprus **23 D12** 35 12N 33 53 E
Ayios Theodhoros, Cyprus **23 D13** 35 22N 34 1 E
Aykino, Russia **24 B8** 62 15N 49 56 E
Aylesbury, U.K. **11 F7** 51 49N 0 49W
Aylmer, Canada **78 D4** 42 46N 80 59W
Aylmer, L., Canada **68 B8** 64 0N 110 8W
'Ayn, Wādī al, Oman **45 F7** 22 15N 55 28 E
Ayn Dār, Si. Arabia **45 E7** 25 55N 49 10 E
Ayn Zālah, Iraq **44 B4** 36 45N 42 35 E
Ayolas, Paraguay **94 B4** 27 10S 56 59W
Ayon, Ostrov, Russia **27 C17** 69 50N 169 0 E
'Ayoûn el 'Atroûs, Mauritania **50 E4** 16 40N 9 37W
Ayr, Australia **62 B4** 19 35S 147 25 E
Ayr, Canada **78 C4** 43 17N 80 27W
Ayr, U.K. **12 F4** 55 28N 4 38W
Ayr →, U.K. **12 F4** 55 28N 4 38W
Ayre, Pt. of, U.K. **10 C3** 54 25N 4 21W
Ayton, Australia **62 B4** 15 56S 145 22 E
Aytos, Bulgaria **21 C12** 42 42N 27 16 E
Ayu, Kepulauan, Indonesia **37 D8** 0 35N 131 5 E
Ayutla, Guatemala **88 D1** 14 40N 92 10W
Ayutla, Mexico **87 D5** 16 58N 99 17W
Ayvacık, Turkey **21 E12** 39 36N 26 24 E
Ayvalık, Turkey **21 E12** 39 20N 26 46 E
Az Zabadānī, Syria **47 B5** 33 43N 36 5 E
Aẓ Ẓāhirīyah, West Bank **47 D3** 31 25N 34 58 E
Aẓ Ẓahrān, Si. Arabia **45 E6** 26 10N 50 7 E
Az Zarqā, Jordan **47 C5** 32 5N 36 4 E
Az Zarqā', U.A.E. **45 E7** 24 53N 53 4 E
Az Zāwiyah, Libya **51 B8** 32 52N 12 56 E
Az Zībār, Iraq **44 B5** 36 52N 44 4 E
Az-Zilfī, Si. Arabia **44 E5** 26 12N 44 52 E
Az Zubayr, Iraq **44 D5** 30 26N 47 40 E
Azamgarh, India **43 F10** 26 5N 83 13 E
Azangaro, Peru **92 F4** 14 55S 70 13W
Āzār Shahr, Iran **44 B5** 37 45N 45 59 E
Azarān, Iran **44 B5** 37 25N 47 16 E
Azärbayjan = Azerbaijan ■, Asia **25 F8** 40 20N 48 0 E
Āzarbāyjān-e Gharbī □, Iran **44 B5** 37 0N 44 30 E
Āzarbāyjān-e Sharqī □, Iran **44 B5** 37 20N 47 0 E
Azare, Nigeria **50 F8** 11 55N 10 10 E
A'zāz, Syria **44 B3** 36 36N 37 4 E
Azbine = Aïr, Niger **50 E7** 18 30N 8 0 E
Azerbaijan ■, Asia **25 F8** 40 20N 48 0 E
Azerbaijchan = Azerbaijan ■, Asia **25 F8** 40 20N 48 0 E
Azimganj, India **43 G13** 24 14N 88 16 E
Azogues, Ecuador **92 D3** 2 35S 78 0W
Azores, Atl. Oc. **50 A1** 38 44N 29 0W
Azov, Russia **25 E6** 47 3N 39 25 E
Azov, Sea of, Europe **25 E6** 46 0N 36 30 E
Azovskoye More = Azov, Sea of, Europe **25 E6** 46 0N 36 30 E
Azraq ash Shīshān, Jordan **47 D5** 31 50N 36 49 E
Aztec, U.S.A. **83 H10** 36 49N 107 59W
Azúa de Compostela, Dom. Rep. **89 C5** 18 25N 70 44W
Azuaga, Spain **19 C3** 38 16N 5 39W
Azuero, Pen. de, Panama **88 E3** 7 30N 80 30W
Azul, Argentina **94 D4** 36 42S 59 43W
Azusa, U.S.A. **85 L9** 34 8N 117 52W

B

Ba Don, Vietnam **38 D6** 17 45N 106 26 E
Ba Dong, Vietnam **39 H6** 9 40N 106 33 E
Ba Ngoi = Cam Lam, Vietnam **39 G7** 11 54N 109 10 E
Ba Tri, Vietnam **39 G6** 10 2N 106 36 E
Ba Xian = Bazhou, China **34 E9** 39 8N 116 22 E
Baa, Indonesia **37 F6** 10 50S 123 0 E
Baarle-Nassau, Belgium **15 C4** 51 27N 4 56 E
Bab el Mandeb, Red Sea **46 E3** 12 35N 43 25 E
Baba Burnu, Turkey **21 E12** 39 29N 26 2 E
Bābā Kalū, Iran **45 D6** 30 7N 50 49 E
Babadag, Romania **17 F15** 44 53N 28 44 E
Babadayhan, Turkmenistan **26 F7** 37 42N 60 23 E
Babaeski, Turkey **21 D12** 41 26N 27 6 E
Babahoyo, Ecuador **92 D3** 1 40S 79 30W
Babai = Sarju →, India **43 F9** 27 21N 81 23 E
Babar, Indonesia **37 F7** 8 0S 129 30 E
Babar, Pakistan **42 D3** 31 7N 69 32 E
Babarkach, Pakistan **42 E3** 29 45N 68 0 E
Babb, U.S.A. **82 B7** 48 51N 113 27W
Babelthuap, Pac. Oc. **37 C8** 7 30N 134 30 E
Baberu, India **43 G9** 25 33N 80 43 E
Babi Besar, Pulau, Malaysia **39 L4** 2 25N 103 59 E
Babinda, Australia **62 B4** 17 20S 145 56 E
Babine, Canada **72 B3** 55 22N 126 37W
Babine →, Canada **72 B3** 55 45N 127 44W
Babine L., Canada **72 C3** 54 48N 126 0W
Babo, Indonesia **37 E8** 2 30S 133 30 E
Bābol, Iran **45 B7** 36 40N 52 50 E
Bābol Sar, Iran **45 B7** 36 45N 52 45 E
Babruysk, Belarus **17 B15** 53 10N 29 15 E
Babuhri, India **42 F3** 26 49N 69 43 E
Babusar Pass, Pakistan **43 B5** 35 12N 73 59 E
Babuyan Chan., Phil. **37 A6** 18 40N 121 30 E
Babylon, Iraq **44 C5** 32 34N 44 22 E
Bac Lieu, Vietnam **39 H5** 9 17N 105 43 E
Bac Phan, Vietnam **38 B5** 22 0N 105 0 E
Bacabal, Brazil **93 D10** 4 15S 44 45W
Bacalar, Mexico **87 D7** 18 50N 87 27W
Bacan, Kepulauan, Indonesia **37 E7** 0 35S 127 30 E
Bacarra, Phil. **37 A6** 18 15N 120 37 E
Bacău, Romania **17 E14** 46 35N 26 55 E
Bacerac, Mexico **86 A3** 30 18N 108 50W
Bach Long Vi, Dao, Vietnam **38 B6** 20 10N 107 40 E
Bachelina, Russia **26 D7** 57 45N 67 20 E
Bachhwara, India **43 G11** 25 35N 85 54 E
Back →, Canada **68 B9** 65 10N 104 0W
Bacolod, Phil. **37 B6** 10 40N 122 57 E
Bacuk, Malaysia **39 J4** 6 4N 102 25 E
Bād, Iran **45 C7** 33 41N 52 1 E
Bad →, U.S.A. **80 C4** 44 21N 100 22W
Bad Axe, U.S.A. **78 C2** 43 48N 83 0W
Bad Ischl, Austria **16 E7** 47 44N 13 38 E
Bad Kissingen, Germany **16 C6** 50 11N 10 4 E
Bad Lands, U.S.A. **80 D3** 43 40N 102 10W
Bada Barabil, India **43 H11** 22 7N 85 24 E
Badagara, India **40 P9** 11 35N 75 40 E
Badajós, L., Brazil **92 D6** 3 15S 62 50W
Badajoz, Spain **19 C2** 38 50N 6 59W
Badalona, Spain **19 B7** 41 26N 2 15 E
Badalzai, Afghan. **42 E1** 29 50N 65 35 E
Badampahar, India **41 H15** 22 10N 86 10 E
Badanah, Si. Arabia **44 D4** 30 58N 41 30 E
Badarinath, India **43 D8** 30 45N 79 30 E
Badas, Kepulauan, Indonesia **36 D3** 0 45N 107 5 E
Baddo →, Pakistan **40 F4** 28 0N 64 20 E
Bade, Indonesia **37 F9** 7 10S 139 35 E
Baden, Austria **16 D9** 48 1N 16 13 E
Baden, U.S.A. **78 F4** 40 38N 80 14W
Baden-Baden, Germany **16 D5** 48 44N 8 13 E
Baden-Württemberg □, Germany **16 D5** 48 20N 8 40 E
Badgastein, Austria **16 E7** 47 7N 13 9 E
Badger, Canada **71 C8** 49 0N 56 4W
Badger, U.S.A. **84 J7** 36 38N 119 1W
Bādghīsāt □, Afghan. **40 B3** 35 0N 63 0 E
Badgom, India **43 B6** 34 1N 74 45 E
Badin, Pakistan **42 G3** 24 38N 68 54 E
Badlands National Park, U.S.A. **80 D3** 43 38N 102 56W
Badrah, Iraq **44 C5** 33 6N 45 58 E
Badrinath, India **43 D8** 30 44N 79 29 E
Badulla, Sri Lanka **40 R12** 7 1N 81 7 E
Baena, Spain **19 D3** 37 37N 4 20W
Baeza, Spain **19 D4** 37 57N 3 25W
Baffin B., Canada **4 B4** 72 0N 64 0W
Baffin I., Canada **69 B12** 68 0N 75 0W
Bafing →, Mali **50 F3** 13 49N 10 50W
Bafliyūn, Syria **44 B3** 36 37N 36 59 E
Bafoulabé, Mali **50 F3** 13 50N 10 55W
Bafoussam, Cameroon **52 C2** 5 28N 10 25 E
Bāfq, Iran **45 D7** 31 40N 55 25 E
Bafra, Turkey **25 F6** 41 34N 35 54 E
Bāft, Iran **45 D8** 29 15N 56 38 E
Bafwasende, Dem. Rep. of the Congo **54 B2** 1 3N 27 5 E
Bagamoyo, Tanzania **54 D4** 6 28S 38 55 E
Bagan Datoh, Malaysia **39 L3** 3 59N 100 47 E
Bagan Serai, Malaysia **39 K3** 5 1N 100 32 E
Baganga, Phil. **37 C7** 7 34N 126 33 E
Bagani, Namibia **56 B3** 18 7S 21 41 E
Bagansiapiapi, Indonesia **36 D2** 2 12N 100 50 E
Bagasra, India **42 J4** 21 30N 71 0 E
Bagaud, India **42 H6** 22 19N 75 53 E
Bagdad, U.S.A. **85 L11** 34 35N 115 53W
Bagdarin, Russia **27 D12** 54 26N 113 36 E
Bagé, Brazil **95 C5** 31 20S 54 15W
Bagenalstown = Muine Bheag, Ireland **13 D5** 52 42N 6 58W
Baggs, U.S.A. **82 F10** 41 2N 107 39W
Bagh, Pakistan **43 C5** 33 59N 73 45 E
Baghain →, India **43 G9** 25 32N 81 1 E
Baghdād, Iraq **44 C5** 33 20N 44 30 E
Bagheria, Italy **20 E5** 38 5N 13 30 E
Baghlān, Afghan. **40 A6** 36 12N 69 0 E
Bagley, U.S.A. **80 B7** 47 32N 95 24W
Bagodar, India **43 G11** 24 5N 85 52 E
Bagrationovsk, Russia **9 J19** 54 23N 20 39 E
Baguio, Phil. **37 A6** 16 26N 120 34 E
Bah, India **43 F8** 26 53N 78 36 E
Bahadurganj, India **43 F12** 26 16N 87 49 E
Bahadurgarh, India **42 E7** 28 40N 76 57 E
Bahama, Canal Viejo de, W. Indies **88 B4** 22 10N 77 30W
Bahamas ■, N. Amer. **89 B5** 24 0N 75 0W
Baharampur, India **43 G13** 24 2N 88 27 E
Bahawalnagar, Pakistan **42 E5** 30 0N 73 15 E
Bahawalpur, Pakistan **42 E4** 29 24N 71 40 E
Baheri, India **43 E8** 28 45N 79 34 E
Bahgul →, India **43 F8** 27 45N 79 36 E
Bahi, Tanzania **54 D4** 5 58S 35 21 E
Bahi Swamp, Tanzania **54 D4** 6 10S 35 0 E
Bahía = Salvador, Brazil **93 F11** 13 0S 38 30W
Bahía □, Brazil **93 F10** 12 0S 42 0W
Bahía, Is. de la, Honduras **88 C2** 16 45N 86 15W
Bahía Blanca, Argentina **94 D3** 38 35S 62 13W
Bahía de Caráquez, Ecuador **92 D2** 0 40S 80 27W
Bahía Honda, Cuba **88 B3** 22 54N 83 10W
Bahía Laura, Argentina **96 F3** 48 10S 66 30W
Bahía Negra, Paraguay **92 H7** 20 5S 58 5W

Bardstown

Bahir Dar, Ethiopia 46 E2 11 37N 37 10 E
Bahmanzād, Iran 45 D6 31 15N 51 47 E
Bahr el Ghazâl □, Sudan 51 G11 7 0N 28 0 E
Bahraich, India 43 F9 27 38N 81 37 E
Bahrain ■, Asia 45 E6 26 0N 50 35 E
Bahror, India 42 F7 27 51N 76 20 E
Bāhū Kalāt, Iran 45 E9 25 43N 61 25 E
Bai Bung, Mui = Ca Mau, Mui, Vietnam 39 H5 8 38N 104 44 E
Bai Duc, Vietnam 38 C5 18 3N 105 49 E
Bai Thuong, Vietnam 38 C5 19 54N 105 23 E
Baia Mare, Romania 17 E12 47 40N 23 35 E
Baião, Brazil 93 D9 2 40S 49 40W
Baïbokoum, Chad 51 G9 7 46N 15 43 E
Baicheng, China 35 B12 45 38N 122 42 E
Baidoa, Somali Rep. 46 G3 3 8N 43 30 E
Baie Comeau, Canada 71 C6 49 12N 68 10W
Baie-St-Paul, Canada 71 C5 47 28N 70 32W
Baie Trinité, Canada 71 C6 49 25N 67 20W
Baie Verte, Canada 71 C8 49 55N 56 12W
Baihar, India 43 H9 22 6N 80 33 E
Baihe, China 34 H6 32 50N 110 5 E
Ba'ījī, Iraq 44 C4 35 0N 43 30 E
Baijnath, India 43 E8 29 55N 79 37 E
Baikal, L. = Baykal, Oz., Russia 27 D11 53 0N 108 0 E
Baikunthpur, India 43 H10 23 15N 82 33 E
Baile Atha Cliath = Dublin, Ireland 13 C5 53 21N 6 15W
Băileşti, Romania 17 F12 44 1N 23 20 E
Bainbridge, Ga., U.S.A. 77 K3 30 55N 84 35W
Bainbridge, N.Y., U.S.A. 79 D9 42 18N 75 29W
Baing, Indonesia 37 F6 10 14S 120 34 E
Bainiu, China 34 H7 32 50N 112 15 E
Bā'ir, Jordan 47 E5 30 45N 36 55 E
Bairin Youqi, China 35 C10 43 30N 118 35 E
Bairin Zuoqi, China 35 C10 43 58N 119 15 E
Bairnsdale, Australia 63 F4 37 48S 147 36 E
Baisha, China 34 G7 34 20N 112 32 E
Baitadi, Nepal 43 E9 29 35N 80 25 E
Baiyin, China 34 F3 36 45N 104 14 E
Baiyu Shan, China 34 F4 37 15N 107 30 E
Baj Baj, India 43 H13 22 30N 88 5 E
Baja, Hungary 17 E10 46 12N 18 59 E
Baja, Pta., Mexico 86 B1 29 50N 116 0W
Baja California, Mexico 86 A1 31 10N 115 12W
Baja California □, Mexico 86 B2 30 0N 115 0W
Baja California Sur □, Mexico 86 B2 25 50N 111 50W
Bajag, India 43 H9 22 40N 81 21 E
Bajamar, Canary Is. 22 F3 28 33N 16 20W
Bajana, India 42 H4 23 7N 71 49 E
Bājgīrān, Iran 45 B8 37 36N 58 24 E
Bajimba, Mt., Australia 63 D5 29 17S 152 6 E
Bajo Nuevo, Caribbean 88 C4 15 40N 78 50W
Bajoga, Nigeria 51 F8 10 57N 11 20 E
Bajool, Australia 62 C5 23 40S 150 35 E
Bakel, Senegal 50 F3 14 56N 12 20W
Baker, Calif., U.S.A. 85 K10 35 16N 116 4W
Baker, Mont., U.S.A. 80 B2 46 22N 104 17W
Baker, L., Canada 68 B10 64 0N 96 0W
Baker City, U.S.A. 82 D5 44 47N 117 50W
Baker I., Pac. Oc. 64 G10 0 10N 176 35W
Baker I., U.S.A. 72 B2 55 20N 133 40W
Baker L., Australia 61 E4 26 54S 126 5 E
Baker Lake, Canada 68 B10 64 20N 96 3W
Baker Mt., U.S.A. 82 B3 48 50N 121 49W
Bakers Creek, Australia 62 C4 21 13S 149 7 E
Baker's Dozen Is., Canada 70 A4 56 45N 78 45W
Bakersfield, Calif., U.S.A. 85 K8 35 23N 119 1W
Bakersfield, Vt., U.S.A. 79 B12 44 45N 72 48W
Bākhtarān, Iran 44 C5 34 23N 47 0 E
Bākhtarān □, Iran 44 C5 34 0N 46 30 E
Bakı, Azerbaijan 25 F8 40 29N 49 56 E
Bakkafjörður, Iceland 8 C6 66 2N 14 48W
Bakony, Hungary 17 E9 47 10N 17 30 E
Bakony Forest = Bakony, Hungary 17 E9 47 10N 17 30 E
Bakouma, C.A.R. 52 C4 5 40N 22 56 E
Bakswaho, India 43 G8 24 15N 79 18 E
Baku = Bakı, Azerbaijan 25 F8 40 29N 49 56 E
Bakutis Coast, Antarctica 5 D15 74 0S 120 0W
Baky = Bakı, Azerbaijan 25 F8 40 29N 49 56 E
Bala, Canada 78 A5 45 1N 79 37W
Bala, U.K. 10 E4 52 54N 3 36W
Bala, L., U.K. 10 E4 52 53N 3 37W
Balabac I., Phil. 36 C5 8 0N 117 0 E
Balabac Str., E. Indies 36 C5 7 53N 117 5 E
Balabagh, Afghan. 42 B4 34 25N 70 12 E
Ba'labakk, Lebanon 47 B5 34 0N 36 10 E
Balabalangan, Kepulauan, Indonesia 36 E5 2 20S 117 30 E
Balad, Iraq 44 C5 34 1N 44 9 E
Balad Rūz, Iraq 44 C5 33 42N 45 5 E
Bālādeh, Fārs, Iran 45 D6 29 17N 51 56 E
Bālādeh, Māzandaran, Iran 45 B6 36 12N 51 48 E
Balaghat, India 40 J12 21 49N 80 12 E
Balaghat Ra., India 40 K10 18 50N 76 30 E
Balaguer, Spain 19 B6 41 50N 0 50 E
Balaklava, Ukraine 25 F5 44 30N 33 30 E
Balakovo, Russia 24 D8 52 4N 47 55 E
Balamau, India 43 F9 27 10N 80 21 E
Balancán, Mexico 87 D6 17 48N 91 32W
Balashov, Russia 25 D7 51 30N 43 10 E
Balasinor, India 42 H5 22 57N 73 23 E
Balasore = Baleshwar, India 41 J15 21 35N 87 3 E
Balaton, Hungary 17 E9 46 50N 17 40 E
Balbina, Reprêsa de, Brazil 92 D7 2 0S 59 30W
Balboa, Panama 88 E4 8 57N 79 34W
Balbriggan, Ireland 13 C5 53 37N 6 11W
Balcarce, Argentina 94 D4 38 0S 58 10W
Balcarres, Canada 73 C8 50 50N 103 35W
Balchik, Bulgaria 21 C13 43 28N 28 11 E
Balclutha, N.Z. 59 M2 46 15S 169 45 E
Balcones Escarpment, U.S.A. 81 L5 29 30N 99 15W
Bald Hd., Australia 61 G2 35 6S 118 1 E
Bald I., Australia 61 F2 34 57S 118 27 E
Bald Knob, U.S.A. 81 H9 35 19N 91 34W
Baldock L., Canada 73 B9 56 33N 97 57W
Baldwin, Mich., U.S.A. 76 D3 43 54N 85 51W
Baldwin, Pa., U.S.A. 78 F5 40 23N 79 59W
Baldwinsville, U.S.A. 79 C8 43 10N 76 20W
Baldy Mt., U.S.A. 82 B9 48 9N 109 39W
Baldy Peak, U.S.A. 83 K9 33 54N 109 34W
Baleares, Is., Spain 22 B10 39 30N 3 0 E
Balearic Is. = Baleares, Is., Spain 22 B10 39 30N 3 0 E
Baleine = Whale →, Canada 71 A6 58 15N 67 40W
Baler, Phil. 37 A6 15 46N 121 34 E
Baleshare, U.K. 12 D1 57 31N 7 22W
Baleshwar, India 41 J15 21 35N 87 3 E
Balfate, Honduras 88 C2 15 48N 86 25W
Bali, Greece 23 D6 35 25N 24 47 E
Bali, India 42 G5 25 11N 73 17 E
Bali □, Indonesia 36 F5 8 20S 115 0 E
Bali, Selat, Indonesia 37 H16 8 18S 114 25 E
Baliapal, India 43 J12 21 40N 87 17 E
Balikeşir, Turkey 21 E12 39 39N 27 53 E
Balikpapan, Indonesia 36 E5 1 10S 116 55 E
Balimbing, Phil. 37 C5 5 5N 119 58 E
Baling, Malaysia 39 K3 5 41N 100 55 E
Balipara, India 41 F18 26 50N 92 45 E
Balkan Mts. = Stara Planina, Bulgaria 21 C10 43 15N 23 0 E
Balkhash = Balqash, Kazakstan 26 E8 46 50N 74 50 E
Balkhash, Ozero = Balqash Köl, Kazakstan 26 E8 46 0N 74 50 E
Balla, Bangla. 41 G17 24 10N 91 35 E
Ballachulish, U.K. 12 E3 56 41N 5 8W
Balladonia, Australia 61 F3 32 27S 123 51 E
Ballaghaderreen, Ireland 13 C3 53 55N 8 34W
Ballarat, Australia 63 F3 37 33S 143 50 E
Ballard, L., Australia 61 E3 29 20S 120 40 E
Ballater, U.K. 12 D5 57 3N 3 3W
Ballenas, Canal de, Mexico 86 B2 29 10N 113 45W
Balleny Is., Antarctica 5 C11 66 30S 163 0 E
Ballia, India 43 G11 25 46N 84 12 E
Ballina, Australia 63 D5 28 50S 153 31 E
Ballina, Ireland 13 B2 54 7N 9 9W
Ballinasloe, Ireland 13 C3 53 20N 8 13W
Ballinger, U.S.A. 81 K5 31 45N 99 57W
Ballinrobe, Ireland 13 C2 53 38N 9 13W
Ballinskelligs B., Ireland 13 E1 51 48N 10 13W
Ballston Spa, U.S.A. 79 D11 43 0N 73 51W
Ballycastle, U.K. 13 A5 55 12N 6 15W
Ballyclare, U.K. 13 B5 54 46N 6 0W
Ballyhaunis, Ireland 13 C3 53 46N 8 46W
Ballymena, U.K. 13 B5 54 52N 6 17W
Ballymoney, U.K. 13 A5 55 5N 6 31W
Ballymote, Ireland 13 B3 54 5N 8 31W
Ballynahinch, U.K. 13 B6 54 24N 5 54W
Ballyquintin Pt., U.K. 13 B6 54 20N 5 30W
Ballyshannon, Ireland 13 B3 54 30N 8 11W
Balmaceda, Chile 96 F2 46 0S 71 50W
Balmertown, Canada 73 C10 51 4N 93 41W
Balmoral, Australia 63 F3 37 15S 141 48 E
Balmorhea, U.S.A. 81 K3 30 59N 103 45W
Balonne →, Australia 63 D4 28 47S 147 56 E
Balotra, India 42 G5 25 50N 72 14 E
Balqash, Kazakstan 26 E8 46 50N 74 50 E
Balqash Köl, Kazakstan 26 E8 46 0N 74 50 E
Balrampur, India 43 F10 27 30N 82 20 E
Balranald, Australia 63 E3 34 38S 143 33 E
Balsas, Mexico 87 D5 18 0N 99 40W
Balsas →, Brazil 93 E9 7 15S 44 35W
Balsas →, Mexico 86 D4 17 55N 102 10W
Balston Spa, U.S.A. 79 D11 43 0N 73 52W
Balta, Ukraine 17 D15 48 2N 29 45 E
Bălţi, Moldova 17 E14 47 48N 27 58 E
Baltic Sea, Europe 9 H18 57 0N 19 0 E
Baltimore, Ireland 13 E2 51 29N 9 22W
Baltimore, Md., U.S.A. 76 F7 39 17N 76 37W
Baltimore, Ohio, U.S.A. 78 G2 39 51N 82 36W
Baltit, Pakistan 43 A6 36 15N 74 40 E
Baltiysk, Russia 9 J18 54 41N 19 58 E
Baluchistan □, Pakistan 40 F4 27 30N 65 0 E
Balurghat, India 43 G13 25 15N 88 44 E
Balvi, Latvia 9 H22 57 8N 27 15 E
Balya, Turkey 21 E12 39 44N 27 35 E
Bam, Iran 45 D8 29 7N 58 14 E
Bama, Nigeria 51 F8 11 33N 13 41 E
Bamaga, Australia 62 A3 10 50S 142 25 E
Bamaji L., Canada 70 B1 51 9N 91 25W
Bamako, Mali 50 F4 12 34N 7 55W
Bambari, C.A.R. 52 C4 5 40N 20 35 E
Bambaroo, Australia 62 B4 18 50S 146 10 E
Bamberg, Germany 16 D6 49 54N 10 54 E
Bamberg, U.S.A. 77 J5 33 18N 81 2W
Bambili, Dem. Rep. of the Congo 54 B2 3 40N 26 0 E
Bamenda, Cameroon 52 C1 5 57N 10 11 E
Bamfield, Canada 72 D3 48 45N 125 10W
Bāmīān □, Afghan. 40 B5 35 0N 67 0 E
Bamiancheng, China 35 C13 43 15N 124 2 E
Bampūr, Iran 45 E9 27 15N 60 21 E
Ban Ban, Laos 38 C4 19 31N 103 30 E
Ban Bang Hin, Thailand 39 H2 9 32N 98 35 E
Ban Chiang Klang, Thailand 38 C3 19 25N 100 55 E
Ban Chik, Laos 38 D4 17 15N 102 22 E
Ban Choho, Thailand 38 E4 15 2N 102 9 E
Ban Dan Lan Hoi, Thailand 38 D2 17 0N 99 35 E
Ban Don = Surat Thani, Thailand 39 H2 9 6N 99 20 E
Ban Don, Vietnam 38 F6 12 53N 107 48 E
Ban Don, Ao →, Thailand 39 H2 9 20N 99 25 E
Ban Dong, Thailand 38 C3 19 30N 100 59 E
Ban Hong, Thailand 38 C2 18 18N 98 50 E
Ban Kaeng, Thailand 38 D3 17 29N 100 7 E
Ban Kantang, Thailand 39 J2 7 25N 99 31 E
Ban Keun, Laos 38 C4 18 22N 102 35 E
Ban Khai, Thailand 38 F3 12 46N 101 18 E
Ban Kheun, Laos 38 B3 20 13N 101 7 E
Ban Khlong Kua, Thailand 39 J3 6 57N 100 8 E
Ban Khuan Mao, Thailand 39 J2 7 50N 99 37 E
Ban Ko Yai Chim, Thailand 39 G2 11 17N 99 26 E
Ban Kok, Thailand 38 D4 16 40N 103 40 E
Ban Laem, Thailand 38 F2 13 13N 99 59 E
Ban Lao Ngam, Laos 38 E6 15 28N 106 10 E
Ban Le Kathe, Thailand 38 E2 15 49N 98 53 E
Ban Mae Chedi, Thailand 38 C2 19 11N 99 31 E
Ban Mae Laeng, Thailand 38 B2 20 1N 99 17 E
Ban Mae Sariang, Thailand 38 C1 18 10N 97 56 E
Ban Mê Thuôt = Buon Ma Thuot, Vietnam 38 F7 12 40N 108 3 E
Ban Mi, Thailand 38 E3 15 3N 100 32 E
Ban Muong Mo, Laos 38 C4 19 4N 103 58 E
Ban Na Mo, Laos 38 D5 17 7N 105 40 E
Ban Na San, Thailand 39 H2 8 53N 99 52 E
Ban Na Tong, Laos 38 B3 20 56N 101 47 E
Ban Nam Bac, Laos 38 B4 20 38N 102 20 E
Ban Nam Ma, Laos 38 A3 22 2N 101 37 E
Ban Ngang, Laos 38 E6 15 59N 106 11 E
Ban Nong Bok, Laos 38 D5 17 5N 104 48 E
Ban Nong Boua, Laos 38 E6 15 40N 106 33 E
Ban Nong Pling, Thailand 38 E3 15 40N 100 10 E
Ban Pak Chan, Thailand 39 G2 10 32N 98 51 E
Ban Phai, Thailand 38 D4 16 4N 102 44 E
Ban Pong, Thailand 38 F2 13 50N 99 55 E
Ban Ron Phibun, Thailand 39 H2 8 9N 99 51 E
Ban Sanam Chai, Thailand 39 J3 7 33N 100 25 E
Ban Sangkha, Thailand 38 E4 14 37N 103 52 E
Ban Tak, Thailand 38 D2 17 2N 99 4 E
Ban Tako, Thailand 38 E4 14 5N 102 40 E
Ban Tha Dua, Thailand 38 D2 17 59N 98 39 E
Ban Tha Li, Thailand 38 D3 17 37N 101 25 E
Ban Tha Nun, Thailand 39 H2 8 12N 98 18 E
Ban Thahine, Laos 38 E5 14 12N 105 33 E
Ban Xien Kok, Laos 38 B3 20 54N 100 39 E
Ban Yen Nhan, Vietnam 38 B6 20 57N 106 2 E
Banaba, Kiribati 64 H8 0 45S 169 50 E
Banalia, Dem. Rep. of the Congo 54 B2 1 32N 25 5 E
Banam, Cambodia 39 G5 11 20N 105 17 E
Bananal, I. do, Brazil 93 F8 11 30S 50 30W
Banaras = Varanasi, India 43 G10 25 22N 83 0 E
Banas →, Gujarat, India 42 H4 23 45N 71 25 E
Banas →, Mad. P., India 43 G9 24 15N 81 30 E
Bânâs, Ras, Egypt 51 D13 23 57N 35 59 E
Banbān, Si. Arabia 44 E5 25 1N 46 35 E
Banbridge, U.K. 13 B5 54 22N 6 16W
Banbury, U.K. 11 E6 52 4N 1 20W
Banchory, U.K. 12 D6 57 3N 2 29W
Bancroft, Canada 78 A7 45 3N 77 51W
Band Bonī, Iran 45 E8 25 30N 59 33 E
Band Qīr, Iran 45 D6 31 39N 48 53 E
Banda, India 43 G9 25 30N 80 26 E
Banda, Mad. P., India 43 G8 24 3N 78 57 E
Banda, Kepulauan, Indonesia 37 E7 4 37S 129 50 E
Banda Aceh, Indonesia 36 C1 5 35N 95 20 E
Banda Banda, Mt., Australia 63 E5 31 10S 152 28 E
Banda Elat, Indonesia 37 F8 5 40S 133 5 E
Banda Is. = Banda, Kepulauan, Indonesia 37 E7 4 37S 129 50 E
Banda Sea, Indonesia 37 F8 6 0S 130 0 E
Bandai-San, Japan 30 F10 37 36N 140 4 E
Bandān, Iran 45 D9 31 23N 60 44 E
Bandanaira, Indonesia 37 E7 4 32S 129 54 E
Bandanwara, India 42 F6 26 9N 74 38 E
Bandar = Machilipatnam, India 41 L12 16 12N 81 8 E
Bandār 'Abbās, Iran 45 E8 27 15N 56 15 E
Bandar-e Anzalī, Iran 45 B6 37 30N 49 30 E
Bandar-e Bushehr = Būshehr, Iran 45 D6 28 55N 50 55 E
Bandar-e Chārak, Iran 45 E7 26 45N 54 20 E
Bandar-e Deylam, Iran 45 D6 30 5N 50 10 E
Bandar-e Khomeynı, Iran 45 D6 30 30N 49 5 E
Bandar-e Lengeh, Iran 45 E7 26 35N 54 58 E
Bandar-e Maqām, Iran 45 E7 26 56N 53 29 E
Bandar-e Ma'shur, Iran 45 D6 30 35N 49 10 E
Bandar-e Nakhīlū, Iran 45 E7 26 58N 53 30 E
Bandar-e Rīg, Iran 45 D6 29 29N 50 38 E
Bandar-e Torkeman, Iran 45 B7 37 0N 54 10 E
Bandar Maharani = Muar, Malaysia 39 L4 2 3N 102 34 E
Bandar Penggaram = Batu Pahat, Malaysia 39 M4 1 50N 102 56 E
Bandar Seri Begawan, Brunei 36 D5 4 52N 115 0 E
Bandar Sri Aman, Malaysia 36 D4 1 15N 111 32 E
Bandawe, Malawi 55 E3 11 58S 34 5 E
Bandeira, Pico da, Brazil 95 A7 20 26S 41 47W
Bandera, Argentina 94 B3 28 55S 62 20W
Banderas, B. de, Mexico 86 C3 20 40N 105 30W
Bandhogarh, India 43 H9 23 40N 81 2 E
Bandi →, India 42 F6 26 12N 75 47 E
Bandikui, India 42 F7 27 3N 76 34 E
Bandırma, Turkey 21 D13 40 20N 28 0 E
Bandon, Ireland 13 E3 51 44N 8 44W
Bandon →, Ireland 13 E3 51 43N 8 37W
Bandula, Mozam. 55 F3 19 0S 33 7 E
Bandundu, Dem. Rep. of the Congo 52 E3 3 15S 17 22 E
Bandung, Indonesia 37 G12 6 54S 107 36 E
Bāneh, Iran 44 C5 35 59N 45 53 E
Banes, Cuba 89 B4 21 0N 75 42W
Banff, Canada 72 C5 51 10N 115 34W
Banff, U.K. 12 D6 57 40N 2 33W
Banff Nat. Park, Canada 72 C5 51 30N 116 15W
Bang Fai →, Laos 38 D5 16 57N 104 45 E
Bang Hieng →, Laos 38 D5 16 10N 105 10 E
Bang Krathum, Thailand 38 D3 16 34N 100 18 E
Bang Lamung, Thailand 38 F3 13 3N 100 56 E
Bang Mun Nak, Thailand 38 D3 16 2N 100 23 E
Bang Pa In, Thailand 38 E3 14 14N 100 35 E
Bang Rakam, Thailand 38 D3 16 45N 100 7 E
Bang Saphan, Thailand 39 G2 11 14N 99 28 E
Bangaduni I., India 43 J13 21 34N 88 52 E
Bangala Dam, Zimbabwe 55 G3 21 7S 31 25 E
Bangalore, India 40 N10 12 59N 77 40 E
Banganga →, India 42 F6 27 6N 77 25 E
Bangaon, India 43 H13 23 0N 88 47 E
Bangassou, C.A.R. 52 D4 4 55N 23 7 E
Banggai, Indonesia 37 E6 1 34S 123 30 E
Banggai, Kepulauan, Indonesia 37 E6 1 40S 123 30 E
Banggai Arch. = Banggai, Kepulauan, Indonesia 37 E6 1 40S 123 30 E
Banggi, Malaysia 36 C5 7 17N 117 12 E
Banghāzī, Libya 51 B10 32 11N 20 3 E
Bangka, Sulawesi, Indonesia 37 D7 1 50N 125 5 E
Bangka, Sumatera, Indonesia 36 E3 2 0S 105 50 E
Bangka, Selat, Indonesia 36 E3 2 30S 105 30 E
Bangkalan, Indonesia 37 G15 7 2S 112 46 E
Bangkinang, Indonesia 36 D2 0 18N 101 5 E
Bangko, Indonesia 36 E2 2 5S 102 9 E
Bangkok, Thailand 38 F3 13 45N 100 35 E
Bangladesh ■, Asia 41 H17 24 0N 90 0 E
Bangong Co, India 43 B8 35 50N 79 20 E
Bangor, Down, U.K. 13 B6 54 40N 5 40W
Bangor, Gwynedd, U.K. 10 D3 53 14N 4 8W
Bangor, Maine, U.S.A. 69 D13 44 48N 68 46W
Bangor, Pa., U.S.A. 79 F9 40 52N 75 13W
Bangued, Phil. 37 A6 17 40N 120 37 E
Bangui, C.A.R. 52 D3 4 23N 18 35 E
Banguru, Dem. Rep. of the Congo 54 B2 0 30N 27 10 E
Bangweulu, L., Zambia 55 E3 11 0S 30 0 E
Bangweulu Swamp, Zambia 55 E3 11 20S 30 15 E
Bani, Dom. Rep. 89 C5 18 16N 70 22W
Banī Sa'd, Iraq 44 C5 33 34N 44 32 E
Banihal Pass, India 43 C6 33 30N 75 12 E
Bāniyās, Syria 44 C3 35 10N 36 0 E
Banja Luka, Bos.-H. 20 B7 44 49N 17 11 E
Banjar, India 42 D7 31 38N 77 21 E
Banjar →, India 43 H9 22 36N 80 22 E
Banjarmasin, Indonesia 36 E4 3 20S 114 35 E
Banjul, Gambia 50 F2 13 28N 16 40W
Banka, India 43 G12 24 53N 86 55 E
Banket, Zimbabwe 55 F3 17 27S 30 19 E
Bankipore, India 41 G14 25 35N 85 10 E
Banks I., B.C., Canada 72 C3 53 20N 130 0W
Banks I., N.W.T., Canada 68 A7 73 15N 121 30W
Banks Pen., N.Z. 59 K4 43 45S 173 15 E
Banks Str., Australia 62 G4 40 40S 148 10 E
Bankura, India 43 H12 23 11N 87 18 E
Banmankhi, India 43 G12 25 53N 87 11 E
Bann →, Arm., U.K. 13 B5 54 30N 6 31W
Bann →, L'derry., U.K. 13 A5 55 8N 6 41W
Bannang Sata, Thailand 39 J3 6 16N 101 16 E
Banning, U.S.A. 85 M10 33 56N 116 53W
Banningville = Bandundu, Dem. Rep. of the Congo 52 E3 3 15S 17 22 E
Bannockburn, Canada 78 B7 44 39N 77 33W
Bannockburn, U.K. 12 E5 56 5N 3 55W
Bannockburn, Zimbabwe 55 G2 20 17S 29 48 E
Bannu, Pakistan 40 C7 33 0N 70 18 E
Bano, India 43 H11 22 40N 84 55 E
Bansgaon, India 43 F10 26 33N 83 21 E
Banská Bystrica, Slovak Rep. 17 D10 48 46N 19 14 E
Banswara, India 42 H6 23 32N 74 24 E
Bantaeng, Indonesia 37 F5 5 32S 119 56 E
Bantry, Ireland 13 E2 51 41N 9 27W
Bantry B., Ireland 13 E2 51 37N 9 44W
Bantul, Indonesia 37 G14 7 55S 110 19 E
Bantva, India 42 J4 21 29N 70 12 E
Banu, Afghan. 40 B6 35 35N 69 5 E
Banyak, Kepulauan, Indonesia 36 D1 2 10N 97 10 E
Banyalbufar, Spain 22 B9 39 42N 2 31 E
Banyo, Cameroon 52 C2 6 52N 11 45 E
Banyumas, Indonesia 37 G13 7 32S 109 18 E
Banyuwangi, Indonesia 37 H16 8 13S 114 21 E
Banzare Coast, Antarctica 5 C9 68 0S 125 0 E
Banzyville = Mobayi, Dem. Rep. of the Congo 52 D4 4 15N 21 8 E
Bao Lac, Vietnam 38 A5 22 57N 105 40 E
Bao Loc, Vietnam 39 G6 11 32N 107 48 E
Baocheng, China 34 H4 33 12N 106 56 E
Baode, China 34 E6 39 1N 111 5 E
Baodi, China 35 E9 39 38N 117 20 E
Baoding, China 34 E8 38 50N 115 28 E
Baoji, China 34 G4 34 20N 107 5 E
Baoshan, China 32 D4 25 10N 99 5 E
Baotou, China 34 D6 40 32N 110 2 E
Baoying, China 35 H10 33 17N 119 20 E
Bap, India 42 F5 27 23N 72 18 E
Bapatla, India 41 M12 15 55N 80 30 E
Bāqerābād, Iran 45 C6 33 2N 51 58 E
Ba'qūbah, Iraq 44 C5 33 45N 44 50 E
Baquedano, Chile 94 A2 23 20S 69 52W
Bar, Montenegro, Yug. 21 C8 42 8N 19 6 E
Bar, Ukraine 17 D14 49 4N 27 40 E
Bar Bigha, India 43 G11 25 21N 85 47 E
Bar Harbor, U.S.A. 77 C11 44 23N 68 13W
Bar-le-Duc, France 18 B6 48 47N 5 10 E
Bara, India 43 G9 25 16N 81 43 E
Bara Banki, India 43 F9 26 55N 81 12 E
Barabai, Indonesia 36 E5 2 32S 115 34 E
Baraboo, U.S.A. 80 D10 43 28N 89 45W
Baracoa, Cuba 89 B5 20 20N 74 30W
Baradā →, Syria 47 B5 33 33N 36 34 E
Baradero, Argentina 94 C4 33 52S 59 29W
Baradine, Australia 63 E4 30 56S 149 4 E
Baraga, U.S.A. 80 B10 46 47N 88 30W
Barah →, India 42 F6 27 42N 77 5 E
Barahona, Dom. Rep. 89 C5 18 13N 71 7W
Barail Range, India 41 G18 25 15N 93 20 E
Barakaldo, Spain 19 A4 43 18N 2 59W
Barakar →, India 43 G12 24 7N 86 14 E
Barakhola, India 41 G18 25 0N 92 45 E
Barakot, India 43 J11 21 33N 84 59 E
Barakpur, India 43 H13 22 44N 88 30 E
Baralaba, Australia 62 C4 24 13S 149 50 E
Baralzon L., Canada 73 B9 60 0N 98 3W
Baramula, India 43 B6 34 15N 74 20 E
Baran, India 42 G7 25 9N 76 40 E
Baran →, Pakistan 42 G3 25 13N 68 17 E
Baranavichy, Belarus 17 B14 53 10N 26 0 E
Baranof, U.S.A. 72 B2 57 5N 134 50W
Baranof I., U.S.A. 68 C6 57 0N 135 0W
Barapasi, Indonesia 37 E9 2 15S 137 5 E
Barasat, India 43 H13 22 46N 88 31 E
Barat Daya, Kepulauan, Indonesia 37 F7 7 30S 128 0 E
Barataria B., U.S.A. 81 L10 29 20N 89 55W
Barauda, India 42 H6 23 33N 75 15 E
Baraut, India 42 E7 29 13N 77 7 E
Barbacena, Brazil 95 A7 21 15S 43 56W
Barbados ■, W. Indies 89 D8 13 10N 59 30W
Barbària, C. de, Spain 22 C7 38 39N 1 24 E
Barbastro, Spain 19 A6 42 2N 0 5 E
Barberton, S. Africa 57 D5 25 42S 31 2 E
Barberton, U.S.A. 78 E3 41 0N 81 39W
Barbosa, Colombia 92 B4 5 57N 73 37W
Barbourville, U.S.A. 77 G4 36 52N 83 53W
Barbuda, W. Indies 89 C7 17 30N 61 40W
Barcaldine, Australia 62 C4 23 43S 145 6 E
Barcellona Pozzo di Gotto, Italy 20 E6 38 9N 15 13 E
Barcelona, Spain 19 B7 41 21N 2 10 E
Barcelona, Venezuela 92 A6 10 10N 64 40W
Barcelos, Brazil 92 D6 1 0S 63 0W
Barcoo →, Australia 62 D3 25 30S 142 50 E
Bardaï, Chad 51 D9 21 25N 17 0 E
Bardas Blancas, Argentina 94 D2 35 49S 69 45W
Barddhaman, India 43 H12 23 14N 87 39 E
Bardejov, Slovak Rep. 17 D11 49 18N 21 15 E
Bardera, Somali Rep. 46 G3 2 20N 42 27 E
Bardīyah, Libya 51 B10 31 45N 25 5 E
Bardsey I., U.K. 10 E3 52 45N 4 47W
Bardstown, U.S.A. 76 G3 37 49N 85 28W

Bareilly

Bareilly, *India* **43 E8** 28 22N 79 27 E
Barela, *India* **43 H9** 23 6N 80 3 E
Barents Sea, *Arctic* **4 B9** 73 0N 39 0 E
Barfleur, Pte. de, *France* **18 B3** 49 42N 1 16W
Bargara, *Australia* **62 C5** 24 50S 152 25 E
Barguzin, *Russia* **27 D11** 53 37N 109 37 E
Barh, *India* **43 G11** 25 29N 85 46 E
Barhaj, *India* **43 F10** 26 18N 83 44 E
Barham, *Australia* **63 F3** 35 36S 144 8 E
Barharwa, *India* **43 G12** 24 52N 87 47 E
Barhi, *India* **43 G11** 24 15N 85 25 E
Bari, *India* **42 F7** 26 39N 77 39 E
Bari, *Italy* **20 D7** 41 8N 16 51 E
Bari Doab, *Pakistan* **42 D5** 30 20N 73 0 E
Bari Sadri, *India* **42 G6** 24 28N 74 30 E
Barīdī, Ra's, *Si. Arabia* **44 E3** 24 17N 37 31 E
Barīm, *Yemen* **48 E8** 12 39N 43 25 E
Barinas, *Venezuela* **92 B4** 8 36N 70 15W
Baring, C., *Canada* **68 B8** 70 0N 117 30W
Baringo, *Kenya* **54 B4** 0 47N 36 16 E
Baringo, L., *Kenya* **54 B4** 0 47N 36 16 E
Barisal, *Bangla.* **41 H17** 22 45N 90 20 E
Barisan, Bukit, *Indonesia* **36 E2** 3 30S 102 15 E
Barito →, *Indonesia* **36 E4** 4 0S 114 50 E
Bark L., *Canada* **78 A7** 45 27N 77 51W
Barkakana, *India* **43 H11** 23 37N 85 29 E
Barker, *U.S.A.* **78 C6** 43 20N 78 33W
Barkley, L., *U.S.A.* **77 G2** 37 1N 88 14W
Barkley Sound, *Canada* **72 D3** 48 50N 125 10W
Barkly East, *S. Africa* **56 E4** 30 58S 27 33 E
Barkly Roadhouse, *Australia* **62 B2** 19 52S 135 50 E
Barkly Tableland, *Australia* **62 B2** 17 50S 136 40 E
Barkly West, *S. Africa* **56 D3** 28 5S 24 31 E
Barkol Kazak Zizhixian, *China* **32 B4** 43 37N 93 2 E
Bârlad, *Romania* **17 E14** 46 15N 27 38 E
Bârlad →, *Romania* **17 F14** 45 38N 27 32 E
Barlee, L., *Australia* **61 E2** 29 15S 119 30 E
Barlee, Mt., *Australia* **61 D4** 24 38S 128 13 E
Barletta, *Italy* **20 D7** 41 19N 16 17 E
Barlovento, *Canary Is.* **22 F2** 28 48N 17 48W
Barlow L., *Canada* **73 A8** 62 0N 103 0W
Barmedman, *Australia* **63 E4** 34 9S 147 21 E
Barmer, *India* **42 G4** 25 45N 71 20 E
Barmera, *Australia* **63 E3** 34 15S 140 28 E
Barmouth, *U.K.* **10 E3** 52 44N 4 4W
Barna →, *India* **43 G10** 25 21N 83 3 E
Barnagar, *India* **42 H6** 23 7N 75 19 E
Barnala, *India* **42 D6** 30 23N 75 33 E
Barnard Castle, *U.K.* **10 C6** 54 33N 1 55W
Barnaul, *Russia* **26 D9** 53 20N 83 40 E
Barnesville, *U.S.A.* **77 J3** 33 3N 84 9W
Barnet, *U.K.* **11 F7** 51 38N 0 9W
Barneveld, *Neths.* **15 B5** 52 7N 5 36 E
Barneveld, *U.S.A.* **79 C9** 43 16N 75 14W
Barnhart, *U.S.A.* **81 K4** 31 8N 101 10W
Barnsley, *U.K.* **10 D6** 53 34N 1 27W
Barnstaple, *U.K.* **11 F3** 51 5N 4 4W
Barnstaple Bay = Bideford Bay, *U.K.* **11 F3** 51 5N 4 20W
Barnsville, *U.S.A.* **80 B6** 46 43N 96 28W
Barnwell, *U.S.A.* **77 J5** 33 15N 81 23W
Baro, *Nigeria* **50 G7** 8 35N 6 18 E
Baroda = Vadodara, *India* **42 H5** 22 20N 73 10 E
Baroda, *India* **42 G7** 25 29N 76 35 E
Baroe, *S. Africa* **56 E3** 33 13S 24 33 E
Baron Ra., *Australia* **60 D4** 23 30S 127 45 E
Barotseland, *Zambia* **53 H4** 15 0S 24 0 E
Barpeta, *India* **41 F17** 26 20N 91 10 E
Barques, Pt. Aux, *U.S.A.* **78 B2** 44 4N 82 58W
Barquísimeto, *Venezuela* **92 A5** 10 4N 69 19W
Barr Smith Range, *Australia* **61 E3** 27 4S 120 20 E
Barra, *Brazil* **93 F10** 11 5S 43 10W
Barra, *U.K.* **12 E1** 57 0N 7 29W
Barra, Sd. of, *U.K.* **12 D1** 57 4N 7 25W
Barra de Navidad, *Mexico* **86 D4** 19 12N 104 41W
Barra do Corda, *Brazil* **93 E9** 5 30S 45 10W
Barra do Piraí, *Brazil* **95 A7** 22 30S 43 50W
Barra Falsa, Pta. da, *Mozam.* **57 C6** 22 58S 35 37 E
Barra Hd., *U.K.* **12 E1** 56 47N 7 40W
Barra Mansa, *Brazil* **95 A7** 22 35S 44 12W
Barraba, *Australia* **63 E5** 30 21S 150 35 E
Barrackpur = Barakpur, *India* **43 H13** 22 44N 88 30 E
Barradale Roadhouse, *Australia* **60 D1** 22 42S 114 58 E
Barraigh = Barra, *U.K.* **12 E1** 57 0N 7 29W
Barranca, *Lima, Peru* **92 F3** 10 45S 77 50W
Barranca, *Loreto, Peru* **92 D3** 4 50S 76 50W
Barrancabermeja, *Colombia* **92 B4** 7 0N 73 50W
Barrancas, *Venezuela* **92 B6** 8 55N 62 5W
Barrancos, *Portugal* **19 C2** 38 10N 6 58W
Barranqueras, *Argentina* **94 B4** 27 30S 59 0W
Barranquilla, *Colombia* **92 A4** 11 0N 74 50W
Barraute, *Canada* **70 C4** 48 26N 77 38W
Barre, *Mass., U.S.A.* **79 D12** 42 25N 72 6W
Barre, *Vt., U.S.A.* **79 B12** 44 12N 72 30W
Barreal, *Argentina* **94 C2** 31 33S 69 28W
Barreiras, *Brazil* **93 F10** 12 8S 45 0W
Barreirinhas, *Brazil* **93 D10** 2 30S 42 50W
Barreiro, *Portugal* **19 C1** 38 40N 9 6W
Barren, Nosy, *Madag.* **57 B7** 18 25S 43 40 E
Barretos, *Brazil* **93 H9** 20 30S 48 35W
Barrhead, *Canada* **72 C6** 54 10N 114 24W
Barrie, *Canada* **78 B5** 44 24N 79 40W
Barrier Ra., *Australia* **63 E3** 31 0S 141 30 E
Barrière, *Canada* **72 C4** 51 12N 120 7W
Barrington, *U.S.A.* **79 E13** 41 44N 71 18W
Barrington L., *Canada* **73 B8** 56 55N 100 15W
Barrington Tops, *Australia* **63 E5** 32 6S 151 28 E
Barringun, *Australia* **63 D4** 29 1S 145 41 E
Barro do Garças, *Brazil* **93 G8** 15 54S 52 16W
Barron, *U.S.A.* **80 C9** 45 24N 91 51W
Barrow, *U.S.A.* **68 A4** 71 18N 156 47W
Barrow →, *Ireland* **13 D5** 52 25N 6 58W
Barrow Creek, *Australia* **62 C1** 21 30S 133 55 E
Barrow I., *Australia* **60 D2** 20 45S 115 20 E
Barrow-in-Furness, *U.K.* **10 C4** 54 7N 3 14W
Barrow Pt., *Australia* **62 A3** 14 20S 144 40 E
Barrow Pt., *U.S.A.* **66 B4** 71 24N 156 29W
Barrow Ra., *Australia* **61 E4** 26 0S 127 40 E
Barrow Str., *Canada* **4 B3** 74 20N 95 0W
Barry, *U.K.* **11 F4** 51 24N 3 16W
Barry's Bay, *Canada* **78 A7** 45 29N 77 41W
Barsat, *Pakistan* **43 A5** 36 10N 72 45 E
Barsham, *Syria* **44 C4** 35 21N 40 33 E
Barsi, *India* **40 K9** 18 10N 75 50 E
Barsoi, *India* **41 G15** 25 48N 87 57 E
Barstow, *U.S.A.* **85 L9** 34 54N 117 1W
Barthélemy, Col, *Vietnam* **38 C5** 19 26N 104 6 E
Bartica, *Guyana* **92 B7** 6 25N 58 40W
Bartlesville, *U.S.A.* **81 G7** 36 45N 95 59W
Bartlett, *U.S.A.* **84 J8** 36 29N 118 2W
Bartlett, L., *Canada* **72 A5** 63 5N 118 20W
Bartolomeu Dias, *Mozam.* **55 G4** 21 10S 35 8 E
Barton, *U.S.A.* **79 B12** 44 45N 72 11W
Barton upon Humber, *U.K.* **10 D7** 53 41N 0 25W
Bartow, *U.S.A.* **77 M5** 27 54N 81 50W
Barú, Volcan, *Panama* **88 E3** 8 55N 82 35W
Barumba, *Dem. Rep. of the Congo* **54 B1** 1 3N 23 37 E
Baruunsuu, *Mongolia* **34 C3** 43 43N 105 35 E
Barwani, *India* **42 H6** 22 2N 74 57 E
Barysaw, *Belarus* **17 A15** 54 17N 28 28 E
Barzān, *Iraq* **44 B5** 36 55N 44 3 E
Bāsa'idū, *Iran* **45 E7** 26 35N 55 20 E
Basal, *Pakistan* **42 C5** 33 33N 72 13 E
Basankusa, *Dem. Rep. of the Congo* **52 D3** 1 5N 19 50 E
Basarabeasca, *Moldova* **17 E15** 46 21N 28 58 E
Basawa, *Afghan.* **42 B4** 34 15N 70 50 E
Bascuñán, C., *Chile* **94 B1** 28 52S 71 35W
Basel, *Switz.* **18 C7** 47 35N 7 35 E
Bashākerd, Kūhhā-ye, *Iran* **45 E8** 26 42N 58 35 E
Bashaw, *Canada* **72 C6** 52 35N 112 58W
Bāshī, *Iran* **45 D6** 28 41N 51 4 E
Bashkir Republic = Bashkortostan □, *Russia* **24 D10** 54 0N 57 0 E
Bashkortostan □, *Russia* **24 D10** 54 0N 57 0 E
Basilan, *Phil.* **37 C6** 6 35N 122 0 E
Basilan Str., *Phil.* **37 C6** 6 50N 122 0 E
Basildon, *U.K.* **11 F8** 51 34N 0 28 E
Basim = Washim, *India* **40 J10** 20 3N 77 0 E
Basin, *U.S.A.* **82 D9** 44 23N 108 2W
Basingstoke, *U.K.* **11 F6** 51 15N 1 5W
Baskatong, Rés., *Canada* **70 C4** 46 46N 75 50W
Basle = Basel, *Switz.* **18 C7** 47 35N 7 35 E
Basoda, *India* **42 H7** 23 52N 77 54 E
Basoka, *Dem. Rep. of the Congo* **54 B1** 1 16N 23 40 E
Basque Provinces = País Vasco □, *Spain* **19 A4** 42 50N 2 45W
Basra = Al Başrah, *Iraq* **44 D5** 30 30N 47 50 E
Bass Str., *Australia* **62 F4** 39 15S 146 30 E
Bassano, *Canada* **72 C6** 50 48N 112 20W
Bassano del Grappa, *Italy* **20 B4** 45 46N 11 44 E
Bassas da India, *Ind. Oc.* **53 J7** 22 0S 39 0 E
Basse-Terre, *Guadeloupe* **89 C7** 16 0N 61 44W
Bassein, *Burma* **41 L19** 16 45N 94 30 E
Basseterre, *St. Kitts & Nevis* **89 C7** 17 17N 62 43W
Bassett, *U.S.A.* **80 D5** 42 35N 99 32W
Bassi, *India* **42 D7** 30 44N 76 21 E
Bastak, *Iran* **45 E7** 27 15N 54 25 E
Baştām, *Iran* **45 B7** 36 29N 55 4 E
Bastar, *India* **41 K12** 19 15N 81 40 E
Basti, *India* **43 F10** 26 52N 82 55 E
Bastia, *France* **18 E8** 42 40N 9 30 E
Bastogne, *Belgium* **15 D5** 50 1N 5 43 E
Bastrop, *La., U.S.A.* **81 J9** 32 47N 91 55W
Bastrop, *Tex., U.S.A.* **81 K6** 30 7N 97 19W
Bat Yam, *Israel* **47 C3** 32 2N 34 44 E
Bata, *Eq. Guin.* **52 D1** 1 57N 9 50 E
Bataan, *Phil.* **37 B6** 14 40N 120 25 E
Batabanó, *Cuba* **88 B3** 22 40N 82 20W
Batabanó, G. de, *Cuba* **88 B3** 22 30N 82 30W
Batac, *Phil.* **37 A6** 18 3N 120 34 E
Batagai, *Russia* **27 C14** 67 38N 134 38 E
Batala, *India* **42 D6** 31 48N 75 12 E
Batama, *Dem. Rep. of the Congo* **54 B2** 0 58N 26 33 E
Batamay, *Russia* **27 C13** 63 30N 129 15 E
Batang, *Indonesia* **37 G13** 6 55S 109 45 E
Batangas, *Phil.* **37 B6** 13 35N 121 10 E
Batanta, *Indonesia* **37 E8** 0 55S 130 40 E
Batatais, *Brazil* **95 A6** 20 54S 47 37W
Batavia, *U.S.A.* **78 D6** 43 0N 78 11W
Batchelor, *Australia* **60 B5** 13 4S 131 1 E
Batdambang, *Cambodia* **38 F4** 13 7N 103 12 E
Bateman's B., *Australia* **63 F5** 35 40S 150 12 E
Batemans Bay, *Australia* **63 F5** 35 44S 150 11 E
Bates Ra., *Australia* **61 E3** 27 27S 121 5 E
Batesburg, *U.S.A.* **77 J5** 33 54N 81 33W
Batesville, *Ark., U.S.A.* **81 H9** 35 46N 91 39W
Batesville, *Miss., U.S.A.* **81 H10** 34 19N 89 57W
Batesville, *Tex., U.S.A.* **81 L5** 28 58N 99 37W
Bath, *Canada* **79 B8** 44 11N 76 47W
Bath, *U.K.* **11 F5** 51 23N 2 22W
Bath, *Maine, U.S.A.* **77 D11** 43 55N 69 49W
Bath, *N.Y., U.S.A.* **78 D7** 42 20N 77 19W
Bath & North East Somerset □, *U.K.* **11 F5** 51 21N 2 27W
Batheay, *Cambodia* **39 G5** 11 59N 104 57 E
Bathurst = Banjul, *Gambia* **50 F2** 13 28N 16 40W
Bathurst, *Australia* **63 E4** 33 25S 149 31 E
Bathurst, *Canada* **71 C6** 47 37N 65 43W
Bathurst, *S. Africa* **56 E4** 33 30S 26 50 E
Bathurst, C., *Canada* **68 A7** 70 34N 128 0W
Bathurst B., *Australia* **62 A3** 14 16S 144 25 E
Bathurst Harb., *Australia* **62 G4** 43 15S 146 10 E
Bathurst I., *Australia* **60 B5** 11 30S 130 10 E
Bathurst I., *Canada* **4 B2** 76 0N 100 30W
Bathurst Inlet, *Canada* **68 B9** 66 50N 108 1W
Batlow, *Australia* **63 F4** 35 31S 148 9 E
Batman, *Turkey* **25 G7** 37 55N 41 5 E
Baţn al Ghūl, *Jordan* **47 F4** 29 36N 35 56 E
Batna, *Algeria* **50 A7** 35 34N 6 15 E
Batoka, *Zambia* **55 F2** 16 45S 27 15 E
Baton Rouge, *U.S.A.* **81 K9** 30 27N 91 11W
Batong, Ko, *Thailand* **39 J2** 6 32N 99 12 E
Batopilas, *Mexico* **86 B3** 27 0N 107 45W
Batouri, *Cameroon* **52 D2** 4 30N 14 25 E
Båtsfjord, *Norway* **8 A23** 70 38N 29 39 E
Battambang = Batdambang, *Cambodia* **38 F4** 13 7N 103 12 E
Batticaloa, *Sri Lanka* **40 R12** 7 43N 81 45 E
Battipáglia, *Italy* **20 D6** 40 37N 14 58 E
Battle, *U.K.* **11 G8** 50 55N 0 30 E
Battle →, *Canada* **73 C7** 52 43N 108 15W
Battle Creek, *U.S.A.* **76 D3** 42 19N 85 11W
Battle Ground, *U.S.A.* **84 E4** 45 47N 122 32W
Battle Harbour, *Canada* **71 B8** 52 16N 55 35W
Battle Lake, *U.S.A.* **80 B7** 46 17N 95 43W
Battle Mountain, *U.S.A.* **82 F5** 40 38N 116 56W
Battlefields, *Zimbabwe* **55 F2** 18 37S 29 47 E
Battleford, *Canada* **73 C7** 52 45N 108 15W
Batu, Kepulauan, *Indonesia* **36 E1** 0 30S 98 25 E
Batu, Mt., *Ethiopia* **46 F2** 6 55N 39 45 E
Batu Caves, *Malaysia* **39 L3** 3 15N 101 40 E
Batu Gajah, *Malaysia* **39 K3** 4 28N 101 3 E
Batu Is. = Batu, Kepulauan, *Indonesia* **36 E1** 0 30S 98 25 E
Batu Pahat, *Malaysia* **39 M4** 1 50N 102 56 E
Batuata, *Indonesia* **37 F6** 6 12S 122 42 E
Batumi, *Georgia* **25 F7** 41 39N 41 44 E
Baturaja, *Indonesia* **36 E2** 4 11S 104 15 E
Baturité, *Brazil* **93 D11** 4 28S 38 45W
Bau, *Malaysia* **36 D4** 1 25N 110 9 E
Baubau, *Indonesia* **37 F6** 5 25S 122 38 E
Bauchi, *Nigeria* **50 F7** 10 22N 9 48 E
Baudette, *U.S.A.* **80 A7** 48 43N 94 36W
Bauer, C., *Australia* **63 E1** 32 44S 134 4 E
Bauhinia, *Australia* **62 C4** 24 35S 149 18 E
Baukau, *Indonesia* **37 F7** 8 27S 126 27 E
Bauld, C., *Canada* **69 C14** 51 38N 55 26W
Bauru, *Brazil* **95 A6** 22 10S 49 0W
Bausi, *India* **43 G12** 24 48N 87 1 E
Bauska, *Latvia* **9 H21** 56 24N 24 15 E
Bautzen, *Germany* **16 C8** 51 10N 14 26 E
Bavānāt, *Iran* **45 D7** 30 28N 53 27 E
Bavaria = Bayern □, *Germany* **16 D6** 48 50N 12 0 E
Bavispe →, *Mexico* **86 B3** 29 30N 109 11W
Bawdwin, *Burma* **41 H20** 23 5N 97 20 E
Bawean, *Indonesia* **36 F4** 5 46S 112 35 E
Bawku, *Ghana* **50 F5** 11 3N 0 19W
Bawlake, *Burma* **41 K20** 19 11N 97 21 E
Baxley, *U.S.A.* **77 K4** 31 47N 82 21W
Baxter, *U.S.A.* **80 B7** 46 21N 94 17W
Baxter Springs, *U.S.A.* **81 G7** 37 2N 94 44W
Bay City, *Mich., U.S.A.* **76 D4** 43 36N 83 54W
Bay City, *Tex., U.S.A.* **81 L7** 28 59N 95 58W
Bay Minette, *U.S.A.* **77 K2** 30 53N 87 46W
Bay Roberts, *Canada* **71 C9** 47 36N 53 16W
Bay St. Louis, *U.S.A.* **81 K10** 30 19N 89 20W
Bay Springs, *U.S.A.* **81 K10** 31 59N 89 17W
Bay View, *N.Z.* **59 H6** 39 25S 176 50 E
Baya, *Dem. Rep. of the Congo* **55 E2** 11 53S 27 25 E
Bayamo, *Cuba* **88 B4** 20 20N 76 40W
Bayamón, *Puerto Rico* **89 C6** 18 24N 66 10W
Bayan Har Shan, *China* **32 C4** 34 0N 98 0 E
Bayan Hot = Alxa Zuoqi, *China* **34 E3** 38 50N 105 40 E
Bayan Obo, *China* **34 D5** 41 52N 109 59 E
Bayan-Ovoo = Erdenetsogt, *Mongolia* **34 C4** 42 55N 106 5 E
Bayana, *India* **42 F7** 26 55N 77 18 E
Bayanaūyl, *Kazakstan* **26 D8** 50 45N 75 45 E
Bayandalay, *Mongolia* **34 C2** 43 30N 103 29 E
Bayanhongor, *Mongolia* **32 B5** 46 8N 102 43 E
Bayard, *N. Mex., U.S.A.* **83 K9** 32 46N 108 8W
Bayard, *Nebr., U.S.A.* **80 E3** 41 45N 103 20W
Baybay, *Phil.* **37 B6** 10 40N 124 55 E
Bayern □, *Germany* **16 D6** 48 50N 12 0 E
Bayeux, *France* **18 B3** 49 17N 0 42W
Bayfield, *Canada* **78 C3** 43 34N 81 42W
Bayfield, *U.S.A.* **80 B9** 46 49N 90 49W
Bayındır, *Turkey* **21 E12** 38 13N 27 39 E
Baykal, Oz., *Russia* **27 D11** 53 0N 108 0 E
Baykan, *Turkey* **44 B4** 38 7N 41 44 E
Baykonur = Bayqongyr, *Kazakstan* **26 E7** 47 48N 65 50 E
Baymak, *Russia* **24 D10** 52 36N 58 19 E
Baynes Mts., *Namibia* **56 B1** 17 15S 13 0 E
Bayombong, *Phil.* **37 A6** 16 30N 121 10 E
Bayonne, *France* **18 E3** 43 30N 1 28W
Bayonne, *U.S.A.* **79 F10** 40 40N 74 7W
Bayovar, *Peru* **92 E2** 5 50S 81 0W
Bayqongyr, *Kazakstan* **26 E7** 47 48N 65 50 E
Bayram-Ali = Bayramaly, *Turkmenistan* **26 F7** 37 37N 62 10 E
Bayramaly, *Turkmenistan* **26 F7** 37 37N 62 10 E
Bayramiç, *Turkey* **21 E12** 39 48N 26 36 E
Bayreuth, *Germany* **16 D6** 49 56N 11 35 E
Bayrūt, *Lebanon* **47 B4** 33 53N 35 31 E
Bays, L. of, *Canada* **78 A5** 45 15N 79 4W
Baysville, *Canada* **78 A5** 45 9N 79 7W
Bayt Lahm, *West Bank* **47 D4** 31 43N 35 12 E
Baytown, *U.S.A.* **81 L7** 29 43N 94 59W
Baza, *Spain* **19 D4** 37 30N 2 47W
Bazaruto, I. do, *Mozam.* **57 C6** 21 40S 35 28 E
Bazhou, *China* **34 E9** 39 8N 116 22 E
Bazmān, Kūh-e, *Iran* **45 D9** 28 4N 60 1 E
Beach, *U.S.A.* **80 B3** 46 58N 104 0W
Beach City, *U.S.A.* **78 F3** 40 39N 81 35W
Beachport, *Australia* **63 F3** 37 29S 140 0 E
Beachy Hd., *U.K.* **11 G8** 50 44N 0 15 E
Beacon, *Australia* **61 F2** 30 26S 117 52 E
Beacon, *U.S.A.* **79 E11** 41 30N 73 58W
Beaconsfield, *Australia* **62 G4** 41 11S 146 48 E
Beagle, Canal, *S. Amer.* **96 H3** 55 0S 68 30W
Beagle Bay, *Australia* **60 C3** 16 58S 122 40 E
Bealanana, *Madag.* **57 A8** 14 33S 48 44 E
Beals Cr. →, *U.S.A.* **81 J4** 32 10N 100 51W
Beamsville, *Canada* **78 C5** 43 12N 79 28W
Bear →, *Calif., U.S.A.* **84 G5** 38 56N 121 36W
Bear →, *Utah, U.S.A.* **74 B4** 41 30N 112 8W
Bear I., *Ireland* **13 E2** 51 38N 9 50W
Bear L., *Canada* **73 B9** 55 8N 96 0W
Bear L., *U.S.A.* **82 F8** 41 59N 111 21W
Beardmore, *Canada* **70 C2** 49 36N 87 57W
Beardmore Glacier, *Antarctica* **5 E11** 84 30S 170 0 E
Beardstown, *U.S.A.* **80 F9** 40 1N 90 26W
Bearma →, *India* **43 G8** 24 20N 79 51 E
Béarn, *France* **18 E3** 43 20N 0 30W
Bearpaw Mts., *U.S.A.* **82 B9** 48 12N 109 30W
Bearskin Lake, *Canada* **70 B1** 53 58N 91 2W
Beas →, *India* **42 D6** 31 10N 74 59 E
Beata, C., *Dom. Rep.* **89 C5** 17 40N 71 30W
Beata, I., *Dom. Rep.* **89 C5** 17 34N 71 31W
Beatrice, *U.S.A.* **80 E6** 40 16N 96 45W
Beatrice, *Zimbabwe* **55 F3** 18 15S 30 55 E
Beatrice, C., *Australia* **62 A2** 14 20S 136 55 E
Beatton →, *Canada* **72 B4** 56 15N 120 45W
Beatton River, *Canada* **72 B4** 57 26N 121 20W
Beatty, *U.S.A.* **84 J10** 36 54N 116 46W
Beauce, Plaine de la, *France* **18 B4** 48 10N 1 45 E
Beauceville, *Canada* **71 C5** 46 13N 70 46W
Beaudesert, *Australia* **63 D5** 27 59S 153 0 E
Beaufort, *Malaysia* **36 C5** 5 30N 115 40 E
Beaufort, *N.C., U.S.A.* **77 H7** 34 43N 76 40W
Beaufort, *S.C., U.S.A.* **77 J5** 32 26N 80 40W
Beaufort Sea, *Arctic* **4 B1** 72 0N 140 0W
Beaufort West, *S. Africa* **56 E3** 32 18S 22 36 E
Beauharnois, *Canada* **79 A11** 45 20N 73 52W
Beaulieu →, *Canada* **72 A6** 62 3N 113 11W
Beauly, *U.K.* **12 D4** 57 30N 4 28W
Beauly →, *U.K.* **12 D4** 57 29N 4 27W
Beaumaris, *U.K.* **10 D3** 53 16N 4 6W
Beaumont, *Belgium* **15 D4** 50 15N 4 14 E
Beaumont, *U.S.A.* **81 K7** 30 5N 94 6W
Beaune, *France* **18 C6** 47 2N 4 50 E
Beaupré, *Canada* **71 C5** 47 3N 70 54W
Beauraing, *Belgium* **15 D4** 50 7N 4 57 E
Beauséjour, *Canada* **73 C9** 50 5N 96 35W
Beauvais, *France* **18 B5** 49 25N 2 8 E
Beauval, *Canada* **73 B7** 55 9N 107 37W
Beaver, *Okla., U.S.A.* **81 G4** 36 49N 100 31W
Beaver, *Pa., U.S.A.* **78 F4** 40 42N 80 19W
Beaver, *Utah, U.S.A.* **83 G7** 38 17N 112 38W
Beaver →, *B.C., Canada* **72 B4** 59 52N 124 20W
Beaver →, *Ont., Canada* **70 A2** 55 55N 87 48W
Beaver →, *Sask., Canada* **73 B7** 55 26N 107 45W
Beaver →, *U.S.A.* **81 G5** 36 35N 99 30W
Beaver City, *U.S.A.* **80 E5** 40 8N 99 50W
Beaver Creek, *Canada* **68 B5** 63 0N 141 0W
Beaver Dam, *U.S.A.* **80 D10** 43 28N 88 50W
Beaver Falls, *U.S.A.* **78 F4** 40 46N 80 20W
Beaver Hill L., *Canada* **73 C10** 54 5N 94 50W
Beaver I., *U.S.A.* **76 C3** 45 40N 85 33W
Beaverhill L., *Canada* **72 C6** 53 27N 112 32W
Beaverlodge, *Canada* **72 B5** 55 11N 119 29W
Beaverstone →, *Canada* **70 B2** 54 59N 89 25W
Beaverton, *Canada* **78 B5** 44 26N 79 9W
Beaverton, *U.S.A.* **84 E4** 45 29N 122 48W
Beawar, *India* **42 F6** 26 3N 74 18 E
Bebedouro, *Brazil* **95 A6** 21 0S 48 25W
Beboa, *Madag.* **57 B7** 17 22S 44 33 E
Beccles, *U.K.* **11 E9** 52 27N 1 35 E
Bečej, *Serbia, Yug.* **21 B9** 45 36N 20 3 E
Béchar, *Algeria* **50 B5** 31 38N 2 18W
Beckley, *U.S.A.* **76 G5** 37 47N 81 11W
Beddouza, Ras, *Morocco* **50 B4** 32 33N 9 9W
Bedford, *Canada* **79 A12** 45 7N 72 59W
Bedford, *S. Africa* **56 E4** 32 40S 26 10 E
Bedford, *U.K.* **11 E7** 52 8N 0 28W
Bedford, *Ind., U.S.A.* **76 F2** 38 52N 86 29W
Bedford, *Iowa, U.S.A.* **80 E7** 40 40N 94 44W
Bedford, *Ohio, U.S.A.* **78 E3** 41 23N 81 32W
Bedford, *Pa., U.S.A.* **78 F6** 40 1N 78 30W
Bedford, *Va., U.S.A.* **76 G6** 37 20N 79 31W
Bedford, C., *Australia* **62 B4** 15 14S 145 21 E
Bedfordshire □, *U.K.* **11 E7** 52 4N 0 28W
Bedourie, *Australia* **62 C2** 24 30S 139 30 E
Bedum, *Neths.* **15 A6** 53 18N 6 36 E
Beebe Plain, *Canada* **79 A12** 45 1N 72 9W
Beech Creek, *U.S.A.* **78 E7** 41 5N 77 36W
Beenleigh, *Australia* **63 D5** 27 43S 153 10 E
Be'er Menuha, *Israel* **44 D2** 30 19N 35 8 E
Be'er Sheva, *Israel* **47 D3** 31 15N 34 48 E
Beersheba = Be'er Sheva, *Israel* **47 D3** 31 15N 34 48 E
Beeston, *U.K.* **10 E6** 52 56N 1 14W
Beeville, *U.S.A.* **81 L6** 28 24N 97 45W
Befale, *Dem. Rep. of the Congo* **52 D4** 0 25N 20 45 E
Befandriana, *Madag.* **57 C7** 21 55S 44 0 E
Befotaka, *Madag.* **57 C8** 23 49S 47 0 E
Bega, *Australia* **63 F4** 36 41S 149 51 E
Begusarai, *India* **43 G12** 25 24N 86 9 E
Behābād, *Iran* **45 C8** 32 24N 59 47 E
Behala, *India* **43 H13** 22 30N 88 20 E
Behara, *Madag.* **57 C8** 24 55S 46 20 E
Behbehān, *Iran* **45 D6** 30 30N 50 15 E
Behm Canal, *U.S.A.* **72 B2** 55 10N 131 0W
Behshahr, *Iran* **45 B7** 36 45N 53 35 E
Bei Jiang →, *China* **33 D6** 23 2N 112 58 E
Bei'an, *China* **33 B7** 48 10N 126 20 E
Beihai, *China* **33 D5** 21 28N 109 6 E
Beijing, *China* **34 E9** 39 55N 116 20 E
Beijing □, *China* **34 E9** 39 55N 116 20 E
Beilen, *Neths.* **15 B6** 52 52N 6 27 E
Beilpajah, *Australia* **63 E3** 32 54S 143 52 E
Beinn na Faoghla = Benbecula, *U.K.* **12 D1** 57 26N 7 21W
Beipiao, *China* **35 D11** 41 52N 120 32 E
Beira, *Mozam.* **55 F3** 19 50S 34 52 E
Beirut = Bayrūt, *Lebanon* **47 B4** 33 53N 35 31 E
Beiseker, *Canada* **72 C6** 51 23N 113 32W
Beitaolaizhao, *China* **35 B13** 44 58N 125 58 E
Beitbridge, *Zimbabwe* **55 G3** 22 12S 30 0 E
Beizhen = Binzhou, *China* **35 F10** 37 20N 118 2 E
Beizhen, *China* **35 D11** 41 38N 121 54 E
Beizhengzhen, *China* **35 B12** 44 31N 123 30 E
Beja, *Portugal* **19 C2** 38 2N 7 53W
Béja, *Tunisia* **51 A7** 36 43N 9 12 E
Bejaia, *Algeria* **50 A7** 36 42N 5 2 E
Béjar, *Spain* **19 B3** 40 23N 5 46W
Bejestān, *Iran* **45 C8** 34 30N 58 5 E
Békéscsaba, *Hungary* **17 E11** 46 40N 21 5 E
Bekily, *Madag.* **57 C8** 24 13S 45 19 E
Bekok, *Malaysia* **39 L4** 2 20N 103 7 E
Bela, *India* **43 G10** 25 50N 82 0 E
Bela, *Pakistan* **42 F2** 26 12N 66 20 E
Bela Crkva, *Serbia, Yug.* **21 B9** 44 55N 21 27 E
Bela Vista, *Brazil* **94 A4** 22 12S 56 20W
Bela Vista, *Mozam.* **57 D5** 26 10S 32 44 E
Belan →, *India* **43 G9** 24 2N 81 45 E
Belarus ■, *Europe* **17 B14** 53 30N 27 0 E
Belau = Palau ■, *Pac. Oc.* **28 J17** 7 30N 134 30 E
Belavenona, *Madag.* **57 C8** 24 50S 47 4 E
Belawan, *Indonesia* **36 D1** 3 33N 98 32 E
Belaya →, *Russia* **24 C9** 54 40N 56 0 E
Belaya Tserkov = Bila Tserkva, *Ukraine* **17 D16** 49 45N 30 10 E
Belcher Is., *Canada* **70 A3** 56 15N 78 45W
Belden, *U.S.A.* **84 E5** 40 2N 121 17W
Belebey, *Russia* **24 D9** 54 7N 54 7 E
Belém, *Brazil* **93 D9** 1 20S 48 30W
Belén, *Argentina* **94 B2** 27 40S 67 5W
Belén, *Paraguay* **94 A4** 23 30S 57 6W
Belen, *U.S.A.* **83 J10** 34 40N 106 46W
Belet Uen, *Somali Rep.* **46 G4** 4 30N 45 5 E
Belev, *Russia* **24 D6** 53 50N 36 5 E
Belfair, *U.S.A.* **84 C4** 47 27N 122 50W
Belfast, *S. Africa* **57 D5** 25 42S 30 2 E
Belfast, *U.K.* **13 B6** 54 37N 5 56W

Big Timber

elfast, Maine, U.S.A. 77 C11 44 26N 69 1W
elfast, N.Y., U.S.A. 78 D6 42 21N 78 7W
elfast L., U.K. 13 B6 54 40N 5 50W
elfield, U.S.A. 80 B3 46 53N 103 12W
elfort, France 18 C7 47 38N 6 50 E
elfry, U.S.A. 82 D9 45 9N 109 1W
elgaum, India 40 M9 15 55N 74 35 E
elgium ■, Europe 15 D4 50 30N 5 0 E
elgorod, Russia 25 D6 50 35N 36 35 E
elgorod-Dnestrovskiy = Bilhorod-Dnistrovskyy, Ukraine 25 E5 46 11N 30 23 E
elgrade = Beograd, Serbia, Yug. 21 B9 44 50N 20 37 E
elgrade, U.S.A. 82 D8 45 47N 111 11W
elhaven, U.S.A. 77 H7 35 33N 76 37W
eli Drim →, Europe 21 C9 42 6N 20 25 E
elinyu, Indonesia 36 E3 1 35S 105 50 E
eliton Is. = Belitung, Indonesia 36 E3 3 10S 107 50 E
elitung, Indonesia 36 E3 3 10S 107 50 E
elize ■, Cent. Amer. 87 D7 17 0N 88 30W
elize City, Belize 87 D7 17 25N 88 0W
elkovskiy, Ostrov, Russia 27 B14 75 32N 135 44 E
ell →, Canada 70 C4 49 48N 77 38W
ell I., Canada 71 B8 50 46N 55 35W
ell-Irving →, Canada 72 B3 56 12N 129 5W
ell Peninsula, Canada 69 B11 63 50N 82 0W
ell Ville, Argentina 94 C3 32 40S 62 40W
ella Bella, Canada 72 C3 52 10N 128 10W
ella Coola, Canada 72 C3 52 25N 126 40W
ella Unión, Uruguay 94 C4 30 15S 57 40W
ella Vista, Corrientes, Argentina 94 B4 28 33S 59 0W
ella Vista, Tucuman, Argentina 94 B2 27 10S 65 25W
ellaire, U.S.A. 78 F4 40 1N 80 45W
ellary, India 40 M10 15 10N 76 56 E
ellata, Australia 63 D4 29 53S 149 46 E
elle-Chasse, U.S.A. 81 L10 29 51N 89 59W
elle Fourche, U.S.A. 80 C3 44 40N 103 51W
elle Fourche →, U.S.A. 80 C3 44 26N 102 18W
elle Glade, U.S.A. 77 M5 26 41N 80 40W
elle-Île, France 18 C2 47 20N 3 10W
elle Isle, Canada 71 B8 51 57N 55 25W
elle Isle, Str. of, Canada 71 B8 51 30N 56 30W
elle Plaine, U.S.A. 80 E8 41 54N 92 17W
ellefontaine, U.S.A. 76 E4 40 22N 83 46W
ellefonte, U.S.A. 78 F7 40 55N 77 47W
elleoram, Canada 71 C8 47 31N 55 25W
elleville, Canada 78 B7 44 10N 77 23W
elleville, Ill., U.S.A. 80 F10 38 31N 89 59W
elleville, Kans., U.S.A. 80 F6 39 50N 97 38W
elleville, N.Y., U.S.A. 79 C8 43 46N 76 10W
ellevue, Canada 72 D6 49 35N 114 22W
ellevue, Idaho, U.S.A. 82 E6 43 28N 114 16W
ellevue, Nebr., U.S.A. 80 E7 41 8N 95 53W
ellevue, Ohio, U.S.A. 78 E2 41 17N 82 51W
ellevue, Wash., U.S.A. 84 C4 47 37N 122 12W
ellin = Kangirsuk, Canada 69 C13 60 0N 70 0W
ellingen, Australia 63 E5 30 25S 152 50 E
ellingham, U.S.A. 68 D7 48 46N 122 29W
ellingshausen Sea, Antarctica 5 C17 66 0S 80 0W
ellinzona, Switz. 18 C8 46 11N 9 1 E
ello, Colombia 92 B3 6 20N 75 33W
ellows Falls, U.S.A. 79 C12 43 8N 72 27W
ellpat, Pakistan 42 E3 29 0N 68 5 E
elluno, Italy 20 A5 46 9N 12 13 E
ellwood, U.S.A. 78 F6 40 36N 78 20W
elmont, Canada 78 D3 42 53N 81 5W
elmont, S. Africa 56 D3 29 28S 24 22 E
elmont, U.S.A. 78 D6 42 14N 78 2W
elmonte, Brazil 93 G11 16 0S 39 0W
elmopan, Belize 87 D7 17 18N 88 30W
elmullet, Ireland 13 B2 54 14N 9 58W
elo Horizonte, Brazil 93 G10 19 55S 43 56W
elo-sur-Mer, Madag. 57 C7 20 42S 44 0 E
elo-Tsiribihina, Madag. 57 B7 19 40S 44 30 E
elogorsk, Russia 27 D13 51 0N 128 20 E
eloha, Madag. 57 D8 25 10S 45 3 E
eloit, Kans., U.S.A. 80 F5 39 28N 98 6W
eloit, Wis., U.S.A. 80 D10 42 31N 89 2W
elokorovichi, Ukraine 17 C15 51 7N 28 2 E
elomorsk, Russia 24 B5 64 35N 34 54 E
elonia, India 41 H17 23 15N 91 30 E
eloretsk, Russia 24 D10 53 58N 58 24 E
elorussia = Belarus ■, Europe 17 B14 53 30N 27 0 E
elovo, Russia 26 D9 54 30N 86 0 E
eloye, Ozero, Russia 24 B6 60 10N 37 35 E
eloye More, Russia 24 A6 66 30N 38 0 E
elozersk, Russia 24 B6 60 1N 37 45 E
elpre, U.S.A. 76 F5 39 17N 81 34W
elrain, India 43 E9 28 23N 80 55 E
elt, U.S.A. 82 C8 47 23N 110 55W
eltana, Australia 63 E2 30 48S 138 25 E
elterra, Brazil 93 D8 2 45S 55 0W
elton, U.S.A. 81 K6 31 3N 97 28W
elton L., U.S.A. 81 K6 31 8N 97 32W
eltsy = Bălţi, Moldova 17 E14 47 48N 27 58 E
elturbet, Ireland 13 B4 54 6N 7 26W
elukha, Russia 26 E9 49 50N 86 50 E
eluran, Malaysia 36 C5 5 48N 117 35 E
elvidere, Ill., U.S.A. 80 D10 42 15N 88 50W
elvidere, N.J., U.S.A. 79 F9 40 50N 75 5W
elyando →, Australia 62 C4 21 38S 146 50 E
elyy, Ostrov, Russia 26 B8 73 30N 71 0 E
elyy Yar, Russia 26 D9 58 26N 84 39 E
elzoni, U.S.A. 81 J9 33 11N 90 29W
emaraha, Lembalemban' i, Madag. 57 B7 18 40S 44 45 E
emarivo, Madag. 57 C7 21 45S 44 45 E
emarivo →, Madag. 57 B8 15 27S 47 40 E
emavo, Madag. 57 C8 21 33S 45 25 E
embéréke, Benin 50 F6 10 11N 2 43 E
embesi, Zimbabwe 55 G2 20 0S 28 58 E
embesi →, Zimbabwe 55 F2 18 57S 27 47 E
emetara, India 43 J9 21 42N 81 32 E
emidji, U.S.A. 80 B7 47 28N 94 53W
en, Iran 45 C6 32 32N 50 45 E
en Cruachan, U.K. 12 E3 56 26N 5 8W
en Dearg, U.K. 12 D4 57 47N 4 56W
en Hope, U.K. 12 C4 58 25N 4 36W
en Lawers, U.K. 12 E4 56 32N 4 14W
en Lomond, N.S.W., Australia 63 E5 30 1S 151 43 E
Ben Lomond, Tas., Australia 62 G4 41 38S 147 42 E
Ben Lomond, U.K. 12 E4 56 11N 4 38W
Ben Luc, Vietnam 39 G6 10 39N 106 29 E
Ben Macdhui, U.K. 12 D5 57 4N 3 40W
Ben Mhor, U.K. 12 D1 57 15N 7 18W
Ben More, Arg. & Bute, U.K. 12 E2 56 26N 6 1W
Ben More, Stirl., U.K. 12 E4 56 23N 4 32W
Ben More Assynt, U.K. 12 C4 58 8N 4 52W
Ben Nevis, U.K. 12 E3 56 48N 5 1W
Ben Quang, Vietnam 38 D6 17 3N 106 55 E
Ben Vorlich, U.K. 12 E4 56 21N 4 14W
Ben Wyvis, U.K. 12 D4 57 40N 4 35W
Bena, Nigeria 50 F7 11 20N 5 50 E
Benalla, Australia 63 F4 36 30S 146 0 E
Benares = Varanasi, India 43 G10 25 22N 83 0 E
Benavente, Spain 19 A3 42 2N 5 43W
Benavides, U.S.A. 81 M5 27 36N 98 25W
Benbecula, U.K. 12 D1 57 26N 7 21W
Benbonyathe, Australia 63 E2 30 25S 139 11 E
Bend, U.S.A. 82 D3 44 4N 121 19W
Bendemeer, Australia 63 E5 30 53S 151 8 E
Bender Beila, Somali Rep. 46 F5 9 30N 50 48 E
Bendery = Tighina, Moldova 17 E15 46 50N 29 30 E
Bendigo, Australia 63 F3 36 40S 144 15 E
Benē Beraq, Israel 47 C3 32 6N 34 51 E
Benenitra, Madag. 57 C8 23 27S 45 5 E
Benevento, Italy 20 D6 41 8N 14 45 E
Benga, Mozam. 55 F3 16 11S 33 40 E
Bengal, Bay of, Ind. Oc. 41 M17 15 0N 90 0 E
Bengbu, China 35 H9 32 58N 117 20 E
Benghazi = Banghāzī, Libya 51 B10 32 11N 20 3 E
Bengkalis, Indonesia 36 D2 1 30N 102 10 E
Bengkulu, Indonesia 36 E2 3 50S 102 12 E
Bengkulu □, Indonesia 36 E2 3 48S 102 16 E
Bengough, Canada 73 D7 49 25N 105 10W
Benguela, Angola 53 G2 12 37S 13 25 E
Benguérua, I., Mozam. 57 C6 21 58S 35 28 E
Beni, Dem. Rep. of the Congo 54 B2 0 30N 29 27 E
Beni →, Bolivia 92 F5 10 23S 65 24W
Beni Mellal, Morocco 50 B4 32 21N 6 21W
Beni Suef, Egypt 51 C12 29 5N 31 6 E
Beniah L., Canada 72 A6 63 23N 112 17W
Benicia, U.S.A. 84 G4 38 3N 122 9W
Benidorm, Spain 19 C5 38 33N 0 9W
Benin ■, Africa 50 G6 10 0N 2 0 E
Benin, Bight of, W. Afr. 50 H6 5 0N 3 0 E
Benin City, Nigeria 50 G7 6 20N 5 31 E
Benitses, Greece 23 A3 39 32N 19 55 E
Benjamin Aceval, Paraguay 94 A4 24 58S 57 34W
Benjamin Constant, Brazil 92 D4 4 40S 70 15W
Benjamin Hill, Mexico 86 A2 30 10N 111 10W
Benkelman, U.S.A. 80 E4 40 3N 101 32W
Bennett, Canada 72 B2 59 56N 134 53W
Bennett, L., Australia 60 D5 22 50S 131 2 E
Bennetta, Ostrov, Russia 27 B15 76 21N 148 56 E
Bennettsville, U.S.A. 77 H6 34 37N 79 41W
Bennington, N.H., U.S.A. 79 D11 43 0N 71 55W
Bennington, Vt., U.S.A. 79 D11 42 53N 73 12W
Benoni, S. Africa 57 D4 26 11S 28 18 E
Benque Viejo, Belize 87 D7 17 5N 89 8W
Benson, Ariz., U.S.A. 83 L8 31 58N 110 18W
Benson, Minn., U.S.A. 80 C7 45 19N 95 36W
Bent, Iran 45 E8 26 20N 59 31 E
Benteng, Indonesia 37 F6 6 10S 120 30 E
Bentinck I., Australia 62 B2 17 3S 139 35 E
Bento Gonçalves, Brazil 95 B5 29 10S 51 31W
Benton, Ark., U.S.A. 81 H8 34 34N 92 35W
Benton, Calif., U.S.A. 84 H8 37 48N 118 32W
Benton, Ill., U.S.A. 80 G10 38 0N 88 55W
Benton, Pa., U.S.A. 79 E8 41 12N 76 23W
Benton Harbor, U.S.A. 76 D2 42 6N 86 27W
Bentonville, U.S.A. 81 G7 36 22N 94 13W
Bentung, Malaysia 39 L3 3 31N 101 55 E
Benue →, Nigeria 50 G7 7 48N 6 46 E
Benxi, China 35 D12 41 20N 123 48 E
Beo, Indonesia 37 D7 4 25N 126 50 E
Beograd, Serbia, Yug. 21 B9 44 50N 20 37 E
Beppu, Japan 31 H5 33 15N 131 30 E
Beqaa Valley = Al Biqā, Lebanon 47 A5 34 10N 36 10 E
Ber Mota, India 42 H3 23 27N 68 34 E
Berach →, India 42 G6 25 15N 75 2 E
Berati, Albania 21 D8 40 43N 19 59 E
Berau, Teluk, Indonesia 37 E8 2 30S 132 30 E
Berber, Sudan 51 E12 18 0N 34 0 E
Berbera, Somali Rep. 46 E4 10 30N 45 2 E
Berbérati, C.A.R. 52 D3 4 15N 15 40 E
Berbice →, Guyana 92 B7 6 20N 57 32W
Berdichev = Berdychiv, Ukraine 17 D15 49 57N 28 30 E
Berdsk, Russia 26 D9 54 47N 83 2 E
Berdyansk, Ukraine 25 E6 46 45N 36 50 E
Berdychiv, Ukraine 17 D15 49 57N 28 30 E
Berea, U.S.A. 76 G3 37 34N 84 17W
Berebere, Indonesia 37 D7 2 25N 128 45 E
Bereda, Somali Rep. 46 E5 11 45N 51 0 E
Berehove, Ukraine 17 D12 48 15N 22 35 E
Berekum, Ghana 50 G5 7 29N 2 34W
Berens →, Canada 73 C9 52 25N 97 2W
Berens I., Canada 73 C9 52 18N 97 18W
Berens River, Canada 73 C9 52 25N 97 0W
Beresford, U.S.A. 80 D6 43 5N 96 47W
Berestechko, Ukraine 17 C13 50 22N 25 5 E
Berevo, Mahajanga, Madag. 57 B7 17 14S 44 17 E
Berevo, Toliara, Madag. 57 B7 19 44S 44 58 E
Bereza, Belarus 17 B13 52 31N 24 51 E
Berezhany, Ukraine 17 D13 49 26N 24 58 E
Berezina = Byarezina →, Belarus 17 B16 52 33N 30 14 E
Bereznik, Russia 24 B7 62 51N 42 40 E
Berezniki, Russia 24 C10 59 24N 56 46 E
Berezovo, Russia 26 C7 64 0N 65 0 E
Berga, Spain 19 A6 42 6N 1 48 E
Bergama, Turkey 21 E12 39 8N 27 11 E
Bérgamo, Italy 18 D8 45 41N 9 43 E
Bergen, Neths. 15 B4 52 40N 4 43 E
Bergen, Norway 9 F11 60 20N 5 20 E
Bergen, U.S.A. 78 C7 43 5N 77 57W
Bergen op Zoom, Neths. 15 C4 51 28N 4 18 E
Bergerac, France 18 D4 44 51N 0 30 E
Bergholz, U.S.A. 78 F4 40 31N 80 53W
Bergisch Gladbach, Germany 15 D7 50 59N 7 8 E
Bergville, S. Africa 57 D4 28 52S 29 18 E
Berhala, Selat, Indonesia 36 E2 1 0S 104 15 E
Berhampore = Baharampur, India 43 G13 24 2N 88 27 E
Berhampur = Brahmapur, India 41 K14 19 15N 84 54 E
Bering Sea, Pac. Oc. 68 C1 58 0N 171 0 E
Bering Strait, Pac. Oc. 68 B3 65 30N 169 0W
Beringovskiy, Russia 27 C18 63 3N 179 19 E
Berisso, Argentina 94 C4 34 56S 57 50W
Berja, Spain 19 D4 36 50N 2 56W
Berkeley, U.S.A. 84 H4 37 52N 122 16W
Berkner I., Antarctica 5 D18 79 30S 50 0W
Berkshire, U.S.A. 79 D8 42 19N 76 11W
Berkshire Downs, U.K. 11 F6 51 33N 1 29W
Berlin, Germany 16 B7 52 30N 13 25 E
Berlin, Md., U.S.A. 76 F8 38 20N 75 13W
Berlin, N.H., U.S.A. 79 B13 44 28N 71 11W
Berlin, N.Y., U.S.A. 79 D11 42 42N 73 23W
Berlin, Wis., U.S.A. 76 D1 43 58N 88 57W
Berlin L., U.S.A. 78 E4 41 3N 81 0W
Bermejo →, Formosa, Argentina 94 B4 26 51S 58 23W
Bermejo →, San Juan, Argentina 94 C2 32 30S 67 30W
Bermen, L., Canada 71 B6 53 35N 68 55W
Bermuda ■, Atl. Oc. 66 F13 32 45N 65 0W
Bern, Switz. 18 C7 46 57N 7 28 E
Bernalillo, U.S.A. 83 J10 35 18N 106 33W
Bernardo de Irigoyen, Argentina 95 B5 26 15S 53 40W
Bernardo O'Higgins □, Chile 94 C1 34 15S 70 45W
Bernardsville, U.S.A. 79 F10 40 43N 74 34W
Bernasconi, Argentina 94 D3 37 55S 63 44W
Bernburg, Germany 16 C6 51 47N 11 44 E
Berne = Bern, Switz. 18 C7 46 57N 7 28 E
Berneray, U.K. 12 D1 57 43N 7 11W
Bernier I., Australia 61 D1 24 50S 113 12 E
Bernina, Piz, Switz. 18 C8 46 20N 9 54 E
Beroroha, Madag. 57 C8 21 40S 45 10 E
Beroun, Czech Rep. 16 D8 49 57N 14 5 E
Berri, Australia 63 E3 34 14S 140 35 E
Berriane, Algeria 50 B6 32 50N 3 46 E
Berrigan, Australia 63 F4 35 38S 145 49 E
Berry, Australia 63 E5 34 46S 150 43 E
Berry, France 18 C5 46 50N 2 0 E
Berry Is., Bahamas 88 A4 25 40N 77 50W
Berryessa L., U.S.A. 84 G4 38 31N 122 6W
Berryville, U.S.A. 81 G8 36 22N 93 34W
Bershad, Ukraine 17 D15 48 22N 29 31 E
Berthold, U.S.A. 80 A4 48 19N 101 44W
Berthoud, U.S.A. 80 E2 40 19N 105 5W
Bertoua, Cameroon 52 D2 4 30N 13 45 E
Bertraghboy B., Ireland 13 C2 53 22N 9 54W
Berwick, U.S.A. 79 E8 41 3N 76 14W
Berwick-upon-Tweed, U.K. 10 B6 55 46N 2 0W
Berwyn Mts., U.K. 10 E4 52 54N 3 26W
Besal, Pakistan 43 B5 35 4N 73 56 E
Besalampy, Madag. 57 B7 16 43S 44 29 E
Besançon, France 18 C7 47 15N 6 2 E
Besar, Indonesia 36 E5 2 40S 116 0 E
Besnard L., Canada 73 B7 55 25N 106 0W
Besni, Turkey 44 B3 37 41N 37 52 E
Besor, N. →, Egypt 47 D3 31 28N 34 22 E
Bessarabiya, Moldova 17 E15 47 0N 28 10 E
Bessarabka = Basarabeasca, Moldova 17 E15 46 21N 28 58 E
Bessemer, Ala., U.S.A. 77 J2 33 24N 86 58W
Bessemer, Mich., U.S.A. 80 B9 46 29N 90 3W
Bessemer, Pa., U.S.A. 78 F4 40 59N 80 30W
Beswick, Australia 60 B5 14 34S 132 53 E
Bet She'an, Israel 47 C4 32 30N 35 30 E
Bet Shemesh, Israel 47 D4 31 44N 35 0 E
Betafo, Madag. 57 B8 19 50S 46 51 E
Betancuria, Canary Is. 22 F5 28 25N 14 3W
Betanzos, Spain 19 A1 43 15N 8 12W
Bétaré Oya, Cameroon 52 C2 5 40N 14 5 E
Bethal, S. Africa 57 D4 26 27S 29 28 E
Bethanien, Namibia 56 D2 26 31S 17 8 E
Bethany, Canada 78 B6 44 11N 78 34W
Bethany, U.S.A. 80 E7 40 16N 94 2W
Bethel, Alaska, U.S.A. 68 B3 60 48N 161 45W
Bethel, Conn., U.S.A. 79 E11 41 22N 73 25W
Bethel, Maine, U.S.A. 79 B14 44 25N 70 47W
Bethel, Vt., U.S.A. 79 C12 43 50N 72 38W
Bethel Park, U.S.A. 78 F4 40 20N 80 1W
Bethlehem = Bayt Lahm, West Bank 47 D4 31 43N 35 12 E
Bethlehem, S. Africa 57 D4 28 14S 28 18 E
Bethlehem, U.S.A. 79 F9 40 37N 75 23W
Bethulie, S. Africa 56 E4 30 30S 25 59 E
Béthune, France 18 A5 50 30N 2 38 E
Betioky, Madag. 57 C7 23 48S 44 20 E
Betong, Thailand 39 K3 5 45N 101 5 E
Betoota, Australia 62 D3 25 45S 140 42 E
Betroka, Madag. 57 C8 23 16S 46 0 E
Betsiamites, Canada 71 C6 48 56N 68 40W
Betsiamites →, Canada 71 C6 48 56N 68 38W
Betsiboka →, Madag. 57 B8 16 3S 46 36 E
Bettendorf, U.S.A. 80 E9 41 32N 90 30W
Bettiah, India 43 F11 26 48N 84 33 E
Betul, India 40 J10 21 58N 77 59 E
Betung, Malaysia 36 D4 1 24N 111 31 E
Betws-y-Coed, U.K. 10 D4 53 5N 3 48W
Beulah, Mich., U.S.A. 76 C2 44 38N 86 6W
Beulah, N. Dak., U.S.A. 80 B4 47 16N 101 47W
Beveren, Belgium 15 C4 51 12N 4 16 E
Beverley, Australia 61 F2 32 9S 116 56 E
Beverley, U.K. 10 D7 53 51N 0 26W
Beverley Hills, U.S.A. 77 L4 28 56N 82 28W
Beverly, U.S.A. 79 D14 42 33N 70 53W
Beverly Hills, U.S.A. 85 L8 34 4N 118 25W
Bewas →, India 43 H8 23 59N 79 21 E
Bexhill, U.K. 11 G8 50 51N 0 29 E
Beyānlū, Iran 44 C5 36 0N 47 51 E
Beyneu, Kazakstan 25 E10 45 18N 55 9 E
Beypazarı, Turkey 25 F5 40 10N 31 56 E
Beyşehir Gölü, Turkey 25 G5 37 41N 31 33 E
Béziers, France 18 E5 43 20N 3 12 E
Bezwada = Vijayawada, India 41 L12 16 31N 80 39 E
Bhabua, India 43 G10 25 3N 83 37 E
Bhachau, India 40 H7 23 20N 70 16 E
Bhadar →, Gujarat, India 42 H5 22 17N 72 20 E
Bhadar →, Gujarat, India 42 J3 21 27N 69 47 E
Bhadarwah, India 43 C6 32 58N 75 46 E
Bhadohi, India 43 G10 25 25N 82 34 E
Bhadra, India 42 E6 29 8N 75 14 E
Bhadrakh, India 41 J15 21 10N 86 30 E
Bhadran, India 42 H5 22 19N 72 6 E
Bhadravati, India 40 N9 13 49N 75 40 E
Bhag, Pakistan 42 E2 29 2N 67 49 E
Bhagalpur, India 43 G12 25 10N 87 0 E
Bhagirathi →, Ut. P., India 43 D8 30 8N 78 35 E
Bhagirathi →, W. Bengal, India 43 H13 23 25N 88 23 E
Bhakkar, Pakistan 42 D4 31 40N 71 5 E
Bhakra Dam, India 42 D7 31 30N 76 45 E
Bhamo, Burma 41 G20 24 15N 97 15 E
Bhandara, India 40 J11 21 5N 79 42 E
Bhanpura, India 42 G6 24 31N 75 44 E
Bhanrer Ra., India 43 H8 23 40N 79 45 E
Bhaptiahi, India 43 F12 26 19N 86 44 E
Bharat = India ■, Asia 40 K11 20 0N 78 0 E
Bharatpur, Mad. P., India 43 H9 23 44N 81 46 E
Bharatpur, Raj., India 42 F7 27 15N 77 30 E
Bharno, India 43 H11 23 14N 84 53 E
Bhatinda, India 42 D6 30 15N 74 57 E
Bhatpara, India 43 H13 22 50N 88 25 E
Bhattu, India 42 E6 29 36N 75 19 E
Bhaun, Pakistan 42 C5 32 55N 72 40 E
Bhaunagar = Bhavnagar, India 40 J8 21 45N 72 10 E
Bhavnagar, India 40 J8 21 45N 72 10 E
Bhawanipatna, India 41 K12 19 55N 80 10 E
Bhawari, India 42 G5 25 42N 73 4 E
Bhayavadar, India 42 J4 21 51N 70 15 E
Bhera, Pakistan 42 C5 32 29N 72 57 E
Bhikangaon, India 42 J6 21 52N 75 57 E
Bhilsa = Vidisha, India 42 H7 23 28N 77 53 E
Bhilwara, India 42 G6 25 25N 74 38 E
Bhima →, India 40 L10 16 25N 77 17 E
Bhimavaram, India 41 L12 16 30N 81 30 E
Bhimbar, Pakistan 43 C6 32 59N 74 3 E
Bhind, India 43 F8 26 30N 78 46 E
Bhinga, India 43 F9 27 43N 81 56 E
Bhinmal, India 42 G5 25 0N 72 15 E
Bhiwandi, India 40 K8 19 20N 73 0 E
Bhiwani, India 42 E7 28 50N 76 9 E
Bhogava →, India 42 H5 22 26N 72 20 E
Bhola, Bangla. 41 H17 22 45N 90 35 E
Bholari, Pakistan 42 G3 25 19N 68 13 E
Bhopal, India 42 H7 23 20N 77 30 E
Bhubaneshwar, India 41 J14 20 15N 85 50 E
Bhuj, India 42 H3 23 15N 69 49 E
Bhusaval, India 40 J9 21 3N 75 46 E
Bhutan ■, Asia 41 F17 27 25N 90 30 E
Biafra, B. of = Bonny, Bight of, Africa 52 D1 3 30N 9 20 E
Biak, Indonesia 37 E9 1 10S 136 6 E
Biała Podlaska, Poland 17 B12 52 4N 23 6 E
Białogard, Poland 16 A8 54 2N 15 58 E
Białystok, Poland 17 B12 53 10N 23 10 E
Biaora, India 42 H7 23 56N 76 56 E
Bīārjmand, Iran 45 B7 36 6N 55 53 E
Biaro, Indonesia 37 D7 2 5N 125 26 E
Biarritz, France 18 E3 43 29N 1 33W
Bibai, Japan 30 C10 43 19N 141 52 E
Bibby I., Canada 73 A10 61 55N 93 0W
Biberach, Germany 16 D5 48 5N 9 47 E
Bibungwa, Dem. Rep. of the Congo 54 C2 2 40S 28 15 E
Bic, Canada 71 C6 48 20N 68 41W
Bicester, U.K. 11 F6 51 54N 1 9W
Bicheno, Australia 62 G4 41 52S 148 18 E
Bichia, India 43 H9 22 27N 80 42 E
Bickerton I., Australia 62 A2 13 45S 136 10 E
Bida, Nigeria 50 G7 9 3N 5 58 E
Bidar, India 40 L10 17 55N 77 35 E
Biddeford, U.S.A. 77 D10 43 30N 70 28W
Bideford, U.K. 11 F3 51 1N 4 13W
Bideford Bay, U.K. 11 F3 51 5N 4 20W
Bidhuna, India 43 F8 26 49N 79 31 E
Bidor, Malaysia 39 K3 4 6N 101 15 E
Bié, Planalto de, Angola 53 G3 12 0S 16 0 E
Bieber, U.S.A. 82 F3 41 7N 121 8W
Biel, Switz. 18 C7 47 8N 7 14 E
Bielefeld, Germany 16 B5 52 1N 8 33 E
Biella, Italy 18 D8 45 34N 8 3 E
Bielsk Podlaski, Poland 17 B12 52 47N 23 12 E
Bielsko-Biała, Poland 17 D10 49 50N 19 2 E
Bien Hoa, Vietnam 39 G6 10 57N 106 49 E
Bienne = Biel, Switz. 18 C7 47 8N 7 14 E
Bienville, L., Canada 70 A5 55 5N 72 40W
Biesiesfontein, S. Africa 56 E2 30 57S 17 58 E
Big →, Canada 71 B8 54 50N 58 55W
Big B., Canada 71 A7 55 43N 60 35W
Big Bear City, U.S.A. 85 L10 34 16N 116 51W
Big Bear Lake, U.S.A. 85 L10 34 15N 116 56W
Big Belt Mts., U.S.A. 82 C8 46 30N 111 25W
Big Bend, Swaziland 57 D5 26 50S 31 58 E
Big Bend National Park, U.S.A. 81 L3 29 20N 103 5W
Big Black →, U.S.A. 81 K9 32 3N 91 4W
Big Blue →, U.S.A. 80 F6 39 35N 96 34W
Big Creek, U.S.A. 84 H7 37 11N 119 14W
Big Cypress National Preserve, U.S.A. 77 M5 26 0N 81 10W
Big Cypress Swamp, U.S.A. 77 M5 26 12N 81 10W
Big Falls, U.S.A. 80 A8 48 12N 93 48W
Big Fork →, U.S.A. 80 A8 48 31N 93 43W
Big Horn Mts. = Bighorn Mts., U.S.A. 82 D10 44 30N 107 30W
Big I., Canada 72 A5 61 7N 116 45W
Big Lake, U.S.A. 81 K4 31 12N 101 28W
Big Moose, U.S.A. 79 C10 43 49N 74 58W
Big Muddy Cr. →, U.S.A. 80 A2 48 8N 104 36W
Big Pine, U.S.A. 84 H8 37 10N 118 17W
Big Piney, U.S.A. 82 E8 42 32N 110 7W
Big Rapids, U.S.A. 76 D3 43 42N 85 29W
Big Rideau L., Canada 79 B8 44 40N 76 15W
Big River, Canada 73 C7 53 50N 107 0W
Big Run, U.S.A. 78 F6 40 57N 78 55W
Big Sable Pt., U.S.A. 76 C2 44 3N 86 1W
Big Salmon →, Canada 72 A2 61 52N 134 55W
Big Sand L., Canada 73 B9 57 45N 99 45W
Big Sandy, U.S.A. 82 B8 48 11N 110 7W
Big Sandy →, U.S.A. 76 F4 38 25N 82 36W
Big Sandy Cr. →, U.S.A. 80 F3 38 7N 102 29W
Big Sioux →, U.S.A. 80 D6 42 29N 96 27W
Big Spring, U.S.A. 81 J4 32 15N 101 28W
Big Stone City, U.S.A. 80 C6 45 18N 96 28W
Big Stone Gap, U.S.A. 77 G4 36 52N 82 47W
Big Stone L., U.S.A. 80 C6 45 30N 96 35W
Big Sur, U.S.A. 84 J5 36 15N 121 48W
Big Timber, U.S.A. 82 D9 45 50N 109 57W

Broad

olton, U.K. 10 D5 53 35N 2 26W
olton Landing, U.S.A. 79 C11 43 32N 73 35W
olu, Turkey 25 F5 40 45N 31 35 E
olungavík, Iceland 8 C2 66 9N 23 15W
olvadin, Turkey 25 G5 38 45N 31 4 E
olzano, Italy 20 A4 46 31N 11 22 E
om Jesus da Lapa, Brazil 93 F10 13 15S 43 25W
oma,
Dem. Rep. of the Congo 52 F2 5 50S 13 4 E
ombala, Australia 63 F4 36 56S 149 15 E
ombay = Mumbai, India 40 K8 18 55N 72 50 E
omboma,
Dem. Rep. of the Congo 52 D3 2 25N 18 55 E
ombombwa,
Dem. Rep. of the Congo 54 B2 1 40N 25 40 E
omili,
Dem. Rep. of the Congo 54 B2 1 45N 27 5 E
ømlo, Norway 9 G11 59 37N 5 13 E
omokandi →,
Dem. Rep. of the Congo 54 B2 3 39N 26 8 E
omu →, C.A.R. 52 D4 4 40N 22 30 E
on, C., Tunisia 48 C5 37 1N 11 2 E
on Sar Pa, Vietnam 38 F6 12 24N 107 35 E
onaigarh, India 43 J11 21 50N 84 57 E
onaire, Neth. Ant. 89 D6 12 10N 68 15W
onang, Australia 63 F4 37 11S 148 41 E
onanza, Nic. 88 D3 13 54N 84 35W
onaparte Arch., Australia 60 B3 14 0S 124 30 E
onaventure, Canada 71 C6 48 5N 65 32W
onavista, Canada 71 C9 48 40N 53 5W
onavista, C., Canada 71 C9 48 42N 53 5W
onavista B., Canada 71 C9 48 45N 53 25W
ondo,
Dem. Rep. of the Congo 54 B1 3 55N 23 53 E
ondoukou, Ivory C. 50 G5 8 2N 2 47W
ondowoso, Indonesia 37 G15 7 55S 113 49 E
one, Teluk, Indonesia 37 E6 4 10S 120 50 E
onerate, Indonesia 37 F6 7 25S 121 5 E
onerate, Kepulauan,
Indonesia 37 F6 6 30S 121 10 E
o'ness, U.K. 12 E5 56 1N 3 37W
onete, Cerro, Argentina 94 B2 27 55S 68 40W
ong Son = Hoai Nhon,
Vietnam 38 E7 14 28N 109 1 E
ongor, Chad 51 F9 10 35N 15 20 E
onham, U.S.A. 81 J6 33 35N 96 11W
onifacio, France 18 F8 41 24N 9 10 E
onifacio, Bouches de,
Medit. S. 20 D3 41 12N 9 15 E
onin Is. = Ogasawara
Gunto, Pac. Oc. 28 G18 27 0N 142 0 E
onn, Germany 16 C4 50 46N 7 6 E
onne Terre, U.S.A. 81 G9 37 55N 90 33W
onners Ferry, U.S.A. 82 B5 48 42N 116 19W
onney, L., Australia 63 F3 37 50S 140 20 E
onnie Rock, Australia 61 F2 30 29S 118 22 E
onny, Bight of, Africa 52 D1 3 30N 9 20 E
onnyrigg, U.K. 12 F5 55 53N 3 6W
onnyville, Canada 73 C6 54 20N 110 45W
onoi, Indonesia 37 E9 1 45S 137 41 E
onsall, U.S.A. 85 M9 33 16N 117 14W
ontang, Indonesia 36 D5 0 10N 117 30 E
onthe, S. Leone 50 G3 7 30N 12 33W
ontoc, Phil. 37 A6 17 7N 120 58 E
onython Ra., Australia 60 D4 23 40S 128 45 E
ookabie, Australia 61 F5 31 50S 132 41 E
ooker, U.S.A. 81 G4 36 27N 100 32W
ooligal, Australia 63 E3 33 58S 144 53 E
oonah, Australia 63 D5 27 58S 152 41 E
oone, Iowa, U.S.A. 80 D8 42 4N 93 53W
oone, N.C., U.S.A. 77 G5 36 13N 81 41W
ooneville, Ark., U.S.A. 81 H8 35 8N 93 55W
ooneville, Miss., U.S.A. 77 H1 34 39N 88 34W
oonville, Calif., U.S.A. 84 F3 39 1N 123 22W
oonville, Ind., U.S.A. 76 F2 38 3N 87 16W
oonville, Mo., U.S.A. 80 F8 38 58N 92 44W
oonville, N.Y., U.S.A. 79 C9 43 29N 75 20W
oorindal, Australia 63 E4 30 22S 146 11 E
oorowa, Australia 63 E4 34 28S 148 44 E
oothia, Gulf of, Canada 69 A11 71 0N 90 0W
oothia Pen., Canada 68 A10 71 0N 94 0W
ootle, U.K. 10 D4 53 28N 3 1W
oué, Gabon 52 E2 0 5S 11 55 E
oquete, Panama 88 E3 8 46N 82 27W
oquilla, Presa de la,
Mexico 86 B3 27 40N 105 30W
oquillas del Carmen,
Mexico 86 B4 29 17N 102 53W
or, Serbia, Yug. 21 B10 44 5N 22 7 E
ôr, Sudan 51 G12 6 10N 31 40 E
or Mashash, Israel 47 D3 31 7N 34 50 E
orah Peak, U.S.A. 82 D7 44 8N 113 47W
orås, Sweden 9 H15 57 43N 12 56 E
orāzjān, Iran 45 D6 29 22N 51 10 E
orba, Brazil 92 D7 4 12S 59 34W
orborema, Planalto da,
Brazil 90 D7 7 0S 37 0W
ord Khūn-e Now, Iran 45 D6 28 3N 51 28 E
orda, C., Australia 63 F2 35 45S 136 34 E
ordeaux, France 18 D3 44 50N 0 36W
orden, Australia 61 F2 34 3S 118 12 E
orden, Canada 71 C7 46 18N 63 47W
orden I., Canada 4 B2 78 30N 111 30W
orden Pen., Canada 69 A11 73 0N 83 0W
orders = Scottish
Borders □, U.K. 12 F6 55 35N 2 50W
ordertown, Australia 63 F3 36 19S 140 45 E
orðeyri, Iceland 8 D3 65 12N 21 6W
ordj Fly Ste. Marie, Algeria 50 C5 27 19N 2 32W
ordj-in-Eker, Algeria 50 D7 24 9N 5 3 E
ordj Omar Driss, Algeria 50 C7 28 10N 6 40 E
orehamwood, U.K. 11 F7 51 40N 0 15W
orgå = Porvoo, Finland 9 F21 60 24N 25 40 E
orgarfjörður, Iceland 8 D7 65 31N 13 49W
orgarnes, Iceland 8 D3 64 32N 21 55W
ørgefjellet, Norway 8 D15 65 20N 13 45 E
orger, Neths. 15 B6 52 54N 6 44 E
orger, U.S.A. 81 H4 35 39N 101 24W
orgholm, Sweden 9 H17 56 52N 16 39 E
orhoyn Tal, Mongolia 34 C6 43 50N 111 58 E
orikhane, Laos 38 C4 18 33N 103 43 E
orisoglebsk, Russia 25 D7 51 27N 42 5 E
orisov = Barysaw, Belarus 17 A15 54 17N 28 28 E
orja, Peru 92 D3 4 20S 77 40W
orkou, Chad 51 E9 18 15N 18 50 E
orkum, Germany 16 B4 53 34N 6 40 E
orlänge, Sweden 9 F16 60 29N 15 26 E
Borley, C., Antarctica 5 C5 66 15S 52 30 E
Borneo, E. Indies 36 D5 1 0N 115 0 E
Bornholm, Denmark 9 J16 55 10N 15 0 E
Borogontsy, Russia 27 C14 62 42N 131 8 E
Boron, U.S.A. 85 L9 35 0N 117 39W
Borongan, Phil. 37 B7 11 37N 125 26 E
Borovichi, Russia 24 C5 58 25N 33 55 E
Borrego Springs, U.S.A. 85 M10 33 15N 116 23W
Borroloola, Australia 62 B2 16 4S 136 17 E
Borşa, Romania 17 E13 47 41N 24 50 E
Borsad, India 42 H5 22 25N 72 54 E
Borth, U.K. 11 E3 52 29N 4 2W
Borūjerd, Iran 45 C6 33 55N 48 50 E
Boryslav, Ukraine 17 D12 49 18N 23 28 E
Borzya, Russia 27 D12 50 24N 116 31 E
Bosa, Italy 20 D3 40 18N 8 30 E
Bosanska Gradiška, Bos.-H. 20 B7 45 10N 17 15 E
Bosaso, Somali Rep. 46 E4 11 12N 49 18 E
Boscastle, U.K. 11 G3 50 41N 4 42W
Boshan, China 35 F9 36 28N 117 49 E
Boshof, S. Africa 56 D4 28 31S 25 13 E
Boshrūyeh, Iran 45 C8 33 50N 57 30 E
Bosna →, Bos.-H. 21 B8 45 4N 18 29 E
Bosna i Hercegovina =
Bosnia-Herzegovina ■,
Europe 20 B7 44 0N 18 0 E
Bosnia-Herzegovina ■,
Europe 20 B7 44 0N 18 0 E
Bosnik, Indonesia 37 E9 1 5S 136 10 E
Bosobolo,
Dem. Rep. of the Congo 52 D3 4 15N 19 50 E
Bosporus = İstanbul Boğazı,
Turkey 21 D13 41 10N 29 10 E
Bosque Farms, U.S.A. 83 J10 34 53N 106 40W
Bossangoa, C.A.R. 52 C3 6 35N 17 30 E
Bossier City, U.S.A. 81 J8 32 31N 93 44W
Bosso, Niger 51 F8 13 43N 13 19 E
Bostan, Pakistan 42 D2 30 26N 67 2 E
Bostānābād, Iran 44 B5 37 50N 46 50 E
Bosten Hu, China 32 B3 41 55N 87 40 E
Boston, U.K. 10 E7 52 59N 0 2W
Boston, U.S.A. 79 D13 42 22N 71 4W
Boston Bar, Canada 72 D4 49 52N 121 30W
Boston Mts., U.S.A. 81 H8 35 42N 93 15W
Boswell, Canada 72 D5 49 28N 116 45W
Boswell, U.S.A. 78 F5 40 10N 79 2W
Botad, India 42 H4 22 15N 71 40 E
Botene, Laos 38 D3 17 35N 101 12 E
Bothaville, S. Africa 56 D4 27 23S 26 34 E
Bothnia, G. of, Europe 8 E19 63 0N 20 15 E
Bothwell, Australia 62 G4 42 20S 147 1 E
Bothwell, Canada 78 D3 42 38N 81 52W
Botletle →, Botswana 56 C3 20 10S 23 15 E
Botoşani, Romania 17 E14 47 42N 26 41 E
Botou, Burkina Faso 50 F6 12 40N 2 3 E
Botswana ■, Africa 56 C3 22 0S 24 0 E
Bottineau, U.S.A. 80 A4 48 50N 100 27W
Bottrop, Germany 15 C6 51 31N 6 58 E
Botucatu, Brazil 95 A6 22 55S 48 30W
Botwood, Canada 71 C8 49 6N 55 23W
Bouaflé, Ivory C. 50 G4 7 1N 5 47W
Bouaké, Ivory C. 50 G4 7 40N 5 2W
Bouar, C.A.R. 52 C3 6 0N 15 40 E
Bouârfa, Morocco 50 B5 32 32N 1 58W
Boucaut B., Australia 62 A1 12 0S 134 25 E
Bougainville, C., Australia 60 B4 13 57S 126 4 E
Bougainville I., Papua N. G. 64 H7 6 0S 155 0 E
Bougainville Reef, Australia 62 B4 15 30S 147 5 E
Bougie = Bejaia, Algeria 50 A7 36 42N 5 2 E
Bougouni, Mali 50 F4 11 30N 7 20W
Bouillon, Belgium 15 E5 49 44N 5 3 E
Boulder, Colo., U.S.A. 80 E2 40 1N 105 17W
Boulder, Mont., U.S.A. 82 C7 46 14N 112 7W
Boulder City, U.S.A. 85 K12 35 59N 114 50W
Boulder Creek, U.S.A. 84 H4 37 7N 122 7W
Boulder Dam = Hoover
Dam, U.S.A. 85 K12 36 1N 114 44W
Boulia, Australia 62 C2 22 52S 139 51 E
Boulogne-sur-Mer, France 18 A4 50 42N 1 36 E
Boultoum, Niger 51 F8 14 45N 10 25 E
Boun Neua, Laos 38 B3 21 38N 101 54 E
Boun Tai, Laos 38 B3 21 23N 101 58 E
Bouna, Ivory C. 50 G5 9 10N 3 0W
Boundary Peak, U.S.A. 84 H8 37 51N 118 21W
Boundiali, Ivory C. 50 G4 9 30N 6 20W
Bountiful, U.S.A. 82 F8 40 53N 111 53W
Bounty Is., Pac. Oc. 64 M9 48 0S 178 30 E
Bourbonnais, France 18 C5 46 28N 3 0 E
Bourdel L., Canada 70 A5 56 43N 74 10W
Bourem, Mali 50 E5 17 0N 0 24W
Bourg-en-Bresse, France 18 C6 46 13N 5 12 E
Bourg-St-Maurice, France 18 D7 45 35N 6 46 E
Bourges, France 18 C5 47 9N 2 25 E
Bourget, Canada 79 A9 45 26N 75 9W
Bourgogne, France 18 C6 47 0N 4 50 E
Bourke, Australia 63 E4 30 8S 145 55 E
Bourne, U.K. 10 E7 52 47N 0 22W
Bournemouth, U.K. 11 G6 50 43N 1 52W
Bournemouth □, U.K. 11 G6 50 43N 1 52W
Bouse, U.S.A. 85 M13 33 56N 114 0W
Bouvet I. = Bouvetøya,
Antarctica 3 G10 54 26S 3 24 E
Bouvetøya, Antarctica 3 G10 54 26S 3 24 E
Bovill, U.S.A. 82 C5 46 51N 116 24W
Bovril, Argentina 94 C4 31 21S 59 26W
Bow →, Canada 72 C6 49 57N 111 41W
Bow Island, Canada 72 D6 49 50N 111 23W
Bowbells, U.S.A. 80 A3 48 48N 102 15W
Bowdle, U.S.A. 80 C5 45 27N 99 39W
Bowelling, Australia 61 F2 33 25S 116 30 E
Bowen, Argentina 94 D2 35 0S 67 31W
Bowen, Australia 62 C4 20 0S 148 16 E
Bowen Mts., Australia 63 F4 37 0S 147 50 E
Bowie, Ariz., U.S.A. 83 K9 32 19N 109 29W
Bowie, Tex., U.S.A. 81 J6 33 34N 97 51W
Bowkān, Iran 44 B5 36 31N 46 12 E
Bowland, Forest of, U.K. 10 D5 54 0N 2 30W
Bowling Green, Ky., U.S.A. 76 G2 36 59N 86 27W
Bowling Green, Ohio, U.S.A. 76 E4 41 23N 83 39W
Bowling Green, C., Australia 62 B4 19 19S 147 25 E
Bowman, U.S.A. 80 B3 46 11N 103 24W
Bowman I., Antarctica 5 C8 65 0S 104 0 E
Bowmanville, Canada 78 C6 43 55N 78 41W
Bowmore, U.K. 12 F2 55 45N 6 17W
Bowral, Australia 63 E5 34 26S 150 27 E
Bowraville, Australia 63 E5 30 37S 152 52 E
Bowron →, Canada 72 C4 54 3N 121 50W
Bowron Lake Prov. Park,
Canada 72 C4 53 10N 121 5W
Bowser L., Canada 72 B3 56 30N 129 30W
Bowsman, Canada 73 C8 52 14N 101 12W
Bowwood, Zambia 55 F2 17 5S 26 20 E
Box Cr. →, Australia 63 E3 34 10S 143 50 E
Boxmeer, Neths. 15 C5 51 38N 5 56 E
Boxtel, Neths. 15 C5 51 36N 5 20 E
Boyce, U.S.A. 81 K8 31 23N 92 40W
Boyd L., Canada 70 B4 52 46N 76 42W
Boyle, Canada 72 C6 54 35N 112 49W
Boyle, Ireland 13 C3 53 59N 8 18W
Boyne →, Ireland 13 C5 53 43N 6 15W
Boyne City, U.S.A. 76 C3 45 13N 85 1W
Boynton Beach, U.S.A. 77 M5 26 32N 80 4W
Boyolali, Indonesia 37 G14 7 32S 110 35 E
Boyoma, Chutes,
Dem. Rep. of the Congo 54 B2 0 35N 25 23 E
Boysen Reservoir, U.S.A. 82 E9 43 25N 108 11W
Boyuibe, Bolivia 92 G6 20 25S 63 17W
Boyup Brook, Australia 61 F2 33 50S 116 23 E
Boz Dağları, Turkey 21 E13 38 20N 28 0 E
Bozburun, Turkey 21 F13 36 43N 28 4 E
Bozcaada, Turkey 21 E12 39 49N 26 3 E
Bozdoğan, Turkey 21 F13 37 40N 28 17 E
Bozeman, U.S.A. 82 D8 45 41N 111 2W
Bozen = Bolzano, Italy 20 A4 46 31N 11 22 E
Bozhou, China 34 H8 33 55N 115 41 E
Bozoum, C.A.R. 52 C3 6 25N 16 35 E
Bra, Italy 18 D7 44 42N 7 51 E
Brabant □, Belgium 15 D4 50 46N 4 30 E
Brabant L., Canada 73 B8 55 58N 103 43W
Brač, Croatia 20 C7 43 20N 16 40 E
Bracadale, L., U.K. 12 D2 57 20N 6 30W
Bracciano, L. di, Italy 20 C5 42 7N 12 14 E
Bracebridge, Canada 78 A5 45 2N 79 19W
Brach, Libya 51 C8 27 31N 14 20 E
Bräcke, Sweden 9 E16 62 45N 15 26 E
Brackettville, U.S.A. 81 L4 29 19N 100 25W
Bracknell, U.K. 11 F7 51 25N 0 43W
Bracknell Forest □, U.K. 11 F7 51 25N 0 44W
Brad, Romania 17 E12 46 10N 22 50 E
Bradenton, U.S.A. 77 M4 27 30N 82 34W
Bradford, Canada 78 B5 44 7N 79 34W
Bradford, U.K. 10 D6 53 47N 1 45W
Bradford, Pa., U.S.A. 78 E6 41 58N 78 38W
Bradford, Vt., U.S.A. 79 C12 43 59N 72 9W
Bradley, Ark., U.S.A. 81 J8 33 6N 93 39W
Bradley, Calif., U.S.A. 84 K6 35 52N 120 48W
Bradley Institute, Zimbabwe 55 F3 17 7S 31 25 E
Brady, U.S.A. 81 K5 31 9N 99 20W
Braemar, U.K. 12 D5 57 0N 3 23W
Braeside, Canada 79 A8 45 28N 76 24W
Braga, Portugal 19 B1 41 35N 8 25W
Bragado, Argentina 94 D3 35 2S 60 27W
Bragança, Brazil 93 D9 1 0S 47 2W
Bragança, Portugal 19 B2 41 48N 6 50W
Bragança Paulista, Brazil 95 A6 22 55S 46 32W
Brahmanbaria, Bangla. 41 H17 23 58N 91 15 E
Brahmani →, India 41 J15 20 39N 86 46 E
Brahmapur, India 41 K14 19 15N 84 54 E
Brahmaputra →, India 43 H13 23 58N 89 50 E
Braich-y-pwll, U.K. 10 E3 52 47N 4 46W
Braidwood, Australia 63 F4 35 27S 149 49 E
Brăila, Romania 17 F14 45 19N 27 59 E
Brainerd, U.S.A. 80 B7 46 22N 94 12W
Braintree, U.K. 11 F8 51 53N 0 34 E
Braintree, U.S.A. 79 D14 42 13N 71 0W
Brak →, S. Africa 56 D3 29 35S 22 55 E
Brakwater, Namibia 56 C2 22 28S 17 3 E
Brampton, Canada 78 C5 43 45N 79 45W
Brampton, U.K. 10 C5 54 57N 2 44W
Branco →, Brazil 92 D6 1 20S 61 50W
Brandenburg =
Neubrandenburg,
Germany 16 B7 53 33N 13 15 E
Brandenburg, Germany 16 B7 52 25N 12 33 E
Brandenburg □, Germany 16 B6 52 50N 13 0 E
Brandfort, S. Africa 56 D4 28 40S 26 30 E
Brandon, Canada 73 D9 49 50N 99 57W
Brandon, U.S.A. 79 C11 43 48N 73 4W
Brandon B., Ireland 13 D1 52 17N 10 8W
Brandon Mt., Ireland 13 D1 52 15N 10 15W
Brandsen, Argentina 94 D4 35 10S 58 15W
Brandvlei, S. Africa 56 E3 30 25S 20 30 E
Branford, U.S.A. 79 E12 41 17N 72 49W
Braniewo, Poland 17 A10 54 25N 19 50 E
Bransfield Str., Antarctica 5 C18 63 0S 59 0W
Branson, U.S.A. 81 G8 36 39N 93 13W
Brantford, Canada 78 C4 43 10N 80 15W
Bras d'Or L., Canada 71 C7 45 50N 60 50W
Brasher Falls, U.S.A. 79 B10 44 49N 74 47W
Brasil, Planalto, Brazil 90 E6 18 0S 46 30W
Brasiléia, Brazil 92 F5 11 0S 68 45W
Brasília, Brazil 93 G9 15 47S 47 55W
Brasília Legal, Brazil 93 D7 3 49S 55 36W
Braslaw, Belarus 9 J22 55 38N 27 0 E
Braşov, Romania 17 F13 45 38N 25 35 E
Brasschaat, Belgium 15 C4 51 19N 4 27 E
Brassey, Banjaran, Malaysia 36 D5 5 0N 117 15 E
Brassey Ra., Australia 61 E3 25 8S 122 15 E
Brasstown Bald, U.S.A. 77 H4 34 53N 83 49W
Brastad, Sweden 9 G14 58 23N 11 30 E
Bratislava, Slovak Rep. 17 D9 48 10N 17 7 E
Bratsk, Russia 27 D11 56 10N 101 30 E
Brattleboro, U.S.A. 79 D12 42 51N 72 34W
Braunau, Austria 16 D7 48 15N 13 3 E
Braunschweig, Germany 16 B6 52 15N 10 31 E
Braunton, U.K. 11 F3 51 7N 4 10W
Bravo del Norte, Rio =
Grande, Rio →, U.S.A. 81 N6 25 58N 97 9W
Brawley, U.S.A. 85 N11 32 59N 115 31W
Bray, Ireland 13 C5 53 13N 6 7W
Bray, Mt., Australia 62 A1 14 0S 134 30 E
Bray, Pays de, France 18 B4 49 46N 1 26 E
Brazeau →, Canada 72 C5 52 55N 115 14W
Brazil, U.S.A. 76 F2 39 32N 87 8W
Brazil ■, S. Amer. 93 F9 12 0S 50 0W
Brazilian Highlands = Brasil,
Planalto, Brazil 90 E6 18 0S 46 30W
Brazo Sur →, S. Amer. 94 B4 25 21S 57 42W
Brazos →, U.S.A. 81 L7 28 53N 95 23W
Brazzaville, Congo 52 E3 4 9S 15 12 E
Brčko, Bos.-H. 21 B8 44 54N 18 46 E
Breaden, L., Australia 61 E4 25 51S 125 28 E
Breaksea Sd., N.Z. 59 L1 45 35S 166 35 E
Bream B., N.Z. 59 F5 35 56S 174 28 E
Bream Hd., N.Z. 59 F5 35 51S 174 36 E
Breas, Chile 94 B1 25 29S 70 24W
Brebes, Indonesia 37 G13 6 52S 109 3 E
Brechin, Canada 78 B5 44 32N 79 10W
Brechin, U.K. 12 E6 56 44N 2 39W
Brecht, Belgium 15 C4 51 21N 4 38 E
Breckenridge, Colo., U.S.A. 82 G10 39 29N 106 3W
Breckenridge, Minn., U.S.A. 80 B6 46 16N 96 35W
Breckenridge, Tex., U.S.A. 81 J5 32 45N 98 54W
Breckland, U.K. 11 E8 52 30N 0 40 E
Brecon, U.K. 11 F4 51 57N 3 23W
Brecon Beacons, U.K. 11 F4 51 53N 3 26W
Breda, Neths. 15 C4 51 35N 4 45 E
Bredasdorp, S. Africa 56 E3 34 33S 20 2 E
Bree, Belgium 15 C5 51 8N 5 35 E
Bregenz, Austria 16 E5 47 30N 9 45 E
Breiðafjörður, Iceland 8 D2 65 15N 23 15W
Brejo, Brazil 93 D10 3 41S 42 47W
Bremen, Germany 16 B5 53 4N 8 47 E
Bremer Bay, Australia 61 F2 34 21S 119 20 E
Bremer I., Australia 62 A2 12 5S 136 45 E
Bremerhaven, Germany 16 B5 53 33N 8 36 E
Bremerton, U.S.A. 84 C4 47 34N 122 38W
Brenham, U.S.A. 81 K6 30 10N 96 24W
Brennerpass, Austria 16 E6 47 2N 11 30 E
Brent, U.S.A. 77 J2 32 56N 87 10W
Brentwood, U.K. 11 F8 51 37N 0 19 E
Brentwood, Calif., U.S.A. 84 H5 37 56N 121 42W
Brentwood, N.Y., U.S.A. 79 F11 40 47N 73 15W
Bréscia, Italy 18 D9 45 33N 10 15 E
Breskens, Neths. 15 C3 51 23N 3 33 E
Breslau = Wrocław, Poland 17 C9 51 5N 17 5 E
Bressanone, Italy 20 A4 46 43N 11 39 E
Bressay, U.K. 12 A7 60 9N 1 6W
Brest, Belarus 17 B12 52 10N 23 40 E
Brest, France 18 B1 48 24N 4 31W
Brest-Litovsk = Brest,
Belarus 17 B12 52 10N 23 40 E
Bretagne, France 18 B2 48 10N 3 0W
Breton, Canada 72 C6 53 7N 114 28W
Breton Sd., U.S.A. 81 L10 29 35N 89 15W
Brett, C., N.Z. 59 F5 35 10S 174 20 E
Brevard, U.S.A. 77 H4 35 14N 82 44W
Breves, Brazil 93 D8 1 40S 50 29W
Brewarrina, Australia 63 E4 30 0S 146 51 E
Brewer, U.S.A. 77 C11 44 48N 68 46W
Brewer, Mt., U.S.A. 84 J8 36 44N 118 28W
Brewster, N.Y., U.S.A. 79 E11 41 23N 73 37W
Brewster, Ohio, U.S.A. 78 F3 40 43N 81 36W
Brewster, Wash., U.S.A. 82 B4 48 6N 119 47W
Brewster, Kap, Greenland 4 B6 70 7N 22 0W
Brewton, U.S.A. 77 K2 31 7N 87 4W
Breyten, S. Africa 57 D5 26 16S 30 0 E
Brezhnev = Naberezhnyye
Chelny, Russia 24 C9 55 42N 52 19 E
Briançon, France 18 D7 44 54N 6 39 E
Bribie I., Australia 63 D5 27 0S 153 10 E
Bribri, Costa Rica 88 E3 9 38N 82 50W
Bridgehampton, U.S.A. 79 F12 40 56N 72 19W
Bridgend, U.K. 11 F4 51 30N 3 34W
Bridgend □, U.K. 11 F4 51 36N 3 36W
Bridgeport, Calif., U.S.A. 84 G7 38 15N 119 14W
Bridgeport, Conn., U.S.A. 79 E11 41 11N 73 12W
Bridgeport, Nebr., U.S.A. 80 E3 41 40N 103 6W
Bridgeport, Tex., U.S.A. 81 J6 33 13N 97 45W
Bridger, U.S.A. 82 D9 45 18N 108 55W
Bridgeton, U.S.A. 76 F8 39 26N 75 14W
Bridgetown, Australia 61 F2 33 58S 116 7 E
Bridgetown, Barbados 89 D8 13 5N 59 30W
Bridgetown, Canada 71 D6 44 55N 65 18W
Bridgewater, Canada 71 D7 44 25N 64 31W
Bridgewater, Mass., U.S.A. 79 E14 41 59N 70 58W
Bridgewater, N.Y., U.S.A. 79 D9 42 53N 75 15W
Bridgewater, C., Australia 63 F3 38 23S 141 23 E
Bridgewater-Gagebrook,
Australia 62 G4 42 44S 147 14 E
Bridgnorth, U.K. 11 E5 52 32N 2 25W
Bridgton, U.S.A. 79 B14 44 3N 70 42W
Bridgwater, U.K. 11 F5 51 8N 2 59W
Bridgwater B., U.K. 11 F4 51 15N 3 15W
Bridlington, U.K. 10 C7 54 5N 0 12W
Bridlington B., U.K. 10 C7 54 4N 0 10W
Bridport, Australia 62 G4 40 59S 147 23 E
Bridport, U.K. 11 G5 50 44N 2 45W
Brig, Switz. 18 C7 46 18N 7 59 E
Brigg, U.K. 10 D7 53 34N 0 28W
Brigham City, U.S.A. 82 F7 41 31N 112 1W
Bright, Australia 63 F4 36 42S 146 56 E
Brighton, Australia 63 F2 35 5S 138 30 E
Brighton, Canada 78 B7 44 2N 77 44W
Brighton, U.K. 11 G7 50 49N 0 7W
Brighton, Colo., U.S.A. 80 F2 39 59N 104 49W
Brighton, N.Y., U.S.A. 78 C7 43 8N 77 34W
Brilliant, U.S.A. 78 F4 40 15N 80 39W
Bríndisi, Italy 21 D7 40 39N 17 55 E
Brinkley, U.S.A. 81 H9 34 53N 91 12W
Brinnon, U.S.A. 84 C4 47 41N 122 54W
Brion, I., Canada 71 C7 47 46N 61 26W
Brisbane, Australia 63 D5 27 25S 153 2 E
Brisbane →, Australia 63 D5 27 24S 153 9 E
Bristol, U.K. 11 F5 51 26N 2 35W
Bristol, Conn., U.S.A. 79 E12 41 40N 72 57W
Bristol, Pa., U.S.A. 79 F10 40 6N 74 51W
Bristol, R.I., U.S.A. 79 E13 41 40N 71 16W
Bristol, Tenn., U.S.A. 77 G4 36 36N 82 11W
Bristol, City of □, U.K. 11 F5 51 27N 2 36W
Bristol B., U.S.A. 68 C4 58 0N 160 0W
Bristol Channel, U.K. 11 F3 51 18N 4 30W
Bristol I., Antarctica 5 B1 58 45S 28 0W
Bristol L., U.S.A. 83 J5 34 23N 116 50W
Bristow, U.S.A. 81 H6 35 50N 96 23W
Britain = Great Britain,
Europe 6 E5 54 0N 2 15W
British Columbia □, Canada 72 C3 55 0N 125 15W
British Indian Ocean Terr. =
Chagos Arch., Ind. Oc. 29 K11 6 0S 72 0 E
British Isles, Europe 6 E5 54 0N 4 0W
Brits, S. Africa 57 D4 25 37S 27 48 E
Britstown, S. Africa 56 E3 30 37S 23 30 E
Britt, Canada 70 C3 45 46N 80 34W
Brittany = Bretagne, France 18 B2 48 10N 3 0W
Britton, U.S.A. 80 C6 45 48N 97 45W
Brive-la-Gaillarde, France 18 D4 45 10N 1 32 E
Brixen = Bressanone, Italy 20 A4 46 43N 11 39 E
Brixham, U.K. 11 G4 50 23N 3 31W
Brno, Czech Rep. 17 D9 49 10N 16 35 E
Broad →, U.S.A. 77 J5 34 1N 81 4W

Broad Arrow

Broad Arrow, *Australia* .... **61 F3** 30 23S 121 15 E
Broad B., *U.K.* **12 C2** 58 14N 6 18W
Broad Haven, *Ireland* **13 B2** 54 20N 9 55W
Broad Law, *U.K.* **12 F5** 55 30N 3 21W
Broad Sd., *Australia* ..... **62 C4** 22 0S 149 45 E
Broadalbin, *U.S.A.* **79 C10** 43 4N 74 12W
Broadback → , *Canada* .. **70 B4** 51 21N 78 52W
Broadford, *Australia* ..... **63 F4** 37 14S 145 4 E
Broadhurst Ra., *Australia* . **60 D3** 22 30S 122 30 E
Broads, The, *U.K.* .... **10 E9** 52 45N 1 30 E
Broadus, *U.S.A.* **80 C2** 45 27N 105 25W
Brochet, *Canada* **73 B8** 57 53N 101 40W
Brochet, L., *Canada* **73 B8** 58 36N 101 35W
Brocken, *Germany* .... **16 C6** 51 47N 10 37 E
Brockport, *U.S.A.* **78 C7** 43 13N 77 56W
Brockton, *U.S.A.* **79 D13** 42 5N 71 1W
Brockville, *Canada* **79 B9** 44 35N 75 41W
Brockway, Mont., *U.S.A.* . **80 B2** 47 18N 105 45W
Brockway, Pa., *U.S.A.* **78 E6** 41 15N 78 47W
Brocton, *U.S.A.* **78 D5** 42 23N 79 26W
Brodeur Pen., *Canada* **69 A11** 72 30N 88 10W
Brodhead, Mt., *U.S.A.* **78 E7** 41 39N 77 47W
Brodick, *U.K.* **12 F3** 55 35N 5 9W
Brodnica, *Poland* .... **17 B10** 53 15N 19 25 E
Brody, *Ukraine* .... **17 C13** 50 5N 25 10 E
Brogan, *U.S.A.* **82 D5** 44 15N 117 31W
Broken Arrow, *U.S.A.* **81 G7** 36 3N 95 48W
Broken Bow, Nebr., *U.S.A.* **80 E5** 41 24N 99 38W
Broken Bow, Okla., *U.S.A.* **81 H7** 34 2N 94 44W
Broken Bow Lake, *U.S.A.* . **81 H7** 34 9N 94 40W
Broken Hill = Kabwe,
  Zambia .... **55 E2** 14 30S 28 29 E
Broken Hill, *Australia* .... **63 E3** 31 58S 141 29 E
Bromley, *U.K.* .... **11 F8** 51 24N 0 2 E
Bromsgrove, *U.K.* **11 E5** 52 21N 2 2W
Brønderslev, *Denmark* .... **9 H13** 57 16N 9 57 E
Bronkhorstspruit, *S. Africa* **57 D4** 25 46S 28 45 E
Brønnøysund, *Norway* .... **8 D15** 65 28N 12 14 E
Brook Park, *U.S.A.* **78 E4** 41 24N 81 51W
Brookhaven, *U.S.A.* **81 K9** 31 35N 90 26W
Brookings, Oreg., *U.S.A.* .. **82 E1** 42 3N 124 17W
Brookings, S. Dak., *U.S.A.* . **80 C6** 44 19N 96 48W
Brooklin, *Canada* **78 C6** 43 55N 78 55W
Brooklyn Park, *U.S.A.* **80 C8** 45 6N 93 23W
Brooks, *Canada* **72 C6** 50 35N 111 55W
Brooks Range, *U.S.A.* **68 B5** 68 0N 152 0W
Brooksville, *U.S.A.* **77 L4** 28 33N 82 23W
Brookton, *Australia* ...... **61 F2** 32 22S 117 0 E
Brookville, *U.S.A.* **78 E5** 41 10N 79 5W
Broom, L., *U.K.* **12 D3** 57 55N 5 15W
Broome, *Australia* .... **60 C3** 18 0S 122 15 E
Brora, *U.K.* **12 C5** 58 0N 3 52W
Brora → , *U.K.* **12 C5** 58 0N 3 51W
Brosna → , *Ireland* **13 C4** 53 14N 7 58W
Brothers, *U.S.A.* **82 E3** 43 49N 120 36W
Brough, *U.K.* **10 C5** 54 32N 2 18W
Brough Hd., *U.K.* **12 B5** 59 8N 3 20W
Broughton Island =
  Qikiqtarjuaq, *Canada* ... **69 B13** 67 33N 63 0W
Brown, L., *Australia* ...... **61 F2** 31 5S 118 15 E
Brown, Pt., *Australia* ..... **63 E1** 32 32S 133 50 E
Brown City, *U.S.A.* **78 C2** 43 13N 82 59W
Brown Willy, *U.K.* **11 G3** 50 35N 4 37W
Brownfield, *U.S.A.* **81 J3** 33 11N 102 17W
Browning, *U.S.A.* **82 B7** 48 34N 113 1W
Brownsville, Oreg., *U.S.A.* . **82 D2** 44 24N 122 59W
Brownsville, Pa., *U.S.A.* .. **78 F5** 40 1N 79 53W
Brownsville, Tenn., *U.S.A.* . **81 H10** 35 36N 89 16W
Brownsville, Tex., *U.S.A.* .. **81 N6** 25 54N 97 30W
Brownville, *U.S.A.* **79 C9** 44 0N 75 59W
Brownwood, *U.S.A.* **81 K5** 31 43N 98 59W
Browse I., *Australia* ...... **60 B3** 14 7S 123 33 E
Bruas, *Malaysia* .... **39 K3** 4 30N 100 47 E
Bruay-la-Buissière, *France* . **18 A5** 50 29N 2 33 E
Bruce, Mt., *Australia* ..... **60 D2** 22 37S 118 8 E
Bruce Pen., *Canada* **78 B3** 45 0N 81 30W
Bruce Rock, *Australia* .... **61 F2** 31 52S 118 8 E
Bruck an der Leitha, *Austria* **17 D9** 48 1N 16 47 E
Bruck an der Mur, *Austria* . **16 E8** 47 24N 15 16 E
Brue → , *U.K.* **11 F5** 51 13N 2 59W
Bruges = Brugge, *Belgium* . **15 C3** 51 13N 3 13 E
Brugge, *Belgium* .... **15 C3** 51 13N 3 13 E
Bruin, *U.S.A.* **78 E5** 41 3N 79 43W
Brûlé, *Canada* **72 C5** 53 15N 117 58W
Brumado, *Brazil* **93 F10** 14 14S 41 40W
Brumunddal, *Norway* ..... **9 F14** 60 53N 10 56 E
Bruneau, *U.S.A.* **82 E6** 42 53N 115 48W
Bruneau → , *U.S.A.* **82 E6** 42 56N 115 57W
Brunei = Bandar Seri
  Begawan, *Brunei* .... **36 D5** 4 52N 115 0 E
Brunei ■, *Asia* .... **36 D5** 4 50N 115 0 E
Brunner, L., *N.Z.* .... **59 K3** 42 37S 171 27 E
Brunssum, *Neths.* .... **15 D5** 50 57N 5 59 E
Brunswick = Braunschweig,
  Germany .... **16 B6** 52 15N 10 31 E
Brunswick, Ga., *U.S.A.* ... **77 K5** 31 10N 81 30W
Brunswick, Maine, *U.S.A.* . **77 D11** 43 55N 69 58W
Brunswick, Md., *U.S.A.* ... **76 F7** 39 19N 77 38W
Brunswick, Mo., *U.S.A.* ... **80 F8** 39 26N 93 8W
Brunswick, Ohio, *U.S.A.* .. **78 E3** 41 14N 81 51W
Brunswick, Pen. de, *Chile* . **96 G2** 53 30S 71 30W
Brunswick B., *Australia* ... **60 C3** 15 15S 124 50 E
Brunswick Junction,
  Australia .... **61 F2** 33 15S 115 50 E
Bruny I., *Australia* .... **62 G4** 43 20S 147 15 E
Brus Laguna, *Honduras* ... **88 C3** 15 47N 84 35W
Brush, *U.S.A.* **80 E3** 40 15N 103 37W
Brushton, *U.S.A.* **79 B10** 44 50N 74 31W
Brusque, *Brazil* **95 B6** 27 5S 49 0W
Brussel, *Belgium* .... **15 D4** 50 51N 4 21 E
Brussels = Brussel, *Belgium* **15 D4** 50 51N 4 21 E
Brussels, *Canada* **78 C3** 43 44N 81 15W
Bruthen, *Australia* .... **63 F4** 37 42S 147 50 E
Bruxelles = Brussel,
  Belgium .... **15 D4** 50 51N 4 21 E
Bryan, Ohio, *U.S.A.* **76 E3** 41 28N 84 33W
Bryan, Tex., *U.S.A.* **81 K6** 30 40N 96 22W
Bryan, Mt., *Australia* ..... **63 E2** 33 30S 139 0 E
Bryansk, *Russia* .... **24 D5** 53 13N 34 25 E
Bryce Canyon National Park,
  U.S.A. **83 H7** 37 30N 112 10W
Bryne, *Norway* .... **9 G11** 58 44N 5 38 E
Bryson City, *U.S.A.* **77 H4** 35 26N 83 27W
Bsharri, *Lebanon* .... **47 A5** 34 15N 36 0 E
Bū Baqarah, *U.A.E.* ...... **45 E8** 25 35N 56 25 E
Bu Craa, *W. Sahara* **50 C3** 26 45N 12 50W
Bū Ḥasā, *U.A.E.* .... **45 F7** 23 30N 53 20 E

Bua Yai, *Thailand* .... **38 E4** 15 33N 102 26 E
Buapinang, *Indonesia* .... **37 E6** 4 40S 121 30 E
Buabanza, *Burundi* .... **54 C2** 3 6S 29 23 E
Būbiyān, *Kuwait* .... **45 D6** 29 45N 48 15 E
Bucaramanga, *Colombia* .. **92 B4** 7 0N 73 0W
Bucasia, *Australia* .... **62 C4** 21 2S 149 10 E
Buccaneer Arch., *Australia* . **60 C3** 16 7S 123 20 E
Buchach, *Ukraine* .... **17 D13** 49 5N 25 25 E
Buchan, *U.K.* **12 D6** 57 32N 2 21W
Buchan Ness, *U.K.* **12 D7** 57 29N 1 46W
Buchanan, *Canada* **73 C8** 51 40N 102 45W
Buchanan, *Liberia* **50 G3** 5 57N 10 2W
Buchanan, L., Queens.,
  Australia .... **62 C4** 21 35S 145 52 E
Buchanan, L., W. Austral.,
  Australia .... **61 E3** 25 33S 123 2 E
Buchanan, L., *U.S.A.* **81 K5** 30 45N 98 25W
Buchanan Cr. → , *Australia* **62 B2** 19 13S 136 33 E
Buchans, *Canada* **71 C8** 48 50N 56 52W
Bucharest = Bucureşti,
  Romania .... **17 F14** 44 27N 26 10 E
Buchon, Pt., *U.S.A.* **84 K6** 35 15N 120 54W
Buck Hill Falls, *U.S.A.* **79 E9** 41 11N 75 16W
Buckeye, *U.S.A.* **83 K7** 33 22N 112 35W
Buckeye Lake, *U.S.A.* **78 G2** 39 55N 82 29W
Buckhannon, *U.S.A.* **76 F5** 39 0N 80 8W
Buckhaven, *U.K.* **12 E5** 56 11N 3 3W
Buckhorn L., *Canada* **78 B6** 44 29N 78 23W
Buckie, *U.K.* **12 D6** 57 41N 2 58W
Buckingham, *Canada* **70 C4** 45 37N 75 24W
Buckingham, *U.K.* **11 F7** 51 59N 0 57W
Buckingham B., *Australia* . **62 A2** 12 10S 135 40 E
Buckinghamshire □, *U.K.* . **11 F7** 51 53N 0 55W
Buckle Hd., *Australia* ..... **60 B4** 14 26S 127 52 E
Buckleboo, *Australia* ..... **63 E2** 32 54S 136 12 E
Buckley, *U.K.* **10 D4** 53 10N 3 5W
Buckley → , *Australia* .... **62 C2** 20 10S 138 49 E
Bucklin, *U.S.A.* **81 G5** 37 33N 99 38W
Bucks L., *U.S.A.* **84 F5** 39 54N 121 12W
Buctouche, *Canada* **71 C7** 46 30N 64 45W
Bucureşti, *Romania* ...... **17 F14** 44 27N 26 10 E
Bucyrus, *U.S.A.* **76 E4** 40 48N 82 59W
Budalin, *Burma* .... **41 H19** 22 20N 95 10 E
Budapest, *Hungary* ...... **17 E10** 47 29N 19 5 E
Budaun, *India* .... **43 E8** 28 5N 79 10 E
Budd Coast, *Antarctica* ... **5 C8** 68 0S 112 0 E
Bude, *U.K.* **11 G3** 50 49N 4 34W
Budennovsk, *Russia* ...... **25 F7** 44 50N 44 10 E
Budge Budge = Baj Baj,
  India .... **43 H13** 22 30N 88 5 E
Budgewoi, *Australia* ..... **63 E5** 33 13S 151 34 E
Budjala,
  Dem. Rep. of the Congo . **52 D3** 2 50N 19 40 E
Buellton, *U.S.A.* **85 L6** 34 37N 120 12W
Buena Esperanza, *Argentina* **94 C2** 34 45S 65 15W
Buena Park, *U.S.A.* **85 M9** 33 52N 117 59W
Buena Vista, Colo., *U.S.A.* . **83 G10** 38 51N 106 8W
Buena Vista, Va., *U.S.A.* .. **76 G6** 37 44N 79 21W
Buena Vista Lake Bed,
  U.S.A. **85 K7** 35 12N 119 18W
Buenaventura, *Colombia* .. **92 C3** 3 53N 77 4W
Buenaventura, *Mexico* ... **86 B3** 29 50N 107 30W
Buenos Aires, *Argentina* .. **94 C4** 34 30S 58 20W
Buenos Aires, Costa Rica .. **88 E3** 9 10N 83 20W
Buenos Aires □, *Argentina* **94 D4** 36 30S 60 0W
Buenos Aires, L., *Chile* **96 F2** 46 35S 72 30W
Buffalo, Mo., *U.S.A.* **81 G8** 37 39N 93 6W
Buffalo, N.Y., *U.S.A.* **78 D6** 42 53N 78 53W
Buffalo, Okla., *U.S.A.* **81 G5** 36 50N 99 38W
Buffalo, S. Dak., *U.S.A.* ... **80 C3** 45 35N 103 33W
Buffalo, Wyo., *U.S.A.* **82 D10** 44 21N 106 42W
Buffalo → , *Canada* **72 A5** 60 5N 115 5W
Buffalo Head Hills, *Canada* **72 B5** 57 25N 115 55W
Buffalo L., *Canada* **72 A5** 60 12N 115 25W
Buffalo L., Alta., *Canada* .. **72 C6** 52 27N 112 54W
Buffalo Narrows, *Canada* . **73 B7** 55 51N 108 29W
Buffels → , S. Africa ...... **56 D2** 29 36S 17 3 E
Buford, *U.S.A.* **77 H4** 34 10N 84 0W
Bug → , Poland .... **17 B11** 52 31N 21 5 E
Buga, *Colombia* **92 C3** 4 0N 76 15W
Buganda, *Uganda* .... **54 C3** 0 0 31 30 E
Buganga, *Uganda* .... **54 C3** 0 3S 32 0 E
Bugel, Tanjung, *Indonesia* . **37 G14** 6 26S 111 3 E
Bugibba, *Malta* .... **23 D1** 35 57N 14 25 E
Bugsuk, Phil. .... **36 C5** 8 15N 117 15 E
Bugulma, *Russia* .... **24 D9** 54 33N 52 48 E
Bugun Shara, *Mongolia* ... **32 B5** 49 0N 104 0 E
Buguruslan, *Russia* ...... **24 D9** 53 39N 52 26 E
Buh → , *Ukraine* .... **25 E5** 46 59N 31 58 E
Buhl, *U.S.A.* **82 E6** 42 36N 114 46W
Buick → , Mongolia ...... **33 B6** 47 50N 117 42 E
Bujumbura, *Burundi* ..... **54 C2** 3 16S 29 18 E
Bukachacha, *Russia* ...... **27 D12** 52 55N 116 50 E
Bukama,
  Dem. Rep. of the Congo . **55 D2** 9 10S 25 50 E
Bukavu,
  Dem. Rep. of the Congo . **54 C2** 2 20S 28 52 E
Bukene, Tanzania .... **54 C3** 4 15S 32 48 E
Bukhara = Bukhoro,
  Uzbekistan .... **26 F7** 39 48N 64 25 E
Bukhoro, Uzbekistan ..... **26 F7** 39 48N 64 25 E
Bukima, Tanzania .... **54 C3** 1 50S 33 25 E
Bukit Mertajam, Malaysia .. **39 K3** 5 22N 100 28 E
Bukittinggi, Indonesia .... **36 E2** 0 20S 100 20 E
Bukoba, Tanzania .... **54 C3** 1 20S 31 49 E
Bukuya, Uganda .... **54 B3** 0 40N 31 52 E
Būl, Kuh-e, Iran .... **45 D7** 30 48N 52 45 E
Bula, Indonesia .... **37 E8** 3 6S 130 30 E
Bulahdelah, Australia ..... **63 E5** 32 23S 152 13 E
Bulan, Phil. .... **37 B6** 12 40N 123 52 E
Bulandshahr, India .... **42 E7** 28 28N 77 51 E
Bulawayo, Zimbabwe ..... **55 G2** 20 7S 28 32 E
Buldan, Turkey .... **21 E13** 38 2N 28 50 E
Bulgar, Russia .... **24 C9** 54 57N 49 4 E
Bulgaria ■, Europe ...... **21 C11** 42 35N 25 30 E
Buli, Teluk, Indonesia .... **37 D7** 1 5N 128 25 E
Buliluyan, C., Phil. .... **36 C5** 8 20N 117 15 E
Bulkley → , Canada **72 B3** 55 15N 127 40W
Bull Shoals L., U.S.A. **81 G8** 36 22N 92 35W
Bullhead City, U.S.A. **85 K12** 35 8N 114 32W
Büllingen, Belgium ...... **15 D6** 50 25N 6 16 E
Bullock Creek, Australia .. **62 B3** 17 43S 144 31 E
Bulloo → , Australia ..... **63 D3** 28 43S 142 30 E
Bulloo L., Australia ...... **63 D3** 28 43S 142 25 E
Bulls, N.Z. .... **59 J5** 40 10S 175 24 E

Bulnes, Chile **94 D1** 36 42S 72 19W
Bulsar = Valsad, India .... **40 J8** 20 40N 72 58 E
Bultfontein, S. Africa ..... **56 D4** 28 18S 26 10 E
Bulukumba, Indonesia ... **37 F6** 5 33S 120 11 E
Bulun, Russia .... **27 B13** 70 37N 127 30 E
Bumba,
  Dem. Rep. of the Congo . **52 D4** 2 13N 22 30 E
Bumbiri I., Tanzania ...... **54 C3** 1 40S 31 55 E
Bumhpa Bum, Burma .... **41 F20** 26 51N 97 14 E
Bumi → , Zimbabwe .... **55 F2** 17 0S 28 20 E
Buna, Kenya .... **54 B4** 2 58N 39 30 E
Bunazi, Tanzania .... **54 C3** 1 3S 31 23 E
Bunbury, Australia .... **61 F2** 33 20S 115 35 E
Bunclody, Ireland **13 D5** 52 39N 6 40W
Buncrana, Ireland **13 A4** 55 8N 7 27W
Bundaberg, Australia .... **63 C5** 24 54S 152 22 E
Bundey → , Australia ... **62 C2** 21 46S 135 37 E
Bundi, India .... **42 G6** 25 30N 75 35 E
Bundoran, Ireland **13 B3** 54 28N 8 16W
Bung Kan, Thailand ..... **38 C4** 18 23N 103 37 E
Bungay, U.K. .... **11 E9** 52 27N 1 28 E
Bungil Cr. → , Australia .. **63 D4** 27 5S 149 5 E
Bungo-Suidō, Japan ..... **31 H6** 33 0N 132 15 E
Bungoma, Kenya .... **54 B3** 0 34N 34 34 E
Bungu, Tanzania .... **54 D4** 7 35S 39 0 E
Bunia,
  Dem. Rep. of the Congo . **54 B3** 1 35N 30 20 E
Bunji, Pakistan .... **43 B6** 35 45N 74 40 E
Bunkie, U.S.A. **81 K8** 30 57N 92 11W
Buntok, Indonesia .... **36 E4** 1 40S 114 58 E
Bunyu, Indonesia .... **36 D5** 3 35N 117 50 E
Buol, Indonesia .... **37 D6** 1 15N 121 32 E
Buon Brieng, Vietnam ... **38 F7** 13 9N 108 12 E
Buon Ma Thuot, Vietnam . **38 F7** 12 40N 108 3 E
Buong Long, Cambodia .. **38 F6** 13 44N 106 59 E
Buorkhaya, Mys, Russia .. **27 B14** 71 50N 132 40 E
Buqayq, Si. Arabia ...... **45 E6** 26 0N 49 45 E
Bur Acaba, Somali Rep. .. **46 G3** 3 12N 44 20 E
Bûr Safâga, Egypt ...... **44 E2** 26 43N 33 57 E
Bûr Sa'îd, Egypt .... **51 B12** 31 16N 32 18 E
Bûr Sûdân, Sudan .... **51 E13** 19 32N 37 9 E
Bura, Kenya .... **54 C4** 1 4S 39 58 E
Burakin, Australia .... **61 F2** 30 31S 117 10 E
Burao, Somali Rep. ...... **47 F4** 9 32N 45 32 E
Buraydah, Si. Arabia ..... **44 E5** 26 20N 44 8 E
Burbank, U.S.A. **85 L8** 34 11N 118 19W
Burda, India .... **42 G6** 25 50N 77 35 E
Burdekin → , Australia .. **62 B4** 19 38S 147 25 E
Burdur, Turkey .... **25 G5** 37 45N 30 17 E
Burdwan = Barddhaman,
  India .... **43 H12** 23 14N 87 39 E
Bure, Ethiopia .... **46 E2** 10 40N 37 4 E
Bure → , U.K. .... **10 E9** 52 38N 1 43 E
Bureya → , Russia ...... **27 E13** 49 27N 129 30 E
Burford, Canada **78 C4** 43 7N 80 27W
Burgas, Bulgaria .... **21 C12** 42 33N 27 29 E
Burgeo, Canada **71 C8** 47 37N 57 38W
Burgersdorp, S. Africa ... **56 E4** 31 0S 26 20 E
Burges, Mt., Australia ... **61 F3** 30 50S 121 5 E
Burgos, Spain **19 A4** 42 21N 3 41W
Burgsvik, Sweden .... **9 H18** 57 3N 18 19 E
Burgundy = Bourgogne,
  France .... **18 C6** 47 0N 4 50 E
Burhaniye, Turkey .... **21 E12** 39 30N 26 58 E
Burhanpur, India .... **40 J10** 21 18N 76 14 E
Burhi Gandak → , India . **43 G12** 25 20N 86 37 E
Burhner → , India ...... **43 H9** 22 43N 80 31 E
Burias, Phil. .... **37 B6** 12 55N 123 5 E
Burica, Pta., Costa Rica .. **88 E3** 8 3N 82 51W
Burigi, L., Tanzania ...... **54 C3** 2 2S 31 22 E
Burin, Canada **71 C8** 47 1N 55 14W
Buriram, Thailand .... **38 E4** 15 0N 103 0 E
Burj Säfita, Syria .... **44 C3** 34 48N 36 7 E
Burkburnett, U.S.A. **81 H5** 34 6N 98 34W
Burke → , Australia ..... **62 C2** 23 12S 139 33 E
Burke Chan., Canada **72 C3** 52 10N 127 30W
Burketown, Australia .... **62 B2** 17 45S 139 33 E
Burkina Faso ■, Africa ... **50 F5** 12 0N 1 0W
Burk's Falls, Canada **70 C4** 45 37N 79 24W
Burleigh Falls, Canada ... **78 B6** 44 33N 78 12W
Burley, U.S.A. **82 E7** 42 32N 113 48W
Burlingame, U.S.A. **84 H4** 37 35N 122 21W
Burlington, Canada **78 C5** 43 18N 79 45W
Burlington, Colo., U.S.A. . **80 F3** 39 18N 102 16W
Burlington, Iowa, U.S.A. . **80 E9** 40 49N 91 14W
Burlington, Kans., U.S.A. . **80 F7** 38 12N 95 45W
Burlington, N.C., U.S.A. .. **77 G6** 36 6N 79 26W
Burlington, N.J., U.S.A. .. **79 F10** 40 4N 74 51W
Burlington, Vt., U.S.A. ... **79 B11** 44 29N 73 12W
Burlington, Wash., U.S.A. . **84 B4** 48 28N 122 20W
Burlington, Wis., U.S.A. .. **76 D1** 42 41N 88 17W
Burlyu-Tyube, Kazakstan . **26 E8** 46 30N 79 10 E
Burma ■, Asia .... **41 J20** 21 0N 96 30 E
Burnaby I., Canada **72 C2** 52 25N 131 19W
Burnet, U.S.A. **81 K5** 30 45N 98 14W
Burney, U.S.A. **82 F3** 40 53N 121 40W
Burnham, U.S.A. **78 F7** 40 38N 77 34W
Burnham-on-Sea, U.K. .. **11 F5** 51 14N 3 0W
Burnie, Australia .... **62 G4** 41 4S 145 56 E
Burnley, U.K. **10 D5** 53 47N 2 14W
Burns, U.S.A. **82 E4** 43 35N 119 3W
Burns Lake, Canada **72 C3** 54 20N 125 45W
Burnside → , Canada ... **68 B9** 66 51N 108 4W
Burnside, L., Australia ... **61 E3** 25 22S 123 0 E
Burnsville, U.S.A. **80 C8** 44 47N 93 17W
Burnt L., Canada **71 B7** 53 35N 64 4W
Burnt River, Canada **78 B6** 44 41N 78 42W
Burntwood → , Canada . **73 B9** 56 8N 96 34W
Burntwood L., Canada ... **73 B8** 55 22N 100 26W
Burqān, Kuwait .... **44 D5** 29 0N 47 57 E
Burra, Australia .... **63 E2** 33 40S 138 55 E
Burray, U.K. **12 C6** 58 51N 2 54W
Burren Junction, Australia . **63 E4** 30 7S 148 59 E
Burriniuck Res., Australia . **63 F4** 35 0S 148 36 E
Burro, Serranías del, Mexico **86 B4** 29 0N 102 0W
Burrow Hd., U.K. **12 G4** 54 41N 4 24W
Burruyacú, Argentina **94 B3** 26 30S 64 40W
Bursa, Turkey .... **21 D13** 40 15N 29 5 E
Burstall, Canada **73 C7** 50 39N 109 54W
Burton, Ohio, U.S.A. **78 E3** 41 28N 81 8W
Burton, S.C., U.S.A. **77 J5** 32 25N 80 45W
Burton, L., Canada **70 B4** 54 45N 78 20W
Burton upon Trent, U.K. .. **10 E6** 52 48N 1 38W

Buru, Indonesia .... **37 E7** 3 30S 126 30 E
Burûn, Râs, Egypt .... **47 D2** 31 14N 33 7 E
Burundi ■, Africa .... **54 C3** 3 15S 30 0 E
Bururi, Burundi .... **54 C2** 3 57S 29 37 E
Burutu, Nigeria .... **50 G7** 5 20N 5 29 E
Burwell, U.S.A. **80 E5** 41 47N 99 8W
Burwick, U.K. **12 C5** 58 45N 2 58W
Bury, U.K. **10 D5** 53 35N 2 17W
Bury St. Edmunds, U.K. .. **11 E8** 52 15N 0 43 E
Buryatia □, Russia ...... **27 D12** 53 0N 110 0 E
Busango Swamp, Zambia . **55 E2** 14 15S 25 45 E
Buşayrah, Syria .... **44 C4** 35 9N 40 26 E
Būshehr, Iran .... **45 D6** 28 55N 50 55 E
Būshehr □, Iran .... **45 D6** 28 20N 51 45 E
Bushell, Canada **73 B7** 59 31N 108 45W
Bushenyi, Uganda .... **54 C3** 0 35S 30 10 E
Bushire = Būshehr, Iran .. **45 D6** 28 55N 50 55 E
Businga,
  Dem. Rep. of the Congo . **52 D4** 3 16N 20 59 E
Buşra ash Shām, Syria ... **47 C5** 32 30N 36 25 E
Busselton, Australia ..... **61 F2** 33 42S 115 15 E
Bussum, Neths. .... **15 B5** 52 16N 5 10 E
Busto Arsízio, Italy ...... **18 D8** 45 37N 8 51 E
Busu-Djanoa,
  Dem. Rep. of the Congo . **52 D4** 1 43N 21 23 E
Busuanga, Phil. .... **37 B6** 12 10N 120 0 E
Buta,
  Dem. Rep. of the Congo . **54 B1** 2 50N 24 53 E
Butare, Rwanda .... **54 C2** 2 31S 29 52 E
Butaritari, Kiribati .... **64 G9** 3 30N 174 0 E
Bute, U.K. **12 F3** 55 48N 5 2W
Bute Inlet, Canada **72 C4** 50 40N 124 53W
Butemba, Uganda .... **54 B3** 1 9N 31 37 E
Butembo,
  Dem. Rep. of the Congo . **54 B2** 0 9N 29 18 E
Butha Qi, China .... **33 B7** 48 0N 122 32 E
Butiaba, Uganda .... **54 B3** 1 50N 31 20 E
Butler, Mo., U.S.A. **80 F7** 38 16N 94 20W
Butler, Pa., U.S.A. **78 F5** 40 52N 79 54W
Buton, Indonesia .... **37 E6** 5 0S 122 45 E
Butte, Mont., U.S.A. **82 C7** 46 0N 112 32W
Butte, Nebr., U.S.A. **80 D5** 42 58N 98 51W
Butte Creek → , U.S.A. .. **84 F5** 39 12N 121 56W
Butterworth =
  Gcuwa, S. Africa .... **57 E4** 32 20S 28 11 E
Butterworth, Malaysia ... **39 K3** 5 24N 100 23 E
Buttevant, Ireland **13 D3** 52 14N 8 40W
Buttfield, Mt., Australia .. **61 D4** 24 45S 128 9 E
Button B., Canada **73 B10** 58 45N 94 23W
Buttonwillow, U.S.A. **85 K7** 35 24N 119 28W
Butty Hd., Australia ..... **61 F3** 33 54S 121 39 E
Butuan, Phil. .... **37 C7** 8 57N 125 33 E
Butung = Buton, Indonesia **37 E6** 5 0S 122 45 E
Buturlinovka, Russia ..... **25 D7** 50 50N 40 35 E
Buxa Duar, India .... **43 F13** 26 45N 89 35 E
Buxar, India .... **43 G10** 25 34N 83 58 E
Buxtehude, Germany .... **16 B5** 53 28N 9 39 E
Buxton, U.K. **10 D6** 53 16N 1 54W
Buy, Russia .... **24 C7** 58 28N 41 28 E
Büyük Menderes → ,
  Turkey .... **21 F12** 37 28N 27 11 E
Büyükçekmece, Turkey .. **21 D13** 41 2N 28 35 E
Büzău, Romania .... **17 F14** 45 10N 26 50 E
Büzău → , Romania ..... **17 F14** 45 26N 27 44 E
Buzen, Japan .... **31 H5** 33 35N 131 5 E
Buzi → , Mozam. .... **55 F3** 19 50S 34 43 E
Buzuluk, Russia .... **24 D9** 52 48N 52 12 E
Buzzards B., U.S.A. **79 E14** 41 45N 70 37W
Buzzards Bay, U.S.A. **79 E14** 41 44N 70 37W
Bwana Mkubwe,
  Dem. Rep. of the Congo . **55 E2** 13 8S 28 38 E
Byarezina → , Belarus ... **17 B16** 52 33N 30 14 E
Bydgoszcz, Poland ...... **17 B9** 53 10N 18 0 E
Byelarus = Belarus ■,
  Europe .... **17 B14** 53 30N 27 0 E
Byelorussia = Belarus ■,
  Europe .... **17 B14** 53 30N 27 0 E
Byers, U.S.A. **80 F2** 39 43N 104 14W
Byesville, U.S.A. **78 G3** 39 58N 81 32W
Byford, Australia .... **61 F2** 32 15S 116 0 E
Byhaw, Belarus .... **17 B16** 53 31N 30 14 E
Bykhov = Byhaw, Belarus **17 B16** 53 31N 30 14 E
Bylas, U.S.A. **83 K8** 33 8N 110 7W
Bylot, Canada **73 B10** 58 25N 94 8W
Bylot I., Canada **69 A12** 73 13N 78 34W
Byrd, C., Antarctica **5 C17** 69 38S 76 7W
Byrock, Australia .... **63 E4** 30 40S 146 27 E
Byron Bay, Australia .... **63 D5** 28 43S 153 37 E
Byrranga, Gory, Russia ... **27 B11** 75 0N 100 0 E
Byrranga Mts. = Byrranga,
  Gory, Russia .... **27 B11** 75 0N 100 0 E
Byske, Sweden .... **8 D19** 64 57N 21 11 E
Byske älv → , Sweden .. **8 D19** 64 57N 21 13 E
Bytom, Poland .... **17 C10** 50 25N 18 54 E
Bytów, Poland .... **17 A9** 54 10N 17 30 E
Byumba, Rwanda .... **54 C3** 1 35S 30 4 E

C

Ca → , Vietnam .... **38 C5** 18 45N 105 45 E
Ca Mau, Vietnam .... **39 H5** 9 7N 105 8 E
Ca Mau, Mui, Vietnam ... **39 H5** 8 38N 104 44 E
Ca Na, Vietnam .... **39 G7** 11 20N 108 54 E
Caacupé, Paraguay **94 B4** 25 23S 57 5W
Caála, Angola .... **53 G3** 12 46S 15 30 E
Caamano Sd., Canada ... **72 C3** 52 55N 129 25W
Caazapá, Paraguay **94 B4** 26 8S 56 19W
Caazapá □, Paraguay **95 B4** 26 10S 56 0W
Cabanatuan, Phil. .... **37 A6** 15 30N 120 58 E
Cabano, Canada **71 C6** 47 40N 68 56W
Cabazon, U.S.A. **85 M10** 33 55N 116 47W
Cabedelo, Brazil **93 E12** 7 0S 34 50W
Cabildo, Chile **94 C1** 32 30S 71 5W
Cabimas, Venezuela **92 A4** 10 23N 71 25W
Cabinda, Angola .... **52 F2** 5 33S 12 11 E
Cabinda □, Angola ...... **52 F2** 5 0S 12 30 E
Cabinet Mts., U.S.A. **82 C6** 48 0N 115 30W
Cabo Blanco, Argentina .. **96 F3** 47 15S 65 47W
Cabo Frio, Brazil **95 A7** 22 51S 42 3W
Cabo Pantoja, Peru **92 D3** 1 0S 75 10W
Cabonga, Réservoir, Canada **70 C4** 47 20N 76 40W
Cabool, U.S.A. **81 G8** 37 7N 92 6W
Caboolture, Australia .... **63 D5** 27 5S 152 58 E

Cárdenas

Cárdenas, *Tabasco, Mexico* **87 D6** 17 59N 93 21W
Cardiff, *U.K.* **11 F4** 51 29N 3 10W
Cardiff □, *U.K.* **11 F4** 51 31N 3 12W
Cardiff-by-the-Sea, *U.S.A.* **85 M9** 33 1N 117 17W
Cardigan, *U.K.* **11 E3** 52 5N 4 40W
Cardigan B., *U.K.* **11 E3** 52 30N 4 30W
Cardinal, *Canada* **79 B9** 44 47N 75 23W
Cardona, *Uruguay* **94 C4** 33 53S 57 18W
Cardoso, Ilha do, *Brazil* **95 B5** 25 8S 47 58W
Cardston, *Canada* **72 D6** 49 15N 113 20W
Cardwell, *Australia* **62 B4** 18 14S 146 2 E
Careen L., *Canada* **73 B7** 57 0N 108 11W
Carei, *Romania* **17 E12** 47 40N 22 29 E
Careme = Ciremai, *Indonesia* **37 G13** 6 55S 108 27 E
Carey, *U.S.A.* **82 E7** 43 19N 113 57W
Carey, L., *Australia* **61 E3** 29 0S 122 15 E
Carey L., *Canada* **73 A8** 62 12N 102 55W
Carhué, *Argentina* **94 D3** 37 10S 62 50W
Caria, *Turkey* **21 F13** 37 20N 28 10 E
Cariacica, *Brazil* **93 H10** 20 16S 40 25W
Caribbean Sea, *W. Indies* **89 D5** 15 0N 75 0W
Cariboo Mts., *Canada* **72 C4** 53 0N 121 0W
Caribou, *U.S.A.* **77 B12** 46 52N 68 1W
Caribou →, *Man., Canada* **73 B10** 59 20N 94 44W
Caribou →, *N.W.T., Canada* **72 A3** 61 27N 125 45W
Caribou I., *Canada* **70 C2** 47 22N 85 49W
Caribou Is., *Canada* **72 A6** 61 55N 113 15W
Caribou L., *Man., Canada* **73 B9** 59 21N 96 10W
Caribou L., *Ont., Canada* **70 B2** 50 25N 89 5W
Caribou Mts., *Canada* **72 B5** 59 12N 115 40W
Carichic, *Mexico* **86 B3** 27 56N 107 3W
Carillo, *Mexico* **86 B4** 26 50N 103 55W
Carinda, *Australia* **63 E4** 30 28S 147 41 E
Carinhanha, *Brazil* **93 F10** 14 15S 44 46W
Carinhanha →, *Brazil* **93 F10** 14 20S 43 47W
Carinthia = Kärnten □, *Austria* **16 E8** 46 52N 13 30 E
Caripito, *Venezuela* **92 A6** 10 8N 63 6W
Carleton, Mt., *Canada* **71 C6** 47 23N 66 53W
Carleton Place, *Canada* **79 A8** 45 8N 76 9W
Carletonville, *S. Africa* **56 D4** 26 23S 27 22 E
Carlin, *U.S.A.* **82 F5** 40 43N 116 7W
Carlingford L., *U.K.* **13 B5** 54 3N 6 9W
Carlinville, *U.S.A.* **80 F10** 39 17N 89 53W
Carlisle, *U.K.* **10 C5** 54 54N 2 56W
Carlisle, *U.S.A.* **78 F7** 40 12N 77 12W
Carlos Casares, *Argentina* **94 D3** 35 32S 61 20W
Carlos Tejedor, *Argentina* **94 D3** 35 25S 62 25W
Carlow, *Ireland* **13 D5** 52 50N 6 56W
Carlow □, *Ireland* **13 D5** 52 43N 6 50W
Carlsbad, *Calif., U.S.A.* **85 M9** 33 10N 117 21W
Carlsbad, *N. Mex., U.S.A.* **81 J2** 32 25N 104 14W
Carlsbad Caverns National Park, *U.S.A.* **81 J2** 32 10N 104 35W
Carluke, *U.K.* **12 F5** 55 45N 3 50W
Carlyle, *Canada* **73 D8** 49 40N 102 20W
Carmacks, *Canada* **68 B6** 62 5N 136 16W
Carman, *Canada* **73 D9** 49 30N 98 0W
Carmarthen, *U.K.* **11 F3** 51 52N 4 19W
Carmarthen B., *U.K.* **11 F3** 51 40N 4 30W
Carmarthenshire □, *U.K.* **11 F3** 51 55N 4 13W
Carmaux, *France* **18 D5** 44 3N 2 10 E
Carmel, *U.S.A.* **79 E11** 41 26N 73 41W
Carmel-by-the-Sea, *U.S.A.* **84 J5** 36 33N 121 55W
Carmel Valley, *U.S.A.* **84 J5** 36 29N 121 43W
Carmelo, *Uruguay* **94 C4** 34 0S 58 20W
Carmen, *Colombia* **92 B3** 9 43N 75 8W
Carmen, *Paraguay* **95 B4** 27 13S 56 12W
Carmen →, *Mexico* **86 A3** 30 42N 106 29W
Carmen, I., *Mexico* **86 B2** 26 0N 111 20W
Carmen de Patagones, *Argentina* **96 E4** 40 50S 63 0W
Carmensa, *Argentina* **94 D2** 35 15S 67 40W
Carmi, *Canada* **72 D5** 49 36N 119 8W
Carmi, *U.S.A.* **76 F1** 38 5N 88 10W
Carmichael, *U.S.A.* **84 G5** 38 38N 121 19W
Carmila, *Australia* **62 C4** 21 55S 149 24 E
Carmona, *Costa Rica* **88 E2** 10 0N 85 15W
Carmona, *Spain* **19 D3** 37 28N 5 42W
Carn Ban, *U.K.* **12 D4** 57 7N 4 15W
Carn Eige, *U.K.* **12 D3** 57 17N 5 8W
Carnac, *France* **18 C2** 47 35N 3 6W
Carnamah, *Australia* **61 E2** 29 41S 115 53 E
Carnarvon, *Australia* **61 D1** 24 51S 113 42 E
Carnarvon, *S. Africa* **56 E3** 30 56S 22 8 E
Carnarvon Ra., *Queens., Australia* **62 D4** 25 15S 148 30 E
Carnarvon Ra., *W. Austral., Australia* **61 E3** 25 20S 120 45 E
Carnation, *U.S.A.* **84 C5** 47 39N 121 55W
Carndonagh, *Ireland* **13 A4** 55 16N 7 15W
Carnduff, *Canada* **73 D8** 49 10N 101 50W
Carnegie, *U.S.A.* **78 F4** 40 24N 80 5W
Carnegie, L., *Australia* **61 E3** 26 5S 122 30 E
Carnic Alps = Karnische Alpen, *Europe* **16 E7** 46 36N 13 0 E
Carniche Alpi = Karnische Alpen, *Europe* **16 E7** 46 36N 13 0 E
Carnot, *C.A.R.* **52 D3** 4 59N 15 56 E
Carnot, C., *Australia* **63 E2** 34 57S 135 38 E
Carnot B., *Australia* **60 C3** 17 20S 122 15 E
Carnoustie, *U.K.* **12 E6** 56 30N 2 42W
Carnsore Pt., *Ireland* **13 D5** 52 10N 6 22W
Caro, *U.S.A.* **76 D4** 43 29N 83 24W
Carol City, *U.S.A.* **77 N5** 25 56N 80 16W
Carolina, *Brazil* **93 E9** 7 10S 47 30W
Carolina, *Puerto Rico* **89 C6** 18 23N 65 58W
Carolina, *S. Africa* **57 D5** 26 5S 30 6 E
Caroline I., *Kiribati* **65 H12** 9 15S 150 3W
Caroline Is., *Micronesia* **28 J17** 8 0N 150 0 E
Caroni →, *Venezuela* **92 B6** 8 21N 62 43W
Caronie = Nébrodi, Monti, *Italy* **20 F6** 37 54N 14 35 E
Caroona, *Australia* **63 E5** 31 24S 150 26 E
Carpathians, *Europe* **17 D11** 49 30N 21 0 E
Carpaţii Meridionali, *Romania* **17 F13** 45 30N 25 0 E
Carpentaria, G. of, *Australia* **62 A2** 14 0S 139 0 E
Carpentras, *France* **18 D6** 44 3N 5 2 E
Carpi, *Italy* **20 B4** 44 47N 10 53 E
Carpinteria, *U.S.A.* **85 L7** 34 24N 119 31W
Carr Boyd Ra., *Australia* **60 C4** 16 15S 128 35 E
Carrabelle, *U.S.A.* **77 L3** 29 51N 84 40W
Carranza, Presa V., *Mexico* **86 B4** 27 20N 100 50W
Carrara, *Italy* **18 D9** 44 5N 10 6 E
Carrauntoohill, *Ireland* **13 D2** 52 0N 9 45W
Carrick-on-Shannon, *Ireland* **13 C3** 53 57N 8 5W
Carrick-on-Suir, *Ireland* **13 D4** 52 21N 7 24W
Carrickfergus, *U.K.* **13 B6** 54 43N 5 49W
Carrickmacross, *Ireland* **13 C5** 53 59N 6 43W
Carrieton, *Australia* **63 E2** 32 25S 138 31 E
Carrington, *U.S.A.* **80 B5** 47 27N 99 8W
Carrizal Bajo, *Chile* **94 B1** 28 5S 71 20W
Carrizalillo, *Chile* **94 B1** 29 5S 71 30W
Carrizo Cr. →, *U.S.A.* **81 G3** 36 55N 103 55W
Carrizo Springs, *U.S.A.* **81 L5** 28 31N 99 52W
Carrizozo, *U.S.A.* **83 K11** 33 38N 105 53W
Carroll, *U.S.A.* **80 D7** 42 4N 94 52W
Carrollton, *Ga., U.S.A.* **77 J3** 33 35N 85 5W
Carrollton, *Ill., U.S.A.* **80 F9** 39 18N 90 24W
Carrollton, *Ky., U.S.A.* **76 F3** 38 41N 85 11W
Carrollton, *Mo., U.S.A.* **80 F8** 39 22N 93 30W
Carrollton, *Ohio, U.S.A.* **78 F3** 40 34N 81 5W
Carron →, *U.K.* **12 D4** 57 53N 4 22W
Carron, L., *U.K.* **12 D3** 57 22N 5 35W
Carrot →, *Canada* **73 C8** 53 50N 101 17W
Carrot River, *Canada* **73 C8** 53 17N 103 35W
Carruthers, *Canada* **73 C7** 52 52N 109 16W
Carson, *Calif., U.S.A.* **85 M8** 33 48N 118 17W
Carson, *N. Dak., U.S.A.* **80 B4** 46 25N 101 34W
Carson →, *U.S.A.* **84 F8** 39 45N 118 40W
Carson City, *U.S.A.* **84 F7** 39 10N 119 46W
Carson Sink, *U.S.A.* **82 G4** 39 50N 118 25W
Cartagena, *Colombia* **92 A3** 10 25N 75 33W
Cartagena, *Spain* **19 D5** 37 38N 0 59W
Cartago, *Colombia* **92 C3** 4 45N 75 55W
Cartago, *Costa Rica* **88 E3** 9 50N 83 55W
Cartersville, *U.S.A.* **77 H3** 34 10N 84 48W
Carterton, *N.Z.* **59 J5** 41 2S 175 31 E
Carthage, *Tunisia* **51 A8** 36 50N 10 21 E
Carthage, *Ill., U.S.A.* **80 E9** 40 25N 91 8W
Carthage, *Mo., U.S.A.* **81 G7** 37 11N 94 19W
Carthage, *N.Y., U.S.A.* **76 D8** 43 59N 75 37W
Carthage, *Tex., U.S.A.* **81 J7** 32 9N 94 20W
Cartier I., *Australia* **60 B3** 12 31S 123 29 E
Cartwright, *Canada* **71 B8** 53 41N 56 58W
Caruaru, *Brazil* **93 E11** 8 15S 35 55W
Carúpano, *Venezuela* **92 A6** 10 39N 63 15W
Caruthersville, *U.S.A.* **81 G10** 36 11N 89 39W
Carvoeiro, *Brazil* **92 D6** 1 30S 61 59W
Carvoeiro, C., *Portugal* **19 C1** 39 21N 9 24W
Cary, *U.S.A.* **77 H6** 35 47N 78 46W
Casa Grande, *U.S.A.* **83 K8** 32 53N 111 45W
Casablanca, *Chile* **94 C1** 33 20S 71 25W
Casablanca, *Morocco* **50 B4** 33 36N 7 36W
Cascade, *Idaho, U.S.A.* **82 D5** 44 31N 116 2W
Cascade, *Mont., U.S.A.* **82 C8** 47 16N 111 42W
Cascade Locks, *U.S.A.* **84 E5** 45 40N 121 54W
Cascade Ra., *U.S.A.* **84 D5** 47 0N 121 30W
Cascade Reservoir, *U.S.A.* **82 D5** 44 32N 116 3W
Cascais, *Portugal* **19 C1** 38 41N 9 25W
Cascavel, *Brazil* **95 A5** 24 57S 53 28W
Cáscina, *Italy* **20 C4** 43 41N 10 33 E
Casco B., *U.S.A.* **77 D10** 43 45N 70 0W
Caserta, *Italy* **20 D6** 41 4N 14 20 E
Cashel, *Ireland* **13 D4** 52 30N 7 53W
Casiguran, *Phil.* **37 A6** 16 22N 122 7 E
Casilda, *Argentina* **94 C3** 33 10S 61 10W
Casino, *Australia* **63 D5** 28 52S 153 3 E
Casiquiare →, *Venezuela* **92 C5** 2 1N 67 7W
Casma, *Peru* **92 E3** 9 30S 78 20W
Casmalia, *U.S.A.* **85 L6** 34 50N 120 32W
Caspe, *Spain* **19 B5** 41 14N 0 1W
Casper, *U.S.A.* **82 E10** 42 51N 106 19W
Caspian Depression, *Eurasia* **25 E8** 47 0N 48 0 E
Caspian Sea, *Eurasia* **25 F9** 43 0N 50 0 E
Cass Lake, *U.S.A.* **80 B7** 47 23N 94 37W
Cassadaga, *U.S.A.* **78 D5** 42 20N 79 19W
Casselman, *Canada* **79 A9** 45 19N 75 5W
Casselton, *U.S.A.* **80 B6** 46 54N 97 13W
Cassiar, *Canada* **72 B3** 59 16N 129 40W
Cassiar Mts., *Canada* **72 B2** 59 30N 130 30W
Cassino, *Italy* **20 D5** 41 30N 13 49 E
Cassville, *U.S.A.* **81 G8** 36 41N 93 52W
Castaic, *U.S.A.* **85 L8** 34 30N 118 38W
Castalia, *U.S.A.* **78 E2** 41 24N 82 49W
Castanhal, *Brazil* **93 D9** 1 18S 47 55W
Castellammare di Stábia, *Italy* **20 D6** 40 42N 14 29 E
Castelli, *Argentina* **94 D4** 36 7S 57 47W
Castelló de la Plana, *Spain* **19 C5** 39 58N 0 3W
Castelo, *Brazil* **95 A7** 20 33S 41 14W
Castelo Branco, *Portugal* **19 C2** 39 50N 7 31W
Castelsarrasin, *France* **18 E4** 44 2N 1 7 E
Castelvetrano, *Italy* **20 F5** 37 41N 12 47 E
Casterton, *Australia* **63 F3** 37 30S 141 30 E
Castile, *U.S.A.* **78 D6** 42 38N 78 3W
Castilla-La Mancha □, *Spain* **19 C4** 39 30N 3 30W
Castilla y Leon □, *Spain* **19 B3** 42 0N 5 0W
Castillos, *Uruguay* **95 C5** 34 12S 53 52W
Castle Dale, *U.S.A.* **82 G8** 39 13N 111 1W
Castle Douglas, *U.K.* **12 G5** 54 56N 3 56W
Castle Rock, *Colo., U.S.A.* **80 F2** 39 22N 104 51W
Castle Rock, *Wash., U.S.A.* **84 D4** 46 17N 122 54W
Castlebar, *Ireland* **13 C2** 53 52N 9 18W
Castleblaney, *Ireland* **13 B5** 54 7N 6 44W
Castlederg, *U.K.* **13 B4** 54 42N 7 35W
Castleford, *U.K.* **10 D6** 53 43N 1 21W
Castlegar, *Canada* **72 D5** 49 20N 117 40W
Castlemaine, *Australia* **63 F3** 37 2S 144 12 E
Castlepollard, *Ireland* **13 C4** 53 41N 7 19W
Castlerea, *Ireland* **13 C3** 53 46N 8 29W
Castlereagh →, *Australia* **63 E4** 30 12S 147 32 E
Castlereagh B., *Australia* **62 A2** 12 10S 135 10 E
Castleton, *U.S.A.* **79 C11** 43 37N 73 11W
Castletown, *U.K.* **10 C3** 54 5N 4 38W
Castletown Bearhaven, *Ireland* **13 E2** 51 39N 9 55W
Castor, *Canada* **72 C6** 52 15N 111 50W
Castor →, *Canada* **70 B4** 53 24N 78 58W
Castorland, *U.S.A.* **79 C9** 43 53N 75 31W
Castres, *France* **18 E5** 43 37N 2 13 E
Castricum, *Neths.* **15 B4** 52 33N 4 40 E
Castries, *St. Lucia* **89 D7** 14 2N 60 58W
Castro, *Brazil* **95 A6** 24 45S 50 0W
Castro, *Chile* **96 E2** 42 30S 73 50W
Castro Alves, *Brazil* **93 F11** 12 46S 39 33W
Castroville, *U.S.A.* **84 J5** 36 46N 121 45W
Castuera, *Spain* **19 C3** 38 43N 5 37W
Cat Ba, Dao, *Vietnam* **38 B6** 20 50N 107 0 E
Cat I., *Bahamas* **89 B4** 24 30N 75 30W
Cat L., *Canada* **70 B1** 51 40N 91 50W
Cat Lake, *Canada* **70 B1** 51 40N 91 50W
Catacamas, *Honduras* **88 D2** 14 54N 85 56W
Cataguases, *Brazil* **95 A7** 21 23S 42 39W
Catalão, *Brazil* **93 G9** 18 10S 47 57W
Çatalca, *Turkey* **21 D13** 41 8N 28 27 E
Catalina, *Canada* **71 C9** 48 31N 53 4W
Catalina, *Chile* **94 B2** 25 13S 69 43W
Catalina, *U.S.A.* **83 K8** 32 30N 110 50W
Catalonia = Cataluña □, *Spain* **19 B6** 41 40N 1 15 E
Cataluña □, *Spain* **19 B6** 41 40N 1 15 E
Catamarca, *Argentina* **94 B2** 28 30S 65 50W
Catamarca □, *Argentina* **94 B2** 27 0S 65 50W
Catanduanes, *Phil.* **37 B6** 13 50N 124 20 E
Catanduva, *Brazil* **95 A6** 21 5S 48 58W
Catánia, *Italy* **20 F6** 37 30N 15 6 E
Catanzaro, *Italy* **20 E7** 38 54N 16 35 E
Catarman, *Phil.* **37 B6** 12 28N 124 35 E
Cateel, *Phil.* **37 C7** 7 47N 126 24 E
Caterham, *U.K.* **11 F7** 51 15N 0 4W
Cathcart, *S. Africa* **56 E4** 32 18S 27 10 E
Cathlamet, *U.S.A.* **84 D3** 46 12N 123 23W
Catlettsburg, *U.S.A.* **76 F4** 38 25N 82 36W
Catoche, C., *Mexico* **87 C7** 21 40N 87 8W
Catriló, *Argentina* **94 D3** 36 26S 63 24W
Catrimani, *Brazil* **92 C6** 0 27N 61 41W
Catrimani →, *Brazil* **92 C6** 0 28N 61 44W
Catskill, *U.S.A.* **79 D11** 42 14N 73 52W
Catskill Mts., *U.S.A.* **79 D10** 42 10N 74 25W
Catt, Mt., *Australia* **62 A1** 13 49S 134 23 E
Cattaraugus, *U.S.A.* **78 D6** 42 22N 78 52W
Catuala, *Angola* **56 B2** 16 25S 19 2 E
Catur, *Mozam.* **55 E4** 13 45S 35 30 E
Catwick Is., *Vietnam* **39 H7** 10 0N 109 0 E
Cauca →, *Colombia* **92 B4** 8 54N 74 28W
Caucaia, *Brazil* **93 D11** 3 40S 38 35W
Caucasus Mountains, *Eurasia* **25 F7** 42 50N 44 0 E
Caungula, *Angola* **52 F3** 8 26S 18 38 E
Cauquenes, *Chile* **94 D1** 36 0S 72 22W
Caura →, *Venezuela* **92 B6** 7 38N 64 53W
Cauresi →, *Mozam.* **55 F3** 17 8S 33 0 E
Causapscal, *Canada* **71 C6** 48 19N 67 12W
Cauvery →, *India* **40 P11** 11 9N 78 52 E
Caux, Pays de, *France* **18 B4** 49 38N 0 35 E
Cavalier, *U.S.A.* **80 A6** 48 48N 97 37W
Cavalleria, C. de, *Spain* **22 A11** 40 5N 4 5 E
Cavan, *Ireland* **13 B4** 54 0N 7 22W
Cavan □, *Ireland* **13 C4** 54 1N 7 16W
Cave Creek, *U.S.A.* **83 K7** 33 50N 111 57W
Cavenagh Ra., *Australia* **61 E4** 26 12S 127 55 E
Cavendish, *Australia* **63 F3** 37 31S 142 2 E
Caviana, I., *Brazil* **93 C8** 0 10N 50 10W
Cavite, *Phil.* **37 B6** 14 29N 120 55 E
Cawndilla L., *Australia* **63 E3** 32 30S 142 15 E
Cawnpore = Kanpur, *India* **43 F9** 26 28N 80 20 E
Caxias, *Brazil* **93 D10** 4 55S 43 20W
Caxias do Sul, *Brazil* **95 B5** 29 10S 51 10W
Cay Sal Bank, *Bahamas* **88 B4** 23 45N 80 0W
Cayambe, *Ecuador* **92 C3** 0 3N 78 8W
Cayenne, *Fr. Guiana* **93 B8** 5 5N 52 18W
Cayman Brac, *Cayman Is.* **88 C4** 19 43N 79 49W
Cayman Is. ■, *W. Indies* **88 C3** 19 40N 80 30W
Cayo Romano, *Cuba* **88 B4** 22 0N 78 0W
Cayuga, *Canada* **78 D5** 42 59N 79 50W
Cayuga, *U.S.A.* **79 D8** 42 54N 76 44W
Cayuga L., *U.S.A.* **79 D8** 42 41N 76 41W
Cazenovia, *U.S.A.* **79 D9** 42 56N 75 51W
Cazombo, *Angola* **53 G4** 11 54S 22 56 E
Ceanannus Mor, *Ireland* **13 C5** 53 44N 6 53W
Ceará = Fortaleza, *Brazil* **93 D11** 3 45S 38 35W
Ceará □, *Brazil* **93 E11** 5 0S 40 0W
Ceará Mirim, *Brazil* **93 E11** 5 38S 35 25W
Cebaco, I. de, *Panama* **88 E3** 7 33N 81 9W
Cebollar, *Argentina* **94 B2** 29 10S 66 35W
Cebu, *Phil.* **37 B6** 10 18N 123 54 E
Cecil Plains, *Australia* **63 D5** 27 30S 151 11 E
Cedar →, *U.S.A.* **80 E9** 41 17N 91 21W
Cedar City, *U.S.A.* **83 H7** 37 41N 113 4W
Cedar Creek Reservoir, *U.S.A.* **81 J6** 32 11N 96 4W
Cedar Falls, *Iowa, U.S.A.* **80 D8** 42 32N 92 27W
Cedar Falls, *Wash., U.S.A.* **84 C5** 47 25N 121 45W
Cedar L., *Canada* **73 C9** 53 10N 100 0W
Cedar Rapids, *U.S.A.* **80 E9** 41 59N 91 40W
Cedartown, *U.S.A.* **77 H3** 34 1N 85 15W
Cedarvale, *Canada* **72 B3** 55 1N 128 22W
Cedarville, *S. Africa* **57 E4** 30 23S 29 3 E
Cedral, *Mexico* **86 C4** 23 50N 100 42W
Cedro, *Brazil* **93 E11** 6 34S 39 3W
Cedros, I. de, *Mexico* **86 B1** 28 10N 115 20W
Ceduna, *Australia* **63 E1** 32 7S 133 46 E
Cefalù, *Italy* **20 E6** 38 2N 14 1 E
Cegléd, *Hungary* **17 E10** 47 11N 19 47 E
Celaya, *Mexico* **86 C4** 20 31N 100 37W
Celebes = Sulawesi □, *Indonesia* **37 E6** 2 0S 120 0 E
Celebes Sea, *Indonesia* **37 D6** 3 0N 123 0 E
Celina, *U.S.A.* **76 E3** 40 33N 84 35W
Celje, *Slovenia* **16 E8** 46 16N 15 18 E
Celle, *Germany* **16 B6** 52 37N 10 4 E
Cenderwasih, Teluk, *Indonesia* **37 E9** 3 0S 135 20 E
Center, *N. Dak., U.S.A.* **80 B4** 47 7N 101 18W
Center, *Tex., U.S.A.* **81 K7** 31 48N 94 11W
Centerburg, *U.S.A.* **78 F2** 40 18N 82 42W
Centerville, *Calif., U.S.A.* **84 J7** 36 44N 119 30W
Centerville, *Iowa, U.S.A.* **80 E8** 40 44N 92 52W
Centerville, *Pa., U.S.A.* **78 F5** 40 3N 79 59W
Centerville, *Tenn., U.S.A.* **77 H2** 35 47N 87 28W
Centerville, *Tex., U.S.A.* **81 K7** 31 16N 95 59W
Central □, *Kenya* **54 C4** 0 30S 37 30 E
Central □, *Malawi* **55 E3** 13 30S 33 30 E
Central □, *Zambia* **55 E2** 14 25S 28 50 E
Central, Cordillera, *Colombia* **92 C4** 5 0N 75 0W
Central, Cordillera, *Costa Rica* **88 D3** 10 10N 84 5W
Central, Cordillera, *Dom. Rep.* **89 C5** 19 15N 71 0W
Central African Rep. ■, *Africa* **52 C4** 7 0N 20 0 E
Central America, *America* **66 H11** 12 0N 85 0W
Central Butte, *Canada* **73 C7** 50 48N 106 31W
Central City, *Colo., U.S.A.* **82 G11** 39 48N 105 31W
Central City, *Ky., U.S.A.* **76 G2** 37 18N 87 7W
Central City, *Nebr., U.S.A.* **80 E6** 41 7N 98 0W
Central I., *Kenya* **54 B4** 3 30N 36 0 E
Central Makran Range, *Pakistan* **40 F4** 26 30N 64 15 E
Central Patricia, *Canada* **70 B1** 51 30N 90 9W
Central Point, *U.S.A.* **82 E2** 42 23N 122 55W
Central Russian Uplands, *Europe* **6 E13** 54 0N 36 0 E
Central Siberian Plateau, *Russia* **28 C14** 65 0N 105 0 E
Central Square, *U.S.A.* **79 C8** 43 17N 76 9W
Centralia, *Ill., U.S.A.* **80 F10** 38 32N 89 8W
Centralia, *Mo., U.S.A.* **80 F8** 39 13N 92 8W
Centralia, *Wash., U.S.A.* **84 D4** 46 43N 122 58W
Cephalonia = Kefallinía, *Greece* **21 E9** 38 20N 20 30 E
Cepu, *Indonesia* **37 G14** 7 9S 111 35 E
Ceram = Seram, *Indonesia* **37 E7** 3 10S 129 0 E
Ceram Sea = Seram Sea, *Indonesia* **37 E7** 2 30S 128 30 E
Ceredigion □, *U.K.* **11 E3** 52 16N 4 15W
Ceres, *Argentina* **94 B3** 29 55S 61 55W
Ceres, *S. Africa* **56 E2** 33 21S 19 18 E
Ceres, *U.S.A.* **84 H6** 37 35N 120 57W
Cerignola, *Italy* **20 D6** 41 17N 15 53 E
Cerigo = Kíthira, *Greece* **21 F10** 36 8N 23 0 E
Çerkezköy, *Turkey* **21 D12** 41 17N 28 0 E
Cerralvo, I., *Mexico* **86 C3** 24 20N 109 45W
Cerritos, *Mexico* **86 C4** 22 27N 100 20W
Cerro Chato, *Uruguay* **95 C4** 33 6S 55 8W
Cerventes, *Australia* **61 F2** 30 31S 115 3 E
Cervera, *Spain* **19 B6** 41 40N 1 16 E
Cesena, *Italy* **20 B5** 44 8N 12 15 E
Cēsis, *Latvia* **9 H21** 57 18N 25 15 E
České Budějovice, *Czech Rep.* **16 D8** 48 55N 14 25 E
Českomoravská Vrchovina, *Czech Rep.* **16 D8** 49 30N 15 40 E
Çeşme, *Turkey* **21 E12** 38 20N 26 23 E
Cessnock, *Australia* **63 E5** 32 50S 151 21 E
Cetinje, *Montenegro, Yug.* **21 C8** 42 23N 18 59 E
Cetraro, *Italy* **20 E6** 39 31N 15 55 E
Ceuta, *N. Afr.* **19 E3** 35 52N 5 18W
Cévennes, *France* **18 D5** 44 10N 3 50 E
Ceyhan, *Turkey* **44 B2** 37 4N 35 47 E
Ceylon = Sri Lanka ■, *Asia* **40 R12** 7 30N 80 50 E
Cha-am, *Thailand* **38 F2** 12 48N 99 58 E
Cha Pa, *Vietnam* **38 A4** 22 20N 103 47 E
Chacabuco, *Argentina* **94 C3** 34 40S 60 27W
Chachapoyas, *Peru* **92 E3** 6 15S 77 50W
Chachoengsao, *Thailand* **38 F3** 13 42N 101 5 E
Chachran, *Pakistan* **40 E7** 28 55N 70 30 E
Chachro, *Pakistan* **42 G4** 25 5N 70 15 E
Chaco □, *Argentina* **94 B3** 26 30S 61 0W
Chaco □, *Paraguay* **94 B4** 26 0S 60 0W
Chaco →, *U.S.A.* **83 H9** 36 46N 108 39W
Chaco Austral, *S. Amer.* **96 B4** 27 0S 61 30W
Chaco Boreal, *S. Amer.* **92 H6** 22 0S 60 0W
Chaco Central, *S. Amer.* **96 A4** 24 0S 61 0W
Chacon, C., *U.S.A.* **72 C2** 54 42N 132 0W
Chad ■, *Africa* **51 F8** 15 0N 17 15 E
Chad, L. = Tchad, L., *Chad* **51 F8** 13 30N 14 30 E
Chadan, *Russia* **27 D10** 51 17N 91 35 E
Chadileuvú →, *Argentina* **94 D2** 37 46S 66 0W
Chadiza, *Zambia* **55 E3** 14 45S 32 27 E
Chadron, *U.S.A.* **80 D3** 42 50N 103 0W
Chadyr-Lunga = Ciadâr-Lunga, *Moldova* **17 E15** 46 3N 28 51 E
Chae Hom, *Thailand* **38 C2** 18 43N 99 35 E
Chaem →, *Thailand* **38 C2** 18 11N 98 38 E
Chaeryŏng, *N. Korea* **35 E13** 38 24N 125 36 E
Chagai Hills, *Afghan.* **40 E3** 29 30N 63 0 E
Chagda, *Russia* **27 D14** 58 45N 130 38 E
Chagos Arch., *Ind. Oc.* **29 K11** 6 0S 72 0 E
Chagrin Falls, *U.S.A.* **78 E3** 41 26N 81 24W
Chāh Ākhvor, *Iran* **45 C8** 32 41N 59 40 E
Chāh Bahār, *Iran* **45 E9** 25 20N 60 40 E
Chāh-e Kavīr, *Iran* **45 C8** 34 29N 56 52 E
Chahar Burjak, *Afghan.* **40 D3** 30 15N 62 0 E
Chahār Mahāll va Bakhtīarī □, *Iran* **45 C6** 32 0N 49 0 E
Chaibasa, *India* **41 H14** 22 42N 85 49 E
Chainat, *Thailand* **38 E3** 15 11N 100 8 E
Chaiya, *Thailand* **39 H2** 9 23N 99 14 E
Chaj Doab, *Pakistan* **42 C5** 32 15N 73 0 E
Chajari, *Argentina* **94 C4** 30 42S 58 0W
Chak Amru, *Pakistan* **42 C6** 32 22N 75 11 E
Chakar →, *Pakistan* **42 E3** 29 29N 68 2 E
Chake Chake, *Tanzania* **54 D4** 5 15S 39 45 E
Chakhānsūr, *Afghan.* **40 D3** 31 10N 62 0 E
Chakonipau, L., *Canada* **71 A6** 56 18N 68 30W
Chakradharpur, *India* **43 H11** 22 45N 85 40 E
Chakrata, *India* **42 D7** 30 42N 77 51 E
Chakwal, *Pakistan* **42 C5** 32 56N 72 53 E
Chala, *Peru* **92 G4** 15 48S 74 20W
Chalchihuites, *Mexico* **86 C4** 23 29N 103 53W
Chalcis = Khalkís, *Greece* **21 E10** 38 27N 23 42 E
Chaleur B., *Canada* **71 C6** 47 55N 65 30W
Chalfant, *U.S.A.* **84 H8** 37 32N 118 21W
Chalhuanca, *Peru* **92 F4** 14 15S 73 15W
Chalisgaon, *India* **40 J9** 20 30N 75 10 E
Chalk River, *Canada* **70 C4** 46 1N 77 27W
Chalky Inlet, *N.Z.* **59 M1** 46 3S 166 31 E
Challapata, *Bolivia* **92 G5** 18 53S 66 50W
Challis, *U.S.A.* **82 D6** 44 30N 114 14W
Chalmette, *U.S.A.* **81 L10** 29 56N 89 58W
Chalon-sur-Saône, *France* **18 C6** 46 48N 4 50 E
Châlons-en-Champagne, *France* **18 B6** 48 58N 4 20 E
Chalyaphum, *Thailand* **38 E4** 15 48N 102 2 E
Cham, Cu Lao, *Vietnam* **38 E7** 15 57N 108 30 E
Chama, *U.S.A.* **83 H10** 36 54N 106 35W
Chamaicó, *Argentina* **94 D3** 35 3S 64 58W
Chaman, *Pakistan* **40 D5** 30 58N 66 25 E
Chamba, *India* **42 C7** 32 35N 76 10 E
Chamba, *Tanzania* **55 E4** 11 37S 37 0 E
Chambal →, *India* **43 F8** 26 29N 79 15 E
Chamberlain, *U.S.A.* **80 D5** 43 49N 99 20W
Chamberlain →, *Australia* **60 C4** 15 30S 127 54 E
Chamberlain L., *U.S.A.* **77 B11** 46 14N 69 19W
Chambers, *U.S.A.* **83 J9** 35 11N 109 26W
Chambersburg, *U.S.A.* **76 F7** 39 56N 77 40W
Chambéry, *France* **18 D6** 45 34N 5 55 E
Chambeshi →, *Zambia* **52 G6** 11 53S 29 48 E
Chambly, *Canada* **79 A11** 45 27N 73 17W
Chambord, *Canada* **71 C5** 48 25N 72 6W
Chamchamal, *Iraq* **44 C5** 35 32N 44 50 E
Chamela, *Mexico* **86 D3** 19 32N 105 5W

Chinchilla

amical, Argentina 94 C2 30 22S 66 27W
amkar Luong, Cambodia 39 G4 11 0N 103 45 E
amoli, India 43 D8 30 24N 79 21 E
amonix-Mont Blanc,
France 18 D7 45 55N 6 51 E
amouchouane →,
Canada 70 C5 48 37N 72 20W
ampa, India 43 H10 22 2N 82 43 E
ampagne, Canada 72 A1 60 49N 136 30W
ampagne, France 18 B6 48 40N 4 20 E
ampaign, U.S.A. 76 E1 40 7N 88 15W
ampassak, Laos 38 E5 14 53N 105 52 E
ampawat, India 43 E9 29 20N 80 6 E
ampdoré, L., Canada 71 A6 55 55N 65 49W
ampion, U.S.A. 78 E4 41 19N 80 51W
amplain, U.S.A. 79 B11 44 59N 73 27W
amplain, L., U.S.A. 79 B11 44 40N 73 20W
ampotón, Mexico 87 D6 19 20N 90 50W
ampua, India 43 H11 22 5N 85 40 E
ana, Thailand 39 J3 6 55N 100 44 E
añaral, Chile 94 B1 26 23S 70 40W
anārān, Iran 45 B8 36 39N 59 6 E
anasma, India 42 H5 23 44N 72 5 E
anco, Chile 94 D1 35 44S 72 32W
and, India 43 J8 21 57N 79 7 E
andan, India 43 G12 24 38N 86 40 E
andan Chauki, India 43 E9 28 33N 80 47 E
andannagar, India 43 H13 22 52N 88 24 E
andausi, India 43 E8 28 27N 78 49 E
andeleur Is., U.S.A. 81 L10 29 55N 88 57W
andeleur Sd., U.S.A. 81 L10 29 55N 89 0W
andigarh, India 42 D7 30 43N 76 47 E
andil, India 43 H12 22 58N 86 3 E
andler, Australia 63 D1 27 0S 133 19 E
andler, Canada 71 C7 48 18N 64 46W
andler, Ariz., U.S.A. 83 K8 33 18N 111 50W
andler, Okla., U.S.A. 81 H6 35 42N 96 53W
andod, India 42 J5 21 59N 73 28 E
andpur, Bangla. 41 H17 23 8N 90 45 E
andrapur, India 40 K11 19 57N 79 25 E
ānf, Iran 45 E9 26 38N 60 29 E
ang, Pakistan 42 F3 26 59N 68 30 E
ang, Ko, Thailand 39 G4 12 0N 102 23 E
'ang Chiang = Chang
Jiang →, China 33 C7 31 48N 121 10 E
ang Jiang →, China 33 C7 31 48N 121 10 E
anga, India 43 C7 33 53N 77 35 E
anganacheri, India 40 Q10 9 25N 76 31 E
angane →, Mozam. 57 C5 24 30S 33 30 E
angbai, China 35 D15 41 25N 128 5 E
angbai Shan, China 35 C15 42 20N 129 0 E
angchiak'ou =
Zhangjiakou, China 34 D8 40 48N 114 55 E
'angchou = Changzhou,
China 33 C6 31 47N 119 58 E
angchun, China 35 C13 43 57N 125 17 E
angchunling, China 35 B13 45 18N 125 27 E
angde, China 33 D6 29 4N 111 35 E
angdo-ri, N. Korea 35 E14 38 30N 127 40 E
anghai = Shanghai,
China 33 C7 31 15N 121 26 E
anghua, Taiwan 33 D7 24 2N 120 30 E
anghŭng, S. Korea 35 G14 34 41N 126 52 E
anghŭngni, N. Korea 35 D15 40 24N 128 19 E
angjiang, China 38 C7 19 20N 108 55 E
angjin, N. Korea 35 D14 40 23N 127 15 E
angjin-chŏsuji, N. Korea 35 D14 40 30N 127 15 E
angli, China 35 E10 39 40N 119 13 E
angling, China 35 B12 44 20N 123 58 E
anglun, Malaysia 39 J3 6 25N 100 26 E
angping, China 34 D9 40 14N 116 12 E
angsha, China 33 D6 28 12N 113 0 E
angwu, China 34 G4 35 10N 107 45 E
angyi, China 35 F10 36 40N 119 30 E
angyŏn, N. Korea 35 E13 38 15N 125 6 E
angyuan, China 34 G8 35 15N 114 42 E
angzhi, China 34 F7 36 10N 113 6 E
angzhou, China 33 C6 31 47N 119 58 E
anhanga, Angola 56 B1 16 0S 14 8 E
annapatna, India 40 N10 12 40N 77 15 E
annel Is., U.K. 11 H5 49 19N 2 24W
annel Is., U.S.A. 85 M7 33 40N 119 15W
annel Islands National
Park, U.S.A. 85 M8 33 30N 119 0W
annel-Port aux Basques,
Canada 71 C8 47 30N 59 9W
annel Tunnel, Europe 11 F9 51 0N 1 30 E
anning, U.S.A. 81 H3 35 41N 102 20W
antada, Spain 19 A2 42 36N 7 46W
anthaburi, Thailand 38 F4 12 38N 102 12 E
antrey Inlet, Canada 68 B10 67 48N 96 20W
anute, U.S.A. 81 G7 37 41N 95 27W
ao Phraya →, Thailand 38 F3 13 32N 100 36 E
ao Phraya Lowlands,
Thailand 38 E3 15 30N 100 0 E
aocheng, China 34 F8 36 4N 115 37 E
aoyang, China 35 D11 41 35N 120 22 E
aozhou, China 33 D6 23 42N 116 32 E
apais, Canada 70 C5 49 47N 74 51W
apala, Mozam. 55 F4 15 50S 37 35 E
apala, L. de, Mexico 86 C4 20 10N 103 20W
apayev, Kazakstan 25 D9 50 25N 51 10 E
apayevsk, Russia 24 D8 53 0N 49 40 E
apecó, Brazil 95 B5 27 14S 52 41W
apel Hill, U.S.A. 77 H6 35 55N 79 4W
apleau, Canada 70 C3 47 50N 83 24W
aplin, Canada 73 C7 50 28N 106 40W
aplin L., Canada 73 C7 50 22N 106 36W
appell, U.S.A. 80 E3 41 6N 102 28W
apra = Chhapra, India 43 G11 25 48N 84 44 E
ara, Russia 27 D12 56 54N 118 20 E
aradai, Argentina 94 B4 27 35S 59 55W
araguá, Bolivia 92 G6 19 45S 63 10W
arambirá, Punta,
Colombia 92 C3 4 16N 77 32W
araña, Bolivia 92 G5 17 30S 69 25W
aranwala, India 42 F5 27 51N 72 10 E
arata, Argentina 94 B3 27 13S 61 14W
arcas, Mexico 86 C4 23 10N 101 20W
ard, U.K. 11 G5 50 52N 2 58W
ardon, U.S.A. 78 E3 41 35N 81 12W
ardzhou = Chärjew,
Turkmenistan 26 F7 39 6N 63 34 E
arente →, France 18 D3 45 57N 1 5W
ari →, Chad 51 F8 12 58N 14 31 E
ārīkār, Afghan. 40 B6 35 0N 69 10 E
ariton →, U.S.A. 80 F8 39 19N 92 58W
Chärjew, Turkmenistan 26 F7 39 6N 63 34 E
Charkhari, India 43 G8 25 24N 79 45 E
Charkhi Dadri, India 42 E7 28 37N 76 17 E
Charleroi, Belgium 15 D4 50 24N 4 27 E
Charleroi, U.S.A. 78 F5 40 9N 79 57W
Charles, C., U.S.A. 76 G8 37 7N 75 58W
Charles City, U.S.A. 80 D8 43 4N 92 41W
Charles L., Canada 73 B6 59 50N 110 33W
Charles Town, U.S.A. 76 F7 39 17N 77 52W
Charleston, Ill., U.S.A. 76 F1 39 30N 88 10W
Charleston, Miss., U.S.A. 81 H9 34 1N 90 4W
Charleston, Mo., U.S.A. 81 G10 36 55N 89 21W
Charleston, S.C., U.S.A. 77 J6 32 46N 79 56W
Charleston, W. Va., U.S.A. 76 F5 38 21N 81 38W
Charleston L., Canada 79 B9 44 32N 76 0W
Charleston Peak, U.S.A. 85 J11 36 16N 115 42W
Charlestown, Ireland 13 C3 53 58N 8 48W
Charlestown, S. Africa 57 D4 27 26S 29 53 E
Charlestown, Ind., U.S.A. 76 F3 38 27N 85 40W
Charlestown, N.H., U.S.A. 79 C12 43 14N 72 25W
Charleville = Rath Luirc,
Ireland 13 D3 52 21N 8 40W
Charleville, Australia 63 D4 26 24S 146 15 E
Charleville-Mézières, France 18 B6 49 44N 4 40 E
Charlevoix, U.S.A. 76 C3 45 19N 85 16W
Charlotte, Mich., U.S.A. 76 D3 42 34N 84 50W
Charlotte, N.C., U.S.A. 77 H5 35 13N 80 51W
Charlotte, Vt., U.S.A. 79 B11 44 19N 73 14W
Charlotte Amalie, Virgin Is. 89 C7 18 21N 64 56W
Charlotte Harbor, U.S.A. 77 M4 26 50N 82 10W
Charlotte L., Canada 72 C3 52 12N 125 19W
Charlottesville, U.S.A. 76 F6 38 2N 78 30W
Charlottetown, Nfld.,
Canada 71 B8 52 46N 56 7W
Charlottetown, P.E.I.,
Canada 71 C7 46 14N 63 8W
Charlton, Australia 63 F3 36 16S 143 24 E
Charlton, U.S.A. 80 E8 40 59N 93 20W
Charlton I., Canada 70 B4 52 0N 79 20W
Charny, Canada 71 C5 46 43N 71 15W
Charolles, France 18 C6 46 27N 4 16 E
Charre, Mozam. 55 F4 17 13S 35 10 E
Charsadda, Pakistan 42 B4 34 7N 71 45 E
Charters Towers, Australia 62 C4 20 5S 146 13 E
Chartres, France 18 B4 48 29N 1 30 E
Chascomús, Argentina 94 D4 35 30S 58 0W
Chasefu, Zambia 55 E3 11 55S 33 8 E
Chashma Barrage, Pakistan 42 C4 32 27N 71 20 E
Chāt, Iran 45 B7 37 59N 55 16 E
Châteaubriant, France 18 C3 47 43N 1 23W
Chateaugay, U.S.A. 79 B10 44 56N 74 5W
Châteauguay, L., Canada 71 A5 56 26N 70 3W
Châteaulin, France 18 B1 48 11N 4 8W
Châteauroux, France 18 C4 46 50N 1 40 E
Châtellerault, France 18 C4 46 50N 0 30 E
Chatham = Miramichi,
Canada 71 C6 47 2N 65 28W
Chatham, Canada 78 D2 42 24N 82 11W
Chatham, U.K. 11 F8 51 22N 0 32 E
Chatham, U.S.A. 79 D11 42 21N 73 36W
Chatham Is., Pac. Oc. 64 M10 44 0S 176 40W
Chatmohar, Bangla. 43 G13 24 15N 89 15 E
Chatra, India 43 G11 24 12N 84 56 E
Chatrapur, India 41 K14 19 22N 85 2 E
Chats, L. des, Canada 79 A8 45 30N 76 20W
Chatsu, India 42 F6 26 36N 75 57 E
Chatsworth, Canada 78 B4 44 27N 80 54W
Chatsworth, Zimbabwe 55 F3 19 38S 31 13 E
Chattahoochee, U.S.A. 77 K3 30 42N 84 51W
Chattahoochee →, U.S.A. 77 K3 30 54N 84 57W
Chattanooga, U.S.A. 77 H3 35 3N 85 19W
Chatteris, U.K. 11 E8 52 28N 0 2 E
Chaturat, Thailand 38 E3 15 40N 101 51 E
Chau Doc, Vietnam 39 G5 10 42N 105 7 E
Chauk, Burma 41 J19 20 53N 94 49 E
Chaukan La, Burma 41 F20 27 0N 97 15 E
Chaumont, France 18 B6 48 7N 5 8 E
Chaumont, U.S.A. 79 B8 44 4N 76 8W
Chautauqua L., U.S.A. 78 D5 42 10N 79 24W
Chauvin, Canada 73 C6 52 45N 110 10W
Chaves, Brazil 93 D9 0 15S 49 55W
Chaves, Portugal 19 B2 41 45N 7 32W
Chawang, Thailand 39 H2 8 25N 99 30 E
Chaykovskiy, Russia 24 C9 56 47N 54 9 E
Chazy, U.S.A. 79 B11 44 53N 73 26W
Cheb, Czech Rep. 16 C7 50 9N 12 28 E
Cheboksary, Russia 24 C8 56 8N 47 12 E
Cheboygan, U.S.A. 76 C3 45 39N 84 29W
Chech, Erg, Africa 50 D5 25 0N 2 15W
Chechenia □, Russia 25 F8 43 30N 45 29 E
Checheno-Ingush Republic
= Chechenia □, Russia 25 F8 43 30N 45 29 E
Chechnya = Chechenia □,
Russia 25 F8 43 30N 45 29 E
Chech'ŏn, S. Korea 35 F15 37 8N 128 12 E
Checotah, U.S.A. 81 H7 35 28N 95 31W
Chedabucto B., Canada 71 C7 45 25N 61 8W
Cheduba I., Burma 41 K18 18 45N 93 40 E
Cheepie, Australia 63 D4 26 33S 145 1 E
Chegdomyn, Russia 27 D14 51 7N 133 1 E
Chegga, Mauritania 50 C4 25 27N 5 40W
Chegutu, Zimbabwe 55 F3 18 10S 30 14 E
Chehalis, U.S.A. 84 D4 46 40N 122 58W
Chehalis →, U.S.A. 84 D3 46 57N 123 50W
Cheju do, S. Korea 35 H14 33 29N 126 34 E
Chekiang = Zhejiang □,
China 33 D7 29 0N 120 0 E
Chela, Sa. da, Angola 56 B1 16 20S 13 20 E
Chelan, U.S.A. 82 C4 47 51N 120 1W
Chelan, L., U.S.A. 82 B3 48 11N 120 30W
Cheleken, Turkmenistan 25 G9 39 34N 53 16 E
Cheleken Yarymadasy,
Turkmenistan 45 B7 39 30N 53 15 E
Chelforó, Argentina 96 D3 39 0S 66 33W
Chelkar = Shalqar,
Kazakstan 26 E6 47 48N 59 39 E
Chelkar Tengiz, Solonchak,
Kazakstan 26 E7 48 5N 63 7 E
Chełm, Poland 17 C12 51 8N 23 30 E
Chełmno, Poland 17 B10 53 20N 18 30 E
Chelmsford, U.K. 11 F8 51 44N 0 29 E
Chelsea, U.S.A. 79 C12 43 59N 72 27W
Cheltenham, U.K. 11 F5 51 54N 2 4W
Chelyabinsk, Russia 26 D7 55 10N 61 24 E
Chelyuskin, C., Russia 28 B14 77 30N 103 0 E
Chemainus, Canada 84 B3 48 55N 123 42W
Chemba, Mozam. 53 H6 17 9S 34 53 E
Chemnitz, Germany 16 C7 50 51N 12 54 E
Chemult, U.S.A. 82 E3 43 14N 121 47W
Chen, Gora, Russia 27 C15 65 16N 141 50 E
Chenab →, Pakistan 42 D4 30 23N 71 2 E
Chenango Forks, U.S.A. 79 D9 42 15N 75 51W
Cheney, U.S.A. 82 C5 47 30N 117 35W
Cheng Xian, China 34 H3 33 43N 105 42 E
Chengcheng, China 34 G5 35 8N 109 56 E
Chengchou = Zhengzhou,
China 34 G7 34 45N 113 34 E
Chengde, China 35 D9 40 59N 117 58 E
Chengdu, China 32 C5 30 38N 104 2 E
Chenggu, China 34 H4 33 10N 107 21 E
Chengjiang, China 32 D5 24 39N 103 0 E
Ch'engmai, China 38 C7 19 50N 109 58 E
Ch'engtu = Chengdu, China 32 C5 30 38N 104 2 E
Chengwu, China 34 G8 34 58N 115 50 E
Chengyang, China 35 F11 36 18N 120 21 E
Chenjiagang, China 35 G10 34 23N 119 47 E
Chenkán, Mexico 87 D6 19 8N 90 58W
Chennai, India 40 N12 13 8N 80 19 E
Cheo Reo, Vietnam 36 B3 13 25N 108 28 E
Cheom Ksan, Cambodia 38 E5 14 13N 104 56 E
Chepén, Peru 92 E3 7 15S 79 23W
Chepes, Argentina 94 C2 31 20S 66 35W
Chepo, Panama 88 E4 9 10N 79 6W
Chepstow, U.K. 11 F5 51 38N 2 41W
Cheptulil, Mt., Kenya 54 B4 1 25N 35 35 E
Chequamegon B., U.S.A. 80 B9 46 40N 90 30W
Cher →, France 18 C4 47 21N 0 29 E
Cheraw, U.S.A. 77 H6 34 42N 79 53W
Cherbourg, France 18 B3 49 39N 1 40W
Cherdyn, Russia 24 B10 60 24N 56 29 E
Cheremkhovo, Russia 27 D11 53 8N 103 1 E
Cherepanovo, Russia 26 D9 54 15N 83 30 E
Cherepovets, Russia 24 C6 59 5N 37 55 E
Chergui, Chott ech, Algeria 50 B6 34 21N 0 25 E
Cherikov = Cherykaw,
Belarus 17 B16 53 32N 31 20 E
Cherkasy, Ukraine 25 E5 49 27N 32 4 E
Cherkessk, Russia 25 F7 44 15N 42 5 E
Cherlak, Russia 26 D8 54 15N 74 55 E
Chernaya, Russia 27 B9 70 30N 89 10 E
Chernigov = Chernihiv,
Ukraine 24 D5 51 28N 31 20 E
Chernihiv, Ukraine 24 D5 51 28N 31 20 E
Chernivtsi, Ukraine 17 D13 48 15N 25 52 E
Chernobyl = Chornobyl,
Ukraine 17 C16 51 20N 30 15 E
Chernogorsk, Russia 27 D10 53 49N 91 18 E
Chernovtsy = Chernivtsi,
Ukraine 17 D13 48 15N 25 52 E
Chernyakhovsk, Russia 9 J19 54 36N 21 48 E
Chernysheyskiy, Russia 27 C12 63 0N 112 30 E
Cherokee, Iowa, U.S.A. 80 D7 42 45N 95 33W
Cherokee, Okla., U.S.A. 81 G5 36 45N 98 21W
Cherokee Village, U.S.A. 81 G9 36 17N 91 30W
Cherokees, Grand Lake O'
The, U.S.A. 81 G7 36 28N 95 2W
Cherrapunji, India 41 G17 25 17N 91 47 E
Cherry Valley, Calif., U.S.A. 85 M10 33 59N 116 57W
Cherry Valley, N.Y., U.S.A. 79 D10 42 48N 74 45W
Cherskiy, Russia 27 C17 68 45N 161 18 E
Cherskogo Khrebet, Russia 27 C15 65 0N 143 0 E
Cherven, Belarus 17 B15 53 45N 28 28 E
Chervonohrad, Ukraine 17 C13 50 25N 24 10 E
Cherwell →, U.K. 11 F6 51 44N 1 14W
Cherykaw, Belarus 17 B16 53 32N 31 20 E
Chesapeake, U.S.A. 76 G7 36 50N 76 17W
Chesapeake B., U.S.A. 76 G7 38 0N 76 10W
Cheshire □, U.K. 10 D5 53 14N 2 30W
Cheshskaya Guba, Russia 24 A8 67 20N 47 0 E
Cheshunt, U.K. 11 F7 51 43N 0 1W
Chesil Beach, U.K. 11 G5 50 37N 2 33W
Chesley, Canada 78 B3 44 17N 81 5W
Chester, U.K. 10 D5 53 12N 2 53W
Chester, Calif., U.S.A. 82 F3 40 19N 121 14W
Chester, Ill., U.S.A. 81 G10 37 55N 89 49W
Chester, Mont., U.S.A. 82 B8 48 31N 110 58W
Chester, Pa., U.S.A. 76 F8 39 51N 75 22W
Chester, S.C., U.S.A. 77 H5 34 43N 81 12W
Chester, Vt., U.S.A. 79 C12 43 16N 72 36W
Chester, W. Va., U.S.A. 78 F4 40 37N 80 34W
Chester-le-Street, U.K. 10 C6 54 51N 1 34W
Chesterfield, U.K. 10 D6 53 15N 1 25W
Chesterfield, Is., N. Cal. 64 J7 19 52S 158 15 E
Chesterfield Inlet, Canada 68 B10 63 30N 90 45W
Chesterton Ra., Australia 63 D4 25 30S 147 27 E
Chestertown, U.S.A. 79 C11 43 40N 73 48W
Chesterville, Canada 79 A9 45 6N 75 14W
Chestnut Ridge, U.S.A. 78 F5 40 20N 79 10W
Chesuncook L., U.S.A. 77 C11 46 0N 69 21W
Chéticamp, Canada 71 C7 46 37N 60 59W
Chetumal, Mexico 87 D7 18 30N 88 20W
Chetumal, B. de, Mexico 87 D7 18 40N 88 10W
Chetwynd, Canada 72 B4 55 45N 121 36W
Cheviot, The, U.K. 10 B5 55 29N 2 9W
Cheviot Hills, U.K. 10 B5 55 20N 2 30W
Cheviot Ra., Australia 62 D3 25 20S 143 45 E
Chew Bahir, Ethiopia 46 G2 4 40N 36 50 E
Chewelah, U.S.A. 82 B5 48 17N 117 43W
Cheyenne, Okla., U.S.A. 81 H5 35 37N 99 40W
Cheyenne, Wyo., U.S.A. 80 E2 41 8N 104 49W
Cheyenne →, U.S.A. 80 C4 44 41N 101 18W
Cheyenne Wells, U.S.A. 80 F3 38 49N 102 21W
Cheyne B., Australia 61 F2 34 35S 118 50 E
Chhabra, India 42 G7 24 40N 76 54 E
Chhaktala, India 42 H6 22 6N 74 11 E
Chhapra, India 43 G11 25 48N 84 44 E
Chhata, India 42 F7 27 42N 77 30 E
Chhatarpur, Bihar, India 43 G11 24 23N 84 11 E
Chhatarpur, Mad. P., India 43 G8 24 55N 79 35 E
Chhep, Cambodia 38 F5 13 45N 105 24 E
Chhindwara, Mad. P., India 43 H8 23 3N 79 29 E
Chhindwara, Mad. P., India 43 H8 22 2N 78 59 E
Chhlong, Cambodia 39 F5 12 15N 105 58 E
Chhota Tawa →, India 42 H7 22 14N 76 36 E
Chhoti Kali Sindh →, India 42 G6 24 2N 75 31 E
Chhuikhadan, India 43 J9 21 32N 80 59 E
Chhuk, Cambodia 39 G5 10 46N 104 28 E
Chi →, Thailand 38 E5 15 11N 104 43 E
Chiai, Taiwan 33 D7 23 29N 120 25 E
Chiamboni, Somali Rep. 52 E8 1 39S 41 35 E
Chiamussu = Jiamusi,
China 33 B8 46 40N 130 26 E
Chiang Dao, Thailand 38 C2 19 22N 98 58 E
Chiang Kham, Thailand 38 C3 19 32N 100 18 E
Chiang Khan, Thailand 38 D3 17 52N 101 36 E
Chiang Mai, Thailand 38 C2 18 47N 98 59 E
Chiang Rai, Thailand 38 C2 19 52N 99 50 E
Chiapa →, Mexico 87 D6 16 42N 93 0W
Chiapa de Corzo, Mexico 87 D6 16 42N 93 0W
Chiapas □, Mexico 87 D6 17 0N 92 45W
Chiautla, Mexico 87 D5 18 18N 98 34W
Chiávari, Italy 18 D8 44 19N 9 19 E
Chiavenna, Italy 18 C8 46 19N 9 24 E
Chiba, Japan 31 G10 35 30N 140 7 E
Chiba □, Japan 31 G10 35 30N 140 20 E
Chibabava, Mozam. 57 C5 20 17S 33 35 E
Chibemba, Cunene, Angola 53 H2 15 48S 14 8 E
Chibemba, Huila, Angola 56 B2 16 20S 15 20 E
Chibia, Angola 53 H2 15 10S 13 42 E
Chibougamau, Canada 70 C5 49 56N 74 24W
Chibougamau, L., Canada 70 C5 49 50N 74 20W
Chic-Chocs, Mts., Canada 71 C6 48 55N 66 0W
Chicacole = Srikakulam,
India 41 K13 18 14N 83 58 E
Chicago, U.S.A. 76 E2 41 53N 87 38W
Chicago Heights, U.S.A. 76 E2 41 30N 87 38W
Chichagof I., U.S.A. 68 C6 57 30N 135 30W
Chichén-Itzá, Mexico 87 C7 20 40N 88 36W
Chicheng, China 34 D8 40 55N 115 55 E
Chichester, U.K. 11 G7 50 50N 0 47W
Chichester Ra., Australia 60 D2 22 12S 119 15 E
Chichibu, Japan 31 F9 36 5N 139 10 E
Ch'ich'ihaerh = Qiqihar,
China 27 E13 47 26N 124 0 E
Chicholi, India 42 H8 22 1N 77 40 E
Chickasha, U.S.A. 81 H6 35 3N 97 58W
Chiclana de la Frontera,
Spain 19 D2 36 26N 6 9W
Chiclayo, Peru 92 E3 6 42S 79 50W
Chico, U.S.A. 84 F5 39 44N 121 50W
Chico →, Chubut,
Argentina 96 E3 44 0S 67 0W
Chico →, Santa Cruz,
Argentina 96 G3 50 0S 68 30W
Chicomo, Mozam. 57 C5 24 31S 34 6 E
Chicontepec, Mexico 87 C5 20 58N 98 10W
Chicopee, U.S.A. 79 D12 42 9N 72 37W
Chicoutimi, Canada 71 C5 48 28N 71 5W
Chicualacuala, Mozam. 57 C5 22 6S 31 42 E
Chidambaram, India 40 P11 11 20N 79 45 E
Chidenguele, Mozam. 57 C5 24 55S 34 11 E
Chidley, C., Canada 69 B13 60 23N 64 26W
Chiede, Angola 56 B2 17 15S 16 22 E
Chiefs Pt., Canada 78 B3 44 41N 81 18W
Chiem Hoa, Vietnam 38 A5 22 12N 105 17 E
Chiemsee, Germany 16 E7 47 53N 12 28 E
Chiengi, Zambia 55 D2 8 45S 29 10 E
Chiengmai = Chiang Mai,
Thailand 38 C2 18 47N 98 59 E
Chiese →, Italy 18 D9 45 8N 10 25 E
Chieti, Italy 20 C6 42 21N 14 10 E
Chifeng, China 35 C10 42 18N 118 58 E
Chignecto B., Canada 71 C7 45 30N 64 40W
Chiguana, Bolivia 94 A2 21 0S 67 58W
Chigwell, U.K. 11 F8 51 37N 0 5 E
Chiha-ri, N. Korea 35 E14 38 40N 126 30 E
Chihli, G. of = Bo Hai, China 35 E10 39 0N 119 0 E
Chihuahua, Mexico 86 B3 28 40N 106 3W
Chihuahua □, Mexico 86 B3 28 40N 106 3W
Chiili, Kazakstan 26 E7 44 20N 66 15 E
Chik Bollapur, India 40 N10 13 25N 77 45 E
Chikmagalur, India 40 N9 13 15N 75 45 E
Chikwawa, Malawi 55 F3 16 2S 34 50 E
Chilac, Mexico 87 D5 18 20N 97 24W
Chilam Chavki, Pakistan 43 B6 35 5N 75 5 E
Chilanga, Zambia 55 F2 15 33S 28 16 E
Chilapa, Mexico 87 D5 17 40N 99 11W
Chilas, Pakistan 43 B6 35 25N 74 5 E
Chilaw, Sri Lanka 40 R11 7 30N 79 50 E
Chilcotin →, Canada 72 C4 51 44N 122 23W
Childers, Australia 63 D5 25 15S 152 17 E
Childress, U.S.A. 81 H4 34 25N 100 13W
Chile ■, S. Amer. 96 D2 35 0S 72 0W
Chile Rise, Pac. Oc. 65 L18 38 0S 92 0W
Chilecito, Argentina 94 B2 29 10S 67 30W
Chilete, Peru 92 E3 7 10S 78 50W
Chililabombwe, Zambia 55 E2 12 18S 27 43 E
Chilin = Jilin, China 35 C14 43 44N 126 30 E
Chilka L., India 41 K14 19 40N 85 25 E
Chilko →, Canada 72 C4 52 0N 123 40W
Chilko L., Canada 72 C4 51 20N 124 10W
Chillagoe, Australia 62 B3 17 7S 144 33 E
Chillán, Chile 94 D1 36 40S 72 10W
Chillicothe, Ill., U.S.A. 80 E10 40 55N 89 29W
Chillicothe, Mo., U.S.A. 80 F8 39 48N 93 33W
Chillicothe, Ohio, U.S.A. 76 F4 39 20N 82 59W
Chilliwack, Canada 72 D4 49 10N 121 54W
Chilo, India 42 F5 27 25N 73 32 E
Chiloane, I., Mozam. 57 C5 20 40S 34 55 E
Chiloé, I. de, Chile 96 E2 42 30S 73 50W
Chilpancingo, Mexico 87 D5 17 30N 99 30W
Chiltern Hills, U.K. 11 F7 51 40N 0 53W
Chilton, U.S.A. 76 C1 44 2N 88 10W
Chilubi, Zambia 55 E2 11 5S 29 58 E
Chilubula, Zambia 55 E3 10 14S 30 51 E
Chilumba, Malawi 55 E3 10 28S 34 12 E
Chilung, Taiwan 33 D7 25 3N 121 45 E
Chilwa, L., Malawi 55 F4 15 15S 35 40 E
Chimaltitán, Mexico 86 C4 21 46N 103 50W
Chimán, Panama 88 E4 8 45N 78 40W
Chimay, Belgium 15 D4 50 3N 4 20 E
Chimayo, U.S.A. 83 H11 36 0N 105 56W
Chimbay, Uzbekistan 26 E6 42 57N 59 47 E
Chimborazo, Ecuador 92 D3 1 29S 78 55W
Chimbote, Peru 92 E3 9 0S 78 35W
Chimkent = Shymkent,
Kazakstan 26 E7 42 18N 69 36 E
Chimoio, Mozam. 55 F3 19 4S 33 30 E
Chimpembe, Zambia 55 D2 9 31S 29 33 E
Chin □, Burma 41 J18 22 0N 93 0 E
Chin Ling Shan = Qinling
Shandi, China 34 H5 33 50N 108 10 E
China, Mexico 87 B5 25 40N 99 20W
China ■, Asia 33 D6 30 0N 110 0 E
China Lake, U.S.A. 85 K9 35 44N 117 37W
Chinan = Jinan, China 34 F9 36 38N 117 1 E
Chinandega, Nic. 88 D2 12 35N 87 12W
Chinati Peak, U.S.A. 81 L2 29 57N 104 29W
Chincha Alta, Peru 92 F3 13 25S 76 7W
Chinchaga →, Canada 72 B5 58 53N 118 20W
Chinchilla, Australia 63 D5 26 45S 150 38 E

Chinchorro, Banco

Chinchorro, Banco, Mexico 87 D7 18 35N 87 20W
Chinchou = Jinzhou, China 35 D11 41 5N 121 3 E
Chincoteague, U.S.A. 76 G8 37 56N 75 23W
Chinde, Mozam. 55 F4 18 35S 36 30 E
Chindo, S. Korea 35 G14 34 28N 126 15 E
Chindwin →, Burma 41 J19 21 26N 95 15 E
Chineni, India 43 C6 33 2N 75 15 E
Chinga, Mozam. 55 F4 15 13S 38 35 E
Chingola, Zambia 55 E2 12 31S 27 53 E
Chingole, Malawi 55 E3 13 4S 34 17 E
Ch'ingtao = Qingdao, China 35 F11 36 5N 120 20 E
Chinguar, Angola 53 G3 12 25S 16 45 E
Chinguetti, Mauritania 50 D3 20 25N 12 24W
Chingune, Mozam. 57 C5 20 33S 34 58 E
Chinhae, S. Korea 35 G15 35 9N 128 47 E
Chinhanguanine, Mozam. 57 D5 25 21S 32 30 E
Chinhoyi, Zimbabwe 55 F3 17 20S 30 8 E
Chini, India 42 D8 31 32N 78 15 E
Chiniot, Pakistan 42 D5 31 45N 73 0 E
Chínipas, Mexico 86 B3 27 22N 108 32W
Chinji, Pakistan 42 C5 32 42N 72 22 E
Chinju, S. Korea 35 G15 35 12N 128 2 E
Chinle, U.S.A. 83 H9 36 9N 109 33W
Chinnampo = Namp'o, N. Korea 35 E13 38 52N 125 10 E
Chino, Japan 31 G9 35 59N 138 9 E
Chino, U.S.A. 85 L9 34 1N 117 41W
Chino Valley, U.S.A. 83 J7 34 45N 112 27W
Chinon, France 18 C4 47 10N 0 15 E
Chinook, U.S.A. 82 B9 48 35N 109 14W
Chinsali, Zambia 55 E3 10 30S 32 2 E
Chióggia, Italy 20 B5 45 13N 12 17 E
Chíos = Khíos, Greece 21 E12 38 27N 26 9 E
Chipata, Zambia 55 E3 13 38S 32 28 E
Chipinge, Zimbabwe 55 G3 20 13S 32 28 E
Chipley, U.S.A. 77 K3 30 47N 85 32W
Chipman, Canada 71 C6 46 6N 65 53W
Chipoka, Malawi 55 E3 13 57S 34 28 E
Chippenham, U.K. 11 F5 51 27N 2 6W
Chippewa →, U.S.A. 80 C8 44 25N 92 5W
Chippewa Falls, U.S.A. 80 C9 44 56N 91 24W
Chipping Norton, U.K. 11 F6 51 56N 1 32W
Chiputneticook Lakes, U.S.A. 77 C11 45 35N 67 35W
Chiquián, Peru 92 F3 10 10S 77 0W
Chiquimula, Guatemala 88 D2 14 51N 89 37W
Chiquinquira, Colombia 92 B4 5 37N 73 50W
Chirala, India 40 M12 15 50N 80 26 E
Chiramba, Mozam. 55 F3 16 55S 34 39 E
Chirawa, India 42 E6 28 14N 75 42 E
Chirchiq, Uzbekistan 26 E7 41 29N 69 35 E
Chiredzi, Zimbabwe 57 C5 21 0S 31 38 E
Chirfa, Niger 51 D8 20 55N 12 22 E
Chiricahua Peak, U.S.A. 83 L9 31 51N 109 18W
Chiriquí, G. de, Panama 88 E3 8 0N 82 10W
Chiriquí, L. de, Panama 88 E3 9 10N 82 0W
Chirivira Falls, Zimbabwe 55 G3 21 10S 32 12 E
Chirmiri, India 41 H13 23 15N 82 20 E
Chirripó Grande, Cerro, Costa Rica 88 E3 9 29N 83 29W
Chisamba, Zambia 55 E2 14 55S 28 20 E
Chisapani Garhi, Nepal 41 F14 27 30N 84 2 E
Chisasibi, Canada 70 B4 53 50N 79 0W
Chisholm, Canada 72 C6 54 55N 114 10W
Chisholm, U.S.A. 80 B8 47 29N 92 53W
Chishtian Mandi, Pakistan 42 E5 29 50N 72 55 E
Chisimaio, Somali Rep. 49 G8 0 22S 42 32 E
Chisimba Falls, Zambia 55 E3 10 12S 30 56 E
Chişinău, Moldova 17 E15 47 2N 28 50 E
Chisos Mts., U.S.A. 81 L3 29 5N 103 15W
Chistopol, Russia 24 C9 55 25N 50 38 E
Chita, Russia 27 D12 52 0N 113 35 E
Chitipa, Malawi 55 D3 9 41S 33 19 E
Chitose, Japan 30 C10 42 49N 141 39 E
Chitral, Pakistan 40 B7 35 50N 71 56 E
Chitré, Panama 88 E3 7 59N 80 27W
Chittagong, Bangla. 41 H17 22 19N 91 48 E
Chittagong □, Bangla. 41 G17 24 5N 91 0 E
Chittaurgarh, India 42 G6 24 52N 74 38 E
Chittoor, India 40 N11 13 15N 79 5 E
Chitungwiza, Zimbabwe 55 F3 18 0S 31 6 E
Chiusi, Italy 20 C4 43 1N 11 57 E
Chivasso, Italy 18 D7 45 11N 7 53 E
Chivhu, Zimbabwe 55 F3 19 2S 30 52 E
Chivilcoy, Argentina 94 C4 34 55S 60 0W
Chiwanda, Tanzania 55 E3 11 23S 34 55 E
Chizera, Zambia 55 E2 13 10S 25 0 E
Chkalov = Orenburg, Russia 24 D10 51 45N 55 6 E
Chloride, U.S.A. 85 K12 35 25N 114 12W
Cho-do, N. Korea 35 E13 38 30N 124 40 E
Cho Phuoc Hai, Vietnam 39 G6 10 26N 107 18 E
Choba, Kenya 54 B4 2 30N 38 5 E
Chobe National Park, Botswana 56 B4 18 0S 25 0 E
Choch'iwŏn, S. Korea 35 F14 36 37N 127 18 E
Chocolate Mts., U.S.A. 85 M11 33 15N 115 15W
Choctawatchee →, U.S.A. 77 K3 30 25N 86 8W
Choctawhatchee B., U.S.A. 75 D9 30 20N 86 20W
Choele Choel, Argentina 96 D3 39 11S 65 40W
Choix, Mexico 86 B3 26 40N 108 23W
Chojnice, Poland 17 B9 53 42N 17 32 E
Chōkai-San, Japan 30 E10 39 6N 140 3 E
Choke Canyon L., U.S.A. 81 L5 28 30N 98 20W
Chokurdakh, Russia 27 B15 70 38N 147 55 E
Cholame, U.S.A. 84 K6 35 44N 120 18W
Cholet, France 18 C3 47 4N 0 52W
Cholguan, Chile 94 D1 37 10S 72 3W
Choluteca, Honduras 88 D2 13 20N 87 14W
Choluteca →, Honduras 88 D2 13 0N 87 20W
Chom Bung, Thailand 38 F2 13 37N 99 36 E
Chom Thong, Thailand 38 C2 18 25N 98 41 E
Choma, Zambia 55 F2 16 48S 26 59 E
Chomun, India 42 F6 27 15N 75 40 E
Chomutov, Czech Rep. 16 C7 50 28N 13 23 E
Chon Buri, Thailand 38 F3 13 21N 101 1 E
Chon Thanh, Vietnam 39 G6 11 24N 106 36 E
Ch'onan, S. Korea 35 F14 36 48N 127 9 E
Chone, Ecuador 92 D3 0 40S 80 0W
Chong Kai, Cambodia 38 F4 13 57N 103 35 E
Chong Mek, Thailand 38 E5 15 10N 105 27 E
Chŏngdo, S. Korea 35 G15 35 38N 128 42 E
Chŏngha, S. Korea 35 F15 36 12N 129 21 E
Chŏngjin, N. Korea 35 D15 41 47N 129 50 E
Chŏngjiu, S. Korea 35 F14 36 39N 127 27 E
Chŏngju, N. Korea 35 E13 39 40N 125 5 E
Chongli, China 34 D8 40 58N 115 15 E
Chongqing, China 32 D5 29 35N 106 25 E
Chongqing □, China 32 C5 30 0N 108 0 E
Chŏngŭp, S. Korea 35 G14 35 35N 126 50 E
Chŏnju, S. Korea 35 G14 35 50N 127 4 E
Chonos, Arch. de los, Chile 96 F2 45 0S 75 0W
Chop, Ukraine 17 D12 48 26N 22 12 E
Chopim →, Brazil 95 B5 25 35S 53 5W
Chor, Pakistan 42 G3 25 31N 69 46 E
Chorbat La, India 43 B7 34 42N 76 37 E
Chorley, U.K. 10 D5 53 39N 2 38W
Chornobyl, Ukraine 17 C16 51 20N 30 15 E
Chorolque, Cerro, Bolivia 94 A2 20 59S 66 5W
Chorregon, Australia 62 C3 22 40S 143 32 E
Chortkiv, Ukraine 17 D13 49 2N 25 46 E
Ch'ŏrwon, S. Korea 35 E14 38 15N 127 10 E
Chorzów, Poland 17 C10 50 18N 18 57 E
Chos-Malal, Argentina 94 D1 37 20S 70 15W
Ch'osan, N. Korea 35 D13 40 50N 125 47 E
Choszczno, Poland 16 B8 53 7N 15 25 E
Choteau, U.S.A. 82 C7 47 49N 112 11W
Chotila, India 42 H4 22 23N 71 15 E
Chotta Udepur, India 42 H6 22 19N 74 1 E
Chowchilla, U.S.A. 84 H6 37 7N 120 16W
Choybalsan, Mongolia 33 B6 48 4N 114 30 E
Christchurch, N.Z. 59 K4 43 33S 172 47 E
Christchurch, U.K. 11 G6 50 44N 1 47W
Christian I., Canada 78 B4 44 50N 80 12W
Christiana, S. Africa 56 D4 27 52S 25 8 E
Christiansted, Virgin Is. 89 C7 17 45N 64 42W
Christie B., Canada 73 A6 62 32N 111 10W
Christina →, Canada 73 B6 56 40N 111 3W
Christmas Cr. →, Australia 60 C4 18 29S 125 23 E
Christmas I. = Kiritimati, Kiribati 65 G12 1 58N 157 27W
Christmas I., Ind. Oc. 64 J2 10 30S 105 40 E
Christopher L., Australia 61 D4 24 49S 127 42 E
Chtimba, Malawi 55 E3 10 35S 34 13 E
Chu = Shu, Kazakstan 26 E8 43 36N 73 42 E
Chu = Shu →, Kazakstan 28 E10 45 0N 67 44 E
Chu →, Vietnam 38 C5 19 53N 105 45 E
Chu Lai, Vietnam 38 E7 15 28N 108 45 E
Ch'uanchou = Quanzhou, China 33 D6 24 55N 118 34 E
Chuankou, China 34 G6 34 20N 110 59 E
Chubbuck, U.S.A. 82 E7 42 55N 112 28W
Chūbu □, Japan 31 F8 36 45N 137 30 E
Chubut →, Argentina 96 E3 43 20S 65 5W
Chuchi L., Canada 72 B4 55 12N 124 30W
Chuda, India 42 H4 22 29N 71 41 E
Chudskoye, Ozero, Russia 9 G22 58 13N 27 30 E
Chūgoku □, Japan 31 G6 35 0N 133 0 E
Chūgoku-Sanchi, Japan 31 G6 35 0N 133 0 E
Chugwater, U.S.A. 80 E2 41 46N 104 50W
Chukchi Sea, Russia 27 C19 68 0N 175 0W
Chukotskoye Nagorye, Russia 27 C18 68 0N 175 0 E
Chula Vista, U.S.A. 85 N9 32 39N 117 5W
Chulucanas, Peru 92 E2 5 8S 80 10W
Chulym →, Russia 26 D9 57 43N 83 51 E
Chum Phae, Thailand 38 D4 16 40N 102 6 E
Chum Saeng, Thailand 38 E3 15 55N 100 15 E
Chumar, India 43 C8 32 40N 78 35 E
Chumbicha, Argentina 94 B2 29 0S 66 10W
Chumikan, Russia 27 D14 54 40N 135 10 E
Chumphon, Thailand 39 G2 10 35N 99 14 E
Chumuare, Mozam. 55 E3 14 31S 31 50 E
Chumunjin, S. Korea 35 F15 37 55N 128 54 E
Chuna →, Russia 27 D10 57 47N 94 37 E
Ch'unch'ŏn, S. Korea 35 F14 37 58N 127 44 E
Chunchura, India 43 H13 22 53N 88 27 E
Chunga, Zambia 55 F2 15 0S 26 2 E
Chunggang-ŭp, N. Korea 35 D14 41 48N 126 48 E
Chunghwa, N. Korea 35 E13 38 52N 125 47 E
Ch'ungju, S. Korea 35 F14 36 58N 127 58 E
Chungking = Chongqing, China 32 D5 29 35N 106 25 E
Ch'ungmu, S. Korea 35 G15 34 50N 128 20 E
Chungt'iaoshan = Zhongtiao Shan, China 34 G6 35 0N 111 10 E
Chunian, Pakistan 42 D6 30 57N 74 0 E
Chunya, Tanzania 55 D3 8 30S 33 27 E
Chunyang, China 35 C15 43 38N 129 23 E
Chuquibamba, Peru 92 G4 15 47S 72 44W
Chuquicamata, Chile 94 A2 22 15S 69 0W
Chur, Switz. 18 C8 46 52N 9 32 E
Churachandpur, India 41 G18 24 20N 93 40 E
Churchill, Canada 73 B10 58 47N 94 11W
Churchill →, Man., Canada 73 B10 58 47N 94 12W
Churchill →, Nfld., Canada 71 B7 53 19N 60 10W
Churchill, C., Canada 73 B10 58 46N 93 12W
Churchill Falls, Canada 71 B7 53 36N 64 19W
Churchill L., Canada 73 B7 55 55N 108 20W
Churchill Pk., Canada 72 B3 58 10N 125 10W
Churki, India 43 H10 23 50N 83 12 E
Churu, India 42 E6 28 20N 74 50 E
Churún Merú = Angel Falls, Venezuela 92 B6 5 57N 62 30W
Chushal, India 43 C8 33 40N 78 40 E
Chuska Mts., U.S.A. 83 H9 36 15N 108 50W
Chusovoy, Russia 24 C10 58 22N 57 50 E
Chute-aux-Outardes, Canada 71 C6 49 7N 68 24W
Chuuronjang, N. Korea 35 D15 41 35N 129 40 E
Chuvash Republic = Chuvashia □, Russia 24 C8 55 30N 47 0 E
Chuvashia □, Russia 24 C8 55 30N 47 0 E
Chuwārtah, Iraq 44 C5 35 43N 45 34 E
Chuy, Uruguay 95 C5 33 41S 53 27W
Ci Xian, China 34 F8 36 20N 114 25 E
Ciadâr-Lunga, Moldova 17 E15 46 3N 28 51 E
Ciamis, Indonesia 37 G13 7 20S 108 21 E
Cianjur, Indonesia 37 G12 6 49S 107 8 E
Cianorte, Brazil 95 A5 23 37S 52 37W
Cibola, U.S.A. 85 M12 33 17N 114 42W
Cicero, U.S.A. 76 E2 41 48N 87 48W
Ciechanów, Poland 17 B11 52 52N 20 38 E
Ciego de Avila, Cuba 88 B4 21 50N 78 50W
Ciénaga, Colombia 92 A4 11 1N 74 15W
Cienfuegos, Cuba 88 B3 22 10N 80 30W
Cieszyn, Poland 17 D10 49 45N 18 35 E
Cieza, Spain 19 C5 38 17N 1 23W
Cihuatlán, Mexico 86 D4 19 14N 104 35W
Cijara, Embalse de, Spain 19 C3 39 18N 4 52W
Cijulang, Indonesia 37 G13 7 42S 108 27 E
Cilacap, Indonesia 37 G13 7 43S 109 0 E
Cill Chainnigh = Kilkenny, Ireland 13 D4 52 39N 7 15W
Cilo Dağı, Turkey 25 G7 37 28N 43 55 E
Cima, U.S.A. 85 K11 35 14N 115 30W
Cimarron, Kans., U.S.A. 81 G4 37 48N 100 21W
Cimarron, N. Mex., U.S.A. 81 G2 36 31N 104 55W
Cimarron →, U.S.A. 81 G6 36 10N 96 17W
Cimişlia, Moldova 17 E15 46 34N 28 44 E
Cimone, Mte., Italy 20 B4 44 12N 10 42 E
Cinca →, Spain 19 B6 41 26N 0 21 E
Cincar, Bos.-H. 20 C7 43 55N 17 5 E
Cincinnati, U.S.A. 76 F3 39 6N 84 31W
Cincinnatus, U.S.A. 79 D9 42 33N 75 54W
Çine, Turkey 21 F13 37 37N 28 2 E
Ciney, Belgium 15 D5 50 18N 5 5 E
Cinto, Mte., France 18 E8 42 24N 8 54 E
Circle, Alaska, U.S.A. 68 B5 65 50N 144 4W
Circle, Mont., U.S.A. 80 B2 47 25N 105 35W
Circleville, U.S.A. 76 F4 39 36N 82 57W
Cirebon, Indonesia 37 G13 6 45S 108 32 E
Ciremai, Indonesia 37 G13 6 55S 108 27 E
Cirencester, U.K. 11 F6 51 43N 1 57W
Cirium, Cyprus 23 E11 34 40N 32 53 E
Cisco, U.S.A. 81 J5 32 23N 98 59W
Citlaltépetl, Mexico 87 D5 19 0N 97 20W
Citrus Heights, U.S.A. 84 G5 38 42N 121 17W
Citrusdal, S. Africa 56 E2 32 35S 19 0 E
Città di Castello, Italy 20 C5 43 27N 12 14 E
City of Edinburgh □, U.K. 12 F5 55 57N 3 17W
City of Glasgow □, U.K. 12 F4 55 51N 4 12W
Ciudad Altamirano, Mexico 86 D4 18 20N 100 40W
Ciudad Bolívar, Venezuela 92 B6 8 5N 63 36W
Ciudad Camargo, Mexico 86 B3 27 41N 105 10W
Ciudad de Valles, Mexico 87 C5 22 0N 99 0W
Ciudad del Carmen, Mexico 87 D6 18 38N 91 50W
Ciudad del Este, Paraguay 95 B5 25 30S 54 50W
Ciudad Delicias = Delicias, Mexico 86 B3 28 10N 105 30W
Ciudad Guayana, Venezuela 92 B6 8 0N 62 30W
Ciudad Guerrero, Mexico 86 B3 28 33N 107 28W
Ciudad Guzmán, Mexico 86 D4 19 40N 103 30W
Ciudad Juárez, Mexico 86 A3 31 40N 106 28W
Ciudad Madero, Mexico 87 C5 22 19N 97 50W
Ciudad Mante, Mexico 87 C5 22 50N 99 0W
Ciudad Obregón, Mexico 86 B3 27 28N 109 59W
Ciudad Real, Spain 19 C4 38 59N 3 55W
Ciudad Rodrigo, Spain 19 B2 40 35N 6 32W
Ciudad Trujillo = Santo Domingo, Dom. Rep. 89 C6 18 30N 69 59W
Ciudad Victoria, Mexico 87 C5 23 41N 99 9W
Ciudadela, Spain 22 B10 40 0N 3 50 E
Civitanova Marche, Italy 20 C5 43 18N 13 44 E
Civitavécchia, Italy 20 C4 42 6N 11 48 E
Cizre, Turkey 25 G7 37 19N 42 10 E
Clackmannanshire □, U.K. 12 E5 56 10N 3 43W
Clacton-on-Sea, U.K. 11 F9 51 47N 1 11 E
Claire, L., Canada 72 B6 58 35N 112 5W
Clairton, U.S.A. 78 F5 40 18N 79 53W
Clallam Bay, U.S.A. 84 B2 48 15N 124 16W
Clanton, U.S.A. 77 J2 32 51N 86 38W
Clanwilliam, S. Africa 56 E2 32 11S 18 52 E
Clara, Ireland 13 C4 53 21N 7 37W
Claraville, U.S.A. 85 K8 35 24N 118 20W
Clare, Australia 63 E2 33 50S 138 37 E
Clare, U.S.A. 76 D3 43 49N 84 46W
Clare □, Ireland 13 D3 52 45N 9 0W
Clare →, Ireland 13 C2 53 20N 9 2W
Clare I., Ireland 13 C1 53 49N 10 0W
Claremont, Calif., U.S.A. 85 L9 34 6N 117 43W
Claremont, N.H., U.S.A. 79 C12 43 23N 72 20W
Claremont Pt., Australia 62 A3 14 1S 143 41 E
Claremore, U.S.A. 81 G7 36 19N 95 36W
Claremorris, Ireland 13 C3 53 45N 9 0W
Clarence →, Australia 63 D5 29 25S 153 22 E
Clarence →, N.Z. 59 K4 42 10S 173 56 E
Clarence, I., Chile 96 G2 54 0S 72 0W
Clarence I., Antarctica 5 C18 61 10S 54 0W
Clarence Str., Australia 60 B5 12 0S 131 0 E
Clarence Town, Bahamas 89 B5 23 6N 74 59W
Clarendon, Pa., U.S.A. 78 E5 41 47N 79 6W
Clarendon, Tex., U.S.A. 81 H4 34 56N 100 53W
Clarenville, Canada 71 C9 48 10N 54 1W
Claresholm, Canada 72 D6 50 0N 113 33W
Clarie Coast, Antarctica 5 C9 68 0S 135 0 E
Clarinda, U.S.A. 80 E7 40 44N 95 2W
Clarion, Iowa, U.S.A. 80 D8 42 44N 93 44W
Clarion, Pa., U.S.A. 78 E5 41 13N 79 23W
Clarion →, U.S.A. 78 E5 41 7N 79 41W
Clark, U.S.A. 80 C6 44 53N 97 44W
Clark, Pt., Canada 78 B3 44 4N 81 45W
Clark Fork, U.S.A. 82 B5 48 9N 116 11W
Clark Fork →, U.S.A. 82 B5 48 9N 116 15W
Clark Hill L., U.S.A. 77 J4 33 40N 82 12W
Clarkdale, U.S.A. 83 J7 34 46N 112 3W
Clarke City, Canada 71 B6 50 12N 66 38W
Clarke I., Australia 62 G4 40 32S 148 10 E
Clarke Ra., Australia 62 C4 20 40S 148 30 E
Clark's Fork →, U.S.A. 82 D9 45 39N 108 43W
Clark's Harbour, Canada 71 D6 43 25N 65 38W
Clarks Summit, U.S.A. 79 E9 41 30N 75 42W
Clarksburg, U.S.A. 76 F5 39 17N 80 30W
Clarksdale, U.S.A. 81 H9 34 12N 90 35W
Clarksville, Ark., U.S.A. 81 H8 35 28N 93 28W
Clarksville, Tenn., U.S.A. 77 G2 36 32N 87 21W
Clarksville, Tex., U.S.A. 81 J7 33 37N 95 3W
Clatskanie, U.S.A. 84 D3 46 6N 123 12W
Claude, U.S.A. 81 H4 35 7N 101 22W
Claveria, Phil. 37 A6 18 37N 121 4 E
Clay, U.S.A. 84 G5 38 17N 121 10W
Clay Center, U.S.A. 80 F6 39 23N 97 8W
Claypool, U.S.A. 83 K8 33 25N 110 51W
Claysburg, U.S.A. 78 F6 40 17N 78 27W
Claysville, U.S.A. 78 F4 40 7N 80 25W
Clayton, N. Mex., U.S.A. 81 G3 36 27N 103 11W
Clayton, N.Y., U.S.A. 79 B8 44 14N 76 5W
Clear, C., Ireland 13 E2 51 25N 9 32W
Clear, L., Canada 78 A7 45 26N 77 12W
Clear Hills, Canada 72 B5 56 40N 119 30W
Clear I., Ireland 13 E2 51 26N 9 30W
Clear L., U.S.A. 84 F4 39 2N 122 47W
Clear Lake, Iowa, U.S.A. 80 D8 43 8N 93 23W
Clear Lake, S. Dak., U.S.A. 80 C6 44 45N 96 41W
Clear Lake Reservoir, U.S.A. 82 F3 41 56N 121 5W
Clearfield, Pa., U.S.A. 78 E6 41 2N 78 27W
Clearfield, Utah, U.S.A. 82 F8 41 7N 112 2W
Clearlake, U.S.A. 82 G2 38 57N 122 38W
Clearlake Highlands, U.S.A. 84 G4 38 57N 122 38W
Clearwater, Canada 72 C4 51 38N 120 2W
Clearwater, U.S.A. 77 M4 27 58N 82 48W
Clearwater →, Alta., Canada 72 C6 52 22N 114 57W
Clearwater →, Alta., Canada 73 B6 56 44N 111 23
Clearwater L., Canada 73 C9 53 34N 99 49
Clearwater Mts., U.S.A. 82 C6 46 5N 115 20
Clearwater Prov. Park, Canada 73 C8 54 0N 101 0
Clearwater River Prov. Park, Canada 73 B7 56 55N 109 10
Cleburne, U.S.A. 81 J6 32 21N 97 23
Clee Hills, U.K. 11 E5 52 26N 2 35
Cleethorpes, U.K. 10 D7 53 33N 0 3
Cleeve Cloud, U.K. 11 F6 51 56N 2 0
Clemson, U.S.A. 77 H4 34 41N 82 50
Clerke Reef, Australia 60 C2 17 22S 119 20
Clermont, Australia 62 C4 22 49S 147 39
Clermont, U.S.A. 77 L5 28 33N 81 46
Clermont-Ferrand, France 18 D5 45 46N 3 4
Clervaux, Lux. 15 D6 50 4N 6 2
Cleve, Australia 63 E2 33 43S 136 30
Clevedon, U.K. 11 F5 51 26N 2 52
Cleveland, Miss., U.S.A. 81 J9 33 45N 90 43
Cleveland, Ohio, U.S.A. 78 E3 41 30N 81 42
Cleveland, Okla., U.S.A. 81 G6 36 19N 96 28
Cleveland, Tenn., U.S.A. 77 H3 35 10N 84 53
Cleveland, Tex., U.S.A. 81 K7 30 21N 95 5
Cleveland, C., Australia 62 B4 19 11S 147 1
Cleveland, Mt., U.S.A. 82 B7 48 56N 113 51
Cleveland Heights, U.S.A. 78 E3 41 30N 81 34
Clevelândia, Brazil 95 B5 26 24S 52 23
Clew B., Ireland 13 C2 53 50N 9 49
Clewiston, U.S.A. 77 M5 26 45N 80 56
Clifden, Ireland 13 C1 53 29N 10 1
Clifden, N.Z. 59 M1 46 1S 167 42
Cliffdell, U.S.A. 84 D5 46 56N 121 5
Cliffy Hd., Australia 61 G2 35 1S 116 29
Clifton, Australia 63 D5 27 59S 151 53
Clifton, Ariz., U.S.A. 83 K9 33 3N 109 18
Clifton, Colo., U.S.A. 83 G9 39 7N 108 25
Clifton, Tex., U.S.A. 81 K6 31 47N 97 35
Clifton Beach, Australia 62 B4 16 46S 145 39
Climax, Canada 73 D7 49 10N 108 20
Clinch →, U.S.A. 77 H3 35 53N 84 29
Clingmans Dome, U.S.A. 77 H4 35 34N 83 30
Clint, U.S.A. 83 L10 31 35N 106 14
Clinton, B.C., Canada 72 C4 51 6N 121 35
Clinton, Ont., Canada 78 C3 43 37N 81 32
Clinton, N.Z. 59 M2 46 12S 169 23
Clinton, Ark., U.S.A. 81 H8 35 36N 92 28
Clinton, Conn., U.S.A. 79 E12 41 17N 72 32
Clinton, Ill., U.S.A. 80 E10 40 9N 88 57
Clinton, Ind., U.S.A. 76 F2 39 40N 87 24
Clinton, Iowa, U.S.A. 80 E9 41 51N 90 12
Clinton, Mass., U.S.A. 79 D13 42 25N 71 41
Clinton, Miss., U.S.A. 81 J9 32 20N 90 20
Clinton, Mo., U.S.A. 80 F8 38 22N 93 46
Clinton, N.C., U.S.A. 77 H6 35 0N 78 22
Clinton, Okla., U.S.A. 81 H5 35 31N 98 58
Clinton, S.C., U.S.A. 77 H5 34 29N 81 53
Clinton, Tenn., U.S.A. 77 G3 36 6N 84 8
Clinton, Wash., U.S.A. 84 C4 47 59N 122 21
Clinton C., Australia 62 C5 22 30S 150 45
Clinton Colden L., Canada 68 B9 63 58N 107 27
Clintonville, U.S.A. 80 C10 44 37N 88 46
Clipperton, I., Pac. Oc. 65 F17 10 18N 109 13
Clisham, U.K. 12 D2 57 57N 6 49
Clitheroe, U.K. 10 D5 53 53N 2 22
Clo-oose, Canada 84 B2 48 39N 124 49
Cloates, Pt., Australia 60 D1 22 43S 113 40
Clocolan, S. Africa 57 D4 28 55S 27 34
Clodomira, Argentina 94 B3 27 35S 64 14
Clogher Hd., Ireland 13 C5 53 48N 6 14
Clonakilty, Ireland 13 E3 51 37N 8 53
Clonakilty B., Ireland 13 E3 51 35N 8 51
Cloncurry, Australia 62 C3 20 40S 140 28
Cloncurry →, Australia 62 B3 18 37S 140 40
Clondalkin, Ireland 13 C5 53 19N 6 25
Clones, Ireland 13 B4 54 11N 7 15
Clonmel, Ireland 13 D4 52 21N 7 42
Cloquet, U.S.A. 80 B8 46 43N 92 28
Clorinda, Argentina 94 B4 25 16S 57 45
Cloud Bay, Canada 70 C2 48 5N 89 26
Cloud Peak, U.S.A. 82 D10 44 23N 107 11
Cloudcroft, U.S.A. 83 K11 32 58N 105 45
Cloverdale, U.S.A. 84 G4 38 48N 123 1
Clovis, Calif., U.S.A. 84 J7 36 49N 119 42
Clovis, N. Mex., U.S.A. 81 H3 34 24N 103 12
Cloyne, Canada 78 B7 44 49N 77 11
Cluj-Napoca, Romania 17 E12 46 47N 23 38
Clunes, Australia 63 F3 37 20S 143 45
Clutha →, N.Z. 59 M2 46 20S 169 49
Clwyd →, U.K. 10 D4 53 19N 3 31
Clyde, Canada 72 C6 54 9N 113 39
Clyde, N.Z. 59 L2 45 12S 169 20
Clyde, U.S.A. 78 C8 43 5N 76 52
Clyde →, U.K. 12 F4 55 55N 4 30
Clyde, Firth of, U.K. 12 F3 55 22N 5 1
Clyde River, Canada 69 A13 70 30N 68 30
Clydebank, U.K. 12 F4 55 54N 4 23
Clymer, N.Y., U.S.A. 78 D5 42 1N 79 37
Clymer, Pa., U.S.A. 78 D5 40 40N 79 1
Coachella, U.S.A. 85 M10 33 41N 116 10
Coachella Canal, U.S.A. 85 N12 32 43N 114 57
Coahoma, U.S.A. 81 J4 32 18N 101 18
Coahuayana →, Mexico 86 D4 18 41N 103 45
Coahuila □, Mexico 86 B4 27 0N 103 0
Coal →, Canada 72 B3 59 39N 126 57
Coalane, Mozam. 55 F4 17 48S 37 2
Coalcomán, Mexico 86 D4 18 40N 103 10
Coaldale, Canada 72 D6 49 45N 112 35
Coalgate, U.S.A. 81 H6 34 32N 96 13
Coalinga, U.S.A. 84 J6 36 9N 120 21
Coalisland, U.K. 13 B5 54 33N 6 42
Coalville, U.K. 10 E6 52 44N 1 23
Coalville, U.S.A. 82 F8 40 55N 111 24
Coari, Brazil 92 D6 4 8S 63 7
Coast □, Kenya 54 C4 2 40S 39 45
Coast Mts., Canada 72 C3 55 0N 129 20
Coast Ranges, U.S.A. 84 G4 39 0N 123 0
Coatbridge, U.K. 12 F4 55 52N 4 6
Coatepec, Mexico 87 D5 19 27N 96 58
Coatepeque, Guatemala 88 D1 14 46N 91 55
Coatesville, U.S.A. 76 F8 39 59N 75 50
Coaticook, Canada 79 A13 45 10N 71 46
Coats I., Canada 69 B11 62 30N 83 0
Coats Land, Antarctica 5 D1 77 0S 25 0
Coatzacoalcos, Mexico 87 D6 18 7N 94 25
Cobalt, Canada 70 C4 47 25N 79 42

Corrientes

114

115

Despeñaperros, Paso

Despeñaperros, Paso, *Spain* **19 C4** 38 24N 3 30W
Dessau, *Germany* **16 C7** 51 51N 12 14 E
Dessye = Dese, *Ethiopia* **46 E2** 11 5N 39 40 E
D'Estrees B., *Australia* **63 F2** 35 55S 137 45 E
Desuri, *India* **42 G5** 25 18N 73 35 E
Det Udom, *Thailand* **38 E5** 14 54N 105 5 E
Dete, *Zimbabwe* **55 F2** 18 38S 26 50 E
Detmold, *Germany* **16 C5** 51 56N 8 52 E
Detour, Pt., *U.S.A.* **76 C2** 45 40N 86 40W
Detroit, *U.S.A.* **78 D1** 42 20N 83 3W
Detroit Lakes, *U.S.A.* **80 B7** 46 49N 95 51W
Deurne, *Neths.* **15 C5** 51 27N 5 49 E
Deutsche Bucht, *Germany* **16 A5** 54 15N 8 0 E
Deva, *Romania* **17 F12** 45 53N 22 55 E
Devakottai, *India* **40 Q11** 9 55N 78 45 E
Devaprayag, *India* **43 D8** 30 13N 78 35 E
Deventer, *Neths.* **15 B6** 52 15N 6 10 E
Deveron →, *U.K.* **12 D6** 57 41N 2 32W
Devgadh Bariya, *India* **42 H5** 22 40N 73 55 E
Devikot, *India* **42 F4** 26 42N 71 12 E
Devils Den, *U.S.A.* **84 K7** 35 46N 119 58W
Devils Lake, *U.S.A.* **80 A5** 48 7N 98 52W
Devils Paw, *Canada* **72 B2** 58 47N 134 0W
Devils Tower Junction, *U.S.A.* **80 C2** 44 31N 104 57W
Devine, *U.S.A.* **81 L5** 29 8N 98 54W
Devizes, *U.K.* **11 F6** 51 22N 1 58W
Devli, *India* **42 G6** 25 50N 75 20 E
Devon, *Canada* **72 C6** 53 24N 113 44W
Devon □, *U.K.* **11 G4** 50 50N 3 40W
Devon I., *Canada* **4 B3** 75 10N 85 0W
Devonport, *Australia* **62 G4** 41 10S 146 22 E
Devonport, *N.Z.* **59 G5** 36 49S 174 49 E
Dewas, *India* **42 H7** 22 59N 76 3 E
Dewetsdorp, *S. Africa* **56 D4** 29 33S 26 39 E
Dexter, *Maine, U.S.A.* **77 C11** 45 1N 69 18W
Dexter, *Mo., U.S.A.* **81 G10** 36 48N 89 57W
Dexter, *N. Mex., U.S.A.* **81 J2** 33 12N 104 22W
Dey-Dey, L., *Australia* **61 E5** 29 12S 131 4 E
Deyhūk, *Iran* **45 C8** 33 15N 57 30 E
Deyyer, *Iran* **45 E6** 27 55N 51 55 E
Dezadeash L., *Canada* **72 A1** 60 28N 136 58W
Dezfūl, *Iran* **45 C6** 32 20N 48 30 E
Dezhneva, Mys, *Russia* **27 C19** 66 5N 169 40W
Dezhou, *China* **34 F9** 37 26N 116 18 E
Dhadhar →, *India* **43 G11** 24 56N 85 24 E
Dháfni, *Greece* **23 D7** 35 13N 25 3 E
Dhahiriya = Az Zāhirīyah, *West Bank* **47 D3** 31 25N 34 58 E
Dhahran = Az Zahrān, *Si. Arabia* **45 E6** 26 10N 50 7 E
Dhak, *Pakistan* **42 C5** 32 25N 72 33 E
Dhaka, *Bangla.* **43 H14** 23 43N 90 26 E
Dhaka □, *Bangla.* **43 G14** 24 25N 90 25 E
Dhali, *Cyprus* **23 D12** 35 1N 33 25 E
Dhampur, *India* **43 E8** 29 19N 78 33 E
Dhamtari, *India* **41 J12** 20 42N 81 35 E
Dhanbad, *India* **43 H12** 23 50N 86 30 E
Dhangarhi, *Nepal* **41 E12** 28 55N 80 40 E
Dhankuta, *Nepal* **43 F12** 26 55N 87 40 E
Dhar, *India* **42 H6** 22 35N 75 26 E
Dharampur, *India* **42 H6** 22 13N 75 18 E
Dharamsala = Dharmsala, *India* **42 C7** 32 16N 76 23 E
Dhariwal, *India* **42 D6** 31 57N 75 19 E
Dharla →, *Bangla.* **43 G13** 25 46N 89 42 E
Dharmapuri, *India* **40 N11** 12 10N 78 10 E
Dharmjaygarh, *India* **43 H10** 22 28N 83 13 E
Dharmsala, *India* **42 C7** 32 16N 76 23 E
Dharni, *India* **42 J7** 21 33N 76 53 E
Dhasan →, *India* **43 G8** 25 48N 79 24 E
Dhaulagiri, *Nepal* **43 E10** 28 39N 83 28 E
Dhebar, L., *India* **42 G6** 24 10N 74 0 E
Dheftera, *Cyprus* **23 D12** 35 5N 33 16 E
Dhenkanal, *India* **41 J14** 20 45N 85 35 E
Dherinia, *Cyprus* **23 D12** 35 3N 33 57 E
Dhiarrizos →, *Cyprus* **23 E11** 34 41N 32 34 E
Dhībān, *Jordan* **47 D4** 31 30N 35 46 E
Dhíkti Óros, *Greece* **23 D7** 35 8N 25 30 E
Dhilwan, *India* **42 D6** 31 31N 75 21 E
Dhimarkhera, *India* **43 H9** 23 28N 80 22 E
Dhírfis = Dhírfis Óros, *Greece* **21 E10** 38 40N 23 54 E
Dhírfis Óros, *Greece* **21 E10** 38 40N 23 54 E
Dhodhekánisos, *Greece* **21 F12** 36 35N 27 0 E
Dholka, *India* **42 H5** 22 44N 72 29 E
Dhoraji, *India* **42 J4** 21 45N 70 37 E
Dhráhstis, Ákra, *Greece* **23 A3** 39 48N 19 40 E
Dhrangadhra, *India* **42 H4** 22 59N 71 31 E
Dhrápanon, Ákra, *Greece* **23 D6** 35 28N 24 14 E
Dhrol, *India* **42 H4** 22 33N 70 25 E
Dhuburi, *India* **41 F16** 26 2N 89 59 E
Dhule, *India* **40 J9** 20 58N 74 50 E
Di Linh, *Vietnam* **39 G7** 11 35N 108 4 E
Di Linh, Cao Nguyen, *Vietnam* **39 G7** 11 30N 108 0 E
Día, *Greece* **23 D7** 35 28N 25 14 E
Diablo, Mt., *U.S.A.* **84 H5** 37 53N 121 56W
Diablo Range, *U.S.A.* **84 J5** 37 20N 121 25W
Diafarabé, *Mali* **50 F5** 14 9N 4 57W
Diamante, *Argentina* **94 C3** 32 5S 60 40W
Diamante →, *Argentina* **94 C2** 34 30S 66 46W
Diamantina, *Brazil* **93 G10** 18 17S 43 40W
Diamantina →, *Australia* **63 D2** 26 45S 139 10 E
Diamantino, *Brazil* **93 F7** 14 30S 56 30W
Diamond Bar, *U.S.A.* **85 L9** 34 1N 117 48W
Diamond Harbour, *India* **43 H13** 22 11N 88 14 E
Diamond Is., *Australia* **62 B5** 17 25S 151 5 E
Diamond Mts., *U.S.A.* **82 G6** 39 50N 115 30W
Diamond Springs, *U.S.A.* **84 G6** 38 42N 120 49W
Dībā, *Oman* **45 E8** 25 45N 56 16 E
Dibai, *India* **42 E8** 28 13N 78 15 E
Dibaya-Lubue, *Dem. Rep. of the Congo* **52 E3** 4 12S 19 54 E
Dibete, *Botswana* **56 C4** 23 45S 26 32 E
Dibrugarh, *India* **41 F19** 27 29N 94 55 E
Dickens, *U.S.A.* **81 J4** 33 37N 100 50W
Dickinson, *U.S.A.* **80 B3** 46 53N 102 47W
Dickson = Dikson, *Russia* **26 B9** 73 40N 80 5 E
Dickson, *U.S.A.* **77 G2** 36 5N 87 23W
Dickson City, *U.S.A.* **79 E9** 41 29N 75 40W
Didiéni, *Mali* **50 F4** 13 53N 8 6W
Didsbury, *Canada* **72 C6** 51 35N 114 10W
Didwana, *India* **42 F6** 27 23N 74 36 E
Diefenbaker, L., *Canada* **73 C7** 51 0N 106 55W
Diego de Almagro, *Chile* **94 B1** 26 22S 70 3W
Diego Garcia, *Ind. Oc.* **3 E13** 7 50S 72 50 E
Diekirch, *Lux.* **15 E6** 49 52N 6 10 E
Dien Ban, *Vietnam* **38 E7** 15 53N 108 16 E
Dien Khanh, *Vietnam* **39 F7** 12 15N 109 6 E
Dieppe, *France* **18 B4** 49 54N 1 4 E
Dierks, *U.S.A.* **81 H8** 34 7N 94 1W
Diest, *Belgium* **15 D5** 50 58N 5 4 E
Dif, *Somali Rep.* **46 G3** 0 59N 0 56 E
Differdange, *Lux.* **15 E5** 49 31N 5 54 E
Dig, *India* **42 F7** 27 28N 77 20 E
Digba, *Dem. Rep. of the Congo* **54 B2** 4 25N 25 48 E
Digby, *Canada* **71 D6** 44 38N 65 50W
Diggi, *India* **42 F6** 26 22N 75 26 E
Dighinala, *Bangla.* **41 H18** 23 15N 92 5 E
Dighton, *U.S.A.* **80 F4** 38 29N 100 28W
Digne-les-Bains, *France* **18 D7** 44 5N 6 12 E
Digos, *Phil.* **37 C7** 6 45N 125 20 E
Digranes, *Iceland* **8 C6** 66 4N 14 44W
Digul →, *Indonesia* **37 F9** 7 7S 138 42 E
Dihang →, *India* **41 F19** 27 48N 95 30 E
Dijlah, Nahr →, *Asia* **44 D5** 31 0N 47 25 E
Dijon, *France* **18 C6** 47 20N 5 3 E
Dikkil, *Djibouti* **46 E3** 11 8N 42 20 E
Dikomu di Kai, *Botswana* **56 C3** 24 58S 24 36 E
Diksmuide, *Belgium* **15 C2** 51 2N 2 52 E
Dikson, *Russia* **26 B9** 73 40N 80 5 E
Dila, *Ethiopia* **46 F2** 6 21N 38 22 E
Dili, *Indonesia* **37 F7** 8 39S 125 34 E
Dilley, *U.S.A.* **81 L5** 28 40N 99 10W
Dillingham, *U.S.A.* **68 C4** 59 3N 158 28W
Dillon, *Canada* **73 B7** 55 56N 108 35W
Dillon, *Mont., U.S.A.* **82 D7** 45 13N 112 38W
Dillon, *S.C., U.S.A.* **77 H6** 34 25N 79 22W
Dillon →, *Canada* **73 B7** 55 56N 108 56W
Dillsburg, *U.S.A.* **78 F7** 40 7N 77 2W
Dilolo, *Dem. Rep. of the Congo* **52 G4** 10 28S 22 18 E
Dimas, *Mexico* **86 C3** 23 43N 106 47W
Dimashq, *Syria* **47 B5** 33 30N 36 18 E
Dimashq □, *Syria* **47 B5** 33 30N 36 30 E
Dimbaza, *S. Africa* **57 E4** 32 50S 27 14 E
Dimboola, *Australia* **63 F3** 36 28S 142 7 E
Dîmboviţa = Dâmboviţa →, *Romania* **17 F14** 44 12N 26 26 E
Dimbulah, *Australia* **62 B4** 17 8S 145 4 E
Dimitrovgrad, *Bulgaria* **21 C11** 42 5N 25 35 E
Dimitrovgrad, *Russia* **24 D8** 54 14N 49 39 E
Dimitrovo = Pernik, *Bulgaria* **21 C10** 42 35N 23 2 E
Dimmitt, *U.S.A.* **81 H3** 34 33N 102 19W
Dimona, *Israel* **47 D4** 31 2N 35 1 E
Dinagat, *Phil.* **37 B7** 10 10N 125 40 E
Dinajpur, *Bangla.* **41 G16** 25 33N 88 43 E
Dinan, *France* **18 B2** 48 28N 2 2W
Dīnān Āb, *Iran* **45 C8** 32 4N 56 49 E
Dinant, *Belgium* **15 D4** 50 16N 4 55 E
Dinapur, *India* **43 G11** 25 38N 85 5 E
Dīnār, Kūh-e, *Iran* **45 D6** 30 42N 51 46 E
Dinara Planina, *Croatia* **20 C7** 44 0N 16 30 E
Dinard, *France* **18 B2** 48 38N 2 6W
Dinaric Alps = Dinara Planina, *Croatia* **20 C7** 44 0N 16 30 E
Dindigul, *India* **40 P11** 10 25N 78 0 E
Dindori, *India* **43 H9** 22 57N 81 5 E
Ding Xian = Dingzhou, *China* **34 E8** 38 30N 114 59 E
Dinga, *Pakistan* **42 G2** 25 26N 67 10 E
Dingbian, *China* **34 F4** 37 35N 107 32 E
Dingle, *Ireland* **13 D1** 52 9N 10 17W
Dingle B., *Ireland* **13 D1** 52 3N 10 20W
Dingmans Ferry, *U.S.A.* **79 E10** 41 13N 74 55W
Dingo, *Australia* **62 C4** 23 38S 149 19 E
Dingtao, *China* **34 G8** 35 5N 115 35 E
Dingwall, *U.K.* **12 D4** 57 36N 4 26W
Dingxi, *China* **34 G3** 35 30N 104 33 E
Dingxiang, *China* **34 E7** 38 30N 112 58 E
Dingzhou, *China* **34 E8** 38 30N 114 59 E
Dinh, Mui, *Vietnam* **39 G7** 11 22N 109 1 E
Dinokwe, *Botswana* **56 C4** 23 29S 26 37 E
Dinorwic, *Canada* **73 D10** 49 41N 92 30W
Dinosaur National Monument, *U.S.A.* **82 F9** 40 30N 108 45W
Dinosaur Prov. Park, *Canada* **72 C6** 50 47N 111 30W
Dinuba, *U.S.A.* **84 J7** 36 32N 119 23W
Dipalpur, *Pakistan* **42 D5** 30 40N 73 39 E
Diplo, *Pakistan* **42 G3** 24 35N 69 35 E
Dipolog, *Phil.* **37 C6** 8 36N 123 20 E
Dir, *Pakistan* **40 B7** 35 8N 71 59 E
Dire Dawa, *Ethiopia* **46 F3** 9 35N 41 45 E
Diriamba, *Nic.* **88 D2** 11 51N 86 19W
Dirk Hartog I., *Australia* **61 E1** 25 50S 113 5 E
Dirranbandi, *Australia* **63 D4** 28 33S 148 17 E
Disa, *India* **42 G5** 24 18N 72 10 E
Disappointment, C., *U.S.A.* **82 C2** 46 18N 124 5W
Disappointment, L., *Australia* **60 D3** 23 20S 122 40 E
Disaster B., *Australia* **63 F4** 37 15S 149 58 E
Discovery B., *Australia* **63 F3** 38 10S 140 40 E
Disko, *Greenland* **4 C5** 69 45N 53 30W
Disko Bugt, *Greenland* **4 C5** 69 10N 52 0W
Diss, *U.K.* **11 E9** 52 23N 1 7 E
Disteghil Sar, *Pakistan* **43 A6** 36 20N 75 12 E
Distrito Federal □, *Brazil* **93 G9** 15 45S 47 45W
Distrito Federal □, *Mexico* **87 D5** 19 15N 99 10W
Diu, *India* **42 J4** 20 45N 70 58 E
Divāndarreh, *Iran* **44 C5** 35 55N 47 2 E
Divide, *U.S.A.* **82 D7** 45 45N 112 45W
Dividing Ra., *Australia* **61 E2** 27 45S 116 0 E
Divinópolis, *Brazil* **93 H10** 20 10S 44 54W
Divnoye, *Russia* **25 E7** 45 55N 43 21 E
Divo, *Ivory C.* **50 G4** 5 48N 5 15W
Dīwāl Kol, *Afghan.* **42 B2** 34 23N 67 52 E
Dixie Mt., *U.S.A.* **84 F6** 39 55N 120 16W
Dixon, *Calif., U.S.A.* **84 G5** 38 27N 121 49W
Dixon, *Ill., U.S.A.* **80 E10** 41 50N 89 29W
Dixon Entrance, *U.S.A.* **68 C6** 54 30N 132 0W
Dixville, *Canada* **79 A13** 45 4N 71 46W
Diyālā →, *Iraq* **44 C5** 33 14N 44 31 E
Diyarbakır, *Turkey* **25 G7** 37 55N 40 18 E
Diyodar, *India* **42 G4** 24 8N 71 50 E
Djakarta = Jakarta, *Indonesia* **37 G12** 6 9S 106 49 E
Djamba, *Angola* **56 B1** 16 45S 13 58 E
Djambala, *Congo* **52 E2** 2 32S 14 30 E
Djanet, *Algeria* **50 D7** 24 35N 9 32 E
Djawa = Jawa, *Indonesia* **37 G14** 7 0S 110 0 E
Djelfa, *Algeria* **50 B6** 34 40N 3 15 E
Djema, *C.A.R.* **54 A2** 6 3N 25 15 E
Djerba, I. de, *Tunisia* **51 B8** 33 50N 10 48 E
Djerid, Chott, *Tunisia* **50 B7** 33 42N 8 30 E
Djibouti, *Djibouti* **46 E3** 11 30N 43 5 E
Djibouti ■, *Africa* **46 E3** 12 0N 43 0 E
Djolu, *Dem. Rep. of the Congo* **52 D4** 0 35N 22 5 E
Djoum, *Cameroon* **52 D2** 2 41N 12 35 E
Djourab, Erg du, *Chad* **51 E9** 16 40N 18 50 E
Djugu, *Dem. Rep. of the Congo* **54 B3** 1 55N 30 35 E
Djúpivogur, *Iceland* **8 D6** 64 39N 14 17W
Dmitriya Lapteva, Proliv, *Russia* **27 B15** 73 0N 140 0 E
Dnepr = Dnipro →, *Ukraine* **25 E5** 46 30N 32 18 E
Dneprodzerzhinsk = Dniprodzerzhynsk, *Ukraine* **25 E5** 48 32N 34 37 E
Dnepropetrovsk = Dnipropetrovsk, *Ukraine* **25 E6** 48 30N 35 0 E
Dnestr = Dnister →, *Europe* **17 E16** 46 18N 30 17 E
Dnestrovski = Belgorod, *Russia* **25 D6** 50 35N 36 35 E
Dnieper = Dnipro →, *Ukraine* **25 E5** 46 30N 32 18 E
Dniester = Dnister →, *Europe* **17 E16** 46 18N 30 17 E
Dnipro →, *Ukraine* **25 E5** 46 30N 32 18 E
Dniprodzerzhynsk, *Ukraine* **25 E5** 48 32N 34 37 E
Dnipropetrovsk, *Ukraine* **25 E6** 48 30N 35 0 E
Dnister →, *Europe* **17 E16** 46 18N 30 17 E
Dnistrovskyy Lyman, *Ukraine* **17 E16** 46 15N 30 17 E
Dno, *Russia* **24 C4** 57 50N 29 58 E
Dnyapro = Dnipro →, *Ukraine* **25 E5** 46 30N 32 18 E
Doaktown, *Canada* **71 C6** 46 33N 66 8W
Doba, *Chad* **51 G9** 8 40N 16 50 E
Dobandi, *Pakistan* **42 D2** 31 13N 66 50 E
Dobbyn, *Australia* **62 B3** 19 44S 140 2 E
Dobele, *Latvia* **9 H20** 56 37N 23 16 E
Doberai, Jazirah, *Indonesia* **37 E8** 1 25S 133 0 E
Doblas, *Argentina* **94 D3** 37 5S 64 0W
Dobo, *Indonesia* **37 F8** 5 45S 134 15 E
Doboj, *Bos.-H.* **21 B8** 44 46N 18 4 E
Dobreta-Turnu Severin, *Romania* **17 F12** 44 39N 22 41 E
Dobrich, *Bulgaria* **21 C12** 43 37N 27 49 E
Dobruja, *Europe* **17 F15** 44 30N 28 15 E
Dobrush, *Belarus* **17 B16** 52 25N 31 22 E
Doc, Mui, *Vietnam* **38 D6** 17 58N 106 30 E
Docker River, *Australia* **61 D4** 24 52S 129 5 E
Doctor Arroyo, *Mexico* **86 C4** 23 40N 100 11W
Doda, *India* **43 C6** 33 10N 75 34 E
Doda, L., *Canada* **70 C4** 49 25N 75 13W
Dodecanese = Dhodhekánisos, *Greece* **21 F12** 36 35N 27 0 E
Dodge City, *U.S.A.* **81 G5** 37 45N 100 1W
Dodge L., *Canada* **73 B7** 59 50N 105 36W
Dodgeville, *U.S.A.* **80 D9** 42 58N 90 8W
Dodoma, *Tanzania* **54 D4** 6 8S 35 45 E
Dodoma □, *Tanzania* **54 D4** 6 0S 36 0 E
Dodsland, *Canada* **73 C7** 51 50N 108 45W
Dodson, *U.S.A.* **82 B9** 48 24N 108 15W
Doesburg, *Neths.* **15 B6** 52 1N 6 9 E
Doetinchem, *Neths.* **15 C6** 51 59N 6 18 E
Dog Creek, *Canada* **72 C4** 51 35N 122 14W
Dog L., *Man., Canada* **73 C9** 51 2N 98 31W
Dog L., *Ont., Canada* **70 C2** 48 48N 89 30W
Dogi, *Afghan.* **40 C3** 32 20N 62 50 E
Dogran, *Pakistan* **42 D5** 31 48N 73 35 E
Doğubayazıt, *Turkey* **44 B5** 39 31N 44 5 E
Doha = Ad Dawḩah, *Qatar* **45 E6** 25 15N 51 35 E
Dohazari, *Bangla.* **41 H18** 22 10N 92 5 E
Dohrighat, *India* **43 F10** 26 16N 83 31 E
Doi, *Indonesia* **37 D7** 2 14N 127 49 E
Doi Luang, *Thailand* **38 C3** 18 30N 101 0 E
Doi Saket, *Thailand* **38 C2** 18 52N 99 9 E
Dois Irmãos, Sa., *Brazil* **93 E10** 9 0S 42 30W
Dokkum, *Neths.* **15 A5** 53 20N 5 59 E
Dokri, *Pakistan* **42 F3** 27 25N 68 7 E
Dolak, Pulau, *Indonesia* **37 F9** 8 0S 138 30 E
Dolbeau, *Canada* **71 C5** 48 53N 72 18W
Dole, *France* **18 C6** 47 7N 5 31 E
Dolgellau, *U.K.* **10 E4** 52 45N 3 53W
Dolgelley = Dolgellau, *U.K.* **10 E4** 52 45N 3 53W
Dollard, *Neths.* **15 A7** 53 20N 7 10 E
Dolo, *Ethiopia* **46 G3** 4 11N 42 3 E
Dolomites = Dolomiti, *Italy* **20 A4** 46 23N 11 51 E
Dolomiti, *Italy* **20 A4** 46 23N 11 51 E
Dolores, *Argentina* **94 D4** 36 20S 57 40W
Dolores, *Uruguay* **94 C4** 33 34S 58 15W
Dolores, *U.S.A.* **83 H9** 37 28N 108 30W
Dolores →, *U.S.A.* **83 G9** 38 49N 109 17W
Dolphin, C., *Falk. Is.* **96 G5** 51 10S 59 0W
Dolphin and Union Str., *Canada* **68 B8** 69 5N 114 45W
Dom Pedrito, *Brazil* **95 C5** 31 0S 54 40W
Domariaganj →, *India* **43 F10** 26 17N 83 44 E
Domasi, *Malawi* **55 F4** 15 15S 35 22 E
Dombarovskiy, *Russia* **26 D6** 50 46N 59 32 E
Dombås, *Norway* **9 E13** 62 4N 9 8 E
Domel I. = Letsôk-aw Kyun, *Burma* **39 G2** 11 30N 98 25 E
Domeyko, *Chile* **94 B1** 29 0S 71 0W
Domeyko, Cordillera, *Chile* **94 A2** 24 30S 69 0W
Dominador, *Chile* **94 A2** 24 21S 69 20W
Dominica ■, *W. Indies* **89 C7** 15 20N 61 20W
Dominica Passage, *W. Indies* **89 C7** 15 10N 61 20W
Dominican Rep. ■, *W. Indies* **89 C5** 19 0N 70 30W
Domodóssola, *Italy* **18 C8** 46 7N 8 17 E
Domville, Mt., *Australia* **63 D5** 28 1S 151 15 E
Don →, *Russia* **25 E6** 47 4N 39 18 E
Don →, *Aberds., U.K.* **12 D6** 57 11N 2 5W
Don →, *S. Yorks., U.K.* **10 D7** 53 41N 0 52W
Don, C., *Australia* **60 B5** 11 18S 131 46 E
Don Benito, *Spain* **19 C3** 38 53N 5 51W
Dona Ana = Nhamaabué, *Mozam.* **55 F4** 17 25S 35 5 E
Donaghadee, *U.K.* **13 B6** 54 39N 5 33W
Donald, *Australia* **63 F3** 36 23S 143 0 E
Donaldsonville, *U.S.A.* **81 K9** 30 6N 90 59W
Donalsonville, *U.S.A.* **77 K3** 31 3N 84 53W
Donau = Dunărea →, *Europe* **17 F15** 45 20N 29 40 E
Donau →, *Austria* **15 D3** 48 10N 17 0 E
Donauwörth, *Germany* **16 D6** 48 43N 10 47 E
Doncaster, *U.K.* **10 D6** 53 32N 1 6W
Dondo, *Mozam.* **55 F3** 19 33S 34 46 E
Dondo, Teluk, *Indonesia* **37 D6** 0 50N 120 30 E
Dondra Head, *Sri Lanka* **40 S12** 5 55N 80 40 E
Donegal, *Ireland* **13 B3** 54 39N 8 5W
Donegal □, *Ireland* **13 B4** 54 53N 8 0W
Donegal B., *Ireland* **13 B3** 54 31N 8 49W
Donets →, *Russia* **25 E7** 47 33N 40 55 E
Donetsk, *Ukraine* **25 E6** 48 0N 37 45 E
Dong Ba Thin, *Vietnam* **39 F7** 12 8N 109 13 E
Dong Giam, *Vietnam* **38 C5** 19 25N 105 31 E
Dong Ha, *Vietnam* **38 D6** 16 55N 107 8 E
Dong Hene, *Laos* **38 D5** 16 40N 105 18 E
Dong Hoi, *Vietnam* **38 D6** 17 29N 106 36 E
Dong Khe, *Vietnam* **38 A6** 22 26N 106 27 E
Dong Ujimqin Qi, *China* **34 B9** 45 32N 116 55 E
Dong Van, *Vietnam* **38 A5** 23 16N 105 22 E
Dong Xoai, *Vietnam* **39 G6** 11 32N 106 55 E
Dongara, *Australia* **61 E1** 29 14S 114 57 E
Dongbei, *China* **35 D13** 45 0N 125 0 E
Dongchuan, *China* **32 D5** 26 8N 103 1 E
Dongfang, *China* **38 C7** 18 50N 108 33 E
Dongfeng, *China* **35 C13** 42 40N 125 34 E
Donggala, *Indonesia* **37 E5** 0 30S 119 40 E
Donggou, *China* **35 E13** 39 52N 124 10 E
Dongguang, *China* **34 F9** 37 50N 116 30 E
Dongjingcheng, *China* **35 B15** 44 5N 129 10 E
Dongning, *China* **35 B16** 44 2N 131 5 E
Dongola, *Sudan* **51 E12** 19 9N 30 22 E
Dongping, *China* **34 G9** 35 55N 116 20 E
Dongsheng, *China* **34 E6** 39 50N 110 0 E
Dongtai, *China* **35 H11** 32 51N 120 21 E
Dongting Hu, *China* **33 D6** 29 18N 112 45 E
Donington, C., *Australia* **63 E2** 34 45S 136 0 E
Doniphan, *U.S.A.* **81 G9** 36 37N 90 50W
Dønna, *Norway* **8 C15** 66 6N 12 30 E
Donna, *U.S.A.* **81 M5** 26 9N 98 4W
Donnaconna, *Canada* **71 C5** 46 41N 71 41W
Donnelly's Crossing, *N.Z.* **59 F4** 35 42S 173 38 E
Donnybrook, *Australia* **61 F2** 33 34S 115 48 E
Donnybrook, *S. Africa* **57 D4** 29 59S 29 48 E
Donora, *U.S.A.* **78 F5** 40 11N 79 52W
Donostia = Donostia-San Sebastián, *Spain* **19 A5** 43 17N 1 58W
Donostia-San Sebastián, *Spain* **19 A5** 43 17N 1 58W
Doon →, *U.K.* **12 F4** 55 27N 4 39W
Dora, L., *Australia* **60 D3** 22 0S 123 0 E
Dora Báltea →, *Italy* **18 D8** 45 11N 8 3 E
Doran L., *Canada* **73 A7** 61 13N 108 6W
Dorchester, *U.K.* **11 G5** 50 42N 2 27W
Dorchester, C., *Canada* **69 B12** 65 27N 77 27W
Dordogne →, *France* **18 D3** 45 2N 0 36W
Dordrecht, *Neths.* **15 C4** 51 48N 4 39 E
Dordrecht, *S. Africa* **56 E4** 31 20S 27 3 E
Doré L., *Canada* **73 C7** 54 46N 107 17W
Doré Lake, *Canada* **73 C7** 54 38N 107 36W
Dori, *Burkina Faso* **50 F5** 14 3N 0 2W
Doring →, *S. Africa* **56 E2** 31 54S 18 39 E
Doringbos, *S. Africa* **56 E2** 31 59S 19 16 E
Dorion, *Canada* **79 A10** 45 23N 74 3W
Dornbirn, *Austria* **16 E5** 47 25N 9 45 E
Dornie, *U.K.* **12 D3** 57 17N 5 31W
Dornoch, *U.K.* **12 D4** 57 53N 4 2W
Dornoch Firth, *U.K.* **12 D4** 57 51N 4 4W
Dornogovĭ □, *Mongolia* **34 C6** 44 0N 110 0 E
Dorohoi, *Romania* **17 E14** 47 56N 26 23 E
Döröö Nuur, *Mongolia* **32 B4** 48 0N 93 0 E
Dorr, *Iran* **45 C6** 33 17N 50 38 E
Dorre I., *Australia* **61 E1** 25 13S 113 12 E
Dorrigo, *Australia* **63 E5** 30 20S 152 44 E
Dorris, *U.S.A.* **82 F3** 41 58N 121 55W
Dorset, *Canada* **78 A6** 45 14N 78 54W
Dorset, *U.S.A.* **78 E4** 41 40N 80 40W
Dorset □, *U.K.* **11 G5** 50 45N 2 26W
Dortmund, *Germany* **16 C4** 51 30N 7 28 E
Doruma, *Dem. Rep. of the Congo* **54 B2** 4 42N 27 33 E
Dorūneh, *Iran* **45 C8** 35 10N 57 18 E
Dos Bahías, C., *Argentina* **96 E3** 44 58S 65 32W
Dos Hermanas, *Spain* **19 D3** 37 16N 5 55W
Dos Palos, *U.S.A.* **84 J6** 36 59N 120 37W
Dosso, *Niger* **50 F6** 13 0N 3 13 E
Dothan, *U.S.A.* **77 K3** 31 13N 85 24W
Doty, *U.S.A.* **84 D3** 46 38N 123 17W
Douai, *France* **18 A5** 50 21N 3 4 E
Douala, *Cameroon* **52 D1** 4 0N 9 45 E
Douarnenez, *France* **18 B1** 48 6N 4 21W
Double Island Pt., *Australia* **63 D5** 25 56S 153 11 E
Double Mountain Fork →, *U.S.A.* **81 J4** 33 16N 100 0W
Doubs →, *France* **18 C6** 46 53N 5 1 E
Doubtful Sd., *N.Z.* **59 L1** 45 20S 166 49 E
Doubtless B., *N.Z.* **59 F4** 34 55S 173 26 E
Douglas, *S. Africa* **56 D3** 29 4S 23 46 E
Douglas, *U.K.* **10 C3** 54 10N 4 28W
Douglas, *Ariz., U.S.A.* **83 L9** 31 21N 109 33W
Douglas, *Ga., U.S.A.* **77 K4** 31 31N 82 51W
Douglas, *Wyo., U.S.A.* **80 D2** 42 45N 105 24W
Douglas Chan., *Canada* **72 C3** 53 40N 129 20W
Douglas Pt., *Canada* **78 B3** 44 19N 81 37W
Douglasville, *U.S.A.* **77 J3** 33 45N 84 45W
Dounreay, *U.K.* **12 C5** 58 35N 3 44W
Dourada, Serra, *Brazil* **93 F9** 13 10S 48 45W
Dourados, *Brazil* **95 A5** 22 9S 54 50W
Dourados →, *Brazil* **95 A5** 21 58S 54 18W
Dourados, Serra dos, *Brazil* **95 A5** 23 30S 53 30W
Douro →, *Europe* **19 B1** 41 8N 8 40W
Dove →, *U.K.* **10 E6** 52 51N 1 36W
Dove Creek, *U.S.A.* **83 H9** 37 46N 108 54W
Dover, *Australia* **62 G4** 43 18S 147 2 E
Dover, *U.K.* **11 F9** 51 7N 1 19 E
Dover, *Del., U.S.A.* **76 F8** 39 10N 75 32W
Dover, *N.H., U.S.A.* **79 C14** 43 12N 70 56W
Dover, *N.J., U.S.A.* **79 F10** 40 53N 74 34W
Dover, *Ohio, U.S.A.* **78 F3** 40 32N 81 29W
Dover, Pt., *Australia* **61 F4** 32 32S 125 32 E
Dover, Str. of, *Europe* **11 G9** 51 0N 1 30 E
Dover-Foxcroft, *U.S.A.* **77 C11** 45 11N 69 13W
Dover Plains, *U.S.A.* **79 E11** 41 43N 73 35W
Dovey = Dyfi →, *U.K.* **11 E3** 52 32N 4 3W
Dovrefjell, *Norway* **9 E13** 62 15N 9 33 E
Dow Rūd, *Iran* **45 C6** 33 28N 49 4 E
Dowa, *Malawi* **55 E3** 13 38S 33 58 E
Dowagiac, *U.S.A.* **76 E2** 41 59N 86 6W

Eddystone Pt.

Dowerin, Australia 61 F2 31 12S 117 2 E
Dowgha'i, Iran 45 B8 36 54N 58 32 E
Dowlatābād, Iran 45 D8 28 20N 56 40 E
Down □, U.K. 13 B5 54 23N 6 2W
Downey, Calif., U.S.A. 85 M8 33 56N 118 7W
Downey, Idaho, U.S.A. 82 E7 42 26N 112 7W
Downham Market, U.K. 11 E8 52 37N 0 23 E
Downieville, U.S.A. 84 F6 39 34N 120 50W
Downpatrick, U.K. 13 B6 54 20N 5 43W
Downpatrick Hd., Ireland 13 B2 54 20N 9 21W
Downsville, U.S.A. 79 D10 42 5N 74 50W
Downton, Mt., Canada 72 C4 52 42N 124 52W
Dowsārī, Iran 45 D8 28 25N 57 59 E
Doyle, U.S.A. 84 E6 40 2N 120 6W
Doylestown, U.S.A. 79 F9 40 21N 75 10W
Dozois, Rés., Canada 70 C4 47 30N 77 5W
Dra Khel, Pakistan 42 F2 27 58N 66 45 E
Drachten, Neths. 15 A6 53 7N 6 5 E
Drăgăşani, Romania 17 F13 44 39N 24 17 E
Dragichyn, Belarus 17 B13 52 15N 25 8 E
Dragoman, Prokhod, Bulgaria 21 C10 42 58N 22 53 E
Draguignan, France 18 E7 43 32N 6 27 E
Drain, U.S.A. 82 E2 43 40N 123 19W
Drake, U.S.A. 80 B4 47 55N 100 23W
Drake Passage, S. Ocean 5 B17 58 0S 68 0W
Drakensberg, S. Africa 57 E4 31 0S 28 0 E
Dráma, Greece 21 D11 41 9N 24 10 E
Drammen, Norway 9 G14 59 42N 10 12 E
Drangajökull, Iceland 8 C2 66 9N 22 15W
Dras, India 43 B6 34 25N 75 48 E
Drau = Drava —►, Croatia 21 B8 45 33N 18 55 E
Drava —►, Croatia 21 B8 45 33N 18 55 E
Drayton Valley, Canada 72 C6 53 12N 114 58W
Drenthe □, Neths. 15 B6 52 52N 6 40 E
Drepanum, C., Cyprus 23 E11 34 54N 32 19 E
Dresden, Canada 78 D2 42 35N 82 11W
Dresden, Germany 16 C7 51 3N 13 44 E
Dreux, France 18 B4 48 44N 1 23 E
Driffield, U.K. 10 C7 54 0N 0 26W
Driftwood, U.S.A. 78 E6 41 20N 78 8W
Driggs, U.S.A. 82 E8 43 44N 111 6W
Drina —►, Bos.-H. 21 B8 44 53N 19 21 E
Drini —►, Albania 21 C8 42 1N 19 38 E
Drøbak, Norway 9 G14 59 39N 10 39 E
Drochia, Moldova 17 D14 48 2N 27 48 E
Drogheda, Ireland 13 C5 53 43N 6 22W
Drogichin = Dragichyn, Belarus 17 B13 52 15N 25 8 E
Drogobych = Drohobych, Ukraine 17 D12 49 20N 23 30 E
Drohobych, Ukraine 17 D12 49 20N 23 30 E
Droichead Atha = Drogheda, Ireland 13 C5 53 43N 6 22W
Droichead Nua, Ireland 13 C5 53 11N 6 48W
Droitwich, U.K. 11 E5 52 16N 2 8W
Dromedary, C., Australia 63 F5 36 17S 150 10 E
Dromore, U.K. 13 B4 54 31N 7 28W
Dromore West, Ireland 13 B3 54 15N 8 52W
Dronfield, U.K. 10 D6 53 19N 1 27W
Dronten, Neths. 15 B5 52 32N 5 43 E
Drumbo, Canada 78 C4 43 16N 80 35W
Drumheller, Canada 72 C6 51 25N 112 40W
Drummond, U.S.A. 82 C7 46 40N 113 9W
Drummond I., U.S.A. 76 C4 46 1N 83 39W
Drummond Pt., Australia 63 E2 34 9S 135 16 E
Drummond Ra., Australia 62 C4 23 45S 147 10 E
Drummondville, Canada 70 C5 45 55N 72 25W
Drumright, U.S.A. 81 H6 35 59N 96 36W
Druskininkai, Lithuania 9 J20 54 3N 23 58 E
Drut —►, Belarus 17 B16 53 8N 30 5 E
Druzhina, Russia 27 C15 68 14N 145 18 E
Dry Tortugas, U.S.A. 88 B3 24 38N 82 55W
Dryden, Canada 73 D10 49 47N 92 50W
Dryden, U.S.A. 79 D8 42 30N 76 18W
Drygalski I., Antarctica 5 C7 66 0S 92 0 E
Drysdale —►, Australia 60 B4 13 59S 126 51 E
Drysdale I., Australia 62 A2 11 41S 136 0 E
Du Bois, U.S.A. 78 E6 41 8N 78 46W
Du Gué —►, Canada 70 A5 57 21N 70 45W
Du Quoin, U.S.A. 80 G10 38 1N 89 14W
Duanesburg, U.S.A. 79 D10 42 45N 74 11W
Duaringa, Australia 62 C4 23 42S 149 42 E
Ḑubā, Si. Arabia 44 E2 27 10N 35 40 E
Dubai = Dubayy, U.A.E. 45 E7 25 18N 55 20 E
Dubăsari, Moldova 17 E15 47 15N 29 10 E
Dubăsari Vdkhr., Moldova 17 E15 47 30N 29 0 E
Dubawnt —►, Canada 73 A8 64 33N 100 6W
Dubawnt, L., Canada 73 A8 63 4N 101 42W
Dubayy, U.A.E. 45 E7 25 18N 55 20 E
Dubbo, Australia 63 E4 32 11S 148 35 E
Dubele, Dem. Rep. of the Congo 54 B2 2 56N 29 35 E
Dublin, Ireland 13 C5 53 21N 6 15W
Dublin, Ga., U.S.A. 77 J4 32 32N 82 54W
Dublin, Tex., U.S.A. 81 J5 32 5N 98 21W
Dublin □, Ireland 13 C5 53 24N 6 20W
Dubno, Ukraine 17 C13 50 25N 25 45 E
Dubois, U.S.A. 82 D7 44 10N 112 14W
Dubossary = Dubăsari, Moldova 17 E15 47 15N 29 10 E
Dubossary Vdkhr. = Dubăsari Vdkhr., Moldova 17 E15 47 30N 29 0 E
Dubovka, Russia 25 E7 49 5N 44 50 E
Dubrajpur, India 43 H12 23 48N 87 25 E
Dubréka, Guinea 50 G3 9 46N 13 31W
Dubrovitsa = Dubrovytsya, Ukraine 17 C14 51 31N 26 35 E
Dubrovnik, Croatia 21 C8 42 39N 18 6 E
Dubrovytsya, Ukraine 17 C14 51 31N 26 35 E
Dubuque, U.S.A. 80 D9 42 30N 90 41W
Duchesne, U.S.A. 82 F8 40 10N 110 24W
Duchess, Australia 62 C2 21 20S 139 50 E
Ducie I., Pac. Oc. 65 K15 24 40S 124 48W
Duck —►, U.S.A. 77 G2 36 2N 87 52W
Duck Cr. —►, Australia 60 D2 22 37S 116 53 E
Duck Lake, Canada 73 C7 52 50N 106 16W
Duck Mountain Prov. Park, Canada 73 C8 51 45N 101 0W
Duckwall, Mt., U.S.A. 84 H6 37 58N 120 7W
Dudhi, India 41 G13 24 15N 83 10 E
Dudinka, Russia 27 C9 69 30N 86 13 E
Dudley, U.K. 11 E5 52 31N 2 5W
Dudwa, India 43 E9 28 30N 80 41 E
Duero = Douro —►, Europe 19 B1 41 8N 8 40W
Dufftown, U.K. 12 D5 57 27N 3 8W
Dugi Otok, Croatia 16 G8 44 0N 15 3 E
Duifken Pt., Australia 62 A3 12 33S 141 38 E
Duisburg, Germany 16 C4 51 26N 6 45 E
Duiwelskloof, S. Africa 57 C5 23 42S 30 10 E
Dūkdamīn, Iran 45 C8 35 59N 57 43 E
Dukelský Průsmyk, Slovak Rep. 17 D11 49 25N 21 42 E
Dukhān, Qatar 45 E6 25 25N 50 50 E
Duki, Pakistan 40 D6 30 14N 68 25 E
Duku, Nigeria 51 F8 10 43N 10 43 E
Dulce, U.S.A. 83 H10 36 56N 107 0W
Dulce —►, Argentina 94 C3 30 32S 62 33W
Dulce, G., Costa Rica 88 E3 8 40N 83 20W
Dulf, Iraq 44 C5 35 7N 45 51 E
Dulit, Banjaran, Malaysia 36 D4 3 15N 114 30 E
Duliu, China 34 E9 39 2N 116 55 E
Dullewala, Pakistan 42 D4 31 50N 71 25 E
Dulq Maghār, Syria 44 B3 36 22N 38 39 E
Duluth, U.S.A. 80 B8 46 47N 92 6W
Dum Dum, India 43 H13 22 39N 88 33 E
Dum Duma, India 41 F19 27 40N 95 40 E
Dūmā, Syria 47 B5 33 34N 36 24 E
Dumaguete, Phil. 37 C6 9 17N 123 15 E
Dumai, Indonesia 36 D2 1 35N 101 28 E
Dumaran, Phil. 37 B5 10 33N 119 50 E
Dumas, Ark., U.S.A. 81 J9 33 53N 91 29W
Dumas, Tex., U.S.A. 81 H4 35 52N 101 58W
Ḑumayr, Syria 47 B5 33 39N 36 42 E
Dumbarton, U.K. 12 F4 55 57N 4 33W
Dumbleyung, Australia 61 F2 33 17S 117 42 E
Dumfries, U.K. 12 F5 55 4N 3 37W
Dumfries & Galloway □, U.K. 12 F5 55 9N 3 58W
Dumka, India 43 G12 24 12N 87 15 E
Dumoine —►, Canada 70 C4 46 13N 77 51W
Dumoine, L., Canada 70 C4 46 55N 77 55W
Dumraon, India 43 G11 25 33N 84 8 E
Dumyât, Egypt 51 B12 31 24N 31 48 E
Dún Dealgan = Dundalk, Ireland 13 B5 54 1N 6 24W
Dun Laoghaire, Ireland 13 C5 53 17N 6 8W
Duna = Dunărea —►, Europe 17 F15 45 20N 29 40 E
Dunagiri, India 43 D8 30 31N 79 52 E
Dunaj = Dunărea —►, Europe 17 F15 45 20N 29 40 E
Dunakeszi, Hungary 17 E10 47 37N 19 8 E
Dunărea —►, Europe 17 F15 45 20N 29 40 E
Dunaújváros, Hungary 17 E10 46 58N 18 57 E
Dunav = Dunărea —►, Europe 17 F15 45 20N 29 40 E
Dunay, Russia 30 C6 42 52N 132 22 E
Dunback, N.Z. 59 L3 45 23S 170 36 E
Dunbar, U.K. 12 E6 56 0N 2 31W
Dunblane, U.K. 12 E5 56 11N 3 58W
Duncan, Canada 72 D4 48 45N 123 40W
Duncan, Ariz., U.S.A. 83 K9 32 43N 109 6W
Duncan, Okla., U.S.A. 81 H6 34 30N 97 57W
Duncan, L., Canada 70 B4 53 29N 77 58W
Duncan L., Canada 72 A6 62 51N 113 58W
Duncan Town, Bahamas 88 B4 22 15N 75 45W
Duncannon, U.S.A. 78 F7 40 23N 77 2W
Duncansby Head, U.K. 12 C5 58 38N 3 1W
Duncansville, U.S.A. 78 F6 40 25N 78 26W
Dundalk, Canada 78 B4 44 10N 80 24W
Dundalk, Ireland 13 B5 54 1N 6 24W
Dundalk, U.S.A. 76 F7 39 16N 76 32W
Dundalk Bay, Ireland 13 C5 53 55N 6 15W
Dundas, Canada 78 C5 43 17N 79 59W
Dundas, L., Australia 61 F3 32 35S 121 50 E
Dundas I., Canada 72 C2 54 30N 130 50W
Dundas Str., Australia 60 B5 11 15S 131 35 E
Dundee, S. Africa 57 D5 28 11S 30 15 E
Dundee, U.K. 12 E6 56 28N 2 59W
Dundee, U.S.A. 78 D8 42 32N 76 59W
Dundee City □, U.K. 12 E6 56 30N 2 58W
Dundgovĭ □, Mongolia 34 B4 45 10N 106 0 E
Dundrum, U.K. 13 B6 54 16N 5 52W
Dundrum B., U.K. 13 B6 54 13N 5 47W
Dunedin, N.Z. 59 L3 45 50S 170 33 E
Dunedin, U.S.A. 77 L4 28 1N 82 47W
Dunedoo, Australia 63 E4 32 0S 149 25 E
Dunfermline, U.K. 12 E5 56 5N 3 27W
Dungannon, Canada 78 C3 43 51N 81 36W
Dungannon, U.K. 13 B5 54 31N 6 46W
Dungarpur, India 42 H5 23 52N 73 45 E
Dungarvan, Ireland 13 D4 52 5N 7 37W
Dungarvan Harbour, Ireland 13 D4 52 4N 7 35W
Dungeness, U.K. 11 G8 50 54N 0 59 E
Dungo, L. do, Angola 56 B2 17 15S 19 0 E
Dungog, Australia 63 E5 32 22S 151 46 E
Dungu, Dem. Rep. of the Congo 54 B2 3 40N 28 32 E
Dungun, Malaysia 39 K4 4 45N 103 25 E
Dunhua, China 35 C15 43 20N 128 14 E
Dunhuang, China 32 B4 40 8N 94 36 E
Dunk I., Australia 62 B4 17 59S 146 29 E
Dunkeld, Australia 63 E4 33 25S 149 29 E
Dunkeld, U.K. 12 E5 56 34N 3 35W
Dunkerque, France 18 A5 51 2N 2 20 E
Dunkery Beacon, U.K. 11 F4 51 9N 3 36W
Dunkirk = Dunkerque, France 18 A5 51 2N 2 20 E
Dunkirk, U.S.A. 78 D5 42 29N 79 20W
Dúnleary = Dun Laoghaire, Ireland 13 C5 53 17N 6 8W
Dunleer, Ireland 13 C5 53 50N 6 24W
Dunmanus B., Ireland 13 E2 51 31N 9 50W
Dunmanway, Ireland 13 E2 51 43N 9 6W
Dunmara, Australia 62 B1 16 42S 133 25 E
Dunmore, U.S.A. 79 E9 41 25N 75 38W
Dunmore Hd., Ireland 13 D1 52 10N 10 35W
Dunmore Town, Bahamas 88 A4 25 30N 76 39W
Dunn, U.S.A. 77 H6 35 19N 78 37W
Dunnet Hd., U.K. 12 C5 58 40N 3 21W
Dunning, U.S.A. 80 E4 41 50N 100 6W
Dunnville, Canada 78 D5 42 54N 79 36W
Dunolly, Australia 63 F3 36 51S 143 44 E
Dunoon, U.K. 12 F4 55 57N 4 56W
Dunphy, U.S.A. 82 F5 40 42N 116 31W
Duns, U.K. 12 F6 55 47N 2 20W
Dunseith, U.S.A. 80 A4 48 50N 100 3W
Dunsmuir, U.S.A. 82 F2 41 13N 122 16W
Dunstable, U.K. 11 F7 51 53N 0 32W
Dunstan Mts., N.Z. 59 L2 44 53S 169 35 E
Dunster, Canada 72 C5 53 8N 119 50W
Dunvegan L., Canada 73 A7 60 8N 107 10W
Duolun, China 34 C9 42 12N 116 28 E
Duong Dong, Vietnam 39 G4 10 13N 103 58 E
Dupree, U.S.A. 80 C4 45 4N 101 35W
Dupuyer, U.S.A. 82 B7 48 13N 112 30W
Duque de Caxias, Brazil 95 A7 22 45S 43 19W
Durack —►, Australia 60 C4 15 33S 127 52 E
Durack Ra., Australia 60 C4 16 50S 127 40 E
Durance —►, France 18 E6 43 55N 4 45 E
Durand, U.S.A. 80 C9 44 38N 91 58W
Durango, Mexico 86 C4 24 3N 104 39W
Durango, U.S.A. 83 H10 37 16N 107 53W
Durango □, Mexico 86 C4 25 0N 105 0W
Durant, Miss., U.S.A. 81 J10 33 4N 89 51W
Durant, Okla., U.S.A. 81 J6 33 59N 96 25W
Durazno, Uruguay 94 C4 33 25S 56 31W
Durazzo = Durrësi, Albania 21 D8 41 19N 19 28 E
Durban, S. Africa 57 D5 29 49S 31 1 E
Durbuy, Belgium 15 D5 50 21N 5 28 E
Düren, Germany 16 C4 50 48N 6 29 E
Durg, India 41 J12 21 15N 81 22 E
Durgapur, India 43 H12 23 30N 87 20 E
Durham, Canada 78 B4 44 10N 80 49W
Durham, U.K. 10 C6 54 47N 1 34W
Durham, Calif., U.S.A. 84 F5 39 39N 121 48W
Durham, N.C., U.S.A. 77 H6 35 59N 78 54W
Durham, N.H., U.S.A. 79 C14 43 8N 70 56W
Durham □, U.K. 10 C6 54 42N 1 45W
Ḑurmā, Si. Arabia 44 E5 24 37N 46 8 E
Durmitor, Montenegro, Yug. 21 C8 43 10N 19 0 E
Durness, U.K. 12 C4 58 34N 4 45W
Durrësi, Albania 21 D8 41 19N 19 28 E
Durrow, Ireland 13 D4 52 51N 7 24W
Dursey I., Ireland 13 E1 51 36N 10 12W
Dursunbey, Turkey 21 E13 39 35N 28 37 E
Duru, Dem. Rep. of the Congo 54 B2 4 14N 28 50 E
Durūz, Jabal ad, Jordan 47 C5 32 35N 36 40 E
D'Urville, Tanjung, Indonesia 37 E9 1 28S 137 54 E
D'Urville I., N.Z. 59 J4 40 50S 173 55 E
Duryea, U.S.A. 79 E9 41 20N 75 45W
Dushak, Turkmenistan 26 F7 37 13N 60 1 E
Dushanbe, Tajikistan 26 F7 38 33N 68 48 E
Dushore, U.S.A. 79 E8 41 31N 76 24W
Dusky Sd., N.Z. 59 L1 45 47S 166 30 E
Dussejour, C., Australia 60 B4 14 45S 128 13 E
Düsseldorf, Germany 16 C4 51 14N 6 47 E
Dutch Harbor, U.S.A. 68 C3 53 53N 166 32W
Dutlwe, Botswana 56 C3 23 58S 23 46 E
Dutton, Canada 78 D3 42 39N 81 30W
Dutton —►, Australia 62 C3 20 44S 143 10 E
Duwayhin, Khawr, U.A.E. 45 E6 24 20N 51 25 E
Duyun, China 32 D5 26 18N 107 29 E
Duzdab = Zāhedān, Iran 45 D9 29 30N 60 50 E
Dvina, Severnaya —►, Russia 24 B7 64 32N 40 30 E
Dvinsk = Daugavpils, Latvia 9 J22 55 53N 26 32 E
Dvinskaya Guba, Russia 24 B6 65 0N 39 0 E
Dwarka, India 42 H3 22 18N 69 8 E
Dwellingup, Australia 61 F2 32 43S 116 4 E
Dwight, Canada 78 A5 45 20N 79 1W
Dwight, U.S.A. 76 E1 41 5N 88 26W
Dyatlovo = Dzyatlava, Belarus 17 B13 53 28N 25 28 E
Dyce, U.K. 12 D6 57 13N 2 12W
Dyer, C., Canada 69 B13 66 40N 61 0W
Dyer Bay, Canada 78 A3 45 10N 81 20W
Dyer Plateau, Antarctica 5 D17 70 45S 65 30W
Dyersburg, U.S.A. 81 G10 36 3N 89 23W
Dyfi —►, U.K. 11 E3 52 32N 4 3W
Dymer, Ukraine 17 C16 50 47N 30 18 E
Dysart, Australia 62 C4 22 32S 148 23 E
Dzamin Üüd = Borhoyn Tal, Mongolia 34 C6 43 50N 111 58 E
Dzerzhinsk, Russia 24 C7 56 14N 43 30 E
Dzhalinda, Russia 27 D13 53 26N 124 0 E
Dzhambul = Zhambyl, Kazakstan 26 E8 42 54N 71 22 E
Dzhankoy, Ukraine 25 E5 45 40N 34 20 E
Dzhezkazgan = Zhezqazghan, Kazakstan 26 E7 47 44N 67 40 E
Dzhizak = Jizzakh, Uzbekistan 26 E7 40 6N 67 50 E
Dzhugdzur, Khrebet, Russia 27 D14 57 30N 138 0 E
Dzhungarskiye Vorota = Dzungarian Gates, Kazakstan 32 B3 45 0N 82 0 E
Działdowo, Poland 17 B11 53 15N 20 15 E
Dzibilchaltun, Mexico 87 C7 21 5N 89 36W
Dzierżoniów, Poland 17 C9 50 45N 16 39 E
Dzilam de Bravo, Mexico 87 C7 21 24N 88 53W
Dzungaria = Junggar Pendi, China 32 B3 44 30N 86 0 E
Dzungarian Gates, Kazakstan 32 B3 45 0N 82 0 E
Dzuumod, Mongolia 32 B5 47 45N 106 58 E
Dzyarzhynsk, Belarus 17 B14 53 40N 27 1 E
Dzyatlava, Belarus 17 B13 53 28N 25 28 E

E

Eabamet L., Canada 70 B2 51 30N 87 46W
Eads, U.S.A. 80 F3 38 29N 102 47W
Eagar, U.S.A. 83 J9 34 6N 109 17W
Eagle, Alaska, U.S.A. 68 B5 64 47N 141 12W
Eagle, Colo., U.S.A. 82 G10 39 39N 106 50W
Eagle —►, Canada 71 B8 53 36N 57 26W
Eagle Butte, U.S.A. 80 C4 45 0N 101 10W
Eagle Grove, U.S.A. 80 D8 42 40N 93 54W
Eagle L., Canada 73 D10 49 42N 93 13W
Eagle L., Calif., U.S.A. 82 F3 40 39N 120 45W
Eagle L., Maine, U.S.A. 77 B11 46 20N 69 22W
Eagle Lake, Canada 78 A6 45 8N 78 29W
Eagle Lake, Maine, U.S.A. 77 B11 47 3N 68 36W
Eagle Lake, Tex., U.S.A. 81 L6 29 35N 96 20W
Eagle Mountain, U.S.A. 85 M11 33 49N 115 27W
Eagle Nest, U.S.A. 83 H11 36 33N 105 16W
Eagle Pass, U.S.A. 81 L4 28 43N 100 30W
Eagle Pk., U.S.A. 84 G7 38 10N 119 25W
Eagle Pt., Australia 60 C3 16 11S 124 23 E
Eagle River, Mich., U.S.A. 76 B1 47 24N 88 18W
Eagle River, Wis., U.S.A. 80 C10 45 55N 89 15W
Eaglehawk, Australia 63 F3 36 44S 144 15 E
Eagles Mere, U.S.A. 79 E8 41 25N 76 33W
Ealing, U.K. 11 F7 51 31N 0 20W
Ear Falls, Canada 73 C10 50 38N 93 13W
Earle, U.S.A. 81 H9 35 16N 90 28W
Earlimart, U.S.A. 85 K7 35 53N 119 16W
Earn —►, U.K. 12 E5 56 21N 3 18W
Earn, L., U.K. 12 E4 56 23N 4 13W
Earnslaw, Mt., N.Z. 59 L2 44 32S 168 27 E
Earth, U.S.A. 81 H3 34 14N 102 24W
Easley, U.S.A. 77 H4 34 50N 82 36W
East Anglia, U.K. 10 E9 52 30N 1 0 E
East Angus, Canada 71 C5 45 30N 71 40W
East Aurora, U.S.A. 78 D6 42 46N 78 37W
East Ayrshire □, U.K. 12 F4 55 26N 4 11W
East Bengal, Bangla. 41 H17 24 0N 90 0 E
East Beskids = Vychodné Beskydy, Europe 17 D11 49 20N 22 0 E
East Brady, U.S.A. 78 F5 40 59N 79 36W
East C., N.Z. 59 G7 37 42S 178 35 E
East Chicago, U.S.A. 76 E2 41 38N 87 27W
East China Sea, Asia 33 D7 30 0N 126 0 E
East Coulee, Canada 72 C6 51 23N 112 27W
East Dereham, U.K. 11 E8 52 41N 0 57 E
East Dunbartonshire □, U.K. 12 F4 55 57N 4 13W
East Falkland, Falk. Is. 96 G5 51 30S 58 30W
East Grand Forks, U.S.A. 80 B6 47 56N 97 1W
East Greenwich, U.S.A. 79 E13 41 40N 71 27W
East Grinstead, U.K. 11 F8 51 7N 0 0 E
East Hartford, U.S.A. 79 E12 41 46N 72 39W
East Helena, U.S.A. 82 C8 46 35N 111 56W
East Indies, Asia 28 K15 0 0 120 0 E
East Kilbride, U.K. 12 F4 55 47N 4 11W
East Lansing, U.S.A. 76 D3 42 44N 84 29W
East Liverpool, U.S.A. 78 F4 40 37N 80 35W
East London, S. Africa 57 E4 33 0S 27 55 E
East Lothian □, U.K. 12 F6 55 58N 2 44W
East Main = Eastmain, Canada 70 B4 52 10N 78 30W
East Northport, U.S.A. 79 F11 40 53N 73 20W
East Orange, U.S.A. 79 F10 40 46N 74 13W
East Pacific Ridge, Pac. Oc. 65 J17 15 0S 110 0W
East Palestine, U.S.A. 78 F4 40 50N 80 33W
East Pine, Canada 72 B4 55 48N 120 12W
East Point, U.S.A. 77 J3 33 41N 84 27W
East Providence, U.S.A. 79 E13 41 49N 71 23W
East Pt., Canada 71 C7 46 27N 61 58W
East Renfrewshire □, U.K. 12 F4 55 46N 4 21W
East Retford = Retford, U.K. 10 D7 53 19N 0 56W
East Riding of Yorkshire □, U.K. 10 D7 53 55N 0 30W
East Rochester, U.S.A. 78 C7 43 7N 77 29W
East St. Louis, U.S.A. 80 F9 38 37N 90 9W
East Schelde = Oosterschelde —►, Neths. 15 C4 51 33N 4 0 E
East Siberian Sea, Russia 27 B17 73 0N 160 0 E
East Stroudsburg, U.S.A. 79 E9 41 1N 75 11W
East Sussex □, U.K. 11 G8 50 56N 0 19 E
East Tawas, U.S.A. 76 C4 44 17N 83 29W
East Timor = Timor Timur □, Indonesia 37 F7 9 0S 125 0 E
East Toorale, Australia 63 E4 30 27S 145 28 E
East Walker —►, U.S.A. 84 G7 38 52N 119 10W
East Windsor, U.S.A. 79 F10 40 17N 74 34W
Eastbourne, N.Z. 59 J5 41 19S 174 55 E
Eastbourne, U.K. 11 G8 50 46N 0 18 E
Eastend, Canada 73 D7 49 32N 108 50W
Easter I. = Pascua, I. de, Pac. Oc. 65 K17 27 0S 109 0W
Eastern □, Kenya 54 C4 0 0 38 30 E
Eastern □, Uganda 54 B3 1 50N 33 45 E
Eastern Cape □, S. Africa 56 E4 32 0S 26 0 E
Eastern Cr. —►, Australia 62 C3 20 40S 141 35 E
Eastern Ghats, India 40 N11 14 0N 78 50 E
Eastern Group = Lau Group, Fiji 59 C9 17 0S 178 30W
Eastern Group, Australia 61 F3 33 30S 124 30 E
Eastern Transvaal = Mpumalanga □, S. Africa 57 B5 26 0S 30 0 E
Easterville, Canada 73 C9 53 8N 99 49W
Easthampton, U.S.A. 79 D12 42 16N 72 40W
Eastlake, U.S.A. 78 E3 41 40N 81 26W
Eastland, U.S.A. 81 J5 32 24N 98 49W
Eastleigh, U.K. 11 G6 50 58N 1 21W
Eastmain, Canada 70 B4 52 10N 78 30W
Eastmain —►, Canada 70 B4 52 27N 78 26W
Eastman, Canada 79 A12 45 18N 72 19W
Eastman, U.S.A. 77 J4 32 12N 83 11W
Easton, Md., U.S.A. 76 F7 38 47N 76 5W
Easton, Pa., U.S.A. 79 F9 40 41N 75 13W
Easton, Wash., U.S.A. 84 C5 47 14N 121 11W
Eastpointe, U.S.A. 78 D2 42 27N 82 56W
Eastport, U.S.A. 77 C12 44 56N 67 0W
Eastsound, U.S.A. 84 B4 48 42N 122 55W
Eaton, U.S.A. 80 E2 40 32N 104 42W
Eatonia, Canada 73 C7 51 13N 109 25W
Eatonton, U.S.A. 77 J4 33 20N 83 23W
Eatontown, U.S.A. 79 F10 40 19N 74 4W
Eatonville, U.S.A. 84 D4 46 52N 122 16W
Eau Claire, U.S.A. 80 C9 44 49N 91 30W
Eau Claire, L. à l', Canada 70 A5 56 10N 74 25W
Ebbw Vale, U.K. 11 F4 51 46N 3 12W
Ebeltoft, Denmark 9 H14 56 12N 10 41 E
Ebensburg, U.S.A. 78 F6 40 29N 78 44W
Eberswalde-Finow, Germany 16 B7 52 50N 13 49 E
Ebetsu, Japan 30 C10 43 7N 141 34 E
Ebolowa, Cameroon 52 D2 2 55N 11 10 E
Ebro —►, Spain 19 B6 40 43N 0 54 E
Eceabat, Turkey 21 D12 40 11N 26 21 E
Ech Cheliff, Algeria 50 A6 36 10N 1 20 E
Echigo-Sammyaku, Japan 31 F9 36 50N 139 50 E
Echizen-Misaki, Japan 31 G7 35 59N 135 57 E
Echo Bay, N.W.T., Canada 68 B8 66 5N 117 55W
Echo Bay, Ont., Canada 70 C3 46 29N 84 4W
Echoing —►, Canada 70 B1 55 51N 92 5W
Echternach, Lux. 15 E6 49 49N 6 25 E
Echuca, Australia 63 F3 36 10S 144 20 E
Ecija, Spain 19 D3 37 30N 5 10W
Eclipse Is., Australia 60 B4 13 54S 126 19 E
Eclipse Sd., Canada 69 A11 72 38N 79 0W
Ecuador ■, S. Amer. 92 D3 2 0S 78 0W
Ed Damazin, Sudan 51 F12 11 46N 34 21 E
Ed Debba, Sudan 51 E12 18 0N 30 51 E
Ed Dueim, Sudan 51 F12 14 0N 32 10 E
Edam, Canada 73 C7 53 11N 108 46W
Edam, Neths. 15 B5 52 31N 5 3 E
Eday, U.K. 12 B6 59 11N 2 47W
Eddrachillis B., U.K. 12 C3 58 17N 5 14W
Eddystone Pt., Australia 62 G4 40 59S 148 20 E

Ede, *Neths.* **15 B5** 52 4N 5 40 E
Edehon L., *Canada* **73 A9** 60 25N 97 15W
Eden, *Australia* **63 F4** 37 3S 149 55 E
Eden, *N.C., U.S.A.* **77 G6** 36 29N 79 53W
Eden, *N.Y., U.S.A.* **78 D6** 42 39N 78 55W
Eden, *Tex., U.S.A.* **81 K5** 31 13N 99 51W
Eden →, *U.K.* **10 C4** 54 57N 3 1W
Edenburg, *S. Africa* **56 D4** 29 43S 25 58 E
Edendale, *S. Africa* **57 D5** 29 39S 30 18 E
Edenderry, *Ireland* **13 C4** 53 21N 7 4W
Edenhope, *Australia* **63 F3** 37 4S 141 19 E
Edenton, *U.S.A.* **77 G7** 36 4N 76 39W
Edenville, *S. Africa* **57 D4** 27 37S 27 34 E
Eder →, *Germany* **16 C5** 51 12N 9 28 E
Edgar, *U.S.A.* **80 E6** 40 22N 97 58W
Edgartown, *U.S.A.* **79 E14** 41 23N 70 31W
Edge Hill, *U.K.* **11 E6** 52 8N 1 26W
Edgefield, *U.S.A.* **77 J5** 33 47N 81 56W
Edgeley, *U.S.A.* **80 B5** 46 22N 98 43W
Edgemont, *U.S.A.* **80 D3** 43 18N 103 50W
Edgeøya, *Svalbard* **4 B9** 77 45N 22 30 E
Édhessa, *Greece* **21 D10** 40 48N 22 5 E
Edievale, *N.Z.* **59 L2** 45 49S 169 22 E
Edina, *U.S.A.* **80 E8** 40 10N 92 11W
Edinboro, *U.S.A.* **78 E4** 41 52N 80 8W
Edinburg, *U.S.A.* **81 M5** 26 18N 98 10W
Edinburgh, *U.K.* **12 F5** 55 57N 3 13W
Edineţ, *Moldova* **17 D14** 48 9N 27 18 E
Edirne, *Turkey* **21 D12** 41 40N 26 34 E
Edison, *U.S.A.* **84 B4** 48 33N 122 27W
Edithburgh, *Australia* **63 F2** 35 5S 137 43 E
Edmeston, *U.S.A.* **79 D9** 42 42N 75 15W
Edmond, *U.S.A.* **81 H6** 35 39N 97 29W
Edmonds, *U.S.A.* **84 C4** 47 49N 122 23W
Edmonton, *Australia* **62 B4** 17 2S 145 46 E
Edmonton, *Canada* **72 C6** 53 30N 113 30W
Edmund L., *Canada* **70 B1** 54 45N 93 17W
Edmundston, *Canada* **71 C6** 47 23N 68 20W
Edna, *U.S.A.* **81 L6** 28 59N 96 39W
Edremit, *Turkey* **21 E12** 39 34N 27 0 E
Edremit Körfezi, *Turkey* **21 E12** 39 30N 26 45 E
Edson, *Canada* **72 C5** 53 35N 116 28W
Eduardo Castex, *Argentina* **94 D3** 35 50S 64 18W
Edward →, *Australia* **63 F3** 35 5S 143 30 E
Edward, L., *Africa* **54 C2** 0 25S 29 40 E
Edward River, *Australia* **62 A3** 14 59S 141 26 E
Edward VII Land, *Antarctica* **5 E13** 80 0S 150 0W
Edwards, *Calif., U.S.A.* **85 L9** 34 55N 117 51W
Edwards, *N.Y., U.S.A.* **79 B9** 44 20N 75 15W
Edwards Air Force Base, *U.S.A.* **85 L9** 34 50N 117 40W
Edwards Plateau, *U.S.A.* **81 K4** 30 45N 101 20W
Edwardsville, *U.S.A.* **79 E9** 41 15N 75 56W
Edzo, *Canada* **72 A5** 62 49N 116 4W
Eeklo, *Belgium* **15 C3** 51 11N 3 33 E
Effingham, *U.S.A.* **76 F1** 39 7N 88 33W
Égadi, Ísole, *Italy* **20 F5** 37 55N 12 16 E
Egan Range, *U.S.A.* **82 G6** 39 35N 114 55W
Eganville, *Canada* **78 A7** 45 32N 77 5W
Eger = Cheb, *Czech Rep.* **16 C7** 50 9N 12 28 E
Eger, *Hungary* **17 E11** 47 53N 20 27 E
Egersund, *Norway* **9 G12** 58 26N 6 1 E
Egg L., *Canada* **73 B7** 55 5N 105 30W
Éghezée, *Belgium* **15 D4** 50 35N 4 55 E
Egmont, *Canada* **72 D4** 49 45N 123 56W
Egmont, C., *N.Z.* **59 H4** 39 16S 173 45 E
Egmont, Mt., *N.Z.* **59 H5** 39 17S 174 5 E
Egra, *India* **43 J12** 21 54N 87 32 E
Eğridir, *Turkey* **25 G5** 37 52N 30 51 E
Eğridir Gölü, *Turkey* **25 G5** 37 53N 30 50 E
Egvekinot, *Russia* **27 C19** 66 19N 179 50W
Egypt ■, *Africa* **51 C12** 28 0N 31 0 E
Ehime □, *Japan* **31 H6** 33 30N 132 40 E
Ehrenberg, *U.S.A.* **85 M12** 33 36N 114 31W
Eibar, *Spain* **19 A4** 43 11N 2 28W
Eidsvold, *Australia* **63 D5** 25 25S 151 12 E
Eidsvoll, *Norway* **9 F14** 60 19N 11 14 E
Eifel, *Germany* **16 C4** 50 15N 6 50 E
Eiffel Flats, *Zimbabwe* **55 F3** 18 20S 30 0 E
Eigg, *U.K.* **12 E2** 56 54N 6 10W
Eighty Mile Beach, *Australia* **60 C3** 19 30S 120 40 E
Eil, *Somali Rep.* **46 F4** 8 0N 49 50 E
Eil, L., *U.K.* **12 E3** 56 51N 5 16W
Eildon, *Australia* **63 F4** 37 14S 145 55 E
Eildon, L., *Australia* **63 F4** 37 10S 146 0 E
Einasleigh, *Australia* **62 B3** 18 32S 144 5 E
Einasleigh →, *Australia* **62 B3** 17 30S 142 17 E
Eindhoven, *Neths.* **15 C5** 51 26N 5 28 E
Eire = Ireland ■, *Europe* **13 C4** 53 50N 7 52W
Eiríksjökull, *Iceland* **8 D3** 64 46N 20 24W
Eirunepé, *Brazil* **92 E5** 6 35S 69 53W
Eisenach, *Germany* **16 C6** 50 58N 10 19 E
Eisenerz, *Austria* **16 E8** 47 32N 14 54 E
Eivissa, *Spain* **22 C7** 38 54N 1 26 E
Ejutla, *Mexico* **87 D5** 16 34N 96 44W
Ekalaka, *U.S.A.* **80 C2** 45 53N 104 33W
Eketahuna, *N.Z.* **59 J5** 40 38S 175 43 E
Ekibastuz, *Kazakstan* **26 D8** 51 50N 75 10 E
Ekoli, *Dem. Rep. of the Congo* **54 C1** 0 23S 24 13 E
Eksjö, *Sweden* **9 H16** 57 40N 14 58 E
Ekwan →, *Canada* **70 B3** 53 12N 82 15W
Ekwan Pt., *Canada* **70 B3** 53 16N 82 7W
El Aaiún, *W. Sahara* **50 C3** 27 9N 13 12W
El Abanico, *Chile* **94 D1** 37 20S 71 31W
El 'Agrûd, *Egypt* **47 E3** 30 14N 34 24 E
El Alamein, *Egypt* **51 B11** 30 48N 28 58 E
El 'Aqaba, W. →, *Egypt* **47 E2** 30 7N 33 54 E
El Arīḥā, *West Bank* **47 D4** 31 52N 35 27 E
El 'Arîsh, *Egypt* **47 D2** 31 8N 33 50 E
El 'Arîsh, W. →, *Egypt* **47 D2** 31 8N 33 47 E
El Asnam = Ech Cheliff, *Algeria* **50 A6** 36 10N 1 20 E
El Bayadh, *Algeria* **50 B6** 33 40N 1 1 E
El Bluff, *Nic.* **88 D3** 11 59N 83 40W
El Brûk, W. →, *Egypt* **47 E2** 30 15N 33 50 E
El Cajon, *U.S.A.* **85 N10** 32 48N 116 58W
El Campo, *U.S.A.* **81 L6** 29 12N 96 16W
El Centro, *U.S.A.* **85 N11** 32 48N 115 34W
El Cerro, *Bolivia* **92 G6** 17 30S 61 40W
El Compadre, *Mexico* **85 N10** 32 20N 116 14W
El Cuy, *Argentina* **96 D3** 39 55S 68 25W
El Cuyo, *Mexico* **87 C7** 21 30N 87 40W
El Daheir, *Egypt* **47 D3** 31 13N 34 10 E
El Dátil, *Mexico* **86 B2** 30 7N 112 15W
El Dere, *Somali Rep.* **46 G4** 3 50N 47 8 E
El Descanso, *Mexico* **85 N10** 32 12N 116 58W
El Desemboque, *Mexico* **86 A2** 30 30N 112 57W
El Diviso, *Colombia* **92 C3** 1 22N 78 14W
El Djouf, *Mauritania* **50 D4** 20 0N 9 0W
El Dorado, *Ark., U.S.A.* **81 J8** 33 12N 92 40W
El Dorado, *Kans., U.S.A.* **81 G6** 37 49N 96 52W
El Dorado, *Venezuela* **92 B6** 6 55N 61 37W
El Escorial, *Spain* **19 B3** 40 35N 4 7W
El Faiyûm, *Egypt* **51 C12** 29 19N 30 50 E
El Fâsher, *Sudan* **51 F11** 13 33N 25 26 E
El Ferrol = Ferrol, *Spain* **19 A1** 43 29N 8 15W
El Fuerte, *Mexico* **86 B3** 26 30N 108 40W
El Gal, *Somali Rep.* **46 E5** 10 58N 50 20 E
El Geneina = Al Junaynah, *Sudan* **51 F10** 13 27N 22 45 E
El Gîza, *Egypt* **51 C12** 30 0N 31 10 E
El Goléa, *Algeria* **50 B6** 30 30N 2 50 E
El Iskandarîya, *Egypt* **51 B11** 31 13N 29 58 E
El Istiwa'iya, *Sudan* **51 G11** 5 0N 28 0 E
El Jadida, *Morocco* **50 B4** 33 11N 8 17W
El Jardal, *Honduras* **88 D2** 14 54N 88 50W
El Kabrît, G., *Egypt* **47 F2** 29 42N 33 16 E
El Khârga, *Egypt* **51 C12** 25 30N 30 33 E
El Khartûm, *Sudan* **51 E12** 15 31N 32 35 E
El Kuntilla, *Egypt* **47 E3** 30 1N 34 45 E
El Maestrazgo, *Spain* **19 B5** 40 30N 0 25W
El Mahalla el Kubra, *Egypt* **51 B12** 31 0N 31 0 E
El Mansûra, *Egypt* **51 B12** 31 0N 31 19 E
El Medano, *Canary Is.* **22 F3** 28 3N 16 32W
El Milagro, *Argentina* **94 C2** 30 59S 65 59W
El Minyâ, *Egypt* **51 C12** 28 7N 30 33 E
El Monte, *U.S.A.* **85 L8** 34 4N 118 1W
El Obeid, *Sudan* **51 F12** 13 8N 30 10 E
El Odaiya, *Sudan* **51 F11** 12 8N 28 12 E
El Oro, *Mexico* **87 D4** 19 48N 100 8W
El Oued, *Algeria* **50 B7** 33 20N 6 58 E
El Palmito, Presa, *Mexico* **86 B3** 25 40N 105 30W
El Paso, *U.S.A.* **83 L10** 31 45N 106 29W
El Paso Robles, *U.S.A.* **84 K6** 35 38N 120 41W
El Portal, *U.S.A.* **84 H7** 37 41N 119 47W
El Porvenir, *Mexico* **86 A3** 31 15N 105 51W
El Prat de Llobregat, *Spain* **19 B7** 41 18N 2 3 E
El Progreso, *Honduras* **88 C2** 15 26N 87 51W
El Pueblito, *Mexico* **86 B3** 29 3N 105 4W
El Pueblo, *Canary Is.* **22 F2** 28 36N 17 47W
El Puerto de Santa María, *Spain* **19 D2** 36 36N 6 13W
El Qâhira, *Egypt* **51 B12** 30 1N 31 14 E
El Qantara, *Egypt* **47 E1** 30 51N 32 20 E
El Quseima, *Egypt* **47 E3** 30 40N 34 15 E
El Real, *Panama* **92 B3** 8 0N 77 40W
El Reno, *U.S.A.* **81 H6** 35 32N 97 57W
El Rio, *U.S.A.* **85 L7** 34 14N 119 10W
El Roque, Pta., *Canary Is.* **22 F4** 28 10N 15 25W
El Rosarito, *Mexico* **86 B2** 28 38N 114 4W
El Saheira, W. →, *Egypt* **47 E2** 30 5N 33 25 E
El Salto, *Mexico* **86 C3** 23 47N 105 22W
El Salvador ■, *Cent. Amer.* **88 D2** 13 50N 89 0W
El Sauce, *Nic.* **88 D2** 13 0N 86 40W
El Sueco, *Mexico* **86 B3** 29 54N 106 24W
El Suweis, *Egypt* **51 C12** 29 58N 32 31 E
El Tamarâni, W. →, *Egypt* **47 E3** 30 7N 34 43 E
El Thamad, *Egypt* **47 F3** 29 40N 34 28 E
El Tigre, *Venezuela* **92 B6** 8 44N 64 15W
El Tîh, Gebal, *Egypt* **47 F2** 29 40N 33 50 E
El Tîna, Khalîg, *Egypt* **47 D1** 31 10N 32 40 E
El Tofo, *Chile* **94 B1** 29 22S 71 18W
El Tránsito, *Chile* **94 B1** 28 52S 70 17W
El Tûr, *Egypt* **44 D2** 28 14N 33 36 E
El Turbio, *Argentina* **96 G2** 51 45S 72 5W
El Uqsur, *Egypt* **51 C12** 25 41N 32 38 E
El Venado, *Mexico* **86 C4** 22 56N 101 10W
El Vergel, *Mexico* **86 B3** 26 28N 106 22W
El Vigía, *Venezuela* **92 B4** 8 38N 71 39W
El Wabeira, *Egypt* **47 F2** 29 34N 33 6 E
El Wak, *Kenya* **54 B5** 2 49N 40 56 E
El Wuz, *Sudan* **51 E12** 15 5N 30 7 E
Elat, *Israel* **47 F3** 29 30N 34 56 E
Elâzığ, *Turkey* **25 G6** 38 37N 39 14 E
Elba, *Italy* **20 C4** 42 46N 10 17 E
Elba, *U.S.A.* **77 K2** 31 25N 86 4W
Elbasani, *Albania* **21 D9** 41 9N 20 9 E
Elbe, *U.S.A.* **84 D4** 46 45N 122 10W
Elbe →, *Europe* **16 B5** 53 50N 9 0 E
Elbert, Mt., *U.S.A.* **83 G10** 39 7N 106 27W
Elberton, *U.S.A.* **77 H4** 34 7N 82 52W
Elbeuf, *France* **18 B4** 49 17N 1 2 E
Elbidtan, *Turkey* **44 B3** 38 13N 37 12 E
Elbing = Elbląg, *Poland* **17 A10** 54 10N 19 25 E
Elbląg, *Poland* **17 A10** 54 10N 19 25 E
Elbow, *Canada* **73 C7** 51 7N 106 35W
Elbrus, *Asia* **25 F7** 43 21N 42 30 E
Elburz Mts. = Alborz, Reshteh-ye Kūhhā-ye, *Iran* **45 C7** 36 0N 52 0 E
Elche, *Spain* **19 C5** 38 15N 0 42W
Elcho I., *Australia* **62 A2** 11 55S 135 45 E
Elda, *Spain* **19 C5** 38 29N 0 47W
Elde →, *Germany* **16 B6** 53 7N 11 15 E
Eldon, *Mo., U.S.A.* **80 F8** 38 21N 92 35W
Eldon, *Wash., U.S.A.* **84 C3** 47 33N 123 3W
Eldora, *U.S.A.* **80 D8** 42 22N 93 5W
Eldorado, *Argentina* **95 B5** 26 28S 54 43W
Eldorado, *Canada* **78 B7** 44 35N 77 31W
Eldorado, *Mexico* **86 C3** 24 20N 107 22W
Eldorado, *Ill., U.S.A.* **76 G1** 37 49N 88 26W
Eldorado, *Tex., U.S.A.* **81 K4** 30 52N 100 36W
Eldorado Springs, *U.S.A.* **81 G8** 37 52N 94 1W
Eldoret, *Kenya* **54 B4** 0 30N 35 17 E
Eldred, *U.S.A.* **78 E6** 41 58N 78 23W
Elea, C., *Cyprus* **23 D13** 35 19N 34 4 E
Eleanora, Pk., *Australia* **61 F3** 32 57S 121 9 E
Electra, *U.S.A.* **74 D7** 34 2N 98 55W
Elefantes →, *Mozam.* **57 C5** 24 10S 32 40 E
Elektrostal, *Russia* **24 C6** 55 41N 38 32 E
Elephant Butte Reservoir, *U.S.A.* **83 K10** 33 9N 107 11W
Elephant I., *Antarctica* **5 C18** 61 0S 55 0W
Eleuthera, *Bahamas* **88 B4** 25 0N 76 20W
Elgin, *Canada* **79 B8** 44 36N 76 13W
Elgin, *U.K.* **12 D5** 57 39N 3 19W
Elgin, *Ill., U.S.A.* **76 D1** 42 2N 88 17W
Elgin, *N. Dak., U.S.A.* **80 B4** 46 24N 101 51W
Elgin, *Oreg., U.S.A.* **82 D5** 45 34N 117 55W
Elgin, *Tex., U.S.A.* **81 K6** 30 21N 97 22W
Elgon, Mt., *Africa* **54 B3** 1 10N 34 30 E
Eliase, *Indonesia* **37 F8** 8 21S 130 48 E
Elim, *S. Africa* **56 E2** 34 35S 19 45 E
Elisabethville = Lubumbashi, *Dem. Rep. of the Congo* **55 E2** 11 40S 27 28 E
Elista, *Russia* **25 E7** 46 16N 44 14 E
Elizabeth, *Australia* **63 E2** 34 42S 138 41 E
Elizabeth, *N.J., U.S.A.* **79 F10** 40 39N 74 13W
Elizabeth, *N.J., U.S.A.* **79 F10** 40 40N 74 13W
Elizabeth City, *U.S.A.* **77 G7** 36 18N 76 14W
Elizabethton, *U.S.A.* **77 G4** 36 21N 82 13W
Elizabethtown, *Ky., U.S.A.* **76 G3** 37 42N 85 52W
Elizabethtown, *N.Y., U.S.A.* **79 B11** 44 13N 73 36W
Elizabethtown, *Pa., U.S.A.* **79 F8** 40 9N 76 36W
Ełk, *Poland* **17 B12** 53 50N 22 21 E
Elk →, *Canada* **72 C5** 49 11N 115 14W
Elk →, *U.S.A.* **77 H2** 34 46N 87 16W
Elk City, *U.S.A.* **81 H5** 35 25N 99 25W
Elk Creek, *U.S.A.* **84 F4** 39 36N 122 32W
Elk Grove, *U.S.A.* **84 G5** 38 25N 121 22W
Elk Island Nat. Park, *Canada* **72 C6** 53 35N 112 59W
Elk Lake, *Canada* **70 C3** 47 40N 80 25W
Elk Point, *Canada* **73 C6** 53 54N 110 55W
Elk River, *Idaho, U.S.A.* **82 C5** 46 47N 116 11W
Elk River, *Minn., U.S.A.* **80 C8** 45 18N 93 35W
Elkedra →, *Australia* **62 C2** 21 8S 136 22 E
Elkhart, *Ind., U.S.A.* **76 E3** 41 41N 85 58W
Elkhart, *Kans., U.S.A.* **81 G4** 37 0N 101 54W
Elkhorn, *Canada* **73 D8** 49 59N 101 14W
Elkhorn →, *U.S.A.* **80 E6** 41 8N 96 19W
Elkhovo, *Bulgaria* **21 C12** 42 10N 26 35 E
Elkin, *U.S.A.* **77 G5** 36 15N 80 51W
Elkins, *U.S.A.* **76 F6** 38 55N 79 51W
Elkland, *U.S.A.* **78 E7** 41 59N 77 19W
Elko, *Canada* **72 D5** 49 20N 115 10W
Elko, *U.S.A.* **82 F6** 40 50N 115 46W
Elkton, *U.S.A.* **78 C1** 43 49N 83 11W
Ell, L., *Australia* **61 E4** 29 13S 127 46 E
Ellef Ringnes I., *Canada* **4 B2** 78 30N 102 2W
Ellen, Mt., *U.S.A.* **79 B12** 44 9N 72 56W
Ellenburg, *U.S.A.* **79 B11** 44 54N 73 48W
Ellendale, *U.S.A.* **80 B5** 46 0N 98 32W
Ellensburg, *U.S.A.* **82 C3** 46 59N 120 34W
Ellenville, *U.S.A.* **79 E10** 41 43N 74 24W
Ellery, Mt., *Australia* **63 F4** 37 28S 148 47 E
Ellesmere, L., *N.Z.* **59 M4** 47 47S 172 28 E
Ellesmere I., *Canada* **4 B4** 79 30N 80 0W
Ellesmere Port, *U.K.* **10 D5** 53 17N 2 54W
Ellice Is. = Tuvalu ■, *Pac. Oc.* **64 H9** 8 0S 178 0 E
Ellicottville, *U.S.A.* **78 D6** 42 17N 78 40W
Elliot, *Australia* **62 B1** 17 33S 133 32 E
Elliot, *S. Africa* **57 E4** 31 22S 27 48 E
Elliot Lake, *Canada* **70 C3** 46 25N 82 35W
Elliotdale = Xhora, *S. Africa* **57 E4** 31 55S 28 38 E
Ellis, *U.S.A.* **80 F5** 38 56N 99 34W
Elliston, *Australia* **63 E1** 33 39S 134 53 E
Ellisville, *U.S.A.* **81 K10** 31 36N 89 12W
Ellon, *U.K.* **12 D6** 57 22N 2 4W
Ellore = Eluru, *India* **41 L12** 16 48N 81 8 E
Ellsworth, *Kans., U.S.A.* **80 F5** 38 44N 98 14W
Ellsworth, *Maine, U.S.A.* **77 C11** 44 33N 68 25W
Ellsworth Land, *Antarctica* **5 D16** 76 0S 89 0W
Ellsworth Mts., *Antarctica* **5 D16** 78 30S 85 0W
Ellwood City, *U.S.A.* **78 F4** 40 52N 80 17W
Elma, *Canada* **73 D9** 49 52N 95 55W
Elma, *U.S.A.* **84 D3** 47 0N 123 25W
Elmalı, *Turkey* **25 G4** 36 44N 29 56 E
Elmhurst, *U.S.A.* **76 E2** 41 53N 87 56W
Elmira, *Canada* **78 C4** 43 36N 80 33W
Elmira, *U.S.A.* **78 D8** 42 6N 76 48W
Elmira Heights, *U.S.A.* **78 D8** 42 8N 76 50W
Elmore, *Australia* **63 F3** 36 30S 144 37 E
Elmore, *U.S.A.* **85 M11** 33 7N 115 49W
Elmshorn, *Germany* **16 B5** 53 43N 9 40 E
Elmvale, *Canada* **78 B5** 44 35N 79 52W
Elora, *Canada* **78 C4** 43 41N 80 26W
Eloúnda, *Greece* **23 D7** 35 16N 25 42 E
Eloy, *U.S.A.* **83 K8** 32 45N 111 33W
Elrose, *Canada* **73 C7** 51 12N 108 0W
Elsie, *U.S.A.* **84 E3** 45 52N 123 36W
Elsinore = Helsingør, *Denmark* **9 H15** 56 2N 12 35 E
Eltham, *N.Z.* **59 H5** 39 26S 174 19 E
Eluru, *India* **41 L12** 16 48N 81 8 E
Elvas, *Portugal* **19 C2** 38 50N 7 10W
Elverum, *Norway* **9 F14** 60 53N 11 34 E
Elvire →, *Australia* **60 C4** 17 51S 128 11 E
Elvire, Mt., *Australia* **61 E2** 29 22S 119 36 E
Elwell, L., *U.S.A.* **82 B8** 48 22N 111 17W
Elwood, *Ind., U.S.A.* **76 E3** 40 17N 85 50W
Elwood, *Nebr., U.S.A.* **80 E5** 40 36N 99 52W
Elx = Elche, *Spain* **19 C5** 38 15N 0 42W
Ely, *U.K.* **11 E8** 52 24N 0 16 E
Ely, *Minn., U.S.A.* **80 B9** 47 55N 91 51W
Ely, *Nev., U.S.A.* **82 G6** 39 15N 114 54W
Elyria, *U.S.A.* **78 E2** 41 22N 82 7W
Emāmrūd, *Iran* **45 B7** 36 30N 55 0 E
Emba, *Kazakstan* **26 E6** 48 50N 58 8 E
Emba →, *Kazakstan* **25 E9** 46 55N 53 28 E
Embarcación, *Argentina* **94 A3** 23 10S 64 0W
Embarras Portage, *Canada* **73 B6** 58 27N 111 28W
Embetsu, *Japan* **30 B10** 44 44N 141 47 E
Embi = Emba, *Kazakstan* **26 E6** 48 50N 58 8 E
Embi = Emba →, *Kazakstan* **25 E9** 46 55N 53 28 E
Embóna, *Greece* **23 C9** 36 13N 27 51 E
Embrun, *France* **18 D7** 44 34N 6 30 E
Embu, *Kenya* **54 C4** 0 32S 37 38 E
Emden, *Germany* **16 B4** 53 21N 7 12 E
Emerald, *Australia* **62 C4** 23 32S 148 10 E
Emerson, *Canada* **73 D9** 49 0N 97 10W
Emet, *Turkey* **21 E13** 39 20N 29 15 E
Emi Koussi, *Chad* **51 E9** 19 45N 18 55 E
Eminabad, *Pakistan* **42 C6** 32 2N 74 8 E
Emine, Nos, *Bulgaria* **21 C12** 42 40N 27 56 E
Emlenton, *U.S.A.* **78 E5** 41 11N 79 43W
Emmaus, *U.S.A.* **79 F9** 40 32N 75 30W
Emmeloord, *Neths.* **15 B5** 52 44N 5 46 E
Emmen, *Neths.* **15 B6** 52 48N 6 57 E
Emmet, *Australia* **62 C3** 24 45S 144 30 E
Emmetsburg, *U.S.A.* **80 D7** 43 7N 94 41W
Emmett, *Idaho, U.S.A.* **82 E5** 43 52N 116 30W
Emmett, *Mich., U.S.A.* **78 D2** 42 59N 82 46W
Emmonak, *U.S.A.* **68 B3** 62 46N 164 30W
Emo, *Canada* **73 D10** 48 38N 93 50W
Empalme, *Mexico* **86 B2** 28 1N 110 49W
Empangeni, *S. Africa* **57 D5** 28 50S 31 52 E
Empedrado, *Argentina* **94 B4** 28 0S 58 46W
Emperor Seamount Chain, *Pac. Oc.* **64 D9** 40 0N 170 0 E
Emporia, *Kans., U.S.A.* **80 F6** 38 25N 96 11W
Emporia, *Va., U.S.A.* **77 G7** 36 42N 77 32W
Emporium, *U.S.A.* **78 E6** 41 31N 78 14W
Empress, *Canada* **73 C7** 50 57N 110 0W
Empty Quarter = Rub' al Khālī, *Si. Arabia* **46 D4** 18 0N 48 0 E
Ems →, *Germany* **16 B4** 53 20N 7 12 E
Emsdale, *Canada* **78 A5** 45 32N 79 19W
Emu, *China* **35 C15** 43 40N 128 6 E
Emu Park, *Australia* **62 C5** 23 13S 150 50 E
'En 'Avrona, *Israel* **47 F4** 29 43N 35 0 E
En Nahud, *Sudan* **51 F11** 12 45N 28 25 E
Ena, *Japan* **31 G8** 35 25N 137 25 E
Enana, *Namibia* **56 B2** 17 30S 16 23 E
Enaratoli, *Indonesia* **37 E9** 3 55S 136 21 E
Enard B., *U.K.* **12 C3** 58 5N 5 20W
Enare = Inarijärvi, *Finland* **8 B22** 69 0N 28 0 E
Encampment, *U.S.A.* **82 F10** 41 12N 106 47W
Encantadas, Serra, *Brazil* **95 C5** 30 40S 53 0W
Encarnación, *Paraguay* **95 B4** 27 15S 55 50W
Encarnación de Diaz, *Mexico* **86 C4** 21 30N 102 13W
Encinitas, *U.S.A.* **85 M9** 33 3N 117 17W
Encino, *U.S.A.* **83 J11** 34 39N 105 28W
Encounter B., *Australia* **63 F2** 35 45S 138 45 E
Endako, *Canada* **72 C3** 54 6N 125 2W
Ende, *Indonesia* **37 F6** 8 45S 121 40 E
Endeavour Str., *Australia* **62 A3** 10 45S 142 0 E
Enderbury I., *Kiribati* **64 H10** 3 8S 171 5W
Enderby, *Canada* **72 C5** 50 35N 119 10W
Enderby I., *Australia* **60 D2** 20 35S 116 30 E
Enderby Land, *Antarctica* **5 C5** 66 0S 53 0 E
Enderlin, *U.S.A.* **80 B6** 46 38N 97 36W
Endicott, *U.S.A.* **79 D8** 42 6N 76 4W
Endwell, *U.S.A.* **79 D8** 42 6N 76 2W
Endyalgout I., *Australia* **60 B5** 11 40S 132 35 E
Eneabba, *Australia* **61 E2** 29 49S 115 16 E
Enewetak Atoll, *Marshall Is.* **64 F8** 11 30N 162 15 E
Enez, *Turkey* **21 D12** 40 45N 26 5 E
Enfield, *Canada* **71 D7** 44 56N 63 32W
Enfield, *Conn., U.S.A.* **79 E12** 41 58N 72 36W
Enfield, *N.H., U.S.A.* **79 C12** 43 39N 72 9W
Engadin, *Switz.* **18 C9** 46 45N 10 10 E
Engaño, C., *Dom. Rep.* **89 C6** 18 30N 68 20W
Engaño, C., *Phil.* **37 A6** 18 35N 122 23 E
Engaru, *Japan* **30 B11** 44 3N 143 31 E
Engcobo, *S. Africa* **57 E4** 31 37S 28 0 E
Engels, *Russia* **25 D8** 51 28N 46 6 E
Engemann L., *Canada* **73 B7** 58 0N 106 55W
Enggano, *Indonesia* **36 F2** 5 20S 102 40 E
England, *U.S.A.* **81 H9** 34 33N 91 58W
England □, *U.K.* **10 D7** 53 0N 2 0W
Englee, *Canada* **71 B8** 50 45N 56 5W
Englehart, *Canada* **70 C4** 47 49N 79 52W
Englewood, *U.S.A.* **80 F2** 39 39N 104 59W
English →, *Canada* **73 C10** 50 35N 93 30W
English Bazar = Ingraj Bazar, *India* **43 G13** 24 58N 88 10 E
English Channel, *Europe* **11 G6** 50 0N 2 0W
English River, *Canada* **70 C1** 49 14N 91 0W
Enid, *U.S.A.* **81 G6** 36 24N 97 53W
Enkhuizen, *Neths.* **15 B5** 52 42N 5 17 E
Enna, *Italy* **20 F6** 37 34N 14 16 E
Ennadai, *Canada* **73 A8** 61 8N 100 53W
Ennadai L., *Canada* **73 A8** 61 0N 101 0W
Ennedi, *Chad* **51 E10** 17 15N 22 0 E
Enngonia, *Australia* **63 D4** 29 21S 145 50 E
Ennis, *Ireland* **13 D3** 52 51N 8 59W
Ennis, *Mont., U.S.A.* **82 D8** 45 21N 111 44W
Ennis, *Tex., U.S.A.* **81 J6** 32 20N 96 38W
Enniscorthy, *Ireland* **13 D5** 52 30N 6 34W
Enniskillen, *U.K.* **13 B4** 54 21N 7 39W
Ennistimon, *Ireland* **13 D2** 52 57N 9 17W
Enns →, *Austria* **16 D8** 48 14N 14 32 E
Enontekiö, *Finland* **8 B20** 68 23N 23 37 E
Enosburg Falls, *U.S.A.* **79 B12** 44 55N 72 48W
Enriquillo, L., *Dom. Rep.* **89 C5** 18 20N 72 5W
Enschede, *Neths.* **15 B6** 52 13N 6 53 E
Ensenada, *Argentina* **94 C4** 34 55S 57 55W
Ensenada, *Mexico* **86 A1** 31 50N 116 50W
Ensenada de los Muertos, *Mexico* **86 C2** 23 59N 109 50W
Ensiola, Pta. de n', *Spain* **22 B9** 39 7N 2 55 E
Entebbe, *Uganda* **54 B3** 0 4N 32 28 E
Enterprise, *Canada* **72 A5** 60 47N 115 45W
Enterprise, *Ala., U.S.A.* **77 K3** 31 19N 85 51W
Enterprise, *Oreg., U.S.A.* **82 D5** 45 25N 117 17W
Entre Ríos, *Bolivia* **94 A3** 21 30S 64 25W
Entre Ríos □, *Argentina* **94 C4** 30 30S 58 30W
Entroncamento, *Portugal* **19 C1** 39 28N 8 28W
Enugu, *Nigeria* **50 G7** 6 20N 7 30 E
Enumclaw, *U.S.A.* **84 C5** 47 12N 121 59W
Eólie, Ís., *Italy* **20 E6** 38 30N 14 57 E
Epe, *Neths.* **15 B5** 52 21N 5 59 E
Épernay, *France* **18 B5** 49 3N 3 56 E
Ephesus, *Turkey* **21 F12** 37 55N 27 22 E
Ephraim, *U.S.A.* **82 G8** 39 22N 111 35W
Ephrata, *Pa., U.S.A.* **79 F8** 40 11N 76 11W
Ephrata, *Wash., U.S.A.* **82 C4** 47 19N 119 33W
Épinal, *France* **18 B7** 48 10N 6 27 E
Episkopi, *Cyprus* **23 E11** 34 40N 32 54 E
Episkopí, *Greece* **23 D6** 35 20N 24 20 E
Episkopi Bay, *Cyprus* **23 E11** 34 35N 32 50 E
Epsom, *U.K.* **11 F7** 51 19N 0 16W
Epukiro, *Namibia* **56 C2** 21 40S 19 9 E
Equatorial Guinea ■, *Africa* **52 D1** 2 0N 8 0 E
Er Rahad, *Sudan* **51 F12** 12 45N 30 32 E
Er Rif, *Morocco* **50 A5** 35 1N 4 1W
Erāwadī Myit = Irrawaddy →, *Burma* **41 M19** 15 50N 95 6 E
Erbil = Arbīl, *Iraq* **44 B5** 36 15N 44 5 E
Erçek, *Turkey* **44 B4** 38 39N 43 36 E
Erciyaş Dağı, *Turkey* **25 G6** 38 30N 35 30 E
Érd, *Hungary* **17 E10** 47 22N 18 56 E
Erdao Jiang →, *China* **35 C14** 43 0N 127 0 E
Erdek, *Turkey* **21 D12** 40 23N 27 47 E
Erdene = Ulaan-Uul, *Mongolia* **34 B6** 44 13N 111 10 E
Erdenetsogt, *Mongolia* **34 C4** 42 55N 106 5 E
Erebus, Mt., *Antarctica* **5 D11** 77 35S 167 0 E
Erechim, *Brazil* **95 B5** 27 35S 52 15W
Ereğli, *Konya, Turkey* **25 G5** 37 31N 34 4 E
Ereğli, *Zonguldak, Turkey* **25 F5** 41 15N 31 24 E
Erenhot, *China* **34 C7** 43 48N 112 2 E
Eresma →, *Spain* **19 B3** 41 26N 4 45W
Erewadi Myitwanya, *Burma* **41 M19** 15 30N 95 0 E

Feldkirch

Erfenisdam, S. Africa 56 D4 28 30S 26 50 E
Erfurt, Germany 16 C6 50 58N 11 2 E
Erg Iguidi, Africa 50 C4 27 0N 7 0 E
Ergani, Turkey 44 B3 38 17N 39 49 E
Ergel, Mongolia 34 C5 43 8N 109 5 E
Ergeni Vozvyshennost, Russia 25 E7 47 0N 44 0 E
Ērgli, Latvia 9 H21 56 54N 25 38 E
Eriboll, L., U.K. 12 C4 58 30N 4 42W
Érice, Italy 20 E5 38 2N 12 35 E
Erie, U.S.A. 78 D4 42 8N 80 5W
Erie, L., N. Amer. 78 D4 42 15N 81 0W
Erie Canal, U.S.A. 78 C7 43 5N 78 43W
Erieau, Canada 78 D3 42 16N 81 57W
Erigavo, Somali Rep. 46 E4 10 35N 47 20 E
Erikoúsa, Greece 23 A3 39 53N 19 34 E
Eriksdale, Canada 73 C9 50 52N 98 7W
Erímanthos, Greece 21 F9 37 57N 21 50 E
Erimo-misaki, Japan 30 D11 41 50N 143 15 E
Erinpura, India 42 G5 25 9N 73 3 E
Eriskay, U.K. 12 D1 57 4N 7 18W
Eritrea ■, Africa 46 D2 14 0N 38 30 E
Erlangen, Germany 16 D6 49 36N 11 0 E
Erldunda, Australia 62 D1 25 14S 133 12 E
Ermelo, Neths. 15 B5 52 18N 5 35 E
Ermelo, S. Africa 57 D4 26 31S 29 59 E
Ermenek, Turkey 44 B2 36 38N 33 0 E
Ermones, Greece 23 A3 39 37N 19 46 E
Ermoúpolis = Síros, Greece 21 F11 37 28N 24 57 E
Ernakulam = Cochin, India 40 Q10 9 59N 76 22 E
Erne →, Ireland 13 B3 54 30N 8 16W
Erne, Lower L., U.K. 13 B4 54 28N 7 47W
Erne, Upper L., U.K. 13 B4 54 14N 7 32W
Ernest Giles Ra., Australia 61 E3 27 0S 123 45 E
Erode, India 40 P10 11 24N 77 45 E
Eromanga, Australia 63 D3 26 40S 143 11 E
Erongo, Namibia 56 C2 21 39S 15 58 E
Erramala Hills, India 40 M11 15 30N 78 15 E
Errigal, Ireland 13 A3 55 2N 8 6W
Erris Hd., Ireland 13 B1 54 19N 10 0W
Erskine, U.S.A. 80 B7 47 40N 96 0W
Ertis = Irtysh →, Russia 26 C7 61 4N 68 52 E
Erwin, U.S.A. 77 G4 36 9N 82 25W
Erzgebirge, Germany 16 C7 50 27N 12 55 E
Erzin, Russia 27 D10 50 15N 95 10 E
Erzincan, Turkey 25 G6 39 46N 39 30 E
Erzurum, Turkey 25 G7 39 57N 41 15 E
Es Caló, Spain 22 C8 38 40N 1 30 E
Es Canar, Spain 22 B8 39 2N 1 36 E
Es Mercadal, Spain 22 B11 39 59N 4 5 E
Es Migjorn Gran, Spain 22 B11 39 57N 4 3 E
Es Sahrâ' Esh Sharqîya, Egypt 51 C12 27 30N 32 30 E
Es Sînâ', Egypt 47 F3 29 0N 34 0 E
Es Vedrà, Spain 22 C7 38 52N 1 12 E
Esambo, Dem. Rep. of the Congo 54 C1 3 48S 23 30 E
Esan-Misaki, Japan 30 D10 41 40N 141 10 E
Esashi, Hokkaidō, Japan 30 B11 44 56N 142 35 E
Esashi, Hokkaidō, Japan 30 D10 41 52N 140 7 E
Esbjerg, Denmark 9 J13 55 29N 8 29 E
Escalante, U.S.A. 83 H8 37 47N 111 36W
Escalante →, U.S.A. 83 H8 37 24N 110 57W
Escalón, Mexico 86 B4 26 46N 104 20W
Escambia →, U.S.A. 77 K2 30 32N 87 11W
Escanaba, U.S.A. 76 C2 45 45N 87 4W
Esch-sur-Alzette, Lux. 18 B6 49 32N 6 0 E
Escondido, U.S.A. 85 M9 33 7N 117 5W
Escuinapa, Mexico 86 C3 22 50N 105 50W
Escuintla, Guatemala 88 D1 14 20N 90 48W
Esenguly, Turkmenistan 26 F6 37 37N 53 59 E
Eşfahān, Iran 45 C6 32 39N 51 43 E
Eşfahān □, Iran 45 C6 32 50N 51 50 E
Esfarāyen, Iran 45 B8 37 4N 57 30 E
Esfideh, Iran 45 C8 33 39N 59 46 E
Esh Sham = Dimashq, Syria 47 B5 33 30N 36 18 E
Esha Ness, U.K. 12 A7 60 29N 1 38W
Esher, U.K. 11 F7 51 21N 0 20W
Eshowe, S. Africa 57 D5 28 50S 31 30 E
Esil = Ishim →, Russia 26 D8 57 45N 71 10 E
Esk →, Cumb., U.K. 12 G5 54 58N 3 2W
Esk →, N. Yorks., U.K. 10 C7 54 30N 0 37W
Eskān, Iran 45 E9 26 48N 63 9 E
Esker, Canada 71 B6 53 53N 66 25W
Eskifjörður, Iceland 8 D7 65 3N 13 55W
Eskilstuna, Sweden 9 G17 59 22N 16 32 E
Eskimo Pt., Canada 68 B10 61 10N 94 15W
Eskişehir, Turkey 25 G5 39 50N 30 30 E
Esla →, Spain 19 B2 41 29N 6 3W
Eslāmābād-e Gharb, Iran 44 C5 34 10N 46 30 E
Eslāmshahr, Iran 45 C6 35 40N 51 10 E
Eşme, Turkey 21 E13 38 23N 28 58 E
Esmeraldas, Ecuador 92 C3 1 0N 79 40W
Esnagi L., Canada 70 C3 48 36N 84 33W
Espanola, Canada 70 C3 46 15N 81 46W
Espanola, U.S.A. 83 H10 35 59N 106 5W
Esparta, Costa Rica 88 E3 9 59N 84 40W
Esperance, Australia 61 F3 33 45S 121 55 E
Esperance B., Australia 61 F3 33 48S 121 55 E
Esperanza, Argentina 94 C3 31 29S 61 3W
Espichel, C., Portugal 19 C1 38 22N 9 16W
Espigão, Serra do, Brazil 95 B5 26 35S 50 30W
Espinazo, Sierra del = Espinhaço, Serra do, Brazil 93 G10 17 30S 43 30W
Espinhaço, Serra do, Brazil 93 G10 17 30S 43 30W
Espinilho, Serra do, Brazil 95 B5 28 30S 55 0W
Espírito Santo □, Brazil 93 H10 20 0S 40 45W
Espíritu Santo, Vanuatu 64 J8 15 15S 166 50 E
Espíritu Santo, B. del, Mexico 87 D7 19 15N 87 0W
Espíritu Santo, I., Mexico 86 C2 24 30N 110 23W
Espita, Mexico 87 C7 21 1N 88 19W
Espoo, Finland 9 F21 60 12N 24 40 E
Espungabera, Mozam. 57 C5 20 29S 32 45 E
Esquel, Argentina 96 E2 42 55S 71 20W
Esquimalt, Canada 72 D4 48 26N 123 25W
Esquina, Argentina 94 C4 30 0S 59 30W
Essaouira, Morocco 50 B4 31 32N 9 42W
Essebie, Dem. Rep. of the Congo 54 B3 2 58N 30 40 E
Essen, Belgium 15 C4 51 28N 4 28 E
Essen, Germany 16 C4 51 28N 7 2 E
Essendon, Mt., Australia 61 E3 25 0S 120 29 E
Essequibo →, Guyana 92 B7 6 50N 58 30W
Essex, Canada 78 D2 42 10N 82 49W
Essex, Calif., U.S.A. 85 L11 34 44N 115 15W
Essex, N.Y., U.S.A. 79 B11 44 19N 73 21W
Essex □, U.K. 11 F8 51 54N 0 27 E
Essex Junction, U.S.A. 79 B11 44 29N 73 7W
Esslingen, Germany 16 D5 48 44N 9 18 E
Estados, I. de Los, Argentina 96 G4 54 40S 64 30W
Eşţahbānāt, Iran 45 D7 29 8N 54 4 E
Estância, Brazil 93 F11 11 16S 37 26W
Estancia, U.S.A. 83 J10 34 46N 106 4W
Estārm, Iran 45 D8 28 21N 58 21 E
Estcourt, S. Africa 57 D4 29 0S 29 53 E
Estelí, Nic. 88 D2 13 9N 86 22W
Estellencs, Spain 22 B9 39 39N 2 29 E
Esterhazy, Canada 73 C8 50 37N 102 5W
Estevan, Canada 73 D8 49 10N 102 59W
Estevan Group, Canada 72 C3 53 3N 129 38W
Estherville, U.S.A. 80 D7 43 24N 94 50W
Eston, Canada 73 C7 51 8N 108 40W
Estonia ■, Europe 9 G21 58 30N 25 30 E
Estreito, Brazil 93 E9 6 32S 47 25W
Estrela, Serra da, Portugal 19 B2 40 10N 7 45W
Estremoz, Portugal 19 C2 38 51N 7 39W
Estrondo, Serra do, Brazil 93 E9 7 20S 48 0W
Esztergom, Hungary 17 E10 47 47N 18 44 E
Etah, India 43 F8 27 35N 78 40 E
Étampes, France 18 B5 48 26N 2 10 E
Etanga, Namibia 56 B1 17 55S 13 0 E
Etawah, India 43 F8 26 48N 79 6 E
Etawney L., Canada 73 B9 57 50N 96 50W
Ethel, U.S.A. 84 D4 46 32N 122 46W
Ethelbert, Canada 73 C8 51 32N 100 25W
Ethiopia ■, Africa 46 F3 8 0N 40 0 E
Ethiopian Highlands, Ethiopia 28 J7 10 0N 37 0 E
Etive, L., U.K. 12 E3 56 29N 5 10W
Etna, Italy 20 F6 37 50N 14 55 E
Etoile, Dem. Rep. of the Congo 55 E2 11 33S 27 30 E
Etosha Pan, Namibia 56 B2 18 40S 16 30 E
Etowah, U.S.A. 77 H3 35 20N 84 32W
Ettelbruck, Lux. 15 E6 49 51N 6 5 E
Ettrick Water →, U.K. 12 F6 55 31N 2 55W
Etuku, Dem. Rep. of the Congo 54 C2 3 42S 25 45 E
Etzatlán, Mexico 86 C4 20 48N 104 5W
Etzná, Mexico 87 D6 19 35N 90 15W
Euboea = Évvoia, Greece 21 E11 38 30N 24 0 E
Eucla, Australia 61 F4 31 41S 128 52 E
Euclid, U.S.A. 78 E3 41 34N 81 32W
Eucumbene, L., Australia 63 F4 36 2S 148 40 E
Eudora, U.S.A. 81 J9 33 7N 91 16W
Eufaula, Ala., U.S.A. 77 K3 31 54N 85 9W
Eufaula, Okla., U.S.A. 81 H7 35 17N 95 35W
Eufaula L., U.S.A. 81 H7 35 18N 95 21W
Eugene, U.S.A. 82 E2 44 5N 123 4W
Eugowra, Australia 63 E4 33 22S 148 24 E
Eulo, Australia 63 D4 28 10S 145 3 E
Eunice, La., U.S.A. 81 K8 30 30N 92 25W
Eunice, N. Mex., U.S.A. 81 J3 32 26N 103 10W
Eupen, Belgium 15 D6 50 37N 6 3 E
Euphrates = Furāt, Nahr al →, Asia 44 D5 31 0N 47 25 E
Eureka, Canada 4 B3 80 0N 85 56W
Eureka, Calif., U.S.A. 82 F1 40 47N 124 9W
Eureka, Kans., U.S.A. 81 G6 37 49N 96 17W
Eureka, Mont., U.S.A. 82 B6 48 53N 115 3W
Eureka, Nev., U.S.A. 82 G5 39 31N 115 58W
Eureka, S. Dak., U.S.A. 80 C5 45 46N 99 38W
Eureka, Mt., Australia 61 E3 26 35S 121 35 E
Euroa, Australia 63 F4 36 44S 145 35 E
Europa, Île, Ind. Oc. 53 J8 22 20S 40 22 E
Europa, Picos de, Spain 19 A3 43 10N 4 49W
Europa, Pta. de, Gib. 19 D3 36 3N 5 21W
Europe 6 E10 50 0N 20 0 E
Europoort, Neths. 15 C4 51 57N 4 10 E
Eustis, U.S.A. 77 L5 28 51N 81 41W
Euston, Australia 63 E3 34 30S 142 46 E
Eutsuk L., Canada 72 C3 53 20N 126 45W
Evale, Angola 56 B2 16 33S 15 44 E
Evans, U.S.A. 80 E2 40 23N 104 41W
Evans, L., Canada 70 B4 50 50N 77 0W
Evans City, U.S.A. 78 F4 40 46N 80 4W
Evans Head, Australia 63 D5 29 7S 153 27 E
Evans Mills, U.S.A. 79 B9 44 6N 75 48W
Evansburg, Canada 72 C5 53 36N 114 59W
Evanston, Ill., U.S.A. 76 E2 42 3N 87 41W
Evanston, Wyo., U.S.A. 82 F8 41 16N 110 58W
Evansville, U.S.A. 76 G2 37 58N 87 35W
Evaz, Iran 45 E7 27 46N 53 59 E
Eveleth, U.S.A. 80 B8 47 28N 92 32W
Evensk, Russia 27 C16 62 12N 159 30 E
Everard, L., Australia 63 E2 31 30S 135 0 E
Everard Ranges, Australia 61 E5 27 5S 132 28 E
Everest, Mt., Nepal 43 E12 28 5N 86 58 E
Everett, Pa., U.S.A. 78 F6 40 1N 78 23W
Everett, Wash., U.S.A. 84 C4 47 59N 122 12W
Everglades, The, U.S.A. 77 N5 25 50N 81 0W
Everglades National Park, U.S.A. 77 N5 25 30N 81 0W
Evergreen, Ala., U.S.A. 77 K2 31 26N 86 57W
Evergreen, Mont., U.S.A. 82 B6 48 9N 114 13W
Evesham, U.K. 11 E6 52 6N 1 56W
Evje, Norway 9 G12 58 36N 7 51 E
Évora, Portugal 19 C2 38 33N 7 57W
Evowghlī, Iran 44 B5 38 43N 45 13 E
Évreux, France 18 B4 49 3N 1 8 E
Évros →, Bulgaria 21 D12 41 40N 26 34 E
Évry, France 18 B5 48 38N 2 27 E
Évvoia, Greece 21 E11 38 30N 24 0 E
Ewe, L., U.K. 12 D3 57 49N 5 38W
Ewing, U.S.A. 80 D5 42 16N 98 21W
Ewo, Congo 52 E2 0 48S 14 45 E
Exaltación, Bolivia 92 F5 13 10S 65 20W
Excelsior Springs, U.S.A. 80 F7 39 20N 94 13W
Exe →, U.K. 11 G4 50 41N 3 29W
Exeter, Canada 78 C3 43 21N 81 29W
Exeter, U.K. 11 G4 50 43N 3 31W
Exeter, Calif., U.S.A. 84 J7 36 18N 119 9W
Exeter, N.H., U.S.A. 79 D14 42 59N 70 57W
Exmoor, U.K. 11 F4 51 12N 3 45W
Exmouth, Australia 60 D1 21 54S 114 10 E
Exmouth, U.K. 11 G4 50 37N 3 25W
Exmouth G., Australia 60 D1 22 15S 114 15 E
Expedition Ra., Australia 62 C4 24 30S 149 12 E
Extremadura □, Spain 19 C2 39 30N 6 5W
Exuma Sound, Bahamas 88 B4 24 30N 76 20W
Eyasi, L., Tanzania 54 C4 3 30S 35 0 E
Eye Pen., U.K. 12 C2 58 13N 6 10W
Eyemouth, U.K. 12 F6 55 52N 2 5W
Eyjafjörður, Iceland 8 C4 66 15N 18 30W
Eyre (North), L., Australia 63 D2 28 30S 137 20 E
Eyre (South), L., Australia 63 D2 29 18S 137 25 E
Eyre Mts., N.Z. 59 L2 45 25S 168 25 E
Eyre Pen., Australia 63 E2 33 30S 136 17 E
Eysturoy, Færoe Is. 8 E9 62 13N 6 54W
Eyvānkī, Iran 45 C6 35 24N 51 56 E
Ezine, Turkey 21 E12 39 48N 26 20 E
Ezouza →, Cyprus 23 E11 34 44N 32 27 E

F

F.Y.R.O.M. = Macedonia ■, Europe 21 D9 41 53N 21 40 E
Fabala, Guinea 50 G4 9 44N 9 5W
Fabens, U.S.A. 83 L10 31 30N 106 10W
Fabriano, Italy 20 C5 43 20N 12 54 E
Fachi, Niger 51 E8 18 6N 11 34 E
Fada, Chad 51 E10 17 13N 21 34 E
Fada-n-Gourma, Burkina Faso 50 F6 12 10N 0 30 E
Faddeyevskiy, Ostrov, Russia 27 B15 76 0N 144 0 E
Fadghāmī, Syria 44 C4 35 53N 40 52 E
Faenza, Italy 20 B4 44 17N 11 53 E
Færoe Is. = Føroyar, Atl. Oc. 8 F9 62 0N 7 0W
Făgăras, Romania 17 F13 45 48N 24 58 E
Fagersta, Sweden 9 F16 60 1N 15 46 E
Fagnano, L., Argentina 96 G3 54 30S 68 0W
Fahlīān, Iran 45 D6 30 11N 51 28 E
Fahraj, Kermān, Iran 45 D8 29 0N 59 0 E
Fahraj, Yazd, Iran 45 D7 31 46N 54 36 E
Faial, Madeira 22 D3 32 47N 16 53W
Fair Haven, U.S.A. 76 D9 43 36N 73 16W
Fair Hd., U.K. 13 A5 55 14N 6 9W
Fair Oaks, U.S.A. 84 G5 38 39N 121 16W
Fairbanks, U.S.A. 68 B5 64 51N 147 43W
Fairbury, U.S.A. 80 E6 40 8N 97 11W
Fairfax, U.S.A. 79 B11 44 40N 73 1W
Fairfield, Ala., U.S.A. 77 J2 33 29N 86 55W
Fairfield, Calif., U.S.A. 84 G4 38 15N 122 3W
Fairfield, Conn., U.S.A. 79 E11 41 9N 73 16W
Fairfield, Idaho, U.S.A. 82 E6 43 21N 114 44W
Fairfield, Ill., U.S.A. 76 F1 38 23N 88 22W
Fairfield, Iowa, U.S.A. 80 E9 40 56N 91 57W
Fairfield, Tex., U.S.A. 81 K7 31 44N 96 10W
Fairford, Canada 73 C9 51 37N 98 38W
Fairhope, U.S.A. 77 K2 30 31N 87 54W
Fairlie, N.Z. 59 L3 44 5S 170 49 E
Fairmead, U.S.A. 84 H6 37 5N 120 10W
Fairmont, Minn., U.S.A. 80 D7 43 39N 94 28W
Fairmont, W. Va., U.S.A. 76 F5 39 29N 80 9W
Fairmount, Calif., U.S.A. 85 L8 34 45N 118 26W
Fairmount, N.Y., U.S.A. 79 C8 43 5N 76 12W
Fairplay, U.S.A. 83 G11 39 15N 106 2W
Fairport, U.S.A. 78 C7 43 6N 77 27W
Fairport Harbor, U.S.A. 78 E3 41 45N 81 17W
Fairview, Canada 72 B5 56 5N 118 25W
Fairview, Mont., U.S.A. 80 B2 47 51N 104 3W
Fairview, Okla., U.S.A. 81 G5 36 16N 98 29W
Fairweather, Mt., U.S.A. 72 B1 58 55N 137 32W
Faisalabad, Pakistan 42 D5 31 30N 73 5 E
Faith, U.S.A. 80 C3 45 2N 102 2W
Faizabad, India 43 F10 26 45N 82 10 E
Fajardo, Puerto Rico 89 C6 18 20N 65 39W
Fajr, Wādī, Si. Arabia 44 D3 29 10N 38 10 E
Fakenham, U.K. 10 E8 52 51N 0 51 E
Fakfak, Indonesia 37 E8 3 0S 132 15 E
Faku, China 35 C12 42 32N 123 21 E
Falaise, France 18 B3 48 54N 0 12W
Falaise, Mui, Vietnam 38 C5 19 6N 105 45 E
Falam, Burma 41 H18 23 0N 93 45 E
Falcó, C. des, Spain 22 C7 38 50N 1 23 E
Falcón, Presa, Mexico 87 B5 26 35N 99 10W
Falcon Lake, Canada 73 D9 49 42N 95 15W
Falcon Reservoir, U.S.A. 81 M5 26 34N 99 10W
Falconara Marittima, Italy 20 C5 43 37N 13 24 E
Falcone, C. del, Italy 20 D3 40 58N 8 12 E
Falconer, U.S.A. 78 D5 42 7N 79 13W
Faleshty = Făleşti, Moldova 17 E14 47 32N 27 44 E
Făleşti, Moldova 17 E14 47 32N 27 44 E
Falfurrias, U.S.A. 81 M5 27 14N 98 9W
Falher, Canada 72 B5 55 44N 117 15W
Falirakí, Greece 23 C10 36 22N 28 12 E
Falkenberg, Sweden 9 H15 56 54N 12 30 E
Falkirk, U.K. 12 F5 56 0N 3 47W
Falkirk □, U.K. 12 F5 55 58N 3 49W
Falkland, U.K. 12 E5 56 16N 3 12W
Falkland Is. □, Atl. Oc. 96 G5 51 30S 59 0W
Falkland Sd., Falk. Is. 96 G5 52 0S 60 0W
Falköping, Sweden 9 G15 58 12N 13 33 E
Fall River, U.S.A. 79 E13 41 43N 71 10W
Fallbrook, U.S.A. 85 M9 33 23N 117 15W
Fallon, U.S.A. 82 G4 39 28N 118 47W
Falls City, U.S.A. 80 E7 40 3N 95 36W
Falls Creek, U.S.A. 78 E6 41 9N 78 48W
Falmouth, Jamaica 88 C4 18 30N 77 40W
Falmouth, U.K. 11 G2 50 9N 5 5W
Falmouth, U.S.A. 79 E14 41 33N 70 37W
Falsa, Pta., Mexico 86 B1 27 51N 115 3W
False B., S. Africa 56 E2 34 15S 18 40 E
Falso, C., Honduras 88 C3 15 12N 83 21W
Falster, Denmark 9 J14 54 45N 11 55 E
Falsterbo, Sweden 9 J15 55 23N 12 50 E
Fălticeni, Romania 17 E14 47 21N 26 20 E
Falun, Sweden 9 F16 60 37N 15 37 E
Famagusta, Cyprus 23 D12 35 8N 33 55 E
Famagusta Bay, Cyprus 23 D13 35 15N 34 0 E
Famalé, Niger 50 F6 14 33N 1 5 E
Famatina, Sierra de, Argentina 94 B2 27 30S 68 0W
Family L., Canada 73 C9 51 54N 95 27W
Famoso, U.S.A. 85 K7 35 37N 119 12W
Fan Xian, China 34 G8 35 55N 115 38 E
Fanad Hd., Ireland 13 A4 55 17N 7 38W
Fandriana, Madag. 57 C8 20 14S 47 21 E
Fangcheng, China 34 H7 33 18N 112 59 E
Fangshan, China 34 E6 38 3N 111 25 E
Fangzi, China 35 F10 36 33N 119 10 E
Fanjiatun, China 35 C13 43 40N 125 15 E
Fannich, L., U.K. 12 D4 57 38N 4 59W
Fannūj, Iran 45 E8 26 35N 59 38 E
Fanø, Denmark 9 J13 55 25N 8 25 E
Fano, Italy 20 C5 43 50N 13 1 E
Fanshi, China 34 E7 39 12N 113 20 E
Fao = Al Fāw, Iraq 45 D6 30 0N 48 30 E
Faqirwali, Pakistan 42 E5 29 27N 73 0 E
Faradje, Dem. Rep. of the Congo 54 B2 3 50N 29 45 E
Farafangana, Madag. 57 C8 22 49S 47 50 E
Farāh, Afghan. 40 C3 32 20N 62 7 E
Farāh □, Afghan. 40 C3 32 25N 62 10 E
Farahalana, Madag. 57 A9 14 26S 50 10 E
Faranah, Guinea 50 F3 10 3N 10 45W
Farasān, Jazā'ir, Si. Arabia 46 D3 16 45N 41 55 E
Farasan Is. = Farasān, Jazā'ir, Si. Arabia 46 D3 16 45N 41 55 E
Faratsiho, Madag. 57 B8 19 24S 46 57 E
Fareham, U.K. 11 G6 50 51N 1 11W
Farewell, C., N.Z. 59 J4 40 29S 172 43 E
Farewell C. = Farvel, Kap, Greenland 4 D5 59 48N 43 55W
Farghona, Uzbekistan 26 E8 40 23N 71 19 E
Fargo, U.S.A. 80 B6 46 53N 96 48W
Fār'iah, W. al →, West Bank 47 C4 32 12N 35 27 E
Faribault, U.S.A. 80 C8 44 18N 93 16W
Faridabad, India 42 E6 28 26N 77 19 E
Faridkot, India 42 D6 30 44N 74 45 E
Faridpur, Bangla. 43 H13 23 15N 89 55 E
Faridpur, India 43 E8 28 13N 79 33 E
Farīmān, Iran 45 C8 35 40N 59 49 E
Farina, Australia 63 E2 30 3S 138 15 E
Fariones, Pta., Canary Is. 22 E6 29 13N 13 28W
Farmerville, U.S.A. 81 J8 32 47N 92 24W
Farmingdale, U.S.A. 79 F10 40 12N 74 10W
Farmington, Canada 72 B4 55 54N 120 30W
Farmington, Calif., U.S.A. 84 H6 37 55N 120 59W
Farmington, Maine, U.S.A. 77 C10 44 40N 70 9W
Farmington, Mo., U.S.A. 81 G9 37 47N 90 25W
Farmington, N.H., U.S.A. 79 C13 43 24N 71 4W
Farmington, N. Mex., U.S.A. 83 H9 36 44N 108 12W
Farmington, Utah, U.S.A. 82 F8 41 0N 111 12W
Farmington →, U.S.A. 79 E12 41 51N 72 38W
Farmville, U.S.A. 76 G6 37 18N 78 24W
Farne Is., U.K. 10 B6 55 38N 1 37W
Farnham, Canada 79 A12 45 17N 72 59W
Farnham, Mt., Canada 72 C5 50 29N 116 30W
Faro, Brazil 93 D7 2 10S 56 39W
Faro, Canada 68 B6 62 11N 133 22W
Faro, Portugal 19 D2 37 2N 7 55W
Fårö, Sweden 9 H18 57 55N 19 5 E
Farquhar, C., Australia 61 D1 23 50S 113 36 E
Farrars Cr. →, Australia 62 D3 25 35S 140 43 E
Farrāshband, Iran 45 D7 28 57N 52 5 E
Farrell, U.S.A. 78 E4 41 13N 80 30W
Farrokhī, Iran 45 C8 33 50N 59 31 E
Farruch, C. = Ferrutx, C., Spain 22 B10 39 47N 3 21 E
Farrukhabad-cum-Fatehgarh, India 40 F11 27 30N 79 32 E
Fārs □, Iran 45 D7 29 30N 55 0 E
Fársala, Greece 21 E10 39 17N 22 23 E
Farson, U.S.A. 82 E9 42 6N 109 27W
Farsund, Norway 9 G12 58 5N 6 55 E
Fartak, Râs, Si. Arabia 44 D2 28 5N 34 34 E
Fartak, Ra's, Yemen 46 D5 15 38N 52 15 E
Fartura, Serra da, Brazil 95 B5 26 21S 52 52W
Fārūj, Iran 45 B8 37 14N 58 14 E
Farvel, Kap, Greenland 4 D5 59 48N 43 55W
Farwell, U.S.A. 81 H3 34 23N 103 2W
Fasā, Iran 45 D7 29 0N 53 39 E
Fasano, Italy 20 D7 40 50N 17 22 E
Fastiv, Ukraine 17 C15 50 7N 29 57 E
Fastov = Fastiv, Ukraine 17 C15 50 7N 29 57 E
Fatagar, Tanjung, Indonesia 37 E8 2 46S 131 57 E
Fatehabad, Haryana, India 42 E6 29 31N 75 27 E
Fatehabad, Ut. P., India 42 F8 27 1N 78 19 E
Fatehgarh, India 43 F8 27 25N 79 35 E
Fatehpur, Bihar, India 43 G11 24 38N 85 14 E
Fatehpur, Raj., India 42 F6 28 0N 74 40 E
Fatehpur, Ut. P., India 43 G9 25 56N 81 13 E
Fatehpur, Ut. P., India 43 F9 27 10N 81 13 E
Fatehpur Sikri, India 42 F6 27 6N 77 40 E
Fatima, Canada 71 C7 47 24N 61 53W
Faulkton, U.S.A. 80 C5 45 2N 99 8W
Faure I., Australia 61 E1 25 52S 113 50 E
Fauresmith, S. Africa 56 D4 29 44S 25 17 E
Fauske, Norway 8 C16 67 17N 15 25 E
Favara, Italy 20 F5 37 19N 13 39 E
Faváritx, C. de, Spain 22 B11 40 0N 4 15 E
Favignana, Italy 20 F5 37 56N 12 20 E
Fawcett, Pt., Australia 60 B5 11 46S 130 2 E
Fawn →, Canada 70 A2 55 20N 87 35W
Fawnskin, U.S.A. 85 L10 34 16N 116 56W
Faxaflói, Iceland 8 D2 64 29N 23 0W
Faya-Largeau, Chad 51 E9 17 58N 19 6 E
Fayd, Si. Arabia 44 E4 27 1N 42 52 E
Fayette, Ala., U.S.A. 77 J2 33 41N 87 50W
Fayette, Mo., U.S.A. 80 F8 39 9N 92 41W
Fayetteville, Ark., U.S.A. 81 G7 36 4N 94 10W
Fayetteville, N.C., U.S.A. 77 H6 35 3N 78 53W
Fayetteville, Tenn., U.S.A. 77 H2 35 9N 86 34W
Fazilka, India 42 D6 30 27N 74 2 E
Fazilpur, Pakistan 42 E4 29 18N 70 29 E
Fdérik, Mauritania 50 D3 22 40N 12 45W
Feale →, Ireland 13 D2 52 27N 9 37W
Fear, C., U.S.A. 77 J7 33 50N 77 58W
Feather →, U.S.A. 82 G3 38 47N 121 36W
Feather Falls, U.S.A. 84 F5 39 36N 121 16W
Featherston, N.Z. 59 J5 41 6S 175 20 E
Featherstone, Zimbabwe 55 F3 18 42S 30 55 E
Fécamp, France 18 B4 49 45N 0 22 E
Fedala = Mohammedia, Morocco 50 B4 33 44N 7 21W
Federación, Argentina 94 C4 31 0S 57 55W
Féderal, Argentina 96 C5 30 57S 58 48W
Federal Way, U.S.A. 84 C4 47 18N 122 19W
Fedeshkūh, Iran 45 D7 28 49N 53 50 E
Fehmarn, Germany 16 A6 54 27N 11 7 E
Fehmarn Bælt, Europe 9 J14 54 35N 11 20 E
Fehmarn Belt = Fehmarn Bælt, Europe 9 J14 54 35N 11 20 E
Fei Xian, China 35 G9 35 18N 117 59 E
Feijó, Brazil 92 E4 8 9S 70 21W
Feilding, N.Z. 59 J5 40 13S 175 35 E
Feira de Santana, Brazil 93 F11 12 15S 38 57W
Feixiang, China 34 F8 36 30N 114 45 E
Felanitx, Spain 22 B10 39 28N 3 9 E
Feldkirch, Austria 16 E5 47 15N 9 37 E

Felipe Carrillo Puerto

Felipe Carrillo Puerto, *Mexico* **87 D7** 19 38N 88 3W
Felixstowe, *U.K.* **11 F9** 51 58N 1 23 E
Felton, *U.S.A.* **84 H4** 37 3N 122 4W
Femer Bælt = Fehmarn Bælt, *Europe* **9 J14** 54 35N 11 20 E
Femunden, *Norway* **9 E14** 62 10N 11 53 E
Fen He ➝, *China* **34 G6** 35 36N 110 42 E
Fenelon Falls, *Canada* **78 B6** 44 32N 78 45W
Feng Xian, *Jiangsu, China* **34 G9** 34 43N 116 35 E
Feng Xian, *Shaanxi, China* **34 H4** 33 54N 106 40 E
Fengcheng, *China* **35 D13** 40 28N 124 5 E
Fengfeng, *China* **34 F8** 36 28N 114 8 E
Fengjie, *China* **33 C5** 31 5N 109 36 E
Fengning, *China* **34 D9** 41 10N 116 33 E
Fengqiu, *China* **34 G8** 35 2N 114 25 E
Fengrun, *China* **35 E10** 39 48N 118 8 E
Fengtai, *China* **34 E9** 39 50N 116 18 E
Fengxiang, *China* **34 G4** 34 29N 107 25 E
Fengyang, *China* **35 H9** 32 51N 117 29 E
Fengzhen, *China* **34 D7** 40 25N 113 2 E
Fenoarivo Afovoany, *Madag.* **57 B8** 18 26S 46 34 E
Fenoarivo Atsinanana, *Madag.* **57 B8** 17 22S 49 25 E
Fens, The, *U.K.* **10 E7** 52 38N 0 2W
Fenton, *U.S.A.* **76 D4** 42 48N 83 42W
Fenxi, *China* **34 F6** 36 40N 111 31 E
Fenyang, *China* **34 F6** 37 18N 111 48 E
Feodosiya, *Ukraine* **25 E6** 45 2N 35 16 E
Ferdows, *Iran* **45 C8** 33 58N 58 2 E
Ferfer, *Somali Rep.* **46 F4** 5 4N 45 9 E
Fergana = Farghona, *Uzbekistan* **26 E8** 40 23N 71 19 E
Fergus, *Canada* **78 C4** 43 43N 80 24W
Fergus Falls, *U.S.A.* **80 B6** 46 17N 96 4W
Ferkéssédougou, *Ivory C.* **50 G4** 9 35N 5 6W
Ferland, *Canada* **70 B2** 50 19N 88 27W
Fermanagh □, *U.K.* **13 B4** 54 21N 7 40W
Fermo, *Italy* **20 C5** 43 9N 13 43 E
Fermont, *Canada* **71 B6** 52 47N 67 5W
Fermont, *Qué., Canada* **69 C13** 50 28N 67 29W
Fermoy, *Ireland* **13 D3** 52 9N 8 16W
Fernández, *Argentina* **94 B3** 27 55S 63 50W
Fernandina Beach, *U.S.A.* **77 K5** 30 40N 81 27W
Fernando de Noronha, *Brazil* **93 D12** 4 0S 33 10W
Fernando Póo = Bioko, *Eq. Guin.* **52 D1** 3 30N 8 40 E
Ferndale, *U.S.A.* **84 B4** 48 51N 122 36W
Fernie, *Canada* **72 D5** 49 30N 115 5W
Fernlees, *Australia* **62 C4** 23 51S 148 7 E
Fernley, *U.S.A.* **82 G4** 39 36N 119 15W
Ferozepore = Firozpur, *India* **42 D6** 30 55N 74 40 E
Ferrara, *Italy* **20 B4** 44 50N 11 35 E
Ferreñafe, *Peru* **92 E3** 6 42S 79 50W
Ferrerías, *Spain* **22 B11** 39 59N 4 1 E
Ferret, C., *France* **18 D3** 44 38N 1 15W
Ferriday, *U.S.A.* **81 K9** 31 38N 91 33W
Ferrol, *Spain* **19 A1** 43 29N 8 15W
Ferron, *U.S.A.* **83 G8** 39 5N 111 8W
Ferrutx, C., *Spain* **22 B10** 39 47N 3 21 E
Ferryland, *Canada* **71 C9** 47 2N 52 53W
Fertile, *U.S.A.* **80 B6** 47 32N 96 17W
Fès, *Morocco* **50 B5** 34 0N 5 0W
Fessenden, *U.S.A.* **80 B5** 47 39N 99 38W
Festus, *U.S.A.* **80 F9** 38 13N 90 24W
Feteşti, *Romania* **17 F14** 44 22N 27 51 E
Fethiye, *Turkey* **25 G4** 36 36N 29 6 E
Fetlar, *U.K.* **12 A8** 60 36N 0 52W
Feuilles ➝, *Canada* **69 C12** 58 47N 70 4W
Fez = Fès, *Morocco* **50 B5** 34 0N 5 0W
Fezzan, *Libya* **51 C8** 27 0N 13 0 E
Fiambalá, *Argentina* **94 B2** 27 45S 67 37W
Fianarantsoa, *Madag.* **57 C8** 21 26S 47 5 E
Fianarantsoa □, *Madag.* **57 B8** 19 30S 47 0 E
Ficksburg, *S. Africa* **57 D4** 28 51S 27 53 E
Field ➝, *Australia* **62 C2** 23 48S 138 0 E
Field I., *Australia* **60 B5** 12 5S 132 23 E
Fieri, *Albania* **21 D8** 40 43N 19 33 E
Fife □, *U.K.* **12 E5** 56 16N 3 1W
Fife Ness, *U.K.* **12 E6** 56 17N 2 35W
Fifth Cataract, *Sudan* **51 E12** 18 23N 33 47 E
Figeac, *France* **18 D5** 44 37N 2 2 E
Figtree, *Zimbabwe* **55 G2** 20 22S 28 20 E
Figueira da Foz, *Portugal* **19 B1** 40 7N 8 54W
Figueres, *Spain* **19 A7** 42 18N 2 58 E
Figuig, *Morocco* **50 B5** 32 5N 1 11W
Fihaonana, *Madag.* **57 B8** 18 36S 47 12 E
Fiherenana, *Madag.* **57 B8** 18 29S 48 24 E
Fiherenana ➝, *Madag.* **57 C7** 23 19S 43 37 E
Fiji ■, *Pac. Oc.* **59 C8** 17 20S 179 0 E
Filey, *U.K.* **10 C7** 54 12N 0 18W
Filey B., *U.K.* **10 C7** 54 12N 0 15W
Filfla, *Malta* **23 D1** 35 47N 14 24 E
Filiatrá, *Greece* **21 F9** 37 9N 21 35 E
Filingué, *Niger* **50 F6** 14 21N 3 22 E
Filipstad, *Sweden* **9 G16** 59 43N 14 9 E
Fillmore, *Calif., U.S.A.* **85 L8** 34 24N 118 55W
Fillmore, *Utah, U.S.A.* **83 G7** 38 58N 112 20W
Finch, *Canada* **79 A9** 45 11N 75 7W
Findhorn ➝, *U.K.* **12 D5** 57 38N 3 38W
Findlay, *U.S.A.* **76 E4** 41 2N 83 39W
Finger L., *Canada* **70 B1** 53 33N 93 30W
Finger Lakes, *U.S.A.* **79 D8** 42 40N 76 30W
Fíngoè, *Mozam.* **55 E3** 14 55S 31 50 E
Finisterre, C. = Fisterra, C., *Spain* **19 A1** 42 50N 9 19W
Finke, *Australia* **62 D1** 25 34S 134 35 E
Finland ■, *Europe* **8 E22** 63 0N 27 0 E
Finland, G. of, *Europe* **9 G21** 60 0N 26 0 E
Finlay ➝, *Canada* **72 B3** 57 0N 125 10W
Finley, *Australia* **63 F4** 35 38S 145 35 E
Finley, *U.S.A.* **80 B6** 47 31N 97 50W
Finn ➝, *Ireland* **13 B4** 54 51N 7 28W
Finnigan, Mt., *Australia* **62 B4** 15 49S 145 17 E
Finniss, C., *Australia* **63 E1** 33 8S 134 51 E
Finnmark, *Norway* **8 B20** 69 37N 23 57 E
Finnsnes, *Norway* **8 B18** 69 14N 18 0 E
Finspång, *Sweden* **9 G16** 58 43N 15 47 E
Fiora ➝, *Italy* **20 C4** 42 20N 11 34 E
Fīq, *Syria* **47 C4** 32 46N 35 41 E
Firat = Furāt, Nahr al ➝, *Asia* **44 D5** 31 0N 47 25 E
Firebag ➝, *Canada* **73 B6** 57 45N 111 21W
Firebaugh, *U.S.A.* **84 J6** 36 52N 120 27W
Firedrake L., *Canada* **73 A8** 61 25N 104 30W
Firenze, *Italy* **20 C4** 43 46N 11 15 E
Firk ➝, *Iraq* **44 D5** 30 59N 44 34 E
Firozabad, *India* **43 F8** 27 10N 78 25 E
Firozpur, *India* **42 D6** 30 55N 74 40 E
Firozpur-Jhirka, *India* **42 F7** 27 48N 76 57 E
Fīrūzābād, *Iran* **45 D7** 28 52N 52 35 E
Fīrūzkūh, *Iran* **45 C7** 35 50N 52 50 E
Firvale, *Canada* **72 C3** 52 27N 126 13W
Fish ➝, *Namibia* **56 D2** 28 7S 17 10 E
Fish ➝, *S. Africa* **56 E3** 31 30S 20 16 E
Fisher, *Australia* **61 F5** 30 30S 131 0 E
Fisher B., *Canada* **73 C9** 51 35N 97 13W
Fishers I., *U.S.A.* **79 E13** 41 15N 72 0W
Fishguard, *U.K.* **11 E3** 52 0N 4 58W
Fishing L., *Canada* **73 C9** 52 10N 95 24W
Fishkill, *U.S.A.* **79 E11** 41 32N 73 53W
Fisterra, C., *Spain* **19 A1** 42 50N 9 19W
Fitchburg, *U.S.A.* **79 D13** 42 35N 71 48W
Fitz Roy, *Argentina* **96 F3** 47 0S 67 0W
Fitzgerald, *Canada* **72 B6** 59 51N 111 36W
Fitzgerald, *U.S.A.* **77 K4** 31 43N 83 15W
Fitzmaurice ➝, *Australia* **60 B5** 14 45S 130 5 E
Fitzroy ➝, *Queens., Australia* **62 C5** 23 32S 150 52 E
Fitzroy ➝, *W. Austral., Australia* **60 C3** 17 31S 123 35 E
Fitzroy, Mte., *Argentina* **96 F2** 49 17S 73 5W
Fitzroy Crossing, *Australia* **60 C4** 18 9S 125 38 E
Fitzwilliam I., *Canada* **78 A3** 45 30N 81 45W
Fiume = Rijeka, *Croatia* **16 F8** 45 20N 14 21 E
Five Points, *U.S.A.* **84 J6** 36 26N 120 6W
Fizi, *Dem. Rep. of the Congo* **54 C2** 4 17S 28 55 E
Flagstaff, *U.S.A.* **83 J8** 35 12N 111 39W
Flagstaff L., *Maine, U.S.A.* **77 C10** 45 12N 70 19W
Flagstaff L., *Maine, U.S.A.* **79 A14** 45 12N 70 18W
Flaherty I., *Canada* **70 A4** 56 15N 79 15W
Flåm, *Norway* **9 F12** 60 50N 7 7 E
Flambeau ➝, *U.S.A.* **80 C9** 45 18N 91 14W
Flamborough Hd., *U.K.* **10 C7** 54 7N 0 5W
Flaming Gorge Reservoir, *U.S.A.* **82 F9** 41 10N 109 25W
Flamingo, Teluk, *Indonesia* **37 F9** 5 30S 138 0 E
Flanders = Flandre, *Europe* **18 A5** 50 50N 2 30 E
Flandre, *Europe* **18 A5** 50 50N 2 30 E
Flandre Occidentale = West-Vlaanderen □, *Belgium* **15 D2** 51 0N 3 0 E
Flandre Orientale = Oost-Vlaanderen □, *Belgium* **15 C3** 51 5N 3 50 E
Flandreau, *U.S.A.* **80 C6** 44 3N 96 36W
Flanigan, *U.S.A.* **84 E7** 40 10N 119 53W
Flannan Is., *U.K.* **12 C1** 58 9N 7 52W
Flåsjön, *Sweden* **8 D16** 64 5N 15 40 E
Flat ➝, *Canada* **72 A3** 61 33N 125 18W
Flathead L., *U.S.A.* **82 C7** 47 51N 114 8W
Flattery, C., *Australia* **62 A4** 14 58S 145 21 E
Flattery, C., *U.S.A.* **84 B2** 48 23N 124 29W
Flatwoods, *U.S.A.* **76 F4** 38 31N 82 43W
Fleetwood, *U.K.* **10 D4** 53 55N 3 1W
Fleetwood, *U.S.A.* **79 F9** 40 27N 75 49W
Flekkefjord, *Norway* **9 G12** 58 18N 6 39 E
Flemington, *U.S.A.* **78 E7** 41 7N 77 28W
Flensburg, *Germany* **16 A5** 54 47N 9 27 E
Flers, *France* **18 B3** 48 47N 0 33W
Flesherton, *Canada* **78 B4** 44 16N 80 33W
Flesko, Tanjung, *Indonesia* **37 D6** 0 29N 124 30 E
Fleurieu Pen., *Australia* **63 F2** 35 40S 138 5 E
Flevoland □, *Neths.* **15 B5** 52 30N 5 30 E
Flin Flon, *Canada* **73 C8** 54 46N 101 53W
Flinders ➝, *Australia* **62 B3** 17 36S 140 36 E
Flinders B., *Australia* **61 F2** 34 19S 115 19 E
Flinders Group, *Australia* **62 A3** 14 11S 144 15 E
Flinders I., *S. Austral., Australia* **63 E1** 33 44S 134 41 E
Flinders I., *Tas., Australia* **62 G4** 40 0S 148 0 E
Flinders Ranges, *Australia* **63 E2** 31 30S 138 30 E
Flinders Reefs, *Australia* **62 B4** 17 37S 148 31 E
Flint, *U.K.* **10 D4** 53 15N 3 8W
Flint, *U.S.A.* **76 D4** 43 1N 83 41W
Flint ➝, *U.S.A.* **77 K3** 30 57N 84 34W
Flint I., *Kiribati* **65 J12** 11 26S 151 48W
Flintshire □, *U.K.* **10 D4** 53 17N 3 17W
Flodden, *U.K.* **10 B5** 55 37N 2 8W
Floodwood, *U.S.A.* **80 B8** 46 55N 92 55W
Flora, *U.S.A.* **76 F1** 38 40N 88 29W
Florala, *U.S.A.* **77 K2** 31 0N 86 20W
Florence = Firenze, *Italy* **20 C4** 43 46N 11 15 E
Florence, *Ala., U.S.A.* **77 H2** 34 48N 87 41W
Florence, *Ariz., U.S.A.* **83 K8** 33 2N 111 23W
Florence, *Colo., U.S.A.* **80 F2** 38 23N 105 8W
Florence, *Oreg., U.S.A.* **82 E1** 43 58N 124 7W
Florence, *S.C., U.S.A.* **77 H6** 34 12N 79 46W
Florence, L., *Australia* **63 D2** 28 53S 138 9 E
Florencia, *Colombia* **92** 1 36N 75 36W
Florennes, *Belgium* **15 D4** 50 15N 4 35 E
Florenville, *Belgium* **15 E5** 49 40N 5 19 E
Flores, *Guatemala* **88 C2** 16 59N 89 50W
Flores, *Indonesia* **37 F6** 8 35S 121 0 E
Flores I., *Canada* **72 D3** 49 20N 126 10W
Flores Sea, *Indonesia* **37 F6** 6 30S 120 0 E
Floreşti, *Moldova* **17 E15** 47 53N 28 17 E
Floresville, *U.S.A.* **81 L5** 29 8N 98 10W
Floriano, *Brazil* **93 E10** 6 50S 43 0W
Florianópolis, *Brazil* **95 B6** 27 30S 48 30W
Florida, *Cuba* **88 B4** 21 32N 78 14W
Florida, *Uruguay* **95 C4** 34 7S 56 10W
Florida □, *U.S.A.* **77 L5** 28 0N 82 0W
Florida, Straits of, *U.S.A.* **88 B4** 25 0N 80 0W
Florida B., *U.S.A.* **88 B3** 25 0N 80 45W
Florida Keys, *U.S.A.* **77 N5** 24 40N 81 0W
Flórina, *Greece* **21 D9** 40 48N 21 26 E
Florø, *Norway* **9 F11** 61 35N 5 1 E
Flower Station, *Canada* **79 A8** 45 10N 76 41W
Flowerpot I., *Canada* **78 A3** 45 18N 81 38W
Floydada, *U.S.A.* **81 J4** 33 59N 101 20W
Fluk, *Indonesia* **37 E7** 1 42S 127 44 E
Flushing = Vlissingen, *Neths.* **15 C3** 51 26N 3 34 E
Flying Fish, C., *Antarctica* **5 D15** 72 6S 102 29W
Foam Lake, *Canada* **73 C8** 51 40N 103 32W
Foça, *Turkey* **21 E12** 38 39N 26 46 E
Focşani, *Romania* **17 F14** 45 41N 27 15 E
Fóggia, *Italy* **20 D6** 41 27N 15 34 E
Fogo, *Canada* **71 C9** 49 43N 54 17W
Fogo I., *Canada* **71 C9** 49 40N 54 5W
Föhr, *Germany* **16 A5** 54 43N 8 30 E
Foix, *France* **18 E4** 42 58N 1 38 E
Folda, *Nord-Trøndelag, Norway* **8 D14** 64 32N 10 30 E
Folda, *Nordland, Norway* **8 C16** 67 38N 14 50 E
Foley, *U.S.A.* **77 K2** 30 24N 87 41W
Foleyet, *Canada* **70 C3** 48 15N 82 25W
Folgefonni, *Norway* **9 F12** 60 3N 6 23 E
Foligno, *Italy* **20 C5** 42 57N 12 42 E
Folkestone, *U.K.* **11 F9** 51 5N 1 12 E
Folkston, *U.S.A.* **77 K5** 30 50N 82 0W
Follansbee, *U.S.A.* **78 F4** 40 19N 80 35W
Folsom L., *U.S.A.* **84 G5** 38 42N 121 9W
Fond-du-Lac, *Canada* **73 B7** 59 19N 107 12W
Fond du Lac, *U.S.A.* **80 D10** 43 47N 88 27W
Fond-du-Lac ➝, *Canada* **73 B7** 59 17N 106 0W
Fonda, *U.S.A.* **79 D10** 42 57N 74 22W
Fondi, *Italy* **20 D5** 41 21N 13 25 E
Fongafale, *Tuvalu* **64 H9** 8 31S 179 13 E
Fonsagrada = A Fonsagrada, *Spain* **19 A2** 43 8N 7 4W
Fonseca, G. de, *Cent. Amer.* **88 D2** 13 10N 87 40W
Fontainebleau, *France* **18 B5** 48 24N 2 40 E
Fontana, *U.S.A.* **85 L9** 34 6N 117 26W
Fontas ➝, *Canada* **72 B4** 58 14N 121 48W
Fonte Boa, *Brazil* **92 D5** 2 33S 66 0W
Fontenay-le-Comte, *France* **18 C3** 46 28N 0 48W
Fontenelle Reservoir, *U.S.A.* **82 E8** 42 1N 110 3W
Fontur, *Iceland* **8 C6** 66 23N 14 32W
Foochow = Fuzhou, *China* **33 D6** 26 5N 119 16 E
Foping, *China* **34 H5** 33 41N 108 0 E
Forbes, *Australia* **63 E4** 33 22S 148 0 E
Forbesganj, *India* **43 F12** 26 17N 87 18 E
Ford City, *Calif., U.S.A.* **85 K7** 35 9N 119 27W
Ford City, *Pa., U.S.A.* **78 F5** 40 46N 79 32W
Førde, *Norway* **9 F11** 61 27N 5 53 E
Ford's Bridge, *Australia* **63 D4** 29 41S 145 29 E
Fordyce, *U.S.A.* **81 J8** 33 49N 92 25W
Forel, Mt., *Greenland* **4 C6** 66 52N 36 55W
Foremost, *Canada* **72 D6** 49 26N 111 34W
Forest, *Canada* **78 C3** 43 6N 82 0W
Forest, *U.S.A.* **81 J10** 32 22N 89 29W
Forest City, *Iowa, U.S.A.* **80 D8** 43 16N 93 39W
Forest City, *N.C., U.S.A.* **77 H5** 35 20N 81 52W
Forest City, *Pa., U.S.A.* **79 E9** 41 39N 75 28W
Forest Grove, *U.S.A.* **84 E3** 45 31N 123 7W
Forestburg, *Canada* **72 C6** 52 35N 112 1W
Foresthill, *U.S.A.* **84 F6** 39 1N 120 49W
Forestier Pen., *Australia* **62 G4** 43 0S 148 0 E
Forestville, *Canada* **71 C6** 48 48N 69 2W
Forestville, *Calif., U.S.A.* **84 G4** 38 28N 122 54W
Forestville, *N.Y., U.S.A.* **78 D5** 42 28N 79 10W
Forfar, *U.K.* **12 E6** 56 39N 2 53W
Forks, *U.S.A.* **84 C2** 47 57N 124 23W
Forksville, *U.S.A.* **79 E8** 41 29N 76 35W
Forlì, *Italy* **20 B5** 44 13N 12 3 E
Forman, *U.S.A.* **80 B6** 46 7N 97 38W
Formby Pt., *U.K.* **10 D4** 53 33N 3 6W
Formentera, *Spain* **22 C7** 38 43N 1 27 E
Formentor, C. de, *Spain* **22 B10** 39 58N 3 13 E
Former Yugoslav Republic of Macedonia = Macedonia ■, *Europe* **21 D9** 41 53N 21 40 E
Fórmia, *Italy* **20 D5** 41 15N 13 37 E
Formosa = Taiwan ■, *Asia* **33 D7** 23 30N 121 0 E
Formosa, *Argentina* **94 B4** 26 15S 58 10W
Formosa, *Brazil* **93 G9** 15 32S 47 20W
Formosa □, *Argentina* **94 B4** 25 0S 60 0W
Formosa, Serra, *Brazil* **93 F8** 12 0S 55 0W
Formosa Bay, *Kenya* **54 C5** 2 40S 40 20 E
Fornells, *Spain* **22 A11** 40 3N 4 7 E
Føroyar, *Atl. Oc.* **8 F9** 62 0N 7 0W
Forres, *U.K.* **12 D5** 57 37N 3 37W
Forrest, *Australia* **61 F4** 30 51S 128 6 E
Forrest, Mt., *Australia* **61 D4** 24 48S 127 45 E
Forrest City, *U.S.A.* **81 H9** 35 1N 90 47W
Forsayth, *Australia* **62 B3** 18 33S 143 34 E
Forssa, *Finland* **9 F20** 60 49N 23 38 E
Forst, *Germany* **16 C8** 51 45N 14 37 E
Forsyth, *U.S.A.* **82 C10** 46 16N 106 41W
Fort Abbas, *Pakistan* **42 E5** 29 12N 72 52 E
Fort Albany, *Canada* **70 B3** 52 15N 81 35W
Fort Ann, *U.S.A.* **79 C11** 43 25N 73 30W
Fort Assiniboine, *Canada* **72 C6** 54 20N 114 45W
Fort Augustus, *U.K.* **12 D4** 57 9N 4 42W
Fort Beaufort, *S. Africa* **56 E4** 32 46S 26 40 E
Fort Benton, *U.S.A.* **82 C8** 47 49N 110 40W
Fort Bragg, *U.S.A.* **82 G2** 39 26N 123 48W
Fort Bridger, *U.S.A.* **82 F8** 41 19N 110 23W
Fort Chipewyan, *Canada* **73 B6** 58 42N 111 8W
Fort Collins, *U.S.A.* **80 E2** 40 35N 105 5W
Fort-Coulonge, *Canada* **70 C4** 45 50N 76 45W
Fort Covington, *U.S.A.* **79 B10** 44 59N 74 29W
Fort Davis, *U.S.A.* **81 K3** 30 35N 103 54W
Fort-de-France, *Martinique* **89 D7** 14 36N 61 2W
Fort Defiance, *U.S.A.* **83 J9** 35 45N 109 5W
Fort Dodge, *U.S.A.* **80 D7** 42 30N 94 11W
Fort Edward, *U.S.A.* **79 C11** 43 16N 73 35W
Fort Erie, *Canada* **78 D6** 42 54N 78 56W
Fort Fairfield, *U.S.A.* **77 B12** 46 46N 67 50W
Fort Frances, *Canada* **73 D10** 48 36N 93 24W
Fort Garland, *U.S.A.* **83 H11** 37 26N 105 26W
Fort George = Chisasibi, *Canada* **70 B4** 53 50N 79 0W
Fort Good-Hope, *Canada* **68 B7** 66 14N 128 40W
Fort Hancock, *U.S.A.* **83 L11** 31 18N 105 51W
Fort Hertz = Putao, *Burma* **41 F20** 27 28N 97 30 E
Fort Hope, *Canada* **70 B2** 51 30N 88 0W
Fort Irwin, *U.S.A.* **85 K10** 35 16N 116 34W
Fort Jameson = Chipata, *Zambia* **55 E3** 13 38S 32 28 E
Fort Kent, *U.S.A.* **77 B11** 47 15N 68 36W
Fort Klamath, *U.S.A.* **82 E3** 42 42N 122 0W
Fort-Lamy = Ndjamena, *Chad* **51 F8** 12 10N 14 59 E
Fort Laramie, *U.S.A.* **80 D2** 42 13N 104 31W
Fort Lauderdale, *U.S.A.* **77 M5** 26 7N 80 8W
Fort Liard, *Canada* **72 A4** 60 14N 123 30W
Fort Liberté, *Haiti* **89 C5** 19 42N 71 51W
Fort Lupton, *U.S.A.* **80 E2** 40 5N 104 49W
Fort Mackay, *Canada* **72 B6** 57 12N 111 41W
Fort Macleod, *Canada* **72 D6** 49 45N 113 30W
Fort McMurray, *Canada* **72 B6** 56 44N 111 7W
Fort McPherson, *Canada* **68 B6** 67 30N 134 55W
Fort Madison, *U.S.A.* **80 E9** 40 38N 91 27W
Fort Meade, *U.S.A.* **77 M5** 27 45N 81 48W
Fort Morgan, *U.S.A.* **80 E3** 40 15N 103 48W
Fort Munro, *Pakistan* **42 E3** 29 54N 69 58 E
Fort Myers, *U.S.A.* **77 M5** 26 39N 81 52W
Fort Nelson, *Canada* **72 B4** 58 50N 122 44W
Fort Nelson ➝, *Canada* **72 B4** 59 32N 124 0W
Fort Norman = Tulita, *Canada* **68 B7** 64 57N 125 30W
Fort Payne, *U.S.A.* **77 H3** 34 26N 85 43W
Fort Peck, *U.S.A.* **82 B10** 48 1N 106 27W
Fort Peck Dam, *U.S.A.* **82 C10** 48 0N 106 26W
Fort Peck L., *U.S.A.* **82 C10** 48 0N 106 26W
Fort Pierce, *U.S.A.* **77 M5** 27 27N 80 20W
Fort Pierre, *U.S.A.* **80 C4** 44 21N 100 22W
Fort Plain, *U.S.A.* **79 D10** 42 56N 74 37W
Fort Portal, *Uganda* **54 B3** 0 40N 30 20 E
Fort Providence, *Canada* **72 A5** 61 3N 117 40W
Fort Qu'Appelle, *Canada* **73 C8** 50 45N 103 50W
Fort Resolution, *Canada* **72 A6** 61 10N 113 40W
Fort Rixon, *Zimbabwe* **55 G2** 20 2S 29 17 E
Fort Rosebery = Mansa, *Zambia* **55 E2** 11 13S 28 55 E
Fort Ross, *U.S.A.* **84 G3** 38 32N 123 13W
Fort Rousset = Owando, *Congo* **52 E3** 0 29S 15 55 E
Fort Rupert = Waskaganish, *Canada* **70 B4** 51 30N 78 40W
Fort St. James, *Canada* **72 C4** 54 30N 124 10W
Fort St. John, *Canada* **72 B4** 56 15N 120 50W
Fort Sandeman = Zhob, *Pakistan* **42 D3** 31 20N 69 31 E
Fort Saskatchewan, *Canada* **72 C6** 53 40N 113 15W
Fort Scott, *U.S.A.* **81 G7** 37 50N 94 42W
Fort Severn, *Canada* **70 A2** 56 0N 87 40W
Fort Shevchenko, *Kazakstan* **25 F9** 44 35N 50 23 E
Fort Simpson, *Canada* **72 A4** 61 45N 121 15W
Fort Smith, *Canada* **72 B6** 60 0N 111 51W
Fort Smith, *U.S.A.* **81 H7** 35 23N 94 25W
Fort Stockton, *U.S.A.* **81 K3** 30 53N 102 53W
Fort Sumner, *U.S.A.* **81 H2** 34 28N 104 15W
Fort Thompson, *U.S.A.* **80 C5** 44 3N 99 26W
Fort Trinquet = Bir Mogreïn, *Mauritania* **50 C3** 25 10N 11 25W
Fort Valley, *U.S.A.* **77 J4** 32 33N 83 53W
Fort Vermilion, *Canada* **72 B5** 58 24N 116 0W
Fort Walton Beach, *U.S.A.* **77 K2** 30 25N 86 36W
Fort Wayne, *U.S.A.* **76 E3** 41 4N 85 9W
Fort William, *U.K.* **12 E3** 56 49N 5 7W
Fort Worth, *U.S.A.* **81 J6** 32 45N 97 18W
Fort Yates, *U.S.A.* **80 B4** 46 5N 100 38W
Fort Yukon, *U.S.A.* **68 B5** 66 34N 145 16W
Fortaleza, *Brazil* **93 D11** 3 45S 38 35W
Forteau, *Canada* **71 B8** 51 28N 56 58W
Fortescue ➝, *Australia* **60 D2** 21 0S 116 4 E
Forth ➝, *U.K.* **12 E5** 56 9N 3 50W
Forth, Firth of, *U.K.* **12 E6** 56 5N 2 55W
Fortrose, *U.K.* **12 D4** 57 35N 4 9W
Fortuna, *Calif., U.S.A.* **82 F1** 40 36N 124 9W
Fortuna, *N. Dak., U.S.A.* **80 A3** 48 55N 103 47W
Fortune, *Canada* **71 C8** 47 4N 55 50W
Fortune B., *Canada* **71 C8** 47 30N 55 22W
Forūr, *Iran* **45 E7** 26 17N 54 32 E
Foshan, *China* **33 D6** 23 4N 113 5 E
Fosna, *Norway* **8 E14** 63 50N 10 20 E
Fosnavåg, *Norway* **9 E11** 62 22N 5 38 E
Fossano, *Italy* **18 D7** 44 33N 7 43 E
Fossil, *U.S.A.* **82 D3** 45 0N 120 9W
Foster, *Australia* **63 F4** 38 40S 146 15 E
Foster, *Canada* **79 A12** 45 17N 72 30W
Foster ➝, *Canada* **73 B7** 55 47N 105 49W
Fosters Ra., *Australia* **62 C1** 21 35S 133 48 E
Fostoria, *U.S.A.* **76 E4** 41 10N 83 25W
Fougères, *France* **18 B3** 48 21N 1 14W
Foul Pt., *Sri Lanka* **40 Q12** 8 35N 81 18 E
Foula, *U.K.* **12 A6** 60 10N 2 5W
Foulness I., *U.K.* **11 F8** 51 36N 0 55 E
Foulpointe, *Madag.* **57 B8** 17 41S 49 31 E
Foulweather, C., *U.S.A.* **74 B2** 44 50N 124 5W
Foumban, *Cameroon* **52 C2** 5 45N 10 50 E
Fountain, *U.S.A.* **80 F2** 38 41N 104 42W
Fountain Springs, *U.S.A.* **85 K8** 35 54N 118 51W
Fouriesburg, *S. Africa* **56 D4** 28 38S 28 14 E
Foúrnoi, *Greece* **21 F12** 37 36N 26 32 E
Fourth Cataract, *Sudan* **51 E12** 18 47N 32 3 E
Fouta Djalon, *Guinea* **50 F3** 11 20N 12 10W
Foux, Cap-à-, *Haiti* **89 C5** 19 43N 73 27W
Foveaux Str., *N.Z.* **59 M2** 46 42S 168 10 E
Fowey, *U.K.* **11 G3** 50 20N 4 39W
Fowler, *Calif., U.S.A.* **84 J7** 36 38N 119 41W
Fowler, *Colo., U.S.A.* **80 F3** 38 8N 104 2W
Fowlers B., *Australia* **61 F5** 31 59S 132 34 E
Fowman, *Iran* **45 B6** 37 13N 49 19 E
Fox ➝, *Canada* **73 B10** 56 3N 93 18W
Fox Creek, *Canada* **72 C5** 54 24N 116 48W
Fox Lake, *Canada* **72 B6** 58 28N 114 31W
Fox Valley, *Canada* **73 C7** 50 30N 109 25W
Foxboro, *U.S.A.* **79 D13** 42 4N 71 16W
Foxe Basin, *Canada* **69 B12** 66 0N 77 0W
Foxe Chan., *Canada* **69 B12** 65 0N 80 0W
Foxe Pen., *Canada* **69 B12** 65 0N 76 0W
Foxton, *N.Z.* **59 J5** 40 29S 175 18 E
Foyle, Lough, *U.K.* **13 A4** 55 7N 7 4W
Foynes, *Ireland* **13 D2** 52 37N 9 7W
Fóz do Cunene, *Angola* **56 B1** 17 15S 11 48 E
Foz do Iguaçu, *Brazil* **95 B5** 25 30S 54 30W
Frackville, *U.S.A.* **79 F8** 40 47N 76 14W
Fraile Muerto, *Uruguay* **95 C5** 32 31S 54 32W
Framingham, *U.S.A.* **79 D13** 42 17N 71 25W
Franca, *Brazil* **93 H9** 20 33S 47 30W
Francavilla Fontana, *Italy* **21 D7** 40 32N 17 35 E
France ■, *Europe* **18 C5** 47 0N 3 0 E
Frances, *Australia* **63 F3** 36 41S 140 55 E
Frances ➝, *Canada* **72 A3** 60 16N 129 10W
Frances L., *Canada* **72 A3** 61 23N 129 30W
Franceville, *Gabon* **52 E2** 1 40S 13 32 E
Franche-Comté, *France* **18 C6** 46 50N 5 55 E
Francis Case, L., *U.S.A.* **80 D5** 43 4N 98 34W
Francisco Beltrão, *Brazil* **95 B5** 26 5S 53 4W
Francisco I. Madero, *Coahuila, Mexico* **86 B4** 25 48N 103 18W
Francisco I. Madero, *Durango, Mexico* **86 C4** 24 32N 104 22W
Francistown, *Botswana* **57 C4** 21 7S 27 33 E
François, *Canada* **71 C8** 47 35N 56 45W
François L., *Canada* **72 C3** 54 0N 125 30W
Franeker, *Neths.* **15 A5** 53 12N 5 33 E
Frankford, *Canada* **78 B7** 44 12N 77 36W
Frankfort, *S. Africa* **57 D4** 27 17S 28 30 E
Frankfort, *Ind., U.S.A.* **76 E2** 40 17N 86 31W
Frankfort, *Kans., U.S.A.* **80 F6** 39 42N 96 25W
Frankfort, *Ky., U.S.A.* **76 F3** 38 12N 84 52W
Frankfort, *N.Y., U.S.A.* **79 C9** 43 2N 75 4W

Gatton

rankfurt, Brandenburg, Germany **16 B8** 52 20N 14 32 E
rankfurt, Hessen, Germany **16 C5** 50 7N 8 41 E
ränkische Alb, Germany **16 D6** 49 10N 11 23 E
rankland →, Australia **61 G2** 35 0S 116 48 E
ranklin, Ky., U.S.A. **77 G2** 36 43N 86 35W
ranklin, La., U.S.A. **81 L9** 29 48N 91 30W
ranklin, Mass., U.S.A. **79 D13** 42 5N 71 24W
ranklin, N.H., U.S.A. **79 C13** 43 27N 71 39W
ranklin, Nebr., U.S.A. **80 E5** 40 6N 98 57W
ranklin, Pa., U.S.A. **78 E5** 41 24N 79 50W
ranklin, Va., U.S.A. **77 G7** 36 41N 76 56W
ranklin, W. Va., U.S.A. **76 F6** 38 39N 79 20W
ranklin B., Canada **68 B7** 69 45N 126 0W
ranklin D. Roosevelt L., U.S.A. **82 B4** 48 18N 118 9W
ranklin I., Antarctica **5 D11** 76 10S 168 30 E
ranklin L., U.S.A. **82 F6** 40 25N 115 22W
ranklin Mts., Canada **68 B7** 65 0N 125 0W
ranklin Str., Canada **68 A10** 72 0N 96 0W
ranklinton, U.S.A. **81 K9** 30 51N 90 9W
ranklinville, U.S.A. **78 D6** 42 20N 78 27W
ranks Pk., U.S.A. **82 E9** 43 58N 109 18W
rankston, Australia **63 F4** 38 8S 145 8 E
rantsa Iosifa, Zemlya, Russia **26 A6** 82 0N 55 0 E
ranz, Canada **70 C3** 48 25N 84 30W
ranz Josef Land = Frantsa Iosifa, Zemlya, Russia **26 A6** 82 0N 55 0 E
raser, U.S.A. **78 D2** 42 32N 82 57W
raser →, B.C., Canada **72 D4** 49 7N 123 11W
raser →, Nfld., Canada **71 A7** 56 39N 62 10W
raser, Mt., Australia **61 E2** 25 35S 118 20 E
raser I., Australia **63 D5** 25 15S 153 10 E
raser Lake, Canada **72 C4** 54 0N 124 50W
raserburg, S. Africa **56 E3** 31 55S 21 30 E
raserburgh, U.K. **12 D6** 57 42N 2 1W
raserdale, Canada **70 C3** 49 55N 81 37W
ray Bentos, Uruguay **94 C4** 33 10S 58 15W
redericia, Denmark **9 J13** 55 34N 9 45 E
rederick, Md., U.S.A. **76 F7** 39 25N 77 25W
rederick, Okla., U.S.A. **81 H5** 34 23N 99 1W
rederick, S. Dak., U.S.A. **80 C5** 45 50N 98 31W
redericksburg, Pa., U.S.A. **79 F8** 40 27N 76 26W
redericksburg, Tex., U.S.A. **81 K5** 30 16N 98 52W
redericksburg, Va., U.S.A. **76 F7** 38 18N 77 28W
redericktown, Mo., U.S.A. **81 G9** 37 34N 90 18W
redericktown, Ohio, U.S.A. **78 F2** 40 29N 82 33W
rederico I. Madero, Presa, Mexico **86 B3** 28 7N 105 40W
rederico Westphalen, Brazil **95 B5** 27 22S 53 24W
redericton, Canada **71 C6** 45 57N 66 40W
redericton Junction, Canada **71 C6** 45 41N 66 40W
rederikshåb, Greenland **4 C5** 62 0N 49 43W
rederikshavn, Denmark **9 H14** 57 28N 10 31 E
rederiksted, Virgin Is. **89 C7** 17 43N 64 53W
redonia, Ariz., U.S.A. **83 H7** 36 57N 112 32W
redonia, Kans., U.S.A. **81 G7** 37 32N 95 49W
redonia, N.Y., U.S.A. **78 D5** 42 26N 79 20W
redrikstad, Norway **9 G14** 59 13N 10 57 E
ree State □, S. Africa **56 D4** 28 30S 27 0 E
reehold, U.S.A. **79 F10** 40 16N 74 17W
reel Peak, U.S.A. **84 G7** 38 52N 119 54W
reeland, U.S.A. **79 E9** 41 1N 75 54W
reels, C., Canada **71 C9** 49 15N 53 30W
reeman, Calif., U.S.A. **85 K9** 35 35N 117 53W
reeman, S. Dak., U.S.A. **80 D6** 43 21N 97 26W
reeport, Bahamas **88 A4** 26 30N 78 47W
reeport, Ill., U.S.A. **80 D10** 42 17N 89 36W
reeport, N.Y., U.S.A. **79 F11** 40 39N 73 35W
reeport, Ohio, U.S.A. **78 F3** 40 12N 81 15W
reeport, Pa., U.S.A. **78 F5** 40 41N 79 41W
reeport, Tex., U.S.A. **81 L7** 28 57N 95 21W
reetown, S. Leone **50 G3** 8 30N 13 17W
régate, L., Canada **70 B5** 53 15N 74 45W
regenal de la Sierra, Spain **19 C2** 38 10N 6 39W
reibourg = Fribourg, Switz. **18 C7** 46 49N 7 9 E
reiburg, Germany **16 E4** 47 59N 7 51 E
reire, Chile **96 D2** 38 54S 72 38W
reirina, Chile **94 B1** 28 30S 71 10W
reising, Germany **16 D6** 48 24N 11 45 E
reistadt, Austria **16 D8** 48 30N 14 30 E
réjus, France **18 E7** 43 25N 6 44 E
remantle, Australia **61 F2** 32 7S 115 47 E
remont, Calif., U.S.A. **84 H4** 37 32N 121 57W
remont, Mich., U.S.A. **76 D3** 43 28N 85 57W
remont, Nebr., U.S.A. **80 E6** 41 26N 96 30W
remont, Ohio, U.S.A. **76 E4** 41 21N 83 7W
remont →, U.S.A. **83 G8** 38 24N 110 42W
rench Camp, U.S.A. **84 H5** 37 53N 121 16W
rench Creek →, U.S.A. **78 E5** 41 24N 79 50W
rench Guiana ■, S. Amer. **93 C8** 4 0N 53 0W
rench Pass, N.Z. **59 J4** 40 55S 173 55 E
rench Polynesia ■, Pac. Oc. **65 K13** 20 0S 145 0W
renchman Cr. →, N. Amer. **82 B10** 48 31N 107 10W
renchman Cr. →, U.S.A. **80 E4** 40 14N 100 50W
resco →, Brazil **93 E8** 7 15S 51 30W
reshfield, C., Antarctica **5 C10** 68 25S 151 10 E
resnillo, Mexico **86 C4** 23 10N 103 0W
resno, U.S.A. **84 J7** 36 44N 119 47W
resno Reservoir, U.S.A. **82 B9** 48 36N 109 57W
rew →, Australia **62 C2** 20 0S 135 38 E
rewsburg, U.S.A. **78 D5** 42 3N 79 10W
reycinet Pen., Australia **62 G4** 42 10S 148 25 E
ria, C., Namibia **56 B1** 18 0S 12 0 E
riant, U.S.A. **84 J7** 36 59N 119 43W
rías, Argentina **94 B2** 28 40S 65 5W
ribourg, Switz. **18 C7** 46 49N 7 9 E
riday Harbor, U.S.A. **84 B3** 48 32N 123 1W
riedens, U.S.A. **78 F6** 40 3N 78 59W
riedrichshafen, Germany **16 E5** 47 39N 9 30 E
riendly Is. = Tonga ■, Pac. Oc. **59 D11** 19 50S 174 30W
riendship, U.S.A. **78 D6** 42 12N 78 8W
riesland □, Neths. **15 A5** 53 5N 5 50 E
rio →, U.S.A. **81 L5** 28 26N 98 11W
rio, C., Brazil **90 F6** 22 50S 41 50W
riona, U.S.A. **81 H3** 34 38N 102 43W
ritch, U.S.A. **81 H4** 35 38N 101 36W
robisher B., Canada **69 B13** 62 30N 66 0W
robisher Bay = Iqaluit, Canada **69 B13** 63 44N 68 31W
robisher L., Canada **73 B7** 56 20N 108 15W
rohavet, Norway **8 E13** 64 0N 9 30 E
rome, U.K. **11 F5** 51 14N 2 19W
Frome →, U.K. **11 G5** 50 41N 2 6W
Frome, L., Australia **63 E2** 30 45S 139 45 E
Front Range, U.S.A. **74 C5** 40 25N 105 45W
Front Royal, U.S.A. **76 F6** 38 55N 78 12W
Frontera, Canary Is. **22 G2** 27 47N 17 59W
Frontera, Mexico **87 D6** 18 30N 92 40W
Fronteras, Mexico **86 A3** 30 56N 109 31W
Frosinone, Italy **20 D5** 41 38N 13 19 E
Frostburg, U.S.A. **76 F6** 39 39N 78 56W
Frostisen, Norway **8 B17** 68 14N 17 10 E
Frøya, Norway **8 E13** 63 43N 8 40 E
Frunze = Bishkek, Kyrgyzstan **26 E8** 42 54N 74 46 E
Frutal, Brazil **93 H9** 20 0S 49 0W
Frýdek-Místek, Czech Rep. **17 D10** 49 40N 18 20 E
Fryeburg, U.S.A. **79 B14** 44 1N 70 59W
Fu Xian = Wafangdian, China **35 E11** 39 38N 121 58 E
Fu Xian, China **34 G5** 36 0N 109 20 E
Fucheng, China **34 F9** 37 50N 116 10 E
Fuchou = Fuzhou, China **33 D6** 26 5N 119 16 E
Fuchū, Japan **31 G6** 34 34N 133 14 E
Fuencaliente, Canary Is. **22 F2** 28 28N 17 50W
Fuencaliente, Pta., Canary Is. **22 F2** 28 27N 17 51W
Fuengirola, Spain **19 D3** 36 32N 4 41W
Fuentes de Oñoro, Spain **19 B2** 40 33N 6 52W
Fuerte →, Mexico **86 B3** 25 50N 109 25W
Fuerte Olimpo, Paraguay **94 A4** 21 0S 57 51W
Fuerteventura, Canary Is. **22 F6** 28 30N 14 0W
Fufeng, China **34 G5** 34 22N 108 0 E
Fugou, China **34 G8** 34 3N 114 25 E
Fugu, China **34 E6** 39 2N 111 3 E
Fuhai, China **32 B3** 47 2N 87 25 E
Fuḩaymī, Iraq **44 C4** 34 16N 42 10 E
Fuji, Japan **31 G9** 35 9N 138 39 E
Fuji-San, Japan **31 G9** 35 22N 138 44 E
Fuji-yoshida, Japan **31 G9** 35 30N 138 46 E
Fujian □, China **33 D6** 26 0N 118 0 E
Fujinomiya, Japan **31 G9** 35 10N 138 40 E
Fujisawa, Japan **31 G9** 35 22N 139 29 E
Fujiyama, Mt. = Fuji-San, Japan **31 G9** 35 22N 138 44 E
Fukien = Fujian □, China **33 D6** 26 0N 118 0 E
Fukuchiyama, Japan **31 G7** 35 19N 135 9 E
Fukue-Shima, Japan **31 H4** 32 40N 128 45 E
Fukui, Japan **31 F8** 36 5N 136 10 E
Fukui □, Japan **31 G8** 36 0N 136 12 E
Fukuoka, Japan **31 H5** 33 39N 130 21 E
Fukuoka □, Japan **31 H5** 33 30N 131 0 E
Fukushima, Japan **30 F10** 37 44N 140 28 E
Fukushima □, Japan **30 F10** 37 30N 140 15 E
Fukuyama, Japan **31 G6** 34 35N 133 20 E
Fulda, Germany **16 C5** 50 32N 9 40 E
Fulda →, Germany **16 C5** 51 25N 9 39 E
Fulford Harbour, Canada **84 B3** 48 47N 123 27W
Fullerton, Calif., U.S.A. **85 M9** 33 53N 117 56W
Fullerton, Nebr., U.S.A. **80 E6** 41 22N 97 58W
Fulongquan, China **35 B13** 44 20N 124 42 E
Fulton, Mo., U.S.A. **80 F9** 38 52N 91 57W
Fulton, N.Y., U.S.A. **79 C8** 43 19N 76 25W
Funabashi, Japan **31 G10** 35 45N 140 0 E
Funchal, Madeira **22 D3** 32 38N 16 54W
Fundación, Colombia **92 A4** 10 31N 74 11W
Fundão, Portugal **19 B2** 40 8N 7 30W
Fundy, B. of, Canada **71 D6** 45 0N 66 0W
Funing, Hebei, China **35 E10** 39 53N 119 12 E
Funing, Jiangsu, China **35 H10** 33 45N 119 50 E
Funiu Shan, China **34 H7** 33 30N 112 20 E
Funtua, Nigeria **50 F7** 11 30N 7 18 E
Fuping, Hebei, China **34 E8** 38 48N 114 12 E
Fuping, Shaanxi, China **34 G5** 34 42N 109 10 E
Furano, Japan **30 C11** 43 21N 142 23 E
Furāt, Nahr al →, Asia **44 D5** 31 0N 47 25 E
Fūrg, Iran **45 D7** 28 18N 55 13 E
Furnás, Spain **22 B8** 39 3N 1 32 E
Furnas, Reprêsa de, Brazil **95 A6** 20 50S 45 30W
Furneaux Group, Australia **62 G4** 40 10S 147 50 E
Furqlus, Syria **47 A6** 34 36N 37 8 E
Fürstenwalde, Germany **16 B8** 52 22N 14 3 E
Fürth, Germany **16 D6** 49 28N 10 59 E
Furukawa, Japan **30 E10** 38 34N 140 58 E
Fury and Hecla Str., Canada **69 B11** 69 56N 84 0W
Fusagasuga, Colombia **92 C4** 4 21N 74 22W
Fushan, Shandong, China **35 F11** 37 30N 121 15 E
Fushan, Shanxi, China **34 G6** 35 58N 111 51 E
Fushun, China **35 D12** 41 50N 123 56 E
Fusong, China **35 C14** 42 20N 127 15 E
Futuna, Wall. & F. Is. **59 B8** 14 25S 178 20 E
Fuxin, China **35 C11** 42 5N 121 48 E
Fuyang, China **34 H8** 33 0N 115 48 E
Fuyang He →, China **34 E9** 38 12N 117 0 E
Fuyu, China **35 B13** 45 12N 124 43 E
Fuzhou, China **33 D6** 26 5N 119 16 E
Fylde, U.K. **10 D5** 53 50N 2 58W
Fyn, Denmark **9 J14** 55 20N 10 30 E
Fyne, L., U.K. **12 F3** 55 59N 5 23W

G

Gabela, Angola **52 G2** 11 0S 14 24 E
Gabès, Tunisia **51 B8** 33 53N 10 2 E
Gabès, G. de, Tunisia **51 B8** 34 0N 10 30 E
Gabon ■, Africa **52 E2** 0 10S 10 0 E
Gaborone, Botswana **56 C4** 24 45S 25 57 E
Gabriels, U.S.A. **79 B10** 44 26N 74 12W
Gābrīk, Iran **45 E8** 25 44N 58 28 E
Gabrovo, Bulgaria **21 C11** 42 52N 25 19 E
Gāch Sār, Iran **45 B6** 36 7N 51 19 E
Gachsārān, Iran **45 D6** 30 15N 50 45 E
Gadag, India **40 M9** 15 30N 75 45 E
Gadap, Pakistan **42 G2** 25 5N 67 28 E
Gadarwara, India **43 H8** 22 50N 78 50 E
Gadhada, India **42 J4** 22 0N 71 35 E
Gadra, Pakistan **42 G4** 25 40N 70 38 E
Gadsden, U.S.A. **77 H3** 34 1N 86 1W
Gadwal, India **40 L10** 16 10N 77 50 E
Gaffney, U.S.A. **77 H5** 35 5N 81 39W
Gafsa, Tunisia **50 B7** 34 24N 8 43 E
Gagaria, India **42 G4** 25 43N 70 46 E
Gagnoa, Ivory C. **50 G4** 6 56N 5 16W
Gagnon, Canada **71 B6** 51 50N 68 5W
Gagnon, L., Canada **73 A6** 62 3N 110 27W
Gahini, Rwanda **54 C3** 1 50S 30 30 E
Gahmar, India **43 G10** 25 27N 83 49 E
Gai Xian = Gaizhou, China **35 D12** 40 22N 122 20 E
Gaïdhouronísi, Greece **23 E7** 34 53N 25 41 E
Gail, U.S.A. **81 J4** 32 46N 101 27W
Gaillimh = Galway, Ireland **13 C2** 53 17N 9 3W
Gaines, U.S.A. **78 E7** 41 46N 77 35W
Gainesville, Fla., U.S.A. **77 L4** 29 40N 82 20W
Gainesville, Ga., U.S.A. **77 H4** 34 18N 83 50W
Gainesville, Mo., U.S.A. **81 G8** 36 36N 92 26W
Gainesville, Tex., U.S.A. **81 J6** 33 38N 97 8W
Gainsborough, U.K. **10 D7** 53 24N 0 46W
Gairdner, L., Australia **63 E2** 31 30S 136 0 E
Gairloch, L., U.K. **12 D3** 57 43N 5 45W
Gaizhou, China **35 D12** 40 22N 122 20 E
Gaj →, Pakistan **42 F2** 26 26N 67 21 E
Gakuch, Pakistan **43 A5** 36 7N 73 45 E
Galán, Cerro, Argentina **94 B2** 25 55S 66 52W
Galana →, Kenya **54 C5** 3 9S 40 8 E
Galápagos, Pac. Oc. **90 D1** 0 0 91 0W
Galashiels, U.K. **12 F6** 55 37N 2 49W
Galaţi, Romania **17 F15** 45 27N 28 2 E
Galatina, Italy **21 D8** 40 10N 18 10 E
Galax, U.S.A. **77 G5** 36 40N 80 56W
Galcaio, Somali Rep. **46 F4** 6 30N 47 30 E
Galdhøpiggen, Norway **9 F12** 61 38N 8 18 E
Galeana, Mexico **86 C4** 24 50N 100 4W
Galeana, Nuevo León, Mexico **86 A3** 24 50N 100 4W
Galela, Indonesia **37 D7** 1 50N 127 49 E
Galena, U.S.A. **68 B4** 64 44N 156 56W
Galera Point, Trin. & Tob. **89 D7** 10 8N 61 0W
Galesburg, U.S.A. **80 E9** 40 57N 90 22W
Galeton, U.S.A. **78 E7** 41 44N 77 39W
Galich, Russia **24 C7** 58 22N 42 24 E
Galicia □, Spain **19 A2** 42 43N 7 45W
Galilee = Hagalil, Israel **47 C4** 32 53N 35 18 E
Galilee, L., Australia **62 C4** 22 20S 145 50 E
Galilee, Sea of = Yam Kinneret, Israel **47 C4** 32 45N 35 35 E
Galinoporni, Cyprus **23 D13** 35 31N 34 18 E
Galion, U.S.A. **78 F2** 40 44N 82 47W
Galiuro Mts., U.S.A. **83 K8** 32 30N 110 20W
Galiwinku, Australia **62 A2** 12 2S 135 34 E
Gallan Hd., U.K. **12 C1** 58 15N 7 2W
Gallatin, U.S.A. **77 G2** 36 24N 86 27W
Galle, Sri Lanka **40 R12** 6 5N 80 10 E
Gállego →, Spain **19 B5** 41 39N 0 51W
Gallegos →, Argentina **96 G3** 51 35S 69 0W
Galley Hd., Ireland **13 E3** 51 32N 8 55W
Gallinas, Pta., Colombia **92 A4** 12 28N 71 40W
Gallipoli = Gelibolu, Turkey **21 D12** 40 28N 26 43 E
Gallípoli, Italy **21 D8** 40 3N 17 58 E
Gallipolis, U.S.A. **76 F4** 38 49N 82 12W
Gällivare, Sweden **8 C19** 67 9N 20 40 E
Galloo I., U.S.A. **79 C8** 43 55N 76 25W
Galloway, U.K. **12 F4** 55 1N 4 29W
Galloway, Mull of, U.K. **12 G4** 54 39N 4 52W
Gallup, U.S.A. **83 J9** 35 32N 108 45W
Galoya, Sri Lanka **40 Q12** 8 10N 80 55 E
Galt, U.S.A. **84 G5** 38 15N 121 18W
Galty Mts., Ireland **13 D3** 52 22N 8 10W
Galtymore, Ireland **13 D3** 52 21N 8 11W
Galva, U.S.A. **80 E9** 41 10N 90 3W
Galveston, U.S.A. **81 L7** 29 18N 94 48W
Galveston B., U.S.A. **81 L7** 29 36N 94 50W
Gálvez, Argentina **94 C3** 32 0S 61 14W
Galway, Ireland **13 C2** 53 17N 9 3W
Galway □, Ireland **13 C2** 53 22N 9 1W
Galway B., Ireland **13 C2** 53 13N 9 10W
Gam →, Vietnam **38 B5** 21 55N 105 12 E
Gamagori, Japan **31 G8** 34 50N 137 14 E
Gambat, Pakistan **42 F3** 27 17N 68 26 E
Gambhir →, India **42 F6** 26 58N 77 27 E
Gambia ■, W. Afr. **50 F2** 13 25N 16 0W
Gambia →, W. Afr. **50 F2** 13 28N 16 34W
Gambier, U.S.A. **78 F2** 40 22N 82 23W
Gambier, C., Australia **60 B5** 11 56S 130 57 E
Gambier Is., Australia **63 F2** 35 3S 136 30 E
Gambo, Canada **71 C9** 48 47N 54 13W
Gamboli, Pakistan **42 E3** 29 53N 68 24 E
Gamboma, Congo **52 E3** 1 55S 15 52 E
Gamlakarleby = Kokkola, Finland **8 E20** 63 50N 23 8 E
Gammon →, Canada **73 C9** 51 24N 95 44W
Gan Jiang →, China **33 D6** 29 15N 116 0 E
Ganado, U.S.A. **83 J9** 35 43N 109 33W
Gananoque, Canada **79 B8** 44 20N 76 10W
Ganāveh, Iran **45 D6** 29 35N 50 35 E
Gäncä, Azerbaijan **25 F8** 40 45N 46 20 E
Gancheng, China **38 C7** 18 51N 108 37 E
Gand = Gent, Belgium **15 C3** 51 2N 3 42 E
Ganda, Angola **53 G2** 13 3S 14 35 E
Gandajika, Dem. Rep. of the Congo **52 F4** 6 45S 23 57 E
Gandak →, India **43 G11** 25 39N 85 13 E
Gandava, Pakistan **42 E2** 28 32N 67 32 E
Gander, Canada **71 C9** 48 58N 54 35W
Gander L., Canada **71 C9** 48 58N 54 35W
Ganderowe Falls, Zimbabwe **55 F2** 17 20S 29 10 E
Gandhi Sagar, India **42 G6** 24 40N 75 40 E
Gandhinagar, India **42 H5** 23 15N 72 45 E
Gandía, Spain **19 C5** 38 58N 0 9W
Gando, Pta., Canary Is. **22 G4** 27 55N 15 22W
Ganedidalem = Gani, Indonesia **37 E7** 0 48S 128 14 E
Ganga →, India **43 H14** 23 20N 90 30 E
Ganga Sagar, India **43 J13** 21 38N 88 5 E
Gangan →, India **43 E8** 28 38N 78 58 E
Ganganagar, India **42 E5** 29 56N 73 56 E
Gangapur, India **42 F7** 26 32N 76 49 E
Gangaw, Burma **41 H19** 22 5N 94 5 E
Gangdisê Shan, China **41 D12** 31 20N 81 0 E
Ganges = Ganga →, India **43 H14** 23 20N 90 30 E
Ganges, Canada **72 D4** 48 51N 123 31W
Ganges, Mouths of the, India **43 J14** 21 30N 90 0 E
Gangoh, India **42 E7** 29 46N 77 18 E
Gangroti, India **43 D8** 30 50N 79 10 E
Gangtok, India **41 F16** 27 20N 88 37 E
Gangu, China **34 G3** 34 40N 105 15 E
Gangyao, China **35 B14** 44 12N 126 37 E
Gani, Indonesia **37 E7** 0 48S 128 14 E
Ganj, India **43 F8** 27 45N 78 57 E
Gannett Peak, U.S.A. **82 E9** 43 11N 109 39W
Ganquan, China **34 F5** 36 20N 109 20 E
Gansu □, China **34 G3** 36 0N 104 0 E
Ganta, Liberia **50 G4** 7 15N 8 59W
Gantheaume, C., Australia **63 F2** 36 4S 137 32 E
Gantheaume B., Australia **61 E1** 27 40S 114 10 E
Gantsevichi = Hantsavichy, Belarus **17 B14** 52 49N 26 30 E
Ganyem = Genyem, Indonesia **37 E10** 2 46S 140 12 E
Ganyu, China **35 G10** 34 50N 119 8 E
Ganzhou, China **33 D6** 25 51N 114 56 E
Gao, Mali **50 E5** 16 15N 0 5W
Gaomi, China **35 F10** 36 20N 119 42 E
Gaoping, China **34 G7** 35 45N 112 55 E
Gaotang, China **34 F9** 36 50N 116 15 E
Gaoua, Burkina Faso **50 F5** 10 20N 3 8W
Gaoual, Guinea **50 F3** 11 45N 13 25W
Gaoxiong = Kaohsiung, Taiwan **33 D7** 22 35N 120 16 E
Gaoyang, China **34 E8** 38 40N 115 45 E
Gaoyou Hu, China **35 H10** 32 45N 119 20 E
Gaoyuan, China **35 F9** 37 8N 117 58 E
Gap, France **18 D7** 44 33N 6 5 E
Gapat →, India **43 G10** 24 30N 82 28 E
Gapuwiyak, Australia **62 A2** 12 25S 135 43 E
Gar, China **32 C2** 32 10N 79 58 E
Garabogazköl Aylagy, Turkmenistan **25 F9** 41 0N 53 30 E
Garachico, Canary Is. **22 F3** 28 22N 16 46W
Garachiné, Panama **88 E4** 8 0N 78 12W
Garafia, Canary Is. **22 F2** 28 48N 17 57W
Garah, Australia **63 D4** 29 5S 149 38 E
Garajonay, Canary Is. **22 F2** 28 7N 17 14W
Garanhuns, Brazil **93 E11** 8 50S 36 30W
Garautha, India **43 G8** 25 34N 79 18 E
Garba Tula, Kenya **54 B4** 0 30N 38 32 E
Garberville, U.S.A. **82 F2** 40 6N 123 48W
Garbiyang, India **43 D9** 30 8N 80 54 E
Garda, L. di, Italy **20 B4** 45 40N 10 41 E
Garde L., Canada **73 A7** 62 50N 106 13W
Garden City, Ga., U.S.A. **77 J5** 32 6N 81 9W
Garden City, Kans., U.S.A. **81 G4** 37 58N 100 53W
Garden City, Tex., U.S.A. **81 K4** 31 52N 101 29W
Garden Grove, U.S.A. **85 M9** 33 47N 117 55W
Gardēz, Afghan. **42 C3** 33 37N 69 9 E
Gardiner, Maine, U.S.A. **77 C11** 44 14N 69 47W
Gardiner, Mont., U.S.A. **82 D8** 45 2N 110 22W
Gardiners I., U.S.A. **79 E12** 41 6N 72 6W
Gardner, U.S.A. **79 D13** 42 34N 71 59W
Gardner Canal, Canada **72 C3** 53 27N 128 8W
Gardnerville, U.S.A. **84 G7** 38 56N 119 45W
Gardo, Somali Rep. **46 F4** 9 30N 49 6 E
Garey, U.S.A. **85 L6** 34 53N 120 19W
Garfield, U.S.A. **82 C5** 47 1N 117 9W
Garforth, U.K. **10 D6** 53 47N 1 24W
Gargano, Mte., Italy **20 D6** 41 43N 15 43 E
Garibaldi Prov. Park, Canada **72 D4** 49 50N 122 40W
Garies, S. Africa **56 E2** 30 32S 17 59 E
Garigliano →, Italy **20 D5** 41 13N 13 45 E
Garissa, Kenya **54 C4** 0 25S 39 40 E
Garland, Tex., U.S.A. **81 J6** 32 55N 96 38W
Garland, Utah, U.S.A. **82 F7** 41 47N 112 10W
Garm, Tajikistan **26 F8** 39 0N 70 20 E
Garmāb, Iran **45 C8** 35 25N 56 45 E
Garmisch-Partenkirchen, Germany **16 E6** 47 30N 11 6 E
Garmsār, Iran **45 C7** 35 20N 52 25 E
Garner, U.S.A. **80 D8** 43 6N 93 36W
Garnett, U.S.A. **80 F7** 38 17N 95 14W
Garo Hills, India **43 G14** 25 30N 90 30 E
Garoe, Somali Rep. **46 F4** 8 25N 48 33 E
Garonne →, France **18 D3** 45 2N 0 36W
Garot, India **42 G6** 24 19N 75 41 E
Garoua, Cameroon **51 G8** 9 19N 13 21 E
Garrauli, India **43 G8** 25 5N 79 22 E
Garrison, Mont., U.S.A. **82 C7** 46 31N 112 49W
Garrison, N. Dak., U.S.A. **80 B4** 47 40N 101 25W
Garrison Res. = Sakakawea, L., U.S.A. **80 B4** 47 30N 101 25W
Garron Pt., U.K. **13 A6** 55 3N 5 59W
Garry →, U.K. **12 E5** 56 44N 3 47W
Garry, L., Canada **68 B9** 65 58N 100 18W
Garsen, Kenya **54 C5** 2 20S 40 5 E
Garson L., Canada **73 B6** 56 19N 110 2W
Garu, India **43 H11** 23 40N 84 14 E
Garub, Namibia **56 D2** 26 37S 16 0 E
Garut, Indonesia **37 G12** 7 14S 107 53 E
Garvie Mts., N.Z. **59 L2** 45 30S 168 50 E
Garwa = Garoua, Cameroon **51 G8** 9 19N 13 21 E
Garwa, India **43 G10** 24 11N 83 47 E
Gary, U.S.A. **76 E2** 41 36N 87 20W
Garzê, China **32 C5** 31 38N 100 1 E
Garzón, Colombia **92 C3** 2 10N 75 40W
Gas-San, Japan **30 E10** 38 32N 140 1 E
Gasan Kuli = Esenguly, Turkmenistan **26 F6** 37 37N 53 59 E
Gascogne, France **18 E4** 43 45N 0 20 E
Gascogne, G. de, Europe **18 D2** 44 0N 2 0W
Gascony = Gascogne, France **18 E4** 43 45N 0 20 E
Gascoyne →, Australia **61 D1** 24 52S 113 37 E
Gascoyne Junction, Australia **61 E2** 25 2S 115 17 E
Gashaka, Nigeria **51 G8** 7 20N 11 29 E
Gasherbrum, Pakistan **43 B7** 35 40N 76 40 E
Gashua, Nigeria **51 F8** 12 54N 11 0 E
Gaspé, Canada **71 C7** 48 52N 64 30W
Gaspé, C. de, Canada **71 C7** 48 48N 64 7W
Gaspé, Pén. de, Canada **71 C6** 48 45N 65 40W
Gaspésie, Parc de Conservation de la, Canada **71 C6** 48 55N 65 50W
Gasteiz = Vitoria-Gasteiz, Spain **19 A4** 42 50N 2 41W
Gastonia, U.S.A. **77 H5** 35 16N 81 11W
Gastre, Argentina **96 E3** 42 20S 69 15W
Gata, C., Cyprus **23 E12** 34 34N 33 2 E
Gata, C. de, Spain **19 D4** 36 41N 2 13W
Gata, Sierra de, Spain **19 B2** 40 20N 6 45W
Gataga →, Canada **72 B3** 58 35N 126 59W
Gatehouse of Fleet, U.K. **12 G4** 54 53N 4 12W
Gates, U.S.A. **78 C7** 43 9N 77 42W
Gateshead, U.K. **10 C6** 54 57N 1 35W
Gatesville, U.S.A. **81 K6** 31 26N 97 45W
Gaths, Zimbabwe **55 G3** 20 2S 30 32 E
Gatico, Chile **94 A1** 22 29S 70 20W
Gatineau, Canada **79 A9** 45 29N 75 38W
Gatineau →, Canada **70 C4** 45 27N 75 42W
Gatineau, Parc Nat. de la, Canada **70 C4** 45 40N 76 0W
Gatton, Australia **63 D5** 27 32S 152 17 E

Gatun, L.

Gatun, L., Panama 88 E4 9 7N 79 56W
Gatyana, S. Africa 57 E4 32 16S 28 31 E
Gau, Fiji 59 D8 18 2S 179 18 E
Gauer L., Canada 73 B9 57 0N 97 50W
Gauhati, India 41 F17 26 10N 91 45 E
Gauja →, Latvia 9 H21 57 10N 24 16 E
Gaula →, Norway 8 E14 63 21N 10 14 E
Gauri Phanta, India 43 E9 28 41N 80 36 E
Gausta, Norway 9 G13 59 48N 8 40 E
Gauteng □, S. Africa 57 D4 26 0S 28 0 E
Gāv Koshī, Iran 45 D8 28 38N 57 12 E
Gāvakān, Iran 45 D7 29 37N 53 10 E
Gavāter, Iran 45 E9 25 10N 61 31 E
Gāvbandī, Iran 45 E7 27 12N 53 4 E
Gavdhopoúla, Greece 23 E6 34 56N 24 0 E
Gávdhos, Greece 23 E6 34 50N 24 5 E
Gaviota, U.S.A. 85 L6 34 29N 120 13W
Gāvkhūnī, Bāţlāq-e, Iran 45 C7 32 6N 52 52 E
Gävle, Sweden 9 F17 60 40N 17 9 E
Gawachab, Namibia 56 D2 27 4S 17 55 E
Gawilgarh Hills, India 40 J10 21 15N 76 45 E
Gawler, Australia 63 E2 34 30S 138 42 E
Gaxun Nur, China 32 B5 42 22N 100 30 E
Gay, Russia 24 D10 51 27N 58 27 E
Gaya, India 43 G11 24 47N 85 4 E
Gaya, Niger 50 F6 11 52N 3 28 E
Gaylord, U.S.A. 76 C3 45 2N 84 41W
Gayndah, Australia 63 D5 25 35S 151 32 E
Gaysin = Haysyn, Ukraine 17 D15 48 57N 29 25 E
Gayvoron = Hayvoron, Ukraine 17 D15 48 22N 29 52 E
Gaza, Gaza Strip 47 D3 31 30N 34 28 E
Gaza □, Mozam. 57 C5 23 10S 32 45 E
Gaza Strip □, Asia 47 D3 31 29N 34 25 E
Gazanjyk, Turkmenistan 45 B7 39 16N 55 32 E
Gāzbor, Iran 45 D8 28 5N 58 51 E
Gazi, Dem. Rep. of the Congo 54 B1 1 3N 24 30 E
Gaziantep, Turkey 25 G6 37 6N 37 23 E
Gcuwa, S. Africa 57 E4 32 20S 28 11 E
Gdańsk, Poland 17 A10 54 22N 18 40 E
Gdańska, Zatoka, Poland 17 A10 54 30N 19 20 E
Gdov, Russia 9 G22 58 48N 27 55 E
Gdynia, Poland 17 A10 54 35N 18 33 E
Gebe, Indonesia 37 D7 0 5N 129 25 E
Gebze, Turkey 21 D13 40 47N 29 25 E
Gedaref, Sudan 51 F13 14 2N 35 28 E
Gediz →, Turkey 21 E12 38 35N 26 48 E
Gedser, Denmark 9 J14 54 35N 11 55 E
Geegully Cr. →, Australia 60 C3 18 32S 123 41 E
Geel, Belgium 15 C4 51 10N 4 59 E
Geelong, Australia 63 F3 38 10S 144 22 E
Geelvink B. = Cenderwasih, Teluk, Indonesia 37 E9 3 0S 135 20 E
Geelvink Chan., Australia 61 E1 28 30S 114 0 E
Geesthacht, Germany 16 B6 53 26N 10 22 E
Geidam, Nigeria 51 F8 12 57N 11 57 E
Geikie →, Canada 73 B8 57 45N 103 52W
Geistown, U.S.A. 78 F6 40 18N 78 52W
Geita, Tanzania 54 C3 2 48S 32 12 E
Gejiu, China 32 D5 23 20N 103 10 E
Gel, Meydān-e, Iran 45 D7 29 4N 54 50 E
Gela, Italy 20 F6 37 4N 14 15 E
Gelderland □, Neths. 15 B6 52 5N 6 10 E
Geldrop, Neths. 15 C5 51 25N 5 32 E
Geleen, Neths. 15 D5 50 57N 5 49 E
Gelibolu, Turkey 21 D12 40 28N 26 43 E
Gelsenkirchen, Germany 16 C4 51 32N 7 6 E
Gemas, Malaysia 39 L4 2 37N 102 36 E
Gembloux, Belgium 15 D4 50 34N 4 43 E
Gemena, Dem. Rep. of the Congo 52 D3 3 13N 19 48 E
Gemerek, Turkey 44 B3 39 15N 36 10 E
Gemlik, Turkey 21 D13 40 26N 29 9 E
Genale, Ethiopia 46 F2 6 0N 39 30 E
General Acha, Argentina 94 D3 37 20S 64 38W
General Alvear, Buenos Aires, Argentina 94 D4 36 0S 60 0W
General Alvear, Mendoza, Argentina 94 D2 35 0S 67 40W
General Artigas, Paraguay 94 B4 26 52S 56 16W
General Belgrano, Argentina 94 D4 36 35S 58 47W
General Cabrera, Argentina 94 C3 32 53S 63 52W
General Cepeda, Mexico 86 B4 25 23N 101 27W
General Guido, Argentina 94 D4 36 40S 57 50W
General Juan Madariaga, Argentina 94 D4 37 0S 57 0W
General La Madrid, Argentina 94 D3 37 17S 61 20W
General MacArthur, Phil. 37 B7 11 18N 125 28 E
General Martin Miguel de Güemes, Argentina 94 A3 24 50S 65 0W
General Paz, Argentina 94 B4 27 45S 57 36W
General Pico, Argentina 94 D3 35 45S 63 50W
General Pinedo, Argentina 94 B3 27 15S 61 20W
General Pinto, Argentina 94 C3 34 45S 61 50W
General Roca, Argentina 96 D3 39 2S 67 35W
General Santos, Phil. 37 C7 6 5N 125 14 E
General Trevino, Mexico 87 B5 26 14N 99 29W
General Trías, Mexico 86 B3 28 21N 106 22W
General Viamonte, Argentina 94 D3 35 1S 61 3W
General Villegas, Argentina 94 D3 35 5S 63 0W
Genesee, Idaho, U.S.A. 82 C5 46 33N 116 56W
Genesee, Pa., U.S.A. 78 E7 41 59N 77 54W
Genesee →, U.S.A. 78 C7 43 16N 77 36W
Geneseo, Ill., U.S.A. 80 E9 41 27N 90 9W
Geneseo, N.Y., U.S.A. 78 D7 42 48N 77 49W
Geneva = Genève, Switz. 18 C7 46 12N 6 9 E
Geneva, Ala., U.S.A. 77 K3 31 2N 85 52W
Geneva, N.Y., U.S.A. 78 D8 42 52N 76 59W
Geneva, Nebr., U.S.A. 80 E6 40 32N 97 36W
Geneva, Ohio, U.S.A. 78 E4 41 48N 80 57W
Geneva, L. = Léman, L., Europe 18 C7 46 26N 6 30 E
Geneva, L., U.S.A. 76 D1 42 38N 88 30W
Genève, Switz. 18 C7 46 12N 6 9 E
Genil →, Spain 19 D3 37 42N 5 19W
Genk, Belgium 15 D5 50 58N 5 32 E
Gennargentu, Mti. del, Italy 20 D3 40 1N 9 19 E
Genoa = Génova, Italy 18 D8 44 25N 8 57 E
Genoa, Australia 63 F4 37 29S 149 35 E
Genoa, N.Y., U.S.A. 79 D8 42 40N 76 32W
Genoa, Nebr., U.S.A. 80 E6 41 27N 97 44W
Genoa, Nev., U.S.A. 84 F7 39 2N 119 50W
Génova, Italy 18 D8 44 25N 8 57 E
Génova, G. di, Italy 20 C3 44 0N 9 0 E
Genriyetty, Ostrov, Russia 27 B16 77 6N 156 30 E
Gent, Belgium 15 C3 51 2N 3 42 E
Genteng, Indonesia 37 G12 7 22S 106 24 E
Genyem, Indonesia 37 E10 2 46S 140 12 E
Geographe B., Australia 61 F2 33 30S 115 15 E
Geographe Chan., Australia 61 D1 24 30S 113 0 E
Georga, Zemlya, Russia 26 A5 80 30N 49 0 E
George, S. Africa 56 E3 33 58S 22 29 E
George →, Canada 71 A6 58 49N 66 10W
George, L., N.S.W., Australia 63 F4 35 10S 149 25 E
George, L., S. Austral., Australia 63 F3 37 25S 140 0 E
George, L., W. Austral., Australia 60 D3 22 45S 123 40 E
George, L., Uganda 54 B3 0 5N 30 10 E
George, L., Fla., U.S.A. 77 L5 29 17N 81 36W
George, L., N.Y., U.S.A. 79 C11 43 37N 73 33W
George Gill Ra., Australia 60 D5 24 22S 131 45 E
George River = Kangiqsualujjuaq, Canada 69 C13 58 30N 65 59W
George Sound, N.Z. 59 L1 44 52S 167 25 E
George Town, Australia 62 G4 41 6S 146 49 E
George Town, Bahamas 88 B4 23 33N 75 47W
George Town, Malaysia 39 K3 5 25N 100 15 E
George V Land, Antarctica 5 C10 69 0S 148 0 E
George VI Sound, Antarctica 5 D17 71 0S 68 0W
George West, U.S.A. 81 L5 28 20N 98 7W
Georgetown, Australia 62 B3 18 17S 143 33 E
Georgetown, Ont., Canada 78 C5 43 40N 79 56W
Georgetown, P.E.I., Canada 71 C7 46 13N 62 24W
Georgetown, Cayman Is. 88 C3 19 20N 81 24W
Georgetown, Gambia 50 F3 13 30N 14 47W
Georgetown, Guyana 92 B7 6 50N 58 12W
Georgetown, Calif., U.S.A. 84 G6 38 54N 120 50W
Georgetown, Colo., U.S.A. 82 G11 39 42N 105 42W
Georgetown, Ky., U.S.A. 76 F3 38 13N 84 33W
Georgetown, N.Y., U.S.A. 79 D9 42 46N 75 44W
Georgetown, Ohio, U.S.A. 76 F4 38 52N 83 54W
Georgetown, S.C., U.S.A. 77 J6 33 23N 79 17W
Georgetown, Tex., U.S.A. 81 K6 30 38N 97 41W
Georgia □, U.S.A. 77 K5 32 50N 83 15W
Georgia ■, Asia 25 F7 42 0N 43 0 E
Georgia, Str. of, Canada 72 D4 49 25N 124 0W
Georgian B., Canada 78 A4 45 15N 81 0W
Georgina →, Australia 62 C2 23 30S 139 47 E
Georgina I., Canada 78 B5 44 22N 79 17W
Georgiu-Dezh = Liski, Russia 25 D6 51 3N 39 30 E
Georgiyevsk, Russia 25 F7 44 12N 43 28 E
Gera, Germany 16 C7 50 53N 12 4 E
Geraardsbergen, Belgium 15 D3 50 45N 3 53 E
Geral, Serra, Brazil 95 B6 26 25S 50 0W
Geral de Goiás, Serra, Brazil 93 F9 12 0S 46 0W
Geraldine, U.S.A. 82 C8 47 36N 110 16W
Geraldton, Australia 61 E1 28 48S 114 32 E
Geraldton, Canada 70 C2 49 44N 86 59W
Gereshk, Afghan. 40 D4 31 47N 64 35 E
Gerik, Malaysia 39 K3 5 50N 101 15 E
Gering, U.S.A. 80 E3 41 50N 103 40W
Gerlach, U.S.A. 82 F4 40 39N 119 21W
Germansen Landing, Canada 72 B4 55 43N 124 40W
Germantown, U.S.A. 81 M10 35 5N 89 49W
Germany ■, Europe 16 C6 51 0N 10 0 E
Germī, Iran 45 B6 39 1N 48 3 E
Germiston, S. Africa 57 D4 26 15S 28 10 E
Gernika-Lumo, Spain 19 A4 43 19N 2 40W
Gero, Japan 31 G8 35 48N 137 14 E
Gerona = Girona, Spain 19 B7 41 58N 2 46 E
Gerrard, Canada 72 C5 50 30N 117 17W
Geser, Indonesia 37 E8 3 50S 130 54 E
Getafe, Spain 19 B4 40 18N 3 44W
Gettysburg, Pa., U.S.A. 76 F7 39 50N 77 14W
Gettysburg, S. Dak., U.S.A. 80 C5 45 1N 99 57W
Getxo, Spain 19 A4 43 21N 2 59W
Getz Ice Shelf, Antarctica 5 D14 75 0S 130 0W
Geyser, U.S.A. 82 C8 47 16N 110 30W
Geyserville, U.S.A. 84 G4 38 42N 122 54W
Ghaggar →, India 42 E6 29 30N 74 53 E
Ghaghara →, India 43 G11 25 45N 84 40 E
Ghaghat →, Bangla. 43 G13 25 19N 89 38 E
Ghagra, India 43 H11 23 17N 84 33 E
Ghagra →, India 43 F9 27 29N 81 9 E
Ghana ■, W. Afr. 50 G5 8 0N 1 0W
Ghansor, India 43 H9 22 39N 80 1 E
Ghanzi, Botswana 56 C3 21 50S 21 34 E
Ghanzi □, Botswana 56 C3 21 50S 21 45 E
Ghardaïa, Algeria 50 B6 32 20N 3 37 E
Gharyān, Libya 51 B8 32 10N 13 0 E
Ghāt, Libya 51 D8 24 59N 10 11 E
Ghatal, India 43 H12 22 40N 87 46 E
Ghatampur, India 43 F9 26 8N 80 13 E
Ghatsila, India 43 H12 22 36N 86 29 E
Ghaţţī, Si. Arabia 44 D3 31 16N 37 31 E
Ghawdex = Gozo, Malta 23 C1 36 3N 14 13 E
Ghazal, Bahr el →, Chad 51 F9 13 0N 15 47 E
Ghazâl, Bahr el →, Sudan 51 G12 9 31N 30 25 E
Ghaziabad, India 42 E7 28 42N 77 26 E
Ghazipur, India 43 G10 25 38N 83 35 E
Ghaznī, Afghan. 42 C3 33 30N 68 28 E
Ghaznī □, Afghan. 40 C6 32 10N 68 20 E
Ghent = Gent, Belgium 15 C3 51 2N 3 42 E
Ghīnah, Wādī al, Si. Arabia 44 D3 30 27N 38 14 E
Ghizao, Afghan. 42 C1 33 20N 65 44 E
Ghizar →, Pakistan 43 A5 36 15N 73 43 E
Ghotaru, India 42 F4 27 20N 70 1 E
Ghotki, Pakistan 42 E3 28 5N 69 21 E
Ghowr □, Afghan. 40 C4 34 0N 64 20 E
Ghudaf, W. al →, Iraq 44 C4 32 56N 43 30 E
Ghudāmis, Libya 51 B7 30 11N 9 29 E
Ghughri, India 43 H9 22 39N 80 41 E
Ghugus, India 40 K11 19 58N 79 12 E
Ghulam Mohammad Barrage, Pakistan 42 G3 25 30N 68 20 E
Ghūrīān, Afghan. 40 B2 34 17N 61 25 E
Gia Dinh, Vietnam 39 G6 10 49N 106 42 E
Gia Lai = Plei Ku, Vietnam 38 F7 13 57N 108 0 E
Gia Nghia, Vietnam 39 G6 11 58N 107 42 E
Gia Ngoc, Vietnam 38 E7 14 50N 108 58 E
Gia Vuc, Vietnam 38 E7 14 42N 108 34 E
Giant Forest, U.S.A. 84 J8 36 36N 118 43W
Giants Causeway, U.K. 13 A5 55 16N 6 29W
Giarabub = Al Jaghbūb, Libya 51 C10 29 42N 24 38 E
Giarre, Italy 20 F6 37 43N 15 11 E
Gibara, Cuba 88 B4 21 9N 76 11W
Gibb River, Australia 60 C4 16 26S 126 26 E
Gibbon, U.S.A. 80 E5 40 45N 98 51W
Gibeon, Namibia 53 K3 25 7S 17 40 E
Gibraltar ■, Europe 19 D3 36 7N 5 22W
Gibraltar, Str. of, Medit. S. 19 E3 35 55N 5 40W
Gibson Desert, Australia 60 D4 24 0S 126 0 E
Gibsons, Canada 72 D4 49 24N 123 32W
Gibsonville, U.S.A. 84 F6 39 46N 120 54W
Giddings, U.S.A. 81 K6 30 11N 96 56W
Giessen, Germany 16 C5 50 34N 8 41 E
Gīfān, Iran 45 B8 37 54N 57 28 E
Gift Lake, Canada 72 B5 55 53N 115 49W
Gifu, Japan 31 G8 35 30N 136 45 E
Gifu □, Japan 31 G8 35 40N 137 0 E
Giganta, Sa. de la, Mexico 86 B2 25 30N 111 30W
Gigha, U.K. 12 F3 55 42N 5 44W
Giglio, Italy 20 C4 42 20N 10 52 E
Gijón, Spain 19 A3 43 32N 5 42W
Gil I., Canada 72 C3 53 12N 129 15W
Gila →, U.S.A. 83 K6 32 43N 114 33W
Gila Bend, U.S.A. 83 K7 32 57N 112 43W
Gila Bend Mts., U.S.A. 83 K7 33 10N 113 0W
Gīlān □, Iran 45 B6 37 0N 50 0 E
Gilbert →, Australia 62 B3 16 35S 141 15 E
Gilbert Is., Kiribati 64 G9 1 0N 172 0 E
Gilbert River, Australia 62 B3 18 9S 142 52 E
Gilead, U.S.A. 79 B14 44 24N 70 59W
Gilford I., Canada 72 C3 50 40N 126 30W
Gilgandra, Australia 63 E4 31 43S 148 39 E
Gilgil, Kenya 54 C4 0 30S 36 20 E
Gilgit, India 43 B6 35 50N 74 15 E
Gilgit →, Pakistan 43 B6 35 44N 74 37 E
Gilgunnia, Australia 63 E4 32 26S 146 2 E
Gillam, Canada 73 B10 56 20N 94 40W
Gillen, L., Australia 61 E3 26 11S 124 38 E
Gilles, L., Australia 63 E2 32 50S 136 45 E
Gillette, U.S.A. 80 C2 44 18N 105 30W
Gilliat, Australia 62 C3 20 40S 141 28 E
Gillingham, U.K. 11 F8 51 23N 0 33 E
Gilmer, U.S.A. 81 J7 32 44N 94 57W
Gilmore, L., Australia 61 F3 32 29S 121 37 E
Gilroy, U.S.A. 84 H5 37 1N 121 34W
Gimli, Canada 73 C9 50 40N 97 0W
Gin Gin, Australia 63 D5 25 0S 151 58 E
Gingin, Australia 61 F2 31 22S 115 54 E
Ginir, Ethiopia 46 F3 7 6N 40 40 E
Gióna, Óros, Greece 21 E10 38 38N 22 14 E
Gippsland, Australia 63 F4 37 52S 147 0 E
Gir Hills, India 42 J4 21 0N 71 0 E
Girab, India 42 F4 26 2N 70 38 E
Girâfi, W. →, Egypt 47 F3 29 58N 34 39 E
Girard, Kans., U.S.A. 81 G7 37 31N 94 51W
Girard, Ohio, U.S.A. 78 E4 41 9N 80 42W
Girard, Pa., U.S.A. 78 D4 42 0N 80 19W
Girard, Pa., U.S.A. 78 E4 42 0N 80 19W
Girdle Ness, U.K. 12 D6 57 9N 2 3W
Giresun, Turkey 25 F6 40 55N 38 30 E
Girga, Egypt 51 C12 26 17N 31 55 E
Giri →, India 42 D7 30 28N 77 41 E
Giridih, India 43 G12 24 10N 86 21 E
Girne = Kyrenia, Cyprus 23 D12 35 20N 33 20 E
Girona, Spain 19 B7 41 58N 2 46 E
Gironde →, France 18 D3 45 32N 1 7W
Giru, Australia 62 B4 19 30S 147 5 E
Girvan, U.K. 12 F4 55 14N 4 51W
Gisborne, N.Z. 59 H7 38 39S 178 5 E
Gisenyi, Rwanda 54 C2 1 41S 29 15 E
Gislaved, Sweden 9 H15 57 19N 13 32 E
Gitega, Burundi 54 C2 3 26S 29 56 E
Giuba →, Somali Rep. 46 G3 1 30N 42 35 E
Giurgiu, Romania 17 G13 43 52N 25 57 E
Giza = El Gîza, Egypt 51 C12 30 0N 31 10 E
Gizhiga, Russia 27 C17 62 3N 160 30 E
Gizhiginskaya Guba, Russia 27 C16 61 0N 158 0 E
Giżycko, Poland 17 A11 54 2N 21 48 E
Gjirokastra, Albania 21 D9 40 7N 20 10 E
Gjoa Haven, Canada 68 B10 68 20N 96 8W
Gjøvik, Norway 9 F14 60 47N 10 43 E
Glace Bay, Canada 71 C8 46 11N 59 58W
Glacier Bay National Park and Preserve, U.S.A. 72 B1 58 45N 136 30W
Glacier National Park, Canada 72 C5 51 15N 117 30W
Glacier National Park, U.S.A. 82 B7 48 30N 113 18W
Glacier Peak, U.S.A. 82 B3 48 7N 121 7W
Gladewater, U.S.A. 81 J7 32 33N 94 56W
Gladstone, Queens., Australia 62 C5 23 52S 151 16 E
Gladstone, S. Austral., Australia 63 E2 33 15S 138 22 E
Gladstone, Canada 73 C9 50 13N 98 57W
Gladstone, U.S.A. 76 C2 45 51N 87 1W
Gladwin, U.S.A. 76 D3 43 59N 84 29W
Glåma = Glomma →, Norway 9 G14 59 12N 10 57 E
Gláma, Iceland 8 D2 65 48N 23 0W
Glamis, U.S.A. 85 N11 32 55N 115 5W
Glasco, Kans., U.S.A. 80 F6 39 22N 97 50W
Glasco, N.Y., U.S.A. 79 D11 42 3N 73 57W
Glasgow, U.K. 12 F4 55 51N 4 15W
Glasgow, Ky., U.S.A. 76 G3 37 0N 85 55W
Glasgow, Mont., U.S.A. 82 B10 48 12N 106 38W
Glaslyn, Canada 73 C7 53 22N 108 21W
Glastonbury, U.K. 11 F5 51 9N 2 43W
Glastonbury, U.S.A. 79 E12 41 43N 72 37W
Glazov, Russia 24 C9 58 9N 52 40 E
Gleichen, Canada 72 C6 50 52N 113 3W
Gleiwitz = Gliwice, Poland 17 C10 50 22N 18 41 E
Glen, U.S.A. 79 B13 44 7N 71 11W
Glen Affric, U.K. 12 D3 57 17N 5 1W
Glen Canyon, U.S.A. 83 H8 37 30N 110 40W
Glen Canyon Dam, U.S.A. 83 H8 36 57N 111 29W
Glen Canyon National Recreation Area, U.S.A. 83 H8 37 15N 111 0W
Glen Coe, U.K. 12 E3 56 40N 5 0W
Glen Cove, U.S.A. 79 F11 40 52N 73 38W
Glen Garry, U.K. 12 D3 57 3N 5 7W
Glen Innes, Australia 63 D5 29 44S 151 44 E
Glen Lyon, U.S.A. 79 E8 41 10N 76 5W
Glen Mor, U.K. 12 D4 57 9N 4 37W
Glen Moriston, U.K. 12 D4 57 11N 4 52W
Glen Robertson, Canada 79 A10 45 22N 74 30W
Glen Spean, U.K. 12 E4 56 53N 4 40W
Glen Ullin, U.S.A. 80 B4 46 49N 101 50W
Glencoe, Canada 78 D3 42 45N 81 43W
Glencoe, S. Africa 57 D5 28 11S 30 11 E
Glencoe, U.S.A. 80 C7 44 46N 94 9W
Glendale, Ariz., U.S.A. 83 K7 33 32N 112 11W
Glendale, Calif., U.S.A. 85 L8 34 9N 118 15W
Glendale, Zimbabwe 55 F3 17 22S 31 5
Glendive, U.S.A. 80 B2 47 7N 104 43W
Glendo, U.S.A. 80 D2 42 30N 105 2W
Glenelg →, Australia 63 F3 38 4S 140 59
Glenfield, U.S.A. 79 C9 43 43N 75 24W
Glengarriff, Ireland 13 E2 51 45N 9 34W
Glenmont, U.S.A. 78 F2 40 31N 82 6W
Glenmorgan, Australia 63 D4 27 14S 149 42
Glenn, U.S.A. 84 F4 39 31N 122 1W
Glennallen, U.S.A. 68 B5 62 0N 145 50W
Glennamaddy, Ireland 13 C3 53 37N 8 33W
Glenns Ferry, U.S.A. 82 E6 42 57N 115 18W
Glenore, Australia 62 B3 17 50S 141 12
Glenreagh, Australia 63 E5 30 2S 153 1
Glenrock, U.S.A. 82 E11 42 52N 105 52W
Glenrothes, U.K. 12 E5 56 12N 3 10W
Glens Falls, U.S.A. 79 C11 43 19N 73 39W
Glenside, U.S.A. 79 F9 40 6N 75 9W
Glenties, Ireland 13 B3 54 49N 8 16W
Glenville, U.S.A. 76 F5 38 56N 80 50W
Glenwood, Canada 71 C9 49 0N 54 58W
Glenwood, Ark., U.S.A. 81 H8 34 20N 93 33W
Glenwood, Hawaii, U.S.A. 74 J17 19 29N 155 9W
Glenwood, Iowa, U.S.A. 80 E7 41 3N 95 45W
Glenwood, Minn., U.S.A. 80 C7 45 39N 95 23W
Glenwood, Wash., U.S.A. 84 D5 46 1N 121 17W
Glenwood Springs, U.S.A. 82 G10 39 33N 107 19W
Glettinganes, Iceland 8 D7 65 30N 13 37W
Gliwice, Poland 17 C10 50 22N 18 41
Globe, U.S.A. 83 K8 33 24N 110 47W
Głogów, Poland 16 C9 51 37N 16 5
Glomma →, Norway 9 G14 59 12N 10 57
Glorieuses, Is., Ind. Oc. 57 A8 11 30S 47 20
Glossop, U.K. 10 D6 53 27N 1 56W
Gloucester, Australia 63 E5 32 0S 151 59
Gloucester, U.K. 11 F5 51 53N 2 15W
Gloucester, U.S.A. 79 D14 42 37N 70 40W
Gloucester I., Australia 62 C4 20 0S 148 30
Gloucester Point, U.S.A. 76 G7 37 15N 76 29W
Gloucestershire □, U.K. 11 F5 51 46N 2 15W
Gloversville, U.S.A. 79 C10 43 3N 74 21W
Glovertown, Canada 71 C9 48 40N 54 3W
Glusk, Belarus 17 B15 52 53N 28 41
Gmünd, Austria 16 D8 48 45N 15 0
Gmunden, Austria 16 E7 47 55N 13 48
Gniezno, Poland 17 B9 52 30N 17 35
Gnowangerup, Australia 61 F2 33 58S 117 59
Go Cong, Vietnam 39 G6 10 22N 106 40
Gō-no-ura, Japan 31 H4 33 44N 129 40
Goa, India 40 M8 15 33N 73 59
Goa □, India 40 M8 15 33N 73 59
Goalen Hd., Australia 63 F5 36 33S 150 4
Goalpara, India 41 F17 26 10N 90 40
Goaltor, India 43 H12 22 43N 87 10
Goalundo Ghat, Bangla. 43 H13 23 50N 89 47
Goat Fell, U.K. 12 F3 55 38N 5 11W
Goba, Ethiopia 46 F2 7 1N 39 59
Goba, Mozam. 57 D5 26 15S 32 13
Gobabis, Namibia 56 C2 22 30S 19 0
Gobi, Asia 34 C6 44 0N 110 0
Gobō, Japan 31 H7 33 53N 135 10
Gochas, Namibia 56 C2 24 59S 18 55
Godavari →, India 41 L13 16 25N 82 18
Godavari Pt., India 41 L13 17 0N 82 20
Godbout, Canada 71 C6 49 20N 67 38W
Godda, India 43 G12 24 50N 87 13
Goderich, Canada 78 C3 43 45N 81 41W
Godfrey Ra., Australia 61 D2 24 0S 117 0
Godhavn, Greenland 4 C5 69 15N 53 38W
Godhra, India 42 H5 22 49N 73 40
Godoy Cruz, Argentina 94 C2 32 56S 68 52W
Gods →, Canada 70 A1 56 22N 92 51W
Gods L., Canada 70 B1 54 40N 94 15W
Gods River, Canada 73 C10 54 50N 94 5W
Godthåb = Nuuk, Greenland 69 B14 64 10N 51 35W
Godwin Austen = K2, Pakistan 43 B7 35 58N 76 32
Goeie Hoop, Kaap die = Good Hope, C. of, S. Africa 56 E2 34 24S 18 30
Goéland, L. au, Canada 70 C4 49 50N 76 48W
Goeree, Neths. 15 C3 51 50N 4 0
Goes, Neths. 15 C3 51 30N 3 55
Goffstown, U.S.A. 79 C13 43 1N 71 36W
Gogama, Canada 70 C3 47 35N 81 43W
Gogebic, L., U.S.A. 80 B10 46 30N 89 35W
Gogra = Ghaghara →, India 43 G11 25 45N 84 40
Gogriâl, Sudan 51 G11 8 30N 28 8
Gohana, India 42 E7 29 8N 76 42
Goharganj, India 42 H7 23 1N 77 41
Goi →, India 42 H6 22 4N 74 46
Goiânia, Brazil 93 G9 16 43S 49 20W
Goiás, Brazil 93 G8 15 55S 50 10W
Goiás □, Brazil 93 F9 12 10S 48 0W
Goio-Ere, Brazil 95 A5 24 12S 53 1W
Gojō, Japan 31 G7 34 21N 135 42
Gojra, Pakistan 42 D5 31 10N 72 40
Gökçeada, Turkey 21 D11 40 10N 25 50
Gökova Körfezi, Turkey 21 F12 36 55N 27 50
Gokteik, Burma 41 H20 22 26N 97 0
Gokurt, Pakistan 42 E2 29 40N 67 26
Gol Gol, Australia 63 E3 34 12S 142 14
Gola, India 43 E9 28 3N 80 32
Golakganj, India 43 F13 26 8N 89 52
Golan Heights = Hagolan, Syria 47 C4 33 0N 35 45
Golāshkerd, Iran 45 E8 27 59N 57 16
Golchikha, Russia 4 B12 71 45N 83 30
Golconda, U.S.A. 82 F5 40 58N 117 30W
Gold, U.S.A. 78 E7 41 52N 77 50W
Gold Beach, U.S.A. 82 E1 42 25N 124 25W
Gold Coast, W. Afr. 50 H5 4 0N 1 40W
Gold Hill, U.S.A. 82 E2 42 26N 123 3W
Gold River, Canada 72 D3 49 46N 126 3W
Golden, Canada 72 C5 51 20N 116 59W
Golden B., N.Z. 59 J4 40 40S 172 50
Golden Gate, U.S.A. 82 H2 37 54N 122 30W
Golden Hinde, Canada 72 D3 49 40N 125 44W
Golden Lake, Canada 78 A7 45 34N 77 21W
Golden Vale, Ireland 13 D3 52 33N 8 17W
Goldendale, U.S.A. 82 D3 45 49N 120 50W
Goldfield, U.S.A. 83 H5 37 42N 117 14W
Goldsand L., Canada 73 B8 57 2N 101 8W
Goldsboro, U.S.A. 77 H7 35 23N 77 59W
Goldsmith, U.S.A. 81 K3 31 59N 102 37W

Grenen

Grenen, *Denmark* **9 H14** 57 44N 10 40 E
Grenfell, *Australia* **63 E4** 33 52S 148 8 E
Grenfell, *Canada* **73 C8** 50 30N 102 56W
Grenoble, *France* **18 D6** 45 12N 5 42 E
Grenville, C., *Australia* **62 A3** 12 0S 143 13 E
Grenville Chan., *Canada* **72 C3** 53 40N 129 46W
Gresham, *U.S.A.* **84 E4** 45 30N 122 26W
Gresik, *Indonesia* **37 G15** 7 13S 112 38 E
Gretna, *U.K.* **12 F5** 55 0N 3 3W
Grevenmacher, *Lux.* **15 E6** 49 41N 6 26 E
Grey →, *Canada* **71 C8** 47 34N 57 6W
Grey →, *N.Z.* **59 K3** 42 27S 171 12 E
Grey, C., *Australia* **62 A2** 13 0S 136 35 E
Grey Ra., *Australia* **63 D3** 27 0S 143 30 E
Greybull, *U.S.A.* **82 D9** 44 30N 108 3W
Greymouth, *N.Z.* **59 K3** 42 29S 171 13 E
Greystones, *Ireland* **13 C5** 53 9N 6 5W
Greytown, *N.Z.* **59 J5** 41 5S 175 29 E
Greytown, *S. Africa* **57 D5** 29 1S 30 36 E
Gribbell I., *Canada* **72 C3** 53 23N 129 0W
Gridley, *U.S.A.* **84 F5** 39 22N 121 42W
Griekwastad, *S. Africa* **56 D3** 28 49S 23 15 E
Griffin, *U.S.A.* **77 J3** 33 15N 84 16W
Griffith, *Australia* **63 E4** 34 18S 146 2 E
Griffith, *Canada* **78 A7** 45 15N 77 10W
Griffith I., *Canada* **78 B4** 44 50N 80 55W
Grimaylov = Hrymayliv, *Ukraine* **17 D14** 49 20N 26 5 E
Grimes, *U.S.A.* **84 F5** 39 4N 121 54W
Grimsay, *U.K.* **12 D1** 57 29N 7 14W
Grimsby, *Canada* **78 C5** 43 12N 79 34W
Grimsby, *U.K.* **10 D7** 53 34N 0 5W
Grímsey, *Iceland* **8 C5** 66 33N 17 58W
Grimshaw, *Canada* **72 B5** 56 10N 117 40W
Grimstad, *Norway* **9 G13** 58 20N 8 35 E
Grindstone I., *Canada* **79 B8** 44 43N 76 14W
Grinnell, *U.S.A.* **80 E8** 41 45N 92 43W
Gris-Nez, C., *France* **18 A4** 50 52N 1 35 E
Groais I., *Canada* **71 B8** 50 55N 55 35W
Groblersdal, *S. Africa* **57 D4** 25 15S 29 25 E
Grodno = Hrodna, *Belarus* **17 B12** 53 42N 23 52 E
Grodzyanka = Hrodzyanka, *Belarus* **17 B15** 53 31N 28 42 E
Groesbeck, *U.S.A.* **81 K6** 30 48N 96 31W
Grójec, *Poland* **17 C11** 51 50N 20 58 E
Grong, *Norway* **8 D15** 64 25N 12 8 E
Groningen, *Neths.* **15 A6** 53 15N 6 35 E
Groningen □, *Neths.* **15 A6** 53 16N 6 40 E
Groom, *U.S.A.* **81 H4** 35 12N 101 6W
Groot →, *S. Africa* **56 E3** 33 45S 24 36 E
Groot Berg →, *S. Africa* **56 E2** 32 47S 18 8 E
Groot-Brakrivier, *S. Africa* **56 E3** 34 2S 22 18 E
Groot-Kei →, *S. Africa* **57 E4** 32 41S 28 22 E
Groot Vis →, *S. Africa* **56 E4** 33 28S 27 5 E
Groote Eylandt, *Australia* **62 A2** 14 0S 136 40 E
Grootfontein, *Namibia* **56 B2** 19 31S 18 6 E
Grootlaagte →, *Africa* **56 C3** 20 55S 21 27 E
Grootvloer, *S. Africa* **56 E3** 30 0S 20 40 E
Gros C., *Canada* **72 A6** 61 59N 113 32W
Gros Morne Nat. Park, *Canada* **71 C8** 49 40N 57 50W
Grossa, Pta., *Spain* **22 B8** 39 6N 1 36 E
Grosser Arber, *Germany* **16 D7** 49 6N 13 8 E
Grosseto, *Italy* **20 C4** 42 46N 11 8 E
Grossglockner, *Austria* **16 E7** 47 5N 12 40 E
Groswater B., *Canada* **71 B8** 54 20N 57 40W
Groton, *Conn., U.S.A.* **79 E12** 41 21N 72 5W
Groton, *N.Y., U.S.A.* **79 D8** 42 36N 76 22W
Groton, *S. Dak., U.S.A.* **80 C5** 45 27N 98 6W
Grouard Mission, *Canada* **72 B5** 55 33N 116 9W
Groundhog →, *Canada* **70 C3** 48 45N 82 58W
Grouw, *Neths.* **15 A5** 53 5N 5 51 E
Grove City, *U.S.A.* **78 E4** 41 10N 80 5W
Grove Hill, *U.S.A.* **77 K2** 31 42N 87 47W
Groveland, *U.S.A.* **84 H6** 37 50N 120 14W
Grover City, *U.S.A.* **85 K6** 35 7N 120 37W
Groves, *U.S.A.* **81 L8** 29 57N 93 54W
Groveton, *U.S.A.* **79 B13** 44 36N 71 31W
Groznyy, *Russia* **25 F8** 43 20N 45 45 E
Grudziądz, *Poland* **17 B10** 53 30N 18 47 E
Gruinard B., *U.K.* **12 D3** 57 56N 5 35W
Grundy Center, *U.S.A.* **80 D8** 42 22N 92 47W
Gruver, *U.S.A.* **81 G4** 36 16N 101 24W
Gryazi, *Russia* **24 D6** 52 30N 39 58 E
Gryazovets, *Russia* **24 C7** 58 50N 40 10 E
Gua, *India* **41 H14** 22 18N 85 20 E
Gua Musang, *Malaysia* **39 K3** 4 53N 101 58 E
Guacanayabo, G. de, *Cuba* **88 B4** 20 40N 77 20W
Guachípas →, *Argentina* **94 B2** 25 40S 65 30W
Guadalajara, *Mexico* **86 C4** 20 40N 103 20W
Guadalajara, *Spain* **19 B4** 40 37N 3 12W
Guadalcanal, *Solomon Is.* **64 H8** 9 32S 160 12 E
Guadales, *Argentina* **94 C2** 34 30S 67 55W
Guadalete →, *Spain* **19 D2** 36 35N 6 13W
Guadalquivir →, *Spain* **19 D2** 36 47N 6 22W
Guadalupe = Guadeloupe ■, *W. Indies* **89 C7** 16 20N 61 40W
Guadalupe, *Mexico* **85 N10** 32 4N 116 32W
Guadalupe, *U.S.A.* **85 L6** 34 59N 120 33W
Guadalupe →, *Mexico* **85 N10** 32 6N 116 51W
Guadalupe →, *U.S.A.* **81 L6** 28 27N 96 47W
Guadalupe, Sierra de, *Spain* **19 C3** 39 28N 5 30W
Guadalupe Bravos, *Mexico* **86 A3** 31 20N 106 10W
Guadalupe I., *Pac. Oc.* **66 G8** 29 0N 118 50W
Guadalupe Mts. Nat. Park, *U.S.A.* **81 K2** 32 0N 104 30W
Guadalupe Peak, *U.S.A.* **81 K2** 31 50N 104 52W
Guadalupe y Calvo, *Mexico* **86 B3** 26 6N 106 58W
Guadarrama, Sierra de, *Spain* **19 B4** 41 0N 4 0W
Guadeloupe ■, *W. Indies* **89 C7** 16 20N 61 40W
Guadeloupe Passage, *W. Indies* **89 C7** 16 50N 62 15W
Guadiana →, *Portugal* **19 D2** 37 14N 7 22W
Guadix, *Spain* **19 D4** 37 18N 3 11W
Guafo, Boca del, *Chile* **96 E2** 43 35S 74 0W
Guainía →, *Colombia* **92 C5** 2 1N 67 7W
Guaíra, *Brazil* **95 A5** 24 5S 54 10W
Guaíra □, *Paraguay* **94 B4** 25 45S 56 30W
Guaitecas, Is., *Chile* **96 E2** 44 0S 74 30W
Guajará-Mirim, *Brazil* **92 F5** 10 50S 65 20W
Guajira, Pen. de la, *Colombia* **92 A4** 12 0N 72 0W
Gualán, *Guatemala* **88 C2** 15 8N 89 22W
Gualeguay, *Argentina* **94 C4** 33 10S 59 14W
Gualeguaychú, *Argentina* **94 C4** 33 3S 59 31W
Gualequay →, *Argentina* **94 C4** 33 19S 59 39W
Guam ■, *Pac. Oc.* **64 F6** 13 27N 144 45 E
Guaminí, *Argentina* **94 D3** 37 1S 62 28W
Guamúchil, *Mexico* **86 B3** 25 25N 108 3W
Guanabacoa, *Cuba* **88 B3** 23 8N 82 18W
Guanacaste, Cordillera del, *Costa Rica* **88 D2** 10 40N 85 4W
Guanaceví, *Mexico* **86 B3** 25 40N 106 0W
Guanahani = San Salvador I., *Bahamas* **89 B5** 24 0N 74 40W
Guanajay, *Cuba* **88 B3** 22 56N 82 42W
Guanajuato, *Mexico* **86 C4** 21 0N 101 20W
Guanajuato □, *Mexico* **86 C4** 20 40N 101 20W
Guandacol, *Argentina* **94 B2** 29 30S 68 40W
Guane, *Cuba* **88 B3** 22 10N 84 7W
Guangdong □, *China* **33 D6** 23 0N 113 0 E
Guangling, *China* **34 E8** 39 47N 114 22 E
Guangrao, *China* **35 F10** 37 5N 118 25 E
Guangwu, *China* **34 F3** 37 48N 105 57 E
Guangxi Zhuangzu Zizhiqu □, *China* **33 D5** 24 0N 109 0 E
Guangzhou, *China* **33 D6** 23 5N 113 10 E
Guanipa →, *Venezuela* **92 B6** 9 56N 62 26W
Guannan, *China* **35 G10** 34 8N 119 21 E
Guantánamo, *Cuba* **89 B4** 20 10N 75 14W
Guantao, *China* **34 F8** 36 42N 115 25 E
Guanyun, *China* **35 G10** 34 20N 119 18 E
Guápiles, *Costa Rica* **88 D3** 10 10N 83 46W
Guaporé, *Brazil* **95 B5** 28 51S 51 54W
Guaporé →, *Brazil* **92 F5** 11 55S 65 4W
Guaqui, *Bolivia* **92 G5** 16 41S 68 54W
Guarapari, *Brazil* **95 A7** 20 40S 40 30W
Guarapuava, *Brazil* **95 B5** 25 20S 51 30W
Guaratinguetá, *Brazil* **95 A6** 22 49S 45 9W
Guaratuba, *Brazil* **95 B6** 25 53S 48 38W
Guarda, *Portugal* **19 B2** 40 32N 7 20W
Guardafui, C. = Asir, Ras, *Somali Rep.* **46 E5** 11 55N 51 10 E
Guárico □, *Venezuela* **92 B5** 8 40N 66 35W
Guarujá, *Brazil* **95 A6** 24 2S 46 25W
Guarus, *Brazil* **95 A7** 21 44S 41 20W
Guasave, *Mexico* **86 B3** 25 34N 108 27W
Guasdualito, *Venezuela* **92 B4** 7 15N 70 44W
Guatemala, *Guatemala* **88 D1** 14 40N 90 22W
Guatemala ■, *Cent. Amer.* **88 C1** 15 40N 90 30W
Guaviare →, *Colombia* **92 C5** 4 3N 67 44W
Guaxupé, *Brazil* **95 A6** 21 10S 47 5W
Guayama, *Puerto Rico* **89 C6** 17 59N 66 7W
Guayaquil, *Ecuador* **92 D3** 2 15S 79 52W
Guayaquil, G. de, *Ecuador* **92 D2** 3 10S 81 0W
Guaymas, *Mexico* **86 B2** 27 59N 110 54W
Guba, *Dem. Rep. of the Congo* **55 E2** 10 38S 26 27 E
Gubkin, *Russia* **25 D6** 51 17N 37 32 E
Gudbrandsdalen, *Norway* **9 F14** 61 33N 10 10 E
Guddu Barrage, *Pakistan* **40 E6** 28 30N 69 50 E
Gudivada, *India* **41 L12** 16 30N 81 3 E
Gudur, *India* **40 M11** 14 12N 79 55 E
Guecho = Getxo, *Spain* **19 A4** 43 21N 2 59W
Guelph, *Canada* **78 C4** 43 35N 80 20W
Guéret, *France* **18 C4** 46 11N 1 51 E
Guerneville, *U.S.A.* **84 G4** 38 30N 123 0W
Guernica = Gernika-Lumo, *Spain* **19 A4** 43 19N 2 40W
Guernsey, *U.K.* **11 H5** 49 26N 2 35W
Guernsey, *U.S.A.* **80 D2** 42 19N 104 45W
Guerrero □, *Mexico* **87 D5** 17 30N 100 0W
Gügher, *Iran* **45 D8** 29 28N 56 27 E
Guhakolak, Tanjung, *Indonesia* **37 G11** 6 50S 105 14 E
Guia, *Canary Is.* **22 F4** 28 8N 15 38W
Guia de Isora, *Canary Is.* **22 F3** 28 12N 16 46W
Guia Lopes da Laguna, *Brazil* **95 A4** 21 26S 56 7W
Guiana, *S. Amer.* **90 C4** 5 10N 60 40W
Guider, *Cameroon* **51 G8** 9 56N 13 57 E
Guidónia-Montecélio, *Italy* **20 C5** 42 1N 12 45 E
Guijá, *Mozam.* **57 C5** 24 27S 33 0 E
Guildford, *U.K.* **11 F7** 51 14N 0 34W
Guilford, *U.S.A.* **79 E12** 41 17N 72 41W
Guilin, *China* **33 D6** 25 18N 110 15 E
Guillaume-Delisle L., *Canada* **70 A4** 56 15N 76 17W
Güimar, *Canary Is.* **22 F3** 28 18N 16 24W
Guimarães, *Portugal* **19 B1** 41 28N 8 24W
Guimaras, *Phil.* **37 B6** 10 35N 122 37 E
Guinda, *U.S.A.* **84 G4** 38 50N 122 12W
Guinea, *Africa* **48 F4** 8 0N 8 0 E
Guinea ■, *W. Afr.* **50 F3** 10 20N 11 30W
Guinea, Gulf of, *Atl. Oc.* **48 F4** 3 0N 2 30 E
Guinea-Bissau ■, *Africa* **50 F3** 12 0N 15 0W
Güines, *Cuba* **88 B3** 22 50N 82 0W
Guingamp, *France* **18 B2** 48 34N 3 10W
Güiria, *Venezuela* **92 A6** 10 32N 62 18W
Guiuan, *Phil.* **37 B7** 11 5N 125 55 E
Guiyang, *China* **32 D5** 26 32N 106 40 E
Guizhou □, *China* **32 D5** 27 0N 107 0 E
Gujar Khan, *Pakistan* **42 C5** 33 16N 73 19 E
Gujarat □, *India* **42 H4** 23 20N 71 0 E
Gujranwala, *Pakistan* **42 C6** 32 10N 74 12 E
Gujrat, *Pakistan* **42 C6** 32 40N 74 2 E
Gulargambone, *Australia* **63 E4** 31 20S 148 30 E
Gulbarga, *India* **40 L10** 17 20N 76 50 E
Gulbene, *Latvia* **9 H22** 57 8N 26 52 E
Gulf, The, *Asia* **45 E6** 27 0N 50 0 E
Gulfport, *U.S.A.* **81 K10** 30 22N 89 6W
Gulgong, *Australia* **63 E4** 32 20S 149 49 E
Gulistan, *Pakistan* **42 D2** 30 30N 66 35 E
Gull Lake, *Canada* **73 C7** 50 10N 108 29W
Güllük, *Turkey* **21 F12** 37 14N 27 35 E
Gulmarg, *India* **43 B6** 34 3N 74 25 E
Gulshad, *Kazakstan* **26 E8** 46 45N 74 25 E
Gulu, *Uganda* **54 B3** 2 48N 32 17 E
Gulwe, *Tanzania* **54 D4** 6 30S 36 25 E
Gumal →, *Pakistan* **42 D4** 31 40N 71 50 E
Gumbaz, *Pakistan* **42 D3** 30 2N 69 0 E
Gumel, *Nigeria* **50 F7** 12 39N 9 22 E
Gumla, *India* **43 H11** 23 3N 84 33 E
Gumlu, *Australia* **62 B4** 19 53S 147 41 E
Gumma □, *Japan* **31 F9** 36 30N 138 20 E
Gumzai, *Indonesia* **37 F8** 5 28S 134 42 E
Guna, *India* **42 G7** 24 40N 77 19 E
Gunisao →, *Canada* **73 C9** 53 56N 97 53W
Gunisao L., *Canada* **73 C9** 53 33N 96 15W
Gunjyal, *Pakistan* **42 C4** 32 20N 71 55 E
Gunnbjørn Fjeld, *Greenland* **4 C6** 68 55N 29 47W
Gunnedah, *Australia* **63 E5** 30 59S 150 15 E
Gunnewin, *Australia* **63 D4** 25 59S 148 33 E
Gunningbar Cr. →, *Australia* **63 E4** 31 14S 147 6 E
Gunnison, *Colo., U.S.A.* **83 G10** 38 33N 106 56W
Gunnison, *Utah, U.S.A.* **82 G8** 39 9N 111 49W
Gunnison →, *U.S.A.* **83 G9** 39 4N 108 35W
Gunpowder, *Australia* **62 B2** 19 42S 139 22 E
Guntakal, *India* **40 M10** 15 11N 77 27 E
Guntersville, *U.S.A.* **77 H2** 34 21N 86 18W
Guntong, *Malaysia* **39 K3** 4 36N 101 3 E
Guntur, *India* **41 L12** 16 23N 80 30 E
Gunungapi, *Indonesia* **37 F7** 6 45S 126 30 E
Gunungsitoli, *Indonesia* **36 D1** 1 15N 97 30 E
Gunza, *Angola* **52 G2** 10 50S 13 50 E
Guo He →, *China* **35 H9** 32 59N 117 10 E
Guoyang, *China* **34 H9** 33 32N 116 12 E
Gupis, *Pakistan* **43 A5** 36 15N 73 20 E
Gurdaspur, *India* **42 C6** 32 5N 75 31 E
Gurdon, *U.S.A.* **81 J8** 33 55N 93 9W
Gurgaon, *India* **42 E7** 28 27N 77 1 E
Gurgueia →, *Brazil* **93 E10** 6 50S 43 24W
Gurha, *India* **42 G4** 25 12N 71 39 E
Guri, Embalse de, *Venezuela* **92 B6** 7 50N 62 52W
Gurkha, *Nepal* **43 E11** 28 5N 84 40 E
Gurley, *Australia* **63 D4** 29 45S 149 48 E
Gurnet Point, *U.S.A.* **79 D14** 42 1N 70 34W
Gurué, *Mozam.* **55 F4** 15 25S 36 58 E
Gurun, *Malaysia* **39 K3** 5 49N 100 27 E
Gürün, *Turkey* **25 G6** 38 43N 37 15 E
Gurupá, *Brazil* **93 D8** 1 25S 51 35W
Gurupá, I. Grande de, *Brazil* **93 D8** 1 25S 51 45W
Gurupi, *Brazil* **93 F9** 11 43S 49 4W
Gurupi →, *Brazil* **93 D9** 1 13S 46 6W
Guryev = Atyraū, *Kazakstan* **25 E9** 47 5N 52 0 E
Gusau, *Nigeria* **50 F7** 12 12N 6 40 E
Gusev, *Russia* **9 J20** 54 35N 22 10 E
Gushan, *China* **35 E12** 39 50N 123 35 E
Gushgy, *Turkmenistan* **26 F7** 35 20N 62 18 E
Gusinoozersk, *Russia* **27 D11** 51 16N 106 27 E
Gustavus, *U.S.A.* **72 B1** 58 25N 135 44W
Gustine, *U.S.A.* **84 H6** 37 16N 121 0W
Güstrow, *Germany* **16 B7** 53 47N 12 10 E
Gütersloh, *Germany* **16 C5** 51 54N 8 24 E
Gutha, *Australia* **61 E2** 28 58S 115 55 E
Guthalungra, *Australia* **62 B4** 19 52S 147 50 E
Guthrie, *Okla., U.S.A.* **81 H6** 35 53N 97 25W
Guthrie, *Tex., U.S.A.* **81 J4** 33 37N 100 19W
Guttenberg, *U.S.A.* **80 D9** 42 47N 91 6W
Guyana ■, *S. Amer.* **92 C7** 5 0N 59 0W
Guyane française = French Guiana ■, *S. Amer.* **93 C8** 4 0N 53 0W
Guyang, *China* **34 D6** 41 0N 110 5 E
Guyenne, *France* **18 D4** 44 30N 0 40 E
Guymon, *U.S.A.* **81 G4** 36 41N 101 29W
Guyra, *Australia* **63 E5** 30 15S 151 40 E
Guyuan, *Hebei, China* **34 D8** 41 37N 115 40 E
Guyuan, *Ningxia Huizu, China* **34 G4** 36 0N 106 20 E
Guzhen, *China* **35 H9** 33 22N 117 18 E
Guzmán, L. de, *Mexico* **86 A3** 31 25N 107 25W
Gvardeysk, *Russia* **9 J19** 54 39N 21 5 E
Gwa, *Burma* **41 L19** 17 36N 94 34 E
Gwaai, *Zimbabwe* **55 F2** 19 15S 27 45 E
Gwabegar, *Australia* **63 E4** 30 31S 149 0 E
Gwādar, *Pakistan* **40 G3** 25 10N 62 18 E
Gwalior, *India* **42 F8** 26 12N 78 10 E
Gwanda, *Zimbabwe* **55 G2** 20 55S 29 0 E
Gwane, *Dem. Rep. of the Congo* **54 B2** 4 45N 25 48 E
Gweebarra B., *Ireland* **13 B3** 54 51N 8 23W
Gweedore, *Ireland* **13 A3** 55 3N 8 13W
Gweru, *Zimbabwe* **55 F2** 19 28S 29 45 E
Gwinn, *U.S.A.* **76 B2** 46 19N 87 27W
Gwydir →, *Australia* **63 D4** 29 27S 149 48 E
Gwynedd □, *U.K.* **10 E3** 52 52N 4 10W
Gyandzha = Gäncä, *Azerbaijan* **25 F8** 40 45N 46 20 E
Gyaring Hu, *China* **32 C4** 34 50N 97 40 E
Gydanskiy Poluostrov, *Russia* **26 C8** 70 0N 78 0 E
Gympie, *Australia* **63 D5** 26 11S 152 38 E
Gyöngyös, *Hungary* **17 E10** 47 48N 19 56 E
Győr, *Hungary* **17 E9** 47 41N 17 40 E
Gypsum Pt., *Canada* **72 A6** 61 53N 114 35W
Gypsumville, *Canada* **73 C9** 51 45N 98 40W
Gyula, *Hungary* **17 E11** 46 38N 21 17 E
Gyumri, *Armenia* **25 F7** 40 47N 43 50 E
Gyzylarbat, *Turkmenistan* **26 F6** 39 4N 56 23 E
Gyzyletrek, *Turkmenistan* **45 B7** 37 36N 54 46 E

H

Ha 'Arava →, *Israel* **47 E4** 30 50N 35 20 E
Ha Tien, *Vietnam* **39 G5** 10 23N 104 29 E
Ha Tinh, *Vietnam* **38 C5** 18 20N 105 54 E
Ha Trung, *Vietnam* **38 C5** 19 58N 105 50 E
Haaksbergen, *Neths.* **15 B6** 52 9N 6 45 E
Haapsalu, *Estonia* **9 G20** 58 56N 23 30 E
Haarlem, *Neths.* **15 B4** 52 23N 4 39 E
Haast →, *N.Z.* **59 K2** 43 50S 169 2 E
Haast Bluff, *Australia* **60 D5** 23 22S 132 0 E
Hab →, *Pakistan* **42 G3** 24 53N 66 41 E
Hab Nadi Chauki, *Pakistan* **42 G2** 25 0N 66 50 E
Habaswein, *Kenya* **54 B4** 1 2N 39 30 E
Habay, *Canada* **72 B5** 58 50N 118 44W
Ḩabbānīyah, *Iraq* **44 C4** 33 17N 43 29 E
Haboro, *Japan* **30 B10** 44 22N 141 42 E
Ḩabshān, *U.A.E.* **45 F7** 23 50N 53 37 E
Hachijō-Jima, *Japan* **31 H9** 33 5N 139 45 E
Hachinohe, *Japan* **30 D10** 40 30N 141 29 E
Hachiōji, *Japan* **31 G9** 35 40N 139 20 E
Hachŏn, *N. Korea* **35 D15** 41 29N 129 2 E
Hackensack, *U.S.A.* **79 F10** 40 53N 74 3W
Hackettstown, *U.S.A.* **79 F10** 40 51N 74 50W
Hadali, *Pakistan* **42 C5** 32 16N 72 11 E
Hadarba, Ras, *Sudan* **51 D13** 22 4N 36 51 E
Hadarom □, *Israel* **47 E4** 31 0N 35 0 E
Hadd, Ra's al, *Oman* **46 C6** 22 35N 59 50 E
Hadejia, *Nigeria* **50 F7** 12 30N 10 5 E
Hadera, *Israel* **47 C3** 32 27N 34 55 E
Hadera, N. →, *Israel* **47 C3** 32 28N 34 52 E
Haderslev, *Denmark* **9 J13** 55 15N 9 30 E
Hadhramaut = Haḑramawt, *Yemen* **46 D4** 15 30N 49 30 E
Hadibu, *Yemen* **46 E5** 12 39N 54 2 E
Hadong, *S. Korea* **35 G14** 35 5N 127 44
Haḑramawt, *Yemen* **46 D4** 15 30N 49 30
Ḩadrānīyah, *Iraq* **44 C4** 35 38N 43 14
Hadrian's Wall, *U.K.* **10 B5** 55 0N 2 30
Haeju, *N. Korea* **35 E13** 38 3N 125 45
Haenam, *S. Korea* **35 G14** 34 34N 126 35
Haerhpin = Harbin, *China* **35 B14** 45 48N 126 40
Hafar al Bāţin, *Si. Arabia* **44 D5** 28 32N 45 52
Ḩafirat al 'Aydā, *Si. Arabia* **44 E3** 26 26N 39 12
Ḩafit, *Oman* **45 F7** 23 59N 55 49
Ḩafit, Jabal, *Oman* **45 E7** 24 3N 55 46
Hafizabad, *Pakistan* **42 C5** 32 5N 73 40
Haflong, *India* **41 G18** 25 10N 93 5
Hafnarfjörður, *Iceland* **8 D3** 64 4N 21 57
Haft Gel, *Iran* **45 D6** 31 30N 49 32
Hafun, Ras, *Somali Rep.* **46 E5** 10 29N 51 30
Hagalil, *Israel* **47 C4** 32 53N 35 18
Hagen, *Germany* **16 C4** 51 21N 7 27
Hagerman, *U.S.A.* **81 J2** 33 7N 104 20
Hagerstown, *U.S.A.* **76 F7** 39 39N 77 43
Hagersville, *Canada* **78 D4** 42 58N 80 3
Hagfors, *Sweden* **9 F15** 60 3N 13 45
Hagi, *Japan* **31 G5** 34 30N 131 22
Hagolan, *Syria* **47 C4** 33 0N 35 45
Hagondange, *France* **18 B7** 49 16N 6 11
Hags Hd., *Ireland* **13 D2** 52 57N 9 28
Hague, C. de la, *France* **18 B3** 49 44N 1 56
Hague, The = 's-Gravenhage, *Neths.* **15 B4** 52 7N 4 17
Haguenau, *France* **18 B7** 48 49N 7 47
Haicheng, *China* **35 D12** 40 50N 122 45
Haidar Khel, *Afghan.* **42 C3** 33 58N 68 38
Haidargarh, *India* **43 F9** 26 37N 81 22
Haifa = Hefa, *Israel* **47 C4** 32 46N 35 0
Haikou, *China* **33 D6** 20 1N 110 16
Ḩā'il, *Si. Arabia* **44 E4** 27 28N 41 45
Hailar, *China* **33 B6** 49 10N 119 38
Hailey, *U.S.A.* **82 E6** 43 31N 114 19
Haileybury, *Canada* **70 C4** 47 30N 79 38
Hailin, *China* **35 B15** 44 37N 129 30
Hailong, *China* **35 C13** 42 32N 125 40
Hailuoto, *Finland* **8 D21** 65 3N 24 45
Hainan □, *China* **33 E5** 19 0N 109 30
Hainaut □, *Belgium* **15 D4** 50 30N 4 0
Haines, *Alaska, U.S.A.* **72 B1** 59 14N 135 26
Haines, *Oreg., U.S.A.* **82 D5** 44 55N 117 56
Haines City, *U.S.A.* **77 L5** 28 7N 81 38
Haines Junction, *Canada* **72 A1** 60 45N 137 30
Haiphong, *Vietnam* **32 D5** 20 47N 106 41
Haiti ■, *W. Indies* **89 C5** 19 0N 72 30
Haiya, *Sudan* **51 E13** 18 20N 36 21
Haiyang, *China* **35 F11** 36 47N 121 9
Haiyuan, *China* **34 F3** 36 35N 105 52
Haizhou, *China* **35 G10** 34 37N 119 7
Haizhou Wan, *China* **35 G10** 34 50N 119 20
Hajdúböszörmény, *Hungary* **17 E11** 47 40N 21 30
Hajipur, *India* **43 G11** 25 45N 85 13
Hājjī Muḩsin, *Iraq* **44 C5** 32 35N 45 29
Ḩājjīābād, *Iran* **45 D7** 28 19N 55 55
Ḩājjīābād-e Zarrīn, *Iran* **45 C7** 33 9N 54 51
Hajnówka, *Poland* **17 B12** 52 47N 23 35
Hakansson, Mts., *Dem. Rep. of the Congo* **55 D2** 8 40S 25 45
Hakkâri, *Turkey* **44 B4** 37 34N 43 44
Hakken-Zan, *Japan* **31 G7** 34 10N 135 54
Hakodate, *Japan* **30 D10** 41 45N 140 44
Haku-San, *Japan* **31 F8** 36 9N 136 46
Hakui, *Japan* **31 F8** 36 53N 136 47
Hala, *Pakistan* **40 G6** 25 43N 68 20
Ḩalab, *Syria* **44 B3** 36 10N 37 15
Ḩalabjah, *Iraq* **44 C5** 35 10N 45 58
Halaib, *Sudan* **51 D13** 22 12N 36 30
Hālat 'Ammār, *Si. Arabia* **44 D3** 29 10N 36 4
Halbā, *Lebanon* **47 A5** 34 34N 36 6
Halberstadt, *Germany* **16 C6** 51 54N 11 3
Halcombe, *N.Z.* **59 J5** 40 8S 175 30
Halcon, *Phil.* **37 B6** 13 0N 121 30
Halden, *Norway* **9 G14** 59 9N 11 23
Haldia, *India* **41 H16** 22 5N 88 3
Haldwani, *India* **43 E8** 29 31N 79 30
Hale →, *Australia* **62 C2** 24 56S 135 53
Haleakala Crater, *U.S.A.* **74 H16** 20 43N 156 16
Halesowen, *U.K.* **11 E5** 52 27N 2 3
Haleyville, *U.S.A.* **77 H2** 34 14N 87 37
Halfway →, *Canada* **72 B4** 56 12N 121 32
Halia, *India* **43 G10** 24 50N 82 19
Haliburton, *Canada* **78 A6** 45 3N 78 30
Halifax, *Australia* **62 B4** 18 32S 146 22
Halifax, *Canada* **71 D7** 44 38N 63 35
Halifax, *U.K.* **10 D6** 53 43N 1 52
Halifax, *U.S.A.* **78 F8** 40 25N 76 55
Halifax B., *Australia* **62 B4** 18 50S 147 0
Halifax I., *Namibia* **56 D2** 26 38S 15 4
Halīl →, *Iran* **45 E8** 27 40N 58 30
Halkirk, *U.K.* **12 C5** 58 30N 3 29
Hall Beach = Sanirajak, *Canada* **69 B11** 68 46N 81 12
Hall Pen., *Canada* **69 B13** 63 30N 66 0
Hall Pt., *Australia* **60 C3** 15 40S 124 23
Halland, *Sweden* **9 H15** 57 8N 12 47
Halle, *Belgium* **15 D4** 50 44N 4 13
Halle, *Germany* **16 C6** 51 30N 11 56
Hällefors, *Sweden* **9 G16** 59 47N 14 31
Hallett, *Australia* **63 E2** 33 25S 138 55
Hallettsville, *U.S.A.* **81 L6** 29 27N 96 57
Hallim, *S. Korea* **35 H14** 33 24N 126 15
Hallingdalselvi →, *Norway* **9 F13** 60 23N 9 35
Halls Creek, *Australia* **60 C4** 18 16S 127 38
Hallsberg, *Sweden* **9 G16** 59 5N 15 7
Hallstead, *U.S.A.* **79 E9** 41 58N 75 45
Halmahera, *Indonesia* **37 D7** 0 40N 128 0
Halmstad, *Sweden* **9 H15** 56 41N 12 52
Hälsingborg = Helsingborg, *Sweden* **9 H15** 56 3N 12 42
Hälsingland, *Sweden* **9 F16** 61 40N 16 5
Halstead, *U.K.* **11 F8** 51 57N 0 40
Halti, *Finland* **8 B19** 69 17N 21 18
Halton □, *U.K.* **10 D5** 53 22N 2 45
Haltwhistle, *U.K.* **10 C5** 54 58N 2 26
Halul, *Qatar* **45 E7** 25 40N 52 40
Halvad, *India* **42 H4** 23 1N 71 11
Ḩalvān, *Iran* **45 C8** 33 57N 56 15
Ham Tan, *Vietnam* **39 G6** 10 40N 107 45
Ham Yen, *Vietnam* **38 A5** 22 4N 105 3
Hamab, *Namibia* **56 D2** 28 7S 19 16
Hamada, *Japan* **31 G6** 34 56N 132 4
Hamadān, *Iran* **45 C6** 34 52N 48 32

125

Hensall

Hensall, *Canada* **78 C3** 43 26N 81 30W
Hentiyn Nuruu, *Mongolia* **33 B5** 48 30N 108 30 E
Henty, *Australia* **63 F4** 35 30S 147 0 E
Henzada, *Burma* **41 L19** 17 38N 95 26 E
Heppner, *U.S.A.* **82 D4** 45 21N 119 33W
Hepworth, *Canada* **78 B3** 44 37N 81 9W
Hequ, *China* **34 E6** 39 20N 111 15 E
Héraðsflói, *Iceland* **8 D6** 65 42N 14 12W
Héraðsvötn →, *Iceland* **8 D4** 65 45N 19 25W
Herald Cays, *Australia* **62 B4** 16 58S 149 9 E
Herāt, *Afghan.* **40 B3** 34 20N 62 7 E
Herāt □, *Afghan.* **40 B3** 35 0N 62 0 E
Herbert →, *Australia* **62 B4** 18 31S 146 17 E
Herberton, *Australia* **62 B4** 17 20S 145 25 E
Herceg-Novi, *Montenegro, Yug.* **21 C8** 42 30N 18 33 E
Herchmer, *Canada* **73 B10** 57 22N 94 10W
Herðubreið, *Iceland* **8 D5** 65 11N 16 21W
Hereford, *U.K.* **11 E5** 52 4N 2 43W
Hereford, *U.S.A.* **81 H3** 34 49N 102 24W
Herefordshire □, *U.K.* **11 E5** 52 8N 2 40W
Herentals, *Belgium* **15 C4** 51 12N 4 51 E
Herford, *Germany* **16 B5** 52 7N 8 39 E
Herington, *U.S.A.* **80 F6** 38 40N 96 57W
Herkimer, *U.S.A.* **79 D10** 43 0N 74 59W
Herlong, *U.S.A.* **84 E6** 40 8N 120 8W
Herm, *U.K.* **11 H5** 49 30N 2 28W
Hermann, *U.S.A.* **80 F9** 38 42N 91 27W
Hermannsburg, *Australia* **60 D5** 23 57S 132 45 E
Hermanus, *S. Africa* **56 E2** 34 27S 19 12 E
Hermidale, *Australia* **63 E4** 31 30S 146 42 E
Hermiston, *U.S.A.* **82 D4** 45 51N 119 17W
Hermitage, *N.Z.* **59 K3** 43 44S 170 5 E
Hermite, I., *Chile* **96 H3** 55 50S 68 0W
Hermon, *U.S.A.* **79 B9** 44 28N 75 14W
Hermon, Mt. = Shaykh, J. ash, *Lebanon* **47 B4** 33 25N 35 50 E
Hermosillo, *Mexico* **86 B2** 29 10N 111 0W
Hernád →, *Hungary* **17 D11** 47 56N 21 8 E
Hernandarias, *Paraguay* **95 B5** 25 20S 54 40W
Hernandez, *U.S.A.* **84 J6** 36 24N 120 46W
Hernando, *Argentina* **94 C3** 32 28S 63 40W
Hernando, *U.S.A.* **81 H10** 34 50N 90 0W
Herndon, *U.S.A.* **78 F8** 40 43N 76 51W
Herne, *Germany* **15 C7** 51 32N 7 14 E
Herne Bay, *U.K.* **11 F9** 51 21N 1 8 E
Herning, *Denmark* **9 H13** 56 8N 8 58 E
Heroica = Caborca, *Mexico* **86 A2** 30 40N 112 10W
Heroica Nogales = Nogales, *Mexico* **86 A2** 31 20N 110 56W
Heron Bay, *Canada* **70 C2** 48 40N 86 25W
Herradura, Pta. de la, *Canary Is.* **22 F5** 28 26N 14 8W
Herreid, *U.S.A.* **80 C4** 45 50N 100 4W
Herrin, *U.S.A.* **81 G10** 37 48N 89 2W
Herriot, *Canada* **73 B8** 56 22N 101 16W
Hershey, *U.S.A.* **79 F8** 40 17N 76 39W
Hersonissos, *Greece* **23 D7** 35 18N 25 22 E
Herstal, *Belgium* **15 D5** 50 40N 5 38 E
Hertford, *U.K.* **11 F7** 51 48N 0 4W
Hertfordshire □, *U.K.* **11 F7** 51 51N 0 5W
's-Hertogenbosch, *Neths.* **15 C5** 51 42N 5 17 E
Hertzogville, *S. Africa* **56 D4** 28 9S 25 30 E
Hervey B., *Australia* **62 C5** 25 0S 152 52 E
Herzliyya, *Israel* **47 C3** 32 10N 34 50 E
Ḥeşār, *Fārs, Iran* **45 D6** 29 52N 50 16 E
Ḥeşār, *Markazī, Iran* **45 C6** 35 50N 49 12 E
Heshui, *China* **34 G5** 35 48N 108 0 E
Heshun, *China* **34 F7** 37 22N 113 32 E
Hesperia, *U.S.A.* **85 L9** 34 25N 117 18W
Hesse = Hessen □, *Germany* **16 C5** 50 30N 9 0 E
Hessen □, *Germany* **16 C5** 50 30N 9 0 E
Hetch Hetchy Aqueduct, *U.S.A.* **84 H5** 37 29N 122 19W
Hettinger, *U.S.A.* **80 C3** 46 0N 102 42W
Heuvelton, *U.S.A.* **79 B9** 44 37N 75 25W
Hewitt, *U.S.A.* **81 K6** 31 27N 97 11W
Hexham, *U.K.* **10 C5** 54 58N 2 4W
Hexigten Qi, *China* **35 C9** 43 18N 117 30 E
Ḥeydarābād, *Iran* **45 D7** 30 33N 55 38 E
Heysham, *U.K.* **10 C5** 54 3N 2 53W
Heywood, *Australia* **63 F3** 38 8S 141 37 E
Heze, *China* **34 G8** 35 14N 115 20 E
Hi Vista, *U.S.A.* **85 L9** 34 45N 117 46W
Hialeah, *U.S.A.* **77 N5** 25 50N 80 17W
Hiawatha, *U.S.A.* **80 F7** 39 51N 95 32W
Hibbing, *U.S.A.* **80 B8** 47 25N 92 56W
Hibbs B., *Australia* **62 G4** 42 35S 145 15 E
Hibernia Reef, *Australia* **60 B3** 12 0S 123 23 E
Hickman, *U.S.A.* **81 G10** 36 34N 89 11W
Hickory, *U.S.A.* **77 H5** 35 44N 81 21W
Hicks, Pt., *Australia* **63 F4** 37 49S 149 17 E
Hicks L., *Canada* **73 A9** 61 25N 100 0W
Hicksville, *U.S.A.* **79 F11** 40 46N 73 32W
Hida-Gawa →, *Japan* **31 G8** 35 26N 137 3 E
Hida-Sammyaku, *Japan* **31 F8** 36 30N 137 40 E
Hidaka-Sammyaku, *Japan* **30 C11** 42 35N 142 45 E
Hidalgo, *Mexico* **87 C5** 24 15N 99 26W
Hidalgo □, *Mexico* **87 C5** 20 30N 99 10W
Hidalgo, Presa M., *Mexico* **86 B3** 26 30N 108 35W
Hidalgo, Pta. del, *Canary Is.* **22 F3** 28 33N 16 19W
Hidalgo del Parral, *Mexico* **86 B3** 26 58N 105 40W
Hierro, *Canary Is.* **22 G1** 27 44N 18 0W
Higashiajima-San, *Japan* **30 F10** 37 40N 140 10 E
Higashiōsaka, *Japan* **31 G7** 34 40N 135 37 E
Higgins, *U.S.A.* **81 G4** 36 7N 100 2W
Higgins Corner, *U.S.A.* **84 F5** 39 2N 121 5W
High Atlas = Haut Atlas, *Morocco* **50 B4** 32 30N 5 0W
High Bridge, *U.S.A.* **79 F10** 40 40N 74 54W
High Level, *Canada* **72 B5** 58 31N 117 8W
High Point, *U.S.A.* **77 H6** 35 57N 80 0W
High Prairie, *Canada* **72 B5** 55 30N 116 30W
High River, *Canada* **72 C6** 50 30N 113 50W
High Tatra = Tatry, *Slovak Rep.* **17 D11** 49 20N 20 0 E
High Veld, *Africa* **48 J6** 27 0S 27 0 E
High Wycombe, *U.K.* **11 F7** 51 37N 0 45W
Highland □, *U.K.* **12 D4** 57 17N 4 21W
Highland Park, *U.S.A.* **76 D2** 42 11N 87 48W
Highmore, *U.S.A.* **80 C5** 44 31N 99 27W
Highrock L., *Canada* **73 B8** 55 45N 100 30W
Highrock L., *Sask., Canada* **73 B7** 57 5N 105 32W
Higüey, *Dom. Rep.* **89 C6** 18 37N 68 42W
Hiiumaa, *Estonia* **9 G20** 58 50N 22 45 E
Ḥijāz □, *Si. Arabia* **46 C3** 24 0N 40 0 E
Hijo = Tagum, *Phil.* **37 C7** 7 33N 125 53 E
Hikari, *Japan* **31 H5** 33 58N 131 58 E
Hiko, *U.S.A.* **84 H11** 37 32N 115 14W
Hikone, *Japan* **31 G8** 35 15N 136 10 E
Hikurangi, *N.Z.* **59 F5** 35 36S 174 17 E
Hikurangi, Mt., *N.Z.* **59 H6** 38 21S 176 52 E
Hildesheim, *Germany* **16 B5** 52 9N 9 56 E
Hill →, *Australia* **61 F2** 30 23S 115 3 E
Hill City, *Idaho, U.S.A.* **82 E6** 43 18N 115 3W
Hill City, *Kans., U.S.A.* **80 F5** 39 22N 99 51W
Hill City, *S. Dak., U.S.A.* **80 D3** 43 56N 103 35W
Hill Island L., *Canada* **73 A7** 60 30N 109 50W
Hillcrest Center, *U.S.A.* **85 K8** 35 23N 118 57W
Hillegom, *Neths.* **15 B4** 52 18N 4 35 E
Hillerød, *Denmark* **9 J15** 55 56N 12 19 E
Hillsboro, *Kans., U.S.A.* **80 F6** 38 21N 97 12W
Hillsboro, *N. Dak., U.S.A.* **80 B6** 47 26N 97 3W
Hillsboro, *N.H., U.S.A.* **79 C13** 43 7N 71 54W
Hillsboro, *Ohio, U.S.A.* **76 F4** 39 12N 83 37W
Hillsboro, *Oreg., U.S.A.* **84 E4** 45 31N 122 59W
Hillsboro, *Tex., U.S.A.* **81 J6** 32 1N 97 8W
Hillsborough, *Grenada* **89 D7** 12 28N 61 28W
Hillsdale, *Mich., U.S.A.* **76 E3** 41 56N 84 38W
Hillsdale, *N.Y., U.S.A.* **79 D11** 42 11N 73 30W
Hillsport, *Canada* **70 C2** 49 27N 85 34W
Hillston, *Australia* **63 E4** 33 30S 145 31 E
Hilo, *U.S.A.* **74 J17** 19 44N 155 5W
Hilton, *U.S.A.* **78 C7** 43 17N 77 48W
Hilton Head Island, *U.S.A.* **77 J5** 32 13N 80 45W
Hilversum, *Neths.* **15 B5** 52 14N 5 10 E
Himachal Pradesh □, *India* **42 D7** 31 30N 77 0 E
Himalaya, *Asia* **43 E11** 29 0N 84 0 E
Himatnagar, *India* **40 H8** 23 37N 72 57 E
Himeji, *Japan* **31 G7** 34 50N 134 40 E
Himi, *Japan* **31 F8** 36 50N 136 55 E
Ḥimş, *Syria* **47 A5** 34 40N 36 45 E
Ḥimş □, *Syria* **47 A6** 34 30N 37 0 E
Hinche, *Haiti* **89 C5** 19 9N 72 1W
Hinchinbrook I., *Australia* **62 B4** 18 20S 146 15 E
Hinckley, *U.K.* **11 E6** 52 33N 1 22W
Hinckley, *U.S.A.* **80 B8** 46 1N 92 56W
Hindaun, *India* **42 F7** 26 44N 77 5 E
Hindmarsh, L., *Australia* **63 F3** 36 5S 141 55 E
Hindu Bagh, *Pakistan* **42 D2** 30 56N 67 50 E
Hindu Kush, *Asia* **40 B7** 36 0N 71 0 E
Hindubagh, *Pakistan* **40 D5** 30 56N 67 57 E
Hindupur, *India* **40 N10** 13 49N 77 32 E
Hines Creek, *Canada* **72 B5** 56 20N 118 40W
Hinesville, *U.S.A.* **77 K5** 31 51N 81 36W
Hinganghat, *India* **40 J11** 20 30N 78 52 E
Hingham, *U.S.A.* **82 B8** 48 33N 110 25W
Hingir, *India* **43 J10** 21 57N 83 41 E
Hingoli, *India* **40 K10** 19 41N 77 15 E
Hinna = Imi, *Ethiopia* **46 F3** 6 28N 42 10 E
Hinnøya, *Norway* **8 B16** 68 35N 15 50 E
Hinojosa del Duque, *Spain* **19 C3** 38 30N 5 9W
Hinsdale, *U.S.A.* **79 D12** 42 47N 72 29W
Hinton, *Canada* **72 C5** 53 26N 117 34W
Hinton, *U.S.A.* **76 G5** 37 40N 80 54W
Hirado, *Japan* **31 H4** 33 22N 129 33 E
Hirakud Dam, *India* **41 J13** 21 32N 83 45 E
Hiran →, *India* **43 H8** 23 6N 79 21 E
Hirapur, *India* **43 G8** 24 22N 79 13 E
Hiratsuka, *Japan* **31 G9** 35 19N 139 21 E
Hiroo, *Japan* **30 C11** 42 17N 143 19 E
Hirosaki, *Japan* **30 D10** 40 34N 140 28 E
Hiroshima, *Japan* **31 G6** 34 24N 132 30 E
Hiroshima □, *Japan* **31 G6** 34 50N 133 0 E
Hisar, *India* **42 E6** 29 12N 75 45 E
Hisb →, *Iraq* **44 D5** 31 45N 44 17 E
Ḥismá, *Si. Arabia* **44 D3** 28 30N 36 0 E
Hispaniola, *W. Indies* **89 C5** 19 0N 71 0W
Hīt, *Iraq* **44 C4** 33 38N 42 49 E
Hita, *Japan* **31 H5** 33 20N 130 58 E
Hitachi, *Japan* **31 F10** 36 36N 140 39 E
Hitchin, *U.K.* **11 F7** 51 58N 0 16W
Hitoyoshi, *Japan* **31 H5** 32 13N 130 45 E
Hitra, *Norway* **8 E13** 63 30N 8 45 E
Hixon, *Canada* **72 C4** 53 25N 122 35W
Hiyyon, N. →, *Israel* **47 E4** 30 25N 35 10 E
Hjalmar L., *Canada* **73 A7** 61 33N 109 25W
Hjälmaren, *Sweden* **9 G16** 59 18N 15 40 E
Hjørring, *Denmark* **9 H13** 57 29N 9 59 E
Hluhluwe, *S. Africa* **57 D5** 28 1S 32 15 E
Hlyboka, *Ukraine* **17 D13** 48 5N 25 56 E
Ho Chi Minh City = Phanh Bho Ho Chi Minh, *Vietnam* **39 G6** 10 58N 106 40 E
Ho Thuong, *Vietnam* **38 C5** 19 32N 105 48 E
Hoa Da, *Vietnam* **39 G7** 11 16N 108 40 E
Hoa Hiep, *Vietnam* **39 G5** 11 34N 105 51 E
Hoai Nhon, *Vietnam* **38 E7** 14 28N 109 1 E
Hoang Lien Son, *Vietnam* **38 A4** 22 0N 104 0 E
Hoare B., *Canada* **69 B13** 65 17N 62 30W
Hobart, *Australia* **62 G4** 42 50S 147 21 E
Hobart, *U.S.A.* **81 H5** 35 1N 99 6W
Hobbs, *U.S.A.* **81 J3** 32 42N 103 8W
Hobbs Coast, *Antarctica* **5 D14** 74 50S 131 0W
Hobe Sound, *U.S.A.* **77 M5** 27 4N 80 8W
Hoboken, *U.S.A.* **79 F10** 40 45N 74 4W
Hobro, *Denmark* **9 H13** 56 39N 9 46 E
Hoburgen, *Sweden* **9 H18** 56 55N 18 7 E
Hodaka-Dake, *Japan* **31 F8** 36 17N 137 39 E
Hodgeville, *Canada* **73 C7** 50 7N 106 58W
Hodgson, *Canada* **73 C9** 51 13N 97 36W
Hódmezővásárhely, *Hungary* **17 E11** 46 28N 20 22 E
Hodna, Chott el, *Algeria* **50 A6** 35 26N 4 43 E
Hodonín, *Czech Rep.* **17 D9** 48 50N 17 10 E
Hoeamdong, *N. Korea* **35 C16** 42 30N 130 16 E
Hoek van Holland, *Neths.* **15 C4** 52 0N 4 7 E
Hoengsŏng, *S. Korea* **35 F14** 37 29N 127 59 E
Hoeryong, *N. Korea* **35 C15** 42 30N 129 45 E
Hoeyang, *N. Korea* **35 E14** 38 43N 127 36 E
Hof, *Germany* **16 C6** 50 19N 11 55 E
Hofmeyr, *S. Africa* **56 E4** 31 39S 25 50 E
Höfn, *Iceland* **8 D6** 64 15N 15 13W
Hofors, *Sweden* **9 F17** 60 31N 16 15 E
Hofsjökull, *Iceland* **8 D4** 64 49N 18 48W
Hōfu, *Japan* **31 G5** 34 3N 131 34 E
Hogan Group, *Australia* **63 F4** 39 13S 147 1 E
Hogarth, Mt., *Australia* **62 C2** 21 48S 136 58 E
Hoggar = Ahaggar, *Algeria* **50 D7** 23 0N 6 30 E
Hogsty Reef, *Bahamas* **89 B5** 21 41N 73 48W
Hoh →, *U.S.A.* **84 C2** 47 45N 124 29W
Hohe Venn, *Belgium* **15 D6** 50 30N 6 5 E
Hohenwald, *U.S.A.* **77 H2** 35 33N 87 33W
Hohhot, *China* **34 D6** 40 52N 111 40 E
Hóhlakas, *Greece* **23 D9** 35 57N 27 53 E
Hoi An, *Vietnam* **38 E7** 15 30N 108 19 E
Hoisington, *U.S.A.* **80 F5** 38 31N 98 47W
Hōjō, *Japan* **31 H6** 33 58N 132 46 E
Hokianga Harbour, *N.Z.* **59 F4** 35 31S 173 22 E
Hokitika, *N.Z.* **59 K3** 42 42S 171 0 E
Hokkaidō □, *Japan* **30 C11** 43 30N 143 0 E
Holbrook, *Australia* **63 F4** 35 42S 147 18 E
Holbrook, *U.S.A.* **83 J8** 34 54N 110 10W
Holden, *U.S.A.* **82 G7** 39 6N 112 16W
Holdenville, *U.S.A.* **81 H6** 35 5N 96 24W
Holdrege, *U.S.A.* **80 E5** 40 26N 99 23W
Holguín, *Cuba* **88 B4** 20 50N 76 20W
Hollams Bird I., *Namibia* **56 C1** 24 40S 14 30 E
Holland, *Mich., U.S.A.* **76 D2** 42 47N 86 7W
Holland, *N.Y., U.S.A.* **78 D6** 42 38N 78 32W
Hollandale, *U.S.A.* **81 J9** 33 10N 90 51W
Hollandia = Jayapura, *Indonesia* **37 E10** 2 28S 140 38 E
Holley, *U.S.A.* **78 C6** 43 14N 78 2W
Hollidaysburg, *U.S.A.* **78 F6** 40 26N 78 24W
Hollis, *U.S.A.* **81 H5** 34 41N 99 55W
Hollister, *Calif., U.S.A.* **84 J5** 36 51N 121 24W
Hollister, *Idaho, U.S.A.* **82 E6** 42 21N 114 35W
Holly Hill, *U.S.A.* **77 L5** 29 16N 81 3W
Holly Springs, *U.S.A.* **81 H10** 34 46N 89 27W
Hollywood, *Calif., U.S.A.* **74 D3** 34 7N 118 25W
Hollywood, *Fla., U.S.A.* **77 N5** 26 1N 80 9W
Holman, *Canada* **68 A8** 70 42N 117 41W
Holman, *N.W.T., Canada* **68 A8** 70 44N 117 44W
Hólmavík, *Iceland* **8 D3** 65 42N 21 40W
Holmen, *U.S.A.* **80 D9** 43 58N 91 15W
Holmes Reefs, *Australia* **62 B4** 16 27S 148 0 E
Holmsund, *Sweden* **8 E19** 63 41N 20 20 E
Holroyd →, *Australia* **62 A3** 14 10S 141 36 E
Holstebro, *Denmark* **9 H13** 56 22N 8 37 E
Holsworthy, *U.K.* **11 G3** 50 48N 4 22W
Holton, *Canada* **71 B8** 54 31N 57 12W
Holton, *U.S.A.* **80 F7** 39 28N 95 44W
Holtville, *U.S.A.* **85 N11** 32 49N 115 23W
Holwerd, *Neths.* **15 A5** 53 22N 5 54 E
Holy I., *Angl., U.K.* **10 D3** 53 17N 4 37W
Holy I., *Northumb., U.K.* **10 B6** 55 40N 1 47W
Holyhead, *U.K.* **10 D3** 53 18N 4 38W
Holyoke, *Colo., U.S.A.* **80 E3** 40 35N 102 18W
Holyoke, *Mass., U.S.A.* **79 D12** 42 12N 72 37W
Holyrood, *Canada* **71 C9** 47 27N 53 8W
Homa Bay, *Kenya* **54 C3** 0 36S 34 30 E
Homalin, *Burma* **41 G19** 24 55N 95 0 E
Homand, *Iran* **45 C8** 32 28N 59 37 E
Homathko →, *Canada* **72 C4** 51 0N 124 56W
Hombori, *Mali* **50 E5** 15 20N 1 38W
Home B., *Canada* **69 B13** 68 40N 67 10W
Home Hill, *Australia* **62 B4** 19 43S 147 25 E
Homedale, *U.S.A.* **82 E5** 43 37N 116 56W
Homer, *Alaska, U.S.A.* **68 C4** 59 39N 151 33W
Homer, *La., U.S.A.* **81 J8** 32 48N 93 4W
Homer City, *U.S.A.* **78 F5** 40 32N 79 10W
Homestead, *Australia* **62 C4** 20 20S 145 40 E
Homestead, *U.S.A.* **77 N5** 25 28N 80 29W
Homewood, *U.S.A.* **84 F6** 39 4N 120 8W
Homoine, *Mozam.* **57 C6** 23 55S 35 8 E
Homs = Ḥimş, *Syria* **47 A5** 34 40N 36 45 E
Homyel, *Belarus* **17 B16** 52 28N 31 0 E
Hon Chong, *Vietnam* **39 G5** 10 25N 104 30 E
Hon Me, *Vietnam* **38 C5** 19 23N 105 56 E
Honan = Henan □, *China* **34 H8** 34 0N 114 0 E
Honbetsu, *Japan* **30 C11** 43 7N 143 37 E
Honcut, *U.S.A.* **84 F5** 39 20N 121 32W
Hondeklipbaai, *S. Africa* **56 E2** 30 19S 17 17 E
Hondo, *Japan* **31 H5** 32 27N 130 12 E
Hondo, *U.S.A.* **81 L5** 29 21N 99 9W
Hondo →, *Belize* **87 D7** 18 25N 88 21W
Honduras ■, *Cent. Amer.* **88 D2** 14 40N 86 30W
Honduras, G. de, *Caribbean* **88 C2** 16 50N 87 0W
Hønefoss, *Norway* **9 F14** 60 10N 10 18 E
Honesdale, *U.S.A.* **79 E9** 41 34N 75 16W
Honey L., *U.S.A.* **84 E6** 40 15N 120 19W
Honfleur, *France* **18 B4** 49 25N 0 13 E
Hong →, *Vietnam* **32 D5** 22 0N 104 0 E
Hong He →, *China* **34 H8** 32 25N 115 35 E
Hong Kong □, *China* **33 D6** 22 11N 114 14 E
Hongch'ŏn, *S. Korea* **35 F14** 37 44N 127 53 E
Hongjiang, *China* **33 D5** 27 7N 109 59 E
Hongliu He →, *China* **34 F5** 38 0N 109 50 E
Hongor, *Mongolia* **34 B7** 45 45N 112 50 E
Hongsa, *Laos* **38 C3** 19 43N 101 20 E
Hongshui He →, *China* **33 D5** 23 48N 109 30 E
Hongsŏng, *S. Korea* **35 F14** 36 37N 126 38 E
Hongtong, *China* **34 F6** 36 16N 111 40 E
Honguedo, Détroit d', *Canada* **71 C7** 49 15N 64 0W
Hongwon, *N. Korea* **35 E14** 40 0N 127 56 E
Hongze Hu, *China* **35 H10** 33 15N 118 35 E
Honiara, *Solomon Is.* **64 H7** 9 27S 159 57 E
Honiton, *U.K.* **11 G4** 50 47N 3 11W
Honjō, *Japan* **30 E10** 39 23N 140 3 E
Honningsvåg, *Norway* **8 A21** 70 59N 25 59 E
Honolulu, *U.S.A.* **74 H16** 21 19N 157 52W
Honshū, *Japan* **31 G9** 36 0N 138 0 E
Hood, Mt., *U.S.A.* **82 D3** 45 23N 121 42W
Hood, Pt., *Australia* **61 F2** 34 23S 119 34 E
Hood River, *U.S.A.* **82 D3** 45 43N 121 31W
Hoodsport, *U.S.A.* **84 C3** 47 24N 123 9W
Hoogeveen, *Neths.* **15 B6** 52 44N 6 28 E
Hoogezand-Sappemeer, *Neths.* **15 A6** 53 9N 6 45 E
Hooghly = Hugli →, *India* **43 J13** 21 56N 88 4 E
Hooghly-Chinsura = Chunchura, *India* **43 H13** 22 53N 88 27 E
Hook Hd., *Ireland* **13 D5** 52 7N 6 56W
Hook I., *Australia* **62 C4** 20 4S 149 0 E
Hook of Holland = Hoek van Holland, *Neths.* **15 C4** 52 0N 4 7 E
Hooker, *U.S.A.* **81 G4** 36 52N 101 13W
Hooker Creek, *Australia* **60 C5** 18 23S 130 38 E
Hoonah, *U.S.A.* **72 B1** 58 7N 135 27W
Hooper Bay, *U.S.A.* **68 B3** 61 32N 166 6W
Hoopeston, *U.S.A.* **76 E2** 40 28N 87 40W
Hoopstad, *S. Africa* **56 D4** 27 50S 25 55 E
Hoorn, *Neths.* **15 B5** 52 38N 5 4 E
Hoover, *U.S.A.* **77 J2** 33 20N 86 11W
Hoover Dam, *U.S.A.* **85 K12** 36 1N 114 44W
Hooversville, *U.S.A.* **78 F6** 40 9N 78 55W
Hop Bottom, *U.S.A.* **79 E9** 41 42N 75 46W
Hope, *Canada* **72 D4** 49 25N 121 25W
Hope, *Ariz., U.S.A.* **85 M13** 33 43N 113 42W
Hope, *Ark., U.S.A.* **81 J8** 33 40N 93 36
Hope, L., *S. Austral., Australia* **63 D2** 28 24S 139 18
Hope, L., *W. Austral., Australia* **61 F3** 32 35S 120 15
Hope I., *Canada* **78 B4** 44 55N 80 11
Hope Town, *Bahamas* **88 A4** 26 35N 76 57
Hopedale, *Canada* **71 A7** 55 28N 60 13
Hopedale, *U.S.A.* **79 D13** 42 8N 71 33
Hopefield, *S. Africa* **56 E2** 33 3S 18 22
Hopei = Hebei □, *China* **34 E9** 39 0N 116 0
Hopelchén, *Mexico* **87 D7** 19 46N 89 50
Hopetoun, *Vic., Australia* **63 F3** 35 42S 142 22
Hopetoun, *W. Austral., Australia* **61 F3** 33 57S 120 7
Hopetown, *S. Africa* **56 D3** 29 34S 24 3
Hopevale, *Australia* **62 B4** 15 16S 145 20
Hopewell, *U.S.A.* **76 G7** 37 18N 77 17
Hopkins, L., *Australia* **60 D4** 24 15S 128 35
Hopkinsville, *U.S.A.* **77 G2** 36 52N 87 29
Hopland, *U.S.A.* **84 G3** 38 58N 123 7
Hoquiam, *U.S.A.* **84 D3** 46 59N 123 53
Horden Hills, *Australia* **60 D5** 20 15S 130 0
Horinger, *China* **34 D6** 40 28N 111 48
Horlick Mts., *Antarctica* **5 E15** 84 0S 102 0
Horlivka, *Ukraine* **25 E6** 48 19N 38 5
Hormak, *Iran* **45 D9** 29 58N 60 51
Hormoz, *Iran* **45 E7** 27 35N 55 0
Hormoz, Jaz.-ye, *Iran* **45 E8** 27 8N 56 28
Hormozgān □, *Iran* **45 E8** 27 30N 56 0
Hormuz, Kūh-e, *Iran* **45 E7** 27 27N 55 10
Hormuz, Str. of, *The Gulf* **45 E8** 26 30N 56 30
Horn, *Austria* **16 D8** 48 39N 15 40
Horn, *Iceland* **8 C2** 66 28N 22 28
Horn →, *Canada* **72 A5** 61 30N 118 1
Horn, Cape = Hornos, C. de, *Chile* **96 H3** 55 50S 67 30
Horn Head, *Ireland* **13 A3** 55 14N 8 0
Horn I., *Australia* **62 A3** 10 37S 142 17
Horn Mts., *Canada* **72 A5** 62 15N 119 15
Hornavan, *Sweden* **8 C17** 66 15N 17 30
Hornbeck, *U.S.A.* **81 K8** 31 20N 93 24
Hornbrook, *U.S.A.* **82 F2** 41 55N 122 33
Horncastle, *U.K.* **10 D7** 53 13N 0 7
Hornell, *U.S.A.* **78 D7** 42 20N 77 40
Hornell L., *Canada* **72 A5** 62 20N 119 25
Hornepayne, *Canada* **70 C3** 49 14N 84 48
Hornings Mills, *Canada* **78 B4** 44 9N 80 12
Hornitos, *U.S.A.* **84 H6** 37 30N 120 14
Hornos, C. de, *Chile* **96 H3** 55 50S 67 30
Hornsea, *U.K.* **10 D7** 53 55N 0 11
Horobetsu, *Japan* **30 C10** 42 24N 141 6
Horodenka, *Ukraine* **17 D13** 48 41N 25 29
Horodok, *Khmelnytskyy, Ukraine* **17 D14** 49 10N 26 34
Horodok, *Lviv, Ukraine* **17 D12** 49 46N 23 32
Horokhiv, *Ukraine* **17 C13** 50 30N 24 45
Horqin Youyi Qianqi, *China* **35 A12** 46 5N 122 3
Horqueta, *Paraguay* **94 A4** 23 15S 56 55
Horse Creek, *U.S.A.* **80 E3** 41 57N 105 10
Horse Is., *Canada* **71 B8** 50 15N 55 50
Horsefly L., *Canada* **72 C4** 52 25N 121 0
Horseheads, *U.S.A.* **78 D8** 42 10N 76 49
Horsens, *Denmark* **9 J13** 55 52N 9 51
Horsham, *Australia* **63 F3** 36 44S 142 13
Horsham, *U.K.* **11 F7** 51 4N 0 20
Horten, *Norway* **9 G14** 59 25N 10 32
Horton, *U.S.A.* **80 F7** 39 40N 95 32
Horton →, *Canada* **68 B7** 69 56N 126 52
Horwood L., *Canada* **70 C3** 48 5N 82 20
Hose, Gunung-Gunung, *Malaysia* **36 D4** 2 5N 114 6
Ḥoseynābād, *Khuzestān, Iran* **45 C6** 32 45N 48 20
Ḥoseynābād, *Kordestān, Iran* **44 C5** 35 33N 47 8
Hoshangabad, *India* **42 H7** 22 45N 77 45
Hoshiarpur, *India* **42 D6** 31 30N 75 58
Hospet, *India* **40 M10** 15 15N 76 20
Hoste, I., *Chile* **96 H3** 55 0S 69 0
Hot, *Thailand* **38 C2** 18 8N 98 29
Hot Creek Range, *U.S.A.* **82 G6** 38 40N 116 20
Hot Springs, *Ark., U.S.A.* **81 H8** 34 31N 93 3
Hot Springs, *S. Dak., U.S.A.* **80 D3** 43 26N 103 29
Hotagen, *Sweden* **8 E16** 63 50N 14 30
Hotan, *China* **32 C2** 37 25N 79 55
Hotazel, *S. Africa* **56 D3** 27 17S 22 58
Hotchkiss, *U.S.A.* **83 G10** 38 48N 107 43
Hotham, C., *Australia* **60 B5** 12 2S 131 18
Hoting, *Sweden* **8 D17** 64 8N 16 15
Hotte, Massif de la, *Haiti* **89 C5** 18 30N 73 45
Hottentotsbaai, *Namibia* **56 D1** 26 8S 14 59
Houffalize, *Belgium* **15 D5** 50 8N 5 48
Houghton, *Mich., U.S.A.* **80 B10** 47 7N 88 34
Houghton, *N.Y., U.S.A.* **78 D6** 42 25N 78 10
Houghton L., *U.S.A.* **76 C3** 44 21N 84 44
Houhora Heads, *N.Z.* **59 F4** 34 49S 173 9
Houlton, *U.S.A.* **77 B12** 46 8N 67 51
Houma, *U.S.A.* **81 L9** 29 36N 90 43
Housatonic →, *U.S.A.* **79 E11** 41 10N 73 7
Houston, *Canada* **72 C3** 54 25N 126 39
Houston, *Mo., U.S.A.* **81 G9** 37 22N 91 58
Houston, *Tex., U.S.A.* **81 L7** 29 46N 95 22
Houtman Abrolhos, *Australia* **61 E1** 28 43S 113 48
Hovd, *Mongolia* **32 B4** 48 2N 91 37
Hove, *U.K.* **11 G7** 50 50N 0 10
Hoveyzeh, *Iran* **45 D6** 31 27N 48 4
Hövsgöl, *Mongolia* **34 C5** 43 37N 109 39
Hövsgöl Nuur, *Mongolia* **32 A5** 51 0N 100 30
Howard, *Australia* **63 D5** 25 16S 152 32
Howard, *Pa., U.S.A.* **78 F7** 41 1N 77 40
Howard, *S. Dak., U.S.A.* **80 C6** 44 1N 97 32
Howe, *U.S.A.* **82 E7** 43 48N 113 0
Howe, C., *Australia* **63 F5** 37 30S 150 0
Howe I., *Canada* **79 B8** 44 16N 76 17
Howell, *U.S.A.* **76 D4** 42 36N 83 56
Howick, *Canada* **79 A11** 45 11N 73 51
Howick, *S. Africa* **57 D5** 29 28S 30 14
Howick Group, *Australia* **62 A4** 14 20S 145 30
Howitt, L., *Australia* **63 D2** 27 40S 138 40
Howland I., *Pac. Oc.* **64 G10** 0 48N 176 38
Howrah = Haora, *India* **43 H13** 22 37N 88 20
Howth Hd., *Ireland* **13 C5** 53 22N 6 3
Höxter, *Germany* **16 C5** 51 46N 9 22
Hoy, *U.K.* **12 C5** 58 50N 3 15
Høyanger, *Norway* **9 F12** 61 13N 6 4

Indonesia

yerswerda, *Germany* **16 C8** 51 26N 14 14 E
ylake, *U.K.* **10 D4** 53 24N 3 10W
ungan Pass, *Burma* **41 F20** 27 30N 96 55 E
adec Králové, *Czech Rep.* **16 C8** 50 15N 15 50 E
odna, *Belarus* **17 B12** 53 42N 23 52 E
odzyanka, *Belarus* **17 B15** 53 31N 28 42 E
on →, *Slovak Rep.* **17 E10** 47 49N 18 45 E
vatska = Croatia ■, *Europe* **16 F9** 45 20N 16 0 E
ymayliv, *Ukraine* **17 D14** 49 20N 26 5 E
enwi, *Burma* **41 H20** 23 22N 97 55 E
iamen = Xiamen, *China* **33 D6** 24 25N 118 4 E
ian = Xi'an, *China* **34 G5** 34 15N 109 0 E
inchu, *Taiwan* **33 D7** 24 48N 120 58 E
inhailien = Lianyungang, *China* **35 G10** 34 40N 119 11 E
üchou = Xuzhou, *China* **35 G9** 34 18N 117 10 E
Xian, *China* **34 G5** 34 8N 108 42 E
a Hin, *Thailand* **38 F2** 12 34N 99 58 E
a Xian, *Henan, China* **34 G8** 35 30N 114 30 E
a Xian, *Shaanxi, China* **34 G5** 34 30N 109 48 E
achinera, *Mexico* **86 A3** 30 9N 108 55W
acho, *Peru* **92 F3** 11 10S 77 35W
ade, *China* **34 D7** 41 55N 113 59 E
adian, *China* **35 C14** 43 0N 126 40 E
ai He →, *China* **33 C6** 33 0N 118 30 E
ai Yot, *Thailand* **39 J2** 7 45N 99 37 E
ai'an, *Hebei, China* **34 D8** 40 30N 114 20 E
ai'an, *Jiangsu, China* **35 H10** 33 30N 119 10 E
aibei, *China* **34 G9** 34 0N 116 48 E
aide = Gongzhuling, *China* **35 C13** 43 30N 124 40 E
aidezhen, *China* **35 C13** 43 48N 124 50 E
ainan, *China* **33 C6** 32 38N 116 58 E
airen, *China* **34 E7** 39 48N 113 20 E
airou, *China* **34 D9** 40 20N 116 35 E
aiyang, *China* **34 H8** 33 40N 114 52 E
aiyin, *China* **35 H10** 33 30N 119 2 E
aiyuan, *China* **35 H9** 32 55N 117 10 E
ajianzi, *China* **35 D13** 41 23N 125 20 E
ajuapan de Leon, *Mexico* **87 D5** 17 50N 97 48W
alapai Peak, *U.S.A.* **83 J7** 35 5N 113 54W
allaga →, *Peru* **92 E3** 5 15S 75 30W
ambo, *Angola* **53 G3** 12 42S 15 54 E
an Jiang →, *China* **34 G5** 34 28N 109 0 E
an Xian, *China* **34 F4** 36 33N 107 7 E
ancabamba, *Peru* **92 E3** 5 10S 79 15W
ancane, *Peru* **92 G5** 15 10S 69 44W
ancavelica, *Peru* **92 F3** 12 50S 75 5W
ancayo, *Peru* **92 F3** 12 5S 75 12W
anchaca, *Bolivia* **92 H5** 20 15S 66 40W
ang Hai = Yellow Sea, *China* **35 G12** 35 0N 123 0 E
ang He →, *China* **35 F10** 37 55N 118 50 E
ang Xian, *China* **35 F11** 37 38N 120 30 E
angling, *China* **34 G5** 35 34N 109 15 E
anglong, *China* **34 G5** 35 30N 109 59 E
angshan, *China* **33 D6** 29 42N 118 25 E
angshi, *China* **33 C6** 30 10N 115 3 E
angsongdian, *China* **35 C14** 43 45N 127 25 E
antai, *China* **35 F9** 36 58N 117 56 E
ánuco, *Peru* **92 E3** 9 55S 76 15W
araz, *Peru* **92 E3** 9 30S 77 32W
armey, *Peru* **92 F3** 10 5S 78 5W
ascarán, *Peru* **92 E3** 9 8S 77 36W
asco, *Chile* **94 B1** 28 30S 71 15W
asco →, *Chile* **94 B1** 28 27S 71 13W
asna, *U.S.A.* **85 K6** 35 6N 120 24W
atabampo, *Mexico* **86 B3** 26 50N 109 50W
auchinango, *Mexico* **87 C5** 20 11N 98 3W
autla de Jiménez, *Mexico* **87 D5** 18 8N 96 51W
ay Namota, *Mexico* **86 C4** 21 56N 104 30W
ayin, *China* **34 G6** 34 35N 110 5 E
bbard, *Ohio, U.S.A.* **78 E4** 41 9N 80 34W
bbard, *Tex., U.S.A.* **81 K6** 31 51N 96 48W
bbart Pt., *Canada* **73 B10** 59 21N 94 41W
bei □, *China* **33 C6** 31 0N 112 0 E
bli, *India* **40 M9** 15 22N 75 15 E
ch'ang, *N. Korea* **35 D14** 41 25N 127 2 E
cknall, *U.K.* **10 D6** 53 3N 1 13W
ddersfield, *U.K.* **10 D6** 53 39N 1 47W
diksvall, *Sweden* **9 F17** 61 43N 17 10 E
dson, *Canada* **70 B1** 50 6N 92 9W
dson, *Mass., U.S.A.* **79 D13** 42 23N 71 34W
dson, *N.Y., U.S.A.* **79 D11** 42 15N 73 46W
dson, *Wis., U.S.A.* **80 C8** 44 58N 92 45W
dson, *Wyo., U.S.A.* **82 E9** 42 54N 108 35W
dson →, *U.S.A.* **79 F10** 40 42N 74 2W
dson Bay, *N.W.T., Canada* **69 C11** 60 0N 86 0W
dson Bay, *Sask., Canada* **73 C8** 52 51N 102 23W
dson Falls, *U.S.A.* **79 C11** 43 18N 73 35W
dson Mts., *Antarctica* **5 D16** 74 32S 99 20W
dson Str., *Canada* **69 B13** 62 0N 70 0W
dson's Hope, *Canada* **72 B4** 56 0N 121 54W
e, *Vietnam* **38 D6** 16 30N 107 35 E
ehuetenango, *Guatemala* **88 C1** 15 20N 91 28W
ejúcar, *Mexico* **86 C4** 22 21N 103 13W
elva, *Spain* **19 D2** 37 18N 6 57W
entelauquén, *Chile* **94 C1** 31 38S 71 33W
erta, Sa. de la, *Argentina* **94 C2** 31 10S 67 30W
esca, *Spain* **19 A5** 42 8N 0 25W
etamo, *Mexico* **86 D4** 18 36N 100 54W
gh →, *Australia* **62 D1** 25 1S 134 1 E
ghenden, *Australia* **62 C3** 20 52S 144 10 E
ghes, *Australia* **61 F4** 30 42S 129 31 E
ghesville, *U.S.A.* **79 E8** 41 14N 76 44W
gli →, *India* **43 J13** 21 56N 88 4 E
go, *Colo., U.S.A.* **80 F3** 39 8N 103 28W
go, *Okla., U.S.A.* **81 H7** 34 1N 95 31W
goton, *U.S.A.* **81 G4** 37 11N 101 21W
Xian = Huixian, *China* **34 G7** 35 27N 113 12 E
Xian, *China* **34 H4** 33 50N 106 4 E
'anbu, *China* **34 F4** 37 28N 106 38 E
chapán, *Mexico* **87 C5** 20 24N 99 40W
fa He →, *China* **35 C14** 43 0N 127 50 E
la, Nevado del, *Colombia* **92 C3** 3 0N 76 0W
min, *China* **35 F9** 37 27N 117 28 E
inan, *China* **35 C14** 42 40N 126 2 E
inca Renancó, *Argentina* **94 C3** 34 51S 64 22W
ining, *China* **34 G3** 35 38N 105 0 E
inong, *China* **34 E4** 39 5N 106 35 E
isache, *Mexico* **86 C4** 22 55N 100 25W
iting, *China* **34 G9** 34 5N 116 5 E
ixian, *China* **34 G7** 35 27N 113 12 E
ixtla, *Mexico* **87 D6** 15 9N 92 28W
Huize, *China* **32 D5** 26 24N 103 15 E
Hukawng Valley, *Burma* **41 F20** 26 30N 96 30 E
Hukuntsi, *Botswana* **56 C3** 23 58S 21 45 E
Ḥulayfā', *Si. Arabia* **44 E4** 25 58N 40 45 E
Huld = Ulaanjirem, *Mongolia* **34 B3** 45 5N 105 30 E
Hulin He →, *China* **35 B12** 45 0N 122 10 E
Hull = Kingston upon Hull, *U.K.* **10 D7** 53 45N 0 21W
Hull, *Canada* **79 A9** 45 25N 75 44W
Hull →, *U.K.* **10 D7** 53 44N 0 20W
Hulst, *Neths.* **15 C4** 51 17N 4 2 E
Hulun Nur, *China* **33 B6** 49 0N 117 30 E
Humahuaca, *Argentina* **94 A2** 23 10S 65 25W
Humaitá, *Brazil* **92 E6** 7 35S 63 1W
Humaitá, *Paraguay* **94 B4** 27 2S 58 31W
Humansdorp, *S. Africa* **56 E3** 34 2S 24 46 E
Humbe, *Angola* **56 B1** 16 40S 14 55 E
Humber →, *U.K.* **10 D7** 53 42N 0 27W
Humboldt, *Canada* **73 C7** 52 15N 105 9W
Humboldt, *Iowa, U.S.A.* **80 D7** 42 44N 94 13W
Humboldt, *Tenn., U.S.A.* **81 H10** 35 50N 88 55W
Humboldt →, *U.S.A.* **82 F4** 39 59N 118 36W
Humboldt Gletscher, *Greenland* **4 B4** 79 30N 62 0W
Hume, *U.S.A.* **84 J8** 36 48N 118 54W
Hume, L., *Australia* **63 F4** 36 0S 147 5 E
Humenné, *Slovak Rep.* **17 D11** 48 55N 21 50 E
Humphreys, Mt., *U.S.A.* **84 H8** 37 17N 118 40W
Humphreys Peak, *U.S.A.* **83 J8** 35 21N 111 41W
Humptulips, *U.S.A.* **84 C3** 47 14N 123 57W
Hūn, *Libya* **51 C9** 29 2N 16 0 E
Hun Jiang →, *China* **35 D13** 40 50N 125 38 E
Húnaflói, *Iceland* **8 D3** 65 50N 20 50W
Hunan □, *China* **33 D6** 27 30N 112 0 E
Hunchun, *China* **35 C16** 42 52N 130 28 E
Hundewali, *Pakistan* **42 D5** 31 55N 72 38 E
Hundred Mile House, *Canada* **72 C4** 51 38N 121 18W
Hunedoara, *Romania* **17 F12** 45 40N 22 50 E
Hungary ■, *Europe* **17 E10** 47 20N 19 20 E
Hungary, Plain of, *Europe* **6 F10** 47 0N 20 0 E
Hungerford, *Australia* **63 D3** 28 58S 144 24 E
Hŭngnam, *N. Korea* **35 E14** 39 49N 127 45 E
Hunsberge, *Namibia* **56 D2** 27 45S 17 12 E
Hunsrück, *Germany* **16 D4** 49 56N 7 27 E
Hunstanton, *U.K.* **10 E8** 52 56N 0 29 E
Hunter, *U.S.A.* **79 D10** 42 13N 74 13W
Hunter I., *Australia* **62 G3** 40 30S 144 45 E
Hunter I., *Canada* **72 C3** 51 55N 128 0W
Hunter Ra., *Australia* **63 E5** 32 45S 150 15 E
Hunters Road, *Zimbabwe* **55 F2** 19 9S 29 49 E
Hunterville, *N.Z.* **59 H5** 39 56S 175 35 E
Huntingburg, *U.S.A.* **76 F2** 38 18N 86 57W
Huntingdon, *Canada* **70 C5** 45 6N 74 10W
Huntingdon, *U.K.* **11 E7** 52 20N 0 11W
Huntingdon, *U.S.A.* **78 F6** 40 30N 78 1W
Huntington, *Ind., U.S.A.* **76 E3** 40 53N 85 30W
Huntington, *Oreg., U.S.A.* **82 D5** 44 21N 117 16W
Huntington, *Utah, U.S.A.* **82 G8** 39 20N 110 58W
Huntington, *W. Va., U.S.A.* **76 F4** 38 25N 82 27W
Huntington Beach, *U.S.A.* **85 M9** 33 40N 118 5W
Huntington Station, *U.S.A.* **79 F11** 40 52N 73 26W
Huntly, *N.Z.* **59 G5** 37 34S 175 11 E
Huntly, *U.K.* **12 D6** 57 27N 2 47W
Huntsville, *Canada* **78 A5** 45 20N 79 14W
Huntsville, *Ala., U.S.A.* **77 H2** 34 44N 86 35W
Huntsville, *Tex., U.S.A.* **81 K7** 30 43N 95 33W
Hunyani →, *Zimbabwe* **55 F3** 15 57S 30 39 E
Hunyuan, *China* **34 E7** 39 42N 113 42 E
Hunza →, *India* **43 B6** 35 54N 74 20 E
Huo Xian = Huozhou, *China* **34 F6** 36 36N 111 42 E
Huong Hoa, *Vietnam* **38 D6** 16 37N 106 45 E
Huong Khe, *Vietnam* **38 C5** 18 13N 105 41 E
Huonville, *Australia* **62 G4** 43 0S 147 5 E
Huozhou, *China* **34 F6** 36 36N 111 42 E
Hupeh = Hubei □, *China* **33 C6** 31 0N 112 0 E
Ḥūr, *Iran* **45 D8** 30 50N 57 7 E
Hurd, C., *Canada* **78 A3** 45 13N 81 44W
Hure Qi, *China* **35 C11** 42 45N 121 45 E
Hurghada, *Egypt* **51 C12** 27 15N 33 50 E
Hurley, *N. Mex., U.S.A.* **83 K9** 32 42N 108 8W
Hurley, *Wis., U.S.A.* **80 B9** 46 27N 90 11W
Huron, *Calif., U.S.A.* **84 J6** 36 12N 120 6W
Huron, *Ohio, U.S.A.* **78 E2** 41 24N 82 33W
Huron, *S. Dak., U.S.A.* **80 C5** 44 22N 98 13W
Huron, L., *U.S.A.* **78 B2** 44 30N 82 40W
Hurricane, *U.S.A.* **83 H7** 37 11N 113 17W
Hurunui →, *N.Z.* **59 K4** 42 54S 173 18 E
Húsavík, *Iceland* **8 C5** 66 3N 17 21W
Huşi, *Romania* **17 E15** 46 41N 28 7 E
Huskvarna, *Sweden* **9 H16** 57 47N 14 15 E
Hustadvika, *Norway* **8 E12** 63 0N 7 0 E
Hustontown, *U.S.A.* **78 F6** 40 3N 78 2W
Hutchinson, *Kans., U.S.A.* **81 F6** 38 5N 97 56W
Hutchinson, *Minn., U.S.A.* **80 C7** 44 54N 94 22W
Hutte Sauvage, L. de la, *Canada* **71 A7** 56 15N 64 45W
Hutton, Mt., *Australia* **63 D4** 25 51S 148 20 E
Huy, *Belgium* **15 D5** 50 31N 5 15 E
Huzhou, *China* **33 C7** 30 51N 120 8 E
Hvammstangi, *Iceland* **8 D3** 65 24N 20 57W
Hvar, *Croatia* **20 C7** 43 11N 16 28 E
Hvítá →, *Iceland* **8 D3** 64 30N 21 58W
Hwachŏn-chŏsuji, *S. Korea* **35 E14** 38 5N 127 50 E
Hwang Ho = Huang He →, *China* **35 F10** 37 55N 118 50 E
Hwange, *Zimbabwe* **55 F2** 18 18S 26 30 E
Hwange Nat. Park, *Zimbabwe* **56 B4** 19 0S 26 30 E
Hyannis, *Mass., U.S.A.* **76 E10** 41 39N 70 17W
Hyannis, *Nebr., U.S.A.* **80 E4** 42 0N 101 46W
Hyargas Nuur, *Mongolia* **32 B4** 49 0N 93 0 E
Hydaburg, *U.S.A.* **72 B2** 55 15N 132 50W
Hyde Park, *U.S.A.* **79 E11** 41 47N 73 56W
Hyden, *Australia* **61 F2** 32 24S 118 53 E
Hyder, *U.S.A.* **72 B2** 55 55N 130 5W
Hyderabad, *India* **40 L11** 17 22N 78 29 E
Hyderabad, *Pakistan* **42 G3** 25 23N 68 24 E
Hyères, *France* **18 E7** 43 8N 6 9 E
Hyères, Îs. d', *France* **18 E7** 43 0N 6 20 E
Hyesan, *N. Korea* **35 D15** 41 20N 128 10 E
Hyland →, *Canada* **72 B3** 59 52N 128 12W
Hymia, *India* **43 C8** 33 40N 78 2 E
Hyndman Peak, *U.S.A.* **82 E6** 43 45N 114 8W
Hyōgo □, *Japan* **31 G7** 35 15N 134 50 E
Hyrum, *U.S.A.* **82 F8** 41 38N 111 51W
Hysham, *U.S.A.* **82 C10** 46 18N 107 14W
Hythe, *U.K.* **11 F9** 51 4N 1 5 E
Hyūga, *Japan* **31 H5** 32 25N 131 35 E
Hyvinge = Hyvinkää, *Finland* **9 F21** 60 38N 24 50 E
Hyvinkää, *Finland* **9 F21** 60 38N 24 50 E

I

I-n-Gall, *Niger* **50 E7** 16 51N 7 1 E
Iaco →, *Brazil* **92 E5** 9 3S 68 34W
Iakora, *Madag.* **57 C8** 23 6S 46 40 E
Ialomiţa →, *Romania* **17 F14** 44 42N 27 51 E
Iaşi, *Romania* **17 E14** 47 10N 27 40 E
Ib →, *India* **43 J10** 21 34N 83 48 E
Iba, *Phil.* **37 A6** 15 22N 120 0 E
Ibadan, *Nigeria* **50 G6** 7 22N 3 58 E
Ibagué, *Colombia* **92 C3** 4 20N 75 20W
Ibar →, *Serbia, Yug.* **21 C9** 43 43N 20 45 E
Ibaraki □, *Japan* **31 F10** 36 10N 140 10 E
Ibarra, *Ecuador* **92 C3** 0 21N 78 7W
Ibembo, *Dem. Rep. of the Congo* **54 B1** 2 35N 23 35 E
Ibera, L., *Argentina* **94 B4** 28 30S 57 9W
Iberian Peninsula, *Europe* **6 H5** 40 0N 5 0W
Iberville, *Canada* **79 A11** 45 19N 73 17W
Iberville, Lac d', *Canada* **70 A5** 55 55N 73 15W
Ibiá, *Brazil* **93 G9** 19 30S 46 30W
Ibicuí →, *Brazil* **95 B4** 29 25S 56 47W
Ibicuy, *Argentina* **94 C4** 33 55S 59 10W
Ibioapaba, Sa. da, *Brazil* **93 D10** 4 0S 41 30W
Ibiza = Eivissa, *Spain* **22 C7** 38 54N 1 26 E
Ibo, *Mozam.* **55 E5** 12 22S 40 40 E
Ibonma, *Indonesia* **37 E8** 3 29S 133 31 E
Ibotirama, *Brazil* **93 F10** 12 13S 43 12W
Ibrāhīm →, *Lebanon* **47 A4** 34 4N 35 38 E
'Ibrī, *Oman* **45 F8** 23 14N 56 30 E
Ibu, *Indonesia* **37 D7** 1 35N 127 33 E
Ibusuki, *Japan* **31 J5** 31 12N 130 40 E
Ica, *Peru* **92 F3** 14 0S 75 48W
Içá →, *Brazil* **92 D5** 2 55S 67 58W
Içana, *Brazil* **92 C5** 0 21N 67 19W
Içana →, *Brazil* **92 C5** 0 26N 67 19W
Içel = Mersin, *Turkey* **25 G5** 36 51N 34 36 E
Iceland ■, *Europe* **8 D4** 64 45N 19 0W
Ich'ang = Yichang, *China* **33 C6** 30 40N 111 20 E
Ichchapuram, *India* **41 K14** 19 10N 84 40 E
Ichhawar, *India* **42 H7** 23 1N 77 1 E
Ichihara, *Japan* **31 G10** 35 28N 140 5 E
Ichikawa, *Japan* **31 G9** 35 44N 139 55 E
Ichilo →, *Bolivia* **92 G6** 15 57S 64 50W
Ichinohe, *Japan* **30 D10** 40 13N 141 17 E
Ichinomiya, *Japan* **31 G8** 35 18N 136 48 E
Ichinoseki, *Japan* **30 E10** 38 55N 141 8 E
Ichŏn, *S. Korea* **35 F14** 37 17N 127 27 E
Icod, *Canary Is.* **22 F3** 28 22N 16 43W
Ida Grove, *U.S.A.* **80 D7** 42 21N 95 28W
Idabel, *U.S.A.* **81 J7** 33 54N 94 50W
Idaho □, *U.S.A.* **82 D7** 45 0N 115 0W
Idaho City, *U.S.A.* **82 E6** 43 50N 115 50W
Idaho Falls, *U.S.A.* **82 E7** 43 30N 112 2W
Idar-Oberstein, *Germany* **16 D4** 49 43N 7 16 E
Idfû, *Egypt* **51 D12** 24 55N 32 49 E
Ídhi Óros, *Greece* **23 D6** 35 15N 24 45 E
Ídhra, *Greece* **21 F10** 37 20N 23 28 E
Idi, *Indonesia* **36 C1** 5 2N 97 37 E
Idiofa, *Dem. Rep. of the Congo* **52 E3** 4 55S 19 42 E
Idlib, *Syria* **44 C3** 35 55N 36 36 E
Idria, *U.S.A.* **84 J6** 36 25N 120 41W
Idutywa, *S. Africa* **57 E4** 32 8S 28 18 E
Ieper, *Belgium* **15 D2** 50 51N 2 53 E
Ierápetra, *Greece* **23 E7** 35 1N 25 44 E
Iesi, *Italy* **20 C5** 43 31N 13 14 E
Ifakara, *Tanzania* **52 F7** 8 8S 36 41 E
'Ifāl, W. al →, *Si. Arabia* **44 D2** 28 7N 35 3 E
Ifanadiana, *Madag.* **57 C8** 21 19S 47 39 E
Ife, *Nigeria* **50 G6** 7 30N 4 31 E
Iférouâne, *Niger* **50 E7** 19 5N 8 24 E
Iffley, *Australia* **62 B3** 18 53S 141 12 E
Ifni, *Morocco* **50 C3** 29 29N 10 12W
Iforas, Adrar des, *Mali* **50 E6** 19 40N 1 40 E
Ifould, L., *Australia* **61 F5** 30 52S 132 6 E
Iganga, *Uganda* **54 B3** 0 37N 33 28 E
Igarapava, *Brazil* **93 H9** 20 3S 47 47W
Igarka, *Russia* **26 C9** 67 30N 86 33 E
Igatimi, *Paraguay* **95 A4** 24 5S 55 40W
Iggesund, *Sweden* **9 F17** 61 39N 17 10 E
Iglésias, *Italy* **20 E3** 39 19N 8 32 E
Igloolik, *Canada* **69 B11** 69 20N 81 49W
Igluligaarjuk, *Canada* **69 B10** 63 21N 90 42W
Ignace, *Canada* **70 C1** 49 30N 91 40W
İğneada Burnu, *Turkey* **21 D13** 41 53N 28 2 E
Igoumenítsa, *Greece* **21 E9** 39 32N 20 18 E
Iguaçu →, *Brazil* **95 B5** 25 36S 54 36W
Iguaçu, Cat. del, *Brazil* **95 B5** 25 41S 54 26W
Iguaçu Falls = Iguaçu, Cat. del, *Brazil* **95 B5** 25 41S 54 26W
Iguala, *Mexico* **87 D5** 18 20N 99 40W
Igualada, *Spain* **19 B6** 41 37N 1 37 E
Iguassu = Iguaçu →, *Brazil* **95 B5** 25 36S 54 36W
Iguatu, *Brazil* **93 E11** 6 20S 39 18W
Iharana, *Madag.* **57 A9** 13 25S 50 0 E
Ihbulag, *Mongolia* **34 C4** 43 11N 107 10 E
Iheya-Shima, *Japan* **31 L3** 27 4N 127 58 E
Ihosy, *Madag.* **57 C8** 22 24S 46 8 E
Ihotry, L., *Madag.* **57 C7** 21 56S 43 41 E
Ii, *Finland* **8 D21** 65 19N 25 22 E
Ii-Shima, *Japan* **31 L3** 26 43N 127 47 E
Iida, *Japan* **31 G8** 35 35N 137 50 E
Iijoki →, *Finland* **8 D21** 65 20N 25 20 E
Iisalmi, *Finland* **8 E22** 63 32N 27 10 E
Iiyama, *Japan* **31 F9** 36 51N 138 22 E
Iizuka, *Japan* **31 H5** 33 38N 130 42 E
Ijebu-Ode, *Nigeria* **50 G6** 6 47N 3 58 E
IJmuiden, *Neths.* **15 B4** 52 28N 4 35 E
IJssel →, *Neths.* **15 B5** 52 35N 5 50 E
IJsselmeer, *Neths.* **15 B5** 52 45N 5 20 E
Ijuí, *Brazil* **95 B5** 28 23S 53 55W
Ijuí →, *Brazil* **95 B4** 27 58S 55 20W
Ikaluktutiak, *Canada* **68 B9** 69 10N 105 0W
Ikare, *Nigeria* **50 G7** 7 32N 5 40 E
Ikaría, *Greece* **21 F12** 37 35N 26 10 E
Ikeda, *Japan* **31 G6** 34 1N 133 48 E
Ikela, *Dem. Rep. of the Congo* **52 E4** 1 6S 23 6 E
Iki, *Japan* **31 H4** 33 45N 129 42 E
Ikimba L., *Tanzania* **54 C3** 1 30S 31 20 E
Ikopa →, *Madag.* **57 B8** 16 45S 46 40 E
Ikungu, *Tanzania* **54 C3** 1 33S 33 42 E
Ilagan, *Phil.* **37 A6** 17 7N 121 53 E
Īlām, *Iran* **44 C5** 33 36N 46 36 E
Ilam, *Nepal* **43 F12** 26 58N 87 58 E
Ilam □, *Iran* **44 C5** 33 0N 47 0 E
Ilanskiy, *Russia* **27 D10** 56 14N 96 3 E
Iława, *Poland* **17 B10** 53 36N 19 34 E
Ile-à-la-Crosse, *Canada* **73 B7** 55 27N 107 53W
Ile-à-la-Crosse, Lac, *Canada* **73 B7** 55 40N 107 45W
Île-de-France □, *France* **18 B5** 49 0N 2 20 E
Ilebo, *Dem. Rep. of the Congo* **52 E4** 4 17S 20 55 E
Ilek, *Russia* **26 D6** 51 32N 53 21 E
Ilek →, *Russia* **24 D9** 51 30N 53 22 E
Ilesha, *Nigeria* **50 G6** 7 37N 4 40 E
Ilford, *Canada* **73 B9** 56 4N 95 35W
Ilfracombe, *Australia* **62 C3** 23 30S 144 30 E
Ilfracombe, *U.K.* **11 F3** 51 12N 4 8W
Ilhéus, *Brazil* **93 F11** 14 49S 39 2W
Ili →, *Kazakstan* **26 E8** 45 53N 77 10 E
Iliamna L., *U.S.A.* **68 C4** 59 30N 155 0W
Iligan, *Phil.* **37 C6** 8 12N 124 13 E
Ilion, *U.S.A.* **79 D9** 43 1N 75 2W
Ilkeston, *U.K.* **10 E6** 52 58N 1 19W
Ilkley, *U.K.* **10 D6** 53 56N 1 48W
Illampu = Ancohuma, Nevada, *Bolivia* **92 G5** 16 0S 68 50W
Illana B., *Phil.* **37 C6** 7 35N 123 45 E
Illapel, *Chile* **94 C1** 32 0S 71 10W
Iller →, *Germany* **16 D6** 48 23N 9 58 E
Illetas, *Spain* **22 B9** 39 32N 2 35 E
Illimani, Nevado, *Bolivia* **92 G5** 16 30S 67 50W
Illinois □, *U.S.A.* **80 E10** 40 15N 89 30W
Illinois →, *U.S.A.* **75 C8** 38 58N 90 28W
Illium = Troy, *Turkey* **21 E12** 39 57N 26 12 E
Illizi, *Algeria* **50 C7** 26 31N 8 32 E
Ilmajoki, *Finland* **9 E20** 62 44N 22 34 E
Ilmen, Ozero, *Russia* **24 C5** 58 15N 31 10 E
Ilo, *Peru* **92 G4** 17 40S 71 20W
Iloilo, *Phil.* **37 B6** 10 45N 122 33 E
Ilorin, *Nigeria* **50 G6** 8 30N 4 35 E
Ilwaco, *U.S.A.* **84 D2** 46 19N 124 3W
Ilwaki, *Indonesia* **37 F7** 7 55S 126 30 E
Imabari, *Japan* **31 G6** 34 4N 133 0 E
Imaloto →, *Madag.* **57 C8** 23 27S 45 13 E
Imandra, Ozero, *Russia* **24 A5** 67 30N 33 0 E
Imari, *Japan* **31 H4** 33 15N 129 52 E
Imatra, *Finland* **24 B4** 61 12N 28 48 E
Imbil, *Australia* **63 D5** 26 22S 152 32 E
imeni 26 Bakinskikh Komissarov = Neftçala, *Azerbaijan* **25 G8** 39 19N 49 12 E
Imeri, Serra, *Brazil* **92 C5** 0 50N 65 25W
Imerimandroso, *Madag.* **57 B8** 17 26S 48 35 E
Imi, *Ethiopia* **46 F3** 6 28N 42 10 E
Imlay, *U.S.A.* **82 F4** 40 40N 118 9W
Imlay City, *U.S.A.* **78 D1** 43 2N 83 5W
Immingham, *U.K.* **10 D7** 53 37N 0 13W
Immokalee, *U.S.A.* **77 M5** 26 25N 81 25W
Ímola, *Italy* **20 B4** 44 20N 11 42 E
Imperatriz, *Brazil* **93 E9** 5 30S 47 29W
Impéria, *Italy* **18 E8** 43 53N 8 3 E
Imperial, *Canada* **73 C7** 51 21N 105 28W
Imperial, *Calif., U.S.A.* **85 N11** 32 51N 115 34W
Imperial, *Nebr., U.S.A.* **80 E4** 40 31N 101 39W
Imperial Beach, *U.S.A.* **85 N9** 32 35N 117 8W
Imperial Dam, *U.S.A.* **85 N12** 32 55N 114 25W
Imperial Reservoir, *U.S.A.* **85 N12** 32 53N 114 28W
Imperial Valley, *U.S.A.* **85 N11** 33 0N 115 30W
Imperieuse Reef, *Australia* **60 C2** 17 36S 118 50 E
Impfondo, *Congo* **52 D3** 1 40N 18 0 E
Imphal, *India* **41 G18** 24 48N 93 56 E
İmroz = Gökçeada, *Turkey* **21 D11** 40 10N 25 50 E
Imuris, *Mexico* **86 A2** 30 47N 110 52W
Imuruan B., *Phil.* **37 B5** 10 40N 119 10 E
In Salah, *Algeria* **50 C6** 27 10N 2 32 E
Ina, *Japan* **31 G8** 35 50N 137 55 E
Inangahua Junction, *N.Z.* **59 J3** 41 52S 171 59 E
Inanwatan, *Indonesia* **37 E8** 2 10S 132 14 E
Iñapari, *Peru* **92 F5** 11 0S 69 40W
Inari, *Finland* **8 B22** 68 54N 27 5 E
Inarijärvi, *Finland* **8 B22** 69 0N 28 0 E
Inawashiro-Ko, *Japan* **30 F10** 37 29N 140 6 E
Inca, *Spain* **22 B9** 39 43N 2 54 E
Inca de Oro, *Chile* **94 B2** 26 45S 69 54W
Incaguasi, *Chile* **94 B1** 29 12S 71 5W
İnce Burun, *Turkey* **25 F5** 42 7N 34 56 E
İncesu, *Turkey* **44 B2** 38 38N 35 11 E
Inch'ŏn, *S. Korea* **35 F14** 37 27N 126 40 E
İncirliova, *Turkey* **21 F12** 37 50N 27 41 E
Incline Village, *U.S.A.* **82 G4** 39 10N 119 58W
Incomáti →, *Mozam.* **57 D5** 25 46S 32 43 E
Indalsälven →, *Sweden* **9 E17** 62 36N 17 30 E
Indaw, *Burma* **41 G20** 24 15N 96 5 E
Independence, *Calif., U.S.A.* **84 J8** 36 48N 118 12W
Independence, *Iowa, U.S.A.* **80 D9** 42 28N 91 54W
Independence, *Kans., U.S.A.* **81 G7** 37 14N 95 42W
Independence, *Ky., U.S.A.* **76 F3** 38 57N 84 33W
Independence, *Mo., U.S.A.* **80 F7** 39 6N 94 25W
Independence Fjord, *Greenland* **4 A6** 82 10N 29 0W
Independence Mts., *U.S.A.* **82 F5** 41 20N 116 0W
Index, *U.S.A.* **84 C5** 47 50N 121 33W
India ■, *Asia* **40 K11** 20 0N 78 0 E
Indian →, *U.S.A.* **77 M5** 27 59N 80 34W
Indian Cabins, *Canada* **72 B5** 59 52N 117 40W
Indian Harbour, *Canada* **71 B8** 54 27N 57 13W
Indian Head, *Canada* **73 C8** 50 30N 103 41W
Indian Lake, *U.S.A.* **79 C10** 43 47N 74 16W
Indian Ocean **28 K11** 5 0S 75 0 E
Indian Springs, *U.S.A.* **85 J11** 36 35N 115 40W
Indiana, *U.S.A.* **78 F5** 40 37N 79 9W
Indiana □, *U.S.A.* **76 F3** 40 0N 86 0W
Indianapolis, *U.S.A.* **76 F2** 39 46N 86 9W
Indianola, *Iowa, U.S.A.* **80 E8** 41 22N 93 34W
Indianola, *Miss., U.S.A.* **81 J9** 33 27N 90 39W
Indiga, *Russia* **24 A8** 67 38N 49 9 E
Indigirka →, *Russia* **27 B15** 70 48N 148 54 E
Indio, *U.S.A.* **85 M10** 33 43N 116 13W
Indo-China, *Asia* **28 H14** 15 0N 102 0 E
Indonesia ■, *Asia* **36 F5** 5 0S 115 0 E

Juruena

alūlā, Iraq 44 C5 34 16N 45 10 E
amaica ■, W. Indies 88 C4 18 10N 77 30W
amalpur, Bangla. 41 G16 24 52N 89 56 E
amalpur, India 43 G12 25 18N 86 28 E
amalpurganj, India 43 H13 23 2N 87 59 E
amanxim →, Brazil 93 D7 4 43S 56 18W
ambi, Indonesia 36 E2 1 38S 103 30 E
ambi □, Indonesia 36 E2 1 30S 102 30 E
ambusar, India 42 H5 22 3N 72 51 E
ames →, S. Dak., U.S.A. 80 D6 42 52N 97 18W
ames →, Va., U.S.A. 76 G7 36 56N 76 27W
ames B., Canada 70 B3 54 0N 80 0W
ames Ranges, Australia 60 D5 24 10S 132 30 E
ames Ross I., Antarctica 5 C18 63 58S 57 50W
amesabad, Pakistan 42 G3 25 17N 69 15 E
amestown, Australia 63 E2 33 10S 138 32 E
amestown, S. Africa 56 E4 31 6S 26 45 E
amestown, N. Dak., U.S.A. 80 B5 46 54N 98 42W
amestown, N.Y., U.S.A. 78 D5 42 6N 79 14W
amestown, Pa., U.S.A. 78 E4 41 29N 80 27W
amīlābād, Iran 45 C6 34 24N 48 28 E
amiltepec, Mexico 87 D5 16 17N 97 49W
amira →, India 43 J13 21 35N 88 28 E
amkhandi, India 40 L9 16 30N 75 15 E
ammu, India 42 C6 32 43N 74 54 E
ammu & Kashmir □, India 43 B7 34 25N 77 0 E
amnagar, India 42 H4 22 30N 70 6 E
amni →, India 43 G8 25 13N 78 35 E
ampur, Pakistan 42 E4 29 39N 70 40 E
amrud, Pakistan 42 C4 33 59N 71 24 E
ämsä, Finland 9 F21 61 53N 25 10 E
amshedpur, India 43 H12 22 44N 86 12 E
amtara, India 43 H12 23 59N 86 49 E
ämtland, Sweden 8 E15 63 31N 14 0 E
an L., Canada 73 C8 54 56N 102 55W
an Mayen, Arctic 4 B7 71 0N 9 0W
anakkala, Finland 9 F21 60 54N 24 36 E
anaúba, Brazil 93 G10 15 48S 43 19W
and, Pakistan 42 C5 33 30N 72 6 E
andaq, Iran 45 C7 34 3N 54 22 E
andia, Canary Is. 22 F5 28 6N 14 21W
andia, Pta. de, Canary Is. 22 F5 28 3N 14 31W
andola, Pakistan 42 C4 32 20N 70 9 E
andowae, Australia 63 D5 26 45S 151 7 E
anesville, U.S.A. 80 D10 42 41N 89 1W
anghai, India 43 G10 25 33N 82 19 E
anīn, West Bank 47 C4 32 28N 35 18 E
anjgir, India 43 J10 22 1N 82 34 E
anos, Mexico 86 A3 30 45N 108 10W
anuária, Brazil 93 G10 15 25S 44 25W
anubio, Canary Is. 22 F6 28 56N 13 50W
aora, India 42 H6 23 40N 75 10 E
apan ■, Asia 31 G8 36 0N 136 0 E
apan, Sea of, Asia 30 E7 40 0N 135 0 E
apan Trench, Pac. Oc. 28 F18 32 0N 142 0 E
apen = Yapen, Indonesia 37 E9 1 50S 136 0 E
apla, India 43 G11 24 33N 84 1 E
apurá →, Brazil 92 D5 3 8S 65 46W
aquarão, Brazil 95 C5 32 34S 53 23W
aqué, Panama 88 E4 7 27N 78 8W
arābulus, Syria 44 B3 36 49N 38 1 E
arama →, Spain 19 B4 40 24N 3 32W
aranwala, Pakistan 42 D5 31 15N 73 26 E
arash, Jordan 47 C4 32 17N 35 54 E
ardim, Brazil 94 A4 21 28S 56 2W
ardines de la Reina, Arch.
  de los, Cuba 88 B4 20 50N 78 50W
argalang, China 35 C12 43 5N 122 55 E
argalant = Hovd, Mongolia 32 B4 48 2N 91 37 E
ari →, Brazil 93 D8 1 9S 51 54W
arīr, W. al →, Si. Arabia 44 E4 25 38N 42 30 E
arosław, Poland 17 C12 50 2N 22 42 E
arrahdale, Australia 61 F2 32 24S 116 5 E
arrahi →, Iran 45 D6 30 49N 48 48 E
arres, Plaine des, Laos 38 C4 19 27N 103 10 E
artai, China 34 E3 39 45N 105 48 E
arud Qi, China 35 B11 44 28N 120 50 E
ärvenpää, Finland 9 F21 60 29N 25 5 E
arvis, Canada 78 D4 42 53N 80 6W
arvis I., Pac. Oc. 65 H12 0 15S 159 55W
arwa, India 43 F10 27 38N 82 30 E
asdan, India 42 H4 22 2N 71 12 E
ashpurnagar, India 43 H11 22 54N 84 9 E
asidih, India 43 G12 24 31N 86 39 E
āsimīyah, Iraq 44 C5 33 45N 44 41 E
asin, Malaysia 39 L4 2 20N 102 26 E
āsk, Iran 45 E8 25 38N 57 45 E
asło, Poland 17 D11 49 45N 21 30 E
aso, India 43 G9 24 30N 80 29 E
asper, Alta., Canada 72 C5 52 55N 118 5W
asper, Ont., Canada 79 B9 44 52N 75 57W
asper, Ala., U.S.A. 77 J2 33 50N 87 17W
asper, Fla., U.S.A. 77 K4 30 31N 82 57W
asper, Ind., U.S.A. 76 F2 38 24N 86 56W
asper, Tex., U.S.A. 81 K8 30 56N 94 1W
asper Nat. Park, Canada 72 C5 52 50N 118 8W
asrasar, India 42 F5 27 43N 73 49 E
ászberény, Hungary 17 E10 47 30N 19 55 E
ataí, Brazil 93 G8 17 58S 51 48W
atí, Pakistan 42 G3 24 20N 68 19 E
atibarang, Indonesia 37 G13 6 28S 108 18 E
atinegara, Indonesia 37 G12 6 13S 106 52 E
átiva = Xátiva, Spain 19 C5 38 59N 0 32W
aú, Brazil 95 A6 22 10S 48 30W
auja, Peru 92 F3 11 45S 75 15W
aunpur, India 43 G10 25 46N 82 44 E
ava = Jawa, Indonesia 37 G14 7 0S 110 0 E
ava Barat □, Indonesia 37 G12 7 0S 107 0 E
ava Sea, Indonesia 36 E3 4 35S 107 15 E
ava Tengah □, Indonesia 37 G14 7 0S 110 0 E
ava Timur □, Indonesia 37 G15 8 0S 113 0 E
ava Trench, Ind. Oc. 36 F3 9 0S 105 0 E
avhlant = Uliastay,
  Mongolia 32 B4 47 56N 97 28 E
awa, Indonesia 37 G14 7 0S 110 0 E
awad, India 42 G6 24 36N 74 51 E
ay Peak, U.S.A. 79 B12 44 55N 72 32W
aya, Puncak, Indonesia 37 E9 3 57S 137 17 E
ayanti, India 41 F16 26 45N 89 40 E
ayapura, Indonesia 37 E10 2 28S 140 38 E
ayawijaya, Pegunungan,
  Indonesia 37 F9 5 0S 139 0 E
aynagar, India 41 F15 26 43N 86 9 E
ayrūd, Syria 44 C3 33 49N 36 44 E
ayton, U.S.A. 81 J4 33 15N 100 34W
āz Mūrīān, Hāmūn-e, Iran 45 E8 27 20N 58 55 E
azīreh-ye Shīf, Iran 45 D6 29 4N 50 54 E
Jazminal, Mexico 86 C4 24 56N 101 25W
Jazzīn, Lebanon 47 B4 33 31N 35 35 E
Jean, U.S.A. 85 K11 35 47N 115 20W
Jean Marie River, Canada 72 A4 61 32N 120 38W
Jean Rabel, Haiti 89 C5 19 50N 73 5W
Jeanerette, U.S.A. 81 L9 29 55N 91 40W
Jeanette, Ostrov =
  Zhannetty, Ostrov, Russia 27 B16 76 43N 158 0 E
Jeannette, U.S.A. 78 F5 40 20N 79 36W
Jebāl Bārez, Kūh-e, Iran 45 D8 28 30N 58 20 E
Jebel, Bahr el →, Sudan 51 G12 9 30N 30 25 E
Jedburgh, U.K. 12 F6 55 29N 2 33W
Jedda = Jiddah, Si. Arabia 46 C2 21 29N 39 10 E
Jeddore L., Canada 71 C8 48 3N 55 55W
Jędrzejów, Poland 17 C11 50 35N 20 15 E
Jefferson, Iowa, U.S.A. 80 D7 42 1N 94 23W
Jefferson, Ohio, U.S.A. 78 E4 41 44N 80 46W
Jefferson, Tex., U.S.A. 81 J7 32 46N 94 21W
Jefferson, Mt., Nev., U.S.A. 82 G5 38 51N 117 0W
Jefferson, Mt., Oreg., U.S.A. 82 D3 44 41N 121 48W
Jefferson City, Mo., U.S.A. 80 F8 38 34N 92 10W
Jefferson City, Tenn., U.S.A. 77 G4 36 7N 83 30W
Jeffersontown, U.S.A. 76 F3 38 12N 85 35W
Jeffersonville, U.S.A. 76 F3 38 17N 85 44W
Jeffrey City, U.S.A. 82 E10 42 30N 107 49W
Jega, Nigeria 50 F6 12 15N 4 23 E
Jēkabpils, Latvia 9 H21 56 29N 25 57 E
Jekyll I., U.S.A. 77 K5 31 4N 81 25W
Jelenia Góra, Poland 16 C8 50 50N 15 45 E
Jelgava, Latvia 9 H20 56 41N 23 49 E
Jemaja, Indonesia 39 L5 3 5N 105 45 E
Jemaluang, Malaysia 39 L4 2 16N 103 52 E
Jember, Indonesia 37 H15 8 11S 113 41 E
Jembongan, Malaysia 36 C5 6 45N 117 20 E
Jena, Germany 16 C6 50 54N 11 35 E
Jena, U.S.A. 81 K8 31 41N 92 8W
Jenkins, U.S.A. 76 G4 37 10N 82 38W
Jenner, U.S.A. 84 G3 38 27N 123 7W
Jennings, U.S.A. 81 K8 30 13N 92 40W
Jepara, Indonesia 37 G14 7 40S 109 14 E
Jeparit, Australia 63 F3 36 8S 142 1 E
Jequié, Brazil 93 F10 13 51S 40 5W
Jequitinhonha, Brazil 93 G10 16 30S 41 0W
Jequitinhonha →, Brazil 93 G11 15 51S 38 53W
Jerantut, Malaysia 39 L4 3 56N 102 22 E
Jérémie, Haiti 89 C5 18 40N 74 10W
Jerez, Punta, Mexico 87 C5 22 58N 97 40W
Jerez de García Salinas,
  Mexico 86 C4 22 39N 103 0W
Jerez de la Frontera, Spain 19 D2 36 41N 6 7W
Jerez de los Caballeros,
  Spain 19 C2 38 20N 6 45W
Jericho = El Arīḥā,
  West Bank 47 D4 31 52N 35 27 E
Jericho, Australia 62 C4 23 38S 146 6 E
Jerilderie, Australia 63 F4 35 20S 145 41 E
Jermyn, U.S.A. 79 E9 41 31N 75 31W
Jerome, U.S.A. 82 E6 42 44N 114 31W
Jerramungup, Australia 61 F2 33 55S 118 55 E
Jersey, U.K. 11 H5 49 11N 2 7W
Jersey City, U.S.A. 79 F10 40 44N 74 4W
Jersey Shore, U.S.A. 78 E7 41 12N 77 15W
Jerseyville, U.S.A. 80 F9 39 7N 90 20W
Jerusalem, Israel 47 D4 31 47N 35 10 E
Jervis B., Australia 63 F5 35 8S 150 46 E
Jervis Inlet, Canada 72 C4 50 0N 123 57W
Jesselton = Kota Kinabalu,
  Malaysia 36 C5 6 0N 116 4 E
Jessore, Bangla. 41 H16 23 10N 89 10 E
Jesup, U.S.A. 77 K5 31 36N 81 53W
Jesús Carranza, Mexico 87 D5 17 28N 95 1W
Jesús María, Argentina 94 C3 30 59S 64 5W
Jetmore, U.S.A. 81 F5 38 4N 99 54W
Jetpur, India 42 J4 21 45N 70 10 E
Jevnaker, Norway 9 F14 60 15N 10 26 E
Jewett, U.S.A. 78 F3 40 22N 81 2W
Jewett City, U.S.A. 79 E13 41 36N 72 0W
Jeyḥūnābād, Iran 45 C6 34 58N 48 59 E
Jeypore, India 41 K13 18 50N 82 38 E
Jha Jha, India 43 G12 24 46N 86 22 E
Jhabua, India 42 H6 22 46N 74 36 E
Jhajjar, India 42 E7 28 37N 76 42 E
Jhal, Pakistan 42 E2 28 17N 67 27 E
Jhal Jhao, Pakistan 40 F4 26 20N 65 35 E
Jhalawar, India 42 G7 24 40N 76 10 E
Jhalida, India 43 H11 23 22N 85 58 E
Jhalrapatan, India 42 G7 24 33N 76 10 E
Jhang Maghiana, Pakistan 42 D5 31 15N 72 22 E
Jhansi, India 43 G8 25 30N 78 36 E
Jhargram, India 43 H12 22 27N 86 59 E
Jharia, India 43 H12 23 45N 86 26 E
Jharsuguda, India 41 J14 21 56N 84 5 E
Jhelum, Pakistan 42 C5 33 0N 73 45 E
Jhelum →, Pakistan 42 D5 31 20N 72 10 E
Jhilmilli, India 43 H10 23 24N 82 51 E
Jhudo, Pakistan 42 G3 24 58N 69 18 E
Jhunjhunu, India 42 E6 28 10N 75 30 E
Ji-Paraná, Brazil 92 F6 10 52S 62 57W
Ji Xian, Hebei, China 34 F8 37 35N 115 30 E
Ji Xian, Henan, China 34 G8 35 22N 114 5 E
Ji Xian, Shanxi, China 34 F6 36 7N 110 40 E
Jia Xian, Henan, China 34 H7 33 59N 113 12 E
Jia Xian, Shaanxi, China 34 E6 38 12N 110 28 E
Jiamusi, China 33 B8 46 40N 130 26 E
Ji'an, Jiangxi, China 33 D6 27 6N 114 59 E
Ji'an, Jilin, China 35 D14 41 5N 126 10 E
Jianchang, China 35 D11 40 55N 120 35 E
Jianchangying, China 35 D10 40 10N 118 50 E
Jiangcheng, China 32 D5 22 36N 101 52 E
Jiangmen, China 33 D6 22 32N 113 0 E
Jiangsu □, China 35 H11 33 0N 120 0 E
Jiangxi □, China 33 D6 27 30N 116 0 E
Jiao Xian = Jiaozhou, China 35 F11 36 18N 120 1 E
Jiaohe, Hebei, China 34 E9 38 2N 116 20 E
Jiaohe, Jilin, China 35 C14 43 40N 127 22 E
Jiaozhou, China 35 F11 36 18N 120 1 E
Jiaozhou Wan, China 35 F11 36 5N 120 10 E
Jiaozuo, China 34 G7 35 16N 113 12 E
Jiawang, China 35 G9 34 28N 117 26 E
Jiaxiang, China 34 G9 35 25N 116 20 E
Jiaxing, China 33 C7 30 49N 120 45 E
Jiayi = Chiai, Taiwan 33 D7 23 29N 120 25 E
Jibuti = Djibouti ■, Africa 46 E3 12 0N 43 0 E
Jicarón, I., Panama 88 E3 7 10N 81 50W
Jiddah, Si. Arabia 46 C2 21 29N 39 10 E
Jido, India 41 E19 29 2N 94 58 E
Jieshou, China 34 H8 33 18N 115 22 E
Jiexiu, China 34 F6 37 2N 111 55 E
Jiggalong, Australia 60 D3 23 21S 120 47 E
Jigni, India 43 G8 25 45N 79 25 E
Jihlava, Czech Rep. 16 D8 49 28N 15 35 E
Jihlava →, Czech Rep. 17 D9 48 55N 16 36 E
Jijiga, Ethiopia 46 F3 9 20N 42 50 E
Jilin, China 35 C14 43 44N 126 30 E
Jilin □, China 35 C14 44 0N 127 0 E
Jilong = Chilung, Taiwan 33 D7 25 3N 121 45 E
Jim Thorpe, U.S.A. 79 F9 40 52N 75 44W
Jima, Ethiopia 46 F2 7 40N 36 47 E
Jiménez, Mexico 86 B4 27 10N 104 54W
Jimo, China 35 F11 36 23N 120 30 E
Jin Xian = Jinzhou, China 34 E8 38 2N 115 2 E
Jin Xian, China 35 E11 38 55N 121 42 E
Jinan, China 34 F9 36 38N 117 1 E
Jincheng, China 34 G7 35 29N 112 50 E
Jind, India 42 E7 29 19N 76 22 E
Jindabyne, Australia 63 F4 36 25S 148 35 E
Jindřichův Hradec,
  Czech Rep. 16 D8 49 10N 15 2 E
Jing He →, China 34 G5 34 27N 109 4 E
Jingbian, China 34 F5 37 20N 108 30 E
Jingchuan, China 34 G4 35 20N 107 20 E
Jingdezhen, China 33 D6 29 20N 117 11 E
Jinggu, China 32 D5 23 35N 100 41 E
Jinghai, China 34 E9 38 55N 116 55 E
Jingle, China 34 E6 38 20N 111 55 E
Jingning, China 34 G3 35 30N 105 43 E
Jingpo Hu, China 35 C15 43 55N 128 55 E
Jingtai, China 34 F3 37 10N 104 6 E
Jingxing, China 34 E8 38 2N 114 8 E
Jingyang, China 34 G5 34 30N 108 50 E
Jingyu, China 35 C14 42 25N 126 45 E
Jingyuan, China 34 F3 36 30N 104 40 E
Jingziguan, China 34 H6 33 15N 111 0 E
Jinhua, China 33 D6 29 8N 119 38 E
Jining, Nei Mongol Zizhiqu,
  China 34 D7 41 5N 113 0 E
Jining, Shandong, China 34 G9 35 22N 116 34 E
Jinja, Uganda 54 B3 0 25N 33 12 E
Jinjang, Malaysia 39 L3 3 13N 101 39 E
Jinji, China 34 F4 37 58N 106 8 E
Jinnah Barrage, Pakistan 40 C7 32 58N 71 33 E
Jinotega, Nic. 88 D2 13 6N 85 59W
Jinotepe, Nic. 88 D2 11 50N 86 10W
Jinsha Jiang →, China 32 D5 28 50N 104 36 E
Jinxi, China 35 D11 40 52N 120 50 E
Jinxiang, China 34 G9 35 5N 116 22 E
Jinzhou, Hebei, China 34 E8 38 2N 115 2 E
Jinzhou, Liaoning, China 35 D11 41 5N 121 3 E
Jiparaná →, Brazil 92 E6 8 3S 62 52W
Jipijapa, Ecuador 92 D2 1 0S 80 40W
Jiquilpan, Mexico 86 D4 19 57N 102 42W
Jishan, China 34 G6 35 34N 110 58 E
Jisr ash Shughūr, Syria 44 C3 35 49N 36 18 E
Jitarning, Australia 61 F2 32 48S 117 57 E
Jitra, Malaysia 39 J3 6 16N 100 25 E
Jiu →, Romania 17 F12 43 47N 23 48 E
Jiudengkou, China 34 E4 39 56N 106 40 E
Jiujiang, China 33 D6 29 42N 115 58 E
Jiutai, China 35 B13 44 10N 125 50 E
Jiuxiangcheng, China 34 H8 33 12N 114 50 E
Jiuxincheng, China 34 E8 39 17N 115 59 E
Jixi, China 35 B16 45 20N 130 50 E
Jiyang, China 35 F9 37 0N 117 12 E
Jiyuan, China 34 G7 35 7N 112 57 E
Jīzān, Si. Arabia 46 D3 17 0N 42 20 E
Jize, China 34 F8 36 54N 114 56 E
Jizl, Wādī al, Si. Arabia 44 E3 25 39N 38 25 E
Jizō-Zaki, Japan 31 G6 35 34N 133 20 E
Jizzakh, Uzbekistan 26 E7 40 6N 67 50 E
Joaçaba, Brazil 95 B5 27 5S 51 31W
João Pessoa, Brazil 93 E12 7 10S 34 52W
Joaquín V. González,
  Argentina 94 B3 25 10S 64 0W
Jobat, India 42 H6 22 25N 74 34 E
Jodhpur, India 42 F5 26 23N 73 8 E
Jodiya, India 42 H4 22 42N 70 18 E
Joensuu, Finland 24 B4 62 37N 29 49 E
Jōetsu, Japan 31 F9 37 12N 138 10 E
Jofane, Mozam. 57 C5 21 15S 34 18 E
Jogbani, India 43 F12 26 25N 87 15 E
Jõgeva, Estonia 9 G22 58 45N 26 24 E
Jogjakarta = Yogyakarta,
  Indonesia 37 G14 7 49S 110 22 E
Johannesburg, S. Africa 57 D4 26 10S 28 2 E
Johannesburg, U.S.A. 85 K9 35 22N 117 38W
Johilla →, India 43 H9 23 37N 81 14 E
John Day, U.S.A. 82 D4 44 25N 118 57W
John Day →, U.S.A. 82 D3 45 44N 120 39W
John D'Or Prairie, Canada 72 B5 58 30N 115 8W
John H. Kerr Reservoir,
  U.S.A. 77 G6 36 36N 78 18W
John o' Groats, U.K. 12 C5 58 38N 3 4W
Johnnie, U.S.A. 85 J10 36 25N 116 5W
John's Ra., Australia 62 C1 21 55S 133 23 E
Johnson, Kans., U.S.A. 81 G4 37 34N 101 45W
Johnson, Vt., U.S.A. 79 B12 44 38N 72 41W
Johnson City, N.Y., U.S.A. 79 D9 42 7N 75 58W
Johnson City, Tenn., U.S.A. 77 G4 36 19N 82 21W
Johnson City, Tex., U.S.A. 81 K5 30 17N 98 25W
Johnsonburg, U.S.A. 78 E6 41 29N 78 41W
Johnsondale, U.S.A. 85 K8 35 58N 118 32W
Johnson's Crossing, Canada 72 A2 60 29N 133 18W
Johnston, L., Australia 61 F3 32 25S 120 30 E
Johnston Falls =
  Mambilima Falls, Zambia 55 E2 10 31S 28 45 E
Johnston I., Pac. Oc. 65 F11 17 10N 169 8W
Johnstone Str., Canada 72 C3 50 28N 126 0W
Johnstown, N.Y., U.S.A. 79 C10 43 0N 74 22W
Johnstown, Ohio, U.S.A. 78 F2 40 9N 82 41W
Johnstown, Pa., U.S.A. 78 F6 40 20N 78 55W
Johor Baharu, Malaysia 39 M4 1 28N 103 46 E
Jõhvi, Estonia 9 G22 59 22N 27 27 E
Joinville, Brazil 95 B6 26 15S 48 55W
Joinville I., Antarctica 5 C18 65 0S 55 30W
Jojutla, Mexico 87 D5 18 37N 99 11W
Jokkmokk, Sweden 8 C18 66 35N 19 50 E
Jökulsá á Bru →, Iceland 8 D6 65 40N 14 16W
Jökulsá á Fjöllum →,
  Iceland 8 C5 66 10N 16 30W
Jolfā, Āzarbājān-e Sharqī,
  Iran 44 B5 38 57N 45 38 E
Jolfā, Eşfahan, Iran 45 C6 32 58N 51 37 E
Joliet, U.S.A. 76 E1 41 32N 88 5W
Joliette, Canada 70 C5 46 3N 73 24W
Jolo, Phil. 37 C6 6 0N 121 0 E
Jolon, U.S.A. 84 K5 35 58N 121 9W
Jombang, Indonesia 37 G15 7 33S 112 14 E
Jonava, Lithuania 9 J21 55 8N 24 12 E
Jones Sound, Canada 4 B3 76 0N 85 0W
Jonesboro, Ark., U.S.A. 81 H9 35 50N 90 42W
Jonesboro, La., U.S.A. 81 J8 32 15N 92 43W
Joniškis, Lithuania 9 H20 56 13N 23 35 E
Jönköping, Sweden 9 H16 57 45N 14 8 E
Jonquière, Canada 71 C5 48 27N 71 14W
Joplin, U.S.A. 81 G7 37 6N 94 31W
Jora, India 42 F6 26 20N 77 49 E
Jordan, Mont., U.S.A. 82 C10 47 19N 106 55W
Jordan, N.Y., U.S.A. 79 C8 43 4N 76 29W
Jordan ■, Asia 47 E5 31 0N 36 0 E
Jordan →, Asia 47 D4 31 48N 35 32 E
Jordan Valley, U.S.A. 82 E5 42 59N 117 3W
Jorhat, India 41 F19 26 45N 94 12 E
Jörn, Sweden 8 D19 65 4N 20 1 E
Jorong, Indonesia 36 E4 3 58S 114 56 E
Jørpeland, Norway 9 G11 59 3N 6 1 E
Jorquera →, Chile 94 B2 28 3S 69 58W
Jos, Nigeria 50 G7 9 53N 8 51 E
José Batlle y Ordóñez,
  Uruguay 95 C4 33 20S 55 10W
Joseph, L., Nfld., Canada 71 B6 52 45N 65 18W
Joseph, L., Ont., Canada 78 A5 45 10N 79 44W
Joseph Bonaparte G.,
  Australia 60 B4 14 35S 128 50 E
Joshinath, India 43 D8 30 34N 79 34 E
Joshua Tree, U.S.A. 85 L10 34 8N 116 19W
Joshua Tree National Park,
  U.S.A. 85 M10 33 55N 116 0W
Jostedalsbreen, Norway 9 F12 61 40N 6 59 E
Jotunheimen, Norway 9 F13 61 35N 8 25 E
Jourdanton, U.S.A. 81 L5 28 55N 98 33W
Jovellanos, Cuba 88 B3 22 40N 81 10W
Ju Xian, China 35 F10 36 35N 118 20 E
Juan Aldama, Mexico 86 C4 24 20N 103 23W
Juan Bautista Alberdi,
  Argentina 94 C3 34 26S 61 48W
Juan de Fuca Str., Canada 84 B3 48 15N 124 0W
Juan de Nova, Ind. Oc. 57 B7 17 3S 43 45 E
Juan Fernández, Arch. de,
  Pac. Oc. 90 G2 33 50S 80 0W
Juan José Castelli,
  Argentina 94 B3 25 27S 60 57W
Juan L. Lacaze, Uruguay 94 C4 34 26S 57 25W
Juankoski, Finland 8 E23 63 3N 28 19 E
Juárez, Argentina 94 D4 37 40S 59 43W
Juárez, Mexico 85 N11 32 20N 115 57W
Juárez, Sierra de, Mexico 86 A1 32 0N 116 0W
Juàzeiro, Brazil 93 E10 9 30S 40 30W
Juàzeiro do Norte, Brazil 93 E11 7 10S 39 18W
Juba, Sudan 51 H12 4 50N 31 35 E
Jubayl, Lebanon 47 A4 34 5N 35 39 E
Jubbah, Si. Arabia 44 D4 28 2N 40 56 E
Jubbal, India 42 D7 31 5N 77 40 E
Jubbulpore = Jabalpur,
  India 43 H8 23 9N 79 58 E
Jubilee L., Australia 61 E4 29 0S 126 50 E
Juby, C., Morocco 50 C3 28 0N 12 59W
Júcar = Xúquer →, Spain 19 C5 39 5N 0 10W
Júcaro, Cuba 88 B4 21 37N 78 51W
Juchitán, Mexico 87 D5 16 27N 95 5W
Judaea = Har Yehuda, Israel 47 D3 31 35N 34 57 E
Judith →, U.S.A. 82 C9 47 44N 109 39W
Judith, Pt., U.S.A. 79 E13 41 22N 71 29W
Judith Gap, U.S.A. 82 C9 46 41N 109 45W
Jugoslavia = Yugoslavia ■,
  Europe 21 B9 43 20N 20 0 E
Juigalpa, Nic. 88 D2 12 6N 85 26W
Juiz de Fora, Brazil 95 A7 21 43S 43 19W
Jujuy □, Argentina 94 A2 23 20S 65 40W
Julesburg, U.S.A. 80 E3 40 59N 102 16W
Juli, Peru 92 G5 16 10S 69 25W
Julia Cr. →, Australia 62 C3 20 0S 141 11 E
Julia Creek, Australia 62 C3 20 39S 141 44 E
Juliaca, Peru 92 G4 15 25S 70 10W
Julian, U.S.A. 85 M10 33 4N 116 38W
Julian L., Canada 70 B4 54 25N 77 57W
Julianatop, Surinam 93 C7 3 40N 56 30W
Julianehåb, Greenland 4 C5 60 43N 46 0W
Julimes, Mexico 86 B3 28 25N 105 27W
Jullundur, India 42 D6 31 20N 75 40 E
Julu, China 34 F8 37 15N 115 2 E
Jumbo, Zimbabwe 55 F3 17 30S 30 58 E
Jumbo Pk., U.S.A. 85 J12 36 12N 114 11W
Jumentos Cays, Bahamas 88 B4 23 0N 75 40W
Jumilla, Spain 19 C5 38 28N 1 19W
Jumla, Nepal 43 E10 29 15N 82 13 E
Jumna = Yamuna →,
  India 43 G9 25 30N 81 53 E
Junagadh, India 42 J4 21 30N 70 30 E
Junction, Tex., U.S.A. 81 K5 30 29N 99 46W
Junction, Utah, U.S.A. 83 G7 38 14N 112 13W
Junction B., Australia 62 A1 11 52S 133 55 E
Junction City, Kans., U.S.A. 80 F6 39 2N 96 50W
Junction City, Oreg., U.S.A. 82 D2 44 13N 123 12W
Junction Pt., Australia 62 A1 11 45S 133 50 E
Jundah, Australia 62 C3 24 46S 143 2 E
Jundiaí, Brazil 95 A6 24 30S 47 0W
Juneau, U.S.A. 72 B2 58 18N 134 25W
Junee, Australia 63 E4 34 53S 147 35 E
Jungfrau, Switz. 18 C7 46 32N 7 58 E
Junggar Pendi, China 32 B3 44 30N 86 0 E
Jungshahi, Pakistan 42 G2 24 52N 67 44 E
Juniata →, U.S.A. 78 F7 40 30N 77 40W
Junín, Argentina 94 C3 34 33S 60 57W
Junín de los Andes,
  Argentina 96 D2 39 45S 71 0W
Jūniyah, Lebanon 47 B4 33 59N 35 38 E
Juntas, Chile 94 B2 28 24S 69 58W
Juntura, U.S.A. 82 E4 43 45N 118 5W
Jur, Nahr el →, Sudan 51 G11 8 45N 29 15 E
Jura = Jura, Mts. du,
  Europe 18 C7 46 40N 6 5 E
Jura = Schwäbische Alb,
  Germany 16 D5 48 20N 9 30 E
Jura, U.K. 12 F3 56 0N 5 50W
Jura, Mts. du, Europe 18 C7 46 40N 6 5 E
Jura, Sd. of, U.K. 12 F3 55 57N 5 45W
Jurbarkas, Lithuania 9 J20 55 4N 22 46 E
Jurien, Australia 61 F2 30 18S 115 2 E
Jūrmala, Latvia 9 H20 56 58N 23 34 E
Juruá →, Brazil 92 D5 2 37S 65 44W
Juruena, Brazil 92 F7 13 0S 58 10W

Juruena

Juruena →, Brazil 92 E7 7 20S 58 3W
Juruti, Brazil 93 D7 2 9S 56 4W
Justo Daract, Argentina 94 C2 33 52S 65 12W
Jutaí →, Brazil 92 D5 2 43S 66 57W
Juticalpa, Honduras 88 D2 14 40N 86 12W
Jutland = Jylland, Denmark 9 H13 56 25N 9 30 E
Juventud, I. de la, Cuba 88 B3 21 40N 82 40W
Juwain, Afghan. 40 D2 31 45N 61 30 E
Jūy Zar, Iran 44 C5 33 50N 46 18 E
Juye, China 34 G9 35 22N 116 5 E
Jwaneng, Botswana 53 J4 24 45S 24 50 E
Jylland, Denmark 9 H13 56 25N 9 30 E
Jyväskylä, Finland 9 E21 62 14N 25 50 E

K

K2, Pakistan 43 B7 35 58N 76 32 E
Kaap Plateau, S. Africa 56 D3 28 30S 24 0 E
Kaapkruis, Namibia 56 C1 21 55S 13 57 E
Kaapstad = Cape Town, S. Africa 56 E2 33 55S 18 22 E
Kabaena, Indonesia 37 F6 5 15S 122 0 E
Kabala, S. Leone 50 G3 9 38N 11 37W
Kabale, Uganda 54 C3 1 15S 30 0 E
Kabalo, Dem. Rep. of the Congo 54 D2 6 0S 27 0 E
Kabambare, Dem. Rep. of the Congo 54 C2 4 41S 27 39 E
Kabango, Dem. Rep. of the Congo 55 D2 8 35S 28 30 E
Kabanjahe, Indonesia 36 D1 3 6N 98 30 E
Kabardino-Balkar Republic = Kabardino-Balkaria □, Russia 25 F7 43 30N 43 30 E
Kabardino-Balkaria □, Russia 25 F7 43 30N 43 30 E
Kabarega Falls = Murchison Falls, Uganda 54 B3 2 15N 31 30 E
Kabasalan, Phil. 37 C6 7 47N 122 44 E
Kabetogama, U.S.A. 80 A8 48 28N 92 59W
Kabin Buri, Thailand 38 F3 13 57N 101 43 E
Kabinakagami L., Canada 70 C3 48 54N 84 25W
Kabinda, Dem. Rep. of the Congo 52 F4 6 19S 24 20 E
Kabompo, Zambia 55 E1 13 36S 24 14 E
Kabompo →, Zambia 53 G4 14 10S 23 11 E
Kabondo, Dem. Rep. of the Congo 55 D2 8 58S 25 40 E
Kabongo, Dem. Rep. of the Congo 54 D2 7 22S 25 33 E
Kabūd Gonbad, Iran 45 B8 37 5N 59 45 E
Kābul, Afghan. 42 B3 34 28N 69 11 E
Kābul □, Afghan. 40 B6 34 30N 69 0 E
Kabul →, Pakistan 42 C5 33 55N 72 14 E
Kabunga, Dem. Rep. of the Congo 54 C2 1 38S 28 3 E
Kaburuang, Indonesia 37 D7 3 50N 126 30 E
Kabwe, Zambia 55 E2 14 30S 28 29 E
Kachchh, Gulf of, India 42 H3 22 50N 69 15 E
Kachchh, Rann of, India 42 H4 24 0N 70 0 E
Kachchhidhana, India 43 J8 21 44N 78 46 E
Kachebera, Zambia 55 E3 13 50S 32 50 E
Kachin □, Burma 41 G20 26 0N 97 30 E
Kachira, L., Uganda 54 C3 0 40S 31 7 E
Kachiry, Kazakstan 26 D8 53 10N 75 50 E
Kachnara, India 42 H6 23 50N 75 6 E
Kachot, Cambodia 39 G4 11 30N 103 3 E
Kaçkar, Turkey 25 F7 40 45N 41 10 E
Kadan Kyun, Burma 38 F2 12 30N 98 20 E
Kadanai →, Afghan. 42 D1 31 22N 65 45 E
Kadi, India 42 H5 23 18N 72 23 E
Kadina, Australia 63 E2 33 55S 137 43 E
Kadipur, India 43 F10 26 10N 82 23 E
Kadirli, Turkey 44 B3 37 23N 36 5 E
Kadiyevka = Stakhanov, Ukraine 25 E6 48 35N 38 40 E
Kadoka, U.S.A. 80 D4 43 50N 101 31W
Kadoma, Zimbabwe 55 F2 18 20S 29 52 E
Kâdugli, Sudan 51 F11 11 0N 29 45 E
Kaduna, Nigeria 50 F7 10 30N 7 21 E
Kaédi, Mauritania 50 E3 16 9N 13 28W
Kaeng Khoï, Thailand 38 E3 14 35N 101 0 E
Kaesŏng, N. Korea 35 F14 37 58N 126 35 E
Kāf, Si. Arabia 44 D3 31 25N 37 29 E
Kafan = Kapan, Armenia 25 G8 39 18N 46 27 E
Kafanchan, Nigeria 50 G7 9 40N 8 20 E
Kafinda, Zambia 55 E3 12 32S 30 20 E
Kafirévs, Ákra, Greece 21 E11 38 9N 24 38 E
Kafue, Zambia 55 F2 15 46S 28 9 E
Kafue →, Zambia 53 H5 15 30S 29 0 E
Kafue Flats, Zambia 55 F2 15 40S 27 25 E
Kafue Nat. Park, Zambia 55 F2 15 0S 25 30 E
Kafulwe, Zambia 55 D2 9 0S 29 1 E
Kaga, Afghan. 42 B4 34 14N 70 10 E
Kaga Bandoro, C.A.R. 52 C3 7 0N 19 10 E
Kagan, Uzbekistan 26 F7 39 43N 64 33 E
Kagawa □, Japan 31 G7 34 15N 134 0 E
Kagera □, Tanzania 54 C3 2 0S 31 30 E
Kagera →, Uganda 54 C3 0 57S 31 47 E
Kağızman, Turkey 44 A4 40 5N 43 10 E
Kagoshima, Japan 31 J5 31 35N 130 33 E
Kagoshima □, Japan 31 J5 31 30N 130 30 E
Kagul = Cahul, Moldova 17 F15 45 50N 28 15 E
Kahak, Iran 45 B6 36 6N 49 46 E
Kahama, Tanzania 54 C3 4 8S 32 30 E
Kahan, Pakistan 42 E3 29 18N 68 54 E
Kahang, Malaysia 39 L4 2 12N 103 32 E
Kahayan →, Indonesia 36 E4 3 40S 114 0 E
Kahe, Tanzania 54 C4 3 30S 37 25 E
Kahnūj, Iran 45 E8 27 55N 57 40 E
Kahoka, U.S.A. 80 E9 40 25N 91 44W
Kahoolawe, U.S.A. 74 H16 20 33N 156 37W
Kahramanmaraş, Turkey 25 G6 37 37N 36 53 E
Kahuta, Pakistan 42 C5 33 35N 73 24 E
Kai, Kepulauan, Indonesia 37 F8 5 55S 132 45 E
Kai Besar, Indonesia 37 F8 5 35S 133 0 E
Kai Is. = Kai, Kepulauan, Indonesia 37 F8 5 55S 132 45 E
Kai Kecil, Indonesia 37 F8 5 45S 132 40 E
Kaiapoi, N.Z. 59 K4 43 24S 172 40 E
Kaieteur Falls, Guyana 92 B7 5 1N 59 10W
Kaifeng, China 34 G8 34 48N 114 21 E
Kaikohe, N.Z. 59 F4 35 25S 173 49 E
Kaikoura, N.Z. 59 K4 42 25S 173 43 E
Kaikoura Ra., N.Z. 59 J4 41 59S 173 41 E
Kailu, China 35 C11 43 38N 121 18 E
Kailua Kona, U.S.A. 74 J17 19 39N 155 59W
Kaimana, Indonesia 37 E8 3 39S 133 45 E
Kaimanawa Mts., N.Z. 59 H5 39 15S 175 56 E
Kaimganj, India 43 F8 27 33N 79 24 E
Kaimur Hills, India 43 G10 24 30N 82 0 E
Kaingaroa Forest, N.Z. 59 H6 38 24S 176 30 E
Kainji Res., Nigeria 50 F6 10 1N 4 40 E
Kainuu, Finland 8 D23 64 30N 29 7 E
Kaipara Harbour, N.Z. 59 G5 36 25S 174 14 E
Kaipokok B., Canada 71 B8 54 54N 59 47W
Kaira, India 42 H5 22 45N 72 50 E
Kairana, India 42 E7 29 24N 77 15 E
Kaironi, Indonesia 37 E8 0 47S 133 40 E
Kairouan, Tunisia 51 A8 35 45N 10 5 E
Kaiserslautern, Germany 16 D4 49 26N 7 45 E
Kaitaia, N.Z. 59 F4 35 8S 173 17 E
Kaitangata, N.Z. 59 M2 46 17S 169 51 E
Kaithal, India 42 E7 29 48N 76 26 E
Kaitu →, Pakistan 42 C4 33 10N 70 30 E
Kaiwi Channel, U.S.A. 74 H16 21 15N 157 30W
Kaiyuan, China 35 C13 42 28N 124 1 E
Kajaani, Finland 8 D22 64 17N 27 46 E
Kajabbi, Australia 62 C3 20 0S 140 1 E
Kajana = Kajaani, Finland 8 D22 64 17N 27 46 E
Kajang, Malaysia 39 L3 2 59N 101 48 E
Kajiado, Kenya 54 C4 1 53S 36 48 E
Kajo Kaji, Sudan 51 H12 3 58N 31 40 E
Kakabeka Falls, Canada 70 C2 48 24N 89 37W
Kakadu Nat. Park, Australia 60 B5 12 30S 132 5 E
Kakamas, S. Africa 56 D3 28 45S 20 33 E
Kakamega, Kenya 54 B3 0 20N 34 46 E
Kakanui Mts., N.Z. 59 L3 45 10S 170 30 E
Kakdwip, India 43 J13 21 53N 88 11 E
Kake, Japan 31 G6 34 36N 132 19 E
Kake, U.S.A. 72 B2 56 59N 133 57W
Kakegawa, Japan 31 G9 34 45N 138 1 E
Kakeroma-Jima, Japan 31 K4 28 8N 129 14 E
Kakhovka, Ukraine 25 E5 46 45N 33 30 E
Kakhovske Vdskh., Ukraine 25 E5 47 5N 34 0 E
Kakinada, India 41 L13 16 57N 82 11 E
Kakisa →, Canada 72 A5 61 3N 118 10W
Kakisa L., Canada 72 A5 60 56N 117 43W
Kakogawa, Japan 31 G7 34 46N 134 51 E
Kakwa →, Canada 72 C5 54 37N 118 28W
Kāl Gūsheh, Iran 45 D8 30 59N 58 12 E
Kal Safīd, Iran 44 C5 34 52N 47 23 E
Kalabagh, Pakistan 42 C4 33 0N 71 28 E
Kalabahi, Indonesia 37 F6 8 13S 124 31 E
Kalach, Russia 25 D7 50 22N 41 0 E
Kaladan →, Burma 41 J18 20 20N 93 5 E
Kaladar, Canada 78 B7 44 37N 77 5W
Kalahari, Africa 56 C3 24 0S 21 30 E
Kalahari Gemsbok Nat. Park, S. Africa 56 D3 25 30S 20 30 E
Kalajoki, Finland 8 D20 64 12N 24 10 E
Kālak, Iran 45 E8 25 29N 59 22 E
Kalakamati, Botswana 57 C4 20 40S 27 25 E
Kalakan, Russia 27 D12 55 15N 116 45 E
K'alak'unlun Shank'ou, Pakistan 43 B7 35 33N 77 46 E
Kalam, Pakistan 43 B5 35 34N 72 30 E
Kalama, Dem. Rep. of the Congo 54 C2 2 52S 28 35 E
Kalama, U.S.A. 84 E4 46 1N 122 51W
Kalámai, Greece 21 F10 37 3N 22 10 E
Kalamata = Kalámai, Greece 21 F10 37 3N 22 10 E
Kalamazoo, U.S.A. 76 D3 42 17N 85 35W
Kalamazoo →, U.S.A. 76 D2 42 40N 86 10W
Kalambo Falls, Tanzania 55 D3 8 37S 31 35 E
Kalan, Turkey 44 B3 39 7N 39 32 E
Kalannie, Australia 61 F2 30 22S 117 5 E
Kalāntarī, Iran 45 C7 32 10N 54 8 E
Kalao, Indonesia 37 F6 7 21S 121 0 E
Kalaotoa, Indonesia 37 F6 7 20S 121 50 E
Kalasin, Thailand 38 D4 16 26N 103 30 E
Kalat, Pakistan 40 E5 29 8N 66 31 E
Kalāteh, Iran 45 B7 36 33N 55 41 E
Kalāteh-ye Ganj, Iran 45 E8 27 31N 57 55 E
Kalbarri, Australia 61 E1 27 40S 114 10 E
Kalce, Slovenia 16 F8 45 54N 14 13 E
Kale, Turkey 21 F13 37 27N 28 49 E
Kalegauk Kyun, Burma 41 M20 15 33N 97 35 E
Kalehe, Dem. Rep. of the Congo 54 C2 2 6S 28 50 E
Kalema, Tanzania 54 C3 1 12S 31 55 E
Kalemie, Dem. Rep. of the Congo 54 D2 5 55S 29 9 E
Kalewa, Burma 41 H19 23 10N 94 15 E
Kaleybar, Iran 44 B5 38 47N 47 2 E
Kalgan = Zhangjiakou, China 34 D8 40 48N 114 55 E
Kalgoorlie-Boulder, Australia 61 F3 30 40S 121 22 E
Kali →, India 43 F8 27 6N 79 55 E
Kali Sindh →, India 42 G6 25 32N 76 17 E
Kaliakra, Nos, Bulgaria 21 C13 43 21N 28 30 E
Kalianda, Indonesia 36 F3 5 50S 105 45 E
Kalibo, Phil. 37 B6 11 43N 122 22 E
Kalima, Dem. Rep. of the Congo 54 C2 2 33S 26 32 E
Kalimantan □, Indonesia 36 E4 0 0 114 0 E
Kalimantan Barat □, Indonesia 36 E4 0 0 110 30 E
Kalimantan Selatan □, Indonesia 36 E5 2 30S 115 30 E
Kalimantan Tengah □, Indonesia 36 E4 2 0S 113 30 E
Kalimantan Timur □, Indonesia 36 D5 1 30N 116 30 E
Kálimnos, Greece 21 F12 37 0N 27 0 E
Kalimpong, India 43 F13 27 4N 88 35 E
Kalinin = Tver, Russia 24 C6 56 55N 35 55 E
Kaliningrad, Russia 9 J19 54 42N 20 32 E
Kalinkavichy, Belarus 17 B15 52 12N 29 20 E
Kalinkovichi = Kalinkavichy, Belarus 17 B15 52 12N 29 20 E
Kaliro, Uganda 54 B3 0 56N 33 30 E
Kalispell, U.S.A. 82 B6 48 12N 114 19W
Kalisz, Poland 17 C10 51 45N 18 8 E
Kaliua, Tanzania 54 D3 5 5S 31 48 E
Kalix, Sweden 8 D20 65 53N 23 12 E
Kalix →, Sweden 8 D20 65 50N 23 11 E
Kalka, India 42 D7 30 46N 76 57 E
Kalkarindji, Australia 60 C5 17 30S 130 47 E
Kalkaska, U.S.A. 76 C3 44 44N 85 11W
Kalkfeld, Namibia 56 C2 20 57S 16 14 E
Kalkfontein, Botswana 56 C3 22 4S 20 57 E
Kalkrand, Namibia 56 C2 24 1S 17 35 E
Kallavesi, Finland 8 E22 62 58N 27 30 E
Kallsjön, Sweden 8 E15 63 38N 13 0 E
Kalmar, Sweden 9 H17 56 40N 16 20 E
Kalmyk Republic = Kalmykia □, Russia 25 E8 46 5N 46 1 E
Kalmykia □, Russia 25 E8 46 5N 46 1 E
Kalmykovo, Kazakstan 25 E9 49 0N 51 47 E
Kalna, India 43 H13 23 13N 88 25 E
Kalnai, India 43 H10 22 46N 83 30 E
Kalocsa, Hungary 17 E10 46 32N 19 0 E
Kalokhorio, Cyprus 23 E12 34 51N 33 2 E
Kaloko, Dem. Rep. of the Congo 54 D2 6 47S 25 48 E
Kalol, Gujarat, India 42 H5 22 37N 73 31 E
Kalol, Gujarat, India 42 H5 23 15N 72 33 E
Kalomo, Zambia 55 F2 17 0S 26 30 E
Kalpi, India 43 F8 26 8N 79 47 E
Kalu, Pakistan 42 G2 25 5N 67 39 E
Kaluga, Russia 24 D6 54 35N 36 10 E
Kalulushi, Zambia 55 E2 12 50S 28 3 E
Kalundborg, Denmark 9 J14 55 41N 11 5 E
Kalush, Ukraine 17 D13 49 3N 24 23 E
Kalutara, Sri Lanka 40 R12 6 35N 80 0 E
Kalya, Russia 24 B10 60 15N 59 59 E
Kama, Dem. Rep. of the Congo 54 C2 3 30S 27 5 E
Kama →, Russia 24 C9 55 45N 52 0 E
Kamachumu, Tanzania 54 C3 1 37S 31 37 E
Kamaishi, Japan 30 E10 39 16N 141 53 E
Kamalia, Pakistan 42 D5 30 44N 72 42 E
Kaman, India 42 F6 27 39N 77 16 E
Kamapanda, Zambia 55 E1 12 5S 24 0 E
Kamaran, Yemen 46 D3 15 21N 42 35 E
Kamativi, Zimbabwe 55 F2 18 15S 27 27 E
Kambalda, Australia 61 F3 31 10S 121 37 E
Kambar, Pakistan 42 F3 27 37N 68 1 E
Kambarka, Russia 24 C9 56 15N 54 11 E
Kambolé, Zambia 55 D3 8 47S 30 48 E
Kambos, Cyprus 23 D11 35 2N 32 44 E
Kambove, Dem. Rep. of the Congo 55 E2 10 51S 26 33 E
Kamchatka, Poluostrov, Russia 27 D17 57 0N 160 0 E
Kamchatka Pen. = Kamchatka, Poluostrov, Russia 27 D17 57 0N 160 0 E
Kamchiya →, Bulgaria 21 C12 43 4N 27 44 E
Kamen, Russia 26 D9 53 50N 81 30 E
Kamen-Rybolov, Russia 30 B6 44 46N 132 2 E
Kamenjak, Rt., Croatia 16 F7 44 47N 13 55 E
Kamenka, Russia 24 A7 65 58N 44 0 E
Kamenka Bugskaya = Kamyanka-Buzka, Ukraine 17 C13 50 8N 24 16 E
Kamensk Uralskiy, Russia 26 D7 56 25N 62 2 E
Kamenskoye, Russia 27 C17 62 45N 165 30 E
Kameoka, Japan 31 G7 35 0N 135 35 E
Kamiah, U.S.A. 82 C5 46 14N 116 2W
Kamieskroon, S. Africa 56 E2 30 9S 17 56 E
Kamilukuak, L., Canada 73 A8 62 22N 101 40W
Kamin-Kashyrskyy, Ukraine 17 C13 51 39N 24 56 E
Kamina, Dem. Rep. of the Congo 55 D2 8 45S 25 0 E
Kaminak L., Canada 73 A10 62 10N 95 0W
Kaministiquia, Canada 70 C1 48 32N 89 35W
Kaminoyama, Japan 30 E10 38 9N 140 17 E
Kamiros, Greece 23 C9 36 20N 27 56 E
Kamituga, Dem. Rep. of the Congo 54 C2 3 2S 28 10 E
Kamla →, India 43 G12 25 35N 86 36 E
Kamloops, Canada 72 C4 50 40N 120 20W
Kamo, Japan 30 F9 37 39N 139 3 E
Kamoke, Pakistan 42 C6 32 4N 74 4 E
Kampala, Uganda 54 B3 0 20N 32 30 E
Kampang Chhnang, Cambodia 39 F5 12 20N 104 35 E
Kampar, Malaysia 39 K3 4 18N 101 9 E
Kampar →, Indonesia 36 D2 0 30N 103 8 E
Kampen, Neths. 15 B5 52 33N 5 53 E
Kampene, Dem. Rep. of the Congo 52 E5 3 36S 26 40 E
Kamphaeng Phet, Thailand 38 D2 16 28N 99 30 E
Kampolombo, L., Zambia 55 E2 11 37S 29 42 E
Kampong Saom, Cambodia 39 G4 10 38N 103 30 E
Kampong Saom, Chaak, Cambodia 36 B2 10 45N 103 30 E
Kampong Saom, Chaak, Cambodia 39 G4 10 50N 103 32 E
Kampong To, Thailand 39 J3 6 3N 101 13 E
Kampot, Cambodia 39 G5 10 36N 104 10 E
Kampuchea = Cambodia ■, Asia 38 F5 12 15N 105 0 E
Kampung Air Putih, Malaysia 39 K4 4 15N 103 10 E
Kampung Jerangau, Malaysia 39 K4 4 50N 103 10 E
Kampung Raja, Malaysia 39 K4 5 45N 102 35 E
Kampungbaru = Tolitoli, Indonesia 37 D6 1 5N 120 50 E
Kamrau, Teluk, Indonesia 37 E8 3 30S 133 36 E
Kamsack, Canada 73 C8 51 34N 101 54W
Kamskoye Vdkhr., Russia 24 C10 58 41N 56 7 E
Kamuchawie L., Canada 73 B8 56 18N 101 59W
Kamuela, U.S.A. 74 H17 20 1N 155 41W
Kamui-Misaki, Japan 30 C10 43 20N 140 21 E
Kamyanets-Podilskyy, Ukraine 17 D14 48 45N 26 40 E
Kamyanka-Buzka, Ukraine 17 C13 50 8N 24 16 E
Kāmyārān, Iran 44 C5 34 47N 46 56 E
Kamyshin, Russia 25 D8 50 10N 45 24 E
Kanaaupscow, Canada 70 B4 54 2N 76 30W
Kanaaupscow →, Canada 69 C12 53 39N 77 9W
Kanab, U.S.A. 83 H7 37 3N 112 32W
Kanab →, U.S.A. 83 H7 36 24N 112 38W
Kanagi, Japan 30 D10 40 54N 140 27 E
Kanairiktok →, Canada 71 A7 55 2N 60 18W
Kananga, Dem. Rep. of the Congo 52 F4 5 55S 22 18 E
Kanash, Russia 24 C8 55 30N 47 32 E
Kanaskat, U.S.A. 84 C5 47 19N 121 54W
Kanastraíon, Ákra = Palioúrion, Ákra, Greece 21 E10 39 57N 23 45 E
Kanawha →, U.S.A. 76 F4 38 50N 82 9W
Kanazawa, Japan 31 F8 36 30N 136 38 E
Kanchanaburi, Thailand 38 E2 14 2N 99 31 E
Kanchenjunga, Nepal 43 F13 27 50N 88 10 E
Kanchipuram, India 40 N11 12 52N 79 45 E
Kandaghat, India 42 D7 30 59N 77 7 E
Kandahar = Qandahār, Afghan. 40 D4 31 32N 65 30 E
Kandalaksha, Russia 24 A5 67 9N 32 30 E
Kandalakshkiy Zaliv, Russia 24 A6 66 0N 35 0 E
Kandalu, Afghan. 40 E3 29 55N 63 20 E
Kandangan, Indonesia 36 E5 2 50S 115 20 E
Kandanghaur, Indonesia 37 G13 6 21S 108 6 E
Kandanos, Greece 23 D5 35 19N 23 44 E
Kandhkot, Pakistan 42 E3 28 16N 69 8 E
Kandhla, India 42 E7 29 18N 77 19 E
Kandi, Benin 50 F6 11 7N 2 55 E
Kandi, India 43 H13 23 58N 88 5 E
Kandiaro, Pakistan 42 F3 27 4N 68 13 E
Kandla, India 42 H4 23 0N 70 10 E
Kandos, Australia 63 E4 32 45S 149 58 E
Kandy, Sri Lanka 40 R12 7 18N 80 43 E
Kane, U.S.A. 78 E6 41 40N 78 49W
Kane Basin, Greenland 4 B4 79 1N 70 0W
Kaneohe, U.S.A. 74 H16 21 25N 157 48W
Kangān, Fārs, Iran 45 E7 27 50N 52 3 E
Kangān, Hormozgān, Iran 45 E8 25 48N 57 28 E
Kangar, Malaysia 39 J3 6 27N 100 12 E
Kangaroo I., Australia 63 F2 35 45S 137 0 E
Kangaroo Mts., Australia 62 C3 23 29S 141 51 E
Kangasala, Finland 9 F21 61 28N 24 4 E
Kangāvar, Iran 45 C6 34 40N 48 0 E
Kangdong, N. Korea 35 E14 39 9N 126 5 E
Kangean, Kepulauan, Indonesia 36 F5 6 55S 115 23 E
Kangean Is. = Kangean, Kepulauan, Indonesia 36 F5 6 55S 115 23 E
Kanggye, N. Korea 35 D14 41 0N 126 35 E
Kanggyŏng, S. Korea 35 F14 36 10N 127 0 E
Kanghwa, S. Korea 35 F14 37 45N 126 30 E
Kangiqsualujjuaq, Canada 69 C13 58 30N 65 59W
Kangiqsujuaq, Canada 69 B12 61 30N 72 0W
Kangirsuk, Canada 69 C13 60 0N 70 0W
Kangnŭng, S. Korea 35 F15 37 45N 128 54 E
Kangping, China 35 C12 42 43N 123 18 E
Kangra, India 42 C7 32 6N 76 16 E
Kangto, India 41 F18 27 50N 92 35 E
Kanhar →, India 43 G10 24 28N 83 8 E
Kaniama, Dem. Rep. of the Congo 54 D1 7 30S 24 12 E
Kaniapiskau = Caniapiscau →, Canada 71 A6 56 40N 69 30W
Kaniapiskau, Res. = Caniapiscau Rés. de, Canada 71 B6 54 10N 69 55W
Kanin, Poluostrov, Russia 24 A8 68 0N 45 0 E
Kanin Nos, Mys, Russia 24 A7 68 39N 43 32 E
Kanin Pen. = Kanin, Poluostrov, Russia 24 A8 68 0N 45 0 E
Kaniva, Australia 63 F3 36 22S 141 18 E
Kanjut Sar, Pakistan 43 A6 36 7N 75 25 E
Kankaanpää, Finland 9 F20 61 44N 22 50 E
Kankakee, U.S.A. 76 E2 41 7N 87 52W
Kankakee →, U.S.A. 76 E1 41 23N 88 15W
Kankan, Guinea 50 F4 10 23N 9 15W
Kankendy = Xankändi, Azerbaijan 25 G8 39 52N 46 49 E
Kanker, India 41 J12 20 10N 81 40 E
Kankroli, India 42 G5 25 4N 73 53 E
Kannapolis, U.S.A. 77 H5 35 30N 80 37W
Kannauj, India 43 F8 27 3N 79 56 E
Kannod, India 40 H10 22 45N 76 40 E
Kano, Nigeria 50 F7 12 2N 8 30 E
Kan'onji, Japan 31 G6 34 7N 133 39 E
Kanowit, Malaysia 36 D4 2 14N 112 20 E
Kanoya, Japan 31 J5 31 25N 130 50 E
Kanpetlet, Burma 41 J18 21 10N 93 59 E
Kanpur, India 43 F9 26 28N 80 20 E
Kansas □, U.S.A. 80 F6 38 30N 99 0W
Kansas →, U.S.A. 80 F7 39 7N 94 37W
Kansas City, Kans., U.S.A. 80 F7 39 7N 94 38W
Kansas City, Mo., U.S.A. 80 F7 39 6N 94 35W
Kansenia, Dem. Rep. of the Congo 55 E2 10 20S 26 0 E
Kansk, Russia 27 D10 56 20N 95 37 E
Kansŏng, S. Korea 35 E15 38 24N 128 30 E
Kansu = Gansu □, China 34 G3 36 0N 104 0 E
Kantaphor, India 42 H7 22 35N 76 34 E
Kantharalak, Thailand 38 E5 14 39N 104 39 E
Kantli →, India 42 E6 28 20N 75 30 E
Kantō □, Japan 31 F9 36 15N 139 30 E
Kantō-Sanchi, Japan 31 G9 35 59N 138 50 E
Kanturk, Ireland 13 D3 52 11N 8 54W
Kanuma, Japan 31 F9 36 34N 139 42 E
Kanus, Namibia 56 D2 27 50S 18 39 E
Kanye, Botswana 56 C4 24 55S 25 28 E
Kanzenze, Dem. Rep. of the Congo 55 E2 10 30S 25 12 E
Kanzi, Ras, Tanzania 54 D4 7 1S 39 33 E
Kaohsiung, Taiwan 33 D7 22 35N 120 16 E
Kaokoveld, Namibia 56 B1 19 15S 14 30 E
Kaolack, Senegal 50 F2 14 5N 16 8W
Kaoshan, China 35 B13 44 38N 124 50 E
Kapaa, U.S.A. 74 G15 22 5N 159 19W
Kapadvanj, India 42 H5 23 5N 73 0 E
Kapan, Armenia 25 G8 39 18N 46 27 E
Kapanga, Dem. Rep. of the Congo 52 F4 8 30S 22 40 E
Kapchagai = Qapshaghay, Kazakstan 26 E8 43 51N 77 14 E
Kapela = Velika Kapela, Croatia 16 F8 45 10N 15 5 E
Kapema, Dem. Rep. of the Congo 55 E2 10 45S 28 22 E
Kapfenberg, Austria 16 E8 47 26N 15 18 E
Kapiri Mposhi, Zambia 55 E2 13 59S 28 43 E
Kapiskau →, Canada 70 B3 52 47N 81 55W
Kapit, Malaysia 36 D4 2 0N 112 55 E
Kapiti I., N.Z. 59 J5 40 50S 174 56 E
Kaplan, U.S.A. 81 K8 30 0N 92 17W
Kapoe, Thailand 39 H2 9 34N 98 32 E
Kapoeta, Sudan 51 H12 4 50N 33 35 E
Kaposvár, Hungary 17 E9 46 25N 17 47 E
Kapowsin, U.S.A. 84 D4 46 59N 122 13W
Kapps, Namibia 56 C2 22 32S 17 18 E
Kapsan, N. Korea 35 D15 41 4N 128 19 E
Kapsukas = Marijampole, Lithuania 9 J20 54 33N 23 19 E
Kapuas →, Indonesia 36 E3 0 25S 109 20 E
Kapuas Hulu, Pegunungan, Malaysia 36 D4 1 30N 113 30 E

Kentville

Kentville, *Canada* **71 C7** 45 6N 64 29W
Kentwood, *U.S.A.* **81 K9** 30 56N 90 31W
Kenya ■, *Africa* **54 B4** 1 0N 38 0 E
Kenya, Mt., *Kenya* **54 C4** 0 10S 37 18 E
Keo Neua, Deo, *Vietnam* **38 C5** 18 23N 105 10 E
Keokuk, *U.S.A.* **80 E9** 40 24N 91 24W
Keonjhargarh, *India* **43 J11** 21 28N 85 35 E
Kep, *Cambodia* **39 G5** 10 29N 104 19 E
Kep, *Vietnam* **38 B6** 21 24N 106 16 E
Kepi, *Indonesia* **37 F9** 6 32S 139 19 E
Kerala □, *India* **40 P10** 11 0N 76 15 E
Kerama-Rettō, *Japan* **31 L3** 26 5N 127 15 E
Keran, *Pakistan* **43 B5** 34 35N 73 59 E
Kerang, *Australia* **63 F3** 35 40S 143 55 E
Keraudren, C., *Australia* **60 C2** 19 58S 119 45 E
Kerava, *Finland* **9 F21** 60 25N 25 5 E
Kerch, *Ukraine* **25 E6** 45 20N 36 20 E
Kerguelen, *Ind. Oc.* **3 G13** 49 15S 69 10 E
Kericho, *Kenya* **54 C4** 0 22S 35 15 E
Kerinci, *Indonesia* **36 E2** 1 40S 101 15 E
Kerki, *Turkmenistan* **26 F7** 37 50N 65 12 E
Kérkira, *Greece* **23 A3** 39 38N 19 50 E
Kerkrade, *Neths.* **15 D6** 50 53N 6 4 E
Kermadec Is., *Pac. Oc.* **64 L10** 30 0S 178 15W
Kermadec Trench, *Pac. Oc.* **64 L10** 30 30S 176 0W
Kermān, *Iran* **45 D8** 30 15N 57 1 E
Kerman, *U.S.A.* **84 J6** 36 43N 120 4W
Kermān □, *Iran* **45 D8** 30 0N 57 0 E
Kermān, Bīābān-e, *Iran* **45 D8** 28 45N 59 45 E
Kermānshāh = Bākhtarān, *Iran* **44 C5** 34 23N 47 0 E
Kermit, *U.S.A.* **81 K3** 31 52N 103 6W
Kern →, *U.S.A.* **85 K7** 35 16N 119 18W
Kernville, *U.S.A.* **85 K8** 35 45N 118 26W
Keroh, *Malaysia* **39 K3** 5 43N 101 1 E
Kerrera, *U.K.* **12 E3** 56 24N 5 33W
Kerrobert, *Canada* **73 C7** 51 56N 109 8W
Kerrville, *U.S.A.* **81 K5** 30 3N 99 8W
Kerry □, *Ireland* **13 D2** 52 7N 9 35W
Kerry Hd., *Ireland* **13 D2** 52 25N 9 56W
Kerulen →, *Asia* **33 B6** 48 48N 117 0 E
Kerzaz, *Algeria* **50 C5** 29 29N 1 37W
Kesagami →, *Canada* **70 B4** 51 40N 79 45W
Kesagami L., *Canada* **70 B3** 50 23N 80 15W
Keşan, *Turkey* **21 D12** 40 49N 26 38 E
Kesennuma, *Japan* **30 E10** 38 54N 141 35 E
Keshit, *Iran* **45 D8** 29 43N 58 17 E
Kestell, *S. Africa* **57 D4** 28 17S 28 42 E
Kestenga, *Russia* **24 A5** 65 50N 31 45 E
Keswick, *U.K.* **10 C4** 54 36N 3 8W
Ket →, *Russia* **26 D9** 58 55N 81 32 E
Ketapang, *Indonesia* **36 E4** 1 55S 110 0 E
Ketchikan, *U.S.A.* **72 B2** 55 21N 131 39W
Ketchum, *U.S.A.* **82 E6** 43 41N 114 22W
Ketef, Khalîg Umm el, *Egypt* **44 F2** 23 40N 35 35 E
Keti Bandar, *Pakistan* **42 G2** 24 8N 67 27 E
Ketri, *India* **42 E6** 28 1N 75 50 E
Kętrzyn, *Poland* **17 A11** 54 7N 21 22 E
Kettering, *U.K.* **11 E7** 52 24N 0 43W
Kettering, *U.S.A.* **76 F3** 39 41N 84 10W
Kettle →, *Canada* **73 B11** 56 40N 89 34W
Kettle Falls, *U.S.A.* **82 B4** 48 37N 118 3W
Kettle Pt., *Canada* **78 C2** 43 13N 82 1W
Kettleman City, *U.S.A.* **84 J7** 36 1N 119 58W
Keuka L., *U.S.A.* **78 D7** 42 30N 77 9W
Keuruu, *Finland* **9 E21** 62 16N 24 41 E
Kewanee, *U.S.A.* **80 E10** 41 14N 89 56W
Kewaunee, *U.S.A.* **76 C2** 44 27N 87 31W
Keweenaw B., *U.S.A.* **76 B1** 47 0N 88 15W
Keweenaw Pen., *U.S.A.* **76 B2** 47 30N 88 0W
Keweenaw Pt., *U.S.A.* **76 B2** 47 25N 87 43W
Key Largo, *U.S.A.* **77 N5** 25 5N 80 27W
Key West, *U.S.A.* **75 F10** 24 33N 81 48W
Keynsham, *U.K.* **11 F5** 51 24N 2 29W
Keyser, *U.S.A.* **76 F6** 39 26N 78 59W
Kezhma, *Russia* **27 D11** 58 59N 101 9 E
Khabarovsk, *Russia* **27 E14** 48 30N 135 5 E
Khabr, *Iran* **45 D8** 28 51N 56 22 E
Khābūr →, *Syria* **44 C4** 35 17N 40 35 E
Khachmas = Xaçmaz, *Azerbaijan* **25 F8** 41 31N 48 42 E
Khachrod, *India* **42 H6** 23 25N 75 20 E
Khadro, *Pakistan* **42 F3** 26 11N 68 50 E
Khadzhilyangar, *India* **43 B8** 35 45N 79 20 E
Khaga, *India* **43 G9** 25 47N 81 7 E
Khagaria, *India* **43 G12** 25 30N 86 32 E
Khaipur, *Pakistan* **42 E5** 29 34N 72 17 E
Khair, *India* **42 F7** 27 57N 77 46 E
Khairabad, *India* **43 F9** 27 33N 80 47 E
Khairagarh, *India* **43 J9** 21 27N 81 2 E
Khairpur, *Pakistan* **40 F6** 27 32N 68 49 E
Khairpur, *Hyderabad, Pakistan* **42 F3** 27 32N 68 49 E
Khairpur Nathan Shah, *Pakistan* **42 F2** 27 6N 67 44 E
Khairwara, *India* **42 H5** 23 58N 73 38 E
Khaisor →, *Pakistan* **42 D3** 31 17N 68 59 E
Khajuri Kach, *Pakistan* **42 C3** 32 4N 69 51 E
Khakassia □, *Russia* **26 D9** 53 0N 90 0 E
Khakhea, *Botswana* **56 C3** 24 48S 23 22 E
Khalafābād, *Iran* **45 D6** 30 54N 49 24 E
Khalilabad, *India* **43 F10** 26 48N 83 5 E
Khalīlī, *Iran* **45 E7** 27 38N 53 17 E
Khalkhāl, *Iran* **45 B6** 37 37N 48 32 E
Khalkís, *Greece* **21 E10** 38 27N 23 42 E
Khalmer-Sede = Tazovskiy, *Russia* **26 C8** 67 30N 78 44 E
Khalmer Yu, *Russia* **26 C7** 67 58N 65 1 E
Khalturin, *Russia* **24 C8** 58 40N 48 50 E
Khalūf, *Oman* **46 C6** 20 30N 58 13 E
Kham Keut, *Laos* **38 C5** 18 15N 104 43 E
Khamaria, *India* **43 H9** 23 5N 80 48 E
Khamas Country, *Botswana* **56 C4** 21 45S 26 30 E
Khambhaliya, *India* **42 H3** 22 14N 69 41 E
Khambhat, *India* **42 H5** 22 23N 72 33 E
Khambhat, G. of, *India* **40 J8** 20 45N 72 30 E
Khamīr, *Iran* **45 E7** 26 57N 55 36 E
Khamir, *Yemen* **46 D3** 16 2N 44 0 E
Khamsa, *Egypt* **47 E1** 30 27N 32 23 E
Khān Abū Shāmat, *Syria* **47 B5** 33 39N 36 53 E
Khān Azād, *Iraq* **44 C5** 33 7N 44 22 E
Khān Mujiddah, *Iraq* **44 C4** 32 21N 43 48 E
Khān Shaykhūn, *Syria* **44 C3** 35 26N 36 38 E
Khān Yūnis, *Gaza Strip* **47 D3** 31 21N 34 18 E
Khanai, *Pakistan* **42 D2** 30 30N 67 8 E
Khānaqīn, *Iraq* **44 C5** 34 23N 45 25 E
Khānbāghī, *Iran* **45 B7** 36 10N 55 25 E
Khandwa, *India* **40 J10** 21 49N 76 22 E
Khandyga, *Russia* **27 C14** 62 42N 135 35 E
Khāneh, *Iran* **44 B5** 36 41N 45 8 E
Khanewal, *Pakistan* **42 D4** 30 20N 71 55 E
Khangah Dogran, *Pakistan* **42 D5** 31 50N 73 37 E
Khanh Duong, *Vietnam* **38 F7** 12 44N 108 44 E
Khaniá, *Greece* **23 D6** 35 30N 24 4 E
Khaniá □, *Greece* **23 D6** 35 30N 24 0 E
Khaniadhana, *India* **42 G8** 25 1N 78 8 E
Khaníon, Kólpos, *Greece* **23 D5** 35 33N 23 55 E
Khanka, L., *Asia* **27 E14** 45 0N 132 24 E
Khankendy = Xankändi, *Azerbaijan* **25 G8** 39 52N 46 49 E
Khanna, *India* **42 D7** 30 42N 76 16 E
Khanozai, *Pakistan* **42 D2** 30 37N 67 19 E
Khanpur, *Pakistan* **42 E4** 28 42N 70 35 E
Khanty-Mansiysk, *Russia* **26 C7** 61 0N 69 0 E
Khapalu, *Pakistan* **43 B7** 35 10N 76 20 E
Khapcheranga, *Russia* **27 E12** 49 42N 112 24 E
Kharaghoda, *India* **42 H4** 23 11N 71 46 E
Kharagpur, *India* **43 H12** 22 20N 87 25 E
Khárakas, *Greece* **23 D7** 35 1N 25 7 E
Kharan Kalat, *Pakistan* **40 E4** 28 34N 65 21 E
Kharānaq, *Iran* **45 C7** 32 20N 54 45 E
Kharda, *India* **40 K9** 18 40N 75 34 E
Khardung La, *India* **43 B7** 34 20N 77 43 E
Khârga, El Wâhât el, *Egypt* **51 C12** 25 10N 30 35 E
Khargon, *India* **40 J9** 21 45N 75 40 E
Khari →, *India* **42 G6** 25 54N 74 31 E
Kharian, *Pakistan* **42 C5** 32 49N 73 52 E
Khārk, Jazīreh-ye, *Iran* **45 D6** 29 15N 50 28 E
Kharkiv, *Ukraine* **25 E6** 49 58N 36 20 E
Kharkov = Kharkiv, *Ukraine* **25 E6** 49 58N 36 20 E
Kharovsk, *Russia* **24 C7** 59 56N 40 13 E
Kharsawangarh, *India* **43 H11** 22 48N 85 50 E
Kharta, *Turkey* **21 D13** 40 55N 29 7 E
Khartoum = El Khartûm, *Sudan* **51 E12** 15 31N 32 35 E
Khasan, *Russia* **30 C5** 42 25N 130 40 E
Khāsh, *Iran* **40 E2** 28 15N 61 15 E
Khashm el Girba, *Sudan* **51 F13** 14 59N 35 58 E
Khaskovo, *Bulgaria* **21 D11** 41 56N 25 30 E
Khatanga, *Russia* **27 B11** 72 0N 102 20 E
Khatanga →, *Russia* **27 B11** 72 55N 106 0 E
Khatauli, *India* **42 E7** 29 17N 77 43 E
Khatra, *India* **43 H12** 22 59N 86 51 E
Khātūnābād, *Iran* **45 D7** 30 1N 55 25 E
Khatyrka, *Russia* **27 C18** 62 3N 175 15 E
Khavda, *India* **42 H3** 23 51N 69 43 E
Khaybar, Harrat, *Si. Arabia* **44 E4** 25 45N 40 0 E
Khayelitsha, *S. Africa* **53 L3** 34 5S 18 42 E
Khāzimiyah, *Iraq* **44 C4** 34 46N 43 37 E
Khe Bo, *Vietnam* **38 C5** 19 8N 104 41 E
Khe Long, *Vietnam* **38 B5** 21 29N 104 46 E
Khed Brahma, *India* **40 G8** 24 7N 73 5 E
Khekra, *India* **42 E7** 28 52N 77 20 E
Khemarak Phouminville, *Cambodia* **39 G4** 11 37N 102 59 E
Khemisset, *Morocco* **50 B4** 33 50N 6 1W
Khemmarat, *Thailand* **38 D5** 16 10N 105 15 E
Khenāmān, *Iran* **45 D8** 30 27N 56 29 E
Khenchela, *Algeria* **50 A7** 35 28N 7 11 E
Khersān →, *Iran* **45 D6** 31 33N 50 22 E
Kherson, *Ukraine* **25 E5** 46 35N 32 35 E
Khersónisos Akrotíri, *Greece* **23 D6** 35 30N 24 10 E
Kheta →, *Russia* **27 B11** 71 54N 102 6 E
Khewari, *Pakistan* **42 F3** 26 36N 68 52 E
Khilchipur, *India* **42 G7** 24 2N 76 34 E
Khilok, *Russia* **27 D12** 51 30N 110 45 E
Khíos, *Greece* **21 E12** 38 27N 26 9 E
Khirsadoh, *India* **43 H8** 22 11N 78 47 E
Khiuma = Hiiumaa, *Estonia* **9 G20** 58 50N 22 45 E
Khiva, *Uzbekistan* **26 E7** 41 30N 60 18 E
Khīyāv, *Iran* **44 B5** 38 30N 47 45 E
Khlong Khlung, *Thailand* **38 D2** 16 12N 99 43 E
Khmelnik, *Ukraine* **17 D14** 49 33N 27 58 E
Khmelnitskiy = Khmelnytskyy, *Ukraine* **17 D14** 49 23N 27 0 E
Khmelnytskyy, *Ukraine* **17 D14** 49 23N 27 0 E
Khmer Rep. = Cambodia ■, *Asia* **38 F5** 12 15N 105 0 E
Khoai, Hon, *Vietnam* **39 H5** 8 26N 104 50 E
Khodoriv, *Ukraine* **17 D13** 49 24N 24 19 E
Khodzent = Khudzhand, *Tajikistan* **26 E7** 40 17N 69 37 E
Khojak Pass, *Afghan.* **42 D2** 30 51N 66 34 E
Khok Kloi, *Thailand* **39 H2** 8 17N 98 19 E
Khok Pho, *Thailand* **39 J3** 6 43N 101 6 E
Kholm, *Russia* **24 C5** 57 10N 31 15 E
Kholmsk, *Russia* **27 E15** 47 40N 142 5 E
Khomas Hochland, *Namibia* **56 C2** 22 40S 16 0 E
Khomeyn, *Iran* **45 C6** 33 40N 50 7 E
Khomeynī Shahr, *Iran* **45 C6** 32 41N 51 31 E
Khon Kaen, *Thailand* **38 D4** 16 30N 102 47 E
Khong →, *Cambodia* **38 F5** 13 32N 105 58 E
Khong Sedone, *Laos* **38 E5** 15 34N 105 49 E
Khonuu, *Russia* **27 C15** 66 30N 143 12 E
Khoper →, *Russia* **25 D6** 49 30N 42 20 E
Khóra Sfakíon, *Greece* **23 D6** 35 15N 24 9 E
Khorāsān □, *Iran* **45 C8** 34 0N 58 0 E
Khorat = Nakhon Ratchasima, *Thailand* **38 E4** 14 59N 102 12 E
Khorat, Cao Nguyen, *Thailand* **38 E4** 15 30N 102 50 E
Khorixas, *Namibia* **56 C1** 20 16S 14 59 E
Khorramābād, *Khorāsān, Iran* **45 C8** 35 6N 57 57 E
Khorramābād, *Lorestān, Iran* **45 C6** 33 30N 48 25 E
Khorrāmshahr, *Iran* **45 D6** 30 29N 48 15 E
Khorugh, *Tajikistan* **26 F8** 37 30N 71 36 E
Khosravī, *Iran* **45 D6** 30 48N 51 28 E
Khosrowābād, *Khuzestān, Iran* **45 D6** 30 10N 48 25 E
Khosrowābād, *Kordestān, Iran* **44 C5** 35 31N 47 38 E
Khost, *Pakistan* **42 D2** 30 13N 67 35 E
Khosūyeh, *Iran* **45 D7** 28 32N 54 26 E
Khotyn, *Ukraine* **17 D14** 48 31N 26 27 E
Khouribga, *Morocco* **50 B4** 32 58N 6 57W
Khowai, *Bangla.* **41 G17** 24 5N 91 40 E
Khowst, *Afghan.* **42 C3** 33 22N 69 58 E
Khoyniki, *Belarus* **17 C15** 51 54N 29 55 E
Khrysokhou B., *Cyprus* **23 D11** 35 6N 32 25 E
Khu Khan, *Thailand* **38 E5** 14 42N 104 12 E
Khudzhand, *Tajikistan* **26 E7** 40 17N 69 37 E
Khuff, *Si. Arabia* **44 E5** 24 55N 44 53 E
Khūgīānī, *Afghan.* **42 D1** 31 28N 65 14 E
Khuiyala, *India* **42 F4** 27 9N 70 25 E
Khujner, *India* **42 H7** 23 47N 76 36 E
Khulna, *Bangla.* **41 H16** 22 45N 89 34 E
Khulna □, *Bangla.* **41 H16** 22 25N 89 35 E
Khumago, *Botswana* **56 C3** 20 26S 24 32 E
Khūnsorkh, *Iran* **45 E8** 27 9N 56 7 E
Khunti, *India* **43 H11** 23 5N 85 17 E
Khūr, *Iran* **45 C8** 32 55N 58 18 E
Khurai, *India* **42 G8** 24 3N 78 23 E
Khurayş, *Si. Arabia* **45 E6** 25 6N 48 2 E
Khurīyā Murīyā, Jazā 'ir, *Oman* **46 D6** 17 30N 55 58 E
Khurja, *India* **42 E7** 28 15N 77 58 E
Khūrmāl, *Iraq* **44 C5** 35 18N 46 2 E
Khurr, Wādī al, *Iraq* **44 C4** 32 3N 43 52 E
Khūsf, *Iran* **45 C8** 32 46N 58 53 E
Khush, *Afghan.* **40 C3** 32 55N 62 10 E
Khushab, *Pakistan* **42 C5** 32 20N 72 20 E
Khust, *Ukraine* **17 D12** 48 10N 23 18 E
Khuzdar, *Pakistan* **42 F2** 27 52N 66 30 E
Khūzestān □, *Iran* **45 D6** 31 0N 49 0 E
Khvāf, *Iran* **45 C9** 34 33N 60 8 E
Khvājeh, *Iran* **44 B5** 38 9N 46 35 E
Khvānsār, *Iran* **45 D7** 29 56N 54 8 E
Khvor, *Iran* **45 C7** 33 45N 55 0 E
Khvorgū, *Iran* **45 E8** 27 34N 56 27 E
Khvormūj, *Iran* **45 D6** 28 40N 51 30 E
Khvoy, *Iran* **44 B5** 38 35N 45 0 E
Khyber Pass, *Afghan.* **42 B4** 34 10N 71 8 E
Kiabukwa, *Dem. Rep. of the Congo* **55 D1** 8 40S 24 48 E
Kiama, *Australia* **63 E5** 34 40S 150 50 E
Kiamba, *Phil.* **37 C6** 6 2N 124 46 E
Kiambi, *Dem. Rep. of the Congo* **54 D2** 7 15S 28 0 E
Kiambu, *Kenya* **54 C4** 1 8S 36 50 E
Kiangsi = Jiangxi □, *China* **33 D6** 27 30N 116 0 E
Kiangsu = Jiangsu □, *China* **35 H11** 33 0N 120 0 E
Kibanga Port, *Uganda* **54 B3** 0 10N 32 58 E
Kibara, *Tanzania* **54 C3** 2 8S 33 30 E
Kibare, Mts., *Dem. Rep. of the Congo* **54 D2** 8 25S 27 10 E
Kibombo, *Dem. Rep. of the Congo* **54 C2** 3 57S 25 53 E
Kibondo, *Tanzania* **54 C3** 3 35S 30 45 E
Kibre Mengist, *Ethiopia* **46 F2** 5 53N 38 59 E
Kibumbu, *Burundi* **54 C2** 3 32S 29 45 E
Kibungo, *Rwanda* **54 C3** 2 10S 30 32 E
Kibuye, *Burundi* **54 C2** 3 39S 29 59 E
Kibuye, *Rwanda* **54 C2** 2 3S 29 21 E
Kibwesa, *Tanzania* **54 D2** 6 30S 29 58 E
Kibwezi, *Kenya* **54 C4** 2 27S 37 57 E
Kichha, *India* **43 E8** 28 53N 79 30 E
Kichha →, *India* **43 E8** 28 41N 79 18 E
Kichmengskiy Gorodok, *Russia* **24 B8** 59 59N 45 48 E
Kicking Horse Pass, *Canada* **72 C5** 51 28N 116 16W
Kidal, *Mali* **50 E6** 18 26N 1 22 E
Kidderminster, *U.K.* **11 E5** 52 24N 2 15W
Kidete, *Tanzania* **54 D4** 6 25S 37 17 E
Kidnappers, C., *N.Z.* **59 H6** 39 38S 177 5 E
Kidsgrove, *U.K.* **10 D5** 53 5N 2 14W
Kidston, *Australia* **62 B3** 18 52S 144 8 E
Kidugallo, *Tanzania* **54 D4** 6 49S 38 15 E
Kiel, *Germany* **16 A6** 54 19N 10 8 E
Kiel Canal = Nord-Ostsee-Kanal, *Germany* **16 A5** 54 12N 9 32 E
Kielce, *Poland* **17 C11** 50 52N 20 42 E
Kielder Water, *U.K.* **10 B5** 55 11N 2 31W
Kieler Bucht, *Germany* **16 A6** 54 35N 10 25 E
Kien Binh, *Vietnam* **39 H5** 9 55N 105 19 E
Kien Tan, *Vietnam* **39 G5** 10 7N 105 17 E
Kienge, *Dem. Rep. of the Congo* **55 E2** 10 30S 27 30 E
Kiev = Kyyiv, *Ukraine* **17 C16** 50 30N 30 28 E
Kiffa, *Mauritania* **50 E3** 16 37N 11 24W
Kifrī, *Iraq* **44 C5** 34 45N 45 0 E
Kigali, *Rwanda* **54 C3** 1 59S 30 4 E
Kigarama, *Tanzania* **54 C3** 1 1S 31 50 E
Kigoma □, *Tanzania* **54 D3** 5 0S 30 0 E
Kigoma-Ujiji, *Tanzania* **54 C2** 4 55S 29 36 E
Kigomasha, Ras, *Tanzania* **54 C4** 4 58S 38 58 E
Kığzı, *Turkey* **44 B4** 38 18N 43 25 E
Kihei, *U.S.A.* **74 H16** 20 47N 156 28W
Kihnu, *Estonia* **9 G21** 58 9N 24 1 E
Kii-Sanchi, *Japan* **31 G8** 34 20N 136 0 E
Kii-Suidō, *Japan* **31 H7** 33 40N 134 45 E
Kikaiga-Shima, *Japan* **31 K4** 28 19N 129 59 E
Kikinda, *Serbia, Yug.* **21 B9** 45 50N 20 30 E
Kikládhes, *Greece* **21 F11** 37 0N 24 30 E
Kikwit, *Dem. Rep. of the Congo* **52 F3** 5 0S 18 45 E
Kilar, *India* **42 C7** 33 6N 76 25 E
Kilauea, *U.S.A.* **74 J14** 22 13N 159 25W
Kilauea Crater, *U.S.A.* **74 J17** 19 25N 155 17W
Kilbrannan Sd., *U.K.* **12 F3** 55 37N 5 26W
Kilchu, *N. Korea* **35 D15** 40 57N 129 25 E
Kilcoy, *Australia* **63 D5** 26 59S 152 30 E
Kildare, *Ireland* **13 C5** 53 9N 6 55W
Kildare □, *Ireland* **13 C5** 53 10N 6 50W
Kilfinnane, *Ireland* **13 D3** 52 21N 8 28W
Kilgore, *U.S.A.* **81 J7** 32 23N 94 53W
Kilifi, *Kenya* **54 C4** 3 40S 39 48 E
Kilimanjaro, *Tanzania* **54 C4** 3 7S 37 20 E
Kilimanjaro □, *Tanzania* **54 C4** 4 0S 38 0 E
Kilindini, *Kenya* **54 C4** 4 4S 39 40 E
Kilis, *Turkey* **44 B3** 36 42N 37 6 E
Kiliya, *Ukraine* **17 F15** 45 28N 29 16 E
Kilkee, *Ireland* **13 D2** 52 41N 9 39W
Kilkeel, *U.K.* **13 B5** 54 4N 6 0W
Kilkenny, *Ireland* **13 D4** 52 39N 7 15W
Kilkenny □, *Ireland* **13 D4** 52 35N 7 15W
Kilkieran B., *Ireland* **13 C2** 53 20N 9 41W
Kilkís, *Greece* **21 D10** 40 58N 22 57 E
Killala, *Ireland* **13 B2** 54 13N 9 12W
Killala B., *Ireland* **13 B2** 54 16N 9 8W
Killaloe, *Ireland* **13 D3** 52 48N 8 28W
Killaloe Sta., *Canada* **78 A7** 45 33N 77 25W
Killarney, *Australia* **63 D5** 28 20S 152 18 E
Killarney, *Canada* **73 D9** 49 10N 99 40W
Killarney, *Ireland* **13 D2** 52 4N 9 30W
Killary Harbour, *Ireland* **13 C2** 53 38N 9 52W
Killdeer, *U.S.A.* **80 B3** 47 26N 102 48W
Killeen, *U.S.A.* **81 K6** 31 7N 97 44W
Killin, *U.K.* **12 E4** 56 28N 4 19W
Killíni, *Greece* **21 F10** 37 54N 22 25 E
Killorglin, *Ireland* **13 D2** 52 6N 9 47W
Killybegs, *Ireland* **13 B3** 54 38N 8 26W
Kilmarnock, *U.K.* **12 F4** 55 37N 4 29W
Kilmore, *Australia* **63 F3** 37 25S 144 53 E
Kilondo, *Tanzania* **55 D3** 9 45S 34 20 E
Kilosa, *Tanzania* **54 D4** 6 48S 37 0 E
Kilrush, *Ireland* **13 D2** 52 38N 9 29W
Kilwa Kisiwani, *Tanzania* **55 D4** 8 58S 39 32 E
Kilwa Kivinje, *Tanzania* **55 D4** 8 45S 39 25 E
Kilwa Masoko, *Tanzania* **55 D4** 8 55S 39 30 E
Kilwinning, *U.K.* **12 F4** 55 39N 4 43W
Kim, *U.S.A.* **81 G3** 37 15N 103 21W
Kimaam, *Indonesia* **37 F9** 7 58S 138 53 E
Kimamba, *Tanzania* **54 D4** 6 45S 37 10 E
Kimba, *Australia* **63 E2** 33 8S 136 23 E
Kimball, *Nebr., U.S.A.* **80 E3** 41 14N 103 40W
Kimball, *S. Dak., U.S.A.* **80 D5** 43 45N 98 57W
Kimberley, *Australia* **60 C4** 16 20S 127 0 E
Kimberley, *Canada* **72 D5** 49 40N 115 59W
Kimberley, *S. Africa* **56 D3** 28 43S 24 46 E
Kimberly, *U.S.A.* **82 E6** 42 32N 114 22W
Kimch'aek, *N. Korea* **35 D15** 40 40N 129 10 E
Kimch'ŏn, *S. Korea* **35 F15** 36 11N 128 4 E
Kimje, *S. Korea* **35 G14** 35 48N 126 45 E
Kimmirut, *Canada* **69 B13** 62 50N 69 50W
Kimpese, *Dem. Rep. of the Congo* **52 F2** 5 35S 14 26 E
Kimry, *Russia* **24 C6** 56 55N 37 15 E
Kinabalu, Gunong, *Malaysia* **36 C5** 6 3N 116 14 E
Kinaskan L., *Canada* **72 B2** 57 38N 130 8W
Kinbasket L., *Canada* **72 C5** 52 0N 118 10W
Kincardine, *Canada* **78 B3** 44 10N 81 40W
Kincolith, *Canada* **72 B3** 55 0N 129 57W
Kinda, *Dem. Rep. of the Congo* **55 D2** 9 18S 25 4 E
Kinde, *U.S.A.* **78 C2** 43 56N 83 0W
Kinder Scout, *U.K.* **10 D6** 53 24N 1 52W
Kindersley, *Canada* **73 C7** 51 30N 109 10W
Kindia, *Guinea* **50 F3** 10 0N 12 52W
Kindu, *Dem. Rep. of the Congo* **54 C2** 2 55S 25 50 E
Kineshma, *Russia* **24 C7** 57 30N 42 5 E
Kinesi, *Tanzania* **54 C3** 1 25S 33 50 E
King, L., *Australia* **61 F2** 33 10S 119 35 E
King, Mt., *Australia* **62 D4** 25 10S 147 30 E
King City, *U.S.A.* **84 J5** 36 13N 121 8W
King Cr. →, *Australia* **62 C2** 24 35S 139 30 E
King Edward →, *Australia* **60 B4** 14 14S 126 35 E
King Frederick VI Land = Kong Frederik VI.s Kyst, *Greenland* **4 C5** 63 0N 43 0W
King George B., *Falk. Is.* **96 G4** 51 30S 60 30W
King George I., *Antarctica* **5 C18** 60 0S 60 0W
King George Is., *Canada* **69 C11** 57 20N 80 30W
King I. = Kadan Kyun, *Burma* **38 F2** 12 30N 98 20 E
King I., *Australia* **62 F3** 39 50S 144 0 E
King I., *Canada* **72 C3** 52 10N 127 40W
King Leopold Ranges, *Australia* **60 C4** 17 30S 125 45 E
King of Prussia, *U.S.A.* **79 F9** 40 5N 75 23W
King Sd., *Australia* **60 C3** 16 50S 123 20 E
King William I., *Canada* **68 B10** 69 10N 97 25W
King William's Town, *S. Africa* **56 E4** 32 51S 27 22 E
Kingaroy, *Australia* **63 D5** 26 32S 151 51 E
Kingfisher, *U.S.A.* **81 H6** 35 52N 97 56W
Kingirbān, *Iraq* **44 C5** 34 40N 44 54 E
Kingisepp = Kuressaare, *Estonia* **9 G20** 58 15N 22 30 E
Kingman, *Ariz., U.S.A.* **85 K12** 35 12N 114 4W
Kingman, *Kans., U.S.A.* **81 G5** 37 39N 98 7W
Kingoonya, *Australia* **63 E2** 30 55S 135 19 E
Kingri, *Pakistan* **42 D3** 30 27N 69 49 E
Kings →, *U.S.A.* **84 J7** 36 3N 119 50W
Kings Canyon National Park, *U.S.A.* **84 J8** 36 50N 118 40W
King's Lynn, *U.K.* **10 E8** 52 45N 0 24 E
Kings Mountain, *U.S.A.* **77 H5** 35 15N 81 20W
Kings Park, *U.S.A.* **79 F11** 40 53N 73 16W
King's Peak, *U.S.A.* **82 F8** 40 46N 110 27W
Kingsbridge, *U.K.* **11 G4** 50 17N 3 47W
Kingsburg, *U.S.A.* **84 J7** 36 31N 119 33W
Kingscote, *Australia* **63 F2** 35 40S 137 38 E
Kingscourt, *Ireland* **13 C5** 53 55N 6 48W
Kingsford, *U.S.A.* **76 C1** 45 48N 88 4W
Kingsland, *U.S.A.* **77 K5** 30 48N 81 41W
Kingsley, *U.S.A.* **80 D7** 42 35N 95 58W
Kingsport, *U.S.A.* **77 G4** 36 33N 82 33W
Kingston, *Canada* **79 B8** 44 14N 76 30W
Kingston, *Jamaica* **88 C4** 18 0N 76 50W
Kingston, *N.Z.* **59 L2** 45 20S 168 43 E
Kingston, *N.H., U.S.A.* **79 D13** 42 56N 71 3W
Kingston, *N.Y., U.S.A.* **79 E11** 41 56N 73 59W
Kingston, *Pa., U.S.A.* **79 E9** 41 16N 75 54W
Kingston, *R.I., U.S.A.* **79 E13** 41 29N 71 30W
Kingston Pk., *U.S.A.* **85 K11** 35 45N 115 54W
Kingston South East, *Australia* **63 F2** 36 51S 139 55 E
Kingston upon Hull, *U.K.* **10 D7** 53 45N 0 21W
Kingston upon Hull □, *U.K.* **10 D7** 53 45N 0 21W
Kingston-upon-Thames, *U.K.* **11 F7** 51 24N 0 17W
Kingstown, *St. Vincent* **89 D7** 13 10N 61 10W
Kingstree, *U.S.A.* **77 J6** 33 40N 79 50W
Kingsville, *Canada* **78 D2** 42 2N 82 45W
Kingsville, *U.S.A.* **81 M6** 27 31N 97 52W
Kingussie, *U.K.* **12 D4** 57 6N 4 2W
Kingwood, *U.S.A.* **81 K7** 29 54N 95 18W
Kınık, *Turkey* **21 E12** 39 6N 27 24 E
Kinistino, *Canada* **73 C7** 52 57N 105 2W
Kinkala, *Congo* **52 E2** 4 18S 14 49 E
Kinki □, *Japan* **31 H8** 33 45N 136 0 E
Kinleith, *N.Z.* **59 H5** 38 20S 175 56 E
Kinmount, *Canada* **78 B6** 44 48N 78 45W
Kinna, *Sweden* **9 H15** 57 32N 12 42 E
Kinnairds Hd., *U.K.* **12 D6** 57 43N 2 1W
Kinnarodden, *Norway* **6 A11** 71 8N 27 40 E
Kino, *Mexico* **86 B2** 28 45N 111 59W
Kinoje →, *Canada* **70 B3** 52 8N 81 25W
Kinomoto, *Japan* **31 G8** 35 30N 136 13 E
Kinoni, *Uganda* **54 C3** 0 41S 30 28 E
Kinoosao, *Canada* **73 B8** 57 5N 102 1W
Kinross, *U.K.* **12 E5** 56 13N 3 25W
Kinsale, *Ireland* **13 E3** 51 42N 8 31W

Kościan

Kinsale, Old Hd. of, *Ireland* **13 E3** 51 37N 8 33W
Kinsha = Chang Jiang →, *China* **33 C7** 31 48N 121 10 E
Kinshasa, *Dem. Rep. of the Congo* **52 E3** 4 20S 15 15 E
Kinsley, *U.S.A.* **81 G5** 37 55N 99 25W
Kinsman, *U.S.A.* **78 E4** 41 26N 80 35W
Kinston, *U.S.A.* **77 H7** 35 16N 77 35W
Kintore Ra., *Australia* **60 D4** 23 15S 128 47 E
Kintyre, *U.K.* **12 F3** 55 30N 5 35W
Kintyre, Mull of, *U.K.* **12 F3** 55 17N 5 47W
Kinushseo →, *Canada* **70 A3** 55 15N 83 45W
Kinuso, *Canada* **72 B5** 55 20N 115 25W
Kinyangiri, *Tanzania* **54 C3** 4 25S 34 37 E
Kinzua, *U.S.A.* **78 E6** 41 52N 78 58W
Kinzua Dam, *U.S.A.* **78 E6** 41 53N 79 0W
Kiosk, *Canada* **70 C4** 46 6N 78 53W
Kiowa, *Kans., U.S.A.* **81 G5** 37 1N 98 29W
Kiowa, *Okla., U.S.A.* **81 H7** 34 43N 95 54W
Kipahigan L., *Canada* **73 B8** 55 20N 101 55W
Kipanga, *Tanzania* **54 D4** 6 15S 35 20 E
Kiparissía, *Greece* **21 F9** 37 15N 21 40 E
Kiparissiakós Kólpos, *Greece* **21 F9** 37 25N 21 25 E
Kipawa, L., *Canada* **70 C4** 46 50N 79 0W
Kipembawe, *Tanzania* **54 D3** 7 38S 33 27 E
Kipengere Ra., *Tanzania* **55 D3** 9 12S 34 15 E
Kipili, *Tanzania* **54 D3** 7 28S 30 32 E
Kipini, *Kenya* **54 C5** 2 30S 40 32 E
Kipling, *Canada* **73 C8** 50 6N 102 38W
Kippure, *Ireland* **13 C5** 53 11N 6 21W
Kipushi, *Dem. Rep. of the Congo* **55 E2** 11 48S 27 12 E
Kirensk, *Russia* **27 D11** 57 50N 107 55 E
Kirghizia = Kyrgyzstan ■, *Asia* **26 E8** 42 0N 75 0 E
Kirghizstan = Kyrgyzstan ■, *Asia* **26 E8** 42 0N 75 0 E
Kirgiziya Steppe, *Eurasia* **25 E10** 50 0N 55 0 E
Kiribati ■, *Pac. Oc.* **64 H10** 5 0S 180 0 E
Kırıkkale, *Turkey* **25 G5** 39 51N 33 32 E
Kirillov, *Russia* **24 C6** 59 49N 38 24 E
Kirin = Jilin, *China* **35 C14** 43 44N 126 30 E
Kiritimati, *Kiribati* **65 G12** 1 58N 157 27W
Kirkby, *U.K.* **10 D5** 53 30N 2 54W
Kirkby Lonsdale, *U.K.* **10 C5** 54 12N 2 36W
Kirkcaldy, *U.K.* **12 E5** 56 7N 3 9W
Kirkcudbright, *U.K.* **12 G4** 54 50N 4 2W
Kirkee, *India* **40 K8** 18 34N 73 56 E
Kirkenes, *Norway* **8 B23** 69 40N 30 5 E
Kirkfield, *Canada* **78 B6** 44 34N 78 59W
Kirkjubæjarklaustur, *Iceland* **8 E4** 63 47N 18 4W
Kirkkonummi, *Finland* **9 F21** 60 8N 24 26 E
Kirkland Lake, *Canada* **70 C3** 48 9N 80 2W
Kırklareli, *Turkey* **21 D12** 41 44N 27 15 E
Kirksville, *U.S.A.* **80 E8** 40 12N 92 35W
Kirkūk, *Iraq* **44 C5** 35 30N 44 21 E
Kirkwall, *U.K.* **12 C6** 58 59N 2 58W
Kirkwood, *S. Africa* **56 E4** 33 22S 25 15 E
Kirov, *Russia* **24 C8** 58 35N 49 40 E
Kirovabad = Gäncä, *Azerbaijan* **25 F8** 40 45N 46 20 E
Kirovakan = Vanadzor, *Armenia* **25 F7** 40 48N 44 30 E
Kirovograd = Kirovohrad, *Ukraine* **25 E5** 48 35N 32 20 E
Kirovohrad, *Ukraine* **25 E5** 48 35N 32 20 E
Kirovsk = Babadayhan, *Turkmenistan* **26 F7** 37 42N 60 23 E
Kirovsk, *Russia* **24 A5** 67 32N 33 41 E
Kirovskiy, *Kamchatka, Russia* **27 D16** 54 27N 155 42 E
Kirovskiy, *Primorsk, Russia* **30 B6** 45 7N 133 30 E
Kirriemuir, *U.K.* **12 E5** 56 41N 3 1W
Kirsanov, *Russia* **24 D7** 52 35N 42 40 E
Kırşehir, *Turkey* **25 G5** 39 14N 34 5 E
Kirthar Range, *Pakistan* **42 F2** 27 0N 67 0 E
Kirtland, *U.S.A.* **83 H9** 36 44N 108 21W
Kiruna, *Sweden* **8 C19** 67 52N 20 15 E
Kirundu, *Dem. Rep. of the Congo* **54 C2** 0 50S 25 35 E
Kiryū, *Japan* **31 F9** 36 24N 139 20 E
Kisaga, *Tanzania* **54 C3** 4 30S 34 23 E
Kisalaya, *Nic.* **88 D3** 14 40N 84 3W
Kisámou, Kólpos, *Greece* **23 D5** 35 30N 23 38 E
Kisanga, *Dem. Rep. of the Congo* **54 B2** 2 30N 26 35 E
Kisangani, *Dem. Rep. of the Congo* **54 B2** 0 35N 25 15 E
Kisar, *Indonesia* **37 F7** 8 5S 127 10 E
Kisarawe, *Tanzania* **54 D4** 6 53S 39 0 E
Kisarazu, *Japan* **31 G9** 35 23N 139 55 E
Kishanganga →, *Pakistan* **43 B5** 34 18N 73 28 E
Kishanganj, *India* **43 F13** 26 3N 88 14 E
Kishangarh, *Raj., India* **42 F6** 26 34N 74 52 E
Kishangarh, *Raj., India* **42 F4** 27 50N 70 30 E
Kishinev = Chişinău, *Moldova* **17 E15** 47 2N 28 50 E
Kishiwada, *Japan* **31 G7** 34 28N 135 22 E
Kishtwar, *India* **43 C6** 33 20N 75 48 E
Kisii, *Kenya* **54 C3** 0 40S 34 45 E
Kisiju, *Tanzania* **54 D4** 7 23S 39 19 E
Kisizi, *Uganda* **54 C2** 1 0S 29 58 E
Kiskőrös, *Hungary* **17 E10** 46 37N 19 20 E
Kiskunfélegyháza, *Hungary* **17 E10** 46 42N 19 53 E
Kiskunhalas, *Hungary* **17 E10** 46 28N 19 37 E
Kislovodsk, *Russia* **25 F7** 43 50N 42 45 E
Kismayu = Chisimaio, *Somali Rep.* **49 G8** 0 22S 42 32 E
Kiso-Gawa →, *Japan* **31 G8** 35 20N 136 45 E
Kiso-Sammyaku, *Japan* **31 G8** 35 45N 137 45 E
Kisofukushima, *Japan* **31 G8** 35 52N 137 43 E
Kisoro, *Uganda* **54 C2** 1 17S 29 48 E
Kissidougou, *Guinea* **50 G3** 9 5N 10 5W
Kissimmee, *U.S.A.* **77 L5** 28 18N 81 24W
Kissimmee →, *U.S.A.* **77 M5** 27 9N 80 52W
Kississing L., *Canada* **73 B8** 55 10N 101 20W
Kissónerga, *Cyprus* **23 E11** 34 49N 32 24 E
Kisumu, *Kenya* **54 C3** 0 3S 34 45 E
Kiswani, *Tanzania* **54 C4** 4 5S 37 57 E
Kiswere, *Tanzania* **55 D4** 9 27S 39 30 E
Kit Carson, *U.S.A.* **80 F3** 38 46N 102 48W
Kita, *Mali* **50 F4** 13 5N 9 25W
Kitaibaraki, *Japan* **31 F10** 36 50N 140 45 E
Kitakami, *Japan* **30 E10** 39 20N 141 10 E
Kitakami-Gawa →, *Japan* **30 E10** 38 25N 141 19 E
Kitakami-Sammyaku, *Japan* **30 E10** 39 30N 141 30 E
Kitakata, *Japan* **30 F9** 37 39N 139 52 E
Kitakyūshū, *Japan* **31 H5** 33 50N 130 50 E
Kitale, *Kenya* **54 B4** 1 0N 35 0 E
Kitami, *Japan* **30 C11** 43 48N 143 54 E
Kitami-Sammyaku, *Japan* **30 B11** 44 22N 142 43 E
Kitangiri, L., *Tanzania* **54 C3** 4 5S 34 20 E
Kitaya, *Tanzania* **55 E5** 10 38S 40 8 E
Kitchener, *Canada* **78 C4** 43 27N 80 29W
Kitega = Gitega, *Burundi* **54 C2** 3 26S 29 56 E
Kitengo, *Dem. Rep. of the Congo* **54 D1** 7 26S 24 8 E
Kitgum, *Uganda* **54 B3** 3 17N 32 52 E
Kíthira, *Greece* **21 F10** 36 8N 23 0 E
Kíthnos, *Greece* **21 F11** 37 26N 24 27 E
Kiti, *Cyprus* **23 E12** 34 50N 33 34 E
Kiti, C., *Cyprus* **23 E12** 34 48N 33 36 E
Kitimat, *Canada* **72 C3** 54 3N 128 38W
Kitinen →, *Finland* **8 C22** 67 14N 27 27 E
Kitsuki, *Japan* **31 H5** 33 25N 131 37 E
Kittakittaooloo, L., *Australia* **63 D2** 28 3S 138 14 E
Kittanning, *U.S.A.* **78 F5** 40 49N 79 31W
Kittatinny Mts., *U.S.A.* **79 F10** 41 0N 75 0W
Kittery, *U.S.A.* **77 D10** 43 5N 70 45W
Kittilä, *Finland* **8 C21** 67 40N 24 51 E
Kitui, *Kenya* **54 C4** 1 17S 38 0 E
Kitwanga, *Canada* **72 B3** 55 6N 128 4W
Kitwe, *Zambia* **55 E2** 12 54S 28 13 E
Kivarli, *India* **42 G5** 24 33N 72 46 E
Kivertsi, *Ukraine* **17 C13** 50 50N 25 28 E
Kividhes, *Cyprus* **23 E11** 34 46N 32 51 E
Kivu, L., *Dem. Rep. of the Congo* **54 C2** 1 48S 29 0 E
Kiyev = Kyyiv, *Ukraine* **17 C16** 50 30N 30 28 E
Kiyevskoye Vdkhr. = Kyyivske Vdskh., *Ukraine* **17 C16** 51 0N 30 25 E
Kizel, *Russia* **24 C10** 59 3N 57 40 E
Kiziguru, *Rwanda* **54 C3** 1 46S 30 23 E
Kızıl Irmak →, *Turkey* **25 F6** 41 44N 35 58 E
Kizil Jilga, *India* **43 B8** 35 26N 78 50 E
Kızıltepe, *Turkey* **44 B4** 37 12N 40 35 E
Kizimkazi, *Tanzania* **54 D4** 6 28S 39 30 E
Kizlyar, *Russia* **25 F8** 43 51N 46 40 E
Kizyl-Arvat = Gyzylarbat, *Turkmenistan* **26 F6** 39 4N 56 23 E
Kjölur, *Iceland* **8 D4** 64 50N 19 25W
Kladno, *Czech Rep.* **16 C8** 50 10N 14 7 E
Klaeng, *Thailand* **38 F3** 12 47N 101 39 E
Klagenfurt, *Austria* **16 E8** 46 38N 14 20 E
Klaipėda, *Lithuania* **9 J19** 55 43N 21 10 E
Klaksvík, *Færoe Is.* **8 E9** 62 14N 6 35W
Klamath →, *U.S.A.* **82 F1** 41 33N 124 5W
Klamath Falls, *U.S.A.* **82 E3** 42 13N 121 46W
Klamath Mts., *U.S.A.* **82 F2** 41 20N 123 0W
Klamono, *Indonesia* **37 E8** 1 8S 131 30 E
Klappan →, *Canada* **72 B3** 58 0N 129 43W
Klarälven →, *Sweden* **9 G15** 59 23N 13 32 E
Klatovy, *Czech Rep.* **16 D7** 49 23N 13 18 E
Klawer, *S. Africa* **56 E2** 31 44S 18 36 E
Klazienaveen, *Neths.* **15 B6** 52 44N 7 0 E
Kleena Kleene, *Canada* **72 C4** 52 0N 124 59W
Klein-Karas, *Namibia* **56 D2** 27 33S 18 7 E
Klerksdorp, *S. Africa* **56 D4** 26 53S 26 38 E
Kletsk = Klyetsk, *Belarus* **17 B14** 53 5N 26 45 E
Kletskiy, *Russia* **25 E7** 49 16N 43 11 E
Klickitat, *U.S.A.* **82 D3** 45 49N 121 9W
Klickitat →, *U.S.A.* **84 E5** 45 42N 121 17W
Klidhes, *Cyprus* **23 D13** 35 42N 34 36 E
Klinaklini →, *Canada* **72 C3** 51 21N 125 40W
Klipdale, *S. Africa* **56 E2** 34 19S 19 57 E
Klipplaat, *S. Africa* **56 E3** 33 1S 24 22 E
Kłodzko, *Poland* **17 C9** 50 28N 16 38 E
Klouto, *Togo* **50 G6** 6 57N 0 44 E
Kluane L., *Canada* **68 B6** 61 15N 138 40W
Kluane Nat. Park, *Canada* **72 A1** 60 45N 139 30W
Kluczbork, *Poland* **17 C10** 50 58N 18 12 E
Klukwan, *U.S.A.* **72 B1** 59 24N 135 54W
Klyetsk, *Belarus* **17 B14** 53 5N 26 45 E
Klyuchevskaya, Gora, *Russia* **27 D17** 55 50N 160 30 E
Knaresborough, *U.K.* **10 C6** 54 1N 1 28W
Knee L., *Man., Canada* **70 A1** 55 3N 94 45W
Knee L., *Sask., Canada* **73 B7** 55 51N 107 0W
Knight Inlet, *Canada* **72 C3** 50 45N 125 40W
Knighton, *U.K.* **11 E4** 52 21N 3 3W
Knights Ferry, *U.S.A.* **84 H6** 37 50N 120 40W
Knights Landing, *U.S.A.* **84 G5** 38 48N 121 43W
Knob, C., *Australia* **61 F2** 34 32S 119 16 E
Knock, *Ireland* **13 C3** 53 48N 8 55W
Knockmealdown Mts., *Ireland* **13 D4** 52 14N 7 56W
Knokke-Heist, *Belgium* **15 C3** 51 21N 3 17 E
Knossós, *Greece* **23 D7** 35 16N 25 10 E
Knowlton, *Canada* **79 A12** 45 13N 72 31W
Knox, *U.S.A.* **76 E2** 41 18N 86 37W
Knox Coast, *Antarctica* **5 C8** 66 30S 108 0 E
Knoxville, *Iowa, U.S.A.* **80 E8** 41 19N 93 6W
Knoxville, *Pa., U.S.A.* **78 E7** 41 57N 77 27W
Knoxville, *Tenn., U.S.A.* **77 H4** 35 58N 83 55W
Knysna, *S. Africa* **56 E3** 34 2S 23 2 E
Ko Kha, *Thailand* **38 C2** 18 11N 99 24 E
Koartac = Quaqtaq, *Canada* **69 B13** 60 55N 69 40W
Koba, *Indonesia* **37 F8** 6 37S 134 37 E
Kobarid, *Slovenia* **16 E7** 46 15N 13 30 E
Kobayashi, *Japan* **31 J5** 31 56N 130 59 E
Kobdo = Hovd, *Mongolia* **32 B4** 48 2N 91 37 E
Kōbe, *Japan* **31 G7** 34 45N 135 10 E
København, *Denmark* **9 J15** 55 41N 12 34 E
Kōbi-Sho, *Japan* **31 M1** 25 56N 123 41 E
Koblenz, *Germany* **16 C4** 50 21N 7 36 E
Kobryn, *Belarus* **17 B13** 52 15N 24 22 E
Kocaeli, *Turkey* **25 F4** 40 45N 29 50 E
Kočani, *Macedonia* **21 D10** 41 55N 22 25 E
Koch Bihar, *India* **41 F16** 26 22N 89 29 E
Kochang, *S. Korea* **35 G14** 35 41N 127 55 E
Kochas, *India* **43 G10** 25 15N 83 56 E
Kōchi, *Japan* **31 H6** 33 30N 133 35 E
Kōchi □, *Japan* **31 H6** 33 40N 133 30 E
Kochiu = Gejiu, *China* **32 D5** 23 20N 103 10 E
Kodarma, *India* **43 G11** 24 28N 85 36 E
Kodiak, *U.S.A.* **68 C4** 57 47N 152 24W
Kodiak I., *U.S.A.* **68 C4** 57 30N 152 45W
Kodinar, *India* **42 J4** 20 46N 70 46 E
Koes, *Namibia* **56 D2** 26 0S 19 15 E
Koffiefontein, *S. Africa* **56 D4** 29 30S 25 0 E
Kofiau, *Indonesia* **37 E7** 1 11S 129 50 E
Koforidua, *Ghana* **50 G5** 6 3N 0 17W
Kōfu, *Japan* **31 G9** 35 40N 138 30 E
Koga, *Japan* **31 F9** 36 11N 139 43 E
Kogaluk →, *Canada* **71 A7** 56 12N 61 44W
Køge, *Denmark* **9 J15** 55 27N 12 11 E
Koh-i-Bābā, *Afghan.* **40 B5** 34 30N 67 0 E
Koh-i-Khurd, *Afghan.* **42 C1** 33 30N 65 59 E
Koh-i-Maran, *Pakistan* **42 E2** 29 18N 66 50 E
Kohat, *Pakistan* **42 C4** 33 40N 71 29 E
Kohima, *India* **41 G19** 25 35N 94 10 E
Kohkīlūyeh va Būyer Aḥmadi □, *Iran* **45 D6** 31 30N 50 30 E
Kohler Ra., *Antarctica* **5 D15** 77 0S 110 0W
Kohlu, *Pakistan* **42 E3** 29 54N 69 15 E
Kohtla-Järve, *Estonia* **9 G22** 59 20N 27 20 E
Koillismaa, *Finland* **8 D23** 65 44N 28 36 E
Koin-dong, *N. Korea* **35 D14** 40 28N 126 18 E
Kojŏ, *N. Korea* **35 E14** 38 58N 127 58 E
Kojonup, *Australia* **61 F2** 33 48S 117 10 E
Kojūr, *Iran* **45 B6** 36 23N 51 43 E
Kokand = Qŭqon, *Uzbekistan* **26 E8** 40 30N 70 57 E
Kokas, *Indonesia* **37 E8** 2 42S 132 26 E
Kokchetav = Kökshetaū, *Kazakstan* **26 D7** 53 20N 69 25 E
Kokemäenjoki →, *Finland* **9 F19** 61 32N 21 44 E
Kokkola, *Finland* **8 E20** 63 50N 23 8 E
Koko Kyunzu, *Burma* **41 M18** 14 10N 93 25 E
Kokomo, *U.S.A.* **76 E2** 40 29N 86 8W
Koksan, *N. Korea* **35 E14** 38 46N 126 40 E
Kökshetaū, *Kazakstan* **26 D7** 53 20N 69 25 E
Koksoak →, *Canada* **69 C13** 58 30N 68 10W
Kokstad, *S. Africa* **57 E4** 30 32S 29 29 E
Kokubu, *Japan* **31 J5** 31 44N 130 46 E
Kola, *Indonesia* **37 F8** 5 35S 134 30 E
Kola, *Russia* **24 A5** 68 45N 33 8 E
Kola Pen. = Kolskiy Poluostrov, *Russia* **24 A6** 67 30N 38 0 E
Kolachi →, *Pakistan* **42 F2** 27 8N 67 2 E
Kolahoi, *India* **43 B6** 34 12N 75 22 E
Kolaka, *Indonesia* **37 E6** 4 3S 121 46 E
Kolar, *India* **40 N11** 13 12N 78 15 E
Kolar Gold Fields, *India* **40 N11** 12 58N 78 16 E
Kolaras, *India* **42 G6** 25 14N 77 36 E
Kolari, *Finland* **8 C20** 67 20N 23 48 E
Kolayat, *India* **40 F8** 27 50N 72 50 E
Kolchugino = Leninsk-Kuznetskiy, *Russia* **26 D9** 54 44N 86 10 E
Kolding, *Denmark* **9 J13** 55 30N 9 29 E
Kolepom = Dolak, Pulau, *Indonesia* **37 F9** 8 0S 138 30 E
Kolguyev, Ostrov, *Russia* **24 A8** 69 20N 48 30 E
Kolhapur, *India* **40 L9** 16 43N 74 15 E
Kolín, *Czech Rep.* **16 C8** 50 2N 15 9 E
Kolkas rags, *Latvia* **9 H20** 57 46N 22 37 E
Kollum, *Neths.* **15 A6** 53 17N 6 10 E
Kolmanskop, *Namibia* **56 D2** 26 45S 15 14 E
Köln, *Germany* **16 C4** 50 56N 6 57 E
Koło, *Poland* **17 B10** 52 14N 18 40 E
Kołobrzeg, *Poland* **16 A8** 54 10N 15 35 E
Kolomna, *Russia* **24 C6** 55 8N 38 45 E
Kolomyya, *Ukraine* **17 D13** 48 31N 25 2 E
Kolonodale, *Indonesia* **37 E6** 2 3S 121 25 E
Kolosib, *India* **41 G18** 24 15N 92 45 E
Kolpashevo, *Russia* **26 D9** 58 20N 83 5 E
Kolpino, *Russia* **24 C5** 59 44N 30 39 E
Kolskiy Poluostrov, *Russia* **24 A6** 67 30N 38 0 E
Kolskiy Zaliv, *Russia* **24 A5** 69 23N 34 0 E
Kolwezi, *Dem. Rep. of the Congo* **55 E2** 10 40S 25 25 E
Kolyma →, *Russia* **27 C17** 69 30N 161 0 E
Kolymskoye Nagorye, *Russia* **27 C16** 63 0N 157 0 E
Kôm Ombo, *Egypt* **51 D12** 24 25N 32 52 E
Komandorskiye Is. = Komandorskiye Ostrova, *Russia* **27 D17** 55 0N 167 0 E
Komandorskiye Ostrova, *Russia* **27 D17** 55 0N 167 0 E
Komárno, *Slovak Rep.* **17 E10** 47 49N 18 5 E
Komatipoort, *S. Africa* **57 D5** 25 25S 31 55 E
Komatou Yialou, *Cyprus* **23 D13** 35 25N 34 8 E
Komatsu, *Japan* **31 F8** 36 25N 136 30 E
Komatsujima, *Japan* **31 H7** 34 0N 134 35 E
Komi □, *Russia* **24 B10** 64 0N 55 0 E
Kommunarsk = Alchevsk, *Ukraine* **25 E6** 48 30N 38 45 E
Kommunizma, Pik, *Tajikistan* **26 F8** 39 0N 72 2 E
Komodo, *Indonesia* **37 F5** 8 37S 119 20 E
Komoran, Pulau, *Indonesia* **37 F9** 8 18S 138 45 E
Komoro, *Japan* **31 F9** 36 19N 138 26 E
Komotini, *Greece* **21 D11** 41 9N 25 26 E
Kompasberg, *S. Africa* **56 E3** 31 45S 24 32 E
Kompong Bang, *Cambodia* **39 F5** 12 24N 104 40 E
Kompong Cham, *Cambodia* **39 G5** 12 0N 105 30 E
Kompong Chhnang = Kampang Chhnang, *Cambodia* **39 F5** 12 20N 104 35 E
Kompong Chikreng, *Cambodia* **38 F5** 13 5N 104 18 E
Kompong Kleang, *Cambodia* **38 F5** 13 6N 104 8 E
Kompong Luong, *Cambodia* **39 G5** 11 49N 104 48 E
Kompong Pranak, *Cambodia* **38 F5** 13 35N 104 55 E
Kompong Som = Kampong Saom, *Cambodia* **39 G4** 10 38N 103 30 E
Kompong Som, Chhung = Kampong Saom, Chaak, *Cambodia* **39 G4** 10 50N 103 32 E
Kompong Speu, *Cambodia* **39 G5** 11 26N 104 32 E
Kompong Sralao, *Cambodia* **38 E5** 14 5N 105 46 E
Kompong Thom, *Cambodia* **38 F5** 12 35N 104 51 E
Kompong Trabeck, *Cambodia* **38 F5** 13 6N 105 14 E
Kompong Trabeck, *Cambodia* **39 G5** 11 9N 105 28 E
Kompong Trach, *Cambodia* **39 G5** 11 25N 105 48 E
Kompong Tralach, *Cambodia* **39 G5** 11 54N 104 47 E
Komrat = Comrat, *Moldova* **17 E15** 46 18N 28 40 E
Komsberg, *S. Africa* **56 E3** 32 40S 20 45 E
Komsomolets, Ostrov, *Russia* **27 A10** 80 30N 95 0 E
Komsomolsk, *Russia* **27 D14** 50 30N 137 0 E
Kon Tum, *Vietnam* **38 E7** 14 24N 108 0 E
Kon Tum, Plateau du, *Vietnam* **38 E7** 14 30N 108 30 E
Konarhā □, *Afghan.* **40 B7** 35 30N 71 3 E
Konārī, *Iran* **45 D6** 28 13N 51 36 E
Konch, *India* **43 G8** 26 0N 79 10 E
Konde, *Tanzania* **54 C4** 4 57S 39 45 E
Kondinin, *Australia* **61 F2** 32 34S 118 8 E
Kondoa, *Tanzania* **54 C4** 4 55S 35 50 E
Kondókali, *Greece* **23 A3** 39 38N 19 51 E
Kondopaga, *Russia* **24 B5** 62 12N 34 17 E
Kondratyevo, *Russia* **27 D10** 57 22N 98 15 E
Köneürgench, *Turkmenistan* **26 E6** 42 19N 59 10 E
Konevo, *Russia* **24 B6** 62 8N 39 20 E
Kong = Khong →, *Cambodia* **38 F5** 13 32N 105 58 E
Kong, *Ivory C.* **50 G5** 8 54N 4 36W
Kong, Koh, *Cambodia* **39 G4** 11 20N 103 0 E
Kong Christian IX.s Land, *Greenland* **4 C6** 68 0N 36 0W
Kong Christian X.s Land, *Greenland* **4 B6** 74 0N 29 0W
Kong Franz Joseph Fd., *Greenland* **4 B6** 73 30N 24 30W
Kong Frederik IX.s Land, *Greenland* **4 C5** 67 0N 52 0W
Kong Frederik VI.s Kyst, *Greenland* **4 C5** 63 0N 43 0W
Kong Frederik VIII.s Land, *Greenland* **4 B6** 78 30N 26 0W
Kong Oscar Fjord, *Greenland* **4 B6** 72 20N 24 0W
Kongju, *S. Korea* **35 F14** 36 30N 127 0 E
Konglu, *Burma* **41 F20** 27 13N 97 57 E
Kongolo, *Kasai-Or., Dem. Rep. of the Congo* **54 D1** 5 26S 24 49 E
Kongolo, *Katanga, Dem. Rep. of the Congo* **54 D2** 5 22S 27 0 E
Kongsberg, *Norway* **9 G13** 59 39N 9 39 E
Kongsvinger, *Norway* **9 F15** 60 12N 12 2 E
Kongwa, *Tanzania* **54 D4** 6 11S 36 26 E
Koni, *Dem. Rep. of the Congo* **55 E2** 10 40S 27 11 E
Koni, Mts., *Dem. Rep. of the Congo* **55 E2** 10 36S 27 10 E
Königsberg = Kaliningrad, *Russia* **9 J19** 54 42N 20 32 E
Konin, *Poland* **17 B10** 52 12N 18 15 E
Konjic, *Bos.-H.* **21 C7** 43 42N 17 58 E
Konkiep, *Namibia* **56 D2** 26 49S 17 15 E
Konosha, *Russia* **24 B7** 61 0N 40 5 E
Kōnosu, *Japan* **31 F9** 36 3N 139 31 E
Konotop, *Ukraine* **25 D5** 51 12N 33 7 E
Końskie, *Poland* **17 C11** 51 15N 20 23 E
Konstanz, *Germany* **16 E5** 47 40N 9 10 E
Kont, *Iran* **45 E9** 26 55N 61 50 E
Kontagora, *Nigeria* **50 F7** 10 23N 5 27 E
Konya, *Turkey* **25 G5** 37 52N 32 35 E
Konza, *Kenya* **54 C4** 1 45S 37 7 E
Koocanusa, L., *Canada* **82 B6** 49 20N 115 15W
Kookynie, *Australia* **61 E3** 29 17S 121 22 E
Koolyanobbing, *Australia* **61 F2** 30 48S 119 36 E
Koonibba, *Australia* **63 E1** 31 54S 133 25 E
Koorawatha, *Australia* **63 E4** 34 2S 148 33 E
Koorda, *Australia* **61 F2** 30 48S 117 35 E
Kooskia, *U.S.A.* **82 C6** 46 9N 115 59W
Kootenay →, *U.S.A.* **72 D5** 49 19N 117 39W
Kootenay L., *Canada* **72 D5** 49 45N 116 50W
Kootenay Nat. Park, *Canada* **72 C5** 51 0N 116 0W
Kootjieskolk, *S. Africa* **56 E3** 31 15S 20 21 E
Kopaonik, *Serbia, Yug.* **21 C9** 43 10N 20 50 E
Kópavogur, *Iceland* **8 D3** 64 6N 21 55W
Koper, *Slovenia* **16 F7** 45 31N 13 44 E
Kopervik, *Norway* **9 G11** 59 17N 5 17 E
Kopet Dagh, *Asia* **45 B8** 38 0N 58 0 E
Kopi, *Australia* **63 E2** 33 24S 135 40 E
Köping, *Sweden* **9 G17** 59 31N 16 3 E
Koppeh Dāgh = Kopet Dagh, *Asia* **45 B8** 38 0N 58 0 E
Koppies, *S. Africa* **57 D4** 27 20S 27 30 E
Koprivnica, *Croatia* **20 A7** 46 12N 16 45 E
Kopychyntsi, *Ukraine* **17 D13** 49 7N 25 58 E
Korab, *Macedonia* **21 D9** 41 44N 20 40 E
Korakiána, *Greece* **23 A3** 39 42N 19 45 E
Koral, *India* **42 J5** 21 50N 73 12 E
Korba, *India* **43 H10** 22 20N 82 45 E
Korbu, G., *Malaysia* **39 K3** 4 41N 101 18 E
Korça, *Albania* **21 D9** 40 37N 20 50 E
Korce = Korça, *Albania* **21 D9** 40 37N 20 50 E
Korčula, *Croatia* **20 C7** 42 56N 16 57 E
Kord Kūy, *Iran* **45 B7** 36 48N 54 7 E
Kord Sheykh, *Iran* **45 D7** 28 31N 52 53 E
Kordestān □, *Iran* **44 C5** 36 0N 47 0 E
Kordofân, *Sudan* **51 F11** 13 0N 29 0 E
Korea, North ■, *Asia* **35 E14** 40 0N 127 0 E
Korea, South ■, *Asia* **35 G15** 36 0N 128 0 E
Korea Bay, *Korea* **35 E13** 39 0N 124 0 E
Korea Strait, *Asia* **35 H15** 34 0N 129 30 E
Korets, *Ukraine* **17 C14** 50 40N 27 5 E
Korhogo, *Ivory C.* **50 G4** 9 29N 5 28W
Korinthiakós Kólpos, *Greece* **21 E10** 38 16N 22 30 E
Kórinthos, *Greece* **21 F10** 37 56N 22 55 E
Koríssa, Límni, *Greece* **23 B3** 39 27N 19 53 E
Kōriyama, *Japan* **30 F10** 37 24N 140 23 E
Korla, *China* **32 B3** 41 45N 86 4 E
Kormakiti, C., *Cyprus* **23 D11** 35 23N 32 56 E
Korneshty = Corneşti, *Moldova* **17 E15** 47 21N 28 1 E
Koro, *Fiji* **59 C8** 17 19S 179 23 E
Koro, *Ivory C.* **50 G4** 8 32N 7 30W
Koro Sea, *Fiji* **59 C9** 17 30S 179 45W
Korogwe, *Tanzania* **54 D4** 5 5S 38 25 E
Koronadal, *Phil.* **37 C6** 6 12N 125 1 E
Koror, *Palau* **37 C8** 7 20N 134 28 E
Körös →, *Hungary* **17 E11** 46 43N 20 12 E
Korosten, *Ukraine* **17 C15** 50 54N 28 36 E
Korostyshev, *Ukraine* **17 C15** 50 19N 29 4 E
Korraraika, Helodranon' i, *Madag.* **57 B7** 17 45S 43 57 E
Korsakov, *Russia* **27 E15** 46 36N 142 42 E
Korshunovo, *Russia* **27 D12** 58 37N 110 10 E
Korsør, *Denmark* **9 J14** 55 20N 11 9 E
Kortrijk, *Belgium* **15 D3** 50 50N 3 17 E
Korwai, *India* **42 G8** 24 7N 78 5 E
Koryakskoye Nagorye, *Russia* **27 C18** 61 0N 171 0 E
Koryŏng, *S. Korea* **35 G15** 35 44N 128 15 E
Kos, *Greece* **21 F12** 36 50N 27 15 E
Koschagyl, *Kazakstan* **25 E9** 46 40N 54 0 E
Kościan, *Poland* **17 B9** 52 5N 16 40 E

Kosciusko

134

Laporte

Kyustendil, *Bulgaria* . . . . . . **21 C10** 42 16N 22 41 E
Kyusyur, *Russia* . . . . **27 B13** 70 19N 127 30 E
Kyyiv, *Ukraine* . . . . **17 C16** 50 30N 30 28 E
Kyyivske Vdskh., *Ukraine* . . **17 C16** 51 0N 30 25 E
Kyzyl, *Russia* . . . . **27 D10** 51 50N 94 30 E
Kyzyl Kum, *Uzbekistan* . . . . **26 E7** 42 30N 65 0 E
Kyzyl-Kyya, *Kyrgyzstan* . . . **26 E8** 40 16N 72 8 E
Kzyl-Orda = Qyzylorda, *Kazakstan* . . . . **26 E7** 44 48N 65 28 E

L

La Alcarria, *Spain* **19 B4** 40 31N 2 45W
La Asunción, *Venezuela* . . . **92 A6** 11 2N 63 53W
La Baie, *Canada* **71 C5** 48 19N 70 53W
La Banda, *Argentina* **94 B3** 27 45S 64 10W
La Barca, *Mexico* **86 C4** 20 20N 102 40W
La Barge, *U.S.A.* **82 E8** 42 16N 110 12W
La Belle, *U.S.A.* **77 M5** 26 46N 81 26W
La Biche →, *Canada* **72 B4** 59 57N 123 50W
La Biche, L., *Canada* **72 C6** 54 50N 112 5W
La Bomba, *Mexico* **86 A1** 31 53N 115 2W
La Calera, *Chile* **94 C1** 32 50S 71 10W
La Canal = Sa Canal, *Spain* **22 C7** 38 51N 1 23 E
La Carlota, *Argentina* **94 C3** 33 30S 63 20W
La Ceiba, *Honduras* **88 C2** 15 40N 86 50W
La Chaux-de-Fonds, *Switz.* . **18 C7** 47 7N 6 50 E
La Chorrera, *Panama* **88 E4** 8 53N 79 47W
La Cocha, *Argentina* **94 B2** 27 50S 65 40W
La Concepción, *Panama* . . . **88 E3** 8 31N 82 37W
La Concordia, *Mexico* **87 D6** 16 8N 92 38W
La Coruña = A Coruña, *Spain* **19 A1** 43 20N 8 25W
La Crescent, *U.S.A.* **80 D9** 43 50N 91 18W
La Crete, *Canada* **72 B5** 58 11N 116 24W
La Crosse, *Kans., U.S.A.* . . . **80 F5** 38 32N 99 18W
La Crosse, *Wis., U.S.A.* **80 D9** 43 48N 91 15W
La Cruz, *Costa Rica* **88 D2** 11 4N 85 39W
La Cruz, *Mexico* **86 C3** 23 55N 106 54W
La Désirade, *Guadeloupe* . . **89 C7** 16 18N 61 3W
La Escondida, *Mexico* **86 C5** 24 6N 99 55W
La Esmeralda, *Paraguay* . . . **94 A3** 22 16S 62 33W
La Esperanza, *Cuba* **88 B3** 22 46N 83 44W
La Esperanza, *Honduras* . . . **88 D2** 14 15N 88 10W
La Estrada = A Estrada, *Spain* **19 A1** 42 43N 8 27W
La Fayette, *U.S.A.* **77 H3** 34 42N 85 17W
La Fé, *Cuba* **88 B3** 22 2N 84 15W
La Follette, *U.S.A.* **77 G3** 36 23N 84 7W
La Grande, *U.S.A.* **82 D4** 45 20N 118 5W
La Grande →, *Canada* . . . **70 B5** 53 50N 79 0W
La Grande Deux, Rés., *Canada* **70 B4** 53 40N 76 55W
La Grande Quatre, Rés., *Canada* **70 B5** 54 0N 73 15W
La Grande Trois, Rés., *Canada* **70 B4** 53 40N 75 10W
La Grange, *Calif., U.S.A.* . . . **84 H6** 37 42N 120 27W
La Grange, *Ga., U.S.A.* **77 J3** 33 2N 85 2W
La Grange, *Ky., U.S.A.* **76 F3** 38 25N 85 23W
La Grange, *Tex., U.S.A.* . . . **81 L6** 29 54N 96 52W
La Guaira, *Venezuela* **92 A5** 10 36N 66 56W
La Habana, *Cuba* **88 B3** 23 8N 82 22W
La Independencia, *Mexico* . **87 D6** 16 31N 91 47W
La Isabela, *Dom. Rep.* **89 C5** 19 58N 71 2W
La Junta, *U.S.A.* **81 F3** 37 59N 103 33W
La Laguna, *Canary Is.* **22 F3** 28 28N 16 18W
La Libertad, *Guatemala* . . . **88 C1** 16 47N 90 7W
La Libertad, *Mexico* **86 B2** 29 55N 112 41W
La Ligua, *Chile* **94 C1** 32 30S 71 16W
La Línea de la Concepción, *Spain* **19 D3** 36 15N 5 23W
La Loche, *Canada* **73 B7** 56 29N 109 26W
La Louvière, *Belgium* . . . . . **15 D4** 50 27N 4 10 E
La Malbaie, *Canada* **71 C5** 47 40N 70 10W
La Mancha, *Spain* **19 C4** 39 10N 2 54W
La Martre, L., *Canada* **72 A5** 63 15N 117 55W
La Mesa, *U.S.A.* **85 N9** 32 46N 117 3W
La Misión, *Mexico* **86 A1** 32 5N 116 50W
La Moure, *U.S.A.* **80 B5** 46 21N 98 18W
La Negra, *Chile* **94 A1** 23 46S 70 18W
La Oliva, *Canary Is.* **22 F6** 28 36N 13 57W
La Orotava, *Canary Is.* **22 F3** 28 22N 16 31W
La Oroya, *Peru* **92** 11 32S 75 54W
La Palma, *Canary Is.* **22 F2** 28 40N 17 50W
La Palma, *Panama* **88 E4** 8 15N 78 0W
La Palma del Condado, *Spain* **19 D2** 37 21N 6 38W
La Paloma, *Chile* **94 C1** 30 35S 71 0W
La Pampa □, *Argentina* . . . **94 D2** 36 50S 66 0W
La Paragua, *Venezuela* **92 B6** 6 50N 63 20W
La Paz, *Entre Ríos, Argentina* **94 C4** 30 50S 59 45W
La Paz, *San Luis, Argentina* **94 C2** 33 30S 67 20W
La Paz, *Bolivia* **92 G5** 16 20S 68 10W
La Paz, *Honduras* **88 D2** 14 20N 87 47W
La Paz, *Mexico* **86 C2** 24 10N 110 20W
La Paz Centro, *Nic.* **88 D2** 12 20N 86 41W
La Pedrera, *Colombia* **92 D5** 1 18S 69 43W
La Pérade, *Canada* **71 C5** 46 35N 72 12W
La Perouse Str., *Asia* . . . . . **30 B11** 45 40N 142 0 E
La Pesca, *Mexico* **87 C5** 23 46N 97 47W
La Piedad, *Mexico* **86 C4** 20 20N 102 1W
La Pine, *U.S.A.* **82 E3** 43 40N 121 30W
La Plata, *Argentina* **94 D4** 35 0S 57 55W
La Pocatière, *Canada* **71 C5** 47 22N 70 2W
La Porte, *Ind., U.S.A.* **76 E2** 41 36N 86 43W
La Porte, *Tex., U.S.A.* **81 L7** 29 39N 95 1W
La Purísima, *Mexico* **86 B2** 26 10N 112 4W
La Push, *U.S.A.* **84 C2** 47 55N 124 38W
La Quiaca, *Argentina* **94 A2** 22 5S 65 35W
La Restinga, *Canary Is.* **22 G2** 27 38N 17 59W
La Rioja, *Argentina* **94 B2** 29 20S 67 0W
La Rioja □, *Argentina* **94 B2** 29 30S 67 0W
La Rioja □, *Spain* **19 A4** 42 20N 2 20W
La Robla, *Spain* **19 A3** 42 50N 5 41W
La Roche-en-Ardenne, *Belgium* . . . . **15 D5** 50 11N 5 35 E
La Roche-sur-Yon, *France* . . **18 C3** 46 40N 1 25W
La Rochelle, *France* **18 C3** 46 10N 1 9W
La Roda, *Spain* **19 C4** 39 13N 2 15W
La Romana, *Dom. Rep.* **89 C6** 18 27N 68 57W
La Ronge, *Canada* **73 B7** 55 5N 105 20W
La Rumorosa, *Mexico* **85 N10** 32 33N 116 4W
La Sabina = Sa Savina, *Spain* . . . . **22 C7** 38 44N 1 25 E
La Salle, *U.S.A.* **80 E10** 41 20N 89 6W
La Santa, *Canary Is.* **22 E6** 29 5N 13 40W
La Sarre, *Canada* **70 C4** 48 45N 79 15W
La Scie, *Canada* **71 C8** 49 57N 55 36W
La Selva Beach, *U.S.A.* **84 J5** 36 56N 121 51W
La Serena, *Chile* **94 B1** 29 55S 71 10W
La Seu d'Urgell, *Spain* . . . . **19 A6** 42 22N 1 23 E
La Seyne-sur-Mer, *France* . . **18 E6** 43 7N 5 52 E
La Soufrière, *St. Vincent* . . **89 D7** 13 20N 61 11W
La Spézia, *Italy* . . . . **18 D8** 44 7N 9 50 E
La Tagua, *Colombia* **92 C4** 0 3N 74 40W
La Tortuga, *Venezuela* **89 D6** 11 0N 65 22W
La Tuque, *Canada* **70 C5** 47 30N 72 50W
La Unión, *Chile* **96 E2** 40 10S 73 0W
La Unión, *El Salv.* **88 D2** 13 20N 87 50W
La Unión, *Mexico* **86 D4** 17 58N 101 49W
La Urbana, *Venezuela* **92 B5** 7 8N 66 56W
La Vall d'Uixó, *Spain* **19 C5** 39 49N 0 15W
La Vega, *Dom. Rep.* **89 C5** 19 20N 70 30W
La Vela de Coro, *Venezuela* **92 A5** 11 27N 69 34W
La Venta, *Mexico* **87 D6** 18 8N 94 3W
La Ventura, *Mexico* **86 C4** 24 38N 100 54W
Labe = Elbe →, *Europe* . . **16 B5** 53 50N 9 0 E
Labé, *Guinea* **50 F3** 11 24N 12 16W
Laberge, L., *Canada* **72 A1** 61 11N 135 12W
Labinsk, *Russia* . . . . **25 F7** 44 40N 40 48 E
Labis, *Malaysia* . . . . **39 L4** 2 22N 103 2 E
Laboulaye, *Argentina* **94 C3** 34 10S 63 30W
Labrador, *Canada* **71 B7** 53 20N 61 0W
Labrador City, *Canada* **71 B6** 52 57N 66 55W
Labrador Sea, *Atl. Oc.* **69 C14** 57 0N 54 0W
Lábrea, *Brazil* **92 E6** 7 15S 64 51W
Labuan, *Malaysia* . . . . **36 C5** 5 20N 115 14 E
Labuan, Pulau, *Malaysia* . . . **36 C5** 5 21N 115 13 E
Labuha, *Indonesia* . . . . **37 E7** 0 30S 127 30 E
Labuhan, *Indonesia* . . . . . . **37 G11** 6 22S 105 50 E
Labuhanbajo, *Indonesia* . . . **37 F6** 8 28S 120 1 E
Labuk, Telok, *Malaysia* . . . . **36 C5** 6 10N 117 50 E
Labyrinth, L., *Australia* . . . **63 E2** 30 40S 135 11 E
Labytnangi, *Russia* . . . . **26 C7** 66 39N 66 21 E
Lac Bouchette, *Canada* **71 C5** 48 16N 72 11W
Lac Édouard, *Canada* **70 C5** 47 40N 72 16W
Lac La Biche, *Canada* **72 C6** 54 45N 111 58W
Lac la Martre = Wha Ti, *Canada* **68 B8** 63 8N 117 16W
Lac La Ronge Prov. Park, *Canada* **73 B7** 55 9N 104 41W
Lac-Mégantic, *Canada* **71 C5** 45 35N 70 53W
Lac Seul, Res., *Canada* **70 B1** 50 25N 92 30W
Lac Thien, *Vietnam* . . . . **38 F7** 12 25N 108 11 E
Lacanau, *France* **18 D3** 44 58N 1 5W
Lacantúm →, *Mexico* **87 D6** 16 36N 90 40W
Laccadive Is. = Lakshadweep Is., *Ind. Oc.* . **28 H11** 10 0N 72 30 E
Lacepede B., *Australia* . . . . **63 F2** 36 40S 139 40 E
Lacepede Is., *Australia* . . . . **60 C3** 16 55S 122 0 E
Lacerdónia, *Mozam.* . . . . . . **55 F4** 18 3S 35 35 E
Lacey, *U.S.A.* **84 C4** 47 7N 122 49W
Lachhmangarh, *India* . . . . . **42 F6** 27 50N 75 4 E
Lachi, *Pakistan* . . . . **42 C4** 33 25N 71 20 E
Lachine, *Canada* **79 A11** 45 30N 73 40W
Lachlan →, *Australia* . . . . . **63 E3** 34 22S 143 55 E
Lachute, *Canada* **70 C5** 45 39N 74 21W
Lackawanna, *U.S.A.* **78 D6** 42 50N 78 50W
Lackawaxen, *U.S.A.* **79 E10** 41 29N 74 59W
Lacolle, *Canada* **79 A11** 45 5N 73 22W
Lacombe, *Canada* **72 C6** 52 30N 113 44W
Lacona, *U.S.A.* **79 C8** 43 39N 76 10W
Laconia, *U.S.A.* **79 C13** 43 32N 71 28W
Ladakh Ra., *India* . . . . **43 C8** 34 0N 78 0 E
Ladismith, *S. Africa* . . . . . . **56 E3** 33 28S 21 15 E
Ladnun, *India* . . . . **42 F6** 27 38N 74 25 E
Ladoga, L. = Ladozhskoye Ozero, *Russia* . . . . **24 B5** 61 15N 30 30 E
Ladozhskoye Ozero, *Russia* **24 B5** 61 15N 30 30 E
Lady Elliott I., *Australia* . . . **62 C5** 24 7S 152 42 E
Lady Grey, *S. Africa* . . . . . . **56 E4** 30 43S 27 13 E
Ladybrand, *S. Africa* . . . . . . **56 D4** 29 9S 27 29 E
Ladysmith, *Canada* **72 D4** 49 0N 123 49W
Ladysmith, *S. Africa* . . . . . . **57 D4** 28 32S 29 46 E
Ladysmith, *U.S.A.* **80 C9** 45 28N 91 12W
Lae, *Papua N. G.* . . . . **64 H6** 6 40S 147 2 E
Laem Ngop, *Thailand* . . . . . **39 F4** 12 10N 102 26 E
Laem Pho, *Thailand* . . . . . . **39 J3** 6 55N 101 19 E
Læsø, *Denmark* . . . . **9 H14** 57 15N 11 5 E
Lafayette, *Colo., U.S.A.* **80 F2** 39 58N 105 12W
Lafayette, *Ind., U.S.A.* **76 E2** 40 25N 86 54W
Lafayette, *La., U.S.A.* **81 K9** 30 14N 92 1W
Lafayette, *Tenn., U.S.A.* . . . **77 G2** 36 31N 86 2W
Laferte →, *Canada* **72 A5** 61 53N 117 44W
Lafia, *Nigeria* . . . . **50 G7** 8 30N 8 34 E
Lafleche, *Canada* **73 D7** 49 45N 106 40W
Lagan →, *U.K.* **13 B6** 54 36N 5 55W
Lagarfljót →, *Iceland* **8 D6** 65 40N 14 18W
Lågen →, *Oppland, Norway* . . . . **9 F14** 61 8N 10 25 E
Lågen →, *Vestfold, Norway* . . . . **9 G14** 59 3N 10 3 E
Laghouat, *Algeria* . . . . **50 B6** 33 50N 2 59 E
Lagoa Vermelha, *Brazil* **95 B5** 28 13S 51 32W
Lagonoy G., *Phil.* . . . . **37 B6** 13 50N 123 50 E
Lagos, *Nigeria* . . . . **50 G6** 6 25N 3 27 E
Lagos, *Portugal* **19 D1** 37 5N 8 41W
Lagos de Moreno, *Mexico* . . **86 C4** 21 21N 101 55W
Lagrange, *Australia* . . . . . . **60 C3** 18 45S 121 43 E
Lagrange B., *Australia* . . . . **60 C3** 18 38S 121 42 E
Laguna, *Brazil* **95 B6** 28 30S 48 50W
Laguna, *U.S.A.* **83 J10** 35 2N 107 25W
Laguna Beach, *U.S.A.* **85 M9** 33 33N 117 47W
Laguna Limpia, *Argentina* . . **94 B4** 26 32S 59 45W
Laguna Madre, *U.S.A.* **87 B5** 27 0N 97 20W
Lagunas, *Chile* **94 A2** 21 0S 69 45W
Lagunas, *Peru* **92 E3** 5 10S 75 35W
Lahad Datu, *Malaysia* . . . . . **37 D5** 5 0N 118 20 E
Lahad Datu, Teluk, *Malaysia* **37 D5** 4 50N 118 20 E
Lahan Sai, *Thailand* . . . . . . **38 E4** 14 25N 102 52 E
Lahanam, *Laos* . . . . **38 D5** 16 16N 105 16 E
Lahar, *India* . . . . **43 F8** 26 12N 78 57 E
Laharpur, *India* . . . . **43 F9** 27 43N 80 56 E
Lahat, *Indonesia* . . . . **36 E2** 3 45S 103 30 E
Lahewa, *Indonesia* . . . . **36 D1** 1 22N 97 12 E
Lāhījān, *Iran* . . . . **45 B6** 37 10N 50 6 E
Lahn →, *Germany* . . . . **16 C4** 50 19N 7 37 E
Laholm, *Sweden* . . . . **9 H15** 56 30N 13 2 E
Lahore, *Pakistan* . . . . **42 D6** 31 32N 74 22 E
Lahri, *Pakistan* . . . . **42 E3** 29 11N 68 13 E
Lahti, *Finland* . . . . **9 F21** 60 58N 25 40 E
Lahtis = Lahti, *Finland* . . . . **9 F21** 60 58N 25 40 E
Laï, *Chad* . . . . **51 G9** 9 25N 16 18 E
Laila = Laylá, *Si. Arabia* . . . **46 C4** 22 10N 46 40 E
Laingsburg, *S. Africa* . . . . . **56 E3** 33 9S 20 52 E
Lainio älv →, *Sweden* . . . **8 C20** 67 35N 22 40 E
Lairg, *U.K.* **12 C4** 58 2N 4 24W
Laishui, *China* . . . . **34 E8** 39 23N 115 45 E
Laiwu, *China* . . . . **35 F9** 36 15N 117 40 E
Laixi, *China* . . . . **35 F11** 36 50N 120 31 E
Laiyang, *China* . . . . **35 F11** 36 59N 120 45 E
Laiyuan, *China* . . . . **34 E8** 39 20N 114 40 E
Laizhou, *China* . . . . **35 F10** 37 8N 119 57 E
Laizhou Wan, *China* . . . . . . **35 F10** 37 30N 119 30 E
Laja →, *Mexico* **86 C4** 20 55N 100 46W
Lajes, *Brazil* **95 B5** 27 48S 50 20W
Lak Sao, *Laos* . . . . **38 C5** 18 11N 104 59 E
Lakaband, *Pakistan* . . . . **42 D3** 31 2N 69 15 E
Lake Alpine, *U.S.A.* **84 G7** 38 29N 120 0W
Lake Andes, *U.S.A.* **80 D5** 43 9N 98 32W
Lake Arthur, *U.S.A.* **81 K8** 30 5N 92 41W
Lake Cargelligo, *Australia* . . **63 E4** 33 15S 146 22 E
Lake Charles, *U.S.A.* **81 K8** 30 14N 93 13W
Lake City, *Colo., U.S.A.* **83 G10** 38 2N 107 19W
Lake City, *Fla., U.S.A.* **77 K4** 30 11N 82 38W
Lake City, *Mich., U.S.A.* **76 C3** 44 20N 85 13W
Lake City, *Minn., U.S.A.* **80 C8** 44 27N 92 16W
Lake City, *Pa., U.S.A.* **78 D4** 42 1N 80 21W
Lake City, *S.C., U.S.A.* **77 J6** 33 52N 79 45W
Lake Cowichan, *Canada* **72 D4** 48 49N 124 3W
Lake District, *U.K.* . . . . **10 C4** 54 35N 3 20 E
Lake Elsinore, *U.S.A.* **85 M9** 33 38N 117 20W
Lake George, *U.S.A.* **79 C11** 43 26N 73 43W
Lake Grace, *Australia* . . . . . **61 F2** 33 7S 118 28 E
Lake Harbour = Kimmirut, *Canada* **69 B13** 62 50N 69 50W
Lake Havasu City, *U.S.A.* . . **85 L12** 34 27N 114 22W
Lake Hughes, *U.S.A.* **85 L8** 34 41N 118 26W
Lake Isabella, *U.S.A.* **85 K8** 35 38N 118 28W
Lake Jackson, *U.S.A.* **81 L7** 29 3N 95 27W
Lake Junction, *U.S.A.* **82 D8** 44 35N 110 28W
Lake King, *Australia* . . . . . . **61 F2** 33 5S 119 45 E
Lake Lenore, *Canada* **73 C8** 52 24N 104 59W
Lake Louise, *Canada* **72 C5** 51 30N 116 10W
Lake Mead National Recreation Area, *U.S.A.* . **85 K12** 36 15N 114 30W
Lake Mills, *U.S.A.* **80 D8** 43 25N 93 32W
Lake Placid, *U.S.A.* **79 B11** 44 17N 73 59W
Lake Pleasant, *U.S.A.* **79 C10** 43 28N 74 25W
Lake Providence, *U.S.A.* . . . **81 J9** 32 48N 91 10W
Lake St. Peter, *Canada* **78 A6** 45 18N 78 2W
Lake Superior Prov. Park, *Canada* **70 C3** 47 45N 84 45W
Lake Village, *U.S.A.* **81 J9** 33 20N 91 17W
Lake Wales, *U.S.A.* **77 M5** 27 54N 81 35W
Lake Worth, *U.S.A.* **77 M5** 26 37N 80 3W
Lakefield, *Canada* **78 B6** 44 25N 78 16W
Lakehurst, *U.S.A.* **79 F10** 40 1N 74 19W
Lakeland, *Australia* . . . . **62 B3** 15 49S 144 57 E
Lakeland, *U.S.A.* **77 M5** 28 3N 81 57W
Lakemba, *Fiji* **59 D9** 18 13S 178 47W
Lakeport, *Calif., U.S.A.* **84 F4** 39 3N 122 55W
Lakeport, *Mich., U.S.A.* **78 C2** 43 7N 82 30W
Lakes Entrance, *Australia* . . **63 F4** 37 50S 148 0 E
Lakeside, *Ariz., U.S.A.* **83 J9** 34 9N 109 58W
Lakeside, *Calif., U.S.A.* **85 N10** 32 52N 116 55W
Lakeside, *Nebr., U.S.A.* **80 D3** 42 3N 102 26W
Lakeside, *Ohio, U.S.A.* **78 E2** 41 32N 82 46W
Lakeview, *U.S.A.* **82 E3** 42 11N 120 21W
Lakeville, *U.S.A.* **80 C8** 44 39N 93 14W
Lakewood, *Colo., U.S.A.* **80 F2** 39 44N 105 5W
Lakewood, *N.J., U.S.A.* **79 F10** 40 6N 74 13W
Lakewood, *N.Y., U.S.A.* **78 D5** 42 6N 79 19W
Lakewood, *Ohio, U.S.A.* **78 E3** 41 29N 81 48W
Lakewood, *Wash., U.S.A.* . . . **84 C4** 47 11N 122 32W
Lakha, *India* . . . . **42 F4** 26 9N 70 54 E
Lakhaniá, *Greece* . . . . **23 D9** 35 58N 27 54 E
Lakhimpur, *India* . . . . **43 F9** 27 57N 80 46 E
Lakhnadon, *India* . . . . **43 H8** 22 36N 79 36 E
Lakhonpheng, *Laos* . . . . **38 E5** 15 54N 105 34 E
Lakhpat, *India* . . . . **42 H3** 23 48N 68 47 E
Lakin, *U.S.A.* **81 G4** 37 57N 101 15W
Lakitusaki →, *Canada* **70 B3** 54 21N 82 25W
Lakki, *Pakistan* . . . . **42 C4** 32 36N 70 55 E
Lákkoi, *Greece* . . . . **23 D5** 35 24N 23 57 E
Lakonikós Kólpos, *Greece* . . **21 F10** 36 40N 22 40 E
Lakor, *Indonesia* . . . . **37 F7** 8 15S 128 17 E
Lakota, *Ivory C.* **50 G4** 5 50N 5 30W
Lakota, *U.S.A.* **80 A5** 48 2N 98 21W
Laksar, *India* . . . . **42 E8** 29 46N 78 3 E
Laksefjorden, *Norway* . . . . . **8 A22** 70 45N 26 50 E
Lakselv, *Norway* . . . . **8 A21** 70 2N 25 0 E
Lakshadweep Is., *Ind. Oc.* . . **28 H11** 10 0N 72 30 E
Lakshmanpur, *India* . . . . **43 H10** 22 58N 83 3 E
Lakshmikantapur, *India* . . . . **43 H13** 22 5N 88 20 E
Lala Ghat, *India* . . . . **41 G18** 24 30N 92 40 E
Lala Musa, *Pakistan* . . . . . . **42 C5** 32 40N 73 57 E
Lalago, *Tanzania* . . . . **54 C3** 3 28S 33 58 E
Lalapanzi, *Zimbabwe* . . . . . **55 F3** 19 20S 30 15 E
L'Albufera, *Spain* **19 C5** 39 20N 0 27W
Lalganj, *India* . . . . **43 G11** 25 52N 85 13 E
Lalgola, *India* . . . . **43 G13** 24 25N 88 15 E
Lālī, *Iran* . . . . **45 C6** 32 21N 49 6 E
Lalibela, *Ethiopia* . . . . **46 E2** 12 2N 39 2 E
Lalin, *China* . . . . **35 B14** 45 12N 127 0 E
Lalín, *Spain* **19 A1** 42 40N 8 5W
Lalin He →, *China* . . . . **35 B13** 45 32N 125 40 E
Lalitapur = Patan, *Nepal* . . **41 F14** 27 40N 85 20 E
Lalitpur, *India* . . . . **43 G8** 24 42N 78 28 E
Lalkua, *India* . . . . **43 E8** 29 5N 79 31 E
Lalsot, *India* . . . . **42 F7** 26 34N 76 20 E
Lam, *Vietnam* . . . . **38 B6** 21 21N 106 31 E
Lam Pao Res., *Thailand* . . . . **38 D4** 16 50N 103 15 E
Lamaing, *Burma* . . . . **41 M20** 15 25N 97 53 E
Lamar, *Colo., U.S.A.* **80 F3** 38 5N 102 37W
Lamar, *Mo., U.S.A.* **81 G7** 37 30N 94 16W
Lamas, *Peru* **92 E3** 6 28S 76 31W
Lambaréné, *Gabon* . . . . **52 E2** 0 41S 10 12 E
Lambasa, *Fiji* . . . . **59 C8** 16 30S 179 10 E
Lambay I., *Ireland* **13 C5** 53 29N 6 1W
Lambert Glacier, *Antarctica* . **5 D6** 71 0S 70 0 E
Lamberts Bay, *S. Africa* . . . . **56 E2** 32 5S 18 17 E
Lambeth, *Canada* **78 D3** 42 54N 81 18W
Lambi Kyun, *Burma* . . . . **39 G2** 10 50N 98 20 E
Lame Deer, *U.S.A.* **82 D10** 45 37N 106 40W
Lamego, *Portugal* **19 B2** 41 5N 7 52W
Lamèque, *Canada* **71 C7** 47 45N 64 38W
Lameroo, *Australia* . . . . **63 F3** 35 19S 140 33 E
Lamesa, *U.S.A.* **81 J4** 32 44N 101 58W
Lamía, *Greece* . . . . **21 E10** 38 55N 22 26 E
Lammermuir Hills, *U.K.* **12 F6** 55 50N 2 40W
Lamoille →, *U.S.A.* **79 B11** 44 38N 73 13W
Lamon B., *Phil.* . . . . **37 B6** 14 30N 122 20 E
Lamont, *Canada* **72 C6** 53 46N 112 50W
Lamont, *Calif., U.S.A.* **85 K8** 35 15N 118 55W
Lamont, *Wyo., U.S.A.* **82 E10** 42 13N 107 29W
Lampa, *Peru* **92 G4** 15 22S 70 22W
Lampang, *Thailand* . . . . **38 C2** 18 16N 99 32 E
Lampasas, *U.S.A.* **81 K5** 31 4N 98 11W
Lampazos de Naranjo, *Mexico* **86 B4** 27 2N 100 32W
Lampedusa, *Medit. S.* . . . . . . **20 G5** 35 36N 12 40 E
Lampeter, *U.K.* **11 E3** 52 7N 4 4W
Lampione, *Medit. S.* . . . . **20 G5** 35 33N 12 20 E
Lampman, *Canada* **73 D8** 49 25N 102 50W
Lampung □, *Indonesia* . . . . . **36 F2** 5 30S 104 30 E
Lamta, *India* . . . . **43 H9** 22 8N 80 7 E
Lamu, *Kenya* . . . . **54 C5** 2 16S 40 55 E
Lamy, *U.S.A.* **83 J11** 35 29N 105 53W
Lan Xian, *China* . . . . **34 E6** 38 15N 111 35 E
Lanai, *U.S.A.* **74 H16** 20 50N 156 55W
Lanak La, *India* . . . . **43 B8** 34 27N 79 32 E
Lanak'o Shank'ou = Lanak La, *India* . . . . **43 B8** 34 27N 79 32 E
Lanark, *Canada* **79 A8** 45 1N 76 22W
Lanark, *U.K.* **12 F5** 55 40N 3 47W
Lancang Jiang →, *China* . . **32 D5** 21 40N 101 10 E
Lancashire □, *U.K.* **10 D5** 53 50N 2 48W
Lancaster, *Canada* **79 A10** 45 10N 74 30W
Lancaster, *U.K.* **10 C5** 54 3N 2 48W
Lancaster, *Calif., U.S.A.* **85 L8** 34 42N 118 8W
Lancaster, *Ky., U.S.A.* **76 G3** 37 37N 84 35W
Lancaster, *N.H., U.S.A.* **79 B13** 44 29N 71 34W
Lancaster, *N.Y., U.S.A.* **78 D6** 42 54N 78 40W
Lancaster, *Ohio, U.S.A.* **76 F4** 39 43N 82 36W
Lancaster, *Pa., U.S.A.* **79 F8** 40 2N 76 19W
Lancaster, *S.C., U.S.A.* **77 H5** 34 43N 80 46W
Lancaster, *Wis., U.S.A.* **80 D9** 42 51N 90 43W
Lancaster Sd., *Canada* **69 A11** 74 13N 84 0W
Lancelin, *Australia* . . . . **61 F2** 31 0S 115 18 E
Lanchow = Lanzhou, *China* . **34 F2** 36 1N 103 52 E
Lanciano, *Italy* . . . . **20 C6** 42 14N 14 23 E
Lancun, *China* . . . . **35 F11** 36 25N 120 10 E
Landeck, *Austria* . . . . **16 E6** 47 9N 10 34 E
Lander, *U.S.A.* **82 E9** 42 50N 108 44W
Lander →, *Australia* . . . . . . **60 D5** 22 0S 132 0 E
Landes, *France* **18 D3** 44 0N 1 0W
Landi Kotal, *Pakistan* . . . . . . **42 B4** 34 7N 71 6 E
Landisburg, *U.S.A.* **78 F7** 40 21N 77 19W
Land's End, *U.K.* **11 G2** 50 4N 5 44W
Landsborough Cr. →, *Australia* . . . . **62 C3** 22 28S 144 35 E
Landshut, *Germany* . . . . **16 D7** 48 34N 12 8 E
Landskrona, *Sweden* . . . . . . **9 J15** 55 53N 12 50 E
Lanesboro, *U.S.A.* **79 E9** 41 57N 75 34W
Lanett, *U.S.A.* **77 J3** 32 52N 85 12W
Lang Qua, *Vietnam* . . . . **38 A5** 22 16N 104 27 E
Lang Shan, *China* . . . . **34 D4** 41 0N 106 30 E
Lang Suan, *Thailand* . . . . **39 H2** 9 57N 99 4 E
La'nga Co, *China* . . . . **41 D12** 30 45N 81 15 E
Langar, *Iran* . . . . **45 C9** 35 23N 60 25 E
Langara I., *Canada* **72 C2** 54 14N 133 1W
Langdon, *U.S.A.* **80 A5** 48 45N 98 22W
Langeberg, *S. Africa* . . . . **56 E3** 33 55S 21 0 E
Langeberge, *S. Africa* . . . . . . **56 D3** 28 15S 22 33 E
Langeland, *Denmark* . . . . **9 J14** 54 56N 10 48 E
Langenburg, *Canada* **73 C8** 50 51N 101 43W
Langholm, *U.K.* **12 F5** 55 9N 3 0W
Langjökull, *Iceland* **8 D3** 64 39N 20 12W
Langkawi, Pulau, *Malaysia* . . **39 J2** 6 25N 99 45 E
Langklip, *S. Africa* . . . . **56 D3** 28 12S 20 20 E
Langkon, *Malaysia* . . . . **36 C5** 6 30N 116 40 E
Langlade, *St- P. & M.* **71 C8** 46 50N 56 20W
Langley, *Canada* **84 A4** 49 7N 122 39W
Langøya, *Norway* . . . . **8 B16** 68 45N 14 50 E
Langreo, *Spain* **19 A3** 43 18N 5 40W
Langres, *France* . . . . **18 C6** 47 52N 5 20 E
Langres, Plateau de, *France* **18 C6** 47 45N 5 3 E
Langsa, *Indonesia* . . . . **36 D1** 4 30N 97 57 E
Langtry, *U.S.A.* **81 L4** 29 49N 101 34W
Langu, *Thailand* . . . . **39 J2** 6 53N 99 47 E
Languedoc, *France* . . . . **18 E5** 43 58N 3 55 E
Langxiangzhen, *China* . . . . . **34 E9** 39 43N 116 8 E
Lanigan, *Canada* **73 C7** 51 51N 105 2W
Lankao, *China* . . . . **34 G8** 34 48N 114 50 E
Länkäran, *Azerbaijan* . . . . . . **25 G8** 38 48N 48 52 E
Lannion, *France* **18 B2** 48 46N 3 29W
L'Annonciation, *Canada* **70 C5** 46 25N 74 55W
Lansdale, *U.S.A.* **79 F9** 40 14N 75 17W
Lansdowne, *Australia* . . . . . . **63 E5** 31 48S 152 30 E
Lansdowne, *Canada* **79 B8** 44 24N 76 1W
Lansdowne, *India* . . . . **43 E8** 29 50N 78 41 E
Lansdowne House, *Canada* . . **70 B2** 52 14N 87 53W
L'Anse, *Mich., U.S.A.* **76 B1** 46 42N 88 25W
L'Anse, *Mich., U.S.A.* **80 B10** 46 45N 88 27W
L'Anse au Loup, *Canada* . . . **71 B8** 51 32N 56 50W
L'Anse aux Meadows, *Canada* **71 B8** 51 36N 55 32W
Lansford, *U.S.A.* **79 F9** 40 50N 75 53W
Lansing, *U.S.A.* **76 D3** 42 44N 84 33W
Lanta Yai, Ko, *Thailand* . . . . . **39 J2** 7 35N 99 3 E
Lantian, *China* . . . . **34 G5** 34 11N 109 20 E
Lanus, *Argentina* **94 C4** 34 44S 58 27W
Lanusei, *Italy* . . . . **20 E3** 39 52N 9 34 E
Lanzarote, *Canary Is.* **22 F6** 29 0N 13 40W
Lanzhou, *China* . . . . **34 F2** 36 1N 103 52 E
Lao Bao, *Laos* . . . . **38 D6** 16 35N 106 30 E
Laoag, *Phil.* . . . . **37 A6** 18 7N 120 34 E
Laoang, *Phil.* . . . . **37 B7** 12 32N 125 8 E
Laoha He →, *China* . . . . **35 C11** 43 25N 120 35 E
Laois □, *Ireland* **13 D4** 52 57N 7 36W
Laon, *France* . . . . **18 B5** 49 33N 3 35 E
Laona, *U.S.A.* **76 C1** 45 34N 88 40W
Laos ■, *Asia* . . . . **38 D5** 17 45N 105 0 E
Lapa, *Brazil* **95 B6** 25 46S 49 44W
Lapeer, *U.S.A.* **76 D4** 43 3N 83 19W
Lapithos, *Cyprus* . . . . **23 D12** 35 21N 33 11 E
Lapland = Lappland, *Europe* **8 B21** 68 7N 24 0 E
Laporte, *U.S.A.* **79 E8** 41 25N 76 30W

Mehr Jān

Mehr Jān, *Iran* **45 C7** 33 50N 55 6 E
Mehrābād, *Iran* **44 B5** 36 53N 47 55 E
Mehrān, *Iran* **44 C5** 33 7N 46 10 E
Mehrīz, *Iran* **45 D7** 31 35N 54 28 E
Mei Xian, *China* **34 G4** 34 18N 107 55 E
Meiktila, *Burma* **41 J19** 20 53N 95 54 E
Meissen, *Germany* **16 C7** 51 9N 13 29 E
Meizhou, *China* **33 D6** 24 16N 116 6 E
Meja, *India* **43 G10** 25 9N 82 7 E
Mejillones, *Chile* **94 A1** 23 10S 70 30W
Mekele, *Ethiopia* **46 E2** 13 33N 39 30 E
Mekhtar, *Pakistan* **40 D6** 30 30N 69 15 E
Meknès, *Morocco* **50 B4** 33 57N 5 33W
Mekong →, *Asia* **39 H6** 9 30N 106 15 E
Mekongga, *Indonesia* **37 E6** 3 39S 121 15 E
Mekvari = Kür →, *Azerbaijan* **25 G8** 39 29N 49 15 E
Melagiri Hills, *India* **40 N10** 12 20N 77 30 E
Melaka, *Malaysia* **39 L4** 2 15N 102 15 E
Melalap, *Malaysia* **36 C5** 5 10N 116 5 E
Mélambes, *Greece* **23 D6** 35 8N 24 40 E
Melanesia, *Pac. Oc.* **64 H7** 4 0S 155 0 E
Melbourne, *Australia* **63 F4** 37 50S 145 0 E
Melbourne, *U.S.A.* **77 L5** 28 5N 80 37W
Melchor Múzquiz, *Mexico* **86 B4** 27 50N 101 30W
Melchor Ocampo, *Mexico* **86 C4** 24 52N 101 40W
Mélèzes →, *Canada* **69 C12** 57 30N 71 0W
Mélèzes →, *Qué., Canada* **70 A5** 57 40N 69 29W
Melfort, *Canada* **73 C8** 52 50N 104 37W
Melfort, *Zimbabwe* **55 F3** 18 0S 31 25 E
Melhus, *Norway* **8 E14** 63 17N 10 18 E
Melilla, *N. Afr.* **19 E4** 35 21N 2 57W
Melipilla, *Chile* **94 C1** 33 42S 71 15W
Mélissa, Ákra, *Greece* **23 D6** 35 6N 24 33 E
Melita, *Canada* **73 D8** 49 15N 101 0W
Melitopol, *Ukraine* **25 E6** 46 50N 35 22 E
Melk, *Austria* **16 D8** 48 13N 15 20 E
Mellansel, *Sweden* **8 E18** 63 25N 18 17 E
Mellen, *U.S.A.* **80 B9** 46 20N 90 40W
Mellerud, *Sweden* **9 G15** 58 41N 12 28 E
Mellette, *U.S.A.* **80 C5** 45 9N 98 30W
Mellieha, *Malta* **23 D1** 35 57N 14 21 E
Melo, *Uruguay* **95 C5** 32 20S 54 10W
Melolo, *Indonesia* **37 F6** 9 53S 120 40 E
Melouprey, *Cambodia* **38 F5** 13 48N 105 16 E
Melrose, *Australia* **63 E4** 32 42S 146 57 E
Melrose, *U.K.* **12 F6** 55 36N 2 43W
Melrose, *Minn., U.S.A.* **80 C7** 45 40N 94 49W
Melrose, *N. Mex., U.S.A.* **81 H3** 34 26N 103 38W
Melstone, *U.S.A.* **82 C10** 46 36N 107 52W
Melton Mowbray, *U.K.* **10 E7** 52 47N 0 54W
Melun, *France* **18 B5** 48 32N 2 39 E
Melville, *Canada* **73 C8** 50 55N 102 50W
Melville, C., *Australia* **62 A3** 14 11S 144 30 E
Melville, L., *Canada* **71 B8** 53 30N 60 0W
Melville B., *Australia* **62 A2** 12 0S 136 45 E
Melville I., *Australia* **60 B5** 11 30S 131 0 E
Melville I., *Canada* **4 B2** 75 30N 112 0W
Melville Pen., *Canada* **69 B11** 68 0N 84 0W
Memba, *Mozam.* **55 E5** 14 11S 40 30 E
Memboro, *Indonesia* **37 F5** 9 30S 119 30 E
Memel = Klaìpeda, *Lithuania* **9 J19** 55 43N 21 10 E
Memel, *S. Africa* **57 D4** 27 38S 29 36 E
Memmingen, *Germany* **16 E6** 47 58N 10 10 E
Mempawah, *Indonesia* **36 D3** 0 30N 109 5 E
Memphis, *Mich., U.S.A.* **78 D2** 42 54N 82 46W
Memphis, *Tenn., U.S.A.* **81 H10** 35 8N 90 3W
Memphis, *Tex., U.S.A.* **81 H4** 34 44N 100 33W
Memphremagog, L., *U.S.A.* **79 B12** 45 0N 72 12W
Mena, *U.S.A.* **81 H7** 34 35N 94 15W
Menai Strait, *U.K.* **10 D3** 53 11N 4 13W
Ménaka, *Mali* **50 E6** 15 59N 2 18 E
Menan = Chao Phraya →, *Thailand* **38 F3** 13 32N 100 36 E
Menarandra →, *Madag.* **57 D7** 25 17S 44 30 E
Menard, *U.S.A.* **81 K5** 30 55N 99 47W
Mendawai →, *Indonesia* **36 E4** 3 30S 113 0 E
Mende, *France* **18 D5** 44 31N 3 30 E
Mendez, *Mexico* **87 B5** 25 7N 98 34W
Mendhar, *India* **43 C6** 33 35N 74 10 E
Mendip Hills, *U.K.* **11 F5** 51 17N 2 40W
Mendocino, *U.S.A.* **82 G2** 39 19N 123 48W
Mendocino, C., *U.S.A.* **82 F1** 40 26N 124 25W
Mendooran, *Australia* **63 E4** 31 50S 149 6 E
Mendota, *Calif., U.S.A.* **84 J6** 36 45N 120 23W
Mendota, *Ill., U.S.A.* **80 E10** 41 33N 89 7W
Mendoza, *Argentina* **94 C2** 32 50S 68 52W
Mendoza □, *Argentina* **94 C2** 33 0S 69 0W
Mene Grande, *Venezuela* **92 B4** 9 49N 70 56W
Menemen, *Turkey* **21 E12** 38 34N 27 3 E
Menen, *Belgium* **15 D3** 50 47N 3 7 E
Menggala, *Indonesia* **36 E3** 4 30S 105 15 E
Mengjin, *China* **34 G7** 34 55N 112 45 E
Mengyin, *China* **35 G9** 35 40N 117 58 E
Mengzi, *China* **32 D5** 23 20N 103 22 E
Menihek, *Canada* **71 B6** 54 28N 56 36W
Menihek L., *Canada* **71 B6** 54 0N 67 0W
Menin = Menen, *Belgium* **15 D3** 50 47N 3 7 E
Menindee, *Australia* **63 E3** 32 20S 142 25 E
Menindee L., *Australia* **63 E3** 32 20S 142 25 E
Meningie, *Australia* **63 F2** 35 50S 139 18 E
Menlo Park, *U.S.A.* **84 H4** 37 27N 122 12W
Menominee, *U.S.A.* **76 C2** 45 6N 87 37W
Menominee →, *U.S.A.* **76 C2** 45 6N 87 36W
Menomonie, *U.S.A.* **80 C9** 44 53N 91 55W
Menongue, *Angola* **53 G3** 14 48S 17 52 E
Menorca, *Spain* **22 B11** 40 0N 4 0 E
Mentakab, *Malaysia* **39 L4** 3 29N 102 21 E
Mentawai, Kepulauan, *Indonesia* **36 E1** 2 0S 99 0 E
Menton, *France* **18 E7** 43 50N 7 29 E
Mentor, *U.S.A.* **78 E3** 41 40N 81 21W
Menzelinsk, *Russia* **24 C9** 55 47N 53 11 E
Menzies, *Australia* **61 E3** 29 40S 121 2 E
Me'ona, *Israel* **47 B4** 33 1N 35 15 E
Meoqui, *Mexico* **86 B3** 28 17N 105 29W
Mepaco, *Mozam.* **55 F3** 15 57S 30 48 E
Meppel, *Neths.* **15 B6** 52 42N 6 12 E
Merabéllou, Kólpos, *Greece* **23 D7** 35 10N 25 50 E
Merak, *Indonesia* **37 F12** 6 10N 106 26 E
Meramangye, L., *Australia* **61 E5** 28 25S 132 13 E
Meran = Merano, *Italy* **20 A4** 46 40N 11 9 E
Merano, *Italy* **20 A4** 46 40N 11 9 E
Merauke, *Indonesia* **37 F10** 8 29S 140 24 E
Merbein, *Australia* **63 E3** 34 10S 142 2 E
Merca, *Somali Rep.* **46 G3** 1 48N 44 50 E
Merced, *U.S.A.* **84 H6** 37 18N 120 29W
Merced →, *U.S.A.* **84 H6** 37 21N 120 59W
Merced Pk., *U.S.A.* **84 H7** 37 36N 119 24W
Mercedes, *Buenos Aires, Argentina* **94 C4** 34 40S 59 30W
Mercedes, *Corrientes, Argentina* **94 B4** 29 10S 58 5W
Mercedes, *San Luis, Argentina* **94 C2** 33 40S 65 21W
Mercedes, *Uruguay* **94 C4** 33 12S 58 0W
Mercedes, *U.S.A.* **81 M6** 26 9N 97 55W
Merceditas, *Chile* **94 B1** 28 20S 70 35W
Mercer, *N.Z.* **59 G5** 37 16S 175 5 E
Mercer, *U.S.A.* **78 E4** 41 14N 80 15W
Mercer Island, *U.S.A.* **84 C4** 47 35N 122 15W
Mercury, *U.S.A.* **85 J11** 36 40N 115 58W
Mercy C., *Canada* **69 B13** 65 0N 63 30W
Mere, *U.K.* **11 F5** 51 6N 2 16W
Meredith, C., *Falk. Is.* **96 G4** 52 15S 60 40W
Meredith, L., *U.S.A.* **81 H4** 35 43N 101 33W
Mergui, *Burma* **38 F2** 12 26N 98 34 E
Mergui Arch. = Myeik Kyunzu, *Burma* **39 G1** 11 30N 97 30 E
Mérida, *Mexico* **87 C7** 20 58N 89 37W
Mérida, *Spain* **19 C2** 38 55N 6 25W
Mérida, *Venezuela* **92 B4** 8 24N 71 8W
Mérida, Cord. de, *Venezuela* **90 C3** 9 0N 71 0W
Meriden, *U.K.* **11 E6** 52 26N 1 38W
Meriden, *U.S.A.* **79 E12** 41 32N 72 48W
Meridian, *Calif., U.S.A.* **84 F5** 39 9N 121 55W
Meridian, *Idaho, U.S.A.* **82 E5** 43 37N 116 24W
Meridian, *Miss., U.S.A.* **77 J1** 32 22N 88 42W
Merimbula, *Australia* **63 F4** 36 53S 149 54 E
Merinda, *Australia* **62 C4** 20 2S 148 11 E
Meringur, *Australia* **63 E3** 34 20S 141 19 E
Merir, *Pac. Oc.* **37 D8** 4 10N 132 30 E
Merirumã, *Brazil* **93 C8** 1 15N 54 50W
Merkel, *U.S.A.* **81 J5** 32 28N 100 1W
Mermaid Reef, *Australia* **60 C2** 17 6S 119 36 E
Merredin, *Australia* **61 F2** 31 28S 118 18 E
Merrick, *U.K.* **12 F4** 55 8N 4 28W
Merrickville, *Canada* **79 B9** 44 55N 75 50W
Merrill, *Oreg., U.S.A.* **82 E3** 42 1N 121 36W
Merrill, *Wis., U.S.A.* **80 C10** 45 11N 89 41W
Merrimack →, *U.S.A.* **79 D14** 42 49N 70 49W
Merriman, *U.S.A.* **80 D4** 42 55N 101 42W
Merritt, *Canada* **72 C4** 50 10N 120 45W
Merritt Island, *U.S.A.* **77 L5** 28 21N 80 42W
Merriwa, *Australia* **63 E5** 32 6S 150 22 E
Merry I., *Canada* **70 A4** 55 29N 77 31W
Merryville, *U.S.A.* **81 K8** 30 45N 93 33W
Mersch, *Lux.* **15 E6** 49 44N 6 7 E
Mersea I., *U.K.* **11 F8** 51 47N 0 58 E
Merseburg, *Germany* **16 C6** 51 22N 11 59 E
Mersey →, *U.K.* **10 D4** 53 25N 3 1W
Merseyside □, *U.K.* **10 D4** 53 31N 3 2W
Mersin, *Turkey* **25 G5** 36 51N 34 36 E
Mersing, *Malaysia* **39 L4** 2 25N 103 50 E
Merta, *India* **42 F6** 26 39N 74 4 E
Merta Road, *India* **42 F5** 26 43N 73 55 E
Merthyr Tydfil, *U.K.* **11 F4** 51 45N 3 22W
Merthyr Tydfil □, *U.K.* **11 F4** 51 46N 3 21W
Mértola, *Portugal* **19 D2** 37 40N 7 40W
Mertzon, *U.S.A.* **81 K4** 31 16N 100 49W
Meru, *Kenya* **54 B4** 0 3N 37 40 E
Meru, *Tanzania* **54 C4** 3 15S 36 46 E
Mesa, *U.S.A.* **83 K8** 33 25N 111 50W
Mesa Verde National Park, *U.S.A.* **83 H9** 37 11N 108 29W
Mesanagrós, *Greece* **23 C9** 36 1N 27 49 E
Mesaoría □, *Cyprus* **23 D12** 35 12N 33 14 E
Mesarás, Kólpos, *Greece* **23 D6** 35 6N 24 47 E
Mesgouez, L., *Canada* **70 B5** 51 20N 75 0W
Meshed = Mashhad, *Iran* **45 B8** 36 20N 59 35 E
Meshoppen, *U.S.A.* **79 E8** 41 36N 76 3W
Mesilinka →, *Canada* **72 B4** 56 6N 124 30W
Mesilla, *U.S.A.* **83 K10** 32 16N 106 48W
Mesolóngion, *Greece* **21 E9** 38 21N 21 28 E
Mesopotamia = Al Jazirah, *Iraq* **44 C5** 33 30N 44 0 E
Mesopotamia, *U.S.A.* **78 E4** 41 27N 80 57W
Mesquite, *U.S.A.* **83 H6** 36 47N 114 6W
Messad, *Algeria* **50 B6** 34 8N 3 30 E
Messalo →, *Mozam.* **55 E4** 12 25S 39 15 E
Messina, *Italy* **20 E6** 38 11N 15 34 E
Messina, *S. Africa* **57 C5** 22 20S 30 5 E
Messina, Str. di, *Italy* **20 F6** 38 15N 15 35 E
Messíni, *Greece* **21 F10** 37 4N 22 1 E
Messiniakós Kólpos, *Greece* **21 F10** 36 45N 22 5 E
Messonghi, *Greece* **23 B3** 39 29N 19 56 E
Mesta →, *Bulgaria* **21 D11** 40 54N 24 49 E
Meta →, *S. Amer.* **92 B5** 6 12N 67 28W
Meta Incognita Peninsula, *Canada* **69 B13** 62 40N 68 0W
Metabetchouan, *Canada* **71 C5** 48 26N 71 52W
Metairie, *U.S.A.* **81 L9** 29 58N 90 10W
Metaline Falls, *U.S.A.* **82 B5** 48 52N 117 22W
Metán, *Argentina* **94 B3** 25 30S 65 0W
Metangula, *Mozam.* **55 E3** 12 40S 34 50 E
Metengobalame, *Mozam.* **55 E3** 14 49S 34 30 E
Methven, *N.Z.* **59 K3** 43 38S 171 40 E
Metil, *Mozam.* **55 F4** 16 24S 39 0 E
Metlakatla, *U.S.A.* **68 C6** 55 8N 131 35W
Metropolis, *U.S.A.* **81 G10** 37 9N 88 44W
Mettur Dam, *India* **40 P10** 11 45N 77 45 E
Metu, *Ethiopia* **46 F2** 8 18N 35 35 E
Metz, *France* **18 B7** 49 8N 6 10 E
Meulaboh, *Indonesia* **36 D1** 4 11N 96 3 E
Meureudu, *Indonesia* **36 C1** 5 19N 96 10 E
Meuse →, *Europe* **18 A6** 50 45N 5 41 E
Mexia, *U.S.A.* **81 K6** 31 41N 96 29W
Mexiana, I., *Brazil* **93 D9** 0 0 49 30W
Mexicali, *Mexico* **85 N11** 32 40N 115 30W
Mexican Plateau, *Mexico* **66 G9** 25 0N 104 0W
Mexican Water, *U.S.A.* **83 H9** 36 57N 109 32W
México, *Mexico* **87 D5** 19 20N 99 10W
Mexico, *Maine, U.S.A.* **79 B14** 44 34N 70 33W
Mexico, *Mo., U.S.A.* **80 F9** 39 10N 91 53W
Mexico, *N.Y., U.S.A.* **79 C8** 43 28N 76 18W
México □, *Mexico* **87 D5** 19 20N 99 10W
Mexico ■, *Cent. Amer.* **86 C4** 25 0N 105 0W
Mexico, G. of, *Cent. Amer.* **87 C7** 25 0N 90 0W
Mexico B., *U.S.A.* **79 C8** 43 35N 76 20W
Meydān-e Naftūn, *Iran* **45 D6** 31 56N 49 18 E
Meydani, Ra's-e, *Iran* **45 E8** 25 24N 59 6 E
Meymaneh, *Afghan.* **40 B4** 35 53N 64 38 E
Mezen, *Russia* **24 A7** 65 50N 44 20 E
Mezen →, *Russia* **24 A7** 65 44N 44 22 E
Mézenc, Mt., *France* **18 D6** 44 54N 4 11 E
Mezhdurechenskiy, *Russia* **26 D7** 59 36N 65 56 E
Mezökövesd, *Hungary* **17 E11** 47 49N 20 35 E
Mezőtúr, *Hungary* **17 E11** 47 1N 20 41 E
Mezquital, *Mexico* **86 C4** 23 29N 104 23W
Mgeta, *Tanzania* **55 D4** 8 22S 36 6 E
Mhlaba Hills, *Zimbabwe* **55 F3** 18 30S 30 30 E
Mhow, *India* **42 H6** 22 33N 75 50 E
Miahuatlán, *Mexico* **87 D5** 16 21N 96 36W
Miami, *Fla., U.S.A.* **77 N5** 25 47N 80 11W
Miami, *Okla., U.S.A.* **81 G7** 36 53N 94 53W
Miami, *Tex., U.S.A.* **81 H4** 35 42N 100 38W
Miami Beach, *U.S.A.* **77 N5** 25 47N 80 8W
Mian Xian, *China* **34 H4** 33 10N 106 32 E
Mianchi, *China* **34 G6** 34 48N 111 48 E
Mīāndarreh, *Iran* **45 C7** 35 37N 53 39 E
Mīāndowāb, *Iran* **44 B5** 37 0N 46 5 E
Miandrivazo, *Madag.* **57 B8** 19 31S 45 29 E
Mīāneh, *Iran* **44 B5** 37 30N 47 40 E
Mianwali, *Pakistan* **42 C4** 32 38N 71 28 E
Miarinarivo, *Madag.* **57 B8** 18 57S 46 55 E
Miass, *Russia* **24 D11** 54 59N 60 6 E
Michalovce, *Slovak Rep.* **17 D11** 48 47N 21 58 E
Michigan □, *U.S.A.* **76 C3** 44 0N 85 0W
Michigan, L., *U.S.A.* **76 D2** 44 0N 87 0W
Michigan City, *U.S.A.* **76 E2** 41 43N 86 54W
Michipicoten I., *Canada* **70 C2** 47 40N 85 40W
Michoacan □, *Mexico* **86 D4** 19 0N 102 0W
Michurin, *Bulgaria* **21 C12** 42 9N 27 51 E
Michurinsk, *Russia* **24 D7** 52 58N 40 27 E
Mico, Pta., *Nic.* **88 D3** 12 0N 83 30W
Micronesia, *Pac. Oc.* **64 G7** 11 0N 160 0 E
Micronesia, Federated States of ■, *Pac. Oc.* **64 G7** 9 0N 150 0 E
Midai, *Indonesia* **39 L6** 3 0N 107 47 E
Midale, *Canada* **73 D8** 49 25N 103 20W
Middelburg, *Neths.* **15 C3** 51 30N 3 36 E
Middelburg, *Eastern Cape, S. Africa* **56 E4** 31 30S 25 0 E
Middelburg, *Mpumalanga, S. Africa* **57 D4** 25 49S 29 28 E
Middelwit, *S. Africa* **56 C4** 24 51S 27 3 E
Middle Alkali L., *U.S.A.* **82 F3** 41 27N 120 5W
Middle Bass I., *U.S.A.* **78 E2** 41 41N 82 49W
Middle East, *Asia* **28 F7** 38 0N 40 0 E
Middle Fork Feather →, *U.S.A.* **84 F5** 38 33N 121 30W
Middle I., *Australia* **61 F3** 34 6S 123 11 E
Middle Loup →, *U.S.A.* **80 E5** 41 17N 98 24W
Middle Sackville, *Canada* **71 D7** 44 47N 63 42W
Middleboro, *U.S.A.* **79 E14** 41 54N 70 55W
Middleburg, *Fla., U.S.A.* **77 K5** 30 4N 81 52W
Middleburg, *N.Y., U.S.A.* **79 D10** 42 36N 74 20W
Middleburg, *Pa., U.S.A.* **78 F7** 40 47N 77 3W
Middlebury, *U.S.A.* **79 B11** 44 1N 73 10W
Middlemount, *Australia* **62 C4** 22 50S 148 40 E
Middleport, *N.Y., U.S.A.* **78 C6** 43 13N 78 29W
Middleport, *Ohio, U.S.A.* **76 F4** 39 0N 82 3W
Middlesboro, *U.S.A.* **77 G4** 36 36N 83 43W
Middlesbrough, *U.K.* **10 C6** 54 35N 1 13W
Middlesbrough □, *U.K.* **10 C6** 54 28N 1 13W
Middlesex, *Belize* **88 C2** 17 2N 88 31W
Middlesex, *N.J., U.S.A.* **79 F10** 40 36N 74 30W
Middlesex, *N.Y., U.S.A.* **78 D7** 42 42N 77 16W
Middleton, *Australia* **62 C3** 22 22S 141 32 E
Middleton, *Canada* **71 D6** 44 57N 65 4W
Middleton Cr. →, *Australia* **62 C3** 22 35S 141 51 E
Middletown, *U.K.* **13 B5** 54 17N 6 51W
Middletown, *Calif., U.S.A.* **84 G4** 38 45N 122 37W
Middletown, *Conn., U.S.A.* **79 E12** 41 34N 72 39W
Middletown, *N.Y., U.S.A.* **79 E10** 41 27N 74 25W
Middletown, *Ohio, U.S.A.* **76 F3** 39 31N 84 24W
Middletown, *Pa., U.S.A.* **79 F8** 40 12N 76 44W
Midhurst, *U.K.* **11 G7** 50 59N 0 44W
Midi, Canal du →, *France* **18 E4** 43 45N 1 21 E
Midland, *Canada* **78 B5** 44 45N 79 50W
Midland, *Calif., U.S.A.* **85 M12** 33 52N 114 48W
Midland, *Mich., U.S.A.* **76 D3** 43 37N 84 14W
Midland, *Pa., U.S.A.* **78 F4** 40 39N 80 27W
Midland, *Tex., U.S.A.* **81 K3** 32 0N 102 3W
Midlands □, *Zimbabwe* **55 F2** 19 40S 29 0 E
Midleton, *Ireland* **13 E3** 51 55N 8 10W
Midlothian, *U.S.A.* **81 J6** 32 30N 97 0W
Midlothian □, *U.K.* **12 F5** 55 51N 3 5W
Midongy, Tangorombohitr' i, *Madag.* **57 C8** 23 30S 47 0 E
Midongy Atsimo, *Madag.* **57 C8** 23 35S 47 1 E
Midway Is., *Pac. Oc.* **64 E10** 28 13N 177 22W
Midway Wells, *U.S.A.* **85 N11** 32 41N 115 7W
Midwest, *U.S.A.* **75 B9** 42 0N 90 0W
Midwest, *Wyo., U.S.A.* **82 E10** 43 25N 106 16W
Midwest City, *U.S.A.* **81 H6** 35 27N 97 24W
Midyat, *Turkey* **44 B4** 37 25N 41 23 E
Midzŏr, *Bulgaria* **21 C10** 43 24N 22 40 E
Mie □, *Japan* **31 G8** 34 30N 136 10 E
Międzychód, *Poland* **16 B8** 52 35N 15 53 E
Międzyrzec Podlaski, *Poland* **17 C12** 51 58N 22 45 E
Mielec, *Poland* **17 C11** 50 15N 21 25 E
Mienga, *Angola* **56 B2** 17 12S 19 48 E
Miercurea-Ciuc, *Romania* **17 E13** 46 21N 25 48 E
Mieres, *Spain* **19 A3** 43 18N 5 48W
Mifflintown, *U.S.A.* **78 F7** 40 34N 77 24W
Mifraz Hefa, *Israel* **47 C4** 32 52N 35 0 E
Miguel Alemán, Presa, *Mexico* **87 D5** 18 15N 96 40W
Mihara, *Japan* **31 G6** 34 24N 133 5 E
Mikese, *Tanzania* **54 D4** 6 48S 37 55 E
Mikhaylovgrad = Montana, *Bulgaria* **21 C10** 43 27N 23 16 E
Mikhaylovka, *Russia* **25 D7** 50 3N 43 5 E
Mikkeli, *Finland* **9 F22** 61 43N 27 15 E
Mikkwa →, *Canada* **72 B6** 58 25N 114 46W
Míkonos, *Greece* **21 F11** 37 30N 25 25 E
Mikumi, *Tanzania* **54 D4** 7 26S 37 0 E
Mikun, *Russia* **24 B9** 62 20N 50 0 E
Milaca, *U.S.A.* **80 C8** 45 45N 93 39W
Milagro, *Ecuador* **92 D3** 2 11S 79 36W
Milan = Milano, *Italy* **18 D8** 45 28N 9 12 E
Milan, *Mo., U.S.A.* **80 E8** 40 12N 93 7W
Milan, *Tenn., U.S.A.* **77 H1** 35 55N 88 46W
Milang, *Australia* **63 F2** 35 24S 138 58 E
Milange, *Mozam.* **55 F4** 16 3S 35 45 E
Milano, *Italy* **18 D8** 45 28N 9 12 E
Milâs, *Turkey* **21 F12** 37 20N 27 50 E
Mílatos, *Greece* **23 D7** 35 18N 25 34 E
Milazzo, *Italy* **20 E6** 38 13N 15 15 E
Milbank, *U.S.A.* **80 C6** 45 13N 96 38W
Milbanke Sd., *Canada* **72 C3** 52 15N 128 35W
Milden, *Canada* **73 C7** 51 29N 107 32W
Mildenhall, *U.K.* **11 E8** 52 21N 0 32 E
Mildmay, *Canada* **78 B3** 44 3N 81 7W
Mildura, *Australia* **63 E3** 34 13S 142 9 E
Miles, *Australia* **63 D5** 26 40S 150 9 E
Miles City, *U.S.A.* **80 B2** 46 25N 105 51W
Milestone, *Canada* **73 D8** 49 59N 104 31W
Miletus, *Turkey* **21 F12** 37 30N 27 18 E
Milford, *Calif., U.S.A.* **84 E6** 40 10N 120 22W
Milford, *Conn., U.S.A.* **79 E11** 41 14N 73 3W
Milford, *Del., U.S.A.* **76 F8** 38 55N 75 26W
Milford, *Mass., U.S.A.* **79 D13** 42 8N 71 31W
Milford, *N.H., U.S.A.* **79 D13** 42 50N 71 39W
Milford, *Pa., U.S.A.* **79 E10** 41 19N 74 48W
Milford, *Utah, U.S.A.* **83 G7** 38 24N 113 1W
Milford Haven, *U.K.* **11 F2** 51 42N 5 7W
Milford Sd., *N.Z.* **59 L1** 44 41S 167 47 E
Milḩ, Baḩr al, *Iraq* **44 C4** 32 40N 43 35 E
Milikapiti, *Australia* **60 B5** 11 26S 130 40 E
Miling, *Australia* **61 F2** 30 30S 116 17 E
Milk →, *U.S.A.* **82 B10** 48 4N 106 19W
Milk River, *Canada* **72 D6** 49 10N 112 5W
Mill I., *Antarctica* **5 C8** 66 0S 101 30 E
Mill Valley, *U.S.A.* **84 H4** 37 54N 122 32W
Millau, *France* **18 D5** 44 8N 3 4 E
Millbridge, *Canada* **78 B7** 44 41N 77 36W
Millbrook, *Canada* **78 B6** 44 10N 78 29W
Millbrook, *U.S.A.* **79 E11** 41 47N 73 42W
Mille Lacs, L. des, *Canada* **70 C1** 48 45N 90 35W
Mille Lacs L., *U.S.A.* **80 B8** 46 15N 93 39W
Milledgeville, *U.S.A.* **77 J4** 33 5N 83 14W
Millen, *U.S.A.* **77 J5** 32 48N 81 57W
Miller, *U.S.A.* **80 C5** 44 31N 98 59W
Millersburg, *Ohio, U.S.A.* **78 F3** 40 33N 81 55W
Millersburg, *Pa., U.S.A.* **78 F8** 40 32N 76 58W
Millerton, *U.S.A.* **79 E11** 41 57N 73 31W
Millerton L., *U.S.A.* **84 J7** 37 1N 119 41W
Millheim, *U.S.A.* **78 F7** 40 54N 77 29W
Millicent, *Australia* **63 F3** 37 34S 140 21 E
Millington, *U.S.A.* **81 H10** 35 20N 89 53W
Millinocket, *U.S.A.* **77 C11** 45 39N 68 43W
Millmerran, *Australia* **63 D5** 27 53S 151 16 E
Millom, *U.K.* **10 C4** 54 13N 3 16W
Mills L., *Canada* **72 A5** 61 30N 118 20W
Millsboro, *U.S.A.* **78 G5** 40 0N 80 0W
Milltown Malbay, *Ireland* **13 D2** 52 52N 9 24W
Millville, *N.J., U.S.A.* **76 F8** 39 24N 75 2W
Millville, *Pa., U.S.A.* **79 E8** 41 7N 76 32W
Millwood L., *U.S.A.* **81 J8** 33 42N 93 58W
Milne →, *Australia* **62 C2** 21 10S 137 33 E
Milo, *U.S.A.* **77 C11** 45 15N 68 59W
Mílos, *Greece* **21 F11** 36 44N 24 25 E
Milparinka, *Australia* **63 D3** 29 46S 141 57 E
Milton, *N.S., Canada* **71 D7** 44 4N 64 45W
Milton, *Ont., Canada* **78 C5** 43 31N 79 53W
Milton, *N.Z.* **59 M2** 46 7S 169 59 E
Milton, *Calif., U.S.A.* **84 G6** 38 3N 120 51W
Milton, *Fla., U.S.A.* **77 K2** 30 38N 87 3W
Milton, *Pa., U.S.A.* **78 F8** 41 1N 76 51W
Milton, *Vt., U.S.A.* **79 B11** 44 38N 73 7W
Milton-Freewater, *U.S.A.* **82 D4** 45 56N 118 23W
Milton Keynes, *U.K.* **11 E7** 52 1N 0 44W
Milton Keynes □, *U.K.* **11 E7** 52 1N 0 44W
Milverton, *Canada* **78 C4** 43 34N 80 55W
Milwaukee, *U.S.A.* **76 D2** 43 2N 87 55W
Milwaukee Deep, *Atl. Oc.* **89 C6** 19 50N 68 0W
Milwaukie, *U.S.A.* **84 E4** 45 27N 122 38W
Min Jiang →, *Fujian, China* **33 D6** 26 0N 119 35 E
Min Jiang →, *Sichuan, China* **32 D5** 28 45N 104 40 E
Min Xian, *China* **34 G3** 34 25N 104 5 E
Mina Pirquitas, *Argentina* **94 A2** 22 40S 66 30W
Mīnā Su'ud, *Si. Arabia* **45 D6** 28 45N 48 28 E
Mīnā'al Aḩmadī, *Kuwait* **45 D6** 29 5N 48 10 E
Minago →, *Canada* **73 C9** 54 33N 98 59W
Minaki, *Canada* **73 D10** 49 59N 94 40W
Minamata, *Japan* **31 H5** 32 10N 130 30 E
Minami-Tori-Shima, *Pac. Oc.* **64 E7** 24 20N 153 58 E
Minas, *Uruguay* **95 C4** 34 20S 55 10W
Minas, Sierra de las, *Guatemala* **88 C2** 15 9N 89 31W
Minas Basin, *Canada* **71 C7** 45 20N 64 12W
Minas Gerais □, *Brazil* **93 G9** 18 50S 46 0W
Minatitlán, *Mexico* **87 D6** 17 59N 94 31W
Minbu, *Burma* **41 J19** 20 10N 94 52 E
Minchinabad, *Pakistan* **42 D5** 30 10N 73 34 E
Mindanao, *Phil.* **37 C7** 8 0N 125 0 E
Mindanao Sea = Bohol Sea, *Phil.* **37 C6** 9 0N 124 0 E
Mindanao Trench, *Pac. Oc.* **37 B7** 12 0N 126 6 E
Minden, *Canada* **78 B6** 44 55N 78 43W
Minden, *Germany* **16 B5** 52 17N 8 55 E
Minden, *La., U.S.A.* **81 J8** 32 37N 93 17W
Minden, *Nev., U.S.A.* **84 G7** 38 57N 119 46W
Mindiptana, *Indonesia* **37 F10** 5 55S 140 22 E
Mindoro, *Phil.* **37 B6** 13 0N 121 0 E
Mindoro Str., *Phil.* **37 B6** 12 30N 120 30 E
Mine, *Japan* **31 G5** 34 12N 131 7 E
Minehead, *U.K.* **11 F4** 51 12N 3 29W
Mineola, *N.Y., U.S.A.* **79 F11** 40 45N 73 39W
Mineola, *Tex., U.S.A.* **81 J7** 32 40N 95 29W
Mineral King, *U.S.A.* **84 J8** 36 27N 118 36W
Mineral Wells, *U.S.A.* **81 J5** 32 48N 98 7W
Minersville, *U.S.A.* **79 F8** 40 41N 76 16W
Minerva, *U.S.A.* **78 F3** 40 44N 81 6W
Minetto, *U.S.A.* **79 C8** 43 24N 76 28W
Mingäçevir Su Anbarı, *Azerbaijan* **25 F8** 40 57N 46 50 E
Mingan, *Canada* **71 B7** 50 20N 64 0W
Mingechaurskoye Vdkhr. = Mingäçevir Su Anbarı, *Azerbaijan* **25 F8** 40 57N 46 50 E
Mingela, *Australia* **62 B4** 19 52S 146 38 E
Mingenew, *Australia* **61 E2** 29 12S 115 21 E
Mingera Cr. →, *Australia* **62 C2** 20 38S 137 45 E
Mingin, *Burma* **41 H19** 22 50N 94 30 E
Mingo Junction, *U.S.A.* **78 F4** 40 19N 80 37W
Mingyuegue, *China* **35 C15** 43 2N 128 50 E
Minho = Miño →, *Spain* **19 A2** 41 52N 8 40W
Minho, *Portugal* **19 B1** 41 25N 8 20W
Minidoka, *U.S.A.* **82 E7** 42 45N 113 29W

Montour Falls

nigwal, L., Australia 61 E3 29 31S 123 14 E
nilya →, Australia 61 D1 23 45S 114 0 E
nilya Roadhouse, Australia 61 D1 23 55S 114 0 E
nipi L., Canada 71 B7 52 25N 60 45W
nk L., Canada 72 A5 61 54N 117 40W
nna, Nigeria 50 G7 9 37N 6 30 E
nneapolis, Kans., U.S.A. 80 F6 39 8N 97 42W
nneapolis, Minn., U.S.A. 80 C8 44 59N 93 16W
nnedosa, Canada 73 C9 50 14N 99 50W
nnesota □, U.S.A. 80 B8 46 0N 94 15W
nnesota →, U.S.A. 80 C8 44 54N 93 9W
nnewaukan, U.S.A. 80 A5 48 4N 99 15W
nnipa, Australia 63 E2 32 51S 135 9 E
nnitaki L., Canada 70 C1 49 57N 92 10W
no, Japan 31 G8 35 32N 136 55 E
ño →, Spain 19 A2 41 52N 8 40W
norca = Menorca, Spain 22 B11 40 0N 4 0 E
not, U.S.A. 80 A4 48 14N 101 18W
nqin, China 34 E2 38 38N 103 20 E
nsk, Belarus 17 B14 53 52N 27 30 E
ńsk Mazowiecki, Poland 17 B11 52 10N 21 33 E
ntabie, Australia 63 D1 27 15S 133 7 E
ntaka Pass, Pakistan 43 A6 37 0N 74 58 E
nteke Daban = Mintaka Pass, Pakistan 43 A6 37 0N 74 58 E
nto, Canada 71 C6 46 5N 66 5W
nto, L., Canada 70 A5 57 13N 75 0W
nton, Canada 73 D8 49 10N 104 35W
nturn, U.S.A. 82 G10 39 35N 106 26W
nusinsk, Russia 27 D10 53 43N 91 20 E
nutang, India 41 E20 28 15N 96 30 E
quelon, Canada 70 C4 49 25N 76 27W
quelon, St- P. & M. 71 C8 47 8N 56 22W
Kūh, Iran 45 E8 26 22N 58 55 E
Shahdād, Iran 45 E8 26 15N 58 29 E
a, Italy 20 B5 45 26N 12 8 E
a por vos Cay, Bahamas 89 B5 22 9N 74 30W
aj, India 40 L9 16 50N 74 45 E
am Shah, Pakistan 42 C4 33 0N 70 2 E
amar, Argentina 94 D4 38 15S 57 50W
amar, Mozam. 57 C6 23 50S 35 35 E
amichi, Canada 71 C6 47 2N 65 28W
amichi B., Canada 71 C7 47 15N 65 0W
anda, Brazil 93 H7 20 10S 56 15W
anda →, Brazil 92 G7 19 25S 57 20W
anda de Ebro, Spain 19 A4 42 41N 2 57W
anda do Douro, Portugal 19 B2 41 30N 6 16W
andópolis, Brazil 95 A5 21 9S 51 6W
ango, Malawi 55 E3 13 32S 34 58 E
assol, Brazil 95 A6 20 46S 49 28W
bāţ, Oman 46 D5 17 0N 54 45 E
i, Malaysia 36 D4 4 23N 113 59 E
iam Vale, Australia 62 C5 24 20S 151 33 E
im, L., S. Amer. 95 C5 32 45S 52 50W
nyy, Russia 27 C12 62 33N 113 53 E
okhan, Pakistan 42 F3 27 46N 68 6 E
ond L., Canada 73 B8 55 6N 102 47W
pur, Pakistan 43 C5 33 32N 73 56 E
pur Batoro, Pakistan 42 G3 24 44N 68 16 E
pur Bibiwari, Pakistan 42 E2 28 33N 67 44 E
pur Khas, Pakistan 42 G3 25 30N 69 0 E
pur Sakro, Pakistan 42 G2 24 33N 67 41 E
tağ, Turkey 44 B4 38 23N 41 56 E
yang, S. Korea 35 G15 35 31N 128 44 E
zapur, India 43 G10 25 10N 82 34 E
zapur-cum-Vindhyachal = Mirzapur, India 43 G10 25 10N 82 34 E
santla, Mexico 87 D5 19 56N 96 50W
sawa, Japan 30 D10 40 41N 141 24 E
scou I., Canada 71 C7 47 57N 64 31W
sh'āb, Ra's al, Si. Arabia 45 D6 28 15N 48 43 E
shan, China 33 B8 45 37N 131 48 E
shawaka, U.S.A. 76 E2 41 40N 86 11W
shima, Japan 31 G9 35 10N 138 52 E
sión, Mexico 85 N10 32 6N 116 53W
siones □, Argentina 95 B5 27 0S 55 0W
siones □, Paraguay 94 B4 27 0S 56 0W
skah, Si. Arabia 44 E4 24 49N 42 56 E
skitos, Cayos, Nic. 88 D3 14 26N 82 50W
skolc, Hungary 17 D11 48 7N 20 50 E
soke, Dem. Rep. of the Congo 54 C2 0 42S 28 2 E
sool, Indonesia 37 E8 1 52S 130 10 E
srātah, Libya 51 B9 32 24N 15 3 E
ssanabie, Canada 70 C3 48 20N 84 6W
ssinaibi →, Canada 70 B3 50 43N 81 29W
ssinaibi L., Canada 70 C3 48 23N 83 40W
ssion, Canada 72 D4 49 10N 122 15W
ssion, S. Dak., U.S.A. 80 D4 43 18N 100 39W
ssion, Tex., U.S.A. 81 M5 26 13N 98 20W
ssion Beach, Australia 62 B4 17 53S 146 6 E
ssion Viejo, U.S.A. 85 M9 33 36N 117 40W
ssisa L., Canada 70 B2 52 20N 85 7W
ssisicabi →, Canada 70 B4 51 14N 79 31W
ssissagi →, Canada 70 C3 46 15N 83 9W
ssissauga, Canada 78 C5 43 32N 79 35W
ssissippi □, U.S.A. 81 J10 33 0N 90 0W
ssissippi →, U.S.A. 81 L10 29 9N 89 15W
ssissippi L., Canada 79 A8 45 5N 76 10W
ssissippi River Delta, U.S.A. 81 L9 29 10N 89 15W
ssissippi Sd., U.S.A. 81 K10 30 20N 89 0W
ssoula, U.S.A. 82 C7 46 52N 114 1W
ssouri □, U.S.A. 80 F8 38 25N 92 30W
ssouri →, U.S.A. 80 F9 38 49N 90 7W
ssouri City, U.S.A. 81 L7 29 37N 95 32W
ssouri Valley, U.S.A. 80 E7 41 34N 95 53W
st, U.S.A. 84 E3 45 59N 123 15W
stassibi →, Canada 71 B5 48 53N 72 13W
stassini, Canada 71 C5 48 53N 72 12W
stassini →, Canada 71 C5 48 42N 72 20W
stassini, L., Canada 70 B5 51 0N 73 30W
stastin L., Canada 71 A7 55 57N 63 20W
stinibi, L., Canada 71 A7 55 56N 64 17W
sty L., Canada 73 B8 58 53N 101 40W
surata = Misrātah, Libya 51 B9 32 24N 15 3 E
chell, Australia 63 D4 26 29S 147 58 E
chell, Canada 78 C3 43 28N 81 12W
chell, Nebr., U.S.A. 80 E3 41 57N 103 49W
chell, Oreg., U.S.A. 82 D3 44 34N 120 9W
chell, S. Dak., U.S.A. 80 D6 43 43N 98 2W
chell →, Australia 62 B3 15 12S 141 35 E
chell, Mt., U.S.A. 77 H4 35 46N 82 16W
chell Ranges, Australia 62 A2 12 49S 135 36 E
chelstown, Ireland 13 D3 52 15N 8 16W
Mitha Tiwana, Pakistan 42 C5 32 13N 72 6 E
Mithi, Pakistan 42 G3 24 44N 69 48 E
Mithrao, Pakistan 42 F3 27 28N 69 40 E
Mitilíni, Greece 21 E12 39 6N 26 35 E
Mito, Japan 31 F10 36 20N 140 30 E
Mitrovica = Kosovska Mitrovica, Serbia, Yug. 21 C9 42 54N 20 52 E
Mitsinjo, Madag. 57 B8 16 1S 45 52 E
Mitsiwa, Eritrea 46 D2 15 35N 39 25 E
Mitsukaidō, Japan 31 F9 36 1N 139 59 E
Mittagong, Australia 63 E5 34 28S 150 29 E
Mitú, Colombia 92 C4 1 15N 70 13W
Mitumba, Tanzania 54 D3 7 8S 31 2 E
Mitumba, Mts., Dem. Rep. of the Congo 54 D2 7 0S 27 30 E
Mitwaba, Dem. Rep. of the Congo 55 D2 8 2S 27 17 E
Mityana, Uganda 54 B3 0 23N 32 2 E
Mixteco →, Mexico 87 D5 18 11N 98 30W
Miyagi □, Japan 30 E10 38 15N 140 45 E
Miyah, W. el →, Syria 44 C3 34 44N 39 57 E
Miyake-Jima, Japan 31 G9 34 5N 139 30 E
Miyako, Japan 30 E10 39 40N 141 59 E
Miyako-Jima, Japan 31 M2 24 45N 125 20 E
Miyako-Rettō, Japan 31 M2 24 24N 125 0 E
Miyakonojō, Japan 31 J5 31 40N 131 5 E
Miyani, India 42 J3 21 50N 69 26 E
Miyanoura-Dake, Japan 31 J5 30 20N 130 31 E
Miyazaki, Japan 31 J5 31 56N 131 30 E
Miyazaki □, Japan 31 H5 32 30N 131 30 E
Miyazu, Japan 31 G7 35 35N 135 10 E
Miyet, Bahr el = Dead Sea, Asia 47 D4 31 30N 35 30 E
Miyoshi, Japan 31 G6 34 48N 132 51 E
Miyun, China 34 D9 40 28N 116 50 E
Miyun Shuiku, China 35 D9 40 30N 117 0 E
Mizdah, Libya 51 B8 31 30N 13 0 E
Mizen Hd., Cork, Ireland 13 E2 51 27N 9 50W
Mizen Hd., Wick., Ireland 13 D5 52 51N 6 4W
Mizhi, China 34 F6 37 47N 110 12 E
Mizoram □, India 41 H18 23 30N 92 40 E
Mizpe Ramon, Israel 47 E3 30 34N 34 49 E
Mizusawa, Japan 30 E10 39 8N 141 8 E
Mjölby, Sweden 9 G16 58 20N 15 10 E
Mjøsa, Norway 9 F14 60 40N 11 0 E
Mkata, Tanzania 54 D4 5 45S 38 20 E
Mkokotoni, Tanzania 54 D4 5 55S 39 15 E
Mkomazi, Tanzania 54 C4 4 40S 38 7 E
Mkomazi →, S. Africa 57 E5 30 12S 30 50 E
Mkulwe, Tanzania 55 D3 8 37S 32 20 E
Mkumbi, Ras, Tanzania 54 D4 7 38S 39 55 E
Mkushi, Zambia 55 E2 14 25S 29 15 E
Mkushi River, Zambia 55 E2 13 32S 29 45 E
Mkuze, S. Africa 57 D5 27 10S 32 0 E
Mladá Boleslav, Czech Rep. 16 C8 50 27N 14 53 E
Mlala Hills, Tanzania 54 D3 6 50S 31 40 E
Mlange = Mulanje, Malawi 55 F4 16 2S 35 33 E
Mlanje, Pic, Malawi 53 H7 15 57S 35 38 E
Mława, Poland 17 B11 53 9N 20 25 E
Mljet, Croatia 20 C7 42 43N 17 30 E
Mmabatho, S. Africa 56 D4 25 49S 25 30 E
Mo i Rana, Norway 8 C16 66 20N 14 7 E
Moa, Cuba 89 B4 20 40N 74 56W
Moa, Indonesia 37 F7 8 0S 128 0 E
Moab, U.S.A. 83 G9 38 35N 109 33W
Moala, Fiji 59 D8 18 36S 179 53 E
Moama, Australia 63 F3 36 7S 144 46 E
Moapa, U.S.A. 85 J12 36 40N 114 37W
Moate, Ireland 13 C4 53 24N 7 44W
Moba, Dem. Rep. of the Congo 54 D2 7 0S 29 48 E
Mobārakābād, Iran 45 D7 28 24N 53 20 E
Mobaye, C.A.R. 52 D4 4 25N 21 5 E
Mobayi, Dem. Rep. of the Congo 52 D4 4 15N 21 8 E
Moberley Lake, Canada 72 B4 55 50N 121 44W
Moberly, U.S.A. 80 F8 39 25N 92 26W
Mobile, U.S.A. 77 K1 30 41N 88 3W
Mobile B., U.S.A. 77 K2 30 30N 88 0W
Mobridge, U.S.A. 80 C4 45 32N 100 26W
Mobutu Sese Seko, L. = Albert L., Africa 54 B3 1 30N 31 0 E
Moc Chau, Vietnam 38 B5 20 50N 104 38 E
Moc Hoa, Vietnam 39 G5 10 46N 105 56 E
Mocabe Kasari, Dem. Rep. of the Congo 55 D2 9 58S 26 12 E
Moçambique, Mozam. 55 F5 15 3S 40 42 E
Moçâmedes = Namibe, Angola 53 H2 15 7S 12 11 E
Mocanaqua, U.S.A. 79 E8 41 9N 76 8W
Mochudi, Botswana 56 C4 24 27S 26 7 E
Mocimboa da Praia, Mozam. 55 E5 11 25S 40 20 E
Moclips, U.S.A. 84 C2 47 14N 124 13W
Mocoa, Colombia 92 C3 1 7N 76 35W
Mococa, Brazil 95 A6 21 28S 47 0W
Mocorito, Mexico 86 B3 25 30N 107 53W
Moctezuma, Mexico 86 B3 29 50N 109 0W
Moctezuma →, Mexico 87 C5 21 59N 98 34W
Mocuba, Mozam. 55 F4 16 54S 36 57 E
Mocúzari, Presa, Mexico 86 B3 27 10N 109 10W
Modane, France 18 D7 45 12N 6 40 E
Modasa, India 42 H5 23 30N 73 21 E
Modder →, S. Africa 56 D3 29 2S 24 37 E
Modderrivier, S. Africa 56 D3 29 2S 24 38 E
Módena, Italy 20 B4 44 40N 10 55 E
Modena, U.S.A. 83 H7 37 48N 113 56W
Modesto, U.S.A. 84 H6 37 39N 121 0W
Módica, Italy 20 F6 36 52N 14 46 E
Moe, Australia 63 F4 38 12S 146 19 E
Moebase, Mozam. 55 F4 17 3S 38 41 E
Moengo, Surinam 93 B8 5 45N 54 20W
Moffat, U.K. 12 F5 55 21N 3 27W
Moga, India 42 D6 30 48N 75 8 E
Mogadishu = Muqdisho, Somali Rep. 46 G4 2 2N 45 25 E
Mogador = Essaouira, Morocco 50 B4 31 32N 9 42W
Mogalakwena →, S. Africa 57 C4 22 38S 28 40 E
Mogami-Gawa →, Japan 30 E10 38 45N 140 0 E
Mogán, Canary Is. 22 G4 27 53N 15 43W
Mogaung, Burma 41 G20 25 20N 97 0 E
Mogi das Cruzes, Brazil 95 A6 23 31S 46 11W
Mogi-Guaçu →, Brazil 95 A6 20 53S 48 10W
Mogi-Mirim, Brazil 95 A6 22 29S 47 0W
Mogilev = Mahilyow, Belarus 17 B16 53 55N 30 18 E
Mogilev-Podolskiy = Mohyliv-Podilskyy, Ukraine 17 D14 48 26N 27 48 E
Mogincual, Mozam. 55 F5 15 35S 40 25 E
Mogocha, Russia 27 D12 53 40N 119 50 E
Mogok, Burma 41 H20 23 0N 96 40 E
Mogollon Rim, U.S.A. 83 J8 34 10N 110 50W
Mogumber, Australia 61 F2 31 2S 116 3 E
Mohács, Hungary 17 F10 45 58N 18 41 E
Mohales Hoek, Lesotho 56 E4 30 7S 27 26 E
Mohall, U.S.A. 80 A4 48 46N 101 31W
Moḩammadābād, Iran 45 B8 37 52N 59 5 E
Mohammedia, Morocco 50 B4 33 44N 7 21W
Mohana →, India 43 G11 24 43N 85 0 E
Mohanlalganj, India 43 F9 26 41N 80 58 E
Mohave, L., U.S.A. 85 K12 35 12N 114 34W
Mohawk →, U.S.A. 79 D11 42 47N 73 41W
Mohenjodaro, Pakistan 42 F3 27 19N 68 7 E
Mohicanville Reservoir, U.S.A. 78 F3 40 45N 82 0W
Mohoro, Tanzania 54 D4 8 6S 39 8 E
Mohyliv-Podilskyy, Ukraine 17 D14 48 26N 27 48 E
Moidart, L., U.K. 12 E3 56 47N 5 52W
Moira →, Canada 78 B7 44 21N 77 24W
Moíres, Greece 23 D6 35 4N 24 56 E
Moisaküla, Estonia 9 G21 58 3N 25 12 E
Moisie, Canada 71 B6 50 12N 66 1W
Moisie →, Canada 71 B6 50 14N 66 5W
Mojave, U.S.A. 85 K8 35 3N 118 10W
Mojave Desert, U.S.A. 85 L10 35 0N 116 30W
Mojo, Bolivia 94 A2 21 48S 65 33W
Mojokerto, Indonesia 37 G15 7 28S 112 26 E
Mokai, N.Z. 59 H5 38 32S 175 56 E
Mokambo, Dem. Rep. of the Congo 55 E2 12 25S 28 20 E
Mokameh, India 43 G11 25 24N 85 55 E
Mokelumne →, U.S.A. 84 G5 38 13N 121 28W
Mokelumne Hill, U.S.A. 84 G6 38 18N 120 43W
Mokhós, Greece 23 D7 35 16N 25 27 E
Mokhotlong, Lesotho 57 D4 29 22S 29 2 E
Mokokchung, India 41 F19 26 15N 94 30 E
Mokp'o, S. Korea 35 G14 34 50N 126 25 E
Mokra Gora, Serbia, Yug. 21 C9 42 50N 20 30 E
Mol, Belgium 15 C5 51 11N 5 5 E
Molchanovo, Russia 26 D9 57 40N 83 50 E
Mold, U.K. 10 D4 53 9N 3 8W
Moldavia = Moldova ■, Europe 17 E15 47 0N 28 0 E
Molde, Norway 8 E12 62 45N 7 9 E
Moldova ■, Europe 17 E15 47 0N 28 0 E
Moldoveana, Vf., Romania 17 F13 45 36N 24 45 E
Mole →, U.K. 11 F7 51 24N 0 21W
Mole Creek, Australia 62 G4 41 34S 146 24 E
Molepolole, Botswana 56 C4 24 28S 25 28 E
Molfetta, Italy 20 D7 41 12N 16 36 E
Moline, U.S.A. 80 E9 41 30N 90 31W
Molinos, Argentina 94 B2 25 28S 66 15W
Moliro, Dem. Rep. of the Congo 54 D3 8 12S 30 30 E
Mollendo, Peru 92 G4 17 0S 72 0W
Mollerin, L., Australia 61 F2 30 30S 117 35 E
Molodechno = Maladzyechna, Belarus 17 A14 54 20N 26 50 E
Molokai, U.S.A. 74 H16 21 8N 157 0W
Molong, Australia 63 E4 33 5S 148 54 E
Molopo →, Africa 56 D3 27 30S 20 13 E
Molotov = Perm, Russia 24 C10 58 0N 56 10 E
Molson L., Canada 73 C9 54 22N 96 40W
Molteno, S. Africa 56 E4 31 22S 26 22 E
Molu, Indonesia 37 F8 6 45S 131 40 E
Molucca Sea, Indonesia 37 E6 2 0S 124 0 E
Moluccas = Maluku, Indonesia 37 E7 1 0S 127 0 E
Moma, Dem. Rep. of the Congo 54 C1 1 35S 23 52 E
Moma, Mozam. 55 F4 16 47S 39 4 E
Mombasa, Kenya 54 C4 4 2S 39 43 E
Mombetsu, Japan 30 B11 44 21N 143 22 E
Momchilgrad, Bulgaria 21 D11 41 33N 25 23 E
Momi, Dem. Rep. of the Congo 54 C2 1 42S 27 0 E
Mompós, Colombia 92 B4 9 14N 74 26W
Møn, Denmark 9 J15 54 57N 12 20 E
Mon →, Burma 41 J19 20 25N 94 30 E
Mona, Canal de la, W. Indies 89 C6 18 30N 67 45W
Mona, Isla, Puerto Rico 89 C6 18 5N 67 54W
Mona, Pta., Costa Rica 88 E3 9 37N 82 36W
Monaca, U.S.A. 78 F4 40 41N 80 17W
Monaco ■, Europe 18 E7 43 46N 7 23 E
Monadhliath Mts., U.K. 12 D4 57 10N 4 4W
Monadnock, Mt., U.S.A. 79 D12 42 52N 72 7W
Monaghan, Ireland 13 B5 54 15N 6 57W
Monaghan □, Ireland 13 B5 54 11N 6 56W
Monahans, U.S.A. 81 K3 31 36N 102 54W
Monapo, Mozam. 55 E5 14 56S 40 19 E
Monar, L., U.K. 12 D3 57 26N 5 8W
Monarch Mt., Canada 72 C3 51 55N 125 57W
Monashee Mts., Canada 72 C5 51 0N 118 43W
Monasterevin, Ireland 13 C4 53 8N 7 4W
Monastir = Bitola, Macedonia 21 D9 41 1N 21 20 E
Moncayo, Sierra del, Spain 19 B5 41 48N 1 50W
Monchegorsk, Russia 24 A5 67 54N 32 58 E
Mönchengladbach, Germany 16 C4 51 11N 6 27 E
Monchique, Portugal 19 D1 37 19N 8 38W
Moncks Corner, U.S.A. 77 J5 33 12N 80 1W
Monclova, Mexico 86 B4 26 50N 101 30W
Moncton, Canada 71 C7 46 7N 64 51W
Mondego →, Portugal 19 B1 40 9N 8 52W
Mondeodo, Indonesia 37 E6 3 34S 122 9 E
Mondovì, Italy 18 D7 44 23N 7 49 E
Mondrain I., Australia 61 F3 34 9S 122 14 E
Monessen, U.S.A. 78 F5 40 9N 79 54W
Monett, U.S.A. 81 G8 36 55N 93 55W
Moneymore, U.K. 13 B5 54 41N 6 40W
Monforte de Lemos, Spain 19 A2 42 31N 7 33W
Mong Hsu, Burma 41 J21 21 54N 98 30 E
Mong Kung, Burma 41 J20 21 35N 97 35 E
Mong Nai, Burma 41 J20 20 32N 97 46 E
Mong Pawk, Burma 41 H21 22 4N 99 16 E
Mong Ton, Burma 41 J21 20 17N 98 45 E
Mong Wa, Burma 41 J22 21 26N 100 27 E
Mong Yai, Burma 41 H21 22 21N 98 3 E
Mongalla, Sudan 51 G12 5 8N 31 42 E
Mongers, L., Australia 61 E2 29 25S 117 5 E
Monghyr = Munger, India 43 G12 25 23N 86 30 E
Mongibello = Etna, Italy 20 F6 37 50N 14 55 E
Mongo, Chad 51 F9 12 14N 18 43 E
Mongolia ■, Asia 27 E10 47 0N 103 0 E
Mongu, Zambia 53 H4 15 16S 23 12 E
Môngua, Angola 56 B2 16 43S 15 20 E
Monifieth, U.K. 12 E6 56 30N 2 48W
Monkey Bay, Malawi 55 E4 14 7S 35 1 E
Monkey Mia, Australia 61 E1 25 48S 113 43 E
Monkey River, Belize 87 D7 16 22N 88 29W
Monkoto, Dem. Rep. of the Congo 52 E4 1 38S 20 35 E
Monkton, Canada 78 C3 43 35N 81 5W
Monmouth, U.K. 11 F5 51 48N 2 42W
Monmouth, Ill., U.S.A. 80 E9 40 55N 90 39W
Monmouth, Oreg., U.S.A. 82 D2 44 51N 123 14W
Monmouthshire □, U.K. 11 F5 51 48N 2 54W
Mono L., U.S.A. 84 H7 38 1N 119 1W
Monolith, U.S.A. 85 K8 35 7N 118 22W
Monólithos, Greece 23 C9 36 7N 27 45 E
Monongahela, U.S.A. 78 F5 40 12N 79 56W
Monópoli, Italy 20 D7 40 57N 17 18 E
Monroe, Ga., U.S.A. 77 J4 33 47N 83 43W
Monroe, La., U.S.A. 81 J8 32 30N 92 7W
Monroe, Mich., U.S.A. 76 E4 41 55N 83 24W
Monroe, N.C., U.S.A. 77 H5 34 59N 80 33W
Monroe, N.Y., U.S.A. 79 E10 41 20N 74 11W
Monroe, Utah, U.S.A. 83 G7 38 38N 112 7W
Monroe, Wash., U.S.A. 84 C5 47 51N 121 58W
Monroe, Wis., U.S.A. 80 D10 42 36N 89 38W
Monroe City, U.S.A. 80 F9 39 39N 91 44W
Monroeton, U.S.A. 79 E8 41 43N 76 29W
Monroeville, Ala., U.S.A. 77 K2 31 31N 87 20W
Monroeville, Pa., U.S.A. 78 F5 40 26N 79 45W
Monrovia, Liberia 50 G3 6 18N 10 47W
Mons, Belgium 15 D3 50 27N 3 58 E
Monse, Indonesia 37 E6 4 0S 123 10 E
Mont-de-Marsan, France 18 E3 43 54N 0 31W
Mont-Joli, Canada 71 C6 48 37N 68 10W
Mont-Laurier, Canada 70 C4 46 35N 75 30W
Mont-Louis, Canada 71 C6 49 15N 65 44W
Mont-St-Michel, Le = Le Mont-St-Michel, France 18 B3 48 40N 1 30W
Mont Tremblant, Parc Recr. du, Canada 70 C5 46 30N 74 30W
Montagu, S. Africa 56 E3 33 45S 20 8 E
Montagu I., Antarctica 5 B1 58 25S 26 20W
Montague, Canada 71 C7 46 10N 62 39W
Montague, I., Mexico 86 A2 31 40N 114 56W
Montague Ra., Australia 61 E2 27 15S 119 30 E
Montague Sd., Australia 60 B4 14 28S 125 20 E
Montalbán, Spain 19 B5 40 50N 0 45W
Montalvo, U.S.A. 85 L7 34 15N 119 12W
Montana, Bulgaria 21 C10 43 27N 23 16 E
Montaña, Peru 92 E4 6 0S 73 0W
Montana □, U.S.A. 82 C9 47 0N 110 0W
Montaña Clara, I., Canary Is. 22 E6 29 17N 13 33W
Montargis, France 18 C5 47 59N 2 43 E
Montauban, France 18 D4 44 2N 1 21 E
Montauk, U.S.A. 79 E13 41 3N 71 57W
Montauk Pt., U.S.A. 79 E13 41 4N 71 52W
Montbéliard, France 18 C7 47 31N 6 48 E
Montceau-les-Mines, France 18 C6 46 40N 4 23 E
Montclair, U.S.A. 79 F10 40 49N 74 13W
Monte Albán, Mexico 87 D5 17 2N 96 45W
Monte Alegre, Brazil 93 D8 2 0S 54 0W
Monte Azul, Brazil 93 G10 15 9S 42 53W
Monte Bello Is., Australia 60 D2 20 30S 115 45 E
Monte-Carlo, Monaco 18 E7 43 46N 7 23 E
Monte Caseros, Argentina 94 C4 30 10S 57 50W
Monte Comán, Argentina 94 C2 34 40S 67 53W
Monte Cristi, Dom. Rep. 89 C5 19 52N 71 39W
Monte Lindo →, Paraguay 94 A4 23 56S 57 12W
Monte Patria, Chile 94 C1 30 42S 70 58W
Monte Quemado, Argentina 94 B3 25 53S 62 41W
Monte Rio, U.S.A. 84 G4 38 28N 123 0W
Monte Santu, C. di, Italy 20 D3 40 5N 9 44 E
Monte Vista, U.S.A. 83 H10 37 35N 106 9W
Monteagudo, Argentina 95 B5 27 14S 54 8W
Montebello, Canada 70 C5 45 40N 74 55W
Montecito, U.S.A. 85 L7 34 26N 119 40W
Montecristo, Italy 20 C4 42 20N 10 19 E
Montego Bay, Jamaica 88 C4 18 30N 78 0W
Montélimar, France 18 D6 44 33N 4 45 E
Montello, U.S.A. 80 D10 43 48N 89 20W
Montemorelos, Mexico 87 B5 25 11N 99 42W
Montenegro, Brazil 95 B5 29 39S 51 29W
Montenegro □, Yugoslavia 21 C8 42 40N 19 20 E
Montepuez, Mozam. 55 E4 13 8S 38 59 E
Montepuez →, Mozam. 55 E5 12 32S 40 27 E
Monterey, U.S.A. 84 J5 36 37N 121 55W
Monterey B., U.S.A. 84 J5 36 45N 122 0W
Montería, Colombia 92 B3 8 46N 75 53W
Monteros, Argentina 94 B2 27 11S 65 30W
Monterrey, Mexico 86 B4 25 40N 100 30W
Montes Claros, Brazil 93 G10 16 30S 43 50W
Montesano, U.S.A. 84 D3 46 59N 123 36W
Montesilvano, Italy 20 C6 42 29N 14 8 E
Montevideo, Uruguay 95 C4 34 50S 56 11W
Montevideo, U.S.A. 80 C7 44 57N 95 43W
Montezuma, U.S.A. 80 E8 41 35N 92 32W
Montgomery = Sahiwal, Pakistan 42 D5 30 45N 73 8 E
Montgomery, U.K. 11 E4 52 34N 3 8W
Montgomery, Ala., U.S.A. 77 J2 32 23N 86 19W
Montgomery, Pa., U.S.A. 78 E8 41 10N 76 53W
Montgomery, W. Va., U.S.A. 76 F5 38 11N 81 19W
Montgomery City, U.S.A. 80 F9 38 59N 91 30W
Monticello, Ark., U.S.A. 81 J9 33 38N 91 47W
Monticello, Fla., U.S.A. 77 K4 30 33N 83 52W
Monticello, Ind., U.S.A. 76 E2 40 45N 86 46W
Monticello, Iowa, U.S.A. 80 D9 42 15N 91 12W
Monticello, Ky., U.S.A. 77 G3 36 50N 84 51W
Monticello, Minn., U.S.A. 80 C8 45 18N 93 48W
Monticello, Miss., U.S.A. 81 K9 31 33N 90 7W
Monticello, N.Y., U.S.A. 79 E10 41 39N 74 42W
Monticello, Utah, U.S.A. 83 H9 37 52N 109 21W
Montijo, Portugal 19 C1 38 41N 8 54W
Montilla, Spain 19 D3 37 36N 4 40W
Montluçon, France 18 C5 46 22N 2 36 E
Montmagny, Canada 71 C5 46 58N 70 34W
Montmartre, Canada 73 C8 50 14N 103 27W
Montmorillon, France 18 C4 46 26N 0 50 E
Monto, Australia 62 C5 24 52S 151 6 E
Montoro, Spain 19 C3 38 1N 4 27W
Montour Falls, U.S.A. 78 D8 42 21N 76 51W

Montoursville

Montoursville, *U.S.A.* **78 E8** 41 15N 76 55W
Montpelier, *Idaho, U.S.A.* **82 E8** 42 19N 111 18W
Montpelier, *Vt., U.S.A.* **79 B12** 44 16N 72 35W
Montpellier, *France* **18 E5** 43 37N 3 52 E
Montréal, *Canada* **79 A11** 45 31N 73 34W
Montreal →, *Canada* **70 C3** 47 14N 84 39W
Montreal L., *Canada* **73 C7** 54 20N 105 45W
Montreal Lake, *Canada* **73 C7** 54 3N 105 46W
Montreux, *Switz.* **18 C7** 46 26N 6 55 E
Montrose, *U.K.* **12 E6** 56 44N 2 27W
Montrose, *Colo., U.S.A.* **83 G10** 38 29N 107 53W
Montrose, *Pa., U.S.A.* **79 E9** 41 50N 75 53W
Monts, Pte. des, *Canada* **71 C6** 49 20N 67 12W
Montserrat ■, *W. Indies* **89 C7** 16 40N 62 10W
Montuiri, *Spain* **22 B9** 39 34N 2 59 E
Monywa, *Burma* **41 H19** 22 7N 95 11 E
Monza, *Italy* **18 D8** 45 35N 9 16 E
Monze, *Zambia* **55 F2** 16 17S 27 29 E
Monze, C., *Pakistan* **42 G2** 24 47N 66 37 E
Monzón, *Spain* **19 B6** 41 52N 0 10 E
Mooers, *U.S.A.* **79 B11** 44 58N 73 35W
Mooi River, *S. Africa* **57 D4** 29 13S 29 50 E
Moonah →, *Australia* **62 C2** 22 3S 138 33 E
Moonda, L., *Australia* **62 D3** 25 52S 140 25 E
Moonie, *Australia* **63 D5** 27 46S 150 20 E
Moonie →, *Australia* **63 D4** 29 19S 148 43 E
Moonta, *Australia* **63 E2** 34 6S 137 32 E
Moora, *Australia* **61 F2** 30 37S 115 58 E
Moorcroft, *U.S.A.* **80 C2** 44 16N 104 57W
Moore →, *Australia* **61 F2** 31 22S 115 30 E
Moore, L., *Australia* **61 E2** 29 50S 117 35 E
Moore Park, *Australia* **62 C5** 24 43S 152 17 E
Moore Reefs, *Australia* **62 B4** 16 0S 149 5 E
Moorefield, *U.S.A.* **76 F6** 39 5N 78 59W
Moores Res., *U.S.A.* **79 B13** 44 45N 71 50W
Moorfoot Hills, *U.K.* **12 F5** 55 44N 3 8W
Moorhead, *U.S.A.* **80 B6** 46 53N 96 45W
Moorpark, *U.S.A.* **85 L8** 34 17N 118 53W
Moorreesburg, *S. Africa* **56 E2** 33 6S 18 38 E
Moose →, *Canada* **70 B3** 51 20N 80 25W
Moose →, *U.S.A.* **79 C9** 43 38N 75 24W
Moose Creek, *Canada* **79 A10** 45 15N 74 58W
Moose Factory, *Canada* **70 B3** 51 16N 80 32W
Moose Jaw, *Canada* **73 C7** 50 24N 105 30W
Moose Jaw →, *Canada* **73 C7** 50 34N 105 18W
Moose Lake, *Canada* **73 C8** 53 43N 100 20W
Moose Lake, *U.S.A.* **80 B8** 46 27N 92 46W
Moose Mountain Prov. Park, *Canada* **73 D8** 49 48N 102 25W
Moosehead L., *U.S.A.* **77 C11** 45 38N 69 40W
Mooselookmeguntic L., *U.S.A.* **77 C10** 44 55N 70 49W
Moosilauke, Mt., *U.S.A.* **79 B13** 44 3N 71 40W
Moosomin, *Canada* **73 C8** 50 9N 101 40W
Moosonee, *Canada* **70 B3** 51 17N 80 39W
Moosup, *U.S.A.* **79 E13** 41 43N 71 53W
Mopeia Velha, *Mozam.* **55 F4** 17 30S 35 40 E
Mopipi, *Botswana* **56 C3** 21 6S 24 55 E
Mopoi, *C.A.R.* **54 A2** 5 6N 26 54 E
Mopti, *Mali* **50 F5** 14 30N 4 0W
Moqor, *Afghan.* **42 C2** 32 50N 67 42 E
Moquegua, *Peru* **92 G4** 17 15S 70 46W
Mora, *Sweden* **9 F16** 61 2N 14 38 E
Mora, *Minn., U.S.A.* **80 C8** 45 53N 93 18W
Mora, *N. Mex., U.S.A.* **83 J11** 35 58N 105 20W
Mora →, *U.S.A.* **81 H2** 35 35N 104 25W
Moradabad, *India* **43 E8** 28 50N 78 50 E
Morafenobe, *Madag.* **57 B7** 17 50S 44 53 E
Moramanga, *Madag.* **57 B8** 18 56S 48 12 E
Moran, *Kans., U.S.A.* **81 G7** 37 55N 95 10W
Moran, *Wyo., U.S.A.* **82 E8** 43 53N 110 37W
Moranbah, *Australia* **62 C4** 22 1S 148 6 E
Morant Cays, *Jamaica* **88 C4** 17 22N 76 0W
Morant Pt., *Jamaica* **88 C4** 17 55N 76 12W
Morar, *India* **42 F8** 26 14N 78 14 E
Morar, L., *U.K.* **12 E3** 56 57N 5 40W
Moratuwa, *Sri Lanka* **40 R11** 6 45N 79 55 E
Morava →, *Serbia, Yug.* **21 B9** 44 36N 21 4 E
Morava →, *Slovak Rep.* **17 D9** 48 10N 16 59 E
Moravia, *U.S.A.* **79 D8** 42 43N 76 25W
Moravian Hts. = Českomoravská Vrchovina, *Czech Rep.* **16 D8** 49 30N 15 40 E
Morawa, *Australia* **61 E2** 29 13S 116 0 E
Morawhanna, *Guyana* **92 B7** 8 30N 59 40W
Moray □, *U.K.* **12 D5** 57 31N 3 18W
Moray Firth, *U.K.* **12 D5** 57 40N 3 52W
Morbi, *India* **42 H4** 22 50N 70 42 E
Morden, *Canada* **73 D9** 49 15N 98 10W
Mordovian Republic = Mordvinia □, *Russia* **24 D7** 54 20N 44 30 E
Mordvinia □, *Russia* **24 D7** 54 20N 44 30 E
Morea, *Greece* **6 H10** 37 45N 22 10 E
Moreau →, *U.S.A.* **80 C4** 45 18N 100 43W
Morecambe, *U.K.* **10 C5** 54 5N 2 52W
Morecambe B., *U.K.* **10 C5** 54 7N 3 0W
Moree, *Australia* **63 D4** 29 28S 149 54 E
Morehead, *U.S.A.* **76 F4** 38 11N 83 26W
Morehead City, *U.S.A.* **77 H7** 34 43N 76 43W
Morel →, *India* **42 F7** 26 13N 76 36 E
Morelia, *Mexico* **86 D4** 19 42N 101 7W
Morella, *Australia* **62 C3** 23 0S 143 52 E
Morella, *Spain* **19 B5** 40 35N 0 5W
Morelos, *Mexico* **86 B3** 26 42N 107 40W
Morelos □, *Mexico* **87 D5** 18 40N 99 10W
Morena, *India* **42 F8** 26 30N 78 4 E
Morena, Sierra, *Spain* **19 C3** 38 20N 4 0W
Moreno Valley, *U.S.A.* **85 M10** 33 56N 117 15W
Moresby I., *Canada* **72 C2** 52 30N 131 40W
Moreton I., *Australia* **63 D5** 27 10S 153 25 E
Morey, *Spain* **22 B10** 39 44N 3 20 E
Morgan, *U.S.A.* **82 F8** 41 2N 111 41W
Morgan City, *U.S.A.* **81 L9** 29 42N 91 12W
Morgan Hill, *U.S.A.* **84 H5** 37 8N 121 39W
Morganfield, *U.S.A.* **76 G2** 37 41N 87 55W
Morganton, *U.S.A.* **77 H5** 35 45N 81 41W
Morgantown, *U.S.A.* **76 F6** 39 38N 79 57W
Morgenzon, *S. Africa* **57 D4** 26 45S 29 36 E
Morghak, *Iran* **45 D8** 29 7N 57 54 E
Morhar →, *India* **43 G11** 25 29N 85 11 E
Moriarty, *U.S.A.* **83 J10** 34 59N 106 3W
Morice L., *Canada* **72 C3** 53 50N 127 40W
Morinville, *Canada* **72 C6** 53 49N 113 41W
Morioka, *Japan* **30 E10** 39 45N 141 8 E
Moris, *Mexico* **86 B3** 28 8N 108 32W
Morlaix, *France* **18 B2** 48 36N 3 52W
Mornington, *Australia* **63 F4** 38 15S 145 5 E
Mornington, I., *Chile* **96 F1** 49 50S 75 30W
Mornington I., *Australia* **62 B2** 16 30S 139 30 E
Moro, *Pakistan* **42 F2** 26 40N 68 0 E
Moro →, *Pakistan* **42 E2** 29 42N 67 22 E
Moro G., *Phil.* **37 C6** 6 30N 123 0 E
Morocco ■, *N. Afr.* **50 B4** 32 0N 5 50W
Morogoro, *Tanzania* **54 D4** 6 50S 37 40 E
Morogoro □, *Tanzania* **54 D4** 8 0S 37 0 E
Moroleón, *Mexico* **86 C4** 20 8N 101 32W
Morombe, *Madag.* **57 C7** 21 45S 43 22 E
Moron, *Argentina* **94 C4** 34 39S 58 37W
Morón, *Cuba* **88 B4** 22 8N 78 39W
Morón de la Frontera, *Spain* **19 D3** 37 6N 5 28W
Morona →, *Peru* **92 D3** 4 40S 77 10W
Morondava, *Madag.* **57 C7** 20 17S 44 17 E
Morongo Valley, *U.S.A.* **85 L10** 34 3N 116 37W
Moroni, *Comoros Is.* **49 H8** 11 40S 43 16 E
Moroni, *U.S.A.* **82 G8** 39 32N 111 35W
Morotai, *Indonesia* **37 D7** 2 10N 128 30 E
Moroto, *Uganda* **54 B3** 2 28N 34 42 E
Moroto Summit, *Kenya* **54 B3** 2 30N 34 43 E
Morpeth, *U.K.* **10 B6** 55 10N 1 41W
Morphou, *Cyprus* **23 D11** 35 12N 32 59 E
Morphou Bay, *Cyprus* **23 D11** 35 15N 32 50 E
Morrilton, *U.S.A.* **81 H8** 35 9N 92 44W
Morrinhos, *Brazil* **93 G9** 17 45S 49 10W
Morrinsville, *N.Z.* **59 G5** 37 40S 175 32 E
Morris, *Canada* **73 D9** 49 25N 97 22W
Morris, *Minn., U.S.A.* **80 C7** 45 35N 95 55W
Morris, *N.Y., U.S.A.* **79 D9** 42 33N 75 15W
Morris, *Pa., U.S.A.* **78 E7** 41 35N 77 17W
Morris, Mt., *Australia* **61 E5** 26 9S 131 4 E
Morrisburg, *Canada* **79 B9** 44 55N 75 7W
Morristown, *Ariz., U.S.A.* **83 K7** 33 51N 112 37W
Morristown, *N.J., U.S.A.* **79 F10** 40 48N 74 29W
Morristown, *N.Y., U.S.A.* **79 B9** 44 35N 75 39W
Morristown, *Tenn., U.S.A.* **77 G4** 36 13N 83 18W
Morrisville, *N.Y., U.S.A.* **79 D9** 42 53N 75 35W
Morrisville, *Pa., U.S.A.* **79 F10** 40 13N 74 47W
Morrisville, *Vt., U.S.A.* **79 B12** 44 34N 72 36W
Morro, Pta., *Chile* **94 B1** 27 6S 71 0W
Morro Bay, *U.S.A.* **84 K6** 35 22N 120 51W
Morro del Jable, *Canary Is.* **22 F5** 28 3N 14 23W
Morro Jable, Pta. de, *Canary Is.* **22 F5** 28 2N 14 20W
Morrosquillo, G. de, *Colombia* **88 E4** 9 35N 75 40W
Morrumbene, *Mozam.* **57 C6** 23 31S 35 16 E
Morshansk, *Russia* **24 D7** 53 28N 41 50 E
Morteros, *Argentina* **94 C3** 30 50S 62 0W
Mortlach, *Canada* **73 C7** 50 27N 106 4W
Mortlake, *Australia* **63 F3** 38 5S 142 50 E
Morton, *Tex., U.S.A.* **81 J3** 33 44N 102 46W
Morton, *Wash., U.S.A.* **84 D4** 46 34N 122 17W
Morundah, *Australia* **63 E4** 34 57S 146 19 E
Moruya, *Australia* **63 F5** 35 58S 150 3 E
Morvan, *France* **18 C6** 47 5N 4 3 E
Morven, *Australia* **63 D4** 26 22S 147 5 E
Morvern, *U.K.* **12 E3** 56 38N 5 44W
Morwell, *Australia* **63 F4** 38 10S 146 22 E
Morzhovets, Ostrov, *Russia* **24 A7** 66 44N 42 35 E
Moscos Is. = Maungmagan Is., *Burma* **38 F1** 14 0N 97 30 E
Moscow = Moskva, *Russia* **24 C6** 55 45N 37 35 E
Moscow, *Idaho, U.S.A.* **82 C5** 46 44N 117 0W
Moscow, *Pa., U.S.A.* **79 E9** 41 20N 75 31W
Mosel →, *Europe* **18 A7** 50 22N 7 36 E
Moselle = Mosel →, *Europe* **18 A7** 50 22N 7 36 E
Moses Lake, *U.S.A.* **82 C4** 47 8N 119 17W
Mosgiel, *N.Z.* **59 L3** 45 53S 170 21 E
Moshi, *Tanzania* **54 C4** 3 22S 37 18 E
Moshupa, *Botswana* **56 C4** 24 46S 25 29 E
Mosjøen, *Norway* **8 D15** 65 51N 13 12 E
Moskenesøya, *Norway* **8 C15** 67 58N 13 0 E
Moskenstraumen, *Norway* **8 C15** 67 47N 12 45 E
Moskva, *Russia* **24 C6** 55 45N 37 35 E
Mosomane, *Botswana* **56 C4** 24 2S 26 19 E
Moson-magyaróvár, *Hungary* **17 E9** 47 52N 17 18 E
Mosquera, *Colombia* **92 C3** 2 35N 78 24W
Mosquero, *U.S.A.* **81 H3** 35 47N 103 58W
Mosquitia, *Honduras* **88 C3** 15 20N 84 10W
Mosquito Coast = Mosquitia, *Honduras* **88 C3** 15 20N 84 10W
Mosquito Creek L., *U.S.A.* **78 E4** 41 18N 80 46W
Mosquito L., *Canada* **73 A8** 62 35N 103 20W
Mosquitos, G. de los, *Panama* **88 E3** 9 15N 81 10W
Moss, *Norway* **9 G14** 59 27N 10 40 E
Moss Vale, *Australia* **63 E5** 34 32S 150 25 E
Mossbank, *Canada* **73 D7** 49 56N 105 56W
Mossburn, *N.Z.* **59 L2** 45 41S 168 15 E
Mosselbaai, *S. Africa* **56 E3** 34 11S 22 8 E
Mossendjo, *Congo* **52 E2** 2 55S 12 42 E
Mossgiel, *Australia* **63 E3** 33 15S 144 5 E
Mossman, *Australia* **62 B4** 16 21S 145 15 E
Mossoró, *Brazil* **93 E11** 5 10S 37 15W
Mossuril, *Mozam.* **55 E5** 14 58S 40 42 E
Most, *Czech Rep.* **16 C7** 50 31N 13 38 E
Mosta, *Malta* **23 D1** 35 54N 14 24 E
Moşţafáābād, *Iran* **45 C7** 33 39N 54 53 E
Mostaganem, *Algeria* **50 A6** 35 54N 0 5 E
Mostar, *Bos.-H.* **21 C7** 43 22N 17 50 E
Mostardas, *Brazil* **95 C5** 31 2S 50 51W
Mostiska = Mostyska, *Ukraine* **17 D12** 49 48N 23 4 E
Mosty = Masty, *Belarus* **17 B13** 53 27N 24 38 E
Mostyska, *Ukraine* **17 D12** 49 48N 23 4 E
Mosul = Al Mawşil, *Iraq* **44 B4** 36 15N 43 5 E
Mosŭlpo, *S. Korea* **35 H14** 33 20N 126 17 E
Motagua →, *Guatemala* **88 C2** 15 44N 88 14W
Motala, *Sweden* **9 G16** 58 32N 15 1 E
Moth, *India* **43 G8** 25 43N 78 57 E
Motherwell, *U.K.* **12 F5** 55 47N 3 58W
Motihari, *India* **43 F11** 26 30N 84 55 E
Motozintla de Mendoza, *Mexico* **87 D6** 15 21N 92 14W
Motril, *Spain* **19 D4** 36 31N 3 37W
Mott, *U.S.A.* **80 B3** 46 23N 102 20W
Motueka, *N.Z.* **59 J4** 41 7S 173 1 E
Motueka →, *N.Z.* **59 J4** 41 5S 173 1 E
Motul, *Mexico* **87 C7** 21 0N 89 20W
Mouchalagane →, *Canada* **71 B6** 50 56N 68 41W
Moúdhros, *Greece* **21 E11** 39 50N 25 18 E
Mouila, *Gabon* **52 E2** 1 50S 11 0 E
Moulamein, *Australia* **63 F3** 35 3S 144 1 E
Moulianá, *Greece* **23 D7** 35 10N 25 59 E
Moulins, *France* **18 C5** 46 35N 3 19 E
Moulmein, *Burma* **41 L20** 16 30N 97 40 E
Moulouya, O. →, *Morocco* **50 B5** 35 5N 2 25W
Moultrie, *U.S.A.* **77 K4** 31 11N 83 47W
Moultrie, L., *U.S.A.* **77 J5** 33 20N 80 5W
Mound City, *Mo., U.S.A.* **80 E7** 40 7N 95 14W
Mound City, *S. Dak., U.S.A.* **80 C4** 45 44N 100 4W
Moundou, *Chad* **51 G9** 8 40N 16 10 E
Moundsville, *U.S.A.* **78 G4** 39 55N 80 44W
Moung, *Cambodia* **38 F4** 12 46N 103 27 E
Mount Airy, *U.S.A.* **77 G5** 36 31N 80 37W
Mount Albert, *Canada* **78 B5** 44 8N 79 19W
Mount Barker, *S. Austral., Australia* **63 F2** 35 5S 138 52 E
Mount Barker, *W. Austral., Australia* **61 F2** 34 38S 117 40 E
Mount Beauty, *Australia* **63 F4** 36 47S 147 10 E
Mount Brydges, *Canada* **78 D3** 42 54N 81 29W
Mount Burr, *Australia* **63 F3** 37 34S 140 26 E
Mount Carmel, *Ill., U.S.A.* **76 F2** 38 25N 87 46W
Mount Carmel, *Pa., U.S.A.* **79 F8** 40 47N 76 24W
Mount Charleston, *U.S.A.* **85 J11** 36 16N 115 37W
Mount Clemens, *U.S.A.* **78 D2** 42 35N 82 53W
Mount Coolon, *Australia* **62 C4** 21 25S 147 25 E
Mount Darwin, *Zimbabwe* **55 F3** 16 47S 31 38 E
Mount Desert I., *U.S.A.* **77 C11** 44 21N 68 20W
Mount Dora, *U.S.A.* **77 L5** 28 48N 81 38W
Mount Edziza Prov. Park, *Canada* **72 B2** 57 30N 130 45W
Mount Fletcher, *S. Africa* **57 E4** 30 40S 28 30 E
Mount Forest, *Canada* **78 C4** 43 59N 80 43W
Mount Gambier, *Australia* **63 F3** 37 50S 140 46 E
Mount Garnet, *Australia* **62 B4** 17 37S 145 6 E
Mount Holly, *U.S.A.* **79 G10** 39 59N 74 47W
Mount Holly Springs, *U.S.A.* **78 F7** 40 7N 77 12W
Mount Hope, *N.S.W., Australia* **63 E4** 32 51S 145 51 E
Mount Hope, *S. Austral., Australia* **63 E2** 34 7S 135 23 E
Mount Isa, *Australia* **62 C2** 20 42S 139 26 E
Mount Jewett, *U.S.A.* **78 E6** 41 44N 78 39W
Mount Kisco, *U.S.A.* **79 E11** 41 12N 73 44W
Mount Laguna, *U.S.A.* **85 N10** 32 52N 116 25W
Mount Larcom, *Australia* **62 C5** 23 48S 150 59 E
Mount Lofty Ra., *Australia* **63 E2** 34 35S 139 5 E
Mount Magnet, *Australia* **61 E2** 28 2S 117 47 E
Mount Maunganui, *N.Z.* **59 G6** 37 40S 176 14 E
Mount Molloy, *Australia* **62 B4** 16 42S 145 20 E
Mount Morgan, *Australia* **62 C5** 23 40S 150 25 E
Mount Morris, *U.S.A.* **78 D7** 42 44N 77 52W
Mount Pearl, *Canada* **71 C9** 47 31N 52 47W
Mount Penn, *U.S.A.* **79 F9** 40 20N 75 54W
Mount Perry, *Australia* **63 D5** 25 13S 151 42 E
Mount Pleasant, *Iowa, U.S.A.* **80 E9** 40 58N 91 33W
Mount Pleasant, *Mich., U.S.A.* **76 D3** 43 36N 84 46W
Mount Pleasant, *Pa., U.S.A.* **78 F5** 40 9N 79 33W
Mount Pleasant, *S.C., U.S.A.* **77 J6** 32 47N 79 52W
Mount Pleasant, *Tenn., U.S.A.* **77 H2** 35 32N 87 12W
Mount Pleasant, *Tex., U.S.A.* **81 J7** 33 9N 94 58W
Mount Pleasant, *Utah, U.S.A.* **82 G8** 39 33N 111 27W
Mount Pocono, *U.S.A.* **79 E9** 41 7N 75 22W
Mount Rainier Nat. Park, *U.S.A.* **84 D5** 46 55N 121 50W
Mount Revelstoke Nat. Park, *Canada* **72 C5** 51 5N 118 30W
Mount Robson Prov. Park, *Canada* **72 C5** 53 0N 119 0W
Mount Shasta, *U.S.A.* **82 F2** 41 19N 122 19W
Mount Signal, *U.S.A.* **85 N11** 32 39N 115 37W
Mount Sterling, *Ill., U.S.A.* **80 F9** 39 59N 90 45W
Mount Sterling, *Ky., U.S.A.* **76 F4** 38 4N 83 56W
Mount Surprise, *Australia* **62 B3** 18 10S 144 17 E
Mount Union, *U.S.A.* **78 F7** 40 23N 77 53W
Mount Upton, *U.S.A.* **79 D9** 42 26N 75 23W
Mount Vernon, *Ill., U.S.A.* **76 F1** 38 19N 88 55W
Mount Vernon, *Ind., U.S.A.* **80 F10** 38 17N 88 57W
Mount Vernon, *N.Y., U.S.A.* **79 F11** 40 55N 73 50W
Mount Vernon, *Ohio, U.S.A.* **78 F2** 40 23N 82 29W
Mount Vernon, *Wash., U.S.A.* **84 B4** 48 25N 122 20W
Mountain Ash, *U.K.* **11 F4** 51 40N 3 23W
Mountain Center, *U.S.A.* **85 M10** 33 42N 116 44W
Mountain City, *Nev., U.S.A.* **82 F6** 41 50N 115 58W
Mountain City, *Tenn., U.S.A.* **77 G5** 36 29N 81 48W
Mountain Dale, *U.S.A.* **79 E10** 41 41N 74 32W
Mountain Grove, *U.S.A.* **81 G8** 37 8N 92 16W
Mountain Home, *Ark., U.S.A.* **81 G8** 36 20N 92 23W
Mountain Home, *Idaho, U.S.A.* **82 E6** 43 8N 115 41W
Mountain Iron, *U.S.A.* **80 B8** 47 32N 92 37W
Mountain Pass, *U.S.A.* **85 K11** 35 29N 115 35W
Mountain View, *Ark., U.S.A.* **81 H8** 35 52N 92 7W
Mountain View, *Calif., U.S.A.* **84 H4** 37 23N 122 5W
Mountain View, *Hawaii, U.S.A.* **74 J17** 19 33N 155 7W
Mountainair, *U.S.A.* **83 J10** 34 31N 106 15W
Mountlake Terrace, *U.S.A.* **84 C4** 47 47N 122 19W
Mountmellick, *Ireland* **13 C4** 53 7N 7 20W
Mountrath, *Ireland* **13 D4** 53 0N 7 28W
Moura, *Australia* **62 C4** 24 35S 149 58 E
Moura, *Brazil* **92 D6** 1 32S 61 38W
Moura, *Portugal* **19 C2** 38 7N 7 30W
Mourdi, Dépression du, *Chad* **51 E10** 18 10N 23 0 E
Mourilyan, *Australia* **62 B4** 17 35S 146 3 E
Mourne →, *U.K.* **13 B4** 54 52N 7 26W
Mourne Mts., *U.K.* **13 B5** 54 10N 6 0W
Mourniaí, *Greece* **23 D6** 35 29N 24 1 E
Mournies = Mourniaí, *Greece* **23 D6** 35 29N 24 1 E
Mouscron, *Belgium* **15 D3** 50 45N 3 12 E
Moussoro, *Chad* **51 F9** 13 41N 16 35 E
Moutohara, *N.Z.* **59 H6** 38 27S 177 32 E
Moutong, *Indonesia* **37 D6** 0 28N 121 13 E
Movas, *Mexico* **86 B3** 28 10N 109 25W
Moville, *Ireland* **13 A4** 55 11N 7 3W
Mowandjum, *Australia* **60 C3** 17 22S 123 40 E
Moy →, *Ireland* **13 B2** 54 8N 9 8W
Moyale, *Kenya* **54 B4** 3 30N 39 0
Moyen Atlas, *Morocco* **50 B4** 33 0N 5 0W
Moyne, L. le, *Canada* **71 A6** 56 45N 68 47W
Moyo, *Indonesia* **36 F5** 8 10S 117 40
Moyobamba, *Peru* **92 E3** 6 0S 77 0W
Moyyero →, *Russia* **27 C11** 68 44N 103 42
Moyynty, *Kazakstan* **26 E8** 47 10N 73 18
Mozambique = Moçambique, *Mozam.* **55 F5** 15 3S 40 42
Mozambique ■, *Africa* **55 F4** 19 0S 35 0
Mozambique Chan., *Africa* **57 B7** 17 30S 42 30
Mozdok, *Russia* **25 F7** 43 45N 44 48
Mozdūrān, *Iran* **45 B9** 36 9N 60 35
Mozhnābād, *Iran* **45 C9** 34 7N 60 6
Mozyr = Mazyr, *Belarus* **17 B15** 51 59N 29 15
Mpanda, *Tanzania* **54 D3** 6 23S 31 1
Mpika, *Zambia* **55 E3** 11 51S 31 25
Mpulungu, *Zambia* **55 D3** 8 51S 31 5
Mpumalanga, *S. Africa* **57 D5** 29 50S 30 33
Mpumalanga □, *S. Africa* **57 B5** 26 0S 30 0
Mpwapwa, *Tanzania* **54 D4** 6 23S 36 30
Msambansovu, *Zimbabwe* **55 F3** 15 50S 30 3
M'sila →, *Algeria* **50 A6** 35 30N 4 29
Msoro, *Zambia* **55 E3** 13 35S 31 50
Mstislavl = Mstsislaw, *Belarus* **17 A16** 54 0N 31 50
Mstsislaw, *Belarus* **17 A16** 54 0N 31 50
Mtama, *Tanzania* **55 E4** 10 17S 39 21
Mtilikwe →, *Zimbabwe* **55 G3** 21 9S 31 30
Mtubatuba, *S. Africa* **57 D5** 28 30S 32 8
Mtwara-Mikindani, *Tanzania* **55 E5** 10 20S 40 20
Mu Gia, Deo, *Vietnam* **38 D5** 17 40N 105 47
Mu Us Shamo, *China* **34 E5** 39 0N 109 0
Muang Chiang Rai = Chiang Rai, *Thailand* **38 C2** 19 52N 99 50
Muang Khong, *Laos* **36 B3** 14 5N 105 52
Muang Khong, *Laos* **38 E5** 14 7N 105 51
Muang Lamphun, *Thailand* **38 C2** 18 40N 99 2
Muar, *Malaysia* **39 L4** 2 3N 102 34
Muarabungo, *Indonesia* **36 E2** 1 28S 102 52
Muaraenim, *Indonesia* **36 E2** 3 40S 103 50
Muarajuloi, *Indonesia* **36 E4** 0 12S 114 3
Muarakaman, *Indonesia* **36 E5** 0 2S 116 45
Muaratebo, *Indonesia* **36 E2** 1 30S 102 26
Muaratembesi, *Indonesia* **36 E2** 1 42S 103 8
Muaratewe, *Indonesia* **36 E4** 0 58S 114 52
Mubarakpur, *India* **43 F10** 26 6N 83 18
Mubarraz = Al Mubarraz, *Si. Arabia* **45 E6** 25 30N 49 40
Mubende, *Uganda* **54 B3** 0 33N 31 22
Mubi, *Nigeria* **51 F8** 10 18N 13 16
Mubur, Pulau, *Indonesia* **39 L6** 3 20N 106 12
Mucajaí →, *Brazil* **92 C6** 2 25N 60 52W
Muchachos, Roque de los, *Canary Is.* **22 F2** 28 44N 17 52W
Muchinga Mts., *Zambia* **55 E3** 11 30S 31 30
Muck, *U.K.* **12 E2** 56 50N 6 15W
Muckadilla, *Australia* **63 D4** 26 35S 148 23
Mucuri, *Brazil* **93 G11** 18 0S 39 36W
Mucusso, *Angola* **56 B3** 18 1S 21 25
Muda, *Canary Is.* **22 F6** 28 34N 13 57W
Mudanjiang, *China* **35 B15** 44 38N 129 30
Mudanya, *Turkey* **21 D13** 40 25N 28 50
Muddy Cr. →, *U.S.A.* **83 H8** 38 24N 110 42W
Mudgee, *Australia* **63 E4** 32 32S 149 31
Mudjatik →, *Canada* **73 B7** 56 1N 107 36W
Muecate, *Mozam.* **55 E4** 14 55S 39 40
Mueda, *Mozam.* **55 E4** 11 36S 39 28
Mueller Ra., *Australia* **60 C4** 18 18S 126 46
Muende, *Mozam.* **55 E3** 14 28S 33 0
Muerto, Mar, *Mexico* **87 D6** 16 10N 94 10W
Mufulira, *Zambia* **55 E2** 12 32S 28 15
Mufumbiro Range, *Africa* **54 C2** 1 25S 29 30
Mughal Sarai, *India* **43 G10** 25 18N 83 7
Mughayrā', *Si. Arabia* **44 D3** 29 17N 37 41
Mugi, *Japan* **31 H7** 33 40N 134 25
Mugila, Mts., *Dem. Rep. of the Congo* **54 D2** 7 0S 28 50
Muğla, *Turkey* **21 F13** 37 15N 28 22
Mugu, *Nepal* **43 E10** 29 45N 82 30
Muhammad, Râs, *Egypt* **44 E2** 27 44N 34 16
Muhammad Qol, *Sudan* **51 D13** 20 53N 37 9
Muhammadabad, *India* **43 F10** 26 4N 83 25
Muhesi →, *Tanzania* **54 D4** 7 0S 35 20
Mühlhausen, *Germany* **16 C6** 51 12N 10 27
Mühlig Hofmann fjell, *Antarctica* **5 D3** 72 30S 5 0
Muhos, *Finland* **8 D22** 64 47N 25 59
Muhu, *Estonia* **9 G20** 58 36N 23 11
Muhutwe, *Tanzania* **54 C3** 1 35S 31 45
Muine Bheag, *Ireland* **13 D5** 52 42N 6 58W
Muir, L., *Australia* **61 F2** 34 30S 116 40
Mukacheve, *Ukraine* **17 D12** 48 27N 22 45
Mukachevo = Mukacheve, *Ukraine* **17 D12** 48 27N 22 45
Mukah, *Malaysia* **36 D4** 2 55N 112 5
Mukandwara, *India* **42 G6** 24 49N 75 59
Mukdahan, *Thailand* **38 D5** 16 32N 104 43
Mukden = Shenyang, *China* **35 D12** 41 48N 123 27
Mukerian, *India* **42 D6** 31 57N 75 37
Mukhtuya = Lensk, *Russia* **27 C12** 60 48N 114 55
Mukinbudin, *Australia* **61 F2** 30 55S 118 5
Mukishi, *Dem. Rep. of the Congo* **55 D1** 8 30S 24 44
Mukomuko, *Indonesia* **36 E2** 2 30S 101 10
Mukomwenze, *Dem. Rep. of the Congo* **54 D2** 6 49S 27 15
Muktsar, *India* **42 D6** 30 30N 74 30
Mukur = Moqor, *Afghan.* **42 C2** 32 50N 67 42
Mukutawa →, *Canada* **73 C9** 53 10N 97 24
Mukwela, *Zambia* **55 F2** 17 0S 26 40
Mula, *Spain* **19 C5** 38 3N 1 33
Mula →, *Pakistan* **42 F2** 27 57N 67 36
Mulange, *Dem. Rep. of the Congo* **54 C2** 3 40S 27 10
Mulanje, *Malawi* **55 F4** 16 2S 35 33
Mulchén, *Chile* **94 D1** 37 45S 72 20
Mulde →, *Germany* **16 C7** 51 53N 12 15
Mule Creek Junction, *U.S.A.* **80 D2** 43 19N 104 8
Muleba, *Tanzania* **54 C3** 1 50S 31 37
Mulejé, *Mexico* **86 B2** 26 53N 112 1
Muleshoe, *U.S.A.* **81 H3** 34 13N 102 43
Mulgrave, *Canada* **71 C7** 45 38N 61 31
Mulhacén, *Spain* **19 D4** 37 4N 3 20
Mülheim, *Germany* **33 C6** 51 25N 6 54

Nanching

Mulhouse, France 18 C7 47 40N 7 20 E
Muling, China 35 B16 44 35N 130 10 E
Mull, U.K. 12 E3 56 25N 5 56W
Mull, Sound of, U.K. 12 E3 56 30N 5 50W
Mullaittivu, Sri Lanka 40 Q12 9 15N 80 49 E
Mullen, U.S.A. 80 D4 42 3N 101 1W
Mullens, U.S.A. 76 G5 37 35N 81 23W
Muller, Pegunungan, Indonesia 36 D4 0 30N 113 30 E
Mullet Pen., Ireland 13 B1 54 13N 10 2W
Mullewa, Australia 61 E2 28 29S 115 30 E
Mulligan →, Australia 62 D2 25 0S 139 0 E
Mullingar, Ireland 13 C4 53 31N 7 21W
Mullins, U.S.A. 77 H6 34 12N 79 15W
Mullumbimby, Australia 63 D5 28 30S 153 30 E
Mulobezi, Zambia 55 F2 16 45S 25 7 E
Mulroy B., Ireland 13 A4 55 15N 7 46W
Multan, Pakistan 42 D4 30 15N 71 36 E
Mulumbe, Mts., Dem. Rep. of the Congo 55 D2 8 40S 27 30 E
Mulungushi Dam, Zambia 55 E2 14 48S 28 48 E
Mulvane, U.S.A. 81 G6 37 29N 97 15W
Mumbai, India 40 K8 18 55N 72 50 E
Mumbwa, Zambia 55 F2 15 0S 27 0 E
Mun →, Thailand 38 E5 15 19N 105 30 E
Muna, Indonesia 37 F6 5 0S 122 30 E
Munabao, India 42 G4 25 45N 70 17 E
Munamagi, Estonia 9 H22 57 43N 27 4 E
München, Germany 16 D6 48 8N 11 34 E
München-Gladbach = Mönchengladbach, Germany 16 C4 51 11N 6 27 E
Muncho Lake, Canada 72 B3 59 0N 125 50W
Munch'ŏn, N. Korea 35 E14 39 14N 127 19 E
Muncie, U.S.A. 76 E3 40 12N 85 23W
Muncoonie, L., Australia 62 D2 25 12S 138 40 E
Mundabbera, Australia 63 D5 25 36S 151 18 E
Munday, U.S.A. 81 J5 33 27N 99 38W
Münden, Germany 16 C5 51 25N 9 38 E
Mundiwindi, Australia 60 D3 23 47S 120 9 E
Mundo Novo, Brazil 93 F10 11 50S 40 29W
Mundra, India 42 H3 22 54N 69 48 E
Mundrabilla, Australia 61 F4 31 52S 127 51 E
Mungallala, Australia 63 D4 26 28S 147 34 E
Mungallala Cr. →, Australia 63 D4 28 53S 147 5 E
Mungana, Australia 62 B3 17 8S 144 27 E
Mungaoli, India 42 G8 24 24N 78 7 E
Mungari, Mozam. 55 F3 17 12S 33 30 E
Mungbere, Dem. Rep. of the Congo 54 B2 2 36N 28 28 E
Mungeli, India 43 H9 22 4N 81 41 E
Munger, India 43 G12 25 23N 86 30 E
Munich = München, Germany 16 D6 48 8N 11 34 E
Munising, U.S.A. 76 B2 46 25N 86 40W
Munku-Sardyk, Russia 27 D11 51 45N 100 20 E
Muñoz Gamero, Pen., Chile 96 G2 52 30S 73 5W
Munroe L., Canada 73 B9 59 13N 98 35W
Munsan, S. Korea 35 F14 37 51N 126 48 E
Münster, Germany 16 C4 51 58N 7 37 E
Munster □, Ireland 13 D3 52 18N 8 44W
Muntadgin, Australia 61 F2 31 45S 118 33 E
Muntok, Indonesia 36 E3 2 5S 105 10 E
Munyama, Zambia 55 F2 16 5S 28 31 E
Muong Et, Laos 38 B5 20 49N 104 1 E
Muong Hiem, Laos 38 B4 20 5N 103 22 E
Muong Kau, Laos 38 E5 15 6N 105 47 E
Muong Khao, Laos 38 C4 19 38N 103 32 E
Muong Liep, Laos 38 C3 18 29N 101 40 E
Muong May, Laos 38 E6 14 49N 106 56 E
Muong Nong, Laos 38 D6 16 22N 106 30 E
Muong Oua, Laos 38 C3 18 18N 101 20 E
Muong Phalane, Laos 38 D5 16 39N 105 34 E
Muong Phieng, Laos 38 C3 19 6N 101 32 E
Muong Phine, Laos 38 D6 16 32N 106 2 E
Muong Saiapoun, Laos 38 C3 18 24N 101 31 E
Muong Sen, Vietnam 38 C5 19 24N 104 8 E
Muong Soui, Laos 38 C4 19 33N 102 52 E
Muong Xia, Vietnam 38 B5 20 19N 104 50 E
Muonio, Finland 8 C20 67 57N 23 40 E
Muonionjoki →, Finland 8 C20 67 11N 23 34 E
Muping, China 35 F11 37 22N 121 36 E
Muqdisho, Somali Rep. 46 G4 2 2N 45 25 E
Mur →, Austria 17 E9 46 18N 16 52 E
Murakami, Japan 30 E9 38 14N 139 29 E
Murallón, Cerro, Chile 96 F2 49 48S 73 30W
Muranda, Rwanda 54 C2 1 52S 29 20 E
Murang'a, Kenya 54 C4 0 45S 37 9 E
Murashi, Russia 24 C8 59 30N 49 0 E
Murat →, Turkey 25 G7 38 46N 40 0 E
Muratlı, Turkey 21 D12 41 10N 27 29 E
Murayama, Japan 30 E10 38 30N 140 25 E
Murban, U.A.E. 45 F7 23 50N 53 45 E
Murchison →, Australia 61 E1 27 45S 114 0 E
Murchison, Mt., Antarctica 5 D11 73 0S 168 0 E
Murchison Falls, Uganda 54 B3 2 15N 31 30 E
Murchison Ra., Australia 62 C1 20 0S 134 10 E
Murchison Rapids, Malawi 55 F3 15 55S 34 35 E
Murcia, Spain 19 D5 38 5N 1 10W
Murcia □, Spain 19 D5 37 50N 1 30W
Murdo, U.S.A. 80 D4 43 53N 100 43W
Murdoch Pt., Australia 62 A3 14 37S 144 55 E
Mureş →, Romania 17 E11 46 15N 20 13 E
Mureşul = Mureş →, Romania 17 E11 46 15N 20 13 E
Murfreesboro, N.C., U.S.A. 77 G7 36 27N 77 6W
Murfreesboro, Tenn., U.S.A. 77 H2 35 51N 86 24W
Murgab = Murghob, Tajikistan 26 F8 38 10N 74 2 E
Murgab →, Turkmenistan 45 B9 38 18N 61 12 E
Murgenella, Australia 60 B5 11 34S 132 56 E
Murgha Kibzai, Pakistan 42 D3 30 44N 69 25 E
Murghob, Tajikistan 26 F8 38 10N 74 2 E
Murgon, Australia 63 D5 26 15S 151 54 E
Muri, India 43 H11 23 22N 85 52 E
Muria, Indonesia 37 G14 6 36S 110 53 E
Muriaé, Brazil 95 A7 21 8S 42 23W
Muriel Mine, Zimbabwe 55 F3 17 14S 30 40 E
Müritz, Germany 16 B7 53 25N 12 42 E
Murka, Kenya 54 C4 3 27S 38 0 E
Murliganj, India 43 G12 25 54N 86 59 E
Murmansk, Russia 24 A5 68 57N 33 10 E
Muro, Spain 22 B10 39 44N 3 3 E
Murom, Russia 24 C7 55 35N 42 3 E
Muroran, Japan 30 C10 42 25N 141 0 E
Muroto, Japan 31 H7 33 18N 134 9 E
Muroto-Misaki, Japan 31 H7 33 15N 134 10 E
Murphy, U.S.A. 82 E5 43 13N 116 33W
Murphys, U.S.A. 84 G6 38 8N 120 28W
Murray, Ky., U.S.A. 77 G1 36 37N 88 19W
Murray, Utah, U.S.A. 82 F8 40 40N 111 53W
Murray →, Australia 63 F2 35 20S 139 22 E
Murray, L., U.S.A. 77 H5 34 3N 81 13W
Murray Bridge, Australia 63 F2 35 6S 139 14 E
Murray Harbour, Canada 71 C7 46 0N 62 28W
Murraysburg, S. Africa 56 E3 31 58S 23 47 E
Murree, Pakistan 42 C5 33 56N 73 28 E
Murrieta, U.S.A. 85 M9 33 33N 117 13W
Murrumbidgee →, Australia 63 E3 34 43S 143 12 E
Murrumburrah, Australia 63 E4 34 32S 148 22 E
Murrurundi, Australia 63 E5 31 42S 150 51 E
Murshidabad, India 43 G13 24 11N 88 19 E
Murtle L., Canada 72 C5 52 8N 119 38W
Murtoa, Australia 63 F3 36 35S 142 28 E
Murungu, Tanzania 54 C3 4 12S 31 10 E
Mururoa, Pac. Oc. 65 K14 21 52S 138 55W
Murwara, India 43 H9 23 46N 80 28 E
Murwillumbah, Australia 63 D5 28 18S 153 27 E
Mürzzuschlag, Austria 16 E8 47 36N 15 41 E
Muş, Turkey 25 G7 38 45N 41 30 E
Mûsa, Gebel, Egypt 44 D2 28 33N 33 59 E
Musa Khel, Pakistan 42 D3 30 59N 69 52 E
Mūsá Qal'eh, Afghan. 40 C4 32 20N 64 50 E
Musaffargarh, Pakistan 40 D7 30 10N 71 10 E
Musafirkhana, India 43 F9 26 22N 81 48 E
Musala, Bulgaria 21 C10 42 13N 23 37 E
Musala, Indonesia 36 D1 1 41N 98 28 E
Musan, N. Korea 35 C15 42 12N 129 12 E
Musangu, Dem. Rep. of the Congo 55 E1 10 28S 23 55 E
Musasa, Tanzania 54 C3 3 25S 31 30 E
Musay'īd, Qatar 45 E6 25 0N 51 33 E
Muscat = Masqat, Oman 46 C6 23 37N 58 36 E
Muscat & Oman = Oman ■, Asia 46 C6 23 0N 58 0 E
Muscatine, U.S.A. 80 E9 41 25N 91 3W
Musgrave Harbour, Canada 71 C9 49 27N 53 58W
Musgrave Ranges, Australia 61 E5 26 0S 132 0 E
Mushie, Dem. Rep. of the Congo 52 E3 2 56S 16 55 E
Musi →, Indonesia 36 E2 2 20S 104 56 E
Muskeg →, Canada 72 A4 60 20N 123 20W
Muskegon, U.S.A. 76 D2 43 14N 86 16W
Muskegon →, U.S.A. 76 D2 43 14N 86 21W
Muskegon Heights, U.S.A. 76 D2 43 12N 86 16W
Muskogee, U.S.A. 81 H7 35 45N 95 22W
Muskoka, L., Canada 78 B5 45 0N 79 25W
Muskwa →, Canada 72 B4 58 47N 122 48W
Muslīmiyah, Syria 44 B3 36 19N 37 12 E
Musofu, Zambia 55 E2 13 30S 29 0 E
Musoma, Tanzania 54 C3 1 30S 33 48 E
Musquaro, L., Canada 71 B7 50 38N 61 5W
Musquodoboit Harbour, Canada 71 D7 44 50N 63 9W
Musselburgh, U.K. 12 F5 55 57N 3 2W
Musselshell →, U.S.A. 82 C10 47 21N 107 57W
Mussoorie, India 42 D8 30 27N 78 6 E
Mussuco, Angola 56 B2 17 2S 19 3 E
Mustafakemalpaşa, Turkey 21 D13 40 2N 28 24 E
Mustang, Nepal 43 E10 29 10N 83 55 E
Musters, L., Argentina 96 F3 45 20S 69 25W
Musudan, N. Korea 35 D15 40 50N 129 43 E
Muswellbrook, Australia 63 E5 32 16S 150 56 E
Mût, Egypt 51 C11 25 28N 28 58 E
Mut, Turkey 44 B2 36 40N 33 28 E
Mutanda, Mozam. 57 C5 21 0S 33 34 E
Mutanda, Zambia 55 E2 12 24S 26 13 E
Mutare, Zimbabwe 55 F3 18 58S 32 38 E
Muting, Indonesia 37 F10 7 23S 140 20 E
Mutoray, Russia 27 C11 60 56N 101 0 E
Mutshatsha, Dem. Rep. of the Congo 55 E1 10 35S 24 20 E
Mutsu, Japan 30 D10 41 5N 140 55 E
Mutsu-Wan, Japan 30 D10 41 5N 140 55 E
Muttaburra, Australia 62 C3 22 38S 144 29 E
Mutton I., Ireland 13 D2 52 49N 9 32W
Mutuáli, Mozam. 55 E4 14 55S 37 0 E
Muweilih, Egypt 47 E3 30 42N 34 19 E
Muy Muy, Nic. 88 D2 12 39N 85 36W
Muyinga, Burundi 54 C3 3 14S 30 33 E
Muynak, Uzbekistan 26 E6 43 44N 59 10 E
Muzaffarabad, Pakistan 43 B5 34 25N 73 30 E
Muzaffargarh, Pakistan 42 D4 30 5N 71 14 E
Muzaffarnagar, India 42 E7 29 26N 77 40 E
Muzaffarpur, India 43 F11 26 7N 85 23 E
Muzafirpur, Pakistan 42 D3 30 58N 69 9 E
Muzhi, Russia 24 A11 65 25N 64 40 E
Mvuma, Zimbabwe 55 F3 19 16S 30 30 E
Mvurwi, Zimbabwe 55 F3 17 0S 30 57 E
Mwadui, Tanzania 54 C3 3 26S 33 32 E
Mwambo, Tanzania 55 E5 10 30S 40 22 E
Mwandi, Zambia 55 F1 17 30S 24 51 E
Mwanza, Dem. Rep. of the Congo 54 D2 7 55S 26 43 E
Mwanza, Tanzania 54 C3 2 30S 32 58 E
Mwanza, Zambia 55 F1 16 58S 24 28 E
Mwanza □, Tanzania 54 C3 2 0S 33 0 E
Mwaya, Tanzania 55 D3 9 32S 33 55 E
Mweelrea, Ireland 13 C2 53 39N 9 49W
Mweka, Dem. Rep. of the Congo 52 E4 4 50S 21 34 E
Mwene-Ditu, Dem. Rep. of the Congo 52 F4 6 35S 22 27 E
Mwenezi, Zimbabwe 55 G3 21 15S 30 48 E
Mwenezi →, Mozam. 55 G3 22 40S 31 50 E
Mwenga, Dem. Rep. of the Congo 54 C2 3 1S 28 28 E
Mweru, L., Zambia 55 D2 9 0S 28 40 E
Mweza Range, Zimbabwe 55 G3 21 0S 30 0 E
Mwilambwe, Dem. Rep. of the Congo 54 D2 8 7S 25 5 E
Mwimbi, Tanzania 55 D3 8 38S 31 39 E
Mwinilunga, Zambia 55 E1 11 43S 24 25 E
My Tho, Vietnam 39 G6 10 29N 106 23 E
Myajlar, India 42 F4 26 15N 70 20 E
Myanaung, Burma 41 K19 18 18N 95 22 E
Myanmar = Burma ■, Asia 41 J20 21 0N 96 30 E
Myaungmya, Burma 41 L19 16 30N 94 40 E
Mycenæ, Greece 21 F10 37 39N 22 52 E
Myeik Kyunzu, Burma 39 G1 11 30N 97 30 E
Myers Chuck, U.S.A. 72 B2 55 44N 132 11W
Myerstown, U.S.A. 79 F8 40 22N 76 19W
Myingyan, Burma 41 J19 21 30N 95 20 E
Myitkyina, Burma 41 G20 25 24N 97 26 E
Mykines, Færoe Is. 8 E9 62 7N 7 35W
Mykolayiv, Ukraine 25 E5 46 58N 32 0 E
Mymensingh, Bangla. 41 G17 24 45N 90 24 E
Mynydd Du, U.K. 11 F4 51 52N 3 50W
Mýrdalsjökull, Iceland 8 E4 63 40N 19 6W
Myrtle Beach, U.S.A. 77 J6 33 42N 78 53W
Myrtle Creek, U.S.A. 82 E2 43 1N 123 17W
Myrtle Point, U.S.A. 82 E1 43 4N 124 8W
Myrtou, Cyprus 23 D12 35 18N 33 4 E
Mysia, Turkey 21 E12 39 50N 27 0 E
Mysore = Karnataka □, India 40 N10 13 15N 77 0 E
Mysore, India 40 N10 12 17N 76 41 E
Mystic, U.S.A. 79 E13 41 21N 71 58W
Myszków, Poland 17 C10 50 45N 19 22 E
Mytishchi, Russia 24 C6 55 50N 37 50 E
Mývatn, Iceland 8 D5 65 36N 17 0W
Mzimba, Malawi 55 E3 11 55S 33 39 E
Mzimkulu →, S. Africa 57 E5 30 44S 30 28 E
Mzimvubu →, S. Africa 57 E4 31 38S 29 33 E
Mzuzu, Malawi 55 E3 11 30S 33 55 E

N

Na Hearadh = Harris, U.K. 12 D2 57 50N 6 55W
Na Noi, Thailand 38 C3 18 19N 100 43 E
Na Phao, Laos 38 D5 17 35N 105 44 E
Na San, Vietnam 38 B5 21 12N 104 2 E
Naab →, Germany 16 D6 49 1N 12 2 E
Naantali, Finland 9 F19 60 29N 22 2 E
Naas, Ireland 13 C5 53 12N 6 40W
Nababiep, S. Africa 56 D2 29 36S 17 46 E
Nabadwip = Navadwip, India 43 H13 23 34N 88 20 E
Nabari, Japan 31 G8 34 37N 136 5 E
Nabawa, Australia 61 E1 28 30S 114 48 E
Nabberu, L., Australia 61 E3 25 50S 120 30 E
Naberezhnyye Chelny, Russia 24 C9 55 42N 52 19 E
Nabeul, Tunisia 51 A8 36 30N 10 44 E
Nabha, India 42 D7 30 26N 76 14 E
Nabīd, Iran 45 D8 29 40N 57 38 E
Nabire, Indonesia 37 E9 3 15S 135 26 E
Nabisar, Pakistan 42 G3 25 8N 69 40 E
Nabisipi →, Canada 71 B7 50 14N 62 13W
Nabiswera, Uganda 54 B3 1 27N 32 15 E
Nablus = Nābulus, West Bank 47 C4 32 14N 35 15 E
Naboomspruit, S. Africa 57 C4 24 32S 28 40 E
Nābulus, West Bank 47 C4 32 14N 35 15 E
Nacala, Mozam. 55 E5 14 31S 40 34 E
Nacala-Velha, Mozam. 55 E5 14 32S 40 34 E
Nacaome, Honduras 88 D2 13 31N 87 30W
Nacaroa, Mozam. 55 E4 14 22S 39 56 E
Naches, U.S.A. 82 C3 46 44N 120 42W
Naches →, U.S.A. 84 D6 46 38N 120 31W
Nachicapau, L., Canada 71 A6 56 40N 68 5W
Nachingwea, Tanzania 55 E4 10 23S 38 49 E
Nachna, India 42 F4 27 34N 71 41 E
Nacimiento L., U.S.A. 84 K6 35 46N 120 53W
Naco, Mexico 86 A3 31 20N 109 56W
Nacogdoches, U.S.A. 81 K7 31 36N 94 39W
Nácori Chico, Mexico 86 B3 29 39N 109 1W
Nacozari, Mexico 86 A3 30 24N 109 39W
Nadiad, India 42 H5 22 41N 72 56 E
Nador, Morocco 50 B5 35 14N 2 58W
Nadur, Malta 23 C1 36 2N 14 17 E
Nadūshan, Iran 45 C7 32 2N 53 35 E
Nadvirna, Ukraine 17 D13 48 37N 24 30 E
Nadvoitsy, Russia 24 B5 63 52N 34 14 E
Nadvornaya = Nadvirna, Ukraine 17 D13 48 37N 24 30 E
Nadym, Russia 26 C8 65 35N 72 42 E
Nadym →, Russia 26 C8 66 12N 72 0 E
Nærbø, Norway 9 G11 58 40N 5 39 E
Næstved, Denmark 9 J14 55 13N 11 44 E
Naft-e Safīd, Iran 45 D6 31 40N 49 17 E
Naftshahr, Iran 44 C5 34 0N 45 30 E
Nafud Desert = An Nafūd, Si. Arabia 44 D4 28 15N 41 0 E
Naga, Phil. 37 B6 13 38N 123 15 E
Nagahama, Japan 31 G8 35 23N 136 16 E
Nagai, Japan 30 E10 38 6N 140 2 E
Nagaland □, India 41 G19 26 0N 94 30 E
Nagano, Japan 31 F9 36 40N 138 10 E
Nagano □, Japan 31 F9 36 15N 138 0 E
Nagaoka, Japan 31 F9 37 27N 138 51 E
Nagappattinam, India 40 P11 10 46N 79 51 E
Nagar →, Bangla. 43 G13 24 27N 89 12 E
Nagar Parkar, Pakistan 42 G4 24 28N 70 46 E
Nagasaki, Japan 31 H4 32 47N 129 50 E
Nagasaki □, Japan 31 H4 32 50N 129 40 E
Nagato, Japan 31 G5 34 19N 131 5 E
Nagaur, India 42 F5 27 15N 73 45 E
Nagda, India 42 H6 23 27N 75 25 E
Nagercoil, India 40 Q10 8 12N 77 26 E
Nagina, India 43 E8 29 30N 78 30 E
Nagīneh, Iran 45 C8 34 20N 57 15 E
Nagir, Pakistan 43 A6 36 12N 74 42 E
Nagod, India 43 G9 24 34N 80 36 E
Nagoorin, Australia 62 C5 24 17S 151 15 E
Nagorno-Karabakh, Azerbaijan 25 F8 39 55N 46 45 E
Nagornyy, Russia 27 D13 55 58N 124 57 E
Nagoya, Japan 31 G8 35 10N 136 50 E
Nagpur, India 40 J11 21 8N 79 10 E
Nagua, Dom. Rep. 89 C6 19 23N 69 50W
Nagykanizsa, Hungary 17 E9 46 28N 17 0 E
Nagykőrös, Hungary 17 E10 47 5N 19 48 E
Naha, Japan 31 L3 26 13N 127 42 E
Nahan, India 42 D7 30 33N 77 18 E
Nahanni Butte, Canada 72 A4 61 2N 123 31W
Nahanni Nat. Park, Canada 72 A4 61 15N 125 0W
Nahargarh, Mad. P., India 42 G6 24 10N 75 14 E
Nahargarh, Raj., India 42 G7 24 55N 76 50 E
Nahariyya, Israel 44 C2 33 1N 35 5 E
Nahāvand, Iran 45 C6 34 10N 48 22 E
Naicá, Mexico 86 B3 27 53N 105 31W
Naicam, Canada 73 C8 52 30N 104 30W
Naikoon Prov. Park, Canada 72 C2 53 55N 131 55W
Naimisharanya, India 43 F9 27 21N 80 30 E
Nain, Canada 71 A7 56 34N 61 40W
Nā'īn, Iran 45 C7 32 54N 53 0 E
Naini Tal, India 43 E8 29 30N 79 30 E
Nainpur, India 40 H12 22 30N 80 10 E
Nainwa, India 42 G6 25 46N 75 51 E
Nairn, U.K. 12 D5 57 35N 3 53W
Nairobi, Kenya 54 C4 1 17S 36 48 E
Naissaar, Estonia 9 G21 59 34N 24 29 E
Naivasha, Kenya 54 C4 0 40S 36 30 E
Naivasha, L., Kenya 54 C4 0 48S 36 20 E
Najafābād, Iran 45 C6 32 40N 51 15 E
Najd, Si. Arabia 46 B3 26 30N 42 0 E
Najibabad, India 42 E8 29 40N 78 20 E
Najin, N. Korea 35 C16 42 12N 130 15 E
Najmah, Si. Arabia 45 E6 26 42N 50 6 E
Naju, S. Korea 35 G14 35 3N 126 43 E
Nakadōri-Shima, Japan 31 H4 32 57N 129 4 E
Nakalagba, Dem. Rep. of the Congo 54 B2 2 50N 27 58 E
Nakaminato, Japan 31 F10 36 21N 140 36 E
Nakamura, Japan 31 H6 32 59N 132 56 E
Nakano, Japan 31 F9 36 45N 138 22 E
Nakano-Shima, Japan 31 K4 29 51N 129 52 E
Nakashibetsu, Japan 30 C12 43 33N 144 59 E
Nakfa, Eritrea 46 D2 16 40N 38 32 E
Nakhfar al Buşayyah, Iraq 44 D5 30 0N 46 10 E
Nakhichevan = Naxçıvan, Azerbaijan 25 G8 39 12N 45 15 E
Nakhichevan Republic = Naxçıvan □, Azerbaijan 25 G8 39 25N 45 26 E
Nakhl, Egypt 47 F2 29 55N 33 43 E
Nakhl-e Taqī, Iran 45 E7 27 28N 52 36 E
Nakhodka, Russia 27 E14 42 53N 132 54 E
Nakhon Nayok, Thailand 38 E3 14 12N 101 13 E
Nakhon Pathom, Thailand 38 F3 13 49N 100 3 E
Nakhon Phanom, Thailand 38 D5 17 23N 104 43 E
Nakhon Ratchasima, Thailand 38 E4 14 59N 102 12 E
Nakhon Sawan, Thailand 38 E3 15 35N 100 10 E
Nakhon Si Thammarat, Thailand 39 H3 8 29N 100 0 E
Nakhon Thai, Thailand 38 D3 17 5N 100 44 E
Nakhtarana, India 42 H3 23 20N 69 15 E
Nakina, Canada 70 B2 50 10N 86 40W
Nakodar, India 42 D6 31 8N 75 31 E
Nakskov, Denmark 9 J14 54 50N 11 8 E
Naktong →, S. Korea 35 G15 35 7N 128 57 E
Nakuru, Kenya 54 C4 0 15S 36 4 E
Nakuru, L., Kenya 54 C4 0 23S 36 5 E
Nakusp, Canada 72 C5 50 20N 117 45W
Nal, Pakistan 42 F2 27 40N 66 12 E
Nal →, Pakistan 42 G1 25 20N 65 30 E
Nalchik, Russia 25 F7 43 30N 43 33 E
Nalgonda, India 40 L11 17 6N 79 15 E
Nalhati, India 43 G12 24 17N 87 52 E
Naliya, India 42 H3 23 16N 68 50 E
Nallamalai Hills, India 40 M11 15 30N 78 50 E
Nam Can, Vietnam 39 H5 8 46N 104 59 E
Nam-ch'on, N. Korea 35 E14 38 15N 126 26 E
Nam Co, China 32 C4 30 30N 90 45 E
Nam Du, Hon, Vietnam 39 H5 9 41N 104 21 E
Nam Ngum Dam, Laos 38 C4 18 35N 102 34 E
Nam-Phan = Cochin China, Vietnam 39 G6 10 30N 106 0 E
Nam Phong, Thailand 38 D4 16 42N 102 52 E
Nam Tok, Thailand 38 E2 14 21N 99 4 E
Namacunde, Angola 56 B2 17 18S 15 50 E
Namacurra, Mozam. 57 B6 17 30S 36 50 E
Namak, Daryācheh-ye, Iran 45 C7 34 30N 52 0 E
Namak, Kavir-e, Iran 45 C8 34 30N 57 30 E
Namakzār, Daryācheh-ye, Iran 45 C9 34 0N 60 30 E
Namaland, Namibia 56 C2 26 0S 17 0 E
Namangan, Uzbekistan 26 E8 41 0N 71 40 E
Namapa, Mozam. 55 E4 13 43S 39 50 E
Namaqualand, S. Africa 56 E2 30 0S 17 25 E
Namasagali, Uganda 54 B3 1 2N 33 0 E
Namber, Indonesia 37 E8 1 2S 134 49 E
Nambour, Australia 63 D5 26 32S 152 58 E
Nambucca Heads, Australia 63 E5 30 37S 153 0 E
Namcha Barwa, China 32 D4 29 40N 95 10 E
Namche Bazar, Nepal 43 F12 27 51N 86 47 E
Namchonjŏm = Nam-ch'on, N. Korea 35 E14 38 15N 126 26 E
Namecunda, Mozam. 55 E4 14 54S 37 37 E
Nameponda, Mozam. 55 F4 15 50S 39 50 E
Nametil, Mozam. 55 F4 15 40S 39 21 E
Namew L., Canada 73 C8 54 14N 101 56W
Namgia, India 43 D8 31 48N 78 40 E
Namib Desert = Namibwoestyn, Namibia 56 C2 22 30S 15 0 E
Namibe, Angola 53 H2 15 7S 12 11 E
Namibe □, Angola 56 B1 16 35S 12 30 E
Namibia ■, Africa 56 C2 22 0S 18 9 E
Namibwoestyn, Namibia 56 C2 22 30S 15 0 E
Namlea, Indonesia 37 E7 3 18S 127 5 E
Namoi →, Australia 63 E4 30 12S 149 30 E
Nampa, U.S.A. 82 E5 43 34N 116 34W
Namp'o, N. Korea 35 E13 38 52N 125 10 E
Nampō-Shotō, Japan 31 J10 32 0N 140 0 E
Nampula, Mozam. 55 F4 15 6S 39 15 E
Namrole, Indonesia 37 E7 3 46S 126 46 E
Namse Shankou, China 41 E13 30 0N 82 25 E
Namsen →, Norway 8 D14 64 28N 11 37 E
Namsos, Norway 8 D14 64 29N 11 30 E
Namtsy, Russia 27 C13 62 43N 129 37 E
Namtu, Burma 41 H20 23 5N 97 28 E
Namtumbo, Tanzania 55 E4 10 30S 36 4 E
Namu, Canada 72 C3 51 52N 127 50W
Namur, Belgium 15 D4 50 27N 4 52 E
Namur □, Belgium 15 D4 50 17N 5 0 E
Namutoni, Namibia 56 B2 18 49S 16 55 E
Namwala, Zambia 55 F2 15 44S 26 30 E
Namwŏn, S. Korea 35 G14 35 23N 127 23 E
Nan, Thailand 38 C3 18 48N 100 46 E
Nan →, Thailand 38 E3 15 42N 100 9 E
Nan-ch'ang = Nanchang, China 33 D6 28 42N 115 55 E
Nanaimo, Canada 72 D4 49 10N 124 0W
Nanam, N. Korea 35 D15 41 44N 129 40 E
Nanango, Australia 63 D5 26 40S 152 0 E
Nanao, Japan 31 F8 37 0N 137 0 E
Nanchang, China 33 D6 28 42N 115 55 E
Nanching = Nanjing, China 33 C6 32 2N 118 47 E

Oshmyany

Oshmyany = Ashmyany, *Belarus* **9 J21** 54 26N 25 52 E
Oshnovīyeh, *Iran* **44 B5** 37 2N 45 6 E
Oshogbo, *Nigeria* **50 G6** 7 48N 4 37 E
Oshtorīnān, *Iran* **45 C6** 34 1N 48 38 E
Oshwe, *Dem. Rep. of the Congo* **52 E3** 3 25S 19 28 E
Osijek, *Croatia* **21 B8** 45 34N 18 41 E
Osipenko = Berdyansk, *Ukraine* **25 E6** 46 45N 36 50 E
Osipovichi = Asipovichy, *Belarus* **17 B15** 53 19N 28 33 E
Osiyan, *India* **42 F5** 26 43N 72 55 E
Osizweni, *S. Africa* **57 D5** 27 49S 30 7 E
Oskaloosa, *U.S.A.* **80 E8** 41 18N 92 39W
Oskarshamn, *Sweden* **9 H17** 57 15N 16 27 E
Oskélanéo, *Canada* **70 C4** 48 5N 75 15W
Öskemen, *Kazakstan* **26 E9** 50 0N 82 36 E
Oslo, *Norway* **9 G14** 59 55N 10 45 E
Oslofjorden, *Norway* **9 G14** 59 20N 10 35 E
Osmanabad, *India* **40 K10** 18 5N 76 10 E
Osmaniye, *Turkey* **25 G6** 37 5N 36 10 E
Osnabrück, *Germany* **16 B5** 52 17N 8 3 E
Osorio, *Brazil* **95 B5** 29 53S 50 17W
Osorno, *Chile* **96 E2** 40 25S 73 0W
Osoyoos, *Canada* **72 D5** 49 0N 119 30W
Osøyro, *Norway* **9 F11** 60 9N 5 30 E
Ospika →, *Canada* **72 B4** 56 20N 124 0W
Osprey Reef, *Australia* **62 A4** 13 52S 146 36 E
Oss, *Neths.* **15 C5** 51 46N 5 32 E
Ossa, Mt., *Australia* **62 G4** 41 52S 146 3 E
Óssa, Óros, *Greece* **21 E10** 39 47N 22 42 E
Ossabaw I., *U.S.A.* **77 K5** 31 50N 81 5W
Ossining, *U.S.A.* **79 E11** 41 10N 73 55W
Ossipee, *U.S.A.* **79 C13** 43 41N 71 7W
Ossokmanuan L., *Canada* **71 B7** 53 25N 65 0W
Ossora, *Russia* **27 D17** 59 20N 163 13 E
Ostend = Oostende, *Belgium* **15 C2** 51 15N 2 54 E
Oster, *Ukraine* **17 C16** 50 57N 30 53 E
Osterburg, *U.S.A.* **78 F6** 40 16N 78 31W
Österdalälven, *Sweden* **9 F16** 61 30N 13 45 E
Østerdalen, *Norway* **9 F14** 61 40N 10 50 E
Östersund, *Sweden* **8 E16** 63 10N 14 38 E
Ostfriesische Inseln, *Germany* **16 B4** 53 42N 7 0 E
Ostrava, *Czech Rep.* **17 D10** 49 51N 18 18 E
Ostróda, *Poland* **17 B10** 53 42N 19 58 E
Ostroh, *Ukraine* **17 C14** 50 20N 26 30 E
Ostrołęka, *Poland* **17 B11** 53 4N 21 32 E
Ostrów Mazowiecka, *Poland* **17 B11** 52 50N 21 51 E
Ostrów Wielkopolski, *Poland* **17 C9** 51 36N 17 44 E
Ostrowiec-Świętokrzyski, *Poland* **17 C11** 50 55N 21 22 E
Ostuni, *Italy* **21 D7** 40 44N 17 35 E
Ōsumi-Kaikyō, *Japan* **31 J5** 30 55N 131 0 E
Ōsumi-Shotō, *Japan* **31 J5** 30 30N 130 0 E
Osuna, *Spain* **19 D3** 37 14N 5 8W
Oswegatchie →, *U.S.A.* **79 B9** 44 42N 75 30W
Oswego, *U.S.A.* **79 C8** 43 27N 76 31W
Oswego →, *U.S.A.* **79 C8** 43 27N 76 30W
Oswestry, *U.K.* **10 E4** 52 52N 3 3W
Oświęcim, *Poland* **17 C10** 50 2N 19 11 E
Otago □, *N.Z.* **59 L2** 45 15S 170 0 E
Otago Harbour, *N.Z.* **59 L3** 45 47S 170 42 E
Ōtake, *Japan* **31 G6** 34 12N 132 13 E
Otaki, *N.Z.* **59 J5** 40 45S 175 10 E
Otaru, *Japan* **30 C10** 43 10N 141 0 E
Otaru-Wan = Ishikari-Wan, *Japan* **30 C10** 43 25N 141 1 E
Otavalo, *Ecuador* **92 C3** 0 13N 78 20W
Otavi, *Namibia* **56 B2** 19 40S 17 24 E
Otchinjau, *Angola* **56 B1** 16 30S 13 56 E
Otelnuk L., *Canada* **71 A6** 56 9N 68 12W
Othello, *U.S.A.* **82 C4** 46 50N 119 10W
Otira Gorge, *N.Z.* **59 K3** 42 53S 171 33 E
Otjiwarongo, *Namibia* **56 C2** 20 30S 16 33 E
Otoineppu, *Japan* **30 B11** 44 44N 142 16 E
Otorohanga, *N.Z.* **59 H5** 38 12S 175 14 E
Otoskwin →, *Canada* **70 B2** 52 13N 88 6W
Otra →, *Norway* **9 G13** 58 9N 8 1 E
Otranto, *Italy* **21 D8** 40 9N 18 28 E
Otranto, C. d', *Italy* **21 D8** 40 7N 18 30 E
Otranto, Str. of, *Italy* **21 D8** 40 15N 18 40 E
Otse, *S. Africa* **56 D4** 25 2S 25 45 E
Ōtsu, *Japan* **31 G7** 35 0N 135 50 E
Ōtsuki, *Japan* **31 G9** 35 36N 138 57 E
Ottawa = Outaouais →, *Canada* **70 C5** 45 27N 74 8W
Ottawa, *Canada* **79 A9** 45 27N 75 42W
Ottawa, *Ill., U.S.A.* **80 E10** 41 21N 88 51W
Ottawa, *Kans., U.S.A.* **80 F7** 38 37N 95 16W
Ottawa Is., *Canada* **69 C11** 59 35N 80 10W
Otter Cr. →, *U.S.A.* **79 B11** 44 13N 73 17W
Otter L., *Canada* **73 B8** 55 35N 104 39W
Otterville, *Canada* **78 D4** 42 55N 80 36W
Ottery St. Mary, *U.K.* **11 G4** 50 44N 3 17W
Otto Beit Bridge, *Zimbabwe* **55 F2** 15 59S 28 56 E
Ottosdal, *S. Africa* **56 D4** 26 46S 25 59 E
Ottumwa, *U.S.A.* **80 E8** 41 1N 92 25W
Oturkpo, *Nigeria* **50 G7** 7 16N 8 8 E
Otway, B., *Chile* **96 G2** 53 30S 74 0W
Otway, C., *Australia* **63 F3** 38 52S 143 30 E
Otwock, *Poland* **17 B11** 52 5N 21 20 E
Ou →, *Laos* **38 B4** 20 4N 102 13 E
Ou-Sammyaku, *Japan* **30 E10** 39 20N 140 35 E
Ouachita →, *U.S.A.* **81 K9** 31 38N 91 49W
Ouachita, L., *U.S.A.* **81 H8** 34 34N 93 12W
Ouachita Mts., *U.S.A.* **81 H7** 34 40N 94 25W
Ouagadougou, *Burkina Faso* **50 F5** 12 25N 1 30W
Ouahran = Oran, *Algeria* **50 A5** 35 45N 0 39W
Ouallene, *Algeria* **50 D6** 24 41N 1 11 E
Ouargla, *Algeria* **50 B7** 31 59N 5 16 E
Ouarzazate, *Morocco* **50 B4** 30 55N 6 50W
Oubangi →, *Dem. Rep. of the Congo* **52 E3** 0 30S 17 50 E
Ouddorp, *Neths.* **15 C3** 51 50N 3 57 E
Oude Rijn →, *Neths.* **15 B4** 52 12N 4 24 E
Oudenaarde, *Belgium* **15 D3** 50 50N 3 37 E
Oudtshoorn, *S. Africa* **56 E3** 33 35S 22 14 E
Ouessant, Î. d', *France* **18 B1** 48 28N 5 6W
Ouesso, *Congo* **52 D3** 1 37N 16 5 E
Ouest, Pte. de l', *Canada* **71 C7** 49 52N 64 40W
Ouezzane, *Morocco* **50 B4** 34 51N 5 35W
Oughterard, *Ireland* **13 C2** 53 26N 9 18W
Oujda, *Morocco* **50 B5** 34 41N 1 55W
Oulainen, *Finland* **8 D21** 64 17N 24 47 E
Oulu, *Finland* **8 D21** 65 1N 25 29 E
Oulujärvi, *Finland* **8 D22** 64 25N 27 15 E
Oulujoki →, *Finland* **8 D21** 65 1N 25 30 E
Oum Chalouba, *Chad* **51 E10** 15 48N 20 46 E
Oum Hadjer, *Chad* **51 F9** 13 18N 19 41 E
Ounasjoki →, *Finland* **8 C21** 66 31N 25 40 E
Ounguati, *Namibia* **56 C2** 22 0S 15 46 E
Ounianga Sérir, *Chad* **51 E10** 18 54N 20 51 E
Our →, *Lux.* **15 E6** 49 55N 6 5 E
Ouray, *U.S.A.* **83 G10** 38 1N 107 40W
Ourense, *Spain* **19 A2** 42 19N 7 55W
Ouricuri, *Brazil* **93 E10** 7 53S 40 5W
Ourinhos, *Brazil* **95 A6** 23 0S 49 54W
Ouro Fino, *Brazil* **95 A6** 22 16S 46 25W
Ouro Prêto, *Brazil* **95 A7** 20 20S 43 30W
Ourthe →, *Belgium* **15 D5** 50 29N 5 35 E
Ouse →, *E. Susx., U.K.* **11 G8** 50 47N 0 4 E
Ouse →, *N. Yorks., U.K.* **10 D7** 53 44N 0 55W
Outaouais →, *Canada* **70 C5** 45 27N 74 8W
Outardes →, *Canada* **71 C6** 49 24N 69 30W
Outer Hebrides, *U.K.* **12 D1** 57 30N 7 40W
Outjo, *Namibia* **56 C2** 20 5S 16 7 E
Outlook, *Canada* **73 C7** 51 30N 107 0W
Outokumpu, *Finland* **8 E23** 62 43N 29 1 E
Ouyen, *Australia* **63 F3** 35 1S 142 22 E
Ovalau, *Fiji* **59 C8** 17 40S 178 48 E
Ovalle, *Chile* **94 C1** 30 33S 71 18W
Ovamboland, *Namibia* **56 B2** 18 30S 16 0 E
Overflakkee, *Neths.* **15 C4** 51 44N 4 10 E
Overijssel □, *Neths.* **15 B6** 52 25N 6 35 E
Overland Park, *U.S.A.* **80 F7** 38 55N 94 50W
Overton, *U.S.A.* **85 J12** 36 33N 114 27W
Övertorneå, *Sweden* **8 C20** 66 23N 23 38 E
Ovid, *U.S.A.* **79 D8** 42 41N 76 49W
Oviedo, *Spain* **19 A3** 43 25N 5 50W
Oviši, *Latvia* **9 H19** 57 33N 21 44 E
Ovoot, *Mongolia* **34 B7** 45 21N 113 45 E
Övör Hangay □, *Mongolia* **34 B2** 45 0N 102 30 E
Øvre Årdal, *Norway* **9 F12** 61 19N 7 48 E
Ovruch, *Ukraine* **17 C15** 51 25N 28 45 E
Owaka, *N.Z.* **59 M2** 46 27S 169 40 E
Owambo = Ovamboland, *Namibia* **56 B2** 18 30S 16 0 E
Owando, *Congo* **52 E3** 0 29S 15 55 E
Owasco L., *U.S.A.* **79 D8** 42 50N 76 31W
Owase, *Japan* **31 G8** 34 7N 136 12 E
Owatonna, *U.S.A.* **80 C8** 44 5N 93 14W
Owbeh, *Afghan.* **40 B3** 34 28N 63 10 E
Owego, *U.S.A.* **79 D8** 42 6N 76 16W
Owen Falls Dam, *Uganda* **54 B3** 0 30N 33 5 E
Owen Sound, *Canada* **78 B4** 44 35N 80 55W
Owens →, *U.S.A.* **84 J9** 36 32N 117 59W
Owens L., *U.S.A.* **85 J9** 36 26N 117 57W
Owensboro, *U.S.A.* **76 G2** 37 46N 87 7W
Owl →, *Canada* **73 B10** 57 51N 92 44W
Owo, *Nigeria* **50 G7** 7 10N 5 39 E
Owosso, *U.S.A.* **76 D3** 43 0N 84 10W
Owyhee, *U.S.A.* **82 F5** 41 57N 116 6W
Owyhee →, *U.S.A.* **82 E5** 43 49N 117 2W
Owyhee, L., *U.S.A.* **82 E5** 43 38N 117 14W
Ox Mts. = Slieve Gamph, *Ireland* **13 B3** 54 6N 9 0W
Öxarfjörður, *Iceland* **8 C5** 66 15N 16 45W
Oxbow, *Canada* **73 D8** 49 14N 102 10W
Oxelösund, *Sweden* **9 G17** 58 43N 17 5 E
Oxford, *N.Z.* **59 K4** 43 18S 172 11 E
Oxford, *U.K.* **11 F6** 51 46N 1 15W
Oxford, *Mass., U.S.A.* **79 D13** 42 7N 71 52W
Oxford, *Miss., U.S.A.* **81 H10** 34 22N 89 31W
Oxford, *N.C., U.S.A.* **77 G6** 36 19N 78 35W
Oxford, *N.Y., U.S.A.* **79 D9** 42 27N 75 36W
Oxford, *Ohio, U.S.A.* **76 F3** 39 31N 84 45W
Oxford L., *Canada* **73 C9** 54 51N 95 37W
Oxfordshire □, *U.K.* **11 F6** 51 48N 1 16W
Oxnard, *U.S.A.* **85 L7** 34 12N 119 11W
Oxus = Amudarya →, *Uzbekistan* **26 E6** 43 58N 59 34 E
Oya, *Malaysia* **36 D4** 2 55N 111 55 E
Oyama, *Japan* **31 F9** 36 18N 139 48 E
Oyem, *Gabon* **52 D2** 1 34N 11 31 E
Oyen, *Canada* **73 C6** 51 22N 110 28W
Oykel →, *U.K.* **12 D4** 57 56N 4 26W
Oymyakon, *Russia* **27 C15** 63 25N 142 44 E
Oyo, *Nigeria* **50 G6** 7 46N 3 56 E
Oyster Bay, *U.S.A.* **79 F11** 40 52N 73 32W
Ōyūbari, *Japan* **30 C11** 43 1N 142 5 E
Ozamiz, *Phil.* **37 C6** 8 15N 123 50 E
Ozark, *Ala., U.S.A.* **77 K3** 31 28N 85 39W
Ozark, *Ark., U.S.A.* **81 H8** 35 29N 93 50W
Ozark, *Mo., U.S.A.* **81 G8** 37 1N 93 12W
Ozark Plateau, *U.S.A.* **81 G9** 37 20N 91 40W
Ozarks, L. of the, *U.S.A.* **80 F8** 38 12N 92 38W
Ózd, *Hungary* **17 D11** 48 14N 20 15 E
Ozette L., *U.S.A.* **84 B2** 48 6N 124 38W
Ozona, *U.S.A.* **81 K4** 30 43N 101 12W
Ozuluama, *Mexico* **87 C5** 21 40N 97 50W

P

Pa-an, *Burma* **41 L20** 16 51N 97 40 E
Pa Mong Dam, *Thailand* **38 D4** 18 0N 102 22 E
Pa Sak →, *Thailand* **36 B2** 15 30N 101 0 E
Paamiut = Frederikshåb, *Greenland* **4 C5** 62 0N 49 43W
Paarl, *S. Africa* **56 E2** 33 45S 18 56 E
Paauilo, *U.S.A.* **74 H17** 20 2N 155 22W
Pab Hills, *Pakistan* **42 F2** 26 30N 66 45 E
Pabbay, *U.K.* **12 D1** 57 46N 7 14W
Pabianice, *Poland* **17 C10** 51 40N 19 20 E
Pabna, *Bangla.* **41 G16** 24 1N 89 18 E
Pabo, *Uganda* **54 B3** 3 1N 32 10 E
Pacaja →, *Brazil* **93 D8** 1 56S 50 50W
Pacaraima, Sa., *S. Amer.* **92 C6** 4 0N 62 30W
Pacasmayo, *Peru* **92 E3** 7 20S 79 35W
Pachhar, *India* **42 G7** 24 40N 77 42 E
Pachitea →, *Peru* **92 E4** 8 46S 74 33W
Pachmarhi, *India* **43 H8** 22 28N 78 26 E
Pachpadra, *India* **40 G8** 25 58N 72 10 E
Pachuca, *Mexico* **87 C5** 20 10N 98 40W
Pacific, *Canada* **72 C3** 54 48N 128 28W
Pacific-Antarctic Ridge, *Pac. Oc.* **65 M16** 43 0S 115 0W
Pacific Grove, *U.S.A.* **84 J5** 36 38N 121 56W
Pacific Ocean, *Pac. Oc.* **65 G14** 10 0N 140 0W
Pacific Rim Nat. Park, *Canada* **84 B2** 48 40N 124 45W
Pacifica, *U.S.A.* **84 H4** 37 36N 122 30W
Pacitan, *Indonesia* **37 H14** 8 12S 111 7 E
Packwood, *U.S.A.* **84 D5** 46 36N 121 40W
Padaido, Kepulauan, *Indonesia* **37 E9** 1 5S 138 0 E
Padang, *Indonesia* **36 E2** 1 0S 100 20 E
Padang Endau, *Malaysia* **39 L4** 2 40N 103 38 E
Padangpanjang, *Indonesia* **36 E2** 0 40S 100 20 E
Padangsidempuan, *Indonesia* **36 D1** 1 30N 99 15 E
Paddle Prairie, *Canada* **72 B5** 57 57N 117 29W
Paddockwood, *Canada* **73 C7** 53 30N 105 30W
Paderborn, *Germany* **16 C5** 51 42N 8 45 E
Padma, *India* **43 G11** 24 12N 85 22 E
Pádova, *Italy* **20 B4** 45 25N 11 53 E
Padra, *India* **42 H5** 22 15N 73 7 E
Padrauna, *India* **43 F10** 26 54N 83 59 E
Padre I., *U.S.A.* **81 M6** 27 10N 97 25W
Padstow, *U.K.* **11 G3** 50 33N 4 58W
Padua = Pádova, *Italy* **20 B4** 45 25N 11 53 E
Paducah, *Ky., U.S.A.* **76 G1** 37 5N 88 37W
Paducah, *Tex., U.S.A.* **81 H4** 34 1N 100 18W
Paengnyŏng-do, *S. Korea* **35 F13** 37 57N 124 40 E
Paeroa, *N.Z.* **59 G5** 37 23S 175 41 E
Pafúri, *Mozam.* **57 C5** 22 28S 31 17 E
Pag, *Croatia* **16 F8** 44 25N 15 3 E
Pagadian, *Phil.* **37 C6** 7 55N 123 30 E
Pagai Selatan, Pulau, *Indonesia* **36 E2** 3 0S 100 15 E
Pagai Utara, Pulau, *Indonesia* **36 E2** 2 35S 100 0 E
Pagalu = Annobón, *Atl. Oc.* **49 G4** 1 25S 5 36 E
Pagara, *India* **43 G9** 24 22N 80 1 E
Pagastikós Kólpos, *Greece* **21 E10** 39 15N 23 0 E
Pagatan, *Indonesia* **36 E5** 3 33S 115 59 E
Page, *U.S.A.* **83 H8** 36 57N 111 27W
Pago Pago, *Amer. Samoa* **59 B13** 14 16S 170 43W
Pagosa Springs, *U.S.A.* **83 H10** 37 16N 107 1W
Pagwa River, *Canada* **70 B2** 50 2N 85 14W
Pahala, *U.S.A.* **74 J17** 19 12N 155 29W
Pahang →, *Malaysia* **39 L4** 3 30N 103 9 E
Pahiatua, *N.Z.* **59 J5** 40 27S 175 50 E
Pahokee, *U.S.A.* **77 M5** 26 50N 80 40W
Pahrump, *U.S.A.* **85 J11** 36 12N 115 59W
Pahute Mesa, *U.S.A.* **84 H10** 37 20N 116 45W
Pai, *Thailand* **38 C2** 19 19N 98 27 E
Paia, *U.S.A.* **74 H16** 20 54N 156 22W
Paicines, *U.S.A.* **84 J5** 36 44N 121 17W
Paide, *Estonia* **9 G21** 58 57N 25 31 E
Paignton, *U.K.* **11 G4** 50 26N 3 35W
Päijänne, *Finland* **9 F21** 61 30N 25 30 E
Pailani, *India* **43 G9** 25 45N 80 26 E
Pailin, *Cambodia* **38 F4** 12 46N 102 36 E
Painan, *Indonesia* **36 E2** 1 21S 100 34 E
Painesville, *U.S.A.* **78 E3** 41 43N 81 15W
Paint Hills = Wemindji, *Canada* **70 B4** 53 0N 78 49W
Paint L., *Canada* **73 B9** 55 28N 97 57W
Painted Desert, *U.S.A.* **83 J8** 36 0N 111 0W
Paintsville, *U.S.A.* **76 G4** 37 49N 82 48W
País Vasco □, *Spain* **19 A4** 42 50N 2 45W
Paisley, *Canada* **78 B3** 44 18N 81 16W
Paisley, *U.K.* **12 F4** 55 50N 4 25W
Paisley, *U.S.A.* **82 E3** 42 42N 120 32W
Paita, *Peru* **92 E2** 5 11S 81 9W
Pajares, Puerto de, *Spain* **19 A3** 42 58N 5 46W
Pak Lay, *Laos* **38 C3** 18 15N 101 27 E
Pak Phanang, *Thailand* **39 H3** 8 21N 100 12 E
Pak Sane, *Laos* **38 C4** 18 22N 103 39 E
Pak Song, *Laos* **38 E6** 15 11N 106 14 E
Pakaur, *India* **43 G12** 24 38N 87 51 E
Pakenham, *Canada* **79 A8** 45 18N 76 18W
Pákhnes, *Greece* **23 D6** 35 16N 24 4 E
Pakistan ■, *Asia* **42 E4** 30 0N 70 0 E
Pakkading, *Laos* **38 C4** 18 19N 103 59 E
Pakokku, *Burma* **41 J19** 21 20N 95 0 E
Pakowki L., *Canada* **73 D6** 49 20N 111 0W
Pakpattan, *Pakistan* **42 D5** 30 25N 73 27 E
Paktīā □, *Afghan.* **40 C6** 33 0N 69 15 E
Pakwach, *Uganda* **54 B3** 2 28N 31 27 E
Pakxe, *Laos* **38 E5** 15 5N 105 52 E
Pal Lahara, *India* **43 J11** 21 27N 85 11 E
Pala, *Chad* **51 G9** 9 25N 15 5 E
Pala, *Dem. Rep. of the Congo* **54 D2** 6 45S 29 30 E
Pala, *U.S.A.* **85 M9** 33 22N 117 5W
Palabek, *Uganda* **54 B3** 3 22N 32 33 E
Palacios, *U.S.A.* **81 L6** 28 42N 96 13W
Palagruža, *Croatia* **20 C7** 42 24N 16 15 E
Palaiókastron, *Greece* **23 D8** 35 12N 26 15 E
Palaiokhóra, *Greece* **23 D5** 35 16N 23 39 E
Palam, *India* **40 K10** 19 0N 77 0 E
Palampur, *India* **42 C7** 32 10N 76 30 E
Palana, *Australia* **62 F4** 39 45S 147 55 E
Palana, *Russia* **27 D16** 59 10N 159 59 E
Palanan, *Phil.* **37 A6** 17 8N 122 29 E
Palanan Pt., *Phil.* **37 A6** 17 17N 122 30 E
Palandri, *Pakistan* **43 C5** 33 42N 73 40 E
Palanga, *Lithuania* **9 J19** 55 58N 21 3 E
Palangkaraya, *Indonesia* **36 E4** 2 16S 113 56 E
Palani Hills, *India* **40 P10** 10 14N 77 33 E
Palanpur, *India* **42 G5** 24 10N 72 25 E
Palapye, *Botswana* **56 C4** 22 30S 27 7 E
Palas, *Pakistan* **43 B5** 35 4N 73 14 E
Palashi, *India* **43 H13** 23 47N 88 15 E
Palasponga, *India* **43 J11** 21 47N 85 34 E
Palatka, *Russia* **27 C16** 60 6N 150 54 E
Palatka, *U.S.A.* **77 L5** 29 39N 81 38W
Palau ■, *Pac. Oc.* **28 J17** 7 30N 134 30 E
Palauk, *Burma* **38 F2** 13 10N 98 40 E
Palawan, *Phil.* **36 C5** 9 30N 118 30 E
Palayankottai, *India* **40 Q10** 8 45N 77 45 E
Paldiski, *Estonia* **9 G21** 59 23N 24 9 E
Paleleh, *Indonesia* **37 D6** 1 10N 121 50 E
Palembang, *Indonesia* **36 E2** 3 0S 104 50 E
Palencia, *Spain* **19 A3** 42 1N 4 34W
Palenque, *Mexico* **87 D6** 17 31N 91 58W
Paleokastrítsa, *Greece* **23 A3** 39 40N 19 41 E
Paleometokho, *Cyprus* **23 D12** 35 7N 33 11 E
Palermo, *Italy* **20 E5** 38 7N 13 22 E
Palermo, *U.S.A.* **82 G3** 39 26N 121 33W
Palestina, *Chile* **96 A3** 23 50S 69 47W
Palestine, *Asia* **47 D4** 32 0N 35 0 E
Palestine, *U.S.A.* **81 K7** 31 46N 95 38W
Paletwa, *Burma* **41 J18** 21 10N 92 50 E
Palghat, *India* **40 P10** 10 46N 76 42 E
Palgrave, Mt., *Australia* **60 D2** 23 22S 115 58 E
Pali, *India* **42 G5** 25 50N 73 20 E
Palikir, *Micronesia* **64 G7** 6 55N 158 9 E
Palioúrion, Ákra, *Greece* **21 E10** 39 57N 23 45 E
Palisades Reservoir, *U.S.A.* **82 E8** 43 20N 111 12W
Paliseul, *Belgium* **15 E5** 49 54N 5 8 E
Palitana, *India* **42 J4** 21 32N 71 49 E
Palizada, *Mexico* **87 D6** 18 18N 92 8W
Palk Bay, *Asia* **40 Q11** 9 30N 79 15 E
Palk Strait, *Asia* **40 Q11** 10 0N 79 45 E
Palkānah, *Iraq* **44 C5** 35 49N 44 26 E
Palkot, *India* **43 H11** 22 53N 84 39 E
Palla Road = Dinokwe, *Botswana* **56 C4** 23 29S 26 37 E
Pallanza = Verbánia, *Italy* **18 D8** 45 56N 8 33 E
Pallarenda, *Australia* **62 B4** 19 12S 146 46 E
Pallinup →, *Australia* **61 F2** 34 27S 118 50 E
Pallisa, *Uganda* **54 B3** 1 12N 33 43 E
Pallu, *India* **42 E6** 28 59N 74 14 E
Palm Bay, *U.S.A.* **77 L5** 28 2N 80 35W
Palm Beach, *U.S.A.* **77 M6** 26 43N 80 2W
Palm Coast, *U.S.A.* **77 L5** 29 32N 81 10W
Palm Desert, *U.S.A.* **85 M10** 33 43N 116 22W
Palm Is., *Australia* **62 B4** 18 40S 146 35 E
Palm Springs, *U.S.A.* **85 M10** 33 50N 116 33W
Palma, *Mozam.* **55 E5** 10 46S 40 29 E
Palma, B. de, *Spain* **22 B9** 39 30N 2 39 E
Palma de Mallorca, *Spain* **22 B9** 39 35N 2 39 E
Palma Soriano, *Cuba* **88 B4** 20 15N 76 0W
Palmares, *Brazil* **93 E11** 8 41S 35 28W
Palmas, *Brazil* **95 B5** 26 29S 52 0W
Palmas, C., *Liberia* **50 H4** 4 27N 7 46W
Pálmas, G. di, *Italy* **20 E3** 39 0N 8 30 E
Palmdale, *U.S.A.* **85 L8** 34 35N 118 7W
Palmeira das Missões, *Brazil* **95 B5** 27 55S 53 17W
Palmeira dos Índios, *Brazil* **93 E11** 9 25S 36 37W
Palmer, *U.S.A.* **68 B5** 61 36N 149 7W
Palmer →, *Australia* **62 B3** 16 0S 142 26 E
Palmer Arch., *Antarctica* **5 C17** 64 15S 65 0W
Palmer Lake, *U.S.A.* **80 F2** 39 7N 104 55W
Palmer Land, *Antarctica* **5 D18** 73 0S 63 0W
Palmerston, *Canada* **78 C4** 43 50N 80 51W
Palmerston, *N.Z.* **59 L3** 45 29S 170 43 E
Palmerston North, *N.Z.* **59 J5** 40 21S 175 39 E
Palmerton, *U.S.A.* **79 F9** 40 48N 75 37W
Palmetto, *U.S.A.* **77 M4** 27 31N 82 34W
Palmi, *Italy* **20 E6** 38 21N 15 51 E
Palmira, *Argentina* **94 C2** 32 59S 68 34W
Palmira, *Colombia* **92 C3** 3 32N 76 16W
Palmyra = Tudmur, *Syria* **44 C3** 34 36N 38 15 E
Palmyra, *Mo., U.S.A.* **80 F9** 39 48N 91 32W
Palmyra, *N.J., U.S.A.* **79 F9** 40 1N 75 1W
Palmyra, *N.Y., U.S.A.* **78 C7** 43 5N 77 18W
Palmyra, *Pa., U.S.A.* **79 F8** 40 18N 76 36W
Palmyra Is., *Pac. Oc.* **65 G11** 5 52N 162 5W
Palo Alto, *U.S.A.* **84 H4** 37 27N 122 10W
Palo Verde, *U.S.A.* **85 M12** 33 26N 114 44W
Palopo, *Indonesia* **37 E6** 3 0S 120 16 E
Palos, C. de, *Spain* **19 D5** 37 38N 0 40W
Palos Verdes, *U.S.A.* **85 M8** 33 48N 118 23W
Palos Verdes, Pt., *U.S.A.* **85 M8** 33 43N 118 26W
Palu, *Indonesia* **37 E5** 1 0S 119 52 E
Palu, *Turkey* **25 G7** 38 45N 40 0 E
Palwal, *India* **42 E7** 28 8N 77 19 E
Pamanukan, *Indonesia* **37 G12** 6 16S 107 49 E
Pamiers, *France* **18 E4** 43 7N 1 39 E
Pamir, *Tajikistan* **26 F8** 37 40N 73 0 E
Pamlico →, *U.S.A.* **77 H7** 35 20N 76 28W
Pamlico Sd., *U.S.A.* **77 H8** 35 20N 76 0W
Pampa, *U.S.A.* **81 H4** 35 32N 100 58W
Pampa de las Salinas, *Argentina* **94 C2** 32 1S 66 58W
Pampanua, *Indonesia* **37 E6** 4 16S 120 8 E
Pampas, *Argentina* **94 D3** 35 0S 63 0W
Pampas, *Peru* **92 F4** 12 20S 74 50W
Pamplona, *Colombia* **92 B4** 7 23N 72 39W
Pamplona, *Spain* **19 A5** 42 48N 1 38W
Pampoenpoort, *S. Africa* **56 E3** 31 3S 22 40 E
Pana, *U.S.A.* **80 F10** 39 23N 89 5W
Panaca, *U.S.A.* **83 H6** 37 47N 114 23W
Panaitan, *Indonesia* **37 G11** 6 36S 105 12 E
Panaji, *India* **40 M8** 15 25N 73 50 E
Panamá, *Panama* **88 E4** 9 0N 79 25W
Panama ■, *Cent. Amer.* **88 E4** 8 48N 79 55W
Panamá, G. de, *Panama* **88 E4** 8 4N 79 20W
Panama Canal, *Panama* **88 E4** 9 10N 79 37W
Panama City, *U.S.A.* **77 K3** 30 10N 85 40W
Panamint Range, *U.S.A.* **85 J9** 36 20N 117 20W
Panamint Springs, *U.S.A.* **85 J9** 36 20N 117 28W
Panão, *Peru* **92 E3** 9 55S 75 55W
Panare, *Thailand* **39 J3** 6 51N 101 30 E
Panay, *Phil.* **37 B6** 11 10N 122 30 E
Panay, G., *Phil.* **37 B6** 11 0N 122 30 E
Pančevo, *Serbia, Yug.* **21 B9** 44 52N 20 41 E
Pandan, *Phil.* **37 B6** 11 45N 122 10 E
Pandegelang, *Indonesia* **37 G12** 6 25S 106 5 E
Pandhana, *India* **42 J7** 21 42N 76 13 E
Pandharpur, *India* **40 L9** 17 41N 75 20 E
Pando, *Uruguay* **95 C4** 34 44S 56 0W
Pando, L. = Hope, L., *Australia* **63 D2** 28 24S 139 18 E
Pandokrátor, *Greece* **23 A3** 39 45N 19 50 E
Pandora, *Costa Rica* **88 E3** 9 43N 83 3W
Panevežys, *Lithuania* **9 J21** 55 42N 24 25 E
Panfilov, *Kazakstan* **26 E9** 44 10N 80 0 E
Pang-Long, *Burma* **41 H21** 23 11N 98 45 E
Pang-Yang, *Burma* **41 H21** 22 7N 98 48 E
Panga, *Dem. Rep. of the Congo* **54 B2** 1 52N 26 18 E
Pangalanes, Canal des, *Madag.* **57 C8** 22 48S 47 50 E
Pangani, *Tanzania* **54 D4** 5 25S 38 58 E
Pangani →, *Tanzania* **54 D4** 5 26S 38 58 E
Pangfou = Bengbu, *China* **35 H9** 32 58N 117 20 E
Pangil, *Dem. Rep. of the Congo* **54 C2** 3 10S 26 35 E
Pangkah, Tanjung, *Indonesia* **37 G15** 6 51S 112 33 E
Pangkajene, *Indonesia* **37 E5** 4 46S 119 34 E
Pangkalanbrandan, *Indonesia* **36 D1** 4 1N 98 20 E
Pangkalanbuun, *Indonesia* **36 E4** 2 41S 111 37 E

Penn Hills

Pangkalpinang, *Indonesia* . **36 E3** 2 0S 106 0 E
Pangnirtung, *Canada* **69 B13** 66 8N 65 54W
Pangong Tso, *India* . . . . . . **42 B8** 34 40N 78 40 E
Panguitch, *U.S.A.* **83 H7** 37 50N 112 26W
Pangutaran Group, *Phil.* . . . **37 C6** 6 18N 120 34 E
Panhandle, *U.S.A.* **81 H4** 35 21N 101 23W
Pani Mines, *India* . . . . **42 H5** 22 29N 73 50 E
Pania-Mutombo,
Dem. Rep. of the Congo . **54 D1** 5 11S 23 51 E
Panikota I., *India* . . . . **42 J4** 20 46N 71 21 E
Panipat, *India* . . . . **42 E7** 29 25N 77 2 E
Panjal Range, *India* . . . . . . **42 C7** 32 30N 76 50 E
Panjang, Hon, *Vietnam* . . . . **39 H4** 9 20N 103 28 E
Panjgur, *Pakistan* . . . . **40 F4** 27 0N 64 5 E
Panjim = Panaji, *India* . . . . **40 M8** 15 25N 73 50 E
Panjin, *China* . . . . **35 D12** 41 3N 122 2 E
Panjinad Barrage, *Pakistan* **40 E7** 29 22N 71 15 E
Panjnad →, *Pakistan* . . . . **42 E4** 28 57N 70 30 E
Panjwai, *Afghan.* . . . . **42 D1** 31 26N 65 27 E
Panmunjŏm, *N. Korea* . . . . **35 F14** 37 59N 126 38 E
Panna, *India* . . . . **43 G9** 24 40N 80 15 E
Panna Hills, *India* . . . . **43 G9** 24 40N 81 15 E
Pannawonica, *Australia* . . . **60 D2** 21 39S 116 19 E
Pano Akil, *Pakistan* . . . . . . **42 F3** 27 51N 69 7 E
Pano Lefkara, *Cyprus* . . . . . **23 E12** 34 53N 33 20 E
Pano Panayia, *Cyprus* . . . . . **23 E11** 34 55N 32 38 E
Panorama, *Brazil* **95 A5** 21 21S 51 51W
Pánormon, *Greece* . . . . **23 D6** 35 25N 24 41 E
Pansemal, *India* . . . . **42 J6** 21 39N 74 42 E
Panshan = Panjin, *China* . . **35 D12** 41 3N 122 2 E
Panshi, *China* . . . . **35 C14** 42 58N 126 5 E
Pantanal, *Brazil* **92 H7** 17 30S 57 40W
Pantar, *Indonesia* . . . . **37 F6** 8 28S 124 10 E
Pante Macassar, *Indonesia* **37 F6** 9 30S 123 58 E
Pantelleria, *Italy* . . . . **20 F4** 36 50N 11 57 E
Pánuco, *Mexico* **87 C5** 22 0N 98 15W
Paola, *Malta* . . . . **23 D2** 35 52N 14 30 E
Paola, *U.S.A.* **80 F7** 38 35N 94 53W
Paonia, *U.S.A.* **83 G10** 38 52N 107 36W
Paoting = Baoding, *China* . . **34 E8** 38 50N 115 28 E
Paot'ou = Baotou, *China* . . **34 D6** 40 32N 110 2 E
Paoua, *C.A.R.* . . . . **52 C3** 7 9N 16 20 E
Pápa, *Hungary* . . . . **17 E9** 47 22N 17 30 E
Papa Stour, *U.K.* **12 A7** 60 20N 1 42W
Papa Westray, *U.K.* **12 B6** 59 20N 2 55W
Papagayo →, *Mexico* **87 D5** 16 36N 99 43W
Papagayo, G. de, *Costa Rica* **88 D2** 10 30N 85 50W
Papakura, *N.Z.* . . . . **59 G5** 37 4S 174 59 E
Papantla, *Mexico* **87 C5** 20 30N 97 30W
Papar, *Malaysia* . . . . **36 C5** 5 45N 116 0 E
Papeete, *Tahiti* **65 J13** 17 32S 149 34W
Paphos, *Cyprus* . . . . **23 E11** 34 46N 32 25 E
Papigochic →, *Mexico* **86 B3** 29 9N 109 40W
Paposo, *Chile* **94 B1** 25 0S 70 30W
Papoutsa, *Cyprus* . . . . **23 E12** 34 54N 33 4 E
Papua New Guinea ■,
Oceania . . . . **64 H6** 8 0S 145 0 E
Papudo, *Chile* **94 C1** 32 29S 71 27W
Papun, *Burma* . . . . **41 K20** 18 2N 97 30 E
Papunya, *Australia* . . . . **60 D5** 23 15S 131 54 E
Pará = Belém, *Brazil* **93 D9** 1 20S 48 30W
Pará □, *Brazil* **93 D8** 3 20S 52 0W
Paraburdoo, *Australia* . . . . . **60 D2** 23 14S 117 32 E
Paracatu, *Brazil* **93 G9** 17 10S 46 50W
Paracel Is., *S. China Sea* . . **36 A4** 15 50N 112 0 E
Parachilna, *Australia* . . . . . **63 E2** 31 10S 138 21 E
Parachinar, *Pakistan* . . . . . . **42 C4** 33 55N 70 5 E
Paradhísi, *Greece* . . . . **23 C10** 36 18N 28 7 E
Paradip, *India* . . . . **41 J15** 20 15N 86 35 E
Paradise, *Calif., U.S.A.* **84 F5** 39 46N 121 37W
Paradise, *Nev., U.S.A.* **85 J11** 36 9N 115 10W
Paradise →, *Canada* **71 B8** 53 27N 57 19W
Paradise Hill, *Canada* **73 C7** 53 32N 109 28W
Paradise River, *Canada* **71 B8** 53 27N 57 17W
Paradise Valley, *U.S.A.* **82 F5** 41 30N 117 32W
Parado, *Indonesia* . . . . **37 F5** 8 42S 118 30 E
Paragould, *U.S.A.* **81 G9** 36 3N 90 29W
Paragua →, *Venezuela* **92 B6** 6 55N 62 55W
Paraguaçu →, *Brazil* **93 F11** 12 45S 38 54W
Paraguaçu Paulista, *Brazil* . **95 A5** 22 22S 50 35W
Paraguaná, Pen. de,
Venezuela **92 A5** 12 0N 70 0W
Paraguarí, *Paraguay* **94 B4** 25 36S 57 0W
Paraguarí □, *Paraguay* **94 B4** 26 0S 57 10W
Paraguay ■, *S. Amer.* **94 A4** 23 0S 57 0W
Paraguay →, *Paraguay* . . . **94 B4** 27 18S 58 38W
Paraíba = João Pessoa,
Brazil **93 E12** 7 10S 34 52W
Paraíba □, *Brazil* **93 E11** 7 0S 36 0W
Paraíba do Sul →, *Brazil* . **95 A7** 21 37S 41 3W
Parainen, *Finland* . . . . **9 F20** 60 18N 22 18 E
Paraiso, *Mexico* **87 D6** 18 24N 93 14W
Parak, *Iran* . . . . **45 E7** 27 38N 52 25 E
Parakou, *Benin* . . . . **50 G6** 9 25N 2 40 E
Paralimni, *Cyprus* . . . . **23 D12** 35 2N 33 58 E
Paramaribo, *Surinam* **93 B7** 5 50N 55 10W
Paramushir, Ostrov, *Russia* **27 D16** 50 24N 156 0 E
Paran →, *Israel* . . . . **47 E4** 30 20N 35 10 E
Paraná, *Argentina* **94 C3** 31 45S 60 30W
Paranã, *Brazil* **93 F9** 12 30S 47 48W
Paraná □, *Brazil* **95 A5** 24 30S 51 0W
Paraná →, *Argentina* **94 C4** 33 43S 59 15W
Paranaguá, *Brazil* **95 B6** 25 30S 48 30W
Paranaíba, *Brazil* **93 G8** 19 40S 51 11W
Paranaíba →, *Brazil* **93 H8** 20 6S 51 4W
Paranapanema →, *Brazil* . **95 A5** 22 40S 53 9W
Paranapiacaba, Serra do,
Brazil **95 A6** 24 31S 48 35W
Paranavaí, *Brazil* **95 A5** 23 4S 52 56W
Parang, *Jolo, Phil.* . . . . **37 C6** 5 55N 120 54 E
Parang, *Mindanao, Phil.* . . . **37 C6** 7 23N 124 16 E
Parângul Mare, Vf., *Romania* **17 F12** 45 20N 23 37 E
Parbati →, *India* . . . . **42 F6** 26 54N 77 53 E
Parbati →, *India* . . . . **42 G7** 25 50N 76 30 E
Parbhani, *India* . . . . **40 K10** 19 8N 76 52 E
Parchim, *Germany* . . . . **16 B6** 53 26N 11 52 E
Pardes Hanna-Karkur, *Israel* **47 C3** 32 28N 34 57 E
Pardo →, *Bahia, Brazil* . . . **93 G11** 15 40S 39 0W
Pardo →, *Mato Grosso,*
Brazil **95 A5** 21 46S 52 9W
Pardubice, *Czech Rep.* . . . . **16 C8** 50 3N 15 45 E
Pare, *Indonesia* . . . . **37 G15** 7 43S 112 12 E
Pare Mts., *Tanzania* . . . . . . **54 C4** 4 0S 37 45 E
Parecis, Serra dos, *Brazil* . . **92 F7** 13 0S 60 0W
Paren, *Russia* . . . . **27 C17** 62 30N 163 15 E
Parent, *Canada* **70 C5** 47 55N 74 35W
Parent, L., *Canada* **70 C4** 48 31N 77 1W
Parepare, *Indonesia* . . . . . . **37 E5** 4 0S 119 40 E
Párga, *Greece* . . . . **21 E9** 39 15N 20 29 E
Pargo, Pta. do, *Madeira* . . . **22 D2** 32 49N 17 17W
Pariaguán, *Venezuela* **92 B6** 8 51N 64 34W
Paricutín, Cerro, *Mexico* . . . **86 D4** 19 28N 102 15W
Parigi, *Indonesia* . . . . **37 E6** 0 50S 120 5 E
Parika, *Guyana* **92 B7** 6 50N 58 20W
Parima, Serra, *Brazil* **92 C6** 2 30N 64 0W
Parinari, *Peru* **92 D4** 4 35S 74 25W
Pariñas, Pta., *S. Amer.* **90 D2** 4 30S 82 0W
Parintins, *Brazil* **93 D7** 2 40S 56 50W
Pariparit Kyun, *Burma* . . . . **41 M18** 14 55N 93 45 E
Paris, *Canada* **78 C4** 43 12N 80 25W
Paris, *France* . . . . **18 B5** 48 50N 2 20 E
Paris, *Idaho, U.S.A.* **82 E8** 42 14N 111 24W
Paris, *Ky., U.S.A.* **76 F3** 38 13N 84 15W
Paris, *Tenn., U.S.A.* **77 G1** 36 18N 88 19W
Paris, *Tex., U.S.A.* **81 J7** 33 40N 95 33W
Parish, *U.S.A.* **79 C8** 43 25N 76 8W
Parishville, *U.S.A.* **79 B10** 44 38N 74 49W
Park, *U.S.A.* **84 B4** 48 45N 122 18W
Park City, *U.S.A.* **81 G6** 37 48N 97 20W
Park Falls, *U.S.A.* **80 C9** 45 56N 90 27W
Park Head, *Canada* **78 B3** 44 36N 81 9W
Park Hills, *U.S.A.* **81 G9** 37 53N 90 28W
Park Range, *U.S.A.* **82 G10** 40 0N 106 30W
Park Rapids, *U.S.A.* **80 B7** 46 55N 95 4W
Park River, *U.S.A.* **80 A6** 48 24N 97 45W
Park Rynie, *S. Africa* . . . . . . **57 E5** 30 25S 30 45 E
Parkā Bandar, *Iran* . . . . **45 E8** 25 55N 59 35 E
Parkano, *Finland* . . . . **9 E20** 62 1N 23 0 E
Parker, *Ariz., U.S.A.* **85 L12** 34 9N 114 17W
Parker, *Pa., U.S.A.* **78 E5** 41 5N 79 41W
Parker Dam, *U.S.A.* **85 L12** 34 18N 114 8W
Parkersburg, *U.S.A.* **76 F5** 39 16N 81 34W
Parkes, *Australia* . . . . **63 E4** 33 9S 148 11 E
Parkfield, *U.S.A.* **84 K6** 35 54N 120 26W
Parkhill, *Canada* **78 C3** 43 15N 81 38W
Parkland, *U.S.A.* **84 C4** 47 9N 122 26W
Parkston, *U.S.A.* **80 D6** 43 24N 97 59W
Parksville, *Canada* **72 D4** 49 20N 124 21W
Parla, *Spain* **19 B4** 40 14N 3 46W
Parma, *Italy* . . . . **18 D9** 44 48N 10 20 E
Parma, *Idaho, U.S.A.* **82 E5** 43 47N 116 57W
Parma, *Ohio, U.S.A.* **78 E3** 41 23N 81 43W
Parnaguá, *Brazil* **93 F10** 10 10S 44 38W
Parnaíba, *Brazil* **93 D10** 2 54S 41 47W
Parnaíba →, *Brazil* **93 D10** 3 0S 41 50W
Parnassós, *Greece* . . . . **21 E10** 38 35N 22 30 E
Pärnu, *Estonia* . . . . **9 G21** 58 28N 24 33 E
Paroo →, *Australia* . . . . . . **63 E3** 31 28S 143 32 E
Páros, *Greece* . . . . **21 F11** 37 5N 25 12 E
Parowan, *U.S.A.* **83 H7** 37 51N 112 50W
Parral, *Chile* **94 D1** 36 10S 71 52W
Parras, *Mexico* **86 B4** 25 30N 102 20W
Parrett →, *U.K.* **11 F4** 51 12N 3 1W
Parris I., *U.S.A.* **77 J5** 32 20N 80 41W
Parrsboro, *Canada* **71 C7** 45 30N 64 25W
Parry I., *Canada* **78 A4** 45 18N 80 10W
Parry Is., *Canada* **4 B2** 77 0N 110 0W
Parry Sound, *Canada* **78 A5** 45 20N 80 0W
Parsnip →, *Canada* **72 B4** 55 10N 123 2W
Parsons, *U.S.A.* **81 G7** 37 20N 95 16W
Parsons Ra., *Australia* . . . . . **62 A2** 13 30S 135 15 E
Partinico, *Italy* . . . . **20 E5** 38 3N 13 7 E
Partridge I., *Canada* **70 A2** 55 59N 87 37W
Paru →, *Brazil* **93 D8** 1 33S 52 38W
Parvān □, *Afghan.* . . . . **40 B6** 35 0N 69 0 E
Parvatipuram, *India* . . . . **41 K13** 18 50N 83 25 E
Parvatsar, *India* . . . . **42 F6** 26 52N 74 49 E
Parys, *S. Africa* . . . . **56 D4** 26 52S 27 29 E
Pas, Pta. des, *Spain* . . . . . . **22 C7** 38 46N 1 26 E
Pasadena, *Canada* **71 C8** 49 1N 57 36W
Pasadena, *Calif., U.S.A.* **85 L8** 34 9N 118 9W
Pasadena, *Tex., U.S.A.* **81 L7** 29 43N 95 13W
Pasaje →, *Argentina* **94 B3** 25 39S 63 56W
Pascagoula, *U.S.A.* **81 K10** 30 21N 88 33W
Pascagoula →, *U.S.A.* **81 K10** 30 23N 88 37W
Paşcani, *Romania* . . . . **17 E14** 47 14N 26 45 E
Pasco, *U.S.A.* **82 C4** 46 14N 119 6W
Pasco, Cerro de, *Peru* **92 F3** 10 45S 76 10W
Pasco I., *Australia* . . . . **60 D2** 20 57S 115 20 E
Pascoag, *U.S.A.* **79 E13** 41 57N 71 42W
Pascua, I. de, *Pac. Oc.* **65 K17** 27 0S 109 0W
Pasfield L., *Canada* **73 B7** 58 24N 105 20W
Pashiwari, *Pakistan* . . . . **43 B6** 34 40N 75 10 E
Pashmakli = Smolyan,
Bulgaria . . . . **21 D11** 41 36N 24 38 E
Pasir Mas, *Malaysia* . . . . **39 J4** 6 2N 102 8 E
Pasir Putih, *Malaysia* . . . . . . **39 K4** 5 50N 102 24 E
Pasirian, *Indonesia* . . . . **37 H15** 8 13S 113 8 E
Pasirkuning, *Indonesia* . . . . **36 E2** 0 30S 104 33 E
Paskūh, *Iran* . . . . **45 E9** 27 34N 61 39 E
Pasley, C., *Australia* . . . . . . **61 F3** 33 52S 123 35 E
Pašman, *Croatia* . . . . **16 G8** 43 58N 15 20 E
Pasni, *Pakistan* . . . . **40 G3** 25 15N 63 27 E
Paso Cantinela, *Mexico* . . . **85 N11** 32 33N 115 47W
Paso de Indios, *Argentina* . **96 E3** 43 55S 69 0W
Paso de los Libres,
Argentina **94 B4** 29 44S 57 10W
Paso de los Toros, *Uruguay* **94 C4** 32 45S 56 30W
Paso Robles, *U.S.A.* **83 J3** 35 38N 120 41W
Paspébiac, *Canada* **71 C6** 48 3N 65 17W
Pasrur, *Pakistan* . . . . **42 C6** 32 16N 74 43 E
Passage West, *Ireland* **13 E3** 51 52N 8 21W
Passaic, *U.S.A.* **79 F10** 40 51N 74 7W
Passau, *Germany* . . . . **16 D7** 48 34N 13 28 E
Passero, C., *Italy* . . . . **20 F6** 36 41N 15 10 E
Passo Fundo, *Brazil* **95 B5** 28 10S 52 20W
Passos, *Brazil* **93 H9** 20 45S 46 37W
Pastavy, *Belarus* . . . . **9 J22** 55 4N 26 50 E
Pastaza →, *Peru* **92 D3** 4 50S 76 52W
Pasto, *Colombia* **92 C3** 1 13N 77 17W
Pasuruan, *Indonesia* . . . . . . **37 G15** 7 40S 112 44 E
Patagonia, *Argentina* **96 F3** 45 0S 69 0W
Patagonia, *U.S.A.* **83 L8** 31 33N 110 45W
Patambar, *Iran* . . . . **45 D9** 29 45N 60 17 E
Patan, *India* . . . . **40 H8** 23 54N 72 14 E
Patan, *Maharashtra, India* . **42 H5** 23 54N 72 14 E
Patan, *Nepal* . . . . **41 F14** 27 40N 85 20 E
Patani, *Indonesia* . . . . **37 D7** 0 20N 128 50 E
Pataudi, *India* . . . . **42 E7** 28 18N 76 48 E
Patchewollock, *Australia* . . **63 F3** 35 22S 142 12 E
Patchogue, *U.S.A.* **79 F11** 40 46N 73 1W
Patea, *N.Z.* . . . . **59 H5** 39 45S 174 30 E
Patensie, *S. Africa* . . . . **56 E3** 33 46S 24 49 E
Paternò, *Italy* . . . . **20 F6** 37 34N 14 54 E
Pateros, *U.S.A.* **82 B4** 48 3N 119 54W
Paterson, *U.S.A.* **79 F10** 40 55N 74 11W
Paterson Ra., *Australia* . . . . **60 D3** 21 45S 122 10 E
Pathankot, *India* . . . . **42 C6** 32 18N 75 45 E
Pathfinder Reservoir, *U.S.A.* **82 E10** 42 28N 106 51W
Pathiu, *Thailand* . . . . **39 G2** 10 42N 99 19 E
Pathum Thani, *Thailand* . . . **38 E3** 14 1N 100 32 E
Pati, *Indonesia* . . . . **37 G14** 6 45S 111 1 E
Patía →, *Colombia* **92 C3** 2 13N 78 40W
Patiala, *India* . . . . **42 D7** 30 23N 76 26 E
Patiala, *India* . . . . **43 F8** 27 43N 79 1 E
Patkai Bum, *India* . . . . **41 F19** 27 0N 95 30 E
Pátmos, *Greece* . . . . **21 F12** 37 21N 26 36 E
Patna, *India* . . . . **43 G11** 25 35N 85 12 E
Pato Branco, *Brazil* **95 B5** 26 13S 52 40W
Patonga, *Uganda* . . . . **54 B3** 2 45N 33 15 E
Patos, *Brazil* **93 E11** 6 55S 37 16W
Patos, L. dos, *Brazil* **95 C5** 31 20S 51 0W
Patos, Río de los →,
Argentina **94 C2** 31 18S 69 25W
Patos de Minas, *Brazil* **93 G9** 18 35S 46 32W
Patquía, *Argentina* **94 C2** 30 2S 66 55W
Pátrai, *Greece* . . . . **21 E9** 38 14N 21 47 E
Pátraikós Kólpos, *Greece* . . **21 E9** 38 17N 21 30 E
Patras = Pátrai, *Greece* . . . **21 E9** 38 14N 21 47 E
Patrocínio, *Brazil* **93 G9** 18 57S 47 0W
Patta, *Kenya* . . . . **54 C5** 2 10S 41 0 E
Pattani, *Thailand* . . . . **39 J3** 6 48N 101 15 E
Pattaya, *Thailand* . . . . **36 B2** 12 52N 100 55 E
Patten, *U.S.A.* **77 C11** 46 0N 68 38W
Patterson, *Calif., U.S.A.* **84 H5** 37 28N 121 8W
Patterson, *La., U.S.A.* **81 L9** 29 42N 91 18W
Patterson, Mt., *U.S.A.* **84 G7** 38 29N 119 20W
Patti, *Punjab, India* . . . . **42 D6** 31 17N 74 54 E
Patti, *Ut. P., India* . . . . **43 G10** 25 55N 82 12 E
Pattoki, *Pakistan* . . . . **42 D5** 31 5N 73 52 E
Patton, *U.S.A.* **78 F6** 40 38N 78 39W
Patuakhali, *Bangla.* . . . . **41 H17** 22 20N 90 25 E
Patuanak, *Canada* **73 B7** 55 55N 107 43W
Patuca →, *Honduras* **88 C3** 15 50N 84 18W
Patuca, Punta, *Honduras* . . **88 C3** 15 49N 84 14W
Pátzcuaro, *Mexico* **86 D4** 19 30N 101 40W
Pau, *France* **18 E3** 43 19N 0 25W
Pauk, *Burma* . . . . **41 J19** 21 27N 94 30 E
Paul I., *Canada* **71 A7** 56 30N 61 20W
Paul Smiths, *U.S.A.* **79 B10** 44 26N 74 15W
Paulatuk, *Canada* **68 B7** 69 25N 124 0W
Paulis = Isiro,
Dem. Rep. of the Congo . **54 B2** 2 53N 27 40 E
Paulistana, *Brazil* **93 E10** 8 9S 41 9W
Paulo Afonso, *Brazil* **93 E11** 9 21S 38 15W
Paulpietersburg, *S. Africa* . **57 D5** 27 23S 30 50 E
Pauls Valley, *U.S.A.* **81 H6** 34 44N 97 13W
Pauma Valley, *U.S.A.* **85 M10** 33 16N 116 58W
Pauri, *India* . . . . **43 D8** 30 9N 78 47 E
Pāveh, *Iran* . . . . **44 C5** 35 3N 46 22 E
Pavia, *Italy* . . . . **18 D8** 45 7N 9 8 E
Pavilion, *U.S.A.* **78 D6** 42 52N 78 1W
Pāvilosta, *Latvia* . . . . **9 H19** 56 53N 21 14 E
Pavlodar, *Kazakstan* . . . . . . **26 D8** 52 33N 77 0 E
Pavlograd = Pavlohrad,
Ukraine . . . . **25 E6** 48 30N 35 52 E
Pavlohrad, *Ukraine* . . . . **25 E6** 48 30N 35 52 E
Pavlovo, *Russia* . . . . **24 C7** 55 58N 43 5 E
Pavlovsk, *Russia* . . . . **25 D7** 50 26N 40 5 E
Pavlovskaya, *Russia* . . . . . . **25 E6** 46 17N 39 47 E
Pawayan, *India* . . . . **43 E9** 28 4N 80 6 E
Pawhuska, *U.S.A.* **81 G6** 36 40N 96 20W
Pawling, *U.S.A.* **79 E11** 41 34N 73 36W
Pawnee, *U.S.A.* **81 G6** 36 20N 96 48W
Pawnee City, *U.S.A.* **80 E6** 40 7N 96 9W
Pawtucket, *U.S.A.* **79 E13** 41 53N 71 23W
Paximádhia, *Greece* . . . . **23 E6** 35 0N 24 35 E
Paxoí, *Greece* . . . . **21 E9** 39 14N 20 12 E
Paxton, *Ill., U.S.A.* **76 E1** 40 27N 88 6W
Paxton, *Nebr., U.S.A.* **80 E4** 41 7N 101 21W
Payakumbuh, *Indonesia* . . . **36 E2** 0 20S 100 35 E
Payette, *U.S.A.* **82 D5** 44 5N 116 56W
Payne Bay = Kangirsuk,
Canada **69 C13** 60 0N 70 0W
Payne L., *Canada* **69 C12** 59 30N 74 30W
Paynes Find, *Australia* . . . . **61 E2** 29 15S 117 42 E
Paynesville, *U.S.A.* **80 C7** 45 23N 94 43W
Paysandú, *Uruguay* **94 C4** 32 19S 58 8W
Payson, *Ariz., U.S.A.* **83 J8** 34 14N 111 20W
Payson, *Utah, U.S.A.* **74 B4** 40 3N 111 44W
Paz →, *Guatemala* **88 D1** 13 44N 90 10W
Paz, B. la, *Mexico* **86 C2** 24 15N 110 25W
Pāzanān, *Iran* . . . . **45 D6** 30 35N 49 59 E
Pazardzhik, *Bulgaria* . . . . . . **21 C11** 42 12N 24 20 E
Pe Ell, *U.S.A.* **84 D3** 46 34N 123 18W
Peabody, *U.S.A.* **79 D14** 42 31N 70 56W
Peace →, *Canada* **72 B6** 59 0N 111 25W
Peace Point, *Canada* **72 B6** 59 7N 112 27W
Peace River, *Canada* **72 B5** 56 15N 117 18W
Peach Springs, *U.S.A.* **83 J7** 35 32N 113 25W
Peachland, *Canada* **72 D5** 49 47N 119 45W
Peachtree City, *U.S.A.* **77 J3** 33 25N 84 35W
Peak, The = Kinder Scout,
U.K. **10 D6** 53 24N 1 52W
Peak District, *U.K.* **10 D6** 53 10N 1 50W
Peak Hill, *N.S.W., Australia* . **63 E4** 32 47S 148 11 E
Peak Hill, *W. Austral.,*
Australia . . . . **61 E2** 25 35S 118 43 E
Peak Ra., *Australia* . . . . **62 C4** 22 50S 148 20 E
Peake Cr. →, *Australia* . . . **63 D2** 28 2S 136 7 E
Peale, Mt., *U.S.A.* **83 G9** 38 26N 109 14W
Pearblossom, *U.S.A.* **85 L9** 34 30N 117 55W
Pearl →, *U.S.A.* **81 K10** 30 11N 89 32W
Pearl City, *U.S.A.* **74 H16** 21 24N 157 59W
Pearl Harbor, *U.S.A.* **74 H16** 21 21N 157 57W
Pearl River, *U.S.A.* **79 E10** 41 4N 74 2W
Pearsall, *U.S.A.* **81 L5** 28 54N 99 6W
Peary Land, *Greenland* **4 A6** 82 40N 33 0W
Pease →, *U.S.A.* **81 H5** 34 12N 99 2W
Peawanuck, *Canada* **69 C11** 55 15N 85 12W
Pebane, *Mozam.* . . . . **55 F4** 17 10S 38 8 E
Pebas, *Peru* **92 D4** 3 10S 71 46W
Pebble Beach, *U.S.A.* **84 J5** 36 34N 121 57W
Peć, *Yugoslavia* . . . . **21 C9** 42 40N 20 17 E
Pechenga, *Russia* . . . . **24 A5** 69 29N 31 4 E
Pechenizhyn, *Ukraine* . . . . . **17 D13** 48 30N 24 48 E
Pechiguera, Pta., *Canary Is.* **22 F6** 28 51N 13 53W
Pechora, *Russia* . . . . **24 A10** 65 10N 57 11 E
Pechora →, *Russia* . . . . **24 A9** 68 13N 54 15 E
Pechorskaya Guba, *Russia* . **24 A9** 68 40N 54 0 E
Pečory, *Russia* . . . . **9 H22** 57 48N 27 40 E
Pecos, *U.S.A.* **81 K3** 31 26N 103 30W
Pecos →, *U.S.A.* **81 L3** 29 42N 101 22W
Pécs, *Hungary* . . . . **17 E10** 46 5N 18 15 E
Pedder, L., *Australia* . . . . . . **62 G4** 42 55S 146 10 E
Peddie, *S. Africa* . . . . **57 E4** 33 14S 27 7 E
Pédernales, *Dom. Rep.* **89 C5** 18 2N 71 44W
Pedieos →, *Cyprus* . . . . **23 D12** 35 10N 33 54 E
Pedirka, *Australia* . . . . **63 D2** 26 40S 135 14 E
Pedra Azul, *Brazil* **93 G10** 16 2S 41 17W
Pedreiras, *Brazil* **93 D10** 4 32S 44 40W
Pedro Afonso, *Brazil* **93 E9** 9 0S 48 10W
Pedro Cays, *Jamaica* **88 C4** 17 5N 77 48W
Pedro de Valdivia, *Chile* . . . **94 A2** 22 55S 69 38W
Pedro Juan Caballero,
Paraguay **95 A4** 22 30S 55 40W
Pee Dee →, *U.S.A.* **77 J6** 33 22N 79 16W
Peebinga, *Australia* . . . . **63 E3** 34 52S 140 57 E
Peebles, *U.K.* **12 F5** 55 40N 3 11W
Peekskill, *U.S.A.* **79 E11** 41 17N 73 55W
Peel, *U.K.* **10 C3** 54 13N 4 40W
Peel →, *Australia* . . . . **63 E5** 30 50S 150 29 E
Peel →, *Canada* **68 B6** 67 0N 135 0W
Peel Sound, *Canada* **68 A10** 73 0N 96 0W
Peera Peera Poolanna L.,
Australia . . . . **63 D2** 26 30S 138 0 E
Peerless Lake, *Canada* **72 B6** 56 37N 114 40W
Peers, *Canada* **72 C5** 53 40N 116 0W
Pegasus Bay, *N.Z.* . . . . **59 K4** 43 20S 173 10 E
Pegu, *Burma* . . . . **41 L20** 17 20N 96 29 E
Pegu Yoma, *Burma* . . . . **41 K20** 19 0N 96 0 E
Pehuajó, *Argentina* **94 D3** 35 45S 62 0W
Pei Xian = Pizhou, *China* . . **34 G9** 34 44N 116 55 E
Peine, *Chile* **94 A2** 23 45S 68 8W
Peine, *Germany* . . . . **16 B6** 52 19N 10 14 E
Peip'ing = Beijing, *China* . . **34 E9** 39 55N 116 20 E
Peipus, L. = Chudskoye,
Ozero, *Russia* . . . . **9 G22** 58 13N 27 30 E
Peixe, *Brazil* **93 F9** 12 0S 48 40W
Peixe →, *Brazil* **93 H8** 21 31S 51 58W
Pekalongan, *Indonesia* . . . . **37 G13** 6 53S 109 40 E
Pekan, *Malaysia* . . . . **39 L4** 3 30N 103 25 E
Pekanbaru, *Indonesia* . . . . . **36 D2** 0 30N 101 15 E
Pekin, *U.S.A.* **80 E10** 40 35N 89 40W
Peking = Beijing, *China* . . . **34 E9** 39 55N 116 20 E
Pelabuhan Kelang, *Malaysia* **39 L3** 3 0N 101 23 E
Pelabuhan Ratu, Teluk,
Indonesia . . . . **37 G12** 7 5S 106 30 E
Pelabuhanratu, *Indonesia* . **37 G12** 7 0S 106 32 E
Pelagie, Is., *Italy* . . . . **20 G5** 35 39N 12 33 E
Pelaihari, *Indonesia* . . . . **36 E4** 3 55S 114 45 E
Peleaga, Vf., *Romania* . . . . **17 F12** 45 22N 22 55 E
Pelée, Mt., *Martinique* **89 D7** 14 48N 61 10W
Pelee, Pt., *Canada* **70 D3** 41 54N 82 31W
Pelee I., *Canada* **78 E2** 41 47N 82 40W
Pelekech, *Kenya* . . . . **54 B4** 3 52N 35 8 E
Peleng, *Indonesia* . . . . **37 E6** 1 20S 123 30 E
Pelican, *U.S.A.* **72 B1** 57 58N 136 14W
Pelican L., *Canada* **73 C8** 52 28N 100 20W
Pelican Narrows, *Canada* . . . **73 B8** 55 10N 102 56W
Pelješac, *Croatia* . . . . **20 C7** 42 55N 17 25 E
Pelkosenniemi, *Finland* . . . **8 C22** 67 6N 27 28 E
Pella, *S. Africa* . . . . **56 D2** 29 1S 19 6 E
Pella, *U.S.A.* **80 E8** 41 25N 92 55W
Pello, *Finland* . . . . **8 C21** 66 47N 23 59 E
Pelly →, *Canada* **68 B6** 62 47N 137 19W
Pelly Bay, *Canada* **69 B11** 68 38N 89 50W
Peloponnese =
Pelopónnisos □, *Greece* . **21 F10** 37 10N 22 0 E
Pelopónnisos □, *Greece* . . **21 F10** 37 10N 22 0 E
Pelorus Sd., *N.Z.* . . . . **59 J4** 40 59S 173 59 E
Pelotas, *Brazil* **95 C5** 31 42S 52 23W
Pelotas →, *Brazil* **95 B5** 27 28S 51 55W
Pelvoux, Massif du, *France* **18 D7** 44 52N 6 20 E
Pemalang, *Indonesia* . . . . . **37 G13** 6 53S 109 23 E
Pemanggil, Pulau, *Malaysia* **39 L5** 2 37N 104 21 E
Pematangsiantar, *Indonesia* **36 D1** 2 57N 99 5 E
Pemba, *Mozam.* . . . . **55 E5** 12 58S 40 30 E
Pemba, *Zambia* . . . . **55 F2** 16 30S 27 28 E
Pemba Channel, *Tanzania* . **54 D4** 5 0S 39 37 E
Pemba I., *Tanzania* . . . . **54 D4** 5 0S 39 45 E
Pemberton, *Australia* . . . . . . **61 F2** 34 30S 116 0 E
Pemberton, *Canada* **72 C4** 50 25N 122 50W
Pembina, *U.S.A.* **80 A6** 48 58N 97 15W
Pembroke, *Canada* **70 C4** 45 50N 77 7W
Pembroke, *U.K.* **11 F3** 51 41N 4 55W
Pembrokeshire □, *U.K.* **11 F3** 51 52N 4 56W
Pen-y-Ghent, *U.K.* **10 C5** 54 10N 2 14W
Penang = Pinang, *Malaysia* **39 K3** 5 25N 100 15 E
Penápolis, *Brazil* **95 A6** 21 30S 50 0W
Peñarroya-Pueblonuevo,
Spain **19 C3** 38 19N 5 16W
Penarth, *U.K.* **11 F4** 51 26N 3 11W
Peñas, C. de, *Spain* **19 A3** 43 42N 5 52W
Penas, G. de, *Chile* **96 F2** 47 0S 75 0W
Peñas del Chache,
Canary Is. **22 E6** 29 6N 13 33W
Pench'i = Benxi, *China* . . . . **35 D12** 41 20N 123 48 E
Pend Oreille →, *U.S.A.* . . . **82 B5** 49 4N 117 37W
Pend Oreille, L., *U.S.A.* **82 C5** 48 10N 116 21W
Pendembu, *S. Leone* **50 G3** 9 7N 11 14W
Pender B., *Australia* . . . . **60 C3** 16 45S 122 42 E
Pendleton, *U.S.A.* **82 D4** 45 40N 118 47W
Pendra, *India* . . . . **43 H9** 22 46N 81 57 E
Penedo, *Brazil* **93 F11** 10 15S 36 36W
Penetanguishene, *Canada* . **78 B5** 44 50N 79 55W
Penfield, *U.S.A.* **78 E6** 41 13N 78 35W
Pengalengan, *Indonesia* . . . **37 G12** 7 9S 107 30 E
Penge, *Kasai-Or.,*
Dem. Rep. of the Congo . **54 D1** 5 30S 24 33 E
Penge, *Sud-Kivu,*
Dem. Rep. of the Congo . **54 C2** 4 27S 28 25 E
Penglai, *China* . . . . **35 F11** 37 48N 120 42 E
Penguin, *Australia* . . . . **62 G4** 41 8S 146 6 E
Penhalonga, *Zimbabwe* . . . . **55 F3** 18 52S 32 40 E
Peniche, *Portugal* **19 C1** 39 19N 9 22W
Penicuik, *U.K.* **12 F5** 55 50N 3 13W
Penida, *Indonesia* . . . . **36 F5** 8 45S 115 30 E
Peninsular Malaysia □,
Malaysia . . . . **39 L4** 4 0N 102 0 E
Penitente, Serra do, *Brazil* . **93 E9** 8 45S 46 20W
Penkridge, *U.K.* **10 E5** 52 44N 2 6W
Penmarch, Pte. de, *France* . **18 C1** 47 48N 4 22W
Penn Hills, *U.S.A.* **78 F5** 40 28N 79 52W

Penn Yan

Penn Yan, *U.S.A.* **78 D7** 42 40N 77 3W
Pennant, *Canada* **73 C7** 50 32N 108 14W
Penner →, *India* **40 M12** 14 35N 80 10 E
Pennines, *U.K.* **10 C5** 54 45N 2 27W
Pennington, *U.S.A.* **84 F5** 39 15N 121 47W
Pennsburg, *U.S.A.* **79 F9** 40 23N 75 29W
Pennsylvania □, *U.S.A.* **76 E7** 40 45N 77 30W
Penny, *Canada* **72 C4** 53 51N 121 20W
Penobscot →, *U.S.A.* **77 C11** 44 30N 68 48W
Penobscot B., *U.S.A.* **77 C11** 44 35N 68 50W
Penola, *Australia* **63 F3** 37 25 S 140 48 E
Penong, *Australia* **61 F5** 31 56 S 133 1 E
Penonomé, *Panama* **88 E3** 8 31N 80 21W
Penrith, *Australia* **63 E5** 33 43 S 150 38 E
Penrith, *U.K.* **10 C5** 54 40N 2 45W
Penryn, *U.K.* **11 G2** 50 9N 5 7W
Pensacola, *U.S.A.* **77 K2** 30 25N 87 13W
Pensacola Mts., *Antarctica* **5 E1** 84 0S 40 0W
Pense, *Canada* **73 C8** 50 25N 104 59W
Penshurst, *Australia* **63 F3** 37 49 S 142 20 E
Penticton, *Canada* **72 D5** 49 30N 119 38W
Pentland, *Australia* **62 C4** 20 32 S 145 25 E
Pentland Firth, *U.K.* **12 C5** 58 43N 3 10W
Pentland Hills, *U.K.* **12 F5** 55 48N 3 25W
Penza, *Russia* **24 D8** 53 15N 45 5 E
Penzance, *U.K.* **11 G2** 50 7N 5 33W
Penzhino, *Russia* **27 C17** 63 30N 167 55 E
Penzhinskaya Guba, *Russia* **27 C17** 61 30N 163 0 E
Peoria, *Ariz., U.S.A.* **83 K7** 33 35N 112 14W
Peoria, *Ill., U.S.A.* **80 E10** 40 42N 89 36W
Pepacton Reservoir, *U.S.A.* **79 D10** 42 5N 74 58W
Pera Hd., *Australia* **62 A3** 12 55 S 141 37 E
Perabumulih, *Indonesia* **36 E2** 3 27 S 104 15 E
Perak →, *Malaysia* **39 K3** 4 0N 100 50 E
Pérama, *Kérkira, Greece* **23 A3** 39 34N 19 54 E
Pérama, *Kríti, Greece* **23 D6** 35 20N 24 40 E
Peräpohjola, *Finland* **8 C22** 66 16N 26 10 E
Percé, *Canada* **71 C7** 48 31N 64 13W
Perche, Collines du, *France* **18 B4** 48 30N 0 40 E
Percival Lakes, *Australia* **60 D4** 21 25 S 125 0 E
Percy Is., *Australia* **62 C5** 21 39 S 150 16 E
Perdido, Mte., *Spain* **19 A6** 42 40N 0 5 E
Perdu, Mt. = Perdido, Mte., *Spain* **19 A6** 42 40N 0 5 E
Pereira, *Colombia* **92 C3** 4 49N 75 43W
Perenjori, *Australia* **61 E2** 29 26 S 116 16 E
Pereyaslav-Khmelnytskyy, *Ukraine* **25 D5** 50 3N 31 28 E
Pérez, I., *Mexico* **87 C7** 22 24N 89 42W
Pergamino, *Argentina* **94 C3** 33 52 S 60 30W
Pergau →, *Malaysia* **39 K3** 5 23N 102 2 E
Perham, *U.S.A.* **80 B7** 46 36N 95 34W
Perhentian, Kepulauan, *Malaysia* **36 C2** 5 54N 102 42 E
Péribonca →, *Canada* **71 C5** 48 45N 72 5W
Péribonca, L., *Canada* **71 B5** 50 1N 71 10W
Perico, *Argentina* **94 A2** 24 20 S 65 5W
Pericos, *Mexico* **86 B3** 25 3N 107 42W
Périgueux, *France* **18 D4** 45 10N 0 42 E
Perijá, Sierra de, *Colombia* **92 B4** 9 30N 73 3W
Peristerona →, *Cyprus* **23 D12** 35 8N 33 5 E
Perito Moreno, *Argentina* **96 F2** 46 36 S 70 56W
Perkasie, *U.S.A.* **79 F9** 40 22N 75 18W
Perlas, Arch. de las, *Panama* **88 E4** 8 41N 79 7W
Perlas, Punta de, *Nic.* **88 D3** 12 30N 83 30W
Perm, *Russia* **24 C10** 58 0N 56 10 E
Pernambuco = Recife, *Brazil* **93 E12** 8 0S 35 0W
Pernambuco □, *Brazil* **93 E11** 8 0S 37 0W
Pernatty Lagoon, *Australia* **63 E2** 31 30 S 137 12 E
Pernik, *Bulgaria* **21 C10** 42 35N 23 2 E
Peron Is., *Australia* **60 B5** 13 9S 130 4 E
Peron Pen., *Australia* **61 E1** 26 0S 113 10 E
Perow, *Canada* **72 C3** 54 35N 126 10W
Perpendicular Pt., *Australia* **63 E5** 31 37 S 152 52 E
Perpignan, *France* **18 E5** 42 42N 2 53 E
Perris, *U.S.A.* **85 M9** 33 47N 117 14W
Perry, *Fla., U.S.A.* **77 K4** 30 7N 83 35W
Perry, *Ga., U.S.A.* **77 J4** 32 28N 83 44W
Perry, *Iowa, U.S.A.* **80 E7** 41 51N 94 6W
Perry, *Okla., U.S.A.* **81 G6** 36 17N 97 14W
Perryton, *U.S.A.* **81 G4** 36 24N 100 48W
Perryville, *U.S.A.* **81 G10** 37 43N 89 52W
Persepolis, *Iran* **45 D7** 29 55N 52 50 E
Pershotravensk, *Ukraine* **17 C14** 50 13N 27 40 E
Persia = Iran ■, *Asia* **45 C7** 33 0N 53 0 E
Persian Gulf = Gulf, The, *Asia* **45 E6** 27 0N 50 0 E
Perth, *Australia* **61 F2** 31 57 S 115 52 E
Perth, *Canada* **79 B8** 44 55N 76 15W
Perth, *U.K.* **12 E5** 56 24N 3 26W
Perth & Kinross □, *U.K.* **12 E5** 56 45N 3 55W
Perth Amboy, *U.S.A.* **79 F10** 40 31N 74 16W
Perth-Andover, *Canada* **71 C6** 46 44N 67 42W
Peru, *Ind., U.S.A.* **76 E2** 40 45N 86 4W
Peru, *N.Y., U.S.A.* **79 B11** 44 35N 73 32W
Peru ■, *S. Amer.* **92 D4** 4 0S 75 0W
Peru-Chile Trench, *Pac. Oc.* **92 G3** 20 0S 72 0W
Perúgia, *Italy* **20 C5** 43 7N 12 23 E
Pervomaysk, *Ukraine* **25 E5** 48 10N 30 46 E
Pervouralsk, *Russia* **24 C10** 56 59N 59 59 E
Pésaro, *Italy* **20 C5** 43 54N 12 55 E
Pescara, *Italy* **20 C6** 42 28N 14 13 E
Peshawar, *Pakistan* **42 B4** 34 2N 71 37 E
Peshkopi, *Albania* **21 D9** 41 41N 20 25 E
Peshtigo, *U.S.A.* **76 C2** 45 4N 87 46W
Pesqueira, *Brazil* **93 E11** 8 20 S 36 42W
Petah Tiqwa, *Israel* **47 C3** 32 6N 34 53 E
Petaling Jaya, *Malaysia* **39 L3** 3 4N 101 42 E
Petaloudhes, *Greece* **23 C10** 36 18N 28 5 E
Petaluma, *U.S.A.* **84 G4** 38 14N 122 39W
Pétange, *Lux.* **15 E5** 49 33N 5 55 E
Petaro, *Pakistan* **42 G3** 25 31N 68 18 E
Petatlán, *Mexico* **86 D4** 17 31N 101 16W
Petauke, *Zambia* **55 E3** 14 14 S 31 20 E
Petawawa, *Canada* **70 C4** 45 54N 77 17W
Petén Itzá, L., *Guatemala* **88 C2** 16 58N 89 50W
Peter I.s Øy, *Antarctica* **5 C16** 69 0S 91 0W
Peter Pond L., *Canada* **73 B7** 55 55N 108 44W
Peterbell, *Canada* **70 C3** 48 36N 83 21W
Peterborough, *Australia* **63 E2** 32 58 S 138 51 E
Peterborough, *Canada* **78 B6** 44 20N 78 20W
Peterborough, *U.K.* **11 E7** 52 35N 0 15W
Peterborough, *U.S.A.* **79 D13** 42 53N 71 57W
Peterborough □, *U.K.* **11 E7** 52 35N 0 15W
Peterculter, *U.K.* **12 D6** 57 6N 2 16W
Peterhead, *U.K.* **12 D7** 57 31N 1 48W
Peterlee, *U.K.* **10 C6** 54 47N 1 20W
Petermann Bjerg, *Greenland* **66 B17** 73 7N 28 25W
Petermann Ranges, *Australia* **60 E5** 26 0S 130 30 E
Petersburg, *Alaska, U.S.A.* **68 C6** 56 48N 132 58W
Petersburg, *Pa., U.S.A.* **78 F6** 40 34N 78 3W
Petersburg, *Va., U.S.A.* **76 G7** 37 14N 77 24W
Petersburg, *W. Va., U.S.A.* **76 F6** 39 1N 79 5W
Petersfield, *U.K.* **11 F7** 51 1N 0 56W
Petit Goâve, *Haiti* **89 C5** 18 27N 72 51W
Petit Jardin, *Canada* **71 C8** 48 28N 59 14W
Petit Lac Manicouagan, *Canada* **71 B6** 51 25N 67 40W
Petit-Mécatina →, *Canada* **71 B8** 50 40N 59 30W
Petit-Mécatina, I. du, *Canada* **71 B8** 50 30N 59 25W
Petitcodiac, *Canada* **71 C6** 45 57N 65 11W
Petite Baleine →, *Canada* **70 A4** 56 0N 76 45W
Petite Saguenay, *Canada* **71 C5** 48 15N 70 4W
Petitot →, *Canada* **72 A4** 60 14N 123 29W
Petitsikapau L., *Canada* **71 B6** 54 37N 66 25W
Petlad, *India* **42 H5** 22 30N 72 45 E
Peto, *Mexico* **87 C7** 20 10N 88 53W
Petone, *N.Z.* **59 J5** 41 13 S 174 53 E
Petorca, *Chile* **94 C1** 32 15 S 70 56W
Petoskey, *U.S.A.* **76 C3** 45 22N 84 57W
Petra, *Jordan* **47 E4** 30 20N 35 22 E
Petra, *Spain* **22 B10** 39 37N 3 6 E
Petra, Ostrova, *Russia* **4 B13** 76 15N 118 30 E
Petra Velikogo, Zaliv, *Russia* **30 C6** 42 40N 132 0 E
Petrich, *Bulgaria* **21 D10** 41 24N 23 13 E
Petrified Forest National Park, *U.S.A.* **83 J9** 35 0N 109 30W
Petrikov = Pyetrikaw, *Belarus* **17 B15** 52 11N 28 29 E
Petrograd = Sankt-Peterburg, *Russia* **24 C5** 59 55N 30 20 E
Petrolândia, *Brazil* **93 E11** 9 5S 38 20W
Petrolia, *Canada* **78 D2** 42 54N 82 9W
Petrolina, *Brazil* **93 E10** 9 24 S 40 30W
Petropavl, *Kazakstan* **26 D7** 54 53N 69 13 E
Petropavlovsk = Petropavl, *Kazakstan* **26 D7** 54 53N 69 13 E
Petropavlovsk-Kamchatskiy, *Russia* **27 D16** 53 3N 158 43 E
Petrópolis, *Brazil* **95 A7** 22 33 S 43 9W
Petroşani, *Romania* **17 F12** 45 28N 23 20 E
Petrovaradin, *Serbia, Yug.* **21 B8** 45 16N 19 55 E
Petrovsk, *Russia* **24 D8** 52 22N 45 19 E
Petrovsk-Zabaykalskiy, *Russia* **27 D11** 51 20N 108 55 E
Petrozavodsk, *Russia* **24 B5** 61 41N 34 20 E
Petrus Steyn, *S. Africa* **57 D4** 27 38 S 28 8 E
Petrusburg, *S. Africa* **56 D4** 29 4S 25 26 E
Peumo, *Chile* **94 C1** 34 21 S 71 12W
Peureulak, *Indonesia* **36 D1** 4 48N 97 45 E
Pevek, *Russia* **27 C18** 69 41N 171 19 E
Pforzheim, *Germany* **16 D5** 48 52N 8 41 E
Phagwara, *India* **40 D9** 31 10N 75 40 E
Phaistós, *Greece* **23 D6** 35 2N 24 50 E
Phala, *Botswana* **56 C4** 23 45 S 26 50 E
Phalera = Phulera, *India* **42 F6** 26 52N 75 16 E
Phalodi, *India* **42 F5** 27 12N 72 24 E
Phan, *Thailand* **38 C2** 19 28N 99 43 E
Phan Rang, *Vietnam* **39 G7** 11 34N 109 0 E
Phan Ri = Hoa Da, *Vietnam* **39 G7** 11 16N 108 40 E
Phan Thiet, *Vietnam* **39 G7** 11 1N 108 9 E
Phanat Nikhom, *Thailand* **38 F3** 13 27N 101 11 E
Phangan, Ko, *Thailand* **39 H3** 9 45N 100 0 E
Phangnga, *Thailand* **39 H2** 8 28N 98 30 E
Phanh Bho Ho Chi Minh, *Vietnam* **39 G6** 10 58N 106 40 E
Phanom Sarakham, *Thailand* **38 F3** 13 45N 101 21 E
Phaphund, *India* **43 F8** 26 36N 79 28 E
Pharenda, *India* **43 F10** 27 5N 83 17 E
Pharr, *U.S.A.* **81 M5** 26 12N 98 11W
Phatthalung, *Thailand* **39 J3** 7 39N 100 6 E
Phayao, *Thailand* **38 C2** 19 11N 99 55 E
Phelps, *U.S.A.* **78 D7** 42 58N 77 3W
Phelps L., *Canada* **73 B8** 59 15N 103 15W
Phenix City, *U.S.A.* **77 J3** 32 28N 85 0W
Phet Buri, *Thailand* **38 F2** 13 1N 99 55 E
Phetchabun, *Thailand* **38 D3** 16 25N 101 8 E
Phetchabun, Thiu Khao, *Thailand* **38 E3** 16 0N 101 20 E
Phetchaburi = Phet Buri, *Thailand* **38 F2** 13 1N 99 55 E
Phi Phi, Ko, *Thailand* **39 J2** 7 45N 98 46 E
Phiafay, *Laos* **38 E6** 14 48N 106 0 E
Phibun Mangsahan, *Thailand* **38 E5** 15 14N 105 14 E
Phichai, *Thailand* **38 D3** 17 22N 100 10 E
Phichit, *Thailand* **38 D3** 16 26N 100 22 E
Philadelphia, *Miss., U.S.A.* **81 J10** 32 46N 89 7W
Philadelphia, *N.Y., U.S.A.* **79 B9** 44 9N 75 43W
Philadelphia, *Pa., U.S.A.* **79 G9** 39 57N 75 10W
Philip, *U.S.A.* **80 C4** 44 2N 101 40W
Philippeville, *Belgium* **15 D4** 50 12N 4 33 E
Philippi, *U.S.A.* **76 F5** 39 9N 80 3W
Philippi L., *Australia* **62 C2** 24 20 S 138 55 E
Philippines ■, *Asia* **37 B6** 12 0N 123 0 E
Philippolis, *S. Africa* **56 E4** 30 15 S 25 16 E
Philippopolis = Plovdiv, *Bulgaria* **21 C11** 42 8N 24 44 E
Philipsburg, *Canada* **79 A11** 45 2N 73 5W
Philipsburg, *Mont., U.S.A.* **82 C7** 46 20N 113 18W
Philipsburg, *Pa., U.S.A.* **78 F6** 40 54N 78 13W
Philipstown = Daingean, *Ireland* **13 C4** 53 18N 7 17W
Philipstown, *S. Africa* **56 E3** 30 28 S 24 30 E
Phillip I., *Australia* **63 F4** 38 30 S 145 12 E
Phillips, *U.S.A.* **80 C9** 45 42N 90 24W
Phillipsburg, *Kans., U.S.A.* **80 F5** 39 45N 99 19W
Phillipsburg, *N.J., U.S.A.* **79 F9** 40 42N 75 12W
Philmont, *U.S.A.* **79 D11** 42 15N 73 39W
Philomath, *U.S.A.* **82 D2** 44 32N 123 22W
Phimai, *Thailand* **38 E4** 15 13N 102 30 E
Phitsanulok, *Thailand* **38 D3** 16 50N 100 12 E
Phnom Dangrek, *Thailand* **36 B2** 14 20N 104 0 E
Phnom Penh, *Cambodia* **39 G5** 11 33N 104 55 E
Phnum Penh = Phnom Penh, *Cambodia* **39 G5** 11 33N 104 55 E
Phoenicia, *U.S.A.* **79 D10** 42 5N 74 14W
Phoenix, *Ariz., U.S.A.* **83 K7** 33 27N 112 4W
Phoenix, *N.Y., U.S.A.* **79 C8** 43 14N 76 18W
Phoenix Is., *Kiribati* **64 H10** 3 30 S 172 0W
Phoenixville, *U.S.A.* **79 F9** 40 8N 75 31W
Phon, *Thailand* **38 E4** 15 49N 102 36 E
Phon Tiou, *Laos* **38 D5** 17 53N 104 37 E
Phong →, *Thailand* **38 D4** 16 23N 102 56 E
Phong Tho, *Vietnam* **38 A4** 22 32N 103 21 E
Phonhong, *Laos* **38 C4** 18 30N 102 25 E
Phonum, *Thailand* **39 H2** 8 49N 98 48 E
Phosphate Hill, *Australia* **62 C2** 21 53 S 139 58 E
Photharam, *Thailand* **38 F2** 13 41N 99 51 E
Phra Nakhon Si Ayutthaya, *Thailand* **38 E3** 14 25N 100 30 E
Phra Thong, Ko, *Thailand* **39 H2** 9 5N 98 17 E
Phrae, *Thailand* **38 C3** 18 7N 100 9 E
Phrom Phiram, *Thailand* **38 D3** 17 2N 100 12 E
Phu Dien, *Vietnam* **38 C5** 18 58N 105 31 E
Phu Loi, *Laos* **38 B4** 20 14N 103 14 E
Phu Quoc, Dao, *Vietnam* **39 G4** 10 20N 104 0 E
Phuket, *Thailand* **39 J2** 7 52N 98 22 E
Phuket, Ko, *Thailand* **39 J2** 8 0N 98 22 E
Phul, *India* **42 D6** 30 19N 75 14 E
Phulad, *India* **42 G5** 25 38N 73 49 E
Phulchari, *Bangla.* **43 G13** 25 11N 89 37 E
Phulera, *India* **42 F6** 26 52N 75 16 E
Phulpur, *India* **43 G10** 25 31N 82 49 E
Phun Phin, *Thailand* **39 H2** 9 7N 99 12 E
Piacenza, *Italy* **18 D8** 45 1N 9 40 E
Pian Cr. →, *Australia* **63 E4** 30 2S 148 12 E
Pianosa, *Italy* **20 C4** 42 35N 10 5 E
Piapot, *Canada* **73 D7** 49 59N 109 8W
Piatra Neamţ, *Romania* **17 E14** 46 56N 26 21 E
Piauí □, *Brazil* **93 E10** 7 0S 43 0W
Piauí →, *Brazil* **93 E10** 6 38 S 42 42W
Piave →, *Italy* **20 B5** 45 32N 12 44 E
Pibor Post, *Sudan* **51 G12** 6 47N 33 3 E
Picardie, *France* **18 B5** 49 50N 3 0 E
Picardy = Picardie, *France* **18 B5** 49 50N 3 0 E
Picayune, *U.S.A.* **81 K10** 30 32N 89 41W
Pichhor, *India* **43 G8** 25 58N 78 20 E
Pichilemu, *Chile* **94 C1** 34 22 S 72 0W
Pichor, *India* **42 G8** 25 11N 78 11 E
Pickerel L., *Canada* **70 C1** 48 40N 91 25W
Pickering, *U.K.* **10 C7** 54 15N 0 46W
Pickering, Vale of, *U.K.* **10 C7** 54 14N 0 45W
Pickle Lake, *Canada* **70 B1** 51 30N 90 12W
Pickwick L., *U.S.A.* **77 H1** 35 4N 88 15W
Pico Truncado, *Argentina* **96 F3** 46 40 S 68 0W
Picos, *Brazil* **93 E10** 7 5S 41 28W
Picton, *Australia* **63 E5** 34 12 S 150 34 E
Picton, *Canada* **78 B7** 44 1N 77 9W
Picton, *N.Z.* **59 J5** 41 18 S 174 3 E
Pictou, *Canada* **71 C7** 45 41N 62 42W
Picture Butte, *Canada* **72 D6** 49 55N 112 45W
Picún Leufú, *Argentina* **96 D3** 39 30 S 69 5W
Pidurutalagala, *Sri Lanka* **40 R12** 7 10N 80 50 E
Piedmont = Piemonte □, *Italy* **18 D7** 45 0N 8 0 E
Piedmont, *Ala., U.S.A.* **77 J3** 33 55N 85 37W
Piedmont, *S.C., U.S.A.* **75 D10** 34 0N 81 30W
Piedras Negras, *Mexico* **86 B4** 28 42N 100 31W
Pieksämäki, *Finland* **9 E22** 62 18N 27 10 E
Piemonte □, *Italy* **18 D7** 45 0N 8 0 E
Piercefield, *U.S.A.* **79 B10** 44 13N 74 35W
Pierceland, *Canada* **73 C7** 54 20N 109 46W
Pierpont, *U.S.A.* **78 E4** 41 45N 80 34W
Pierre, *U.S.A.* **80 C4** 44 22N 100 21W
Piet Retief, *S. Africa* **57 D5** 27 1S 30 50 E
Pietarsaari, *Finland* **8 E20** 63 40N 22 43 E
Pietermaritzburg, *S. Africa* **57 D5** 29 35 S 30 25 E
Pietersburg, *S. Africa* **57 C4** 23 54 S 29 25 E
Pietrosul, Vf., *Maramureş, Romania* **17 E13** 47 35N 24 43 E
Pietrosul, Vf., *Suceava, Romania* **17 E13** 47 12N 25 18 E
Pigeon L., *Canada* **78 B6** 44 27N 78 30W
Piggott, *U.S.A.* **81 G9** 36 23N 90 11W
Pigüe, *Argentina* **94 D3** 37 36 S 62 25W
Pihani, *India* **43 F9** 27 36N 80 15 E
Pihlajavesi, *Finland* **9 F23** 61 45N 28 45 E
Pijijiapan, *Mexico* **87 D6** 15 42N 93 14W
Pikangikum Berens, *Canada* **73 C10** 51 49N 94 0W
Pikes Peak, *U.S.A.* **80 F2** 38 50N 105 3W
Piketberg, *S. Africa* **56 E2** 32 55 S 18 40 E
Pikeville, *U.S.A.* **76 G4** 37 29N 82 31W
Pikou, *China* **35 E12** 39 18N 122 22 E
Pikwitonei, *Canada* **73 B9** 55 35N 97 9W
Piła, *Poland* **17 B9** 53 10N 16 48 E
Pilani, *India* **42 E6** 28 22N 75 33 E
Pilar, *Paraguay* **94 B4** 26 50 S 58 20W
Pilaya →, *Bolivia* **92 H6** 20 55 S 64 4W
Pilbara, *Australia* **60 D2** 23 35 S 117 25 E
Pilcomayo →, *Paraguay* **94 B4** 25 21 S 57 42W
Pilibhit, *India* **43 E8** 28 40N 79 50 E
Pilica →, *Poland* **17 C11** 51 52N 21 17 E
Pilkhawa, *India* **42 E7** 28 43N 77 42 E
Pilliga, *Australia* **63 E4** 30 21 S 148 54 E
Pílos, *Greece* **21 F9** 36 55N 21 42 E
Pilot Mound, *Canada* **73 D9** 49 15N 98 54W
Pilot Point, *U.S.A.* **81 J6** 33 24N 96 58W
Pilot Rock, *U.S.A.* **82 D4** 45 29N 118 50W
Pilsen = Plzeň, *Czech Rep.* **16 D7** 49 45N 13 22 E
Pima, *U.S.A.* **83 K9** 32 54N 109 50W
Pimba, *Australia* **63 E2** 31 18 S 136 46 E
Pimenta Bueno, *Brazil* **92 F6** 11 35 S 61 10W
Pimentel, *Peru* **92 E3** 6 45 S 79 55W
Pinang, *Malaysia* **39 K3** 5 25N 100 15 E
Pinar, C. des, *Spain* **22 B10** 39 53N 3 12 E
Pinar del Río, *Cuba* **88 B3** 22 26N 83 40W
Pınarhisar, *Turkey* **21 D12** 41 37N 27 30 E
Pinatubo, *Phil.* **37 A6** 15 8N 120 21 E
Pincher Creek, *Canada* **72 D6** 49 30N 113 57W
Pinchi L., *Canada* **72 C4** 54 38N 124 30W
Pinckneyville, *U.S.A.* **80 F10** 38 5N 89 23W
Pińczów, *Poland* **17 C11** 50 32N 20 32 E
Pindar, *Australia* **61 E2** 28 30 S 115 47 E
Pindi Gheb, *Pakistan* **42 C5** 33 14N 72 21 E
Pindos Óros, *Greece* **21 E9** 40 0N 21 0 E
Pindus Mts. = Pindos Óros, *Greece* **21 E9** 40 0N 21 0 E
Pine →, *B.C., Canada* **72 B4** 56 8N 120 43W
Pine →, *Sask., Canada* **73 B7** 58 50N 105 38W
Pine, C., *Canada* **71 C9** 46 37N 53 32W
Pine Bluff, *U.S.A.* **81 H9** 34 13N 92 1W
Pine Bluffs, *U.S.A.* **80 E2** 41 11N 104 4W
Pine City, *U.S.A.* **80 C8** 45 50N 92 59W
Pine Cr. →, *U.S.A.* **78 E7** 41 10N 77 16W
Pine Creek, *Australia* **60 B5** 13 50 S 131 50 E
Pine Falls, *Canada* **73 C9** 50 34N 96 11W
Pine Flat Res., *U.S.A.* **84 J7** 36 50N 119 20W
Pine Grove, *U.S.A.* **79 F8** 40 33N 76 23W
Pine Pass, *Canada* **72 B4** 55 25N 122 42W
Pine Point, *Canada* **72 A6** 60 50N 114 28W
Pine Ridge, *U.S.A.* **80 D3** 43 2N 102 33W
Pine River, *Canada* **73 C8** 51 45N 100 30W
Pine River, *U.S.A.* **80 B7** 46 43N 94 24W
Pine Valley, *U.S.A.* **85 N10** 32 50N 116 32W
Pinecrest, *U.S.A.* **84 G6** 38 12N 120 1W
Pinedale, *Calif., U.S.A.* **84 J7** 36 50N 119 48W
Pinedale, *Wyo., U.S.A.* **82 E9** 42 52N 109 52W
Pinega →, *Russia* **24 B8** 64 30N 44 19 E
Pinehill, *Australia* **62 C4** 23 38 S 146 57 E
Pinehouse L., *Canada* **73 B7** 55 32N 106 35W
Pineimuta →, *Canada* **70 B1** 52 8N 88 33W
Pinerolo, *Italy* **18 D7** 44 53N 7 21 E
Pinetop, *U.S.A.* **83 J9** 34 8N 109 56W
Pinetown, *S. Africa* **57 D5** 29 48 S 30 54 E
Pineville, *U.S.A.* **81 K8** 31 19N 92 26W
Ping →, *Thailand* **38 E3** 15 42N 100 9 E
Pingaring, *Australia* **61 F2** 32 40 S 118 32 E
Pingding, *China* **34 F7** 37 47N 113 38 E
Pingdingshan, *China* **34 H7** 33 43N 113 27 E
Pingdong, *Taiwan* **33 D7** 22 39N 120 30 E
Pingdu, *China* **35 F10** 36 42N 119 59 E
Pingelly, *Australia* **61 F2** 32 32 S 117 5 E
Pingliang, *China* **34 G4** 35 35N 106 31 E
Pinglu, *China* **34 E7** 39 31N 112 30 E
Pingluo, *China* **34 E4** 38 52N 106 30 E
Pingquan, *China* **35 D10** 41 1N 118 37 E
Pingrup, *Australia* **61 F2** 33 32 S 118 29 E
P'ingtung, *Taiwan* **33 D7** 22 38N 120 30 E
Pingwu, *China* **34 H3** 32 25N 104 30 E
Pingxiang, *China* **32 D5** 22 6N 106 46 E
Pingyao, *China* **34 F7** 37 12N 112 10 E
Pingyi, *China* **35 G9** 35 30N 117 35 E
Pingyin, *China* **34 F9** 36 20N 116 25 E
Pingyuan, *China* **34 F9** 37 10N 116 22 E
Pinhal, *Brazil* **95 A6** 22 10 S 46 46W
Pinheiro, *Brazil* **93 D9** 2 31 S 45 5W
Pinheiro Machado, *Brazil* **95 C5** 31 34 S 53 23W
Pinhel, *Portugal* **19 B2** 40 50N 7 1W
Pini, *Indonesia* **36 D1** 0 10N 98 40 E
Piniós →, *Greece* **21 E10** 39 55N 22 41 E
Pinjarra, *Australia* **61 F2** 32 37 S 115 52 E
Pink Mountain, *Canada* **72 B4** 57 3N 122 52W
Pinnacles, *U.S.A.* **84 J5** 36 33N 121 19W
Pinnaroo, *Australia* **63 F3** 35 17 S 140 53 E
Pinnes, Ákra, *Greece* **21 D11** 40 5N 24 20 E
Pinon Hills, *U.S.A.* **85 L9** 34 26N 117 39W
Pinos, *Mexico* **86 C4** 22 20N 101 40W
Pinos, Mt., *U.S.A.* **85 L7** 34 49N 119 8W
Pinos Pt., *U.S.A.* **83 H3** 36 38N 121 57W
Pinotepa Nacional, *Mexico* **87 D5** 16 19N 98 3W
Pinrang, *Indonesia* **37 E5** 3 46 S 119 41 E
Pins, Pte. aux, *Canada* **78 D3** 42 15N 81 51W
Pinsk, *Belarus* **17 B14** 52 10N 26 1 E
Pintados, *Chile* **92 H5** 20 35 S 69 40W
Pinyug, *Russia* **24 B8** 60 5N 48 0 E
Pioche, *U.S.A.* **83 H6** 37 56N 114 27W
Piombino, *Italy* **20 C4** 42 55N 10 32 E
Pioner, Ostrov, *Russia* **27 B10** 79 50N 92 0 E
Piorini, L., *Brazil* **92 D6** 3 15 S 62 35W
Piotrków Trybunalski, *Poland* **17 C10** 51 23N 19 43 E
Pīp, *Iran* **45 E9** 26 45N 60 10 E
Pipar, *India* **42 F5** 26 25N 73 31 E
Pipar Road, *India* **42 F5** 26 27N 73 27 E
Piparia, *Mad. P., India* **42 H8** 22 45N 78 23 E
Piparia, *Mad. P., India* **42 J7** 21 49N 77 37 E
Pipestone, *U.S.A.* **80 D6** 44 0N 96 19W
Pipestone →, *Canada* **70 B2** 52 53N 89 23W
Pipestone Cr. →, *Canada* **73 D8** 49 38N 100 15W
Piplan, *Pakistan* **42 C4** 32 17N 71 21 E
Piploda, *India* **42 H6** 23 37N 74 56 E
Pipmuacan, Rés., *Canada* **71 C5** 49 45N 70 30W
Pippingarra, *Australia* **60 D2** 20 27 S 118 42 E
Piqua, *U.S.A.* **76 E3** 40 9N 84 15W
Piquiri →, *Brazil* **95 A5** 24 3S 54 14W
Pīr Sohrāb, *Iran* **45 E9** 25 44N 60 54 E
Piracicaba, *Brazil* **95 A6** 22 45 S 47 40W
Piracuruca, *Brazil* **93 D10** 3 50 S 41 50W
Piræus = Piraiévs, *Greece* **21 F10** 37 57N 23 42 E
Piraiévs, *Greece* **21 F10** 37 57N 23 42 E
Pirajui, *Brazil* **95 A6** 21 59 S 49 29W
Piram I., *India* **42 J5** 21 36N 72 21 E
Pirané, *Argentina* **94 B4** 25 42 S 59 6W
Pirapora, *Brazil* **93 G10** 17 20 S 44 56W
Pirawa, *India* **42 G7** 24 10N 76 2 E
Pirgos, *Greece* **21 F9** 37 40N 21 27 E
Piribebuy, *Paraguay* **94 B4** 25 26 S 57 2W
Pirimapun, *Indonesia* **37 F9** 6 20 S 138 24 E
Pirin Planina, *Bulgaria* **21 D10** 41 40N 23 30 E
Pírineos = Pyrénées, *Europe* **18 E4** 42 45N 0 18 E
Piripiri, *Brazil* **93 D10** 4 15 S 41 46W
Pirmasens, *Germany* **16 D4** 49 12N 7 36 E
Pirot, *Serbia, Yug.* **21 C10** 43 9N 22 33 E
Piru, *Indonesia* **37 E7** 3 4S 128 12 E
Piru, *U.S.A.* **85 L8** 34 25N 118 48W
Pisa, *Italy* **20 C4** 43 43N 10 23 E
Pisagua, *Chile* **92 G4** 19 40 S 70 15W
Pisco, *Peru* **92 F3** 13 50 S 76 12W
Písek, *Czech Rep.* **16 D8** 49 19N 14 10 E
Pishan, *China* **32 C2** 37 30N 78 33 E
Pīshīn, *Iran* **45 E9** 26 6N 61 47 E
Pishin, *Pakistan* **42 D2** 30 35N 67 0 E
Pishin Lora →, *Pakistan* **42 E1** 29 9N 64 5 E
Pising, *Indonesia* **37 F6** 5 8S 121 53 E
Pismo Beach, *U.S.A.* **85 K6** 35 9N 120 38W
Pissis, Cerro, *Argentina* **94 B2** 27 45 S 68 48W
Pissouri, *Cyprus* **23 E11** 34 40N 32 42 E
Pistóia, *Italy* **20 C4** 43 55N 10 54 E
Pistol B., *Canada* **73 A10** 62 25N 92 37W
Pisuerga →, *Spain* **19 B3** 41 33N 4 52W
Pit →, *U.S.A.* **82 F2** 40 47N 122 6W
Pitarpunga, L., *Australia* **63 E3** 34 24 S 143 30 E
Pitcairn I., *Pac. Oc.* **65 K14** 25 5S 130 5W
Pite älv →, *Sweden* **8 D19** 65 20N 21 25 E
Piteå, *Sweden* **8 D19** 65 20N 21 25 E
Piteşti, *Romania* **17 F13** 44 52N 24 54 E
Pithapuram, *India* **41 L13** 17 10N 82 15 E
Pithara, *Australia* **61 F2** 30 20 S 116 35 E
Pithoragarh, *India* **43 E9** 29 35N 80 13 E
Pithoro, *Pakistan* **42 G3** 25 31N 69 23 E
Pitlochry, *U.K.* **12 E5** 56 42N 3 44W

Posse

Posse, Brazil 93 F9 14 4S 46 18W
Possession Is., Antarctica 5 D11 72 4S 172 0 E
Possum Kingdom L., U.S.A. 81 J5 32 52N 98 26W
Post, U.S.A. 81 J4 33 12N 101 23W
Post Falls, U.S.A. 82 C5 47 43N 116 57W
Postavy = Pastavy, Belarus 9 J22 55 4N 26 50 E
Poste-de-la-Baleine = Kuujjuarapik, Canada 70 A4 55 20N 77 35W
Postmasburg, S. Africa 56 D3 28 18S 23 5 E
Postojna, Slovenia 16 F8 45 46N 14 12 E
Poston, U.S.A. 85 M12 34 0N 114 24W
Postville, Canada 71 B8 54 54N 59 47W
Potchefstroom, S. Africa 56 D4 26 41S 27 7 E
Poteau, U.S.A. 81 H7 35 3N 94 37W
Poteet, U.S.A. 81 L5 29 2N 98 35W
Potenza, Italy 20 D6 40 38N 15 48 E
Poteriteri, L., N.Z. 59 M1 46 5S 167 10 E
Potgietersrus, S. Africa 57 C4 24 10S 28 55 E
Poti, Georgia 25 F7 42 10N 41 38 E
Potiskum, Nigeria 51 F8 11 39N 11 2 E
Potomac →, U.S.A. 76 G7 38 0N 76 23W
Potosí, Bolivia 92 G5 19 38S 65 50W
Potosi Mt., U.S.A. 85 K11 35 57N 115 29W
Pototan, Phil. 37 B6 10 54N 122 38 E
Potrerillos, Chile 94 B2 26 30S 69 30W
Potsdam, Germany 16 B7 52 25N 13 4 E
Potsdam, U.S.A. 79 B10 44 40N 74 59W
Pottersville, U.S.A. 79 C11 43 43N 73 50W
Pottstown, U.S.A. 79 F9 40 15N 75 39W
Pottsville, U.S.A. 79 F8 40 41N 76 12W
Pottuvil, Sri Lanka 40 R12 6 55N 81 50 E
Pouce Coupé, Canada 72 B4 55 40N 120 10W
Poughkeepsie, U.S.A. 79 E11 41 42N 73 56W
Poulaphouca Res., Ireland 13 C5 53 8N 6 30W
Poulsbo, U.S.A. 84 C4 47 44N 122 39W
Poultney, U.S.A. 79 C11 43 31N 73 14W
Poulton-le-Fylde, U.K. 10 D5 53 51N 2 58W
Pouso Alegre, Brazil 95 A6 22 14S 45 57W
Pouthisat, Cambodia 38 F4 12 34N 103 50 E
Považská Bystrica, Slovak Rep. 17 D10 49 8N 18 27 E
Povenets, Russia 24 B5 62 50N 34 50 E
Poverty B., N.Z. 59 H7 38 43S 178 2 E
Póvoa de Varzim, Portugal 19 B1 41 25N 8 46W
Povungnituk = Puvirnituq, Canada 69 B12 60 2N 77 10W
Powassan, Canada 70 C4 46 5N 79 25W
Poway, U.S.A. 85 N9 32 58N 117 2W
Powder →, U.S.A. 80 B2 46 45N 105 26W
Powder River, U.S.A. 82 E10 43 2N 106 59W
Powell, U.S.A. 82 D9 44 45N 108 46W
Powell, L., U.S.A. 83 H8 36 57N 111 29W
Powell River, Canada 72 D4 49 50N 124 35W
Powers, U.S.A. 76 C2 45 41N 87 32W
Powys □, U.K. 11 E4 52 20N 3 20W
Poyang Hu, China 33 D6 29 5N 116 20 E
Poyarkovo, Russia 27 E13 49 36N 128 41 E
Poza Rica, Mexico 87 C5 20 33N 97 27W
Požarevac, Serbia, Yug. 21 B9 44 35N 21 18 E
Poznań, Poland 17 B9 52 25N 16 55 E
Pozo, U.S.A. 85 K6 35 20N 120 24W
Pozo Almonte, Chile 92 H5 20 10S 69 50W
Pozo Colorado, Paraguay 94 A4 23 30S 58 45W
Pozoblanco, Spain 19 C3 38 23N 4 51W
Pozzuoli, Italy 20 D6 40 49N 14 7 E
Prachin Buri, Thailand 38 F3 14 0N 101 25 E
Prachuap Khiri Khan, Thailand 39 G2 11 49N 99 48 E
Prado, Brazil 93 G11 17 20S 39 13W
Prague = Praha, Czech Rep. 16 C8 50 5N 14 22 E
Praha, Czech Rep. 16 C8 50 5N 14 22 E
Praia, C. Verde Is. 49 E1 14 55N 23 30W
Prainha, Amazonas, Brazil 92 E6 7 10S 60 30W
Prainha, Pará, Brazil 93 D8 1 45S 53 30W
Prairie, Australia 62 C3 20 50S 144 35 E
Prairie City, U.S.A. 82 D4 44 28N 118 43W
Prairie Dog Town Fork →, U.S.A. 81 H5 34 30N 99 23W
Prairie du Chien, U.S.A. 80 D9 43 3N 91 9W
Prairies, L. of the, Canada 73 C8 51 16N 101 32W
Pran Buri, Thailand 38 F2 12 23N 99 55 E
Prapat, Indonesia 36 D1 2 41N 98 58 E
Prasonísi, Ákra, Greece 23 D9 35 42N 27 46 E
Prata, Brazil 93 G9 19 25S 48 54W
Pratabpur, India 43 H10 23 28N 83 15 E
Pratapgarh, Raj., India 42 G6 24 2N 74 40 E
Pratapgarh, Ut. P., India 43 G9 25 56N 81 59 E
Prato, Italy 20 C4 43 53N 11 6 E
Pratt, U.S.A. 81 G5 37 39N 98 44W
Prattville, U.S.A. 77 J2 32 28N 86 29W
Pravia, Spain 19 A2 43 30N 6 12W
Praya, Indonesia 36 F5 8 39S 116 17 E
Precordillera, Argentina 94 C2 30 0S 69 1W
Preeceville, Canada 73 C8 51 57N 102 40W
Preiļi, Latvia 9 H22 56 18N 26 43 E
Premont, U.S.A. 81 M5 27 22N 98 7W
Prentice, U.S.A. 80 C9 45 33N 90 17W
Preobrazheniye, Russia 30 C6 42 54N 133 54 E
Preparis North Channel, Ind. Oc. 41 M18 15 12N 93 40 E
Preparis South Channel, Ind. Oc. 41 M18 14 36N 93 40 E
Přerov, Czech Rep. 17 D9 49 28N 17 27 E
Prescott, Canada 79 B9 44 45N 75 30W
Prescott, Ariz., U.S.A. 83 J7 34 33N 112 28W
Prescott, Ark., U.S.A. 81 J8 33 48N 93 23W
Prescott Valley, U.S.A. 83 J7 34 40N 112 18W
Preservation Inlet, N.Z. 59 M1 46 8S 166 35 E
Presho, U.S.A. 80 D4 43 54N 100 3W
Presidencia de la Plaza, Argentina 94 B4 27 0S 59 50W
Presidencia Roque Saenz Peña, Argentina 94 B3 26 45S 60 30W
Presidente Epitácio, Brazil 93 H8 21 56S 52 6W
Presidente Hayes □, Paraguay 94 A4 24 0S 59 0W
Presidente Prudente, Brazil 95 A5 22 5S 51 25W
Presidio, Mexico 86 B4 29 29N 104 23W
Presidio, U.S.A. 81 L2 29 34N 104 22W
Prešov, Slovak Rep. 17 D11 49 0N 21 15 E
Prespa, L. = Prespansko Jezero, Macedonia 21 D9 40 55N 21 0 E
Prespansko Jezero, Macedonia 21 D9 40 55N 21 0 E
Presque I., U.S.A. 78 D4 42 9N 80 6W
Presque Isle, U.S.A. 77 B12 46 41N 68 1W
Prestatyn, U.K. 10 D4 53 20N 3 24W
Presteigne, U.K. 11 E5 52 17N 3 0W
Preston, Canada 78 C4 43 23N 80 21W
Preston, U.K. 10 D5 53 46N 2 42W
Preston, Idaho, U.S.A. 82 E8 42 6N 111 53W
Preston, Minn., U.S.A. 80 D8 43 40N 92 5W
Preston, C., Australia 60 D2 20 51S 116 12 E
Prestonburg, U.S.A. 76 G4 37 39N 82 46W
Prestwick, U.K. 12 F4 55 29N 4 37W
Pretoria, S. Africa 57 D4 25 44S 28 12 E
Préveza, Greece 21 E9 38 57N 20 47 E
Prey Veng, Cambodia 39 G5 11 35N 105 29 E
Pribilof Is., U.S.A. 68 C2 57 0N 170 0W
Příbram, Czech Rep. 16 D8 49 41N 14 2 E
Price, U.S.A. 82 G8 39 36N 110 49W
Price I., Canada 72 C3 52 23N 128 41W
Prichard, U.S.A. 77 K1 30 44N 88 5W
Priekule, Latvia 9 H19 56 26N 21 35 E
Prienai, Lithuania 9 J20 54 38N 23 57 E
Prieska, S. Africa 56 D3 29 40S 22 42 E
Priest L., U.S.A. 82 B5 48 35N 116 52W
Priest River, U.S.A. 82 B5 48 10N 116 54W
Priest Valley, U.S.A. 84 J6 36 10N 120 39W
Prievidza, Slovak Rep. 17 D10 48 46N 18 36 E
Prikaspiyskaya Nizmennost = Caspian Depression, Eurasia 25 E8 47 0N 48 0 E
Prilep, Macedonia 21 D9 41 21N 21 32 E
Priluki = Pryluky, Ukraine 25 D5 50 30N 32 24 E
Prime Seal I., Australia 62 G4 40 3S 147 43 E
Primrose L., Canada 73 C7 54 55N 109 45W
Prince Albert, Canada 73 C7 53 15N 105 50W
Prince Albert, S. Africa 56 E3 33 12S 22 2 E
Prince Albert Mts., Antarctica 5 D11 76 0S 161 30 E
Prince Albert Nat. Park, Canada 73 C7 54 0N 106 25W
Prince Albert Pen., Canada 68 A8 72 30N 116 0W
Prince Albert Sd., Canada 68 A8 70 25N 115 0W
Prince Alfred, C., Canada 4 B1 74 20N 124 40W
Prince Charles I., Canada 69 B12 67 47N 76 12W
Prince Charles Mts., Antarctica 5 D6 72 0S 67 0 E
Prince Edward I. □, Canada 71 C7 46 20N 63 20W
Prince Edward Is., Ind. Oc. 3 G11 46 35S 38 0 E
Prince Edward Pt., Canada 78 C8 43 56N 76 52W
Prince George, Canada 72 C4 53 55N 122 50W
Prince of Wales, C., U.S.A. 66 C3 65 36N 168 5W
Prince of Wales I., Australia 62 A3 10 40S 142 10 E
Prince of Wales I., Canada 68 A10 73 0N 99 0W
Prince of Wales I., U.S.A. 68 C6 55 47N 132 50W
Prince Patrick I., Canada 4 B2 77 0N 120 0W
Prince Regent Inlet, Canada 4 B3 73 0N 90 0W
Prince Rupert, Canada 72 C2 54 20N 130 20W
Princess Charlotte B., Australia 62 A3 14 25S 144 0 E
Princess May Ranges, Australia 60 C4 15 30S 125 30 E
Princess Royal I., Canada 72 C3 53 0N 128 40W
Princeton, Canada 72 D4 49 27N 120 30W
Princeton, Calif., U.S.A. 84 F4 39 24N 122 1W
Princeton, Ill., U.S.A. 80 E10 41 23N 89 28W
Princeton, Ind., U.S.A. 76 F2 38 21N 87 34W
Princeton, Ky., U.S.A. 76 G2 37 7N 87 53W
Princeton, Mo., U.S.A. 80 E8 40 24N 93 35W
Princeton, N.J., U.S.A. 79 F10 40 21N 74 39W
Princeton, W. Va., U.S.A. 76 G5 37 22N 81 6W
Principe, I. de, Atl. Oc. 48 F4 1 37N 7 27 E
Principe da Beira, Brazil 92 F6 12 20S 64 30W
Prineville, U.S.A. 82 D3 44 18N 120 51W
Prins Harald Kyst, Antarctica 5 D4 70 0S 35 1 E
Prinsesse Astrid Kyst, Antarctica 5 D3 70 45S 12 30 E
Prinsesse Ragnhild Kyst, Antarctica 5 D4 70 15S 27 30 E
Prinzapolca, Nic. 88 D3 13 20N 83 35W
Priozersk, Russia 24 B5 61 2N 30 7 E
Pripet = Prypyat →, Europe 17 C16 51 20N 30 15 E
Pripet Marshes, Europe 17 B15 52 10N 28 10 E
Pripyat Marshes = Pripet Marshes, Europe 17 B15 52 10N 28 10 E
Pripyats = Prypyat →, Europe 17 C16 51 20N 30 15 E
Priština, Yugoslavia 21 C9 42 40N 21 13 E
Privas, France 18 D6 44 45N 4 37 E
Privolzhskaya Vozvyshennost, Russia 25 D8 51 0N 46 0 E
Prizren, Yugoslavia 21 C9 42 13N 20 45 E
Probolinggo, Indonesia 37 G15 7 46S 113 13 E
Proctor, U.S.A. 79 C11 43 40N 73 2W
Proddatur, India 40 M11 14 45N 78 30 E
Prodhromos, Cyprus 23 E11 34 57N 32 50 E
Profitis Ilias, Greece 23 C9 36 17N 27 56 E
Profondeville, Belgium 15 D4 50 23N 4 52 E
Progreso, Mexico 87 C7 21 20N 89 40W
Progreso, Yucatán, Mexico 86 B4 21 17N 89 40W
Prokopyevsk, Russia 26 D9 54 0N 86 45 E
Prokuplje, Serbia, Yug. 21 C9 43 16N 21 36 E
Prome = Pyè, Burma 41 K19 18 49N 95 13 E
Prophet →, Canada 72 B4 58 48N 122 40W
Prophet River, Canada 72 B4 58 6N 122 43W
Propriá, Brazil 93 F11 10 13S 36 51W
Proserpine, Australia 62 C4 20 21S 148 36 E
Prosna →, Poland 17 B9 52 6N 17 44 E
Prospect, U.S.A. 79 C9 43 18N 75 9W
Prosser, U.S.A. 82 C4 46 12N 119 46W
Prostějov, Czech Rep. 17 D9 49 30N 17 9 E
Proston, Australia 63 D5 26 8S 151 32 E
Provence, France 18 E6 43 40N 5 46 E
Providence, Ky., U.S.A. 76 G2 37 24N 87 46W
Providence, R.I., U.S.A. 79 E13 41 49N 71 24W
Providence Bay, Canada 70 C3 45 41N 82 15W
Providence Mts., U.S.A. 85 K11 35 10N 115 15W
Providencia, I. de, Colombia 88 D3 13 25N 81 26W
Provideniya, Russia 27 C19 64 23N 173 18W
Provins, France 18 B5 48 33N 3 15 E
Provo, U.S.A. 82 F8 40 14N 111 39W
Provost, Canada 73 C6 52 25N 110 20W
Prudhoe Bay, U.S.A. 68 A5 70 18N 148 22W
Prudhoe I., Australia 62 C4 21 19S 149 41 E
Prud'homme, Canada 73 C7 52 20N 105 54W
Pruszków, Poland 17 B11 52 9N 20 49 E
Prut →, Romania 17 F15 45 28N 28 10 E
Pruzhany, Belarus 17 B13 52 33N 24 28 E
Prydz B., Antarctica 5 C6 69 0S 74 0 E
Pryluky, Ukraine 25 D5 50 30N 32 24 E
Pryor, U.S.A. 81 G7 36 19N 95 19W
Prypyat →, Europe 17 C16 51 20N 30 15 E
Przemyśl, Poland 17 D12 49 50N 22 45 E
Przhevalsk, Kyrgyzstan 26 E8 42 30N 78 20 E
Psará, Greece 21 E11 38 37N 25 38 E
Psíra, Greece 23 D7 35 12N 25 52 E
Pskov, Russia 24 C4 57 50N 28 25 E
Pskovskoye, Ozero, Russia 9 H22 58 0N 27 58 E
Ptich = Ptsich →, Belarus 17 B15 52 9N 28 52 E
Ptolemaís, Greece 21 D9 40 30N 21 43 E
Ptsich →, Belarus 17 B15 52 9N 28 52 E
Pu Xian, China 34 F6 36 24N 111 6 E
Pua, Thailand 38 C3 19 11N 100 55 E
Puán, Argentina 94 D3 37 30S 62 45W
Puan, S. Korea 35 G14 35 44N 126 44 E
Pucallpa, Peru 92 E4 8 25S 74 30W
Pudasjärvi, Finland 8 D22 65 23N 26 53 E
Pudozh, Russia 24 B6 61 48N 36 32 E
Pudukkottai, India 40 P11 10 28N 78 47 E
Puebla, Mexico 87 D5 19 3N 98 12W
Puebla □, Mexico 87 D5 18 30N 98 0W
Pueblo, U.S.A. 80 F2 38 16N 104 37W
Pueblo Hundido, Chile 94 B1 26 20S 70 5W
Puelches, Argentina 94 D2 38 5S 65 51W
Puelén, Argentina 94 D2 37 32S 67 38W
Puente Alto, Chile 94 C1 33 32S 70 35W
Puente-Genil, Spain 19 D3 37 22N 4 47W
Puerco →, U.S.A. 83 J10 34 22N 107 50W
Puerto, Canary Is. 22 F2 28 5N 17 20W
Puerto Aisén, Chile 96 F2 45 27S 73 0W
Puerto Ángel, Mexico 87 D5 15 40N 96 29W
Puerto Arista, Mexico 87 D6 15 56N 93 48W
Puerto Armuelles, Panama 88 E3 8 20N 82 51W
Puerto Ayacucho, Venezuela 92 B5 5 40N 67 35W
Puerto Barrios, Guatemala 88 C2 15 40N 88 32W
Puerto Bermejo, Argentina 94 B4 26 55S 58 34W
Puerto Bermúdez, Peru 92 F4 10 20S 74 58W
Puerto Bolívar, Ecuador 92 D3 3 19S 79 55W
Puerto Cabello, Venezuela 92 A5 10 28N 68 1W
Puerto Cabezas, Nic. 88 D3 14 0N 83 30W
Puerto Cabo Gracias á Dios, Nic. 88 D3 15 0N 83 10W
Puerto Carreño, Colombia 92 B5 6 12N 67 22W
Puerto Castilla, Honduras 88 C2 16 0N 86 0W
Puerto Chicama, Peru 92 E3 7 45S 79 20W
Puerto Coig, Argentina 96 G3 50 54S 69 15W
Puerto Cortés, Costa Rica 88 E3 8 55N 84 0W
Puerto Cortés, Honduras 88 C2 15 51N 88 0W
Puerto Cumarebo, Venezuela 92 A5 11 29N 69 30W
Puerto de Alcudia = Port d'Alcúdia, Spain 22 B10 39 50N 3 7 E
Puerto de Andraitx, Spain 22 B9 39 32N 2 23 E
Puerto de Cabrera, Spain 22 B9 39 8N 2 56 E
Puerto de Gran Tarajal, Canary Is. 22 F5 28 13N 14 1W
Puerto de la Cruz, Canary Is. 22 F3 28 24N 16 32W
Puerto de Pozo Negro, Canary Is. 22 F6 28 19N 13 55W
Puerto de Sóller = Port de Sóller, Spain 22 B9 39 48N 2 42 E
Puerto del Carmen, Canary Is. 22 F6 28 55N 13 38W
Puerto del Rosario, Canary Is. 22 F6 28 30N 13 52W
Puerto Deseado, Argentina 96 F3 47 55S 66 0W
Puerto Escondido, Mexico 87 D5 15 50N 97 3W
Puerto Heath, Bolivia 92 F5 12 34S 68 39W
Puerto Inírida, Colombia 92 C5 3 53N 67 52W
Puerto Juárez, Mexico 87 C7 21 11N 86 49W
Puerto La Cruz, Venezuela 92 A6 10 13N 64 38W
Puerto Leguízamo, Colombia 92 D4 0 12S 74 46W
Puerto Limón, Colombia 92 C4 3 23N 73 30W
Puerto Lobos, Argentina 96 E3 42 0S 65 3W
Puerto Madryn, Argentina 96 E3 42 48S 65 4W
Puerto Maldonado, Peru 92 F5 12 30S 69 10W
Puerto Manotí, Cuba 88 B4 21 22N 76 50W
Puerto Montt, Chile 96 E2 41 28S 73 0W
Puerto Morazán, Nic. 88 D2 12 51N 87 11W
Puerto Morelos, Mexico 87 C7 20 49N 86 52W
Puerto Natales, Chile 96 G2 51 45S 72 15W
Puerto Padre, Cuba 88 B4 21 13N 76 35W
Puerto Páez, Venezuela 92 B5 6 13N 67 28W
Puerto Peñasco, Mexico 86 A2 31 20N 113 33W
Puerto Pinasco, Paraguay 94 A4 22 36S 57 50W
Puerto Plata, Dom. Rep. 89 C5 19 48N 70 45W
Puerto Pollensa = Port de Pollença, Spain 22 B10 39 54N 3 4 E
Puerto Princesa, Phil. 37 C5 9 46N 118 45 E
Puerto Quepos, Costa Rica 88 E3 9 29N 84 6W
Puerto Rico, Canary Is. 22 G4 27 47N 15 42W
Puerto Rico ■, W. Indies 89 C6 18 15N 66 45W
Puerto Rico Trench, Atl. Oc. 89 C6 19 50N 66 0W
Puerto San Julián, Argentina 96 F3 49 18S 67 43W
Puerto Sastre, Paraguay 94 A4 22 2S 57 55W
Puerto Suárez, Bolivia 92 G7 18 58S 57 52W
Puerto Vallarta, Mexico 86 C3 20 36N 105 15W
Puerto Wilches, Colombia 92 B4 7 21N 73 54W
Puertollano, Spain 19 C3 38 43N 4 7W
Pueyrredón, L., Argentina 96 F2 47 20S 72 0W
Puffin I., Ireland 13 E1 51 50N 10 24W
Pugachev, Russia 24 D8 52 0N 48 49 E
Pugal, India 42 E5 28 30N 72 48 E
Puge, Tanzania 54 C3 4 45S 33 11 E
Puget Sound, U.S.A. 82 C2 47 50N 122 30W
Pugŏdong, N. Korea 35 C16 42 5N 130 0 E
Pugu, Tanzania 54 D4 6 55S 39 4 E
Pūgūnzi, Iran 45 E8 25 49N 59 10 E
Puig Major, Spain 22 B9 39 48N 2 47 E
Puigcerdà, Spain 19 A6 42 24N 1 50 E
Puigpunyent, Spain 22 B9 39 38N 2 32 E
Pujon-chŏsuji, N. Korea 35 D14 40 35N 127 35 E
Pukaki L., N.Z. 59 L3 44 4S 170 1 E
Pukapuka, Cook Is. 65 J11 10 53S 165 49W
Pukaskwa Nat. Park, Canada 70 C2 48 20N 86 0W
Pukatawagan, Canada 73 B8 55 45N 101 20W
Pukchin, N. Korea 35 D13 40 12N 125 45 E
Pukch'ŏng, N. Korea 35 D15 40 14N 128 10 E
Pukekohe, N.Z. 59 G5 37 12S 174 55 E
Pukhrayan, India 43 F8 26 14N 79 51 E
Pula, Croatia 16 F7 44 54N 13 57 E
Pulacayo, Bolivia 92 H5 20 25S 66 41W
Pulandian, China 35 E11 39 25N 121 58 E
Pularumpi, Australia 60 B5 11 24S 130 26
Pulaski, N.Y., U.S.A. 79 C8 43 34N 76 8W
Pulaski, Tenn., U.S.A. 77 H2 35 12N 87 2W
Pulaski, Va., U.S.A. 76 G5 37 3N 80 47W
Pulau →, Indonesia 37 F9 5 50S 138 15
Puławy, Poland 17 C11 51 23N 21 59
Pulga, U.S.A. 84 F5 39 48N 121 29W
Pulicat L., India 40 N12 13 40N 80 15
Pullman, U.S.A. 82 C5 46 44N 117 10W
Pulo-Anna, Pac. Oc. 37 D8 4 30N 132 5
Pulog, Phil. 37 A6 16 40N 120 50
Pułtusk, Poland 17 B11 52 43N 21 6
Pumlumon Fawr, U.K. 11 E4 52 28N 3 46W
Puná, I., Ecuador 92 D2 2 55S 80 5W
Punakha, Bhutan 41 F16 27 42N 89 52
Punasar, India 42 F5 27 6N 73 6
Punata, Bolivia 92 G5 17 32S 65 50W
Punch, India 43 C6 33 48N 74 4
Punch →, Pakistan 42 C5 33 12N 73 40
Pune, India 40 K8 18 29N 73 57
P'ungsan, N. Korea 35 D15 40 50N 128 9
Pungue, Ponte de, Mozam. 55 F3 19 0S 34 0
Punjab □, India 42 D7 31 0N 76 0
Punjab □, Pakistan 42 E6 32 0N 74 30
Puno, Peru 92 G4 15 55S 70 3W
Punpun →, India 43 G11 25 31N 85 18
Punta Alta, Argentina 96 D4 38 53S 62 4W
Punta Arenas, Chile 96 G2 53 10S 71 0W
Punta de Díaz, Chile 94 B1 28 0S 70 45W
Punta Gorda, Belize 87 D7 16 10N 88 45W
Punta Gorda, U.S.A. 77 M5 26 56N 82 3W
Punta Prieta, Mexico 86 B2 28 58N 114 17W
Punta Prima, Spain 22 B11 39 48N 4 16
Puntarenas, Costa Rica 88 E3 10 0N 84 50W
Punto Fijo, Venezuela 92 A4 11 50N 70 13W
Punxsatawney, U.S.A. 78 F6 40 57N 78 59W
Puquio, Peru 92 F4 14 45S 74 10W
Pur →, Russia 26 C8 67 31N 77 55
Purace, Vol., Colombia 92 C3 2 21N 76 23W
Puralia = Puruliya, India 43 H12 23 17N 86 24
Puranpur, India 43 E9 28 31N 80 9
Purbeck, Isle of, U.K. 11 G6 50 39N 1 59W
Purcell, U.S.A. 81 H6 35 1N 97 22W
Purcell Mts., Canada 72 D5 49 55N 116 15W
Puri, India 41 K14 19 50N 85 58
Purmerend, Neths. 15 B4 52 32N 4 58
Purnia, India 43 G12 25 45N 87 31
Pursat = Pouthisat, Cambodia 38 F4 12 34N 103 50
Purukcahu, Indonesia 36 E4 0 35S 114 35
Puruliya, India 43 H12 23 17N 86 24
Purus →, Brazil 92 D6 3 42S 61 28W
Purvis, U.S.A. 81 K10 31 9N 89 25W
Purwa, India 43 F9 26 28N 80 47
Purwakarta, Indonesia 37 G12 6 35S 107 29
Purwodadi, Indonesia 37 G14 7 7S 110 55
Purwokerto, Indonesia 37 G13 7 25S 109 14
Puryŏng, N. Korea 35 C15 42 5N 129 43
Pusa, India 43 G11 25 59N 85 41
Pusan, S. Korea 35 G15 35 5N 129 0
Pushkino, Russia 25 D8 51 16N 47 0
Putahow L., Canada 73 B8 59 54N 100 40W
Putao, Burma 41 F20 27 28N 97 30
Putaruru, N.Z. 59 H5 38 2S 175 50
Puthein Myit →, Burma 41 M19 15 56N 94 18
Putignano, Italy 20 D7 40 51N 17 7
Puting, Tanjung, Indonesia 36 E4 3 31S 111 46
Putnam, U.S.A. 79 E13 41 55N 71 55W
Putorana, Gory, Russia 27 C10 69 0N 95 0
Puttalam, Sri Lanka 40 Q11 8 1N 79 55
Puttgarden, Germany 16 A6 54 30N 11 10
Putumayo →, S. Amer. 92 D5 3 7S 67 58W
Putussibau, Indonesia 36 D4 0 50N 112 56
Puvirnituq, Canada 69 B12 60 2N 77 10W
Puy-de-Dôme, France 18 D5 45 46N 2 57
Puyallup, U.S.A. 84 C4 47 12N 122 18W
Puyang, China 34 G8 35 40N 115 1
Pūzeh Rīg, Iran 45 E8 27 20N 58 40
Pwani □, Tanzania 54 D4 7 0S 39 0
Pweto, Dem. Rep. of the Congo 55 D2 8 25S 28 51
Pwllheli, U.K. 10 E3 52 53N 4 25W
Pya-ozero, Russia 24 A5 66 5N 30 58
Pyapon, Burma 41 L19 16 20N 95 40
Pyasina →, Russia 27 B9 73 30N 87 0
Pyatigorsk, Russia 25 F7 44 2N 43 6
Pyè, Burma 41 K19 18 49N 95 13
Pyetrikaw, Belarus 17 B15 52 11N 28 29
Pyhäjoki, Finland 8 D21 64 28N 24 14
Pyinmana, Burma 41 K20 19 45N 96 12
Pyla, C., Cyprus 23 E12 34 56N 33 51
Pymatuning Reservoir, U.S.A. 78 E4 41 30N 80 28W
Pyŏktong, N. Korea 35 D13 40 50N 125 50
Pyŏnggang, N. Korea 35 E14 38 24N 127 17
P'yŏngt'aek, S. Korea 35 F14 37 1N 127 4
P'yŏngyang, N. Korea 35 E13 39 0N 125 30
Pyote, U.S.A. 81 K3 31 32N 103 8W
Pyramid L., U.S.A. 82 G4 40 1N 119 35W
Pyramid Pk., U.S.A. 85 J10 36 25N 116 37W
Pyrénées, Europe 18 E4 42 45N 0 18
Pyu, Burma 41 K20 18 30N 96 28

Q

Qaanaaq = Thule, Greenland 4 B4 77 40N 69 0W
Qachasnek, S. Africa 57 E4 30 6S 28 42
Qa'el Jafr, Jordan 47 E5 30 20N 36 25
Qa'emābād, Iran 45 D9 31 44N 60 2
Qā'emshahr, Iran 45 B7 36 30N 52 53
Qagan Nur, China 34 C8 43 30N 114 55
Qahar Youyi Zhongqi, China 34 D7 41 12N 112 40
Qahremānshahr = Bākhtarān, Iran 44 C5 34 23N 47 0
Qaidam Pendi, China 32 C4 37 0N 95 0
Qajarīyeh, Iran 45 D6 31 1N 48 22
Qala, Ras il, Malta 23 C1 36 1N 14 20
Qala-i-Jadid = Spīn Búldak, Afghan. 42 D2 31 1N 66 25
Qala Viala, Pakistan 42 D2 30 49N 67 17
Qala Yangi, Afghan. 42 B2 34 20N 66 30

Rasca, Pta. de la

Rasca, Pta. de la, *Canary Is.* **22 G3** 27 59N 16 41W
Raseiniai, *Lithuania* **9 J20** 55 25N 23 5 E
Rashmi, *India* **42 G6** 25 4N 74 22 E
Rasht, *Iran* **45 B6** 37 20N 49 40 E
Rasi Salai, *Thailand* **38 E5** 15 20N 104 9 E
Rason L., *Australia* **61 E3** 28 45S 124 25 E
Rasra, *India* **43 G10** 25 50N 83 50 E
Rasul, *Pakistan* **42 C5** 32 42N 73 34 E
Rat Buri, *Thailand* **38 F2** 13 30N 99 54 E
Rat Islands, *U.S.A.* **68 C1** 52 0N 178 0 E
Rat L., *Canada* **73 B9** 56 10N 99 40W
Ratangarh, *India* **42 E6** 28 5N 74 35 E
Raţāwī, *Iraq* **44 D5** 30 38N 47 13 E
Ratcatchers L., *Australia* **63 E3** 32 38S 143 10 E
Rath, *India* **43 G8** 25 36N 79 37 E
Rath Luirc, *Ireland* **13 D3** 52 21N 8 40W
Rathdrum, *Ireland* **13 D5** 52 56N 6 14W
Rathenow, *Germany* **16 B7** 52 37N 12 19 E
Rathkeale, *Ireland* **13 D3** 52 32N 8 56W
Rathlin I., *U.K.* **13 A5** 55 18N 6 14W
Rathmelton, *Ireland* **13 A4** 55 2N 7 38W
Ratibor = Racibórz, *Poland* **17 C10** 50 7N 18 18 E
Ratlam, *India* **42 H6** 23 20N 75 0 E
Ratnagiri, *India* **40 L8** 16 57N 73 18 E
Ratodero, *Pakistan* **42 F3** 27 48N 68 18 E
Raton, *U.S.A.* **81 G2** 36 54N 104 24W
Rattaphum, *Thailand* **39 J3** 7 8N 100 16 E
Rattray Hd., *U.K.* **12 D7** 57 38N 1 50W
Ratz, Mt., *Canada* **72 B2** 57 23N 132 12W
Raub, *Malaysia* **39 L3** 3 47N 101 52 E
Rauch, *Argentina* **94 D4** 36 45S 59 5W
Raudales de Malpaso, *Mexico* **87 D6** 17 30N 23 30W
Raufarhöfn, *Iceland* **8 C6** 66 27N 15 57W
Raufoss, *Norway* **9 F14** 60 44N 10 37 E
Raukumara Ra., *N.Z.* **59 H6** 38 5S 177 55 E
Rauma, *Finland* **9 F19** 61 10N 21 30 E
Raurkela, *India* **43 H11** 22 14N 84 50 E
Rausu-Dake, *Japan* **30 B12** 44 4N 145 7 E
Rava-Ruska, *Poland* **17 C12** 50 15N 23 42 E
Rava Russkaya = Rava-Ruska, *Poland* **17 C12** 50 15N 23 42 E
Ravalli, *U.S.A.* **82 C6** 47 17N 114 11W
Ravānsar, *Iran* **44 C5** 34 43N 46 40 E
Rāvar, *Iran* **45 D8** 31 20N 56 51 E
Ravena, *U.S.A.* **79 D11** 42 28N 73 49W
Ravenna, *Italy* **20 B5** 44 25N 12 12 E
Ravenna, *Nebr., U.S.A.* **80 E5** 41 1N 98 55W
Ravenna, *Ohio, U.S.A.* **78 E3** 41 9N 81 15W
Ravensburg, *Germany* **16 E5** 47 46N 9 36 E
Ravenshoe, *Australia* **62 B4** 17 37S 145 29 E
Ravensthorpe, *Australia* **61 F3** 33 35S 120 2 E
Ravenswood, *Australia* **62 C4** 20 6S 146 54 E
Ravenswood, *U.S.A.* **76 F5** 38 57N 81 46W
Ravi →, *Pakistan* **42 D4** 30 35N 71 49 E
Rawalpindi, *Pakistan* **42 C5** 33 38N 73 8 E
Rawāndūz, *Iraq* **44 B5** 36 40N 44 30 E
Rawang, *Malaysia* **39 L3** 3 20N 101 35 E
Rawene, *N.Z.* **59 F4** 35 25S 173 32 E
Rawlinna, *Australia* **61 F4** 30 58S 125 28 E
Rawlins, *U.S.A.* **82 F10** 41 47N 107 14W
Rawlinson Ra., *Australia* **61 D4** 24 40S 128 30 E
Rawson, *Argentina* **96 E3** 43 15S 65 5W
Raxaul, *India* **43 F11** 26 59N 84 51 E
Ray, *U.S.A.* **80 A3** 48 21N 103 10W
Ray, C., *Canada* **71 C8** 47 33N 59 15W
Rayadurg, *India* **40 M10** 14 40N 76 50 E
Rayagada, *India* **41 K13** 19 15N 83 20 E
Raychikhinsk, *Russia* **27 E13** 49 46N 129 25 E
Rāyen, *Iran* **45 D8** 29 34N 57 26 E
Rayleigh, *U.K.* **11 F8** 51 36N 0 37 E
Raymond, *Canada* **72 D6** 49 30N 112 35W
Raymond, *Calif., U.S.A.* **84 H7** 37 13N 119 54W
Raymond, *N.H., U.S.A.* **79 C13** 43 2N 71 11W
Raymond, *Wash., U.S.A.* **84 D3** 46 41N 123 44W
Raymond Terrace, *Australia* **63 E5** 32 45S 151 44 E
Raymondville, *U.S.A.* **81 M6** 26 29N 97 47W
Raymore, *Canada* **73 C8** 51 25N 104 31W
Rayna, *India* **43 H12** 23 5N 87 54 E
Rayón, *Mexico* **86 B2** 29 43N 110 35W
Rayong, *Thailand* **38 F3** 12 40N 101 20 E
Rayville, *U.S.A.* **81 J9** 32 29N 91 46W
Raz, Pte. du, *France* **18 C1** 48 2N 4 47W
Razan, *Iran* **45 C6** 35 23N 49 2 E
Razdel'naya = Rozdilna, *Ukraine* **17 E16** 46 50N 30 2 E
Razdolnoye, *Russia* **30 C5** 43 30N 131 52 E
Razeh, *Iran* **45 C6** 32 47N 48 9 E
Razgrad, *Bulgaria* **21 C12** 43 33N 26 34 E
Razim, Lacul, *Romania* **17 F15** 44 50N 29 0 E
Razmak, *Pakistan* **42 C3** 32 45N 69 50 E
Ré, Î. de, *France* **18 C3** 46 12N 1 30W
Reading, *U.K.* **11 F7** 51 27N 0 58W
Reading, *U.S.A.* **79 F9** 40 20N 75 56W
Reading □, *U.K.* **11 F7** 51 27N 0 58W
Realicó, *Argentina* **94 D3** 35 0S 64 15W
Ream, *Cambodia* **39 G4** 10 34N 103 39 E
Reata, *Mexico* **86 B4** 26 8N 101 5W
Reay Forest, *U.K.* **12 C4** 58 22N 4 55W
Rebi, *Indonesia* **37 F8** 6 23S 134 7 E
Rebiana, *Libya* **51 D10** 24 12N 22 10 E
Rebun-Tō, *Japan* **30 B10** 45 23N 141 2 E
Recherche, Arch. of the, *Australia* **61 F3** 34 15S 122 50 E
Rechna Doab, *Pakistan* **42 D5** 31 35N 73 30 E
Rechytsa, *Belarus* **17 B16** 52 21N 30 24 E
Recife, *Brazil* **93 E12** 8 0S 35 0W
Recklinghausen, *Germany* **15 C7** 51 37N 7 12 E
Reconquista, *Argentina* **94 B4** 29 10S 59 45W
Recreo, *Argentina* **94 B2** 29 25S 65 10W
Red →, *La., U.S.A.* **81 K9** 31 1N 91 45W
Red →, *N. Dak., U.S.A.* **68 C10** 49 0N 97 15W
Red Bank, *U.S.A.* **79 F10** 40 21N 74 5W
Red Bay, *Canada* **71 B8** 51 44N 56 25W
Red Bluff, *U.S.A.* **82 F2** 40 11N 122 15W
Red Bluff L., *U.S.A.* **81 K3** 31 54N 103 55W
Red Cliffs, *Australia* **63 E3** 34 19S 142 11 E
Red Cloud, *U.S.A.* **80 E5** 40 5N 98 32W
Red Creek, *U.S.A.* **79 C8** 43 14N 76 45W
Red Deer, *Canada* **72 C6** 52 20N 113 50W
Red Deer →, *Alta., Canada* **73 C7** 50 58N 110 0W
Red Deer →, *Man., Canada* **73 C8** 52 53N 101 1W
Red Deer L., *Canada* **73 C8** 52 55N 101 20W
Red Hook, *U.S.A.* **79 E11** 41 55N 73 53W
Red Indian L., *Canada* **71 C8** 48 35N 57 0W
Red L., *Canada* **73 C10** 51 3N 93 49W
Red Lake, *Canada* **73 C10** 51 3N 93 49W
Red Lake Falls, *U.S.A.* **80 B6** 47 53N 96 16W
Red Lake Road, *Canada* **73 C10** 49 59N 93 25W
Red Lodge, *U.S.A.* **82 D9** 45 11N 109 15W
Red Mountain, *U.S.A.* **85 K9** 35 37N 117 38W
Red Oak, *U.S.A.* **80 E7** 41 1N 95 14W
Red Rock, *Canada* **70 C2** 48 55N 88 15W
Red Rock, L., *U.S.A.* **80 E8** 41 22N 92 59W
Red Rocks Pt., *Australia* **61 F4** 32 13S 127 32 E
Red Sea, *Asia* **46 C2** 25 0N 36 0 E
Red Slate Mt., *U.S.A.* **84 H8** 37 31N 118 52W
Red Sucker L., *Canada* **70 B1** 54 9N 93 40W
Red Tower Pass = Turnu Roşu, P., *Romania* **17 F13** 45 33N 24 17 E
Red Wing, *U.S.A.* **80 C8** 44 34N 92 31W
Redang, *Malaysia* **36 C2** 5 49N 103 2 E
Redange, *Lux.* **15 E5** 49 46N 5 52 E
Redcar, *U.K.* **10 C6** 54 37N 1 4W
Redcar & Cleveland □, *U.K.* **10 C7** 54 29N 1 0W
Redcliff, *Canada* **73 C6** 50 10N 110 50W
Redcliffe, *Australia* **63 D5** 27 12S 153 0 E
Redcliffe, Mt., *Australia* **61 E3** 28 30S 121 30 E
Reddersburg, *S. Africa* **56 D4** 29 41S 26 10 E
Redding, *U.S.A.* **82 F2** 40 35N 122 24W
Redditch, *U.K.* **11 E6** 52 18N 1 55W
Redfield, *U.S.A.* **80 C5** 44 53N 98 31W
Redford, *U.S.A.* **79 B11** 44 38N 73 48W
Redlands, *U.S.A.* **85 M9** 34 4N 117 11W
Redmond, *Oreg., U.S.A.* **82 D3** 44 17N 121 11W
Redmond, *Wash., U.S.A.* **84 C4** 47 41N 122 7W
Redon, *France* **18 C2** 47 40N 2 6W
Redonda, *Antigua* **89 C7** 16 58N 62 19W
Redondela, *Spain* **19 A1** 42 15N 8 38W
Redondo Beach, *U.S.A.* **85 M8** 33 50N 118 23W
Redruth, *U.K.* **11 G2** 50 14N 5 14W
Redvers, *Canada* **73 D8** 49 35N 101 40W
Redwater, *Canada* **72 C6** 53 55N 113 6W
Redwood, *U.S.A.* **79 B9** 44 18N 75 48W
Redwood City, *U.S.A.* **84 H4** 37 30N 122 15W
Redwood Falls, *U.S.A.* **80 C7** 44 32N 95 7W
Redwood National Park, *U.S.A.* **82 F1** 41 40N 124 5W
Ree, L., *Ireland* **13 C3** 53 35N 8 0W
Reed, L., *Canada* **73 C8** 54 38N 100 30W
Reed City, *U.S.A.* **76 D3** 43 53N 85 31W
Reedley, *U.S.A.* **84 J7** 36 36N 119 27W
Reedsburg, *U.S.A.* **80 D9** 43 32N 90 0W
Reedsport, *U.S.A.* **82 E1** 43 42N 124 6W
Reedsville, *U.S.A.* **78 F7** 40 39N 77 35W
Reefton, *N.Z.* **59 K3** 42 6S 171 51 E
Reese →, *U.S.A.* **82 F5** 40 48N 117 4W
Refugio, *U.S.A.* **81 L6** 28 18N 97 17W
Regensburg, *Germany* **16 D7** 49 1N 12 6 E
Réggio di Calábria, *Italy* **20 E6** 38 6N 15 39 E
Réggio nell'Emília, *Italy* **20 B4** 44 43N 10 36 E
Reghin, *Romania* **17 E13** 46 46N 24 42 E
Regina, *Canada* **73 C8** 50 27N 104 35W
Regina Beach, *Canada* **73 C8** 50 47N 105 0W
Registro, *Brazil* **95 A6** 24 29S 47 49W
Rehar →, *India* **43 H10** 23 55N 82 40 E
Rehli, *India* **43 H8** 23 38N 79 5 E
Rehoboth, *Namibia* **56 C2** 23 15S 17 4 E
Rehovot, *Israel* **47 D3** 31 54N 34 48 E
Reichenbach, *Germany* **16 C7** 50 37N 12 17 E
Reid, *Australia* **61 F4** 30 49S 128 26 E
Reidsville, *U.S.A.* **77 G6** 36 21N 79 40W
Reigate, *U.K.* **11 F7** 51 14N 0 12W
Reims, *France* **18 B6** 49 15N 4 1 E
Reina Adelaida, Arch., *Chile* **96 G2** 52 20S 74 0W
Reindeer →, *Canada* **73 B8** 55 36N 103 11W
Reindeer I., *Canada* **73 C9** 52 30N 98 0W
Reindeer L., *Canada* **73 B8** 57 15N 102 15W
Reinga, C., *N.Z.* **59 F4** 34 25S 172 43 E
Reinosa, *Spain* **19 A3** 43 2N 4 15W
Reitz, *S. Africa* **57 D4** 27 48S 28 29 E
Reivilo, *S. Africa* **56 D3** 27 36S 24 8 E
Reliance, *Canada* **73 A7** 63 0N 109 20W
Remarkable, Mt., *Australia* **63 E2** 32 48S 138 10 E
Rembang, *Indonesia* **37 G14** 6 42S 111 21 E
Remedios, *Panama* **88 E3** 8 15N 81 50W
Remeshk, *Iran* **45 E8** 26 55N 58 50 E
Remich, *Lux.* **15 E6** 49 32N 6 22 E
Remscheid, *Germany* **15 C7** 51 11N 7 12 E
Ren Xian, *China* **34 F8** 37 8N 114 40 E
Rendsburg, *Germany* **16 A5** 54 17N 9 39 E
Renfrew, *Canada* **79 A8** 45 30N 76 40W
Renfrewshire □, *U.K.* **12 F4** 55 49N 4 38W
Rengat, *Indonesia* **36 E2** 0 30S 102 45 E
Rengo, *Chile* **94 C1** 34 24S 70 50W
Reni, *Ukraine* **17 F15** 45 28N 28 15 E
Renmark, *Australia* **63 E3** 34 11S 140 43 E
Rennell Sd., *Canada* **72 C2** 53 23N 132 35W
Renner Springs, *Australia* **62 B1** 18 20S 133 47 E
Rennes, *France* **18 B3** 48 7N 1 41W
Rennie L., *Canada* **73 A7** 61 32N 105 35W
Reno, *U.S.A.* **84 F7** 39 31N 119 48W
Reno →, *Italy* **20 B5** 44 38N 12 16 E
Renovo, *U.S.A.* **78 E7** 41 20N 77 45W
Renqiu, *China* **34 E9** 38 43N 116 5 E
Rensselaer, *Ind., U.S.A.* **76 E2** 40 57N 87 9W
Rensselaer, *N.Y., U.S.A.* **79 D11** 42 38N 73 45W
Rentería, *Spain* **19 A5** 43 19N 1 54W
Renton, *U.S.A.* **84 C4** 47 29N 122 12W
Reotipur, *India* **43 G10** 25 33N 83 45 E
Republic, *Mo., U.S.A.* **81 G8** 37 7N 93 29W
Republic, *Wash., U.S.A.* **82 B4** 48 39N 118 44W
Republican →, *U.S.A.* **80 F6** 39 4N 96 48W
Repulse Bay, *Canada* **69 B11** 66 30N 86 30W
Requena, *Peru* **92 E4** 5 5S 73 52W
Requena, *Spain* **19 C5** 39 30N 1 4W
Reşadiye = Datça, *Turkey* **21 F12** 36 46N 27 40 E
Reserve, *U.S.A.* **83 K9** 33 43N 108 45W
Resht = Rasht, *Iran* **45 B6** 37 20N 49 40 E
Resistencia, *Argentina* **94 B4** 27 30S 59 0W
Reşiţa, *Romania* **17 F11** 45 18N 21 53 E
Resolution I., *Canada* **69 B13** 61 30N 65 0W
Resolution I., *N.Z.* **59 L1** 45 40S 166 40 E
Ressano Garcia, *Mozam.* **57 D5** 25 25S 32 0 E
Reston, *Canada* **73 D8** 49 33N 101 6W
Retalhuleu, *Guatemala* **88 D1** 14 33N 91 46W
Retenue, L. de, *Dem. Rep. of the Congo* **55 E2** 11 0S 27 0 E
Retford, *U.K.* **10 D7** 53 19N 0 56W
Réthímnon, *Greece* **23 D6** 35 18N 24 30 E
Réthímnon □, *Greece* **23 D6** 35 23N 24 28 E
Reti, *Pakistan* **42 E3** 28 5N 69 48 E
Réunion ■, *Ind. Oc.* **49 J9** 21 0S 56 0 E
Reus, *Spain* **19 B6** 41 10N 1 5 E
Reutlingen, *Germany* **16 D5** 48 29N 9 12 E
Reval = Tallinn, *Estonia* **9 G21** 59 22N 24 48 E
Revda, *Russia* **24 C10** 56 48N 59 57 E
Revelganj, *India* **43 G11** 25 50N 84 40 E
Revelstoke, *Canada* **72 C5** 51 0N 118 10W
Reventazón, *Peru* **92 E2** 6 10S 80 58W
Revillagigedo, Is. de, *Pac. Oc.* **86 D2** 18 40N 112 0W
Revuè →, *Mozam.* **55 F3** 19 50S 34 0 E
Rewa, *India* **43 G9** 24 33N 81 25 E
Rewari, *India* **42 E7** 28 15N 76 40 E
Rexburg, *U.S.A.* **82 E8** 43 49N 111 47W
Rey, *Iran* **45 C6** 35 35N 51 25 E
Rey, I. del, *Panama* **88 E4** 8 20N 78 30W
Rey Malabo, *Eq. Guin.* **52 D1** 3 45N 8 50 E
Reyðarfjörður, *Iceland* **8 D6** 65 2N 14 13W
Reyes, Pt., *U.S.A.* **84 H3** 38 0N 123 0W
Reykjahlið, *Iceland* **8 D5** 65 40N 16 55W
Reykjanes, *Iceland* **8 E2** 63 48N 22 40W
Reykjavík, *Iceland* **8 D3** 64 10N 21 57W
Reynolds Ra., *Australia* **60 D5** 22 30S 133 0 E
Reynoldsville, *U.S.A.* **78 E6** 41 5N 78 58W
Reynosa, *Mexico* **87 B5** 26 5N 98 18W
Rēzekne, *Latvia* **9 H22** 56 30N 27 17 E
Rezvān, *Iran* **45 E8** 27 34N 56 6 E
Rhayader, *U.K.* **11 E4** 52 18N 3 29W
Rhein →, *Europe* **15 C6** 51 52N 6 2 E
Rhein-Main-Donau-Kanal, *Germany* **16 D6** 49 15N 11 15 E
Rheine, *Germany* **16 B4** 52 17N 7 26 E
Rheinland-Pfalz □, *Germany* **16 C4** 50 0N 7 0 E
Rhin = Rhein →, *Europe* **15 C6** 51 52N 6 2 E
Rhine = Rhein →, *Europe* **15 C6** 51 52N 6 2 E
Rhinebeck, *U.S.A.* **79 E11** 41 56N 73 55W
Rhineland-Palatinate = Rheinland-Pfalz □, *Germany* **16 C4** 50 0N 7 0 E
Rhinelander, *U.S.A.* **80 C10** 45 38N 89 25W
Rhinns Pt., *U.K.* **12 F2** 55 40N 6 29W
Rhino Camp, *Uganda* **54 B3** 3 0N 31 22 E
Rhir, Cap, *Morocco* **50 B4** 30 38N 9 54W
Rhode Island □, *U.S.A.* **79 E13** 41 40N 71 30W
Rhodes = Ródhos, *Greece* **23 C10** 36 15N 28 10 E
Rhodesia = Zimbabwe ■, *Africa* **55 F3** 19 0S 30 0 E
Rhodope Mts. = Rhodopi Planina, *Bulgaria* **21 D11** 41 40N 24 20 E
Rhodopi Planina, *Bulgaria* **21 D11** 41 40N 24 20 E
Rhön = Rhön, *Germany* **16 C5** 50 24N 9 58 E
Rhön, *Germany* **16 C5** 50 24N 9 58 E
Rhondda, *U.K.* **11 F4** 51 39N 3 31W
Rhondda Cynon Taff □, *U.K.* **11 F4** 51 42N 3 27W
Rhône →, *France* **18 E6** 43 28N 4 42 E
Rhum, *U.K.* **12 E2** 57 0N 6 20W
Rhyl, *U.K.* **10 D4** 53 20N 3 29W
Riachão, *Brazil* **93 E9** 7 20S 46 37W
Riasi, *India* **43 C6** 33 10N 74 50 E
Riau □, *Indonesia* **36 E2** 0 0 102 35 E
Riau, Kepulauan, *Indonesia* **36 D2** 0 30N 104 20 E
Riau Arch. = Riau, Kepulauan, *Indonesia* **36 D2** 0 30N 104 20 E
Ribadeo, *Spain* **19 A2** 43 35N 7 5W
Ribas do Rio Pardo, *Brazil* **93 H8** 20 27S 53 46W
Ribble →, *U.K.* **10 D5** 53 52N 2 25W
Ribe, *Denmark* **9 J13** 55 19N 8 44 E
Ribeira Brava, *Madeira* **22 D2** 32 41N 17 4W
Ribeirão Prêto, *Brazil* **95 A6** 21 10S 47 50W
Riberalta, *Bolivia* **92 F5** 11 0S 66 0W
Riccarton, *N.Z.* **59 K4** 43 32S 172 37 E
Rice, *U.S.A.* **85 L12** 34 5N 114 51W
Rice L., *Canada* **78 B6** 44 12N 78 10W
Rice Lake, *U.S.A.* **80 C9** 45 30N 91 44W
Rich, C., *Canada* **78 B4** 44 43N 80 38W
Richards Bay, *S. Africa* **57 D5** 28 48S 32 6 E
Richardson →, *Canada* **73 B6** 58 25N 111 14W
Richardson Lakes, *U.S.A.* **76 C10** 44 46N 70 58W
Richardson Springs, *U.S.A.* **84 F5** 39 51N 121 46W
Riche, C., *Australia* **61 F2** 34 36S 118 47 E
Richey, *U.S.A.* **80 B2** 47 39N 105 4W
Richfield, *U.S.A.* **83 G8** 38 46N 112 5W
Richfield Springs, *U.S.A.* **79 D10** 42 51N 74 59W
Richford, *U.S.A.* **79 B12** 45 0N 72 40W
Richibucto, *Canada* **71 C7** 46 42N 64 54W
Richland, *Ga., U.S.A.* **77 J3** 32 5N 84 40W
Richland, *Wash., U.S.A.* **82 C4** 46 17N 119 18W
Richland Center, *U.S.A.* **80 D9** 43 21N 90 23W
Richlands, *U.S.A.* **76 G5** 37 6N 81 48W
Richmond, *Australia* **62 C3** 20 43S 143 8 E
Richmond, *N.Z.* **59 J4** 41 20S 173 12 E
Richmond, *U.K.* **10 C6** 54 25N 1 43W
Richmond, *Calif., U.S.A.* **84 H4** 37 56N 122 21W
Richmond, *Ind., U.S.A.* **76 F3** 39 50N 84 53W
Richmond, *Ky., U.S.A.* **76 G3** 37 45N 84 18W
Richmond, *Mich., U.S.A.* **78 D2** 42 49N 82 45W
Richmond, *Mo., U.S.A.* **80 F8** 39 17N 93 58W
Richmond, *Tex., U.S.A.* **81 L7** 29 35N 95 46W
Richmond, *Utah, U.S.A.* **82 F8** 41 56N 111 48W
Richmond, *Va., U.S.A.* **76 G7** 37 33N 77 27W
Richmond, *Vt., U.S.A.* **79 B12** 44 24N 72 59W
Richmond Hill, *Canada* **78 C5** 43 52N 79 27W
Richmond Ra., *Australia* **63 D5** 29 0S 152 45 E
Richwood, *U.S.A.* **76 F5** 38 14N 80 32W
Ridder = Leninogorsk, *Kazakstan* **26 D9** 50 20N 83 30 E
Riddlesburg, *U.S.A.* **78 F6** 40 9N 78 15W
Ridgecrest, *U.S.A.* **85 K9** 35 38N 117 40W
Ridgefield, *Conn., U.S.A.* **79 E11** 41 17N 73 30W
Ridgefield, *Wash., U.S.A.* **84 E4** 45 49N 122 45W
Ridgeland, *U.S.A.* **77 J5** 32 29N 80 59W
Ridgetown, *Canada* **78 D3** 42 26N 81 52W
Ridgewood, *U.S.A.* **79 F10** 40 59N 74 7W
Ridgway, *U.S.A.* **78 E6** 41 25N 78 44W
Riding Mountain Nat. Park, *Canada* **73 C9** 50 50N 100 0W
Ridley, Mt., *Australia* **61 F3** 33 12S 122 7 E
Ried, *Austria* **16 D7** 48 14N 13 30 E
Riesa, *Germany* **16 C7** 51 17N 13 17 E
Riet →, *S. Africa* **56 D3** 29 0S 23 54 E
Rieti, *Italy* **20 C5** 42 24N 12 51 E
Riffe L., *U.S.A.* **84 D4** 46 32N 122 26W
Rifle, *U.S.A.* **82 G10** 39 32N 107 47W
Rift Valley □, *Kenya* **54 B4** 0 20N 36 0 E
Rīga, *Latvia* **9 H21** 56 53N 24 8 E
Riga, G. of, *Latvia* **9 H20** 57 40N 23 45 E
Rīgān, *Iran* **45 D8** 28 37N 58 58
Rīgas Jūras Līcis = Riga, G. of, *Latvia* **9 H20** 57 40N 23 45
Rigaud, *Canada* **79 A10** 45 29N 74 18W
Rigby, *U.S.A.* **82 E8** 43 40N 111 55W
Rīgestān □, *Afghan.* **40 D4** 30 15N 65 0
Riggins, *U.S.A.* **82 D5** 45 25N 116 19W
Rigolet, *Canada* **71 B8** 54 10N 58 23W
Rihand Dam, *India* **43 G10** 24 9N 83 2
Riihimäki, *Finland* **9 F21** 60 45N 24 48
Riiser-Larsen-halvøya, *Antarctica* **5 C4** 68 0S 35 0
Rijeka, *Croatia* **16 F8** 45 20N 14 21
Rijssen, *Neths.* **15 B6** 52 19N 6 31
Rikuzentakada, *Japan* **30 E10** 39 0N 141 40
Riley, *U.S.A.* **82 E4** 43 32N 119 28W
Rimah, Wadi ar →, *Si. Arabia* **44 E4** 26 5N 41 30
Rimbey, *Canada* **72 C6** 52 35N 114 15W
Rimersburg, *U.S.A.* **78 E5** 41 3N 79 30W
Rímini, *Italy* **20 B5** 44 3N 12 33
Rimouski, *Canada* **71 C6** 48 27N 68 30W
Rimrock, *U.S.A.* **84 D5** 46 38N 121 10W
Rinca, *Indonesia* **37 F5** 8 45S 119 35
Rincón de Romos, *Mexico* **86 C4** 22 14N 102 18W
Rinconada, *Argentina* **94 A2** 22 26S 66 10W
Rind →, *India* **43 G9** 25 53N 80 33
Ringas, *India* **42 F6** 27 21N 75 34
Ringkøbing, *Denmark* **9 H13** 56 5N 8 15
Ringvassøy, *Norway* **8 B18** 69 56N 19 15
Ringwood, *U.S.A.* **79 E10** 41 7N 74 15W
Rinjani, *Indonesia* **36 F5** 8 24S 116 28
Rio Branco, *Brazil* **92 E5** 9 58S 67 49W
Río Branco, *Uruguay* **95 C5** 32 40S 53 40W
Río Bravo del Norte →, *Mexico* **87 B5** 25 57N 97 9W
Rio Brilhante, *Brazil* **95 A5** 21 48S 54 33W
Rio Claro, *Brazil* **95 A6** 22 19S 47 35W
Rio Claro, *Trin. & Tob.* **89 D7** 10 20N 61 25W
Río Colorado, *Argentina* **96 D4** 39 0S 64 0W
Río Cuarto, *Argentina* **94 C3** 33 10S 64 25W
Rio das Pedras, *Mozam.* **57 C6** 23 8S 35 28
Rio de Janeiro, *Brazil* **95 A7** 23 0S 43 12W
Rio de Janeiro □, *Brazil* **95 A7** 22 50S 43 0W
Rio do Sul, *Brazil* **95 B6** 27 13S 49 37W
Río Gallegos, *Argentina* **96 G3** 51 35S 69 15W
Rio Grande = Grande, Rio →, *U.S.A.* **81 N6** 25 58N 97 9W
Río Grande, *Argentina* **96 G3** 53 50S 67 45W
Rio Grande, *Brazil* **95 C5** 32 0S 52 20W
Río Grande, *Mexico* **86 C4** 23 50N 103 2W
Río Grande, *Nic.* **88 D3** 12 54N 83 33W
Rio Grande City, *U.S.A.* **81 M5** 26 23N 98 49W
Río Grande de Santiago →, *Mexico* **86 C3** 21 36N 105 26W
Río Grande del Norte →, *N. Amer.* **75 E7** 26 0N 97 0W
Rio Grande do Norte □, *Brazil* **93 E11** 5 40S 36 0W
Rio Grande do Sul □, *Brazil* **95 C5** 30 0S 53 0W
Río Hato, *Panama* **88 E3** 8 22N 80 10W
Rio Lagartos, *Mexico* **87 C7** 21 36N 88 10W
Rio Largo, *Brazil* **93 E11** 9 28S 35 50W
Río Mulatos, *Bolivia* **92 G5** 19 40S 66 50W
Río Muni = Mbini □, *Eq. Guin.* **52 D2** 1 30N 10 0
Rio Negro, *Brazil* **95 B6** 26 0S 49 55W
Rio Pardo, *Brazil* **95 C5** 30 0S 52 30W
Rio Rancho, *U.S.A.* **83 J10** 35 14N 106 38W
Río Segundo, *Argentina* **94 C3** 31 40S 63 59W
Río Tercero, *Argentina* **94 C3** 32 15S 64 8W
Rio Verde, *Brazil* **93 G8** 17 50S 51 0W
Río Verde, *Mexico* **87 C5** 21 56N 99 59W
Rio Vista, *U.S.A.* **84 G5** 38 10N 121 42W
Ríobamba, *Ecuador* **92 D3** 1 50S 78 45W
Ríohacha, *Colombia* **92 A4** 11 33N 72 55W
Ríosucio, *Colombia* **92 B3** 7 27N 77 7W
Riou L., *Canada* **73 B7** 59 7N 106 25W
Ripley, *Canada* **78 B3** 44 4N 81 35W
Ripley, *Calif., U.S.A.* **85 M12** 33 32N 114 39W
Ripley, *N.Y., U.S.A.* **78 D5** 42 16N 79 43W
Ripley, *Tenn., U.S.A.* **81 H10** 35 45N 89 32W
Ripley, *W. Va., U.S.A.* **76 F5** 38 49N 81 43W
Ripon, *U.K.* **10 C6** 54 9N 1 31W
Ripon, *Calif., U.S.A.* **84 H5** 37 44N 121 7W
Ripon, *Wis., U.S.A.* **76 D1** 43 51N 88 50W
Rishā', W. ar →, *Si. Arabia* **44 E5** 25 33N 44 5
Rishiri-Tō, *Japan* **30 B10** 45 11N 141 15
Rishon le Ziyyon, *Israel* **47 D3** 31 58N 34 48
Rison, *U.S.A.* **81 J8** 33 58N 92 11W
Risør, *Norway* **9 G13** 58 43N 9 13
Rita Blanca Cr. →, *U.S.A.* **81 H3** 35 40N 102 29W
Ritter, Mt., *U.S.A.* **84 H7** 37 41N 119 12W
Rittman, *U.S.A.* **78 F3** 40 58N 81 47W
Ritzville, *U.S.A.* **82 C4** 47 8N 118 23W
Riva del Garda, *Italy* **20 B4** 45 53N 10 50
Rivadavia, *Buenos Aires, Argentina* **94 D3** 35 29S 62 59W
Rivadavia, *Mendoza, Argentina* **94 C2** 33 13S 68 30W
Rivadavia, *Salta, Argentina* **94 A3** 24 5S 62 54W
Rivadavia, *Chile* **94 B1** 29 57S 70 35W
Rivas, *Nic.* **88 D2** 11 30N 85 50W
River Cess, *Liberia* **50 G4** 5 30N 9 32W
River Jordan, *Canada* **84 B2** 48 26N 124 3W
Rivera, *Argentina* **94 D3** 37 12S 63 14W
Rivera, *Uruguay* **95 C4** 31 0S 55 50W
Riverbank, *U.S.A.* **84 H6** 37 44N 120 56W
Riverdale, *U.S.A.* **84 J7** 36 26N 119 52W
Riverhead, *U.S.A.* **79 F12** 40 55N 72 40W
Riverhurst, *Canada* **73 C7** 50 55N 106 50W
Rivers, *Canada* **73 C8** 50 2N 100 14W
Rivers Inlet, *Canada* **72 C3** 51 42N 127 15W
Riversdale, *S. Africa* **56 E3** 34 7S 21 15
Riverside, *U.S.A.* **85 M9** 33 59N 117 22W
Riverton, *Australia* **63 E2** 34 10S 138 46
Riverton, *Canada* **73 C9** 51 1N 97 0W
Riverton, *N.Z.* **59 M2** 46 21S 168 0
Riverton, *U.S.A.* **82 E9** 43 2N 108 23W
Riverton Heights, *U.S.A.* **84 C4** 47 28N 122 17W
Riviera, *U.S.A.* **85 K12** 35 4N 114 35W
Riviera di Levante, *Italy* **18 D8** 44 15N 9 30
Riviera di Ponente, *Italy* **18 D8** 44 10N 8 20
Rivière-au-Renard, *Canada* **71 C7** 48 59N 64 23W
Rivière-du-Loup, *Canada* **71 C6** 47 50N 69 30W
Rivière-Pentecôte, *Canada* **71 C6** 49 57N 67 1W

Rzhev

ivière-Pilote, Martinique 89 D7 14 26N 60 53W
ivière St. Paul, Canada 71 B8 51 28N 57 45W
ivne, Ukraine 17 C14 50 40N 26 10 E
ivoli, Italy 18 D7 45 3N 7 31 E
ivoli B., Australia 63 F3 37 32S 140 3 E
iyadh = Ar Riyāḍ,
Si. Arabia 46 C4 24 41N 46 42 E
ize, Turkey 25 F7 41 0N 40 30 E
izhao, China 35 G10 35 25N 119 30 E
izokarpaso, Cyprus 23 D13 35 36N 34 23 E
izzuto, C., Italy 20 E7 38 53N 17 5 E
ukan, Norway 9 G13 59 54N 8 33 E
oad Town, Virgin Is. 89 C7 18 27N 64 37W
oan Plateau, U.S.A. 82 G9 39 20N 109 20W
oanne, France 18 C6 46 3N 4 4 E
oanoke, Ala., U.S.A. 77 J3 33 9N 85 22W
oanoke, Va., U.S.A. 76 G6 37 16N 79 56W
oanoke →, U.S.A. 77 H7 35 57N 76 42W
oanoke I., U.S.A. 77 H8 35 55N 75 40W
oanoke Rapids, U.S.A. 77 G7 36 28N 77 40W
oatán, Honduras 88 C2 16 18N 86 35W
obāt Sang, Iran 45 C8 35 35N 59 10 E
obbins I., Australia 62 G4 40 42S 145 0 E
obe, Australia 63 F2 37 11S 139 45 E
obe →, Australia 60 D2 21 42S 116 15 E
obert Lee, U.S.A. 81 K4 31 54N 100 29W
obertsdale, U.S.A. 78 F6 40 11N 78 6W
obertsganj, India 43 G10 24 44N 83 4 E
obertson, S. Africa 56 E2 33 46S 19 50 E
obertson I., Antarctica 5 C18 65 15S 59 30W
obertson Ra., Australia 60 D3 23 15S 121 0 E
obertstown, Australia 63 E2 33 58S 139 5 E
oberval, Canada 71 C5 48 32N 72 15W
obeson Chan., Greenland 4 A4 82 0N 61 30W
obesonia, U.S.A. 79 F8 40 21N 76 8W
obinson, U.S.A. 76 F2 39 0N 87 44W
obinson →, Australia 62 B2 16 3S 137 16 E
obinson Ra., Australia 61 E2 25 40S 119 0 E
obinvale, Australia 63 E3 34 40S 142 45 E
oblin, Canada 73 C8 51 14N 101 21W
oboré, Bolivia 92 G7 18 10S 59 45W
obson, Canada 72 D5 49 20N 117 41W
obson, Mt., Canada 72 C5 53 10N 119 10W
obstown, U.S.A. 81 M6 27 47N 97 40W
oca, C. da, Portugal 19 C1 38 40N 9 31W
oca Partida, I., Mexico 86 D2 19 1N 112 2W
ocas, I., Brazil 93 D12 4 0S 34 1W
ocha, Uruguay 95 C5 34 30S 54 25W
ochdale, U.K. 10 D5 53 38N 2 9W
ochefort, Belgium 15 D5 50 9N 5 12 E
ochefort, France 18 D3 45 56N 0 57W
ochelle, U.S.A. 80 E10 41 56N 89 4W
ocher River, Canada 72 A6 61 23N 112 44W
ochester, U.K. 11 F8 51 23N 0 31 E
ochester, Ind., U.S.A. 76 E2 41 4N 86 13W
ochester, Minn., U.S.A. 80 C8 44 1N 92 28W
ochester, N.H., U.S.A. 79 C14 43 18N 70 59W
ochester, N.Y., U.S.A. 78 C7 43 10N 77 37W
ock →, Canada 72 A3 60 7N 127 7W
ock Creek, U.S.A. 78 E4 41 40N 80 52W
ock Falls, U.S.A. 80 E10 41 47N 89 41W
ock Hill, U.S.A. 77 H5 34 56N 81 1W
ock Island, U.S.A. 80 E9 41 30N 90 34W
ock Rapids, U.S.A. 80 D6 43 26N 96 10W
ock Sound, Bahamas 88 B4 24 54N 76 12W
ock Springs, Mont., U.S.A. 82 C10 46 49N 106 15W
ock Springs, Wyo., U.S.A. 82 F9 41 35N 109 14W
ock Valley, U.S.A. 80 D6 43 12N 96 18W
ockall, Atl. Oc. 6 D3 57 37N 13 42W
ockdale, Tex., U.S.A. 81 K6 30 39N 97 0W
ockdale, Wash., U.S.A. 84 C5 47 22N 121 28W
ockefeller Plateau,
Antarctica 5 E14 80 0S 140 0W
ockford, U.S.A. 80 D10 42 16N 89 6W
ockglen, Canada 73 D7 49 11N 105 57W
ockhampton, Australia 62 C5 23 22S 150 32 E
ockingham, Australia 61 F2 32 15S 115 38 E
ockingham, U.S.A. 77 H6 34 57N 79 46W
ockingham B., Australia 62 B4 18 5S 146 10 E
ocklake, U.S.A. 80 A5 48 47N 99 15W
ockland, Canada 79 A9 45 33N 75 17W
ockland, Idaho, U.S.A. 82 E7 42 34N 112 53W
ockland, Maine, U.S.A. 77 C11 44 6N 69 7W
ockland, Mich., U.S.A. 80 B10 46 44N 89 11W
ocklin, U.S.A. 84 G5 38 48N 121 14W
ockport, Mass., U.S.A. 79 D14 42 39N 70 37W
ockport, Mo., U.S.A. 80 E7 40 25N 95 31W
ockport, Tex., U.S.A. 81 L6 28 2N 97 3W
ocksprings, U.S.A. 81 K4 30 1N 100 13W
ockville, Conn., U.S.A. 79 E12 41 52N 72 28W
ockville, Md., U.S.A. 76 F7 39 5N 77 9W
ockwall, U.S.A. 81 J6 32 56N 96 28W
ockwell City, U.S.A. 80 D7 42 24N 94 38W
ockwood, Canada 78 C4 43 37N 80 8W
ockwood, Maine, U.S.A. 77 C11 45 41N 69 45W
ockwood, Tenn., U.S.A. 77 H3 35 52N 84 41W
ocky Ford, U.S.A. 80 F3 38 3N 103 43W
ocky Gully, Australia 61 F2 34 30S 116 57 E
ocky Harbour, Canada 71 C8 49 36N 57 55W
ocky Island L., Canada 70 C3 46 55N 83 0W
ocky Lane, Canada 72 B5 58 31N 116 22W
ocky Mount, U.S.A. 77 H7 35 57N 77 48W
ocky Mountain House,
Canada 72 C6 52 22N 114 55W
ocky Mountain National
Park, U.S.A. 82 F11 40 25N 105 45W
ocky Mts., N. Amer. 74 C5 49 0N 115 0W
od, Pakistan 40 E3 28 10N 63 5 E
odbyhavn, Denmark 9 J14 54 39N 11 22 E
oddickton, Canada 71 B8 50 51N 56 8W
odez, France 18 D5 44 21N 2 33 E
odhopoú, Greece 23 D5 35 34N 23 45 E
odhos, Greece 23 C10 36 15N 28 10 E
odney, Canada 78 D3 42 34N 81 41W
odney, C., N.Z. 59 G5 36 17S 174 50 E
odriguez, Ind. Oc. 3 E13 19 45S 63 20 E
oe →, U.K. 13 A5 55 6N 6 59W
oebling, U.S.A. 79 F10 40 7N 74 47W
oebourne, Australia 60 D2 20 44S 117 9 E
oebuck B., Australia 60 C3 18 5S 122 20 E
oermond, Neths. 15 C6 51 12N 6 0 E
oes Welcome Sd., Canada 69 B11 65 0N 87 0W
oeselare, Belgium 15 D3 50 57N 3 7 E
ogachev = Ragachow,
Belarus 17 B16 53 8N 30 5 E
ogagua, L., Bolivia 92 F5 13 43S 66 50W
Rogatyn, Ukraine 17 D13 49 24N 24 36 E
Rogdhia, Greece 23 D7 35 22N 25 1 E
Rogers, U.S.A. 81 G7 36 20N 94 7W
Rogers City, U.S.A. 76 C4 45 25N 83 49W
Rogersville, Canada 71 C6 46 44N 65 26W
Roggan →, Canada 70 B4 54 24N 79 25W
Roggan L., Canada 70 B4 54 8N 77 50W
Roggeveldberge, S. Africa 56 E3 32 10S 20 10 E
Rogoaguado, L., Bolivia 92 F5 13 0S 65 30W
Rogue →, U.S.A. 82 E1 42 26N 124 26W
Róhda, Greece 23 A3 39 48N 19 46 E
Rohnert Park, U.S.A. 84 G4 38 16N 122 40W
Rohri, Pakistan 42 F3 27 45N 68 51 E
Rohri Canal, Pakistan 42 F3 26 15N 68 27 E
Rohtak, India 42 E7 28 55N 76 43 E
Roi Et, Thailand 38 D4 16 4N 103 40 E
Roja, Latvia 9 H20 57 29N 22 43 E
Rojas, Argentina 94 C3 34 10S 60 45W
Rojo, C., Mexico 87 C5 21 33N 97 20W
Rokan →, Indonesia 36 D2 2 0N 100 50 E
Rokiškis, Lithuania 9 J21 55 55N 25 35 E
Rolândia, Brazil 95 A5 23 18S 51 23W
Rolla, U.S.A. 81 G9 37 57N 91 46W
Rolleston, Australia 62 C4 24 28S 148 35 E
Rollingstone, Australia 62 B4 19 2S 146 24 E
Roma, Australia 63 D4 26 32S 148 49 E
Roma, Italy 20 D5 41 54N 12 29 E
Roma, Sweden 9 H18 57 32N 18 26 E
Roma, U.S.A. 81 M5 26 25N 99 1W
Romain C., U.S.A. 77 J6 33 0N 79 22W
Romaine, Canada 71 B7 50 13N 60 40W
Romaine →, Canada 71 B7 50 18N 63 47W
Roman, Romania 17 E14 46 57N 26 55 E
Romang, Indonesia 37 F7 7 30S 127 20 E
Românî, Egypt 47 E1 30 59N 32 38 E
Romania ■, Europe 17 F12 46 0N 25 0 E
Romano, Cayo, Cuba 88 B4 22 0N 77 30W
Romanovka =
Basarabeasca, Moldova 17 E15 46 21N 28 58 E
Romans-sur-Isère, France 18 D6 45 3N 5 3 E
Romblon, Phil. 37 B6 12 33N 122 17 E
Rome = Roma, Italy 20 D5 41 54N 12 29 E
Rome, Ga., U.S.A. 77 H3 34 15N 85 10W
Rome, N.Y., U.S.A. 79 C9 43 13N 75 27W
Rome, Pa., U.S.A. 79 E8 41 51N 76 21W
Romney, U.S.A. 76 F6 39 21N 78 45W
Romney Marsh, U.K. 11 F8 51 2N 0 54 E
Rømø, Denmark 9 J13 55 10N 8 30 E
Romorantin-Lanthenay,
France 18 C4 47 21N 1 45 E
Romsdalen, Norway 9 E12 62 25N 7 52 E
Romsey, U.K. 11 G6 51 0N 1 29W
Ron, Vietnam 38 D6 17 53N 106 27 E
Rona, U.K. 12 D3 57 34N 5 59W
Ronan, U.S.A. 82 C6 47 32N 114 6W
Roncador, Cayos, Caribbean 88 D3 13 32N 80 4W
Roncador, Serra do, Brazil 93 F8 12 30S 52 30W
Ronda, Spain 19 D3 36 46N 5 12W
Rondane, Norway 9 F13 61 57N 9 50 E
Rondônia □, Brazil 92 F6 11 0S 63 0W
Rondonópolis, Brazil 93 G8 16 28S 54 38W
Rong, Koh, Cambodia 39 G4 10 45N 103 15 E
Ronge, L. la, Canada 73 B7 55 6N 105 17W
Rønne, Denmark 9 J16 55 6N 14 43 E
Ronne Ice Shelf, Antarctica 5 D18 78 0S 60 0W
Ronsard, C., Australia 61 D1 24 46S 113 10 E
Ronse, Belgium 15 D3 50 45N 3 35 E
Roodepoort, S. Africa 57 D4 26 11S 27 54 E
Roof Butte, U.S.A. 83 H9 36 28N 109 5W
Roorkee, India 42 E7 29 52N 77 59 E
Roosendaal, Neths. 15 C4 51 32N 4 29 E
Roosevelt, U.S.A. 82 F8 40 18N 109 59W
Roosevelt →, Brazil 92 E6 7 35S 60 20W
Roosevelt, Mt., Canada 72 B3 58 26N 125 20W
Roosevelt I., Antarctica 5 D12 79 30S 162 0W
Roper →, Australia 62 A2 14 43S 135 27 E
Roper Bar, Australia 62 A1 14 44S 134 44 E
Roque Pérez, Argentina 94 D4 35 25S 59 24W
Roquetas de Mar, Spain 19 D4 36 46N 2 36W
Roraima □, Brazil 92 C6 2 0N 61 30W
Roraima, Mt., Venezuela 92 B6 5 10N 60 40W
Røros, Norway 9 E14 62 35N 11 23 E
Rosa, Zambia 55 D3 9 33S 31 15 E
Rosa, L., Bahamas 89 B5 21 0N 73 30W
Rosa, Monte, Europe 18 D7 45 57N 7 53 E
Rosalia, U.S.A. 82 C5 47 14N 117 22W
Rosamond, U.S.A. 85 L8 34 52N 118 10W
Rosario, Argentina 94 C3 33 0S 60 40W
Rosário, Brazil 93 D10 3 0S 44 15W
Rosario, Baja Calif., Mexico 86 B1 30 0N 115 50W
Rosario, Sinaloa, Mexico 86 C3 23 0N 105 52W
Rosario, Paraguay 94 A4 24 30S 57 35W
Rosario de la Frontera,
Argentina 94 B3 25 50S 65 0W
Rosario de Lerma, Argentina 94 A2 24 59S 65 35W
Rosario del Tala, Argentina 94 C4 32 20S 59 10W
Rosário do Sul, Brazil 95 C5 30 15S 54 55W
Rosarito, Mexico 85 N9 32 18N 117 4W
Roscoe, U.S.A. 79 E10 41 56N 74 55W
Roscommon, Ireland 13 C3 53 38N 8 11W
Roscommon □, Ireland 13 C3 53 49N 8 23W
Roscrea, Ireland 13 D4 52 57N 7 49W
Rose →, Australia 62 A2 14 16S 135 45 E
Rose Blanche, Canada 71 C8 47 38N 58 45W
Rose Pt., Canada 72 C2 54 11N 131 39W
Rose Valley, Canada 73 C8 52 19N 103 49W
Roseau, Domin. 89 C7 15 20N 61 24W
Roseau, U.S.A. 80 A7 48 51N 95 46W
Rosebery, Australia 62 G4 41 46S 145 33 E
Rosebud, S. Dak., U.S.A. 80 D4 43 14N 100 51W
Rosebud, Tex., U.S.A. 81 K6 31 4N 96 59W
Roseburg, U.S.A. 82 E2 43 13N 123 20W
Rosedale, U.S.A. 81 J9 33 51N 91 2W
Roseland, U.S.A. 84 G4 38 25N 122 43W
Rosemary, Canada 72 C6 50 46N 112 5W
Rosenberg, U.S.A. 81 L7 29 34N 95 49W
Rosenheim, Germany 16 E7 47 51N 12 7 E
Roses, G. de, Spain 19 A7 42 10N 3 15 E
Rosetown, Canada 73 C7 51 35N 107 59W
Roseville, Calif., U.S.A. 84 G5 38 45N 121 17W
Roseville, Mich., U.S.A. 78 D2 42 30N 82 56W
Rosewood, Australia 63 D5 27 38S 152 36 E
Roshkhvār, Iran 45 C8 34 58N 59 37 E
Rosignano Marittimo, Italy 20 C4 43 24N 10 28 E
Rosignol, Guyana 92 B7 6 15N 57 30W
Roşiori-de-Vede, Romania 17 F13 44 7N 24 59 E
Roskilde, Denmark 9 J15 55 38N 12 3 E
Roslavl, Russia 24 D5 53 57N 32 55 E
Rosmead, S. Africa 56 E4 31 29S 25 8 E
Ross, Australia 62 G4 42 2S 147 30 E
Ross, N.Z. 59 K3 42 53S 170 49 E
Ross I., Antarctica 5 D11 77 30S 168 0 E
Ross Ice Shelf, Antarctica 5 E12 80 0S 180 0 E
Ross L., U.S.A. 82 B3 48 44N 121 4W
Ross-on-Wye, U.K. 11 F5 51 54N 2 34W
Ross River, Australia 62 C1 23 44S 134 30 E
Ross River, Canada 72 A2 62 30N 131 30W
Ross Sea, Antarctica 5 D11 74 0S 178 0 E
Rossall Pt., U.K. 10 D4 53 55N 3 3W
Rossan Pt., Ireland 13 B3 54 42N 8 47W
Rossano, Italy 20 E7 39 36N 16 39 E
Rossburn, Canada 73 C8 50 40N 100 49W
Rosseau, Canada 78 A5 45 16N 79 39W
Rosseau L., Canada 78 A5 45 10N 79 35W
Rosses, The, Ireland 13 A3 55 2N 8 20W
Rossignol, L., Canada 70 B5 52 43N 73 40W
Rossignol Res., Canada 71 D6 44 12N 65 10W
Rossland, Canada 72 D5 49 6N 117 50W
Rosslare, Ireland 13 D5 52 17N 6 24W
Rosso, Mauritania 50 E2 16 40N 15 45W
Rossosh, Russia 25 D6 50 15N 39 28 E
Røssvatnet, Norway 8 D16 65 45N 14 5 E
Røst, Norway 8 C15 67 32N 12 0 E
Rosthern, Canada 73 C7 52 40N 106 20W
Rostock, Germany 16 A7 54 5N 12 8 E
Rostov, Don, Russia 25 E6 47 15N 39 45 E
Rostov, Yaroslavl, Russia 24 C6 57 14N 39 25 E
Roswell, Ga., U.S.A. 77 H3 34 2N 84 22W
Roswell, N. Mex., U.S.A. 81 J2 33 24N 104 32W
Rotan, U.S.A. 81 J4 32 51N 100 28W
Rother →, U.K. 11 G8 50 59N 0 45 E
Rotherham, U.K. 10 D6 53 26N 1 20W
Rothes, U.K. 12 D5 57 32N 3 13W
Rothesay, Canada 71 C6 45 23N 66 0W
Rothesay, U.K. 12 F3 55 50N 5 3W
Roti, Indonesia 37 F6 10 50S 123 0 E
Roto, Australia 63 E4 33 0S 145 30 E
Rotondo Mte., France 18 E8 42 14N 9 8 E
Rotoroa, L., N.Z. 59 J4 41 55S 172 39 E
Rotorua, N.Z. 59 H6 38 9S 176 16 E
Rotorua, L., N.Z. 59 H6 38 5S 176 18 E
Rotterdam, Neths. 15 C4 51 55N 4 30 E
Rotterdam, U.S.A. 79 D10 42 48N 74 1W
Rottnest I., Australia 61 F2 32 0S 115 27 E
Rottumeroog, Neths. 15 A6 53 33N 6 34 E
Rottweil, Germany 16 D5 48 9N 8 37 E
Rotuma, Fiji 64 J9 12 25S 177 5 E
Roubaix, France 18 A5 50 40N 3 10 E
Rouen, France 18 B4 49 27N 1 4 E
Rouleau, Canada 73 C8 50 10N 104 56W
Round Mountain, U.S.A. 82 G5 38 43N 117 4W
Round Mt., Australia 63 E5 30 26S 152 16 E
Round Rock, U.S.A. 81 K6 30 31N 97 41W
Roundup, U.S.A. 82 C9 46 27N 108 33W
Rousay, U.K. 12 B5 59 10N 3 2W
Rouses Point, U.S.A. 79 B11 44 59N 73 22W
Rouseville, U.S.A. 78 E5 41 28N 79 42W
Roussillon, France 18 E5 42 30N 2 35 E
Rouxville, S. Africa 56 E4 30 25S 26 50 E
Rouyn-Noranda, Canada 70 C4 48 20N 79 0W
Rovaniemi, Finland 8 C21 66 29N 25 41 E
Rovereto, Italy 20 B4 45 53N 11 3 E
Rovigo, Italy 20 B4 45 4N 11 47 E
Rovinj, Croatia 16 F7 45 5N 13 40 E
Rovno = Rivne, Ukraine 17 C14 50 40N 26 10 E
Rovuma = Ruvuma →,
Tanzania 55 E5 10 29S 40 28 E
Row'ān, Iran 45 C6 35 8N 48 51 E
Rowena, Australia 63 D4 29 48S 148 55 E
Rowley Shoals, Australia 60 C2 17 30S 119 0 E
Roxas, Phil. 37 B6 11 36N 122 49 E
Roxboro, U.S.A. 77 G6 36 24N 78 59W
Roxburgh, N.Z. 59 L2 45 33S 169 19 E
Roxbury, U.S.A. 78 F7 40 6N 77 39W
Roy, Mont., U.S.A. 82 C9 47 20N 108 58W
Roy, N. Mex., U.S.A. 81 H2 35 57N 104 12W
Roy, Utah, U.S.A. 82 F7 41 10N 112 2W
Royal Canal, Ireland 13 C4 53 30N 7 13W
Royal Leamington Spa, U.K. 11 E6 52 18N 1 31W
Royal Tunbridge Wells, U.K. 11 F8 51 7N 0 16 E
Royan, France 18 D3 45 37N 1 2W
Royston, U.K. 11 E7 52 3N 0 0W
Rozdilna, Ukraine 17 E16 46 50N 30 2 E
Rozhyshche, Ukraine 17 C13 50 54N 25 15 E
Rtishchevo, Russia 24 D7 52 18N 43 46 E
Ruacaná, Angola 56 B1 17 20S 14 12 E
Ruahine Ra., N.Z. 59 H6 39 55S 176 2 E
Ruapehu, N.Z. 59 H5 39 17S 175 35 E
Ruapuke I., N.Z. 59 M2 46 46S 168 31 E
Ruâq, W. →, Egypt 47 F2 30 0N 33 49 E
Rub' al Khālī, Si. Arabia 46 D4 18 0N 48 0 E
Rubeho Mts., Tanzania 54 D4 6 50S 36 25 E
Rubh a' Mhail, U.K. 12 F2 55 56N 6 8W
Rubha Hunish, U.K. 12 D2 57 42N 6 20W
Rubha Robhanais = Lewis,
Butt of, U.K. 12 C2 58 31N 6 16W
Rubicon →, U.S.A. 84 G5 38 53N 121 4W
Rubio, Venezuela 92 B4 7 43N 72 22W
Rubtsovsk, Russia 26 D9 51 30N 81 10 E
Ruby L., U.S.A. 82 F6 40 10N 115 28W
Ruby Mts., U.S.A. 82 F6 40 30N 115 20W
Rubyvale, Australia 62 C4 23 25S 147 42 E
Rūd Sar, Iran 45 B6 37 8N 50 18 E
Rudall, Australia 63 E2 33 43S 136 17 E
Rudall →, Australia 60 D3 22 34S 122 13 E
Rudewa, Tanzania 55 E3 10 7S 34 40 E
Rudnyy, Kazakstan 26 D7 52 57N 63 7 E
Rudolfa, Ostrov, Russia 26 A6 81 45N 58 30 E
Rudyard, U.S.A. 76 B3 46 14N 84 36W
Rufiji →, Tanzania 54 D4 7 50S 39 15 E
Rufino, Argentina 94 C3 34 20S 62 50W
Rufunsa, Zambia 55 F2 15 4S 29 34 E
Rugby, U.K. 11 E6 52 23N 1 16W
Rugby, U.S.A. 80 A5 48 22N 100 0W
Rügen, Germany 16 A7 54 22N 13 24 E
Ruhengeri, Rwanda 54 C2 1 30S 29 36 E
Ruhnu, Estonia 9 H20 57 48N 23 15 E
Ruhr →, Germany 16 C4 51 27N 6 43 E
Ruhuhu →, Tanzania 55 E3 10 31S 34 34 E
Ruidoso, U.S.A. 83 K11 33 20N 105 41W
Ruivo, Pico, Madeira 22 D3 32 45N 16 56W
Rujm Tal'at al Jamā'ah,
Jordan 47 E4 30 24N 35 30 E
Ruk, Pakistan 42 F3 27 50N 68 42 E
Rukhla, Pakistan 42 C4 32 27N 71 57 E
Ruki →,
Dem. Rep. of the Congo 52 E3 0 5N 18 17 E
Rukwa □, Tanzania 54 D3 7 0S 31 30 E
Rukwa, L., Tanzania 54 D3 8 0S 32 20 E
Rulhieres, C., Australia 60 B4 13 56S 127 22 E
Rum = Rhum, U.K. 12 E2 57 0N 6 20W
Rum Cay, Bahamas 89 B5 23 40N 74 58W
Rum Jungle, Australia 60 B5 13 0S 130 59 E
Rumāḥ, Si. Arabia 44 E5 25 29N 47 10 E
Rumania = Romania ■,
Europe 17 F12 46 0N 25 0 E
Rumaylah, Iraq 44 D5 30 47N 47 37 E
Rumbêk, Sudan 51 G11 6 54N 29 37 E
Rumford, U.S.A. 77 C10 44 33N 70 33W
Rumia, Poland 17 A10 54 37N 18 25 E
Rumoi, Japan 30 C10 43 56N 141 39 E
Rumonge, Burundi 54 C2 3 59S 29 26 E
Rumson, U.S.A. 79 F11 40 23N 74 0W
Rumuruti, Kenya 54 B4 0 17N 36 32 E
Runan, China 34 H8 33 0N 114 30 E
Runanga, N.Z. 59 K3 42 25S 171 15 E
Runaway, C., N.Z. 59 G6 37 32S 177 59 E
Runcorn, U.K. 10 D5 53 21N 2 44W
Rundu, Namibia 53 H3 17 52S 19 43 E
Rungwa, Tanzania 54 D3 6 55S 33 32 E
Rungwa →, Tanzania 54 D3 7 36S 31 50 E
Rungwe, Tanzania 55 D3 9 11S 33 32 E
Rungwe, Mt., Tanzania 52 F6 9 8S 33 40 E
Runton Ra., Australia 60 D3 23 31S 123 6 E
Ruoqiang, China 32 C3 38 55N 88 10 E
Rupa, India 41 F18 27 15N 92 21 E
Rupar, India 42 D7 31 2N 76 38 E
Rupat, Indonesia 36 D2 1 45N 101 40 E
Rupen →, India 42 H4 23 28N 71 31 E
Rupert, U.S.A. 82 E7 42 37N 113 41W
Rupert →, Canada 70 B4 51 29N 78 45W
Rupert B., Canada 70 B4 51 35N 79 0W
Rupert House =
Waskaganish, Canada 70 B4 51 30N 78 40W
Rupsa, India 43 J12 21 37N 87 1 E
Rurrenabaque, Bolivia 92 F5 14 30S 67 32W
Rusambo, Zimbabwe 55 F3 16 30S 32 4 E
Rusape, Zimbabwe 55 F3 18 35S 32 8 E
Ruschuk = Ruse, Bulgaria 21 C12 43 48N 25 59 E
Ruse, Bulgaria 21 C12 43 48N 25 59 E
Rush, Ireland 13 C5 53 31N 6 6W
Rushan, China 35 F11 36 56N 121 30 E
Rushden, U.K. 11 E7 52 18N 0 35W
Rushmore, Mt., U.S.A. 80 D3 43 53N 103 28W
Rushville, Ill., U.S.A. 80 E9 40 7N 90 34W
Rushville, Ind., U.S.A. 76 F3 39 37N 85 27W
Rushville, Nebr., U.S.A. 80 D3 42 43N 102 28W
Russas, Brazil 93 D11 4 55S 37 50W
Russell, Canada 73 C8 50 50N 101 20W
Russell, Kans., U.S.A. 80 F5 38 54N 98 52W
Russell, N.Y., U.S.A. 79 B9 44 27N 75 9W
Russell, Pa., U.S.A. 78 E5 41 56N 79 8W
Russell L., Man., Canada 73 B8 56 15N 101 30W
Russell L., N.W.T., Canada 72 A5 63 5N 115 44W
Russellkonda, India 41 K14 19 57N 84 42 E
Russellville, Ala., U.S.A. 77 H2 34 30N 87 44W
Russellville, Ark., U.S.A. 81 H8 35 17N 93 8W
Russellville, Ky., U.S.A. 77 G2 36 51N 86 53W
Russia ■, Eurasia 27 C11 62 0N 105 0 E
Russian →, U.S.A. 84 G3 38 27N 123 8W
Russkoye Ustie, Russia 4 B15 71 0N 149 0 E
Rustam, Pakistan 42 B5 34 25N 72 13 E
Rustam Shahr, Pakistan 42 F2 26 58N 66 6 E
Rustavi, Georgia 25 F8 41 30N 45 0 E
Rustenburg, S. Africa 56 D4 25 41S 27 14 E
Ruston, U.S.A. 81 J8 32 32N 92 38W
Rutana, Burundi 54 C3 3 55S 30 0 E
Ruteng, Indonesia 37 F6 8 35S 120 30 E
Ruth, U.S.A. 78 C2 43 42N 82 45W
Rutherford, U.S.A. 84 G4 38 26N 122 24W
Rutland, U.S.A. 79 C12 43 37N 72 58W
Rutland □, U.K. 11 E7 52 38N 0 40W
Rutland Water, U.K. 11 E7 52 39N 0 38W
Rutledge →, Canada 73 A6 61 4N 112 0W
Rutledge L., Canada 73 A6 61 33N 110 47W
Rutshuru,
Dem. Rep. of the Congo 54 C2 1 13S 29 25 E
Ruvu, Tanzania 54 D4 6 49S 38 43 E
Ruvu →, Tanzania 54 D4 6 23S 38 52 E
Ruvuma □, Tanzania 55 E4 10 20S 36 0 E
Ruvuma →, Tanzania 55 E5 10 29S 40 28 E
Ruwais, U.A.E. 45 E7 24 5N 52 50 E
Ruwenzori, Africa 54 B2 0 30N 29 55 E
Ruyigi, Burundi 54 C3 3 29S 30 15 E
Ružomberok, Slovak Rep. 17 D10 49 3N 19 17 E
Rwanda ■, Africa 54 C3 2 0S 30 0 E
Ryan, L., U.K. 12 G3 55 0N 5 2W
Ryazan, Russia 24 D6 54 40N 39 40 E
Ryazhsk, Russia 24 D7 53 45N 40 3 E
Rybache = Rybachye,
Kazakstan 26 E9 46 40N 81 20 E
Rybachiy Poluostrov, Russia 24 A5 69 43N 32 0 E
Rybachye = Ysyk-Köl,
Kyrgyzstan 28 E11 42 26N 76 12 E
Rybachye, Kazakstan 26 E9 46 40N 81 20 E
Rybinsk, Russia 24 C6 58 5N 38 50 E
Rybinskoye Vdkhr., Russia 24 C6 58 30N 38 25 E
Rybnitsa = Rîbniţa,
Moldova 17 E15 47 45N 29 0 E
Rycroft, Canada 72 B5 55 45N 118 40W
Ryde, U.K. 11 G6 50 43N 1 9W
Ryderwood, U.S.A. 84 D3 46 23N 123 3W
Rye, U.K. 11 G8 50 57N 0 45 E
Rye →, U.K. 10 C7 54 11N 0 44W
Rye Bay, U.K. 11 G8 50 52N 0 49 E
Rye Patch Reservoir, U.S.A. 82 F4 40 28N 118 19W
Ryegate, U.S.A. 82 C9 46 18N 109 15W
Ryley, Canada 72 C6 53 17N 112 26W
Rylstone, Australia 63 E4 32 46S 149 58 E
Ryōtsu, Japan 30 E9 38 5N 138 26 E
Rypin, Poland 17 B10 53 3N 19 25 E
Ryūgasaki, Japan 31 G10 35 54N 140 11 E
Ryūkyū Is. = Ryūkyū-rettō,
Japan 31 M3 26 0N 126 0 E
Ryūkyū-rettō, Japan 31 M3 26 0N 126 0 E
Rzeszów, Poland 17 C11 50 5N 21 58 E
Rzhev, Russia 24 C5 56 20N 34 20 E

S

Sa, *Thailand* **38 C3** 18 34N 100 45 E
Sa Canal, *Spain* **22 C7** 38 51N 1 23 E
Sa Conillera, *Spain* **22 C7** 38 59N 1 13 E
Sa Dec, *Vietnam* **39 G5** 10 20N 105 46 E
Sa Dragonera, *Spain* **22 B9** 39 35N 2 19 E
Sa Mesquida, *Spain* **22 B11** 39 55N 4 16 E
Sa Savina, *Spain* **22 C7** 38 44N 1 25 E
Sa'ādatābād, *Fārs, Iran* **45 D7** 30 10N 53 5 E
Sa'ādatābād, *Hormozgān, Iran* **45 D7** 28 3N 55 53 E
Sa'ādatābād, *Kermān, Iran* **45 D7** 29 40N 55 51 E
Saale →, *Germany* **16 C6** 51 56N 11 54 E
Saalfeld, *Germany* **16 C6** 50 38N 11 21 E
Saar →, *Europe* **18 B7** 49 41N 6 32 E
Saarbrücken, *Germany* **16 D4** 49 14N 6 59 E
Saaremaa, *Estonia* **9 G20** 58 30N 22 30 E
Saarijärvi, *Finland* **9 E21** 62 43N 25 16 E
Saariselkä, *Finland* **8 B23** 68 16N 28 15 E
Sab 'Ābar, *Syria* **44 C3** 33 46N 37 41 E
Saba, *W. Indies* **89 C7** 17 42N 63 26W
Šabac, *Serbia, Yug.* **21 B8** 44 48N 19 42 E
Sabadell, *Spain* **19 B7** 41 28N 2 7 E
Sabah □, *Malaysia* **36 C5** 6 0N 117 0 E
Sabak Bernam, *Malaysia* **39 L3** 3 46N 100 58 E
Sabalān, Kūhhā-ye, *Iran* **44 B5** 38 15N 47 45 E
Sabalana, Kepulauan, *Indonesia* **37 F5** 6 45S 118 50 E
Sábana de la Mar, *Dom. Rep.* **89 C6** 19 7N 69 24W
Sábanalarga, *Colombia* **92 A4** 10 38N 74 55W
Sabang, *Indonesia* **36 C1** 5 50N 95 15 E
Sabará, *Brazil* **93 G10** 19 55S 43 46W
Sabarmati →, *India* **42 H5** 22 18N 72 22 E
Sabattis, *U.S.A.* **79 B10** 44 6N 74 40W
Saberania, *Indonesia* **37 E9** 2 5S 138 18 E
Sabhah, *Libya* **51 C8** 27 9N 14 29 E
Sabi →, *India* **42 E7** 28 29N 76 44 E
Sabie, *S. Africa* **57 D5** 25 10S 30 48 E
Sabinal, *Mexico* **86 A3** 30 58N 107 25W
Sabinal, *U.S.A.* **81 L5** 29 19N 99 28W
Sabinas, *Mexico* **86 B4** 27 50N 101 10W
Sabinas →, *Mexico* **86 B4** 27 37N 100 42W
Sabinas Hidalgo, *Mexico* **86 B4** 26 33N 100 10W
Sabine →, *U.S.A.* **81 L8** 29 59N 93 47W
Sabine L., *U.S.A.* **81 L8** 29 53N 93 51W
Sabine Pass, *U.S.A.* **81 L8** 29 44N 93 54W
Sabinsville, *U.S.A.* **78 E7** 41 52N 77 31W
Sabkhet el Bardawîl, *Egypt* **47 D2** 31 10N 33 15 E
Sablayan, *Phil.* **37 B6** 12 50N 120 50 E
Sable, *Canada* **71 A6** 55 30N 68 21W
Sable, C., *Canada* **71 D6** 43 29N 65 38W
Sable, C., *U.S.A.* **75 E10** 25 9N 81 8W
Sable I., *Canada* **71 D8** 44 0N 60 0W
Sabrina Coast, *Antarctica* **5 C9** 68 0S 120 0 E
Sabulubbek, *Indonesia* **36 E1** 1 36S 98 40 E
Sabzevār, *Iran* **45 B8** 36 15N 57 40 E
Sabzvārān, *Iran* **45 D8** 28 45N 57 50 E
Sac City, *U.S.A.* **80 D7** 42 25N 95 0W
Săcele, *Romania* **17 F13** 45 37N 25 41 E
Sachigo →, *Canada* **70 A2** 55 6N 88 58W
Sachigo, L., *Canada* **70 B1** 53 50N 92 12W
Sachsen □, *Germany* **16 C7** 50 55N 13 10 E
Sachsen-Anhalt □, *Germany* **16 C7** 52 0N 12 0 E
Sackets Harbor, *U.S.A.* **79 C8** 43 57N 76 7W
Sackville, *Canada* **71 C7** 45 54N 64 22W
Saco, *Maine, U.S.A.* **77 D10** 43 30N 70 27W
Saco, *Mont., U.S.A.* **82 B10** 48 28N 107 21W
Sacramento, *U.S.A.* **84 G5** 38 35N 121 29W
Sacramento →, *U.S.A.* **84 G5** 38 3N 121 56W
Sacramento Mts., *U.S.A.* **83 K11** 32 30N 105 30W
Sacramento Valley, *U.S.A.* **84 G5** 39 30N 122 0W
Sada-Misaki, *Japan* **31 H6** 33 20N 132 1 E
Sadabad, *India* **42 F8** 27 27N 78 3 E
Sadani, *Tanzania* **54 D4** 5 58S 38 35 E
Sadao, *Thailand* **39 J3** 6 38N 100 26 E
Sadd el Aali, *Egypt* **51 D12** 23 54N 32 54 E
Saddle Mt., *U.S.A.* **84 E3** 45 58N 123 41W
Sadimi, *Dem. Rep. of the Congo* **55 D1** 9 25S 23 32 E
Sado, *Japan* **30 F9** 38 0N 138 25 E
Sadon, *Burma* **41 G20** 25 28N 97 55 E
Sadra, *India* **42 H5** 23 21N 72 43 E
Sadri, *India* **42 G5** 25 11N 73 26 E
Sæby, *Denmark* **9 H14** 57 21N 10 30 E
Saegertown, *U.S.A.* **78 E4** 41 43N 80 9W
Şafājah, *Si. Arabia* **44 E3** 26 25N 39 0 E
Säffle, *Sweden* **9 G15** 59 8N 12 55 E
Safford, *U.S.A.* **83 K9** 32 50N 109 43W
Saffron Walden, *U.K.* **11 E8** 52 1N 0 16 E
Safi, *Morocco* **50 B4** 32 18N 9 20W
Şafīābād, *Iran* **45 B8** 36 45N 57 58 E
Safīd Dasht, *Iran* **45 C6** 33 27N 48 11 E
Safīd Kūh, *Afghan.* **40 B3** 34 45N 63 0 E
Safīd Rūd →, *Iran* **45 B6** 37 23N 50 11 E
Safipur, *India* **43 F9** 26 44N 80 21 E
Safwān, *Iraq* **44 D5** 30 7N 47 43 E
Sag Harbor, *U.S.A.* **79 F12** 41 0N 72 18W
Saga, *Japan* **31 H5** 33 15N 130 16 E
Saga □, *Japan* **31 H5** 33 15N 130 20 E
Sagae, *Japan* **30 E10** 38 22N 140 17 E
Sagamore, *U.S.A.* **78 F5** 40 46N 79 14W
Sagar, *India* **40 M9** 14 14N 75 6 E
Sagar, *Mad. P., India* **43 H8** 23 50N 78 44 E
Sagara, L., *Tanzania* **54 D3** 5 20S 31 0 E
Saginaw, *U.S.A.* **76 D4** 43 26N 83 56W
Saginaw →, *U.S.A.* **76 D4** 43 39N 83 51W
Saginaw B., *U.S.A.* **76 D4** 43 50N 83 40W
Saglouc = Salluit, *Canada* **69 B12** 62 14N 75 38W
Sagō-ri, *S. Korea* **35 G14** 35 25N 126 49 E
Sagua la Grande, *Cuba* **88 B3** 22 50N 80 10W
Saguache, *U.S.A.* **83 G10** 38 5N 106 8W
Saguaro Nat. Park, *U.S.A.* **83 K8** 32 12N 110 38W
Saguenay →, *Canada* **71 C5** 48 22N 71 0W
Sagunt, *Spain* **19 C5** 39 42N 0 18W
Sagunto = Sagunt, *Spain* **19 C5** 39 42N 0 18W
Sagwara, *India* **42 H6** 23 41N 74 1 E
Sahagún, *Spain* **19 A3** 42 18N 5 2W
Saḩam al Jawlān, *Syria* **47 C4** 32 45N 35 55 E
Sahand, Kūh-e, *Iran* **44 B5** 37 44N 46 27 E
Sahara, *Africa* **50 D6** 23 0N 5 0 E
Saharan Atlas = Saharien, Atlas, *Algeria* **50 B6** 33 30N 1 0 E
Saharanpur, *India* **42 E7** 29 58N 77 33 E
Saharien, Atlas, *Algeria* **50 B6** 33 30N 1 0 E
Saharsa, *India* **43 G12** 25 53N 86 36 E
Sahasinaka, *Madag.* **57 C8** 21 49S 47 49 E
Sahaswan, *India* **43 E8** 28 5N 78 45 E
Sahel, *Africa* **50 E5** 16 0N 5 0 E
Sahibganj, *India* **43 G12** 25 12N 87 40 E
Sāḩilīyah, *Iraq* **44 C4** 33 43N 42 42 E
Sahiwal, *Pakistan* **42 D5** 30 45N 73 8 E
Şaḩneh, *Iran* **44 C5** 34 29N 47 41 E
Sahuaripa, *Mexico* **86 B3** 29 0N 109 13W
Sahuarita, *U.S.A.* **83 L8** 31 57N 110 58W
Sahuayo, *Mexico* **86 C4** 20 4N 102 43W
Sai →, *India* **43 G10** 25 39N 82 47 E
Sai Buri, *Thailand* **39 J3** 6 43N 101 45 E
Sa'id Bundas, *Sudan* **51 G10** 8 24N 24 48 E
Sa'īdābād, *Kermān, Iran* **45 D7** 29 30N 55 45 E
Sa'īdābād, *Semnān, Iran* **45 B7** 36 8N 54 11 E
Sa'īdīyeh, *Iran* **45 B6** 36 20N 48 55 E
Saidpur, *Bangla.* **41 G16** 25 48N 89 0 E
Saidpur, *India* **43 G10** 25 33N 83 11 E
Saidu, *Pakistan* **43 B5** 34 43N 72 24 E
Saigon = Phanh Bho Ho Chi Minh, *Vietnam* **39 G6** 10 58N 106 40 E
Saijō, *Japan* **31 H6** 33 55N 133 11 E
Saikhoa Ghat, *India* **41 F19** 27 50N 95 40 E
Saiki, *Japan* **31 H5** 32 58N 131 51 E
Sailana, *India* **42 H6** 23 28N 74 55 E
Sailolof, *Indonesia* **37 E8** 1 7S 130 46 E
Saimaa, *Finland* **9 F23** 61 15N 28 15 E
Şa'in Dezh, *Iran* **44 B5** 36 40N 46 25 E
St. Abb's Head, *U.K.* **12 F6** 55 55N 2 8W
St. Alban's, *Canada* **71 C8** 47 51N 55 50W
St. Albans, *U.K.* **11 F7** 51 45N 0 19W
St. Albans, *Vt., U.S.A.* **79 B11** 44 49N 73 5W
St. Albans, *W. Va., U.S.A.* **76 F5** 38 23N 81 50W
St. Alban's Head, *U.K.* **11 G5** 50 34N 2 4W
St. Albert, *Canada* **72 C6** 53 37N 113 32W
St. Andrew's, *Canada* **71 C8** 47 45N 59 15W
St. Andrews, *U.K.* **12 E6** 56 20N 2 47W
St-Anicet, *Canada* **79 A10** 45 8N 74 22W
St. Ann B., *Canada* **71 C7** 46 22N 60 25W
St. Ann's Bay, *Jamaica* **88 C4** 18 26N 77 15W
St. Anthony, *Canada* **71 B8** 51 22N 55 35W
St. Anthony, *U.S.A.* **82 E8** 43 58N 111 41W
St. Antoine, *Canada* **71 C7** 46 22N 64 45W
St. Arnaud, *Australia* **63 F3** 36 40S 143 16 E
St-Augustin →, *Canada* **71 B8** 51 16N 58 40W
St-Augustin-Saguenay, *Canada* **71 B8** 51 13N 58 38W
St. Augustine, *U.S.A.* **77 L5** 29 54N 81 19W
St. Austell, *U.K.* **11 G3** 50 20N 4 47W
St. Barbe, *Canada* **71 B8** 51 12N 56 46W
St-Barthélemy, *W. Indies* **89 C7** 17 50N 62 50W
St. Bees Hd., *U.K.* **10 C4** 54 31N 3 38W
St. Bride's, *Canada* **71 C9** 46 56N 54 10W
St. Brides B., *U.K.* **11 F2** 51 49N 5 9W
St-Brieuc, *France* **18 B2** 48 30N 2 46W
St. Catharines, *Canada* **78 C5** 43 10N 79 15W
St. Catherines I., *U.S.A.* **77 K5** 31 40N 81 10W
St. Catherine's Pt., *U.K.* **11 G6** 50 34N 1 18W
St-Chamond, *France* **18 D6** 45 28N 4 31 E
St. Charles, *Ill., U.S.A.* **76 E1** 41 54N 88 19W
St. Charles, *Mo., U.S.A.* **80 F9** 38 47N 90 29W
St. Charles, *Va., U.S.A.* **76 F7** 36 48N 83 4W
St. Christopher-Nevis = St. Kitts & Nevis ■, *W. Indies* **89 C7** 17 20N 62 40W
St. Clair, *Mich., U.S.A.* **78 D2** 42 50N 82 30W
St. Clair, *Pa., U.S.A.* **79 F8** 40 43N 76 12W
St. Clair →, *U.S.A.* **78 D2** 42 38N 82 31W
St. Clair, L., *Canada* **70 D3** 42 30N 82 45W
St. Clair, L., *U.S.A.* **78 D2** 42 27N 82 39W
St. Clairsville, *U.S.A.* **78 F4** 40 5N 80 54W
St. Claude, *Canada* **73 D9** 49 40N 98 20W
St-Clet, *Canada* **79 A10** 45 21N 74 13W
St. Cloud, *Fla., U.S.A.* **77 L5** 28 15N 81 17W
St. Cloud, *Minn., U.S.A.* **80 C7** 45 34N 94 10W
St. Cricq, C., *Australia* **61 E1** 25 17S 113 6 E
St. Croix, *Virgin Is.* **89 C7** 17 45N 64 45W
St. Croix →, *U.S.A.* **80 C8** 44 45N 92 48W
St. Croix Falls, *U.S.A.* **80 C8** 45 24N 92 38W
St. David's, *Canada* **71 C8** 48 12N 58 52W
St. David's, *U.K.* **11 F2** 51 53N 5 16W
St. David's Head, *U.K.* **11 F2** 51 54N 5 19W
St-Denis, *France* **18 B5** 48 56N 2 22 E
St-Dizier, *France* **18 B6** 48 38N 4 56 E
St. Elias, Mt., *U.S.A.* **68 B5** 60 18N 140 56W
St. Elias Mts., *Canada* **72 A1** 60 33N 139 28W
St. Elias Mts., *U.S.A.* **68 C6** 60 0N 138 0W
St-Étienne, *France* **18 D6** 45 27N 4 22 E
St. Eugène, *Canada* **79 A10** 45 30N 74 28W
St. Eustatius, *W. Indies* **89 C7** 17 20N 63 0W
St-Félicien, *Canada* **70 C5** 48 40N 72 25W
St-Flour, *France* **18 D5** 45 2N 3 6 E
St. Francis, *U.S.A.* **80 F4** 39 47N 101 48W
St. Francis →, *U.S.A.* **81 H9** 34 38N 90 36W
St. Francis, C., *S. Africa* **56 E3** 34 14S 24 49 E
St. Francisville, *U.S.A.* **81 K9** 30 47N 91 23W
St-François, L., *Canada* **79 A10** 45 10N 74 22W
St-Gabriel, *Canada* **70 C5** 46 17N 73 24W
St. Gallen = Sankt Gallen, *Switz.* **18 C8** 47 26N 9 22 E
St-Gaudens, *France* **18 E4** 43 6N 0 44 E
St. George, *Australia* **63 D4** 28 1S 148 30 E
St. George, *Canada* **71 C6** 45 11N 66 50W
St. George, *S.C., U.S.A.* **77 J5** 33 11N 80 35W
St. George, *Utah, U.S.A.* **83 H7** 37 6N 113 35W
St. George, C., *Canada* **71 C8** 48 30N 59 16W
St. George, C., *U.S.A.* **77 L3** 29 40N 85 5W
St. George Ra., *Australia* **60 C4** 18 40S 125 0 E
St. George's, *Canada* **71 C8** 48 26N 58 31W
St-Georges, *Canada* **71 C5** 46 8N 70 40W
St. George's, *Grenada* **89 D7** 12 5N 61 43W
St. George's B., *Canada* **71 C8** 48 24N 58 53W
St. Georges Basin, *N.S.W., Australia* **63 F5** 35 7S 150 36 E
St. Georges Basin, *W. Austral., Australia* **60 C4** 15 23S 125 2 E
St. George's Channel, *Europe* **13 E6** 52 0N 6 0W
St. Georges Hd., *Australia* **63 F5** 35 12S 150 42 E
St. Gotthard P. = San Gottardo, P. del, *Switz.* **18 C8** 46 33N 8 33 E
St. Helena, *U.S.A.* **82 G2** 38 30N 122 28W
St. Helena ■, *Atl. Oc.* **49 H3** 15 55S 5 44W
St. Helena, Mt., *U.S.A.* **84 G4** 38 40N 122 36W
St. Helena B., *S. Africa* **56 E2** 32 40S 18 10 E
St. Helens, *Australia* **62 G4** 41 20S 148 15 E
St. Helens, *U.K.* **10 D5** 53 27N 2 44W
St. Helens, *U.S.A.* **84 E4** 45 52N 122 48W
St. Helens, Mt., *U.S.A.* **84 D4** 46 12N 122 12W
St. Helier, *U.K.* **11 H5** 49 10N 2 7W
St-Hubert, *Belgium* **15 D5** 50 2N 5 23 E
St-Hyacinthe, *Canada* **70 C5** 45 40N 72 58W
St. Ignace, *U.S.A.* **76 C3** 45 52N 84 44W
St. Ignace I., *Canada* **70 C2** 48 45N 88 0W
St. Ignatius, *U.S.A.* **82 C6** 47 19N 114 6W
St. Ives, *U.K.* **11 G2** 50 12N 5 30W
St. James, *U.S.A.* **80 D7** 43 59N 94 38W
St-Jean →, *Canada* **71 B7** 50 17N 64 20W
St-Jean, L., *Canada* **71 C5** 48 40N 72 0W
St-Jean-Port-Joli, *Canada* **71 C5** 47 15N 70 13W
St-Jean-sur-Richelieu, *Canada* **79 A11** 45 20N 73 20W
St-Jérôme, *Canada* **70 C5** 45 47N 74 0W
St. John, *Canada* **71 C6** 45 20N 66 8W
St. John, *U.S.A.* **81 G5** 38 0N 98 46W
St. John →, *U.S.A.* **77 C12** 45 12N 66 5W
St. John, C., *Canada* **71 C8** 50 0N 55 32W
St. John's, *Antigua* **89 C7** 17 6N 61 51W
St. John's, *Canada* **71 C9** 47 35N 52 40W
St. Johns, *Ariz., U.S.A.* **83 J9** 34 30N 109 22W
St. Johns, *Mich., U.S.A.* **76 D3** 43 0N 84 33W
St. Johns →, *U.S.A.* **77 K5** 30 24N 81 24W
St. John's Pt., *Ireland* **13 B3** 54 34N 8 27W
St. Johnsbury, *U.S.A.* **79 B12** 44 25N 72 1W
St. Johnsville, *U.S.A.* **79 D10** 43 0N 74 43W
St. Joseph, *La., U.S.A.* **81 K9** 31 55N 91 14W
St. Joseph, *Mich., U.S.A.* **75 B9** 42 6N 86 29W
St. Joseph, *Mo., U.S.A.* **80 F7** 39 46N 94 50W
St. Joseph →, *U.S.A.* **76 D2** 42 7N 86 29W
St. Joseph, I., *Canada* **70 C3** 46 12N 83 58W
St. Joseph, L., *Canada* **70 B1** 51 10N 90 35W
St-Jovite, *Canada* **70 C5** 46 8N 74 38W
St. Kilda, *N.Z.* **59 L3** 45 53S 170 31 E
St. Kitts & Nevis ■, *W. Indies* **89 C7** 17 20N 62 40W
St. Laurent, *Canada* **73 C9** 50 25N 97 58W
St. Lawrence, *Australia* **62 C4** 22 16S 149 31 E
St. Lawrence, *Canada* **71 C8** 46 54N 55 23W
St. Lawrence →, *Canada* **71 C6** 49 30N 66 0W
St. Lawrence, Gulf of, *Canada* **71 C7** 48 25N 62 0W
St. Lawrence I., *U.S.A.* **68 B3** 63 30N 170 30W
St. Leonard, *Canada* **71 C6** 47 12N 67 58W
St. Lewis →, *Canada* **71 B8** 52 26N 56 11W
St-Lô, *France* **18 B3** 49 7N 1 5W
St. Louis, *Senegal* **50 E2** 16 8N 16 27W
St. Louis, *U.S.A.* **80 F9** 38 37N 90 12W
St. Louis →, *U.S.A.* **80 B8** 47 15N 92 45W
St. Lucia ■, *W. Indies* **89 D7** 14 0N 60 50W
St. Lucia, L., *S. Africa* **57 D5** 28 5S 32 30 E
St. Lucia Channel, *W. Indies* **89 D7** 14 15N 61 0W
St. Maarten, *W. Indies* **89 C7** 18 0N 63 5W
St. Magnus B., *U.K.* **12 A7** 60 25N 1 35W
St-Malo, *France* **18 B2** 48 39N 2 1W
St-Marc, *Haiti* **89 C5** 19 10N 72 41W
St. Maries, *U.S.A.* **82 C5** 47 19N 116 35W
St-Martin, *W. Indies* **89 C7** 18 0N 63 0W
St. Martin, L., *Canada* **73 C9** 51 40N 98 30W
St. Mary Pk., *Australia* **63 E2** 31 32S 138 34 E
St. Marys, *Australia* **62 G4** 41 35S 148 11 E
St. Marys, *Canada* **78 C3** 43 20N 81 10W
St. Mary's, *Corn., U.K.* **11 H1** 49 55N 6 18W
St. Mary's, *Orkney, U.K.* **12 C6** 58 54N 2 54W
St. Marys, *Ga., U.S.A.* **77 K5** 30 44N 81 33W
St. Marys, *Pa., U.S.A.* **78 E6** 41 26N 78 34W
St. Mary's, C., *Canada* **71 C9** 46 50N 54 12W
St. Mary's B., *Canada* **71 C9** 46 50N 53 50W
St. Marys Bay, *Canada* **71 D6** 44 25N 66 10W
St-Mathieu, Pte., *France* **18 B1** 48 20N 4 45W
St. Matthew I., *U.S.A.* **68 B2** 60 24N 172 42W
St. Matthews, I. = Zadetkyi Kyun, *Burma* **39 H2** 10 0N 98 25 E
St-Maurice →, *Canada* **70 C5** 46 21N 72 31W
St-Nazaire, *France* **18 C2** 47 17N 2 12W
St. Neots, *U.K.* **11 E7** 52 14N 0 15W
St-Niklaas, *Belgium* **15 C4** 51 10N 4 8 E
St-Omer, *France* **18 A5** 50 45N 2 15 E
St-Pamphile, *Canada* **71 C6** 46 58N 69 48W
St. Pascal, *Canada* **71 C6** 47 32N 69 48W
St. Paul, *Canada* **72 C6** 54 0N 111 17W
St. Paul, *Minn., U.S.A.* **80 C8** 44 57N 93 6W
St. Paul, *Nebr., U.S.A.* **80 E5** 41 13N 98 27W
St-Paul →, *Canada* **71 B8** 51 27N 57 42W
St. Paul, I., *Ind. Oc.* **3 F13** 38 55S 77 34 E
St. Paul I., *Canada* **71 C7** 47 12N 60 9W
St. Peter, *U.S.A.* **80 C8** 44 20N 93 57W
St. Peter Port, *U.K.* **11 H5** 49 26N 2 33W
St. Peters, *N.S., Canada* **71 C7** 45 40N 60 53W
St. Peters, *P.E.I., Canada* **71 C7** 46 25N 62 35W
St. Petersburg = Sankt-Peterburg, *Russia* **24 C5** 59 55N 30 20 E
St. Petersburg, *U.S.A.* **77 M4** 27 46N 82 39W
St-Pie, *Canada* **79 A12** 45 30N 72 54W
St-Pierre, *St- P. & M.* **71 C8** 46 46N 56 12W
St-Pierre, L., *Canada* **70 C5** 46 12N 72 52W
St-Pierre et Miquelon □, *St- P. & M.* **71 C8** 46 55N 56 10W
St. Quentin, *Canada* **71 C6** 47 30N 67 23W
St-Quentin, *France* **18 B5** 49 50N 3 16 E
St. Regis, *U.S.A.* **82 C6** 47 18N 115 6W
St. Sebastien, Tanjon' i, *Madag.* **57 A8** 12 26S 48 44 E
St-Siméon, *Canada* **71 C6** 47 51N 69 54W
St. Simons I., *U.S.A.* **77 K5** 31 12N 81 15W
St. Simons Island, *U.S.A.* **77 K5** 31 9N 81 22W
St. Stephen, *Canada* **71 C6** 45 16N 67 17W
St. Thomas, *Canada* **78 D3** 42 45N 81 10W
St. Thomas I., *Virgin Is.* **89 C7** 18 20N 64 55W
St-Tite, *Canada* **70 C5** 46 45N 72 34W
St-Tropez, *France* **18 E7** 43 17N 6 38 E
St. Troud = St. Truiden, *Belgium* **15 D5** 50 48N 5 10 E
St. Truiden, *Belgium* **15 D5** 50 48N 5 10 E
St. Vincent, G., *Australia* **63 F2** 35 0S 138 0 E
St. Vincent & the Grenadines ■, *W. Indies* **89 D7** 13 0N 61 10W
St. Vincent Passage, *W. Indies* **89 D7** 13 30N 61 0W
St-Vith, *Belgium* **15 D6** 50 17N 6 9 E
St. Walburg, *Canada* **73 C7** 53 39N 109 12W
Ste-Agathe-des-Monts, *Canada* **70 C5** 46 3N 74 17W
Ste-Anne, L., *Canada* **71 B6** 50 0N 67 42W
Ste-Anne-des-Monts, *Canada* **71 C6** 49 8N 66 30W
Ste. Genevieve, *U.S.A.* **80 G9** 37 59N 90 2W
Ste-Marguerite →, *Canada* **71 B6** 50 9N 66 36W
Ste-Marie, *Martinique* **89 D7** 14 48N 61 1W
Ste-Marie de la Madeleine, *Canada* **71 C5** 46 26N 71 0W
Ste-Rose, *Guadeloupe* **89 C7** 16 20N 61 45W
Ste. Rose du Lac, *Canada* **73 C9** 51 4N 99 30W
Saintes, *France* **18 D3** 45 45N 0 37W
Saintes, I. des, *Guadeloupe* **89 C7** 15 50N 61 35W
Saintfield, *U.K.* **13 B6** 54 28N 5 49W
Sainthiya, *India* **43 H12** 23 57N 87 40
Saintonge, *France* **18 D3** 45 40N 0 50
Saipan, *Pac. Oc.* **64 F6** 15 12N 145 45
Sairang, *India* **41 H18** 23 50N 92 45
Sairecábur, Cerro, *Bolivia* **94 A2** 22 43S 67 54
Saitama □, *Japan* **31 F9** 36 25N 139 30
Saiyid, *Pakistan* **42 C5** 33 7N 73 2
Sajama, *Bolivia* **92 G5** 18 7S 69 0
Sajószentpéter, *Hungary* **17 D11** 48 12N 20 44
Sajum, *India* **43 C8** 33 20N 79 0
Sak →, *S. Africa* **56 E3** 30 52S 20 25
Sakai, *Japan* **31 G7** 34 30N 135 30
Sakaide, *Japan* **31 G6** 34 15N 133 50
Sakaiminato, *Japan* **31 G6** 35 38N 133 11
Sakākah, *Si. Arabia* **44 D4** 30 0N 40 8
Sakakawea, L., *U.S.A.* **80 B4** 47 30N 101 25
Sakami →, *Canada* **70 B4** 53 40N 76 40
Sakami, L., *Canada* **70 B4** 53 15N 77 0
Sakania, *Dem. Rep. of the Congo* **55 E2** 12 43S 28 30
Sakarya, *Turkey* **25 F5** 40 48N 30 25
Sakashima-Guntō, *Japan* **31 M2** 24 46N 124 0
Sakata, *Japan* **30 E9** 38 55N 139 50
Sakchu, *N. Korea* **35 D13** 40 23N 125 2
Sakeny →, *Madag.* **57 C8** 20 0S 45 25
Sakha □, *Russia* **27 C14** 66 0N 130 0
Sakhalin, *Russia* **27 D15** 51 0N 143 0
Sakhalinskiy Zaliv, *Russia* **27 D15** 54 0N 141 0
Šakiai, *Lithuania* **9 J20** 54 59N 23 2
Sakon Nakhon, *Thailand* **38 D5** 17 10N 104 9
Sakrand, *Pakistan* **42 F3** 26 10N 68 15
Sakri, *India* **43 F12** 26 13N 86 5
Sakrivier, *S. Africa* **56 E3** 30 54S 20 28
Sakti, *India* **43 H10** 22 2N 82 58
Sakuma, *Japan* **31 G8** 35 3N 137 49
Sakurai, *Japan* **31 G7** 34 30N 135 51
Sala, *Sweden* **9 G17** 59 58N 16 35
Sala Consilina, *Italy* **20 D6** 40 23N 15 36
Sala-y-Gómez, *Pac. Oc.* **65 K17** 26 28S 105 28
Salaberry-de-Valleyfield, *Canada* **79 A10** 45 15N 74 8
Saladas, *Argentina* **94 B4** 28 15S 58 40
Saladillo, *Argentina* **94 D4** 35 40S 59 55
Salado →, *Buenos Aires, Argentina* **94 D4** 35 44S 57 22
Salado →, *La Pampa, Argentina* **96 D3** 37 30S 67 0
Salado →, *Santa Fe, Argentina* **94 C3** 31 40S 60 41
Salado →, *Mexico* **81 M5** 26 52N 99 19
Salaga, *Ghana* **50 G5** 8 31N 0 31
Sālah, *Syria* **47 C5** 32 40N 36 45
Sálakhos, *Greece* **23 C9** 36 17N 27 57
Salālah, *Oman* **46 D5** 16 56N 53 59
Salamanca, *Chile* **94 C1** 31 46S 70 59
Salamanca, *Spain* **19 B3** 40 58N 5 39
Salamanca, *U.S.A.* **78 D6** 42 10N 78 43
Salāmatābād, *Iran* **44 C5** 35 39N 47 50
Salamis, *Cyprus* **23 D12** 35 11N 33 54
Salamís, *Greece* **21 F10** 37 56N 23 30
Salar de Atacama, *Chile* **94 A2** 23 30S 68 25
Salar de Uyuni, *Bolivia* **92 H5** 20 30S 67 45
Salatiga, *Indonesia* **37 G14** 7 19S 110 30
Salavat, *Russia* **24 D10** 53 21N 55 55
Salaverry, *Peru* **92 E3** 8 15S 79 0
Salawati, *Indonesia* **37 E8** 1 7S 130 52
Salaya, *India* **42 H3** 22 19N 69 35
Salayar, *Indonesia* **37 F6** 6 7S 120 30
Salcombe, *U.K.* **11 G4** 50 14N 3 47
Saldanha, *S. Africa* **56 E2** 33 0S 17 58
Saldanha B., *S. Africa* **56 E2** 33 6S 18 0
Saldus, *Latvia* **9 H20** 56 38N 22 30
Sale, *Australia* **63 F4** 38 6S 147 6
Salé, *Morocco* **50 B4** 34 3N 6 48
Sale, *U.K.* **10 D5** 53 26N 2 19
Salekhard, *Russia* **26 C7** 66 30N 66 35
Salem, *India* **40 P11** 11 40N 78 11
Salem, *Ill., U.S.A.* **76 F1** 38 38N 88 57
Salem, *Ind., U.S.A.* **76 F2** 38 36N 86 6
Salem, *Mass., U.S.A.* **79 D14** 42 31N 70 53
Salem, *Mo., U.S.A.* **81 G9** 37 39N 91 32
Salem, *N.H., U.S.A.* **79 D13** 42 45N 71 12
Salem, *N.J., U.S.A.* **76 F8** 39 34N 75 28
Salem, *N.Y., U.S.A.* **79 C11** 43 10N 73 20
Salem, *Ohio, U.S.A.* **78 F4** 40 54N 80 52
Salem, *Oreg., U.S.A.* **82 D2** 44 56N 123 2
Salem, *S. Dak., U.S.A.* **80 D6** 43 44N 97 23
Salem, *Va., U.S.A.* **76 G5** 37 18N 80 3
Salerno, *Italy* **20 D6** 40 41N 14 47
Salford, *U.K.* **10 D5** 53 30N 2 18
Salgótarján, *Hungary* **17 D10** 48 5N 19 47
Salgueiro, *Brazil* **93 E11** 8 4S 39 6
Salibabu, *Indonesia* **37 D7** 3 51N 126 40
Salida, *U.S.A.* **74 C5** 38 32N 106 0
Salihli, *Turkey* **21 E13** 38 28N 28 8
Salihorsk, *Belarus* **17 B14** 52 51N 27 27
Salima, *Malawi* **53 G6** 13 47S 34 28
Salina, *Italy* **20 E6** 38 34N 14 50
Salina, *Kans., U.S.A.* **80 F6** 38 50N 97 37
Salina, *Utah, U.S.A.* **83 G8** 38 58N 111 51
Salina Cruz, *Mexico* **87 D5** 16 10N 95 10
Salinas, *Brazil* **93 G10** 16 10S 42 10
Salinas, *Chile* **94 A2** 23 31S 69 29
Salinas, *Ecuador* **92 D2** 2 10S 80 58
Salinas, *U.S.A.* **84 J5** 36 40N 121 39
Salinas →, *Guatemala* **87 D6** 16 28N 90 31
Salinas →, *U.S.A.* **84 J5** 36 45N 121 48
Salinas, B. de, *Nic.* **88 D2** 11 4N 85 45
Salinas, Pampa de las, *Argentina* **94 C2** 31 58S 66 42
Salinas Ambargasta, *Argentina* **94 B3** 29 0S 65 0

Shafter

Shafter, U.S.A. **85 K7** 35 30N 119 16W
Shaftesbury, U.K. **11 F5** 51 0N 2 11W
Shagram, Pakistan **43 A5** 36 24N 72 20 E
Shah Alizai, Pakistan **42 E2** 29 25N 66 33 E
Shah Bunder, Pakistan **42 G2** 24 13N 67 56 E
Shahabad, Punjab, India **42 D7** 30 10N 76 55 E
Shahabad, Raj., India **42 G7** 25 15N 77 11 E
Shahabad, Ut. P., India **43 F8** 27 36N 79 56 E
Shahadpur, Pakistan **42 G3** 25 55N 68 35 E
Shahba, Syria **47 C5** 32 52N 36 38 E
Shahdād, Iran **45 D8** 30 30N 57 40 E
Shahdād, Namakzār-e, Iran **45 D8** 30 20N 58 20 E
Shahdadkot, Pakistan **42 F2** 27 50N 67 55 E
Shahdol, India **43 H9** 23 19N 81 26 E
Shahe, China **34 F8** 37 0N 114 32 E
Shahganj, India **43 F10** 26 3N 82 44 E
Shahgarh, India **40 F6** 27 15N 69 50 E
Shahjahanpur, India **43 F8** 27 54N 79 57 E
Shahpur, India **42 H7** 22 12N 77 58 E
Shahpur, Baluchistan, Pakistan **42 E3** 28 46N 68 27 E
Shahpur, Punjab, Pakistan **42 C5** 32 17N 72 26 E
Shahpur Chakar, Pakistan **42 F3** 26 9N 68 39 E
Shahpura, Mad. P., India **43 H9** 23 10N 80 45 E
Shahpura, Raj., India **42 G6** 25 38N 74 56 E
Shahr-e Bābak, Iran **45 D7** 30 7N 55 9 E
Shahr-e Kord, Iran **45 C6** 32 15N 50 55 E
Shāhrakht, Iran **45 C9** 33 38N 60 16 E
Shahrig, Pakistan **42 D2** 30 15N 67 40 E
Shahukou, China **34 D7** 40 20N 112 18 E
Shaikhabad, Afghan. **42 B3** 34 2N 68 45 E
Shajapur, India **42 H7** 23 27N 76 21 E
Shakargarh, Pakistan **42 C6** 32 17N 75 10 E
Shakawe, Botswana **56 B3** 18 28S 21 49 E
Shaker Heights, U.S.A. **78 E3** 41 29N 81 32W
Shakhty, Russia **25 E7** 47 40N 40 16 E
Shakhunya, Russia **24 C8** 57 40N 46 46 E
Shaki, Nigeria **50 G6** 8 41N 3 21 E
Shallow Lake, Canada **78 B3** 44 36N 81 5W
Shalqar, Kazakstan **26 E6** 47 48N 59 39 E
Shaluli Shan, China **32 C4** 30 40N 99 55 E
Shām, Iran **45 E8** 26 39N 57 21 E
Shām, Bādiyat ash, Asia **44 C3** 32 0N 40 0 E
Shamâl Kordofân □, Sudan **48 E6** 15 0N 30 0 E
Shamattawa, Canada **70 A1** 55 51N 92 5W
Shamattawa →, Canada **70 A2** 55 1N 85 23W
Shamīl, Iran **45 E8** 27 30N 56 55 E
Shāmkūh, Iran **45 C8** 35 47N 57 50 E
Shamli, India **42 E7** 29 32N 77 18 E
Shammar, Jabal, Si. Arabia **44 E4** 27 40N 41 0 E
Shamo = Gobi, Asia **34 C6** 44 0N 110 0 E
Shamo, L., Ethiopia **46 F2** 5 45N 37 30 E
Shamokin, U.S.A. **79 F8** 40 47N 76 34W
Shamrock, U.S.A. **81 H4** 35 13N 100 15W
Shamva, Zimbabwe **55 F3** 17 20S 31 32 E
Shan □, Burma **41 J21** 21 30N 98 30 E
Shan Xian, China **34 G9** 34 50N 116 5 E
Shanchengzhen, China **35 C13** 42 20N 125 20 E
Shāndak, Iran **45 D9** 28 28N 60 27 E
Shandon, U.S.A. **84 K6** 35 39N 120 23W
Shandong □, China **35 G10** 36 0N 118 0 E
Shandong Bandao, China **35 F11** 37 0N 121 0 E
Shang Xian = Shangzhou, China **34 H5** 33 50N 109 58 E
Shanga, Nigeria **50 F6** 11 12N 4 33 E
Shangalowe, Dem. Rep. of the Congo **55 E2** 10 50S 26 30 E
Shangani →, Zimbabwe **55 F2** 18 41S 27 10 E
Shangbancheng, China **35 D10** 40 50N 118 1 E
Shangdu, China **34 D7** 41 30N 113 30 E
Shanghai, China **33 C7** 31 15N 121 26 E
Shanghe, China **35 F9** 37 20N 117 10 E
Shangnan, China **34 H6** 33 32N 110 50 E
Shangqiu, China **34 G8** 34 26N 115 36 E
Shangrao, China **33 D6** 28 25N 117 59 E
Shangshui, China **34 H8** 33 42N 114 35 E
Shangzhi, China **35 B14** 45 22N 127 56 E
Shangzhou, China **34 H5** 33 50N 109 58 E
Shanhetun, China **35 B14** 44 33N 127 15 E
Shannon, N.Z. **59 J5** 40 33S 175 25 E
Shannon →, Ireland **13 D2** 52 35N 9 30W
Shannon, Mouth of the, Ireland **13 D2** 52 30N 9 55W
Shannon Airport, Ireland **13 D3** 52 42N 8 57W
Shansi = Shanxi □, China **34 F7** 37 0N 112 0 E
Shantar, Ostrov Bolshoy, Russia **27 D14** 55 9N 137 40 E
Shantipur, India **43 H13** 23 17N 88 25 E
Shantou, China **33 D6** 23 18N 116 40 E
Shantung = Shandong □, China **35 G10** 36 0N 118 0 E
Shanxi □, China **34 F7** 37 0N 112 0 E
Shanyang, China **34 H5** 33 31N 109 55 E
Shanyin, China **34 E7** 39 25N 112 56 E
Shaoguan, China **33 D6** 24 48N 113 35 E
Shaoxing, China **33 D7** 30 0N 120 35 E
Shaoyang, China **33 D6** 27 14N 111 25 E
Shap, U.K. **10 C5** 54 32N 2 40W
Shapinsay, U.K. **12 B6** 59 3N 2 51W
Shaqra', Si. Arabia **44 E5** 25 15N 45 16 E
Shaqrā', Yemen **46 E4** 13 22N 45 44 E
Sharafkhāneh, Iran **44 B5** 38 11N 45 29 E
Sharbot Lake, Canada **79 B8** 44 46N 76 41W
Shari, Japan **30 C12** 43 55N 144 40 E
Sharjah = Ash Shāriqah, U.A.E. **45 E7** 25 23N 55 26 E
Shark B., Australia **61 E1** 25 30S 113 32 E
Sharon, Mass., U.S.A. **79 D13** 42 7N 71 11W
Sharon, Pa., U.S.A. **78 E4** 41 14N 80 31W
Sharon Springs, Kans., U.S.A. **80 F4** 38 54N 101 45W
Sharon Springs, N.Y., U.S.A. **79 D10** 42 48N 74 37W
Sharp Pt., Australia **62 A3** 10 58S 142 43 E
Sharpe L., Canada **70 B1** 54 24N 93 40W
Sharpsville, U.S.A. **78 E4** 41 15N 80 29W
Sharya, Russia **24 C8** 58 22N 45 20 E
Shashemene, Ethiopia **46 F2** 7 13N 38 33 E
Shashi, Botswana **57 C4** 21 15S 27 27 E
Shashi, China **33 C6** 30 25N 112 14 E
Shashi →, Africa **55 G2** 21 14S 29 20 E
Shasta, Mt., U.S.A. **82 F2** 41 25N 122 12W
Shasta L., U.S.A. **82 F2** 40 43N 122 25W
Shatt al'Arab →, Iraq **45 D6** 29 57N 48 34 E
Shaunavon, Canada **73 D7** 49 35N 108 25W
Shaver L., U.S.A. **84 H7** 37 9N 119 18W
Shaw →, Australia **60 D2** 20 21S 119 17 E
Shaw I., Australia **62 C4** 20 30S 149 2 E
Shawanaga, Canada **78 A4** 45 31N 80 17W
Shawangunk Mts., U.S.A. **79 E10** 41 35N 74 30W
Shawano, U.S.A. **76 C1** 44 47N 88 36W
Shawinigan, Canada **70 C5** 46 35N 72 50W
Shawnee, U.S.A. **81 H6** 35 20N 96 55W
Shay Gap, Australia **60 D3** 20 30S 120 10 E
Shaybārā, Si. Arabia **44 E3** 25 26N 36 47 E
Shaykh, J. ash, Lebanon **47 B4** 33 25N 35 50 E
Shaykh Miskīn, Syria **47 C5** 32 49N 36 9 E
Shaykh Sa'īd, Iraq **44 C5** 32 34N 46 17 E
Shcherbakov = Rybinsk, Russia **24 C6** 58 5N 38 50 E
Shchuchinsk, Kazakstan **26 D8** 52 56N 70 12 E
She Xian, China **34 F7** 36 30N 113 40 E
Shebele = Scebeli, Wabi →, Somali Rep. **46 G3** 2 0N 44 0 E
Sheboygan, U.S.A. **76 D2** 43 46N 87 45W
Shediac, Canada **71 C7** 46 14N 64 32W
Sheelin, L., Ireland **13 C4** 53 48N 7 20W
Sheep Haven, Ireland **13 A4** 55 11N 7 52W
Sheerness, U.K. **11 F8** 51 26N 0 47 E
Sheet Harbour, Canada **71 D7** 44 56N 62 31W
Sheffield, U.K. **10 D6** 53 23N 1 28W
Sheffield, Ala., U.S.A. **77 H2** 34 46N 87 41W
Sheffield, Mass., U.S.A. **79 D11** 42 5N 73 21W
Sheffield, Pa., U.S.A. **78 E5** 41 42N 79 3W
Sheikhpura, India **43 G11** 25 9N 85 53 E
Shekhupura, Pakistan **42 D5** 31 42N 73 58 E
Shelburne, N.S., Canada **71 D6** 43 47N 65 20W
Shelburne, Ont., Canada **78 B4** 44 4N 80 15W
Shelburne, Vt., U.S.A. **79 B11** 44 22N 73 13W
Shelburne, Vt., U.S.A. **79 B11** 44 23N 73 14W
Shelburne B., Australia **62 A3** 11 50S 142 50 E
Shelburne Falls, U.S.A. **79 D12** 42 36N 72 45W
Shelby, Mich., U.S.A. **76 D2** 43 37N 86 22W
Shelby, Miss., U.S.A. **81 J9** 33 57N 90 46W
Shelby, Mont., U.S.A. **82 B8** 48 30N 111 51W
Shelby, N.C., U.S.A. **77 H5** 35 17N 81 32W
Shelby, Ohio, U.S.A. **78 F2** 40 53N 82 40W
Shelbyville, Ill., U.S.A. **80 F10** 39 24N 88 48W
Shelbyville, Ind., U.S.A. **76 F3** 39 31N 85 47W
Shelbyville, Ky., U.S.A. **76 F3** 38 13N 85 14W
Shelbyville, Tenn., U.S.A. **77 H2** 35 29N 86 28W
Sheldon, U.S.A. **80 D7** 43 11N 95 51W
Sheldrake, Canada **71 B7** 50 20N 64 51W
Shelikhova, Zaliv, Russia **27 D16** 59 30N 157 0 E
Shell Lakes, Australia **61 E4** 29 20S 127 30 E
Shellbrook, Canada **73 C7** 53 13N 106 24W
Shellharbour, Australia **63 E5** 34 31S 150 51 E
Shelter I, U.S.A. **79 E12** 41 5N 72 21W
Shelton, Conn., U.S.A. **79 E11** 41 19N 73 5W
Shelton, Wash., U.S.A. **84 C3** 47 13N 123 6W
Shen Xian, China **34 F8** 36 15N 115 40 E
Shenandoah, Iowa, U.S.A. **80 E7** 40 46N 95 22W
Shenandoah, Pa., U.S.A. **79 F8** 40 49N 76 12W
Shenandoah, Va., U.S.A. **76 F6** 38 29N 78 37W
Shenandoah →, U.S.A. **76 F7** 39 19N 77 44W
Shenandoah National Park, U.S.A. **76 F6** 38 35N 78 22W
Shenchi, China **34 E7** 39 8N 112 10 E
Shendam, Nigeria **50 G7** 8 49N 9 30 E
Shendî, Sudan **51 E12** 16 46N 33 22 E
Shengfang, China **34 E9** 39 3N 116 42 E
Shenjingzi, China **35 B13** 44 40N 124 30 E
Shenmu, China **34 E6** 38 50N 110 29 E
Shenqiu, China **34 H8** 33 25N 115 5 E
Shenqiucheng, China **34 H8** 33 24N 115 2 E
Shensi = Shaanxi □, China **34 G5** 35 0N 109 0 E
Shenyang, China **35 D12** 41 48N 123 27 E
Sheo, India **42 F4** 26 11N 71 15 E
Sheopur Kalan, India **40 G10** 25 40N 76 40 E
Shepetivka, Ukraine **17 C14** 50 10N 27 10 E
Shepetovka = Shepetivka, Ukraine **17 C14** 50 10N 27 10 E
Shepparton, Australia **63 F4** 36 23S 145 26 E
Sheppey, I. of, U.K. **11 F8** 51 25N 0 48 E
Shepton Mallet, U.K. **11 F5** 51 11N 2 33W
Sheqi, China **34 H7** 33 12N 112 57 E
Sher Qila, Pakistan **43 A6** 36 7N 74 2 E
Sherborne, U.K. **11 G5** 50 57N 2 31W
Sherbro I., S. Leone **50 G3** 7 30N 12 40W
Sherbrooke, Canada **71 C7** 45 8N 61 59W
Sherbrooke, Qué., Canada **79 A13** 45 28N 71 57W
Sherburne, U.S.A. **79 D9** 42 41N 75 30W
Shergarh, India **42 F5** 26 20N 72 18 E
Sherghati, India **43 G11** 24 34N 84 47 E
Sheridan, Ark., U.S.A. **81 H8** 34 19N 92 24W
Sheridan, Wyo., U.S.A. **82 D10** 44 48N 106 58W
Sheringham, U.K. **10 E9** 52 56N 1 13 E
Sherkin I., Ireland **13 E2** 51 28N 9 26W
Sherkot, India **43 E8** 29 22N 78 35 E
Sherman, U.S.A. **81 J6** 33 40N 96 35W
Sherpur, India **43 G10** 25 34N 83 47 E
Sherridon, Canada **73 B8** 55 8N 101 5W
Sherwood Forest, U.K. **10 D6** 53 6N 1 7W
Sherwood Park, Canada **72 C6** 53 31N 113 19W
Sheslay →, Canada **72 B2** 58 48N 132 5W
Shethanei L., Canada **73 B9** 58 48N 97 50W
Shetland □, U.K. **12 A7** 60 30N 1 30W
Shetland Is., U.K. **12 A7** 60 30N 1 30W
Shetrunji →, India **42 J5** 21 19N 72 7 E
Sheyenne →, U.S.A. **80 B6** 47 2N 96 50W
Shibām, Yemen **46 D4** 16 0N 48 36 E
Shibata, Japan **30 F9** 37 57N 139 20 E
Shibecha, Japan **30 C12** 43 17N 144 36 E
Shibetsu, Japan **30 B11** 44 10N 142 23 E
Shibogama L., Canada **70 B2** 53 35N 88 15W
Shibushi, Japan **31 J5** 31 25N 131 8 E
Shickshinny, U.S.A. **79 E8** 41 9N 76 9W
Shickshock Mts. = Chic-Chocs, Mts., Canada **71 C6** 48 55N 66 0W
Shidao, China **35 F12** 36 50N 122 25 E
Shido, Japan **31 G7** 34 19N 134 10 E
Shiel, L., U.K. **12 E3** 56 48N 5 34W
Shield, C., Australia **62 A2** 13 20S 136 20 E
Shiga □, Japan **31 G8** 35 20N 136 0 E
Shiguaigou, China **34 D6** 40 52N 110 15 E
Shihchiachuangi = Shijiazhuang, China **34 E8** 38 2N 114 28 E
Shijiazhuang, China **34 E8** 38 2N 114 28 E
Shikarpur, India **42 E8** 28 17N 78 7 E
Shikarpur, Pakistan **42 F3** 27 57N 68 39 E
Shikohabad, India **43 F8** 27 6N 78 36 E
Shikoku □, Japan **31 H6** 33 30N 133 30 E
Shikoku-Sanchi, Japan **31 H6** 33 30N 133 30 E
Shiliguri, India **41 F16** 26 45N 88 25 E
Shilka, Russia **27 D12** 52 0N 115 55 E
Shilka →, Russia **27 D13** 53 20N 121 26 E
Shillelagh, Ireland **13 D5** 52 45N 6 32W
Shillington, U.S.A. **79 F9** 40 18N 75 58W
Shillong, India **41 G17** 25 35N 91 53 E
Shilo, West Bank **47 C4** 32 4N 35 18 E
Shilou, China **34 F6** 37 0N 110 48 E
Shimabara, Japan **31 H5** 32 48N 130 20 E
Shimada, Japan **31 G9** 34 49N 138 10 E
Shimane □, Japan **31 G6** 35 0N 132 30 E
Shimanovsk, Russia **27 D13** 52 15N 127 30 E
Shimizu, Japan **31 G9** 35 0N 138 30 E
Shimodate, Japan **31 F9** 36 20N 139 55 E
Shimoga, India **40 N9** 13 57N 75 32 E
Shimoni, Kenya **54 C4** 4 38S 39 20 E
Shimonoseki, Japan **31 H5** 33 58N 130 55 E
Shimpuru Rapids, Angola **56 B2** 17 45S 19 55 E
Shin, L., U.K. **12 C4** 58 5N 4 30W
Shinano-Gawa →, Japan **31 F9** 36 50N 138 30 E
Shināş, Oman **45 E8** 24 46N 56 28 E
Shīndand, Afghan. **40 C3** 33 12N 62 8 E
Shinglehouse, U.S.A. **78 E6** 41 58N 78 12W
Shingū, Japan **31 H7** 33 40N 135 55 E
Shinjō, Japan **30 E10** 38 46N 140 18 E
Shinshār, Syria **47 A5** 34 36N 36 43 E
Shinyanga, Tanzania **54 C3** 3 45S 33 27 E
Shinyanga □, Tanzania **54 C3** 3 50S 34 0 E
Shio-no-Misaki, Japan **31 H7** 33 25N 135 45 E
Shiogama, Japan **30 E10** 38 19N 141 1 E
Shiojiri, Japan **31 F8** 36 6N 137 58 E
Shipchenski Prokhod, Bulgaria **21 C11** 42 45N 25 15 E
Shiping, China **32 D5** 23 45N 102 23 E
Shipki La, India **40 D11** 31 45N 78 40 E
Shippegan, Canada **71 C7** 47 45N 64 45W
Shippensburg, U.S.A. **78 F7** 40 3N 77 31W
Shippenville, U.S.A. **78 E5** 41 15N 79 28W
Shiprock, U.S.A. **83 H9** 36 47N 108 41W
Shiqma, N. →, Israel **47 D3** 31 37N 34 30 E
Shiquan, China **34 H5** 33 5N 108 15 E
Shiquan He = Indus →, Pakistan **42 G2** 24 20N 67 47 E
Shīr Kūh, Iran **45 D7** 31 39N 54 3 E
Shiragami-Misaki, Japan **30 D10** 41 24N 140 12 E
Shirakawa, Fukushima, Japan **31 F10** 37 7N 140 13 E
Shirakawa, Gifu, Japan **31 F8** 36 17N 136 56 E
Shirane-San, Gumma, Japan **31 F9** 36 48N 139 22 E
Shirane-San, Yamanashi, Japan **31 G9** 35 42N 138 9 E
Shiraoi, Japan **30 C10** 42 33N 141 21 E
Shīrāz, Iran **45 D7** 29 42N 52 30 E
Shire →, Africa **55 F4** 17 42S 35 19 E
Shiretoko-Misaki, Japan **30 B12** 44 21N 145 20 E
Shirinab →, Pakistan **42 D2** 30 15N 66 28 E
Shiriya-Zaki, Japan **30 D10** 41 25N 141 30 E
Shiroishi, Japan **30 F10** 38 0N 140 37 E
Shīrvān, Iran **45 B8** 37 30N 57 50 E
Shirwa, L. = Chilwa, L., Malawi **55 F4** 15 15S 35 40 E
Shivpuri, India **42 G7** 25 26N 77 42 E
Shixian, China **35 C15** 43 5N 129 50 E
Shizuishan, China **34 E4** 39 15N 106 50 E
Shizuoka, Japan **31 G9** 34 57N 138 24 E
Shizuoka □, Japan **31 G9** 35 15N 138 40 E
Shklov = Shklow, Belarus **17 A16** 54 16N 30 15 E
Shklow, Belarus **17 A16** 54 16N 30 15 E
Shkoder = Shkodra, Albania **21 C8** 42 4N 19 32 E
Shkodra, Albania **21 C8** 42 4N 19 32 E
Shkumbini →, Albania **21 D8** 41 2N 19 31 E
Shmidta, Ostrov, Russia **27 A10** 81 0N 91 0 E
Shō-Gawa →, Japan **31 F8** 36 47N 137 4 E
Shoal L., Canada **73 D9** 49 33N 95 1W
Shoal Lake, Canada **73 C8** 50 30N 100 35W
Shōdo-Shima, Japan **31 G7** 34 30N 134 15 E
Sholapur = Solapur, India **40 L9** 17 43N 75 56 E
Shologontsy, Russia **27 C12** 66 13N 114 0 E
Shōmrōn, West Bank **47 C4** 32 15N 35 13 E
Shoreham by Sea, U.K. **11 G7** 50 50N 0 16W
Shori →, Pakistan **42 E3** 28 29N 69 44 E
Shorkot Road, Pakistan **42 D5** 30 47N 72 15 E
Shoshone, Calif., U.S.A. **85 K10** 35 58N 116 16W
Shoshone, Idaho, U.S.A. **82 E6** 42 56N 114 25W
Shoshone L., U.S.A. **82 D8** 44 22N 110 43W
Shoshone Mts., U.S.A. **82 G5** 39 20N 117 25W
Shoshong, Botswana **56 C4** 22 56S 26 31 E
Shoshoni, U.S.A. **82 E9** 43 14N 108 7W
Shouguang, China **35 F10** 37 52N 118 45 E
Shouyang, China **34 F7** 37 54N 113 8 E
Show Low, U.S.A. **83 J9** 34 15N 110 2W
Shreveport, U.S.A. **81 J8** 32 31N 93 45W
Shrewsbury, U.K. **11 E5** 52 43N 2 45W
Shri Mohangarh, India **42 F4** 27 17N 71 18 E
Shrirampur, India **43 H13** 22 44N 88 21 E
Shropshire □, U.K. **11 E5** 52 36N 2 45W
Shu, Kazakstan **26 E8** 43 36N 73 42 E
Shu →, Kazakstan **28 E10** 45 0N 67 44 E
Shuangcheng, China **35 B14** 45 20N 126 15 E
Shuanggou, China **35 G9** 34 2N 117 30 E
Shuangliao, China **35 C12** 43 29N 123 30 E
Shuangshanzi, China **35 D10** 40 20N 119 8 E
Shuangyang, China **35 C13** 43 28N 125 40 E
Shuangyashan, China **33 B8** 46 28N 131 5 E
Shuguri Falls, Tanzania **55 D4** 8 33S 37 22 E
Shuiye, China **34 F8** 36 7N 114 8 E
Shujalpur, India **42 H7** 23 18N 76 46 E
Shukpa Kunzang, India **43 B8** 34 22N 78 22 E
Shulan, China **35 B14** 44 28N 127 0 E
Shule, China **32 C2** 39 25N 76 3 E
Shumagin Is., U.S.A. **68 C4** 55 7N 160 30W
Shumen, Bulgaria **21 C12** 43 18N 26 55 E
Shumikha, Russia **26 D7** 55 10N 63 15 E
Shuo Xian = Shuozhou, China **34 E7** 39 20N 112 33 E
Shuozhou, China **34 E7** 39 20N 112 33 E
Shūr →, Fārs, Iran **45 D7** 28 30N 55 0 E
Shūr →, Kermān, Iran **45 D8** 30 52N 57 37 E
Shūr →, Yazd, Iran **45 D7** 31 45N 55 15 E
Shūr Āb, Iran **45 C6** 34 23N 51 11 E
Shūr Gaz, Iran **45 D8** 29 10N 59 20 E
Shūrāb, Iran **45 C8** 33 43N 56 29 E
Shūrjestān, Iran **45 D7** 31 24N 52 25 E
Shurugwi, Zimbabwe **55 F3** 19 40S 30 0 E
Shūsf, Iran **45 D9** 31 50N 60 5 E
Shūshtar, Iran **45 D6** 32 0N 48 50 E
Shuswap L., Canada **72 C5** 50 55N 119 3W
Shuyang, China **35 G10** 34 10N 118 42 E
Shūzū, Iran **45 D7** 29 52N 54 30 E
Shwebo, Burma **41 H19** 22 30N 95 45 E
Shwegu, Burma **41 G20** 24 15N 96 26 E
Shweli →, Burma **41 H20** 23 45N 96 45 E
Shymkent, Kazakstan **26 E7** 42 18N 69 36 E
Shyok, India **43 B8** 34 13N 78 12 E
Shyok →, Pakistan **43 B6** 35 13N 75 53 E
Si Chon, Thailand **39 H2** 9 0N 99 54 E
Si Kiang = Xi Jiang →, China **33 D6** 22 5N 113 20 E
Si-ngan = Xi'an, China **34 G5** 34 15N 109 0 E
Si Prachan, Thailand **38 E3** 14 37N 100 9 E
Si Racha, Thailand **38 F3** 13 10N 100 48 E
Si Xian, China **35 H9** 33 30N 117 50 E
Siahaf →, Pakistan **42 E3** 29 3N 68 57 E
Siahan Range, Pakistan **40 F4** 27 30N 64 40 E
Siaksriindrapura, Indonesia **36 D2** 0 51N 102 0 E
Sialkot, Pakistan **42 C6** 32 32N 74 30 E
Siam = Thailand ■, Asia **38 E4** 16 0N 102 0 E
Sian = Xi'an, China **34 G5** 34 15N 109 0 E
Siantan, Indonesia **36 D3** 3 10N 106 15 E
Siāreh, Iran **45 D9** 28 5N 60 14 E
Siargao, Phil. **37 C7** 9 52N 126 3 E
Siari, Pakistan **43 B7** 34 55N 76 40 E
Siasi, Phil. **37 C6** 5 34N 120 50 E
Siau, Indonesia **37 D7** 2 50N 125 25 E
Šiauliai, Lithuania **9 J20** 55 56N 23 15 E
Sibâi, Gebel el, Egypt **44 E2** 25 45N 34 10 E
Sibay, Russia **24 D10** 52 42N 58 39 E
Sibayi, L., S. Africa **57 D5** 27 20S 32 45 E
Šibenik, Croatia **20 C6** 43 48N 15 54 E
Siberia, Russia **4 D13** 60 0N 100 0 E
Siberut, Indonesia **36 E1** 1 30S 99 0 E
Sibi, Pakistan **42 E2** 29 30N 67 54 E
Sibil = Oksibil, Indonesia **37 E10** 4 59S 140 35 E
Sibiti, Congo **52 E2** 3 38S 13 19 E
Sibiu, Romania **17 F13** 45 45N 24 9 E
Sibley, U.S.A. **80 D7** 43 24N 95 45W
Sibolga, Indonesia **36 D1** 1 42N 98 45 E
Sibsagar, India **41 F19** 27 0N 94 36 E
Sibu, Malaysia **36 D4** 2 18N 111 49 E
Sibuco, Phil. **37 C6** 7 20N 122 10 E
Sibuguey B., Phil. **37 C6** 7 50N 122 45 E
Sibut, C.A.R. **52 C3** 5 46N 19 10 E
Sibutu, Phil. **37 D5** 4 45N 119 30 E
Sibutu Passage, E. Indies **37 D6** 4 50N 120 0 E
Sibuyan, Phil. **37 B6** 12 25N 122 40 E
Sibuyan Sea, Phil. **37 B6** 12 30N 122 20 E
Sicamous, Canada **72 C5** 50 49N 119 0W
Siccus →, Australia **63 E2** 31 26S 139 30 E
Sichuan □, China **32 C5** 31 0N 104 0 E
Sicilia, Italy **20 F6** 37 30N 14 30 E
Sicily = Sicilia, Italy **20 F6** 37 30N 14 30 E
Sicuani, Peru **92 F4** 14 21S 71 10W
Sidári, Greece **23 A3** 39 47N 19 41 E
Siddhapur, India **42 H5** 23 56N 72 25 E
Siddipet, India **40 K11** 18 5N 78 51 E
Sidhauli, India **43 F9** 27 17N 80 50 E
Sídheros, Ákra, Greece **23 D8** 35 19N 26 19 E
Sidhi, India **43 G9** 24 25N 81 53 E
Sidi-bel-Abbès, Algeria **50 A5** 35 13N 0 39W
Sidlaw Hills, U.K. **12 E5** 56 32N 3 2W
Sidley, Mt., Antarctica **5 D14** 77 2S 126 2W
Sidmouth, U.K. **11 G4** 50 40N 3 15W
Sidmouth, C., Australia **62 A3** 13 25S 143 36 E
Sidney, Canada **72 D4** 48 39N 123 24W
Sidney, Mont., U.S.A. **80 B2** 47 43N 104 9W
Sidney, N.Y., U.S.A. **79 D9** 42 19N 75 24W
Sidney, Nebr., U.S.A. **80 E3** 41 8N 102 59W
Sidney, Ohio, U.S.A. **76 E3** 40 17N 84 9W
Sidney Lanier L., U.S.A. **77 H4** 34 10N 84 4W
Sidoarjo, Indonesia **37 G15** 7 27S 112 43 E
Sidon = Saydā, Lebanon **47 B4** 33 35N 35 25 E
Sidra, G. of = Surt, Khalīj, Libya **51 B9** 31 40N 18 30 E
Siedlce, Poland **17 B12** 52 10N 22 20 E
Sieg →, Germany **16 C4** 50 46N 7 6 E
Siegen, Germany **16 C5** 50 51N 8 0 E
Siem Pang, Cambodia **38 E6** 14 7N 106 23 E
Siem Reap = Siemreab, Cambodia **38 F4** 13 20N 103 52 E
Siemreab, Cambodia **38 F4** 13 20N 103 52 E
Siena, Italy **20 C4** 43 19N 11 21 E
Sieradz, Poland **17 C10** 51 37N 18 41 E
Sierra Blanca, U.S.A. **83 L11** 31 11N 105 22W
Sierra Blanca Peak, U.S.A. **83 K11** 33 23N 105 49W
Sierra City, U.S.A. **84 F6** 39 34N 120 38W
Sierra Colorada, Argentina **96 E3** 40 35S 67 50W
Sierra Gorda, Chile **94 A2** 22 50S 69 15W
Sierra Leone ■, W. Afr. **50 G3** 9 0N 12 0W
Sierra Madre, Mexico **87 D6** 16 0N 93 0W
Sierra Mojada, Mexico **86 B4** 27 19N 103 42W
Sierra Nevada, U.S.A. **84 H8** 37 30N 119 0W
Sierra Vista, U.S.A. **83 L8** 31 33N 110 18W
Sierraville, U.S.A. **84 F6** 39 36N 120 22W
Sífnos, Greece **21 F11** 37 0N 24 45 E
Sifton, Canada **73 C8** 51 21N 100 8W
Sifton Pass, Canada **72 B3** 57 52N 126 15W
Sighetu-Marmaţiei, Romania **17 E12** 47 57N 23 52 E
Sighişoara, Romania **17 E13** 46 12N 24 50 E
Sigli, Indonesia **36 C1** 5 25N 96 0 E
Siglufjörður, Iceland **8 C4** 66 12N 18 55W
Signal, U.S.A. **85 L13** 34 30N 113 38W
Signal Pk., U.S.A. **85 M12** 33 20N 114 2W
Sigsig, Ecuador **92 D3** 3 0S 78 50W
Sigüenza, Spain **19 B4** 41 3N 2 40W
Siguiri, Guinea **50 F4** 11 31N 9 10W
Sigulda, Latvia **9 H21** 57 10N 24 55 E
Sihanoukville = Kampong Saom, Cambodia **39 G4** 10 38N 103 30 E
Sihora, India **43 H9** 23 29N 80 6 E
Siikajoki →, Finland **8 D21** 64 50N 24 43 E
Siilinjärvi, Finland **8 E22** 63 4N 27 39 E
Sijarira Ra., Zimbabwe **55 F2** 17 36S 27 45 E
Sika, India **42 H3** 22 26N 69 47 E
Sikao, Thailand **39 J2** 7 34N 99 21 E
Sikar, India **42 F6** 27 33N 75 10 E
Sikasso, Mali **50 F4** 11 18N 5 35W
Sikeston, U.S.A. **81 G10** 36 53N 89 35W
Sikhote Alin, Khrebet, Russia **27 E14** 45 0N 136 0 E
Sikhote Alin Ra. = Sikhote Alin, Khrebet, Russia **27 E14** 45 0N 136 0 E

Solfonn

Síkinos, Greece **21 F11** 36 40N 25 8 E
Sikkani Chief →, Canada **72 B4** 57 47N 122 15W
Sikkim □, India **41 F16** 27 50N 88 30 E
Sikotu-Ko, Japan **30 C10** 42 45N 141 25 E
Sil →, Spain **19 A2** 42 27N 7 43W
Silacayoapan, Mexico **87 D5** 17 30N 98 9W
Silawad, India **42 J6** 21 54N 74 54 E
Silchar, India **41 G18** 24 49N 92 48 E
Siler City, U.S.A. **77 H6** 35 44N 79 28W
Silesia = Śląsk, Poland **16 C9** 51 0N 16 30 E
Silgarhi Doti, Nepal **43 E9** 29 15N 81 0 E
Silghat, India **41 F18** 26 35N 93 0 E
Silifke, Turkey **25 G5** 36 22N 33 58 E
Siliguri = Shiliguri, India **41 F16** 26 45N 88 25 E
Siling Co, China **32 C3** 31 50N 89 20 E
Silistra, Bulgaria **21 B12** 44 6N 27 19 E
Silivri, Turkey **21 D13** 41 4N 28 14 E
Siljan, Sweden **9 F16** 60 55N 14 45 E
Silkeborg, Denmark **9 H13** 56 10N 9 32 E
Silkwood, Australia **62 B4** 17 45S 146 2 E
Sillajhuay, Cordillera, Chile **92 G5** 19 46S 68 40W
Sillamäe, Estonia **9 G22** 59 24N 27 45 E
Silloth, U.K. **10 C4** 54 52N 3 23W
Siloam Springs, U.S.A. **81 G7** 36 11N 94 32W
Silsbee, U.S.A. **81 K7** 30 21N 94 11W
Šilutė, Lithuania **9 J19** 55 21N 21 33 E
Silva Porto = Kuito, Angola **53 G3** 12 22S 16 55 E
Silvani, India **43 H8** 23 18N 78 25 E
Silver City, U.S.A. **83 K9** 32 46N 108 17W
Silver Cr. →, U.S.A. **82 E4** 43 16N 119 13W
Silver Creek, U.S.A. **78 D5** 42 33N 79 10W
Silver L., U.S.A. **84 G6** 38 39N 120 6W
Silver Lake, Calif., U.S.A. **85 K10** 35 21N 116 7W
Silver Lake, Oreg., U.S.A. **82 E3** 43 8N 121 3W
Silver Streams, S. Africa **56 D3** 28 20S 23 33 E
Silverton, Colo., U.S.A. **83 H10** 37 49N 107 40W
Silverton, Tex., U.S.A. **81 H4** 34 28N 101 19W
Silvies →, U.S.A. **82 E4** 43 34N 119 2W
Simaltala, India **43 G12** 24 43N 86 33 E
Simanggang = Bandar Sri Aman, Malaysia **36 D4** 1 15N 111 32 E
Simard, L., Canada **70 C4** 47 40N 78 40W
Simav, Turkey **21 E13** 39 4N 28 58 E
Simba, Tanzania **54 C4** 2 10S 37 36 E
Simbirsk, Russia **24 D8** 54 20N 48 25 E
Simbo, Tanzania **54 C2** 4 51S 29 41 E
Simcoe, Canada **78 D4** 42 50N 80 20W
Simcoe, L., Canada **78 B5** 44 25N 79 20W
Simdega, India **43 H11** 22 37N 84 31 E
Simeria, Romania **17 F12** 45 51N 23 1 E
Simeulue, Indonesia **36 D1** 2 45N 95 45 E
Simferopol, Ukraine **25 F5** 44 55N 34 3 E
Sími, Greece **21 F12** 36 35N 27 50 E
Simi Valley, U.S.A. **85 L8** 34 16N 118 47W
Simikot, Nepal **43 E9** 30 0N 81 50 E
Simla, India **42 D7** 31 2N 77 9 E
Simmie, Canada **73 D7** 49 56N 108 6W
Simmler, U.S.A. **85 K7** 35 21N 119 59W
Simojoki →, Finland **8 D21** 65 35N 25 1 E
Simojovel, Mexico **87 D6** 17 12N 92 38W
Simonette →, Canada **72 B5** 55 9N 118 15W
Simonstown, S. Africa **56 E2** 34 14S 18 26 E
Simplonpass, Switz. **18 C8** 46 15N 8 3 E
Simpson Desert, Australia **62 D2** 25 0S 137 0 E
Simpson Pen., Canada **69 B11** 68 34N 88 45W
Simpungdong, N. Korea **35 D15** 40 56N 129 29 E
Simrishamn, Sweden **9 J16** 55 33N 14 22 E
Simsbury, U.S.A. **79 E12** 41 53N 72 48W
Simushir, Ostrov, Russia **27 E16** 46 50N 152 30 E
Sin Cowe I., S. China Sea **36 C4** 9 53N 114 19 E
Sinabang, Indonesia **36 D1** 2 30N 96 24 E
Sinadogo, Somali Rep. **46 F4** 5 50N 47 0 E
Sinai = Es Sînâ', Egypt **47 F3** 29 0N 34 0 E
Sinai, Mt. = Mûsa, Gebel, Egypt **44 D2** 28 33N 33 59 E
Sinai Peninsula, Egypt **47 F3** 29 30N 34 0 E
Sinaloa □, Mexico **86 C3** 25 0N 107 30W
Sinaloa de Leyva, Mexico **86 B3** 25 50N 108 20W
Sinarádhes, Greece **23 A3** 39 34N 19 51 E
Sincelejo, Colombia **92 B3** 9 18N 75 24W
Sinch'ang, N. Korea **35 D15** 40 7N 128 28 E
Sinchang-ni, N. Korea **35 E14** 39 24N 126 8 E
Sinclair, U.S.A. **82 F10** 41 47N 107 7W
Sinclair Mills, Canada **72 C4** 54 5N 121 40W
Sinclair's B., U.K. **12 C5** 58 31N 3 5W
Sinclairville, U.S.A. **78 D5** 42 16N 79 16W
Sincorá, Serra do, Brazil **93 F10** 13 30S 41 0W
Sind, Pakistan **42 G3** 26 0N 68 30 E
Sind □, Pakistan **42 G3** 26 0N 69 0 E
Sind →, India **43 F8** 26 26N 79 13 E
Sind →, Jammu & Kashmir, India **43 B6** 34 18N 74 45 E
Sind Sagar Doab, Pakistan **42 D4** 32 0N 71 30 E
Sindangan, Phil. **37 C6** 8 10N 123 5 E
Sindangbarang, Indonesia **37 G12** 7 27S 107 1 E
Sinde, Zambia **55 F2** 17 28S 25 51 E
Sindri, India **43 H12** 23 45N 86 42 E
Sines, Portugal **19 D1** 37 56N 8 51W
Sines, C. de, Portugal **19 D1** 37 58N 8 53W
Sineu, Spain **22 B10** 39 38N 3 1 E
Sing Buri, Thailand **38 E3** 14 53N 100 25 E
Singa, Sudan **51 F12** 13 10N 33 57 E
Singapore ■, Asia **39 M4** 1 17N 103 51 E
Singapore, Straits of, Asia **39 M5** 1 15N 104 0 E
Singaraja, Indonesia **36 F5** 8 6S 115 10 E
Singida, Tanzania **54 C3** 4 49S 34 48 E
Singida □, Tanzania **54 D3** 6 0S 34 30 E
Singitikós Kólpos, Greece **21 D11** 40 6N 24 0 E
Singkaling Hkamti, Burma **41 G19** 26 0N 95 39 E
Singkang, Indonesia **37 E6** 4 8S 120 1 E
Singkawang, Indonesia **36 D3** 1 0N 108 57 E
Singkep, Indonesia **36 E2** 0 30S 104 25 E
Singleton, Australia **63 E5** 32 33S 151 0 E
Singleton, Mt., N. Terr., Australia **60 D5** 22 0S 130 46 E
Singleton, Mt., W. Austral., Australia **61 E2** 29 27S 117 15 E
Singoli, India **42 G6** 25 0N 75 22 E
Singora = Songkhla, Thailand **39 J3** 7 13N 100 37 E
Singosan, N. Korea **35 E14** 38 52N 127 25 E
Sinhung, N. Korea **35 D14** 40 11N 127 34 E
Sînî □, Egypt **47 F3** 30 0N 34 0 E
Sinjai, Indonesia **37 F6** 5 7S 120 20 E
Sinjār, Iraq **44 B4** 36 19N 41 52 E
Sinkat, Sudan **51 E13** 18 55N 36 49 E
Sinkiang Uighur = Xinjiang Uygur Zizhiqu □, China **32 C3** 42 0N 86 0 E
Sinmak, N. Korea **35 E14** 38 25N 126 14 E
Sinnamary, Fr. Guiana **93 B8** 5 25N 53 0W
Sinni →, Italy **20 D7** 40 8N 16 41 E
Sinop, Turkey **25 F6** 42 1N 35 11 E
Sinor, India **42 J5** 21 55N 73 20 E
Sinp'o, N. Korea **35 E15** 40 0N 128 13 E
Sinsk, Russia **27 C13** 61 8N 126 48 E
Sintang, Indonesia **36 D4** 0 5N 111 35 E
Sinton, U.S.A. **81 L6** 28 2N 97 31W
Sintra, Portugal **19 C1** 38 47N 9 25W
Sinŭiju, N. Korea **35 D13** 40 5N 124 24 E
Siocon, Phil. **37 C6** 7 40N 122 10 E
Siófok, Hungary **17 E10** 46 54N 18 3 E
Sioma, Zambia **56 B3** 16 25S 23 28 E
Sion, Switz. **18 C7** 46 14N 7 20 E
Sion Mills, U.K. **13 B4** 54 48N 7 29W
Sioux City, U.S.A. **80 D6** 42 30N 96 24W
Sioux Falls, U.S.A. **80 D6** 43 33N 96 44W
Sioux Lookout, Canada **70 B1** 50 10N 91 50W
Sioux Narrows, Canada **73 D10** 49 25N 94 10W
Siping, China **35 C13** 43 8N 124 21 E
Sipiwesk L., Canada **73 B9** 55 5N 97 35W
Sipra →, India **42 H6** 23 55N 75 28 E
Sipura, Indonesia **36 E1** 2 18S 99 40 E
Siquia →, Nic. **88 D3** 12 10N 84 20W
Siquijor, Phil. **37 C6** 9 12N 123 35 E
Siquirres, Costa Rica **88 D3** 10 6N 83 30W
Şīr Banī Yās, U.A.E. **45 E7** 24 19N 52 37 E
Sir Edward Pellew Group, Australia **62 B2** 15 40S 137 10 E
Sir Graham Moore Is., Australia **60 B4** 13 53S 126 34 E
Sir James MacBrien, Mt., Canada **68 B7** 62 8N 127 40W
Sira →, Norway **9 G12** 58 23N 6 34 E
Siracusa, Italy **20 F6** 37 4N 15 17 E
Sirajganj, Bangla. **43 G13** 24 25N 89 47 E
Sirathu, India **43 G9** 25 39N 81 19 E
Sīrdān, Iran **45 B6** 36 39N 49 12 E
Sirdaryo = Syrdarya →, Kazakstan **26 E7** 46 3N 61 0 E
Siren, U.S.A. **80 C8** 45 47N 92 24W
Sirer, Spain **22 C7** 38 56N 1 22 E
Siret →, Romania **17 F14** 45 24N 28 1 E
Sirghāyā, Syria **47 B5** 33 51N 36 8 E
Sirmaur, India **43 G9** 24 51N 81 23 E
Sirohi, India **42 G5** 24 52N 72 53 E
Sironj, India **42 G7** 24 5N 77 39 E
Síros, Greece **21 F11** 37 28N 24 57 E
Sirretta Pk., U.S.A. **85 K8** 35 56N 118 19W
Sīrrī, Iran **45 E7** 25 55N 54 32 E
Sirsa, India **42 E6** 29 33N 75 4 E
Sirsa →, India **43 F8** 26 51N 79 4 E
Sisak, Croatia **16 F9** 45 30N 16 21 E
Sisaket, Thailand **38 E5** 15 8N 104 23 E
Sishen, S. Africa **56 D3** 27 47S 22 59 E
Sishui, Henan, China **34 G7** 34 48N 113 15 E
Sishui, Shandong, China **35 G9** 35 42N 117 18 E
Sisipuk L., Canada **73 B8** 55 45N 101 50W
Sisophon, Cambodia **38 F4** 13 38N 102 59 E
Sisseton, U.S.A. **80 C6** 45 40N 97 3W
Sīstān, Asia **45 D9** 30 50N 61 0 E
Sīstān, Daryācheh-ye, Iran **45 D9** 31 0N 61 0 E
Sīstān va Balūchestān □, Iran **45 E9** 27 0N 62 0 E
Sisters, U.S.A. **82 D3** 44 18N 121 33W
Siswa Bazar, India **43 F10** 27 9N 83 46 E
Sitamarhi, India **43 F11** 26 37N 85 30 E
Sitapur, India **43 F9** 27 38N 80 45 E
Siteki, Swaziland **57 D5** 26 32S 31 58 E
Sitges, Spain **19 B6** 41 17N 1 47 E
Sitía, Greece **23 D8** 35 13N 26 6 E
Sitka, U.S.A. **72 B1** 57 3N 135 20W
Sitoti, Botswana **56 C3** 23 15S 23 40 E
Sittang Myit →, Burma **41 L20** 17 20N 96 45 E
Sittard, Neths. **15 C5** 51 0N 5 52 E
Sittingbourne, U.K. **11 F8** 51 21N 0 45 E
Sittwe, Burma **41 J18** 20 18N 92 45 E
Situbondo, Indonesia **37 G16** 7 42S 114 0 E
Siuna, Nic. **88 D3** 13 37N 84 45W
Siuri, India **43 H12** 23 50N 87 34 E
Sīvand, Iran **45 D7** 30 5N 52 55 E
Sivas, Turkey **25 G6** 39 43N 36 58 E
Siverek, Turkey **44 B3** 37 50N 39 19 E
Sivomaskinskiy, Russia **24 A11** 66 40N 62 35 E
Sivrihisar, Turkey **25 G5** 39 30N 31 35 E
Sîwa, Egypt **51 C11** 29 11N 25 31 E
Sîwa Oasis, Egypt **48 D6** 29 10N 25 30 E
Siwalik Range, Nepal **43 F10** 28 0N 83 0 E
Siwan, India **43 F11** 26 13N 84 21 E
Siwana, India **42 G5** 25 38N 72 25 E
Sixmilebridge, Ireland **13 D3** 52 44N 8 46W
Sixth Cataract, Sudan **51 E12** 16 20N 32 42 E
Siziwang Qi, China **34 D6** 41 25N 111 40 E
Sjælland, Denmark **9 J14** 55 30N 11 30 E
Sjumen = Shumen, Bulgaria **21 C12** 43 18N 26 55 E
Skadarsko Jezero, Montenegro, Yug. **21 C8** 42 10N 19 20 E
Skaftafell, Iceland **8 D5** 64 1N 17 0W
Skagafjörður, Iceland **8 D4** 65 54N 19 35W
Skagastølstindane, Norway **9 F12** 61 28N 7 52 E
Skagaströnd, Iceland **8 D3** 65 50N 20 19W
Skagen, Denmark **9 H14** 57 43N 10 35 E
Skagerrak, Denmark **9 H13** 57 30N 9 0 E
Skagit →, U.S.A. **84 B4** 48 23N 122 22W
Skagway, U.S.A. **68 C6** 59 28N 135 19W
Skala-Podilska, Ukraine **17 D14** 48 50N 26 15 E
Skala Podolskaya = Skala-Podilska, Ukraine **17 D14** 48 50N 26 15 E
Skalat, Ukraine **17 D13** 49 23N 25 55 E
Skåne, Sweden **9 J15** 55 59N 13 30 E
Skaneateles, U.S.A. **79 D8** 42 57N 76 26W
Skaneateles L., U.S.A. **79 D8** 42 51N 76 22W
Skara, Sweden **9 G15** 58 25N 13 30 E
Skardu, Pakistan **43 B6** 35 20N 75 44 E
Skarżysko-Kamienna, Poland **17 C11** 51 7N 20 52 E
Skeena →, Canada **72 C2** 54 9N 130 5W
Skeena Mts., Canada **72 B3** 56 40N 128 30W
Skegness, U.K. **10 D8** 53 9N 0 20 E
Skeldon, Guyana **92 B7** 5 55N 57 20W
Skellefte älv →, Sweden **8 D19** 64 45N 21 10 E
Skellefteå, Sweden **8 D19** 64 45N 20 50 E
Skelleftehamn, Sweden **8 D19** 64 40N 21 9 E
Skerries, The, U.K. **10 D3** 53 25N 4 36W
Ski, Norway **9 G14** 59 43N 10 52 E
Skíathos, Greece **21 E10** 39 12N 23 30 E
Skibbereen, Ireland **13 E2** 51 33N 9 16W
Skiddaw, U.K. **10 C4** 54 39N 3 9W
Skidegate, Canada **72 C2** 53 15N 132 1W
Skien, Norway **9 G13** 59 12N 9 35 E
Skierniewice, Poland **17 C11** 51 58N 20 10 E
Skikda, Algeria **50 A7** 36 50N 6 58 E
Skilloura, Cyprus **23 D12** 35 14N 33 10 E
Skipton, U.K. **10 D5** 53 58N 2 3W
Skirmish Pt., Australia **62 A1** 11 59S 134 17 E
Skíros, Greece **21 E11** 38 55N 24 34 E
Skive, Denmark **9 H13** 56 33N 9 2 E
Skjálfandafljót →, Iceland **8 D5** 65 59N 17 25W
Skjálfandi, Iceland **8 C5** 66 5N 17 30W
Skoghall, Sweden **9 G15** 59 20N 13 30 E
Skole, Ukraine **17 D12** 49 3N 23 30 E
Skópelos, Greece **21 E10** 39 9N 23 47 E
Skopí, Greece **23 D8** 35 11N 26 2 E
Skopje, Macedonia **21 C9** 42 1N 21 26 E
Skövde, Sweden **9 G15** 58 24N 13 50 E
Skovorodino, Russia **27 D13** 54 0N 124 0 E
Skowhegan, U.S.A. **77 C11** 44 46N 69 43W
Skull, Ireland **13 E2** 51 32N 9 34W
Skunk →, U.S.A. **80 E9** 40 42N 91 7W
Skuodas, Lithuania **9 H19** 56 16N 21 33 E
Skvyra, Ukraine **17 D15** 49 44N 29 40 E
Skye, U.K. **12 D2** 57 15N 6 10W
Skykomish, U.S.A. **82 C3** 47 42N 121 22W
Skyros = Skíros, Greece **21 E11** 38 55N 24 34 E
Slættaratindur, Færoe Is. **8 E9** 62 18N 7 1W
Slagelse, Denmark **9 J14** 55 23N 11 19 E
Slamet, Indonesia **37 G13** 7 16S 109 8 E
Slaney →, Ireland **13 D5** 52 26N 6 33W
Śląsk, Poland **16 C9** 51 0N 16 30 E
Slate Is., Canada **70 C2** 48 40N 87 0W
Slatina, Romania **17 F13** 44 28N 24 22 E
Slatington, U.S.A. **79 F9** 40 45N 75 37W
Slaton, U.S.A. **81 J4** 33 26N 101 39W
Slave →, Canada **72 A6** 61 18N 113 39W
Slave Coast, W. Afr. **50 G6** 6 0N 2 30 E
Slave Lake, Canada **72 B6** 55 17N 114 43W
Slave Pt., Canada **72 A5** 61 11N 115 56W
Slavgorod, Russia **26 D8** 53 1N 78 37 E
Slavonski Brod, Croatia **21 B8** 45 11N 18 1 E
Slavuta, Ukraine **17 C14** 50 15N 27 2 E
Slavyanka, Russia **30 C5** 42 53N 131 21 E
Slavyansk = Slovyansk, Ukraine **25 E6** 48 55N 37 36 E
Slawharad, Belarus **17 B16** 53 27N 31 0 E
Sleaford, U.K. **10 D7** 53 0N 0 24W
Sleaford B., Australia **63 E2** 34 55S 135 45 E
Sleat, Sd. of, U.K. **12 D3** 57 5N 5 47W
Sleeper Is., Canada **69 C11** 58 30N 81 0W
Sleepy Eye, U.S.A. **80 C7** 44 18N 94 43W
Slemon L., Canada **72 A5** 63 13N 116 4W
Slide Mt., U.S.A. **79 E10** 42 0N 74 25W
Slidell, U.S.A. **81 K10** 30 17N 89 47W
Sliema, Malta **23 D2** 35 54N 14 30 E
Slieve Aughty, Ireland **13 C3** 53 4N 8 30W
Slieve Bloom, Ireland **13 C4** 53 4N 7 40W
Slieve Donard, U.K. **13 B6** 54 11N 5 55W
Slieve Gamph, Ireland **13 B3** 54 6N 9 0W
Slieve Gullion, U.K. **13 B5** 54 7N 6 26W
Slieve Mish, Ireland **13 D2** 52 12N 9 50W
Slievenamon, Ireland **13 D4** 52 25N 7 34W
Sligeach = Sligo, Ireland **13 B3** 54 16N 8 28W
Sligo, Ireland **13 B3** 54 16N 8 28W
Sligo, U.S.A. **78 E5** 41 6N 79 29W
Sligo □, Ireland **13 B3** 54 8N 8 42W
Sligo B., Ireland **13 B3** 54 18N 8 40W
Slippery Rock, U.S.A. **78 E4** 41 3N 80 3W
Slite, Sweden **9 H18** 57 42N 18 48 E
Sliven, Bulgaria **21 C12** 42 42N 26 19 E
Sloan, U.S.A. **85 K11** 35 57N 115 13W
Sloansville, U.S.A. **79 D10** 42 45N 74 22W
Slobodskoy, Russia **24 C9** 58 40N 50 6 E
Slobozia, Romania **17 F14** 44 34N 27 23 E
Slocan, Canada **72 D5** 49 48N 117 28W
Slonim, Belarus **17 B13** 53 4N 25 19 E
Slough, U.K. **11 F7** 51 30N 0 36W
Slough □, U.K. **11 F7** 51 30N 0 36W
Sloughhouse, U.S.A. **84 G5** 38 26N 121 12W
Slovak Rep. ■, Europe **17 D10** 48 30N 20 0 E
Slovakia = Slovak Rep. ■, Europe **17 D10** 48 30N 20 0 E
Slovakian Ore Mts. = Slovenské Rudohorie, Slovak Rep. **17 D10** 48 45N 20 0 E
Slovenia ■, Europe **16 F8** 45 58N 14 30 E
Slovenija = Slovenia ■, Europe **16 F8** 45 58N 14 30 E
Slovenské Rudohorie, Slovak Rep. **17 D10** 48 45N 20 0 E
Slovyansk, Ukraine **25 E6** 48 55N 37 36 E
Sluch →, Ukraine **17 C14** 51 37N 26 38 E
Sluis, Neths. **15 C3** 51 18N 3 23 E
Słupsk, Poland **17 A9** 54 30N 17 3 E
Slurry, S. Africa **56 D4** 25 49S 25 42 E
Slutsk, Belarus **17 B14** 53 2N 27 31 E
Slyne Hd., Ireland **13 C1** 53 25N 10 10W
Slyudyanka, Russia **27 D11** 51 40N 103 40 E
Småland, Sweden **9 H16** 57 15N 15 25 E
Smalltree L., Canada **73 A8** 61 0N 105 0W
Smallwood Res., Canada **71 B7** 54 0N 64 0W
Smara, Morocco **50 B4** 32 9N 8 16W
Smarhon, Belarus **17 A14** 54 20N 26 24 E
Smartt Syndicate Dam, S. Africa **56 E3** 30 45S 23 10 E
Smartville, U.S.A. **84 F5** 39 13N 121 18W
Smeaton, Canada **73 C8** 53 30N 104 49W
Smederevo, Serbia, Yug. **21 B9** 44 40N 20 57 E
Smerwick Harbour, Ireland **13 D1** 52 12N 10 23W
Smethport, U.S.A. **78 E6** 41 49N 78 27W
Smidovich, Russia **27 E14** 48 36N 133 49 E
Smith, Canada **72 B6** 55 10N 114 0W
Smith Center, U.S.A. **80 F5** 39 47N 98 47W
Smith Sund, Greenland **4 B4** 78 30N 74 0W
Smithburne →, Australia **62 B3** 17 3S 140 57 E
Smithers, Canada **72 C3** 54 45N 127 10W
Smithfield, S. Africa **57 E4** 30 9S 26 30 E
Smithfield, N.C., U.S.A. **77 H6** 35 31N 78 21W
Smithfield, Utah, U.S.A. **82 F8** 41 50N 111 50W
Smiths Falls, Canada **79 B9** 44 55N 76 0W
Smithton, Australia **62 G4** 40 53S 145 6 E
Smithville, Canada **78 C5** 43 6N 79 33W
Smithville, U.S.A. **81 K6** 30 1N 97 10W
Smoky →, Canada **72 B5** 56 10N 117 21W
Smoky Bay, Australia **63 E1** 32 22S 134 13 E
Smoky Hill →, U.S.A. **80 F6** 39 4N 96 48W
Smoky Hills, U.S.A. **80 F5** 39 15N 99 30W
Smoky Lake, Canada **72 C6** 54 10N 112 30W
Smøla, Norway **8 E13** 63 23N 8 3 E
Smolensk, Russia **24 D5** 54 45N 32 5 E
Smolikas, Óros, Greece **21 D9** 40 9N 20 58 E
Smolyan, Bulgaria **21 D11** 41 36N 24 38 E
Smooth Rock Falls, Canada **70 C3** 49 17N 81 37W
Smoothstone L., Canada **73 C7** 54 40N 106 50W
Smorgon = Smarhon, Belarus **17 A14** 54 20N 26 24 E
Smyrna = İzmir, Turkey **21 E12** 38 25N 27 8 E
Smyrna, U.S.A. **76 F8** 39 18N 75 36W
Snæfell, Iceland **8 D6** 64 48N 15 34W
Snaefell, U.K. **10 C3** 54 16N 4 27W
Snæfellsjökull, Iceland **8 D2** 64 49N 23 46W
Snake →, U.S.A. **82 C4** 46 12N 119 2W
Snake I., Australia **63 F4** 38 47S 146 33 E
Snake Range, U.S.A. **82 G6** 39 0N 114 20W
Snake River Plain, U.S.A. **82 E7** 42 50N 114 0W
Snåsavatnet, Norway **8 D14** 64 12N 12 0 E
Sneek, Neths. **15 A5** 53 2N 5 40 E
Sneeuberge, S. Africa **56 E3** 31 46S 24 20 E
Snelling, U.S.A. **84 H6** 37 31N 120 26W
Sněžka, Europe **16 C8** 50 41N 15 50 E
Snizort, L., U.K. **12 D2** 57 33N 6 28W
Snøhetta, Norway **9 E13** 62 19N 9 16 E
Snohomish, U.S.A. **84 C4** 47 55N 122 6W
Snoul, Cambodia **39 F6** 12 4N 106 26 E
Snow Hill, U.S.A. **76 F8** 38 11N 75 24W
Snow Lake, Canada **73 C8** 54 52N 100 3W
Snow Mt., Calif., U.S.A. **84 F4** 39 23N 122 45W
Snow Mt., Maine, U.S.A. **79 A14** 45 18N 70 48W
Snow Shoe, U.S.A. **78 E7** 41 2N 77 57W
Snowbird L., Canada **73 A8** 60 45N 103 0W
Snowdon, U.K. **10 D3** 53 4N 4 5W
Snowdrift →, Canada **73 A6** 62 24N 110 44W
Snowflake, U.S.A. **83 J8** 34 30N 110 5W
Snowshoe Pk., U.S.A. **82 B6** 48 13N 115 41W
Snowtown, Australia **63 E2** 33 46S 138 14 E
Snowville, U.S.A. **82 F7** 41 58N 112 43W
Snowy →, Australia **63 F4** 37 46S 148 30 E
Snowy Mt., U.S.A. **79 C10** 43 42N 74 23W
Snowy Mts., Australia **63 F4** 36 30S 148 20 E
Snug Corner, Bahamas **89 B5** 22 33N 73 52W
Snyatyn, Ukraine **17 D13** 48 27N 25 38 E
Snyder, Okla., U.S.A. **81 H5** 34 40N 98 57W
Snyder, Tex., U.S.A. **81 J4** 32 44N 100 55W
Soahanina, Madag. **57 B7** 18 42S 44 13 E
Soalala, Madag. **57 B8** 16 6S 45 20 E
Soan →, Pakistan **42 C4** 33 1N 71 44 E
Soanierana-Ivongo, Madag. **57 B8** 16 55S 49 35 E
Sobat, Nahr →, Sudan **51 G12** 9 22N 31 33 E
Sobhapur, India **42 H8** 22 47N 78 17 E
Sobradinho, Represa de, Brazil **93 E10** 9 30S 42 0 E
Sobral, Brazil **93 D10** 3 50S 40 20W
Soc Trang, Vietnam **39 H5** 9 37N 105 50 E
Socastee, U.S.A. **77 J6** 33 41N 79 1W
Soch'e = Shache, China **32 C2** 38 20N 77 10 E
Sochi, Russia **25 F6** 43 35N 39 40 E
Société, Is. de la, Pac. Oc. **65 J12** 17 0S 151 0W
Society Is. = Société, Is. de la, Pac. Oc. **65 J12** 17 0S 151 0W
Socompa, Portezuelo de, Chile **94 A2** 24 27S 68 18W
Socorro, N. Mex., U.S.A. **83 J10** 34 4N 106 54W
Socorro, Tex., U.S.A. **83 L10** 31 39N 106 18W
Socorro, I., Mexico **86 D2** 18 45N 110 58W
Socotra, Ind. Oc. **46 E5** 12 30N 54 0 E
Soda L., U.S.A. **83 J5** 35 10N 116 4W
Soda Plains, India **43 B8** 35 30N 79 0 E
Soda Springs, U.S.A. **82 E8** 42 39N 111 36W
Sodankylä, Finland **8 C22** 67 29N 26 40 E
Soddy-Daisy, U.S.A. **77 H3** 35 17N 85 10W
Söderhamn, Sweden **9 F17** 61 18N 17 10 E
Söderköping, Sweden **9 G17** 58 31N 16 20 E
Södermanland, Sweden **9 G17** 58 56N 16 55 E
Södertälje, Sweden **9 G17** 59 12N 17 39 E
Sodiri, Sudan **51 F11** 14 27N 29 0 E
Sodus, U.S.A. **78 C7** 43 14N 77 4W
Soekmekaar, S. Africa **57 C4** 23 30S 29 55 E
Soest, Neths. **15 B5** 52 9N 5 19 E
Sofia = Sofiya, Bulgaria **21 C10** 42 45N 23 20 E
Sofia →, Madag. **57 B8** 15 27S 47 23 E
Sofiya, Bulgaria **21 C10** 42 45N 23 20 E
Sōfu-Gan, Japan **31 K10** 29 49N 140 21 E
Sogamoso, Colombia **92 B4** 5 43N 72 56W
Sogār, Iran **45 E8** 25 53N 58 6 E
Sogndalsfjøra, Norway **9 F12** 61 14N 7 5 E
Søgne, Norway **9 G12** 58 5N 7 48 E
Sognefjorden, Norway **9 F11** 61 10N 5 50 E
Sŏgwipo, S. Korea **35 H14** 33 13N 126 34 E
Soh, Iran **45 C6** 33 26N 51 27 E
Sohâg, Egypt **51 C12** 26 33N 31 43 E
Sohagpur, India **42 H8** 22 42N 78 12 E
Sŏhori, N. Korea **35 D15** 40 7N 128 23 E
Soignies, Belgium **15 D4** 50 35N 4 5 E
Soissons, France **18 B5** 49 25N 3 19 E
Sōja, Japan **31 G6** 34 40N 133 45 E
Sojat, India **42 G5** 25 55N 73 45 E
Sokal, Ukraine **17 C13** 50 31N 24 15 E
Söke, Turkey **21 F12** 37 48N 27 28 E
Sokelo, Dem. Rep. of the Congo **55 D1** 9 55S 24 36 E
Sokhumi, Georgia **25 F7** 43 0N 41 0 E
Sokodé, Togo **50 G6** 9 0N 1 11 E
Sokol, Russia **24 C7** 59 30N 40 5 E
Sokółka, Poland **17 B12** 53 25N 23 30 E
Sokołów Podlaski, Poland **17 B12** 52 25N 22 15 E
Sokoto, Nigeria **50 F7** 13 2N 5 16 E
Sol Iletsk, Russia **24 D10** 51 10N 55 0 E
Solai, Kenya **54 B4** 0 2N 36 12 E
Solan, India **42 D7** 30 55N 77 7 E
Solano, Phil. **37 A6** 16 31N 121 15 E
Solapur, India **40 L9** 17 43N 75 56 E
Soldotna, U.S.A. **68 B4** 60 29N 151 3W
Soléa □, Cyprus **23 D12** 35 5N 33 4 E
Soledad, Colombia **92 A4** 10 55N 74 46W
Soledad, U.S.A. **84 J5** 36 26N 121 20W
Soledad, Venezuela **92 B6** 8 10N 63 34W
Solent, The, U.K. **11 G6** 50 45N 1 25W
Solfonn, Norway **9 F12** 60 2N 6 57 E

Name	Grid	Coordinates
Solhan, Turkey	44 B4	38 57N 41 3 E
Solikamsk, Russia	24 C7	59 5N 42 10 E
Soligalich, Russia	24 C7	59 5N 42 10 E
Solihull, U.K.	11 E6	52 26N 1 47W
Soligorsk = Salihorsk, Belarus	17 B14	52 51N 27 27 E
Solimões = Amazonas →, S. Amer.	93 D9	0 5S 50 0W
Solingen, Germany	8 D17	51 10N 7 5 E
Sóller, Spain	19 C7	39 46N 2 43 E
Sollefteå, Sweden	8 E17	63 12N 17 20 E
Solna, Sweden	9 G18	59 22N 18 1 E
Sologne, France	18 C5	47 40N 1 45 E
Solok, Indonesia	36 E2	0 45S 100 40 E
Solola, Guatemala	88 D1	14 49N 91 10W
Solomon Is. ■, Pac. Oc.	64 H7	6 0S 155 0 E
Solomon, N. Fork →, U.S.A.	80 F5	39 29N 98 26W
Solon, China	33 B7	46 32N 121 10 E
Solor, Indonesia	37 F6	8 27S 123 0 E
Solothurn, Switz.	18 C7	47 13N 7 32 E
Šolta, Croatia	16 G8	43 24N 16 15 E
Soltānābād, Khorāsān, Iran	45 C8	34 13N 59 58 E
Soltānābād, Khorāsān, Iran	45 B8	36 29N 58 5 E
Solunska Glava, Macedonia	21 D9	41 44N 21 31 E
Solvang, U.S.A.	85 L6	34 36N 120 12W
Solvay, U.S.A.	79 D8	43 3N 76 13W
Sölvesborg, Sweden	9 H16	56 5N 14 35 E
Solvychegodsk, Russia	24 B8	61 21N 46 56 E
Solway Firth, U.K.	10 C4	54 49N 3 35W
Solwezi, Zambia	55 E2	12 11S 26 21 E
Sōma, Japan	30 F10	37 40N 140 50 E
Soma, Turkey	21 E12	39 10N 27 35 E
Somali Pen., Africa	48 F8	7 0N 46 0 E
Somali Rep. ■, Africa	49 F4	7 0N 47 0 E
Somalia = Somali Rep. ■, Africa	49 F4	7 0N 47 0 E
Sombra, Canada	78 D2	42 43N 82 29W
Sombrerete, Mexico	86 C4	23 40N 103 40W
Sombrero, Anguilla	89 C7	18 37N 63 30W
Somdari, India	42 G5	25 47N 72 38 E
Somers, U.S.A.	82 B6	48 5N 114 13W
Somerset, Canada	73 D9	49 25N 98 39W
Somerset, Ky., U.S.A.	76 G3	37 5N 84 36W
Somerset, Mass., U.S.A.	79 E13	41 47N 71 8W
Somerset, Pa., U.S.A.	78 F5	40 1N 79 5W
Somerset □, U.K.	11 F5	51 9N 3 0W
Somerset East, S. Africa	56 E4	32 42S 25 35 E
Somerset I., Canada	68 A10	73 30N 93 0W
Somerset West, S. Africa	56 E2	34 8S 18 50 E
Somersworth, U.S.A.	79 C14	43 16N 70 52W
Somerton, U.S.A.	83 K6	32 36N 114 43W
Somerville, U.S.A.	79 F10	40 35N 74 38W
Somes →, Romania	17 D12	47 49N 22 43 E
Somme →, France	18 A4	50 11N 1 38 E
Somnath, India	42 J4	20 53N 70 22 E
Somosierra, Puerto de, Spain	19 B4	41 4N 3 35W
Somoto, Nic.	88 D2	13 28N 86 37W
Sompom, Puerto de, Spain	18 E3	42 48N 0 31W
Son →, India	43 G11	25 42N 84 52 E
Son Ha, Vietnam	38 E7	15 3N 108 34 E
Son Hoa, Vietnam	38 F7	13 2N 108 58 E
Son La, Vietnam	38 B5	21 20N 103 50 E
Son Serra, Spain	22 B10	39 43N 3 13 E
Soná, Panama	88 E3	8 0N 81 20W
Sonamarg, India	43 B6	34 18N 75 21 E
Sonamukhi, India	43 H12	23 18N 87 27 E
Sŏnch'ŏn, N. Korea	35 E13	39 48N 124 55 E
Sóndrio, Italy	18 C8	46 10N 9 52 E
Sone, Mozam.	55 F3	17 23S 34 55 E
Sonepur, India	41 J13	20 55N 83 50 E
Song, Thailand	38 C3	18 28N 100 11 E
Song Cau, Vietnam	38 F7	13 27N 109 18 E
Song Xian, China	34 G7	34 12N 112 8 E
Songea, Tanzania	55 E4	10 40S 35 40 E
Songgang, China	33 F10	22 46N 113 50 E
Songhua Hu, China	35 C14	43 35N 126 50 E
Songhua Jiang →, China	33 B8	47 45N 132 30 E
Songjin, N. Korea	35 D15	40 40N 129 10 E
Songjŏng-ni, S. Korea	35 G14	35 8N 126 47 E
Songkhla, Thailand	39 J3	7 13N 100 37 E
Songnim, N. Korea	35 E13	38 45N 125 39 E
Songo, Sudan	51 G10	9 47N 24 21 E
Songpan, China	32 C5	32 40N 103 30 E
Songwe, Dem. Rep. of the Congo	54 C2	3 20S 26 16 E
Songwe →, Africa	55 D3	9 44S 33 58 E
Sonid Youqi, China	34 C7	42 45N 112 48 E
Sonipat, India	42 E7	29 0N 77 5 E
Sonkach, India	42 H7	22 59N 76 21 E
Sonmiani B., Pakistan	42 G2	25 15N 66 30 E
Sono →, Brazil	93 E9	9 58S 48 11W
Sonora, Calif., U.S.A.	84 H6	37 59N 120 23W
Sonora □, Mexico	86 B2	29 0N 111 0W
Sonora →, Mexico	86 B2	28 50N 111 33W
Sonora Desert, U.S.A.	85 L12	33 40N 114 15W
Sonsonate, El Salv.	88 D2	13 43N 89 44W
Sonsorol Is., Pac. Oc.	37 C8	5 30N 132 15 E
Soochow = Suzhou, China	33 C7	31 19N 120 38 E
Sop Prap, Thailand	38 D2	17 53N 99 20 E
Sopi, Indonesia	37 D7	2 34N 128 28 E
Sopot, Poland	17 A10	54 27N 18 31 E
Sør-Rondane, Antarctica	5 D4	72 0S 25 0 E
Sorano, India	42 F3	27 13N 69 56 E
Sopron, Hungary	17 E9	47 45N 16 32 E
Sorel, Canada	70 C5	46 0N 73 10W
Sorgono, Italy	20 D3	40 1N 9 6 E
Sorell, India		
South Shields, U.K.	10 C6	55 0N 1 25W
South Shetland Is., Antarctica	5 C18	62 0S 59 0W
South Seal →, Canada	73 B9	58 48N 98 8W
South Saskatchewan →, Canada	73 C7	53 15N 105 5W
South Sandwich Is., Antarctica	5 B1	57 0S 27 0W
South Sandwich Is., Antarctica	2 B9	57 0S 27 0W
South River, Canada	70 C4	45 52N 79 23W
South River, U.S.A.	79 F10	40 27N 74 23W
South Ronaldsay, U.K.	12 C6	58 48N 2 58W
South Porcupine, Canada	70 C3	48 30N 81 12W
South Portland, U.S.A.	77 D10	43 38N 70 15W
South Pole, Antarctica	5 E	90 0S 0 0 E
South Pittsburg, U.S.A.	77 H3	35 1N 85 42W
South Platte →, U.S.A.	80 E4	41 7N 100 42W
South Paris, U.S.A.	79 B14	44 14N 70 31W
South Pass, U.S.A.	82 E9	42 20N 108 58W
South Pagai, I. = Pagai Selatan, Pulau, Indonesia	36 E2	3 0S 100 15 E
South Ossetia □, Georgia	25 F7	42 21N 44 2 E
South Orkney Is., Antarctica	5 C18	63 0S 45 0W
South Negril Pt., Jamaica	88 C4	18 14N 78 30W
South Natuna Is. = Natuna Selatan, Kepulauan, Indonesia	39 L7	2 45N 109 0 E
South Nation →, Canada	79 A9	45 34N 75 6W
South Nahanni →, Canada	72 A4	61 3N 123 21W
South Moose L., Canada	73 C8	53 46N 100 8W
South Molton, U.K.	11 F4	51 1N 3 51W
South Milwaukee, U.S.A.	76 D2	42 55N 87 52W
South Magnetic Pole, Antarctica	5 C9	64 8S 138 8 E
South Loup →, U.S.A.	80 E5	41 4N 98 39W
South Lanarkshire □, U.K.	12 F5	55 37N 3 53W
South Lake Tahoe, U.S.A.	84 G6	38 57N 119 59W
South Korea ■, Asia	35 G15	36 0N 128 0 E
South Koel →, India	43 H11	22 32N 85 14 E
South Knife →, Canada	73 B10	58 55N 94 37W
South Invercargill, N.Z.	59 M2	46 26S 168 23 E
South Indian Lake, Canada	73 B9	56 47N 98 56W
South I., Kenya	54 B4	2 35N 36 35 E
South I., N.Z.	59 L3	44 0S 170 0 E
South Horr, Kenya	54 B4	2 12N 36 56 E
South Honshu Ridge, Pac. Oc.	64 E6	23 0N 143 0 E
South Henik, L., Canada	73 A9	61 30N 97 30W
South Hayle, U.S.A.	79 D12	42 16N 72 35W
South Haven, U.S.A.	76 D2	42 24N 86 16W
South Gloucestershire □, U.K.	11 F5	51 32N 2 28W
South Georgia, Antarctica	80 E4	40 3N 101 31W
South Georgia, Antarctica	96 G9	54 30S 37 0W
South Fork Republican →, U.S.A.	80 C3	45 43N 102 17W
South Fork Grand →, U.S.A.	84 F5	39 17N 121 36W
South Fork Feather →, U.S.A.	84 G5	38 45N 121 5W
South Fork American →, U.S.A.	11 F9	51 8N 1 24 E
South Foreland, U.K.	12 E6	56 43N 3 31W
South Esk →, U.K.	62 G4	43 40S 146 50 E
South East C., Australia	79 D12	42 29N 72 37W
South Deerfield, U.S.A.	80 C5	44 15N 100 0W
South Dakota □, U.S.A.	36 C4	10 0N 113 0 E
South China Sea, Asia	77 C8	34 1N 81 4W
South Carolina □, U.S.A.	70 C3	46 47N 80 55W
South Branch, Canada	76 E2	41 41N 86 15W
South Bend, Ind., U.S.A.	84 D3	46 40N 123 48W
South Bend, Wash., U.S.A.	77 J4	33 55N 83 3W
South Baldy, U.S.A.	83 J10	33 59N 107 11W
South Ayrshire □, U.K.	55 E3	11 55N 4 1W
South Australia □, Australia	63 E2	32 0S 139 0 E
South Aulatsivik I., Canada	71 A7	56 45N 61 30W
South Atlantic Ocean	90 H7	20 0S 10 0W
South Africa ■, Africa	56 E3	32 0S 23 0 E
Soustons, Tunisia	51 A7	36 50N 10 38 E
Sourris →, Canada	80 A5	49 40N 99 34W
Souris, Man., Canada	73 D8	49 40N 100 20W
Souris, P.E.I., Canada	71 C7	46 21N 62 15W
Soure, Brazil	93 D9	0 35S 48 30W
Souris, The, U.K.	11 F6	51 0N 1 20W
Sŏul, S. Korea	35 F14	37 31N 126 58 E
Soufrière, St. Lucia	89 D7	13 51N 61 3W
Soúdha, Greece	23 D6	35 25N 24 10 E
Soúdhas, Kólpos, Greece	23 D6	35 25N 24 10 E
Souk-Ahras, Algeria	51 A7	36 10N 7 50 E

Name	Grid	Coordinates
Spring Hill, U.S.A.	77 L4	28 27N 82 41W
Spring Mts., U.S.A.	83 H6	36 0N 115 45W
Spring Valley, U.S.A.	85 N10	32 45N 117 5W
Springbok, S. Africa	56 D2	29 42S 17 54 E
Springboro, U.S.A.	78 E4	41 48N 80 22W
Springbrook, Canada	78 B7	44 19N 77 56W
Springdale, Canada	71 C8	49 30N 56 6W
Springdale, U.S.A.	81 G7	36 11N 94 8W
Springerville, U.S.A.	83 J9	34 8N 109 17W
Springfield, Canada	78 D4	42 50N 80 56W
Springfield, N.Z.	59 K3	43 19N 171 56 E
Springfield, Colo., U.S.A.	81 G3	37 24N 102 37W
Springfield, Ill., U.S.A.	80 F10	39 48N 89 39W
Springfield, Mass., U.S.A.	79 D12	42 6N 72 35W
Springfield, Mo., U.S.A.	81 G8	37 13N 93 17W
Springfield, Ohio, U.S.A.	76 F4	39 55N 83 49W
Springfield, Oreg., U.S.A.	82 D2	44 3N 123 1W
Springfield, Tenn., U.S.A.	77 G2	36 31N 86 53W
Springfield, Vt., U.S.A.	79 C12	43 18N 72 29W
Springfontein, S. Africa	56 E4	30 15S 25 40 E
Springhill, Canada	71 C7	45 40N 64 4W
Springhouse, Canada	72 C4	51 56N 122 7W
Springs, S. Africa	57 D4	26 13S 28 25 E
Springsure, Australia	62 C4	24 8S 148 6 E
Springvale, U.S.A.	79 C14	43 28N 70 48W
Springville, Calif., U.S.A.	84 J8	36 8N 118 49W
Springville, N.Y., U.S.A.	78 D6	42 31N 78 40W
Springville, Utah, U.S.A.	82 F8	40 10N 111 37W
Springwater, Canada	79 D7	42 38N 77 35W
Spruce-Creek, U.S.A.	78 F6	40 36N 78 9W
Spruce Mt., U.S.A.	79 B12	44 12N 72 19W
Spur, U.S.A.	81 J4	33 28N 100 52W
Spurn Hd., U.K.	10 D8	53 35N 0 8 E
Spuzzum, Canada	72 D4	49 37N 121 23W
Squam L., U.S.A.	79 C13	43 45N 71 32W
Squamish, Canada	72 D4	49 45N 123 10W
Square Islands, Canada	71 B8	52 47N 55 47W
Squires, Mt., Australia	61 E4	26 14S 127 28 E
Srbija = Serbia □, Serbia	21 C9	43 30N 21 0 E
Sre Ambel, Cambodia	39 G4	11 8N 103 46 E
Sre Khtum, Cambodia	39 F6	12 10N 106 52 E
Sre Umbell = Sre Ambel, Cambodia	39 G4	11 8N 103 46 E
Srebrenica, Bos.-H.	21 B8	44 6N 19 18 E
Sredinny Ra. = Sredinnyy Khrebet, Russia	27 D17	57 0N 160 0 E
Sredinnyy Khrebet, Russia	27 D17	57 0N 160 0 E
Srednekolymsk, Russia	27 C16	67 27N 153 40 E
Sredinny = Sredinnyy Khrebet, Russia	27 D17	57 0N 160 0 E
Srem, Poland	17 B9	52 6N 17 2 E
Sremska Mitrovica, Serbia, Yug.	21 B8	44 59N 19 38 E
Srepok →, Cambodia	38 F6	13 33N 106 16 E
Sretensk, Russia	27 D12	52 10N 117 40 E
Sri Lanka ■, Asia	40 R12	7 30N 80 50 E
Srikakulam, India	41 K13	18 14N 83 58 E
Srinagar, India	43 B6	34 5N 74 50 E
Staaten →, Australia	62 B3	16 24S 141 17 E
Stade, Germany	16 B5	53 35N 9 29 E
Stadskanaal, Neths.	15 A6	53 4N 6 55 E
Staffa, U.K.	12 E2	56 27N 6 21W
Stafford, U.K.	10 E5	52 49N 2 7W
Stafford Springs, U.S.A.	79 E12	41 57N 72 18W
Staffordshire □, U.K.	10 E5	52 53N 2 10W
Staines, U.K.	11 F7	51 26N 0 29W
Stakhanov, Ukraine	25 E6	48 35N 38 40 E
Stalingrad = Volgograd, Russia	25 E7	48 40N 44 25 E
Stalino = Donetsk, Ukraine	25 E6	48 0N 37 45 E
Staliniri = Tskhinvali, Georgia	25 F7	42 14N 44 1 E
Stalinogorsk = Novomoskovsk, Russia	24 D6	54 5N 38 15 E
Stalowa Wola, Poland	17 C12	50 34N 22 3 E
Stalybridge, U.K.	10 D5	53 28N 2 3W
Stamford, Australia	62 C3	21 15S 143 46 E
Stamford, Conn., U.S.A.	79 E11	41 3N 73 32W
Stamford, N.Y., U.S.A.	79 D10	42 25N 74 38W
Stamford, Tex., U.S.A.	81 J5	32 57N 99 48W
Stamps, U.S.A.	81 J8	33 22N 93 30W
Standerton, S. Africa	57 D4	26 55S 29 7 E
Standish, U.S.A.	76 D4	43 59N 83 57W
Stanford, U.S.A.	82 C8	47 9N 110 13W
Stanger, S. Africa	57 D5	29 27S 31 14 E
Stanislaus →, U.S.A.	84 H5	37 40N 121 14W
Stanislav = Ivano-Frankivsk, Ukraine	17 D13	48 40N 24 40 E
Stanke Dimitrov, Bulgaria	21 C10	42 17N 23 9 E
Stanley, Australia	62 G4	40 46S 145 19 E
Stanley, Falk. Is.	96 G5	51 40S 59 51W
Stanley, Canada	73 B8	55 24N 104 22W
Stanley, Idaho, U.S.A.	82 D6	44 13N 114 56W
Stanley, N. Dak., U.S.A.	80 A3	48 19N 102 23W
Stanley, N.Y., U.S.A.	78 D7	42 48N 77 6W
Stannum, Kherbet, Russia	27 D14	55 0N 130 0 E
Stanovoy Ra. = Stanovoy Khrebet, Russia	27 D13	55 0N 130 0 E
Stanthorpe, Australia	63 D5	28 36S 151 59 E
Stanton, U.S.A.	81 J4	32 8N 101 48W
Stanwood, U.S.A.	84 B4	48 15N 122 23W
Staples, U.S.A.	80 B7	46 21N 94 48W
Star City, Canada	73 C8	52 50N 104 20W
Star Lake, U.S.A.	79 B9	44 10N 75 2W
Stara Planina, Bulgaria	21 C10	43 15N 23 0 E
Stara Zagora, Bulgaria	21 C11	42 26N 25 39 E
Starachowice, Poland	17 C11	51 3N 21 2 E
Staraya Russa, Russia	24 C5	57 58N 31 23 E
Starbuck I., Kiribati	65 H12	5 37S 155 55W
Stargard Szczeciński, Poland	16 B8	53 20N 15 0 E
Staritsa, Russia	24 C5	56 33N 34 55 E
Starke, U.S.A.	77 L4	29 57N 82 7W
Starogard Gdański, Poland	17 B10	53 59N 18 30 E
Starokonstantinov = Starokostyantyniv, Ukraine	17 D14	49 48N 27 10 E
Starokostyantyniv, Ukraine	17 D14	49 48N 27 10 E
Start Pt., U.K.	11 G4	50 13N 3 38W
Staryy Chartoriysk, Ukraine	17 C13	51 15N 25 54 E
State College, U.S.A.	78 F7	40 48N 77 52W
Staten I., U.S.A.	84 G7	38 57N 119 56W

Name	Grid	Coordinates
South Uist, U.K.	12 D1	57 20N 7 15W
South Twin I., Canada	70 B4	53 7N 79 52W
South Tyne →, U.K.	10 C5	54 59N 2 8W
South West Africa = Namibia ■, Africa	56 C2	22 0S 18 9 E
South West Rocks, Australia	63 E5	30 52S 153 3 E
South West C., Australia	62 G4	43 34S 146 3 E
South Williamsport, U.S.A.	78 E8	41 13N 77 1W
South Yorkshire □, U.K.	10 D6	53 27N 1 36W
Southampton, Canada	78 B3	44 30N 81 25W
Southampton, U.K.	11 G6	50 54N 1 23W
Southampton, U.S.A.	79 F12	40 53N 72 23W
Southampton □, U.K.	11 G6	50 54N 1 23W
Southampton I., Canada	69 B11	64 30N 84 0W
Southbank, Canada	72 C3	54 2N 125 46W
Southbridge, N.Z.	59 K4	43 48S 172 16 E
Southbridge, U.S.A.	79 D12	42 5N 72 2W
Southend, Canada	73 B8	56 19N 103 22W
Southend-on-Sea, U.K.	11 F8	51 32N 0 44 E
Southend-on-Sea □, U.K.	11 F8	51 32N 0 44 E
Southern □, Malawi	55 F4	15 0S 35 0 E
Southern □, Zambia	55 F2	16 20S 26 20 E
Southern □, Uganda	54 C3	0 15S 31 30 E
Southern Alps, N.Z.	59 K3	43 41S 170 11 E
Southern Cross, Australia	61 F2	31 12S 119 15 E
Southern Indian L., Canada	73 B9	57 10N 98 30W
Southern Ocean, Antarctica	5 C6	62 0S 60 0 E
Southern Pines, U.S.A.	77 H6	35 11N 79 24W
Southern Uplands, U.K.	12 F5	55 28N 3 52W
Southington, U.S.A.	79 E12	41 36N 72 53W
Southold, U.S.A.	79 E12	41 4N 72 26W
Southport, Australia	63 D5	27 58S 153 25 E
Southport, U.K.	10 D4	53 39N 3 0W
Southport, Fla., U.S.A.	77 K3	30 17N 85 38W
Southport, N.Y., U.S.A.	78 D8	42 3N 76 49W
Southwest □, N.Z.	59 M1	46 26N 167 28 E
Southwold, U.K.	11 E9	52 20N 1 41 E
Soutpansberg, S. Africa	57 C4	23 0S 29 30 E
Sovetsk, Kaliningd., Russia	9 J19	55 6N 21 50 E
Sovetsk, Kirov, Russia	24 C8	57 38N 48 53 E
Sovetskaya Gavan = Vanino, Russia	27 E15	48 50N 140 5 E
Soweto, S. Africa	57 D4	26 14S 27 54 E
Sōya-Kaikyō = La Perouse Str., Asia	30 B11	45 40N 142 0 E
Sōya-Misaki, Japan	30 B10	45 30N 141 55 E
Sozh →, Belarus	17 B16	51 57N 30 48 E
Spa, Belgium	15 D5	50 29N 5 53 E
Spain ■, Europe	19 B4	39 0N 4 0W
Spalding, U.K.	10 E7	52 48N 0 9W
Spalding, Australia	63 E2	33 30S 138 37 E
Spangler, U.S.A.	78 F6	40 39N 78 48W
Spanish, Canada	70 C3	46 12N 82 20W
Spanish Fork, U.S.A.	82 F8	40 7N 111 39W
Spanish Town, Jamaica	88 C4	18 0N 76 57W
Sparks, U.S.A.	84 F7	39 32N 119 45W
Sparta = Spárti, Greece	23 F10	37 5N 22 25 E
Sparta, Mich., U.S.A.	76 D3	43 10N 85 42W
Sparta, N.J., U.S.A.	79 E10	41 2N 74 38W
Sparta, Wis., U.S.A.	80 D9	43 56N 90 49W
Spartanburg, U.S.A.	77 H5	34 56N 81 57W
Spartansburg, U.S.A.	78 E5	41 49N 79 41W
Spárti, Greece	23 F10	37 5N 22 25 E
Spartivento, C., Calabria, Italy	20 F7	37 55N 16 4 E
Spartivento, C., Sard., Italy	20 E3	38 53N 8 50 E
Sparwood, Canada	72 D6	49 44N 114 53W
Spassk Dalniy, Russia	27 E14	44 40N 132 48 E
Spátha, Ákra, Greece	23 D5	35 42N 23 43 E
Spatsizi →, Canada	72 B3	57 42N 128 7W
Spatsizi Plateau Wilderness Park, Canada	72 B3	57 40N 128 0W
Spean →, U.K.	12 E4	56 55N 4 59W
Spearfish, U.S.A.	80 C3	44 30N 103 52W
Spearman, U.S.A.	81 G4	36 12N 101 12W
Speculator, U.S.A.	79 C10	43 30N 74 22W
Speightstown, Barbados	89 D8	13 15N 59 39W
Speke Gulf, Tanzania	54 C3	2 20S 32 50 E
Spencer, Idaho, U.S.A.	82 D7	44 22N 112 11W
Spencer, Iowa, U.S.A.	80 D7	43 9N 95 9W
Spencer, N.Y., U.S.A.	79 D8	42 13N 76 30W
Spencer, Nebr., U.S.A.	80 D5	42 53N 98 42W
Spencer, C., Australia	63 F2	35 20S 136 53 E
Spencer B., Namibia	56 D1	25 30S 14 47 E
Spencer G., Australia	63 E2	34 0S 137 20 E
Spences Bridge, Canada	72 C4	50 25N 121 20W
Spennymoor, U.K.	10 C6	54 42N 1 36W
Sperrin Mts., U.K.	13 B5	54 50N 7 0W
Spey →, U.K.	12 D5	57 40N 3 6W
Speyer, Germany	16 D5	49 29N 8 25 E
Spezand, Pakistan	42 E2	29 59N 67 0 E
Spili, Greece	23 D6	35 13N 24 31 E
Spin Būldak, Afghan.	42 D2	31 1N 66 25 E
Spīshā Lothe, Greece	23 D7	35 18N 25 44 E
Spirit River, Canada	72 B5	55 45N 118 50W
Spirit Lake, U.S.A.	82 C5	47 58N 116 52W
Spiritwood, Canada	73 C7	53 24N 107 33W
Spithead, U.K.	11 G6	50 45N 1 10W
Spitzbergen = Svalbard, Arctic	4 B8	78 0N 17 0 E
Spjelkavik, Norway	9 E12	62 28N 6 22 E
Split, Croatia	20 C7	43 31N 16 26 E
Split L., Canada	73 B9	56 8N 96 15W
Split Lake, Canada	73 B9	56 8N 96 15W
Spofford, U.S.A.	81 L4	29 10N 100 25W
Spokane, U.S.A.	82 C5	47 40N 117 24W
Spoleto, Italy	20 C5	42 44N 12 44 E
Sporyy Navolok, Mys, Russia	26 B7	75 50N 68 40 E
Spratly I., S. China Sea	36 C4	8 20N 112 0 E
Spratly Is., S. China Sea	36 C4	8 20N 111 55 E
Spray, U.S.A.	82 D4	44 50N 119 48W
Spree →, Germany	16 B7	52 32N 13 13 E
Sprengisandur, Iceland	8 D5	64 52N 18 7W
Spring City, U.S.A.	79 F9	40 11N 75 33W
Spring Creek, U.S.A.	82 F6	40 45N 115 38W
Spring Garden, U.S.A.	84 F6	39 52N 120 47W

Tha Sala

Tanout, *Niger* .... **50 F7** 14 50N 8 55 E
Tanta, *Egypt* .... **51 B12** 30 45N 30 57 E
Tantoyuca, *Mexico* **87 C5** 21 21N 98 10W
Tantung = Dandong, *China* **35 D13** 40 10N 124 20 E
Tanunda, *Australia* .... **63 E2** 34 30S 139 0 E
Tanzania ■, *Africa* .... **54 D3** 6 0S 34 0 E
Tanzilla →, *Canada* **72 B2** 58 8N 130 43W
Tao, Ko, *Thailand* .... **39 G2** 10 5N 99 52 E
Tao'an = Taonan, *China* .. **35 B12** 45 22N 122 40 E
Tao'er He →, *China* ..... **35 B13** 45 45N 124 5 E
Taolanaro, *Madag.* .... **57 D8** 25 2S 47 0 E
Taole, *China* .... **34 E4** 38 48N 106 40 E
Taonan, *China* .... **35 B12** 45 22N 122 40 E
Taos, *U.S.A.* **83 H11** 36 24N 105 35W
Taoudenni, *Mali* **50 D5** 22 40N 3 55W
Tapa, *Estonia* .... **9 G21** 59 15N 25 50 E
Tapa Shan = Daba Shan, *China* .... **33 C5** 32 0N 109 0 E
Tapachula, *Mexico* **87 E6** 14 54N 92 17W
Tapah, *Malaysia* .... **39 K3** 4 12N 101 15 E
Tapajós →, *Brazil* **93 D8** 2 24S 54 41W
Tapaktuan, *Indonesia* ..... **36 D1** 3 15N 97 10 E
Tapanahoni →, *Surinam* . **93 C8** 4 20N 54 25W
Tapanui, *N.Z.* .... **59 L2** 45 56S 169 18 E
Tapauá →, *Brazil* **92 E6** 5 40S 64 21W
Tapes, *Brazil* **95 C5** 30 40S 51 23W
Tapeta, *Liberia* **50 G4** 6 29N 8 52W
Taphan Hin, *Thailand* ..... **38 D3** 16 13N 100 26 E
Tapirapecó, Serra, *Venezuela* **92 C6** 1 10N 65 0W
Tapuaenuku, Mt., *N.Z.* .... **59 K4** 42 0S 173 39 E
Tapul Group, *Phil.* .... **37 C6** 5 35N 120 50 E
Tapurucuará, *Brazil* **92 D5** 0 24S 65 2W
Ṭaqṭaq, *Iraq* .... **44 C5** 35 53N 44 35 E
Taquara, *Brazil* **95 B5** 29 36S 50 46W
Taquari →, *Brazil* **92 G7** 19 15S 57 17W
Tara, *Australia* .... **63 D5** 27 17S 150 31 E
Tara, *Canada* **78 B3** 44 28N 81 9W
Tara, *Russia* .... **26 D8** 56 55N 74 24 E
Tara, *Zambia* .... **55 F2** 16 58S 26 45 E
Tara →, *Montenegro, Yug.* **21 C8** 43 21N 18 51 E
Tarabagatay, Khrebet, *Kazakstan* .... **26 E9** 48 0N 83 0 E
Tarābulus, *Lebanon* ...... **47 A4** 34 31N 35 50 E
Tarābulus, *Libya* .... **51 B8** 32 49N 13 7 E
Taradehi, *India* .... **43 H8** 23 18N 79 21 E
Tarajalejo, *Canary Is.* **22 F5** 28 12N 14 7W
Tarakan, *Indonesia* .... **36 D5** 3 20N 117 35 E
Tarakit, Mt., *Kenya* ...... **54 B4** 2 2N 35 10 E
Tarama-Jima, *Japan* ..... **31 M2** 24 39N 124 42 E
Taran, Mys, *Russia* ...... **9 J18** 54 56N 19 59 E
Taranagar, *India* .... **42 E6** 28 43N 74 50 E
Taranaki □, *N.Z.* .... **59 H5** 39 25S 174 30 E
Tarancón, *Spain* **19 B4** 40 1N 3 0W
Taranga Hill, *India* ...... **40 H8** 24 0N 72 40 E
Taransay, *U.K.* **12 D1** 57 54N 7 0W
Táranto, *Italy* .... **20 D7** 40 28N 17 14 E
Táranto, G. di, *Italy* ..... **20 D7** 40 8N 17 20 E
Tarapacá, *Colombia* **92 D5** 2 56S 69 46W
Tarapacá □, *Chile* **94 A2** 20 45S 69 30W
Tarapoto, *Peru* **92 E3** 6 30S 76 20W
Tararua Ra., *N.Z.* .... **59 J5** 40 45S 175 25 E
Tarashcha, *Ukraine* ...... **17 D16** 49 30N 30 31 E
Tarauacá, *Brazil* **92 E4** 8 6S 70 48W
Tarauacá →, *Brazil* **92 E5** 6 42S 69 48W
Tarawa, *Kiribati* .... **64 G9** 1 30N 173 0 E
Tarawera, *N.Z.* .... **59 H6** 39 2S 176 36 E
Tarawera L., *N.Z.* .... **59 H6** 38 13S 176 27 E
Tarazona, *Spain* **19 B5** 41 55N 1 43W
Tarbat Ness, *U.K.* **12 D5** 57 52N 3 47W
Tarbela Dam, *Pakistan* .... **42 B5** 34 8N 72 52 E
Tarbert, *Arg. & Bute, U.K.* . **12 F3** 55 52N 5 25W
Tarbert, *W. Isles, U.K.* **12 D2** 57 54N 6 49W
Tarbes, *France* .... **18 E4** 43 15N 0 3 E
Tarboro, *U.S.A.* **77 H7** 35 54N 77 32W
Tarcoola, *Australia* ...... **63 E1** 30 44S 134 36 E
Tarcoon, *Australia* .... **63 E4** 30 15S 146 43 E
Taree, *Australia* .... **63 E5** 31 50S 152 30 E
Tarfaya, *Morocco* **50 C3** 27 55N 12 55W
Târgovişte, *Romania* ..... **17 F13** 44 55N 25 27 E
Târgu-Jiu, *Romania* ...... **17 F12** 45 5N 23 19 E
Târgu Mureş, *Romania* .... **17 E13** 46 31N 24 38 E
Ṭarif, *U.A.E.* .... **45 E7** 24 3N 53 46 E
Tarifa, *Spain* **19 D3** 36 1N 5 36W
Tarija, *Bolivia* **94 A3** 21 30S 64 40W
Tarija □, *Bolivia* **94 A3** 21 30S 63 30W
Tariku →, *Indonesia* ..... **37 E9** 2 55S 138 26 E
Tarim Basin = Tarim Pendi, *China* .... **32 B3** 40 0N 84 0 E
Tarim He →, *China* ...... **32 C3** 39 30N 88 30 E
Tarim Pendi, *China* ...... **32 B3** 40 0N 84 0 E
Taritatu →, *Indonesia* .... **37 E9** 2 54S 138 27 E
Tarka →, *S. Africa* ...... **56 E4** 32 10S 26 0 E
Tarkastad, *S. Africa* ..... **56 E4** 32 0S 26 16 E
Tarkhankut, Mys, *Ukraine* . **25 E5** 45 25N 32 30 E
Tarko Sale, *Russia* .... **26 C8** 64 55N 77 50 E
Tarkwa, *Ghana* **50 G5** 5 20N 2 0W
Tarlac, *Phil.* .... **37 A6** 15 29N 120 35 E
Tarma, *Peru* **92 F3** 11 25S 75 45W
Tarn →, *France* .... **18 E4** 44 5N 1 6 E
Târnăveni, *Romania* ...... **17 E13** 46 19N 24 13 E
Tarnobrzeg, *Poland* ...... **17 C11** 50 35N 21 41 E
Tarnów, *Poland* .... **17 C11** 50 3N 21 0 E
Tarnowskie Góry, *Poland* .. **17 C10** 50 27N 18 54 E
Ṭārom, *Iran* .... **45 D7** 28 11N 55 46 E
Taroom, *Australia* .... **63 D4** 25 36S 149 48 E
Taroudannt, *Morocco* **50 B4** 30 30N 8 52W
Tarpon Springs, *U.S.A.* **77 L4** 28 9N 82 45W
Tarragona, *Spain* .... **19 B6** 41 5N 1 17 E
Tarraleah, *Australia* ...... **62 G4** 42 17S 146 26 E
Tarrasa = Terrassa, *Spain* . **19 B7** 41 34N 2 1 E
Tarrytown, *U.S.A.* **79 E11** 41 4N 73 52W
Tarshiha = Me'ona, *Israel* . **47 B4** 33 1N 35 15 E
Tarso Emissi, *Chad* ...... **51 D9** 21 27N 18 36 E
Tarsus, *Turkey* .... **25 G5** 36 58N 34 55 E
Tartagal, *Argentina* **94 A3** 22 30S 63 50W
Tartu, *Estonia* .... **9 G22** 58 20N 26 44 E
Ṭarṭūs, *Syria* .... **44 C2** 34 55N 35 55 E
Tarumizu, *Japan* .... **31 J5** 31 29N 130 42 E
Tarutao, Ko, *Thailand* .... **39 J2** 6 33N 99 40 E
Tarutung, *Indonesia* ...... **36 D1** 2 0N 98 54 E
Taseko →, *Canada* **72 C4** 52 8N 123 45W
Tash-Kömür, *Kyrgyzstan* .. **26 E8** 41 40N 72 10 E
Tash-Kumyr = Tash-Kömür, *Kyrgyzstan* .... **26 E8** 41 40N 72 10 E
Tashauz = Dashhowuz, *Turkmenistan* .... **26 E6** 41 49N 59 58 E
Tashi Chho Dzong = Thimphu, *Bhutan* .... **41 F16** 27 31N 89 45 E
Ṭashk, Daryācheh-ye, *Iran* . **45 D7** 29 45N 53 35 E
Tashkent = Toshkent, *Uzbekistan* .... **26 E7** 41 20N 69 10 E
Tashtagol, *Russia* .... **26 D9** 52 47N 87 53 E
Tasikmalaya, *Indonesia* ... **37 G13** 7 18S 108 12 E
Tåsjön, *Sweden* .... **8 D16** 64 15N 15 40 E
Taskan, *Russia* .... **27 C16** 62 59N 150 20 E
Tasman B., *N.Z.* .... **59 J4** 40 59S 173 25 E
Tasman Mts., *N.Z.* .... **59 J4** 41 3S 172 25 E
Tasman Pen., *Australia* ... **62 G4** 43 10S 148 0 E
Tasman Sea, *Pac. Oc.* ..... **64 L8** 36 0S 160 0 E
Tasmania □, *Australia* .... **62 G4** 42 0S 146 30 E
Tassili n'Ajjer, *Algeria* ... **50 C7** 25 47N 8 1 E
Tatabánya, *Hungary* ...... **17 E10** 47 32N 18 25 E
Tatahouine, *Tunisia* ...... **51 B8** 32 56N 10 27 E
Tatar Republic = Tatarstan □, *Russia* ..... **24 C9** 55 30N 51 30 E
Tatarbunary, *Ukraine* ..... **17 F15** 45 50N 29 39 E
Tatarsk, *Russia* .... **26 D8** 55 14N 76 0 E
Tatarstan □, *Russia* ..... **24 C9** 55 30N 51 30 E
Tateyama, *Japan* .... **31 G9** 35 0N 139 50 E
Tathlina L., *Canada* **72 A5** 60 33N 117 39W
Tathra, *Australia* .... **63 F4** 36 44S 149 59 E
Tati →, *India* .... **40 J8** 21 8N 72 41 E
Tatinnai L., *Canada* **73 A9** 60 55N 97 40W
Tatla L., *Canada* **72 C4** 52 0N 124 20W
Tatnam, C., *Canada* **73 B10** 57 16N 91 0W
Tatra = Tatry, *Slovak Rep.* . **17 D11** 49 20N 20 0 E
Tatry, *Slovak Rep.* .... **17 D11** 49 20N 20 0 E
Tatshenshini →, *Canada* . **72 B1** 59 28N 137 45W
Tatsuno, *Japan* .... **31 G7** 34 52N 134 33 E
Tatta, *Pakistan* .... **42 G2** 24 42N 67 55 E
Tatuí, *Brazil* **95 A6** 23 25S 47 53W
Tatum, *U.S.A.* **81 J3** 33 16N 103 19W
Tat'ung = Datong, *China* .. **34 D7** 40 6N 113 18 E
Tatvan, *Turkey* .... **25 G7** 38 31N 42 15 E
Taubaté, *Brazil* **95 A6** 23 0S 45 36W
Tauern, *Austria* .... **16 E7** 47 15N 12 40 E
Taumarunui, *N.Z.* .... **59 H5** 38 53S 175 15 E
Taumaturgo, *Brazil* **92 E4** 8 54S 72 51W
Taung, *S. Africa* .... **56 D3** 27 33S 24 47 E
Taungdwingyi, *Burma* .... **41 J19** 20 1N 95 40 E
Taunggyi, *Burma* .... **41 J20** 20 50N 97 0 E
Taungup, *Burma* .... **41 K19** 18 51N 94 14 E
Taungup Pass, *Burma* .... **41 K19** 18 40N 94 45 E
Taungup Taunggya, *Burma* **41 K18** 18 20N 93 40 E
Taunsa, *Pakistan* .... **42 D4** 30 42N 70 39 E
Taunsa Barrage, *Pakistan* .. **42 D4** 30 42N 70 50 E
Taunton, *U.K.* **11 F4** 51 1N 3 5W
Taunton, *U.S.A.* **79 E13** 41 54N 71 6W
Taunus, *Germany* .... **16 C5** 50 13N 8 34 E
Taupo, *N.Z.* .... **59 H6** 38 41S 176 7 E
Taupo, L., *N.Z.* .... **59 H5** 38 46S 175 55 E
Tauragė, *Lithuania* ...... **9 J20** 55 14N 22 16 E
Tauranga, *N.Z.* .... **59 G6** 37 42S 176 11 E
Tauranga Harb., *N.Z.* ..... **59 G6** 37 30S 176 5 E
Taureau, Rés., *Canada* **70 C5** 46 46N 73 50W
Taurianova, *Italy* .... **20 E7** 38 21N 16 1 E
Taurus Mts. = Toros Dağlan, *Turkey* .... **25 G5** 37 0N 32 30 E
Tavda, *Russia* .... **26 D7** 58 7N 65 8 E
Tavda →, *Russia* .... **26 D7** 57 47N 67 18 E
Taveta, *Tanzania* .... **54 C4** 3 23S 37 37 E
Taveuni, *Fiji* **59 C9** 16 51S 179 58W
Tavira, *Portugal* **19 D2** 37 8N 7 40W
Tavistock, *Canada* **78 C4** 43 19N 80 50W
Tavistock, *U.K.* **11 G3** 50 33N 4 9W
Tavoy = Dawei, *Burma* ... **38 E2** 14 2N 98 12 E
Taw →, *U.K.* **11 F3** 51 4N 4 4W
Tawa →, *India* .... **42 H8** 22 48N 77 48 E
Tawas City, *U.S.A.* **76 C4** 44 16N 83 31W
Tawau, *Malaysia* .... **36 D5** 4 20N 117 55 E
Tawitawi, *Phil.* .... **37 C6** 5 10N 120 0 E
Taxco de Alarcón, *Mexico* . **87 D5** 18 33N 99 36W
Taxila, *Pakistan* .... **42 C5** 33 42N 72 52 E
Tay →, *U.K.* **12 E5** 56 37N 3 38W
Tay, Firth of, *U.K.* **12 E5** 56 25N 3 8W
Tay, L., *Australia* .... **61 F3** 32 55S 120 48 E
Tay, L., *U.K.* **12 E4** 56 32N 4 8W
Tay Ninh, *Vietnam* .... **39 G6** 11 20N 106 5 E
Tayabamba, *Peru* **92 E3** 8 15S 77 16W
Taylakova, *Russia* .... **26 D8** 59 13N 74 0 E
Taylakovy = Taylakova, *Russia* .... **26 D8** 59 13N 74 0 E
Taylor, *Canada* **72 B4** 56 13N 120 40W
Taylor, *Nebr., U.S.A.* **80 E5** 41 46N 99 23W
Taylor, *Pa., U.S.A.* **79 E9** 41 23N 75 43W
Taylor, *Tex., U.S.A.* **81 K6** 30 34N 97 25W
Taylor, Mt., *U.S.A.* **83 J10** 35 14N 107 37W
Taylorville, *U.S.A.* **80 F10** 39 33N 89 18W
Taymā, *Si. Arabia* .... **44 E3** 27 35N 38 45 E
Taymyr, Oz., *Russia* ..... **27 B11** 74 20N 102 0 E
Taymyr, Poluostrov, *Russia* **27 B11** 75 0N 100 0 E
Tayport, *U.K.* **12 E6** 56 27N 2 52W
Tayshet, *Russia* .... **27 D10** 55 58N 98 1 E
Taytay, *Phil.* .... **37 B5** 10 45N 119 30 E
Taz →, *Russia* .... **26 C8** 67 32N 78 40 E
Taza, *Morocco* **50 B5** 34 16N 4 6W
Ṭāzah Khurmātū, *Iraq* .... **44 C5** 35 18N 44 20 E
Tazawa-Ko, *Japan* .... **30 E10** 39 43N 140 40 E
Tazin, *Canada* **73 B7** 59 48N 109 55W
Tazin L., *Canada* **73 B7** 59 44N 108 42W
Tazovskiy, *Russia* .... **26 C8** 67 30N 78 44 E
Tbilisi, *Georgia* .... **25 F7** 41 43N 44 50 E
Tchad = Chad ■, *Africa* ... **51 F8** 15 0N 17 15 E
Tchad, L., *Chad* .... **51 F8** 13 30N 14 30 E
Tch'eng-tou = Chengdu, *China* .... **32 C5** 30 38N 104 2 E
Tchentlo L., *Canada* **72 B4** 55 15N 125 0W
Tchibanga, *Gabon* .... **52 E2** 2 45S 11 0 E
Tch'ong-k'ing = Chongqing, *China* .... **32 D5** 29 35N 106 25 E
Tczew, *Poland* .... **17 A10** 54 8N 18 50 E
Te Anau, L., *N.Z.* .... **59 L1** 45 15S 167 45 E
Te Aroha, *N.Z.* .... **59 G5** 37 32S 175 44 E
Te Awamutu, *N.Z.* .... **59 H5** 38 1S 175 20 E
Te Kuiti, *N.Z.* .... **59 H5** 38 20S 175 11 E
Te Puke, *N.Z.* .... **59 G6** 37 46S 176 22 E
Te Waewae B., *N.Z.* ...... **59 M1** 46 13S 167 33 E
Teague, *U.S.A.* **81 K6** 31 38N 96 17W
Teapa, *Mexico* **87 D6** 18 35N 92 56W
Tebakang, *Malaysia* ...... **36 D4** 1 6N 110 30 E
Tébessa, *Algeria* .... **50 A7** 35 22N 8 8 E
Tebicuary →, *Paraguay* .. **94 B4** 26 36S 58 16W
Tebingtinggi, *Indonesia* ... **36 D1** 3 20N 99 9 E
Tebintingii, *Indonesia* ..... **36 E2** 1 0N 102 45 E
Tecate, *Mexico* **85 N10** 32 34N 116 38W
Tecka, *Argentina* **96 E2** 43 29S 70 48W
Tecomán, *Mexico* **86 D4** 18 55N 103 53W
Tecopa, *U.S.A.* **85 K10** 35 51N 116 13W
Tecoripa, *Mexico* **86 B3** 28 37N 109 57W
Tecuala, *Mexico* **86 C3** 22 23N 105 27W
Tecuci, *Romania* .... **17 F14** 45 51N 27 27 E
Tecumseh, *Canada* **78 D2** 42 19N 82 54W
Tecumseh, *Mich., U.S.A.* .. **76 D4** 42 0N 83 57W
Tecumseh, *Okla., U.S.A.* ... **81 H6** 35 15N 96 56W
Tedzhen = Tejen, *Turkmenistan* .... **26 F7** 37 23N 60 31 E
Tees →, *U.K.* **10 C6** 54 37N 1 10W
Tees B., *U.K.* **10 C6** 54 40N 1 9W
Teeswater, *Canada* **78 C3** 43 59N 81 17W
Tefé, *Brazil* **92 D6** 3 25S 64 50W
Tegal, *Indonesia* .... **37 G13** 6 52S 109 8 E
Tegid, L. = Bala, L., *U.K.* .. **10 E4** 52 53N 3 37W
Tegucigalpa, *Honduras* ... **88 D2** 14 5N 87 14W
Tehachapi, *U.S.A.* **85 K8** 35 8N 118 27W
Tehachapi Mts., *U.S.A.* **85 L8** 35 0N 118 30W
Tehoru, *Indonesia* .... **37 E7** 3 19S 129 37 E
Tehrān, *Iran* .... **45 C6** 35 44N 51 30 E
Tehri, *India* .... **43 D8** 30 23N 78 29 E
Tehuacán, *Mexico* **87 D5** 18 30N 97 30W
Tehuantepec, *Mexico* **87 D5** 16 21N 95 13W
Tehuantepec, G. de, *Mexico* **87 D5** 15 50N 95 12W
Tehuantepec, Istmo de, *Mexico* **87 D6** 17 0N 94 30W
Teide, *Canary Is.* **22 F3** 28 15N 16 38W
Teifi →, *U.K.* **11 E3** 52 5N 4 41W
Teign →, *U.K.* **11 G4** 50 32N 3 32W
Teignmouth, *U.K.* **11 G4** 50 33N 3 31W
Tejam, *India* .... **43 E9** 29 57N 80 11 E
Tejen, *Turkmenistan* ..... **26 F7** 37 23N 60 31 E
Tejen →, *Turkmenistan* .. **45 B9** 37 24N 60 38 E
Tejo →, *Europe* **19 C1** 38 40N 9 24W
Tejon Pass, *U.S.A.* **85 L8** 34 49N 118 53W
Tekamah, *U.S.A.* **80 E6** 41 47N 96 13W
Tekapo, L., *N.Z.* .... **59 K3** 43 53S 170 33 E
Tekax, *Mexico* **87 C7** 20 11N 89 18W
Tekeli, *Kazakstan* .... **26 E8** 44 50N 79 0 E
Tekirdağ, *Turkey* .... **21 D12** 40 58N 27 30 E
Tekkali, *India* .... **41 K14** 18 37N 84 15 E
Tekoa, *U.S.A.* **82 C5** 47 14N 117 4W
Tel Aviv-Yafo, *Israel* ..... **47 C3** 32 4N 34 48 E
Tel Lakhish, *Israel* .... **47 D3** 31 34N 34 51 E
Tel Megiddo, *Israel* ...... **47 C4** 32 35N 35 11 E
Tela, *Honduras* **88 C2** 15 40N 87 28W
Telanaipura = Jambi, *Indonesia* .... **36 E2** 1 38S 103 30 E
Telavi, *Georgia* .... **25 F8** 42 0N 45 30 E
Telde, *Canary Is.* **22 G4** 27 59N 15 25W
Telegraph Creek, *Canada* .. **72 B2** 58 0N 131 10W
Telekhany = Tsyelyakhany, *Belarus* .... **17 B13** 52 30N 25 46 E
Telemark, *Norway* .... **9 G12** 59 15N 7 40 E
Telén, *Argentina* **94 D2** 36 15S 65 31W
Teleng, *Iran* .... **45 E9** 25 47N 61 3 E
Teles Pires →, *Brazil* **92 E7** 7 21S 58 3W
Telescope Pk., *U.S.A.* **85 J9** 36 10N 117 5W
Telfer Mine, *Australia* .... **60 C3** 21 40S 122 12 E
Telford, *U.K.* **11 E5** 52 40N 2 27W
Telford and Wrekin □, *U.K.* **10 E5** 52 45N 2 27W
Telkwa, *Canada* **72 C3** 54 41N 127 5W
Tell City, *U.S.A.* **76 G2** 37 57N 86 46W
Tellicherry, *India* .... **40 P9** 11 45N 75 30 E
Telluride, *U.S.A.* **83 H10** 37 56N 107 49W
Teloloapán, *Mexico* **87 D5** 18 21N 99 51W
Telpos Iz, *Russia* .... **24 B10** 63 16N 59 13 E
Telsen, *Argentina* **96 E3** 42 30S 66 50W
Telšiai, *Lithuania* .... **9 H20** 55 59N 22 14 E
Teluk Anson = Teluk Intan, *Malaysia* .... **39 K3** 4 3N 101 0 E
Teluk Betung = Tanjungkarang Telukbetung, *Indonesia* . **36 F3** 5 20S 105 10 E
Teluk Intan, *Malaysia* ..... **39 K3** 4 3N 101 0 E
Telukbutun, *Indonesia* .... **39 K7** 4 13N 108 12 E
Telukdalem, *Indonesia* .... **36 D1** 0 33N 97 50 E
Tema, *Ghana* .... **50 G5** 5 41N 0 0 E
Temax, *Mexico* **87 C7** 21 10N 88 50W
Temba, *S. Africa* .... **57 D4** 25 20S 28 17 E
Tembagapura, *Indonesia* .. **37 E9** 4 20S 137 0 E
Tembe, *Dem. Rep. of the Congo* . **54 C2** 0 16S 28 14 E
Temblor Range, *U.S.A.* **85 K7** 35 20N 119 50W
Teme →, *U.K.* **11 E5** 52 11N 2 13W
Temecula, *U.S.A.* **85 M9** 33 30N 117 9W
Temerloh, *Malaysia* ...... **36 D2** 3 27N 102 25 E
Teminabuan, *Indonesia* ... **37 E8** 1 26S 132 1 E
Temir, *Kazakstan* .... **25 E10** 49 1N 57 14 E
Temirtau, *Kazakstan* ..... **26 D8** 50 5N 72 56 E
Temirtau, *Russia* .... **26 D9** 53 10N 87 30 E
Temiscamie →, *Canada* ... **71 B5** 50 59N 73 5W
Témiscaming, *Canada* **70 C4** 46 44N 79 5W
Témiscamingue, L., *Canada* **70 C4** 47 10N 79 25W
Temosachic, *Mexico* **86 B3** 28 58N 107 50W
Tempe, *U.S.A.* **83 K8** 33 25N 111 56W
Tempiute, *U.S.A.* **84 H11** 37 39N 115 38W
Temple, *U.S.A.* **81 K6** 31 6N 97 21W
Temple B., *Australia* ..... **62 A3** 12 15S 143 3 E
Templemore, *Ireland* **13 D4** 52 47N 7 51W
Templeton, *U.S.A.* **84 K6** 35 33N 120 42W
Templeton →, *Australia* .. **62 C2** 21 0S 138 40 E
Tempoal, *Mexico* **87 C5** 21 31N 98 23W
Temuco, *Chile* **96 D2** 38 45S 72 40W
Temuka, *N.Z.* .... **59 L3** 44 14S 171 17 E
Tenabo, *Mexico* **87 C6** 20 2N 90 12W
Tenaha, *U.S.A.* **81 K7** 31 57N 94 15W
Tenakee Springs, *U.S.A.* ... **72 B1** 57 47N 135 13W
Tenali, *India* .... **40 L12** 16 15N 80 35 E
Tenancingo, *Mexico* **87 D5** 19 0N 99 33W
Tenango, *Mexico* **87 D5** 19 7N 99 33W
Tenasserim, *Burma* ...... **39 F2** 12 6N 99 3 E
Tenasserim □, *Burma* .... **38 F2** 14 0N 98 30 E
Tenby, *U.K.* **11 F3** 51 40N 4 42W
Tenda, Colle di, *France* ... **18 D7** 44 7N 7 36 E
Tendaho, *Ethiopia* .... **46 E3** 11 48N 40 54 E
Tendukhera, *India* .... **43 H8** 23 24N 79 33 E
Ténéré, *Niger* .... **50 E7** 19 0N 10 30 E
Tenerife, *Canary Is.* **22 F3** 28 15N 16 35W
Tenerife, Pico, *Canary Is.* .. **22 G1** 27 43N 18 1W
Teng Xian, *China* .... **35 G9** 35 5N 117 10 E
Tengah □, *Indonesia* .... **37 E6** 2 0S 122 0 E
Tengah, Kepulauan, *Indonesia* .... **36 F5** 7 5S 118 15 E
Tengchong, *China* .... **32 D4** 25 0N 98 28 E
Tengchowfu = Penglai, *China* .... **35 F11** 37 48N 120 42 E
Tenggara □, *Indonesia* ... **37 E6** 3 0S 122 0 E
Tenggarong, *Indonesia* ... **36 E5** 0 24S 116 58 E
Tenggol, Pulau, *Malaysia* .. **39 K4** 4 48N 103 41 E
Tengiz, Ozero, *Kazakstan* .. **26 D7** 50 30N 69 0 E
Tenino, *U.S.A.* **84 D4** 46 51N 122 51W
Tenkasi, *India* .... **40 Q10** 8 55N 77 20 E
Tenke, *Katanga, Dem. Rep. of the Congo* . **55 E2** 11 22S 26 40 E
Tenke, *Katanga, Dem. Rep. of the Congo* . **55 E2** 10 32S 26 7 E
Tennant Creek, *Australia* .. **62 B1** 19 30S 134 15 E
Tennessee □, *U.S.A.* **77 H2** 36 0N 86 30W
Tennessee →, *U.S.A.* **76 G1** 37 4N 88 34W
Teno, Pta. de, *Canary Is.* .. **22 F3** 28 21N 16 55W
Tenom, *Malaysia* .... **36 C5** 5 4N 115 57 E
Tenosique, *Mexico* **87 D6** 17 30N 91 24W
Tenryū-Gawa →, *Japan* .. **31 G8** 35 39N 137 48 E
Tenterden, *U.K.* .... **11 F8** 51 4N 0 42 E
Tenterfield, *Australia* .... **63 D5** 29 0S 152 0 E
Teófilo Otoni, *Brazil* **93 G10** 17 50S 41 30W
Tepa, *Indonesia* .... **37 F7** 7 52S 129 31 E
Tepalcatepec →, *Mexico* . **86 D4** 18 35N 101 59W
Tepehuanes, *Mexico* **86 B3** 25 21N 105 44W
Tepetongo, *Mexico* **86 C4** 22 28N 103 9W
Tepic, *Mexico* **86 C4** 21 30N 104 54W
Teplice, *Czech Rep.* ...... **16 C7** 50 40N 13 48 E
Tepoca, C., *Mexico* **86 A2** 30 20N 112 25W
Tequila, *Mexico* **86 C4** 20 54N 103 47W
Ter →, *Spain* .... **19 A7** 42 2N 3 12 E
Ter Apel, *Neths.* .... **15 B7** 52 53N 7 5 E
Teraina, *Kiribati* **65 G11** 4 43N 160 25W
Téramo, *Italy* .... **20 C5** 42 39N 13 42 E
Terang, *Australia* .... **63 F3** 38 15S 142 55 E
Tercero →, *Argentina* **94 C3** 32 58S 61 47W
Terebovlya, *Ukraine* ..... **17 D13** 49 18N 25 44 E
Terek →, *Russia* .... **25 F8** 44 0N 47 30 E
Teresina, *Brazil* **93 E10** 5 9S 42 45W
Terewah, L., *Australia* .... **63 D4** 29 52S 147 35 E
Teridgerie Cr. →, *Australia* **63 E4** 30 25S 148 50 E
Termez = Termiz, *Uzbekistan* .... **26 F7** 37 15N 67 15 E
Términi Imerese, *Italy* .... **20 F5** 37 59N 13 42 E
Términos, L. de, *Mexico* ... **87 D6** 18 35N 91 30W
Termiz, *Uzbekistan* ...... **26 F7** 37 15N 67 15 E
Térmoli, *Italy* .... **20 C6** 42 0N 15 0 E
Ternate, *Indonesia* ...... **37 D7** 0 45N 127 25 E
Terneuzen, *Neths.* .... **15 C3** 51 20N 3 50 E
Terney, *Russia* .... **27 E14** 45 3N 136 37 E
Terni, *Italy* .... **20 C5** 42 34N 12 37 E
Ternopil, *Ukraine* .... **17 D13** 49 30N 25 40 E
Ternopol = Ternopil, *Ukraine* .... **17 D13** 49 30N 25 40 E
Terowie, *Australia* ...... **63 E2** 33 8S 138 55 E
Terra Bella, *U.S.A.* **85 K7** 35 58N 119 3W
Terra Nova Nat. Park, *Canada* **71 C9** 48 33N 53 55W
Terrace, *Canada* **72 C3** 54 30N 128 35W
Terrace Bay, *Canada* **70 C2** 48 47N 87 5W
Terracina, *Italy* .... **20 D5** 41 17N 13 15 E
Terralba, *Italy* .... **20 E3** 39 43N 8 39 E
Terranova = Ólbia, *Italy* ... **20 D3** 40 55N 9 31 E
Terrassa, *Spain* .... **19 B7** 41 34N 2 1 E
Terre Haute, *U.S.A.* **76 F2** 39 28N 87 25W
Terrebonne B., *U.S.A.* **81 L9** 29 5N 90 35W
Terrell, *U.S.A.* **81 J6** 32 44N 96 17W
Terrenceville, *Canada* **71 C9** 47 40N 54 44W
Terry, *U.S.A.* **80 B2** 46 47N 105 19W
Terryville, *U.S.A.* **79 E11** 41 41N 73 3W
Terschelling, *Neths.* ...... **15 A5** 53 25N 5 20 E
Teruel, *Spain* **19 B5** 40 22N 1 8W
Tervola, *Finland* .... **8 C21** 66 6N 24 49 E
Teryaweyna L., *Australia* .. **63 E3** 32 18S 143 22 E
Teshio, *Japan* .... **30 B10** 44 53N 141 44 E
Teshio-Gawa →, *Japan* .. **30 B10** 44 53N 141 45 E
Tesiyn Gol →, *Mongolia* . **32 A4** 50 40N 93 20 E
Teslin, *Canada* **72 A2** 60 10N 132 43W
Teslin →, *Canada* **72 A2** 61 34N 134 35W
Teslin L., *Canada* **72 A2** 60 15N 132 57W
Tessalit, *Mali* .... **50 D6** 20 12N 1 0 E
Test →, *U.K.* **11 G6** 50 56N 1 29W
Testigos, Is. Las, *Venezuela* **89 D7** 11 23N 63 7W
Tetachuck L., *Canada* **72 C3** 53 18N 125 55W
Tetas, Pta., *Chile* **94 A1** 23 31S 70 38W
Tete, *Mozam.* .... **55 F3** 16 13S 33 33 E
Tete □, *Mozam.* .... **55 F3** 15 15S 32 40 E
Teterev →, *Ukraine* ..... **17 C16** 51 1N 30 5 E
Teteven, *Bulgaria* .... **21 C11** 42 58N 24 17 E
Tethul →, *Canada* **72 A6** 60 35N 112 12W
Tetiyev, *Ukraine* .... **17 D15** 49 22N 29 38 E
Teton →, *U.S.A.* **82 C8** 47 56N 110 31W
Tétouan, *Morocco* **50 A4** 35 35N 5 21W
Tetovo, *Macedonia* ...... **21 C9** 42 1N 20 59 E
Teuco →, *Argentina* **94 B3** 25 35S 60 11W
Teulon, *Canada* **73 C9** 50 23N 97 16W
Teun, *Indonesia* .... **37 F7** 6 59S 129 8 E
Teutoburger Wald, *Germany* **16 B5** 52 5N 8 22 E
Tevere →, *Italy* .... **20 D5** 41 44N 12 14 E
Teverya, *Israel* .... **47 C4** 32 47N 35 32 E
Teviot →, *U.K.* **12 F6** 55 29N 2 38W
Tewantin, *Australia* ..... **63 D5** 26 27S 153 3 E
Tewkesbury, *U.K.* **11 F5** 51 59N 2 9W
Texada I., *Canada* **72 D4** 49 40N 124 25W
Texarkana, *Ark., U.S.A.* ... **81 J8** 33 26N 94 2W
Texarkana, *Tex., U.S.A.* ... **81 J7** 33 26N 94 3W
Texas, *Australia* .... **63 D5** 28 49S 151 9 E
Texas □, *U.S.A.* **81 K5** 31 40N 98 30W
Texas City, *U.S.A.* **81 L7** 29 24N 94 54W
Texel, *Neths.* .... **15 A4** 53 5N 4 50 E
Texline, *U.S.A.* **81 G3** 36 23N 103 2W
Texoma, L., *U.S.A.* **81 J6** 33 50N 96 34W
Tezin, *Afghan.* .... **42 B3** 34 24N 69 30 E
Teziutlán, *Mexico* **87 D5** 19 50N 97 22W
Tezpur, *India* .... **41 F18** 26 40N 92 45 E
Tezzeron L., *Canada* **72 C4** 54 43N 124 30W
Tha-anne →, *Canada* **73 A10** 60 31N 94 37W
Tha Deua, *Laos* .... **38 D4** 17 57N 102 53 E
Tha Deua, *Laos* .... **38 C3** 19 26N 101 50 E
Tha Pla, *Thailand* .... **38 D3** 17 48N 100 32 E
Tha Rua, *Thailand* ...... **38 E3** 14 34N 100 44 E
Tha Sala, *Thailand* ...... **39 H2** 8 40N 99 56 E

Tha Song Yang

Tha Song Yang, Thailand 38 D1 17 34N 97 55 E
Thaba Putsoa, Lesotho 57 D4 29 45S 28 0 E
Thabana Ntlenyana, Lesotho 57 D4 29 30S 29 16 E
Thabazimbi, S. Africa 57 C4 24 40S 27 21 E
Thādiq, Si. Arabia 44 E5 25 18N 45 52 E
Thai Muang, Thailand 39 H2 8 24N 98 16 E
Thailand ■, Asia 38 E4 16 0N 102 0 E
Thailand, G. of, Asia 39 G3 11 30N 101 0 E
Thakhek, Laos 38 D5 17 25N 104 45 E
Thal, Pakistan 42 C4 33 28N 70 33 E
Thal Desert, Pakistan 42 D4 31 10N 71 30 E
Thala La, Burma 41 E20 28 25N 97 23 E
Thalabarivat, Cambodia 38 F5 13 33N 105 57 E
Thallon, Australia 63 D4 28 39S 148 49 E
Thames, N.Z. 59 G5 37 7S 175 34 E
Thames →, Canada 78 D2 42 20N 82 25W
Thames →, U.K. 11 F8 51 29N 0 34 E
Thames →, U.S.A. 79 E12 41 18N 72 5W
Thames Estuary, U.K. 11 F8 51 29N 0 52 E
Thamesford, Canada 78 C4 43 4N 81 0W
Thamesville, Canada 78 D3 42 33N 81 59W
Than, India 42 H4 22 34N 71 11 E
Than Uyen, Vietnam 38 B4 22 0N 103 54 E
Thana Gazi, India 42 F7 27 25N 76 19 E
Thandla, India 42 H6 23 0N 74 34 E
Thane, India 40 K8 19 12N 72 59 E
Thanesar, India 42 D7 30 1N 76 52 E
Thanet, I. of, U.K. 11 F9 51 21N 1 20 E
Thangool, Australia 62 C5 24 38S 150 42 E
Thanh Hoa, Vietnam 38 C5 19 48N 105 46 E
Thanh Hung, Vietnam 39 H5 9 55N 105 43 E
Thanh Pho Ho Chi Minh = Phanh Bho Ho Chi Minh, Vietnam 39 G6 10 58N 106 40 E
Thanh Thuy, Vietnam 38 A5 22 55N 104 51 E
Thanjavur, India 40 P11 10 48N 79 12 E
Thano Bula Khan, Pakistan 42 G2 25 22N 67 50 E
Thaolinta L., Canada 73 A9 61 30N 96 25W
Thap Sakae, Thailand 39 G2 11 30N 99 37 E
Thap Than, Thailand 38 E2 15 27N 99 54 E
Thar Desert, India 42 F5 28 0N 72 0 E
Tharad, India 42 G4 24 30N 71 44 E
Thargomindah, Australia 63 D3 27 58S 143 46 E
Tharrawaddy, Burma 41 L19 17 38N 95 48 E
Tharthār, Mileh, Iraq 44 C4 34 0N 43 15 E
Tharthār, W. ath →, Iraq 44 C4 33 59N 43 12 E
Thásos, Greece 21 D11 40 40N 24 40 E
Thatcher, Ariz., U.S.A. 83 K9 32 51N 109 46W
Thatcher, Colo., U.S.A. 81 G2 37 33N 104 7W
Thaton, Burma 41 L20 16 55N 97 22 E
Thaungdut, Burma 41 G19 24 30N 94 40 E
Thayer, U.S.A. 81 G9 36 31N 91 33W
Thayetmyo, Burma 41 K19 19 20N 95 10 E
Thazi, Burma 41 J20 21 0N 96 5 E
The Alberga →, Australia 63 D2 27 6S 135 33 E
The Bight, Bahamas 89 B4 24 19N 75 24W
The Coorong, Australia 63 F2 35 50S 139 20 E
The Dalles, U.S.A. 82 D3 45 36N 121 10W
The English Company's Is., Australia 62 A2 11 50S 136 32 E
The Frome →, Australia 63 D2 29 8S 137 54 E
The Great Divide = Great Dividing Ra., Australia 62 C4 23 0S 146 0 E
The Hague = 's-Gravenhage, Neths. 15 B4 52 7N 4 17 E
The Hamilton →, Australia 63 D2 26 40S 135 19 E
The Macumba →, Australia 63 D2 27 52S 137 12 E
The Neales →, Australia 63 D2 28 8S 136 47 E
The Officer →, Australia 61 E5 27 46S 132 30 E
The Pas, Canada 73 C8 53 45N 101 15W
The Range, Zimbabwe 55 F3 19 2S 31 2 E
The Rock, Australia 63 F4 35 15S 147 2 E
The Salt L., Australia 63 E3 30 6S 142 8 E
The Sandheads, India 43 J13 21 10N 88 20 E
The Stevenson →, Australia 63 D2 27 6S 135 33 E
The Warburton →, Australia 63 D2 28 4S 137 28 E
The Woodlands, U.S.A. 81 K7 30 9N 95 27W
Thebes = Thívai, Greece 21 E10 38 19N 23 19 E
Thebes, Egypt 51 C12 25 40N 32 35 E
Thedford, Canada 78 C3 43 9N 81 51W
Thedford, U.S.A. 80 E4 41 59N 100 35W
Theebine, Australia 63 D5 25 57S 152 34 E
Thekulthili L., Canada 73 A7 61 3N 110 0W
Thelon →, Canada 73 A8 62 35N 104 3W
Theodore, Australia 62 C5 24 55S 150 3 E
Theodore, Canada 73 C8 51 26N 102 55W
Theodore, U.S.A. 77 K1 30 33N 88 10W
Theodore Roosevelt National Memorial Park, U.S.A. 80 B3 47 0N 103 25W
Theodore Roosevelt Res., U.S.A. 83 K8 33 46N 111 0W
Thepha, Thailand 39 J3 6 52N 100 58 E
Theresa, U.S.A. 79 B9 44 13N 75 48W
Thermaïkós Kólpos, Greece 21 D10 40 15N 22 45 E
Thermopolis, U.S.A. 82 E9 43 39N 108 13W
Thermopylae P., Greece 21 E10 38 48N 22 35 E
Thessalon, Canada 70 C3 46 20N 83 30W
Thessaloníki, Greece 21 D10 40 38N 22 58 E
Thessaloniki, Gulf of = Thermaïkós Kólpos, Greece 21 D10 40 15N 22 45 E
Thetford, U.K. 11 E8 52 25N 0 45 E
Thetford Mines, Canada 71 C5 46 8N 71 18W
Theun →, Laos 38 C5 18 19N 104 0 E
Theunissen, S. Africa 56 D4 28 26S 26 43 E
Thevenard, Australia 63 E1 32 9S 133 38 E
Thibodaux, U.S.A. 81 L9 29 48N 90 49W
Thicket Portage, Canada 73 B9 55 19N 97 42W
Thief River Falls, U.S.A. 80 A6 48 7N 96 10W
Thiel Mts., Antarctica 5 E16 85 15S 91 0W
Thiers, France 18 D5 45 52N 3 33 E
Thiès, Senegal 50 F2 14 50N 16 51W
Thika, Kenya 54 C4 1 1S 37 5 E
Thikombia, Fiji 59 B9 15 44S 179 55W
Thimphu, Bhutan 41 F16 27 31N 89 45 E
þingvallavatn, Iceland 8 D3 64 11N 21 9W
Thionville, France 18 B7 49 20N 6 10 E
Thíra, Greece 21 F11 36 23N 25 27 E
Third Cataract, Sudan 51 E12 19 49N 30 19 E
Thirsk, U.K. 10 C6 54 14N 1 19W
Thisted, Denmark 9 H13 56 58N 8 40 E
Thistle I., Australia 63 F2 35 0S 136 8 E
Thívai, Greece 21 E10 38 19N 23 19 E
þjórsá →, Iceland 8 E3 63 47N 20 48W
Thlewiaza →, Man., Canada 73 B8 59 43N 100 5W
Thlewiaza →, N.W.T., Canada 73 A10 60 29N 94 40W
Thmar Puok, Cambodia 38 F4 13 57N 103 4 E
Tho Vinh, Vietnam 38 C5 19 16N 105 42 E
Thoa →, Canada 73 A7 60 31N 109 47W
Thoen, Thailand 38 D2 17 43N 99 12 E
Thoeng, Thailand 38 C3 19 41N 100 12 E
Thohoyandou, S. Africa 53 J6 22 58S 30 29 E
Tholdi, Pakistan 43 B7 35 5N 76 6 E
Thomas, U.S.A. 81 H5 35 45N 98 45W
Thomas, L., Australia 63 D2 26 4S 137 58 E
Thomaston, U.S.A. 77 J3 32 53N 84 20W
Thomasville, Ala., U.S.A. 77 K2 31 55N 87 44W
Thomasville, Ga., U.S.A. 77 K4 30 50N 83 59W
Thomasville, N.C., U.S.A. 77 H5 35 53N 80 5W
Thompson, Canada 73 B9 55 45N 97 52W
Thompson, U.S.A. 79 E9 41 52N 75 31W
Thompson →, Canada 72 C4 50 15N 121 24W
Thompson →, U.S.A. 80 F8 39 46N 93 37W
Thompson Falls, U.S.A. 82 C6 47 36N 115 21W
Thompson Pk., U.S.A. 82 F2 41 0N 123 0W
Thompson Springs, U.S.A. 83 G9 38 58N 109 43W
Thompsontown, U.S.A. 78 F7 40 33N 77 14W
Thomson, U.S.A. 77 J4 33 28N 82 30W
Thomson →, Australia 62 C3 25 11S 142 53 E
Thomson's Falls = Nyahururu, Kenya 54 B4 0 2N 36 27 E
þórisvatn, Iceland 8 D4 64 20N 18 55W
Thornaby on Tees, U.K. 10 C6 54 33N 1 18W
Thornbury, Canada 78 B4 44 34N 80 26W
Thorne, U.K. 10 D7 53 37N 0 57W
Thornhill, Canada 72 C3 54 31N 128 32W
Thorold, Canada 78 C5 43 7N 79 12W
þórshöfn, Iceland 8 C6 66 12N 15 20W
Thouin, C., Australia 60 D2 20 20S 118 10 E
Thousand Oaks, U.S.A. 85 L8 34 10N 118 50W
Thrace, Turkey 21 D12 41 0N 27 0 E
Three Forks, U.S.A. 82 D8 45 54N 111 33W
Three Hills, Canada 72 C6 51 43N 113 15W
Three Hummock I., Australia 62 G3 40 25S 144 55 E
Three Points, C., Ghana 50 H5 4 42N 2 6W
Three Rivers, Calif., U.S.A. 84 J8 36 26N 118 54W
Three Rivers, Tex., U.S.A. 81 L5 28 28N 98 11W
Three Sisters, U.S.A. 82 D3 44 4N 121 51W
Three Springs, Australia 61 E2 29 32S 115 45 E
Throssell, L., Australia 61 E3 27 33S 124 10 E
Throssell Ra., Australia 60 D3 22 3S 121 43 E
Thuan Hoa, Vietnam 39 H5 8 58N 105 30 E
Thubun Lakes, Canada 73 A6 61 30N 112 0W
Thuin, Belgium 15 D4 50 20N 4 17 E
Thule, Greenland 4 B4 77 40N 69 0W
Thun, Switz. 18 C7 46 45N 7 38 E
Thunder B., U.S.A. 78 B1 45 0N 83 20W
Thunder Bay, Canada 70 C2 48 20N 89 15W
Thung Song, Thailand 39 H2 8 10N 99 40 E
Thunkar, Bhutan 41 F17 27 55N 91 0 E
Thuong Tra, Vietnam 38 D6 16 2N 107 42 E
Thüringer Wald, Germany 16 C6 50 35N 11 0 E
Thurles, Ireland 13 D4 52 41N 7 49W
Thurrock □, U.K. 11 F8 51 31N 0 23 E
Thursday I., Australia 62 A3 10 30S 142 3 E
Thurso, Canada 70 C4 45 36N 75 15W
Thurso, U.K. 12 C5 58 36N 3 32W
Thurso →, U.K. 12 C5 58 36N 3 32W
Thurston I., Antarctica 5 D16 72 0S 100 0W
Thutade L., Canada 72 B3 57 0N 126 55W
Thyolo, Malawi 55 F4 16 7S 35 5 E
Thysville = Mbanza Ngungu, Dem. Rep. of the Congo 52 F2 5 12S 14 53 E
Ti Tree, Australia 62 C1 22 5S 133 22 E
Tian Shan, Asia 32 B3 42 0N 76 0 E
Tianjin, China 35 E9 39 8N 117 10 E
Tianshui, China 34 G3 34 32N 105 40 E
Tianzhen, China 34 D8 40 24N 114 5 E
Tianzhuangtai, China 35 D12 40 43N 122 5 E
Tiaret, Algeria 50 A6 35 20N 1 21 E
Tibagi, Brazil 95 A5 24 30S 50 24W
Tibagi →, Brazil 95 A5 22 47S 51 1W
Tiber = Tevere →, Italy 20 D5 41 44N 12 14 E
Tiberias = Teverya, Israel 47 C4 32 47N 35 32 E
Tiberias, L. = Yam Kinneret, Israel 47 C4 32 45N 35 35 E
Tibesti, Chad 51 D9 21 0N 17 30 E
Tibet = Xizang Zizhiqu □, China 32 C3 32 0N 88 0 E
Tibet, Plateau of, Asia 28 F12 32 0N 86 0 E
Tibnī, Syria 44 C3 35 36N 39 50 E
Tibooburra, Australia 63 D3 29 26S 142 1 E
Tiburón, I., Mexico 86 B2 29 0N 112 30W
Ticino →, Italy 18 D8 45 9N 9 14 E
Ticonderoga, U.S.A. 79 C11 43 51N 73 26W
Ticul, Mexico 87 C7 20 20N 89 31W
Tidaholm, Sweden 9 G15 58 12N 13 58 E
Tiddim, Burma 41 H18 23 28N 93 45 E
Tidioute, U.S.A. 78 E5 41 41N 79 24W
Tidjikja, Mauritania 50 E3 18 29N 11 35W
Tidore, Indonesia 37 D7 0 40N 127 25 E
Tiel, Neths. 15 C5 51 53N 5 26 E
Tieling, China 35 C12 42 20N 123 55 E
Tielt, Belgium 15 C3 51 0N 3 20 E
Tien Shan = Tian Shan, Asia 32 B3 42 0N 76 0 E
Tien-tsin = Tianjin, China 35 E9 39 8N 117 10 E
Tien Yen, Vietnam 38 B6 21 20N 107 24 E
T'ienching = Tianjin, China 35 E9 39 8N 117 10 E
Tienen, Belgium 15 D4 50 48N 4 57 E
Tientsin = Tianjin, China 35 E9 39 8N 117 10 E
Tieri, Australia 62 C4 23 2S 148 21 E
Tierra Amarilla, Chile 94 B1 27 28S 70 18W
Tierra Amarilla, U.S.A. 83 H10 36 42N 106 33W
Tierra Colorada, Mexico 87 D5 17 10N 99 35W
Tierra de Campos, Spain 19 A3 42 10N 4 50W
Tierra del Fuego, I. Gr. de, Argentina 96 G3 54 0S 69 0W
Tiétar →, Spain 19 C3 39 50N 6 1W
Tieté →, Brazil 95 A5 20 40S 51 35W
Tiffin, U.S.A. 76 E4 41 7N 83 11W
Tiflis = Tbilisi, Georgia 25 F7 41 43N 44 50 E
Tifton, U.S.A. 77 K4 31 27N 83 31W
Tifu, Indonesia 37 E7 3 39S 126 24 E
Tighina, Moldova 17 E15 46 50N 29 30 E
Tigil, Russia 27 D16 57 49N 158 40 E
Tignish, Canada 71 C7 46 58N 64 2W
Tigre →, Peru 92 D4 4 30S 74 10W
Tigre →, Venezuela 92 B6 9 20N 62 30W
Tigris = Dijlah, Nahr →, Asia 44 D5 31 0N 47 25 E
Tigyaing, Burma 41 H20 23 45N 96 10 E
Tijara, India 42 F7 27 56N 76 31 E
Tijuana, Mexico 85 N9 32 30N 117 10W
Tikal, Guatemala 88 C2 17 13N 89 24W
Tikamgarh, India 43 G8 24 44N 78 50 E
Tikhoretsk, Russia 25 E7 45 56N 40 5 E
Tikhvin, Russia 24 C5 59 35N 33 30 E
Tikrīt, Iraq 44 C4 34 35N 43 37 E
Tiksi, Russia 27 B13 71 40N 128 45 E
Tilamuta, Indonesia 37 D6 0 32N 122 23 E
Tilburg, Neths. 15 C5 51 31N 5 6 E
Tilbury, Canada 78 D2 42 17N 82 23W
Tilbury, U.K. 11 F8 51 27N 0 22 E
Tilcara, Argentina 94 A2 23 36S 65 23W
Tilden, U.S.A. 80 D6 42 3N 97 50W
Tilhar, India 43 F8 28 0N 79 45 E
Tilichiki, Russia 27 C17 60 27N 166 5 E
Tilissos, Greece 23 D7 35 20N 25 1 E
Till →, U.K. 10 B5 55 41N 2 13W
Tillamook, U.S.A. 82 D2 45 27N 123 51W
Tillsonburg, Canada 78 D4 42 53N 80 44W
Tillyeria □, Cyprus 23 D11 35 6N 32 40 E
Tílos, Greece 21 F12 36 27N 27 27 E
Tilpa, Australia 63 E3 30 57S 144 24 E
Tilsit = Sovetsk, Russia 9 J19 55 6N 21 50 E
Tilt →, U.K. 12 E5 56 46N 3 51W
Tilton, U.S.A. 79 C13 43 27N 71 36W
Tiltonsville, U.S.A. 78 F4 40 10N 80 41W
Timagami, L., Canada 70 C3 47 0N 80 10W
Timanskiy Kryazh, Russia 24 A9 65 58N 50 5 E
Timaru, N.Z. 59 L3 44 23S 171 14 E
Timau, Kenya 54 B4 0 4N 37 15 E
Timbákion, Greece 23 D6 35 4N 24 45 E
Timber Creek, Australia 60 C5 15 40S 130 29 E
Timber Lake, U.S.A. 80 C4 45 26N 101 5W
Timber Mt., U.S.A. 84 H10 37 6N 116 28W
Timbuktu = Tombouctou, Mali 50 E5 16 50N 3 0W
Timi, Cyprus 23 E11 34 44N 32 31 E
Timimoun, Algeria 50 C6 29 14N 0 16 E
Timişoara, Romania 17 F11 45 43N 21 15 E
Timmins, Canada 70 C3 48 28N 81 25W
Timok →, Serbia, Yug. 21 B10 44 10N 22 40 E
Timor, Indonesia 37 F7 9 0S 125 0 E
Timor Sea, Ind. Oc. 60 B4 12 0S 127 0 E
Timor Timur □, Indonesia 37 F7 9 0S 125 0 E
Tin Can Bay, Australia 63 D5 25 56S 153 0 E
Tin Mt., U.S.A. 84 J9 36 50N 117 10W
Tinaca Pt., Phil. 37 C7 5 30N 125 25 E
Tinajo, Canary Is. 22 E6 29 4N 13 42W
Tindal, Australia 60 B5 14 31S 132 22 E
Tindouf, Algeria 50 C4 27 42N 8 10W
Tinggi, Pulau, Malaysia 39 L5 2 18N 104 7 E
Tingo Maria, Peru 92 E3 9 10S 75 54W
Tingrela, Ivory C. 50 F4 10 27N 6 25W
Tinh Bien, Vietnam 39 G5 10 36N 104 57 E
Tinnevelly = Tirunelveli, India 40 Q10 8 45N 77 45 E
Tinogasta, Argentina 94 B2 28 5S 67 32W
Tínos, Greece 21 F11 37 33N 25 8 E
Tinpahar, India 43 G12 24 59N 87 44 E
Tintina, Argentina 94 B3 27 2S 62 45W
Tintinara, Australia 63 F3 35 48S 140 2 E
Tioga, N. Dak., U.S.A. 80 A3 48 23N 102 56W
Tioga, Pa., U.S.A. 78 E7 41 55N 77 8W
Tioman, Pulau, Malaysia 39 L5 2 50N 104 10 E
Tionesta, U.S.A. 78 E5 41 30N 79 28W
Tipongpani, India 41 F19 27 20N 95 55 E
Tipperary, Ireland 13 D3 52 28N 8 10W
Tipperary □, Ireland 13 D4 52 37N 7 55W
Tipton, Calif., U.S.A. 84 J7 36 4N 119 19W
Tipton, Iowa, U.S.A. 80 E9 41 46N 91 8W
Tipton Mt., U.S.A. 85 K12 35 32N 114 12W
Tiptonville, U.S.A. 81 G10 36 23N 89 29W
Tīrān, Iran 45 C6 32 45N 51 8 E
Tirana, Albania 21 D8 41 18N 19 49 E
Tiranë = Tirana, Albania 21 D8 41 18N 19 49 E
Tiraspol, Moldova 17 E15 46 55N 29 35 E
Tire, Turkey 21 E12 38 5N 27 45 E
Tirebolu, Turkey 25 F6 40 58N 38 45 E
Tiree, U.K. 12 E2 56 31N 6 55W
Tiree, Passage of, U.K. 12 E2 56 30N 6 30W
Tîrgovişte = Târgovişte, Romania 17 F13 44 55N 25 27 E
Tîrgu-Jiu = Târgu-Jiu, Romania 17 F12 45 5N 23 19 E
Tîrgu Mureş = Târgu Mureş, Romania 17 E13 46 31N 24 38 E
Tirich Mir, Pakistan 40 A7 36 15N 71 55 E
Tírnavos, Greece 21 E10 39 45N 22 18 E
Tirodi, India 40 J11 21 40N 79 44 E
Tirol □, Austria 16 E6 47 3N 10 43 E
Tirso →, Italy 20 E3 39 53N 8 32 E
Tiruchchirappalli, India 40 P11 10 45N 78 45 E
Tirunelveli, India 40 Q10 8 45N 77 45 E
Tirupati, India 40 N11 13 39N 79 25 E
Tiruppur, India 40 P10 11 5N 77 22 E
Tiruvannamalai, India 40 N11 12 15N 79 5 E
Tisa, India 42 C7 32 50N 76 9 E
Tisa →, Serbia, Yug. 21 B9 45 15N 20 17 E
Tisdale, Canada 73 C8 52 50N 104 0W
Tishomingo, U.S.A. 81 H6 34 14N 96 41W
Tisza = Tisa →, Serbia, Yug. 21 B9 45 15N 20 17 E
Tit-Ary, Russia 27 B13 71 55N 127 2 E
Tithwal, Pakistan 43 B5 34 21N 73 50 E
Titicaca, L., S. Amer. 92 G5 15 30S 69 30W
Titograd = Podgorica, Montenegro, Yug. 21 C8 42 30N 19 19 E
Titule, Dem. Rep. of the Congo 54 B2 3 15N 25 31 E
Titusville, Fla., U.S.A. 77 L5 28 37N 80 49W
Titusville, Pa., U.S.A. 78 E5 41 38N 79 41W
Tivaouane, Senegal 50 F2 14 56N 16 45W
Tiverton, U.K. 11 G4 50 54N 3 29W
Tívoli, Italy 20 D5 41 58N 12 45 E
Tizi-Ouzou, Algeria 50 A6 36 42N 4 3 E
Tizimín, Mexico 87 C7 21 0N 88 1W
Tjeggelvas, Sweden 8 C17 66 37N 17 45 E
Tjirebon = Cirebon, Indonesia 37 G13 6 45S 108 32 E
Tjörn, Sweden 9 G14 58 0N 11 35 E
Tlacotalpan, Mexico 87 D5 18 37N 95 40W
Tlahualilo, Mexico 86 B4 26 20N 103 30W
Tlaquepaque, Mexico 86 C4 20 39N 103 19W
Tlaxcala, Mexico 87 D5 19 20N 98 14W
Tlaxcala □, Mexico 87 D5 19 30N 98 20W
Tlaxiaco, Mexico 87 D5 17 18N 97 40W
Tlemcen, Algeria 50 B5 34 52N 1 21W
To Bong, Vietnam 38 F7 12 45N 109 16 E
Toad →, Canada 72 B4 59 25N 124 57W
Toad River, Canada 72 B3 58 51N 125 14W
Toamasina, Madag. 57 B8 18 10S 49 25 E
Toamasina □, Madag. 57 B8 18 0S 49 0 E
Toay, Argentina 94 D3 36 43S 64 38W
Toba, Japan 31 G8 34 30N 136 51 E
Toba, Danau, Indonesia 36 D1 2 30N 97 30 E
Toba Kakar, Pakistan 42 D3 31 30N 69 0 E
Toba Tek Singh, Pakistan 42 D5 30 55N 72 25 E
Tobago, W. Indies 89 D7 11 10N 60 30W
Tobelo, Indonesia 37 D7 1 45N 127 56 E
Tobermory, Canada 78 A3 45 12N 81 40W
Tobermory, U.K. 12 E2 56 38N 6 5W
Tobi, Pac. Oc. 37 D8 2 40N 131 10 E
Tobin, U.S.A. 84 F5 39 55N 121 19W
Tobin, L., Australia 60 D4 21 45S 125 49 E
Tobin L., Canada 73 C8 53 35N 103 30W
Toboali, Indonesia 36 E3 3 0S 106 25 E
Tobol →, Russia 26 D7 58 10N 68 12 E
Toboli, Indonesia 37 E6 0 38S 120 5 E
Tobolsk, Russia 26 D7 58 15N 68 10 E
Tobruk = Tubruq, Libya 51 B10 32 7N 23 55 E
Tobyhanna, U.S.A. 79 E9 41 11N 75 25W
Tobyl = Tobol →, Russia 26 D7 58 10N 68 12 E
Tocantinópolis, Brazil 93 E9 6 20S 47 25W
Tocantins □, Brazil 93 F9 10 0S 48 0W
Tocantins →, Brazil 93 D9 1 45S 49 10W
Toccoa, U.S.A. 77 H4 34 35N 83 19W
Tochi →, Pakistan 42 C4 32 49N 70 41 E
Tochigi, Japan 31 F9 36 25N 139 45 E
Tochigi □, Japan 31 F9 36 45N 139 45 E
Toconao, Chile 94 A2 23 11S 68 1W
Tocopilla, Chile 94 A1 22 5S 70 10W
Tocumwal, Australia 63 F4 35 51S 145 31 E
Tocuyo →, Venezuela 92 A5 11 3N 68 23W
Todd →, Australia 62 C2 24 52S 135 48 E
Todeli, Indonesia 37 E6 1 38S 124 34 E
Todenyang, Kenya 54 B4 4 35N 35 56 E
Todgarh, India 42 G5 25 42N 73 58 E
Todos os Santos, B. de, Brazil 93 F11 12 48S 38 38W
Todos Santos, Mexico 86 C2 23 27N 110 13W
Toe Hd., U.K. 12 D1 57 50N 7 8W
Tofield, Canada 72 C6 53 25N 112 40W
Tofino, Canada 72 D3 49 11N 125 55W
Tofua, Tonga 59 D11 19 45S 175 5W
Tōgane, Japan 31 G10 35 33N 140 22 E
Togian, Kepulauan, Indonesia 37 E6 0 20S 121 50 E
Togliatti, Russia 24 D8 53 32N 49 24 E
Togo ■, W. Afr. 50 G6 8 30N 1 35 E
Togtoh, China 34 D6 40 15N 111 10 E
Tōhoku □, Japan 30 E10 39 50N 141 45 E
Töhöm, Mongolia 34 B5 44 27N 108 2 E
Toinya, Sudan 51 G11 6 17N 29 46 E
Toiyabe Range, U.S.A. 82 G5 39 30N 117 0W
Tojikiston = Tajikistan ■, Asia 26 F8 38 30N 70 0 E
Tojo, Indonesia 37 E6 1 20S 121 15 E
Tōjō, Japan 31 G6 34 53N 133 16 E
Tok, U.S.A. 68 B5 63 20N 142 59W
Tok-do, Japan 31 F5 37 15N 131 52 E
Tokachi-Dake, Japan 30 C11 43 17N 142 5 E
Tokachi-Gawa →, Japan 30 C11 42 44N 143 42 E
Tokala, Indonesia 37 E6 1 30S 121 40 E
Tōkamachi, Japan 31 F9 37 8N 138 43 E
Tokanui, N.Z. 59 M2 46 34S 168 56 E
Tokara-Rettō, Japan 31 K4 29 37N 129 43 E
Tokarahi, N.Z. 59 L3 44 56S 170 39 E
Tokashiki-Shima, Japan 31 L3 26 11N 127 21 E
Tokat □, Turkey 25 F6 40 15N 36 30 E
Tŏkch'ŏn, N. Korea 35 E14 39 45N 126 18 E
Tokeland, U.S.A. 84 D3 46 42N 123 59W
Tokelau Is., Pac. Oc. 64 H10 9 0S 171 45W
Tokmak, Kyrgyzstan 26 E8 42 49N 75 15 E
Toko Ra., Australia 62 C2 23 5S 138 20 E
Tokoro-Gawa →, Japan 30 B12 44 7N 144 5 E
Tokuno-Shima, Japan 31 L4 27 56N 128 55 E
Tokushima, Japan 31 G7 34 4N 134 34 E
Tokushima □, Japan 31 H7 33 55N 134 0 E
Tokuyama, Japan 31 G5 34 3N 131 50 E
Tōkyō, Japan 31 G9 35 45N 139 45 E
Tolaga Bay, N.Z. 59 H7 38 21S 178 20 E
Tolbukhin = Dobrich, Bulgaria 21 C12 43 37N 27 49 E
Toledo, Brazil 95 A5 24 44S 53 45W
Toledo, Spain 19 C3 39 50N 4 2W
Toledo, Ohio, U.S.A. 76 E4 41 39N 83 33W
Toledo, Oreg., U.S.A. 82 D2 44 37N 123 56W
Toledo, Wash., U.S.A. 82 C2 46 26N 122 51W
Toledo, Montes de, Spain 19 C3 39 33N 4 20W
Toledo Bend Reservoir, U.S.A. 81 K8 31 11N 93 34W
Tolga, Australia 62 B4 17 15S 145 29 E
Toliara, Madag. 57 C7 23 21S 43 40 E
Toliara □, Madag. 57 C8 21 0S 45 0 E
Tolima, Colombia 92 C3 4 40N 75 19W
Tolitoli, Indonesia 37 D6 1 5N 120 50 E
Tollhouse, U.S.A. 84 H7 37 1N 119 24W
Tolo, Teluk, Indonesia 37 E6 2 20S 122 10 E
Toluca, Mexico 87 D5 19 20N 99 40W
Tom Burke, S. Africa 57 C4 23 5S 28 0 E
Tom Price, Australia 60 D2 22 40S 117 48 E
Tomah, U.S.A. 80 D9 43 59N 90 30W
Tomahawk, U.S.A. 80 C10 45 28N 89 44W
Tomakomai, Japan 30 C10 42 38N 141 36 E
Tomales, U.S.A. 84 G4 38 15N 122 53W
Tomales B., U.S.A. 84 G3 38 15N 123 58W
Tomar, Portugal 19 C1 39 36N 8 25W
Tomaszów Mazowiecki, Poland 17 C10 51 30N 20 2 E
Tomatlán, Mexico 86 D3 19 56N 105 15W
Tombador, Serra do, Brazil 92 F7 12 0S 58 0W
Tombigbee →, U.S.A. 77 K2 31 8N 87 57W
Tombouctou, Mali 50 E5 16 50N 3 0W
Tombstone, U.S.A. 83 L8 31 43N 110 4W
Tombua, Angola 56 B1 15 55S 11 55 E

Tukums

omé, Chile 94 D1 36 36S 72 57W
omelloso, Spain 19 C4 39 10N 3 2W
omini, Indonesia 37 D6 0 30N 120 30 E
omini, Teluk, Indonesia 37 E6 0 10S 122 0 E
omintoul, U.K. 12 D5 57 15N 3 23W
omkinson Ranges,
Australia 61 E4 26 11S 129 5 E
ommot, Russia 27 D13 59 4N 126 20 E
omnop Ta Suos, Cambodia 39 G5 11 20N 104 15 E
omo →, Colombia 92 B5 5 20N 67 48W
oms Place, U.S.A. 84 H8 37 34N 118 41W
oms River, U.S.A. 79 G10 39 58N 74 12W
omsk, Russia 26 D9 56 30N 85 5 E
onalá, Mexico 87 D6 16 8N 93 41W
onantins, Brazil 92 D5 2 45S 67 45W
onasket, U.S.A. 82 B4 48 42N 119 26W
onawanda, U.S.A. 78 D6 43 1N 78 53W
onbridge, U.K. 11 F8 51 11N 0 17 E
ondano, Indonesia 37 D6 1 35N 124 54 E
one →, Australia 61 F2 34 25S 116 25 E
one-Gawa →, Japan 31 F9 35 44N 140 51 E
onekābon, Iran 45 B6 36 45N 51 12 E
ong Xian, China 34 E9 39 55N 116 35 E
onga ■, Pac. Oc. 59 D11 19 50S 174 30W
onga Trench, Pac. Oc. 64 J10 18 0S 173 0W
ongaat, S. Africa 57 D5 29 33S 31 9 E
ongareva, Cook Is. 65 H12 9 0S 158 0W
ongatapu, Tonga 59 E12 21 10S 174 0W
ongchŏn-ni, N. Korea 35 E14 39 50N 127 25 E
ongchuan, China 34 G5 35 6N 109 3 E
ongeren, Belgium 15 D5 50 47N 5 28 E
ongguan, China 34 G6 34 40N 110 25 E
onghua, China 35 D13 41 42N 125 58 E
ongjosŏn Man, N. Korea 35 E15 39 30N 128 0 E
ongking, G. of, Asia 32 E5 20 0N 108 0 E
ongliao, China 35 C12 43 38N 122 18 E
ongling, China 33 C6 30 55N 117 48 E
ongnae, S. Korea 35 G15 35 12N 129 5 E
ongobory, Madag. 57 C7 23 32S 44 20 E
ongoy, Chile 94 C1 30 16S 71 31W
ongres = Tongeren,
Belgium 15 D5 50 47N 5 28 E
ongsa Dzong, Bhutan 41 F17 27 31N 90 31 E
ongue, U.K. 12 C4 58 29N 4 25W
ongue →, U.S.A. 80 B2 46 25N 105 52W
ongwei, China 34 G3 35 0N 105 5 E
ongxin, China 34 F3 36 59N 105 58 E
ongyang, N. Korea 35 E14 39 9N 126 53 E
ongyu, China 35 B12 44 45N 123 4 E
onj, Sudan 51 G11 7 20N 28 44 E
onk, India 42 F6 26 6N 75 54 E
onkawa, U.S.A. 81 G6 36 41N 97 18W
onkin = Bac Phan, Vietnam 38 B5 22 0N 105 0 E
onle Sap, Cambodia 38 F5 13 0N 104 0 E
ono, Japan 30 E10 39 19N 141 32 E
onopah, U.S.A. 83 G5 38 4N 117 14W
onosí, Panama 88 E3 7 20N 80 20W
ons →, Haryana, India 42 D7 30 30N 77 39 E
ons →, Ut. P., India 43 F10 26 1N 83 33 E
ønsberg, Norway 9 G14 59 19N 10 25 E
oobanna, Australia 62 B4 18 42S 146 9 E
oodyay, Australia 61 F2 31 34S 116 28 E
ooele, U.S.A. 82 F7 40 32N 112 18W
oompine, Australia 63 D3 27 15S 144 19 E
oora, Australia 63 F4 38 39S 146 23 E
oora-Khem, Russia 27 D10 52 28N 96 17 E
oowoomba, Australia 63 D5 27 32S 151 56 E
op-ozero, Russia 24 A5 65 35N 32 0 E
op Springs, Australia 60 C5 16 37S 131 51 E
opaz, U.S.A. 84 G7 38 41N 119 30W
opeka, U.S.A. 80 F7 39 3N 95 40W
opley, Canada 72 C3 54 49N 126 18W
opocalma, Pta., Chile 94 C1 34 10S 72 2W
opock, U.S.A. 85 L12 34 46N 114 29W
opoľčany, Slovak Rep. 17 D10 48 35N 18 12 E
opolobampo, Mexico 86 B3 25 40N 109 4W
oppenish, U.S.A. 82 C3 46 23N 120 19W
oraka Vestale, Madag. 57 B7 16 20S 43 58 E
orata, Peru 92 G4 17 23S 70 1W
orbalı, Turkey 21 E12 38 10N 27 21 E
orbat-e Heydārīyeh, Iran 45 C8 35 15N 59 12 E
orbat-e Jām, Iran 45 C9 35 16N 60 35 E
orbay, Canada 71 C9 47 40N 52 42W
orbay □, U.K. 11 G4 50 26N 3 31W
ordesillas, Spain 19 B3 41 30N 5 0W
orfaen □, U.K. 11 F4 51 43N 3 3W
orgau, Germany 16 C7 51 34N 13 0 E
orhout, Belgium 15 C3 51 5N 3 7 E
ori-Shima, Japan 31 J10 30 29N 140 19 E
orin, Mexico 86 B2 27 33N 110 15W
orino, Italy 18 D7 45 3N 7 40 E
orit, Sudan 51 H12 4 27N 32 31 E
orkamān, Iran 44 B5 37 35N 47 23 E
ormes →, Spain 19 B2 41 18N 6 29W
ornado Mt., Canada 72 D6 49 55N 114 40W
orne älv →, Sweden 8 D21 65 50N 24 12 E
orneå = Tornio, Finland 8 D21 65 50N 24 12 E
orneträsk, Sweden 8 B18 68 24N 19 15 E
ornio, Finland 8 D21 65 50N 24 12 E
ornionjoki →, Finland 8 D21 65 50N 24 12 E
ornquist, Argentina 94 D3 38 8S 62 15W
oro, Spain 22 B11 39 59N 4 8 E
oro, Cerro del, Chile 94 B2 29 10S 69 50W
oro Pk., U.S.A. 85 M10 33 34N 116 24W
oroníos Kólpos, Greece 21 D10 40 5N 23 30 E
oronto, Canada 78 C5 43 39N 79 20W
oronto, U.S.A. 78 F4 40 28N 80 36W
oropets, Russia 24 C5 56 30N 31 40 E
ororo, Uganda 54 B3 0 45N 34 12 E
oros Dağları, Turkey 25 G5 37 0N 32 30 E
orpa, India 43 H11 22 57N 85 6 E
orquay, Australia 63 F3 38 20S 144 19 E
orquay, U.K. 11 G4 50 27N 3 32W
orrance, U.S.A. 85 M8 33 50N 118 19W
orre de Moncorvo,
Portugal 19 B2 41 12N 7 8W
orre del Greco, Italy 20 D6 40 47N 14 22 E
orrejón de Ardoz, Spain 19 B4 40 27N 3 29W
orrelavega, Spain 19 A3 43 20N 4 5W
orremolinos, Spain 19 D3 36 38N 4 30W
orrens, L., Australia 63 E2 31 0S 137 50 E
orrens Cr. →, Australia 62 C4 22 23S 145 9 E
orrens Creek, Australia 62 C4 20 48S 145 3 E
orrent, Spain 19 C5 39 27N 0 28W
orreón, Mexico 86 B4 25 33N 103 26W
orres, Brazil 95 B5 29 21S 49 44W
Torres, Mexico 86 B2 28 46N 110 47W
Torres Strait, Australia 64 H6 9 50S 142 20 E
Torres Vedras, Portugal 19 C1 39 5N 9 15W
Torrevieja, Spain 19 D5 37 59N 0 42W
Torrey, U.S.A. 83 G8 38 18N 111 25W
Torridge →, U.K. 11 G3 51 0N 4 13W
Torridon, L., U.K. 12 D3 57 35N 5 50W
Torrington, Conn., U.S.A. 79 E11 41 48N 73 7W
Torrington, Wyo., U.S.A. 80 D2 42 4N 104 11W
Tórshavn, Færoe Is. 8 E9 62 5N 6 56W
Tortola, Virgin Is. 89 C7 18 19N 64 45W
Tortosa, Spain 19 B6 40 49N 0 31 E
Tortosa, C., Spain 19 B6 40 41N 0 52 E
Tortue, I. de la, Haiti 89 B5 20 5N 72 57W
Torūd, Iran 45 C7 35 25N 55 5 E
Toruń, Poland 17 B10 53 2N 18 39 E
Tory I., Ireland 13 A3 55 16N 8 14W
Tosa, Japan 31 H6 33 24N 133 23 E
Tosa-Shimizu, Japan 31 H6 32 52N 132 58 E
Tosa-Wan, Japan 31 H6 33 15N 133 30 E
Toscana □, Italy 20 C4 43 25N 11 0 E
Toshkent, Uzbekistan 26 E7 41 20N 69 10 E
Tostado, Argentina 94 B3 29 15S 61 50W
Tostón, Pta. de, Canary Is. 22 F5 28 42N 14 2W
Tosu, Japan 31 H5 33 22N 130 31 E
Toteng, Botswana 56 C3 20 22S 22 58 E
Totma, Russia 24 C7 60 0N 42 40 E
Totnes, U.K. 11 G4 50 26N 3 42W
Totness, Surinam 93 B7 5 53N 56 19W
Totonicapán, Guatemala 88 D1 14 58N 91 12W
Totten Glacier, Antarctica 5 C8 66 45S 116 10 E
Tottenham, Australia 63 E4 32 14S 147 21 E
Tottenham, Canada 78 B5 44 1N 79 49W
Tottori, Japan 31 G7 35 30N 134 15 E
Tottori □, Japan 31 G7 35 30N 134 12 E
Toubkal, Djebel, Morocco 50 B4 31 0N 8 0W
Tougan, Burkina Faso 50 F5 13 11N 2 58W
Touggourt, Algeria 50 B7 33 6N 6 4 E
Toul, France 18 B6 48 40N 5 53 E
Toulon, France 18 E6 43 10N 5 55 E
Toulouse, France 18 E4 43 37N 1 27 E
Toummo, Niger 51 D8 22 45N 14 8 E
Toungoo, Burma 41 K20 19 0N 96 30 E
Touraine, France 18 C4 47 20N 0 30 E
Tourane = Da Nang,
Vietnam 38 D7 16 4N 108 13 E
Tourcoing, France 18 A5 50 42N 3 10 E
Touriñán, C., Spain 19 A1 43 3N 9 18W
Tournai, Belgium 15 D3 50 35N 3 25 E
Tournon-sur-Rhône, France 18 D6 45 4N 4 50 E
Tours, France 18 C4 47 22N 0 40 E
Tousidé, Pic, Chad 51 D9 21 1N 16 29 E
Toussora, Mt., C.A.R. 52 C4 9 7N 23 14 E
Touwsrivier, S. Africa 56 E3 33 20S 20 2 E
Towada, Japan 30 D10 40 37N 141 13 E
Towada-Ko, Japan 30 D10 40 28N 140 55 E
Towanda, U.S.A. 79 E8 41 46N 76 27W
Towang, India 41 F17 27 37N 91 50 E
Tower, U.S.A. 80 B8 47 48N 92 17W
Towerhill Cr. →, Australia 62 C3 22 28S 144 35 E
Towner, U.S.A. 80 A4 48 21N 100 25W
Townsend, U.S.A. 82 C8 46 19N 111 31W
Townshend I., Australia 62 C5 22 10S 150 31 E
Townsville, Australia 62 B4 19 15S 146 45 E
Towson, U.S.A. 76 F7 39 24N 76 36W
Towuti, Danau, Indonesia 37 E6 2 45S 121 32 E
Toya-Ko, Japan 30 C10 42 35N 140 51 E
Toyama, Japan 31 F8 36 40N 137 15 E
Toyama □, Japan 31 F8 36 45N 137 30 E
Toyama-Wan, Japan 31 F8 37 0N 137 30 E
Toyohashi, Japan 31 G8 34 45N 137 25 E
Toyokawa, Japan 31 G8 34 48N 137 27 E
Toyonaka, Japan 31 G7 34 50N 135 28 E
Toyooka, Japan 31 G7 35 35N 134 48 E
Toyota, Japan 31 G8 35 3N 137 7 E
Tozeur, Tunisia 50 B7 33 56N 8 8 E
Trá Li = Tralee, Ireland 13 D2 52 16N 9 42W
Tra On, Vietnam 39 H5 9 58N 105 55 E
Trabzon, Turkey 25 F6 41 0N 39 45 E
Tracadie, Canada 71 C7 47 30N 64 55W
Tracy, Calif., U.S.A. 84 H5 37 44N 121 26W
Tracy, Minn., U.S.A. 80 C7 44 14N 95 37W
Trafalgar, C., Spain 19 D2 36 10N 6 2W
Trail, Canada 72 D5 49 5N 117 40W
Trainor L., Canada 72 A4 60 24N 120 17W
Trákhonas, Cyprus 23 D12 35 12N 33 21 E
Tralee, Ireland 13 D2 52 16N 9 42W
Tralee B., Ireland 13 D2 52 17N 9 55W
Tramore, Ireland 13 D4 52 10N 7 10W
Tramore B., Ireland 13 D4 52 9N 7 10W
Tran Ninh, Cao Nguyen,
Laos 38 C4 19 30N 103 10 E
Tranås, Sweden 9 G16 58 3N 14 59 E
Trancas, Argentina 94 B2 26 11S 65 20W
Trang, Thailand 39 J2 7 33N 99 38 E
Trangahy, Madag. 57 B7 19 7S 44 31 E
Trangan, Indonesia 37 F8 6 40S 134 20 E
Trangie, Australia 63 E4 32 4S 148 0 E
Trani, Italy 20 D7 41 17N 16 25 E
Tranoroa, Madag. 57 C8 24 42S 45 4 E
Tranqueras, Uruguay 95 C4 31 13S 55 45W
Transantarctic Mts.,
Antarctica 5 E12 85 0S 170 0W
Transilvania, Romania 17 E12 46 30N 24 0 E
Transilvanian Alps =
Carpaţii Meridionali,
Romania 17 F13 45 30N 25 0 E
Transvaal □, S. Africa 53 K5 25 0S 29 0 E
Transylvania = Transilvania,
Romania 17 E12 46 30N 24 0 E
Trápani, Italy 20 E5 38 1N 12 29 E
Trapper Pk., U.S.A. 82 D6 45 54N 114 18W
Traralgon, Australia 63 F4 38 12S 146 34 E
Trasimeno, L., Italy 20 C5 43 8N 12 6 E
Trat, Thailand 39 F4 12 14N 102 33 E
Tratani →, Pakistan 42 E3 29 19N 68 20 E
Traun, Austria 16 D8 48 14N 14 15 E
Travellers L., Australia 63 E3 33 20S 142 0 E
Travemünde, Germany 16 B6 53 57N 10 52 E
Travers, Mt., N.Z. 59 K4 42 1S 172 45 E
Traverse City, U.S.A. 76 C3 44 46N 85 38W
Travis, L., U.S.A. 81 K5 30 24N 97 55W
Travnik, Bos.-H. 21 B7 44 17N 17 39 E
Trébbia →, Italy 18 D8 45 4N 9 41 E
Třebíč, Czech Rep. 16 D8 49 14N 15 55 E
Trebinje, Bos.-H. 21 C8 42 44N 18 22 E
Trebonne, Australia 62 B4 18 37S 146 5 E
Tregaron, U.K. 11 E4 52 14N 3 56W
Tregrosse Is., Australia 62 B5 17 41S 150 43 E
Treherne, Canada 73 D9 49 38N 98 42W
Treinta y Tres, Uruguay 95 C5 33 16S 54 17W
Trelew, Argentina 96 E3 43 10S 65 20W
Trelleborg, Sweden 9 J15 55 20N 13 10 E
Tremadog Bay, U.K. 10 E3 52 51N 4 18W
Tremonton, U.S.A. 82 F7 41 43N 112 10W
Tremp, Spain 19 A6 42 10N 0 52 E
Trenche →, Canada 70 C5 47 46N 72 53W
Trenčín, Slovak Rep. 17 D10 48 52N 18 4 E
Trenggalek, Indonesia 37 H14 8 3S 111 43 E
Trenque Lauquen, Argentina 94 D3 36 5S 62 45W
Trent →, Canada 78 B7 44 6N 77 34W
Trent →, U.K. 10 D7 53 41N 0 42W
Trento, Italy 20 A4 46 4N 11 8 E
Trenton, Canada 78 B7 44 10N 77 34W
Trenton, Mo., U.S.A. 80 E8 40 5N 93 37W
Trenton, N.J., U.S.A. 79 F10 40 14N 74 46W
Trenton, Nebr., U.S.A. 80 E4 40 11N 101 1W
Trepassey, Canada 71 C9 46 43N 53 25W
Tres Arroyos, Argentina 94 D3 38 26S 60 20W
Três Corações, Brazil 95 A6 21 44S 45 15W
Três Lagoas, Brazil 93 H8 20 50S 51 43W
Tres Lomas, Argentina 94 D3 36 27S 62 51W
Tres Marías, Islas, Mexico 86 C3 21 25N 106 28W
Tres Montes, C., Chile 96 F1 46 50S 75 30W
Tres Pinos, U.S.A. 84 J5 36 48N 121 19W
Três Pontas, Brazil 95 A6 21 23S 45 29W
Tres Puentes, Chile 94 B1 27 50S 70 15W
Tres Puntas, C., Argentina 96 F3 47 0S 66 0W
Três Rios, Brazil 95 A7 22 6S 43 15W
Tres Valles, Mexico 87 D5 18 15N 96 8W
Tresco, U.K. 11 H1 49 57N 6 20W
Treviso, Italy 20 B5 45 40N 12 15 E
Triabunna, Australia 62 G4 42 30S 147 55 E
Triánda, Greece 23 C10 36 25N 28 10 E
Tribulation, C., Australia 62 B4 16 5S 145 29 E
Tribune, U.S.A. 80 F4 38 28N 101 45W
Trichinopoly =
Tiruchchirappalli, India 40 P11 10 45N 78 45 E
Trichur, India 40 P10 10 30N 76 18 E
Trida, Australia 63 E4 33 1S 145 1 E
Trier, Germany 16 D4 49 45N 6 38 E
Trieste, Italy 20 B5 45 40N 13 46 E
Triglav, Slovenia 16 E7 46 21N 13 50 E
Tríkkala, Greece 21 E9 39 34N 21 47 E
Trikomo, Cyprus 23 D12 35 17N 33 52 E
Trikora, Puncak, Indonesia 37 E9 4 15S 138 45 E
Trim, Ireland 13 C5 53 33N 6 48W
Trincomalee, Sri Lanka 40 Q12 8 38N 81 15 E
Trindade, Brazil 93 G9 16 40S 49 30W
Trindade, I., Atl. Oc. 2 F8 20 20S 29 50W
Trinidad, Bolivia 92 F6 14 46S 64 50W
Trinidad, Cuba 88 B4 21 48N 80 0W
Trinidad, Uruguay 94 C4 33 30S 56 50W
Trinidad, U.S.A. 81 G2 37 10N 104 31W
Trinidad, W. Indies 89 D7 10 30N 61 15W
Trinidad →, Mexico 87 D5 17 49N 95 9W
Trinidad & Tobago ■,
W. Indies 89 D7 10 30N 61 20W
Trinity, Canada 71 C9 48 59N 53 55W
Trinity, U.S.A. 81 K7 30 57N 95 22W
Trinity →, Calif., U.S.A. 82 F2 41 11N 123 42W
Trinity →, Tex., U.S.A. 81 L7 29 45N 94 43W
Trinity B., Canada 71 C9 48 20N 53 10W
Trinity Is., U.S.A. 68 C4 56 33N 154 25W
Trinity Range, U.S.A. 82 F4 40 15N 118 45W
Trinkitat, Sudan 51 E13 18 45N 37 51 E
Trinway, U.S.A. 78 F2 40 9N 82 1W
Tripoli = Tarābulus,
Lebanon 47 A4 34 31N 35 50 E
Tripoli = Tarābulus, Libya 51 B8 32 49N 13 7 E
Trípolis, Greece 21 F10 37 31N 22 25 E
Tripolitania, Libya 48 C5 31 0N 12 0 E
Tripolitania, N. Afr. 51 B8 31 0N 13 0 E
Tripura □, India 41 H18 24 0N 92 0 E
Tripylos, Cyprus 23 E11 34 59N 32 41 E
Tristan da Cunha, Atl. Oc. 49 K2 37 6S 12 20W
Trisul, India 43 D8 30 19N 79 47 E
Trivandrum, India 40 Q10 8 41N 77 0 E
Trnava, Slovak Rep. 17 D9 48 23N 17 35 E
Trochu, Canada 72 C6 51 50N 113 13W
Trodely I., Canada 70 B4 52 15N 79 26W
Troglav, Croatia 20 C7 43 56N 16 36 E
Troilus, L., Canada 70 B5 50 50N 74 35W
Trois-Pistoles, Canada 71 C6 48 5N 69 10W
Trois-Rivières, Canada 70 C5 46 25N 72 34W
Troitsk, Russia 26 D7 54 10N 61 35 E
Troitsko Pechorsk, Russia 24 B10 62 40N 56 10 E
Trölladyngja, Iceland 8 D5 64 54N 17 16W
Trollhättan, Sweden 9 G15 58 17N 12 20 E
Trollheimen, Norway 8 E13 62 46N 9 1 E
Trombetas →, Brazil 93 D7 1 55S 55 35W
Tromsø, Norway 8 B18 69 40N 18 56 E
Trona, U.S.A. 85 K9 35 46N 117 23W
Tronador, Mte., Argentina 96 E2 41 10S 71 50W
Trøndelag, Norway 8 D14 64 17N 11 50 E
Trondheim, Norway 8 E14 63 36N 10 25 E
Trondheimsfjorden, Norway 8 E14 63 35N 10 30 E
Troodos, Cyprus 23 E11 34 55N 32 52 E
Troon, U.K. 12 F4 55 33N 4 39W
Tropic, U.S.A. 83 H7 37 37N 112 5W
Trostan, U.K. 13 A5 55 3N 6 10W
Trout →, Canada 72 A5 61 19N 119 51W
Trout L., N.W.T., Canada 72 A4 60 40N 121 14W
Trout L., Ont., Canada 73 C10 51 20N 93 15W
Trout Lake, Canada 72 B6 56 30N 114 32W
Trout Lake, U.S.A. 84 E5 46 0N 121 32W
Trout River, Canada 71 C8 49 29N 58 8W
Trout Run, U.S.A. 78 E7 41 23N 77 3W
Trouville-sur-Mer, France 18 B4 49 21N 0 5 E
Trowbridge, U.K. 11 F5 51 18N 2 12W
Troy, Turkey 21 E12 39 57N 26 12 E
Troy, Ala., U.S.A. 77 K3 31 48N 85 58W
Troy, Kans., U.S.A. 80 F7 39 47N 95 5W
Troy, Mo., U.S.A. 80 F9 38 59N 90 59W
Troy, Mont., U.S.A. 82 B6 48 28N 115 53W
Troy, N.Y., U.S.A. 79 D11 42 44N 73 41W
Troy, Ohio, U.S.A. 76 E3 40 2N 84 12W
Troy, Pa., U.S.A. 79 E8 41 47N 76 47W
Troyes, France 18 B6 48 19N 4 3 E
Truchas Peak, U.S.A. 81 H2 35 58N 105 39W
Trucial States = United
Arab Emirates ■, Asia 45 F7 23 50N 54 0 E
Truckee, U.S.A. 84 F6 39 20N 120 11W
Trudovoye, Russia 30 C6 43 17N 132 5 E
Trujillo, Honduras 88 C2 16 0N 86 0W
Trujillo, Peru 92 E3 8 6S 79 0W
Trujillo, Spain 19 C3 39 28N 5 55W
Trujillo, U.S.A. 81 H2 35 32N 104 42W
Trujillo, Venezuela 92 B4 9 22N 70 38W
Truk, Micronesia 64 G7 7 25N 151 46 E
Trumann, U.S.A. 81 H9 35 41N 90 31W
Trumansburg, U.S.A. 79 D8 42 33N 76 40W
Trumbull, Mt., U.S.A. 83 H7 36 25N 113 8W
Trundle, Australia 63 E4 32 53S 147 35 E
Trung-Phan = Annam,
Vietnam 38 E7 16 0N 108 0 E
Truro, Canada 71 C7 45 21N 63 14W
Truro, U.K. 11 G2 50 16N 5 4W
Truskavets, Ukraine 17 D12 49 17N 23 30 E
Trutch, Canada 72 B4 57 44N 122 57W
Truth or Consequences,
U.S.A. 83 K10 33 8N 107 15W
Trutnov, Czech Rep. 16 C8 50 37N 15 54 E
Truxton, U.S.A. 79 D8 42 45N 76 2W
Tryonville, U.S.A. 78 E5 41 42N 79 48W
Tsaratanana, Madag. 57 B8 16 47S 47 39 E
Tsaratanana, Mt. de, Madag. 57 A8 14 0S 49 0 E
Tsarevo = Michurin,
Bulgaria 21 C12 42 9N 27 51 E
Tsau, Botswana 56 C3 20 8S 22 22 E
Tselinograd = Astana,
Kazakstan 26 D8 51 10N 71 30 E
Tsetserleg, Mongolia 32 B5 47 36N 101 32 E
Tshabong, Botswana 56 D3 26 2S 22 29 E
Tshane, Botswana 56 C3 24 5S 21 54 E
Tshela,
Dem. Rep. of the Congo 52 E2 4 57S 13 4 E
Tshesebe, Botswana 57 C4 21 51S 27 32 E
Tshibeke,
Dem. Rep. of the Congo 54 C2 2 40S 28 35 E
Tshibinda,
Dem. Rep. of the Congo 54 C2 2 23S 28 43 E
Tshikapa,
Dem. Rep. of the Congo 52 F4 6 28S 20 48 E
Tshilenge,
Dem. Rep. of the Congo 54 D1 6 17S 23 48 E
Tshinsenda,
Dem. Rep. of the Congo 55 E2 12 20S 28 0 E
Tshofa,
Dem. Rep. of the Congo 54 D2 5 13S 25 16 E
Tshwane, Botswana 56 C3 22 24S 22 1 E
Tsigara, Botswana 56 C4 20 22S 25 54 E
Tsihombe, Madag. 57 D8 25 10S 45 41 E
Tsiigehtchic, Canada 68 B6 67 15N 134 0W
Tsimlyansk Res. =
Tsimlyanskoye Vdkhr.,
Russia 25 E7 48 0N 43 0 E
Tsimlyanskoye Vdkhr.,
Russia 25 E7 48 0N 43 0 E
Tsinan = Jinan, China 34 F9 36 38N 117 1 E
Tsineng, S. Africa 56 D3 27 5S 23 5 E
Tsinghai = Qinghai □,
China 32 C4 36 0N 98 0 E
Tsingtao = Qingdao, China 35 F11 36 5N 120 20 E
Tsinjomitondraka, Madag. 57 B8 15 40S 47 8 E
Tsiroanomandidy, Madag. 57 B8 18 46S 46 2 E
Tsivory, Madag. 57 C8 24 4S 46 5 E
Tskhinvali, Georgia 25 F7 42 14N 44 1 E
Tsna →, Russia 24 D7 54 55N 41 58 E
Tso Moriri, L., India 43 C8 32 50N 78 20 E
Tsodilo Hill, Botswana 56 B3 18 49S 21 43 E
Tsogttsetsiy = Baruunsuu,
Mongolia 34 C3 43 43N 105 35 E
Tsolo, S. Africa 57 E4 31 18S 28 37 E
Tsomo, S. Africa 57 E4 32 0S 27 42 E
Tsu, Japan 31 G8 34 45N 136 25 E
Tsu L., Canada 72 A6 60 40N 111 52W
Tsuchiura, Japan 31 F10 36 5N 140 15 E
Tsugaru-Kaikyō, Japan 30 D10 41 35N 141 0 E
Tsumeb, Namibia 56 B2 19 9S 17 44 E
Tsumis, Namibia 56 C2 23 39S 17 29 E
Tsuruga, Japan 31 G8 35 45N 136 2 E
Tsurugi-San, Japan 31 H7 33 51N 134 6 E
Tsuruoka, Japan 30 E9 38 44N 139 50 E
Tsushima, Gifu, Japan 31 G8 35 10N 136 43 E
Tsushima, Nagasaki, Japan 31 G4 34 20N 129 20 E
Tsuyama, Japan 31 G7 35 3N 134 0 E
Tsyelyakhany, Belarus 17 B13 52 30N 25 46 E
Tual, Indonesia 37 F8 5 38S 132 44 E
Tuam, Ireland 13 C3 53 31N 8 51W
Tuamotu Arch. = Tuamotu
Is., Pac. Oc. 65 J13 17 0S 144 0W
Tuamotu Is., Pac. Oc. 65 J13 17 0S 144 0W
Tuamotu Ridge, Pac. Oc. 65 K14 20 0S 138 0W
Tuao, Phil. 37 A6 17 55N 121 22 E
Tuapse, Russia 25 F6 44 5N 39 10 E
Tuatapere, N.Z. 59 M1 46 8S 167 41 E
Tuba City, U.S.A. 83 H8 36 8N 111 14W
Tuban, Indonesia 37 G15 6 54S 112 3 E
Tubarão, Brazil 95 B6 28 30S 49 0W
Tūbās, West Bank 47 C4 32 20N 35 22 E
Tübingen, Germany 16 D5 48 31N 9 4 E
Tubruq, Libya 51 B10 32 7N 23 55 E
Tubuai Is., Pac. Oc. 65 K13 25 0S 150 0W
Tuc Trung, Vietnam 39 G6 11 1N 107 12 E
Tucacas, Venezuela 92 A5 10 48N 68 19W
Tuchodi →, Canada 72 B4 58 17N 123 42W
Tuckanarra, Australia 61 E2 27 7S 118 5 E
Tucson, U.S.A. 83 K8 32 13N 110 58W
Tucumán □, Argentina 94 B2 26 48S 66 2W
Tucumcari, U.S.A. 81 H3 35 10N 103 44W
Tucupita, Venezuela 92 B6 9 2N 62 3W
Tucuruí, Brazil 93 D9 3 42S 49 44W
Tucuruí, Represa de, Brazil 93 D9 4 0S 49 30W
Tudela, Spain 19 A5 42 4N 1 39W
Tudmur, Syria 44 C3 34 36N 38 15 E
Tudor, L., Canada 71 A6 55 50N 65 25W
Tugela →, S. Africa 57 D5 29 14S 31 30 E
Tuguegarao, Phil. 37 A6 17 35N 121 42 E
Tugur, Russia 27 D14 53 44N 136 45 E
Tui, Spain 19 A1 42 3N 8 39W
Tuineje, Canary Is. 22 F5 28 19N 14 3W
Tukangbesi, Kepulauan,
Indonesia 37 F6 6 0S 124 0 E
Tukarak I., Canada 70 A4 56 15N 78 45W
Tukayyid, Iraq 44 D5 29 47N 45 36 E
Tuktoyaktuk, Canada 68 B6 69 27N 133 2W
Tukums, Latvia 9 H20 56 58N 23 10 E

Tukuyu

Tukuyu, Tanzania 55 D3 9 17S 33 35 E
Tula, Hidalgo, Mexico 87 C5 20 5N 99 20W
Tula, Tamaulipas, Mexico 87 C5 23 0N 99 40W
Tula, Russia 24 D6 54 13N 37 38 E
Tulancingo, Mexico 87 C5 20 5N 99 22W
Tulare, U.S.A. 84 J7 36 13N 119 21W
Tulare Lake Bed, U.S.A. 84 K7 36 0N 119 48W
Tularosa, U.S.A. 83 K10 33 5N 106 1W
Tulbagh, S. Africa 56 E2 33 16S 19 6 E
Tulcán, Ecuador 92 C3 0 48N 77 43W
Tulcea, Romania 17 F15 45 13N 28 46 E
Tulchyn, Ukraine 17 D15 48 41N 28 49 E
Tūleh, Iran 45 C7 34 35N 52 33 E
Tulemalu L., Canada 73 A9 62 58N 99 25W
Tuli, Zimbabwe 55 G2 21 58S 29 13 E
Tulia, U.S.A. 81 H4 34 32N 101 46W
Tulita, Canada 68 B7 64 57N 125 30W
Ṭūlkarm, West Bank 47 C4 32 19N 35 2 E
Tulla, Ireland 13 D3 52 53N 8 46W
Tullahoma, U.S.A. 77 H2 35 22N 86 13W
Tullamore, Australia 63 E4 32 39S 147 36 E
Tullamore, Ireland 13 C4 53 16N 7 31W
Tulle, France 18 D4 45 16N 1 46 E
Tullow, Ireland 13 D5 52 49N 6 45W
Tully, Australia 62 B4 17 56S 145 55 E
Tully, U.S.A. 79 D8 42 48N 76 7W
Tulsa, U.S.A. 81 G7 36 10N 95 55W
Tulsequah, Canada 72 B2 58 39N 133 35W
Tulua, Colombia 92 C3 4 6N 76 11W
Tulun, Russia 27 D11 54 32N 100 35 E
Tulungagung, Indonesia 37 H14 8 5S 111 54 E
Tuma →, Nic. 88 D3 13 6N 84 35W
Tumaco, Colombia 92 C3 1 50N 78 45W
Tumatumari, Guyana 92 B7 5 20N 58 55W
Tumba, Sweden 9 G17 59 12N 17 48 E
Tumba, L., Dem. Rep. of the Congo 52 E3 0 50S 18 0 E
Tumbarumba, Australia 63 F4 35 44S 148 0 E
Tumbaya, Argentina 94 A2 23 50S 65 26W
Tumbes, Peru 92 D2 3 37S 80 27W
Tumbwe, Dem. Rep. of the Congo 55 E2 11 25S 27 15 E
Tumby Bay, Australia 63 E2 34 21S 136 8 E
Tumd Youqi, China 34 D6 40 30N 110 30 E
Tumen, China 35 C15 43 0N 129 50 E
Tumen Jiang →, China 35 C16 42 20N 130 35 E
Tumeremo, Venezuela 92 B6 7 18N 61 30W
Tumkur, India 40 N10 13 18N 77 6 E
Tump, Pakistan 40 F3 26 7N 62 16 E
Tumpat, Malaysia 39 J4 6 11N 102 10 E
Tumu, Ghana 50 F5 10 56N 1 56W
Tumucumaque, Serra, Brazil 93 C8 2 0N 55 0W
Tumut, Australia 63 F4 35 16S 148 13 E
Tumwater, U.S.A. 84 C4 47 1N 122 54W
Tuna, India 42 H4 22 59N 70 5 E
Tunas de Zaza, Cuba 88 B4 21 39N 79 34W
Tunbridge Wells = Royal Tunbridge Wells, U.K. 11 F8 51 7N 0 16 E
Tuncurry-Forster, Australia 63 E5 32 17S 152 29 E
Tundla, India 42 F8 27 12N 78 17 E
Tunduru, Tanzania 55 E4 11 8S 37 25 E
Tundzha →, Bulgaria 21 C11 41 40N 26 35 E
Tunga Pass, India 41 E19 29 0N 94 14 E
Tungabhadra →, India 40 M11 15 57N 78 15 E
Tungla, Nic. 88 D3 13 24N 84 21W
Tungsten, Canada 72 A3 61 57N 128 16W
Tunguska, Nizhnyaya →, Russia 27 C9 65 48N 88 4 E
Tunguska, Podkamennaya →, Russia 27 C10 61 50N 90 13 E
Tunica, U.S.A. 81 H9 34 41N 90 23W
Tunis, Tunisia 51 A8 36 50N 10 11 E
Tunisia ■, Africa 51 A7 33 30N 9 10 E
Tunja, Colombia 92 B4 5 33N 73 25W
Tunkhannock, U.S.A. 79 E9 41 32N 75 57W
Tunliu, China 34 F7 36 13N 112 52 E
Tunnsjøen, Norway 8 D15 64 45N 13 25 E
Tunungayualok I., Canada 71 A7 56 0N 61 0W
Tunuyán, Argentina 94 C2 33 35S 69 0W
Tunuyán →, Argentina 94 C2 33 33S 67 30W
Tuolumne, U.S.A. 84 H6 37 58N 120 15W
Tuolumne →, U.S.A. 84 H5 37 36N 121 13W
Tūp Āghāj, Iran 44 B5 36 3N 47 50 E
Tupã, Brazil 95 A5 21 57S 50 28W
Tupelo, U.S.A. 77 H1 34 16N 88 43W
Tupinambaranas, Brazil 92 D7 3 0S 58 0W
Tupiza, Bolivia 94 A2 21 30S 65 40W
Tupman, U.S.A. 85 K7 35 18N 119 21W
Tupper, Canada 72 B4 55 32N 120 1W
Tupper Lake, U.S.A. 79 B10 44 14N 74 28W
Tupungato, Cerro, S. Amer. 94 C2 33 15S 69 50W
Tuquan, China 35 B11 45 18N 121 38 E
Túquerres, Colombia 92 C3 1 5N 77 37W
Tura, Russia 27 C11 64 20N 100 17 E
Turabah, Si. Arabia 46 C3 28 20N 43 15 E
Tūrān, Iran 45 C8 35 39N 56 42 E
Turan, Russia 27 D10 51 55N 95 0 E
Ţurayf, Si. Arabia 44 D3 31 41N 38 39 E
Turda, Romania 17 E12 46 34N 23 47 E
Turek, Poland 17 B10 52 3N 18 30 E
Turen, Venezuela 92 B5 9 17N 69 6W
Turfan = Turpan, China 32 B3 43 58N 89 10 E
Turfan Depression = Turpan Hami, China 28 E12 42 40N 89 25 E
Turgeon →, Canada 70 C4 50 0N 78 56W
Tŭrgovishte, Bulgaria 21 C12 43 17N 26 38 E
Turgutlu, Turkey 21 E12 38 30N 27 43 E
Turia →, Spain 19 C5 39 27N 0 19W
Turiaçu, Brazil 93 D9 1 40S 45 19W
Turiaçu →, Brazil 93 D9 1 36S 45 19W
Turin = Torino, Italy 18 D7 45 3N 7 40 E
Turkana, L., Africa 54 B4 3 30N 36 5 E
Turkestan = Türkistan, Kazakstan 26 E7 43 17N 68 16 E
Turkey ■, Eurasia 25 G6 39 0N 36 0 E
Turkey Creek, Australia 60 C4 17 2S 128 12 E
Türkistan, Kazakstan 26 E7 43 17N 68 16 E
Türkmenbashi, Turkmenistan 25 G9 40 5N 53 5 E
Turkmenistan ■, Asia 26 F6 39 0N 59 0 E
Turks & Caicos Is. ■, W. Indies 89 B5 21 20N 71 20W
Turks Island Passage, W. Indies 89 B5 21 30N 71 30W
Turku, Finland 9 F20 60 30N 22 19 E
Turkwel →, Kenya 54 B4 3 6N 36 6 E
Turlock, U.S.A. 84 H6 37 30N 120 51W
Turnagain →, Canada 72 B3 59 12N 127 35W
Turnagain, C., N.Z. 59 J6 40 28S 176 38 E
Turneffe Is., Belize 87 D7 17 20N 87 50W
Turner, U.S.A. 82 B9 48 51N 108 24W
Turner Pt., Australia 62 A1 11 47S 133 32 E
Turner Valley, Canada 72 C6 50 40N 114 17W
Turners Falls, U.S.A. 79 D12 42 36N 72 33W
Turnhout, Belgium 15 C4 51 19N 4 57 E
Turnor L., Canada 73 B7 56 35N 108 35W
Tŭrnovo = Veliko Tŭrnovo, Bulgaria 21 C11 43 5N 25 41 E
Turnu Măgurele, Romania 17 G13 43 46N 24 56 E
Turnu Roşu, P., Romania 17 F13 45 33N 24 17 E
Turpan, China 32 B3 43 58N 89 10 E
Turpan Hami, China 28 E12 42 40N 89 25 E
Turriff, U.K. 12 D6 57 32N 2 27W
Tursăq, Iraq 44 C5 33 27N 45 47 E
Turtle Head I., Australia 62 A3 10 56S 142 37 E
Turtle L., Canada 73 C7 53 36N 108 38W
Turtle Lake, U.S.A. 80 B4 47 31N 100 53W
Turtleford, Canada 73 C7 53 23N 108 57W
Turukhansk, Russia 27 C9 65 21N 88 5 E
Tuscaloosa, U.S.A. 77 J2 33 12N 87 34W
Tuscany = Toscana □, Italy 20 C4 43 25N 11 0 E
Tuscarawas →, U.S.A. 78 F3 40 24N 81 25W
Tuscarora Mt., U.S.A. 78 F7 40 55N 77 55W
Tuscola, Ill., U.S.A. 76 F1 39 48N 88 17W
Tuscola, Tex., U.S.A. 81 J5 32 12N 99 48W
Tuscumbia, U.S.A. 77 H2 34 44N 87 42W
Tuskegee, U.S.A. 77 J3 32 25N 85 42W
Tustin, U.S.A. 85 M9 33 44N 117 49W
Tuticorin, India 40 Q11 8 50N 78 12 E
Tutóia, Brazil 93 D10 2 45S 42 20W
Tutong, Brunei 36 D4 4 47N 114 40 E
Tutrakan, Bulgaria 21 B12 44 2N 26 40 E
Tuttle Creek L., U.S.A. 80 F6 39 22N 96 40W
Tuttlingen, Germany 16 E5 47 58N 8 48 E
Tutuala, Indonesia 37 F7 8 25S 127 15 E
Tutuila, Amer. Samoa 59 B13 14 19S 170 50W
Tutume, Botswana 53 J5 20 30S 27 5 E
Tututepec, Mexico 87 D5 16 9N 97 38W
Tuva □, Russia 27 D10 51 30N 95 0 E
Tuvalu ■, Pac. Oc. 64 H9 8 0S 178 0 E
Tuxpan, Mexico 87 C5 20 58N 97 23W
Tuxtla Gutiérrez, Mexico 87 D6 16 50N 93 10W
Tuy = Tui, Spain 19 A1 42 3N 8 39W
Tuy An, Vietnam 38 F7 13 17N 109 16 E
Tuy Duc, Vietnam 39 F6 12 15N 107 27 E
Tuy Hoa, Vietnam 38 F7 13 5N 109 10 E
Tuy Phong, Vietnam 39 G7 11 14N 108 43 E
Tuya L., Canada 72 B2 59 7N 130 35W
Tuyen Hoa, Vietnam 38 D6 17 50N 106 10 E
Tūysarkān, Iran 45 C6 34 33N 48 27 E
Tuz Gölü, Turkey 25 G5 38 42N 33 18 E
Ţūz Khurmātū, Iraq 44 C5 34 56N 44 38 E
Tuzla, Bos.-H. 21 B8 44 34N 18 41 E
Tver, Russia 24 C6 56 55N 35 55 E
Twain, U.S.A. 84 E5 40 1N 121 3W
Twain Harte, U.S.A. 84 G6 38 2N 120 14W
Tweed, Canada 78 B7 44 29N 77 19W
Tweed →, U.K. 12 F6 55 45N 2 0W
Tweed Heads, Australia 63 D5 28 10S 153 31 E
Tweedsmuir Prov. Park, Canada 72 C3 53 0N 126 20W
Twentynine Palms, U.S.A. 85 L10 34 8N 116 3W
Twillingate, Canada 71 C9 49 42N 54 45W
Twin Bridges, U.S.A. 82 D7 45 33N 112 20W
Twin Falls, Canada 71 B7 53 30N 64 32W
Twin Falls, U.S.A. 82 E6 42 34N 114 28W
Twin Valley, U.S.A. 80 B6 47 16N 96 16W
Twinsburg, U.S.A. 78 E3 41 18N 81 26W
Twitchell Reservoir, U.S.A. 85 L6 34 59N 120 19W
Two Harbors, U.S.A. 80 B9 47 2N 91 40W
Two Hills, Canada 72 C6 53 43N 111 52W
Two Rivers, U.S.A. 76 C2 44 9N 87 34W
Two Rocks, Australia 61 F2 31 30S 115 35 E
Twofold B., Australia 63 F4 37 8S 149 59 E
Tyachiv, Ukraine 17 D12 48 1N 23 35 E
Tychy, Poland 17 C10 50 9N 18 59 E
Tyler, U.S.A. 75 D7 32 18N 95 17W
Tyler, Minn., U.S.A. 80 C6 44 18N 96 8W
Tyler, Tex., U.S.A. 81 J7 32 21N 95 18W
Tynda, Russia 27 D13 55 10N 124 43 E
Tyndall, U.S.A. 80 D6 43 0N 97 50W
Tyne →, U.K. 10 C6 54 59N 1 32W
Tyne & Wear □, U.K. 10 B6 55 6N 1 17W
Tynemouth, U.K. 10 B6 55 1N 1 26W
Tyre = Sūr, Lebanon 47 B4 33 19N 35 16 E
Tyrifjorden, Norway 9 F14 60 2N 10 8 E
Tyrol = Tirol □, Austria 16 E6 47 3N 10 43 E
Tyrone, U.S.A. 78 F6 40 40N 78 14W
Tyrone □, U.K. 13 B4 54 38N 7 11W
Tyrrell →, Australia 63 F3 35 26S 142 51 E
Tyrrell L., Australia 63 F3 35 20S 142 50 E
Tyrrell L., Canada 73 A7 63 7N 105 27W
Tyrrhenian Sea, Medit. S. 20 E5 40 0N 12 30 E
Tysfjorden, Norway 8 B17 68 7N 16 25 E
Tyulgan, Russia 24 D10 52 22N 56 12 E
Tyumen, Russia 26 D7 57 11N 65 29 E
Tywi →, U.K. 11 F3 51 48N 4 21W
Tywyn, U.K. 11 E3 52 35N 4 5W
Tzaneen, S. Africa 57 C5 23 47S 30 9 E
Tzermiádhes, Greece 23 D7 35 12N 25 29 E
Tzukong = Zigong, China 32 D5 29 15N 104 48 E

U

U Taphao, Thailand 38 F3 12 35N 101 0 E
U.S.A. = United States of America ■, N. Amer. 74 C7 37 0N 96 0W
Uatumã →, Brazil 92 D7 2 26S 57 37W
Uaupés, Brazil 92 D5 0 8S 67 5W
Uaupés →, Brazil 92 C5 0 2N 67 16W
Uaxactún, Guatemala 88 C2 17 25N 89 29W
Ubá, Brazil 95 A7 21 8S 43 0W
Ubaitaba, Brazil 93 F11 14 18S 39 20W
Ubangi = Oubangi →, Dem. Rep. of the Congo 52 E3 0 30S 17 50 E
Ubauro, Pakistan 42 E3 28 15N 69 45 E
Ubayyiḑ, W. al →, Iraq 44 C4 32 34N 43 48 E
Ube, Japan 31 H5 33 56N 131 15 E
Úbeda, Spain 19 C4 38 3N 3 23W
Uberaba, Brazil 93 G9 19 50S 47 55W
Uberlândia, Brazil 93 G9 19 0S 48 20W
Ubolratna Res., Thailand 38 D4 16 45N 102 30 E
Ubombo, S. Africa 57 D5 27 31S 32 4 E
Ubon Ratchathani, Thailand 38 E5 15 15N 104 50 E
Ubondo, Dem. Rep. of the Congo 54 C2 0 55S 25 42 E
Ubort →, Belarus 17 B15 52 6N 28 30 E
Ubundu, Dem. Rep. of the Congo 54 C2 0 22S 25 30 E
Ucayali →, Peru 92 D4 4 30S 73 30W
Uchiura-Wan, Japan 30 C10 42 25N 140 40 E
Uchquduq, Uzbekistan 26 E7 41 50N 62 50 E
Uchur →, Russia 27 D14 58 48N 130 35 E
Ucluelet, Canada 72 D3 48 57N 125 32W
Uda →, Russia 27 D14 54 42N 135 14 E
Udagamandalam, India 40 P10 11 30N 76 44 E
Udainagar, India 42 H7 22 33N 76 13 E
Udaipur, India 42 G5 24 36N 73 44 E
Udaipur Garhi, Nepal 43 F12 27 0N 86 35 E
Udala, India 43 J12 21 35N 86 34 E
Uddevalla, Sweden 9 G14 58 21N 11 55 E
Uddjaur, Sweden 8 D17 65 56N 17 49 E
Uden, Neths. 15 C5 51 40N 5 37 E
Udgir, India 40 K10 18 25N 77 5 E
Udhampur, India 43 C6 33 0N 75 5 E
Údine, Italy 20 A5 46 3N 13 14 E
Udmurtia □, Russia 24 C9 57 30N 52 30 E
Udon Thani, Thailand 38 D4 17 29N 102 46 E
Udupi, India 40 N9 13 25N 74 42 E
Udzungwa Range, Tanzania 55 D4 9 30S 35 10 E
Ueda, Japan 31 F9 36 24N 138 16 E
Uedineniya, Os., Russia 4 B12 78 0N 85 0 E
Uele →, Dem. Rep. of the Congo 52 D4 3 45N 24 45 E
Uelen, Russia 27 C19 66 10N 170 0W
Uelzen, Germany 16 B6 52 57N 10 32 E
Ufa, Russia 24 D10 54 45N 55 55 E
Ufa →, Russia 24 D10 54 40N 56 0 E
Ugab →, Namibia 56 C1 20 55S 13 30 E
Ugalla →, Tanzania 54 D3 5 8S 30 42 E
Uganda ■, Africa 54 B3 2 0N 32 0 E
Ugie, S. Africa 57 E4 31 10S 28 13 E
Uglegorsk, Russia 27 E15 49 5N 142 2 E
Ugljan, Croatia 16 F8 44 12N 15 10 E
Uhrichsville, U.S.A. 78 F3 40 24N 81 21W
Uibhist a Deas = South Uist, U.K. 12 D1 57 20N 7 15W
Uibhist a Tuath = North Uist, U.K. 12 D1 57 40N 7 15W
Uig, U.K. 12 D2 57 35N 6 21W
Uíge, Angola 52 F2 7 30S 14 40 E
Uijŏngbu, S. Korea 35 F14 37 48N 127 0 E
Ŭiju, N. Korea 35 D13 40 15N 124 35 E
Uinta Mts., U.S.A. 82 F8 40 45N 110 30W
Uitenhage, S. Africa 56 E4 33 40S 25 28 E
Uithuizen, Neths. 15 A6 53 24N 6 41 E
Ujh →, India 42 C6 32 10N 75 18 E
Ujhani, India 43 F8 28 0N 79 6 E
Uji-guntō, Japan 31 J4 31 15N 129 25 E
Ujjain, India 42 H6 23 9N 75 43 E
Ujung Pandang, Indonesia 37 F5 5 10S 119 20 E
Uka, Russia 27 D17 57 50N 162 0 E
Ukara I., Tanzania 54 C3 1 50S 33 0 E
Uke-Shima, Japan 31 K4 28 2N 129 14 E
Ukerewe I., Tanzania 54 C3 2 0S 33 0 E
Ukhrul, India 41 G19 25 10N 94 25 E
Ukhta, Russia 24 B9 63 34N 53 41 E
Ukiah, U.S.A. 84 F3 39 9N 123 13W
Ukki Fort, India 43 C7 33 28N 76 54 E
Ukmerge, Lithuania 9 J21 55 15N 24 45 E
Ukraine ■, Europe 25 E5 49 0N 32 0 E
Uku, Angola 53 G2 11 24S 14 22 E
Ukwi, Botswana 56 C3 23 29S 20 30 E
Ulaan-Uul, Mongolia 34 B6 44 13N 111 10 E
Ulaanbaatar, Mongolia 27 E11 47 55N 106 53 E
Ulaangom, Mongolia 32 A4 50 5N 92 10 E
Ulaanjirem, Mongolia 34 B3 45 5N 105 30 E
Ulamba, Dem. Rep. of the Congo 55 D1 9 3S 23 38 E
Ulan Bator = Ulaanbaatar, Mongolia 27 E11 47 55N 106 53 E
Ulan Ude, Russia 27 D11 51 45N 107 40 E
Ulaya, Morogoro, Tanzania 54 D4 7 3S 36 55 E
Ulaya, Tabora, Tanzania 54 C3 4 25S 33 30 E
Ulcinj, Montenegro, Yug. 21 D8 41 58N 19 10 E
Ulco, S. Africa 56 D3 28 21S 24 15 E
Ulefoss, Norway 9 G13 59 17N 9 16 E
Ulhasnagar, India 40 K8 19 15N 73 10 E
Uliastay, Mongolia 32 B4 47 56N 97 28 E
Ulithi Atoll, Pac. Oc. 37 B9 10 0N 139 30 E
Uladulla, Australia 63 F5 35 21S 150 29 E
Ullapool, U.K. 12 D3 57 54N 5 9W
Ullswater, U.K. 10 C5 54 34N 2 52W
Ullŭng-do, S. Korea 31 F5 37 30N 130 30 E
Ulm, Germany 16 D5 48 23N 9 58 E
Ulmarra, Australia 63 D5 29 37S 153 4 E
Ulonguè, Mozam. 55 E3 14 37S 34 19 E
Ulricehamn, Sweden 9 H15 57 46N 13 26 E
Ulsan, S. Korea 35 G15 35 20N 129 15 E
Ulsta, U.K. 12 A7 60 30N 1 9W
Ulster □, U.K. 13 B5 54 35N 6 30W
Ulubat Gölü, Turkey 21 D13 40 9N 28 35 E
Uludağ, Turkey 21 D13 40 4N 29 13 E
Uluguru Mts., Tanzania 54 D4 7 15S 37 40 E
Ulungur He →, China 32 B3 47 1N 87 24 E
Uluru = Ayers Rock, Australia 61 E5 25 23S 131 5 E
Uluru Nat. Park, Australia 61 E5 25 15S 131 20 E
Ulutau, Kazakstan 26 E7 48 39N 67 1 E
Ulva, U.K. 12 E2 56 29N 6 13W
Ulverston, U.K. 10 C4 54 13N 3 5W
Ulverstone, Australia 62 G4 41 11S 146 11 E
Ulya, Russia 27 D15 59 10N 142 0 E
Ulyanovsk = Simbirsk, Russia 24 D8 54 20N 48 25 E
Ulyasutay = Uliastay, Mongolia 32 B4 47 56N 97 28 E
Ulysses, U.S.A. 81 G4 37 35N 101 22W
Umala, Bolivia 92 G5 17 25S 68 5W
Uman, Ukraine 17 D16 48 40N 30 12 E
Umaria, India 41 H12 23 35N 80 50 E
Umarkot, Pakistan 40 G6 25 15N 69 40 E
Umarpada, India 42 J5 21 27N 73 30 E
Umatilla, U.S.A. 82 D4 45 55N 119 21W
Umba, Russia 24 A5 66 42N 34 11
Umbagog L., U.S.A. 79 B13 44 46N 71 3
Umbakumba, Australia 62 A2 13 47S 136 50
Umbrella Mts., N.Z. 59 L2 45 35S 169 5
Ume älv →, Sweden 8 E19 63 45N 20 20
Umeå, Sweden 8 E19 63 45N 20 20
Umera, Indonesia 37 E7 0 12S 129 37
Umfuli →, Zimbabwe 55 F2 17 30S 29 23
Umgusa, Zimbabwe 55 F2 19 29S 27 52
Umkomaas, S. Africa 57 E5 30 13S 30 48
Umlazi, S. Africa 53 L6 29 59S 30 54
Umm ad Daraj, J., Jordan 47 C4 32 18N 35 48
Umm al Qaywayn, U.A.E. 45 E7 25 30N 55 35
Umm al Qittayn, Jordan 47 C5 32 18N 36 40
Umm Bāb, Qatar 45 E6 25 12N 50 48
Umm el Fahm, Israel 47 C4 32 31N 35 9
Umm Keddada, Sudan 51 F11 13 36N 26 42
Umm Lajj, Si. Arabia 44 E3 25 0N 37 23
Umm Ruwaba, Sudan 51 F12 12 50N 31 20
Umnak I., U.S.A. 68 C3 53 15N 168 20
Umniati →, Zimbabwe 55 F2 16 49S 28 45
Umpqua →, U.S.A. 82 E1 43 40N 124 12
Umreth, India 42 H5 22 41N 73 4
Umtata, S. Africa 57 E4 31 36S 28 49
Umuarama, Brazil 95 A5 23 45S 53 20
Umvukwe Ra., Zimbabwe 55 F3 16 45S 30 45
Umzimvubu = Port St. Johns, S. Africa 57 E4 31 38S 29 33
Umzingwane →, Zimbabwe 55 G2 22 12S 29 56
Umzinto, S. Africa 57 E5 30 15S 30 45
Una, India 42 J4 20 46N 71 8
Una →, Bos.-H. 16 F9 45 0N 16 20
Unadilla, U.S.A. 79 D9 42 20N 75 19
Unalakleet, U.S.A. 68 B3 63 52N 160 47
Unalaska, U.S.A. 68 C3 53 53N 166 32
Unalaska I., U.S.A. 68 C3 53 35N 166 50
'Unayzah, Si. Arabia 44 E4 26 6N 43 58
'Unâzah, J., Asia 44 C3 32 12N 39 18
Uncía, Bolivia 92 G5 18 25S 66 40
Uncompahgre Peak, U.S.A. 83 G10 38 4N 107 28
Uncompahgre Plateau, U.S.A. 83 G9 38 20N 108 15
Underbool, Australia 63 F3 35 10S 141 51
Ungarie, Australia 63 E4 33 38S 146 56
Ungarra, Australia 63 E2 34 12S 136 2
Ungava, Pén. d', Canada 69 C12 60 0N 74 0
Ungava B., Canada 69 C13 59 30N 67 30
Ungeny = Ungheni, Moldova 17 E14 47 11N 27 51
Unggi, N. Korea 35 C16 42 16N 130 28
Ungheni, Moldova 17 E14 47 11N 27 51
União da Vitória, Brazil 95 B5 26 13S 51 5
Unimak I., U.S.A. 68 C3 54 45N 164 0
Union, Miss., U.S.A. 81 J10 32 34N 89 7
Union, Mo., U.S.A. 80 F9 38 27N 91 0
Union, S.C., U.S.A. 77 H5 34 43N 81 37
Union City, Calif., U.S.A. 84 H4 37 36N 122 1
Union City, N.J., U.S.A. 79 F10 40 45N 74 2
Union City, Pa., U.S.A. 78 E5 41 54N 79 51
Union City, Tenn., U.S.A. 81 G10 36 26N 89 3
Union Gap, U.S.A. 82 C3 46 33N 120 28
Union Springs, U.S.A. 77 J3 32 9N 85 43
Uniondale, S. Africa 56 E3 33 39S 23 7
Uniontown, U.S.A. 76 F6 39 54N 79 44
Unionville, U.S.A. 80 E8 40 29N 93 1
United Arab Emirates ■, Asia 45 F7 23 50N 54 0
United Kingdom ■, Europe 7 E5 53 0N 2 0
United States of America ■, N. Amer. 74 C7 37 0N 96 0
Unity, Canada 73 C7 52 30N 109 5
University Park, U.S.A. 83 K10 32 17N 106 45
Unjha, India 42 H5 23 46N 72 24
Unnao, India 43 F9 26 35N 80 30
Unst, U.K. 12 A8 60 44N 0 53
Unuk →, Canada 72 B2 56 5N 131 3
Uozu, Japan 31 F8 36 48N 137 24
Upata, Venezuela 92 B6 8 1N 62 24
Upemba, L., Dem. Rep. of the Congo 55 D2 8 30S 26 20
Upernavik, Greenland 4 B5 72 49N 56 20
Upington, S. Africa 56 D3 28 25S 21 15
Upleta, India 42 J4 21 46N 70 16
Upolu, W. Samoa 59 A13 13 58S 172 0
Upper Alkali L., U.S.A. 82 F3 41 47N 120 8
Upper Arrow L., Canada 72 C5 50 30N 117 50
Upper Foster L., Canada 73 B7 56 47N 105 20
Upper Hutt, N.Z. 59 J5 41 8S 175 5
Upper Klamath L., U.S.A. 82 E3 42 25N 121 55
Upper Lake, U.S.A. 84 F4 39 10N 122 54
Upper Musquodoboit, Canada 71 C7 45 10N 62 58
Upper Red L., U.S.A. 80 A7 48 8N 94 45
Upper Sandusky, U.S.A. 76 E4 40 50N 83 17
Upper Volta = Burkina Faso ■, Africa 50 F5 12 0N 1 0
Uppland, Sweden 9 F17 59 59N 17 48
Uppsala, Sweden 9 G17 59 53N 17 38
Upshi, India 43 C7 33 48N 77 52
Upstart, C., Australia 62 B4 19 41S 147 45
Upton, U.S.A. 80 C2 44 6N 104 38
Ur, Iraq 44 D5 30 55N 46 25
Urad Qianqi, China 34 D5 40 40N 108 30
Urakawa, Japan 30 C11 42 9N 142 47
Ural = Zhayyq →, Kazakstan 25 E9 47 0N 51 48
Ural, Australia 63 E4 33 21S 146 12
Ural Mts. = Uralskie Gory, Eurasia 24 C10 60 0N 59 0
Uralla, Australia 63 E5 30 37S 151 29
Uralsk = Oral, Kazakstan 25 D9 51 20N 51 20
Uralskie Gory, Eurasia 24 C10 60 0N 59 0
Urambo, Tanzania 54 D3 5 4S 32 0
Urana, Australia 63 F4 35 15S 146 21
Urandangi, Australia 62 C2 21 32S 138 14
Uranium City, Canada 73 B7 59 34N 108 37
Uraricoera →, Brazil 92 C6 3 2N 60 30
Urawa, Japan 31 G9 35 50N 139 40
Uray, Russia 26 C7 60 5N 65 15
'Uray'irah, Si. Arabia 45 E6 25 57N 48 53
Urbana, Ill., U.S.A. 76 E1 40 7N 88 12
Urbana, Ohio, U.S.A. 76 E4 40 7N 83 45
Urbino, Italy 20 C5 43 43N 12 38
Urbión, Picos de, Spain 19 A4 42 1N 2 52
Urcos, Peru 92 F4 13 40S 71 38

Vestfjorden

Vestfjorden, Norway 8 C15 67 55N 14 0 E
Vestmannaeyjar, Iceland 8 E3 63 27N 20 15W
Vestspitsbergen, Svalbard 4 B8 78 40N 17 0 E
Vestvågøy, Norway 8 B15 68 18N 13 50 E
Vesuvio, Italy 20 D6 40 49N 14 26 E
Vesuvius, Mt. = Vesuvio, Italy 20 D6 40 49N 14 26 E
Veszprém, Hungary 17 E9 47 8N 17 57 E
Vetlanda, Sweden 9 H16 57 24N 15 3 E
Vetlugu →, Russia 24 C8 56 36N 46 4 E
Vettore, Mte., Italy 20 C5 42 49N 13 16 E
Veurne, Belgium 15 C2 51 5N 2 40 E
Veys, Iran 45 D6 31 30N 49 0 E
Vezhen, Bulgaria 21 C11 42 50N 24 20 E
Vi Thanh, Vietnam 39 H5 9 42N 105 26 E
Viacha, Bolivia 92 G5 16 39S 68 18W
Viamão, Brazil 95 C5 30 5S 51 0W
Viana, Brazil 93 D10 3 13S 44 55W
Viana do Alentejo, Portugal 19 C2 38 17N 7 59W
Viana do Castelo, Portugal 19 B1 41 42N 8 50W
Vianden, Lux. 15 E6 49 56N 6 12 E
Vianópolis, Brazil 93 G9 16 40S 48 35W
Viaréggio, Italy 20 C4 43 52N 10 14 E
Vibo Valéntia, Italy 20 E7 38 40N 16 6 E
Viborg, Denmark 9 H13 56 27N 9 23 E
Vic, Spain 19 B7 41 58N 2 19 E
Vicenza, Italy 20 B4 45 33N 11 33 E
Vich = Vic, Spain 19 B7 41 58N 2 19 E
Vichada →, Colombia 92 C5 4 55N 67 50W
Vichy, France 18 C5 46 9N 3 26 E
Vicksburg, Ariz., U.S.A. 85 M13 33 45N 113 45W
Vicksburg, Miss., U.S.A. 81 J9 32 21N 90 53W
Victor, India 42 J4 21 0N 71 30 E
Victor, U.S.A. 78 D7 42 58N 77 24W
Victor Harbor, Australia 63 F2 35 30S 138 37 E
Victoria = Labuan, Malaysia 36 C5 5 20N 115 14 E
Victoria, Argentina 94 C3 32 40S 60 10W
Victoria, Canada 72 D4 48 30N 123 25W
Victoria, Chile 96 D2 38 13S 72 20W
Victoria, Malta 23 C1 36 2N 14 14 E
Victoria, Kans., U.S.A. 80 F5 38 52N 99 9W
Victoria, Tex., U.S.A. 81 L6 28 48N 97 0W
Victoria □, Australia 63 F3 37 0S 144 0 E
Victoria →, Australia 60 C4 15 10S 129 40 E
Victoria, Grand L., Canada 70 C4 47 31N 77 30W
Victoria, L., Africa 54 C3 1 0S 33 0 E
Victoria, L., Australia 63 E3 33 57S 141 15 E
Victoria Beach, Canada 73 C9 50 40N 96 35W
Victoria de Durango = Durango, Mexico 86 C4 24 3N 104 39W
Victoria de las Tunas, Cuba 88 B4 20 58N 76 59W
Victoria Falls, Zimbabwe 55 F2 17 58S 25 52 E
Victoria Harbour, Canada 78 B5 44 45N 79 45W
Victoria I., Canada 68 A8 71 0N 111 0W
Victoria L., Canada 71 C8 48 20N 57 27W
Victoria Ld., Antarctica 5 D11 75 0S 160 0 E
Victoria Nile →, Uganda 54 B3 2 14N 31 26 E
Victoria River, Australia 60 C5 16 25S 131 0 E
Victoria Str., Canada 68 B9 69 30N 100 0W
Victoria Taungdeik, Burma 41 J18 21 15N 93 55 E
Victoria West, S. Africa 56 E3 31 25S 23 4 E
Victoriaville, Canada 71 C5 46 4N 71 56W
Victorica, Argentina 94 D2 36 20S 65 30W
Victorville, U.S.A. 85 L9 34 32N 117 18W
Vicuña, Chile 94 C1 30 0S 70 50W
Vicuña Mackenna, Argentina 94 C3 33 53S 64 25W
Vidal, U.S.A. 85 L12 34 7N 114 31W
Vidal Junction, U.S.A. 85 L12 34 11N 114 34W
Vidalia, U.S.A. 77 J4 32 13N 82 25W
Vídho, Greece 23 A3 39 38N 19 55 E
Vidin, Bulgaria 21 C10 43 59N 22 50 E
Vidisha, India 42 H7 23 28N 77 53 E
Vidzy, Belarus 9 J22 55 23N 26 37 E
Viedma, Argentina 96 E4 40 50S 63 0W
Viedma, L., Argentina 96 F2 49 30S 72 30W
Vielsalm, Belgium 15 D5 50 17N 5 54 E
Vienna = Wien, Austria 16 D9 48 12N 16 22 E
Vienna, Ill., U.S.A. 81 G10 37 25N 88 54W
Vienna, Mo., U.S.A. 80 F9 38 11N 91 57W
Vienne, France 18 D6 45 31N 4 53 E
Vienne →, France 18 C4 47 13N 0 5 E
Vientiane, Laos 38 D4 17 58N 102 36 E
Vientos, Paso de los, Caribbean 89 C5 20 0N 74 0W
Vierzon, France 18 C5 47 13N 2 5 E
Vietnam ■, Asia 38 C6 19 0N 106 0 E
Vigan, Phil. 37 A6 17 35N 120 28 E
Vigévano, Italy 18 D8 45 19N 8 51 E
Vigia, Brazil 93 D9 0 50S 48 5W
Vigía Chico, Mexico 87 D7 19 46N 87 35W
Víglas, Ákra, Greece 23 D9 35 54N 27 51 E
Vigo, Spain 19 A1 42 12N 8 41W
Vihowa, Pakistan 42 D4 31 8N 70 30 E
Vihowa →, Pakistan 42 D4 31 8N 70 41 E
Vijayawada, India 41 L12 16 31N 80 39 E
Vík, Iceland 8 E4 63 25N 19 1W
Vikeke, Indonesia 37 F7 8 52S 126 23 E
Viking, Canada 72 C6 53 7N 111 50W
Vikna, Norway 8 D14 64 55N 10 58 E
Vila da Maganja, Mozam. 55 F4 17 18S 37 30 E
Vila de João Belo = Xai-Xai, Mozam. 57 D5 25 6S 33 31 E
Vila do Bispo, Portugal 19 D1 37 5N 8 53W
Vila do Chibuto, Mozam. 57 C5 24 40S 33 33 E
Vila Franca de Xira, Portugal 19 C1 38 57N 8 59W
Vila Gamito, Mozam. 55 E3 14 12S 33 0 E
Vila Gomes da Costa, Mozam. 57 C5 24 20S 33 37 E
Vila Machado, Mozam. 55 F3 19 15S 34 14 E
Vila Mouzinho, Mozam. 55 E3 14 48S 34 25 E
Vila Nova de Gaia, Portugal 19 B1 41 8N 8 37W
Vila Real, Portugal 19 B2 41 17N 7 48W
Vila-real de los Infantes, Spain 19 C5 39 55N 0 3W
Vila Real de Santo António, Portugal 19 D2 37 10N 7 28W
Vila Vasco da Gama, Mozam. 55 E3 14 54S 32 14 E
Vila Velha, Brazil 95 A7 20 20S 40 17W
Vilagarcía de Arousa, Spain 19 A1 42 34N 8 46W
Vilaine →, France 18 C2 47 30N 2 27W
Vilanandro, Tanjona, Madag. 57 B7 16 11S 44 27 E
Vilanculos, Mozam. 57 C6 22 1S 35 17 E
Vilanova i la Geltrú, Spain 19 B6 41 13N 1 40 E
Vileyka, Belarus 17 A14 54 30N 26 53 E
Vilhelmina, Sweden 8 D17 64 35N 16 39 E
Vilhena, Brazil 92 F6 12 40S 60 5W
Viliga, Russia 27 C16 61 36N 156 56 E
Viliya →, Lithuania 9 J21 55 8N 24 16 E
Viljandi, Estonia 9 G21 58 28N 25 30 E
Vilkitskogo, Proliv, Russia 27 B11 78 0N 103 0 E
Vilkovo = Vylkove, Ukraine 17 F15 45 28N 29 32 E
Villa Abecia, Bolivia 94 A2 21 0S 68 18W
Villa Ahumada, Mexico 86 A3 30 38N 106 30W
Villa Ana, Argentina 94 B4 28 28S 59 40W
Villa Ángela, Argentina 94 B3 27 34S 60 45W
Villa Bella, Bolivia 92 F5 10 25S 65 22W
Villa Bens = Tarfaya, Morocco 50 C3 27 55N 12 55W
Villa Cañás, Argentina 94 C3 34 0S 61 35W
Villa Cisneros = Dakhla, W. Sahara 50 D2 23 50N 15 53W
Villa Colón, Argentina 94 C2 31 38S 68 20W
Villa Constitución, Argentina 94 C3 33 15S 60 20W
Villa de María, Argentina 94 B3 29 55S 63 43W
Villa Dolores, Argentina 94 C2 31 58S 65 15W
Villa Frontera, Mexico 86 B4 26 56N 101 27W
Villa Guillermina, Argentina 94 B4 28 15S 59 29W
Villa Hayes, Paraguay 94 B4 25 5S 57 20W
Villa Iris, Argentina 94 D3 38 12S 63 12W
Villa Juárez, Mexico 86 B4 27 37N 100 44W
Villa María, Argentina 94 C3 32 20S 63 10W
Villa Mazán, Argentina 94 B2 28 40S 66 30W
Villa Montes, Bolivia 94 A3 21 10S 63 30W
Villa Ocampo, Argentina 94 B4 28 30S 59 20W
Villa Ocampo, Mexico 86 B3 26 29N 105 30W
Villa Ojo de Agua, Argentina 94 B3 29 30S 63 44W
Villa San José, Argentina 94 C4 32 12S 58 15W
Villa San Martín, Argentina 94 B3 28 15S 64 9W
Villa Unión, Mexico 86 C3 23 12N 106 14W
Villacarlos, Spain 22 B11 39 53N 4 17 E
Villacarrillo, Spain 19 C4 38 7N 3 3W
Villach, Austria 16 E7 46 37N 13 51 E
Villafranca de los Caballeros, Spain 22 B10 39 34N 3 25 E
Villagrán, Mexico 87 C5 24 29N 99 29W
Villaguay, Argentina 94 C4 32 0S 59 0W
Villahermosa, Mexico 87 D6 17 59N 92 55W
Villajoyosa, Spain 19 C5 38 30N 0 12W
Villalba, Spain 19 A2 43 26N 7 40W
Villanueva, U.S.A. 81 H2 35 16N 105 22W
Villanueva de la Serena, Spain 19 C3 38 59N 5 50W
Villanueva y Geltrú = Vilanova i la Geltrú, Spain 19 B6 41 13N 1 40 E
Villarreal = Vila-real de los Infantes, Spain 19 C5 39 55N 0 3W
Villarrica, Chile 96 D2 39 15S 72 15W
Villarrica, Paraguay 94 B4 25 40S 56 30W
Villarrobledo, Spain 19 C4 39 18N 2 36W
Villavicencio, Argentina 94 C2 32 28S 69 0W
Villavicencio, Colombia 92 C4 4 9N 73 37W
Villaviciosa, Spain 19 A3 43 32N 5 27W
Villazón, Bolivia 94 A2 22 0S 65 35W
Ville-Marie, Canada 70 C4 47 20N 79 30W
Ville Platte, U.S.A. 81 K8 30 41N 92 17W
Villena, Spain 19 C5 38 39N 0 52W
Villeneuve-d'Ascq, France 18 A5 50 38N 3 9 E
Villeneuve-sur-Lot, France 18 D4 44 24N 0 42 E
Villiers, S. Africa 57 D4 27 2S 28 36 E
Villingen-Schwenningen, Germany 16 D5 48 3N 8 26 E
Vilna, Canada 72 C6 54 7N 111 55W
Vilnius, Lithuania 9 J21 54 38N 25 19 E
Vilvoorde, Belgium 15 D4 50 56N 4 26 E
Vilyuy →, Russia 27 C13 64 24N 126 26 E
Vilyuysk, Russia 27 C13 63 40N 121 35 E
Viña del Mar, Chile 94 C1 33 0S 71 30W
Vinarós, Spain 19 B6 40 30N 0 27 E
Vincennes, U.S.A. 76 F2 38 41N 87 32W
Vincent, U.S.A. 85 L8 34 33N 118 11W
Vinchina, Argentina 94 B2 28 45S 68 15W
Vindelälven →, Sweden 8 E18 63 55N 19 50 E
Vindeln, Sweden 8 D18 64 12N 19 43 E
Vindhya Ra., India 42 H7 22 50N 77 0 E
Vineland, U.S.A. 76 F8 39 29N 75 2W
Vinh, Vietnam 38 C5 18 45N 105 38 E
Vinh Linh, Vietnam 38 D6 17 4N 107 2 E
Vinh Long, Vietnam 39 G5 10 16N 105 57 E
Vinita, U.S.A. 81 G7 36 39N 95 9W
Vinkovci, Croatia 21 B8 45 19N 18 48 E
Vinnitsa = Vinnytsya, Ukraine 17 D15 49 15N 28 30 E
Vinnytsya, Ukraine 17 D15 49 15N 28 30 E
Vinton, Calif., U.S.A. 84 F6 39 48N 120 10W
Vinton, Iowa, U.S.A. 80 D8 42 10N 92 1W
Vinton, La., U.S.A. 81 K8 30 11N 93 35W
Virac, Phil. 37 B6 13 30N 124 20 E
Virachei, Cambodia 38 F6 13 59N 106 49 E
Virago Sd., Canada 72 C2 54 0N 132 30W
Viramgam, India 42 H5 23 5N 72 0 E
Viranşehir, Turkey 44 B3 37 13N 39 45 E
Virawah, Pakistan 42 G4 24 31N 70 46 E
Virden, Canada 73 D8 49 50N 100 56W
Vire, France 18 B3 48 50N 0 53W
Virgenes, C., Argentina 96 G3 52 19S 68 21W
Virgin →, U.S.A. 83 H6 36 28N 114 21W
Virgin Gorda, Virgin Is. 89 C7 18 30N 64 26W
Virgin Is. (British) ■, W. Indies 89 C7 18 30N 64 30W
Virgin Is. (U.S.) ■, W. Indies 89 C7 18 20N 65 0W
Virginia, S. Africa 56 D4 28 8S 26 55 E
Virginia, U.S.A. 80 B8 47 31N 92 32W
Virginia □, U.S.A. 76 G7 37 30N 78 45W
Virginia Beach, U.S.A. 76 G8 36 51N 75 59W
Virginia City, Mont., U.S.A. 82 D8 45 18N 111 56W
Virginia City, Nev., U.S.A. 84 F7 39 19N 119 39W
Virginia Falls, Canada 72 A3 61 38N 125 42W
Virginiatown, Canada 70 C4 48 9N 79 36W
Viroqua, U.S.A. 80 D9 43 34N 90 53W
Virovitica, Croatia 20 B7 45 51N 17 21 E
Virpur, India 42 J4 21 51N 70 42 E
Virton, Belgium 15 E5 49 35N 5 32 E
Virudunagar, India 40 Q10 9 30N 77 58 E
Vis, Croatia 20 C7 43 4N 16 10 E
Visalia, U.S.A. 84 J7 36 20N 119 18W
Visayan Sea, Phil. 37 B6 11 30N 123 30 E
Visby, Sweden 9 H18 57 37N 18 18 E
Viscount Melville Sd., Canada 4 B2 74 10N 108 0W
Visé, Belgium 15 D5 50 44N 5 41 E
Višegrad, Bos.-H. 21 C8 43 47N 19 17 E
Viseu, Brazil 93 D9 1 10S 46 5W
Viseu, Portugal 19 B2 40 40N 7 55W
Vishakhapatnam, India 41 L13 17 45N 83 20 E
Visnagar, India 42 H5 23 45N 72 32 E
Viso, Mte., Italy 18 D7 44 38N 7 5 E
Visokoi I., Antarctica 5 B1 56 43S 27 15W
Vista, U.S.A. 85 M9 33 12N 117 14W
Vistula = Wisła →, Poland 17 A10 54 22N 18 55 E
Vitebsk = Vitsyebsk, Belarus 24 C5 55 10N 30 15 E
Viterbo, Italy 20 C5 42 25N 12 6 E
Viti Levu, Fiji 59 C7 17 30S 177 30 E
Vitigudino, Spain 19 B2 41 1N 6 26W
Vitim, Russia 27 D12 59 28N 112 35 E
Vitim →, Russia 27 D12 59 26N 112 34 E
Vitória, Brazil 93 H10 20 20S 40 22W
Vitória da Conquista, Brazil 93 F10 14 51S 40 51W
Vitória de São Antão, Brazil 93 E11 8 10S 35 20W
Vitoria-Gasteiz, Spain 19 A4 42 50N 2 41W
Vitsyebsk, Belarus 24 C5 55 10N 30 15 E
Vittória, Italy 20 F6 36 57N 14 32 E
Vittório Véneto, Italy 20 B5 45 59N 12 18 E
Viveiro, Spain 19 A2 43 39N 7 38W
Vivian, U.S.A. 81 J8 32 53N 93 59W
Vizcaíno, Desierto de, Mexico 86 B2 27 40N 113 50W
Vizcaíno, Sierra, Mexico 86 B2 27 30N 114 0W
Vize, Turkey 21 D12 41 34N 27 45 E
Vizianagaram, India 41 K13 18 6N 83 30 E
Vjosa →, Albania 21 D8 40 37N 19 24 E
Vlaardingen, Neths. 15 C4 51 55N 4 21 E
Vladikavkaz, Russia 25 F7 43 0N 44 35 E
Vladimir, Russia 24 C7 56 15N 40 30 E
Vladimir Volynskiy = Volodymyr-Volynskyy, Ukraine 17 C13 50 50N 24 18 E
Vladivostok, Russia 27 E14 43 10N 131 53 E
Vlieland, Neths. 15 A4 53 16N 4 55 E
Vlissingen, Neths. 15 C3 51 26N 3 34 E
Vlóra, Albania 21 D8 40 32N 19 28 E
Vltava →, Czech Rep. 16 D8 50 21N 14 30 E
Vo Dat, Vietnam 39 G6 11 9N 107 31 E
Voe, U.K. 12 A7 60 21N 1 16W
Vogelkop = Doberai, Jazirah, Indonesia 37 E8 1 25S 133 0 E
Vogelsberg, Germany 16 C5 50 31N 9 12 E
Voghera, Italy 18 D8 44 59N 9 1 E
Vohibinany, Madag. 57 B8 18 49S 49 4 E
Vohimarina = Iharana, Madag. 57 A9 13 25S 50 0 E
Vohimena, Tanjon' i, Madag. 57 D8 25 36S 45 8 E
Vohipeno, Madag. 57 C8 22 22S 47 51 E
Voi, Kenya 54 C4 3 25S 38 32 E
Voiron, France 18 D6 45 22N 5 35 E
Voisey B., Canada 71 A7 56 15N 61 50W
Vojmsjön, Sweden 8 D17 64 55N 16 40 E
Vojvodina □, Serbia, Yug. 21 B9 45 20N 20 0 E
Volborg, U.S.A. 80 C2 45 51N 105 41W
Volcano Is. = Kazan-Rettō, Pac. Oc. 64 E6 25 0N 141 0 E
Volda, Norway 9 E12 62 9N 6 5 E
Volga →, Russia 25 E8 46 0N 48 30 E
Volga Hts. = Privolzhskaya Vozvyshennost, Russia 25 D8 51 0N 46 0 E
Volgodonsk, Russia 25 E7 47 33N 42 5 E
Volgograd, Russia 25 E7 48 40N 44 25 E
Volgogradskoye Vdkhr., Russia 25 E8 50 0N 45 20 E
Volkhov →, Russia 24 B5 60 8N 32 20 E
Volkovysk = Vawkavysk, Belarus 17 B13 53 9N 24 30 E
Volksrust, S. Africa 57 D4 27 24S 29 53 E
Volochanka, Russia 27 B10 71 0N 94 28 E
Volodymyr-Volynskyy, Ukraine 17 C13 50 50N 24 18 E
Vologda, Russia 24 C6 59 10N 39 45 E
Vólos, Greece 21 E10 39 24N 22 59 E
Volovets, Ukraine 17 D12 48 43N 23 11 E
Volozhin = Valozhyn, Belarus 17 A14 54 3N 26 30 E
Volsk, Russia 24 D8 52 5N 47 22 E
Volta →, Ghana 48 F4 5 46N 0 41 E
Volta, L., Ghana 50 G6 7 30N 0 0 E
Volta Redonda, Brazil 95 A7 22 31S 44 5W
Voltaire, C., Australia 60 B4 14 16S 125 35 E
Volterra, Italy 20 C4 43 24N 10 51 E
Volturno →, Italy 20 D5 41 1N 13 55 E
Volzhskiy, Russia 25 E7 48 56N 44 46 E
Vondrozo, Madag. 57 C8 22 49S 47 20 E
Vopnafjörður, Iceland 8 D6 65 45N 14 50W
Vóriai Sporádhes, Greece 21 E10 39 15N 23 30 E
Vorkuta, Russia 24 A11 67 48N 64 20 E
Vormsi, Estonia 9 G20 59 1N 23 13 E
Voronezh, Russia 25 D6 51 40N 39 10 E
Voroshilovgrad = Luhansk, Ukraine 25 E6 48 38N 39 15 E
Voroshilovsk = Alchevsk, Ukraine 25 E6 48 30N 38 45 E
Võrts Järv, Estonia 9 G22 58 16N 26 3 E
Võru, Estonia 9 H22 57 48N 26 54 E
Vosges, France 18 B7 48 20N 7 10 E
Voss, Norway 9 F12 60 38N 6 26 E
Vostok I., Kiribati 65 J12 10 5S 152 23W
Votkinsk, Russia 24 C9 57 0N 53 55 E
Votkinskoye Vdkhr., Russia 24 C10 57 22N 55 12 E
Votsuri-Shima, Japan 31 M1 25 45N 123 29 E
Vouga →, Portugal 19 B1 40 41N 8 40W
Voúxa, Ákra, Greece 23 D5 35 37N 23 32 E
Vozhe, Ozero, Russia 24 B6 60 45N 39 0 E
Voznesensk, Ukraine 25 E5 47 35N 31 21 E
Voznesenye, Russia 24 B6 61 0N 35 28 E
Vrangelya, Ostrov, Russia 27 B19 71 0N 180 0 E
Vranje, Serbia, Yug. 21 C9 42 34N 21 54 E
Vratsa, Bulgaria 21 C10 43 15N 23 30 E
Vrbas →, Bos.-H. 20 B7 45 8N 17 29 E
Vrede, S. Africa 57 D4 27 24S 29 6 E
Vredefort, S. Africa 56 D4 27 0S 27 22 E
Vredenburg, S. Africa 56 E2 32 56S 18 0 E
Vredendal, S. Africa 56 E2 31 41S 18 35 E
Vrindavan, India 42 F7 27 37N 77 40 E
Vríses, Greece 23 D6 35 23N 24 13 E
Vršac, Serbia, Yug. 21 B9 45 8N 21 20 E
Vryburg, S. Africa 56 D3 26 55S 24 45 E
Vryheid, S. Africa 57 D5 27 45S 30 47 E
Vu Liet, Vietnam 38 C5 18 43N 105 23 E
Vukovar, Croatia 21 B8 45 21N 18 59 E
Vulcan, Canada 72 C6 50 25N 113 15W
Vulcan, Romania 17 F12 45 23N 23 17 E
Vulcaneşti, Moldova 17 F15 45 41N 28 18 E
Vulcano, Italy 20 E6 38 24N 14 58 E
Vulkaneshty = Vulcaneşti, Moldova 17 F15 45 41N 28 18 E
Vunduzi →, Mozam. 55 F3 18 56S 34 1 E
Vung Tau, Vietnam 39 G6 10 21N 107 4 E
Vyatka = Kirov, Russia 24 C8 58 35N 49 40 E
Vyatka →, Russia 24 C9 55 37N 51 28 E
Vyatskiye Polyany, Russia 24 C9 56 14N 51 5 E
Vyazemskiy, Russia 27 E14 47 32N 134 45 E
Vyazma, Russia 24 C5 55 10N 34 15 E
Vyborg, Russia 24 B4 60 43N 28 47 E
Vychegda →, Russia 24 B8 61 18N 46 36 E
Vychodné Beskydy, Europe 17 D11 49 20N 22 0 E
Vyg-ozero, Russia 24 B5 63 47N 34 29 E
Vylkove, Ukraine 17 F15 45 28N 29 32 E
Vynohradiv, Ukraine 17 D12 48 9N 23 2 E
Vyrnwy, L., U.K. 10 E4 52 48N 3 31W
Vyshniy Volochek, Russia 24 C5 57 30N 34 30 E
Vyškov, Czech Rep. 17 D9 49 17N 17 0 E
Vytegra, Russia 24 B6 61 0N 36 27 E

W

W.A.C. Bennett Dam, Canada 72 B4 56 2N 122 6W
Waal →, Neths. 15 C5 51 37N 5 0 E
Waalwijk, Neths. 15 C5 51 42N 5 4 E
Wabana, Canada 71 C9 47 40N 53 0W
Wabasca →, Canada 72 B5 58 22N 115 20W
Wabasca-Desmarais, Canada 72 B6 55 57N 113 56W
Wabash, U.S.A. 76 E3 40 48N 85 49W
Wabash →, U.S.A. 76 G1 37 48N 88 2W
Wabigoon L., Canada 73 D10 49 44N 92 44W
Wabowden, Canada 73 C9 54 55N 98 38W
Wabuk Pt., Canada 70 A2 55 20N 85 5W
Wabush, Canada 71 B6 52 55N 66 52W
Waco, U.S.A. 81 K6 31 33N 97 9W
Waconichi, L., Canada 70 B5 50 8N 74 0W
Wad Hamid, Sudan 51 E12 16 30N 32 45 E
Wâd Medanî, Sudan 51 F12 14 28N 33 30 E
Wad Thana, Pakistan 42 F2 27 22N 66 23 E
Wadai, Africa 48 E5 12 0N 19 0 E
Wadayama, Japan 31 G7 35 19N 134 52 E
Waddeneilanden, Neths. 15 A5 53 20N 5 10 E
Waddenzee, Neths. 15 A5 53 6N 5 10 E
Waddington, U.S.A. 79 B9 44 52N 75 12W
Waddington, Mt., Canada 72 C3 51 23N 125 15W
Waddy Pt., Australia 63 C5 24 58S 153 21 E
Wadebridge, U.K. 11 G3 50 31N 4 51W
Wadena, Canada 73 C8 51 57N 103 47W
Wadena, U.S.A. 80 B7 46 26N 95 8W
Wadeye, Australia 60 B4 14 28S 129 52 E
Wadhams, Canada 72 C3 51 30N 127 30W
Wādī as Sīr, Jordan 47 D4 31 56N 35 49 E
Wadi Halfa, Sudan 51 D12 21 53N 31 19 E
Wadsworth, Nev., U.S.A. 82 G4 39 38N 119 17W
Wadsworth, Ohio, U.S.A. 78 E3 41 2N 81 44W
Waegwan, S. Korea 35 G15 35 59N 128 23 E
Wafangdian, China 35 E11 39 38N 121 58 E
Wafrah, Si. Arabia 44 D5 28 33N 47 56 E
Wageningen, Neths. 15 C5 51 58N 5 40 E
Wager B., Canada 69 B11 65 26N 88 40W
Wagga Wagga, Australia 63 F4 35 7S 147 24 E
Waghete, Indonesia 37 E9 4 10S 135 50 E
Wagin, Australia 61 F2 33 17S 117 25 E
Wagner, U.S.A. 80 D5 43 5N 98 18W
Wagon Mound, U.S.A. 81 G2 36 1N 104 42W
Wagoner, U.S.A. 81 H7 35 58N 95 22W
Wah, Pakistan 42 C5 33 45N 72 40 E
Wahai, Indonesia 37 E7 2 48S 129 35 E
Wahiawa, U.S.A. 74 H15 21 30N 158 2W
Wâḥid, Egypt 47 E1 30 48N 32 21 E
Wahnai, Afghan. 42 C1 32 40N 65 50 E
Wahoo, U.S.A. 80 E6 41 13N 96 37W
Wahpeton, U.S.A. 80 B6 46 16N 96 36W
Wai, Koh, Cambodia 39 H4 9 55N 102 55 E
Waiau →, N.Z. 59 K4 42 47S 173 22 E
Waibeem, Indonesia 37 E8 0 30S 132 59 E
Waigeo, Indonesia 37 E8 0 20S 130 40 E
Waihi, N.Z. 59 G5 37 23S 175 52 E
Waihou →, N.Z. 59 G5 37 15S 175 40 E
Waika, Dem. Rep. of the Congo 54 C2 2 22S 25 42 E
Waikabubak, Indonesia 37 F5 9 45S 119 25 E
Waikari, N.Z. 59 K4 42 58S 172 41 E
Waikato →, N.Z. 59 G5 37 23S 174 43 E
Waikerie, Australia 63 E3 34 9S 140 0 E
Waikokopu, N.Z. 59 H6 39 3S 177 52 E
Waikouaiti, N.Z. 59 L3 45 36S 170 41 E
Wailuku, U.S.A. 74 H16 20 53N 156 30W
Waimakariri →, N.Z. 59 K4 43 24S 172 42 E
Waimate, N.Z. 59 L3 44 45S 171 3 E
Wainganga →, India 40 K11 18 50N 79 55 E
Waingapu, Indonesia 37 F6 9 35S 120 11 E
Waini →, Guyana 92 B7 8 20N 59 50W
Wainwright, Canada 73 C6 52 50N 110 50W
Waiouru, N.Z. 59 H5 39 28S 175 41 E
Waipara, N.Z. 59 K4 43 3S 172 46 E
Waipawa, N.Z. 59 H6 39 56S 176 38 E
Waipiro, N.Z. 59 H7 38 2S 178 22 E
Waipu, N.Z. 59 F5 35 59S 174 29 E
Waipukurau, N.Z. 59 J6 40 1S 176 33 E
Wairakei, N.Z. 59 H6 38 37S 176 6 E
Wairarapa, L., N.Z. 59 J5 41 14S 175 15 E
Wairoa, N.Z. 59 H6 39 3S 177 25 E
Waitaki →, N.Z. 59 L3 44 56S 171 7 E
Waitara, N.Z. 59 H5 38 59S 174 15 E
Waitsburg, U.S.A. 82 C5 46 16N 118 9W
Waiuku, N.Z. 59 G5 37 15S 174 45 E
Wajima, Japan 31 F8 37 30N 137 0 E
Wajir, Kenya 54 B5 1 42N 40 5 E
Wakasa, Japan 31 G7 35 20N 134 24 E
Wakasa-Wan, Japan 31 G7 35 40N 135 30 E
Wakatipu, L., N.Z. 59 L2 45 5S 168 33 E
Wakaw, Canada 73 C7 52 39N 105 44W
Wakayama, Japan 31 G7 34 15N 135 15 E
Wakayama □, Japan 31 H7 33 50N 135 30 E
Wake Forest, U.S.A. 77 H6 35 59N 78 30W

West Ice Shelf

ake I., *Pac. Oc.* **64 F8** 19 18N 166 36 E
aKeeney, *U.S.A.* **80 F5** 39 1N 99 53W
akefield, *N.Z.* **59 J4** 41 24S 173 5 E
akefield, *U.K.* **10 D6** 53 41N 1 29W
akefield, *Mass., U.S.A.* **79 D13** 42 30N 71 4W
akefield, *Mich., U.S.A.* **80 B10** 46 29N 89 56W
akema, *Burma* **41 L19** 16 30N 95 11 E
akkanai, *Japan* **30 B10** 45 28N 141 35 E
akkerstroom, *S. Africa* **57 D5** 27 24S 30 10 E
akool, *Australia* **63 F3** 35 28S 144 23 E
akool →, *Australia* **63 F3** 35 5S 143 33 E
akre, *Indonesia* **37 E8** 0 19S 131 5 E
akuach, L., *Canada* **71 A6** 55 34N 67 32W
alamba, *Zambia* **55 E2** 13 30S 28 42 E
ałbrzych, *Poland* **16 C9** 50 45N 16 18 E
albury Hill, *U.K.* **11 F6** 51 21N 1 28W
alcha, *Australia* **63 E5** 30 55S 151 31 E
alcheren, *Neths.* **15 C3** 51 30N 3 35 E
alcott, *U.S.A.* **82 F10** 41 46N 106 51W
ałcz, *Poland* **16 B9** 53 17N 16 27 E
aldburg Ra., *Australia* **61 D2** 24 40S 117 35 E
alden, *Colo., U.S.A.* **82 F10** 40 44N 106 17W
alden, *N.Y., U.S.A.* **79 E10** 41 34N 74 11W
aldport, *U.S.A.* **82 D1** 44 26N 124 4W
aldron, *U.S.A.* **81 H7** 34 54N 94 5W
alebing, *Australia* **61 F2** 30 41S 116 13 E
ales □, *U.K.* **11 E3** 52 19N 4 43W
algett, *Australia* **63 E4** 30 0S 148 5 E
algreen Coast, *Antarctica* **5 D15** 75 15S 105 0W
alker, *U.S.A.* **80 B7** 47 6N 94 35W
alker, L., *Canada* **71 B6** 50 20N 67 11W
alker L., *Canada* **73 C9** 54 42N 95 57W
alker L., *U.S.A.* **82 G4** 38 42N 118 43W
alkerston, *Australia* **62 C4** 21 11S 149 8 E
alkerton, *Canada* **78 B3** 44 10N 81 10W
all, *U.S.A.* **80 D3** 44 0N 102 8W
alla Walla, *U.S.A.* **82 C4** 46 4N 118 20W
allace, *Idaho, U.S.A.* **82 C6** 47 28N 115 56W
allace, *N.C., U.S.A.* **77 H7** 34 44N 77 59W
allaceburg, *Canada* **78 D2** 42 34N 82 23W
allachia = Valahia, *Romania* **17 F13** 44 35N 25 0 E
allal, *Australia* **63 D4** 26 32S 146 7 E
allam Cr. →, *Australia* **63 D4** 28 40S 147 20 E
allambin, L., *Australia* **61 F2** 30 57S 117 35 E
allan, *Australia* **63 F3** 37 26S 144 59 E
allangarra, *Australia* **63 D5** 28 56S 151 58 E
allaroo, *Australia* **63 E2** 33 56S 137 39 E
allenpaupack, L., *U.S.A.* **79 E9** 41 25N 75 15W
allingford, *U.S.A.* **79 E12** 41 27N 72 50W
allis & Futuna, Is., *Pac. Oc.* **64 J10** 13 18S 176 10W
allowa, *U.S.A.* **82 D5** 45 34N 117 32W
allowa Mts., *U.S.A.* **82 D5** 45 20N 117 30W
alls, *U.K.* **12 A7** 60 14N 1 33W
allula, *U.S.A.* **82 C4** 46 5N 118 54W
allumbilla, *Australia* **63 D4** 26 33S 149 9 E
almsley, L., *Canada* **73 A7** 63 25N 108 36W
alney, I. of, *U.K.* **10 C4** 54 6N 3 15W
alnut Creek, *U.S.A.* **84 H4** 37 54N 122 4W
alnut Ridge, *U.S.A.* **81 G9** 36 4N 90 57W
alpole, *Australia* **61 F2** 34 58S 116 44 E
alpole, *U.S.A.* **79 D13** 42 9N 71 15W
alsall, *U.K.* **11 E6** 52 35N 1 58W
alsenburg, *U.S.A.* **81 G2** 37 38N 104 47W
alsh, *U.S.A.* **81 G3** 37 23N 102 17W
alsh →, *Australia* **62 B3** 16 31S 143 42 E
alterboro, *U.S.A.* **77 J5** 32 55N 80 40W
alters, *U.S.A.* **81 H5** 34 22N 98 19W
altham, *U.S.A.* **79 D13** 42 23N 71 14W
altman, *U.S.A.* **82 E10** 43 4N 107 12W
alton, *U.S.A.* **79 D9** 42 10N 75 8W
alton-on-the-Naze, *U.K.* **11 F9** 51 51N 1 17 E
alvis Bay, *Namibia* **56 C1** 23 0S 14 28 E
alvisbaai = Walvis Bay, *Namibia* **56 C1** 23 0S 14 28 E
amba, *Dem. Rep. of the Congo* **54 B2** 2 10N 27 57 E
amba, *Kenya* **54 B4** 0 58N 37 19 E
amego, *U.S.A.* **80 F6** 39 12N 96 18W
amena, *Indonesia* **37 E9** 4 4S 138 57 E
amsutter, *U.S.A.* **82 F9** 41 40N 107 58W
amulan, *Indonesia* **37 E7** 3 27S 126 7 E
an Xian, *China* **34 E8** 38 47N 115 7 E
ana, *Pakistan* **42 C3** 32 20N 69 32 E
anaaring, *Australia* **63 D3** 29 38S 144 9 E
anaka, *N.Z.* **59 L2** 44 42S 169 9 E
anaka L., *N.Z.* **59 L2** 44 33S 169 7 E
anapitei L., *Canada* **70 C3** 46 45N 80 40W
andel Sea = McKinley Sea, *Arctic* **4 A7** 82 0N 0 0 E
anderer, *Zimbabwe* **55 F3** 19 36S 30 1 E
andhari, *Pakistan* **42 F2** 27 42N 66 48 E
andoan, *Australia* **63 D4** 26 5S 149 55 E
anfu, *China* **35 D12** 40 8N 122 38 E
ang →, *Thailand* **38 D2** 17 8N 99 2 E
ang Noi, *Thailand* **38 E3** 14 13N 100 44 E
ang Saphung, *Thailand* **38 D3** 17 18N 101 46 E
ang Thong, *Thailand* **38 D3** 16 50N 100 26 E
anga, *Dem. Rep. of the Congo* **54 B2** 2 58N 29 12 E
angal, *Indonesia* **37 F8** 6 8S 134 9 E
anganella, *Australia* **63 F3** 35 6S 144 49 E
anganui, *N.Z.* **59 H5** 39 56S 175 3 E
angaratta, *Australia* **63 F4** 36 21S 146 19 E
angary, *Australia* **63 E2** 34 35S 135 29 E
angdu, *China* **34 E8** 38 40N 115 7 E
angerooge, *Germany* **16 B4** 53 47N 7 54 E
angi, *Kenya* **54 C5** 1 58S 40 58 E
angiwangi, *Indonesia* **37 F6** 5 22S 123 37 E
angqing, *China* **35 C15** 43 12N 129 42 E
ankaner, *India* **42 H4** 22 35N 71 0 E
anless, *Canada* **73 C8** 54 11N 101 21W
anning, *Taiwan* **38 C8** 23 15N 121 17 E
anon Niwat, *Thailand* **38 D4** 17 38N 103 46 E
anquan, *China* **34 D8** 40 50N 114 40 E
anrong, *China* **34 G6** 35 25N 110 50 E
antage, *U.K.* **11 F6** 51 35N 1 25W
anxian, *China* **33 C5** 30 42N 108 20 E
apakoneta, *U.S.A.* **76 E3** 40 34N 84 12W
apato, *U.S.A.* **82 C3** 46 27N 120 25W
apawekka L., *Canada* **73 C8** 54 55N 104 40W
apikopa L., *Canada* **70 B2** 52 56N 87 53W
apiti →, *Canada* **72 B5** 55 5N 118 18W
appingers Falls, *U.S.A.* **79 E11** 41 36N 73 55W
apsipinicon →, *U.S.A.* **80 E9** 41 44N 90 19W
arangal, *India* **40 L11** 17 58N 79 35 E
Waraseoni, *India* **43 J9** 21 45N 80 2 E
Waratah, *Australia* **62 G4** 41 30S 145 30 E
Waratah B., *Australia* **63 F4** 38 54S 146 5 E
Warburton, *Vic., Australia* **63 F4** 37 47S 145 42 E
Warburton, *W. Austral., Australia* **61 E4** 26 8S 126 35 E
Warburton Ra., *Australia* **61 E4** 25 55S 126 28 E
Ward, *N.Z.* **59 J5** 41 49S 174 11 E
Ward →, *Australia* **63 D4** 26 28S 146 6 E
Ward Mt., *U.S.A.* **84 H8** 37 12N 118 54W
Warden, *S. Africa* **57 D4** 27 50S 29 0 E
Wardha, *India* **40 J11** 20 45N 78 39 E
Wardha →, *India* **40 K11** 19 57N 79 11 E
Ware, *Canada* **72 B3** 57 26N 125 41W
Ware, *U.S.A.* **79 D12** 42 16N 72 14W
Waregem, *Belgium* **15 D3** 50 53N 3 27 E
Wareham, *U.S.A.* **79 E14** 41 46N 70 43W
Waremme, *Belgium* **15 D5** 50 43N 5 15 E
Warialda, *Australia* **63 D5** 29 29S 150 33 E
Wariap, *Indonesia* **37 E8** 1 30S 134 5 E
Warin Chamrap, *Thailand* **38 E5** 15 12N 104 53 E
Warkopi, *Indonesia* **37 E8** 1 12S 134 9 E
Warm Springs, *U.S.A.* **83 G5** 38 10N 116 20W
Warman, *Canada* **73 C7** 52 19N 106 30W
Warmbad, *Namibia* **56 D2** 28 25S 18 42 E
Warmbad, *S. Africa* **57 C4** 24 51S 28 19 E
Warminster, *U.K.* **11 F5** 51 12N 2 10W
Warminster, *U.S.A.* **79 F9** 40 12N 75 6W
Warner Mts., *U.S.A.* **82 F3** 41 40N 120 15W
Warner Robins, *U.S.A.* **77 J4** 32 37N 83 36W
Waroona, *Australia* **61 F2** 32 50S 115 58 E
Warracknabeal, *Australia* **63 F3** 36 9S 142 26 E
Warragul, *Australia* **63 F4** 38 10S 145 58 E
Warrego →, *Australia* **63 E4** 30 24S 145 21 E
Warrego Ra., *Australia* **62 C4** 24 58S 146 0 E
Warren, *Australia* **63 E4** 31 42S 147 51 E
Warren, *Ark., U.S.A.* **81 J8** 33 37N 92 4W
Warren, *Mich., U.S.A.* **76 D4** 42 30N 83 0W
Warren, *Minn., U.S.A.* **80 A6** 48 12N 96 46W
Warren, *Ohio, U.S.A.* **78 E4** 41 14N 80 49W
Warren, *Pa., U.S.A.* **78 E5** 41 51N 79 9W
Warrenpoint, *U.K.* **13 B5** 54 6N 6 15W
Warrensburg, *Mo., U.S.A.* **80 F8** 38 46N 93 44W
Warrensburg, *N.Y., U.S.A.* **79 C11** 43 29N 73 46W
Warrenton, *S. Africa* **56 D3** 28 9S 24 47 E
Warrenton, *U.S.A.* **84 D3** 46 10N 123 56W
Warri, *Nigeria* **50 G7** 5 30N 5 41 E
Warrina, *Australia* **63 D2** 28 12S 135 50 E
Warrington, *U.K.* **10 D5** 53 24N 2 35W
Warrington, *U.S.A.* **77 K2** 30 23N 87 17W
Warrington □, *U.K.* **10 D5** 53 24N 2 35W
Warrnambool, *Australia* **63 F3** 38 25S 142 30 E
Warroad, *U.S.A.* **80 A7** 48 54N 95 19W
Warruwi, *Australia* **62 A1** 11 36S 133 20 E
Warsa, *Indonesia* **37 E9** 0 47S 135 55 E
Warsak Dam, *Pakistan* **42 B4** 34 11N 71 19 E
Warsaw = Warszawa, *Poland* **17 B11** 52 13N 21 0 E
Warsaw, *Ind., U.S.A.* **76 E3** 41 14N 85 51W
Warsaw, *N.Y., U.S.A.* **78 D6** 42 45N 78 8W
Warsaw, *Ohio, U.S.A.* **78 F3** 40 20N 82 0W
Warszawa, *Poland* **17 B11** 52 13N 21 0 E
Warta →, *Poland* **16 B8** 52 35N 14 39 E
Warthe = Warta →, *Poland* **16 B8** 52 35N 14 39 E
Waru, *Indonesia* **37 E8** 3 30S 130 36 E
Warwick, *Australia* **63 D5** 28 10S 152 1 E
Warwick, *U.K.* **11 E6** 52 18N 1 35W
Warwick, *N.Y., U.S.A.* **79 E10** 41 16N 74 22W
Warwick, *R.I., U.S.A.* **79 E13** 41 42N 71 28W
Warwickshire □, *U.K.* **11 E6** 52 14N 1 38W
Wasaga Beach, *Canada* **78 B4** 44 31N 80 1W
Wasagaming, *Canada* **73 C9** 50 39N 99 58W
Wasatch Ra., *U.S.A.* **82 F8** 40 30N 111 15W
Wasbank, *S. Africa* **57 D5** 28 15S 30 9 E
Wasco, *Calif., U.S.A.* **85 K7** 35 36N 119 20W
Wasco, *Oreg., U.S.A.* **82 D3** 45 36N 120 42W
Waseca, *U.S.A.* **80 C8** 44 5N 93 30W
Wasekamio L., *Canada* **73 B7** 56 45N 108 45W
Wash, The, *U.K.* **10 E8** 52 58N 0 20 E
Washago, *Canada* **78 B5** 44 45N 79 20W
Washburn, *N. Dak., U.S.A.* **80 B4** 47 17N 101 2W
Washburn, *Wis., U.S.A.* **80 B9** 46 40N 90 54W
Washim, *India* **40 J10** 20 3N 77 0 E
Washington, *U.K.* **10 C6** 54 55N 1 30W
Washington, *D.C., U.S.A.* **76 F7** 38 54N 77 2W
Washington, *Ga., U.S.A.* **77 J4** 33 44N 82 44W
Washington, *Ind., U.S.A.* **76 F2** 38 40N 87 10W
Washington, *Iowa, U.S.A.* **80 E9** 41 18N 91 42W
Washington, *Mo., U.S.A.* **80 F9** 38 33N 91 1W
Washington, *N.C., U.S.A.* **77 H7** 35 33N 77 3W
Washington, *N.J., U.S.A.* **79 F10** 40 46N 74 59W
Washington, *Pa., U.S.A.* **78 F4** 40 10N 80 15W
Washington, *Utah, U.S.A.* **83 H7** 37 8N 113 31W
Washington □, *U.S.A.* **82 C3** 47 30N 120 30W
Washington, Mt., *U.S.A.* **79 B13** 44 16N 71 18W
Washington Court House, *U.S.A.* **76 F4** 39 32N 83 26W
Washington I., *U.S.A.* **76 C2** 45 23N 86 54W
Washougal, *U.S.A.* **84 E4** 45 35N 122 21W
Wasian, *Indonesia* **37 E8** 1 47S 133 19 E
Wasilla, *U.S.A.* **68 B5** 61 35N 149 26W
Wasior, *Indonesia* **37 E8** 2 43S 134 30 E
Waskaganish, *Canada* **70 B4** 51 30N 78 40W
Waskaiowaka, L., *Canada* **73 B9** 56 33N 96 23W
Waskesiu Lake, *Canada* **73 C7** 53 55N 106 5W
Wasserkuppe, *Germany* **16 C5** 50 29N 9 55 E
Waswanipi, *Canada* **70 C4** 49 40N 76 29W
Waswanipi, L., *Canada* **70 C4** 49 35N 76 40W
Watampone, *Indonesia* **37 E6** 4 29S 120 25 E
Water Park Pt., *Australia* **62 C5** 22 56S 150 47 E
Water Valley, *U.S.A.* **81 H10** 34 10N 89 38W
Waterberge, *S. Africa* **57 C4** 24 10S 28 0 E
Waterbury, *Conn., U.S.A.* **79 E11** 41 33N 73 3W
Waterbury, *Vt., U.S.A.* **79 B12** 44 20N 72 46W
Waterbury L., *Canada* **73 B8** 58 10N 104 22W
Waterdown, *Canada* **78 C5** 43 20N 79 53W
Waterford, *Canada* **78 D4** 42 56N 80 17W
Waterford, *Ireland* **13 D4** 52 15N 7 8W
Waterford, *Calif., U.S.A.* **84 H6** 37 38N 120 46W
Waterford, *Pa., U.S.A.* **78 E5** 41 57N 79 59W
Waterford □, *Ireland* **13 D4** 52 10N 7 40W
Waterford Harbour, *Ireland* **13 D5** 52 8N 6 58W
Waterhen L., *Canada* **73 C9** 52 10N 99 40W
Waterloo, *Belgium* **15 D4** 50 43N 4 25 E
Waterloo, *Ont., Canada* **78 C4** 43 30N 80 32W
Waterloo, *Qué., Canada* **79 A12** 45 22N 72 32W
Waterloo, *Ill., U.S.A.* **80 F9** 38 20N 90 9W
Waterloo, *Iowa, U.S.A.* **80 D8** 42 30N 92 21W
Waterloo, *N.Y., U.S.A.* **78 D8** 42 54N 76 52W
Watersmeet, *U.S.A.* **80 B10** 46 16N 89 11W
Waterton Nat. Park, *U.S.A.* **82 B7** 48 45N 115 0W
Watertown, *Conn., U.S.A.* **79 E11** 41 36N 73 7W
Watertown, *N.Y., U.S.A.* **79 C9** 43 59N 75 55W
Watertown, *S. Dak., U.S.A.* **80 C6** 44 54N 97 7W
Watertown, *Wis., U.S.A.* **80 D10** 43 12N 88 43W
Waterval-Boven, *S. Africa* **57 D5** 25 40S 30 18 E
Waterville, *Canada* **79 A13** 45 16N 71 54W
Waterville, *Maine, U.S.A.* **77 C11** 44 33N 69 38W
Waterville, *N.Y., U.S.A.* **79 D9** 42 56N 75 23W
Waterville, *Pa., U.S.A.* **78 E7** 41 19N 77 21W
Waterville, *Wash., U.S.A.* **82 C3** 47 39N 120 4W
Watervliet, *U.S.A.* **79 D11** 42 44N 73 42W
Wates, *Indonesia* **37 G14** 7 51S 110 10 E
Watford, *Canada* **78 D3** 42 57N 81 53W
Watford, *U.K.* **11 F7** 51 40N 0 24W
Watford City, *U.S.A.* **80 B3** 47 48N 103 17W
Wathaman →, *Canada* **73 B8** 57 16N 102 59W
Wathaman L., *Canada* **73 B8** 56 58N 103 44W
Watheroo, *Australia* **61 F2** 30 15S 116 0 E
Wating, *China* **34 G4** 35 40N 106 38 E
Watkins Glen, *U.S.A.* **78 D8** 42 23N 76 52W
Watling I. = San Salvador I., *Bahamas* **89 B5** 24 0N 74 40W
Watonga, *U.S.A.* **81 H5** 35 51N 98 25W
Watrous, *Canada* **73 C7** 51 40N 105 25W
Watrous, *U.S.A.* **81 H2** 35 48N 104 59W
Watsa, *Dem. Rep. of the Congo* **54 B2** 3 4N 29 30 E
Watseka, *U.S.A.* **76 E2** 40 47N 87 44W
Watson, *Australia* **61 F5** 30 29S 131 31 E
Watson, *Canada* **73 C8** 52 10N 104 30W
Watson Lake, *Canada* **72 A3** 60 6N 128 49W
Watsontown, *U.S.A.* **78 E8** 41 5N 76 52W
Watsonville, *U.S.A.* **84 J5** 36 55N 121 45W
Wattiwarriganna Cr. →, *Australia* **63 D2** 28 57S 136 10 E
Watuata = Batuata, *Indonesia* **37 F6** 6 12S 122 42 E
Watubela, Kepulauan, *Indonesia* **37 E8** 4 28S 131 35 E
Watubela Is. = Watubela, Kepulauan, *Indonesia* **37 E8** 4 28S 131 35 E
Wau, *Sudan* **49 F6** 7 45N 28 1 E
Waubamik, *Canada* **78 A4** 45 27N 80 1W
Waubay, *U.S.A.* **80 C6** 45 20N 97 18W
Wauchope, *N.S.W., Australia* **63 E5** 31 28S 152 45 E
Wauchope, *N. Terr., Australia* **62 C1** 20 36S 134 15 E
Waukarlycarly, L., *Australia* **60 D3** 21 18S 121 56 E
Waukegan, *U.S.A.* **75 B9** 42 22N 87 50W
Waukesha, *U.S.A.* **76 D1** 43 1N 88 14W
Waukon, *U.S.A.* **80 D9** 43 16N 91 29W
Waupaca, *U.S.A.* **80 C10** 44 21N 89 5W
Waupun, *U.S.A.* **80 D10** 43 38N 88 44W
Waurika, *U.S.A.* **81 H6** 34 10N 98 0W
Wausau, *U.S.A.* **80 C10** 44 58N 89 38W
Wautoma, *U.S.A.* **80 C10** 44 4N 89 18W
Wauwatosa, *U.S.A.* **76 D2** 43 3N 88 0W
Waveney →, *U.K.* **11 E9** 52 35N 1 39 E
Waverley, *N.Z.* **59 H5** 39 46S 174 37 E
Waverly, *Iowa, U.S.A.* **80 D8** 42 44N 92 29W
Waverly, *N.Y., U.S.A.* **79 E8** 42 1N 76 32W
Wavre, *Belgium* **15 D4** 50 43N 4 38 E
Wâw, *Sudan* **51 G11** 7 45N 28 1 E
Wāw al Kabīr, *Libya* **51 C9** 25 20N 16 43 E
Wawa, *Canada* **70 C3** 47 59N 84 47W
Wawanesa, *Canada* **73 D9** 49 36N 99 40W
Wawona, *U.S.A.* **84 H7** 37 32N 119 39W
Waxahachie, *U.S.A.* **81 J6** 32 24N 96 51W
Way, L., *Australia* **61 E3** 26 45S 120 16 E
Waycross, *U.S.A.* **77 K4** 31 13N 82 21W
Wayland, *U.S.A.* **78 D7** 42 34N 77 35W
Wayne, *Nebr., U.S.A.* **80 D6** 42 14N 97 1W
Wayne, *W. Va., U.S.A.* **76 F4** 38 13N 82 27W
Waynesboro, *Ga., U.S.A.* **77 J4** 33 6N 82 1W
Waynesboro, *Miss., U.S.A.* **77 K1** 31 40N 88 39W
Waynesboro, *Pa., U.S.A.* **76 F7** 39 45N 77 35W
Waynesboro, *Va., U.S.A.* **76 F6** 38 4N 78 53W
Waynesburg, *U.S.A.* **76 F5** 39 54N 80 11W
Waynesville, *U.S.A.* **77 H4** 35 28N 82 58W
Waynoka, *U.S.A.* **81 G5** 36 35N 98 53W
Wazirabad, *Pakistan* **42 C6** 32 30N 74 8 E
We, *Indonesia* **36 C1** 5 51N 95 18 E
Weald, The, *U.K.* **11 F8** 51 4N 0 20 E
Wear →, *U.K.* **10 C6** 54 55N 1 23W
Weatherford, *Okla., U.S.A.* **81 H5** 35 32N 98 43W
Weatherford, *Tex., U.S.A.* **81 J6** 32 46N 97 48W
Weaverville, *U.S.A.* **82 F2** 40 44N 122 56W
Webb City, *U.S.A.* **81 G7** 37 9N 94 28W
Webequie, *Canada* **70 B2** 52 59N 87 21W
Webster, *Mass., U.S.A.* **79 D13** 42 3N 71 53W
Webster, *N.Y., U.S.A.* **78 C7** 43 13N 77 26W
Webster, *S. Dak., U.S.A.* **80 C6** 45 20N 97 31W
Webster City, *U.S.A.* **80 D8** 42 28N 93 49W
Webster Springs, *U.S.A.* **76 F5** 38 29N 80 25W
Weda, *Indonesia* **37 D7** 0 21N 127 50 E
Weda, Teluk, *Indonesia* **37 D7** 0 30N 127 50 E
Weddell I., *Falk. Is.* **96 G4** 51 50S 61 0W
Weddell Sea, *Antarctica* **5 D1** 72 30S 40 0W
Wedderburn, *Australia* **63 F3** 36 26S 143 33 E
Wedgeport, *Canada* **71 D6** 43 44N 65 59W
Wedza, *Zimbabwe* **55 F3** 18 40S 31 33 E
Wee Waa, *Australia* **63 E4** 30 11S 149 26 E
Weed, *U.S.A.* **82 F2** 41 25N 122 23W
Weed Heights, *U.S.A.* **84 G7** 38 59N 119 13W
Weedsport, *U.S.A.* **79 C8** 43 3N 76 35W
Weedville, *U.S.A.* **78 E6** 41 17N 78 30W
Weenen, *S. Africa* **57 D5** 28 48S 30 7 E
Weert, *Neths.* **15 C5** 51 15N 5 43 E
Wei He →, *Hebei, China* **34 F8** 36 10N 115 45 E
Wei He →, *Shaanxi, China* **34 G6** 34 38N 110 15 E
Weichang, *China* **35 D9** 41 58N 117 49 E
Weichuan, *China* **34 G7** 34 20N 113 59 E
Weiden, *Germany* **16 D7** 49 41N 12 10 E
Weifang, *China* **35 F10** 36 44N 119 7 E
Weihai, *China* **35 F12** 37 30N 122 6 E
Weimar, *Germany* **16 C6** 50 58N 11 19 E
Weinan, *China* **34 G5** 34 31N 109 29 E
Weipa, *Australia* **62 A3** 12 40S 141 50 E
Weir →, *Australia* **63 D4** 28 20S 149 50 E
Weir →, *Canada* **73 B10** 56 54N 93 21W
Weir River, *Canada* **73 B10** 56 49N 94 6W
Weirton, *U.S.A.* **78 F4** 40 24N 80 35W
Weiser, *U.S.A.* **82 D5** 44 10N 117 0W
Weishan, *China* **35 G9** 34 47N 117 5 E
Weiyuan, *China* **34 G3** 35 7N 104 10 E
Wejherowo, *Poland* **17 A10** 54 35N 18 12 E
Wekusko L., *Canada* **73 C9** 54 40N 99 50W
Welch, *U.S.A.* **76 G5** 37 26N 81 35W
Welkom, *S. Africa* **56 D4** 28 0S 26 46 E
Welland, *Canada* **78 D5** 43 0N 79 15W
Welland →, *U.K.* **11 E7** 52 51N 0 5W
Wellesley Is., *Australia* **62 B2** 16 42S 139 30 E
Wellingborough, *U.K.* **11 E7** 52 19N 0 41W
Wellington, *Australia* **63 E4** 32 35S 148 59 E
Wellington, *Canada* **78 C7** 43 57N 77 20W
Wellington, *N.Z.* **59 J5** 41 19S 174 46 E
Wellington, *S. Africa* **56 E2** 33 38S 19 1 E
Wellington, *Somst., U.K.* **11 G4** 50 58N 3 13W
Wellington, *Telford & Wrekin, U.K.* **11 E5** 52 42N 2 30W
Wellington, *Colo., U.S.A.* **80 E2** 40 42N 105 0W
Wellington, *Kans., U.S.A.* **81 G6** 37 16N 97 24W
Wellington, *Nev., U.S.A.* **84 G7** 38 45N 119 23W
Wellington, *Ohio, U.S.A.* **78 E2** 41 10N 82 13W
Wellington, *Tex., U.S.A.* **81 H4** 34 51N 100 13W
Wellington, I., *Chile* **96 F2** 49 30S 75 0W
Wellington, L., *Australia* **63 F4** 38 6S 147 20 E
Wells, *U.K.* **11 F5** 51 13N 2 39W
Wells, *Maine, U.S.A.* **79 C14** 43 20N 70 35W
Wells, *N.Y., U.S.A.* **79 C10** 43 24N 74 17W
Wells, *Nev., U.S.A.* **82 F6** 41 7N 114 58W
Wells, L., *Australia* **61 E3** 26 44S 123 15 E
Wells, Mt., *Australia* **60 C4** 17 25S 127 8 E
Wells Gray Prov. Park, *Canada* **72 C4** 52 30N 120 15W
Wells-next-the-Sea, *U.K.* **10 E8** 52 57N 0 51 E
Wells River, *U.S.A.* **79 B12** 44 9N 72 4W
Wellsboro, *U.S.A.* **78 E7** 41 45N 77 18W
Wellsburg, *U.S.A.* **78 F4** 40 16N 80 37W
Wellsville, *N.Y., U.S.A.* **78 D7** 42 7N 77 57W
Wellsville, *Ohio, U.S.A.* **78 F4** 40 36N 80 39W
Wellsville, *Utah, U.S.A.* **82 F8** 41 38N 111 56W
Wellton, *U.S.A.* **83 K6** 32 40N 114 8W
Wels, *Austria* **16 D8** 48 9N 14 1 E
Welshpool, *U.K.* **11 E4** 52 39N 3 8W
Welwyn Garden City, *U.K.* **11 F7** 51 48N 0 12W
Wem, *U.K.* **10 E5** 52 52N 2 44W
Wembere →, *Tanzania* **54 C3** 4 10S 34 15 E
Wemindji, *Canada* **70 B4** 53 0N 78 49W
Wen Xian, *China* **34 G7** 34 55N 113 5 E
Wenatchee, *U.S.A.* **82 C3** 47 25N 120 19W
Wenchang, *China* **38 C8** 19 38N 110 42 E
Wenchi, *Ghana* **50 G5** 7 46N 2 8W
Wenchow = Wenzhou, *China* **33 D7** 28 0N 120 38 E
Wenden, *U.S.A.* **85 M13** 33 49N 113 33W
Wendeng, *China* **35 F12** 37 15N 122 5 E
Wendesi, *Indonesia* **37 E8** 2 30S 134 17 E
Wendover, *U.S.A.* **82 F6** 40 44N 114 2W
Wenlock →, *Australia* **62 A3** 12 2S 141 55 E
Wenshan, *China* **32 D5** 23 20N 104 18 E
Wenshang, *China* **34 G9** 35 45N 116 30 E
Wenshui, *China* **34 F7** 37 26N 112 1 E
Wensleydale, *U.K.* **10 C6** 54 17N 2 0W
Wensu, *China* **32 B3** 41 15N 80 10 E
Wensum →, *U.K.* **10 E8** 52 40N 1 15 E
Wentworth, *Australia* **63 E3** 34 2S 141 54 E
Wentzel L., *Canada* **72 B6** 59 2N 114 28W
Wenut, *Indonesia* **37 E8** 3 11S 133 19 E
Wenxi, *China* **34 G6** 35 20N 111 10 E
Wenxian, *China* **34 H3** 32 43N 104 36 E
Wenzhou, *China* **33 D7** 28 0N 120 38 E
Weott, *U.S.A.* **82 F2** 40 20N 123 55W
Wepener, *S. Africa* **56 D4** 29 42S 27 3 E
Werda, *Botswana* **56 D3** 25 24S 23 15 E
Weri, *Indonesia* **37 E8** 3 10S 132 38 E
Werra →, *Germany* **16 C5** 51 24N 9 39 E
Werrimull, *Australia* **63 E3** 34 25S 141 38 E
Werris Creek, *Australia* **63 E5** 31 18S 150 38 E
Weser →, *Germany* **16 B5** 53 36N 8 28 E
Wesiri, *Indonesia* **37 F7** 7 30S 126 30 E
Weslemkoon L., *Canada* **78 A7** 45 2N 77 25W
Wesleyville, *Canada* **71 C9** 49 8N 53 36W
Wesleyville, *U.S.A.* **78 D4** 42 9N 80 0W
Wessel, C., *Australia* **62 A2** 10 59S 136 46 E
Wessel Is., *Australia* **62 A2** 11 10S 136 45 E
Wessington Springs, *U.S.A.* **80 C5** 44 5N 98 34W
West, *U.S.A.* **81 K6** 31 48N 97 6W
West →, *U.S.A.* **79 D12** 42 52N 72 33W
West Baines →, *Australia* **60 C4** 15 38S 129 59 E
West Bank □, *Asia* **47 C4** 32 6N 35 13 E
West Bend, *U.S.A.* **76 D1** 43 25N 88 11W
West Bengal □, *India* **43 H13** 23 0N 88 0 E
West Berkshire □, *U.K.* **11 F6** 51 25N 1 17W
West Beskids = Západné Beskydy, *Europe* **17 D10** 49 30N 19 0 E
West Branch, *U.S.A.* **76 C3** 44 17N 84 14W
West Branch Susquehanna →, *U.S.A.* **79 F8** 40 53N 76 48W
West Bromwich, *U.K.* **11 E6** 52 32N 1 59W
West Burra, *U.K.* **12 A7** 60 5N 1 21W
West Canada Cr. →, *U.S.A.* **79 C10** 43 1N 74 58W
West Cape Howe, *Australia* **61 G2** 35 8S 117 36 E
West Chazy, *U.S.A.* **79 B11** 44 49N 73 28W
West Chester, *U.S.A.* **79 G9** 39 58N 75 36W
West Columbia, *U.S.A.* **81 L7** 29 9N 95 39W
West Covina, *U.S.A.* **85 L9** 34 4N 117 54W
West Des Moines, *U.S.A.* **80 E8** 41 35N 93 43W
West Dunbartonshire □, *U.K.* **12 F4** 55 59N 4 30W
West End, *Bahamas* **88 A4** 26 41N 78 58W
West Falkland, *Falk. Is.* **96 G5** 51 40S 60 0W
West Fargo, *U.S.A.* **80 B6** 46 52N 96 54W
West Farmington, *U.S.A.* **78 E4** 41 23N 80 58W
West Fjord = Vestfjorden, *Norway* **8 C15** 67 55N 14 0 E
West Fork Trinity →, *U.S.A.* **81 J6** 32 48N 96 54W
West Frankfort, *U.S.A.* **80 G10** 37 54N 88 55W
West Hartford, *U.S.A.* **79 E12** 41 45N 72 44W
West Haven, *U.S.A.* **79 E12** 41 17N 72 57W
West Hazleton, *U.S.A.* **79 F9** 40 58N 76 0W
West Helena, *U.S.A.* **81 H9** 34 33N 90 38W
West Hurley, *U.S.A.* **79 E10** 41 59N 74 7W
West Ice Shelf, *Antarctica* **5 C7** 67 0S 85 0 E

West Indies

Yezd

Z